Encyclopedia
of the
American Constitution

Editorial Board

Encyclopedia
of the
American Constitution

LEONARD W. LEVY, Editor-in-Chief
Claremont Graduate School, Claremont, California

KENNETH L. KARST, Associate Editor
University of California, Los Angeles

DENNIS J. MAHONEY, Assistant Editor
Claremont Graduate School, Claremont, California

MACMILLAN PUBLISHING COMPANY
A Division of Macmillan, Inc.
NEW YORK

Collier Macmillan Publishers
LONDON

Macmillan Publishing Company
A Division of Macmillan, Inc.
866 Third Avenue, New York, NY 10022

Collier Macmillan Canada, Inc.

Printed in the United States of America

printing number
1   2   3   4   5   6   7   8   9   10

Library of Congress Catalog in Publication Data

Encyclopedia of the American Constitution.

   Includes index.
   1. United States—Constitutional Law—Dictionaries.
I. Levy, Leonard Williams, 1923–   II. Karst,
Kenneth L.   III. Mahoney, Dennis J.
KF4548.E53 1986   342.73′023′03   86–3038
ISBN 0–02–918610–2   347.3022303

STAFF:

Charles E. Smith, *Publisher*

Elly Dickason, *Project Editor*

Morton I. Rosenberg, *Production Manager*

Joan Greenfield, *Designer*

Contents

v

Preface

In the summer of 1787 delegates from the various states met in Philadelphia; because they succeeded in their task, we now call their assembly the Constitutional Convention. By September 17 the delegates had completed the framing of the Constitution of the United States. The year 1987 marks the bicentennial of the Constitutional Convention. This Encyclopedia is intended as a scholarly and patriotic enterprise to commemorate the bicentennial. No encyclopedia on the Constitution has heretofore existed. This work seeks to fill the need for a single comprehensive reference work treating the subject in a multidisciplinary way.

The Constitution is a legal document, but it is also an institution: a charter for government, a framework for building a nation, an aspect of the American civic culture. Even in its most limited sense as a body of law, the Constitution includes, in today's understanding, nearly two centuries' worth of court decisions interpreting the charter. Charles Evans Hughes, then governor of New York, made this point pungently in a 1907 speech: "We are under a Constitution, but the Constitution is what the judges say it is." Hughes's remark was, if anything, understated. If the Constitution sometimes seems to be chiefly the product of judicial decisions, it is also what Presidents say it is—and legislators, and police officers, and ordinary citizens, too. In the final analysis today's Constitution is the product of the whole political system and the whole history of the many peoples who have become a nation. "Constitutional law is history," wrote Professor Felix Frankfurter in 1937, "But equally true is it that American history is constitutional law."

Thus an Encyclopedia of the American Constitution would be incomplete if it did not seek to bridge the disciplines of history, law, and political science. Both in identifying subjects and in selecting authors we have sought to build those bridges. The subjects fall into five general categories: doctrinal concepts of constitutional law (about fifty-five percent of the total words); people (about fifteen percent); judicial decisions, mostly of the Supreme Court of the United States (about fifteen percent); public acts, such as statutes, treaties, and executive orders (about five percent); and historical periods (about ten percent). (These percentages are exclusive of the appendices—printed at the end of the final volume—and bibliographies.) The articles vary in length, from brief definitions of terms to treatments of major subjects of constitutional doctrine, which may be as long as 6,000 words, and articles on periods of constitutional history, which may be even longer. A fundamental concept like "due process of law" is the subject of three 6,000-word articles: Procedural Due Process of Law (Civil), Procedural Due Process of Law (Criminal), and Substantive Due Process of Law. In addition, there is a 1,500-word article on the historical background of due process of law. The standard length of an article on a major topic, such as the First Amendment, is 6,000 words; but each principal component of the amendment—Freedom of Speech, Freedom of the Press, Religious Liberty, Separation of Church and State—is also the subject of a 6,000-word article. There are also other, shorter articles on other aspects of the amendment.

The reader will find an article on almost any topic reasonably conceivable. At the beginning of the first volume there is a list of all entries, to spare the reader from paging through the volumes to determine whether particular entries exist. This list, like many another efficiency device, may be a mixed blessing; we commend to our readers the joys of encyclopedia-browsing.

The Encyclopedia's articles are arranged alphabetically and are liberally cross-referenced by the use of small capital letters indicating the titles of related articles. A reader may thus begin with an article focused on one feature of his or her field of inquiry, and move easily to other articles on other aspects of the subject. For example, one who wished to read about the civil rights movement of the 1950s and 1960s might begin with the large-scale subject of Civil Rights itself; or with a particular doctrinal topic (Desegregation, or Miscegenation), or an article focused on a narrower factual setting (Public Accommodations, or Sit-Ins). Alternatively, the reader might start with an important public act (Civil Rights Act of 1964), or with a biographical entry on a particular person (Martin Luther King, Jr., or Earl Warren). Other places to start would be articles on the events in particular eras (Warren Court or Constitutional History, 1945–1961 and 1961–1977). The reader can use any of these articles to find all the others, simply by following the network of cross-references. A Subject Index and a Name Index, at the end of the last volume, list all the pages on which the reader can find, for example, references to the freedom of the press or to Abraham Lincoln. Full citations to all the judicial decisions mentioned in the Encyclopedia are set out in the Case Index, also at the end of the final volume.

The Encyclopedia's approximately 2,100 articles have been written by 262 authors. Most of the authors fall into three groups: 41 historians, 164 lawyers (including academics, practitioners, and judges), and 53 political scientists. The others are identified with the fields of economics and journalism. Our lawyer-authors, who represent about three-fifths of all our writers, have produced about half the words in the Encyclopedia. Historian-authors, although constituting only about sixteen percent of all authors, produced about one-third of the words; political scientists, although responsible for only one-sixth of the words, wrote more than a quarter of the articles. Whether this information is an occasion for surprise may depend on the reader's occupation.

In addition to the interdisciplinary balance, the reader will find geographical balance. Although a large number of contributors is drawn from the School of Law of the University of California, Los Angeles, the Claremont Colleges, and other institutions in California, most come from the Northeast, including twelve from Harvard University, thirteen from Yale University, and nine from Columbia University. Every region of the United States is represented, however, and there are many contributors from the South (Duke University, University of Virginia, University of North Carolina, University of Texas, etc.), from the Midwest (University of Chicago, University of Notre Dame, University of Wisconsin, University of Michigan, etc.), and from the Northwest (University of Oregon, Portland State University, University of Washington, etc.). There are several contributors from foreign countries, including Austria, Canada, and Great Britain.

Every type of academic environment is represented among the eighty-six colleges and universities at which the authors work. The contributors include scholars based at large public universities, smaller state colleges, Ivy League universities, private liberal arts colleges, and religiously affiliated institutions. Not all of the authors are drawn from academia; one is a member of Congress and nine are federal judges. In addition, other government offices, research institutions, libraries, newspaper staffs, and law firms are represented.

Each article is signed by its author; we have encouraged the authors to write commentaries, in essay form, not merely describing and analyzing their subjects but expressing their own views. On the subject of the Constitution, specialists and citizens alike will hold divergent viewpoints. In inviting authors to contribute to the Encyclopedia, we have sought to include a range of views. The reader should be alert to the possibility that a cross-referenced article may discuss similar issues from a different perspective—especially if those issues have been the subject of recent controversy. We hope this awareness will encourage readers to read more widely and to expand the range of their interests concerning the Constitution.

Planning of the Encyclopedia began in 1978, and production began in 1979; nearly all articles were written by 1985. Articles on decisions of the Supreme Court include cases decided during the Court's October 1984 Term, which ended in July 1985. Given the ways in which American constitutional law develops, some of the subjects treated here are moving targets. In a project like this one, some risk of obsolescence is necessarily present; at this writing we can predict with confidence that some of our authors will wish they had one last chance to modify their articles to take account of decisions in the 1985 Term. To minimize these concerns we have asked the authors of articles on doctrinal subjects to concentrate on questions that are fundamental and of enduring significance.

We have insisted that the authors keep to the constitutional aspects of their various topics. There is much to be said about abortion or antitrust law, or about foreign affairs or mental illness, that is not comprehended within the fields of constitutional law and history. In effect, the title of every article might be extended by the phrase ". . . and the Constitution." This statement is emphatically true of the biographical entries; every author was admonished to avoid writing a conventional biography and, instead, to write an appreciation of the subject's significance in American constitutional law and history.

We have also asked authors to remember that the Encyclopedia will be used by readers whose interests and training vary widely, from the specialist in constitutional law or history to the high school student who is writing a paper. Not every article will be within the grasp of that student, but the vast majority of articles are accessible to the general reader who is neither historian nor lawyer not political scientist. Although a constitutional specialist on a particular subject will probably find the articles on that specialty too general, the same specialist may profit from reading articles in other fields. A commerce clause expert may not be an expert on the First Amendment; and First Amendment scholars may know little about criminal justice. The deluge of cases, problems, and information flowing from courts, other agencies of government, law reviews, and scholarly monographs has forced constitutional scholarship to become specialized, like all branches of the liberal arts. Few, if any, can keep in command of it all and remain up to date. The Encyclopedia organizes in readable form an epitome of all that is known and understood on the subject of the Constitution by the nation's specialist scholars.

Because space is limited, no encyclopedia article can pretend to exhaust its subject. Moreover, an encyclopedia is not the same kind of contribution to knowledge as a monograph based on original research in the primary sources is. An encyclopedia is a compendium of knowledge, a reference work addressed to a wide variety of interested audiences: students in secondary school, college, graduate school, and law school; scholars and teachers of constitutional law and history; lawyers; legislators; jurists; government officials; journalists; and educated citizens who care about their Constitution and its history. Typically, an article in this Encyclopedia contains not only cross-references to other articles but also a bibliography that will aid the reader in pursuing his or her own study of the subject.

In addition to the articles, the Encyclopedia comprises several appendices. There is a copy of the complete text of the Constitution as well as of George Washington's Letter of Transmittal. A glossary defines legal terms that may be unfamiliar to readers who are not lawyers. Two chronologies will help put topics in historical perspective; one is a detailed chronology of the framing and ratification of the Constitution and the Bill of Rights, and the other is a more general chronology of American constitutional history. Finally, there are three indices: the first is an index of court cases, with the complete citation to every case mentioned in the Encyclopedia (to which is attached a brief guide to the use of legal citations); the second is an index of names; and the third is a general topical index.

For some readers an encyclopedia article will be a stopping-point, but the articles in this Encyclopedia are intended to be doorways leading to ideas and to additional reading, and perhaps to the reader's development of independent judgment about the Constitution. After all, when the American Constitution's tricentennial is celebrated in 2087, what the Constitution has become will depend less on the views of specialists than on the beliefs and behavior of the nation's citizens.

June 1986

Leonard W. Levy
Kenneth L. Karst
Dennis J. Mahoney

Acknowledgments

The editors are grateful to our authors, to our editorial board, and to our advisory committee (all listed in the early pages of the Encyclopedia) for their labors and advice during these seven years.

The editors acknowledge with utmost appreciation the financial support given to this project by four institutions. The National Endowment for the Humanities made a major grant which the Weingart Foundation of Los Angeles matched. The Macmillan Publishing Company and The Claremont Graduate School also handsomely underwrote this encyclopedia. The earliest private funds came from a small group of southern California attorneys and foundations: The Times Mirror Foundation; James Greene, Judge Dyson William Cox and Janice T. Cox, Robert P. Hastings, James E. Ludlam, and J. Patrick Waley; Musick, Peeler & Garrett; and The Ralph B. Lloyd Foundation.

The Claremont Graduate School and University Center also provided facilities and logistical support for the Encyclopedia. Former President Joseph B. Platt gave the project his encouragement. Executive Vice-President Paul A. Albrecht significantly assisted our grant applications from the outset and remained helpful throughout the project. Associate Dean Christopher N. Oberg has seen to the efficient management of administrative aspects of the project. Sandra Glass, now of the Keck Foundation, provided invaluable aid while she was associated with The Claremont Graduate School. We are also grateful for the unflagging support of the School of Law of the University of California, Los Angeles, and its deans, William D. Warren and Susan Westerberg Prager.

A succession of graduate students at The Claremont Graduate School worked on the project as editorial assistants, research assistants, typists, and proofreaders. First was Dr. David Gordon, who also acted as assistant editor for one year, and who wrote over one hundred of the articles before going on to law school. Dr. Michael E. DeGolyer and Susan Marie Meyer served ably as editorial assistants. Others who worked on the project were Michael Walker, Kenneth V. Benesh, Susan

Orr, Suzanne Kovacs, Dr. Steven Varvis, Dr. Patrick Delana, and Paul R. Huard.

The secretaries in the History Department of The Claremont Graduate School have typed thousands of letters and hundreds of articles, in addition to performing numerous other small tasks to keep the project going; particular thanks are due to Lelah Mullican. The Claremont Graduate School Academic Computing Center and its director, Gunther Freehill, showed us how to automate our record keeping and provided facilities for that purpose.

Most important, we gratefully acknowledge the support of Charles E. Smith, Vice-President and Publisher, Professional Books Division, Macmillan Publishing Company, and of Elly Dickason, our editor at Macmillan. Mr. Smith actively and continuously supported the project from its early days and by his prodding kept us on a Stakhanovite schedule. Ms. Dickason performed arduous labors with supreme professional skill and unfailing good humor.

Finally, we thank Elyse Levy and Smiley Karst for their own indispensable contributions to this project. A personal dedication page seems inappropriate for a reference work, otherwise this Encyclopedia would have been dedicated to them. Natalie Glucklich, Renee Karst, Aaron Harris, and Adam Harris, the grandchildren of the senior editors, entered the world without realizing that the Encyclopedia project was underway. They assisted not a whit, but we acknowledge our pleasure in seeing their names in print.

List of Articles

List of Contributors

Benjamin Aaron
Professor of Law, Emeritus
University of California, Los Angeles

LABOR AND THE ANTITRUST LAWS

Henry J. Abraham
James Hart Professor of Government and Foreign Affairs
University of Virginia

AFFIRMATIVE ACTION
APPOINTMENT OF SUPREME COURT JUSTICES
BIDDLE, FRANCIS
FUNDAMENTAL RIGHTS
HARLAN, JOHN MARSHALL (1833–1911)
ORDERED LIBERTY

Norman Abrams
Professor of Law
University of California, Los Angeles

BALLEW v. GEORGIA
BURCH v. LOUISIANA
JURY SIZE
JURY UNANIMITY
LAW ENFORCEMENT AND FEDERAL-STATE RELATIONS

David Adamany
Professor of Law and Political Science, and President
Wayne State University

CAMPAIGN FINANCING
ELECTIONS, REGULATION OF

* Deceased.

POLITICAL PARTIES IN CONSTITUTIONAL LAW
PRIMARY ELECTIONS

Lee A. Albert
Professor of Law
State University of New York, Buffalo

FEDERAL GRANTS-IN-AID

Francis A. Allen
Edson R. Sunderland Professor of Law
University of Michigan

RIGHT TO COUNSEL

Reginald Alleyne
Professor of Law
University of California, Los Angeles

EMPLOYMENT DISCRIMINATION

George Anastaplo
Professor of Law
Loyola University of Chicago Law School
Lecturer in the Liberal Arts
The University of Chicago

POLITICAL PHILOSOPHY OF THE CONSTITUTION

Alison Grey Anderson
Professor of Law
University of California, Los Angeles

SECURITIES LAW AND THE CONSTITUTION

lxiii

David A. Anderson
Rosenberg Centennial Professor of Law
The University of Texas at Austin

GAG ORDER
NEW YORK TIMES CO. V. SULLIVAN
SEDITIOUS LIBEL

Michael R. Asimow
Professor of Law
University of California, Los Angeles

NATIONAL POLICE POWER
SIXTEENTH AMENDMENT

James R. Asperger
United States Attorney
Los Angeles

ARREST WARRANT
OVERRULING
SEARCH WARRANT
VAGRANCY LAWS

Carl A. Auerbach
Professor of Law
University of Minnesota, Twin Cities

SUBVERSIVE ADVOCACY

Barbara Allen Babcock
Ernest W. McFarland Professor of Law
Stanford Law School

ARGERSINGER V. HAMLIN
ASH, UNITED STATES V.
BETTS V. BRADY
ESCOBEDO V. ILLINOIS
FARETTA V. CALIFORNIA
FRUIT OF THE POISONOUS TREE
JOHNSON V. ZERBST
KIRBY V. ILLINOIS
LINEUP
MASSIAH V. UNITED STATES
POWELL V. ALABAMA
PRETRIAL DISCLOSURE
WADE, UNITED STATES V.

Stewart Abercrombie Baker
Attorney
Steptoe & Johnson, Washington, D.C.

STEVENS, JOHN PAUL

Lance Banning
Professor of History
University of Kentucky

MADISON, JAMES

Sotirios A. Barber
Professor of Government
University of Notre Dame

CHECKS AND BALANCES
DELEGATION OF POWER
ENUMERATED POWERS
GENERAL WELFARE CLAUSE
INHERENT POWERS
INTERGOVERNMENTAL IMMUNITIES
INTERPOSITION
LIMITED GOVERNMENT
NECESSARY AND PROPER CLAUSE
TENTH AMENDMENT
UNWRITTEN CONSTITUTION

Edward L. Barrett, Jr.
Professor of Law
University of California, Davis

DIRECT AND INDIRECT TAXES
EXCISE TAX
FOREIGN COMMERCE
IMPORT-EXPORT CLAUSE
IMPORTS
JURISDICTION TO TAX
ORIGINAL PACKAGE DOCTRINE
STATE REGULATION OF COMMERCE
STATE TAXATION OF COMMERCE
TAKING AND SPENDING POWERS

Paul M. Bator
John P. Wilson Professor of Law
The University of Chicago

JUDICIAL SYSTEM
JUDICIARY ACT OF 1789

Maurice G. Baxter
Professor of History
Indiana University

WEBSTER, DANIEL

Derrick A. Bell, Jr.
Professor of Law
Harvard Law School

DESEGREGATION

Herman Belz
Professor of History
University of Maryland

CONSTITUTIONAL HISTORY, 1861–1865
CONSTITUTIONALISM AND THE AMERICAN FOUNDING
THEORIES OF THE UNION
WAITE, MORRISON R.

Paul Bender
Dean and Professor of Law
Arizona State University

RETROACTIVITY OF JUDICIAL DECISIONS

Michael Les Benedict
Professor of History
The Ohio State University

CONSTITUTIONAL HISTORY, 1865–1877

Raoul Berger
Professor of Law, Emeritus
Harvard Law School

IMPEACHMENT

Walter Berns
*John M. Olin Distinguished Scholar in
    Constitutional and Legal Studies*
American Enterprise Institute
Professorial Lecturer
Georgetown University

CAPITAL PUNISHMENT CASES (1972)
CAPITAL PUNISHMENT CASES (1976)
NATURAL RIGHTS

Richard B. Bernstein
Research Curator, U.S. Constitution Exhibition
The New York Public Library

BALDWIN, ROGER
BOUDIN, LOUIS
BRANT, IRVING
CARR, ROBERT
COHEN, MORRIS R.
CRIMINAL SYNDICALISM LAWS
CROSSKEY, WILLIAM W.
CUSHMAN, ROBERT E.
HAMILTON, WALTER H.
HOWE, MARK DEWOLFE
JENSEN, MERRILL
KELLY, ALFRED H.
MINTON, SHERMAN
ROSSITER, CLINTON
STORY, JOSEPH
SWISHER, CARL BRENT
TEN BROEK, JACOBUS
TUGWELL, REXFORD G.
WIGMORE, JOHN HENRY

Scott H. Bice
Professor of Law and Dean of the Law Center
University of Southern California

LEGISLATIVE INTENT

*Joseph W. Bishop, Jr.
Richard Ely Professor of Law
Yale Law School

DECLARATION OF WAR
MILITARY JUSTICE AND THE CONSTITUTION
POLICE ACTION
STATE OF WAR

Charles L. Black, Jr.
Sterling Professor of Law, Emeritus
Yale Law School
Professor of Law
Columbia University

ADMIRALTY AND MARITIME JURISDICTION
EQUITY
STATE ACTION

Vincent Blasi
Corliss Lamont Professor of Civil Liberties
Columbia University

DEMONSTRATION
PUBLIC FORUM

Albert P. Blaustein
Professor of Law
Rutgers-Camden School of Law

INFLUENCE OF THE AMERICAN CONSTITUTION ABROAD

Maxwell Bloomfield
Professor of History and Law
The Catholic University of America

COMMENTATORS ON THE CONSTITUTION

Grace Ganz Blumberg
Professor of Law
University of California, Los Angeles

HELVERING V. DAVIS
SOCIAL SECURITY ACT
STEWARD MACHINE COMPANY V. DAVIS

Lee C. Bollinger
Professor of Law
University of Michigan

BURGER, WARREN E.

Robert H. Bork
Judge

* Deceased

United States Court of Appeals for the District of
  Columbia Circuit

JUDICIAL REVIEW AND DEMOCRACY

Paul Brest
  *Kenneth and Harle Montgomery Professor of
    Clinical Legal Education*
  Stanford Law School

CONSTITUTIONAL INTERPRETATION
LEGISLATION

Ralph S. Brown
  Simeon E. Baldwin Professor of Law, Emeritus
  Yale Law School

LOYALTY OATH
LOYALTY-SECURITY PROGRAMS

Barbara Brudno
  Attorney
  Former Professor of Law
  University of California, Los Angeles

WEALTH DISCRIMINATION

Harold H. Bruff
  John S. Redditt Professor of Law
  The University of Texas at Austin

OFFICE OF MANAGEMENT AND BUDGET

Robert A. Burt
  Southmayd Professor of Law
  Yale University

FAMILY AND THE CONSTITUTION
MENTAL ILLNESS AND THE CONSTITUTION
MENTAL RETARDATION AND THE CONSTITUTION

Paul D. Carrington
  Professor of Law and Dean of the Law School
  Duke University

TRIAL BY JURY

Robert L. Carter
  Judge
  United States District Court, Southern
    District of New York

UNITED STATES DISTRICT COURTS

Gerhard Casper
  *William B. Graham Professor of Law and Dean
    of the Law School*
  The University of Chicago

CONSTITUTIONALISM

Donald S. Chisum
  Professor of Law
  University of Washington, Seattle

PATENTS

Jesse H. Choper
  Dean and Professor of Law
  University of California, Berkeley

SEPARATION OF CHURCH AND STATE

William Cohen
  *C. Wendell and Edith M. Carlsmith Professor of
    Law*
  Stanford Law School

CLERKS
DOUGLAS, WILLIAM O.
PREEMPTION

Henry Steele Commager
  Professor of History, Emeritus
  Amherst College

STORY, JOSEPH

Richard C. Cortner
  Professor of Political Science
  University of Arizona

CONSTITUTIONAL HISTORY, 1961–1977

*Robert M. Cover
  Chancellor Kent Professor of Law
  Yale Law School

TAFT COURT

Archibald Cox
  Carl M. Loeb University Professor, Emeritus
  Harvard University
  Visiting Professor of Law
  Boston University

FIRST AMENDMENT
HUGHES COURT
STONE COURT

William J. Cuddihy
  Claremont, California

ASSISTANCE, WRIT OF
BONHAM'S CASE
CALVIN'S CASE
FOURTH AMENDMENT (ORIGINS)
GENERAL WARRANT

OTIS, JAMES
PAXTON'S CASE
WILKES CASES

David P. Currie
Harry N. Wyatt Professor of Law
The University of Chicago

JUDICIAL POWER OF THE UNITED STATES

Thomas Curry
Vicar for Priests
Archdiocese of Los Angeles

BACKUS, ISAAC
HOOKER, THOMAS
LELAND, JOHN
WILLIAMS, ROGER

Richard Danzig
Attorney
Latham, Watkins & Hills, Washington, D.C.

CONSCRIPTION

Robert Dawidoff
Associate Professor of History
The Claremont Graduate School

ADAMS, HENRY
RANDOLPH, JOHN

Howard E. Dean
Professor of Political Science
Portland State University

JUDICIAL POLICYMAKING
MECHANICAL JURISPRUDENCE
THAYER, JAMES BRADLEY

Walter Dellinger
Professor of Law
Duke University

AMENDING PROCESS

John P. Diggins
Professor of History
University of California, Irvine

PROGRESSIVE CONSTITUTIONAL THOUGHT

Norman Dorsen
Stokes Professor of Law
New York University
President
American Civil Liberties Union

AMERICAN CIVIL LIBERTIES UNION
CIVIL LIBERTIES
DRAFT CARD BURNING
FLAG DESECRATION

Robert F. Drinan, S. J.
Professor of Law
Georgetown University
Former Member of Congress (1971–1981)

CIVIL DISOBEDIENCE AND THE CONSTITUTION

Murray Dry
Professor of Political Science
Middlebury College

ANTI-FEDERALIST CONSTITUTIONAL THOUGHT
STORING, HERBERT J.

Patrick Dutton
Attorney
Vinnedge, Lance & Glenn, Ontario, California

NEW JERSEY V. T.L.O.

Frank H. Easterbrook
Judge
United States Court of Appeals for the Seventh
  Circuit
*Former Lee and Brena Freeman Professor of
  Law*
The University of Chicago

REHNQUIST, WILLIAM H.

Theodore Eisenberg
Professor of Law
Cornell University

AGE DISCRIMINATION
AGE DISCRIMINATION ACT
ANTIDISCRIMINATION LEGISLATION
ARLINGTON HEIGHTS V. METROPOLITAN HOUSING
  DEVELOPMENT CORP.
BANKRUPTCY ACT
BANKRUPTCY POWER
BANKRUPTCY REFORM ACT
BIVENS V. SIX UNKNOWN NAMED AGENTS
BUTZ V. ECONOMOU
CIVIL RIGHTS ACT OF 1866 (JUDICIAL INTERPRETATION)
CIVIL RIGHTS ACT OF 1957
CIVIL RIGHTS ACT OF 1960
CIVIL RIGHTS ACT OF 1964
CIVIL RIGHTS ACT OF 1968
CIVIL RIGHTS COMMISSION
CIVIL RIGHTS DIVISION
CIVIL RIGHTS REMOVAL

CIVIL RIGHTS REPEAL ACT
CLASSIC, UNITED STATES V.
COLOR OF LAW
DAMAGES
DAVIS V. PASSMAN
DEVELOPMENTALLY DISABLED ACT
DOMBROWSKI V. PFISTER
EDELMAN V. JORDAN
EDUCATION AMENDMENTS
EDUCATION OF HANDICAPPED CHILDREN ACT
EXECUTIVE IMMUNITY
EXECUTIVE ORDER
EXECUTIVE ORDER 11246
EXECUTIVE ORDERS 9980 AND 9981: INTEGRATION
    OF THE FEDERAL GOVERNMENT
EXHAUSTION OF REMEDIES
FEDERAL PROTECTION OF CIVIL RIGHTS
FEDERAL TORT CLAIMS ACT
FITZPATRICK V. BITZER
GRAVEL V. UNITED STATES
GRIFFIN V. BRECKINRIDGE
GRIGGS V. DUKE POWER COMPANY
GUEST, UNITED STATES V.
HAGUE V. C.I.O.
HODGES V. UNITED STATES
HUTCHINSON V. PROXMIRE
IMBLER V. PACHTMAN
IMPLIED CONSTITUTIONAL RIGHTS OF ACTION
INSTITUTIONAL LITIGATION (WITH STEPHEN C. YEA-
    ZELL)
JONES V. ALFRED H. MAYER CO.
JUDICIAL IMMUNITY
KATZENBACH V. MORGAN
LAKE COUNTRY ESTATES V. TAHOE REGIONAL PLANNING
    AGENCY
LARSON V. DOMESTIC AND FOREIGN COMMERCE
    CORP.
LAU V. NICHOLS
LEGISLATIVE IMMUNITY
MITCHUM V. FOSTER
MONELL V. DEPARTMENT OF SOCIAL SERVICES OF NEW
    YORK CITY
MONROE V. PAPE
MUNICIPAL IMMUNITY
OPEN HOUSING LAWS
OREGON V. MITCHELL
OWEN V. CITY OF INDEPENDENCE
PALMER V. THOMPSON
PIERSON V. RAY
QUERN V. JORDAN
REHABILITATION ACT
REVISED STATUTES
SCHEUER V. RHODES
SCREWS V. UNITED STATES
SECTION 1983, TITLE 42, U.S. CODE (JUDICIAL
    INTERPRETATION)
SOUTH CAROLINA V. KATZENBACH

SPEECH OR DEBATE CLAUSE
STRICT CONSTRUCTION
STUMP V. SPARKMAN
TENNEY V. BRANDHOVE
UNITED STEELWORKERS OF AMERICA V. WEBER
VOTING RIGHTS ACT OF 1965
WAIVER OF CONSTITUTIONAL RIGHTS
WASHINGTON V. DAVIS
WOOD V. STRICKLAND

Daniel J. Elazar
    *President, Center for the Study of
        Federalism and Professor of Political Science*
    Temple University

FEDERALISM (THEORY)

Ward E. Y. Elliott
    Professor of Government
    Claremont McKenna College

AVERY V. MIDLAND COUNTY
BAKER V. CARR
COLEGROVE V. GREEN
COLEMAN V. MILLER
DIRECT ELECTIONS
ELECTORAL COLLEGE
FIFTEENTH AMENDMENT (JUDICIAL INTERPRETA-
    TION)
GERRYMANDER
MULTIMEMBER DISTRICT
O'BRIEN V. BROWN
ONE PERSON, ONE VOTE
REPRESENTATION

Richard E. Ellis
    Professor of History
    State University of New York, Buffalo

CHASE, SAMUEL J.
CUSHING, WILLIAM
DUVALL, GABRIEL
ELLSWORTH, OLIVER
IREDELL, JAMES
JAY, JOHN
PATERSON, WILLIAM
TODD, THOMAS
WASHINGTON, BUSHROD

Thomas I. Emerson
    Augustus E. Lines Professor of Law, Emeritus
    Yale Law School

FREEDOM OF SPEECH
FREEDOM OF THE PRESS

David F. Epstein
Analyst
United States Department of Defense,
  Washington, D.C.

THE FEDERALIST

Edward J. Erler
Professor of Political Science
California State University, San Bernardino

CONCURRENT POWERS
DISCRETE AND INSULAR MINORITY
EX POST FACTO
FIREFIGHTERS' LOCAL NO. 1784 v. STOTTS
JUDICIAL LEGISLATION
O'CONNOR, SANDRA DAY
RODGERS v. LODGE

Robert K. Faulkner
Professor of Political Science
Boston College

BICKEL, ALEXANDER M.
LOCKE, JOHN
MARSHALL, JOHN

John D. Feerick
Professor of Law and Dean of the Law School
Fordham University

PRESIDENTIAL SUCCESSION

Don E. Fehrenbacher
Professor of History
Stanford University

CONSTITUTIONAL HISTORY, 1848–1861
DRED SCOTT v. SANDFORD

David Fellman
Vilas Professor of Political Science, Emeritus
University of Wisconsin, Madison

CRIMINAL PROCEDURE
FREEDOM OF ASSEMBLY AND ASSOCIATION

Martha A. Field
Professor of Law
Harvard Law School

ABSTENTION DOCTRINE
FORTAS, ABE

Paul Finkelman
Professor of History
State University of New York, Binghamton

ARTHUR, CHESTER A.
BATES, EDWARD
BENTON, THOMAS HART
BINGHAM, JOHN A.
BINNEY, HORACE
BIRNEY, JAMES
BLACK, JEREMIAH S.
BRECKINRIDGE, JOHN C.
BUCHANAN, JAMES
BUTLER, BENJAMIN F.
CARPENTER, MATTHEW
COMMONWEALTH v. JENNISON
CONKLING, ROSCOE
CRITTENDEN, JOHN J.
CURTIS, GEORGE T.
DAVIS, JEFFERSON
DOUGLAS, STEPHEN A.
FEDERAL TEST ACTS
FESSENDEN, WILLIAM PITT
FILLMORE, MILLARD
GARFIELD, JAMES A.
GARRISON, WILLIAM LLOYD
GRANT, ULYSSES S.
HAYES, RUTHERFORD B.
HAYNE, ROBERT YOUNG
JACKSON'S PROCLAMATION TO THE PEOPLE OF SOUTH
  CAROLINA
JACKSON'S VETO OF THE BANK BILL
JOHNSON, REVERDY
JULIAN, GEORGE
PIERCE, FRANKLIN
PINKNEY, WILLIAM
PRIGG v. PENNSYLVANIA
SEWARD, WILLIAM
STANBERY, HENRY
STANTON, EDWIN M.
STEPHENS, ALEXANDER H.
STEVENS, THADDEUS
SUMNER, CHARLES
TARIFF ACT OF 1828
TAYLOR, ZACHARY
TOOMBS, ROBERT A.
TRUMBULL, LYMAN
TYLER, JOHN
WHEATON, HENRY
WILMOT PROVISO
WIRT, WILLIAM
WOODBURY, LEVI

Louis Fisher
Specialist in American National Government
Congressional Research Service, The Library of
  Congress

CARTER, JIMMY
EMERGENCY POWERS
EXECUTIVE ORDER 10340

LEGISLATIVE VETO
PRESIDENTIAL ORDINANCE-MAKING POWER
PRESIDENTIAL SPENDING POWER
TRUMAN, HARRY S.
VETO POWER
YOUNGSTOWN SHEET & TUBE COMPANY V. SAWYER

Owen M. Fiss
Alexander M. Bickel Professor of Public Law
Yale Law School

FULLER COURT
RACIAL DISCRIMINATION

David H. Flaherty
Professor of History
University of Western Ontario

FUNDAMENTAL LAW (HISTORY)

Caleb Foote
Elizabeth Josselyn Boalt Professor of Law
University of California, Berkeley

BAIL

George Forsyth
Claremont, California

ADAMS, JOHN QUINCY

Marvin E. Frankel
Attorney
Kramer, Levin, Nessen, Kamen & Frankel
Former Judge
United States District Court, Eastern District
    of New York

GRAND JURY

John Hope Franklin
James B. Duke Professor of History, Emeritus
Duke University

SLAVERY AND THE CONSTITUTION

Paul A. Freund
Carl M. Loeb University Professor, Emeritus
Harvard Law School

SUPREME COURT (HISTORY)

Gerald E. Frug
Professor of Law
Harvard Law School

CITIES AND THE CONSTITUTION

Jaime B. Fuster
Member of Congress (Puerto Rico)
Professor of Law
University of Puerto Rico

PUERTO RICO, CONSTITUTIONAL STATUS OF

David J. Garrow
Associate Professor of Political Science
City College of New York and City University
    Graduate School

KING, MARTIN LUTHER, JR.

William Gillette
Professor of History
Rutgers University

FIFTEENTH AMENDMENT (FRAMING)

Ruth Bader Ginsburg
Judge
United States Court of Appeals for the District of
    Columbia Circuit

REPRODUCTIVE AUTONOMY
SEX DISCRIMINATION

Robert Jerome Glennon
Professor of Law
University of Arizona

BROWN, HENRY BILLINGS
FRANK, JEROME

Carole E. Goldberg-Ambrose
Professor of Law
University of California, Los Angeles

AMERICAN INDIANS AND THE CONSTITUTION
CONCURRENT JURISDICTION
DECLARATORY JUDGMENT
DIVERSITY JURISDICTION
FEDERAL QUESTION JURISDICTION
FEDERAL RULES OF CIVIL PROCEDURE
REMOVAL OF CASES

Abraham S. Goldstein
Sterling Professor of Law
Yale Law School

RIGHT TO BE INFORMED OF ACCUSATION

Joel K. Goldstein
Attorney
Goldstein & Price, St. Louis

VICE-PRESIDENCY

David Gordon
Attorney
D'Ancona & Pflaum, Chicago

ACT OF STATE DOCTRINE
ADAMS V. TANNER
ADAMSON EIGHT-HOUR ACT
AGRICULTURAL ADJUSTMENT ACT OF 1933
AGRICULTURAL ADJUSTMENT ACT OF 1938
AGRICULTURAL MARKETING AGREEMENT ACT
ALLEN-BRADLEY LOCAL V. WISCONSIN EMPLOYEE
    RELATIONS BOARD
ALLGEYER V. LOUISIANA
AMES, FISHER
APEX HOSIERY CO. V. LEADER
APPALACHIAN ELECTRIC POWER, UNITED STATES V.
ARNOLD, THURMAN W.
BARTKUS V. ILLINOIS
BATES V. STATE BAR OF ARIZONA
BENTON V. MARYLAND
BIBB V. NAVAJO FREIGHT LINES
BITUMINOUS COAL ACT
BOB-LO EXCURSION COMPANY V. MICHIGAN
BREWSTER V. UNITED STATES
BURBANK V. LOCKHEED AIR TERMINAL
BURNS BAKING COMPANY V. BRYAN
BUSHELL'S CASE
CARTER, JAMES COOLIDGE
CHAE CHAN PING V. UNITED STATES
CHAMPION V. AMES
CHAPMAN V. HOUSTON WELFARE RIGHTS
    ORGANIZATION
CHICAGO, BURLINGTON & QUINCY RAILWAY V. CHICAGO
CHICAGO, MILWAUKEE & ST. PAUL RAILWAY V.
    MINNESOTA
CHILD LABOR TAX ACT
CHINESE EXCLUSION ACT
CHOATE, JOSEPH H.
CIRCUIT COURTS OF APPEALS ACT
CLARK DISTILLING CO. V. WESTERN MARYLAND
    RAILWAY CO.
CLAYTON ACT
CLEVELAND, GROVER
CODISPOTI V. PENNSYLVANIA
COPPAGE V. KANSAS
CORRIGAN V. BUCKLEY
COYLE V. SMITH
CUMMINGS, HOMER S.
DAVIS, JOHN W.
DAYTON-GOOSE CREEK RAILWAY CO. V. UNITED STATES
DEAN MILK COMPANY V. MADISON
DE MINIMIS NON CURAT LEX
DILLON, JOHN F.
DIONISIO, UNITED STATES V.
DISANTO V. PENNSYLVANIA
DISTRICT OF COLUMBIA MINIMUM WAGE LAW
DOREMUS, UNITED STATES V.

DUNCAN V. KAHANAMOKU
DUNCAN V. LOUISIANA
DUPLEX PRINTING PRESS COMPANY V. DEERING
EISNER V. MACOMBER
ELKINS ACT
EMERGENCY BANK ACT
EMPLOYERS' LIABILITY ACTS
EMPLOYERS' LIABILITY CASES
EN BANC
ERDMAN ACT
ERNST, MORRIS L.
ESCH-CUMMINGS TRANSPORTATION ACT
ESTES V. TEXAS
EXECUTIVE ORDER 9066 AND PUBLIC LAW 503
FEDERAL POWER COMMISSION V. HOPE NATURAL GAS
    COMPANY
FEDERAL TRADE COMMISSION V. GRATZ
FEDERAL TRADE COMMISSION ACT
FIELD, DAVID DUDLEY
FOOD, DRUG, AND COSMETIC ACT
FRANK V. MANGUM
FRAZIER-LEMKE ACTS
FREEMAN V. HEWITT
FREUND, ERNST
FROTHINGHAM V. MELLON
GALLOWAY, JOSEPH
GERRY, ELBRIDGE
GOLD CLAUSE CASES
GOLD RESERVE ACT
GOLDFARB V. VIRGINIA STATE BAR
GOMPERS V. BUCKS' STOVE AND RANGE COMPANY
GONG LUM V. RICE
GRIMAUD, UNITED STATES V.
GROSSMAN, EX PARTE
GUTHRIE, WILLIAM
HABEAS CORPUS ACT
HALL V. DECUIR
HARPER, ROBERT G.
HARRIS V. NEW YORK
HARRISON ACT
HARRISON, BENJAMIN
HAYS, ARTHUR GARFIELD
HEPBURN ACT
HILDRETH, RICHARD
HIPOLITE EGG COMPANY V. UNITED STATES
HITCHMAN COAL AND COKE CO. V. MITCHELL
HOKE V. UNITED STATES
HOUSTON, EAST & WEST TEXAS RAILWAY COMPANY V.
    UNITED STATES
HURON PORTLAND CEMENT CO. V. DETROIT
INTERSTATE COMMERCE COMMISSION V. CINCINNATI,
    NEW ORLEANS & TEXAS PACIFIC RAILWAY
INTERSTATE COMMERCE COMMISSION V. ILLINOIS
    CENTRAL RAILROAD
INTERSTATE COMMERCE
INTERSTATE COMMERCE ACT
INTRASTATE COMMERCE

James v. Bowman
Judiciary Act of 1925
Judiciary Reform Act
Knight Co., E. C., United States v.
Knox, Philander C.
Lamar, Joseph R.
Landis, James M.
Lanza, United States v.
Lever Food and Drug Control Act
Long Haul/Short Haul Rate Discrimination
Louisville, New Orleans & Texas Railway v.
  Mississippi
Lurton, Horace H.
Mann Act
Mann-Elkins Act
Martin, Luther
Massachusetts Body of Liberties
Massachusetts General Laws and Liberties
McCray v. United States
McKinley, William
Michelin Tire Company v. Wages
Middendorf v. Henry
Minnesota Rate Cases
Moody, William H.
Moore, Alfred
Mugler v. Kansas
Municipal Bankruptcy Act
Muskrat v. United States
Myers v. United States
National Industrial Recovery Act
New State Ice Company v. Liebmann
New York Central Railroad v. White
Nolo Contendere
Norris-LaGuardia Act
Northern Securities Co. v. United States
Obiter Dictum
Olney, Richard
Olsen v. Nebraska ex rel. Reference & Bond
  Association
Packers and Stockyards Act
Palmer, A. Mitchell
Parker v. Brown
Patton v. United States
Paul v. Virginia
Pell v. Procunier
Per Curiam
Phelps, Edward J.
Pollak, Walter H.
Pollock v. Williams
Prudential Insurance Company v. Benjamin
Pure Food and Drug Act
Railroad Control Act
Railroad Retirement Act
Raymond Motor Transportation v. Rice
Ribnik v. McBride
Robinson-Patman Act
Selden, John

Sherman Antitrust Act
Shreveport Doctrine
Simon v. Eastern Kentucky Welfare Rights
  Organization
Smyth v. Ames
South-Eastern Underwriters Association, United
  States v.
Stafford v. Wallace
Standard Oil Company v. United States
Stettler v. O'Hara
Stream of Commerce Doctrine
Swift & Company v. United States
Tennessee Valley Authority Act
Trans-Missouri Freight Association, United
  States v.
Tyson & Brother v. Banton
Ultra Vires
United Mine Workers v. Coronado Coal
  Company
United Mine Workers, United States v.
Vicinage
Wabash, St. Louis, Pacific Railway v. Illinois
Wagner Act
Walz v. Tax Commission
Water Power Act
Webb-Kenyon Act
Wickersham, George W.
Wilson v. New
Winship, In re
Wolff Packing Co. v. Court of Industrial
  Relations
Woods v. Cloyd W. Miller Co.
Wythe, George
Yakus v. United States
Yamashita, In re

William B. Gould
Charles A. Beardsley Professor of Law
Stanford Law School

  Lochner v. New York
  Workers' Compensation

Henry F. Graff
Professor of History
Columbia University

  Nixon, Richard M.

Kent Greenawalt
Cardozo Professor of Jurisprudence
Columbia University

  Conscientious Objection
  Incitement to Unlawful Conduct

Jack Greenberg
Professor of Law
Columbia University
Former General Counsel
NAACP Legal Defense & Educational Fund

CIVIL RIGHTS
NAACP LEGAL DEFENSE AND EDUCATIONAL FUND

Linda Greenhouse
Staff writer
The New York Times

GOLDBERG, ARTHUR J.

Eugene Gressman
William Rand Kenan, Jr. Professor of Law
The University of North Carolina at
  Chapel Hill

JUDICIAL CODE
MURPHY, FRANK
STAY OF EXECUTION
SUPREME COURT PRACTICE

Thomas C. Grey
Professor of Law
Stanford Law School

HIGHER LAW

Erwin N. Griswold
Partner
Jones, Day, Reavis & Pogue, Washington, D.C.
Former Solicitor General of the United States
Former Dean
Harvard Law School

SOLICITOR GENERAL

Gerald Gunther
William Nelson Cromwell Professor of Law
Stanford Law School

DOWLING, NOEL T.
HAND, LEARNED
JUDICIAL REVIEW

Nathan Hakman
Professor of Political Science
State University of New York, Binghamton

INTEREST GROUP LITIGATION

Kermit L. Hall
Professor of History and Law
University of Florida

BOND, HUGH LENNOX
BREWER, DAVID J.
CAMPBELL, JOHN A.
CIRCUIT COURTS
CRANCH, WILLIAM
GRIER, ROBERT C.
GROSSCUP, PETER
HASTIE, WILLIAM
MORROW, WILLIAM
NELSON, SAMUEL
PARDEE, DON ALBERT
PETERS, RICHARD
POLK, JAMES K.
SAWYER, LORENZO

Catherine Hancock
Associate Professor of Law
Tulane University

CRIMINAL CONSPIRACY
FAY V. NOIA
NO-KNOCK ENTRY
PORNOGRAPHY
TOWNSEND V. SAIN

Louis Henkin
University Professor
Columbia University

FOREIGN AFFAIRS AND THE CONSTITUTION

Harold W. Horowitz
Vice Chancellor for Faculty Relations and Professor
  of Law
University of California, Los Angeles

CHOICE OF LAW

A. E. Dick Howard
White Burkett Miller Professor of Law and Public
  Affairs
University of Virginia

BURGER COURT
MAGNA CARTA

Samuel P. Huntington
Director, Center for International Affairs
Eaton Professor of the Science of Government
Harvard University

CIVIL-MILITARY RELATIONS AND THE CONSTITUTION

James Willard Hurst
Vilas Professor of Law, Emeritus
University of Wisconsin, Madison

CENTRAL HUDSON GAS CO. V. PUBLIC SERVICE
    COMMISSION
CERTIFICATION
CERTIORARI, WRIT OF
CHILLING EFFECT
CITY OF LOS ANGELES V. TAXPAYERS FOR VINCENT
CLAIMS COURT OF THE UNITED STATES
CLEVELAND BOARD OF EDUCATION V. LaFLEUR
COLUMBUS BOARD OF EDUCATION V. PENICK
COMITY
COMMERCE COURT
COMPANION CASE
COMPELLING STATE INTEREST
CONFERENCE
CONSENT DECREE
CONSTITUTIONAL COURTS
COOPER V. AARON
CORNELIUS V. NAACP LEGAL DEFENSE & EDUCATIONAL
    FUND
COURT OF CUSTOMS AND PATENT APPEALS
COURT OF INTERNATIONAL TRADE
COURT OF MILITARY APPEALS
CRAIG V. BOREN
CRAWFORD V. BOARD OF EDUCATION
DANDRIDGE V. WILLIAMS
DE FACTO/DE JURE
DeFUNIS V. ODEGAARD
DEPARTMENT OF AGRICULTURE V. MURRY
DIVORCE AND THE CONSTITUTION
DOCTRINE
DOUGLAS V. CALIFORNIA
DUN & BRADSTREET V. GREENMOSS BUILDERS, INC.
DUNN V. BLUMSTEIN
EDWARDS V. CALIFORNIA
EFFECTS ON COMMERCE
EISENSTADT V. BAIRD
EMERGENCY COURT OF APPEALS
EQUAL EMPLOYMENT OPPORTUNITY COMMISSION V.
    WYOMING
EQUAL PROTECTION OF THE LAWS
ERROR, WRIT OF
EUTHANASIA
EVANS V. ABNEY
EVITTS V. LUCEY
FEDERAL COURTS IMPROVEMENT ACT
FERGUSON V. SKRUPA
FINAL JUDGMENT RULE
FLAGG BROTHERS, INC. V. BROOKS
FOLEY V. CONNELIE
FREEDMAN V. MARYLAND
FREEDOM OF INTIMATE ASSOCIATION
FRONTIERO V. RICHARDSON
FULLILOVE V. KLUTZNICK
FUNDAMENTAL INTERESTS
GARCIA V. SAN ANTONIO METROPOLITAN TRANSIT
    AUTHORITY
GOESAERT V. CLEARY

GOLDBERG V. KELLY
GOLDWATER V. CARTER
GOMILLION V. LIGHTFOOT
GOSS V. LOPEZ
GRACE, UNITED STATES V.
GRAHAM V. RICHARDSON
GRANDFATHER CLAUSE
GRAY V. SANDERS
GREAT ATLANTIC & PACIFIC TEA
    COMPANY V. COTTRELL
GREEN V. NEW KENT COUNTY SCHOOL BOARD
GRIFFIN V. ILLINOIS
GRIFFIN V. SCHOOL BOARD OF PRINCE EDWARD COUNTY
GRISWOLD V. CONNECTICUT
GROVEY V. TOWNSEND
GULF OF TONKIN RESOLUTION
HAMPTON V. MOW SUN WONG
HARPER V. VIRGINIA STATE BOARD OF ELECTIONS
HARRIS V. McCRAE
HART, HENRY M.
HAWAII HOUSING AUTHORITY V. MIDKIFF
HEART OF ATLANTA MOTEL V. UNITED STATES
HEFFRON V. INTERNATIONAL SOCIETY FOR KRISHNA
    CONSCIOUSNESS
HILLS V. GAUTREAUX
HINES V. DAVIDOWITZ
HODEL V. VIRGINIA SURFACE MINING AND
    RECLAMATION ASSOCIATION
HODGSON AND THOMPSON V. BOWERBANK
HOSTILE AUDIENCE
HYDE AMENDMENT
ILLEGITIMACY
IMMIGRATION (with Gerald P. López)
INDIGENT
INGRAHAM V. WRIGHT
INTERLOCUTORY
INVIDIOUS DISCRIMINATION
IRREBUTTABLE PRESUMPTIONS
JACKSON V. METROPOLITAN EDISON COMPANY
JAMES V. VALTIERRA
JAPANESE AMERICAN CASES
JUDICIARY ACT OF 1875
KALVEN, HARRY, JR.
KEYES V. SCHOOL DISTRICT NO. 1 OF DENVER
KRAMER V. UNION FREE SCHOOL DISTRICT
LALLI V. LALLI
LARSON V. VALENTE
LEARY V. UNITED STATES
LEAST RESTRICTIVE MEANS TEST
LEE, UNITED STATES V.
LEGISLATIVE COURTS
LEGISLATIVE FACTS
LEVY V. LOUISIANA
LITERACY TEST
LORETTO V. TELEPROMPTER MANHATTAN
    CATV CO.
LOVING V. VIRGINIA

SUSPECT CLASSIFICATION
SWANN V. CHARLOTTE-MECKLENBURG BOARD OF
   EDUCATION
SWEATT V. PAINTER
TAKAHASHI V. FISH AND GAME COMMISSION
TAX COURT OF THE UNITED STATES
TAYLOR V. LOUISIANA
TERM (SUPREME COURT)
TERRITORIAL COURTS
TERRY V. ADAMS
THIRTEENTH AMENDMENT (JUDICIAL INTERPRETATION)
THOMAS V. INDIANA REVIEW BOARD
THOMAS V. UNION CARBIDE AGRICULTURAL PRODUCTS
   COMPANY
THREE-JUDGE COURTS
TINKER V. DES MOINES SCHOOL DISTRICT
TOOMER V. WITSELL
TOTH, UNITED STATES EX REL., V. QUARLES
TREATY OF GUADALUPE HIDALGO
   (with Gerald P. López)
TRIMBLE V. GORDON
TUCKER ACT
TUITION GRANT
UNCONSTITUTIONALITY
UNITED JEWISH ORGANIZATIONS OF WILLIAMSBURGH
   V. CAREY
UNITED STATES COURT OF APPEALS FOR THE FEDERAL
   CIRCUIT
UNITED STATES TRUST CO. OF NEW YORK V. NEW JERSEY
VACCINATION
VALLEY FORGE CHRISTIAN COLLEGE V. AMERICANS
   UNITED FOR SEPARATION OF CHURCH AND STATE
VENUE
VLANDIS V. KLINE
WAINWRIGHT V. SYKES
WALKER V. BIRMINGHAM
WARD V. ILLINOIS
WATKINS V. UNITED STATES
WAYTE V. UNITED STATES
WENGLER V. DRUGGISTS' MUTUAL INSURANCE CO.
WESBERRY V. SANDERS
WHALEN V. ROE
WIDMAR V. VINCENT
WILLIAMS V. VERMONT
YOUNGER V. HARRIS
ZABLOCKI V. REDHAIL

Don B. Kates, Jr.
   Attorney
   Benenson & Kates, San Francisco

   SECOND AMENDMENT

Andrew L. Kaufman
   Charles Stebbins Fairchild Professor of Law
   Harvard Law School

   CARDOZO, BENJAMIN N.

David Kaye
   Professor of Law
   Arizona State University

   SOCIAL SCIENCE RESEARCH AND CONSTITUTIONAL LAW
   (with Hans Zeisel)

Morton Keller
   Spector Professor of History
   Brandeis University

   CONSTITUTIONAL HISTORY, 1877–1901
   CONSTITUTIONAL HISTORY, 1901–1921

James H. Kettner
   Professor of History
   University of California, Berkeley

   CITIZENSHIP (HISTORICAL DEVELOPMENT)

Edward Keynes
   Professor of Political Science
   Pennsylvania State University

   VIETNAM WAR

Louis W. Koenig
   Professor of Political Science
   New York University

   CABINET

Donald P. Kommers
   Professor of Government and International Studies
   University of Notre Dame

   REGULATORY AGENCIES
   SUBJECTS OF COMMERCE
   SUPREMACY CLAUSE

Sheldon Krantz
   Professor of Law and Dean of the School of Law
   University of San Diego

   CRUEL AND UNUSUAL PUNISHMENT

James E. Krier
   Professor of Law
   University of Michigan

   ENVIRONMENTAL REGULATION AND THE CONSTITUTION

Samuel Krislov
   Professor of Political Science
   University of Minnesota, Twin Cities

   AMICUS CURIAE
   ULYSSES, A BOOK NAMED, UNITED STATES V.

Philip B. Kurland
William R. Kenan Distinguished Service Professor
The University of Chicago

APPOINTING AND REMOVAL POWER, PRESIDENTIAL
EXECUTIVE PRIVILEGE
IMPOUNDMENT OF FUNDS
PARDONING POWER
PRESIDENTIAL POWERS

Stanley I. Kutler
Fox Professor of American Institutions
University of Wisconsin, Madison

BAILEY V. DREXEL FURNITURE COMPANY
BRADLEY, JOSEPH P.
BUNTING V. OREGON
BUTLER, PIERCE
CATRON, JOHN
CHARLES RIVER BRIDGE V. WARREN BRIDGE COMPANY
CHILD LABOR AMENDMENT
CLIFFORD, NATHAN
CURTIS, BENJAMIN R.
DAVIS, DAVID
DAY, WILLIAM R.
EAKIN V. RAUB
EXECUTIVE ORDERS 9835 AND 10450
GIBSON, JOHN BANNISTER
HAMMER V. DAGENHART
HUNT, WARD
KEATING-OWEN CHILD LABOR ACT
KENT V. DULLES
LEGAL TENDER CASES
MATTHEWS, STANLEY
MCREYNOLDS, JAMES C.
MISSISSIPPI V. JOHNSON
MULLER V. OREGON
PITNEY, MAHLON
SANFORD, EDWARD T.
STRONG, WILLIAM
SWAYNE, NOAH H.
TRUAX V. CORRIGAN
VAN DEVANTER, WILLIS
WEST COAST HOTEL CO. V. PARRISH

Wayne R. LaFave
David C. Baum Professor of Law
Professor in the Center for Advanced Study,
University of Illinois

SEARCH AND SEIZURE

Jacob W. Landynski
Professor of Political Science
New School for Social Research

ADMINISTRATIVE SEARCH
AGNELLO V. UNITED STATES
AGUILAR V. TEXAS
ALMEIDA-SANCHEZ V. UNITED STATES
AUTOMOBILE SEARCH
BORDER SEARCH
BRINEGAR V. UNITED STATES
CALANDRA, UNITED STATES V.
CAMARA V. MUNICIPAL COURT
CARROLL V. UNITED STATES
CHIMEL V. CALIFORNIA
CONSENT SEARCH
DRAPER V. UNITED STATES
ELKINS V. UNITED STATES
EXIGENT CIRCUMSTANCES SEARCH
INFORMANT'S TIP
KER V. CALIFORNIA
MAPP V. OHIO
MARSHALL V. BARLOW'S INC.
PLAIN VIEW DOCTRINE
ROBINSON, UNITED STATES V.
SCHNECKLOTH V. BUSTAMONTE
SEARCH INCIDENT TO ARREST
SILVER PLATTER DOCTRINE
SILVERTHORNE LUMBER COMPANY V. UNITED STATES
SPINELLI V. UNITED STATES
STONE V. POWELL
TERRY V. OHIO
UNREASONABLE SEARCH
WEEKS V. UNITED STATES
WOLF V. COLORADO
WONG SUN V. UNITED STATES
WYMAN V. JAMES

Leon Letwin
Professor of Law
University of California, Los Angeles

EVIDENTIARY PRIVILEGES

William Letwin
Professor of Economics
London School of Economics and Political Science

ECONOMIC REGULATION AND THE CONSTITUTION

Betsy Levin
Professor of Law and Dean of the Law School
University of Colorado

EDUCATION AND THE CONSTITUTION

Leonard W. Levy
*Andrew W. Mellon All-Claremont Professor of the
Humanities*
Chairman, Graduate Faculty of History
The Claremont Graduate School

Wendy E. Levy
Deputy District Attorney
Los Angeles County

Anthony Lewis
Columnist
The New York Times
Lecturer on Law
Harvard Law School

Hans A. Linde
Justice
Supreme Court of Oregon

STATE CONSTITUTIONAL LAW

Charles Lister
Attorney
Covington & Burling, Washington, D.C.

HARLAN, JOHN MARSHALL (1899–1971)

Charles A. Lofgren
Crocker Professor of American Politics and History
Claremont McKenna College

CURTISS-WRIGHT EXPORT CORP., UNITED STATES V.
KOREAN WAR
MISSOURI V. HOLLAND
NATIONAL LEAGUE OF CITIES V. USERY
WAR POWERS

Gerald P. López
Professor of Law
Stanford Law School

CITIZENSHIP (THEORY)
IMMIGRATION (with Kenneth L. Karst)
TREATY OF GUADALUPE HIDALGO (with Kenneth L.
   Karst)
TREATY ON EXECUTION OF PENAL SENTENCES

Richard Loss
Evanston, Illinois

CORWIN, EDWARD S.

Daniel H. Lowenstein
Professor of Law
University of California, Los Angeles

HATCH ACTS

Theodore J. Lowi
John L. Senior Professor of American Institutions
Cornell University

POLITICAL PARTIES AND THE CONSTITUTION

Dennis J. Mahoney
Assistant Professor of Political Science
California State University, San Bernardino

ADAMS, SAMUEL
ADVICE AND CONSENT
AMNESTY
APTHEKER V. SECRETARY OF STATE
ARTICLES OF IMPEACHMENT (JOHNSON)

ARTICLES OF IMPEACHMENT (NIXON)
ASSOCIATION, THE
ATTAINDER OF TREASON
BAILEY V. ALABAMA
BALDWIN, ABRAHAM
BAREFOOT V. ESTELLE
BASSETT, RICHARD
BEACON THEATRES, INC. V. WESTOVER
BEARD, CHARLES A.
BECKER AMENDMENT
BEDFORD, GUNNING, JR.
BENIGN RACIAL CLASSIFICATIONS
BEVERIDGE, ALBERT J.
BICAMERALISM
BILL OF ATTAINDER
BILL OF CREDIT
BLAINE AMENDMENT
BLAIR, JOHN
BLOUNT, WILLIAM
BLUE RIBBON JURY
BOB JONES UNIVERSITY V. UNITED STATES
BORROWING POWER
BREARLY, DAVID
BRICKER AMENDMENT
BROAD CONSTRUCTION
BROOM, JACOB
BROWN V. ALLEN
BRYCE, JAMES
BUDGET
BUDGET AND ACCOUNTING ACT
BURGESS, JOHN W.
BURR, AARON
BUTLER, PIERCE
CAPITATION TAXES
CARROLL, DANIEL
CARY, JOHN W.
CEASE-AND-DESIST ORDER
CHIPMAN, NATHANIEL
CLOSED SHOP
CLOTURE
CLYMER, GEORGE
COKER V. GEORGIA
COLLECTIVE BARGAINING
COMMONWEALTH STATUS
COMMUNICATIONS ACT
CONCURRENT RESOLUTION
CONCURRING OPINION
CONFEDERATE CONSTITUTION
CONGRESSIONAL PRIVILEGES AND IMMUNITIES
CONSTITUTIONAL HISTORY, 1977–1985
CORWIN AMENDMENT
CRAMER V. UNITED STATES
CRIMINAL JUSTICE ACT OF 1964
CROLY, HERBERT
DAIRY QUEEN, INC. V. WOOD
DALLAS, ALEXANDER J.
DAYTON, JONATHAN
DECISION

POCKET VETO
POCKET VETO CASE
POLICE POWER
POSSE COMITATUS ACT
POWELL v. MCCORMACK
POWELL, THOMAS REED
PRATT, CHARLES
PREAMBLE
PRIVACY ACT
PRIVILEGE FROM ARREST
PRIVY COUNCIL
PROHIBITION
QUIRIN, EX PARTE
RANDOLPH, EDMUND
RATIFICATION OF CONSTITUTIONAL AMENDMENTS
RATIO DECIDENDI
READ, GEORGE
RECALL
REFERENDUM
REID v. COVERT
RETROACTIVITY OF LEGISLATION
REVENUE SHARING
RIGHT-PRIVILEGE DISTINCTION (with Kenneth L. Karst)
RODNEY, CAESAR AUGUSTUS
ROOSEVELT, THEODORE
RUTLEDGE, JOHN
SCHICK v. REED
SCHNELL v. DAVIS
SCHOULER, JAMES
SEDITION
SELECTIVE DRAFT LAW CASES
SELECTIVE SERVICE ACTS
SERIATIM
SEVENTEENTH AMENDMENT
SEVENTH AMENDMENT
SHAYS' REBELLION
SHERMAN, ROGER
SMITH, J. ALLEN
SOUNDTRUCKS AND AMPLIFIERS
SOVEREIGNTY
SPAIGHT, RICHARD DOBBS
SPOT RESOLUTIONS
STARE DECISIS
STATE
STATES' RIGHTS
SUBVERSIVE ACTIVITY
SWAIN v. ALABAMA
TAFT, ROBERT A.
TAYLOR, JOHN
TERRITORIES
THIRD AMENDMENT
THORPE, FRANCIS NEWTON
TITLES OF NOBILITY
TOCQUEVILLE, ALEXIS DE
TOWNSHEND ACTS
TROP v. DULLES

TUCKER, HENRY ST. GEORGE
TUCKER, JOHN RANDOLPH
TUCKER, N. BEVERLEY
TWELFTH AMENDMENT
TWENTIETH AMENDMENT
TWENTY-FIFTH AMENDMENT
TWENTY-FIRST AMENDMENT
TWENTY-FOURTH AMENDMENT
TWENTY-SECOND AMENDMENT
TWENTY-SIXTH AMENDMENT
TWENTY-THIRD AMENDMENT
VATTEL, EMERICH DE
VOLSTEAD ACT
WAR POWERS ACTS
WASHINGTON, GEORGE
WASHINGTON'S FAREWELL ADDRESS
WEEMS v. UNITED STATES
WELFARE BENEFITS
WILLIAMSON, HUGH
WILLIAMSON v. LEE OPTICAL COMPANY
WILLOUGHBY, WESTEL W.
WILSON, WOODROW
YATES, ROBERT
YOUNG, EX PARTE
ZEMEL v. RUSK

Daniel R. Mandelker
Stamper Professor of Law
Washington University, St. Louis

ZONING (with Barbara Ross)

Everett E. Mann, Jr.
Associate Professor of Public Policy and Administration
California State College, Bakersfield

FREEDOM OF INFORMATION ACT

Burke Marshall
Nicholas deB. Katzenbach Professor of Law
Yale Law School
Former Solicitor General of the United States

ATTORNEY GENERAL AND DEPARTMENT OF JUSTICE

Alpheus Thomas Mason
McCormick Professor of Jurisprudence, Emeritus
Princeton University

ROBERTS, OWEN J.
STONE, HARLAN F.
TAFT, WILLIAM HOWARD

Charles W. McCurdy
Associate Professor of History and Law
University of Virginia

BLATCHFORD, SAMUEL
FIELD, STEPHEN J.
FULLER, MELVILLE W.
GRAY, HORACE
JACKSON, HOWELL E.
LAMAR, L. Q. C.
MILLER, SAMUEL F.
MONETARY POWER
PECKHAM, RUFUS W.
SHIRAS, GEORGE, JR.
WAITE COURT
WOODS, WILLIAM B.

Gary L. McDowell
Associate Professor of Political Science
Newcomb College of Tulane University

CONGRESS AND THE SUPREME COURT

Carl McGowan
Senior Judge
United States Court of Appeals for the
District of Columbia Circuit

UNITED STATES COURTS OF APPEALS

Robert B. McKay
Professor of Law
New York University

REAPPORTIONMENT

Daniel J. Meador
James Monroe Professor of Law
University of Virginia

COKE, EDWARD

Bernard D. Meltzer
Distinguished Service Professor of Law, Emeritus
The University of Chicago

RIGHT TO WORK LAWS

Wallace Mendelson
Professor of Government
The University of Texas at Austin

CONTRACT CLAUSE

Frank I. Michelman
Professor of Law
Harvard Law School

PROCEDURAL DUE PROCESS OF LAW, CIVIL

Abner J. Mikva
Judge
U.S. Court of Appeals for the District of
Columbia Circuit

PREVENTIVE DETENTION

Arthur S. Miller
Professor of Law, Emeritus
The George Washington University

CONSTITUTIONAL REASON OF STATE
CORPORATIONS AND THE CONSTITUTION

Paul J. Mishkin
Emanuel S. Heller Professor of Law
University of California, Berkeley

HABEAS CORPUS

Robert H. Mnookin
Professor of Law
Stanford Law School

CHILDREN'S RIGHTS
GAULT, IN RE
GINSBURG V. NEW YORK
JUVENILE PROCEEDINGS

Henry P. Monaghan
Thomas Macioce Professor of Law
Columbia University

CONSTITUTIONAL COMMON LAW

*Donald G. Morgan
Professor of Politics
Mount Holyoke College

JOHNSON, WILLIAM

Edmund S. Morgan
Sterling Professor of History
Yale University

CONSTITUTIONAL HISTORY BEFORE 1776

Richard E. Morgan
*William Nelson Cromwell Professor of
Constitutional Law and Government*
Bowdoin College

ABINGTON TOWNSHIP SCHOOL DISTRICT V. SCHEMPP
BOARD OF EDUCATION V. ALLEN

* Deceased.

CANTWELL V. CONNECTICUT
CHURCH OF JESUS CHRIST OF LATTER-DAY SAINTS V.
  UNITED STATES
COCHRAN V. LOUISIANA BOARD OF EDUCATION
COMMITTEE FOR PUBLIC EDUCATION & RELIGIOUS
  LIBERTY V. REGAN
DAVIS V. BEASON
DOREMUS V. BOARD OF EDUCATION OF HAWTHORNE
ENGEL V. VITALE
EPPERSON V. ARKANSAS
EVERSON V. BOARD OF EDUCATION OF EWING TOWNSHIP
FLAG SALUTE CASES
GIROUARD V. UNITED STATES
HAMILTON V. REGENTS OF UNIVERSITY OF CALIFORNIA
JACOBSON V. MASSACHUSETTS
LEMON V. KURTZMAN
LOVELL V. GRIFFIN
MCCOLLUM, ILLINOIS EX REL., V. BOARD OF EDUCATION
MURDOCK V. PENNSYLVANIA
PRINCE V. MASSACHUSETTS
SCHWIMMER, UNITED STATES V.
SEEGER, UNITED STATES V.
SHERBERT V. VERNER
TORCASO V. WATKINS
WISCONSIN V. YODER
WOLMAN V. WALTER
ZORACH V. CLAUSEN

Paul L. Murphy
  Professor of History and American Studies
  University of Minnesota

ALIEN REGISTRATION ACT
ATOMIC ENERGY ACT
ATTORNEY GENERAL'S LIST
CHAFEE, ZECHERIAH, JR.
COMMUNIST CONTROL ACT
CONGRESSIONAL BUDGET AND IMPOUNDMENT CONTROL
  ACT
CONSTITUTIONAL HISTORY, 1921–1933
CONSTITUTIONAL HISTORY, 1945–1961
DISTRICT OF COLUMBIA REPRESENTATION AMENDMENT
DISTRICT OF COLUMBIA SELF-GOVERNING AND
  GOVERNMENT REORGANIZATION ACT
ECONOMIC STABILIZATION ACT
ELEMENTARY AND SECONDARY EDUCATION ACT
EMERGENCY PRICE CONTROL ACT
ESPIONAGE ACT
FEDERAL IMMUNITY ACT
FULL EMPLOYMENT ACT
HEALTH INSURANCE FOR THE AGED ACT
HOUSE COMMITTEE ON UN-AMERICAN ACTIVITIES
INTERNAL SECURITY ACT
JENCKS ACT
LANDRUM-GRIFFIN ACT
MUNDT-NIXON BILL
OMNIBUS CRIME CONTROL AND SAFE STREETS ACT
ORGANIZED CRIME CONTROL ACT

PENNSYLVANIA V. NELSON
REPORT OF THE STATE CHIEF JUSTICES
SEDITION ACT
SELECTIVE SERVICE ACT
SHEPPARD-TOWNER MATERNITY ACT
SOUTHERN MANIFESTO
STEEL SEIZURE CONTROVERSY
SUBVERSIVE ACTIVITIES CONTROL BOARD
TAFT-HARTLEY LABOR MANAGEMENT RELATIONS ACT
WATERGATE AND THE CONSTITUTION
YATES V. UNITED STATES

Walter F. Murphy
  McCormick Professor of Jurisprudence
  Princeton University

JUDICIAL STRATEGY
JUDICIAL SUPREMACY

William P. Murphy
  Paul B. Eaton Professor of Law
  The University of North Carolina at Chapel Hill

FAIR LABOR STANDARDS ACT
MAXIMUM HOURS AND MINIMUM WAGES LEGISLATION

John M. Murrin
  Professor of History
  Princeton University

BRITISH CONSTITUTION

William E. Nelson
  Professor of Law
  New York University

FOURTEENTH AMENDMENT (FRAMING)

Ira Nerken
  Attorney
  Latham, Watkins & Hills, Washington, D.C.

CONSCRIPTION (with Richard Danzig)

Burt Neuborne
  Professor of Law
  New York University
  Director of Litigation
  American Civil Liberties Union

BLACKMUN, HARRY A.
LITIGATION STRATEGY

Roger K. Newman
  Attorney
  New York

BLACK, HUGO L.
CAHN, EDMOND

R. Kent Newmyer
Professor of History
University of Connecticut

BALDWIN, HENRY
BARBOUR, PHILIP P.
MCKINLEY, JOHN
MCLEAN, JOHN
TANEY COURT
TRIMBLE, ROBERT

*Melville B. Nimmer
Professor of Law
University of California, Los Angeles

COPYRIGHT
PRIVACY AND THE FIRST AMENDMENT
SYMBOLIC SPEECH

W. John Niven
Professor of History
The Claremont Graduate School

VAN BUREN, MARTIN

John T. Noonan, Jr.
Judge
United States Court of Appeals for the Ninth
Circuit
Former Professor of Law
University of California, Berkeley

REAGAN, RONALD W.

John E. Nowak
Professor of Law
University of Illinois

BREACH OF THE PEACE
FELONY
SUBPOENA
TRESPASS

David M. Oshinsky
Professor of History
Rutgers University

MCCARTHYISM

Lewis J. Paper
Attorney
Washington, D.C.

BRANDEIS, LOUIS D.

* Deceased.

Michael E. Parrish
Professor of History
University of California, San Diego

AFROYIM V. RUSK
BRIDGES V. CALIFORNIA
BURTON, HAROLD H.
BYRNES, JAMES F.
CLARKE, JOHN H.
COMMONWEALTH V. SACCO AND VANZETTI
CONSTITUTIONAL HISTORY, 1933–1945
DEBS V. UNITED STATES
ELFBRANDT V. RUSSELL
FRANKFURTER, FELIX
FROHWERK V. UNITED STATES
GERENDE V. BOARD OF SUPERVISORS OF ELECTIONS OF
    BALTIMORE
GIBONEY V. EMPIRE STORAGE AND ICE COMPANY
HUGHES, CHARLES EVANS
IRVIN V. DOWD
JACKSON, ROBERT H.
JOINT ANTI-FASCIST REFUGEE COMMITTEE V. MCGRATH
KENNEDY, JOHN F.
LINMARK ASSOCIATES V. WILLINGBORO
LOVETT, UNITED STATES V.
MCKENNA, JOSEPH
NIEMOTKO V. MARYLAND
PARKER V. LEVY
PROCUNIER V. MARTINEZ
ROBEL, UNITED STATES V.
ROSENBERG V. UNITED STATES
RUTLEDGE, WILEY B.
SHAUGHNESSY, UNITED STATES EX REL. MEZEI V.
STATE OF TENNESSEE V. SCOPES
STROMBERG V. CALIFORNIA
WHITE, EDWARD D.
WHITTAKER, CHARLES E.
WIEMAN V. UPDEGRAFF

J. Francis Paschal
Professor of Law
Duke University

SUTHERLAND, GEORGE H.

Michael J. Perry
Professor of Law
Northwestern University

ABORTION AND THE CONSTITUTION

Merrill D. Peterson
*Thomas Jefferson Professor of History and
    Former Dean of Faculty*
University of Virginia

ADAMS, JOHN
ALIEN AND SEDITION ACTS

AMERICAN SYSTEM
BANK OF THE UNITED STATES ACTS
CALHOUN, JOHN C.
CLAY, HENRY
CONSTITUTIONAL HISTORY, 1789–1801
CONSTITUTIONAL HISTORY, 1801–1829
INTERNAL IMPROVEMENTS
JACKSON, ANDREW
JEFFERSON, THOMAS
LOUISIANA PURCHASE TREATY
PROCLAMATION OF NEUTRALITY
VIRGINIA AND KENTUCKY RESOLUTIONS
WHISKEY REBELLION

Leo Pfeffer
Professor of Constitutional Law
Long Island University
Former General Counsel
American Jewish Congress

AMERICAN JEWISH CONGRESS
CHILD BENEFIT THEORY
CULTS (RELIGIOUS) AND THE CONSTITUTION
GOVERNMENT AID TO RELIGIOUS INSTITUTIONS
RELEASED TIME
RELIGION AND FRAUD
RELIGION IN PUBLIC SCHOOLS
RELIGIOUS LIBERTY
RELIGIOUS TEST FOR PUBLIC OFFICE
RELIGIOUS USE OF STATE PROPERTY
SUNDAY CLOSING LAWS

Louis H. Pollak
Judge
United States District Court, Eastern
    District of Pennsylvania

VOTING RIGHTS

Robert Post
Professor of Law
University of California, Berkeley

BRENNAN, WILLIAM J.

Monroe E. Price
Professor of Law and Dean
Cardozo School of Law
Yeshiva University of New York

BROADCASTING
FAIRNESS DOCTRINE
PRISONERS' RIGHTS
STEWART, POTTER

C. Herman Pritchett
Professor of Political Science, Emeritus
University of California, Santa Barbara

CONGRESSIONAL MEMBERSHIP
VINSON COURT

A. Kenneth Pye
Samuel Fox Mordecai Professor of Law
Duke University

SPEEDY TRIAL

David M. Rabban
Professor of Law
The University of Texas at Austin

ACADEMIC FREEDOM

Jeremy Rabkin
Professor of Political Science
Cornell University

LEGISLATIVE POWER

Norman Redlich
Dean and Judge Edward Weinfeld Professor of Law
New York University

NINTH AMENDMENT

Willis L. M. Reese
*Charles Evans Hughes Professor of Law, Emeritus
    and Special Service Professor*
Columbia University

FULL FAITH AND CREDIT

Donald H. Regan
Professor of Law and Professor of Philosophy
University of Michigan

PHILOSOPHY AND THE CONSTITUTION

John Phillip Reid
Professor of Law
New York University

COLONIAL CHARTERS
DOE, CHARLES

Deborah L. Rhode
Professor of Law
Stanford Law School

EQUAL RIGHTS AMENDMENT
NINETEENTH AMENDMENT

Charles E. Rice
Professor of Law
University of Notre Dame

FREEDOM OF PETITION

Kenneth F. Ripple
Judge
United States Court of Appeals for the
    Seventh Circuit
Professor of Law
University of Notre Dame

CHIEF JUSTICE, ROLE OF

John P. Roche
*Professor of Civilization and Foreign Affairs
    and Former Dean of the Fletcher
    School of Law and Diplomacy*
Tufts University

CONSTITUTIONAL CONVENTION OF 1787

Donald M. Roper
Professor of History
State University of New York, New Paltz

KENT, JAMES
LIVINGSTON, HENRY BROCKHOLST
THOMPSON, SMITH

Arthur Rosett
Professor of Law
University of California, Los Angeles

ANTITRUST LAW AND THE CONSTITUTION
PLEA BARGAINING
REED, STANLEY F.
UNCONSTITUTIONAL CONDITIONS

Barbara Ross
Attorney
Ross & Hardies, Chicago

ZONING (with Daniel R. Mandelker)

Ralph A. Rossum
Alice Tweed Tuohy Professor of Government
Claremont McKenna College

DENATURALIZATION
DEPORTATION
EXPATRIATION
NATURALIZATION
WILSON, JAMES

Eugene V. Rostow
Sterling Professor of Law, Emeritus
Yale Law School
*Distinguished Visiting Research Professor of Law
    and Diplomacy*
National Defense University

COMMANDER-IN-CHIEF
WAR, FOREIGN AFFAIRS, AND THE CONSTITUTION

W. W. Rostow
Professor of Economics and History
The University of Texas at Austin

JOHNSON, LYNDON BAINES

Wilfrid E. Rumble
Professor of Political Science
Vassar College

LEGAL REALISM
POUND, ROSCOE
SOCIOLOGICAL JURISPRUDENCE

Robert A. Rutland
Editor-in-Chief, Papers of James Madison
University of Virginia

RATIFICATION OF THE CONSTITUTION

Stephen A. Saltzburg
Professor of Law
University of Virginia

REASONABLE DOUBT

Joseph L. Sax
*Philip A. Hart Distinguished University
    Professor of Law*
University of Michigan

TAKING OF PROPERTY

Frederick F. Schauer
Professor of Law
University of Michigan

NEW YORK TIMES COMPANY V. UNITED STATES

Harry N. Scheiber
Professor of Law
University of California, Berkeley

AFFECTED WITH A PUBLIC INTEREST
COMPETITIVE FEDERALISM
COOPERATIVE FEDERALISM
DUAL FEDERALISM
EMINENT DOMAIN
FEDERALISM (HISTORY)
GRANGER CASES
NEBBIA V. NEW YORK
PUBLIC PURPOSE DOCTRINE
STATE POLICE POWER
VESTED RIGHTS DOCTRINE
WEST RIVER BRIDGE COMPANY V. DIX

Arthur Schlesinger, Jr.
Schweitzer Professor in the Humanities
City University of New York

ROOSEVELT, FRANKLIN D.

Benno C. Schmidt, Jr.
President
Yale University

COMMERCIAL SPEECH
FREE PRESS/FAIR TRIAL
LIBEL AND THE FIRST AMENDMENT
PRIOR RESTRAINT AND CENSORSHIP
REPORTER'S PRIVILEGE
SHIELD LAWS
WHITE COURT

Gary T. Schwartz
Professor of Law
University of California, Los Angeles

ECONOMIC ANALYSIS

Herman Schwartz
Professor of Law
Washington College of Law, American University

ALDERMAN V. UNITED STATES
BERGER V. NEW YORK
ELECTRONIC EAVESDROPPING
GELBARD V. UNITED STATES
IRVINE V. CALIFORNIA
KATZ V. UNITED STATES
LOPEZ V. UNITED STATES
NARDONE V. UNITED STATES
NATIONAL SECURITY AND THE FOURTH AMENDMENT
OLMSTEAD V. UNITED STATES
ON LEE V. UNITED STATES
SILVERMAN V. UNITED STATES
UNITED STATES DISTRICT COURT, UNITED STATES V.
WHITE, UNITED STATES V.
WIRETAPPING

Murray L. Schwartz
Professor of Law
University of California, Los Angeles

VINSON, FRED M.

David L. Shapiro
William Nelson Cromwell Professor of Law
Harvard Law School

ERIE RAILROAD V. TOMPKINS
FEDERAL COMMON LAW, CIVIL
SWIFT V. TYSON

Martin Shapiro
Professor of Law
University of California, Berkeley

ABOOD V. DETROIT BOARD OF EDUCATION
ABRAMS V. UNITED STATES
ADDERLEY V. FLORIDA
ADLER V. BOARD OF EDUCATION OF CITY OF NEW YORK
AMERICAN COMMUNICATIONS ASSOCIATION V. DOWDS
BAD TENDENCY TEST
BALANCING TEST
BARENBLATT V. UNITED STATES
BEAUHARNAIS V. ILLINOIS
BRANDENBURG V. OHIO
BUCKLEY V. VALEO
CAPTIVE AUDIENCE
CHAPLINSKY V. NEW HAMPSHIRE
CLEAR AND PRESENT DANGER
COHEN V. CALIFORNIA
COMMUNIST PARTY V. SUBVERSIVE ACTIVITY CONTROL BOARD
COX V. LOUISIANA
COX V. NEW HAMPSHIRE
DE JONGE V. OREGON
DENNIS V. UNITED STATES
FEINER V. NEW YORK
FIGHTING WORDS
FIRST NATIONAL BANK OF BOSTON V. BELLOTTI
GIBSON V. FLORIDA LEGISLATIVE INVESTIGATION COMMISSION
GITLOW V. NEW YORK
HERNDON V. LOWRY
HUDGENS V. N.L.R.B.
KEYISHIAN V. BOARD OF REGENTS
KONIGSBERG V. STATE BAR OF CALIFORNIA
KOVACS V. COOPER
LAIRD V. TATUM
MARSH V. ALABAMA
MASSES PUBLISHING COMPANY V. PATTEN
MCCLOSKEY, ROBERT G.
MCGRAIN V. DAUGHERTY
MIAMI HERALD PUBLISHING COMPANY V. TORNILLO
NAACP V. BUTTON
NEAR V. MINNESOTA EX REL. OLSON
RED LION BROADCASTING CO. V. F.C.C.
SCALES V. UNITED STATES
SCHENCK V. UNITED STATES
SCHWARE V. NEW MEXICO BOARD OF BAR EXAMINERS
SPEISER V. RANDALL
TERMINIELLO V. CHICAGO
THORNHILL V. ALABAMA
UPHAUS V. WYMAN
VIRGINIA STATE BOARD OF PHARMACY V. VIRGINIA CITIZENS CONSUMER COUNCIL
WHITNEY V. CALIFORNIA

Steven H. Shiffrin
Professor of Law
University of California, Los Angeles

BRANZBURG V. HAYES
COLUMBIA BROADCASTING SYSTEM V. DEMOCRATIC
    NATIONAL COMMITTEE
COOLIDGE V. NEW HAMPSHIRE
COX BROADCASTING CORP. V. COHN
FEDERAL COMMUNICATIONS COMMISSION V. PACIFICA
    FOUNDATION
GOVERNMENT SPEECH
GROUP LIBEL
KINGSLEY INTERNATIONAL PICTURES CORP.
    V. REGENTS
LISTENERS' RIGHTS
MARKETPLACE OF IDEAS
OBSCENITY
RIGHT TO KNOW
TWO-LEVEL THEORY

Bernard H. Siegan
Distinguished Professor of Law
University of San Diego

ECONOMIC LIBERTIES AND THE CONSTITUTION

Stanley Siegel
Professor of Law
University of California, Los Angeles

POSTAL POWER

Jay A. Sigler
Distinguished Professor of Political Science
Rutgers University

DOUBLE JEOPARDY

Thomas B. Silver
President
Public Research Syndicated

COOLIDGE, CALVIN
HARDING, WARREN G.

Aviam Soifer
Professor of Law
Boston University

BRANTI V. FINKEL
CAROLENE PRODUCTS CO., UNITED STATES V.
GUILT BY ASSOCIATION
RICHMOND NEWSPAPERS, INC. V. VIRGINIA

Theodore J. St. Antoine
James E. and Sarah A. Degan Professor of Law
University of Michigan

BOYCOTT
PICKETING

Robert L. Stern
Attorney
Mayer, Brown & Platt, Chicago

COMMERCE CLAUSE
DARBY LUMBER COMPANY, UNITED STATES V.
WAGNER ACT CASES

Gerald Stourzh
Professor of History
University of Vienna

HAMILTON, ALEXANDER

Frank R. Strong
*Cary C. Boshamer University Distinguished
    Professor of Law, Emeritus*
University of North Carolina

FUNDAMENTAL LAW AND THE SUPREME COURT
LAW OF THE LAND

Philippa Strum
Professor of Political Science
City University of New York (Brooklyn College and
    the Graduate Center)

POLITICAL QUESTIONS

*William F. Swindler
John Marshall Professor of Law
Marshall-Wythe School of Law
College of William and Mary

BLACKSTONE, WILLIAM

Nathan Tarcov
Associate Professor of Political Science
University of Chicago

POPULAR SOVEREIGNTY (IN DEMOCRATIC POLITICAL
    THEORY)

Telford Taylor
Nash Professor of Law, Emeritus
Columbia University
*Dr. Herman George and Kate Kaiser Professor of
    Constitutional Law*
Cardozo College of Law
Yeshiva University of New York

LEGISLATIVE INVESTIGATIONS

Glen E. Thurow

* Deceased.

Associate Professor of Politics
University of Dallas

DORMANT POWERS
EXCLUSIVE POWERS

Laurence H. Tribe
Tyler Professor of Constitutional Law
Harvard Law School

SUBSTANTIVE DUE PROCESS OF LAW

Phillip R. Trimble
Professor of Law
University of California, Los Angeles

DAMES & MOORE V. REGAN
EXTRATERRITORIALITY

Mark V. Tushnet
Professor of Law
Georgetown University

MARSHALL, THURGOOD

*Arvo Van Alstyne
Professor of Law
University of Utah
Commissioner of Higher Education
State of Utah

INVERSE CONDEMNATION
JUST COMPENSATION
PUBLIC USE

William Van Alstyne
Perkins Professor of Law
Duke University

IMPLIED POWERS
JUDICIAL ACTIVISM AND JUDICIAL RESTRAINT
SUPREME COURT (ROLE IN AMERICAN GOVERNMENT)

Jonathan D. Varat
Professor of Law
University of California, Los Angeles

ADVISORY OPINION
CASES AND CONTROVERSIES
COLLUSIVE SUIT
FLAST V. COHEN
INVALID ON ITS FACE
JUSTICIABILITY
MOOTNESS
OVERBREADTH
PUBLIC EMPLOYEES

* Deceased.

RIPENESS
SIERRA CLUB V. MORTON
STANDING
STOCKHOLDER'S SUIT
STUDENTS CHALLENGING REGULATORY AGENCY
    PROCEDURES (SCRAP), UNITED STATES V.
TAXPAYERS' AND CITIZENS' SUITS
VAGUENESS
WHITE, BYRON R.

Maurice J. C. Vile
Professor of History
University of Kent at Canterbury

SEPARATION OF POWERS

*Clement Ellery Vose
John E. Andrus Professor of Government
Wesleyan University

TEST CASE

Kim McLane Wardlaw
Attorney
O'Melveny & Myers, Los Angeles

BANTAM BOOKS V. SULLIVAN
ERZNOZNIK V. JACKSONVILLE
GANNETT V. DEPASQUALE
HERBERT V. LANDO
JACOBELLIS V. OHIO
KINGSLEY BOOKS, INC. V. BROWN
MEMOIRS V. MASSACHUSETTS
MILLER V. CALIFORNIA
NEBRASKA PRESS ASSOCIATION V. STUART
ROTH V. UNITED STATES
SNEPP V. UNITED STATES
STANLEY V. GEORGIA

Stephen L. Wasby
Professor of Political Science
State University of New York, Albany

IMPACT OF SUPREME COURT DECISIONS

Lloyd L. Weinreb
Professor of Law
Harvard Law School

FAIR TRIAL
WARRANTLESS SEARCH

Robert Weisberg
Professor of Law
Stanford Law School

CAPITAL PUNISHMENT

Harry H. Wellington
Sterling Professor of Law
Yale Law School

LABOR AND THE CONSTITUTION

Peter Westen
Professor of Law
University of Michigan

COMPULSORY PROCESS
CONFRONTATION, RIGHT OF
HEARSAY RULES

Burns H. Weston
Bessie Dutton Murray Professor of Law
University of Iowa

BELMONT, UNITED STATES V.
EXECUTIVE AGREEMENTS
INTERNATIONAL EMERGENCY ECONOMIC POWERS
    ACT
MARSHALL PLAN
NORTH ATLANTIC TREATY
PINK, UNITED STATES V.
STATUS OF FORCES AGREEMENT
TREATY POWER
UNITED NATIONS CHARTER

G. Edward White
Professor of Law
University of Virginia

HOLMES, OLIVER WENDELL
WARREN COURT

James Boyd White
*L. Hart Wright Professor of Law and
Professor of English Language and Literature*
University of Michigan

ARREST
BURDEN OF PROOF
FEDERAL RULES OF CRIMINAL PROCEDURE
JURY DISCRIMINATION

Charles H. Whitebread
George T. Pfleger Professor of Law
University of Southern California

DISCOVERY
INDICTMENT
INFORMATION
MERE EVIDENCE RULE
MIRANDA RULES
MISDEMEANOR
PRESENTMENT
PROBABLE CAUSE

STOP AND FRISK
VOIR DIRE

William M. Wiecek
Congdon Professor of Public Law and Legislation
Syracuse University

ABLEMAN V. BOOTH
ABOLITIONIST CONSTITUTIONAL THEORY
ANNEXATION OF TEXAS
BLACK CODES
CHASE COURT
CIVIL LIBERTIES AND THE ANTISLAVERY CONTROVERSY
COMPROMISE OF 1850
CONFISCATION ACTS
CONQUERED PROVINCES THEORY
CONSTITUTIONAL HISTORY, 1829–1848
DANIEL, PETER V.
FORCE ACT
FORCE ACTS
FREEDMEN'S BUREAU
FUGITIVE SLAVERY
GROVES V. SLAUGHTER
GUARANTEE CLAUSE
JOINT COMMITTEE ON RECONSTRUCTION
KANSAS-NEBRASKA ACT
LECOMPTON CONSTITUTION
LINCOLN'S PLAN OF RECONSTRUCTION
LINCOLN-DOUGLAS DEBATES
LUTHER V. BORDEN
MAYSVILLE ROAD BILL
MCCARDLE, EX PARTE
MILITARY RECONSTRUCTION ACTS
MISSOURI COMPROMISE
MORRILL ACT
NASHVILLE CONVENTION RESOLUTIONS
NULLIFICATION
OMNIBUS ACT
PEONAGE
PERSONAL LIBERTY LAWS
POPULAR SOVEREIGNTY AND SLAVERY IN THE
    TERRITORIES
PRIZE CASES
PROHIBITION OF SLAVE TRADE ACT
REPUBLICAN FORM OF GOVERNMENT
SECESSION
SLAVERY IN THE TERRITORIES
SOMERSET'S CASE
SOUTH CAROLINA ORDINANCE OF NULLIFICATION
SOUTH CAROLINA ORDINANCE OF SECESSION
STATE SUICIDE THEORY
STRADER V. GRAHAM
TANEY, ROGER B.
TENURE OF OFFICE ACT
THREE-FIFTHS CLAUSE
WAYNE, JAMES M.

J. Harvie Wilkinson III
Judge
United States Court of Appeals for the Fourth
    Circuit

POWELL, LEWIS F., JR.

Peter Woll
Professor of Politics
Brandeis University

BUREAUCRACY

C. Vann Woodward
Sterling Professor of History, Emeritus
Yale University

COMPROMISE OF 1877

L. Kinvin Wroth
Professor of Law and Dean of the School of Law
University of Maine

COMMON LAW
RULE OF LAW

Stephen C. Yeazell
Professor of Law
University of California, Los Angeles

ADMINISTRATIVE LAW
CLASS ACTION
COLLATERAL ATTACK
CONTEMPT POWER
FAIR HEARING
INJUNCTION
INSTITUTIONAL LITIGATION (with Theodore Eisenberg)
JURISDICTION
NOTICE

Hans Zeisel
Professor of Law, Emeritus
The University of Chicago

SOCIAL SCIENCE RESEARCH AND CONSTITUTIONAL LAW
    (with David Kaye)

John Zvesper
Professor of Politics
University of East Anglia at Norwich

RIGHT OF REVOLUTION

ABBATE v. UNITED STATES

See: *Bartkus v. Illinois*

ABINGTON TOWNSHIP SCHOOL DISTRICT v. SCHEMPP
374 U.S. 203 (1963)

A Pennsylvania statute required that at least ten verses from the Holy Bible be read, without comment, at the opening of each public school day. A child might be excused from this exercise upon the written request of his parents or guardian.

In ENGEL V. VITALE (1962) the school prayer held unconstitutional had been written by state officials. The question in *Schempp* was whether this made a difference—there being no claim that Pennsylvania was implicated in the authorship of the holy scripture.

Justice TOM C. CLARK concluded that the Pennsylvania exercise suffered from an establishment-clause infirmity every bit as grave as that afflicting New York's prayer. Clark's opinion in *Schempp* was the first strict separationist opinion of the Court not written by Justice HUGO L. BLACK, and Clark formulated a test for establishment clause validity with a precision that had eluded Black. A state program touching upon religion or religious institutions must have a valid secular purpose and must not have the primary effect of advancing or inhibiting religion. The Pennsylvania Bible reading program failed the test on both counts.

Justices WILLIAM O. DOUGLAS and WILLIAM J.

BRENNAN concurred separately in opinions reflecting an even stricter separationism than Clark's. Justice ARTHUR J. GOLDBERG also filed a brief concurring opinion.

Justice POTTER STEWART dissented, as he had in *Engel*, arguing that religious exercises as part of public ceremonies were permissible so long as children were not coerced to participate.

Schempp, along with *Murray v. Curlett* (decided the same day), settled whatever lingering question there may have been about the constitutionality of RELIGION IN PUBLIC SCHOOLS.

RICHARD E. MORGAN

ABLEMAN v. BOOTH
21 Howard 506 (1859)

Ableman v. Booth, Chief Justice ROGER B. TANEY's last major opinion, was part of the dramatic confrontation between the Wisconsin Supreme Court, intent on judicial nullification of the FUGITIVE SLAVE ACTS, and the Supreme Court of the United States, seeking to protect the reach of that statute into the free states.

For his role in organizing a mob that freed Joshua Glover, an alleged fugitive, Sherman Booth was charged with violation of the Fugitive Slave Act of 1850. After trial and conviction, he was released by a writ of habeas corpus from the Wisconsin Supreme Court, which held the Fugitive Slave Act unconstitutional, the first instance in which a state court did so. The Wisconsin court instructed its clerk to make no return to a WRIT OF ERROR from the United States Supreme Court and no entry on the records of the court concerning that writ, thus defying the United States Supreme Court.

The Court took JURISDICTION despite the procedural irregularity. In a magisterial opinion for a unanimous Court, Taney condemned the obstruction of the Wisconsin court and reaffirmed federal JUDICIAL SUPREMACY under section 25 of the JUDICIARY ACT OF 1789. Because the state's sovereignty "is limited and restricted by the Constitution of the United States," no state court process, including habeas corpus, could interfere with the enforcement of federal law. Taney also delivered two significant dicta. He anticipated the later doctrine of DUAL SOVEREIGNTY, which was to hamper state and federal regulatory authority in the early twentieth century, when he wrote that though the powers of the state and federal governments are exercised within the same territorial limits, they "are yet separate and distinct sovereignties, acting separately and independently of each other, within their respective spheres." Taney concluded his opinion by declaring the Fugitive Slave Act of 1850 to be "in all of its provisions, fully authorized by the Constitution."

A reconstituted Wisconsin Supreme Court later conceded the validity of Taney's interpretation of section 25 and apologized to the United States Supreme Court, conceding that its earlier actions were "a breach of that comity, or good behavior, which should be maintained between the courts of the two governments."

WILLIAM M. WIECEK

ABOLITIONIST CONSTITUTIONAL THEORY

American abolitionists developed comprehensive but conflicting theories about the place of slavery in the American constitution. Though these ideas did not positively influence political and legal debate until the 1850s, they exercised profound influence over subsequent constitutional development, merging with constitutional aspirations of nonabolitionist Republicans after the Civil War to provide the basis for what one writer has called the "Third Constitution": the THIRTEENTH through FIFTEENTH AMENDMENTS. From abolitionist constitutional ideals embedded in section 1 of the FOURTEENTH AMENDMENT, there emerged some principal trends of constitutional development in the century after the Civil War: SUB-STANTIVE DUE PROCESS, equality before the law, protection for the privileges of national and state CITIZENSHIP.

By the time abolitionists began systematically to expound constitutional ideas in the 1830s, the constitutional aspects of the controversy over slavery were well developed. Even before American independence, Quakers in the Middle Colonies and some Puritan ministers in New England had attacked slavery on religio-ethical grounds. In SOMERSET'S CASE (1772) WILLIAM MURRAY (Lord Mansfield), Chief Justice of King's Bench, suggested that slavery could be established only by positive law and that, as a legal institution, it was "odious." The American Revolution witnessed the total abolition, exclusion, or disappearance of slavery in some northern jurisdictions (Vermont, Massachusetts and Maine, New Hampshire, the Northwest Territory) and its gradual abolition in the rest (Pennsylvania, New York, New Jersey, Connecticut, Rhode Island). Early antislavery groups, federated as the American Convention of Abolition Societies, worked in legal and paternalistic ways to protect freed blacks and provide them jobs and education. Yet these Revolutionary-era inhibitions on slavery were offset by gains slavery made in the drafting of the United States Constitution, in which ten clauses promoted slavery's security, most notably in the federal number clause (Article I, section 2, clause 3), the slave trade clause (Article I, section 9, clause 1), and the fugitive slave clause (Article IV, section 2, clause 3).

Constitutional controversy flared over slavery in several early episodes: the federal abolition of the international slave trade and its incidents, the Missouri crisis (1819–1821), the disputes over federal aid to colonization of free blacks, Denmark Vesey's slave revolt (Charleston, 1822), and the Negro Seamen's Acts of the southern coastal states (1822–1830). But not until the ideas of immediate abolition rejuvenated the antislavery movement did abolitionists begin a systematic constitutional assault on slavery. When they organized the American Anti-Slavery Society (AASS) in 1833, abolitionists, in a document drafted by WILLIAM LLOYD GARRISON, pledged themselves to tolerate the continued existence of slavery in the states and rejected the possibility that the federal government could abolish it there. But they insisted that slavery should be abolished immediately, that blacks should not suffer legal discrimination because of race, and that Congress should abolish the interstate slave trade, ban slavery in the DISTRICT OF COLUMBIA and the TERRITORIES, and refuse to admit new slave states.

The newly reorganized movement promptly encountered resistance that directed its thinking into constitutional modes. Federal efforts to suppress abolitionist mailings and to gag abolitionists' FREEDOM OF PETITION, together with mobbings throughout the northern states, diverted abolitionists briefly from the pursuit of freedom for blacks to a defense of CIVIL LIBERTIES of whites. At the same time, they assaulted slavery's incidents piecemeal, attempting to protect fugitive slaves from rendition, and seeking repeal of statutes that permitted sojourning masters to keep their slaves with them for limited periods of time in northern states. They secured enactment of PERSONAL LIBERTY LAWS: statutes that protected the freedom of black people in the northern states by providing them HABEAS CORPUS relief when seized as fugitives and by prohibiting state officials or public facilities from being used in the recapture of fugitives.

In 1839–1840, the unified antislavery movement split apart into three factions. Ironically, this organizational disaster stimulated abolitionists' systematic constitutional theorizing and broadcast their ideas widely outside the movement. Because of theological and tactical disagreements, the movement first broke into Garrisonian and political action wings, the Garrisonians condemning conventional electoral politics and the activists organizing a third party, the Liberty party, which ran its own presidential candidate in 1840 and 1844. The political action group subsequently split into those who believed slavery to be everywhere illegitimate and who therefore sought to have the federal government abolish slavery in the states, and those who continued to maintain the position of the original AASS Constitution, namely, that Congress lacked constitutional power to abolish slavery in the states. The Garrisonians, meanwhile, had concluded that the United States Constitution supported slavery and therefore called on northern states to secede from the Union and on individuals to disavow their allegiance to the Constitution.

Those who always maintained slavery's universal illegitimacy relied first on the DUE PROCESS clause of the Fifth Amendment, arguing that slaves were deprived of life, liberty, and property without legal justification, but they soon broadened their attack, ingeniously interpreting nearly a third of the Constitution's clauses, from the PREAMBLE to the TENTH AMENDMENT, to support their untenable thesis that slavery had usurped its preferred constitutional status. The 1840 publication of JAMES MADISON's notes of proceedings at the CONSTITUTIONAL CONVENTION OF 1787 was an embarrassment to them, disclosing as it did the concessions the Framers willingly made to the political power of slavery. Exponents of the universal-illegitimacy theory included Alvan Stewart,

G. W. F. Mellen, Lysander Spooner, Joel Tiffany, and later, Gerrit Smith, JAMES G. BIRNEY, Lewis Tappan, and Frederick Douglass. Their principal contributions to later constitutional development included: their insistence on equality before the law irrespective of race; their vision of national citizenship protecting individuals' rights throughout the Union; their reliance on the PRIVILEGES AND IMMUNITIES clause (Article IV, section 2, clause 1) as a protection for persons of both races; and their uncompromising egalitarianism, which led them to condemn all forms of RACIAL DISCRIMINATION. They were scorned as extremists in their own time, even by fellow abolitionists, and modern scholars such as Robert Cover dismiss their ideas as "utopian."

Political action abolitionists who conceded the legality of slavery in the states remained closest to the mainstream of American politics and established a political alliance with like-minded men outside the abolitionist movement to create the Free Soil party in 1848. Their insistence that, as the federal government could not abolish slavery, neither could it establish it, led them to proclaim the doctrines of "divorce" and "freedom national." "Divorce" called for an immediate and absolute separation of the federal government from the support of slavery (for example, by abolishing the interstate slave trade and repealing the Fugitive Slave Act of 1793), coupled with an aggressive attack on the political bases of slavery's strength (repeal of the federal number clause, refusal to appoint slaveholders to federal posts). "Divorce" provided the doctrinal basis of the three-way Free Soil coalition of 1848, comprised of Conscience Whigs, Barnburner Democrats, and former Libertymen. Liberty leaders in the Free Soil group included SALMON P. CHASE (later Chief Justice of the United States), Gamaliel Bailey, STANLEY MATTHEWS (a future justice of the United States Supreme Court), Representative Owen Lovejoy, and Joshua Leavitt.

Stimulated by the widespread popularity of the WILMOT PROVISO (1846) in the north, which would have excluded slavery from all territories acquired as a result of the Mexican War, the abolitionist Free Soilers demanded "non-extension": the refusal to permit slavery in any American territories, and the nonadmission of new slave states. This became transformed into "freedom national," a constitutional doctrine holding that, under *Somerset*, freedom is the universal condition of humans, and slavery a local aberration created and continued only by local positive law. These ideas were cordially received by Whigs who formed a nucleus of the Republican party after the demise of the Free Soilers and the fragmentation of the regular parties as a result of the KANSAS-NE-BRASKA ACT (1854): Joshua Giddings, CHARLES SUMNER, Charles Francis Adams, and Horace Mann. Other Republicans such as ABRAHAM LINCOLN and WILLIAM SEWARD refused to accept "divorce" but made nonextension the cornerstone of Republican policy. "Freedom national" even influenced anti-abolitionists such as Lewis Cass and then STEPHEN A. DOUGLAS, who promoted a modified version of it as the FREEPORT DOCTRINE of 1858.

Garrisonians dismissed the United States Constitution as the "covenant with death and agreement with hell" denounced by Isaiah, but they too influenced later constitutional development, principally through their insistence that the proslavery clauses of the Constitution would have to be repealed or nullified, and the federal government fumigated of its contamination with support of slavery. Though they included competent lawyers (Wendell Phillips, William I. Bowditch), the Garrisonians were distinguished chiefly by literary and polemical talent (Edmund Quincy, Lydia Maria Child) and consequently made little contribution to systematic constitutional exposition.

The crises of the union in the 1850s, beginning with enactment of the Fugitive Slave Act in 1850, leading through the dramatic fugitive recaptures and rescues, the Kansas-Nebraska Act (1854) and "Bleeding Kansas," and culminating, constitutionally, in DRED SCOTT V. SANDFORD (1857), ABLEMAN V. BOOTH (1859), and the pending appeal of *People v. Lemmon* (1860), together with legislative activity (chiefly enactment of ever broader personal liberty laws, including Vermont's Freedom Act of 1858), enabled abolitionists to work together toward common goals, and to overcome or survive their sectarian quarrels of the 1840s. Though fragmented as a distinct movement, abolitionists permeated the press, parties, and the churches, diffusing their ideas widely among persons who had not been theretofore involved in the antislavery movement. Thus egalitarians like Sumner and THADDEUS STEVENS, conservative lawyers like JOHN BINGHAM and William Lawrence, and political leaders like WILLIAM PITT FESSENDEN and ROSCOE CONKLING were influenced by abolitionist constitutional ideas, appropriating them after the war and injecting them into the Constitution and its interpretation, both in cases and in statutes.

WILLIAM M. WIECEK

Bibliography

DUMOND, DWIGHT L. 1961 *Antislavery.* Ann Arbor: University of Michigan Press.
FEHRENBACHER, DON 1978 *The Dred Scott Case: Its Significance in American Law and Politics.* New York: Oxford University Press.
GRAHAM, HOWARD J. 1968 *Everyman's Constitution.* Madison: State Historical Society of Wisconsin.
TEN BROEK, JACOBUS 1965 *Equal under Law.* New York: Collier Books.
WIECEK, WILLIAM M. 1977 *The Sources of Antislavery Constitutionalism in America, 1760–1848.* Ithaca, N.Y.: Cornell University Press.

ABOLITION OF SLAVERY

See: Slavery and the Constitution; Thirteenth Amendment

ABOOD v. DETROIT BOARD OF EDUCATION
431 U.S. 209 (1977)

Abood is one of the cases where union or agency shop agreements create speech and association problems, because individuals must join unions in order to hold jobs and then must pay dues to support union activities with which the individuals may not agree. Here the union represented public employees. The Supreme Court has consistently held that there is no right *not* to associate in a labor union for the purposes of COLLECTIVE BARGAINING but that a union must develop methods of relieving a member of those portions of union dues devoted to union ideological activities to which he objects.

MARTIN SHAPIRO

(SEE ALSO: *Labor and the Constitution; Freedom of Speech; Freedom of Assembly and Association.*)

ABORTION AND THE CONSTITUTION

The story of abortion and the Constitution is in part an episode in the saga of SUBSTANTIVE DUE PROCESS. During the period from the early 1900s to the mid-1930s, the Supreme Court employed the principle of substantive due process—the principle that governmental action abridging a person's life, liberty, or property interests must serve a legitimate governmental policy—to invalidate much state and federal legislation that offended the Court's views of legitimate policy, particularly socioeconomic policy. In the late 1930s and early 1940s, the Court, with a new majority composed in part of Justices appointed by

President FRANKLIN D. ROOSEVELT, reacted to the perceived judicial excesses of the preceding generation by refusing to employ substantive due process to invalidate any state or federal legislation. During the next quarter century—the period between the demise of the "old" substantive due process and the birth of the "new"—the Court did not formally reject the principle of substantive due process; from time to time the Court inquired whether challenged legislation was consistent with the principle. But the Court's substantive due process review was so deferential to the legislation in question as to be largely inconsequential, as, for example, in WILLIAMSON V. LEE OPTICAL CO. (1955).

Then, in the mid-1960s, the Court changed direction. In GRISWOLD V. CONNECTICUT (1965) the Court relied on a constitutional RIGHT OF PRIVACY to rule that a state could not ban the use of contraceptives by married persons. In *Eisenstadt v. Baird* (1972), on EQUAL PROTECTION grounds, it ruled that a state may not ban the distribution of contraceptives to unmarried persons. Despite the rhetoric of the Court's opinions, there is no doubt that both were substantive due process decisions in the methodological (if not the rhetorical) sense: in each case the Court invalidated legislation that offended not any specific prohibition of the Constitution but simply the Court's views of the governmental policies asserted in justification of the states' regulations.

If any doubt remained about whether the Court had returned to substantive due process, that doubt could not survive the Court's decision in ROE V. WADE (1973), which employed substantive due process in both the rhetorical and the methodological senses. The Court ruled in *Roe* that the due process clause of the FOURTEENTH AMENDMENT prohibited a state from forbidding a woman to obtain an abortion in the period of pregnancy prior to the fetus's viability. Indeed, in *Roe* the Court applied a particularly strong version of the substantive-due-process requirement: because the criminal ban on abortion challenged in *Roe* abridged a "fundamental" liberty interest of the woman—specifically, her "privacy" interest in deciding whether to terminate her pregnancy—the Court insisted that the legislation not merely serve a legitimate governmental policy but that it be *necessary* to serve a COMPELLING STATE INTEREST. The Court concluded that only after viability was government's interest in protecting the life of the fetus sufficiently strong to permit it to ban abortion.

Obviously the written Constitution says nothing about abortion, and no plausible "interpretation" or "application" of any determinate value judgment fairly attributable to the framers of the Fourteenth Amendment prohibits state government from forbidding a woman to obtain an abortion. In that sense, the Supreme Court's decision in *Roe v. Wade* is an exemplar of JUDICIAL ACTIVISM. Thus, it was not surprising that the decision—the Court's constitutionalization of the matter of abortion—ignited one of those periodic explosions about the legitimacy of judicial activism in a democracy. (Earlier such explosions attended the Court's activism in the period from *Lochner v. New York* (1905) to the late 1930s and, more recently, the Court's decision in *Brown v. Board of Education* (1954) outlawing racially segregated public schooling.)

Many critics of the Court's decision in *Roe* complained about the judicial activism underlying the decision. In the view of most such critics, *Roe v. Wade* is simply a contemporary analogue of the almost universally discredited *Lochner v. New York* (1905), and no one who opposes the activist mode of judicial review exemplified by *Lochner* can consistently support the activist mode exemplified by *Roe*. Of course, the force of this argument depends on one's perception of what is wrong with *Lochner*: the activist mode of review exemplified by it or simply the Court's answer in *Lochner* to the question of economic liberty addressed there. There is no inconsistency in opposing *Lochner's* doctrinal conclusions and supporting the activist mode of review exemplified by *Roe* (and by *Lochner*). Indeed, one might support the activist mode of review exemplified by *Roe* and at the same time oppose *Roe's* reasoning and result.

A second, distinct criticism of the Court's decision in *Roe* concerns not the legitimacy of judicial activism but the soundness of the Court's answer to the political-moral question it addressed. Because many persons believe, often on religious grounds, that the Court gave the wrong answer to the question whether state government should be permitted to ban abortion, there was, in the decade following *Roe*, a vigorous political movement to overrule *Roe* legislatively—either by taking away the Court's JURISDICTION to review state abortion laws, or by constitutional amendment or even simple congressional legislation to the effect that a fetus is a person within the meaning of the Fourteenth Amendment and that therefore state government may ban abortion to protect the life of the fetus. The proposals to limit the jurisdiction of the Court and to overrule *Roe* by simple congressional legislation, as opposed to constitutional amendment, became subjects of vigorous political and constitutional controversy.

The vigor of the political controversy over abortion

cannot be fully comprehended—indeed, the Court's decision to constitutionalize the matter of abortion cannot be fully comprehended—without reference to an important development in American society that gained momentum in the 1970s and 1980s: a fundamental shift in attitudes toward the role of women in society. Many of those who opposed abortion and the "liberalization" of public policy regarding abortion did so as part of a larger agenda based on a "traditional" vision of woman's place and of the family. Many of those on the other side of the issue were seeking to implement a different vision—a feminist vision in which women are free to determine for themselves what shapes their lives will take, and therefore free to determine whether, and when, they will bear children.

Not surprisingly, this basic shift in attitudes toward women—from patriarchal to feminist—has been an occasion for deep division in American society. "Abortion politics" was merely one manifestation of that division (although an important one, to be sure). Thus, a controversy that sometimes seemed on the surface to consist mainly of a philosophical-theological dispute over the question, "When does 'life' begin?," actually involved much more. The complexity of the abortion controversy was dramatically evidenced by the fact that even within the Roman Catholic Church in the United States, which was the most powerful institutional opponent of abortion, attitudes toward abortion were deeply divided precisely because attitudes toward women were deeply divided.

As a consequence of its decision in *Roe v. Wade*, the Court has had to resolve many troublesome, controversial issues regarding abortion. For example, in PLANNED PARENTHOOD OF MISSOURI V. DANFORTH (1976) the Court ruled that a state may not require a woman to obtain the consent of her spouse before she terminates her pregnancy. The Court's rulings with respect to parental-consent and parental-notification requirements have not been a model of clarity, in part because the rulings have been fragmented. In *Bellotti v. Baird* (1979), for example, an 8–1 decision striking down the parental consent requirement, the majority split 4–4 as to the proper rationale. This much, however, is clear: state government may not require *every* minor, whatever her level of independence or maturity, to obtain parental consent before she terminates her pregnancy.

Undoubtedly the most controversial issue concerning abortion that the Court has addressed since *Roe v. Wade* involved abortion funding. In MAHER V. ROE (1977), the Court ruled that a state government that spends welfare funds to subsidize medical expenses incident to pregnancy and childbirth may decline to subsidize medical expenses incident to nontherapeutic abortion even if its sole reason for doing so is to discourage abortion. In a companion case, *Poelker v. Doe* (1977), the Court ruled that a public hospital that provides medical services relating to pregnancy and childbirth may decline to provide nontherapeutic abortions even if its sole reason for doing so is to discourage abortion. Three years later, in HARRIS V. MCRAE (1980), the Court sustained the HYDE AMENDMENT (to appropriations for the Medicaid program), which prohibited federal funding of abortion, including therapeutic abortion, even though the sole purpose of the amendment was to discourage abortion.

Some commentators have claimed that, notwithstanding the Court's arguments to the contrary, these abortion-funding cases cannot be reconciled with *Roe v. Wade*. They reason that the Court's decision in *Roe* can be satisfactorily explained only on the ground that government may not take action predicated on the view that abortion (in the pre-viability period) is morally objectionable, but that the governmental policies sustained in *Maher, Poelker,* and *McRae* were all manifestly predicated on just that view. There is probably no final explanation of the Court's decisions in the abortion-funding cases except in terms of judicial *Realpolitik*—that is, as an effort to retrench in the face of vigorous, often bitter, and widespread criticism of its decision in *Roe v. Wade* and threats to overrule *Roe* legislatively.

Its decision, in *Roe v. Wade*, to constitutionalize the deeply controversial issue of abortion represents one of the Supreme Court's most problematic ventures in recent times. Other moves by the Court were as controversial when initially taken—for example, the Court's choice in *Brown v. Board of Education* (1954) to begin to disestablish racially segregated public schooling—but few have been so persistently controversial. Whatever their eventual fate, *Roe* and its progeny have served as an occasion for some of the most fruitful thinking in this century on the proper role of the Supreme Court in American government.

MICHAEL J. PERRY

(SEE ALSO: *Reproductive Autonomy.*)

Bibliography

ELY, JOHN HART 1973 The Wages of Crying Wolf: A Comment on *Roe v. Wade. Yale Law Journal* 82:920.
PERRY, MICHAEL 1980 Why the Supreme Court was

Plainly Wrong in the Hyde Amendment Case: A Brief Comment on *Harris v. McRae. Stanford Law Review* 32:1113–1128.

REGAN, DONALD 1979 Rewriting *Roe v. Wade. Michigan Law Review* 77:1569–1646.

TRIBE, LAURENCE H. 1978 *American Constitutional Law.* Pages 921–934. Mineola, N.Y.: Foundation Press.

ABRAMS v. UNITED STATES
250 U.S. 616 (1919)

In SCHENCK V. UNITED STATES (1919) Justice OLIVER WENDELL HOLMES introduced the CLEAR AND PRESENT DANGER test in upholding the conviction under the ESPIONAGE ACT of a defendant who had mailed circulars opposing military CONSCRIPTION. Only nine months later, in very similar circumstances, the Supreme Court upheld an Espionage Act conviction and Holmes and LOUIS D. BRANDEIS offered the danger test in dissent. *Abrams* is famous for Holmes's dissent which became a classic libertarian pronouncement.

Abrams and three others distributed revolutionary circulars that included calls for a general strike, special appeals to workers in ammunitions factories, and language suggesting armed disturbances as the best means of protecting the Russian revolution against American intervention. These circulars had appeared while the United States was still engaged against the Germans in World War I. Their immediate occasion was the dispatch of an American expeditionary force to Russia at the time of the Russian revolution. The majority reasoned that, whatever their particular occasion, the circulars' purpose was that of hampering the general war effort. Having concluded that "the language of these circulars was obviously intended to provoke and to encourage resistance to the United States in the war" and that they urged munitions workers to strike for the purpose of curtailing the production of war materials, the opinion upheld the convictions without actually addressing any constitutional question. The majority obviously believed that the Espionage Act might constitutionally be applied to speech intended to obstruct the war effort.

Justice Holmes mixed a number of elements in his dissent, and the mixture has bedeviled subsequent commentary. Although it is not clear whether Holmes was focusing on the specific language of the Espionage Act or arguing a more general constitutional standard, his central argument was that speech may not be punished unless it constitutes an attempt at some unlawful act; an essential element in such an attempt must be a specific intent on the part of the speaker to bring about the unlawful act. He did not read the circulars in evidence or the actions of their publishers as showing the specific intent to interfere with the war effort against Germany that would be required to constitute a violation of the Espionage Act.

His *Abrams* opinion shows the extent to which Holmes's invention of the danger rule was a derivation of his thinking about the role of specific intent and surrounding circumstances in the law of attempts. For in the midst of his discussion of specific intent he wrote, "I do not doubt . . . that by the same reasoning that would justify punishing persuasion to murder, the United States constitutionally may punish speech that produces or is intended to produce a clear and imminent danger that it will bring about forthwith certain substantive evils that the United States constitutionally may seek to prevent. . . . It is only the present danger of immediate evil or an intent to bring it about that warrants Congress in setting a limit to the expression of opinion . . . ."

Over time, however, what has survived from Holmes's opinion is not so much the specific intent argument as the more general impression that the "poor and puny anonymities" of the circulars could not possibly have constituted a clear and present danger to the war effort. At least in contexts such as that presented in *Abrams,* the clear and present danger test seems to be a good means of unmasking and constitutionally invalidating prosecutions because of the ideas we hate, when the precautions are undertaken not because the ideas constitute any real danger to our security but simply because we hate them. Although the specific intent aspect of the *Abrams* opinion has subsequently been invoked in a number of cases, particularly those involving membership in the Communist party, the *Abrams* dissent has typically been cited along with *Schenck* as the basic authority for the more general version of the clear and present danger standard that became the dominant FREEDOM OF SPEECH doctrine during the 1940s and has since led a checkered career.

Justice Holmes also argued in *Abrams* that the common law of SEDITIOUS LIBEL has not survived in the United States; the Supreme Court finally adopted that position in NEW YORK TIMES V. SULLIVAN (1964).

The concluding paragraph of the *Abrams* dissent has often been invoked by those who wish to make of Holmes a patron saint of the libertarian movement.

Persecution for the expression of opinions seems to me perfectly logical . . . but when men have realized that time has upset many fighting faiths, they may come to believe even more the very foundations of their own conduct that the ultimate good desired is better reached by free trade in ideas—that the best test of truth is the power of the thought to get itself accepted in the competition of the market, and that truth is the only ground upon which their wishes safely can be carried out. That at any rate is the theory of our Constitution. It is an experiment, as all life is an experiment. Every year if not every day we have to wager our salvation upon some prophecy based upon imperfect knowledge. While that experiment is part of our system I think that we should be eternally vigilant against attempts to check the expression of opinions that we loathe and believe to be fraught with death, unless they so imminently threaten immediate interference with the lawful and pressing purposes of the law that an immediate check is required to save the country. . . . Only the emergency that makes it immediately dangerous to leave the correction of evil counsels to time warrants making any exception to the sweeping command, "Congress shall make no law . . . abridging the freedom of speech."

Sensitized by the destructive powers of such "fighting faiths" as Fascism and communism, subsequent commentators have criticized the muscular, relativistic pragmatism of this pronouncement as at best an inadequate philosophic basis for the libertarian position and at worst an invitation to totalitarianism. The ultimate problem is, of course, what is to be done if a political faith that proposes the termination of freedom of speech momentarily wins the competition in the marketplace of ideas and then shuts down the market. Alternatively it has been argued that Holmes's clear and present danger approach in *Abrams* was basically conditioned by his perception of the ineffectualness of leftist revolutionary rhetoric in the American context of his day. In this view, he was saying no more than that deviant ideas must be tolerated until there is a substantial risk that a large number of Americans will listen to them. The clear and present danger test is often criticized for withdrawing protection of political speech at just the point when the speech threatens to become effective. Other commentators have argued that no matter how persuasive Holmes's comments may be in context, the clear and present danger approach ought not to be uncritically accepted as the single freedom of speech test, uniformly applied to speech situations quite different from those in *Abrams*. Perhaps the most telling criticism of the Holmes approach is that it vests enormous discretion in the judge, for ultimately it depends on the judge's prediction of what will happen rather than on findings of what has happened. Subsequent decisions such as that in FEINER V. NEW YORK (1951) showed that judges less brave than Holmes or less

contemptuously tolerant of dissident ideas, might be quicker to imagine danger.

MARTIN SHAPIRO

Bibliography

CHAFEE, ZECHARIAH 1941 *Free Speech in the United States.* Cambridge, Mass.: Harvard University Press.

ABSOLUTISM
(Freedom of Speech and Press)

In the 1950s and 1960s, some Justices of the Supreme Court and some commentators on the Court's work debated an abstract issue of constitutional theory pressed on it by Justice HUGO L. BLACK: Is the FIRST AMENDMENT an "absolute," totally forbidding government restrictions on speech and the press that fall within the Amendment's scope, or is the FREEDOM OF SPEECH properly subject to BALANCING TESTS that weigh restrictions on speech against governmental interests asserted to justify them? With Black's retirement in 1971, the whole airy question simply collapsed.

The argument that the First Amendment "absolutely" guaranteed speech and press freedoms was first raised in the debate over the Sedition Act (1798) but did not become the focus of debate in Supreme Court opinions for another century and a half. The occasion was presented when the Court confronted a series of cases involving governmental restrictions on SUBVERSIVE ACTIVITIES. For ALEXANDER MEIKLEJOHN, First Amendment absolutism was built into the structure of a self-governing democracy. For Justice Black, it was grounded in the constitutional text.

Black argued that "the Constitution guarantees absolute freedom of speech"—he used the modern locution, including the press when he said "speech"—and, characteristically, he drew support from the First Amendment's words: "Congress shall make no law . . . abridging the freedom of speech, or of the press." He viewed all OBSCENITY and libel laws as unconstitutional; he argued, often supported by Justice WILLIAM O. DOUGLAS, that government could not constitutionally punish discussions of public affairs, even if they incited to illegal action. But Black never claimed that the First Amendment protected all communications, irrespective of context. He distinguished between speech, which was absolutely protected, and conduct, which was subject to reasonable regulation. So it was that the First Amendment absolutist, toward the end of his life, often voted to send marchers and other demonstrators to jail for expressing themselves in places where he said they had no right to be.

First Amendment absolutism fails more fundamentally, on its own terms. A witness who lies under oath surely has no constitutional immunity from prosecution, and yet her perjury is pure speech. Most observers, conceding the force of similar examples, have concluded that even Justice Black, a sophisticated analyst, must have viewed his absolutism as a debating point, not a rigid rule for decision. In the Cold War atmosphere of the 1950s, a debating point was sorely needed; there was truth to Black's charge that the Court was "balancing away the First Amendment." As Judge LEARNED HAND had argued many years previously, in times of stress judges need "a qualitative formula, hard, conventional, difficult to evade," if they are to protect unpopular political expression against hostile majorities. A "definitional" technique has its libertarian advantages. Yet it is also possible to "define away" the First Amendment, as the Court has demonstrated in its dealings with obscenity, FIGHTING WORDS, and some forms of libel and COMMERCIAL SPEECH.

Even when the Court is defining a category of speech out of the First Amendment's scope, it states its reasons. Thus, just as "balancers" must define what it is that they are balancing, "definers" must weigh interests in order to define the boundaries of protected speech. Since Justice Black's departure from the Court, First Amendment inquiry has blended definitional and interest-balancing techniques, focusing— as virtually all constitutional inquiry must ultimately focus—on the justifications asserted for governmental restrictions. Justice Black's enduring legacy to this process is not the theory of First Amendment absolutes, but his lively concern for the values of an open society.

KENNETH L. KARST

Bibliography

KALVEN, HARRY, JR. 1967 Upon Rereading Mr. Justice Black on the First Amendment. *UCLA Law Review* 14:422–453.

ABSTENTION DOCTRINE

All the abstention doctrines refer to circumstances in which federal courts, having JURISDICTION over a case under a congressional enactment, nonetheless may defer to state tribunals as decision makers. Federal courts may not abstain simply because they be-

lieve that particular cases, on their facts, would more appropriately be heard in state courts; they have a general obligation to exercise jurisdiction in cases Congress has placed before them. Abstention is justified only in exceptional circumstances, and then only when it falls within a particular abstention doctrine.

There are several abstention doctrines; they differ in their consequences and in their requirements. *Colorado River Water Conservation District v. United States* (1976) suggests a general doctrine that federal courts have power to defer in favor of ongoing state proceedings raising the same or closely related issues. This type of deference to ongoing proceedings often is not identified as abstention at all, and courts have not spelled out its requirements other than general discretion.

When a federal court does defer under this doctrine, it stays federal proceedings pending completion of the state proceedings. If the state does not proceed expeditiously, or if issues remain for decision, the federal court can reenter the case. When it does not abstain and both state and federal forums exercise their CONCURRENT JURISDICTION over a dispute, the JUDGMENT that controls is the first to become final. Federal courts deferring in favor of ongoing state proceedings avoid this wasteful race to judgment, but the price paid is that the federal plaintiff may lose the federal forum she has chosen and to which federal law entitles her.

In reconciling the competing interests, federal courts are much more likely to defer to prior state proceedings, in which the state plaintiff has won the race to the courthouse, than they are when the federal suit was first filed.

Deference, even to previously commenced state proceedings involving the same parties as the federal suit, is by no means automatic; it is discretionary— justified by the court's INHERENT POWER to control its docket in the interests of efficiency and fairness— and the Supreme Court has said that it is to be invoked sparingly. In *Colorado River Water Conservation District v. United States* the Court stated that the inherent problems in duplicative proceedings are not sufficient to justify deference to the state courts because of "the virtually unflagging obligation of the federal courts to exercise the jurisdiction given them."

This doctrine permitting deference serves as a backdrop to other doctrines that the Supreme Court more consistently calls "abstention." The most important of these today is the doctrine of YOUNGER V. HARRIS (1971). The doctrine started as a principle against enjoining state criminal prosecutions, but it has grown enormously. It has been expanded to bar not only suits for federal injunction but also suits for federal declaratory judgment concerning the constitutionality of an enactment involved in a pending prosecution; and today some believe it goes so far as to bar a federal damage action against state officials that might decide issues that would interfere with a state prosecution. Moreover, the doctrine has grown to protect state civil proceedings as well as criminal ones. Most remarkably, as the Court held in *Hicks v. Miranda* (1975), the doctrine now allows abstention even if the federal action is first filed, so long as the state commences prosecution "before any proceedings of substance on the merits" have occurred in federal court. That rule effectively deters federal suit; a federal plaintiff who wins the race to the courthouse may simply provoke his own criminal prosecution. These developments together have turned *Younger* into a doctrine that permits federal courts to dismiss federal constitutional challenges to state criminal prosecution (or quasi-criminal) enactments whenever a state criminal prosecution (or other enforcement proceeding) provides a forum for the federal constitutional issue. The state forum in theory must be an adequate one, but courts applying the doctrine often overlook this aspect of the inquiry.

Courts abstaining under the *Younger* doctrine generally dismiss the federal suit rather than retaining jurisdiction. Federal plaintiffs who are left to defend state proceedings generally cannot return to federal court for adjudication of the federal or any other issues, and the state court's decision on the constitutional issue and others may control future litigation through collateral estoppel. Litigants do, of course, retain the possibility of Supreme Court review of the federal issues they raise in state court, but the chances that the Supreme Court will hear such cases are slim.

The *Younger* doctrine therefore often deprives the federal plaintiff of any federal forum—prior, concurrent, or subsequent to the state proceeding against him—for his CIVIL RIGHTS action against state officials. This contradicts the apparent purpose of SECTION 1983, TITLE 42, UNITED STATES CODE and its jurisdictional counterpart (section 1343, Title 28) that such a forum be available. Some of those convicted in state criminal prosecutions may later raise federal issues in federal HABEAS CORPUS proceedings, but ACCESS to habeas corpus is itself increasingly limited. (See STONE V. POWELL, 1976; WAINWRIGHT V. SYKES, 1977.)

The *Younger* doctrine does have exceptions. If the federal court finds state courts inadequate on the facts of the particular case (because of what the Court in

Younger termed "bad faith, harassment, or any other unusual circumstance that would call for equitable relief"), it will exercise its jurisdiction. But this approach turns around the usual rule that it takes exceptional circumstances to decline jurisdiction, not to justify its exercise. To avoid this conflict with the usual rules allowing Congress, not the courts, to determine the appropriate cases for federal jurisdiction, *Younger* abstention should be cut back, at least by limiting it to cases in which state proceedings began before the federal one. Such an approach would assimilate *Younger* abstention to the general doctrine of deference to ongoing state proceedings, discussed above.

In the meantime the expanded version of the *Younger* doctrine has largely displaced what had been the key form of abstention, formulated in RAILROAD COMMISSION OF TEXAS V. PULLMAN COMPANY (1941). *Pullman* abstention applies to cases involving federal constitutional challenges to state law. It allows (but does not require) federal judges to refrain from deciding highly uncertain questions of state law when resolution of the questions may avoid or affect the federal constitutional issue.

Pullman today is the only abstention doctrine in which deference to state courts is limited to state law issues. When the federal court abstains under the *Pullman* doctrine, it holds the case while the parties seek declaratory relief on the state law issues in state court. Unless the parties voluntarily submit federal along with state issues to the state court, they have a right to return to federal court after the state adjudication is completed, for decision of the federal issues and for federal factfinding. In this respect *Pullman* abstention is a narrower intrusion on federal court jurisdiction than the *Younger* doctrine is, although the cost of shuttling back and forth from state to federal court dissuades many federal plaintiffs from retaining their federal forum. *Pullman* also differs from *Younger* because the federal plaintiff generally initiates the proceedings in state court, and they are declaratory judgment proceedings rather than criminal prosecutions or civil enforcement proceedings.

As *Younger* has expanded to include some civil enforcement proceedings and to allow abstention in favor of later-filed state proceedings, it has reduced the area for *Pullman* abstention. Both doctrines typically apply to constitutional litigation against state officials. In many cases where *Pullman* abstention could be at issue, *Younger* is operative because a state enforcement proceeding against the federal plaintiff is a possibility as long as the federal plaintiff has violated the law she challenges. If, however, the federal plaintiff has not violated the enactment she challenges, *Youn-*

ger abstention cannot apply, for the state is unable to bring a prosecution or civil enforcement proceeding against her and thereby displace the federal forum. *Pullman,* therefore, is the applicable doctrine for pre-violation suits and for challenges to state enactments that do not involve state enforcement proceedings. Many of those cases, however, will be dismissed before abstention is considered; where the plaintiff has not violated the enactment she complains of, she may have trouble showing that her controversy is justiciable. (See RIPENESS.)

While *Pullman* abstention has therefore become less and less important, a new area has recently been created for a *Pullman*-like abstention. PENNHURST STATE SCHOOL V. HALDERMAN (1984), restricting federal courts' pendent jurisdiction, requires federal litigants in suits against state governments to use state courts to pursue any related state causes of action they do not wish to forfeit. *Pennhurst* thus creates the equivalent of a mandatory *Pullman* abstention category—where state courts must be given certain state law questions to adjudicate even while a federal court exercises jurisdiction over the rest of the case. This new category is not, however, dependent upon uncertainty in state law.

Another abstention doctrine, administrative abstention, was first articulated in *Burford v. Sun Oil Company* (1943). The *Burford* doctrine allows a federal court with jurisdiction of a case to dismiss in favor of state court adjudication, ongoing or not. Like *Younger* abstention, *Burford* abstention displaces federal jurisdiction; if abstention is ordered, state courts adjudicate all issues, subject only to Supreme Court review. The Court has never clearly explained which cases are eligible for administrative abstention. The doctrine is typically employed when a state administrative process has dealt with a controversy in the first instance and the litigant then asks a federal district court to exercise either its federal question or diversity jurisdiction to review that administrative interpretation. The federal court's ability to abstain under this doctrine may be limited to situations in which state statutes concentrate JUDICIAL REVIEW of the administrative process in a particular state court so that it becomes "an integral part of the regulatory process," as the Court said in *Alabama Public Service Commission v. Southern Railway* (1951), or to situations involving complex factual issues. There is no requirement that legal issues, state or federal, be unclear for this abstention to be ordered, or that the case contain any federal issues.

Burford abstention does not apply when state administrative remedies have been skipped altogether

and the litigant has sued first in federal court. The only issue then is whether state administrative remedies must be exhausted. There is no overlap between *Burford* and the *Younger* or *Pullman* abstention doctrines, because exhaustion of administrative remedies has not been required in suits under section 1983, which today includes all constitutional litigation. The Court recently affirmed this exception to the exhaustion requirement in Patsy v. Board of Regents (1982). If the Court were to modify the section 1983 exception to the exhaustion requirement, retreat from the *Burford* doctrine would seem to follow. Otherwise, *Burford* would mandate state judicial review after deference to state administrative proceedings, so federal jurisdiction would be altogether unavailable in section 1983 cases whenever an administrative agency was available.

A final minor category of abstention, which seems to have been limited to EMINENT DOMAIN cases involving unclear state issues, is reflected in *Louisiana Light & Power Company v. Thibodaux* (1959). In contexts other than eminent domain, abstention is not proper simply to clarify difficult state law issues. (In states that provide for certification, however, a federal court without more can certify difficult state issues to the state supreme court.)

All these theories of abstention are judge-made rules, without any statutory authority; they avoid jurisdiction in cases where Congress has given it. By contrast, Congress itself has provided for deference to state processes in narrow categories of cases, most notably cases involving INJUNCTIONS against state rate orders and tax collections. And in the Anti-Injunction Act, Congress has generally prohibited federal injunctions against state proceedings. This prohibition is limited by explicit statutory exceptions, however, and by some judge-made exceptions, and since the area outside the prohibition also is limited, by the judge-made abstention doctrines, the statute apparently has little effect.

MARTHA A. FIELD

Bibliography

FIELD, MARTHA A. 1974 Abstention in Constitutional Cases: The Scope of the Pullman Abstention Doctrine. *University of Pennsylvania Law Review* 122:1071–1087.

—— 1981 The Uncertain Nature of Federal Jurisdiction. *William & Mary Law Review* 22:683–724.

FISS, OWEN 1977 Dombrowksi. *Yale Law Journal* 86:1103–1164.

LAYCOCK, DOUGLAS 1977 Federal Interference with State Prosecutions: The Need for Prospective Relief. *Supreme Court Review* 1977:193–238.

ACADEMIC FREEDOM

Although academic freedom has become a FIRST AMENDMENT principle of special importance, its content and theoretical underpinnings have barely been defined. Most alleged violations of academic freedom can be sorted into three catagories: claims of individual professors against the state, claims of individual professors against the university administration or governing board, and claims of universities against the state. Judicial decisions have upheld claims in all three contexts.

The Supreme Court, however, has not developed a comprehensive theory of academic freedom comparable to its recent elaboration of freedom of association as a distinctive First Amendment DOCTRINE. The relationship between "individual" and "institutional" academic freedom has not been clarified. Nor has the Supreme Court decided whether academic freedom is a separate principle, with its own constitutional contours justified by the unique roles of professors and universities in society, or whether it highlights but is essentially coextensive with the general First Amendment rights of all citizens. Similarly unsettled is the applicability, if any, of academic freedom in primary and secondary schools. While acknowledging that teachers, unlike university professors, are expected to inculcate societal values in their students, the Supreme Court in BOARD OF EDUCATION V. PICO (1982) expressed concern about laws that "cast a pall of orthodoxy" over school as well as university classrooms. Student claims of academic freedom also remain unresolved.

This uncertainty about the constitutional definition of academic freedom contrasts with the internal understanding of the university community, which had elaborated its meaning before any court addressed its legal or constitutional significance. The modern American conception of academic freedom arose during the late nineteenth and early twentieth centuries, when the emerging research university eclipsed the religious college as the model institution of higher education. This structural change reflected an equally profound transformation of educational goals from conserving to searching for truth.

Academic freedom became associated with the search for truth and began to define the very idea of the university. Its content developed under the influence of Darwinism and the German university. The followers of Charles Darwin maintained that all beliefs are subject to the tests of inquiry and that apparent errors must be tolerated, and even expected, in the continuous search for truth. The German academic influence reinforced the growing secular tendencies in the United States. Many attributed the international preeminence of German universities to their traditions of academic freedom. As universities in the United States strove for similar excellence, they adapted these traditions.

This adaptation produced several major changes. The clear German differentiation between great freedom for faculty members within the university and little protection for any citizen outside it did not take hold in America. The ideal of FREEDOM OF SPEECH, including its constitutional expression in the First Amendment, and the philosophy of pragmatism, which encouraged the participation of all citizens in social and political life, prompted American professors to view academic freedom as an aspect of more general CIVIL LIBERTIES. The traditions of powerful administrators and lay boards of governors in American universities posed threats to academic freedom that did not exist in Germany, where universities were largely governed by their faculties. As a result, American professors sought freedom from university authorities as well as from external interference. And academic freedom, which in Germany encompassed freedom for both students and professors, became limited to professors in the United States.

The first major codification of the American conception of academic freedom was produced in 1915 by a committee of the nascent American Association of University Professors (AAUP). Subsequent revisions culminated in the 1940 *Statement of Principles on Academic Freedom and Tenure*, jointly sponsored by the AAUP and the Association of American Colleges, and currently endorsed by over 100 educational organizations. The 1940 *Statement* defines three aspects of academic freedom: freedom in research and publication, freedom in the classroom, and freedom from institutional censorship or discipline when a professor speaks or writes as a citizen. Many colleges and universities have incorporated the 1940 *Statement* into their governing documents. In cases involving the contractual relationship between professors and universities, courts have recently begun to cite it as the COMMON LAW of the academic profession. This contractual theory has provided substantial legal protection for academic freedom without the support of the First Amendment, whose applicability to private universities is limited by the doctrine of STATE ACTION.

The emergence of academic freedom as a constitutional principle did not begin until the McCarthy era of the 1950s, when public and university officials throughout the country challenged and investigated the loyalty of professors. Although earlier decisions had imposed some limitations on governmental intrusions into universities and schools, no Supreme Court opinion explicitly referred to academic freedom until Justice WILLIAM O. DOUGLAS, dissenting in ADLER v. BOARD OF EDUCATION (1952), claimed that it is contained within the First Amendment.

The Supreme Court endorsed this identification of academic freedom with the First Amendment in SWEEZY v. NEW HAMPSHIRE (1957), which reversed the contempt conviction of a Marxist scholar who had refused to answer questions from the state attorney general regarding his political opinions and the contents of his university lecture. A plurality of the Justices concluded that the state had invaded the lecturer's "liberties in the areas of academic freedom and political expression." Both the plurality and concurring opinions in *Sweezy* emphasized the importance to a free society of the search for knowledge within free universities and warned against governmental interference in university life. Justice FELIX FRANKFURTER's concurrence included a particularly influential reference to academic freedom that has often been cited in subsequent decisions. Quoting from a plea by South African scholars for open universities, Frankfurter identified " 'the four essential freedoms of a university'—to determine for itself on academic grounds who may teach, what may be taught, how it shall be taught, and who may be admitted to study."

The opinions in *Sweezy* indicated that academic freedom and political expression are distinct yet related liberties, and that society benefits from the academic freedom of professors as individuals and of universities as institutions. Yet neither in *Sweezy* nor in subsequent decisions did the Supreme Court untangle and clarify these complex relationships. Throughout the 1950s, it alluded only intermittently to academic freedom in cases involving investigations of university professors, and reference to this term did not necessarily lead to protective results. Even the votes and reasoning of individual Justices fluctuated unpredictably. During this period, many within the academic community resisted the advocacy of academic freedom as a constitutional principle, fearing that a judicial definition might both weaken and preempt the one contained in the 1940 *Statement* and widely accepted throughout American universities.

Supreme Court opinions since the 1950s have emphasized that academic freedom is a "transcendent value" and "a special concern of the First Amendment," as the majority observed in KEYISHIAN v. BOARD OF REGENTS (1967). Justice LEWIS F. POWELL's opinion in REGENTS OF THE UNIVERSITY OF CALIFORNIA v. BAKKE (1978) reiterated the university's academic freedom to select its student body, but the Court has held in MINNESOTA STATE BOARD FOR COMMUNITY COLLEGES v. KNIGHT (1984) that academic freedom does not include the right of individual faculty members to participate in institutional governance. By eliminating the RIGHT-PRIVILEGE DISTINCTION, which had allowed dismissal of PUBLIC EMPLOYEES for speech otherwise protected by the First Amendment, the Supreme Court during the 1960s and 1970s dramatically expanded the rights of all public employees, including university professors, to speak in ways that criticize or offend their employers. Yet none of these decisions has refined the relationships between "individual" and "institutional" academic freedom or between "academic freedom" and "political expression," issues posed but not resolved in *Sweezy*. The Supreme Court's continuing reluctance even to recognize issues of academic freedom in cases decided on other grounds underlines the primitive constitutional definition of this term.

Cases since the early 1970s have raised novel issues of academic freedom. University administrators and governing boards have asserted the academic freedom of the university as an institution to resist JUDICIAL REVIEW of their internal policies and practices, which have been challenged by government agencies seeking to enforce CIVIL RIGHTS laws and other statutes of general applicability, by citizens claiming rights to freedom of expression on university property, and by professors maintaining that the university violated their own academic freedom or their statutory protection against employment discrimination. Faculty members have even begun to make contradictory claims of academic freedom against each other. Professors have relied on academic freedom to seek a constitutionally based privilege against compelled disclosure of their deliberations and votes on faculty committees to junior colleagues who want this information to determine whether they were denied reappointment or tenure for impermissible reasons, including reasons that might violate their academic freedom. These difficult issues may force the courts to address more directly the meaning and scope of academic freedom and to resolve many of the lingering ambiguities of previous decisions.

DAVID M. RABBAN

Bibliography
HOFSTADTER, RICHARD and METZGER, WALTER 1955 *The Development of Academic Freedom in the United States.* New York: Columbia University Press.
LOVEJOY, ARTHUR 1937 Academic Freedom. In E. Sel-

igman, ed., *Encyclopedia of the Social Sciences*, Vol. 1, pages 384–388. New York: Macmillan.

SYMPOSIUM 1963 Academic Freedom. *Law & Contemporary Problems* 28:429–671.

VAN ALSTYNE, WILLIAM 1972 The Specific Theory of Academic Freedom and the General Issue of Civil Liberty, In E. Pincoffs, ed., *The Concept of Academic Freedom*, pages 59–85. Austin: University of Texas Press.

ACCESS TO THE COURTS

Writing for the Supreme Court in BOUNDS V. SMITH (1977), Justice THURGOOD MARSHALL spoke confidently of "the fundamental constitutional right of access to the courts." In one sense, such a right has been a traditional and noncontroversial part of our constitutional law; barring unusual circumstances, anyone can bring a lawsuit, or be heard in his or her own defense. Justice Marshall, however, was referring to another kind of access. "Meaningful" access to the courts, *Bounds* held, gave state prisoners a right to legal assistance; the state must provide them either with law libraries or with law-trained persons to help them prepare petitions for HABEAS CORPUS or other legal papers. The modern constitutional law of access to the courts, in other words, is focused on the affirmative obligations of government to provide services to people who cannot afford to pay their costs. In this perspective, Justice Marshall's sweeping characterization goes far beyond the results of the decided cases.

The development began in the WARREN COURT era, with GRIFFIN V. ILLINOIS (1957) (state must provide free transcripts to convicted indigents when transcripts are required for effective APPEAL of their convictions) and DOUGLAS V. CALIFORNIA (1963) (state must provide appellate counsel for convicted indigents). GIDEON V. WAINWRIGHT (1963) interpreted the RIGHT TO COUNSEL to require state-appointed trial counsel in FELONY cases. The *Griffin* plurality had rested on both DUE PROCESS and EQUAL PROTECTION grounds, but by the time of *Douglas* equal protection had become the Court's preferred doctrine: the state, by refusing to pay for appellate counsel for some indigent defendants, had drawn "an unconstitutional line . . . between rich and poor." By the close of the Warren years, the Court seemed well on the way to a broad equal protection principle demanding strict judicial scrutiny of WEALTH DISCRIMINATIONS in the criminal justice system, including simple cases of inability to pay the costs of services needed for effective defense.

The Court remained sharply divided, however; the dissenters in *Griffin* and *Douglas* argued in forceful language that nothing in the Constitution required the states to take affirmative steps to relieve people from the effects of poverty. They saw no principled stopping-place for the majority's equality principle, and they objected to judicial intrusion into state budgetary processes. Even so, the same Justices found no difficulty in joining the 8–1 decision in BODDIE V. CONNECTICUT (1971), holding that a state could not constitutionally bar an indigent plaintiff from its divorce court for failure to pay a $60 filing fee. The *Boddie* majority, however, rested on a due process ground. The marriage relationship was "basic," and the state had monopolized the means for its dissolution; thus fundamental procedural fairness demanded access to the divorce court irrespective of ability to pay the fee.

From *Boddie* forward, the Court has dealt with constitutional claims of access to justice by emphasizing due process considerations of minimal fairness, and deemphasizing the equal protection notion that animated the Warren Court's decisions. At the same time, the Court has virtually ended the expansion of access rights. Thus ROSS V. MOFFITT (1974) pounced on language in *Douglas* about the "first appeal as of right," and refused to require state-appointed counsel to pursue discretionary appeals or Supreme Court review. And in *United States v. Kras* (1971) and *Ortwein v. Schwab* (1971) the Court, emphasizing the "monopoly" aspects of *Boddie*, upheld the application of filing fees to deny indigents access to a bankruptcy court and to judicial review of the denial of WELFARE BENEFITS. A similarly artificial line was drawn in the BURGER COURT's decisions on the right to counsel. The *Gideon* principle was extended, in ARGERSINGER V. HAMLIN (1972), to all prosecutions resulting in imprisonment. Yet in LASSITER V. DEPARTMENT OF SOCIAL SERVICES (1981) a 5–4 Court refused to hold that due process required a state to provide counsel for an indigent mother in a proceeding to terminate her parental rights, absent a showing of complexity or other special circumstances. Behind all these flimsy distinctions surely lay the same considerations urged from the beginning by the *Griffin* and *Douglas* dissenters: keep the "floodgates" closed; keep judges' hands off the allocation of public funds.

An access principle of minimal fairness is better than nothing. Yet in a great many contexts the essence of the access claim is an interest in equality itself. To have one's effective say is to be treated as a respected, participating member of the society. An effective hearing in court is more than a chance to influence a judge's decision; it is a vivid symbol of equal citizenship.

KENNETH L. KARST

Bibliography

GOODPASTER, GARY　1970　The Integration of Equal Protection, Due Process Standards, and the Indigent's Right of Free Access to the Courts. *Iowa Law Review* 56:223–266.

MICHELMAN, FRANK I.　1973, 1974　The Supreme Court and Litigation Access Fees. Part 1, *Duke Law Journal* 1973:1153–1215; Part 2, *Duke Law Journal* 1974:527–570.

ACT OF STATE DOCTRINE

Recognized by English courts as early as 1674, the act of state DOCTRINE prohibits United States courts from examining the validity of foreign acts of state. Chief Justice JOHN MARSHALL mentioned a doctrine of noninvolvement in 1808, but the Supreme Court did not accord it formal recognition until *Underhill v. Hernandez* (1897). Initially, the doctrine strongly resembled the doctrine of SOVEREIGN IMMUNITY which protects the person or acts of a sovereign. In fact, the act of state doctrine may have been invented to deal with technical deficiencies in sovereign immunity.

The act of state doctrine received renewed attention in *Banco Nacional de Cuba v. Sabbatino* (1964) where an 8–1 Supreme Court held that it applied even when the foreign state's sovereign act violated international law. Justice JOHN MARSHALL HARLAN's majority opinion rejected earlier assertions that the "inherent nature of sovereign authority" underlay the doctrine; instead it arose out of the SEPARATION OF POWERS. Justice BYRON R. WHITE, dissenting, read Harlan's opinion to declare "exclusive absolute [executive] control" of foreign relations. Acknowledging executive control, White claimed that "this is far from saying . . . that the validity of a foreign act of state is necessarily a POLITICAL QUESTION." The Court had, in fact, dismissed a specific executive branch request, contending that it need not be bound by executive determinations; the Court repeated this position in *Zschernig v. Miller* (1968) and unequivocally denied such executive control in *First National City Bank v. Banco Nacional de Cuba* (1972) (where two majority Justices joined four dissenters to so argue).

In an effort to harmonize the act of state doctrine with that of sovereign immunity, Justice White tried to create a commercial act exception to the act of state doctrine in *Alfred Dunhill of London, Inc. v. Cuba* (1976), but he failed to convince a majority on this issue. Because the case had involved no formal governmental decree, White would not have allowed the act of state defense. Even had an act of state been shown, White opposed the doctrine's extension to "purely commercial" acts of a sovereign or its commercial instrumentalities. He relied on the notion, accepted ever since *Bank of the United States v. Planters' Bank of Georgia* (1824), that a government's partnership in a commercial business does not confer sovereign status on that business.

Also in 1976, Congress passed the Foreign Sovereign Immunities Act which authorized American courts to determine foreign claims of sovereign immunity, thus approving judicial—as opposed to executive—decisions on the validity of such claims. Although the act established a general rule of immunity of foreign states from the jurisdiction of American courts, its "exceptions" were wide-ranging. Immunity is denied, for example, when the foreign state engages in commercial activity, or takes certain property rights in violation of international law, or is sued for damages for certain kinds of injury to person or property.

DAVID GORDON

Bibliography

GORDON, DAVID　1977　The Origin and Development of the Act of State Doctrine. *Rutgers Law Journal* 8:595–616.

ADAIR v. UNITED STATES
208 U.S. 161 (1908)

After the Pullman strike, which paralyzed the nation's railroads, a federal commission blamed the antiunion activities of the railroads and recommended legislation which Congress enacted in 1898. The ERDMAN ACT sought to free INTERSTATE COMMERCE from railroad strikes by establishing a railroad labor board with arbitration powers and by protecting the right of railroad workers to organize in unions. This second objective was the subject of section ten of the act, which prohibited YELLOW DOG CONTRACTS, blacklisting union members, and discharging employees solely for belonging to a union. The act applied to carriers engaged in interstate commerce. Adair, a manager of a carrier, fired an employee solely because of his union membership; a federal court found Adair guilty of violating section ten. On appeal the Supreme Court, by a vote of 6–2, found section ten unconstitutional for violating the Fifth Amendment's DUE PROCESS clause and for exceeding the powers of Congress under the COMMERCE CLAUSE.

Justice JOHN MARSHALL HARLAN, who spoke for the Court, usually wrote broad commerce clause opinions, but this one was constricted. He could see "no legal or logical connection" between an employee's membership in a labor organization and the carrying on of interstate commerce. The Pullman strike, the federal commission, and Congress's finding that such a connection existed meant nothing to the Court. A week later the Court held, in LOEWE V. LAWLOR (1908), that members of a labor organization who boycotted a manufacturing firm, whose products were intended for interstate commerce, had restrained interstate commerce in violation of the SHERMAN ANTITRUST ACT. In Adair, however, the Court found no constitutional authority for Congress to legislate on the labor affairs of interstate railroads.

Most of Harlan's opinion dealt with the due process issue. He found section ten to be "an invasion of the personal liberty, as well as the right to property," guaranteed by the Fifth Amendment. It embraced the right of employers to contract for labor and the right of labor to contract for its services without government intervention. In his exposition of FREEDOM OF CONTRACT, which is a doctrine derived from SUBSTANTIVE DUE PROCESS, Harlan contended that "it is not within the functions of government . . . to compel any person, in the course of his business and against his will, to accept or retain the personal services of another. . . ." The right of the employee to quit, said Harlan, "is the same as the right of the employer, for whatever reason, to dispense with the services of such employee." The Court forgot the more realistic view it had expressed in HOLDEN V. HARDY (1898), and held that "any legislation" disturbing the "equality of right" arbitrarily interferes with "the liberty of contract which no government can legally justify in a free land." Justice JOSEPH MCKENNA dissented mainly on the ground that the Court "stretched to its extreme" the liberty of contract doctrine. The Court overruled Adair in 1949.

LEONARD W. LEVY

Bibliography
LIEBERMAN, ELIAS 1950 Unions Before the Bar. Pages 44–55. New York: Harper & Row.

ADAMS, HENRY
(1838–1918)

Born to a family whose service to the Constitution was matched by a reverence for it "this side of idolatry," Henry Brooks Adams served the Constitution as a historian of the nation it established. His great *History of the United States during the Administrations of Jefferson and Madison* as well as his biographies of JOHN RANDOLPH and ALBERT GALLATIN and his *Documents Relating to New England Federalism* remain standard sources for the events and characters of the early republican years during which the Constitution was being worked out in practice. Among the highlights of these works are Adams's ironic account of THOMAS JEFFERSON's exercise of his constitutional powers in the face of his particularist scruples, the Republican hostility to the federal judiciary, and the fate of STATES' RIGHTS views. In reply to HERMANN VON HOLST's criticism of the Constitution, Adams wrote in 1876, "the Constitution has done its work. It has made a nation." Adams's own disillusion with this nation affected his writings. Like others of his generation, he became more determinist as he became less sanguine, and the *History* shows this shift in his view as the Constitution is described becoming an engine of American nationalism, democracy, expansion, and centralization. In his novels, historical theory, letters, and *The Education of Henry Adams*, he came to regard the Constitution as almost a figment of human intention in a modern age—an age in which the kind of person it once was possible for an Adams to be has no role.

ROBERT DAWIDOFF

Bibliography
SAMUELS, ERNEST 1948–1964 Henry Adams. 3 Vols. Cambridge, Mass: Harvard University Press.

ADAMS, JOHN
(1735–1826)

Massachusetts lawyer and revolutionary leader, first vice-president and second President of the United States, John Adams was also a distinguished political and constitutional theorist. Born in 1735, the descendant of three generations of hardy independent farmers in Braintree, Massachusetts, near Boston, he attended Harvard College and after graduation studied law for several years, gaining admission to the bar in 1758. The practice of a country lawyer held no charms for him. He took delight in the study of law and government, however, and this scholarly pursuit merged imperceptibly with the polemics of the revolutionary controversy, which probed the nature and history of the English CONSTITUTION. Adams made his political debut in 1765 as the author of Braintree's protest against the Stamp Act. Increasingly, from the pressures of politics as well as of business, he was drawn to Boston, moving there with his young family in 1768. Unlike his cousin SAMUEL ADAMS, he was not an ardent revolutionist. He worried about the "mischievous democratic principles" churned up by the agitation; he braved the popular torrent to defend Captain Thomas Preston and the British soldiers accused of murder in the Boston Massacre. For several years he was torn between Boston and Braintree, and the different worlds they represented. Only in 1773 did he commit himself fully to the Revolution.

The next year, during the crisis produced by the Intolerable Acts, Adams was elected one of the Massachusetts delegates to the FIRST CONTINENTAL CONGRESS, in Philadelphia. Events had shaken his lawyerlike stance on the issues, and he championed the patriots' appeal to "the law of nature," as well as to the English constitution and COLONIAL CHARTERS, in defense of American liberties. He wrote the crucial fourth article of the congress's declaration of rights denying the authority of Parliament to legislate for the colonies, though acquiescing in imperial regulation of trade as a matter of convenience. Back in Boston he expounded his views at length in the series of *Novanglus* letters in the press. TREASON and rebellion, he argued, were on the other side—the advocates of parliamentary supremacy abroad and the Tory oligarchy at home. He had no quarrel with George III, and he lauded the English constitution with its nice balance between king, lords, and commons and its distinctly republican character. Unfortunately, the constitution was not made for colonies. Denied REPRESENTATION in Parliament, they were deprived of the constitution's best feature. The proper relationship between the colonies and the mother country, Adams said, was the same as Scotland's before the Act of Union, that is, as an independent government owing allegiance to a common king. Had America been conquered, like Ireland, imperial rule would be warranted; but America was a discovered, not a conquered, country, and so the people possessed the NATURAL RIGHT to make their own laws as far as compatible with allegiance to the king.

In the Second Continental Congress Adams lost all hope of reconciliation on these terms, and he became a leading advocate of American independence. Although a member of the committee to draft the DECLARATION OF INDEPENDENCE, he made his greatest contribution when it came to the floor for debate. Before this he co-authored and championed the resolution—"a machine to fabricate independence" in opposition eyes—calling upon the colonies to form new governments. Nothing was more important to Adams than the making of new constitutions and the restoration of legitimate authority. He had read all the political theorists from Plato to Rousseau; now he reread them with a view to incorporating their best principles into the foundations of the polity. Government was "the divine science"—"the first in importance"—and American independence opened, in his eyes, a grand "age of political experiments." It was, he declared, "a time when the greatest lawgivers of antiquity would have wished to live. How few of the human race have ever enjoyed an opportunity of making an election of government—more than of air, soil, or climate—for themselves or their children!" To aid this work Adams sketched his ideas in an epistolary essay, *Thoughts on Government*, which was destined to have wide influence. Years later, in his autobiography, Adams said that he wrote to counteract the plan of government advanced by that "disastrous meteor" THOMAS PAINE in *Common Sense*. Paine's ideas, which gave shape to the new PENNSYLVANIA CONSTITUTION OF 1776, were "too democratical," mainly because they concentrated all power in a single representative assembly without mixture or balance. Adams, by contrast, proposed a "complex" government of representative assembly, council (or senate), and governor, each endowed with a negative on the others. The people would glide easily into such a government because of its close resemblance to the colonial governments they had known. It possessed additional merit for Adams as a thoroughly republican adaptation of the idealized balance of the English constitution. Even as he challenged the work of constitution-making, however, Adams was assailed by doubts. The new governments might be too free to survive. The essence of republics was *virtue*, that is, selfless devotion to the common weal, but Adams, still a Puritan under his republican skin, clung to a theory of human nature that emphasized man's capacity for selfishness, ignorance, and vice. The POPULAR SOVEREIGNTY that was the basis of republican government possessed the power to destroy it.

In 1779, after returning to the United States from the first of two diplomatic missions abroad, Adams had the opportunity to amplify his constitutional theory, indeed to become the Solon of his native state. Massachusetts continued to be governed by a revolutionary body, the provincial congress, without legitimate constitutional authority. Only in the previous year the citizenry had rejected a constitution framed by the congress. Now they elected a CONSTITUTIONAL CONVENTION for the specific purpose of framing a FUNDAMENTAL LAW, which would then be referred back to them for approval. (When the process was completed in 1780, the MASSACHUSETTS CONSTITUTION exhibited, for the first time anywhere, all the means by which the theory of "constituent sovereignty," one of the foundations of the American republic, was put into practice.) Elected Braintree's delegate, Adams was assigned the task of preparing a draft constitution for consideration by the convention, and this became, after comparatively few changes, its final product. The preamble reiterated the contractual and consensual basis of government. It was followed by a declaration of rights, derivative of the Virginia model but much more elaborate. Adams was not responsible for Article III—the most disputed provision—making it the duty of the legislature, and thus in turn of the various towns and parishes, to support religion; yet this was consistent with the aim of the constitution as a whole to keep Massachusetts a Christian commonwealth. For Adams religion was as essential to virtue as virtue was to republicanism. Thus he proposed a RELIGIOUS TEST for all elected officials. (The delegates voted to confine the test to the office of governor.) The strength and independence of the executive was an unusual feature of the constitution. Reacting against monarchy, most of the new state constitutions weakened and shackled the governors; but Adams believed that a kingly executive was necessary to control the conflicting passions and interests in the legislature. Accordingly, he proposed to vest the Massachusetts governor with an absolute negative on legislation. The convention declined to follow him, however, conferring a suspensive veto only. Adams ever after felt that the trimming of the governor's legislative power was the one serious error of the convention. Otherwise, with respect to the legislature, his principles were fully embodied in the constitution. Representation in the lower house was based upon population, while representation in the upper house, being proportioned to the taxable wealth of the several senatorial districts, was based upon property. This system of giving representation to property as well as numbers had its principal source in the philosophy of James Harrington, whose axiom "power always follows property," Adams said, "is as infallible a maxim in politics as that action and reaction are equal in mechanics." Property was further joined to office by requiring wealth on an ascending scale of value to make representatives, senators, and governors eligible for their offices. Finally, the constitution retained the freehold qualification for the franchise. In these features it was a distinctly conservative document, and it would, Adams later complained, give him "the reputation of a man of high principles and strong notions in government, scarcely compatible with republicanism."

Adams was in France when the Massachusetts Constitution was ratified in 1780. After helping negotiate the treaty of peace, he was named by Congress the first minister of the United States to Great Britain. He did not return home until 1788. He had, therefore, no direct part in the formation of the United States Constitution. Of course, he took a keen interest in that event. Observing it from his station abroad, he was inevitably influenced by Europe's perception of the terrible weakness of the American confederation and by the tide of democratic revolution that, in his own perception, threatened to inundate the European continent.

Like many of the Americans who would attend the CONSTITUTIONAL CONVENTION OF 1787, Adams was alarmed by SHAYS' REBELLION in Massachusetts, and he took up his pen once again to show the way to constitutional salvation. His three-volume work, *Defence of the American Constitutions* (1787) was devoted to the classical proposition that the *"unum necessarium"* of republican government is the tripartite division of the legislative power, each of the branches embodying a distinctive principle and power—the one, the few, and the many, or monarchy, aristocracy, democracy—and the dynamics of the balance between them securing the equilibrium of the whole. The book's title was misleading. It was not actually a defense of the state constitutions, most of which Adams thought indefensible, but rather a defense of the true republican theory against the criticism of those constitutions by the French *philosophe* Robert Jacques Turgot and his school, who held that instead of collecting all authority at one center, as the logic of equality and popular sovereignty dictated, the American constitutions erred in dividing power among different social orders and principles of government in pale imitation of the English king, lords, and commons. Adams sought to demonstrate, of course, that this balanced government was founded in the law of reason and nature. He ransacked European history, carving huge chunks from the writings of philosophers and historians—about eighty percent of the text—and adding his own argumentative comments to prove his point. All societies are divided between the few and the many, the rich and the poor, aristocrats and commoners; and these two orders, actuated by passion and ambition, are constantly at war with each other. The only escape, the only security, is through the tripartite balance. It involves, primarily, erecting a third power, a monarchical executive, to serve as a balance wheel and umpire between the democracy and the aristocracy. It involves also constituting these two great orders in insulated chambers, wherein each may flourish but neither may dominate or subvert the other. Vice, interest, and ambition are rendered useful when these two orders are made to control each other and a monarchical executive is installed as the presiding genius over the whole.

With the publication of the *Defence,* Adams's political thought hardened into a system that placed him at odds with democratic forces and opinion in both Europe and the United States. In 1789 the French National Assembly rejected his doctrine. At home he was alienated from many former political friends. The subject of his apostasy from republicanism became, it was said, "a kind of political phenomenon." He denied any apostasy, of course, and his use of such galvanizing abstractions as "monarchy" and "aristocracy" undoubtedly opened him to misrepresentation. Nevertheless, the character of his thought had changed. During his sojourn abroad Adams became the captive of Old World political fears, which he then transferred to the United States, where they did not belong. Here, as he sometimes recognized, all men were of one order. Yet for several years after his return to the United States, Adams did not disguise his belief that hereditary monarchy and aristocracy must eventually prove as necessary to the American republic as they had to every other. They were, he said, the only institutions that could preserve the laws and liberties of the people against discord, sedition, and civil war.

These beliefs did not prevent Adams's election as vice-president in 1788. Long a friend of a national government, he approved of the Constitution and even imagined the *Defence* had influenced it. He wished the executive were stronger and feared the recurrent shocks to the system from frequent elections and the factions, turbulence, and intrigue they bred. For a time he toyed with the idea of a second convention to overcome these weaknesses. His concern for the authority and dignity of the government led him to propose in the First Congress a high-sounding title ("His Most Benign Highness") for the President and splendid ceremonies of state in order to awe the people. He reiterated those views and continued the argument of the *Defence* in a series of articles (*Discourses on Davila*) in the *Gazette of the United States,* in Philadelphia. Since the articles also de-

nounced the French Revolution, they were an American parallel to Edmund Burke's *Reflections on the Revolution in France.* When the doctrines were publicly labeled "political heresies" by Adams's old friend, THOMAS JEFFERSON, the secretary of state, the ideological division between them entered into the emerging party conflict. In this conflict Adams proved himself a loyal Federalist. Not wishing to cause further embarrassment to GEORGE WASHINGTON's administration, which the Republicans assailed as Anglican and monarchical, Adams put away his pen in 1791 and withdrew into the recesses of the vice-presidency.

Elected President in 1797, Adams at first sought political reconciliation with his Republican rival, Jefferson, but the effort foundered amidst intense partisanship and foreign crisis. The issue of war and peace with France absorbed his administration. Working to resolve it, Adams was handicapped both by the Republican opposition and by the High Federalists in his cabinet who took their orders from ALEXANDER HAMILTON. The collapse of negotiations with France was followed by frantic preparations for war in the spring of 1798. Adams favored naval defense—and the Navy Department was created. He distrusted Hamilton, who favored a large army, seeing in him a potential Caesar. When General Washington, called out of retirement to command the new army, demanded that the second place be given to Hamilton, Adams resisted, citing his prerogative as COMMANDER-IN-CHIEF, he but was finally forced to yield. He did not recommend and had no direct responsibility for the ALIEN AND SEDITION ACTS passed by Congress in July. Yet he contributed as much as anyone to the war hysteria that provoked this repressive legislation. In his public answers to the addresses of loyalty that poured into Philadelphia, Adams repeatedly condemned "the wild philosophy," "domestic treachery," and "spirit of party, which scruples not to go all lengths of profligacy, falsehood, and malignity in defaming our government." Thus branded disloyal by a President whose philosophy made no place for organized POLITICAL PARTIES, the Republican leaders became easy targets. Moreover, Adams cooperated in the enforcement of these laws. The Alien Law was not fully executed in a single instance, but Adams deserves little credit for this. He apparently approved the numerous prosecutions under the Sedition Law, and showed no mercy for its victims. In retrospect, when the impolicy of the laws was generally conceded, Adams still never doubted their constitutionality.

Despite the prescriptions of his political theory, Adams was not a strong President. Indeed, because of that theory, he continued to consider the office above party and politics, though the conception was already unworkable. In the end he asserted his authority and in one glorious act of statesmanship broke with the High Federalists and made peace with France. The domestic consequences were as important as the foreign. Adams sometimes said he made peace in order to squelch Hamilton and his designs for the army. Standing army, foreign adventurism, mounting debt and taxes—these dangers recalled to Adams the Whig doctrines of his youth. "All the declarations . . . of Trenchard and Gordon [see CATO'S LETTERS], Bolingbroke, Barnard and Walpole, Hume, Burgh, and Burke, rush upon my memory and frighten me out of my wits," he confessed. Patriotic, courageous, and wise, Adams's actions nevertheless split the Federalist party and paved the way for Jefferson's triumph in the election of 1800. Before he left office, Adams signed into law the JUDICIARY ACT OF 1801, creating many new federal courts and judgeships, which he proceeded to fill with faithful partisans. In the Republican view the Federalists retreated to the judiciary as a fortress from which to defeat every popular reform. Less noticed at the time but more important for the nation's constitutional development was the nomination and appointment of JOHN MARSHALL as Chief Justice of the United States.

In retirement at Quincy, Adams slowly made peace with Jeffersonian Republicanism and watched his son JOHN QUINCY ADAMS, who broke with the Federalists in 1808, rise to become the sixth President of the United States. A compulsive and contentious reader, Adams never lost his enthusiasm for political speculation; and although he grew more and more hopeful about the American experiment, he continued to the end to warn the people against their own suicidal tendencies. In 1820 he attended the convention to revise the Massachusetts constitution he had drafted forty years before. When the reformers attacked the "aristocratical principle" of a senate bottomed on property, Adams spoke spiritedly in its defense. And, with most of the original constitution, it survived. The finest literary product of these years—one of the intellectual monuments of the age—was his correspondence with Thomas Jefferson, with whom he was reconciled in friendship in 1812. The correspondence traversed an immense field. In politics, the two men discoursed brilliantly on "natural aristocracy," further defining a fundamental issue of principle between them. Interestingly, Adams's political anxieties, unlike Jefferson's, never fixed upon the Constitution. He did not turn political questions into constitutional questions. He was a nationalist, of course, and spoke highly

of the Union; but for all his work on constitutional government, Adams rarely uttered a complete thought on the United States Constitution. The amiability and learning, the candor and humor, with the occasional banter and abandon of his letters were all perfectly in character. In the often quoted observation of BENJAMIN FRANKLIN, John Adams was "always an honest man, often a wise one, but sometimes, and in some things, absolutely out of his senses." He died, as did Jefferson, on the fiftieth anniversary of American independence, July 4, 1826.

MERRILL D. PETERSON

Bibliography

ADAMS, CHARLES FRANCIS, ED. 1850–1856 *The Works of John Adams.* 10 Vols. Boston: Little, Brown.

BUTTERFIELD, LYMAN C., ED. 1961 *The Diary and Autobiography of John Adams.* 4 Vols. Cambridge, Mass.: Harvard University Press.

HARASZTI, ZOLTAN 1952 *John Adams and the Prophets of Progress.* Cambridge, Mass.: Harvard University Press.

HOWE, JOHN R., JR. 1966 *The Changing Political Thought of John Adams.* Princeton, N.J.: Princeton University Press.

KURTZ, STEPHEN G. 1957 *The Presidency of John Adams.* Philadelphia: University of Pennsylvania Press.

SMITH, PAGE 1962 *John Adams.* 2 Vols. Garden City, N.Y.: Doubleday.

ADAMS, JOHN QUINCY
(1767–1848)

John Quincy Adams served the nation in its earliest days, contributing as diplomat, secretary of state, President, and congressman to the development of constitutional government in America. Throughout his career he sought to be a "man of the whole nation," an ambition that earned him enemies in his native New England and in the South during a period of political sectionalism. As congressman from Massachusetts between 1831 and 1848, he played a decisive role in the development of the Whig theory of the United States Constitution. His speeches in this period inspired a whole generation of Americans to resist the expansion of SLAVERY and to defend the Union.

Adams's political career began at the age of fifteen, when he went as private secretary to his father, JOHN ADAMS, on the diplomatic mission that negotiated the Treaty of Paris (1783). In 1801 he was elected United States senator. He angered Federalists by his support of THOMAS JEFFERON's acquisition of Louisiana and by his cooperation with the administration's policy of countering English and French attacks on American shipping by economic means. This policy resulted in the Embargo (1807) and gave rise to a SECESSION movement in New England (culminating in the HARTFORD CONVENTION of 1814–1815). Eighteen months before his term ended, the legislature elected a replacement and Adams resigned his Senate seat. He returned to private practice of the law, supporting the Yazoo claimants before the Supreme Court in FLETCHER V. PECK (1809). In the same year, President JAMES MADISON appointed him minister to Russia. As secretary of state under JAMES MONROE (1816–1824), Adams secured American territorial claims to the Pacific Northwest and defended ANDREW JACKSON's conduct in Florida during the Seminole Wars. Adams was the principal author of the MONROE DOCTRINE, defending the Latin American republics from fresh incursions by European imperialism.

In 1824 Adams was elected President by the House of Representatives, none of the major candidates (Adams, Jackson, William Crawford, and HENRY CLAY) having achieved a majority in the ELECTORAL COLLEGE. The 1824 election created a political enmity between Adams and Jackson that seriously undermined Adams's presidency. Jackson had received a large plurality of popular votes, and the general's supporters portrayed Adams's election as an antidemocratic "corrupt bargain" between Adams and Clay, whom Adams appointed as secretary of state. In spite of Adams's strong disapproval of partisan politics, his administration gave rise to the second party system: Jacksonian Democrats versus Whigs.

In addition to the conflict between "plain republicans" and "aristocrats"—a popular division recalling the rhetoric of the Jeffersonians—another conflict arising from Adams's presidency was that between partisans of "BROAD CONSTRUCTION" and of "STRICT CONSTRUCTION" of the constitutional powers of the federal government. This division arose from Adams's call for a vigorous program of nationally funded INTERNAL IMPROVEMENTS—roads, canals, harbors, naval facilities, etcetera—a program that Henry Clay named the AMERICAN SYSTEM. But at bottom the division resulted from fundamental disagreements about the character of the Union.

Defeated for reelection in 1828, Adams seemed at the end of his career. In 1829 he wrote the least prudent, if most interesting, of his many essays and pamphlets, an account of the events leading up to the convening of the Hartford Convention, implicating many of New England's most famous men in TREASON. In writing this long essay (published posthumously as *Documents Relating to New England Federalism, 1801–1815*) he developed a THEORY OF THE UNION that constituted the burden of his speeches and public writings until his death in 1848, and that became the political gospel of the new Republican party and its greatest leader, ABRAHAM LINCOLN.

According to Adams, the Constitution was not a compact between sovereign states but was the organic law of the American nation, given by the American people to themselves in the exercise of their inalienable right to consent to the form of government over them. The state governments derived their existence from the same act of consent that created the federal government. They did not exist before the federal government, therefore, and could not have created it themselves by compact. What is more, the state governments, like the federal government, depended decisively on the truth of those first principles of politics enunciated in the DECLARATION OF INDEPENDENCE for their own legitimacy.

This Whig theory of the Constitution was politically provocative. By it slavery was a clear moral evil. Adams, like Lincoln after him, justified the compromise with slavery as necessary in the circumstances to the existence of a constitutional union in America, but Adams vehemently maintained the duty to prevent the spread of what was at best a necessary evil. While he advocated a scrupulous care for the legal rights of slavery where it was established, he insisted that the government of the United States must always speak as a free state in world affairs. He believed it to be a duty of the whole nation to set slavery, as Lincoln would later say, on the course of ultimate extinction.

This theory guided his words and deeds in the House of Representatives from 1831 until his death. For fourteen years he waged an almost single-handed war against the dominant Jacksonian Democratic majority in the House, a struggle focused on the GAG RULE. The gag rule was actually a series of standing rules adopted at every session of Congress from 1836 on. In its final form it read: "No petition, memorial, resolution, or other paper praying the abolition of slavery in the DISTRICT OF COLUMBIA or any State or Territory, or the slave trade between the States or Territories in which it now exists, shall be received by this House, or entertained in any way whatever."

The gag rule was part of a policy followed by the Democratic party in this period, on the advice of JOHN C. CALHOUN, among others, never in the least thing to admit the authority of Congress over slavery. Adams argued that the gag was a patent abrogation of the FIRST AMENDMENT's guarantee of FREEDOM

OF PETITION. His speeches against the gag became a rallying point for the growing free-soil and abolition movements in the North, though Adams himself was cautious about endorsing the program of the radicals.

Through a long and varied career, Adams's statesmanship was guided by the twin principles of liberty and union. As a diplomat and architect of American foreign policy, Adams played a large part in the creation of a continental Republic. He believed that the westward expansion of the country was necessary if the United States was to minimize foreign interference in its domestic politics. Yet expansion brought the most powerful internal forces of disruption of the Union into play and prepared the way for the Civil War.

GEORGE FORSYTH

Bibliography

BEMIS, SAMUEL F. 1949 *John Quincy Adams and the Foundations of American Foreign Policy.* New York: Knopf.
———— 1956 *John Quincy Adams and the Union.* New York: Knopf.
LIPSKY, GEORGE A. 1950 *John Quincy Adams: His Theories and Ideas.* New York: Crowell.

ADAMS, SAMUEL
(1722–1803)

Samuel Adams was one of the greatest leaders of the American Revolution whose career flourished during the long struggle with Great Britain. His strength was in Massachusetts state politics; he was less successful as a national politician. His speeches and writings influenced the shape of American constitutional thought.

Adams's political career began in 1764 when he wrote the instructions of the Boston town meeting to Boston's representatives in the legislature. These included the first formal denial of the right of Parliament to tax the colonists: "If taxes are laid upon us in any shape without our having a legal representation where they are laid, are we not reduced from the character of free subjects to the miserable state of tributary slaves?"

The next year he was elected to the legislature and assumed leadership of the radical popular opposition to the governing clique headed by THOMAS HUTCHINSON. Adams maintained that he was defending not only the rights of British colonists but also the NATURAL RIGHTS of all men: "The leading principles of the British Constitution have their foundation in the Laws of Nature and universal Reason. . . . British rights are in great measure the Rights of the Colonists, and of all men else." Adams led the opposition to the Stamp Act and the TOWNSHEND ACTS. He denounced these acts as unconstitutional, since they involved TAXATION WITHOUT REPRESENTATION.

In the MASSACHUSETTS CIRCULAR LETTER of 1768 Adams wrote of constitutions in general that they should be fixed and unalterable by ordinary legislation, and that under no constitution could subjects be deprived of their property except by their consent, given in person or by elected representatives. Of the British Constitution in particular he argued that, although Parliament might legislate on imperial matters, only the colonial assemblies could legislate on local matters or impose special taxes.

When the British government landed troops at Boston, Adams published a series of letters denouncing as unconstitutional the keeping of a standing army in peacetime without the consent of the people of the colony. "The Americans," he wrote, "as they were not and could not be represented in Parliament, were therefore suffering under military tyranny over which they were allowed to exercise no control."

In the early 1770s, Adams worked to create a network of committees of correspondence. In November 1772, on behalf of the Boston Committee of Correspondence, he drafted a declaration of the rights of the colonists. In three sections it proclaimed the rights of Americans as men, as Christians, and as British subjects. A list of infringements of those rights followed, including the assumption by Parliament of the power to legislate for the colonies in all cases whatsoever and the grant of a royal salary to Governor Thomas Hutchinson and the judges in Massachusetts.

In January 1773 Hutchinson, addressing the legislature, argued for acceptance of the absolute supremacy of the British Parliament and asserted that there was no middle ground between unqualified submission and independence. Samuel Adams, along with JOHN ADAMS, drafted the reply of the Assembly, arguing anew that under the British Constitution the colonial legislature shared power with Parliament.

Samuel Adams was an early proponent of a Continental Congress, and in June 1774 he was elected to the First Continental Congress. There he played a key role in the adoption of the ASSOCIATION. In the Second Continental Congress he moved, in January 1776, for immediate independence and for a federation of the colonies. In July 1776, he signed the DECLARATION OF INDEPENDENCE.

Adams remained a member of the Continental

Congress until 1781. He was a member of the original committee to draft the ARTICLES OF CONFEDERATION. Suspicious of any concentration of power, he opposed creation of the executive departments of finance, war, and foreign affairs. In 1779–1780 he was a delegate to the Massachusetts CONSTITUTIONAL CONVENTION, which produced the first of the Revolutionary state constitutions to be ratified by popular vote.

Throughout the Revolutionary period Adams was a staunch supporter of unified action. When, in 1783, a Massachusetts convention was held to plan resistance to congressional enactment of a pension for army officers, Adams, who had opposed the pension, defended Congress's right to pass it and spoke out against those who would dishonor the state's commitment to pay continental debts.

In 1787, after SHAYS' REBELLION had broken out, Adams, then president of the state senate, proposed to invoke the assistance of the United States as provided in the Articles of Confederation, but his motion failed in the lower house. Later, opposing the pardon of the rebels, he argued that there is a crucial difference between monarchy and self-government and that any "man who dares to rebel against the laws of a republic ought to suffer death."

Adams was not named a delegate to the CONSTITUTIONAL CONVENTION OF 1787, but he was influential at the Massachusetts ratifying convention: "I stumble at the threshold," he wrote to RICHARD HENRY LEE, "I meet with a national government, instead of a federal union of sovereign states." He was troubled by the division of powers in the proposed federal system, which constituted *Imperia in Imperio* [supreme powers within a supreme power] justly deemed a Solecism in Politicks, highly dangerous, and destructive of the Peace Union and Safety of the Nation." Ironically, he echoed the argument of his old enemy Hutchinson that SOVEREIGNTY was indivisible. But, after a meeting of his constituents passed a resolution that "any vote of a delegate from Boston against adopting it would be contrary to the interests, feelings, and wishes of the tradesmen of the town," Adams altered his position. In the end he supported a plan whereby Massachusetts ratified the Constitution unconditionally but also proposed a series of amendments, including a BILL OF RIGHTS.

Adams was defeated by FISHER AMES for election to the first Congress. Thereafter, although he remained active in state politics as a legislator and governor (1794–1797), he never again sought or held national office under the Constitution.

DENNIS J. MAHONEY

Bibliography

MAIER, PAULINE 1980 *The Old Revolutionaries: Political Lives in the Age of Samuel Adams.* New York: Knopf.
MILLER, JOHN C. 1936 *Sam Adams: Pioneer in Propaganda.* Boston: Little, Brown.
WELLS, WILLIAM V. 1865 *Life and Public Services of Samuel Adams . . . With Extracts from His Correspondence, State Papers, and Political Essays.* Boston: Little, Brown.

ADAMS v. TANNER
244 U.S. 590 (1917)

In a 5–4 decision, the Supreme Court declared unconstitutional a Washington state statute prohibiting individuals from paying employment agencies for their services. Although a loophole allowed prospective employers to pay the agencies' fees, Justice JAMES C. MCREYNOLDS nevertheless voided the law as a prohibition, not a regulation, of business. Citing ALLGEYER V. LOUISIANA (1897), McReynolds also declared the statute a violation of DUE PROCESS OF LAW. Justice LOUIS D. BRANDEIS dissented, joined by Justices OLIVER WENDELL HOLMES and JOHN H. CLARKE, demonstrating the "vast evils" that justified the legislature under STATE POLICE POWERS.

DAVID GORDON

(SEE ALSO: *Ribnik v. McBride*, 1928; *Tyson & Brother v. Banton*, 1927; and *Olsen v. Nebraska ex rel. Reference & Bond Association*, 1941.)

ADAMSON v. CALIFORNIA
332 U.S. 46 (1947)

By a 5–4 vote the Supreme Court, speaking through Justice STANLEY F. REED, sustained the constitutionality of provisions of California laws permitting the trial court and prosecutor to call the jury's attention to the accused's failure to explain or deny evidence against him. Adamson argued that the Fifth Amendment's RIGHT AGAINST SELF-INCRIMINATION is a fundamental national privilege protected against state abridgment by the FOURTEENTH AMENDMENT and that the same amendment's DUE PROCESS clause prevented comment on the accused's silence. Reed, relying on TWINING V. NEW JERSEY (1908) and PALKO V. CONNECTICUT (1937), ruled that the Fifth Amendment does not apply to the states and that even adverse comment on the right to silence does not deny due process.

The case is notable less for Reed's opinion, which GRIFFIN V. CALIFORNIA (1965) overruled, than for the classic debate between Justices FELIX FRANK-FURTER, concurring, and HUGO L. BLACK, in dissent, on the INCORPORATION DOCTRINE. Joined by Justice WILLIAM O. DOUGLAS, Black read the history of the origins of the Fourteenth Amendment to mean that its framers and ratifiers intended to make the entire BILL OF RIGHTS applicable to the states, a position that Justice FRANK MURPHY, joined by Justice WILEY RUTLEDGE, surpassed by adding that the Fourteenth Amendment also protected unenumerated rights. Frankfurter, seeking to expose the inconsistency of the dissenters, suggested that they did not mean what they said. They would not fasten on the states the requirement of the SEVENTH AMENDMENT that civil cases involving more than $20 require a TRIAL BY JURY. They really intended only a "selective incorpo-ration," Frankfurter declared, and consequently they offered "a merely subjective test." Black, in turn, pur-porting to be quite literal in his interpretation, ridi-culed Frankfurter's subjective reliance on "civilized decency" to explain due process. History probably supports Frankfurter's argument on the original in-tent of the Fourteenth Amendment, but the Justices on both sides mangled the little historical evidence they knew to make it support preconceived positions.

LEONARD W. LEVY

ADAMSON EIGHT-HOUR ACT
39 Stat. 721 (1916)

In 1916 major railway unions demanded an eight-hour working day and extra pay for overtime work. The railroads' refusal prompted a union call for a nation-wide general strike. President WOODROW WILSON, fearing disastrous consequences, appealed to Con-gress for legislation to avert the strike and to protect "the life and interests of the nation." The Adamson Act mandated an eight-hour day for railroad workers engaged in INTERSTATE COMMERCE. The act also es-tablished a commission to report on the law's opera-tion. Pending that report, the act prohibited reduction in pay rates for the shorter workday. Overtime would be recompensed at regular wages, not time and a half. Congress effectively constituted itself a labor arbitra-tor and vested its award with the force of law. The Supreme Court rejected the argument that Congress exceeded its constitutional authority in WILSON V. NEW (1917), sustaining the act. The Court distin-guished LOCHNER V. NEW YORK (1905) by asserting

that the Adamson Act did no more than supplement the rights of the contracting parties; the act did not interfere with the FREEDOM OF CONTRACT.

DAVID GORDON

ADDERLEY v. FLORIDA
385 U.S. 39 (1966)

A 5–4 Supreme Court, speaking through Justice HUGO L. BLACK, upheld TRESPASS convictions of CIVIL RIGHTS advocates demonstrating in a jail driveway, holding that where public property is devoted to a special use, FREEDOM OF SPEECH constitutionally may be limited in order to "preserve the property . . . for the use to which it is lawfully dedicated." This case signaled a new attention to the extent to which speakers have a right to carry their expressive activity onto private property and non-PUBLIC FORUM public property. It was also one of the first cases in which Justice Black exhibited the increasingly critical atti-tude toward demonstrations and other nontraditional forms of speech that marked his last years.

MARTIN SHAPIRO

ADEQUATE STATE GROUNDS

Although most decisions of state courts falling within the Supreme Court's APPELLATE JURISDICTION in-volve questions of both state and federal law, the Su-preme Court limits its review of such cases to the FEDERAL QUESTIONS. Moreover, the Court will not even decide the federal questions raised by such a case if the decision below rests on a ground of state law that is adequate to support the judgment and is independent of any federal issue. This rule applies to grounds based on both state substantive law and state procedures.

In its substantive-ground aspect, the rule not only protects the state courts' authority as the final arbiters of state law but also bolsters the principle forbidding federal courts to give ADVISORY OPINIONS. If the Su-preme Court were to review the federal issues pre-sented by a decision resting independently on an ade-quate state ground, the Court's pronouncements on the federal issues would be advisory only, having no effect on the resolution of the case. It has been as-sumed that ordinarily no federal policy dictates Su-preme Court review of a decision resting on an inde-pendent state substantive ground; the winner in the state court typically is the same party who has asserted the federal claim. The point is exemplified by a state court decision invalidating a state statute on both state and federal constitutional grounds. This assumption, however, is a hindrance to Justices bent on contracting the reach of particular constitutional guarantees. In *Michigan v. Long* (1983) the BURGER COURT announced that when the independence of a state court's judgment from federal law is in doubt, the Court will assume that the judgment does not rest independently on state law. To insulate a decision from Supreme Court review now requires a plain statement by the state court of the independence of its state law ground.

Obviously, the highest state court retains considerable control over the reviewability of many of its decisions in the Supreme Court. If the state court chooses to rest decision only on grounds of federal law, as the California court did in REGENTS OF THE UNIVERSITY OF CALIFORNIA V. BAKKE (1978), the case is reviewable by the Supreme Court. Correspondingly, the state court can avoid review by the Supreme Court by resting solely on a state-law ground, or by explicitly resting on *both* a state and a federal ground. In the latter case, the state court's pronouncements on federal law are unreviewable. Recently, several state supreme courts (Alaska, California, Massachusetts, New Jersey, and Oregon) have used these devices to make important contributions to the development of both state and federal constitutional law.

When the state court's decision rests on a procedural ground, the usual effect is to cut off a party's right to claim a federal right, because of some procedural default. The Supreme Court generally insists that federal questions be raised in the state courts according to the dictates of state procedure. However, when the state procedural ground itself violates the federal Constitution (and thus is not "independent" of a federal claim), the Supreme Court will consider the federal issues in the case even though state procedure was not precisely followed. Another exception is exemplified in NAACP V. ALABAMA (1964). There the Court reviewed the NAACP's federal claims although the state court had refused to hear them on the transparently phony ground that they had been presented in a brief that departed from the prescribed format. The adequate state ground rule protects judicial federalism, not shamming designed to defeat the claims of federal right.

A similar rule limits the availability of federal HABEAS CORPUS relief for state prisoners. (See FAY V. NOIA, 1963; WAINWRIGHT V. SYKES, 1977.)

KENNETH L. KARST

Bibliography

FALK, JEROME B., JR. 1973 The Supreme Court of California, 1971–1972—Foreword: The State Constitution: A More Than "Adequate" Nonfederal Ground. *California Law Review* 61:273–286.

ADKINS v. CHILDREN'S HOSPITAL
261 U.S. 525 (1923)

The *Adkins* case climaxed the assimilation of laissez-faire economics into constitutional law. At issue was the constitutionality of a congressional minimum wage law for women and children in the District of Columbia. (See DISTRICT OF COLUMBIA MINIMUM WAGE ACT.) The impact of the case was nationwide, affecting all similar state legislation. In the exercise of its police power over the District, Congress in 1918 established an administrative board with investigatory powers over wages and living standards for underprivileged, unorganized workers. After notice and hearing, the board could order wage increases by fixing minima for women and minors. The board followed a general standard set by the legislature: wages had to be reasonably sufficient to keep workers "in good health" and "protect their morals." A corporation maintaining a hospital in the District and a woman who had lost a job paying $35 a month and two meals daily claimed that the statute violated the Fifth Amendment's DUE PROCESS clause which protected their FREEDOM OF CONTRACT on terms mutually desirable.

The constitutionality of minimum wage legislation had come before the Court in STETTLER V. O'HARA (1917) but because Justice LOUIS D. BRANDEIS had disqualified himself, the Court had split evenly, settling nothing. In the same year, however, Professor FELIX FRANKFURTER won from the Court a decision sustaining the constitutionality of a state maximum hours law in BUNTING V. OREGON (1917). Although the Court sustained that law for men as well as for women and children, it neglected to overrule LOCHNER V. NEW YORK (1905). In that case the Court had held that minimum wage laws for bakers violated the freedom of contract protected by due process of law. Nevertheless, *Bunting* seemed to supersede *Lochner* and followed Justice OLIVER WENDELL HOLMES'S *Lochner* dissent. The Court in *Bunting* presumed the constitutionality of the statute, disavowed examination of the legislature's wisdom in exercising its POLICE POWER, and asserted that the reasonableness of the legislation need not be proved;

the burden of proving unreasonableness fell upon those opposed to the social measure.

Because *Bunting* superseded *Lochner* without overruling it, Frankfurter, who again defended the constitutionality of the statute, took no chances in *Adkins*. He relied on the principles of *Bunting*, the plenary powers of Congress over the District, and the overwhelmingly favorable state court precedents. In the main, however, he sought to show the reasonableness of the minimum wage law for women and children in order to rebut the freedom of contract DOCTRINE. In a BRANDEIS BRIEF, he proved the relation between the very low wages that had prevailed before the statute and the high incidences of child neglect, disease, broken homes, prostitution, and death.

A recent appointee, Justice GEORGE SUTHERLAND, spoke for the *Adkins* majority. Chief Justice WILLIAM HOWARD TAFT, joined by Justice EDWARD SANFORD, dissented also, separately. The vote was 5–3. Brandeis disqualified himself from participating because his daughter worked for the minimum wage board. Sutherland dismissed Frankfurter's brief with the comment that his facts were "interesting but only mildly persuasive." Such facts, said Sutherland, were "proper enough for the consideration of lawmaking bodies, since their tendency is to establish the desirability or undesirability of the legislation; but they reflect no legitimate light upon the question of its validity, and that is what we are called upon to decide." The Court then found, on the basis of its own consideration of policy, that the statute was unwise and undesirable. Sutherland assumed that prostitution among the poor was unrelated to income. He claimed that the recently acquired right of women to vote had elevated them to the same status as men, stripping them of any legal protection based on sexual differences. That disposed of the 1908 ruling in MULLER V. OREGON. Consequently, women had the same right of freedom of contract as men, no more or less.

That freedom was not an absolute, Sutherland conceded, but this case did not fall into any of the exceptional categories of cases in which the government might reasonably restrict that freedom. Female elevator operators, scrubwomen, and dishwashers had a constitutional right to work for whatever they pleased, even if for less than a minimum prescribed by an administrative board. Employers had an equal right to pay what they pleased. If the board could fix minimum wages, employers might be forced to pay more than the value of the services rendered and might have to operate at a loss or even go out of business. By comparing the selling of labor with the selling of goods, Sutherland, ironically, supported the claim that

capitalism regarded labor as a commodity on the open market. On such reasoning the Court found that the statute conflicted with the freedom of contract incorporated within the Fifth Amendment's due process clause. Paradoxically the Court distinguished away *Muller* and *Bunting* because they were maximum hours cases irrelevant to a case involving minimum wages, yet it relied heavily on *Lochner* as controlling, though it too was a maximum hours case. (See MAXIMUM HOURS AND MINIMUM WAGES.)

All this was too much for even that stalwart conservative, Chief Justice Taft, who felt bound by precedent to support the statute. Like Holmes, Taft perceived no difference in principle between a maximum hours law, which was valid, and a minimum wages law, which was not. Holmes went further. In addition to showing that both kinds of legislation interfered with freedom of contract to the same extent, he repudiated the freedom of conduct doctrine as he had in his famous *Lochner* dissent. He criticized the Court for expanding an unpretentious assertion of the liberty to follow one's calling into a far-reaching, rigid dogma. Like Taft, Holmes thought that *Bunting* had silently overruled *Lochner*. Both Taft and Holmes took notice of Frankfurter's evidence to make the point that the statute was not unreasonable. Holmes observed that it "does not compel anybody to pay anything. It simply forbids employment at rates below those fixed as the minimum requirement of health and right living." Holmes also remarked that more than a women's suffrage amendment would be required to make him believe that "there are no differences between men and women, or that legislation cannot take those differences into account." Yet, the most caustic line in the dissenting opinions was Taft's: "it is not the function of this court to hold congressional acts invalid simply because they are passed to carry out economic views which the court believes to be unwise or unsound."

By this decision, the Court voided minimum wage laws throughout the country. Per curiam opinions based on *Adkins* disposed of state statutes whose supporters futilely sought to distinguish their administrative standards from the one before the Court in *Adkins*. Samuel Gompers, the leader of American trade unionism, bitterly remarked, "To buy the labor of a woman is not like buying pigs' feet in a butcher shop." A cartoon in the New York *World* showed Sutherland handing a copy of his opinion to a woman wage earner, saying, "This decision affirms your constitutional right to starve." By preventing minimum wage laws, the Court kept labor unprotected when the Depression struck. *Adkins* remained the law of the land controlling decisions as late as 1936; the Court did not overrule it until 1937. (See WEST COAST HOTEL V. PARRISH.)

LEONARD W. LEVY

Bibliography
BERMAN, EDWARD The Supreme Court and the Minimum Wage. *Journal of Political Economy* 31:852–856.
POWELL, THOMAS REED 1924 The Judiciality of Minimum Wage Legislation. *Harvard Law Review* 37:545–573.

ADLER v. BOARD OF EDUCATION OF CITY OF NEW YORK
342 U.S. 485 (1952)

Adler was one of the cases in which state statutes barring members of "subversive" organizations from public school and other public employment were upheld against FIRST AMENDMENT attack on the basis that public employment is a privilege not a right. Most of these decisions were effectively overruled by KEYISHIAN V. BOARD OF REGENTS (1967).

MARTIN SHAPIRO

(SEE ALSO: *Subversive Activities and the Constitution.*)

ADMINISTRATIVE LAW

"Administrative law" describes the legal structure of much of the executive branch of government, particularly the quasi-independent agencies, and the procedural constraints under which they operate. Most of these constraints are statutory; those that do involve the Constitution flow chiefly from the doctrine of SEPARATION OF POWERS and the DUE PROCESS clause. To comprehend the effects of either of these on administrative law one must understand the growth of the administrative agency in the modern American state.

The early years of the twentieth century saw both a growth in the executive branch of the federal government and, perhaps more important, increased expectations about tasks it should perform. Some have seen these changes as a natural concomitant of industrialization; some as a growth in the power of a new professional class claiming to possess a nonpolitical expertise; some as the result of political pressure developed by farmers and small-town residents who looked to government to contain corporate juggernauts; some as the consequence of the desire of those very juggernauts to gain government sanction shielding them from the competitive forces of the marketplace. Whatever the causes, federal, state, and municipal governments took on new tasks in the closing decades of the nineteenth and the opening ones of the twentieth centuries.

Agencies such as the Interstate Commerce Commission, the Federal Trade Commission, the Food and Drug Administration, and the Federal Reserve Board bore witness to national perceptions that the existing economic and social mechanisms left something to be desired and that increased government intervention was the solution. At the local level the rise of social welfare agencies and zoning boards bespoke similar concerns.

With the coming of the Great Depression the federal government sought to revive the economy through numerous public programs designed both to coordinate sectors of the nation's industrial and commercial life (the WAGNER NATIONAL LABOR RELATIONS ACT, the AGRICULTURAL ADJUSTMENT ACT, the NATIONAL INDUSTRIAL RECOVERY ACT) and to create public jobs to reduce unemployment and increase consumer demand (the Civilian Conservation Corps, the Works Progress Administration, the Public Works Administration). Such agencies, generating regulations under the statutory umbrella of broad enabling legislation, came to be a standard feature on the American scene.

In a parallel development state governments created a number of agencies to coordinate and regulate everything from barbers to new car dealers, from avocado marketing to the licensing of physicians. Some of these boards appear to function chiefly as means of controlling entry into occupations and thereby shielding current practitioners from competition, but all function as branches of the government armed with at least some forms of regulatory power.

In some respects such state and national agencies represent not a new form of governmental power but a transfer to state and national levels of what had once been tasks of city government. The functioning of such municipal bureaucracies was, however, largely idiosyncratic and local—defined by the terms of the cities' charters and thus beyond the reach of national law. The migration of regulatory control from city to state and nation both enabled and necessitated the development of a new "administrative" law, which in America is almost entirely a creature of the twentieth century.

Most of that law is statutory, a function of the legislation that creates the board, agency, or commission and defines its tasks and powers. Citizens and enterprises wishing either to invoke or to challenge such powers use the statutorily specified procedures, which often involve both internal agency and external JUDICIAL REVIEW of administrative actions. At two points, however, the Constitution does speak to the structure and conduct of the agencies. In the formative years of the administrative state the Supreme Court expressed doubt about the place of the agency in the divided federal system of government. Since the New Deal the constitutional focus has turned to the processes employed by administrative agencies, and the courts have regularly required agencies' procedures to conform to the due process clause.

The Constitution establishes three branches of the national government, and the courts early decided that no branch should exceed its own powers or intrude on areas designated as the province of another branch. This principle, known as the separation of powers, applies to numerous activities of the federal government, but it impinges particularly on the operation of administrative agencies charged with the formation and enforcement of broad federal policy.

Congress could not possibly specify just what tasks it wishes federal agencies to accomplish and also exactly how to perform them. At the opposite extreme it would just as obviously violate the separation of powers if Congress were to throw up its hands at the task of forming policy and instead direct the President to hit on whatever combination of revenue collection and expenditure he deemed best to fulfill the needs of the country. The concern is that Congress, if it asks an administrative agency not just to carry out defined tasks but also to participate in the formation of policy, has impermissibly given—delegated—its legislative power to the agency (a part of the executive branch).

That concern surfaced in a pair of Supreme Court decisions invalidating New Deal legislation. PANAMA REFINING CO. V. RYAN (1935) struck down a portion of the National Industrial Recovery Act that permitted the President to ban the interstate shipment of petroleum; the Court's ground was that Congress had provided no guidance as to when the President should do so or what aims were to justify the ban. A few months later, in SCHECHTER POULTRY CORP. V. UNITED STATES, the Court held unconstitutional another section of the same act; its DELEGATION OF POWER permitted the President to create codes of fair competition for various industries. Congress had defined neither the content of such codes nor the conditions for their proclamation, and some members of the Court evinced concern that the absence of standards could pave the way for what amounted to a governmentally sanctioned system of industrial cartels.

Since these two cases the Court has not invalidated a congressional delegation of power, but some have argued that the memory of these cases has induced the legislature to indicate more clearly the goals it intends the agency to accomplish, the means by which they are to be accomplished, and the processes that should accompany their implementation.

Even though an administrative agency does not perform tasks that constitutionally belong only to Congress, it might nevertheless violate the constitutional structure of government by performing tasks belonging to the courts. The problem has several guises.

In some instances Congress in creating the agency has given it JURISDICTION that might otherwise have been exercised by the courts (for example, over maritime accidents). Did such congressional action, which could be viewed as a transfer of federal judicial jurisdiction to an agency, violate the constitutional structure of government or the rights of the parties? In *Crowell v. Benson* (1932) the Court concluded that if Congress established fair administrative procedures, the agency could hear and determine cases that might otherwise have been heard by the courts—with the saving proviso that the federal courts might review the agency's determination of questions of law.

That proviso pointed to another difficult question: the extent to which the courts might review agency decisions. Summarizing the history of this question, Louis Jaffe has said that we have moved from a nineteenth-century presumption of unreviewability to a twentieth-century presumption of reviewability. Such reviewability, however, flows from statutory interpretation rather than from constitutional compulsion: if Congress is sufficiently explicit, it can make an agency determination final and unreviewable—either because the statute explicitly says so or because it so clearly makes the decision in question a matter of agency discretion that there is no law to apply. For the most part, however, courts routinely scrutinize agency action for legality and at least minimal rationality and are prepared to give the agencies fairly great leeway in performing their tasks.

One measure of this leeway the agencies enjoy is the set of requirements imposed on litigants seeking to invoke federal judicial review of agency action. Such parties must satisfy the courts that they have STANDING (that is, actual injury caused by the agency action), that the dispute is ripe for judicial review (that is, that the case comes to the courts when it has sufficiently developed to render a judicial decision not merely abstract or hypothetical), and that they have exhausted their administrative remedies (that is, that they have sought such administrative redress as is available). Only the first two of these requirements—standing and RIPENESS—stem from the Constitution; all of them, however, condition the federal courts' exercise of judicial review.

Courts are prepared to grant such leeway, however, only to the extent that they are assured that the agency has complied with the requirements of due process in making its decisions. Due process plays two roles in administrative law. To the extent that agencies make rules only after extensive public participation in their deliberations, they address some of the concerns lying at the base of the delegation doctrine—ill-considered and hasty action. Due process also plays a second, more traditional role of assuring adjudicatory fairness. To the extent that agencies take action against those violating their rules, courts have often required that the agencies afford the violators various procedural protections.

Because an increasing number of Americans, from defense contractors and television broadcasters to mothers of dependent children and disabled veterans, depend on state and federal government for their livelihood, such protections have become increasingly important. In the second half of the twentieth century the courts have held many of those interests to be property, thus giving their holders the right to due process—sometimes including a FAIR HEARING—before suffering their deprivation. Thus state and federal agencies must give welfare recipients an opportunity to know and to contest factual findings before ending benefits; public schools and colleges have to supply students some form of NOTICE and process before suspending or expelling them; and public employers must grant tenured employees an opportunity to contest their dismissal. Courts have left the agencies some discretion as to the form of such procedures, which need not, for example, always include a hearing, but the process must suit the circumstances.

Because such protections flow from the due process clauses, they apply equally to state and to federal government; indeed, an important consequence of the constitutionalization of administrative process is that it has penetrated to state bureaucracies, some of which were perhaps less than exemplary in their concern for those affected by their actions. As a result both state courts and state legislatures have directed attention to the procedures of their agencies.

In a large sense, to understand the relationship of the administrative state to the Constitution, one has to spell constitution with a small "c," for the difficulties

have been less with specific constitutional provisions than with the general picture of how executive action—especially action in new spheres—fits into received understandings of the world. That question is still debatable, but the debates, at least in the last half of the twentieth century, have taken place at the level of desirable policy, not of constitutional legality: so long as the agencies operate fairly, that much, apparently, is assured.

STEPHEN C. YEAZELL

Bibliography

DAVIS, KENNETH C. 1978 *Administrative Law Treatise.* San Diego, Calif.: Davis.
JAFFE, LOUIS 1965 *Judicial Control of Administrative Action.* Boston: Little, Brown.
KOLKO, GABRIEL 1963 *The Triumph of Conservatism: A Reinterpretation of American History, 1900–1916.* New York: Free Press.
WIEBE, ROBERT 1967 *The Search for Order, 1877–1920.* New York: Hill & Wang.

ADMINISTRATIVE SEARCH

Safety inspections of dwellings by government officials, unlike police searches, are conducted to correct hazardous conditions rather than to secure EVIDENCE. Initially, therefore, the Supreme Court regarded such inspection as merely touching interests that were peripheral to the FOURTH AMENDMENT; the RIGHT OF PRIVACY of the householder must give way, even in the absence of a SEARCH WARRANT, to the interest in preserving a safe urban environment. *Frank v. Maryland* (1959) paradoxically granted greater protection under the Fourth Amendment to suspected criminals than to law-abiding citizens.

Later, the Court reversed itself in CAMARA V. MUNICIPAL COURT (1967), holding that the amendment was designed "to safeguard the privacy and security of individuals against arbitrary invasions by government officials," regardless of their purpose. However, because inspections would be crippled if the standard of proof needed for a warrant were the same as that required in a criminal case, the traditional PROBABLE CAUSE standard was discarded in favor of a flexible test based on the condition of the area and the time elapsed since the last inspection, rather than specific knowledge of the condition of the particular dwelling. After WYMAN V. JAMES (1971) WELFARE BENEFITS for support of a dependent child may be made conditional upon periodic visits to the home by a caseworker; a warrant is not required for such a visit.

The requirement of a warrant for inspections generally applies to business premises, as the Court held in *See v. City of Seattle* (1967). But in *Donovan v. Dewey* (1981) the Court held that coal mines, establishments dealing in guns and liquor, and other commercial properties that are comprehensively regulated by government may be inspected without a warrant, because an owner is obviously aware that his property will be subject to inspection.

JACOB W. LANDYNSKI

Bibliography

LAFAVE, WAYNE R. 1967 Administrative Searches and the Fourth Amendment: The *Camara* and *See* Cases. *Supreme Court Review* 1967:2–38.

ADMIRALTY AND MARITIME JURISDICTION

In Article III of the Constitution, the JUDICIAL POWER OF THE UNITED STATES is made to extend "to all cases of admiralty and maritime jurisdiction." ALEXANDER HAMILTON says, in THE FEDERALIST #80, that "the most bigotted idolizers of State authority have not thus far shown a disposition to deny the national judiciary the cognizance of maritime causes." There is no reason not to believe him. The First Congress, in the JUDICIARY ACT OF 1789, gave this JURISDICTION to the UNITED STATES DISTRICT COURTS, which were to have "exclusive original cognizance of all civil causes of admiralty and maritime jurisdiction, saving to suitors, in all cases, the right of a COMMON LAW remedy, where the common law is competent to give it."

This language was verbally changed in the JUDICIAL CODE of 1948, but the change has had no effect, and was pretty surely not meant to have any, so that one may organize the subject (as it has, indeed, organized itself) around the two questions suggested by the original formula: (1) What is the content of the "exclusive cognizance" given the District Court? and (2) What is "saved" to suitors in the saving clause?

There is an admiralty jurisdiction in "prize"—a jurisdiction to condemn and sell, as lawful prize of war, enemy vessels and cargo. This jurisdiction was employed to effect a few condemnations after World War II, but it has on the whole been very little used in this century. There is an admiralty jurisdiction over crime, but the admiralty clause serves in these cases solely as a firm theoretical foundation for American jurisdiction over certain crimes committed outside the country but on navigable waters; these cases are rarely thought of as "admiralty" cases, because IN-DICTMENT and trial are "according to the course of the common law," with such statutory and rule-based changes as affect all federal criminal proceedings. Normally, then, "admiralty jurisdiction" refers to jurisdiction over certain private-law concerns affecting the shipping industry—contracts to carry goods, charters of ships, marine insurance, ship collisions, seamen's or passengers' personal injuries, salvage, and so on.

The courts early followed the English rule limiting the jurisdiction to tidal waters, but a rather tortuous development around the middle of the nineteenth century extended this base to include first, the Great Lakes, then the Mississippi River, and at last all interior waters navigable in INTERSTATE or FOREIGN COMMERCE.

There was an early effort, moreover, to limit the jurisdiction to causes very strictly "arising" on these waters. Suits in marine insurance, for example, were thought to be outside the jurisdiction, because the contracts were made on land, and were to be performed (by payment) on land. On the other hand, some quite late cases extended the admiralty jurisdiction to events having no maritime flavor (e.g., an injury to a bather by a surfboard), on the basis of this same "locality" test. This "test," productive of ludicrous results, has often been abjured by the courts, but has a way of popping up again and again, in context after context.

The "saving clause" has been given an interpretation not at all of obvious correctness. The "common-law remedy" saved to suitors was held to comprise all IN PERSONAM causes of action. Thus, if a shipowner's ship is lost, and he claims indemnity from the insurance company, he is free to sue either in admiralty court or in a regular land-based court—and so on through the whole range of admiralty matters. What is *not* "saved to suitors," and is therefore really "exclusive" to the District Courts, is the suit IN REM, wherein a vessel, or other maritime property, is treated as the defendant party, and sued directly under its own name. In practice, this means that the plaintiff (or "libellant," as he used to be called) enjoys a high-priority security interest in the vessel, an interest called a "maritime lien."

The intricacies of admiralty procedure have been simplified in recent years. But one dominating peculiarity remains. Like EQUITY, admiralty (usually) does not use the jury. This fact is normally determinative of the plaintiff's choice, made under the "saving clause," between the admiralty forum and the land-bound court of law.

CHARLES L. BLACK, JR.

Bibliography

GILMORE, GRANT and BLACK, CHARLES L., JR. 1975 *Admiralty,* 2nd ed. Mineola, N.Y.: Foundation Press.

ROBERTSON, DAVID W. 1970 *Admiralty and Federalism.* Mineola, N.Y.: Foundation Press.

ADVICE AND CONSENT

Under Article II, section 2, of the Constitution, the President's powers to make treaties and to appoint important public officials are to be exercised "by and with the advice and consent of the Senate."

The formula "advice and consent" is an ancient one. It was used in British and American state papers and documents for over a thousand years prior to 1787. The use of these words in the Constitution was proposed by the CONSTITUTIONAL CONVENTION's Committee on Remaining Matters, to which both the TREATY POWER and the APPOINTING POWER had been referred. The first proposal to associate the President and the Senate in the exercise of those powers was made by ALEXANDER HAMILTON, who wanted the Senate to act as a kind of PRIVY COUNCIL. In the debates over RATIFICATION OF THE CONSTITUTION opponents charged that the provision violated the principle of SEPARATION OF POWERS. But in THE FEDERALIST the practice was defended as an instance of CHECKS AND BALANCES and a means of involving the states in the making of important national policy.

In practice, the phrase "advice and consent" has come to have different meanings with respect to the two powers to which it is applied.

In the making of treaties, the advisory function has virtually disappeared. In August 1789, President GEORGE WASHINGTON sought to honor the letter of the Constitution by appearing in person before the Senate to ask its advice prior to negotiating an Indian treaty. When the Senate referred the matter to a committee, Washington walked out, and since that incident, no President has made such a formal request for advice in advance. The common modern practices by which Presidents include senators among American negotiators and consult with influential senators, the party leadership, and members of the Senate Foreign Relations Committee are better understood as political devices to improve the chances of obtaining consent than as deference to the constitutional mandate to obtain advice. In giving its consent to the President's making—or ratification—of a treaty, the Senate is not bound to accept or reject the whole document as submitted. The Senate may amend a treaty or attach reservations to it. Since either of these actions may compel renegotiation, they might be considered perverse forms of giving advice.

In the appointment of officers, the advisory function has become far more important. Nominees to the Supreme Court and to the most important executive and diplomatic posts are normally approved (or rejected) by the Senate on grounds of merit, integrity, and policy. In the case of other executive and judicial appointments, a practice known as "senatorial courtesy" has transformed the requirement for "advice and consent" into an instrument of senatorial control. Nominees cannot expect the Senate's consent to their appointment if it is not supported by senators of the President's party from their home states. If a federal appointee is to serve in a particular state, the senior senator of the President's party from that state (if there is one) customarily makes the actual selection.

DENNIS J. MAHONEY

ADVISORY OPINION

Article III of the Constitution extends the JUDICIAL POWER OF THE UNITED STATES only to the decision of CASES OR CONTROVERSIES. Since 1793, when the Supreme Court declined, in the absence of a concrete dispute, to give legal advice to President GEORGE WASHINGTON on the correct interpretation of treaties with France and Britain, the Court has refused steadfastly to issue advisory opinions, finding them inconsistent with Article III. This refusal is required whether the request seeks advice on interpretation of existing law or on the constitutionality of pending LEGISLATION or anticipated action. The Justices' view is that the federal courts function not as lawyers giving advice but as judges limited to deciding cases presented by adverse parties with a real, not a hypothetical, dispute, one that is subject to judicial resolution and the granting of meaningful relief. The Court held in *Aetna Life Insurance Co. v. Haworth* (1937) that the prohibition against advisory opinions does not preclude declaratory relief, but there must be a concrete controversy between parties of adverse legal positions which a DECLARATORY JUDGMENT can settle.

If doubts exist about the constitutionality of a proposed government policy or the legality of a contemplated application of current law, an advisory opinion could prevent the interim harm that adoption and application of law subsequently found invalid would cause. Moreover, advisory opinions could save time, money, and effort in deliberation and enforcement by clarifying legal limitations before invalid action is taken. Clearing away unlawful options could also contribute to the quality and focus of public debate and accountability.

The rule against advisory opinions responds to different considerations, however. It limits workload, but the dominant concerns involve judicial competence to decide issues in an advisory context and the place of the federal judiciary in a regime characterized by SEPARATION OF POWERS. Fear that decision before a dispute arises would be premature and unwise, that is, made without relevant facts stemming from application of law or other experience and without the benefit of perspectives presented by already affected parties, combined with concern that the advisory opinion may prejudge unfairly the decision of later concrete cases raising the same questions, induces judges to avoid making nonessential and potentially vulnerable decisions that might weaken judicial legitimacy. In addition, the prevailing belief views advisory opinions as likely to stifle rather than clarify the deliberative process, to distort the obligations of legislative or executive officials to evaluate legal questions independently, thereby blurring accountability, and to deprive experimental proposals of an opportunity to prove themselves before being reviewed for the legality of their actual effects.

JONATHAN D. VARAT

Bibliography
FRANKFURTER, FELIX 1924 Note on Advisory Opinions. *Harvard Law Review* 37:1002–1009.

AFFECTED WITH A PUBLIC INTEREST

The phrase "affected with a public interest," first used by the Supreme Court in *Munn v. Illinois* (1877), had a long and distinguished doctrinal lineage in the English COMMON LAW. The fountainhead of the modern development of that phrase was its formulation by Lord Chief Justice Matthew Hale, in his treatise *De Jure Maris*, written about 1670 and first published in 1787. In this work, Lord Hale discussed the basis for distinguishing property that was strictly private, property that was public in ownership, and an intermediate category of property (such as in navigable waters) that was private in ownership but subject to public use and hence a large measure of public control. In cases of business under a servitude to the public, such as wharves and cranes and ferries, according to Hale, it was legitimate for government to regulate

in order to assure that the facilities would be available for "the common use" at rates that would be "reasonable and moderate." Once the public was invited to use such facilities, Hale wrote, "the wharf and the crane and other conveniences are affected with a publick interest, and they cease to be *juris privati* [a matter of private law] only." (See GRANGER CASES.)

When Chief Justice MORRISON R. WAITE, writing for the majority in *Munn*, cited Lord Hale, it was for the purpose of upholding rate regulation of grain elevators against a FOURTEENTH AMENDMENT defense that claimed that the elevator operator's vested property rights were being taken without JUST COMPENSATION. Explaining the *Munn* rule a year later, in his *Sinking Fund Cases* opinion, Justice JOSEPH P. BRADLEY pinned the "affectation" doctrine squarely to the concept of monopoly. The question in *Munn*, Bradley contended, was "the extent of the POLICE POWER in cases where the public interest is affected"; and the Court had concluded that regulation was valid when "an employment or business becomes a matter of such public interest and importance as to create a common charge or burden upon the citizens; in other words, when it becomes a practical monopoly, to which the citizen is compelled to resort. . . ."

In the period immediately following the decision in *Munn*, the Court erected a series of new doctrinal bulwarks for property interests. Among them were the concept of FREEDOM OF CONTRACT, the requirement that regulation must be "reasonable" as judged by the Court, and the notion of PUBLIC PURPOSE as a test for the validity of tax measures. As a result, the concept "affectation with a public interest" was pushed into the background, placing in abeyance such questions as whether only "monopoly" business came within its reach or whether instead it could be invoked to cover regulation of businesses that were not of this character.

In the decade of the 1920s, state legislation directly regulating prices and charges for service was challenged in federal courts and led to revitalization of the "affectation" doctrine by the Supreme Court. The issue, as the Court confronted it, had been set forth succinctly by Justice DAVID J. BREWER in an earlier opinion (*Cotting v. Kansas City Stockyards Co.,* 1901), upholding a state's regulation of stockyard charges on the ground that the business was affected with a public interest no less than a grain elevator or railroad or wharf. Yet the question must be posed, Brewer insisted, "To what extent may this regulation go?" Did any limits pertain, even in clear cases such as a stockyard's operation? Were the yards' owners left in a position, constitutionally, that they could be deprived "altogether of the ordinary privileges of others in mercantile business?"

In the hands of a property-minded, conservative Court the case-by-case development of the principle at issue, responding to Brewer's challenge, resulted in the creation of a closed legal category: only a business "affected with a public interest" might have prices or charges for service regulated; other, "ordinary," businesses were outside that closed category and therefore *not* subject to price or rate regulation. Chief Justice WILLIAM H. TAFT took on the challenge of defining more precisely the closed legal category in his opinion for the Court in WOLFF PACKING CO. V. COURT OF INDUSTRIAL RELATIONS OF KANSAS. Price and rate regulation were constitutional, Taft asserted, in regard to businesses that were public utilities (under an affirmative duty to render service to the public), businesses that historically had been subject to price regulation, and, finally, a rather baffling category, businesses that "though not public at their inception [historically] may be said to have risen to be such." Over strong objections of dissenters—most consistently Justices OLIVER WENDELL HOLMES and LOUIS D. BRANDEIS—the Court in subsequent years relied on this refined "affectation" doctrine to rule that even businesses subject to regulation in other respects could not be regulated as to rates of charge unless they met the criteria set down by Taft in *Wolff*. Mandated price minima or maxima were found unconstitutional with respect to theater ticket agencies, dairy vendors, gasoline retailers, and manufacturers and sellers of ice.

Dissenting Justices objected that the phrase "affected with a public interest" was so "vague and illusory" (as Justice HARLAN F. STONE charged in his dissent in *Tyson v. Banton*, 1927) as to amount to *carte blanche* for the Court to impose arbitrarily its policy preferences. Holmes was more direct: the concept, he stated in his own dissent in *Tyson*, was "little more than a fiction intended to beautify what is disagreeable to the sufferers." In Holmes's view, Lord Hale's language had been misapplied and had become a contrived limitation on the state's legitimate police power. "Subject to compensation when compensation is due," Holmes declared, "the legislature may forbid or restrict any business when it has a force of public opinion behind it."

Along with freedom of contract, the VESTED RIGHTS concept, the public purpose concept, and the doctrine of DUAL FEDERALISM, the "affectation" concept became emblematic of doctrinaire formalism mobilized by practitioners of JUDICIAL ACTIVISM. Such doctrines could undermine entirely, critics argued, the capacity of government to respond to changing objective social conditions or to emergency situations that required sweeping legislative intervention. Building on Justice Holmes's views, for example, the legal scholar WALTON H. HAMILTON wrote a widely noticed, wholesale attack on the Court in 1930. Although Hamilton was wrong in his view of the alleged novelty and obscurity of Lord Hale's treatise when Waite used it in *Munn*, he provided an eloquent argument for abandoning the notion of a closed category of businesses immune from price regulation. It was imperative, he argued, for the law to recognize the transformation of industrial structure and the competitive order in the previous half-century; the "affectation" doctrine was a conceptual straitjacket.

The advent of the Great Depression, along with the enactment of extraordinary legislation to deal with a great variety of emergency situations in a stricken society, lent additional weight to the realist argument that Holmes and commentators such as Hamilton and FELIX FRANKFURTER had set forth. Ruling on the constitutionality of an emergency milk price control law, enacted by New York State at the depth of the Depression spiral, the Supreme Court dramatically terminated the use of the "affectation" doctrine as a defense against price regulation: In NEBBIA V. NEW YORK (1934), the Court concluded that the phrase from Lord Hale meant simply "subject to the exercise of the police power." After *Nebbia*, so long as the procedural requirements of DUE PROCESS were met, the legislature was left "free to adopt whatever economic policy may reasonably be deemed to promote public welfare."

HARRY N. SCHEIBER

Bibliography

HAMILTON, WALTON 1930 Affectation with a Public Interest. *Yale Law Journal* 34:1089–1112.
SCHEIBER, HARRY N. 1971 The Road to *Munn*: Eminent Domain and the Concept of Public Purpose in the State Courts. *Perspectives in American History* 5:327–402.

AFFIRMATIVE ACTION

The Supreme Court's momentous decisions in BROWN V. BOARD OF EDUCATION and BOLLING V. SHARPE (1954), and its subsequent implementation decision in *Brown II* (1955), were followed by a long string of rulings designed to render meaningful and effective the egalitarian promise inherent in the FOURTEENTH AMENDMENT. Compulsory racial SEGREGATION was at last no longer constitutionally permissible; the Fourteenth Amendment's guarantee of the EQUAL PROTECTION OF THE LAWS had become the effective law of the land for all levels of the public sector.

But in the judgment of a good many Americans, equality *qua* equality, even when conscientiously enforced with an even hand, would neither suffice to enable those previously deprived on racial grounds to realize the promises of equality of opportunity, nor would it atone, and provide redress, for the ravages wrought by two centuries of past discrimination. Consequently, as strongly urged by President LYNDON B. JOHNSON, programs were established in both the public and the private realms that were designed to go well beyond "mere" equality of opportunity and provide not only remedial but preferential compensatory action, especially in the worlds of EDUCATION and employment. Labeled "affirmative action"—as distinguished from "neutrality"—these programs were instituted to bring about increased minority employment opportunities, job promotions, and admissions to colleges and universities, among others. Understandably, affirmative action programs quickly became controversial because of their resort to RACIAL QUOTAS, also called euphemistically "goals" or "guidelines." Their proponents' justification has been that to provide an absolute measure of full equality of opportunity based upon individual merit does not suffice; that, given the injustices of the past, both preferential and compensatory treatment must be accorded through "affirmative action" that all but guarantees numerically targeted slots or posts based upon membership in racial groups or upon gender. Most critics of the policy's underlying philosophy have not necessarily objected to "affirmative action" policies such as aggressive recruiting, remedial training (no matter what the expense), and perhaps not even to what Justice LEWIS F. POWELL in REGENTS OF THE UNIVERSITY OF CALIFORNIA V. BAKKE (1978) termed a justifiable "plus" consideration of race along with other equitable factors. They do, however, object strenuously to policies that represent, or may be regarded as sanctioning, "reverse discrimination," generally characterized by the resort to such devices as the *numerus clausus,* that is, rigid quotas set aside to benefit identifiable racial groups, as in the controversial case of UNITED STEELWORKERS OF AMERICA V. WEBER (1979); to double standards in grading, ranking, and similar requirements on the employment,

educational, and other relevant fronts of opportunity; and to "set aside" laws that guarantee specified percentages of contracts to minority groups, as in FULLILOVE V. KLUTZNICK (1980).

The basic issue, while philosophically replete with moral and ethical considerations, was ultimately bound to be fought out on the legal and constitutional front, thus engendering judicial decisions. Several provisions of the CIVIL RIGHTS ACT OF 1964, as amended—for example, Titles IV, VI, VII, and IX— seemed quite specifically not only to forbid racial, sexual, and other discrimination per se but also to proscribe the use of racial and related quotas. The Supreme Court rapidly confronted five major opportunities to address the issue; in each instance it found itself seriously divided. Each of the five decisions involved "affirmative action" and/or "reverse discrimination."

The first and second, DEFUNIS V. ODEGAARD (1974) and *Regents v. Bakke* (1978), dealt with preferential racial admissions quotas that by design advantaged nonwhite applicants and thereby ipso facto disadvantaged whites. In *De Funis* a five-member majority rendered a nondecision on the merits by ruling the case moot, because whatever the outcome of the case, Marco De Funis would be graduated by the University of Washington Law School. Justice WILLIAM O. DOUGLAS, dissenting from the MOOTNESS determination, warned that "the equal protection clause commands the elimination of racial barriers, not their creation in order to satisfy our theory as to how society ought to be organized." In *Bakke* the Court did reach the merits of the racial quota established by the University of California (Davis) medical school, ruling 5–4 (in two diverse lineups, each headed by Justice Powell) that whereas the latter's rigid quota violated Allan Bakke's rights under the Constitution and the Civil Rights Act of 1964, the use of race as a "plus" along with other relevant considerations in admissions decisions did not. The third case, *United Steelworkers v. Weber,* concerned an employer–union craft-training plan that, on its face, directly violated Title VII of the Civil Rights Act of 1964, which clearly, indeed literally, interdicts racial quotas in employment. However, with Justices Powell and JOHN PAUL STEVENS disqualifying themselves from sitting in the cases, Justice WILLIAM J. BRENNAN, speaking for a majority of five, ruled that although the letter of the law appeared to forbid the arrangement, its purpose, as reflected in the legislative history, did not. The fourth case, *Fullilove v. Klutznick,* raised the fundamental question whether Congress, notwithstanding the Fourteenth Amendment's equal protection clause, could constitutionally legislate a ten percent set-aside plan for minority-owned construction companies desirous of obtaining government contracts. "Yes," held a 6–3 plurality—actually, the Court split 3–3–3—finding such legislation to be within the federal legislature's spending and regulatory powers under Article I of the Constitution. In his scathing DISSENTING OPINION, which he read in full from the bench on the day of the decision, Justice Stevens charged that the law represented a "perverse form of reparation," a "slapdash" law that rewards some who may not need rewarding and hurts others who may not deserve hurting. Suggesting that such a law could be used simply as a patronage tool by its authors—it had, in fact, been written on the floor of the House of Representatives without having gone to committee for hearings—he warned that it could breed more resentment and prejudice than it corrected. Echoing the first Justice JOHN MARSHALL HARLAN's memorable phrase in dissent in PLESSY V. FERGUSON (1896), namely, that "our Constitution is color-blind and neither knows nor tolerates classes among citizens," Stevens asked what percentage of "oriental blood or what degree of Spanish-speaking skill is required for membership in the preferred class?" With deep feelings, he suggested sarcastically that now the government must devise its version of the Nazi laws that defined who is a Jew, musing that "our statute books will once again have to contain laws that reflect the odious practice of delineating the qualities that make one person a Negro and make another white." The fifth case, *Memphis Fire Department v. Stotts,* seemed to draw a line (although only by the narrowest of margins, 5–4) when the Justice White-authored majority opinion held that duly established bona fide nondiscriminatory seniority systems supersede affirmative action plans.

Depending upon interpretation, one person's "affirmative action" may well constitute another's "reverse discrimination". Nonetheless, it is possible to essay distinctions. Thus, "affirmative action" may be regarded as encompassing the following five phenomena, all of which would appear to be both legal and constitutional: (1) both governmentally and privately sponsored activity designed to remedy the absence of needed educational preparation by special, even if costly, primary, and/or secondary school level preparatory programs or occupational skill development, always provided that access to these programs is not bottomed upon race or related group criteria or characteristics, but upon educational or economic need; (2) special classes or supplemental training, regardless

of costs, on any level of education or training from the prenursery school bottom to the very top of the professional training ladder; (3) scrupulous enforcement of absolute standards of nondiscrimination on the basis of race, sex, religion, nationality, and age; (4) above-the-table special recruiting efforts to reach out to those members of heretofore underused, deprived, or discriminated-against segments of the citizenry; (5) provided the presence of explicit or implicit merit, of bona fide demonstrated or potential ability, the taking into account of an individual's race, gender, religion as an equitable consideration—the "plus" of which Justice Powell spoke in *Bakke*—but *only* if "all other things are equal."

"Reverse discrimination," on the other hand, which is acceptable neither legally nor constitutionally, would constitute the following quartet: (1) adoption of a *numerus clausus,* the setting aside of quotas, be they rigid or semirigid, on behalf of the admission, recruitment, employment, or promotion of individuals and groups identified and classified by racial, religious, sexual, age, or nationality characteristics; such characteristics are *non sequiturs* on the fronts of individual merit and ability and may well be regarded as an insult to the dignity and intelligence of the quota beneficiaries; (2) slanting of what should be neutral qualification examinations or requirements; double standards in grading and rating; double standards in attendance, retention, and disciplinary requirements; (3) those "goals" and "guidelines" that allegedly differ from rigid quotas, and thus presumably pass legal and constitutional muster, but that, in application, are all but synonymous with enforced quotas; (4) legislative or executive "set aside" programs, such as the one at issue in the *Fullilove* case, that mandate percentage-quotas of awards and activities based upon racial, gender, and related classifications.

"Reverse discrimination" purports to justify itself as atonement for past discrimination. It sanctions the call to children to pay for the sins of their forebears; it embraces a policy that two wrongs make one right, that "temporary" discrimination is "benign" rather than "invidious" when it is designed to remedy past wrongs. Since the "temporary" all too often becomes the "permanent," temporary suspensions of fundamental rights are fraught with permanent dangers and represent prima facie denials of the equal protection of the laws guaranteed by the Fourteenth Amendment and the DUE PROCESS OF LAW guaranteed by the Fifth.

The line between "affirmative action" and "reverse discrimination" may be thin and vexatious, but it does not lie beyond recognition and establishment in our constitutional constellation.

HENRY J. ABRAHAM

Bibliography

DWORKIN, RONALD 1977 *Taking Rights Seriously.* Cambridge, Mass.: Harvard University Press.
GLAZER, NATHAN 1976 *Affirmative Discrimination.* New York: Basic Books.
O'NEILL, ROBERT M. 1975 *Discriminating against Discrimination.* Bloomington: Indiana University Press.
ROCHE, GEORGE C., III 1974 *The Balancing Act: Quota Hiring in Higher Education.* La Salle, Ill.: Open Court.
ROSSUM, RALPH A. 1980 *Reverse Discrimination: The Constitutional Debate.* New York: Marcel Dekker.
SOWELL, THOMAS 1975 *Affirmative Action Reconsidered: Was It Necessary in Academia?* Washington, D.C.: American Enterprise Institute.

AFROYIM v. RUSK
387 U.S. 253 (1967)

A section of the Nationality Act of 1940 stripped Americans of their CITIZENSHIP if they voted in a foreign political election. In PEREZ V. BROWNELL (1957) the Supreme Court upheld the constitutionality of this provision, 5–4. On the authority of *Perez,* the State Department refused a passport to Afroyim, a naturalized citizen, who had voted in an Israeli election. In *Afroyim,* however, a new five-Justice majority, speaking through Justice HUGO L. BLACK, overruled *Perez* and declared that the FOURTEENTH AMENDMENT's citizenship clause denied Congress authority to strip Americans of their citizenship without their consent. "Citizenship in this Nation is a part of a cooperative affair," Black wrote. "Its citizenry is the country and the country is its citizenry."

MICHAEL E. PARRISH

AGE DISCRIMINATION

The racial CIVIL RIGHTS revolution of the 1950s and 1960s generated interest in constitutional protection for groups other than racial and religious minorities. Enhanced constitutional scrutiny of SEX DISCRIMINATION may be a consequence of the civil rights struggle.

Discrimination on the basis of age, however, has not become constitutionally suspect. In MASSACHUSETTS BOARD OF RETIREMENT V. MURGIA (1976) the Supreme Court held that some forms of age classification are not suspect and sustained against EQUAL PROTECTION attack a state statute requiring uniformed

state police officers to retire at age fifty. In a PER CURIAM opinion, the Court concluded that the retirement did not affect a FUNDAMENTAL RIGHT, and characterized the affected class as uniformed police officers over age fifty. Perhaps intending to leave open heightened scrutiny of some age classifications, the Court stated that the requirement in *Murgia* did not discriminate against the elderly. In light of its findings with respect to the nature of the right and the relevant class, the Court held that mere rationality, rather than STRICT SCRUTINY, was the proper STANDARD OF REVIEW in determining whether the statute violated the equal protection clause. It found that the age classification was rationally related to furthering the state's interest of protecting the public by assuring physical preparedness of its uniformed state police.

In *Vance v. Bradley* (1979) the Court, in an opinion by Justice BYRON R. WHITE, again applied the RATIONAL BASIS test and held that Congress may require retirement at age sixty of federal employees covered by the Foreign Service retirement and disability system, even though it imposes no such limit on employees covered by the Civil Service retirement and disability system. In sustaining the mandatory retirement age, the Court emphasized Congress's special consideration of the needs of the Foreign Service. "Congress has legislated separately for the Foreign Service and has gone to great lengths to assure that those conducting our foreign relations will be sufficiently competent and reliable in all respects. If Congress attached special importance to high performance in these positions . . . it was quite rational to avoid the risks connected with having older employees in the Foreign Service but to tolerate those risks in the Civil Service."

But in the legislative arena, age discrimination did feel the effects of the constitutional egalitarian revolution. Section 715 of the CIVIL RIGHTS ACT OF 1964 required the secretary of labor to report to Congress on age discrimination in employment. In 1965 the secretary reported persistent arbitrary discrimination against older Americans. In 1967, upon the recommendation of President LYNDON B. JOHNSON, and relying on its powers under the COMMERCE CLAUSE, Congress passed the Age Discrimination in Employment Act (ADEA). The act, which has been amended several times, prohibits employment discrimination against persons between the ages of forty and seventy.

In EQUAL EMPLOYMENT OPPORTUNITY COMMISSION V. WYOMING (1983), prior to its OVERRULING of NATIONAL LEAGUE OF CITIES V. USERY (1976) in GARCIA V. SAN ANTONIO METROPOLITAN TRANSIT AUTHORITY (1985), the Court sustained against a TENTH AMENDMENT attack the constitutionality of

Congress's 1974 extension of the ADEA to state and local governments. In a 5–4 decision, the Court found that applying the act's prohibition to a Wyoming mandatory retirement age for game wardens would not interfere with integral state functions because the state remained free to apply reasonable standards of fitness to game wardens.

Building on a provision in Title VII of the Civil Rights Act of 1964, the ADEA allows employers to take otherwise prohibited age-based action when age is a "bona fide occupational qualification reasonably necessary to the normal operation of the particular business." In its early interpretations of this provision, the Court has not given the defense an expansive reading. In *Western Air Lines, Inc. v. Criswell* (1985), in an opinion by Justice JOHN PAUL STEVENS, the Court held that Congress's "reasonably necessary" standard requires something more than a showing that an age-based requirement is rationally connected to the employer's business. Relying on the heightened standard, the Court therefore rejected an airline's defense of its requirement that flight engineers retire at age sixty. In *Johnson v. Mayor & City Council of Baltimore* (1985) the Court held that a federal statute generally requiring federal fire fighters to retire at age fifty-five does not establish that being under fifty-five is a bona fide occupational qualification under the ADEA for nonfederal fire fighters.

In the Age Discrimination Act of 1975 (ADA), following the racial antidiscrimination model of Title VI of the Civil Rights Act of 1964, Congress prohibited discrimination on the basis of age in programs or activities receiving federal financial assistance. The ADA thus joins Title IX of the EDUCATION AMENDMENTS OF 1972 and section 504 of the REHABILITATION ACT OF 1973, which prohibit, respectively, sex discrimination and discrimination against the handicapped in federally assisted programs. The ADA vests broad authority in the secretary of health and human services to promulgate regulations to effectuate the statute's antidiscrimination mandate. Like the ADEA, the ADA contains exceptions allowing discrimination on the basis of age when age is reasonably related to the program or activity. Other specific federal spending programs contain their own statutory prohibitions on age discrimination.

THEODORE EISENBERG

Bibliography

SCHUCK, PETER H. 1979 The Graying of Civil Rights Law: The Age Discrimination Act of 1975. *Yale Law Journal* 89:27–93.

UNITED STATES DEPARTMENT OF LABOR 1965 *Report to the Congress on Age Discrimination in Employment under Section 715 of the Civil Rights Act of 1964.* Washington D.C.: Government Printing Office.

AGE DISCRIMINATION ACT
89 Stat. 728 (1975)

Enacted as Title III of the Older Americans Amendments of 1975, the Age Discrimination Act of 1975, like Title VI of the CIVIL RIGHTS ACT OF 1964 and other laws, links ANTIDISCRIMINATION LEGISLATION to Congress's spending power. Subject to important but ambiguous exceptions, the act prohibits exclusion on the basis of age from federally financed programs. In covered programs, the act affords greater protection against AGE DISCRIMINATION than the Supreme Court has held to be required under the EQUAL PROTECTION clause. In MASSACHUSETTS BOARD OF RETIREMENT V. MURGIA (1976), in upholding a statute requiring police officers to retire at age fifty, the Court found age not to be a SUSPECT CLASSIFICATION. The Age Discrimination in Employment Act, as well as some state laws, protect against age discrimination in employment.

THEODORE EISENBERG

Bibliography

SCHUCK, PETER H. 1979 The Graying of Civil Rights Laws: The Age Discrimination Act of 1975. *Yale Law Journal* 89:27–93.

AGNELLO v. UNITED STATES
269 U.S. 20 (1925)

In *Agnello* the Supreme Court extended the scope of SEARCH INCIDENT TO ARREST from the person of the arrestee, previously authorized in WEEKS V. UNITED STATES (1914), to the premises on which the arrest was made. The precise extent of the allowable search was, however, not delineated; it became a matter of great judicial contention in later cases.

JACOB W. LANDYNSKI

AGRICULTURAL ADJUSTMENT ACT OF 1933
48 Stat. 31

This act, the set piece of the New Deal for agriculture, emphasized PRODUCTION controls in an effort to revive farming from its 1920s torpor. Stressing collective action, the act sought to boost farm prices. After World War I ended, American farmers had found stiff new competition in the world market for the tremendously expanded U.S. farm output. As a result, surpluses ballooned and prices deflated. A modest recovery by 1923 had not taken firm hold, and the Depression in 1929 struck hard at farmers. Agricultural prices had dropped four times as far as industrial prices between 1929 and 1933. Shortly after FRANKLIN D. ROOSEVELT's inauguration in March 1933, his secretary of agriculture, Henry Wallace, met with farm leaders to formulate a relief plan. The resulting bill, drafted in part by JEROME FRANK, was ready in five days. To secure wide support, REXFORD TUGWELL and others recommended that this "farm relief" measure comprise elements of plans already proposed. As a result, it established parity prices—a price level that would allow the purchasing power of income from a commodity to equal its purchasing power in the base period, 1909–1914.

The act's avowed purpose, "to relieve the existing national economic emergency by increasing agricultural purchasing power," would be accomplished primarily by raising prices of seven basic commodities to parity levels. Control of production would be the means of achieving this goal. The secretary of agriculture could exert control by regulating benefit payments to farmers who voluntarily reduced production, by imposing marketing quotas, and by providing for government purchase of surpluses. The government would fund these efforts by imposing on the primary processors of agricultural goods an EXCISE TAX based on the difference between farm and parity prices. Benefit payments were designed to entice cooperation although participation was theoretically voluntary.

Senate opposition gave way to substantial public pressure for action and a lack of workable alternatives. The act also granted the secretary of agriculture power to make regulations to enforce the act (subject to presidential approval), assess penalties, and (with the secretary of the treasury) to have ultimate say in issues of payments to farmers. By late 1935 the act and a drought had provided much relief (net farm income rose 250 per cent), forecasting a profitable recovery for American agriculture. In January 1936, however, a 6–3 Supreme Court invalidated the statute in UNITED STATES V. BUTLER. A determined Congress passed a second AGRICULTURAL ADJUSTMENT ACT in 1938.

DAVID GORDON

AGRICULTURAL ADJUSTMENT ACT OF 1938
50 Stat. 246

After the Supreme Court invalidated the AGRICULTURAL ADJUSTMENT ACT (AAA) OF 1933 in UNITED STATES V. BUTLER (1936), Congress passed a second AAA in 1938, citing the effect of farm PRODUCTION on INTERSTATE COMMERCE as the act's basis. Congress once again sought to achieve parity levels for principal commodities and maintain earlier soil conservation payments as well. The act retained voluntary participation and, acknowledging *Butler,* Congress now levied no processing taxes nor did it set up production quotas; instead the act inaugurated a system of marketing quotas. Such a quota applied only when two-thirds of a commodity's producers approved. Once a general quota was authorized, the secretary of agriculture could set specific quotas for individual farms and assess a penalty tax on violators. Moreover, approval of quotas made available special loans to help store surplus production. The 1938 act also provided means of increasing consumption to help alleviate surpluses, and created a Commodity Credit Corporation to make loans when income fell because of low prices, and a Federal Crop Insurance Corporation. The Supreme Court sustained the act in *Mulford v. Smith* (1939) and WICKARD V. FILBURN (1942).

DAVID GORDON

AGRICULTURAL MARKETING AGREEMENT ACT
50 Stat. 246 (1937)

In 1933 the first AGRICULTURAL ADJUSTMENT ACT (AAA) developed programs for marketing various commodities. Congress strengthened that act two years later and, in 1937, reenacted many of the AAA provisions and amended others. The Agricultural Marketing Agreement Act stressed regulation of marketing, not of PRODUCTION. Responding to Supreme Court decisions that cast doubt on the marketing agreement provisions of the AAA, Congress now emphasized the separability of those sections. The act authorized the secretary of agriculture to set marketing quotas and price schedules and to sign voluntary agreements with producers. If fifty percent of the handlers and two-thirds of the producers of a commodity approved, the secretary could issue marketing orders. All such agreements were exempted from federal antitrust laws. The AAA's earlier effort to achieve parity prices (a level providing income with buying power equivalent to that for 1909–1914) by balancing production with consumption was now replaced by maintenance of "orderly marketing conditions for agricultural commodities in INTERSTATE COMMERCE." In addition, the 1937 act contained a broader definition of interstate and FOREIGN COMMERCE, declaring it to include any part of the "current" that is usual in the handling of a commodity. (See STREAM OF COMMERCE DOCTRINE.) The Supreme Court sustained the act in *United States v. Rock Royal Co-operative* (1939), finding that even a local transaction was "inextricably mingled with and directly affect[ed]" marketing in interstate commerce. The Court took similar action in WRIGHTWOOD DAIRY V. UNITED STATES (1942), even though that case involved purely INTRASTATE COMMERCE.

DAVID GORDON

AGRICULTURE

See: *Butler, United States v.*; Subjects of Commerce; *Wickard v. Filburn*

AGUILAR v. FELTON
473 U.S.   (1985)
GRAND RAPIDS SCHOOL DISTRICT v. BALL
473 U.S.   (1985)

In COMPANION CASES a 5–4 Supreme Court held unconstitutional the assignment of public school teachers to parochial schools for special auxiliary services. In the Grand Rapids "shared time" case, Justice WILLIAM J. BRENNAN for the majority concerned himself only with the possibility that the teachers might advance religion by conforming their instruction to the environment of the private sectarian schools. The evidence did not validate his fear. In *Aguilar*, Brennan expressed the same fear but focused on the "excessive entanglement of church and state" which he asserted was present in New York City's program to implement the ELEMENTARY AND SECONDARY EDUCATION ACT passed by Congress in 1965. Advancing religion and excessive entanglement show violations of the FIRST AMENDMENT'S SEPARATION OF CHURCH AND STATE as construed by the Court in LEMON V. KURTZMAN (1971), where it devised a test to determine whether

government has passed a law respecting an ESTABLISHMENT OF RELIGION.

The New York City program employed guidance counselors, psychologists, psychiatrists, social workers, and other specialists to teach remedial reading, mathematics, and English as a second language, and to provide guidance services. They worked part-time on parochial school premises, using only materials and equipment supplied by secular authorities; and, they acted under a ban against participation in religious activities. They worked under supervision similar to that which prevailed in public schools; the city monitored instruction by having supervisory personnel make unannounced "monthly" and "occasional" visits. Almost three-fourths of the educators in the program did not share the religious affiliation of any school in which they taught.

Brennan for the majority traveled a far path to find infirmities in the city's program. He expressed concern that the program might infringe the RELIGIOUS LIBERTY of its intended beneficiaries. He saw government "intrusion into sacred matters" and the necessity of an "ongoing inspection" to ensure the absence of inculcation of religion in the instruction. The need for "a permanent and pervasive State presence in the sectarian schools receiving aid" infringed values protected by the establishment clause.

Thus, if government fails to provide for surveillance to ward off inculcation, its aid unconstitutionally advances the religious mission of the church schools; if government does provide for monitoring, even if only periodically, it gets excessively entangled with religion. Justice SANDRA DAY O'CONNOR, dissenting, declared that the conclusion that the religious mission of the schools would be advanced by auxiliary services provided by the public was "not supported by the facts of this case." The nineteen-year record of the program showed not a single allegation of an attempt to indoctrinate religiously at public expense. The decision adversely affected disadvantaged parochial school children who needed special auxiliary services not provided by their parochial schools.

LEONARD W. LEVY

AGUILAR v. TEXAS
378 U.S. 108 (1964)

The rule that an officer's affidavit supporting an application for a SEARCH WARRANT must contain more than the officer's "mere affirmation of suspicion" was established in *Nathanson v. United States* (1933). Probable cause requires a statement of "facts or circumstances" explaining the affiant's belief that criminal activity is afoot, thus allowing the magistrate to make an independent judgment. In *Aguilar* the same rule was applied to an affidavit based on information supplied by an informant.

The *Aguilar* affidavit stated that the officers "had received reliable information from a credible person" that narcotics were kept on the premises. Nothing in the affidavit allowed the magistrate to determine the accuracy of the informant's conclusion. Though hearsay information can satisfy PROBABLE CAUSE, said the Court, the affidavit must give EVIDENCE that the informant spoke from personal knowledge, and explain the circumstances that led the officer to conclude that he "was 'credible' or his information 'reliable.'" The *Aguilar* rule was discarded in ILLINOIS V. GATES (1983).

JACOB W. LANDYNSKI

AKE v. OKLAHOMA
470 U.S.   (1985)

Following the PRECEDENTS of decisions holding that the RIGHT TO COUNSEL requires a state to provide a lawyer to an INDIGENT defendant, the Supreme Court held, 8–1, that the FOURTEENTH AMENDMENT's guarantee of PROCEDURAL DUE PROCESS requires a state to provide an indigent defendant access to such psychiatric examination and assistance necessary to prepare an effective defense based on the claim of insanity. Justice THURGOOD MARSHALL wrote the OPINION OF THE COURT. Chief Justice WARREN E. BURGER, in a CONCURRING OPINION, said that the decision was limited to capital cases. Justice WILLIAM H. REHNQUIST, dissenting, agreed that some such cases might require the state to provide psychiatric assistance, but argued that in this case, where the burden of proving insanity was on the defendant, the state had no such obligation.

KENNETH L. KARST

AKRON v. AKRON CENTER FOR REPRODUCTIVE CHOICE

See: Reproductive Autonomy

A. L. A. SCHECHTER POULTRY CORP. v. UNITED STATES

See: *Schechter v. United States*

ALBANY PLAN

See: Franklin, Benjamin

ALBERTS v. CALIFORNIA

See: *Roth v. United States*

ALBERTSON v. SUBVERSIVE ACTIVITIES CONTROL BOARD
382 U.S. 70 (1965)

This was one of several cases in which the WARREN COURT, on self-incrimination grounds, struck down compulsory registration provisions aimed at individuals who were members of inherently suspect groups. (See MARCHETTI V. UNITED STATES, 1968.) The Communist party failed to register with the government as required by the SUBVERSIVE ACTIVITIES CONTROL BOARD. The Board's order obligated all members of the party to register. By refusing, Albertson made himself liable to criminal penalties; he offered numerous constitutional objections. The Supreme Court decided only his claim that the order violated his RIGHT AGAINST SELF-INCRIMINATION.

Justice WILLIAM J. BRENNAN for an 8–0 Court observed, "Such an admission of membership may be used to prosecute the registrant under the membership clause of the SMITH ACT . . . or under . . . the Subversive Activities Control Act. . . ." The government relied on an old decision requiring all taxpayers to file returns, but Brennan answered that tax regulations applied to the public, not to "a highly selective group inherently suspect of criminal activities." The government also argued that a grant of immunity from prosecution for registrants supplanted the right against self-incrimination. Relying on COUNSELMAN V. HITCHCOCK (1892), Brennan ruled that unless the government provided "absolute immunity" for all transactions relating to coerced admissions, it failed to supplant the right. In KASTIGAR V. UNITED STATES (1972) the Court switched from transactional to use immunity. (See IMMUNITY GRANTS.)

LEONARD W. LEVY

ALDERMAN v. UNITED STATES
394 U.S. 165 (1969)

During the 1960s, the government admitted it had engaged in illegal electronic surveillance. Criminal defendants overheard in such surveillance sought the transcripts of the conversations to determine whether their convictions had been based on illegal surveillance and were therefore reversible. The government tried to limit the right to challenge electronic surveillance to persons actually overheard and to restrict disclosure of the transcripts to the judge.

The Supreme Court ruled that (1) anyone overheard, or anyone on whose premises conversations were overheard, could challenge the legality of the surveillance, but no one else; and (2) a person found to have been illegally overheard was entitled to see the transcripts to determine whether his conviction was based on illegal surveillance.

HERMAN SCHWARTZ

ALEXANDER, JAMES

See: Zenger's Case

ALEXANDER v. HOLMES COUNTY BOARD OF EDUCATION
396 U.S. 19 (1969)

Part of the "southern strategy" that helped elect President RICHARD M. NIXON had been an assertion that the Supreme Court had been too rigid in its treatment of school SEGREGATION. Thus it was no surprise when, on the eve of the opening of the fall 1969 school year, the Justice Department proposed that thirty-three Mississippi school boards be given an extension until December 1 to present DESEGREGATION plans. The UNITED STATES COURT OF APPEALS agreed, and the next day the plaintiffs sought an order from Justice HUGO L. BLACK staying this decision. Justice Black refused the stay but suggested that the case be brought to the whole Supreme Court for an early decision. The Court promptly granted CERTIORARI, heard the case in late October, and before month's end issued its order. The time for ALL DELIBERATE SPEED in school desegregation had run out; the school boards had an obligation "to terminate dual school systems at once." The BURGER COURT would not be a "Nixon Court" on this issue.

KENNETH L. KARST

ALIEN

The status of aliens—persons who are not citizens of the United States—presented perplexing constitutional problems in this country only after the great waves of IMMIGRATION began in the nineteenth century. The question seems not to have troubled the Framers of the Constitution. JAMES MADISON, in THE FEDERALIST #42, defended the power of Congress to set a uniform rule of NATURALIZATION as a means for easing interstate friction. Absent such a congressional law, he argued, State A might grant CITIZENSHIP to an alien who, on moving to State B, would become entitled to most of the PRIVILEGES AND IMMUNITIES granted by State B to its citizens. Evidently it was assumed from the beginning that aliens were not protected by Article IV's privileges and immunities clause, and it is still the conventional wisdom—although not unchallenged—that aliens cannot claim "the privileges and immunities of citizens of the United States" guaranteed by the FOURTEENTH AMENDMENT.

Alienage has sometimes been treated as synonymous with dissent, or even disloyalty. The ALIEN AND SEDITION ACTS (1798), for example, were aimed not only at American citizens who opposed President JOHN ADAMS but also at their supporters among French and Irish immigrants. The PALMER RAIDS of 1919–1920 culminated in the DEPORTATION of hundreds of alien anarchists and others suspected of SUBVERSIVE ACTIVITIES. At the outbreak of World War II, Attorney General FRANCIS BIDDLE was determined to avoid the mass internment of aliens; in the event, however, Biddle deferred to War Department pressure, and more than 100,000 persons of Japanese ancestry, alien and citizen alike, were removed from their West Coast homes and taken to camps in the interior. (See JAPANESE AMERICAN CASES, 1943–1944.)

When the KENTUCKY RESOLUTIONS (1798) protested against the Alien and Sedition Acts, they defended not so much the rights of aliens as STATES' RIGHTS. Indeed, the *rights* of aliens were not a major concern in the nation's early years. Even the federal courts' DIVERSITY JURISDICTION could be invoked in a case involving aliens only when citizens of a state were on the other side, as HODGSON v. BOWERBANK (1809) held. For this jurisdictional purpose, a "citizen" of a state still means a United States citizen who is also a state citizen. (An alien can sue another alien in a state court.) Thus, while a state can grant "state citizenship"—can allow aliens to vote, hold public office, or receive state benefits—that state citizenship does not qualify a person as a "citizen" within the meaning of the Constitution. Some states have previously allowed aliens to vote; even today, some states allow aliens to hold public office.

Most individual rights protected by the Constitution are not limited to "citizens" but extend to "people" or "persons," including aliens. An exception is the right to vote, protected by the FIFTEENTH, NINETEENTH, and TWENTY-SIXTH AMENDMENTS, which is limited to citizens. Aliens do not, of course, have the constitutional freedom of entry into the country that citizens have; aliens' stay here can be conditioned on conduct—for example, the retention of student status—that could not constitutionally be required of citizens. An alien, but not a citizen, can be deported for certain violations of law. In wartime, the property of enemy aliens can be confiscated. Yet aliens are subject to many of the obligations fastened on citizens: they pay taxes along with the rest of us, and, if Congress so disposes, they are as susceptible as citizens to CONSCRIPTION into the armed forces.

Congress, by authorizing the admission of some aliens for permanent residence, accepts those admittees as at least limited members of the national community. The CIVIL RIGHTS ACT OF 1866, for example, protects a resident alien against state legislation that interferes with the alien's earning a livelihood. The vitality of the PREEMPTION DOCTRINE in such cases no doubt rests on two assumptions: that the national government, not the states, has the primary responsibility for the nation's dealings with foreign countries, and that the regulation of another country's nationals is likely to affect those dealings.

Throughout our history, state laws have discriminated against aliens by disqualifying them from various forms of public and private employment, and from receiving public assistance benefits. Early decisions of the Supreme Court mostly upheld these laws, ignoring their evident tensions with congressional policy and rejecting claims based on the Fourteenth Amendment's EQUAL PROTECTION clause. Two decisions in 1948, OYAMA V. CALIFORNIA and TAKAHASHI V. FISH & GAME COMMISSION, undermined the earlier precedents, and in the 1970s the Court made a frontal assault on state discriminations against aliens.

A legislative classification based on the status of alienage, the Court announced in GRAHAM V. RICHARDSON (1971), was a SUSPECT CLASSIFICATION, analogous to a racial classification. Thus, justifications offered to support the classification must pass the test of STRICT SCRUTINY. State restrictions of WELFARE BENEFITS, on the basis of alienage, were accordingly invalidated. Two years later, this reasoning was extended to invalidate a law disqualifying aliens from a state's civil service, SUGARMAN V. DOUGALL (1973), and a law barring aliens from the practice of law, IN RE GRIFFITHS (1973). The string of invalidations of state laws continued with *Examining Board v.*

Flores de Otero (1976) (disqualification to be a civil engineer) and *Nyquist v. Mauclet* (1977) (limiting eligibility for state scholarship aid).

In the *Sugarman* opinion, the Court had remarked that some state discriminations against aliens would not have to pass strict judicial scrutiny. The right to vote in state elections, or to hold high public office, might be limited to United States citizens on the theory that such rights are closely connected with the idea of membership in a political community. By the end of the decade, these words had become the foundation for a large exception to the principle of strict scrutiny of alienage classifications. The "political community" notion was extended to a broad category of public employees performing "government functions" requiring the exercise of discretion and responsibility. Disqualification of aliens from such jobs would be upheld if it was supported by a RATIONAL BASIS. FOLEY V. CONNELIE (1978) thus upheld a law disqualifying aliens to serve as state troopers, and AMBACH V. NORWICK (1979) upheld a law barring aliens from teaching in public schools unless they had shown an intent to become U.S. citizens. *Cabell v. Chavez-Salido* (1982) extended the same reasoning to state probation officers.

At the same time, the Court made clear that when Congress discriminated against aliens, nothing like strict judicial scrutiny was appropriate. *Mathews v. Diaz* (1976) announced an extremely deferential standard of review for such congressional laws, saying that the strong federal interest in regulating foreign affairs provided a close analogy to the doctrine of POLITICAL QUESTIONS—which suggests, of course, essentially no judicial scrutiny at all.

It was argued for a time that the preemption doctrine provides the most complete explanation of the Court's results in alienage cases. The early 1970s decisions, grounded on equal protection theory, instead might have been rested on congressional laws such as the 1866 act. The decisions on "governmental functions," seen in this light, would amount to a recognition that Congress has not admitted resident aliens to the "political community." On this theory, because Congress has not admitted "undocumented" aliens for any purpose at all, state laws regulating them would be viewed favorably. In PLYLER V. DOE (1982), the Supreme Court rejected this line of reasoning and held, 5–4, that Texas had denied equal protection by refusing free public education to children not lawfully admitted to the country while providing it for all other children. The majority, conceding that Congress might authorize some forms of state discrimination, discerned no such authorization in Congress's silence.

The preemption analysis, no less than an equal protection analysis, leaves the key term ("political community") for manipulation; on either theory, for example, the school teacher case seems wrongly decided. And the equal protection approach has one advantage that is undeniable: it focuses the judiciary on questions that bear some relation to life—substantive questions about degrees of discrimination and proffered justifications—rather than on the metaphysics of preemption.

KENNETH L. KARST

Bibliography

NOTE 1975 Aliens' Right to Teach: Political Socialization and the Public Schools. *Yale Law Journal* 85:90–111.

NOTE 1979 A Dual Standard for State Discrimination Against Aliens. *Harvard Law Review* 92:1516–1537.

NOTE 1979 The Equal Treatment of Aliens: Preemption or Equal Protection? *Stanford Law Review* 31:1069–1091.

NOTE 1980 State Burdens on Resident Aliens: A New Preemption Analysis. *Yale Law Journal* 89:940–961.

PRESTON, WILLIAM, JR. 1963 *Aliens and Dissenters: Federal Suppression of Radicals, 1903–1933.* Cambridge, Mass.: Harvard University Press.

ROSBERG, GERALD M. 1977 The Protection of Aliens from Discriminatory Treatment by the National Government. *Supreme Court Review* 1977:275–339.

ALIEN AND SEDITION ACTS

Naturalization Act
1 Stat. 566 (1798)
Alien Act
1 Stat. 570 (1798)
Alien Enemies Act
1 Stat. 577 (1798)
Sedition Act
1 Stat. 596 (1798)

These acts were provoked by the war crisis with France in 1798. Three of the four acts concerned ALIENS. Federalist leaders feared the French and Irish, in particular, as a potentially subversive force and as an element of strength in the Republican party. The Naturalization Act increased the period of residence required for admission to CITIZENSHIP from five to fourteen years. The Alien Act authorized the President to deport any alien deemed dangerous to the peace and safety of the United States. The Alien Enemies Act authorized incarceration and banishment of aliens in time of war. The Sedition Act, aimed at "domestic traitors," made it a federal crime for anyone to conspire to impede governmental operations or to write or publish "any false, scandalous, and malicious writing" against the government, the Congress, or the President.

While Republicans conceded the constitutionality, though not the necessity, of the Naturalization and Alien Enemies acts, they assailed the others, not only as unnecessary and unconstitutional but as politically designed to cripple or destroy the opposition party under the pretense of foreign menace. The constitutional argument received authoritative statement in the VIRGINIA AND KENTUCKY RESOLUTIONS. In defense of the Alien Act, with its summary procedures, Federalists appealed to the inherent right of the government to protect itself. The same appeal was made for the Sedition Act. Federalists denied, further, that the act violated FIRST AMENDMENT guarantees of FREEDOM OF SPEECH and PRESS, which they interpreted as prohibitions of PRIOR RESTRAINT only. They also claimed that the federal government had JURISDICTION over COMMON LAW crimes, such as SEDITIOUS LIBEL, and so could prosecute without benefit of statute. The statute, they said, liberalized the common law by admitting truth as a defense and authorizing juries to return a general verdict.

Despite the zeal of President JOHN ADAMS's administration, no one was actually deported under the Alien Act. (War not having been declared, the Alien Enemies Act never came into operation.) The Sedition Act, on the other hand, was widely enforced. Twenty-five persons were arrested, fourteen indicted (plus three under common law), ten tried and convicted, all of them Republican printers and publicists. The most celebrated trials were those of Matthew Lyon, Republican congressman and newspaper editor in Vermont; Dr. Thomas Cooper, an English-born scientist and political refugee, in Philadelphia; and James T. Callender, another English refugee, who possessed a vitriolic pen, in Richmond. All were fined upward to $1,000 and imprisoned for as long as nine months. Before partisan judges and juries, in a climate of fear and suspicion, the boasted safeguards of the law proved of no value to the defendants, and all constitutional safeguards were rejected.

The repressive laws recoiled on their sponsors, contributing to the Republican victory in the election of 1800. The Sedition Act expired the day THOMAS JEFFERSON became President. He immediately voided actions pending under it and pardoned the victims. In 1802 the Alien Act expired and Congress returned the NATURALIZATION law to its old footing.

Only the Alien Enemies Act remained on the statute book. Nothing like this legislation would be enacted again until the two world wars of the twentieth century.

MERRILL D. PETERSON

Bibliography

SMITH, JAMES MORTON 1956 *Freedom's Fetters: The Alien and Sedition Laws and American Civil Liberties.* Ithaca, N.Y.: Cornell University Press.

ALIEN REGISTRATION ACT
54 Stat. 670 (1940)

This measure, popularly known as the Smith Act, was destined to become the most famous of the anticommunist measures of the Cold War, McCarthy period. The act required all ALIENS living in the United States to register with the government, be fingerprinted, carry identification cards, and report annually. Persons found to have ties to "subversive organizations" could be deported. The registration requirement was rescinded in 1982.

Such alien registration was only one of the various purposes of the act. It was directed primarily at SUBVERSIVE ACTIVITIES which were causing growing concerns on the eve of war, particularly communist-inspired strikes intended to injure American defense production. As the first federal peacetime SEDITION statute since 1798, the Smith Act in its most significant section made it a crime to "knowingly, or willfully, advocate, abet, advise, or teach the duty, necessity, desirability, or propriety of overthrowing or destroying any government in the United States by force and violence. . . ." Any attempts forcibly to overthrow the government of the United States by publication or display of printed matters, to teach, or to organize any group, or to become a "knowing" member of such an organization were forbidden. Section 3 forbade conspiracy to accomplish any of these ends. The act carried maximum criminal penalties of a $10,000 fine or ten years in prison or both; no one convicted under the law was to be eligible for federal employment during the five years following conviction.

The act, which did not mention the Communist party, attracted little attention at the time of its passage, and initial enforcement was spotty. Although five million aliens were registered and fingerprinted shortly following its passage, its antisubversive sections were not used until 1943, when a small group of Minneapolis Trotskyites were convicted. When the Cold War intensified, following 1947, the HARRY S. TRUMAN administration began a series of dramatic prosecutions of Communist party leaders. These and subsequent prosecutions eventually forced the Supreme Court to clarify the act's terms, starting with DENNIS V. UNITED STATES (1951), and extending through YATES V. UNITED STATES (1957), SCALES V. UNITED STATES (1961), and *Noto v. United States* (1961). As a result of these rulings, the measure's advocacy, organizing, and membership provisions were limited and made more precise.

PAUL L. MURPHY

Bibliography

BELKNAP, MICHAEL R. 1977 *Cold War Political Justice: The Smith Act, the Communist Party, and American Civil Liberties.* Westport, Conn.: Greenwood Press.

ALL DELIBERATE SPEED

Chief Justice EARL WARREN achieved a unanimous decision in BROWN V. BOARD OF EDUCATION (1954) by assuring that enforcement of school DESEGREGATION would be gradual. Ordinarily, state officials found to be violating the Constitution are simply ordered to stop. *Brown II* (1955), however, instructed lower courts to insist only that offending school boards make "a prompt and reasonable start," proceeding toward full desegregation with "all deliberate speed."

This calculatedly elusive phrase was contributed by Justice FELIX FRANKFURTER, who had borrowed it from an old opinion by Justice OLIVER WENDELL HOLMES. Holmes attributed it to English EQUITY practice, but he may also have seen it in Francis Thompson's poem, "The Hound of Heaven." Whatever the phrase's origins, it was a thin cover for compromise. The objective presumably was to allow time for the white South to become accustomed to the end of SEGREGATION, in the hope of avoiding defiance of the courts and even violence. Robert Penn Warren, a southern man of letters who had not studied quantum mechanics, even tried to make gradualism in desegregation a historical necessity: "History, like nature, knows no jumps."

The South responded not with accommodation but with politically orchestrated defiance. A full decade after *Brown I*, two percent of southern black children were attending integrated schools. By 1969, the Supreme Court explicitly abandoned "all deliberate speed"; in ALEXANDER V. HOLMES COUNTY BOARD

OF EDUCATION school boards were told to desegregate "at once."

No one pretends that the Supreme Court could have ended Jim Crow overnight, certainly not without support from Congress or the President. Yet the Court's decisions can command respect only when they are understood to rest on principle. *Brown II*, widely seen to be precisely the political accommodation it was intended to be, did not merely consign a generation of southern black school children to segregated schools. The decision weakened the Court's own moral authority in the very process gradualism was designed to aid.

KENNETH L. KARST

Bibliography

WILKINSON, J. HARVIE, III 1979 *From Brown to Bakke.* New York: Oxford University Press.

ALLEN v. WRIGHT
468 U.S. 737 (1984)

The parents of black school children in districts that were undergoing DESEGREGATION brought suit against officials of the Internal Revenue Service (IRS). Alleging that the IRS had not adopted standards and procedures that would fulfill the agency's obligation to deny tax-exempt status to racially discriminatory private schools, the plaintiffs argued that the IRS in effect subsidized unconstitutional school SEGREGATION. The Supreme Court, 5–3, held that the plaintiffs lacked STANDING to raise this claim.

Justice SANDRA DAY O'CONNOR, for the majority, said that the plaintiffs' claim that they had been stigmatized by the IRS conduct was insufficient as a specification of injury, amounting to little more than a general claim that government must behave according to law. The parents' second claim of injury was that they had been denied the right to have their children attend school in a system that was not segregated. Here the asserted injury was sufficient, Justice O'Connor said, but the injury was not fairly traceable to IRS conduct. The Court thus reinforced the "causation" requirement for standing established in *Warth v. Seldin* (1975). The three dissenters made the familiar charge that the "causation" line of inquiry disguised a rejection of the plaintiffs' claim without really addressing the constitutional issue. As in *Warth*, the Court rejected the plaintiffs' claim of injury without giving them the chance to prove their case.

KENNETH L. KARST

ALLEN-BRADLEY COMPANY v. LOCAL UNION #3
325 U.S. 797 (1945)

An 8–1 Supreme Court, dominated by appointees of FRANKLIN D. ROOSEVELT, held here that union actions that prompted nonlabor market control and business profits violated the SHERMAN ANTITRUST ACT. The union had obtained CLOSED SHOP agreements with New York City manufacturers of electrical equipment in return for a promise to strike or boycott any contractor who did not use the local manufacturers' equipment. Because out-of-city materials were cheaper, these agreements effectively restrained competition. Justice HUGO L. BLACK, for the Court, found that such action could be enjoined under the Sherman Act because neither the CLAYTON ACT nor the NORRIS-LaGUARDIA ACT protected union action not solely in its own interests.

DAVID GORDON

ALLGEYER v. LOUISIANA
165 U.S. 578 (1897)

The Louisiana legislature sought to encourage local business by forbidding state citizens from buying marine insurance from out-of-state companies. Justice RUFUS PECKHAM, building on a long line of dissents by Justice STEPHEN J. FIELD, expounded a broad concept of "liberty" including the idea of FREEDOM OF CONTRACT. Liberty, said the Court, "is deemed to embrace the right of the citizen to be free in the enjoyment of all his faculties." In thus circumscribing state authority over interstate business, *Allgeyer* represents the first invalidation of a state act as a deprivation of freedom of contract without violating the FOURTEENTH AMENDMENT guarantee of DUE PROCESS OF LAW.

DAVID GORDON

ALLIED STRUCTURAL STEEL COMPANY v. SPANNAUS
438 U.S. 234 (1978)

The modern revival of the CONTRACT CLAUSE began with UNITED STATES TRUST COMPANY v. NEW JERSEY (1977), a case in which the Supreme Court showed its willingness to make states live up to their own obligations as contracting parties. *Spannaus* carried the new doctrine further, imposing the contract clause as a significant limitation on the power of a state to regulate relations between private contracting parties.

Minnesota law required certain large employers, when they terminated pension plans or left the state, to provide for the funding of pensions for employees with ten years' service. Allied, in its pension plan, had reserved the right to terminate the plan and distribute the fund's assets to retired and current employees. On closing its Minnesota office, under the law Allied had to provide about $185,000 to fund pensions for its ten-year employees. The Supreme Court, 5–3, held the law unconstitutional as an impairment of the OBLIGATION OF CONTRACTS.

Justice POTTER STEWART wrote for the Court. Much of his opinion was devoted to distinguishing HOME BUILDING & LOAN ASSOCIATION v. BLAISDELL (1934). Here the law did not deal with a "broad, generalized economic or social problem" but focused narrowly, not on all employers or even all who left the state, but on those who previously had voluntarily established pension plans. The law did not merely temporarily alter contractual relationships but "worked a severe, permanent and immediate change in those relationships—irrevocably and retroactively." The law also "invaded an area never before subject to regulation by the State," thus invading reliance interests to a greater degree than would result from a more common (and hence foreseeable) type of regulation.

Justice WILLIAM J. BRENNAN, for the dissenters, correctly noted that the Court's opinion amounted to a major change in the judicial role in supervising state economic regulation, demanding STRICT SCRUTINY under the contract clause to protect contract-based expectations.

Spannaus seemed to invite businesses to challenge all manner of ECONOMIC REGULATIONS on the ground of excessive interference with contractual expectations. In EXXON CORP. V. EAGERTON (1983), however, the Court sought to exorcise the ghost of FREEDOM OF CONTRACT. *Exxon* sharply limited the *Spannaus* principle to laws whose "sole effect" is "to alter contractual duties."

KENNETH L. KARST

ALMEIDA-SANCHEZ v. UNITED STATES
413 U.S. 266 (1973)

A roving United States border patrol, without warrant or PROBABLE CAUSE, stopped and searched an automobile for illegal aliens twenty-five miles from the Mexican border. The Court ruled that while routine searches of persons and vehicles at the border are permissible, this search was conducted too far from the border to be reasonable under the FOURTH AMENDMENT.

JACOB W. LANDYNSKI

AMALGAMATED FOOD EMPLOYEES UNION v. LOGAN VALLEY PLAZA

See: Shopping Centers

AMBACH v. NORWICK
441 U.S. 68 (1979)

Ambach completed the process, begun in FOLEY V. CONNELIE (1978), of carving out a major exception to the principle that discrimination against ALIENS amounts to a SUSPECT CLASSIFICATION, triggering STRICT SCRUTINY of its justifications. New York forbade employment as public school teachers of aliens who had not shown an intention to seek U.S. CITIZENSHIP. The Supreme Court held, 5–4, that this discrimination did not deny its victims the EQUAL PROTECTION OF THE LAWS.

Justice LEWIS F. POWELL, for the majority, concluded that *Foley*, following OBITER DICTA in SUGARMAN V. DOUGALL (1973), implied the exception in question. Where "governmental functions" were involved, the state need show only that the exclusion of aliens had a RATIONAL BASIS. Public school teachers, like police officers, have great individual responsibility and discretion; part of a teacher's function is to transmit our society's values and prepare children to be participating citizens. Under the RATIONAL BASIS standard, the state need not show a close fit between its classification and its objectives; the standard is met if it is rational to conclude that citizens generally would be better able than aliens to transmit citizenship values.

Justice HARRY A. BLACKMUN, author of the *Sugarman* opinion, led the dissenters, pointing out the indiscriminate sweep of the disqualification of aliens, and its tenuous connection with educational goals. (Private schools, for example, were permitted to use alien teachers, even though they were charged with transmitting citizenship values to eighteen percent of New York's children.)

KENNETH L. KARST

AMENDING PROCESS

Article V, which stipulates the methods by which the Constitution may be amended, reflects the Framers' attempt to reconcile the principles of the Revolution with their desire for stable government in the future. Early in the CONSTITUTIONAL CONVENTION OF 1787, GEORGE MASON of Virginia suggested that inclusion in the Constitution of a specified mechanism for future amendments would help channel zeal for change into settled constitutional processes. "Amendments therefore will be necessary," he said, "and it will be better to provide for them, in an easy, regular and constitutional way than to trust to chance and violence." So viewed, the Article V amendment process is a somewhat conservative rendering of the revolutionary spirit that had claimed for the people an inalienable right to alter or abolish an inadequate government.

The Constitution sets out alternative methods both for proposing and for ratifying amendments. Amendments may be proposed by a two-thirds vote of both houses of Congress, or by a national constitutional convention. All of the amendments proposed thus far in our history have emanated from Congress. To become part of the Constitution, proposed amendments must gain the assent of three-fourths of the states. Article V gives Congress the power to choose whether proposed amendments (including any proposed by a constitutional convention) should be submitted to state legislatures or to state conventions for RATIFICATION. Congress has submitted every proposed amendment but one to the state legislatures.

Since 1789, over 5,000 bills proposing amendments to the Constitution have been introduced in Congress. Of these, only thirty-three received the necessary two-thirds vote of both houses of Congress and proceeded to the states for ratification. Twenty-six have been adopted; the remaining seven failed to be ratified. With only a few exceptions, the amendments proposed by Congress have come in clusters; virtually all of them arose during four brief periods.

The first of these periods ran from 1789 to 1804 and produced what may loosely be called the "Anti-Federalist amendments"—the BILL OF RIGHTS, the ELEVENTH AMENDMENT, and the TWELFTH AMENDMENT—each of which was, in part, a concession to Anti-Federalist or Jeffersonian interests. More than half a century passed before the Constitution was again amended. In 1865, sixty-one years after adoption of the Twelfth Amendment, Congress proposed and the states ratified the THIRTEENTH AMENDMENT, the first of the three Reconstruction amendments. The adoption of the FOURTEENTH AMENDMENT and the FIFTEENTH AMENDMENT followed in 1868 and 1870. A gap of almost another half-century intervened between the Reconstruction amendments and the next four amendments. These last grew out of the Populist and Progressive movements and provided for federal income taxation (the SIXTEENTH AMENDMENT, ratified in 1913), DIRECT ELECTION of senators (the SEVENTEENTH AMENDMENT, ratified in 1913), PROHIBITION (the EIGHTEENTH AMENDMENT, ratified in 1919), and women's suffrage (the NINETEENTH AMENDMENT, ratified in 1920). A fifth Progressive amendment, the CHILD LABOR AMENDMENT, was proposed in 1924 but was not ratified.

Together, the first three periods accounted for all but three of the amendments adopted before 1960. (The only amendments that did not fall into one of these clusters were the TWENTIETH AMENDMENT, which limits the lameduck session of Congress and was adopted in 1933; the TWENTY-FIRST AMENDMENT, which repealed prohibition and was adopted in 1933; and the TWENTY-SECOND AMENDMENT, which limits the President to two terms in office and was adopted in 1951). A fourth period of amendment activity lasted from 1961 to 1978. During these years, Congress proposed six amendments, four of which were adopted. The TWENTY-THIRD AMENDMENT gave the DISTRICT OF COLUMBIA three electoral votes in presidential elections. The TWENTY-FOURTH AMENDMENT abolished the POLL TAX for federal elections. The TWENTY-FIFTH AMENDMENT provided rules for presidential disability and PRESIDENTIAL SUCCESSION. The TWENTY-SIXTH AMENDMENT lowered the voting age to eighteen for both state and federal elections.

The fights over adoption of these twenty-six amendments, as well as battles over the proposed amendments that failed to be ratified, have produced conflicts over the proper procedures to be followed under the amendment article. The spare language of Article V leaves a number of questions unanswered. Between 1791 and 1931 the Supreme Court had occasion to address some of these issues. Arguments that there are implicit limits on the kind of amendments that may be adopted have not been accepted. In the *National Prohibition Cases* (1920) the Court rejected the argument that the Eighteenth Amendment (prohibition) was improper because of its interference with the states' exercise of their POLICE POWER. And in *Leser v. Garnett* (1922) the Court held that the Nineteenth Amendment's conferral of VOTING RIGHTS upon women was an appropriate exercise of the amendment power, rejecting the contention that "so great an addition to the electorate if made without the State's consent, destroys its autonomy as a political body."

In several decisions, the Court has given a broad reading to the power of Congress to propose amendments. In *Hollingsworth v. Virginia* (1798) the Court, sustaining the validity of the Eleventh Amendment, held that in spite of the veto clause of Article I, amendments proposed by Congress do not have to be submitted to the President for his signature. In the *National Prohibition Cases* (1920) the Court held that a two-thirds vote of a quorum of each house (rather than two-thirds of the entire membership) is sufficient to propose an amendment. In *Dillon v. Gloss* (1921) the Court held that Congress, when it proposes an amendment, has the power to set a reasonable time limit on ratification, and that seven years is a reasonable limit. The Court also rejected in *United States v. Sprague* (1931) the claim that amendments granting the federal government new, direct powers over the people may properly be ratified only by the people themselves acting through state conventions, and held that the mode of ratification is completely dependent upon congressional discretion. And when Congress does choose to submit an amendment to state legislatures, those legislatures are exercising a federal function under Article V and are not subject to the control of state law. Thus, in *Hawke v. Smith* (1919) the Court held that a state may not make the legislature's ratification of an amendment dependent upon subsequent approval by a voter REFERENDUM.

From 1798 to 1931 the Supreme Court assumed in decisions such as *Hollingsworth, Hawke,* and *Dillon* that issues of constitutional law arising under Article V were to be determined by the Court in the ordinary course of JUDICIAL REVIEW. In COLEMAN V. MILLER (1939), however, the Court refused to address several challenges to Kansas's ratification of the proposed Child Labor Amendment. Issues such as the timeliness of a ratification and the effect of a state's prior rejection of the validity of its ratification were held to be nonjusticiable questions committed to "the ultimate authority in the Congress of its control over the promulgation of the amendment." The *Coleman* decision suggests that judicial review is precluded for all issues that might be considered and resolved by Congress when, at the end of the state ratification process, Congress decides whether or not to "promulgate" the amendment.

Critics of the *Coleman* decision have disputed the Court's conclusion that "congressional promulgation" should preclude the judiciary from resolving challenges to the constitutional validity of an amendment. Critics even question the very notion of "congressional promulgation" as final, necessary step in the amendment process. The text of Article V notes only two stages for the adoption of an amendment: proposal by Congress (or a convention) and ratification by the states. There is no mention of any further action for an amendment to become valid. The Court had expressly held in *Dillon v. Gloss* (1921) what the language of Article V implies: that a proposed amendment becomes part of the Constitution immediately upon ratification by the last necessary state legislature. No further "promulgation" by Congress (or anyone else) appears to be necessary under Article V.

The only occasion upon which Congress ever undertook, at the end of a ratification process, to "promulgate" the adoption of an amendment was during Reconstruction when Congress passed a resolution declaring the Fourteenth Amendment to have been validly adopted despite disputed ratifications from two states that had attempted to rescind. In deciding *Coleman,* the Supreme Court treated the isolated Reconstruction precedent as a settled feature of the amendment process and held that congressional promulgation of an amendment would be binding on the Courts. *Coleman* remains the Court's last word on how disputed amendment process issues are to be resolved. Unless *Coleman* is reconsidered, any challenges to the validity of the procedures used for amendment will be conclusively determined by the Congress sitting when the required number of ratifications are reported to have been received.

It is difficult to predict how unresolved questions concerning the amendment process might be answered. Among the more warmly disputed issues has been the question of whether a state that has ratified an amendment may validly rescind its ratification. The text of Article V is inconclusive; while it does not mention any right of rescission, such a right might be inferred from the right to ratify. However, most treatise writers and scholars of the nineteenth and twentieth centuries have assumed that ratification was final and rescission ineffective. OBITER DICTUM in *Coleman,* moreover, suggests that the Court might have affirmatively approved the decision of the Reconstruction Congress to ignore purported rescissions.

Arguments that rescission by a subsequent legislature ought to nullify a state's earlier ratification, or that ratifications should be considered valid only if they are sufficiently close in time to reflect a "contemporaneous consensus" among ratifying states, may reflect, in part, an unstated assumption that it ought to be very difficult to amend the Constitution. But even without a requirement that ratifications must remain unrescinded or must come within a confined period of time, an amendment will not become part of the Constitution as long as one chamber in thirteen of the fifty state legislatures simply does nothing. An amendment proposed by a supermajority of the national Congress, and formally accepted at some time by the legislatures of three-fourths of the states (even if some state legislatures also pass resolutions of "rescission"), has passed the tests Article V expressly requires. As JAMES MADISON noted in THE FEDERALIST #43, the amendment article was designed to guard "equally against that extreme facility, which would render the constitution too mutable; and that extreme difficulty which might perpetuate its discovered faults."

To insure that the full range of future constitutional changes would be a viable possibility, the Framers sought to provide some means of constitutional change free of the control of existing governmental institutions. The Framers therefore included alternative mechanisms both for proposing and for ratifying amendments. From the earliest days of the Constitutional Convention, the delegates sought to avoid giving Congress the sole authority to propose amendments. If the proposal of all amendments ultimately depended upon Congress, George Mason argued, "no amendments of the proper kind would ever be obtained by the people, if the Government should become oppressive, as he verily believed would be the case." Other delegates, however, were apprehensive about the threat to national authority if state legislatures could effectively propose and ratify amendments without the involvement of some institution reflecting the national interest.

The solution to this dilemma was the "convention of the people." In addition to providing that amendments could be proposed by Congress, the final version of Article V provides that Congress must call "a Convention for proposing Amendments" whenever two-thirds of the state legislatures apply for one. Such a convention would be, like Congress, a deliberative body capable of assessing from a national perspective the need for constitutional change and capable of drafting proposed amendments for submission to the states for ratification. At the same time it would not be Congress itself, and therefore would not pose the threat of legislative self-interest's blocking needed reform of Congress.

No national convention for proposing amendments has ever been called. In recent years, however, a number of state legislatures have petitioned Congress to call a convention limited to proposing a particular amendment specified by the applying state legislatures. Some scholars consider these applications to be valid and argue that if similar applications are received from two-thirds of the state legislatures Congress should call the convention and seek to limit the convention to the particular amendment (or subject) specified in the state legislative applications. Others argue that such state applications are invalid because they erroneously assume that the agenda of the convention can properly be controlled by the applying state legislatures. These scholars argue that the only valid applications are those that recognize that a convention for proposing amendments is to be free to determine for itself what amendments should be proposed.

In addition to providing the alternative of a national convention for proposing amendments, Article V also provides an alternative method of ratifying amendments. For each amendment (whether proposed by Congress or by a national convention) Congress is free to choose whether to submit the amendment for ratification to state legislatures or to "conventions" in each state. By giving Congress this authority, Article V preserves the possibility of reforms restricting the power of state legislatures. The Constitution itself was submitted to ratifying conventions in each state, rather than to state legislatures. For thirty-two of the thirty-three proposed amendments Congress chose to submit its proposal to state legislatures. But the use of the convention method of ratification is not unprecedented: The Twenty-First Amendment repealing prohibition was submitted by Congress in 1933 to state conventions. Virtually every state chose to have delegates to its ratifying convention elected, and in every state the election of delegates was, for all practical purposes, a dispositive referendum on whether or not to ratify the amendment. In every state the voters' wishes were expeditiously carried out by the slate that had won election. In less than ten months from the time it was proposed by Congress, the amendment was ratified by elected conventions in three-fourths of the states.

The "convention of the people" was a familiar device in the eighteenth century. It now seems archaic, and the use of either a national convention for proposing amendments or state conventions for ratification are at present fraught with uncertainties. The convention device was nonetheless an imaginative effort to address a universal problem of constitution drafting: how to provide the means for future reform of governmental institutions when the only institutions readily available for proposing and approving changes are those already in existence, and possibly in need of reform themselves.

WALTER DELLINGER

Bibliography

DELLINGER, WALTER 1984 The Legitimacy of Constitutional Change: Rethinking the Amendment Process. *Harvard Law Review* 97:386–432.

GRIMES, ALLEN P. 1978 *Democracy and the Amendments to the Constitution.* Lexington, Mass.: Lexington Books.

GUNTHER, GERALD 1979 The Convention Method of Amending the United States Constitution. *Georgia Law Review* 14:1–25.

ORFIELD, LESTER BERNHARDT 1942 *The Amending of the Federal Constitution.* Ann Arbor: University of Michigan Press; Chicago: Callaghan & Co.

TRIBE, LAURENCE H. 1984 A *Constitution* We Are Amending: In Defense of a Restrained Judicial Role. *Harvard Law Review* 97:433–445.

AMERICAN CIVIL LIBERTIES UNION

The American Civil Liberties Union (ACLU) is the most important national organization dedicated to the protection of individual liberty. It was founded in 1920 by a distinguished group that included ROGER BALDWIN, Jane Addams, FELIX FRANKFURTER, Helen Keller, Scott Nearing, and Norman Thomas.

The principles of the ACLU are contained in the BILL OF RIGHTS: the right to free expression, above all, the freedom to dissent from the official view and majority opinion; the right to equal treatment regardless of race, sex, religion, national origin, or physical handicap; the right to DUE PROCESS in encounters with government institutions—courts, schools, police, bureaucracy—and with the repositories of great private power; the right to be let alone—to be secure from spying, from the unwarranted collection of personal information, and from interference in private lives.

The ACLU has participated in many controversial cases. It represented John Scopes when he was fired for teaching evolution; it fought for the rights of Sacco and Vanzetti; it defended the Scottsboro Boys, who were denied a FAIR TRIAL for alleged rape (see POWELL V. ALABAMA, 1932; NORRIS V. ALABAMA, 1935); it fought the Customs Bureau when it banned James Joyce's *Ulysses* (see UNITED STATES V. "ULYSSES," (1934); it opposed the censorship of the Pentagon Papers (see NEW YORK TIMES V. UNITED STATES, 1971) and religious exercises in schools.

The ACLU has supported racial and religious minorities, the right of LABOR to organize, and equal treatment for women, and it has opposed arbitrary treatment of persons in closed institutions such as mental patients, prisoners, military personnel, and students.

The concept of CIVIL LIBERTIES, as understood by the ACLU, has developed over the years. For example, in the 1960s it declared that CAPITAL PUNISHMENT violated civil liberties because of the finality and randomness of executions; that military conscription, which substantially restricts individual autonomy, violated civil liberties except during war or national emergency; and that the undeclared VIETNAM WAR was illegal because of failure to abide by constitutional procedures for committing the country to hostilities.

On the other hand, while endorsing many legal protections for poor people, the ACLU has never held that poverty itself violated civil liberties. In addition, since a cardinal precept of the ACLU is political nonpartisanship, it does not endorse or oppose judicial nominees or candidates for public office.

The ACLU has been frequently attacked as subversive, communistic, and even a "criminals' lobby." Its detractors have not recognized that by representing radicals and despised minorities the ACLU does not endorse their causes but rather the primacy and indivisibility of the Bill of Rights. This confusion cost the ACLU many members when in 1977 it secured the right of American Nazis to demonstrate peacefully in Skokie, Illinois.

The ACLU's national headquarters are in New York City; it maintains a legislative office in Washington, D.C., and regional offices in Atlanta and Denver. Its 250,000 members are organized in branches in all fifty states, which are tied to the national organization through revenue-sharing, participation in policy decisions, and united action on common goals. Each affiliate has its own board of directors and hires its own staff. The ACLU participates annually in thousands of court cases and administrative actions, legislative lobbying, and public education.

NORMAN DORSEN

Bibliography

DORSEN, NORMAN 1984 The American Civil Liberties Union: An Institutional Analysis. *Tulane Lawyer* (Spring) 1984:6–14.

AMERICAN COMMUNICATIONS ASSOCIATION v. DOUDS
339 U.S. 382 (1950)

In one of the first cases in which the Supreme Court gave constitutional approval to the anticommunist crusade, Chief Justice FRED VINSON upheld provisions of the TAFT-HARTLEY ACT denying National Labor Relations Board services to unions whose officers had not filed affidavits stating they were not members of the Communist party and that they did "not believe in . . . the overthrow of the . . . Government by force or by any illegal or unconstitutional methods." The opinion of the Court became a model for denying FIRST AMENDMENT protections to alleged subversives through the use of a balancing technique. The Court argued that the statute touched only a few persons and that the only effect even upon them was that they must relinquish their union offices, not their beliefs. It argued that banning communists from NLRB-supported labor negotiations was reasonably related to the legitimate congressional end of protecting INTERSTATE COMMERCE, given the nature of the Communist party and the threat of political strikes. The Court concluded that "Considering the circumstances . . . the statute . . . did not unduly infringe freedoms protected by the First Amendment."

MARTIN SHAPIRO

AMERICAN INDIANS AND THE CONSTITUTION

Indians are mentioned only three times in the Constitution. Yet the Supreme Court has developed a vast body of law defining the status of Indians and tribes in our federal system. This law makes use of constitutional sources but also draws heavily on the history between Indians and the federal government, including wars, conquest, treaties, and the assumption by the government of a protectorate relationship toward the tribes. It reveals that our government is not only, as is popularly believed, one of dual sovereigns, federal and state. There is also a third sovereign, consisting of Indian tribes, operating within a limited but distinct sphere.

The three references to Indians in the Constitution presage this body of law. Two of the three are found in Article I and the FOURTEENTH AMENDMENT, which exclude "Indians not taxed" from the counts for apportioning DIRECT TAXES and representatives to Congress among the states. The third reference is a grant of power to Congress in the COMMERCE CLAUSE of Article I to "regulate Commerce with . . . the Indian Tribes."

The phrase "Indians not taxed" was not a grant of tax exemption. Rather, it described the status of Indians at the time the Constitution was written. Indians were not taxed because generally they were treated as outside the American body politic. They were not United States citizens, and they were not governed by ordinary federal and state legislation. Tribal laws, treaties with the United States, and special federal Indian legislation governed their affairs. Only the few Indians who had severed their tribal relations and come to live in non-Indian communities were treated as appropriate for counting in the constitutionally mandated apportionment.

The phrase probably was chosen because the apportionment served partly to allocate tax burdens. That aspect of the apportionment has lost significance, however, since the SIXTEENTH AMENDMENT made it unnecessary for the federal government to apportion income taxes.

The exclusion of "Indians not taxed" from all aspects of apportionment has, in fact, been mooted by changes in the status of American Indians since ratification of the Fourteenth Amendment in 1868. Treaty-making with Indian tribes ended in 1871, and in 1924 all native-born Indians who had not already been made citizens by federal statute were naturalized. Indians were held subject to federal statutes, including tax laws, except where special Indian legislation or treaties offered exemptions. By 1940 the Department of the Interior officially recognized that there no longer were Indians who can properly be considered "Indians not taxed."

The commerce clause reference to Indians, by contrast, continues to have real force. Since the abandonment of federal treaty-making with Indian tribes in 1871, it has been the primary constitutional provision supporting exercises of federal power over Indians as such. Notwithstanding its reference to commerce "with the Indian Tribes," the clause also applies to transactions with individual tribal Indians, including some off-reservation transactions, and to non-Indians doing business on reservations. Congress's Article I power to regulate "the Territory or other Property belonging to the United States" supplements the treaty and Indian commerce clause powers. Most Indian lands are held in fee by the United States, subject to a beneficial tribal interest in reservations set aside by treaty or EXECUTIVE ORDER, and to the Indians' right of occupancy. Congress's power to make war was also invoked in the early years of dealing with the Indians.

This combination of powers, read together with the NECESSARY AND PROPER CLAUSE of Article I and the SUPREMACY CLAUSE of Article VI, has been the foundation of a complex structure of federal, state, and tribal relations. The federal government's power over Indian affairs is extensive and preemptive of state power. (See CHEROKEE INDIAN CASES, 1831–1832.) In the nineteenth century the courts called the federal power "plenary," and challenges to its exercise were labeled POLITICAL QUESTIONS. In fact this federal authority is a general POLICE POWER, comparable to Congress's power over the DISTRICT OF COLUMBIA and the TERRITORIES. In *Delaware Tribal Business Committee v. Weeks* (1977), the Court held that ordinary constitutional strictures apply to federal Indian legislation, and that, under the Fifth Amendment's DUE PROCESS CLAUSE in particular, such legislation must be reviewed to determine whether it is "tied rationally to the fulfillment of Congress's unique obligation toward the Indians." Even though this trust obligation has not prevented Congress from enacting laws contrary to the best interests of Indians, the Supreme Court now insists upon some determination that Indians will be protected when disadvantageous laws are passed. Thus, for example, Congress may not take Indian property for a non-Indian use without paying JUST COMPENSATION, and it may not arbitrarily give tribal assets to some tribal members but not others.

A law that satisfies the "tied rationally" test is not constitutionally defective under the EQUAL PROTECTION requirement of the Fifth Amendment's due process clause simply because it singles out Indians for special treatment. For example, Congress may establish a preference for employment of tribal Indians with the Bureau of Indian Affairs, or may subject Indians to harsher punishments than non-Indians would suffer in state court for doing the same acts. Such legislation is held not to constitute an otherwise forbidden racial classification, because of the separate status of Indians under the Constitution (*i.e.*, their subjection to federal and tribal rather than state jurisdiction).

Although Congress has enacted laws governing a wide variety of activities on Indian reservations, there is no detailed code comparable to the District of Columbia's. In the absence of such federal legislation, states and Indian tribes have competed for control. The Supreme Court has repeatedly upheld tribal independence from state jurisdiction, basing its decisions on preemptive federal power over Indian affairs and the broad federal policy of setting aside lands for tribal self-government. Although in cases outside Indian law the Supreme Court has refused to apply the PREEMPTION DOCTRINE to exclude the operation of state law where congressional intent was doubtful, in Indian cases it has inferred preemptive intent from the general purposes of treaties and statutes to protect tribal resources and promote tribal sovereignty. Thus, absent clear and express congressional consent, states may not regulate non-Indian activities that affect tribal self-government. Despite their lack of authority over reservation Indians, states are prohibited by the Fourteenth Amendment from denying Indians rights available under state law.

Within their realm of authority, Indian tribes exercise powers of self-government, not because of any DELEGATION OF POWERS, but rather because of their original, unrelinquished tribal sovereignty. The Supreme Court recognized this sovereign status of Indian tribes in *United States v. Wheeler* (1978), which held that it would not constitute DOUBLE JEOPARDY to try an Indian in federal court after he had been convicted in tribal court because the court systems belong to separate sovereigns. The Constitution has never been invoked successfully to prevent Congress from abolishing tribal authority in whole or in part; but the Supreme Court has required a clear and specific expression of congressional intent before recognizing the termination of tribal powers. This canon of construction was established to implement the federal government's obligation to protect the Indian tribes. Some tribal powers were necessarily relinquished when the United States incorporated the tribes, such as the power to carry on foreign relations, the power to transfer Indian land without consent of the United States, and the power to prosecute non-Indians for crimes. These relinquished powers are few, however, and Congress could restore them if it chose.

Because the BILL OF RIGHTS limits only the federal government and the Fourteenth Amendment limits only the states, Indian tribes need not follow their dictates. However, in 1968, Congress enacted the Indian Civil Rights Act, which conferred some but not all protections of the Bill of Rights on individuals subject to tribal authority.

CAROLE E. GOLDBERG-AMBROSE

Bibliography
COHEN, F. 1982 *Handbook of Federal Indian Law.* Indianapolis: Bobbs-Merrill.
GETCHES, D.; ROSENFELT, D.; and WILKINSON, C. 1979 *Federal Indian Law: Cases and Materials.* St. Paul, Minn.: West Publishing Co.
PRICE, M. 1973 *Law and the American Indian: Readings, Notes and Cases.* Indianapolis: Bobbs-Merrill.

AMERICAN INSURANCE COMPANY v. CANTER
1 Peters 511 (1828)

Although the Constitution authorizes Congress to govern the TERRITORIES of the United States, it does not authorize the acquisition of territories. Consequently

THOMAS JEFFERSON had constitutional qualms when he acquired the Louisiana Territory by treaty. This case settled the authority of the United States to acquire territory by the WAR POWERS or TREATY POWER, and sustained the power of Congress to establish LEGISLATIVE COURTS with JURISDICTION extending beyond the JUDICIAL POWER OF THE UNITED STATES as defined by Article III, section 2.

LEONARD W. LEVY

AMERICAN JEWISH CONGRESS

Formed originally in 1918 as a temporary confederation of Jewish organizations to propose a postwar program by the Jewish people for presentation at the Versailles Peace Conference, the American Jewish Congress continued in existence and became fully organized under the chairmanship of Rabbi Stephen S. Wise in 1928. In the 1930s it emerged as a leading force in the anti-Nazi movement and in efforts to aid the victims of Hitlerism.

A new and still continuing chapter in its history was initiated in 1945 when, under the leadership of three socially minded lawyers, Alexander H. Pekelis, Will Maslow, and Leo Pfeffer, it established a Commission on Law and Social Action. The commission was based on two premises: that the security of American Jews is interdependent with that of all religions, races, and other national minorities, and that the security of all is dependent upon the integrity of the BILL OF RIGHTS and the EQUAL PROTECTION clause of the FOURTEENTH AMENDMENT.

Accordingly, the organization's legal staff have instituted litigation or submitted briefs AMICUS CURIAE in a wide variety of constitutional law cases, acquiring a status parallel to that of the AMERICAN CIVIL LIBERTIES UNION and the National Association for the Advancement of Colored People. Typical of these are suits challenging the constitutionality of the death penalty under the Eighth Amendment, racial SEGREGATION in public schools, anti-abortion legislation, racially RESTRICTIVE COVENANTS, LITERACY TESTS for voters, disinheritance of illegitimate children, and denial of tax exemption to organizations advocating overthrow of government.

However, by far the majority of suits in which the organization has participated, either as amicus or as party, have involved either the establishment clause or the free exercise clause of the FIRST AMENDMENT, or the ban in Article VI of RELIGIOUS TESTS for public office. The commission's primacy in this arena is gen-

erally recognized among jurists, organizations, and scholars.

LEO PFEFFER

Bibliography
PEKELIS, ALEXANDER H. 1950 *Law and Social Action.* Ithaca, N.Y.: Cornell University Press.

AMERICAN SYSTEM

"American System" was the name given by HENRY CLAY (in the House of Representatives, March 30–31, 1824) to the national program of economic policy that centered on the protective tariff for the encouragement of domestic manufactures. It assigned the general government a positive role in promoting balanced economic development within the "home market." Each of the great sections would concentrate on the productions for which it was best suited: the South on staples like cotton, the West on grains and livestock, the Northeast on manufacturing. The tariff would protect the market; INTERNAL IMPROVEMENTS would facilitate exchanges and bind the parts together; the national bank would furnish commercial credit and ensure a stable and uniform currency. These measures were implemented in varying degrees, but the system was overtaken by the disintegrating sectionalism of the 1820s and finally buried by Jacksonian Democracy. Constitutionally, the American System posited a broad view of federal powers. It was attacked as dangerously consolidating, indeed unconstitutional in all its leading measures. Although the opposition had other and deeper sources, it tended to become a constitutional opposition, culminating in South Carolina's NULLIFICATION of the tariff in 1832.

MERRILL D. PETERSON

Bibliography
GOODRICH, CARTER, ED. 1967 *The Government and the Economy, 1783–1861.* Indianapolis: Bobbs-Merrill.

AMERICAN TOBACCO COMPANY, UNITED STATES v.

See: *Standard Oil Co. v. United States*

AMES, FISHER
(1758–1808)

An extreme Federalist, Fisher Ames published his "Camillus" essays to promote the idea of the CONSTITUTIONAL CONVENTION OF 1787. The French Revolution inspired his suspicion of democracy—"only the dismal passport to a more dismal hereafter"—and led him to call for a government run by an "aristocracy of talent." Ames also opposed the BILL OF RIGHTS as unnecessary and unwise. Representing Massachusetts in Congress from 1789 to 1797, he vigorously defended JAY'S TREATY and the ALIEN AND SEDITION ACTS, but, by 1802, his radical partisanship left him an embittered STATES' RIGHTS advocate.

DAVID GORDON

AMICUS CURIAE

(Latin: Friend of the Court.) The amicus curiae originally was a lawyer aiding the court. Today in American practice, the lawyers represent an organization, which is the amicus; the group's "friendship" to the court has become an artifice slightly disguising the fact that it is as much an advocate as any party. Although economic interests early employed the amicus brief, CIVIL LIBERTIES groups did not lag far behind. As early as 1904, a group representing Chinese immigrants participated in a Supreme Court case. By the 1940s, the activities of amici were extensive, well coordinated among sister organizations, and highly publicized. In the aftermath of several antisegregation decisions of the mid-1950s, southern legislators and other spokesmen criticized that participation as nonjudicial.

Prior to 1937 the Supreme Court had no formal rule governing amicus briefs. It was standard procedure first to seek consent of the parties to the filing of an amicus brief, but the Court almost invariably accepted an amicus brief irrespective of party consent. The 1937 rule required a request for party consent, but the same easy acceptance of participation continued. In 1949, in the face of criticism, the Court noted that consent of the parties would be expected; without such consent "such motions are not favored." For a decade thereafter denials exceeded granting of motions by a wide margin.

The rule has been retained in subsequent revisions. In practice, however, such motions are now virtually (though not quite) automatically granted, with or without party consent. It is rare for any amicus curiae other than the United States to be given leave to make an ORAL ARGUMENT.

The excitement over use of amicus briefs has died down. Most such presentations are well-coordinated with the main brief, serving chiefly to announce the positions of certain groups. The Court, however, seems well-served by broader sources of information, and some amicus briefs are more cogent or influential than the parties' briefs. Many potential amici curiae qualify for participation through intervention or CLASS ACTIONS. Critics of wider participation, therefore, concentrate their guns on those more significant targets.

SAMUEL KRISLOV

AMNESTY

Amnesty is the blanket forgiveness of a group of people for some offense, usually of a political nature. Although there is a technical distinction between an amnesty, which "forgets" the offense, and a pardon, which remits the penalty, historical practice and common usage have made the terms virtually interchangeable. In the United States, amnesty may be granted by the President (under the PARDONING POWER) or by Congress (as NECESSARY AND PROPER to the carrying out of any of several powers). Amnesty may be granted before or after conviction, and may be conditional or unconditional. But neither Congress nor the President may grant amnesty for offenses against state law.

The first instance of amnesty under the Constitution was extended in 1801 by President THOMAS JEFFERSON to persons convicted or charged under the ALIEN AND SEDITION ACTS. Between 1862 and 1868, Presidents ABRAHAM LINCOLN and ANDREW JOHNSON issued a series of six proclamations of conditional amnesty for southern rebels. Congress specifically authorized the first three but repealed the authorizing statute in 1867; President Johnson issued the last three on his own authority alone. In the TEST OATH CASES (1867), the Supreme Court struck down, as an unconstitutional interference with the pardoning power, an attempt by Congress to limit the effect of Johnson's amnesty. In 1872, exercising its power under section 3 of the FOURTEENTH AMENDMENT, Congress passed the Amnesty Act restoring the CIVIL RIGHTS of most rebels.

President GERALD R. FORD granted conditional amnesty in 1974 to military deserters and draft evaders of the VIETNAM WAR period. The terms of the amnesty required case-by-case determination by a special Presidential Clemency Board empowered to direct performance by applicants of alternative public service. Ford acted on his own authority after Congress failed to approve any of several amnesty proposals.

DENNIS J. MAHONEY

ANCILLARY JURISDICTION

In some cases federal courts hear claims over which no statute confers federal JURISDICTION. Typically, this ancillary jurisdiction has been exercised in cases brought under the federal courts' DIVERSITY JURISDICTION. Suppose a California citizen sues an Arizona citizen in federal court, claiming a right to property. If another Californian claims the same property interest, no state court can take jurisdiction over the property under the federal court's control. It is thus necessary for the federal court to be able to hear that claim, even though the case of one Californian against another would not initially be within its jurisdiction. Similarly, a defendant sued in federal court can file a third-party claim against a co-citizen, which will be heard under the federal court's ancillary jurisdiction.

Ancillary jurisdiction is sometimes confused with PENDENT JURISDICTION, which permits a state *claim* to be heard in federal court along with a closely related FEDERAL QUESTION. Ancillary jurisdiction results in the addition of a *party* who otherwise would not fall within the federal court's jurisdiction. The Supreme Court has not been hospitable to the suggestion that a federal court in a federal question case should take "pendent" jurisdiction over a closely related state law claim against a new party.

KENNETH L. KARST

Bibliography

WRIGHT, CHARLES ALAN 1983 *The Law of Federal Courts*, 4th ed. Pages 28–32. St. Paul, Minn.: West Publishing Co.

ANNEXATION OF TEXAS

American settlers in the Mexican province of Texas revolted against the central government and established the independence of the Lone Star Republic in 1836. President ANDREW JACKSON was unable to effect annexation, however, because many feared war with Mexico and because abolitionists suspected a slaveholders' plot to increase the number of slave states. In 1842, President John Tyler revived annexationist efforts, abetted by a clique of proslavery expansionists, but an annexation treaty failed once again, due in part to the argument that the territories clause (Article IV, section 3) permitted annexation only of dependent TERRITORIES of other nations, not of independent nations themselves. Tyler then recommended annexation by JOINT RESOLUTION of Congress to obviate the constitutional requirement of a

two-thirds Senate vote to ratify a treaty. This aroused further opposition, now including influential southern Whigs, who insisted that the issue involved grave foreign policy risks and hence was precisely the sort of question for which the Framers had required a supermajority. Despite this argument, congressional Democrats enacted a joint resolution in February 1845 declaring the Republic of Texas to be the twenty-eighth state.

WILLIAM M. WIECEK

Bibliography

MERK, FREDERICK 1972 *Slavery and the Annexation of Texas.* New York: Knopf.

ANTIDISCRIMINATION LEGISLATION

From its inception, antidiscrimination legislation has shaped and been shaped by the Constitution. Antidiscrimination legislation's very existence is attributable to developments in constitutional law. Enactment of such legislation usually reflects a relatively favorable atmosphere for the promise of equality embodied in the THIRTEENTH, FOURTEENTH, and FIFTEENTH AMENDMENTS. When the values underlying these amendments are in decline, antidiscrimination legislation is not enacted, and often is not enforced.

Federal antidiscrimination laws have been enacted during two time periods. During the first period, which commenced near the end of the Civil War, Congress enacted the CIVIL RIGHTS ACT OF 1866, the Civil Rights Act of 1870, the FORCE ACT OF 1871, the Civil Rights Act of 1871, and the CIVIL RIGHTS ACT OF 1875. These early provisions, portions of which survive, exemplify two basic forms of antidiscrimination legislation. Some provisions, such as section 1 of the 1871 act (now section 1983) and section 3 of the 1866 act were purely remedial. They provided remedies for violations of federal rights but created no new substantive rights. Other provisions, such as section 1 of the 1866 act and section 16 of the 1870 act (now sections 1981 and 1982), were express efforts to change substantive law by fostering greater equality between black and white Americans.

The COMPROMISE OF 1877 marks the end of the first era during which antidiscrimination legislation flourished. Afterward, congressional and judicial developments favored neither enactment nor enforcement of antidiscrimination legislation. In the CIVIL RIGHTS REPEAL ACT OF 1894 the first Democratic Congress since the Civil War repealed the few effective remnants of post-Civil War antidiscrimination legislation. A favorable climate for legislative implementation of the post-Civil War constitutional amendments did not reemerge until the late 1950s and early 1960s. There were no significant antidiscrimination statutes in the intervening years.

As the constitutional amendments were given new vigor by the WARREN COURT, however, antidiscrimination legislation experienced a renaissance. Modern statutes, including the CIVIL RIGHTS ACTS OF 1957, 1960, 1964, and 1968, protect against discrimination in voting, employment, education, and housing. They represent a second era of federal antidiscrimination legislation, sometimes called part of the second reconstruction.

As in the case of earlier antidiscrimination statutes, the primary reason for enactment was to protect blacks from RACIAL DISCRIMINATION. Again, two kinds of provisions were enacted. Some provisions, such as the 1957 and 1960 Acts and Title VI of the 1964 act, are remedial in tone (though not always so interpreted) and do not purport to create new substantive rights. Others, such as Title VII of the 1964 act, which prohibits private discrimination in employment, confer new substantive rights.

Modern antidiscrimination legislation contains a recognizable subcategory that has been the fastest growing area of antidiscrimination law. Until about 1960 or 1970, antidiscrimination legislation could be equated with laws prohibiting one or more forms of racial discrimination. Subsequently, however, legislation prohibiting discrimination surfaced in many areas. For example, the AGE DISCRIMINATION ACT OF 1975, the Age Discrimination in Employment Act, the REHABILITATION ACT OF 1973, the DEVELOPMENTALLY DISABLED AND BILL OF RIGHTS ACT, the Education of Handicapped Children Acts, the Equal Pay Act, and the EDUCATION AMENDMENTS OF 1972 provide substantial protection to the aged, to the handicapped, and to women. Building on a technique first employed in Title VI of the 1964 act, most of these provisions apply only to programs or entities receiving federal financial assistance.

Although constitutional values can be viewed as the raison d'être of antidiscrimination legislation, the relationship between the Constitution and antidiscrimination laws runs much deeper. Their more complex relationship may be divided into two parts. First, antidiscrimination legislation has been the setting for judicial and congressional decisions concerning the scope of congressional power. One of the few universally agreed upon facts about the history of the Fourteenth Amendment is that it was meant to place the

first major antidiscrimination statute, the Civil Rights Act of 1866, on firm constitutional footing. Before ratification of the Fourteenth Amendment, doubts were expressed about Congress's power under the Thirteenth Amendment to ban racially discriminatory state laws. Many believe that the Fourteenth Amendment was meant primarily to constitutionalize the 1866 Act's prohibitions. With the Fourteenth Amendment in place by 1868, Congress reaffirmed the 1866 Act's bans by reenacting them as part of the Civil Rights Act of 1870. Some claim that the 1866 Act is so akin to a constitutional provision that its surviving remnants should be interpreted more like constitutional provisions than statutory ones.

Soon after this initial interplay between the Constitution and antidiscrimination laws, a foundation of constitutional interpretation grew out of litigation under antidiscrimination statutes. In a line of cases commencing with UNITED STATES V. CRUIKSHANK (1876) and culminating in UNITED STATES V. HARRIS (1883) and the CIVIL RIGHTS CASES (1883), the Court relied on what has come to be known as the STATE ACTION doctrine to invalidate antidiscrimination measures. The *Civil Rights Cases* invalidated the last piece of nineteenth-century civil rights legislation, the Civil Rights Act of 1875. In so doing the Court not only limited the Fourteenth Amendment to prohibiting state action but also rendered a narrow interpretation of the Thirteenth Amendment as a possible source of congressional power to enact antidiscrimination statutes.

The state action doctrine was not the only early limit on antidiscrimination legislation. In UNITED STATES V. REESE (1876) the Court found sections 3 and 4 of the Civil Rights Act of 1870, which prohibited certain interferences with voting, to be beyond Congress's power to enforce the Fifteenth Amendment because the sections were not limited to prohibiting racial discrimination. These limitations on antidiscrimination legislation carried over into the early twentieth century.

But some early antidiscrimination legislation survived constitutional attack and shifting political stances in Congress. For example, in EX PARTE YARBROUGH (1884) the Court sustained use of section 6 of the 1870 act (now section 241) to impose criminal sanctions against private individuals who used force to prevent blacks from voting in federal elections. And in *Ex parte Virginia* (1880), the Court sustained the federal prosecution of a state judge for excluding blacks from juries in violation of section 4 of the 1875 act. (See STRAUDER V. WEST VIRGINIA, 1880.)

The two lines of early constitutional interpretation

of antidiscrimination laws have never been fully reconciled. As a result of the early limits on congressional power to enact antidiscrimination legislation, modern civil rights statutes have been drafted to reduce potential constitutional attacks. Thus, much of the Civil Rights Act of 1964 operates only on individuals and entities engaged in some form of INTERSTATE COMMERCE. Other portions of the 1964 act, and many other modern antidiscrimination laws, are based on Congress's TAXING AND SPENDING POWERS. By tying antidiscrimination legislation to the COMMERCE CLAUSE or the spending power, Congress hoped to avoid some of the constitutional problems that plagued early legislation enacted under the Thirteenth, Fourteenth, and Fifteenth Amendments.

A potential clash between the Court and Congress over the constitutionality of modern antidiscrimination legislation has not surfaced. The modern Court sustains antidiscrimination legislation even in the face of troublesome nineteenth-century precedents. In a landmark holding barely reconcilable with portions of the *Civil Rights Cases,* the Court in JONES V. ALFRED H. MAYER COMPANY (1968) found that Congress has power under the Thirteenth Amendment to ban private racial discrimination in housing. Later, in RUNYON V. MCCRARY (1976), the Court acknowledged Congress's power to outlaw racial discrimination in private contractual relations, including those relations involved in a child's attendance at a private segregated school. In GRIFFIN V. BRECKENRIDGE (1971) the Court relied on the Thirteenth Amendment to sustain a remnant of the 1871 act allowing for causes of action against private conspiracies to violate federal rights. The case undermined *United States v. Harris* and overruled an earlier contrary decision, *Collins v. Hardyman* (1948). Another antidiscrimination statute, the VOTING RIGHTS ACT OF 1965, provided the setting for important decisions in KATZENBACH V. MORGAN (1966) and SOUTH CAROLINA V. KATZENBACH (1966), which found Congress to have broad discretion to interpret and extend Fourteenth Amendment protection to situations which the judiciary had not found violative of the Fourteenth Amendment.

There is a second respect in which constitutional provisions and antidiscrimination legislation influence each other. From the beginning, their relationship has gone beyond one of merely testing the constitutionality of a particular antidiscrimination statute. Interpretation of one set of provisions has shaped the other. This interplay began with the Civil Rights Act of 1866. Soon after ratification of the Fourteenth Amendment, the question arose as to what constituted "the PRIVILEGES AND IMMUNITIES of citizens of the United States" referred to in the Fourteenth Amendment. In the SLAUGHTERHOUSE CASES (1873) the Court's first decision construing the Fourteenth Amendment, Justice STEPHEN J. FIELD argued in dissent that section 1 of the 1866 act provided Congress's interpretation of at least some of the privileges or immunities of United States citizens. Although Field's view did not prevail—the Court limited the privileges or immunities clause to a narrow class of rights—even the majority view of the privileges or immunities clause may have had a profound effect on subsequent development of antidiscrimination legislation.

This effect stems from the strong linguistic parallel between the Fourteenth Amendment's privileges or immunities clause and the rights listed as protected by many antidiscrimination laws. Sections 1983 and 242 protect persons against deprivations of their federal "rights, privileges or immunities." Section 1985(3) refers in part to "equal privileges and immunities." Section 241 refers to any federal "right or privilege." In subsequent cases brought under antidiscrimination statutes, federal courts, relying on the *Slaughterhouse Cases'* narrow interpretation of the Fourteenth Amendment's privileges or immunities clause, plausibly could render a similar narrow interpretation of the antidiscrimination statute. Not until MONROE V. PAPE (1961) did the Court settle that the rights, privileges, and immunities protected by section 1983 include at least all rights secured by the Fourteenth Amendment.

Just as CONSTITUTIONAL INTERPRETATION influenced early antidiscrimination laws and vice versa, modern antidiscrimination legislation influences constitutional interpretation. In GRIGGS V. DUKE POWER COMPANY (1971) the Court found that an employer's selection criteria with unintentional disparate effect on a minority could lead to a violation of Title VII of the Civil Rights Act of 1964. This and earlier Supreme Court cases generated pressure to find violative of the Fourteenth Amendment government action with uneven adverse effects on minorities. Not until WASHINGTON V. DAVIS (1976) and ARLINGTON HEIGHTS V. METROPOLITAN HOUSING DEVELOPMENT CORPORATION (1977) did the Court expressly reject the *Griggs* standard as a basis for constitutional interpretation. And in REGENTS OF THE UNIVERSITY OF CALIFORNIA V. BAKKE (1978), a major theme of the opinions is the relationship between the antidiscrimination standards embodied in Title VI of the Civil Rights Act of 1964 and those of the Fourteenth Amendment.

Judicial hostility to the Reconstruction CIVIL

RIGHTS program and subsequent congressional inaction left much of the civil rights field to the states. Early Massachusetts legislation covered school desegregation and PUBLIC ACCOMMODATIONS, but few other states enacted protective laws prior to 1883 and some laws that had been enacted by southern Reconstruction legislatures were repealed.

The *Civil Rights Cases'* invalidation of the Civil Rights Act of 1875 triggered the first major group of state antidiscrimination laws. Within two years of the decision, eleven states outlawed discrimination in public accommodations. Modest further legislative developments occurred before World War II, including legislation aimed at violence generated by the Ku Klux Klan, some northern prohibitions on school segregation, and some categories of employment discrimination.

The next widespread state civil rights initiative, which covered employment discrimination, drew upon experience under the wartime Committee on Fair Employment Practices. New York's 1945 Law Against Discrimination, the first modern comprehensive fair employment law, established a commission to investigate and adjudicate complaints and became a model for other states' laws. Resort to administrative agencies, now possible in the vast majority of states, remains the primary state method of dealing with many categories of discrimination.

THEODORE EISENBERG

Bibliography

BARDOLPH, RICHARD 1970 *The Civil Rights Record.* New York: Crowell.

KONVITZ, MILTON R. 1961 *A Century of Civil Rights.* New York: Columbia University Press.

MURRAY, PAULI 1961 *States' Laws on Race and Color.* New York: Woman's Division of Christian Service, The Methodist Church.

U.S. COMMISSION ON CIVIL RIGHTS 1970 *Federal Civil Rights Enforcement Effort.* Washington, D.C.: U.S. Government Printing Office.

ANTI-FEDERALIST CONSTITUTIONAL THOUGHT

The men who opposed the Constitution's unconditional RATIFICATION in 1787–1788 were called Anti-Federalists, although they claimed to be the true federalists and the true republicans. Contrary to common opinion, their major contribution to the American founding lies more in their critical examination of the new form of FEDERALISM and the new form of republican government than in their successful argument for a BILL OF RIGHTS.

The federalism issue was complicated by an ambiguity in usage during the Confederation period and by changes in both the Federalist and Anti-Federalist conceptions of federalism during the ratification debates. HERBERT J. STORING has explained the ambiguity by showing how "federal" referred to measures designed to strengthen the national authority, as opposed to state authority, but also to the principle of state supremacy. In the CONSTITUTIONAL CONVENTION, the federal principle meant congressional reliance on state requisitions for armies and taxes, in contrast to the national principle of direct governmental authority over individuals. The Anti-Federalists argued that the Constitution, which strengthened the national authority, went beyond the federal principle by moving away from requisitions and state equality in representation. Supporters of the Constitution were able to take, and keep, the name Federalists by treating any recognition of the state governments in the Constitution (for example, election, apportionment, ratification, amendment) as evidence of federalism, thereby redefining the term. JAMES MADISON, in THE FEDERALIST #39, consequently called the Constitution partly federal, partly national. For their part, the authors of the two best Anti-Federalist writings, who wrote under the pseudonyms Brutus and Federal Farmer, conceded the need for some direct governmental authority over individuals, thereby acknowledging the inadequacy of traditional federalism.

The Anti-Federalists emphasized the need to restrict the national power to what was absolutely necessary to preserve the union. They proposed limiting the national taxing power to imported goods, relying on requisitions if that source was insufficient. Moreover, Brutus proposed limiting standing armies in time of peace to what was necessary for defending the frontiers. If it became necessary to raise an army to repel an attack, he favored a two-thirds vote by both houses of Congress.

As part of their argument that a consolidation of power in the general government was incompatible with republicanism, the Anti-Federalists frequently cited MONTESQUIEU for the proposition that republics must be small, lest the public good be sacrificed. But they agreed with the Federalists, against Montesquieu, that the first principle of republican government was the regulation and protection of individual rights, not the promotion of civic virtue. They also, with rare exceptions, assumed the necessity of representation, while Montesquieu mentioned it only in his discussion of England, not in his discussion of republics.

Defining republican government somewhere between a selfless dedication to the common good, on the one hand, and individualism plus the elective principle, on the other, the Anti-Federalists emphasized mildness in government as essential for public confidence. This mildness required a similarity "in manners, sentiments, and interests" between citizens and officials and among citizens themselves. This, in turn, made possible a genuine REPRESENTATION of the people. Federal Farmer called such representation and local jury trials "the essential parts of a free and good government."

When the Anti-Federalists examined the representation in Congress, they saw an emerging aristocracy. They claimed that the democratic class, especially the middle class or the yeomanry, would have little chance of gaining election against the aristocracy, the men of wealth and of political and professional prominence. Since the middle class was substantially represented in the state governments, the Anti-Federalists argued that the powers of Congress had to be restricted to produce a proper balance between the nation and the states.

The Anti-Federalist objections to the structure of the proposed government related either to federalism or to republicanism. As examples of the former, the Senate, despite state equality, did not satisfy federalism because the legislatures did not pay the senators and could not recall them, and because the voting was by individuals, not by state delegations. And Brutus, who viewed the JUDICIAL POWER as the vehicle of consolidation, objected to Congress's power to ordain and establish lower federal courts. He thought the state courts were adequate to handle every case arising under the Constitution in the first instance, and he favored a limited right of APPEAL to the Supreme Court. As examples of their republicanism, the Anti-Federalists feared the Senate, with its six-year term, plus reeligibility, and its substantial powers, especially regarding appointments and treaty-making, as a special source of aristocracy. The Anti-Federalists were only somewhat less critical of the executive. They favored the proposed mode of election but opposed reeligibility; they generally favored unity but wanted a separately elected council to participate in appointments; some supported and others opposed the qualified executive VETO POWER; and some expressed apprehension about the pardoning power and the COMMANDER-IN-CHIEF power. As for the judi-

ciary, Brutus argued that the combination of tenure for GOOD BEHAVIOR plus a judicial power that extends to "all cases in law and EQUITY, arising under this Constitution," meant not only JUDICIAL REVIEW but JUDICIAL SUPREMACY. He preferred that the legislature interpret the Constitution, since the people could easily correct the errors of their lawmakers.

Finally, the Bill of Rights was as much a Federalist as an Anti-Federalist victory. The Anti-Federalists wanted a bill of rights to curb governmental power. When the Federalists denied the necessity of a federal bill of rights, on the ground that whatever power was not enumerated could not be claimed, the Anti-Federalists pointed to the Constitution's SUPREMACY CLAUSE and to the extensiveness of the enumeration of powers. Paradoxically, this decisive argument resulted in a bill of rights that confirmed the new federalism, with its extended republic. Neither the Anti-Federalist proposals to restrict the tax and WAR POWERS nor their proposal to restrict IMPLIED POWERS was accepted. Nevertheless, the Anti-Federalist concern about "big government" has continued to find occasional constitutional expression in the restrictive interpretation of the ENUMERATED POWERS, along with the TENTH AMENDMENT.

MURRAY DRY

Bibliography

KENYON, CECELIA 1966 *The Antifederalists.* Indianapolis: Bobbs-Merrill.
STORING, HERBERT J. 1981 *The Complete Anti-Federalist.* 7 Vols. Chicago: University of Chicago Press. (Volume 1 separately published in paperback as *What the Anti-Federalists Were For.*)
_____ 1978 The Constitution and the Bill of Rights. Pages 32–48 in M. Judd Harmon, ed., *Essays on the Constitution of the United States.* Port Washington, N.Y.: Kennikat Press Corp.

ANTIPEONAGE ACT OF 1867

See: Peonage

ANTITRUST LAW

Federal antitrust law comprises a set of acts of Congress, administrative regulations, and court decisions that attempt to regulate market structure and competitive behavior in the national economy. The substance of this law is found in the first two sections of the SHERMAN ACT (1890), which forbid concerted action in "restraint of trade" and acts that seek to "monopolize" any part of commerce. The COMMERCE CLAUSE is the nexus between antitrust law and constitutional law.

There are several persistent uncertainties concerning the proper meaning of these prohibitions: the extent to which they embody a particular concept of economic efficiency as a primary value; the degree to which they are designed to protect competition by valuing a market composed of a large number of small competitors rather than a few large units; and the extent to which they embody specific notions of consumer protection. Despite these disagreements, there is general consensus that the antitrust laws express a preference for free and open markets in which prices and production are set by competitive forces and in which neither restraint of trade nor monopolization determines important market conditions. The three most common forms of restraint of trade are competitor agreements to fix prices, to allocate customers and markets, and to exclude parties from the market by a boycott or group refusal to deal. Monopolization is behavior by a dominant firm in the relevant market designed to give the firm power to fix prices, set market conditions, and exclude potential competitors.

The antitrust laws have ancient roots in the English and American COMMON LAW. Most states have comparable laws which complement the congressional scheme with varying degrees of effectiveness. In addition, Congress has amended the original acts, most notably to deal with corporate mergers and consolidations and with price discrimination in the distribution of goods. After a generation of judicial interpretation of the Sherman Act's general prohibitions, Congress in 1914 adopted the CLAYTON ACT and FEDERAL TRADE COMMISSION ACT to supplement the Sherman Act with more specific prohibitions and to supplement judicial interpretation and enforcement with administrative agency rule-making and enforcement. Nonetheless, these additions are largely derivative; the Sherman Act's prohibitions of "restraints of trade" and "monopolization" remain the core of federal antitrust law.

Antitrust law bears a strong resemblance to constitutional law, both in the broad intentions and organic implications of its substantive law and in the methodology of its enforcement and interpretive growth. These laws have long been seen as more than simple statutes. The delphic demands of the Sherman Act are considered a structural imperative with social and political, as well as economic, implications. Justice

HUGO L. BLACK summed up this perspective in *Northern Pacific Railroad v. United States* (1958): "The Sherman Act was designed to be a comprehensive charter of economic liberty aimed at preserving free and unfettered competition as the rule of trade. It rests on the premise that the unrestrained interaction of competitive forces will yield the best allocation of our economic resources, the lowest prices, the highest quality and the greatest material progress, while at the same time providing an environment conducive to the preservation of our democratic political and social institutions."

The Sherman Act was a political response to the threats presented by economic power associated with the industrial revolution in the late nineteenth century. Certainly farmers, industrial workers, and tradespersons suffered from the concentrated economic power of the new order. From their beginning, however, these laws also identified threats presented by concentrated economic power to the social and political fabric. The specifics of the Sherman Act are not demanded by the constitutional text, but they can be seen as the economic corollaries of a constitutional commitment to individual autonomy, free association, and the separation and division of power within society. The antitrust laws seek to prevent economic power from becoming so highly concentrated that political freedom is unworkable.

As units of economic organization have grown in size and markets have become more concentrated over the past century, the antitrust laws have provided one alternative to extensive and detailed governmental ECONOMIC REGULATION. In most of the world's political systems, industrialization has been matched by growing control of the economy by bureaucratic *dirigisme*. Although the American economy has hardly been free from governmental intervention, this involvement has been more modest as a result of the emphasis on private planning and control over enterprises through a competitive market regime. In this perspective, excessive bureaucratic control is seen as the enemy of both economic efficiency and individual liberty.

Not only do antitrust law and constitutional law share comparable legislative approaches; their interpretive processes also show strong similarities—a tendency reinforced by the degree to which the Supreme Court is given broad powers to articulate basic norms in both areas.

The antitrust laws present a uniquely varied set of enforcement procedures. In addition to the sanctions available under state law, the basic federal antitrust norms may be enforced by the Department of Justice in federal court either by criminal prosecution or by civil suit for INJUNCTION relief or DAMAGES. The Federal Trade Commission enforces the same basic norms by administrative CEASE AND DESIST ORDERS backed up by civil penalties. A third level of enforcement is available to any private party aggrieved through a damage action in federal court in which treble damages may be awarded. Finally, legislation enacted in 1976 permits state officials to bring damage actions in federal court on behalf of their citizens.

Antitrust cases may be instituted in any one of the federal district courts and be appealed to a court of appeals. Administrative proceedings may also be reviewed in any one of the courts of appeals. Thus, no single agency has policy control over the bringing of antitrust suits, nor is there any coordination of the often contradictory decisions by local courts and agencies below the level of the Supreme Court. To a degree familiar to constitutional lawyers but atypical in other areas of federal law, a question of antitrust law is not considered settled until the Supreme Court decides it. The Court accepts only a few antitrust cases each year for decision, and the doctrinal impact of these decisions is profound.

Both constitutional and antitrust law generate the "big case," that peculiarly American form of political controversy in the form of litigation. Although there is reason to doubt the actual influence of antitrust law on the grand issues of national economic structure, the bringing of a major case is properly seen as an important political event. The investment of personnel and resources needed to accumulate the economic data necessary to prove a claim under these laws has long presented a major constraint to full enforcement. A big case is likely to exceed the natural lifespan of the national administration that institutes the suit, and may extend beyond the professional career span of government attorneys. As a consequence, charges of monopolization and other abuses of dominant market position are relatively rare. Cases charging specific acts in restraint of trade—particularly price fixing, production limits, and other cartelization—are more common because they are more susceptible to proof within the limits of a judicial trial.

The constraint of the big case produce two kinds of attempts to avoid full trial of cases. First, the great majority of antitrust cases are settled by consent decrees in which the government or private plaintiff is granted substantial relief. Concerned about the consistency of this practice with public interest, Congress

in 1976 amended the law to require fuller judicial examination and public scrutiny of proposed settlements. Second, the problems of the big case have promoted the development of other enforcement techniques. The Federal Trade Commission Act of 1914 and the short-lived COMMERCE COURT represent two efforts to move both legislation and enforcement out of court and into specialized forums. The Federal Trade Commission (FTC) has broad power to proscribe unfair and anticompetitive behavior by rule, but the full potential of this technique has never been realized. Recently a hostile Congress has suspended many of the more important FTC trade rules.

The FTC and the Justice Department have also issued guidelines stating when the government will bring antitrust suits against proposed mergers or other changes in industry structure perceived to threaten overconcentration or monopoly. Because the confidence of securities markets is normally crucial to a successful merger, the threat of a suit often forecloses such a transaction.

The Constitution and the Sherman Act both use language drawn primarily from English common law sources to respond to dimly perceived new social needs that were expected to extend far into the future. In both cases the choice of operative terms served effectively to delegate to the Supreme Court power to pour meaning into common law terms. As few would suggest today that the full meaning of DUE PROCESS OF LAW is found in eighteenth-century common law sources, few would suggest that the meaning of "restraint of trade" is to be found in congressional understanding (actually, misunderstanding) of that common law term at the time the Sherman Act was enacted.

This protean aspect of the Sherman Act has always engendered the complaint that the act provides inadequate guidance to the economic decision makers who are subject to the law's commands. Despite three generations of attempts to contain the law in more specific statutory prohibitions and to delegate its enforcement to administrative experts, antitrust law retains its strong similarity to the process of constitutional adjudication by judicial decision. Even in those few areas of antitrust enforcement marked by heavy reliance on the specifics of the Clayton Act or administrative rules, the Sherman Act's general concepts of restraint of trade and monopolization retain their influence, broadening and reshaping the narrower rules.

As in constitutional litigation, the shifting tides of antitrust interpretation follow major changes in American economic and social thought. The conception of "restraint of trade," for example, has been modified by a RULE OF REASON, which exempts reasonable restraints of trade from the antitrust laws. Most contracts of any duration restrain the freedom of the parties to enter the market by obligating the parties to deal with each other. By the middle of the eighteenth century, the common law prohibition on contracts in restraint of trade had been made into a rule prohibiting only unreasonable restraints. This rule, of course, vastly expanded the potential power of judges, who decide what is reasonable.

When Congress enacted the Sherman Act it certainly had in mind this common law doctrine—although perhaps not the doctrine's specifics. The text declares all contracts in restraint of trade illegal. A persistent interpretive theme from the beginning has been the extent to which the Sherman Act incorporates a rule of reason. During periods when the dominant political thought is permissive of consolidations or economic power, the rule of reason tends to enlarge, thus increasing the power of the lower federal judiciary, who typically have been sympathetic to business interests. This development complicates the trial of cases, for defendants are permitted to enlarge the inquiry with evidence that their behavior, while generally of a prohibited sort, was reasonable under the circumstances. In contrast, during periods of vigorous antitrust enforcement the rule of reason recedes in favor of a per se rule of violation.

The earliest period of interpretation of the Sherman Act was marked by the dominance of a per se approach: competitor agreements fixing prices or allocating markets were per se offenses and could not be justified by evidence that the prices fixed were reasonable, or that conditions in the industry demanded efforts to stabilize market prices. The tone of majority opinions began to change with STANDARD OIL COMPANY V. UNITED STATES (1911), in which a general rule of reason standard was announced. Opposition to this vague standard during WOODROW WILSON's Democratic administration contributed to the enactment of the Clayton Act and the Federal Trade Commission Act. With the arrival of "normalcy" under President WARREN C. HARDING, a permissive rule of reason again flowered, and remained dominant for two decades.

Not until the late 1930s, when a new Supreme Court was in place and the New Deal administration had turned away from unhappy experience with the *dirigisme* of the NATIONAL INDUSTRIAL RECOVERY ACT, did vigorous challenges to anticompetitive private market behavior again become popular. Per se rules forbidding a wide range of competitor collaboration and group refusals to deal were announced by the Court for the first time, or brought down from the attic in which they had lain since the Wilson era. This period lasted for a generation; toward its close in the late 1960s per se rules were extended beyond price fixing and competitor agreements to nonprice market allocations between manufacturers and distributors. The early 1970s brought changes in political climate and in the personnel of the Court, and again the course of antitrust doctrine changed. The new mood was apparent in a more restricted interpretation of merger policy, greater receptivity to distribution agreements, and the reassertion of the rule of reason in peripheral areas. As of the mid-1980s, however, the Court had not adopted the more radical shifts toward permissiveness urged by critics of the antitrust laws.

The Supreme Court's restrictive view of Congress's power under the commerce clause in the years following adoption of the Sherman Act produced an extremely narrow interpretation of the act in UNITED STATES V. E. C. KNIGHT COMPANY (1895). Manufacturing, said the Court, was not commerce; thus the act did not reach the stock transactions that gave one company almost complete control over sugar refining in the United States. Only "direct" restraints of interstate commerce itself were subject to the act, as the Court held in *Addyston Pipe & Steel Company v. United States* (1899). The "constitutional revolution" of the 1930s broadened not only the Court's conception of the commerce power but also its interpretation of the reach of the antitrust laws. By the time of SOUTH-EASTERN UNDERWRITERS ASSOCIATION V. UNITED STATES (1944), both changes were complete.

More recently, courts and commentators have noted a potential conflict between state authority to control alcoholic beverages under the TWENTY-FIRST AMENDMENT and claims that state regulatory authorities have participated in price fixing. This issue illustrates a more basic question: does the Sherman Act decree a national free market, or may the states depart from competitive structures for economic activity otherwise within their regulatory power? The issue has arisen in connection with state utility regulation, control of the legal and medical professions, and agricultural marketing programs, all of which operate on a franchise or monopoly regulation model rather than a free market model. In general, the Supreme Court has held that state action regulating a market does not violate federal law and those complying with state law are not in violation of federal law.

The antitrust laws raise other constitutional questions. The vague language of the Sherman Act has given rise to claims of unconstitutionality when that act is the basis of a felony prosecution. The "big case" raises a variety of due process concerns, for it presses the judicial model to the outer limits of its capacity. The meaning of the right to TRIAL BY JURY, for example, requires clarification in cases presenting the complexity and gargantuan size found in many antitrust suits.

Perhaps the most puzzling set of constitutional concerns involves the connections between the Sherman Act's prohibitions on collective behavior (which it describes as contracts, combinations, and conspiracies in restraint of trade) and the associational rights protected by the FIRST AMENDMENT. An agreement among competitors seeking to exclude other potential competitors from the market is a conspiracy under the Sherman Act, even if the competitors enlist government agencies in their effort. On the other hand, an agreement among members of an industry to petition the government for legal relief from the economic threat of their competitors is constitutionally protected political activity. Supreme Court opinions "distinguishing" between these two kinds of activity have resorted to a pejorative label to explain their results, finding the political activity immune from antitrust claims unless it is a sham.

Comparable tensions exist between the Sherman Act's prohibitions of economic boycotts—which are seen as concerted refusals to deal—and political boycotts. To maintain this distinction requires a worldview in which economics and politics are unconnected spheres. Yet boycotts are per se offenses under the Sherman Act and some courts have held that political boycotts are a protected form of political protest.

A third tension is found in the case of permissible "natural monopolies"—for example, the owners of the railway terminal at the only point on a wide river suitable for a railway crossing. For three quarters of a century the Court has held that such holders of monopoly power are obligated to share it fairly with others. Several of these decisions treat this obligation as one resembling governmental power which carries along with it an obligation of "due process" procedural fairness. These decisions might be said to impose the constitutional obligation of government on those private accumulations of power that are found not to be prohibited outright by the Sherman Act. Together, the Constitution and the Sherman Act thus represent a total response to the problems of concentrated power in modern society: the Constitution controls governmental power, and the antitrust law controls concentrations of private economic power. At the seam between public and private organizations, the two bodies of law combine to limit the excesses of concentrated power.

ARTHUR ROSETT

Bibliography

AREEDA, P. and TURNER, D. 1978–1980 *Antitrust Law: An Analysis of Antitrust Principles and their Application,* 5 vols. Boston: Little, Brown.
NEALE, A. D. and GOYDER, D. G. 1980 *The Antitrust Laws of the USA,* 3rd ed. Cambridge: At the University Press.
SULLIVAN, L. 1977 *Antitrust.* St. Paul, Minn.: West Publishing Co.

APEX HOSIERY COMPANY v. LEADER
310 U.S. 469 (1940)

Destroying the effect of CORONADO COAL COMPANY V. UNITED MINE WORKERS (1925), although not overruling it, this opinion marked the shift toward a prolabor sentiment in the Supreme Court. The Court reaffirmed the application of the SHERMAN ANTITRUST ACT to unions but held that even a strike that effected a reduction of goods in INTERSTATE COMMERCE was no Sherman Act violation if it furthered legitimate union objectives. (See ALLEN-BRADLEY COMPANY V. LOCAL #3, 1945.) A particularly violent sit-down strike at the Apex plant reduced the volume of goods in commerce and resulted in extensive physical damage. Did the act forbid the union's actions? Justice HARLAN FISKE STONE, for a 6–3 Court, condemned the union's conduct, declaring that the company had a remedy under state law, but held that restraints not outlawed by the Sherman Act when accomplished peacefully could not be brought within the law's scope because they were accompanied by violence. The Court also denied that the resulting restraint of trade fell under the act. The union was not proceeding illegally by acting to eliminate nonunion or commercial competition in the market, even though a production halt must accompany a strike and lead to a temporary restraint. Only if the restraint led to a monopoly, price control, or discrimination among consumers would a violation occur. The Court thus substituted a test of restraint in the marketplace for the test of intent previously announced in BEDFORD CUT STONE V. JOURNEYMEN STONECUTTERS (1927). In dissent, Chief

Justice CHARLES EVANS HUGHES, joined by Justices OWEN ROBERTS and JAMES C. MCREYNOLDS, insisted that the earlier decisions governed and that they had not confined the test of restraint to market control. The Court had abandoned its earlier approach; the next year it would supplement *Apex*, excluding both jurisdictional strikes and SECONDARY BOYCOTTS from Sherman Act coverage in *United States v. Hutcheson* (1941).

DAVID GORDON

(SEE ALSO: *Antitrust Law and the Constitution.*)

APODACA v. OREGON

See: *Johnson v. Louisiana*

APPALACHIAN ELECTRIC POWER COMPANY v. UNITED STATES
311 U.S. 377 (1940)

Until this decision, federal authority over waterways extended only to those that were navigable. In this case the Supreme Court agreed to review the scope of federal power over completely nonnavigable waters. The Appalachian Electric Company asserted that the WATER POWER ACT of 1920 did not apply to the New River because its waters were not navigable; moreover, the act imposed conditions dealing with neither navigation nor its protection. Justice STANLEY F. REED, for a 6–2 Court, concluded that it was sufficient that the river might eventually be made navigable, thus broadening the earlier definition of federal authority. The COMMERCE CLAUSE was the constitutional provision involved and navigation was merely one of its parts. "Flood control, watershed development, recovery of the cost of improvements through utilization of power [also renders navigable waters subject] to national planning and control in the broad regulation of commerce granted the Federal Government." Justice OWEN ROBERTS, joined by Justice JAMES C. MCREYNOLDS, dissented from Reed's expansion of the test for navigability: "No authority is cited and I think none can be cited which countenances any such test."

DAVID GORDON

APPEAL

An appeal is the invocation of the JURISDICTION of a higher court to reverse or modify a lower court's decision. Appeal from the decision of a federal district court, for example, is normally taken to a federal court of appeals. In earlier federal practice, an appeal was taken by way of a WRIT OF ERROR; today, the term "appeal" has replaced references to the former writ. In the Supreme Court, "appeal" is a term of art, referring to the Court's obligatory APPELLATE JURISDICTION. In this sense, filing an appeal is distinguished from petitioning for a WRIT OF CERTIORARI, which is the method of invoking the Court's discretionary jurisdiction.

In a case coming to the Supreme Court from a state court, appeal is the appropriate remedy when the highest state court has rejected one of two types of claims based on federal law: either the state court has upheld a state law, rejecting the claim that the law violates the federal Constitution or a federal statute or treaty, or it has held invalid a federal statute or treaty. In those two kinds of cases, the Supreme Court is, in theory, obliged to review state court decisions; in all other cases, only the discretionary remedy of certiorari is available. A similarly obligatory review, by way of appeal, is appropriate when a federal court of appeals holds a state statute invalid. However, the overwhelming majority of court of appeals decisions reviewed by the Supreme Court lie within the Court's discretionary review, on writ of certiorari.

Whether a case is or is not an appropriate case for an appeal lies to some extent within the control of counsel, who may be able to cast the case as a challenge to the constitutionality of a state law as applied to particular facts. Yet some cases lie outside counsel's power to characterize; thus, a claim that a valid statute is being applied in a discriminatory manner, in violation of the equal protection clause, is reviewable only on certiorari.

With each passing year the practical distinction between appeal and certiorari has lessened. The Supreme Court often dismisses an appeal "for want of a substantial federal question" under circumstances strongly indicating the Court's determination, on a discretionary basis, that the appeal is not worthy of being heard. Furthermore, the Court has had the power since 1925 to treat improperly filed appeal papers as if they were a petition for certiorari. The same "RULE OF FOUR" applies to both appeal and certiorari: the vote of four Justices is necessary for a case to be heard. With these factors in mind, commentators have persistently urged Congress to abolish the Supreme Court's appeal jurisdiction entirely, leaving the Court in full discretionary control over the cases it will hear.

KENNETH L. KARST

Bibliography
STERN, ROBERT L. and GRESSMAN, EUGENE 1978 *Supreme Court Practice*, 5th ed. Chaps. 2–5. Washington, D.C.: Bureau of National Affairs.

APPELLATE JURISDICTION

A court's appellate jurisdiction is its power to review the actions of another body, usually a lower court. The appellate jurisdiction of our federal courts lies within the control of Congress. Article III of the Constitution, after establishing the Supreme Court's ORIGINAL JURISDICTION over certain cases, gives the Court appellate jurisdiction over all other types of cases within "the JUDICIAL POWER OF THE UNITED STATES," but empowers Congress to make "exceptions and regulations" governing that jurisdiction. In the JUDICIARY ACT OF 1789 Congress did not, formally, make exceptions to the Supreme Court's appellate jurisdiction; rather it purported to *grant* the Court jurisdiction to hear various types of cases on WRIT OF ERROR. The assumption has been that such an affirmative grant of appellate jurisdiction over specified types of cases is, by implication, an "exception," excluding the Court from taking appellate jurisdiction over cases not mentioned.

The Supreme Court itself accepted this line of reasoning in EX PARTE MCCARDLE (1869), stating that without a statutory grant of appellate jurisdiction it had no power to hear a case. Read broadly, this holding empowers Congress to undermine JUDICIAL REVIEW by withdrawing the Supreme Court's most important functions. Some commentators argue that Congress, in controlling the Supreme Court's appellate jurisdiction, is constitutionally bound to respect the Court's essential role in a system of SEPARATION OF POWERS. Other writers, however, reject this view, and the Supreme Court has been presented with no modern occasion to face the issue. (See JUDICIAL SYSTEM.)

Whatever the Constitution may ultimately require, Congress has acted on the assumption that it need not extend the Supreme Court's appellate jurisdiction to occupy the whole of the judicial power established by Article III. Until 1925, for example, the Court's appellate review of civil cases was limited by a requirement of a certain dollar amount in controversy. For the first century of the Court's existence, it had no general appellate jurisdiction over federal criminal cases, but reviewed such a case only on writ of HABEAS CORPUS or upon a lower court's certification of a division of opinion on an issue of law. Until 1914, the Supreme Court could review state court decisions only when they *denied* claims of federal right, not when they validated those claims. Although all these major limitations on the Court's appellate jurisdiction have now been eliminated, the halls of Congress perennially ring with calls for removing the Court's power over cases involving such emotion-charged subjects as SUBVERSIVE ACTIVITIES, school prayers, or ABORTION.

From the beginning the Supreme Court has reviewed cases coming from the lower federal courts and the state courts. The latter jurisdiction has been the source of political controversy, not only in its exercise but in its very existence. In a doctrinal sense, the power of Congress to establish the Court's appellate jurisdiction over state court decisions was settled early, in MARTIN V. HUNTER'S LESSEE (1816). In the realm of practical politics, the issue was settled when any serious thoughts of INTERPOSITION or NULLIFICATION were laid to rest by the outcome of the Civil War. (Ironically, the CONFEDERATE CONSTITUTION had provided a similar appellate jurisdiction for the Confederacy's own supreme court.) By the late 1950s, when the Court confronted intense opposition to school DESEGREGATION, its appellate jurisdiction was firmly entrenched; southern efforts to curb the Court failed miserably.

The Supreme Court's review of state court decisions is limited to issues of federal law. Even federal questions will not be decided by the Court if the state court's judgment rests on an ADEQUATE STATE GROUND. By congressional statute the Court is instructed to review only FINAL JUDGMENTS of state courts, but this limitation is now riddled with judge-made exceptions. The Court does, however, obey strictly its statutory instruction to review the decision of only the highest state court in which judgment is available in a given case. As THOMPSON V. LOUISVILLE (1960) shows, even a justice of the peace may constitute that "highest court" if state law provides no APPEAL from the justice's decision.

When the Supreme Court reviews a state court decision, all the jurisdictional limitations on the federal courts come into play. For example, although a state court may routinely confer STANDING on any state taxpayer to challenge state governmental action, the Supreme Court can take appellate jurisdiction only if the taxpayer satisfies the federal standards for standing.

Of the 4,000 cases brought to the Court in a typical year, only about 150 will be decided with full opinion. A large number of state criminal convictions raise substantial issues of federal constitutional law, but they largely go unreviewed in the Supreme Court. The WARREN COURT sought to provide a substitute federal remedy, facilitating access for state prisoners to federal habeas corpus. In the 1970s, however, the BURGER COURT drastically limited that access; in practical terms, a great many state convictions now escape review of their federal constitutional issues in any federal forum.

Final judgments of the federal district courts are normally reviewed in the courts of appeals, although direct appeal to the Supreme Court is available in a very few categories of cases. Usually, then, a case brought to the Supreme Court has already been the subject of one appeal. The Court thus can husband its resources for its main appellate functions: nourishing the development of a coherent body of federal law, and promoting that law's uniformity and supremacy.

For the Supreme Court's first century, its appellate jurisdiction was mostly obligatory; when Congress authorized a writ of error, the Court had no discretion to decline. The Court's second century has seen a progressive increase in the use of the discretionary WRIT OF CERTIORARI as a means of invoking Supreme Court review, with a corresponding decline in statutory entitlements to review on appeal. Today the Court has a high degree of discretion to choose which cases it will decide. Some observers think this discretion weakens the theoretical foundation of judicial review, expressed in MARBURY V. MADISON (1803). The Court there based its power to hold an act of Congress unconstitutional on the necessity to decide a case. If the Court has discretion whether to decide, the necessity disappears, and thus (so the argument goes) judicial review's legitimacy. Ultimately, that legitimacy may come to depend, both theoretically and politically, on the very power of congressional control so often seen as a threat to the Supreme Court's appellate jurisdiction.

KENNETH L. KARST

Bibliography

BATOR, PAUL M., MISHKIN, PAUL J., SHAPIRO, DAVID L., and WECHSLER, HERBERT, EDS. 1973 *The Federal Courts and the Federal System*, 2nd ed. Chaps. 5, 11. Mineola, N.Y.: Foundation Press.

APPOINTING AND REMOVAL POWER, PRESIDENTIAL

Article II, section 2, clause 2, of the Constitution provides in part that the President "shall nominate, and by and with the ADVICE AND CONSENT of the Senate, he shall appoint, Ambassadors, other public Ministers and Consuls, Judges of the Supreme Court, and all other Officers of the United States, whose appointments are not herein otherwise provided for, and which shall be established by Law." It goes on to authorize Congress to provide for the appointment of "inferior officers" by the President, the courts, or the heads of departments. The only patent ambiguity is in the distinction between the appointment of "inferior officers" and those presidential appointments requiring advice and consent of the Senate. This problem has given little cause for concern, perhaps because Congress has erred on the side of requiring advice and consent appointments, so that even every officer in the armed forces receives such a presidential appointment.

The processes of the appointment power were canvassed by JOHN MARSHALL in MARBURY V. MADISON (1803), where he also addressed the question that has plagued the construction of Article II, section 2, clause 2, not the meaning of the appointment provisions but what meaning they have for the removal power. The language of the Constitution is silent about removal, except for impeachment and the life tenure it gives to judges. Marshall said:

Where an officer is removable at the will of the executive, the circumstance which completes his appointment is of no concern; because the act is at any time revocable; and the commission may be arrested, if still in the office. But when the officer is not removable at the will of the executive, the appointment is not revocable, and cannot be annulled. It has conferred legal rights which cannot be resumed.

The discretion of the executive is to be exercised until the appointment has been made. But having once made the appointment, his power over the office is terminated in all cases, where by law the officer is not removable by him. The right to the office is *then* in the person appointed, and he has the absolute, and unconditional power of accepting or rejecting it.

Mr. Marbury, then, since his commission was signed by the president, and sealed by the secretary of state, was appointed; and as the law creating the office, gave the officer a right to hold for five years, independent of the executive, the appointment was not revocable, but vested in the officer legal rights, which are protected by the laws of his country.

Obviously, it was to Congress that Marshall ascribed the power to determine the length of the term, and the conditions for removal, except that all officers of the United States were removable by the process of IMPEACHMENT.

The question whether an appointment made by the President with the advice and consent of the Senate could be terminated by the executive without such senatorial approval was soon mooted. ALEXANDER HAMILTON had answered the question in THE FEDERALIST #77:

It has been mentioned as one of the advantages to be expected from the cooperation of the Senate, in the business of appointments, that it would contribute to the stability of the administration. The consent of that body would be necessary to displace as well as to appoint. A change of the Chief Magistrate, therefore, would not occasion so violent or so general a revolution in the officers of the government as might be expected, if he were the sole disposer of offices. Where a man in any station had given satisfactory evidence of his fitness for it, a new President would be restrained from attempting a change in favor of a person more agreeable to him, by the apprehension that a discountenance of the Senate might frustrate the attempt, and bring some discredit upon himself. Those who can best estimate the value of a steady administration, will be most disposed to prize a provision which connects the official existence of public men with the approbation or disapprobation of that body, which from the greater permanence of its own composition, will in all probability be less subject to inconsistency than any other member of the government.

Thus spake the founding father most given to support a strong presidency.

In the very first Congress, however, when it was concerned with the creation of the office of secretary of state, there was extensive debate about whether the removal power was inherently an executive function and therefore not to be encumbered by the necessity for senatorial approval. It was conceded that the appointment power, too, was intrinsically an executive power and, but for constitutional provision to the contrary, would have remained untrammeled by legislative authority. JAMES MADISON thus construed the provision in his lengthy argument in the House of Representatives: the President did not need the acquiescence of the Senate to remove an official who had been appointed with its consent. The impasse that developed in the House was resolved not by choosing one side or the other of the controversial question but rather by omission of any provision concerning the power of removal. Madison's position at the CONSTITUTIONAL CONVENTION OF 1787 had been that the President, like the king, should have the appointment power without condition. He failed to carry the Convention on that point. He sought in the legislature to protect the President's exclusive power of removal. He failed there, too, although the point was not taken definitively against him as it had been at the Convention. But if he failed in 1789, he was nevertheless to be vindicated in MYERS v. UNITED STATES (1926).

The issue had not remained moribund in the in-terim. In 1833, when ANDREW JACKSON removed two secretaries of the treasury for refusing to withdraw government deposits from the BANK OF THE UNITED STATES and put ROGER B. TANEY in their place, motions of censure were moved and passed in the Senate, supported by DANIEL WEBSTER, HENRY CLAY, and JOHN C. CALHOUN. But Jackson had his way, as he usually did. The issue reached proportions of a constitutional crisis in 1867, when President ANDREW JOHNSON was impeached, largely on the ground that he had violated the TENURE OF OFFICE ACT which forbade the removal of a cabinet officer before his successor had been nominated and approved by the Senate. Johnson escaped a guilty verdict in the Senate because the vote fell one shy of the two-thirds necessary for conviction. There were other instances in which the courts were called upon for construction of the removal power, and for the most part the decisions sided with the President, but usually by statutory rather than constitutional construction.

The controlling Supreme Court decision came in the *Myers* case in 1926, which arose out of the removal by the President of a local postmaster. Here Chief Justice WILLIAM HOWARD TAFT, after his experience as chief magistrate, was not prepared to tolerate the suggestion that a President could have foisted on his administration aides that he did not want, even if the aide were only a lowly postmaster. Perhaps Taft's first concern was that Congress would take over the execution of the laws by the creation of independent agencies over whose members the President would have no control at all if he could not exercise the power of removal. That was not the issue in *Myers,* but Taft wished to forestall future problems of independent agencies as well as to lay to rest the canard that the President could not remove those in the direct chain of command, such as a postmaster. He read the debates in the first Congress as establishing Madison's position rather than bypassing it. It took seventy pages of abuse of history to make Taft's point. The presidential power of removal thus became plenary. Justice OLIVER WENDELL HOLMES, in dissent, disposed of the Taft position in less than a page:

We have to deal with an office that owes its existence to Congress and that Congress may abolish tomorrow. Its duration and the pay attached to it while it lasts depend on Congress alone. Congress alone confers on the President the power to appoint to it and at any time may transfer that power to other hands. With such power over its own creation, I have no more trouble in believing that Congress has power to prescribe a term of life for it free from any interference than I have in accepting the undoubted power of Congress to decree its end. I have equally little trouble in accepting its power to prolong the tenure of an incumbent until Congress or the Senate shall have assented to his removal. The duty of the President to see that the laws be executed is a duty that does not go beyond the laws or require him to achieve more than Congress sees fit to leave within his power.

History, however, has been on the side of Taft and Madison rather than on that of Hamilton, Marshall, and Holmes. An exception has been carved by the Court from the President's power of removal where the incumbent is charged with duties that may be called judicial, even if mixed with legislative and executive discretion, such as those involved in HUMPHREY'S EXECUTOR V. UNITED STATES (1935). Thus, Taft's championing of the presidential removal power has been sustained, except in the situation that bothered him most, the independent administrative agencies where legislative, executive, and judicial powers are all exercised by the incumbent.

PHILIP B. KURLAND

Bibliography

CORWIN, EDWARD S. 1927 Tenure of Office and the Removal Power under the Constitution. *Columbia Law Review* 27:353–399.

KURLAND, PHILIP B. 1978 *Watergate and the Constitution*, chap. 5. Chicago: University of Chicago Press.

MILLER, CHARLES A. 1969 *The Supreme Court and the Uses of History.* Chap. 4. Cambridge, Mass.: Harvard University Press.

APPOINTMENT OF SUPREME COURT JUSTICES

Under Article II, section 2, of the Constitution, Supreme Court Justices, like all other federal judges, are nominated and, with the ADVICE AND CONSENT of the Senate, appointed by the President. No other textual mandate, either procedural or substantive, governs the Chief Executive's selection. However, section 1 of Article III—which deals exclusively with the judicial branch of the government—provides GOOD BEHAVIOR tenure for all federal judges; in effect, that means appointment for life. As additional security, that provision of the Constitution provides that the compensation of federal judges "shall not be diminished during their Continuance in Office." But neither the Constitution nor any federal statute provides any clue as to qualifications for office; neither a law degree nor any other proof of professional capability is formally required. But in practice none other than lawyers are appointable to the federal judiciary,

in general, and the Supreme Court, in particular. All of the 102 individuals who sat on that highest tribunal through 1985 held degrees from a school of law or had been admitted to the bar via examination. Indeed, although all the Justices were members of the professional bar in good standing at the time of their appointment, it was not until 1922 that a majority of sitting Justices was composed of law school graduates, and not until 1957 that every Justice was a law school graduate. Once confirmed by the Senate, a Justice is removable only via IMPEACHMENT (by simple majority vote by the House of Representatives) and subsequent conviction (by two-thirds vote of the Senate, there being a quorum on the floor). Only one Justice of the Supreme Court has been impeached by the House—Justice SAMUEL CHASE, by a 72–32 vote in 1804—but he was acquitted on all eight charges by the Senate in 1805. To all intents and purposes, once appointed, a Supreme Court Justice serves as long as he or she wishes—typically until illness or death intervenes.

Theoretically, the President has *carte blanche* in selecting his nominees to the Court. In practice, three facts of political life inform and limit his choices. The first is that it is not realistically feasible for the Chief Executive to designate a Justice and obtain confirmation by the Senate without the at least grudging approval by the two home state senators concerned, especially if the latter are members of the President's own political party. The time-honored practice of "Senatorial courtesy" is an omnipresent phenomenon, because of senatorial camaraderie and the "blue slip" approval system, under which the Judiciary Committee normally will not favorably report a nominee to the floor if an objecting home-state senator has failed to return that slip. (Senator Edward Kennedy, during his two-year tenure as head of the Committee, abandoned the system in 1979, but it was partly restored by his successor, Senator Strom Thurmond, in 1981.) Although nominations to the Supreme Court are regarded as a personal province of presidential choice far more than the appointment of other judges, the Senate's "advice and consent" is neither routine nor perfunctory, to which recent history amply attests. In 1968, despite a favorable Judiciary Committee vote, the Senate refused to consent to President Johnson's promotion of Justice ABE FORTAS to the Chief Justiceship; in 1969 it rejected President RICHARD M. NIXON's nomination of Judge Clement Haynsworth, Jr., by 55 to 45; and in 1970 it turned down that same President's selection of Judge G. Harrold Carswell by 51 to 45. Indeed, to date the Senate, for a variety of reasons, has refused to confirm twenty-seven Supreme Court nominees out of the total of 139 sent to it for its "advice and consent" (twenty-one of these during the nineteenth century).

The second major factor to be taken into account by the President is the evaluative role played by the American Bar Association's fourteen-member Committee on the Federal Judiciary, which has been an unofficial part of the judicial appointments process since 1946. The committee scrutinizes the qualifications of all nominees to the federal bench and normally assigns one of four "grades": Exceptionally Well Qualified, Well Qualified, Qualified, and Not Qualified. In the rare instances of a vacancy on the Supreme Court, however, the committee has in recent years adopted a different, threefold, categorization: "High Standards of Integrity, Judicial Temperament, and Professional Competence"; "Not Opposed"; and "Not Qualified."

The third consideration incumbent upon the Chief Executive is the subtle but demonstrable one of the influence, however *sub rosa* and *sotto voce,* of sitting and retired jurists. Recent research points convincingly to that phenomenon, personified most prominently by Chief Justice WILLIAM HOWARD TAFT. If Taft did not exactly "appoint" colleagues to vacancies that occurred during his nine-year tenure (1921–1930), he assuredly vetoed those unacceptable to him. Among others also involved in advisory or lobbying roles, although on a lesser scale than Taft, were Chief Justices CHARLES EVANS HUGHES, HARLAN F. STONE, FRED VINSON, EARL WARREN, and WARREN E. BURGER and Associate Justices JOHN MARSHALL HARLAN I, SAMUEL F. MILLER, WILLIS VAN DEVANTER, LOUIS D. BRANDEIS, and FELIX FRANKFURTER.

A composite portrait of the 101 men and one woman who have been Justices of the Supreme Court provides the following cross-section: native-born: 96; male: 101 (the first woman, SANDRA DAY O'CONNOR, was appointed by President RONALD REAGAN in the summer of 1981); white: 101 (the first black Justice, THURGOOD MARSHALL, was appointed by President LYNDON B. JOHNSON in 1967); predominantly Protestant: 91 (there have been six Roman Catholic and five Jewish Justices—the first in each category were ANDREW JACKSON's appointment of Chief Justice ROGER B. TANEY in 1836 and WOODROW WILSON's of Louis D. Brandeis in 1916, respectively); 50–55 years of age at time of appointment (the two youngest have been JOSEPH STORY, 33, in 1812 and WILLIAM O. DOUGLAS, 41, in 1939); of Anglo-Saxon ethnic stock (all except fifteen); from an upper middle to high social status (all except a handful); reared in a nonrural but not necessarily urban environment; member of a civic-minded, politically aware, economically comfortable family (all except a handful); holders of B.A. and, in this century, LL.B. or J.D. degrees (with one-third from "Ivy League" institutions); and a background of at least some type of public or community service (all except Justice GEORGE SHIRAS). Contemporary recognition of egalitarianism and "representativeness" may alter this profile, but it is not likely to change radically.

Only the President and his close advisers know the actual motivations for the choice of a particular Supreme Court appointee. But a perusal of the records of the thirty-five Presidents who nominated Justices (four—W. H. Harrison, ZACHARY TAYLOR, ANDREW JOHNSON, and JIMMY CARTER—had no opportunity to do so) points to several predominating criteria, most apparent of which have been: (1) objective merit; (2) personal friendship; (3) considerations of "representativeness"; (4) political ideological compatibility, what THEODORE ROOSEVELT referred to as a selectee's "real politics"; and (5) past judicial experience. Appropriate examples of (1) would be BENJAMIN N. CARDOZO (HERBERT HOOVER) and JOHN MARSHALL HARLAN (DWIGHT D. EISENHOWER); of (2) HAROLD H. BURTON (HARRY S. TRUMAN) and Abe Fortas (Lyndon Johnson); of (4) HUGO BLACK (FRANKLIN D. ROOSEVELT) and William Howard Taft (WARREN G. HARDING); of (5) OLIVER WENDELL HOLMES (Theodore Roosevelt) and DAVID J. BREWER (BENJAMIN HARRISON). Deservedly most contentious is motivation (3), under which Presidents have been moved to weigh such "equitable" factors as geography, religion, gender, race, and perhaps even age in order to provide a "representative" profile of the Court. Of uncertain justification, it is nonetheless a fact of life of the appointive process. Thus geography proved decisive in Franklin D. Roosevelt's selection of WILEY RUTLEDGE of Iowa ("Wiley, you have geography," Roosevelt told him) and ABRAHAM LINCOLN's selection of STEPHEN J. FIELD of California. But given the superb qualifications of Judge Cardozo, despite the presence of two other New Yorkers (Hughes and Stone), the former's selection was all but forced upon Hoover. The notion that there should be a "Roman Catholic" and "Jewish" seat has been present ever since the appointments of Taney and Brandeis. Although there have been periods without such "reserved" seats (for example, 1949–1956 in the former case and since 1965 in the latter), Presidents are aware of the insistent pressures for such "representation." These pressures have increased since the "establishment" of a "black" seat (Marshall in 1967, by Johnson) and a "woman's seat" (O'Connor, by Reagan, in 1981). It has become all but unthinkable that future Supreme Court lineups will not henceforth have "representatives" from such categories. That the Founding Fathers neither considered nor addressed any of these "representative" factors does not gainsay their presence and significance in the political process.

Whatever may be the merits of other criteria motivating presidential Supreme Court appointments, the key factor is the Chief Executive's perception of a candidate's "real" politics—for it is the nominee's likely voting pattern as a Justice that matters most to an incumbent President. To a greater or lesser extent, all Presidents have thus attempted to "pack" the bench. Court-packing has been most closely associated with Franklin D. Roosevelt. Failing a single opportunity to fill a Court vacancy during his first term (and five months of his second), and seeing his domestic programs consistently battered by "the Nine Old Men," Roosevelt moved to get his way in one fell swoop with his "Court Packing Bill" of 1937; however, it was reported unfavorably by the Senate Judiciary Committee and was interred by a decisive recommittal vote. Ultimately, the passage of time enabled him to fill nine vacancies between 1937 and 1943. Yet GEORGE WASHINGTON was able to nominate fourteen, of whom ten chose to serve, and his selectees were measured against a sextet of criteria: (1) support and advocacy of the Constitution; (2) distinguished service in the revolution; (3) active participation in the political life of the new nation; (4) prior judicial experience on lower tribunals; (5) either a "favorable reputation with his fellows" or personal ties with Washington himself; and (6) geographic "suitability." Whatever the specific predispositions may be, concern with a nominee's "real" politics has been and will continue to be crucial in presidential motivations. It even prompted Republican President Taft to award half of his six nominations to the Court to Democrats, who were kindred "real politics" souls (HORACE H. LURTON, EDWARD D. WHITE's promotion to Chief Justice, and JOSEPH R. LAMAR). In ten other instances the appointee came from a formal political affiliation other than that of the appointer, ranging from Whig President JOHN TYLER's appointment of Democrat SAMUEL NELSON in 1845 to Republican Richard M. Nixon's selection of Democrat LEWIS F. POWELL, JR., in 1971.

But to predict the ultimate voting pattern or behavior of a nominee is to lean upon a slender reed. In the characteristically blunt words of President Truman: "Packing the Supreme Court simply can't be done. . . . I've tried and it won't work. . . . Whenever you put a man on the Supreme Court he ceases to

be your friend. I'm sure of that." There is indeed a considerable element of unpredictability in the judicial appointment process. To the question whether a judicial robe makes a person any different, Justice Frankfurter's sharp retort was always, "If he is any good, he does!" In ALEXANDER M. BICKEL's words, "You shoot an arrow into a far-distant future when you appoint a Justice and not the man himself can tell you what he will think about some of the problems that he will face." And late in 1969, reflecting upon his sixteen years as Chief Justice of the United States, Earl Warren pointed out that he, for one, did not "see how a man could be on the Court and not change his views substantially over a period of years . . . for change you must if you are to do your duty on the Supreme Court." It is clear beyond doubt that the Supreme Court appointment process is fraught with imponderables and guesswork, notwithstanding the carefully composed constitutional obligations of President and Senate.

HENRY J. ABRAHAM

Bibliography

ABRAHAM, HENRY J. 1985 *Justices and Presidents: A Political History of Appointments to the Supreme Court*, 2nd ed. New York: Oxford University Press.

_____ 1986 *The Judicial Process: An Introductory Analysis of the Courts of the United States, England and France*, 5th ed. New York: Oxford University Press.

DANELSKI, DAVID J. 1964 *A Supreme Court Justice Is Appointed.* New York: Random House.

SCHMIDHAUSER, JOHN R. 1960 *The Supreme Court: Its Politics, Personalities and Procedures.* New York: Holt, Rinehart & Winston.

_____ 1979 *Judges and Justices: The Federal Appellate Judiciary.* Boston: Little, Brown.

APPORTIONMENT

See: Reapportionment

APTHEKER v. SECRETARY OF STATE
378 U.S. 500 (1959)

Two top leaders of the Communist party appealed the revocation of their passports under section 6 of the Subversive Activities Control Act of 1950.

Justice ARTHUR J. GOLDBERG, in a plurality opinion for a 6–3 Supreme Court, held that that section "too broadly and indiscriminately restrict[ed] the RIGHT TO TRAVEL" and therefore abridged the liberty protected by the Fifth Amendment. The section was overly broad on its face because it did not discriminate between active and inactive members of subversive groups or among the various possible purposes for foreign travel.

Justices HUGO L. BLACK and WILLIAM O. DOUGLAS, concurring, would have held the entire act unconstitutional.

DENNIS J. MAHONEY

ARGERSINGER v. HAMLIN
407 U.S. 25 (1972)

Argersinger culminated four decades of progression in RIGHT TO COUNSEL doctrine: from a DUE PROCESS requirement in CAPITAL PUNISHMENT cases, to application of the Sixth Amendment to the states in serious FELONIES, and finally, in *Argersinger*, to extension of the requirement to any case in which there is a sentence of imprisonment.

Argersinger, unrepresented by counsel, was convicted of a MISDEMEANOR and sentenced by a state court to ninety days in jail. The arguments in the Supreme Court were of an unusually practical rather than doctrinal nature. Much was made of the burden on state criminal justice systems that the extension of the right to counsel would cause. The state also argued that many misdemeanors, though carrying potential jail sentences, are exceedingly straightforward cases that a layperson could handle by him- or herself. Moreover, it was argued that people who can afford lawyers often do not hire them for such simple cases because the cost is not worth what a lawyer could accomplish. The Court rejected all these contentions and established imprisonment as a clear test for requiring the appointment of counsel.

Seven years later, in *Scott v. Illinois* (1979), the Court held that the appointment of counsel was not required for a trial when imprisonment was a possibility but was not actually imposed. The anomalous result is that a judge must predict before the trial whether he will impose imprisonment in order to know whether to appoint counsel.

BARBARA ALLEN BABCOCK

ARLINGTON HEIGHTS v. METROPOLITAN HOUSING DEVELOPMENT CORP.
429 U.S. 252 (1977)

This decision confirmed in another context the previous term's holding in WASHINGTON V. DAVIS (1976) that discriminatory purpose must be shown to establish race-based violations of the EQUAL PROTECTION clause. The Supreme Court declined to strike down a village's refusal to rezone land to allow multiple-family dwellings despite the refusal's racially discriminatory adverse effects. Writing for the Court, Justice LEWIS F. POWELL elaborated on the nature of the showing that must be made to satisfy the purpose requirement announced in *Washington v. Davis*. A plaintiff need not prove that challenged action rested solely on racially discriminatory purposes. Instead, proof that a discriminatory purpose was a motivating factor would require the offending party to prove that it would have taken the challenged action even in the absence of a discriminatory purpose. Powell noted the types of evidence that might lead to a finding of discriminatory purpose: egregious discriminatory effects, the historical background of the governmental action, departures from normal procedure, legislative and administrative history, and, in some instances, testimony by the decision makers themselves.

THEODORE EISENBERG

ARNETT v. KENNEDY
416 U.S. 134 (1974)

A fragmented Supreme Court held, 6–3, that a federal civil service employee had no PROCEDURAL DUE PROCESS right to a full hearing before being dismissed. Justice WILLIAM H. REHNQUIST, for three Justices, concluded that because the governing statute had provided for removal of an employee to "promote the efficiency of the service," the employee's "property" interest was conditioned by this limitation. Thus due process required no predismissal hearing. The other six Justices rejected this view, concluding that the Constitution itself defined the protection required, once the guarantee of procedural due process attached. However, three of the six found no right to a predismissal hearing in the protection defined by the Constitution. The dissenters, led by Justice WILLIAM J. BRENNAN, argued that GOLDBERG V. KELLY (1970) demanded a predismissal hearing, and commented that Justice Rehnquist's view would revive the "right–privilege" distinction that *Goldberg* had rejected. In BISHOP V. WOOD (1976) the Rehnquist position came to command a majority of the Court.

KENNETH L. KARST

ARNOLD, THURMAN
(1891–1969)

Law professor, assistant attorney general, and federal judge, Thurman Arnold of Wyoming was a vigorous champion of both CIVIL LIBERTIES and ANTITRUST regulation. In 1930, when Arnold joined the Yale Law School faculty, which included WILLIAM O. DOUGLAS and WALTON HAMILTON, he had already developed a social and psychological approach to law. He had an extraordinary commitment to the concept of FAIR TRIAL in which he saw ritual significance, and, in *The Symbols of Government* (1935), Arnold described law as a mode of symbolic thinking that conditioned behavior. A witty and sarcastic writer, he described the interplay between CORPORATIONS and antitrust law in *The Folklore of Capitalism* (1937). The following year President FRANKLIN D. ROOSEVELT chose him to head the Antitrust Division of the Justice Department. Arnold was a zealous enforcer of antitrust legislation; he launched over 200 major investigations and saw his budget and personnel quadruple before his departure in 1943 to become a federal judge. Naturally unsuited for judicial office, he resigned within two years to enter private practice where ABE FORTAS soon joined him. Arnold welcomed controversial issues and represented defendants in loyalty cases of the late 1940s and the McCarthy era. Arnold was a spirited libertarian, and his career reflected his belief in the need to erase traditional intellectual boundaries and integrate disciplines and approaches.

DAVID GORDON

Bibliography

KEARNY, EDWARD N. 1970 *Thurman Arnold, Social Critic.* Albuquerque: University of New Mexico Press.

ARREST

The constitutional law of arrest governs every occasion on which a government officer interferes with an individual's freedom, from full-scale custodial arrests at one end of the spectrum to momentary detentions at the other. Its essential principle is that a court, not a police officer or other executive official, shall ultimately decide whether a particular interference with the liberty of an individual is justified. The court may make this judgment either before an arrest, when the police seek a judicial warrant authorizing it, or shortly after an arrest without a warrant, in a hearing held expressly for that purpose. The law of arrest gives practical meaning to the ideal of the liberty of the individual, by defining the circumstances in which, and the degree to which, that liberty may be curtailed by the police or other officers of the government; it is thus a basic part of what we mean by the RULE OF LAW in the United States.

The principal constitutional standard governing arrest is the FOURTH AMENDMENT. This amendment is one article of the original BILL OF RIGHTS, which was held in BARRON V. BALTIMORE (1833) to apply only to the federal government. But in MAPP V. OHIO (1961) the Fourth Amendment was held to be among those provisions of the Bill of Rights that are "incorporated" in the FOURTEENTH AMENDMENT and is thus applicable to arrests by state as well as federal officers. (See INCORPORATION DOCTRINE.) Even without such a holding, of course, the Fourteenth Amendment, which regulates state interference with individual liberty, would have required the development of a body of law governing state arrests. The law so made might have been no less protective of the individual than the law actually made under the Fourth Amendment. As things are, however, the "unreasonableness" standard of the Fourth Amendment has been the basis of the constitutional law governing arrests by both federal and state officers.

What seizures are "unreasonable"? One obvious possibility is that seizures of the person should be held subject to the warrant clause, as searches are, and should accordingly be found "unreasonable" unless a proper warrant has been obtained or, by reason of emergency, excused. For many years the court flirted with such a rule, as in *Trupiano v. United States* (1948) and TERRY V. OHIO (1968), but it never flatly required a warrant for arrests, and in UNITED STATES V. WATSON (1976) it rejected that rule at least for FELONIES. This decision rested partly upon a historical English COMMON LAW rule excusing the warrant for felonies, but despite the similarities of language the analogy is not precise. In English law the term "felony" was reserved for offenses punishable by death and forfeiture, which give rise to a high probability of an attempt to flee; with us "felony" is usually defined by statute as an offense for which the possible punishment exceeds one year's imprisonment. The other basis for *Watson* was a combination of convenience and probability: because a warrant will in fact be excused on emergency grounds in a large class of cases, it is wise to dispense with the requirement entirely, and thus avoid the costs—improper arrests without warrants, delays to obtain unnecessary warrants—necessarily associated with close cases. The Court left open the possibility that arrest warrants may be required for MISDEMEANORS, at least (as at common law) for those not involving a BREACH OF THE PEACE nor committed in the presence of the arresting officer. This question is at present unresolved.

Somewhat more stable as a standard of reasonableness has been the substantive requirement that an arrest must be based upon PROBABLE CAUSE. This is not a term of scientific precision. It means essentially that an officer must demonstrate to a magistrate, before or after the arrest, that he has sufficient reason to believe in the guilt of the suspect to justify his arrest. Although probable cause is not susceptible of precise definition, the cases decided by the Court have gradually given it some content, especially where, as in SPINELLI V. UNITED STATES (1969), an officer's judgment rests on information received from another. In such cases the basic rule is that the officer must give the magistrate reason to trust the honesty of his informant, and reveal the grounds upon which the informant's charge rests—for example, that the informant saw a crime committed, or the suspect told him he had done it.

Probable cause is of course required only when there has been a "seizure" to which the Fourth Amendment speaks. The courts have found that term difficult to define as well, and difficult in ways that make the meaning of "probable cause" itself more uncertain. The world presents a wide range of police interferences with individual liberty, from minor detentions to full-scale incarceration, and it is widely agreed that some of these intrusions, at every level on the scale, are reasonable and appropriate and that others—again at every level—are inappropriate. Were every interference with liberty regarded as a "seizure" requiring demonstration of "probable cause," the Court would thus face a serious delemma: to hold minor intrusions invalid without a showing of traditional probable cause would outlaw an obviously important and generally accepted method of police work; but to permit them on probable cause grounds would water down the probable cause standard, greatly reducing the justification required to support a full-scale arrest. On the other hand, to hold that such intrusions were not "seizures" would seem to say that they are not regulated by the Fourth Amendment at all—nor under present doctrine, by the Fourteenth—and could therefore be inflicted upon a citizen at an officer's whim. In *Terry v. Ohio* the Court tried to deal with this problem by regarding some "seizures" (less than full-scale arrests) as not requiring "probable cause" but as nonetheless subject to the "reasonableness" requirement of the Fourth Amendment. *Terry* involved the detention of persons an officer reasonably suspected to be planning an armed robbery, during which he asked them their identity and frisked them for weapons. The Court took great pains to make clear that it was not establishing a general right to detain on less than probable cause, and that the "reasonableness" of the seizure validated there was closely tied to the protective nature of the officer's measures and to his realistic apprehension of danger. The Court intimated that no detention beyond that necessarily involved in the frisk would be valid. But cases since *Terry* have undercut that position deeply. In *Adams v. Williams* (1972), for example, the Court explicitly talked about a right to detain on suspicion, and in *United States v. Mendenhall* (1980) a plurality of the Court held that there is no seizure when officers merely approach a person and ask him questions, even if they intend to arrest him, unless he can establish "objective grounds" upon which a reasonable person in his position would have believed he was not free to go. On the other hand, *Dunaway v. New York* (1979) expressly refused to adopt the view that increasingly lengthy detentions were permissible on increasingly good justification (which would effectively eliminate the idea that probable cause is required before "arrest," except in the technical sense of full-custody arrest); and *Delaware v. Prouse* (1979) held that a person driving a car may be stopped upon less than probable cause, but only if there is reasonable suspicion of a violation of law.

The precedents come to this: some confrontations between officers and citizens are not seizures at all; others are seizures that must be justified by a "reasonableness" requirement; still others are "arrests" for which probable cause is required. But there are no clear lines between the categories, and the Supreme Court has not given adequate attention to the ways in which a "seizure" can grow into an "arrest," thus defeating the basic aim of the probable cause requirement.

JAMES BOYD WHITE

Bibliography

HALE, MATTHEW (1685)1972 *The Pleas of the Crown.* London: Professional Books.
LaFAVE, WAYNE R. 1978 *Search and Seizure: A Treatise on the Fourth Amendment.* Mineola, N.Y.: Foundation Press.

ARREST WARRANT

Under the FOURTH AMENDMENT, arrest warrants, like SEARCH WARRANTS, may be issued only upon PROBABLE CAUSE, supported by oath or affirmation, and particularly describing the person to be seized. Much of the constitutional doctrine governing search warrants is therefore applicable by analogy to arrest warrants.

At English COMMON LAW, a law enforcement officer was authorized to make a warrantless arrest when he had reasonable grounds to believe that a FELONY had been committed and that the person to be arrested was the perpetrator. A warrantless misdemeanor arrest, however, was permitted only when the misdemeanor was committed in the officer's presence. Consistent with this rule, Congress and almost all states have permitted warrantless arrests in public places since the beginning of the nation.

In view of this history, the Supreme Court held in UNITED STATES V. WATSON (1976) that the Fourth Amendment does not require a law enforcement officer to obtain a warrant for a felony arrest made in a public place even though there may be ample opportunity to obtain the warrant. Although recognizing that the preference for a neutral and detached magistrate applies to the issuance of arrest warrants, the Court reasoned that this judicial preference was insufficient to justify a departure from the common law at the time of the adoption of the Fourth Amendment and from the judgment of Congress and the states.

It may be argued that the preference for a warrant for searches should apply with equal, if not greater, force to arrests because of the significant infringement of personal liberty involved. Unless history is to be regarded as irrelevant in constitutional interpretation, however, the result in *Watson* is correct in view of the unambiguous history relating to warrantless arrests in public places. Moreover, the Court in *Gerstein v. Pugh* (1975) recognized that after a warrantless arrest a timely judicial determination of probable cause is a prerequisite to detention.

The Court has distinguished between arrests made in public places and those made in private homes. Because of, among other things, the historical importance attached to one's privacy at home and the uncertainty in the common law over warrantless arrests in private homes, a law enforcement officer may not enter a person's home to make an arrest without first obtaining a warrant. The distinction has been made in such cases as PAYTON V. NEW YORK (1980) and STEAGALD V. UNITED STATES (1981).

Probable cause in the context of arrest warrants means probable cause to believe that a crime was committed and that the person to be arrested committed it. Unlike a search warrant, an arrest warrant may be issued on the basis of a grand jury INDICTMENT, provided that the GRAND JURY is "properly consti-

tuted" and the indictment is "fair upon its face." The Court's willingness to let a grand jury's judgment substitute for that of a neutral and detached magistrate is attributable to that grand jury's relationship to the courts and its historical role in protecting individuals from unjust prosecution. An INFORMATION filed by a prosecutor, by contrast, will not justify the issuance of an arrest warrant, for the prosecutor's role is inconsistent with that of a neutral and detached magistrate.

The particularity requirement, expressly applied to arrest warrants by the warrant clause, mandates that the warrant contain sufficient information to identify the person to be arrested. It is intended to preclude the use of a general or "dragnet" arrest warrant.

If a person is illegally arrested without a warrant, such an arrest will not prevent the person from being tried or invalidate his conviction. Any EVIDENCE obtained as a result of the arrest, however, including statements made by the person arrested, may be excluded under the FRUIT OF THE POISONOUS TREE DOCTRINE as applied in WONG SUN V. UNITED STATES (1963).

JAMES R. ASPERGER

Bibliography

LaFAVE, WAYNE R. 1978 *Search and Seizure: A Treatise on the Fourth Amendment.* Vol. 2:215–260. St. Paul, Minn.: West Publishing Co.

ARTHUR, CHESTER A.
(1830–1886)

A New York lawyer and politician, Chester Alan Arthur was nominated for vice-president in 1880 to placate the ULYSSES S. GRANT or "stalwart" branch of the Republican party. In September 1881 Arthur became President when President JAMES GARFIELD was assassinated. Although his previous political activities had revolved around the New York customs house and the distribution of Republican patronage, as President Arthur supported civil service reform and opposed unnecessary federal expenditures. He was denied the Republican nomination in 1884 by a combination of reformers, who did not trust him, and by party members opposed to any reforms.

PAUL FINKELMAN

Bibliography

DUENECKE, JUSTIN D. 1981 *The Presidencies of James A. Garfield and Chester A. Arthur.* Lawrence: Regents Press of Kansas.

ARTICLE III

See: Judicial Power of the United States

ARTICLE III COURTS

See: Constitutional Courts

ARTICLES OF CONFEDERATION

On March 1, 1781, Congress proclaimed ratification of the constitution for a confederation named "the United States of America." People celebrated with fireworks and toasts, and a Philadelphia newspaper predicted that the day would forever be memorialized "in the annals of America. . . ." Another newspaper gave thanks because the states had at last made perpetual a union begun by the necessities of war.

The war was only three months old when BENJA-MIN FRANKLIN proposed the first continental constitution. He called it "Articles of Confederation and Perpetual Union," a name that stuck. Because the war was then being fought to achieve a reconciliation with England on American terms, Congress would not even consider Franklin's plan. But a year later, when Congress appointed a committee to frame a DECLA-RATION OF INDEPENDENCE, it also appointed a committee, consisting of one member from each state, to prepare "the form of a confederation to be entered into by these colonies." JOHN DICKINSON of Pennsylvania, whom the committee entrusted to draft the document, borrowed heavily from Franklin's plan and seems not to have been influenced by other committee members. One complained that Dickinson's plan involved "the Idea of destroying all Provincial Distinctions and making every thing of the most minute kind bend to what they call the good of the whole."

Dickinson was a "nationalist" in the sense that he believed that a strong central government was needed to build a union that could effectively manage its own affairs and compete with other nations. Congress, which was directing the war, became the hub of the Confederation. It was a unicameral house in which each state delegation had a single vote, making the states equal, and Dickinson proposed no change. Franklin, by contrast, had recommended that REPRE-SENTATION in Congress be apportioned on the basis of population, with each delegate having one vote. Dickinson carried over Franklin's generous allocation of powers to Congress, except for a power over "gen-

eral commerce." Neither Franklin nor Dickinson recommended a general tax power. Congress requisitioned monies from each state for a common treasury, leaving each state to raise its share by taxation. Congress had exclusive powers over war and peace, armies and navies, foreign affairs, the decision of disputes between states, admiralty and prize courts, the coinage of money and its value, borrowing money on the credit of the United States, Indian affairs, the western boundaries of the states claiming lands to the Pacific, the acquisition of new territory and the creation of new states, standards of weights and measures, and the post office. Dickinson also recommended a "council of state" or permanent executive agency that would enforce congressional measures and administer financial, diplomatic, and military matters. Dickinson proposed many limitations on state power, mainly to secure effective control over matters delegated to Congress. The states could not, for example, levy IM-POSTS or duties that violated treaties of the United States. Even the sovereign power of the states over their internal concerns was limited by the qualification in Article III, the crux of the Dickinson draft: "Each colony [Dickinson always referred to "colony" and not "state"] shall retain and enjoy as much of its present Laws, Rights and Customs, as it may think fit, and reserves to itself the sole and exclusive Regulation and Government of its internal police, in all matters that shall not interfere with the Articles of Confederation." Clearly Dickinson envisioned a confederation in which the states did not master the central government.

Nationalists who supported the Dickinson draft in Congress argued, as did JOHN ADAMS, that the purpose of the confederation was to meld the states into "one common mass. We shall no longer retain our separate individuality" on matters delegated to Congress. The four New England states had the same relation to Congress that "four counties bore to a single state," Adams declared. The states could build roads and enact poor laws but "they have no right to touch upon continental subjects." JAMES WILSON, another centralist, contended that the Congress should represent all the people, not the states, because "As to those matters which are referred to Congress, we are not so many states, we are one large state." Few Congressmen were nationalists, however, and few nationalists were consistent. Congressmen from Virginia, the largest state, rejected state equality in favor of proportional representation in Congress with each delegate voting; but because Virginia claimed a western boundary on the Pacific, it rejected the nationalist contention that Congress had succeeded to British SOVER-

EIGNTY with respect to the West and should govern it for the benefit of all. Congressmen from Maryland, a small state without western claims, adamantly held to that nationalist position but argued for state equality—one state, one vote—on the issue of representation. How requisitions should be determined also provoked dissension based on little principle other than self-interest.

The disputes over representation, western lands, and the basis for requisitions deadlocked the Congress in 1776. The next year, however, state supremacists who feared centralization won a series of victories that decisively altered the character of the confederation proposed by Dickinson and championed by Franklin, Adams, and Wilson. Dickinson's Article III was replaced by a declaration that "Each State retains its sovereignty, freedom, and independence, and every power, jurisdiction, and right, which is not by this confederation expressly delegated to the United States, in Congress assembled." Thus, colonial control over internal police became state sovereignty over all reserved powers, and the central government received only "expressly delegated" powers rather than implied powers to control even internal police involving matters of continental concern. State supremacists also restricted the power of Congress to make commercial treaties: no treaty could prohibit imports or exports, and no treaty could prevent a state from imposing retaliatory imposts. The revised Articles also scrapped Dickinson's executive branch, accepted the state sovereignty principle that each state cast an equal vote, modified Congress's judicial authority to decide all intercolonial disputes, and denied the power of Congress to fix the western boundaries of states.

Maryland, however, refused to accept the decision on the boundary issue. Although Congress completed the Articles in November 1777, unanimous ratification by state legislatures came hard. By the beginning of 1779, however, Maryland stood alone, the only state that had not ratified, and Maryland was unmovable. As unanimity was necessary, Maryland had the advantage as well as a great cause, the creation of a national domain. In 1780 New York and Connecticut ceded their western lands to the United States. Congress then adopted a report recommending the cession of western claims by other states, and in October 1780, Congress yielded to Maryland by resolving that ceded lands should be disposed of for the common benefit of the United States and be formed into "republican states, which shall become members of the federal union" on equal terms with the original states. Virgin-

ia's acceptance in January 1781 was decisive. Maryland ratified.

When Congress had submitted the Articles for ratification its accompanying letter accurately stated that its plan was the best possible under the circumstances; combining "in one general system" the conflicting interests of "a continent divided into so many sovereign . . . communities" was a "difficulty." The Articles were the product of the American Revolution and constituted an extraordinary achievement. Congress had framed the first written constitution that established a federal system of government in which the sovereign powers were distributed between the central and local governments. Those powers that unquestionably belonged to Parliament were delegated to the United States. Under the Articles Congress possessed neither tax nor commerce powers, the two powers that Americans in the final stages of the controversy with Britain refused to recognize in Parliament. Americans were fighting largely because a central government claimed those powers, which Americans demanded for their provincial legislatures. Given the widespread identification of liberty with local autonomy, the commitment to limited government, and the hostility to centralization, the states yielded as much as could be expected at the time. Because Congress represented the states and the people of the states, to deny Congress the power to tax was not logical, but the opposition to centralized powers of taxation was so fierce that even nationalists supported the requisition system. "It takes time," as JOHN JAY remarked, "to make sovereigns of subjects."

The sovereignty claimed by the states existed—within a limited sphere of authority. The Articles made the United States sovereign, too, within its sphere of authority: it possessed "sole and exclusive" power over fundamental matters such as foreign affairs, war and peace, western lands, and Indian affairs. The reservation of some sovereign powers in the states meant the surrender of other sovereign powers to the central government. Americans believed that sovereignty was divisible and divided it. In part, FEDERALISM is a system of divided sovereign powers. The Articles had many defects, the greatest of which was that the United States acted on the states rather than the people and had no way of making the states or anyone but soldiers obey. The failure to create executive and judicial branches, the requirement for unanimity for amendments, and the refusal to concede to Congress what had been denied to Parliament resulted in the eventual breakdown of the Articles. They were, nevertheless, a necessary stage in the evolution of the Constitution of 1787 and contained many provisions that were carried over into that document. (See CONSTITUTIONAL HISTORY, 1776–1789.)

LEONARD W. LEVY

Bibliography

HENDERSON, H. JAMES 1974 *Party Politics in the Continental Congress.* New York: McGraw-Hill.
JENSEN, MERRILL 1963(1940) *Articles of Confederation: An Interpretation of the Social-Constitutional History of the American Revolution.* Madison: University of Wisconsin Press.
RAKOVE, JACK N. 1979 *The Beginnings of National Politics: An Interpretive History of the Continental Congress.* New York: Knopf.

ARTICLES OF IMPEACHMENT OF ANDREW JOHNSON
(1868)

Eleven articles of IMPEACHMENT of President ANDREW JOHNSON were voted by the House of Representatives in March 1868. The impeachment was largely a product of partisan dissatisfaction with Johnson's approach to reconstruction of the South.

Nine of the articles concerned Johnson's attempt to remove Secretary of War EDWIN M. STANTON, supposedly in defiance of the TENURE OF OFFICE ACT of 1867—although, by its letter, the act did not apply to Stanton, who had been appointed by ABRAHAM LINCOLN. The charges ranged from simple violation of the act to conspiracy to seize the property of the War Department and to gain control over its expenditures. However far-fetched, each of the nine articles alleged a specific illegal or criminal act.

The last two articles were overtly political and reflected a different notion of the concept of impeachable offense. Based on accounts of Johnson's speeches, the articles charged that he ridiculed and abused Congress and had questioned the constitutional legitimacy of the Thirty-Ninth Congress.

The impeachment was tried to the Senate which, in May 1868, failed by one vote to give a two-thirds vote for conviction of any of the articles, and so acquitted Johnson.

DENNIS J. MAHONEY

Bibliography

BENEDICT, MICHAEL LES 1973 *The Impeachment and Trial of Andrew Johnson.* New York: W. W. Norton.

ARTICLES OF IMPEACHMENT OF RICHARD M. NIXON
(1974)

Three articles of IMPEACHMENT of President RICHARD M. NIXON were voted by the Committee on the Judiciary of the House of Representatives between July 27 and July 30, 1974. The vote on the articles followed an extended investigation of the so-called WATERGATE affair, the President's knowledge of an involvement in that affair, and a prolonged controversy concerning what constitutes an "impeachable offense." All three articles, as voted, had reference to Watergate, and all charged breach of the oath of office.

The first article charged Nixon with having "prevented, obstructed, and impeded the administration of justice" by withholding evidence and participating in the "cover-up" of the Watergate affair. The nine specifications included making false statements to investigators, approving of others giving false testimony, condoning the payment of "hush money" to potential witnesses, and interfering with the conduct of the investigation.

The second article charged Nixon with misusing the powers of his office and with "repeated conduct violating the constitutional rights of citizens." Five specifications included misusing the Internal Revenue Service, Federal Bureau of Investigation, and Central Intelligence Agency; attempting to prejudice the right to a FAIR TRIAL (of one Daniel Ellsberg); and failing to act against subordinates who engaged in illegal activities.

The third article charged Nixon with disobeying subpoenas issued by the committee itself in the course of its investigation. This article was approved only narrowly since some committee members argued that a good faith assertion of EXECUTIVE PRIVILEGE was not a constitutionally impeachable offense. Two other articles were defeated in the committee vote.

The articles of impeachment never came to a vote in the full House of Representatives. On August 9, 1974, facing the virtual certainty of impeachment and of conviction by the Senate, Richard M. Nixon became the first president ever to resign.

DENNIS J. MAHONEY

Bibliography

UNITED STATES HOUSE OF REPRESENTATIVES, COMMITTEE ON THE JUDICIARY 1974 *Impeachment of Richard Nixon, President of the United States.* Washington, D.C.: Government Printing Office.

ARVER v. UNITED STATES

See: Selective Draft Cases

ASH, UNITED STATES v.
413 U.S. 300 (1973)

The RIGHT TO COUNSEL did not apply when the prosecutor showed eyewitnesses to a crime an array of photographs, including that of the indicted accused. The photographic showing was merely a part of the prosecutor's trial preparation (that is, done in order to refresh recollection) and neither the defendant's nor his lawyer's presence was constitutionally required.

BARBARA ALLEN BABCOCK

ASHTON v. CAMERON COUNTY WATER IMPROVEMENT DISTRICT
298 U.S. 513 (1936)

This is one of the several cases of the period whose decision gave the impression that the United States was constitutionally incapable of combating the Great Depression. Over 2,000 governmental units ranging from big cities to small school districts had defaulted, and the CONTRACT CLAUSE prevented the states from relieving their subdivisions. Congress, responding to pressure from states and creditors, passed the Municipal Bankruptcy Act of 1934, authorizing state subdivisions to apply to federal bankruptcy courts to get their debts scaled down. In accordance with the statute, a Texas water district, supported by state law, applied for a bankruptcy plan that would make possible a final settlement of fifty cents on the dollar, the payment financed by a federal loan. The federal bankruptcy court controlled the bankruptcy plan, which could not be enforced unless approved by creditors holding at least two-thirds of the debt, as required by the statute.

The Supreme Court held the Municipal Bankruptcy Act to be an unconstitutional exercise of Congress's delegated BANKRUPTCY POWER. For a five-member majority, Justice JAMES C. MCREYNOLDS declared that that power was subject to state sovereignty, which cannot be surrendered or impaired by legislation. Congress had violated the TENTH AMENDMENT by infringing on state control over the fiscal affairs of state subdivisions. That the act required state consent, here eagerly given, was irrelevant to the Court. Thus the Court protected the states and even creditors against their will. Justice BENJAMIN N. CARDOZO, for the dissenters, characterizing the majority opinion as "divorced from the realities of life," argued that Congress had framed the statute with sedulous regard for state sovereignty and the structure of the federal system. The Court retreated in *United States v. Bekins* (1938).

LEONARD W. LEVY

ASHWANDER v. TENNESSEE VALLEY AUTHORITY
297 U.S. 288 (1936)

Ashwander was part of a protracted litigation over the constitutionality of the Tennessee Valley Authority (TVA), a government development corporation established by the New Deal. (See CONSTITUTIONAL HISTORY, 1933–1945; TENNESSEE VALLEY AUTHORITY ACT.) TVA was organized to develop the economy of a river valley by improving navigation and flood control and especially by generating cheap electric power for homes, farms, and industry. In *Ashwander* preferred shareholders in an existing power company sued in federal court to enjoin the company and TVA from carrying out a contract under which TVA would purchase much of the company's property and equipment, and TVA would allocate areas for the sale of power. The plaintiffs attacked the whole TVA program as exceeding the scope of congressional power. The district court granted the INJUNCTION, but the court of appeals reversed, upholding the contract. The Supreme Court, 8–1, affirmed the court of appeals.

Chief Justice CHARLES EVANS HUGHES, for the majority, concluded that Wilson Dam, where TVA was generating power, had been built in 1916 to provide power for national defense needs, including the operation of nitrate plants used in the making of munitions, and to improve navigation—both objectives concededly within the powers of Congress. If excess electricity were generated at the dam, Hughes said, Congress had the power to sell it, as it might sell any other property owned by the United States. Justice JAMES C. MCREYNOLDS, dissenting alone on the constitutional merits, pointed out the transparency of the majority's doctrinal clothing: TVA was in the power-generating business for its own sake, not as an adjunct to some military program long since abandoned.

Justice LOUIS D. BRANDEIS, dissenting in part, agreed with the majority's views on congressional power but argued that the plaintiffs' complaint should have been dismissed for want of STANDING. As preferred shareholders, they could show no injury to themselves from the contract. Brandeis went on, in *Ashwander*'s most famous passages, to discuss a series of "rules" under which the Supreme Court had "avoided passing upon a large part of all the constitutional questions pressed upon it for decision." Some of the "rules" flow from Article III of the Constitution, including the standing requirement Brandeis sought to effectuate in *Ashwander* itself. Others, however, express policies of preference for nonconstitutional grounds for decision, for formulating the narrowest possible constitutional grounds, for construing federal statutes to avoid constitutional questions, and the like.

Some modern commentators have read the Brandeis opinion in *Ashwander* to stand for a broad policy of judicial discretion to avoid deciding cases that might place the Court in awkward political positions. Brandeis himself, a stickler for principled application of the Court's jurisdictional requirements, surely had no such generalized discretion in mind. Nonetheless, some of his successors have found it convenient to cite his comments in *Ashwander* in support of far less principled avoidance techniques. (See POE V. ULLMAN, 1961.)

KENNETH L. KARST

ASSISTANCE, WRIT OF

The term "writ of assistance" is applied to several distinct types of legal documents. Of greatest significance to American constitutional history was the writ of assistance issued to customs inspectors by the English Court of the Exchequer authorizing the search of all houses suspected of containing contraband. Such writs were first used no later than 1621, and their form was codified in 1662. They are still used regularly in Britain and in many nations of the British Commonwealth.

In colonial America, writs of assistance were used as GENERAL SEARCH WARRANTS and were authorized by a statute of the British Parliament. In a famous Massachusetts case, PAXTON'S CASE (1761), JAMES OTIS argued that the statute authorizing writs of assistance should be held invalid because it was contrary to MAGNA CARTA and the COMMON LAW; but his argument was rejected. The colonial experience with writs of assistance led to the requirement in the FOURTH AMENDMENT that SEARCH WARRANTS particularly describe the place to be searched and the object of the search.

WILLIAM J. CUDDIHY

Bibliography
SMITH, M. H.   1978   *The Writs of Assistance Case.* Berkeley: University of California Press.

ASSOCIATED PRESS v. N.L.R.B.

See: Wagner Act Cases

ASSOCIATION, THE

The Continental Association was created by the First Continental Congress on October 18, 1774. It was "a non-importation, non-consumption, and non-exportation agreement" undertaken to obtain redress of American grievances against the British Crown and Parliament. The Articles of Association were signed on October 20 by the representatives of twelve colonies, solemnly binding themselves and their constituents to its terms.

The articles listed the most pressing American grievances (TAXATION WITHOUT REPRESENTATION, extension of admiralty court jurisdiction, denial of TRIAL BY JURY in tax cases), enumerated the measures to be taken (cessation of commercial ties to Britain), prescribed the penalty for noncompliance (a total breaking off of communication with offenders), and established the machinery for enforcement (through committees of correspondence).

The Association was a major step toward the creation of a federal union of American states. It was the first prescriptive act of a national Congress to be binding directly on individuals, and the efforts at enforcement of or compliance with its terms certainly contributed to the formation of a national identity. With but little exaggeration the historian RICHARD HILDRETH wrote: "The signature of the Association may be considered as the commencement of the American union."

DENNIS J. MAHONEY

ATASCADERO STATE HOSPITAL v. SCANLON
473 U.S.   (1985)

The opinions in this case made clear that PENNHURST STATE SCHOOL AND HOSPITAL V. HALDERMAN (1984) was a watershed in the Supreme Court's modern treatment of the ELEVENTH AMENDMENT. By the same 5–4 division as in *Pennhurst*, the Court here held that an individual could not obtain relief against a state agency in federal court for harm caused by the agency's violation of the federal REHABILITATION ACT of 1973. In an opinion by Justice LEWIS F. POWELL, the majority concluded that California had not waived its SOVEREIGN IMMUNITY under that amendment, and that Congress, in the act, had not lifted the state's immunity to suit by individual plaintiffs. The latter point carried the Court's restrictive reading of the Eleventh Amendment a step beyond even the *Pennhurst* opinion: a congressional purpose to lift state immunity, the majority said, cannot be found by implication from a statute's purposes, but only in an explicit statement in the statute itself.

The four dissenters, speaking primarily through Justice WILLIAM J. BRENNAN, made a vigorous and broad-ranging attack on the majority's recent approach to Eleventh Amendment issues. Justice Brennan, as before, accused the majority of misconceiving the purposes of the Framers in writing Article III, misreading the text and the purposes of the Eleventh Amendment, and generally twisting the fundamental premises of American FEDERALISM to "put the federal judiciary in the unseemly position of exempting the states from compliance with laws that bind every other legal actor in our nation."

It seems clear that the shock of *Pennhurst* persuaded some of the *Scanlon* dissenters to join Justice Brennan's campaign for a fundamental reorientation of Eleventh Amendment jurisprudence. Four Justices agreed that the recent majority's doctrine "intrudes on the ideal of liberty under law by protecting the States from the consequences of their illegal conduct."

KENNETH L. KARST

ATOMIC ENERGY ACT
68 Stat 919 (1954)

The initial Atomic Energy Act (1946) had created an independent five-person Atomic Energy Commission (AEC) to exercise complete civilian control over the production of atomic energy and associated research programs. By the early 1950s, criticism of the statute mounted because it limited the role of private enterprise in the atomic energy field, overemphasized military phases, and created unwarranted secrecy, precluding the dissemination of technical information to other nations.

The 1954 Amendment addressed these concerns. Its overriding policy objective, strongly supported by President DWIGHT D. EISENHOWER, was to facilitate the commercial development and exploitation of nuclear power by private industry. The key provisions were: private ownership of nuclear facilities; private use of fissionable material (though the AEC still retained title, until revision in 1964); liberalized patenting rights; industrial access to needed technical information; and a program for international cooperation in developing peaceful applications of nuclear energy, particularly nuclear power. The principal focus of the act was to make the nuclear industry economically independent and internally competitive.

Regulatory provisions of the 1954 act authorized the AEC to license facilities and operators producing or using radioactive materials. This licensing process, subject to judicial review by the terms of the act, was to protect the public health, safety, life, and property. Little guidance or standards for licensure was provided, and the question of safety hazards from nuclear technology was not considered. Thus the AEC's administration of the act was slowly hammered out through the regulatory process; that situation continued after the Commission was folded into the Department of Energy in 1974.

PAUL L. MURPHY

Bibliography
ROLPH, ELIZABETH S. 1979 *Nuclear Power and the Public Safety.* Lexington, Mass.: Lexington Books.

ATTAINDER, BILL OF

See: Bill of Attainder

ATTAINDER OF TREASON

Upon conviction of and sentencing for TREASON, a person is attainted: he loses all claim to the protection of the law. Under English law attainder of treason worked "corruption of blood," depriving the traitor's descendants of the right to inherit property from or through him. The second clause of Article III, section 2, of the Constitution virtually abolishes attainder of treason. Because of that clause, ABRAHAM LINCOLN insisted that the forfeiture of ex-Confederates' property under the CONFISCATION ACT of 1862 be only for the lifetime of the owner. Construing the act and the constitutional provision in *Wallach v. Van Riswick* (1872), the Supreme Court held that the limitation on attainder of treason was solely for the benefit of the heirs.

DENNIS J. MAHONEY

ATTORNEY GENERAL AND DEPARTMENT OF JUSTICE

The job of attorney general for the United States, as it was then called, was created by the JUDICIARY ACT OF 1789. The last sentence of that remarkable statute called for the appointment (presumably by the President) of "a meet person, learned in the law, . . . whose duty it shall be to prosecute and conduct all suits in the Supreme Court in which the United States shall be concerned, and to give his advice and opinion upon questions of law when required by the President of the United States, or when requested by the heads of any of the departments, touching any matters that may concern their departments, and [who] shall receive such compensation for his services as shall by law be provided." The first attorney general was EDMUND RANDOLPH, and his salary was $1,500. He had no office or staff provided by his government.

There have been seventy-three attorneys general between Randolph's tenure and that of William French Smith (1981–1985), counting JOHN J. CRITTENDEN twice. From the beginning they have been members of the President's cabinet—fourth in rank after the secretaries of state, treasury, and war (now defense). Since 1870 the attorney general has also been head of the Department of Justice. For the most part, the attorneys general have been citizens of outstanding achievement and public service, although not necessarily of extraordinary professional and intellectual ability; the latter qualities have traditionally been associated with the SOLICITOR GENERAL. Nine attorneys general subsequently sat on the Supreme Court of the United States, two as Chief Justice (ROGER B. TANEY, 1831–1833, and HARLAN F. STONE, 1924–1925); three were nominated to that bench but never confirmed; one was confirmed but never took his seat (EDWIN M. STANTON, 1860–1861); and at least two turned down nominations to the Court (Charles Lee, 1795–1801, as Chief Justice, and LEVI LINCOLN, 1801–1805). Only three attorneys general have had their careers seriously eroded by personal and professional misconduct (Harry M. Daugherty, 1921–1924; John N. Mitchell, 1969–1972; and Richard G. Kleindienst, 1972–1974). Of these, Daugherty was acquitted of charges of attempting to defraud the United States in the Teapot Dome scandal, Mitchell served a prison term for a conspiracy to obstruct justice in connection with the WATERGATE affair, and Kleindienst entered a plea bargain of guilty to a MISDEMEANOR involving his veracity in congressional testimony. The Department of Justice grew with government

after 1870, but at an increasingly accelerated rate, expanding enormously in the 1970s and early 1980s. The budget of the Department for fiscal year 1984 was over three billion dollars; it had increased by almost fifty percent since the beginning of 1981. In addition to the attorney general, top officials now include one deputy attorney general, five deputy associate attorneys general, one associate attorney general, five deputy associate attorneys general, the solicitor general, ten assistant attorneys general, and ninety-four United States attorneys (with coordinate United States marshals), all appointed by the President and all bearing responsibility of some sort in the litigation and advice-giving functions of the Department. These officers are backed by the vast investigative resources of the Federal Bureau of Investigation (FBI). In addition, the Department runs the Immigration and Naturalization Service, the Federal Bureau of Prisons, the Drug Enforcement Agency, and various research and public policy arms.

Public perception of the department as a major instrument of public policy, with a significant effect on the quality of American society, started roughly with the JOHN F. KENNEDY administration in the 1960s, when ROBERT F. KENNEDY (1961–1964) was appointed attorney general by his brother. Before that, the department mostly functioned as a professional law office charged with enforcing the few federal criminal statutes that existed, representing the government in other litigation, and giving advice to the President, especially on questions requiring construction of the Constitution. There had been sporadic periods, however, during which the department temporarily emerged as an important arm of federal government.

The department was established by Congress primarily as the instrument of government to work with the FREEDMEN'S BUREAU in implementing the CIVIL RIGHTS statutes that accompanied the passage of the Civil War amendments. The first attorneys general to run the Department—Amos T. Akerman (1870–1872) and George Henry Williams (1872–1875)—were accordingly deeply engaged in the temporary and unsuccessful efforts then to protect the ideal of racial equality through law. Charles J. Bonaparte (1906–1909), both under President THEODORE ROOSEVELT and in his professional life after that, was also active in the cause of racial justice, using in part the technique of AMICUS CURIAE briefs. Bonaparte also actively enforced the SHERMAN ANTITRUST ACT of 1890, following the traditions of his immediate predecessors, PHILANDER C. KNOX (1901–1904) and WILLIAM H. MOODY (1904–1906). On the darker side, A. MITCH-

ELL PALMER (1919–1921) brought the department into public controversy in the stunning PALMER RAIDS of 1919, in which more than 5,000 persons were taken into custody, their names apparently culled from lists of over 60,000 put together by the agency that became the FBI. No federal criminal charges were lodged against any of them, proposals for federal laws against peacetime SEDITION having failed to pass Congress, and the affair remains a moment of disgrace in the department's history.

The inescapable intertwining of law enforcement priorities and public policy has caused debate over the qualifications that attorneys general should meet. On the one hand, there is the tradition of the even-handed, objective, nonpolitical rule of law, implemented by an impartial Department of Justice. The department's own slogan exemplifies this strand of its work: "The United States wins its case whenever justice is done one of its citizens in the courts." Yet it is not possible to run the department without making choices that have wide public impact; not surprisingly, those choices reflect the political goals of the President. Since the mid-1950s the department's political role has been especially visible in civil rights matters, but it has been marked in antitrust policy, for example, since the passage of the Sherman Act of 1890. Even the work of the Lands Division, which is now also responsible for laws affecting ENVIRONMENTAL REGULATION and the use of natural resources, has strong political effects. The Criminal Division has devoted major energies to the control of organized crime as the result of new policy initiatives of the Kennedy administration in the early 1960s. The FBI, since the death of J. EDGAR HOOVER, has changed not only its direction—away from a concentration on perceived threats to internal security, for one part, and automobile thefts, for another—but also its techniques and training programs, by the initiation of elaborate undercover investigations called "scams."

In the mid-1970s, White House manipulation of the department during the Watergate scandal led Senator Sam J. Ervin of North Carolina seriously to examine, in a series of hearings, the possibility of separating the Department of Justice from presidential control. There were substantial constitutional objections to his plan, stemming from the undoubted constitutional power of the President to run the executive branch with people of his own choosing, at least in policymaking positions. The proposed legislation failed, partly for that reason, and partly because of principled opposition from many lawyers and former government officials who believed it not only inevitable but also appropriate that law enforcement priorities and policies

be part of a presidential candidate's platform and a presidential program. No one, however, supported a presidential right to corruption, and Congress did create the office of a special prosecutor to be filled from time to time by appointment triggered by nonfrivolous charges against any presidential appointee or personal staff member. Such a special prosecutor is, by law, immunized against political accountability to the attorney general or the White House.

The creation of a statutory special prosecutor, in place of the ad hoc use of such a position at the time of Teapot Dome and Watergate, did not, of course, end discussion of the qualifications required of an attorney general. Robert F. Kennedy (1961–1964), John N. Mitchell (1969–1972), and Edwin Meese (1985–   ) had been campaign managers for the Presidents who appointed them, and Herbert Brownell (1953–1957), Griffin B. Bell (1977–1979), and William French Smith (1981–1985) were closely associated with their Presidents' political careers. The argument that close political associates should be disqualified from appointment as the nation's chief law enforcement officer is not borne out by the public careers of these men. Only one, Mitchell, was connected with corruption or scandal. Robert Kennedy, professionally the least qualified of all at the time of his appointment, was a spectacularly successful leader of the department; his tenure was marked by policy innovation and attention to career professionals, and scrupulously devoid of political favoritism. In short, it is difficult to generalize, from the record, on what background is best. A full commitment to the rule of law, an ability to command professional respect, the administrative skill to run a large and diverse bureaucracy, a constitutional regard for an independent judiciary, and the political habit of appropriate deference to the place of Congress in the constitutional scheme are the traits that the Senate must look for in giving its advice and consent. None of these qualifications is necessarily associated with any particular background.

There is implicit in the periodic debate about what qualifications are needed for an attorney general an ambivalence about the identification of his (or her) client. The legal profession has come to realize that the client–lawyer relationship imagined in lawyers' codes of professional responsibility does not fit the corporate-bureaucratic world. Lawyers who are used to concern about whether they represent the managers of a corporation, or some abstract corporate entity, or other financial interests find the problem even more acute in government service. The attorney general is the lawyer for the President, but he is also the lawyer for the United States, which includes the

Congress, and which is governed by a Constitution. The conflicts inherent in this multifaceted responsibility have been reflected, for example, in the department's use of WIRETAPPING and electronic surveillance. Both originated with ambiguous presidential approval, though neither was authorized by Congress nor controlled by explicit legislation. When the Supreme Court applied the exclusionary rule to surveillance by TRESPASS, and then to the product of taps, the response of the department was to confine the use of those devices to investigative work; they were not to be used as EVIDENCE in court. The combining of constitutional constraints on law enforcement behavior, legislative policy, and presidential direction did not take place until decades after the process started. Similar problems of ambiguity of duty are reflected whenever the Congress enacts legislation, or the Supreme Court announces constitutional rules, that the President wants to avoid.

The emergence, in the years since mid-century, of the federal role in ending racial discrimination is largely a product of Justice Department policymaking, mostly with, but sometimes ahead of, the approval of the President. Until recently, the department was consistently in advance of congressional policy. In 1939, without any statutory authority, Attorney General FRANK MURPHY (1939–1940) set up a Civil Rights Section in the Criminal Division to enforce the criminal code's civil rights provisions, which had not been used for years. For the first time, the FBI was thereby drawn, against its will, into the investigation of civil rights violations, particularly in police brutality cases. The section had no authority in civil matters, but its creation immediately created a focus inside the executive branch for the emerging civil rights constituency. The resulting tie between Justice Department policy and the civil rights movement lasted, with some erosion in the early 1970s, until 1981.

In 1948, under TOM C. CLARK (1945–1949), the department initiated a consistent practice of supporting civil rights groups through amicus curiae briefs in private litigation in the Supreme Court. The case was SHELLEY V. KRAEMER (1948), which held racially RESTRICTIVE COVENANTS to be unenforceable in state courts. The solicitor general filed important briefs thereafter in BROWN V. BOARD OF EDUCATION (1954) and its progeny, even though it was far from clear that President DWIGHT D. EISENHOWER supported the positions taken, and it was certain that a majority of Congress did not. In 1960 the department went a step further, although in a technically ambiguous fashion, when it urged reversal in one of the first SIT-IN cases to reach the Court, BOYNTON V. VIRGINIA

(1960). A total of twenty-five amicus curiae briefs were filed between 1955 and 1961. In the meantime, the department took the lead in persuading Congress to give it limited litigation authority in VOTING RIGHTS cases, through the CIVIL RIGHTS ACTS of 1957 and 1960. It seems clear that the 1957 statute at least was drafted and steered through the Congress without the participation, and perhaps without the full understanding, of the President.

Under Robert Kennedy (1961–1964), the department increased its activity in the civil rights field, filing nine amicus curiae briefs in the Supreme Court in 1961, nineteen in 1962, and twenty-eight in 1963. The department at the same time drastically increased not only its own litigation in the lower federal courts in voting rights cases but also its intervention as a party in private suits. In one unusual case, despite the general duty of the attorney general to defend federal legislation, the department attacked the constitutionality of a federal statute that contemplated racially separate hospitals. Civil Rights Division lawyers effectively took over the litigation in crucial cases involving schools in New Orleans, Birmingham, and Montgomery; the University of Mississippi at Oxford in 1962; and the University of Alabama in Huntsville and Tuscaloosa in 1963. They also initiated an INJUNCTION suit to protect the Freedom Riders in 1961, and, following that incident, sought to persuade the Interstate Commerce Commission to require the immediate DESEGREGATION of all interstate bus and rail facilities. All these actions were taken with the approval of the President, but despite congressional refusal to authorize Department of Justice initiatives outside the voting area.

The comprehensive CIVIL RIGHTS ACT OF 1964 finally legitimated the kind of litigating activism the department had undertaken, and the VOTING RIGHTS ACT OF 1965 authorized massive federal intervention, outside the judicial system, into areas where racial discrimination in registration or voting persisted. In the meantime, the department was forced, on its own, to seek to protect the physical security of civil rights workers operating in severely hostile territories. The problem was never quite solved. United States marshals and special temporary deputies volunteering from other branches of the department, especially the Immigration and Naturalization Service, and on one occasion the Bureau of Prisons, served at the direction of the attorney general as ad hoc peace-keeping forces. The FBI, a natural source of manpower for such purposes, never let its people be used for police duty. Several times, starting with Little Rock in 1957, troops were required, with the authorization of the President. At such moments, the department was converted from a law office to a crisis-management center, with consequences for its public responsibility that still persist.

If the Department of Justice is free to participate actively in promoting one direction in the formulation of government policy, and of constitutional rule-making in the courts, it can also undertake to move in the opposite direction. Starting in 1981, the department did just that. In the area of civil rights, it opposed positions previously advocated by the government in school, employment, and voting rights matters, both in its own litigation and through amicus curiae briefs. The civil rights organizations thus found themselves in legal combat with their national government. Further, the department moved far outside the scope of its mandated law enforcement function, filing briefs in constitutional litigation opposing assertions by private citizens of their RIGHT OF PRIVACY in abortion decisions in one line of cases, for example, and their rights under the religion clause of the FIRST AMENDMENT in another. The department's earlier role in civil rights matters had been different, because it had reflected not only the policies of several administrations but also the will of the nation as expressed in the RULE OF LAW, under the Reconstruction amendments, especially the EQUAL PROTECTION clause.

The department's new social mission, announced as official policy by Attorney General Smith in a speech in 1981, fortified the Senate in its questioning of what kind of attorney general is appropriate for a Department of Justice possessing the enormous power it now does. Whether the department should be confined to a traditional role of impartial law enforcement or should continue to press for shifts in social and legal policy is an issue that may never be cleanly and finally resolved. Yet the issue is important in a nation where, in the oft-quoted words of ALEXIS DE TOCQUEVILLE, "scarcely any political question arises . . . that is not resolved, sooner or later, into a judicial question."

BURKE MARSHALL

Bibliography

BIDDLE, FRANCIS BEVERLEY 1962 In Brief Authority. Garden City, N.Y.: Doubleday.
CARR, ROBERT K. (1947)1964 Federal Protection of Civil Rights. Ithaca, N.Y.: Cornell University Press.
CUMMINGS, HOMER STILLE and McFARLAND, CARL 1937 Federal Justice. New York: Macmillan.
DEPARTMENT OF JUSTICE 1980 Attorney General of the United States. Washington, D.C.: Department of Justice.
HUSTON, LUTHER A. 1968 The Department of Justice. New York: Praeger.
HUSTON, LUTHER A., MILLER, ARTHUR SELWYN, KRISLOV, SAMUEL, and DIXON, ROBERT G., JR. 1968 Roles of the Attorney General of the United States. Washington, D.C.: American Enterprise Institute for Public Policy Research.
NAVASKY, VICTOR S. 1971 Kennedy Justice. New York: Atheneum.

ATTORNEY GENERAL'S LIST

President HARRY S. TRUMAN's Executive Order 9835 inaugurated a comprehensive investigation of all federal employees and made any negative information a potential basis for a security dismissal. A list of subversive organizations was to be prepared by the attorney general, and membership in any listed group was a ground for REASONABLE DOUBT as to an employee's loyalty. The only guidelines the order provided were that any designated organization must be "totalitarian, Fascist, Communist, or subversive," or one "approving the commission of acts of force or violence to deny to others their constitutional rights." During the first year under the order, the attorney general so designated 123 organizations. Over time, and frequently as a result of protests, certain organizations were deleted; new ones were also added. By November 1950, 197 organizations had been so listed, eleven of which were labeled subversive, twelve as seeking to overthrow the government by unconstitutional means, and 132 as communist or communist front.

Critics questioned the constitutionality of the list's compilation and use, on FIRST AMENDMENT grounds, as an "executive BILL OF ATTAINDER" and as involving unfair procedures violating the DUE PROCESS CLAUSE of the Fifth Amendment. The Supreme Court in JOINT ANTI-FASCIST REFUGEE COMMITTEE V. McGRATH (1951) raised serious questions regarding the fairness of the compilation procedure, and demands grew for suitable hearings to be granted organizations before their inclusion. No procedural changes were instituted in the Truman years, however, and the list continued to be used under the Eisenhower loyalty program. (See LOYALTY-SECURITY PROGRAMS.)

PAUL L. MURPHY

Bibliography

BONTECOU, ELEANOR 1953 The Federal Loyalty-Security Program. Ithaca, N.Y.: Cornell University Press.

AUTOMOBILE SEARCH

Automobile searches constitute a recognized exception to the FOURTH AMENDMENT's requirement of a SEARCH WARRANT. When police have PROBABLE

CAUSE to believe an automobile is transporting contraband, they may, under CARROLL V. UNITED STATES (1925) and BRINEGAR V. UNITED STATES (1941), conduct a WARRANTLESS SEARCH of the vehicle lest it disappear before a warrant can be obtained. Under CHAMBERS V. MARONEY (1970) the search may be delayed until the vehicle has been removed to a police station, though the emergency that attends a search on the road has dissipated. The rules governing automobile searches apply also to mobile homes, according to *California v. Carney* (1985).

Early cases stressed the vehicle's mobility as justification for a warrantless search, but most recent cases have also emphasized an individual's reduced expectation of privacy in an automobile. In contrast to a dwelling, an automobile usually does not serve as a repository of one's belongings; its interior is plainly visible from the outside; and it is commonly stopped by police enforcing inspection and licensing laws. Nonetheless, as the court held in COOLIDGE V. NEW HAMPSHIRE (1971), a car parked on private property may not be searched without a warrant.

Systematic stopping of automobiles at checkpoints for license and registration checks is permitted, but under the Court's decision in *Delaware v. Prouse* (1979), their random stopping is forbidden absent suspicious circumstances. And under *Opperman v. South Dakota* (1976) a lawfully impounded vehicle may be subjected to a warrantless inventory search to safeguard the owner's possessions and protect police from false property claims.

The scope of the warrantless automobile search is as broad as one a magistrate could authorize with a warrant. As the Court held in UNITED STATES V. ROSS (1982), the search may encompass "every part of the vehicle that might contain the object of the search," including the trunk, glove compartment, and closed containers. Furthermore, the Court has applied lenient standards in automobile search cases as to the EVIDENCE needed to establish probable cause. Justice JOHN MARSHALL HARLAN, dissenting in UNITED STATES V. HARRIS (1971), accurately remarked that the problem of automobile searches "has typically been treated as *sui generis* by this Court."

JACOB W. LANDYNSKI

Bibliography

LAFAVE, WAYNE R. 1978 *Search and Seizure: A Treatise on the Fourth Amendment,* Vol. 2:508–544, 565–581. St. Paul, Minn.: West Publishing Co.
LANDYNSKI, JACOB W. 1971 The Supreme Court's Search for Fourth Amendment Standards: The Warrantless Search. *Connecticut Bar Journal* 45:30–39.

AVERY v. MIDLAND COUNTY
390 U.S. 474 (1968)

In this case, the Supreme Court held that the ONE PERSON, ONE VOTE rule required equal districts in a Texas county commissioners' court election. The decision, in effect, extended the rule's sway from the fifty states to such of the 81,304 units of government as possessed "general responsibility and power for local affairs." Justices JOHN M. HARLAN, ABE FORTAS, and POTTER STEWART dissented, arguing that the Court had overreached its APPELLATE JURISDICTION; that a rigidly uniform one person, one vote rule ignored the special needs functions of most local governments; and that it would discourage joint activity by metropolitan units, thereby undermining the practical benefits of state-level reapportionment.

WARD E. Y. ELLIOTT

B

BACKUS, ISAAC
(1724–1806)

A Baptist minister in Massachusetts from 1756, Isaac Backus gained increasing recognition as an agent, chief spokesman, and campaigner for RELIGIOUS LIBERTY for his New England co-religionists, who were harassed by hostile local officials' narrow interpretation and restrictive implementation of laws exempting Baptists from contributing to the support of Congregational churches. In pamphlets and newspapers, in an appearance before the Massachusetts delegation to the First Continental Congress, and in promoting civil disobedience by encouraging Baptists not to comply with statutes dealing with support of churches, he struggled unsuccessfully to abolish public tax support for religion.

More pietist than civil libertarian, Backus sought religious freedom primarily to prevent state interference with the church. He supported his arguments by citing the Massachusetts Charter's grant of religious liberty to all Protestants and by pointing up the contrast between local oppression of Baptists and New Englanders' charges of English tyranny. By 1780, however, he had come to affirm religious liberty as a NATURAL RIGHT.

As a delegate to the Massachusetts ratifying convention, Backus supported the federal Constitution, convinced that its prohibition against tests precluded any ESTABLISHMENT OF RELIGION. He showed little or no interest in the passage of the FIRST AMENDMENT. Backus equated religious liberty almost entirely with voluntary choice of churches and voluntary support of ministers. He perceived America as a Christian country, did not object to Sabbath laws or to public days of prayer, and approved a Massachusetts law requiring legislators to profess Christianity. Such views typified contemporary evangelical opinion.

THOMAS CURRY

Bibliography

MCLAUGHLIN, WILLIAM G. 1967 *Isaac Backus and the American Pietistic Tradition.* Boston: Little, Brown.
——, ed. 1968 *Isaac Backus on Church, State, and Calvinism—Pamphlets, 1754–1789.* Cambridge, Mass.: Harvard University Press.

BADGES OF SERVITUDE

There was truth in the claim of slavery's defenders that many a northern "wage slave" worked under conditions less favorable than those of his enslaved counterpart down South. The evil of slavery was not primarily its imposition of hard work but its treatment of a person as if he or she were a thing. The laws governing slaves carried out this basic theme by systematically imposing a wide range of legal disabilities on slaves, preventing them not only from entering into the public life of the community (by voting, being members of juries, or speaking in public meetings) but also from owning property, making contracts, or even learning to read and write. All these disabilities were designed not merely to preserve a system of bondage to service, but to serve as badges of servitude, symbolizing the slaves' degraded status. In a moment of racist candor, Chief Justice ROGER B. TANEY extended this view of the stigmatized status of slaves to all black persons, slave or free. His opinion for the Supreme Court in DRED SCOTT V. SANDFORD (1857) spoke of blacks as "a subordinate and inferior class of beings," upon whom had been impressed "deep and enduring marks of inferiority and degradation."

Although slaves were often physically branded, the "marks" of which Taney spoke were metaphorical; they were the aggregate of legal restrictions imposed on slaves. When slavery was abolished by the THIRTEENTH AMENDMENT (1865), those marks did not disappear. The amendment, however, did not stop with the abolition of slavery and involuntary servitude; it also empowered Congress to enforce the abolition. From an early time it was argued that the amendment authorized Congress to enact laws to eradicate not only slavery itself but the "badges of servitude" as well. This view was at first accepted in principle by the Supreme Court, and then rejected in the early twentieth century. However, in JONES V. ALFRED H. MAYER CO. (1968), the Court reverted to the earlier interpretation, concluding that RACIAL DISCRIMINATION was the sort of "badge of servitude" that Congress could prohibit.

In the meanwhile, a parallel doctrinal development has become apparent. The CIVIL RIGHTS ACT OF 1866 and the FOURTEENTH AMENDMENT both recognized the CITIZENSHIP of the freed slaves. Both were designed to end the notion of superior and inferior classes of persons and to replace a system of sociopolitical subordination with the status of equal citizenship. (See EQUAL PROTECTION OF THE LAWS.) Because the principle of equal citizenship protects against the imposition of stigma, it often operates in the same symbolic universe that produced badges of servitude. To give full effect to the symbol and substance of equal citizenship is one of the major challenges of the nation's third century.

KENNETH L. KARST

Bibliography

KINOY, ARTHUR 1967 The Constitutional Right of Negro Freedom. *Rutgers Law Review* 21:387–441.

BAD TENDENCY TEST

In 1920 New York convicted Benjamin Gitlow of violating its statute prohibiting "advocating, advising or teaching the doctrine that organized government should be overthrown by force." Gitlow had published in the journal *Revolutionary Age* a "Left Wing Manifesto," thirty-four pages of Marxist rhetoric calling for class struggle leading to revolution and the dictatorship of the proletariat.

In GITLOW V. NEW YORK (1925) Gitlow's counsel argued in the Supreme Court that since the manifesto contained no direct INCITEMENT to criminal action, Gitlow must have been convicted under the "bad tendency test." That test was borrowed from the eighteenth-century English law of SEDITIOUS LIBEL which made criticism of government criminal because such criticism might tend to contribute to government's eventual collapse.

This bad tendency test ran counter to the CLEAR AND PRESENT DANGER test of SCHENCK V. UNITED STATES (1919). In *Gitlow* Justice EDWARD SANFORD virtually adopted the bad tendency test for instances in which a legislature had decided that a particular variety of speech created a sufficient danger. Even though there was no evidence of any effect resulting from the Manifesto's publication, the Court stressed that its language constituted advocacy of

mass action which shall progressively foment industrial disturbances, and, through . . . mass action, overthrow . . . government. . . . The immediate danger is none the less real and substantial because the effect of a given utterance cannot be accurately foreseen. . . . A single revolutionary spark may kindle a fire that, smoldering for a time, may burst into a sweeping and destructive conflagration. . . . [The State] cannot reasonably be required to defer the adoption of measures for its own peace and safety until the revolutionary utterances lead to . . . imminent and immediate danger of its own destruction.

Justices OLIVER WENDELL HOLMES and LOUIS D. BRANDEIS dissented in *Gitlow*, invoking the clear and present danger test. When that test came to dominate the Court's FIRST AMENDMENT opinions in the 1930s and early 1940s, the bad tendency test seemed to be overthrown.

Nevertheless much of Sanford's approach survived. Judge LEARNED HAND's "discounting formula" as adopted in DENNIS V. UNITED STATES (1951) allows speech to be suppressed "where the gravity of the evil, discounted by its improbability" justifies suppression. As *Dennis* itself illustrates, if the danger is painted as sufficiently grave, speech may be suppressed even if there is a very low probability that the evil will occur or that the particular speech in question will contribute to that occurrence. In *Dennis* the Court replaced the present danger test with the requirement that where an organized subversive group exists, the group intends to bring about overthrow "as speedily as the circumstances would permit." Such an approach echoed Sanford's plea that the government need not wait until the danger of revolution is imminent.

MARTIN SHAPIRO

(SEE ALSO: *Subversive Activities and the Constitution; Freedom of Speech.*)

Bibliography

CHAFEE, ZECHARIAH, JR. (1941)1969 *Free Speech in the United States.* New York: Atheneum.

LINDE, HANS 1970 "Clear and Present Danger" Reexamined: Dissonance in the Brandenburg Concerto. *Stanford Law Review* 22:1163–1186.

BAIL

Bail is the prevailing method by which American law has dealt with a puzzling problem: what to do with a person accused of crime during the time between arrest and trial? Imprisonment imposed before trial subjects one who has not been and may never be convicted to disabilities that have all the attributes of punishment, disrupts employment and family ties, hampers the preparation of a defense, increases pressures to plead guilty, and, compared with bailed defendants, may prejudice trial outcomes and lead to more severe sentences. The development of the institution of bail over centuries of English history and its acceptance and liberalization in colonial America was an attempt to mitigate these handicaps and, by affording an opportunity for pretrial release, to emphasize the values underlying the presumption of innocence while also minimizing the risk that an accused who was not jailed would flee and evade justice. Thus bail makes possible pretrial release if the accused can provide financial security, which is subject to forfeiture if the conditions of the bond are violated.

Traditionally, the amount of security is set in an amount deemed by the court to be sufficient to deter flight and enforce compliance with the court's orders. The defendant's own money or property may be put up for this purpose, but in modern times the prevalent method of providing the required security is the purchase by the defendant of a commercial bail bond for a premium, usually about ten percent of the prescribed security. Conditional release on bail may also be available at later stages of the criminal process, for example, pending APPEAL after conviction or pending a hearing on parole or probation revocation, but the predominant use of bail and the most difficult questions raised by its administration relate to the pretrial period.

A "right to bail" is not a right to pretrial release but merely a right to have a court set the amount of the security to be required. A majority of criminal defendants have little or no financial ability to provide security. Furthermore, bondsmen can and often do refuse to bond those they regard as poor risks even if the amount of the premium is tendered. Thus a high rate of pretrial detention of those unable to provide bail has long been a characteristic feature of American criminal justice. Since the early 1960s a widespread bail reform movement has introduced procedures designed to reduce the dependence of the traditional system on the requirement of financial security, but these changes have supplemented rather than replaced money bail, which remains a dominant feature of the system.

The only direct reference to bail in the Constitution is the brief clause in the Eighth Amendment that "excessive bail shall not be required." There are serious problems in the interpretation of the scope of this limited clause and its application under modern conditions. On its face the language is only a restriction of the amount of security which a judge can require, and poses no constitutional barrier to legislative or judicial denial of bail. Alternatively, the clause has been read as necessarily implying a right to bail, as otherwise the clause is left with little significance.

There is no easy resolution of this problem. To infer from the clause a right to bail that is protected from legislative abrogation reads into it words that are not there and necessarily leaves the scope of such a right uncertain. But a literal interpretation renders the clause superfluous, as PROCEDURAL DUE PROCESS OF LAW would protect against judicial abuse of a legislatively granted right to bail. A narrow reading also takes no account of the long history of what the Supreme court in *Stack v. Boyle* (1951) called the "traditional right to freedom before conviction . . . secured only after centuries of struggle," and leaves in a constitutional vacuum a critical stage of the criminal process which has significant impact on the implementation of other constitutionally protected rights of defendants. For nearly two centuries the question has remained unresolved, for two main reasons. First, the transitory nature of detention and the poverty of most defendants unable to raise bail pose barriers to appellate review. Second, until 1984 federal statutory law and the constitutions or laws of most states guaranteed a pretrial right to bail in all but some capital cases, thereby rendering it unnecessary to reach the constitutional issue. Little direct evidence of what was intended by the framers of the clause can be found in the sparse and inconclusive legislative history of the

Eighth Amendment's proposal by the First Congress. At the same time that Representative JAMES MADISON introduced the amendment in the House, a Senate committee was preparing the JUDICIARY ACT OF 1789, which included a right to bail in all but capital cases. Both bail provisions were uncontroversial and undebated, and both went their separate ways to enactment. There is no indication that anyone in Congress recognized the anomaly of incorporating the basic right governing pretrial practice in a statute while enshrining in the Constitution the derivative protection against judicial abuse of that right. The anomaly is compounded by Madison's insistence, in the House debates on the BILL OF RIGHTS, that whereas England's Bill of Rights raised a barrier only against the power of the Crown, "a different opinion prevails in the United States," where protection against abuse "must be levelled against the Legislative" branch. What we do know, however, about the origin of the clause and the context in which it arose sheds some light relevant to its interpretation.

The words of the bail clause were taken verbatim from the revolutionary VIRGINIA DECLARATION OF RIGHTS of 1776, drafted by GEORGE MASON, and by him taken, with the substitution of "shall" for "ought," from the 1689 English Bill of Rights. Mason states that his purpose in drafting the Virginia Declaration was to provide effectual securities for the essential rights of CIVIL LIBERTY, and it is difficult to believe that he intended to deal with the issue of pretrial liberty by words that, literally construed, offer no security against its denial. Although steeped in English constitutional history, Mason was not a lawyer, may not have understood the complexity of the English law, and may have thought that the clause encapsulated the whole subject. In its English context, however, the excessive bail clause in the 1689 Bill of Rights was the culmination of a chain of events that went back to MAGNA CARTA and of a long succession of detailed statutes that established the scope of the right to bail.

This development was climaxed in the seventeenth century by three important acts of Parliament which had been provoked by abuses in the administration of bail law. In 1628, by the PETITION OF RIGHT, the provision of Magna Carta that "no freeman shall be . . . detained in prison . . . unless by the law of the land" was made applicable to pretrial detention and thus was not limited, as the Crown had maintained in *Darnell's Case* (1627), to imprisonment only after conviction. Next, the HABEAS CORPUS ACT OF 1679, after referring to prolonged detentions caused by the inability of detainees to get any judge to set and take bail, mandated a speedy procedure for this purpose. Finally, the Bill of Rights of 1689 sought to curb the judicial abuse of requiring excessive bail. Thus the English structure was tripartite, and protection against denial of pretrial release through the prohibition of excessive bail must be read in the context not only of the extraordinary procedure provided by HABEAS CORPUS but also with reference to the long history of parliamentary bail statutes. Habeas corpus, of course, was included in the body of the American constitution, but the substantive right to bail was omitted. The argument that this omission seems to have been inadvertent at a time when the Framers were preoccupied with other, more immediately pressing issues, and that such a substantive right must have been the intent of the clause, is the core of the historical case for a broad interpretation.

Beginning with the MASSACHUSETTS BODY OF LIBERTIES in 1641, most of the American colonies reduced the number of capital offenses and otherwise liberalized the English law of bail, and in 1682 Pennsylvania extended the right to bail to those charged with all offenses except those capital cases "where the proof is evident or the presumption great," language that was widely copied in state constitutions after Independence. Besides the Judiciary Act of 1789, the closest contemporary record reflecting what seems to have been a widespread political approach to the right to bail, at the time that the Bill of Rights was before the First Congress, was the enactment two years earlier by the CONTINENTAL CONGRESS of the NORTHWEST ORDINANCE for the governance of the territories beyond the Appalachians. In substantially the same language as that used in Pennsylvania nearly a century earlier, the ordinance made bailable as of right those charged with any except capital offenses.

Given the widespread right to bail that had been provided by federal statute and state law, it is not surprising that until recent years there has been a dearth of litigation asserting an Eighth Amendment constitutional right to pretrial bail. The few occasions on which the Supreme Court has dealt with the subject have not required a resolution of the issue, but there are inconclusive and inconsistent OBITER DICTA in some of the cases. On the one hand, in *Schilb v. Kuebel* (1971), which upheld a bail reform statute, the Court said that "Bail, of course, is basic to our system of law," and earlier a unanimous Court in *Stack v. Boyle* had stressed the importance of providing for pretrial release lest "the presumption of innocence, secured only after centuries of struggle, would lose its meaning." But in *Carlson v. Landon,* decided in the same term as *Stack,* a 5–4 Court held that alien communists were not entitled to bail pending adjudication of DEPORTATION charges against them. Most of the *Carlson* majority's long opinion concerned the limited rights of ALIENS, the classification of deportation as a noncriminal proceeding, and the validity and exercise of the attorney general's discretionary delegated power to bail aliens; but it also included six sentences implying that even in criminal proceedings the Eighth Amendment does not afford a right to bail. Although frequently cited, considering the noncriminal emphasis in the case and the brevity and superficiality of the Eighth Amendment analysis, the *Carlson* obiter dictum warrants little weight. Probably more significant is SCHALL V. MARTIN (1984), upholding PREVENTIVE DETENTION for an accused juvenile delinquent pending a family court fact-finding hearing. The case was decided under the due process clause. The Court stressed the noncriminal classification of the proceeding; it noted the limited rights of juveniles compared with adults and the detention's very limited duration; and it observed that there is no historical tradition of a right to juvenile pretrial release and that the detention practice that was upheld has existed throughout the country. Despite all these distinguishing characteristics, the weight given to the importance of preventing pretrial crime and to the possibility of its prediction is suggestive of how the Court might deal with parallel questions in an adult denial-of-bail criminal case.

A number of other controversial issues in pretrial bail law will remain whether or not the Supreme Court infers some form of a right to bail from the Eighth Amendment. The 1984 federal Bail Reform Act and some state constitutional or statutory amendments permit preventive detention of those charged with noncapital offenses if a court finds that pretrial release would pose a danger of future criminal activity. Besides extending the traditional practice which has denied the right to bail only in some capital cases, these enactments also breach long-standing PRECE-DENT that only the risk of failure to appear for trial or other limited conduct directly impairing the court's processes, such as threats against witnesses, is relevant to the bail decision. Although the change is in some sense more theoretical than real, direct authorization for judges to explore the uncharted waters of predictions of future dangerousness will in practice undermine the values that gave rise to bail and result in further increases in the proportion of defendants jailed pending trial.

Bail is not constitutionally excessive if the amount does not exceed that normally required for the charged offense. These normal amounts are sufficient to result in very high rates of detention and to mask the existence of de facto preventive detention for those unable to post bond. It was a concern for more equal justice in criminal law administration and a reaction against this discrimination against the poor that gave rise to the bail reform movement of the 1960s and the widespread introduction of other incentives and sanctions as substitute deterrents for money bail. Although this reform, unevenly and incompletely implemented, has had some success, the number of those detained has remained high and is growing. The issue of blatant WEALTH DISCRIMINATION in bail law administration remains to be resolved.

CALEB FOOTE

Bibliography

FLEMMING, ROY B. 1982 *Punishment before Trial: An Organizational Perspective of Felony Bail Processes.* New York: Longman's.

FOOTE, CALEB 1985 The Coming Constitutional Crisis in Bail. *University of Pennsylvania Law Review* 113:959–999, 1125–1185.

FREED, DANIEL J. and WALD, PATRICIA M. 1964 *Bail in the United States, 1964.* Washington, D.C.: U.S. Department of Justice.

TRIBE, LAURENCE H. 1970 An Ounce of Detention: Preventive Justice in the World of John Mitchell. *Virginia Law Review* 56:371–407.

BAILEY v. ALABAMA
219 U.S. 219 (1911)

After the demise of the BLACK CODES some southern states resorted to other devices to insure a steady supply of labor. One Alabama statute effectively converted civil breach of contract into the crime of fraud by making it *prima facie* EVIDENCE of intent to defraud that a worker accept an advance on wages and then neither repay the advance nor perform the work contracted for.

In *Bailey* the Supreme Court held (7–2) that the Alabama law constituted a system of PEONAGE in violation of the THIRTEENTH AMENDMENT's prohibition of involuntary servitude. Justice CHARLES EVANS HUGHES, for the majority, argued that involuntary servitude was a broader concept than SLAVERY and included schemes for enforced labor.

Justice OLIVER WENDELL HOLMES, dissenting, argued that Alabama was acting within its power to define crimes and their punishments.

DENNIS J. MAHONEY

BAILEY v. DREXEL FURNITURE CO.
(Child Labor Tax Case)
259 U.S. 20 (1922)

Following the decision invalidating the KEATING-OWEN CHILD LABOR ACT in HAMMER V. DAGENHART (1918), Congress passed a new law in 1919, this time based on its TAXING POWER. The statute levied a ten percent tax on the net profits of mines or factories that employed underage children. Congress had previously used the tax power for social and economic purposes, and the Supreme Court consistently had upheld such enactments, notably in VEAZIE BANK V. FENNO (1869) and MCCRAY V. UNITED STATES (1904).

When the Child Labor Tax Case was decided in 1922, only Justice JOHN H. CLARKE dissented, without opinion, from Chief Justice WILLIAM HOWARD TAFT's opinion for the Court. Taft concluded that the obvious regulatory effect of the law infringed on state JURISDICTION over PRODUCTION and that *Hammer v. Dagenhart* was controlling. Congress, he said, had imposed a tax that was really a penalty for the purpose of reaching a local subject. Like the Justices in *Hammer*, Taft feared the destruction of federalism. "To give such magic to the word 'tax,'" he said, would remove all constitutional limitations upon Congress and abolish "the sovereignty of the States." He distinguished the Court's earlier rulings upholding federal taxes on state bank notes, oleomargarine, and narcotics by insisting that they had involved regulations or prohibitions that were "reasonably adapted to the collection of the tax." Taft, in fact, advanced the unhistorical proposition that the regulatory purposes of the taxes in those cases were only "incidental" to a primary motive of raising revenue.

The Child Labor Tax Case was favorably cited in UNITED STATES V. BUTLER (1936), but a year later, in SONZINSKY V. UNITED STATES, the Court upheld a federal licensing tax on firearms dealers. Justice HARLAN FISKE STONE's opinion sharply repudiated Taft's, contending that the incidental effect of regulation was irrelevant. Courts, he said, were incompetent to question congressional motives; specifically, they should not measure a tax's regulatory effect and use it to argue that Congress had exercised another power denied by the Constitution. Similar arguments were registered in UNITED STATES V. KAHRIGER (1953) when the Court sustained a federal tax on gambling businesses.

STANLEY I. KUTLER

Bibliography

WOOD, STEPHEN 1968 *Constitutional Politics in the Progressive Era: Child Labor and the Law.* Chicago: University of Chicago Press.

BAKER v. CARR
369 U.S. 186 (1962)

Chief Justice EARL WARREN considered *Baker v. Carr* the most important case decided by the Warren Court. Its holding was cryptic: "the right [to equal districts in the Tennessee legislature] is within the reach of judicial protection under the FOURTEENTH AMENDMENT." Many people expected REAPPORTIONMENT under *Baker* to vitalize American democracy. Others feared that it would snare the judiciary in unresolvable questions of political REPRESENTATION, outside the proper bounds of its constitutional authority.

Tennesseans, like others, had moved from countryside to urban and suburban districts, but no redistricting had taken place since 1901. Supporters of reapportionment claimed that the resulting swollen districts made "second-class citizens" of city voters; they blamed "malapportionment" for urban woes and legislative apathy. Finding little legislative sympathy for these claims, they turned to the courts.

But they had several hurdles to clear. The framers of the Fourteenth Amendment had repeatedly denied that it protected the right to vote. Perhaps it protected rights of representation, but the Court had found such rights too cloudy, too sensitive, and too "political" to settle judicially. (See POLITICAL QUESTIONS.)

The central hurdle was the "standards problem" expounded by Justice FELIX FRANKFURTER in COLEGROVE V. GREEN (1946) and in his *Baker* dissent. How could the Court tell lower courts and legislatures the difference between good representation and bad, lacking clear constitutional guidance? The Constitution was a complex blend of competing and countervailing principles, not a mandate for equal districts. "What is actually asked of the Court . . . is to choose among competing bases of representation—ultimately, really, among competing theories of philosophy—in order to establish an appropriate form of government for . . . the states. . . ." Frankfurter accused the Court of sending the lower courts into a "mathematical quagmire."

Writing for the majority, Justice WILLIAM J. BRENNAN argued that the *Colegrove* court had not found apportionment a political question but had declined to hear it using EQUITY discretion. But he did not answer Frankfurter's challenge to lay down workable standards, nor Justice JOHN MARSHALL HARLAN's objection, later reasserted in REYNOLDS V. SIMS (1964), that nothing in the Constitution conveyed a right to equal districts. Brennan merely claimed that "judicial standards under the EQUAL PROTECTION CLAUSE are well developed and familiar," and that "the right asserted is within the reach of judicial protection under the Fourteenth Amendment."

The concurring Justices, WILLIAM O. DOUGLAS and TOM C. CLARK, were not so cautious. Clark felt that "rational" departures from equal districts, such as districts approved by popular referendum, should be permitted. Douglas emphasized that the standards would be flexible (though he would later vote for rigid standards).

These opinions, and *Baker*'s place in history, make sense only in the context of Solicitor General Archibald Cox's AMICUS CURIAE brief supporting intervention. To take on a cause that could, and later did, jeopardize the seats of most of the legislators in the country, and invite formidable political reprisals, the Justices had to move with caution. Cox's brief reassured them that the JOHN F. KENNEDY administration, like its predecessor, favored intervention. The executive support probably swayed the votes of at least two Justices, Clark and POTTER STEWART. Had these voted against intervention, the Court would have divided 4–4, leaving intact the lower court's decision not to hear the case.

Moreover, Cox's brief did address Harlan's and Frankfurter's challenges. As with BROWN V. BOARD OF EDUCATION (1954), he argued, constitutional authority could be demonstrated from social need, as perceived by social scientists, incorporated into a spacious reading of the Fourteenth Amendment. As for standards, there were two possibilities: an absolute, individual right to vote, perhaps grounded on the equal protection clause, and a loose, group right to equal representation, perhaps grounded on the DUE PROCESS CLAUSE. Of the two, Cox seemed to favor the looser one, forbidding "egregious cases" of "gross discrimination." He even showed how such a standard might be drawn on a map of Tennessee. Because he was explicit, Brennan could afford to be cryptic and let the Cox brief draw most of Frankfurter's and Harlan's fire.

Within two years the Court announced in *Reynolds v. Sims* that equal representation for equal numbers was the "fundamental goal" of the Constitution and laid down standards so strict that every state but one, Oregon, was compelled to reapportion. Compliance with *Baker* was widespread and quick. Opposition was strong but late. By 1967 the states had come within a few votes of the two-thirds needed to call a CONSTITUTIONAL CONVENTION to strip courts of redistricting power, but by then reapportionment was largely completed, and the movement died.

Reapportionment added many urban and suburban seats to legislatures, replacing rural ones, but there is little evidence that it produced any of the liberalizing, vitalizing policies its proponents had predicted. What it did bring was a plague of GERRYMANDERING, renewed after each census, because it forced legislators to redistrict without forcing them to be nonpartisan. The Court since *Baker* has been powerless to control gerrymanders. Packing or diluting a group in a district can strengthen or weaken the group, or do both at once. There is no way short of commanding PROPORTIONAL REPRESENTATION to equalize everyone's representation. Nor is there a workable way to equalize representation in the ELECTORAL COLLEGE, the Senate, the national party conventions, party committees, runoff elections, executive appointments, or MULTIMEMBER DISTRICTS. The Court opened these doors when it announced that representation was the fundamental goal of the Constitution, but it closed them when it found that they raised the standards problem too plainly to permit intervention, exactly as Frankfurter had warned.

Baker has left us two legacies. The good one is equalizing district size. The bad one is rhetorical indirection, constitutional fabrication, and a penchant for overriding the wishes of people and their representatives, as for example, in *Lucas v. Forty-fourth General Assembly* (1964). Whether the good legacy is worth the bad, and whether it even added on balance to equal representation, can be told only with reference to the full breadth of representation which was too complicated for the Court to touch.

WARD E. Y. ELLIOTT

Bibliography
Cox, ARCHIBALD 1967 *The Warren Court: Constitutional Decision as an Instrument of Reform.* Cambridge, Mass.: Harvard University Press.

DIXON, ROBERT G., JR. 1968 *Democratic Representation: Reapportionment in Law and Politics.* New York: Oxford University Press.

ELLIOTT, WARD E. Y. 1975 *The Rise of Guardian Democracy: The Supreme Court's Role in Voting Rights Dis-*

putes, 1845–1969. Cambridge, Mass.: Harvard University Press.

NAVASKY, VICTOR 1971 *Kennedy Justice.* New York: Atheneum.

BALANCING TEST

Although the intellectual origins of the balancing of interests formula lie in ROSCOE POUND's sociological jurisprudence, the formula was introduced into constitutional law as a means of implementing the Supreme Court's oft-repeated announcement that FIRST AMENDMENT rights are not absolute. In determining when infringement on speech may be justified constitutionally, the Court may balance the interest in FREEDOM OF SPEECH against the interest that the infringing statute seeks to protect. Thus the Court may conclude that the interests in NATIONAL SECURITY protected by the Smith Act outweigh the interests in speech of those who advocate forcible overthrow of the government, or that the free speech interests of pamphleteers outweigh the interest in clean streets protected by an antilittering ordinance forbidding the distribution of handbills.

The 1950s campaign against alleged subversives brought two interlocking problems to the Supreme Court. The dominant free speech DOCTRINES of the Court were PREFERRED FREEDOMS and the CLEAR AND PRESENT DANGER TEST. Because alleged subversives were exercising preferred speech rights and the government was unprepared to offer evidence that their speech did constitute a present danger of violent overthrow of the government, the Court found it difficult under the existing formulas to uphold government anticommunist action. Because established First Amendment doctrine appeared to be on a collision course with an anticommunist crusade that appeared to enjoy overwhelming popular support, free speech provided the crucial arena for the penultimate crisis of the judicial self-restraint movement. (The ultimate crisis came in BROWN V. BOARD OF EDUCATION, 1954.) Although the logical implication of that movement suggested that the Court ought never declare an act of Congress unconstitutional as a violation of the BILL OF RIGHTS, the Court was not prepared to go so far. The Justices' dilemma was that they were the inheritors of pro-freedom of speech doctrines but wished to uphold infringements upon speech without openly abdicating their constitutional authority.

The way out of this dilemma was the balancing formula. It allowed the Court to vindicate legislative and executive anticommunist measures case by case

without ever flatly announcing that the Court had gone out of the business of enforcing the First Amendment. LEARNED HAND's "clear and probable" or "discounting" formula adopted by the Supreme Court in DENNIS V. UNITED STATES (1951) was the vital bridge in moving from a clear and present danger test that impels judicial action to a balancing test that veils judicial withdrawal. For Hand's test permits conversion of the danger test from an exception to freedom of speech invoked when speech creates an immediate danger of violent crime to a general formula for outweighing speech claims whenever the goals espoused in the speech are sufficiently antithetical to those of the majority. Justice FELIX FRANKFURTER's concurrence in *Dennis* and the majority opinion in BARENBLATT V. UNITED STATES (1959) not only made the antispeech potential of the balancing doctrine clear but also exhibited its great potential for absolute judicial deference to coordinate branches. For if constitutional judgments are ultimately a matter of balancing interests, in a democratic society who is the ultimate balancer? Necessarily, it is the Congress in which all the competing interests are represented. Thus the Court deferred to Congress's judgment that the needs of national security outweighed the speech rights of the enemies of that security.

Proponents of the balancing doctrine argue that no one is really willing to give any constitutional right absolute sway and that the act of judging always involves a weighing of competing claims. Certainly when constitutional rights such as free speech and FAIR TRIAL come into conflict, balancing of the two appears inevitable. The opponents of balancing argue for "principled" versus "ad hoc" or case-by-case balancing. If judges are left free to balance the particular interests in each particular case, they are always free to decide any case for or against the rights claimed by the way they state the interests. Opponents of ad hoc balancing insist that whatever balancing must be done should be done in the course of creating constitutional rules that will then be applied even-handedly in all cases. Thus, if fair trial and free speech values conflict, we may want a rule that upholds the constitutionality of banning prosecutors from pretrial release of confessions, but we do not want the kind of ad hoc balancing in which judges are free to find that in some cases such bans are constitutional and in others they are not.

Balancing has remained a principal doctrine in the freedom of speech area and has spread to other constitutional areas such as PRIVACY. Its capacity as a vehicle for judicial discretion is illustrated by BUCKLEY V. VALEO (1976), in which the Court used the balancing doctrine to march through the complex CAMPAIGN FINANCE ACT, striking down some provisions and upholding others in what was effectively a total legislative redrafting, and by the ABORTION cases (see ROE v. WADE, 1973) in which the Court used the balancing doctrine to invest with constitutional authority the "trimester" scheme it invented.

In GIBSON v. FLORIDA LEGISLATIVE INVESTIGATING COMMITTEE (1963) the Court held that government might infringe upon a First Amendment right only when it could show a COMPELLING STATE INTEREST. This formula may be viewed as weighting the balance of interests in favor of constitutional rights, but any government interests can be stated in such a way as to appear compelling. The Court's employment of the balancing test always leaves us uncertain whether any legislative infringement of free speech or other rights, no matter how direct or how open, will be declared unconstitutional, for the Court may always be prepared to find some state interest sufficiently weighty to justify the infringement.

MARTIN SHAPIRO

(SEE ALSO: *Absolutism; Judicial Activism and Restraint.*)

Bibliography

FRANTZ, LAURENT B. 1963 Is the First Amendment Law? *California Law Review* 51:729–754.

HAND, LEARNED 1958 *The Bill of Rights.* Cambridge, Mass.: Harvard University Press.

MENDELSON, WALLACE 1962 On the Meaning of the First Amendment: Absolutes in the Balance. *California Law Review* 50:821–828.

BALDWIN, ABRAHAM
(1754–1807)

Abraham Baldwin represented Georgia at the CONSTITUTIONAL CONVENTION OF 1787 and signed the Constitution. He served on the Committee on Representation, and, although personally opposed to equal representation of states in the Senate, the Connecticut-born Baldwin played a key role in securing the GREAT COMPROMISE. He later spent eighteen years in Congress.

DENNIS J. MAHONEY

BALDWIN, HENRY
(1780–1844)

Henry Baldwin of Pittsburgh was appointed to the Supreme Court on January 4, 1830, by ANDREW JACKSON. After graduating from Yale College in 1797, he studied law with ALEXANDER J. DALLAS and began his practice in Pittsburgh where he joined the bar in 1801. Law spilled over naturally into politics for Baldwin, and from 1816 to 1822 he served in Congress, where he gained a reputation as an economic nationalist. He also defended Andrew Jackson from charges of misconduct in Spanish Florida and later supported him for President—efforts that won him a seat on the Supreme Court.

Though an unknown judicial quantity, Baldwin was acceptable to the still-dominant JOSEPH STORY-JOHN MARSHALL wing of the Court because of his reputation as a "sound" man and talented lawyer—and because he was not JOHN BANNISTER GIBSON, whom conservatives feared would get the appointment. Baldwin's supporters were soon disappointed, then shocked. Almost immediately the new Justice was out of phase with the Court's nationalism and at odds with several of its members, especially Story, whose scholarly, didactic style Baldwin found offensive and threatening. After serving less than a year on the Court, he wanted off. Worse still, his collapse in 1833 (which caused him to miss that term of the Court) signaled the onset of a mental condition that progressively incapacitated him. Occasionally he rose to the level of his early promise, as for example in *United States v. Arredondo* (1832) where the principle was established that land claims resting on acts of foreign governments (which in the Spanish and Mexican cessions amounted to millions of acres) were presumed valid unless the United States could prove otherwise. Another solid effort was *Holmes v. Jennison* (1840) where he upheld the right of a state to surrender fugitives to a foreign country even though such a power cut into the policymaking authority of the national government in FOREIGN AFFAIRS. His circuit efforts were also well received at first and deservedly so, judging from such opinions as *McGill v. Brown* (1833) where he handled a complicated question of charitable bequests with considerable sophistication.

Baldwin's constitutional philosophy, so far as it can be detected, was set forth in his *General View of the Origin and Nature of the Constitution and Government of the United States,* a rambling, unconvincing treatise published in 1837 (mainly, it would seem, to rescue him from pressing debts). Baldwin presumed to stake out a middle constitutional ground for himself between extreme STATES' RIGHTS constitutional doctrine and the broad nationalism of Marshall and Story which he explicitly condemned as unfounded and usurpatory. He took particular pains to refute the thesis in Story's *Commentaries on the Constitution* (1833) that SOVEREIGNTY devolved on the whole people after 1776. Baldwin's final position on the matter appeared to be little more than a reductionist version of JOHN C. CALHOUN's theories.

The states' rights theory set forth in *General View* was consistent with Baldwin's *Jennison* opinion and his preference for STATE POLICE POWER as stated in the slavery case of GROVES V. SLAUGHTER (1841). On the other hand, in *McCracken v. Hayward* (1844), he did not hesitate to strike down an Illinois stay law that impaired contractual rights. His unpublished opinion in BANK OF AUGUSTA V. EARLE (1839) took the extremely nationalist position that a foreign corporation's right to do business in a state was protected by the PRIVILEGES AND IMMUNITIES clause of Article IV, section 2, of the Constitution.

To say where Baldwin really stood is difficult. He wrote less than forty majority opinions during his fourteen years on the Court. Of those, few were important and fewer still were coherent expositions of constitutional DOCTRINE. He withdrew more and more into paranoiac isolation, carping at his colleagues, criticizing reporter Richard Peters, and pondering his rapidly deteriorating financial situation. He dissented more and more (thirty-some times counting unwritten dissents) and with less and less purpose. That a number of his separate opinions were delivered too late to be included in the reports suggests that his impact in the Court's CONFERENCE was peripheral at best. His effectiveness on the circuit declined, too, if one credits the growing complaints of district judge Joseph Hopkinson who sat with him in Pennsylvania. Baldwin died in 1844, deeply in debt, without friends and with no prospect of being remembered favorably. Illness had taken a heavy toll. His influence on American law was negligible and his presence on the Supreme Court was probably counterproductive.

                                              R. KENT NEWMYER

Bibliography

BALDWIN, HENRY 1837 *A General View of the Origin and Nature of the Constitution and Government of the United States.* . . . Philadelphia: John C. Clark.
GATELL, FRANK O. 1969 Henry Baldwin. In Leon Friedman and Fred L. Israel (eds.), *The Justices of the United States Supreme Court, 1789–1969*, Vol. 1, pages 571–598. New York: Chelsea House.

BALDWIN, ROGER N.
(1884–1981)

Until the United States entered World War I, Roger Nash Baldwin was a social worker and a leading expert on juvenile courts. A pacifist who feared that the war might cause repression of individual rights, Baldwin helped to found the National Civil Liberties Bureau in 1917. The Bureau defended CONSCIENTIOUS OBJECTORS and those prosecuted for allegedly antiwar speeches and publications. Reorganized in 1920 by Baldwin and others as the AMERICAN CIVIL LIBERTIES UNION, it expanded its efforts to include among its many clients leaders of the International Workers of the World and other labor organizations; John T. Scopes, who violated Tennessee's anti-evolution law in 1925 and was prosecuted in the infamous "monkey trial"; the Jehovah's Witnesses; and even those, such as the Ku Klux Klan and the German-American Bund, who opposed FREEDOM OF SPEECH for all but themselves. Baldwin was also committed to efforts on behalf of human rights abroad; despite his sympathy for radical causes, his investigation of the Soviet Union led him to oppose communism. In 1940, at his urging, the ACLU adopted a loyalty resolution barring supporters of totalitarian dictatorships from membership, only to find later that the government LOYALTY OATHS, which it fought in court, were based on its own resolution. Baldwin served as director of the ACLU until 1950, as its chairman from 1950 to 1955, and as its international work adviser until his death. After World War II, Baldwin was counselor on CIVIL LIBERTIES in the reconstruction of the governments of Japan, Korea, and Germany.

                                          RICHARD B. BERNSTEIN

Bibliography

LAMSON, PEGGY 1976 *Roger Baldwin, Founder of the American Civil Liberties Union: A Portrait.* Boston: Houghton Mifflin.

BALDWIN v. FISH & GAME COMMISSION
436 U.S. 371 (1978)

The Supreme Court, 6–3, sustained Montana's exaction of a substantially higher elk-hunting license fee for nonresidents than for residents. Temporarily abandoning the approach of TOOMER V. WITSELL (1948), the Court said that the PRIVILEGES AND IMMUNITIES clause of Article IV of the Constitution protected citizens of other states only as to fundamental rights, a category that did not include the "sport" of killing elk. *Toomer*'s approach returned four weeks later in HICKLIN V. ORBECK (1978), but the Court in Hicklin neither overruled nor distinguished *Baldwin*. (See RESIDENCE REQUIREMENTS.)

                                          KENNETH L. KARST

BALDWIN v. NEW YORK
399 U.S. 66 (1970)

When DUNCAN V. LOUISIANA extended the SIXTH AMENDMENT'S TRIAL BY JURY provision to the states in 1968, the Court said that MISDEMEANORS, crimes punishable by imprisonment for less than six months, may be tried without a jury. Petty offenses have always been exempt from the amendment's guarantee of trial by jury in "all criminal prosecutions." Baldwin, having been sentenced to a year in jail for pickpocketing, claimed on APPEAL that New York City had deprived him of his right to a trial by jury. The Court held that the Constitution requires a trial by jury if an offense can be punished by imprisonment for more than six months. Justice BYRON R. WHITE, for a plurality, found decisive the fact that one city alone in the nation denied trial by jury when the possible punishment exceeded six months. Justices HUGO L. BLACK and WILLIAM O. DOUGLAS, concurring separately, would have ruled that the Constitution requires a jury for all accused persons without exception.

LEONARD W. LEVY

BALLARD, UNITED STATES v.

See: Postal Power; Religion and Fraud

BALLEW v. GEORGIA
435 U.S. 223 (1978)

In *Ballew v. Georgia*, the Supreme Court unanimously held that a five-person jury in a nonpetty criminal case does not satisfy the right to TRIAL BY JURY under the Sixth Amendment as applied to the states through the FOURTEENTH AMENDMENT. *Ballew* involved a misdemeanor conviction for exhibiting an obscene motion picture.

Although all the Justices agreed upon the result, four separate opinions were written on the five-person jury issue. Justice HARRY A. BLACKMUN joined by Justice JOHN PAUL STEVENS relied heavily on SOCIAL SCIENCE RESEARCH in concluding that there was substantial doubt that a five-person jury functioned effectively, was likely to reach accurate results, or truly represented the community. Justice BYRON R. WHITE concluded that a jury of less than six would fail to represent the sense of the community. Justice LEWIS F. POWELL joined by Chief Justice WARREN E. Burger and Justice WILLIAM H. REHNQUIST agreed that five-person juries raised "grave questions of fairness" indicating that "a line has to be drawn somewhere if the substance of jury trial is to be preserved." Since an earlier case, WILLIAMS V. FLORIDA (1970), had upheld the constitutionality of six-person juries, the effect of *Ballew* was to draw the constitutional line between five and six.

NORMAN ABRAMS

(SEE ALSO: *Jury Size.*)

BANCROFT, GEORGE
(1800–1891)

A liberal Democrat from Massachusetts, Bancroft served as JAMES POLK's secretary of the navy and acting secretary of war, as ANDREW JOHNSON's adviser, and as minister to Great Britain and to Germany. He was also the most popular, influential, and respected American historian of the nineteenth century. His twelve-volume epic on American liberty, the *History of the United States from the Discovery of the Continent*, written over half a century, contains 1,700,000 words. The last two volumes, a *History of the Formation of the Constitution of the United States* (1882), covered 1782–1789. The work benefited from Bancroft's notes of his interview with JAMES MADISON in 1836; Madison also opened his private archives to him. Bancroft was an indefatigable researcher. His chronological narrative of the origins, framing, and RATIFICATION OF THE CONSTITUTION was based on manuscript letters as well as public records. He included over 300 pages of letters, many printed for the first time.

Bancroft wrote in a grand style that is today considered florid. His essentially political interpretation remained the standard work of its kind until superseded in 1928 by CHARLES WARREN's *The Making of the Constitution*, although ANDREW C. McLAUGHLIN's *Confederation and Constitution* (1908) exceeded both in judicious analysis. Bancroft's work is remarkably fair, although Madisonian in approach. He viewed the Constitution as a bundle of compromises between nationalists and states' rightists, North and South, large states and small ones. The epigraph to his work was William Gladstone's judgment that "the American Constitution is the most wonderful work ever struck off at a given time by the brain and purpose of man." CHARLES BEARD made Bancroft one of his prime targets because of Bancroft's belief that the Framers were principled patriots who gave their loyalty to a concept of national interest that transcended purse and status without compromising republican ideals.

LEONARD W. LEVY

Bibliography
NYE, RUSSELL 1964 *George Bancroft.* New York: Washington Square Press.

BANK HOLIDAY OF 1933

See: Emergency Bank Act

BANK OF AUGUSTA v. EARLE
13 Peters 519 (1839)

This case was vitally important to CORPORATIONS because it raised the question whether a corporation chartered in one state could do business in another. Justice JOHN MCKINLEY on circuit duty ruled against corporations, provoking Justice JOSEPH STORY to say that McKinley's opinion frightened "all the corporations of the country out of their proprieties. He has held that a corporation created in one State has no power to contract or even to act in any other State. . . . So, banks, insurance companies, manufacturing companies, etc. have no capacity to take or discount notes in another State, or to underwrite policies, or to buy or sell goods." McKinley's decision seemed a death sentence to all interstate corporate business. On APPEAL, DANIEL WEBSTER, representing corporate interests, argued that corporations were citizens entitled to the same rights, under the COMITY CLAUSE in Article IV, section 2, of the Constitution, as natural persons to do business. With only McKinley dissenting, Chief Justice ROGER B. TANEY for the Court steered a middle way between the extremes of McKinley and Webster. He ruled that a corporation, acting through its agents, could do business in other states if they did not expressly prohibit it from doing so. In the absence of such a state prohibition, the Court would presume, from the principle of comity, that out-of-state corporations were invited to transact business. Thus a state might exclude such corporations or admit them conditionally; but the Court overruled McKinley's decision, and corporations as well as Whigs, like Webster and Story, rejoiced.

LEONARD W. LEVY

(SEE ALSO: *Citizenship; Privileges and Immunities.*)

BANK OF THE UNITED STATES ACTS
1 Stat. 191 (1791)
3 Stat. 266 (1816)

The first Bank of the United States (1791–1811) was chartered by Congress on a plan submitted by Secretary of the Treasury ALEXANDER HAMILTON as part of his financial system. Modeled on the century-old Bank of England, the national bank harnessed private interest and profit for public purposes. It received an exclusive twenty-year charter. It was capitalized at $10,000,000, of which the government subscribed one-fifth and private investors the remainder, one-fourth in specie and three-fourths in government stock. Located at Philadelphia and authorized to establish branches, it was to be the financial arm of government (a ready lender, a keeper and tranferrer of funds); through its powers to mount a large paper circulation and advance commercial credit, the bank would also augment the active capital of the country and stimulate enterprise. JAMES MADISON had opposed the bank bill in Congress entirely on constitutional grounds. His arguments, turning on the absence of congressional power and invasion of the reserved rights of the states, were repeated in opinions submitted to President GEORGE WASHINGTON by Attorney General EDMUND RANDOLPH and Secretary of State THOMAS JEFFERSON. They were answered, convincingly in Washington's mind, by Hamilton's argument on the doctrine of IMPLIED POWERS.

The Second Bank of the United States (1816–1836) was an enlarged and revised version of the first. Republican constitutional objections had finally prevailed when Congress refused to recharter the first bank in 1811. But the disorganization of the country's finances during the War of 1812 led the Madison administration to propose a national bank. After several false starts, a plan was agreed upon by Congress in 1816. In 1791, there had been three state-chartered banks; in 1816 there were 260, and Congress acted to recover its abandoned power to regulate the currency. As the constitutional issue receded, controversy shifted to practical and technical questions of banking policy. Inept management, state bank jealousy, and severe financial pressure in 1818–1819 produced demands for revocation of the bank's charter. Aided by the Supreme Court's decision in MCCULLOCH v. MARYLAND (1819), the bank weathered this storm and under the efficient direction of Nicholas Biddle not only prospered but gained widespread public support in the 1820s. Nevertheless, President ANDREW JACK-

SON attacked the bank on financial, political, and constitutional grounds. Biddle and his political friends decided to make the bank the leading issue in the 1832 presidential election by seeking immediate renewal of the charter not due to expire until 1836. Congress obliged, and Jackson vetoed the recharter bill with a powerful indictment of the bank as a privileged moneyed institution that trampled on the Constitution. (See JACKSON'S VETO OF THE BANK BILL.) Asserting the independence of the three branches of government in the interpretation of the Constitution, he declared, "The opinion of the judges has no more authority over Congress than the opinion of Congress has over the judges, and on that point the President is independent of both." After Jackson's reelection, the ties between the government and the bank were quickly severed.

MERRILL D. PETERSON

Bibliography

HAMMOND, BRAY 1957 *Banks and Politics in America from the Revolution to the Civil War.* Princeton, N.J.: Princeton University Press.

BANKRUPTCY (CHANDLER) ACT
52 Stat. 883 (1938)

The Bankruptcy Act of 1938, known as the Chandler Act, represented Congress's first comprehensive revision of the Bankruptcy Act of 1898. (See BANKRUPTCY POWER.) Under the financial strain caused by the Depression, the nation needed supplementary bankruptcy legislation. In a series of measures from 1933 through 1937, Congress sought to foster rehabilitation and reorganization of financially distressed debtors' nonexempt assets. The measures covered individual workers, railroads, farmers, nonrailroad CORPORATIONS, and municipalities. The Chandler Act both revised the basic bankruptcy provisions of the 1898 act and restructured and refined the Depression-era amendments. It segregated the rehabilitation and reorganization provisions into separate chapters, a structure adhered to in the Bankruptcy Reform Act of 1978. But the 1938 act neither sought nor achieved organic changes in bankruptcy law.

THEODORE EISENBERG

Bibliography

WARREN, CHARLES 1935 *Bankruptcy in United States History.* Cambridge, Mass.: Harvard University Press.

BANKRUPTCY POWER

Article I, section 8, of the Constitution authorizes Congress to establish "uniform Laws on the subject of Bankruptcies throughout the United States." As interpreted in the CIRCUIT COURT decision in *In re Klein* (1843), this clause empowers Congress to enact laws covering all aspects of the distribution of a debtor's property and the discharge of his debts. Contrary to some early arguments, Congress's bankruptcy power is not limited to legislating only for the trader class. Commencing in 1800, Congress repeatedly exercised its bankruptcy power during periods of depression or financial unrest, but all early bankruptcy laws were repealed whenever unrest subsided. Since 1898, however, the United States continuously has had a comprehensive bankruptcy law, one completely revised by the BANKRUPTCY REFORM ACT of 1978.

Article I expressly requires bankruptcy legislation to be uniform. As interpreted in *Hanover National Bank v. Moyses* (1902), the uniformity limitation does not prevent incorporation of state law into federal bankruptcy provisions. Bankruptcy law, the Court held in that case, is uniform "when the trustee takes in each state whatever would have been available to the creditor if the bankrupt law had not been passed. The general operation of the law is uniform although it may result in certain particulars differently in different states." And under the *Regional Rail Reorganization Act Cases* (1974) a bankruptcy statute may confine its operations to a single region where all covered bankrupt entities happen to be located. *Railway Executives' Association v. Gibbons* (1982), the only Supreme Court case to invalidate a bankruptcy law for lack of uniformity, struck down the Rock Island Transition and Employee Assistance Act because it covered only one of several railroads then in reorganization.

However many other theoretical limitations restrict Congress's bankruptcy power, only a few have led to invalidation of bankruptcy legislation. As interpreted in reorganization cases, the Fifth Amendment's DUE PROCESS CLAUSE limits Congress's bankruptcy power to alter or interfere with the rights of secured creditors. In LOUISVILLE JOINT STOCK LAND BANK V. RADFORD (1934) the Court found the original FRAZIER-LEMKE ACT unconstitutional because it too drastically interfered with a mortgagee's interest in property. But within months Congress enacted the second Frazier-Lemke Act, with scaled down interference, which the Court upheld in WRIGHT V. VINTON BRANCH OF MOUNTAIN TRUST BANK OF ROANOKE (1937). And in *Continental Illinois National Bank and Trust Co. v. Chicago, Rock Island and Pacific Railway*

Company (1935) the Court held that secured creditors could at least temporarily be enjoined from selling their security. *Van Huffel v. Harkelrode* (1931) allows property to be sold free of a mortage holder's encumbrance where his or her rights are transferred to the proceeds of the sale. The *Regional Rail Reorganization Act Cases* found no constitutional flaw in the government's refusal to permit liquidation of an unsuccessful business where the Tucker Act permitted a suit for damages in the COURT OF CLAIMS.

For a brief period, there was doubt about Congress's authority to regulate municipal bankruptcies. In ASHTON V. CAMERON COUNTY WATER IMPROVEMENT DISTRICT (1937) the Supreme Court invalidated, as an interference with state sovereignty, a 1934 municipal bankruptcy law. But in *United States v. Bekins* (1938), in a shift that may be attributable to changes in Court personnel, the Court sustained a similar law. The Bankruptcy Reform Act of 1978 contains an updated municipal bankruptcy law.

Under STURGES V. CROWNINSHIELD (1819), when no national bankruptcy laws are in effect, states may regulate insolvency. Their effectiveness in doing so is limited by the requirement that states not impair the OBLIGATION OF CONTRACTS. When national bankruptcy legislation is in effect, *Stellwagen v. Clum* (1918) and other cases indicate that state laws are abrogated only to the extent that they undermine federal law.

THEODORE EISENBERG

Bibliography
WARREN, CHARLES 1935 *Bankruptcy in United States History.* Cambridge, Mass.: Harvard University Press.

BANKRUPTCY REFORM ACT
92 Stat. 2549 (1978)

The Bankruptcy Reform Act of 1978 was the first comprehensive revision of federal bankruptcy law since 1938 and the first completely new bankruptcy law since 1898. (See BANKRUPTCY POWER.) Although the 1978 act made many substantive changes in bankruptcy law, its most controversial changes concern the organization of the bankruptcy system. The act expanded the bankruptcy court's authority to include JURISDICTION over virtually all matters relating to the bankrupt and the bankrupt's assets. This expansion, combined with Congress's failure to staff the new bankruptcy courts with life-tenured judges, led the Supreme Court in NORTHERN PIPELINE CONSTRUC-

TION CO. V. MARATHON PIPE LINE CO. (1982) to invalidate portions of the act's jurisdictional scheme. (See JUDICIAL POWER OF THE UNITED STATES.) In an effort to upgrade the bankruptcy courts, the act, in selected pilot districts, creates a system of United States trustees to administer and supervise bankruptcy cases, leaving courts free to perform more traditional adjudicatory functions. One of the statute's most significant changes is to consolidate into a single reorganization proceeding what had been three different methods for reorganizing financially distressed CORPORATIONS.

THEODORE EISENBERG

Bibliography
Selected Articles on the Bankruptcy Reform Act of 1978   1979   *St. Mary's Law Journal* 11:247–501.

BANTAM BOOKS, INC. v. SULLIVAN
372 U.S. 58 (1963)

In *Bantam Books v. Sullivan* the Supreme Court struck down a state system of informal censorship, holding that the regulation of OBSCENITY must meet rigorous procedural safeguards to guard against the repression of constitutionally protected FREEDOM OF SPEECH. Rhode Island had created a commission to educate the public concerning books unsuitable to youths. The commission informed book and magazine distributors that certain publications were "objectionable" for distribution to youths under eighteen years of age and threatened legal sanctions should a distributor fail to "cooperate." Distributors, rather than risk prosecution, had removed books from public circulation, resulting in the suppression of publications the state conceded were not obscene.

KIM MCLANE WARDLAW

BARBOUR, PHILIP P.
(1783–1841)

Philip P. Barbour was appointed to the Supreme Court by ANDREW JACKSON in December 1835 to fill the seat vacated by GABRIEL DUVALL. Born into Virginia's slaveholding plantation elite, Barbour held constitutional values that promoted the interest of that class. His law was largely self-taught, though he attended the College of William and Mary briefly in

1802 before beginning full-time practice in Orange County, Virginia. Beginning in 1812, Barbour served two years in the Virginia Assembly, following which he was elected to Congress where he served until 1825 and then again for two years beginning in 1827. For a brief time he was a Judge of the General Court of Virginia, and in 1830 he was appointed to the federal district court for Eastern Virginia, where he remained until assuming his Supreme Court duties in 1836.

Barbour's views on the Constitution were essentially those of the Richmond Junto of which he was a member. As a STATES' RIGHTS constitutionalist, he was opposed to federally sponsored INTERNAL IMPROVEMENTS, the protective tariff, and the second BANK OF THE UNITED STATES, an institution he viewed as a private CORPORATION whose stock the government should not own. He defended SLAVERY vigorously during the Missouri debates and, at the Virginia Constitutional Convention of 1829–1830, voted consistently with tidewater slaveholders against the democratic forces of the West. Barbour also supported the court-curbing plan of Senator Richard Johnson of Kentucky, prompted by the Court's decision in COHENS V. VIRGINIA (1821), and in 1827 he himself sponsored a measure that would have required a majority of five of seven Justices to hold a law unconstitutional.

Four years on the Court gave Barbour little chance to translate his states' rights philosophy and theory of judicial power into law. He wrote only a handful of opinions, and only in MAYOR OF NEW YORK V. MILN (1837) did he speak for the majority in an important case. There he upheld a New York regulation of immigrants as a STATE POLICE POWER measure, but his exposition of doctrine was inchoate at best and did little to influence future decisions. States' rights thinking also informed his vote in CHARLES RIVER BRIDGE V. WARREN BRIDGE (1837) (where he joined the new Jacksonian majority in refusing to extend by implication the 1819 ruling in DARTMOUTH COLLEGE V. WOODWARD) and in BRISCOE V. BANK OF KENTUCKY, also in 1837 (where the new majority refused to invalidate state bank notes on the ground that they were not BILLS OF CREDIT prohibited by Article I, section 10, of the Constitution).

Although he was a consistent advocate of states' rights, Barbour was not, as JOHN QUINCY ADAMS charged, a "shallow-pated wild-cat" bent on destroying the Union. Indeed, compared to the states' rights views of PETER DANIEL who succeeded him, Barbour's appear moderate and restrained. Even DANIEL

WEBSTER conceded that he was "honest and conscientious," and Justice JOSEPH STORY, for all his objection to Barbour's constitutional notions, thought him a "perspicacious" and "vigorous" judge.

R. KENT NEWMYER

Bibliography

CYNN, P. P. 1913 Philip Pendleton Barbour. *The John P. Branch Historical Papers* (Randolph Macon College) 4:67–77.
GATELL, FRANK O. 1969 Philip Pendleton Barbour. In Leon Friedman and Fred L. Israel (eds.), *The Justices of the United States Supreme Court, 1789–1969*, Vol. 1, pages 717–734. New York: Chelsea House.

BAREFOOT v. ESTELLE
463 U.S. 880 (1983)

In *Barefoot v. Estelle* the Supreme Court gave its approval to expedited federal collateral review of CAPITAL PUNISHMENT cases. In a 6–3 decision the Court approved the consolidation of hearings on procedural and substantive motions, the separate arguing of which had frustrated imposition of the death penalty even when the claims supporting the appeal were without merit. The opinion by Justice BYRON R. WHITE declared that no constitutional right of the convict was impaired by the one-step appeals process.

DENNIS J. MAHONEY

BARENBLATT v. UNITED STATES
360 U.S. 109 (1959)

In a 5–4 decision, Justice JOHN MARSHALL HARLAN writing for the majority, the Supreme Court upheld Barenblatt's conviction for contempt of Congress based on his refusal to answer questions of the House Committee on Un-American Activities about his membership in the Communist party. He argued that such questions violated his rights of FREEDOM OF SPEECH and association by publically exposing his political beliefs. In an earlier decision, WATKINS V. UNITED STATES (1957), the Court had offered some procedural protections to witnesses before such committees and held out hope that it would offer even greater protections in the future. *Barenblatt* ended that hope.

The Court did follow the *Watkins* approach of denouncing "exposure for the exposure's sake" and requiring that Congress have a legislative purpose for its investigations. But it presumed that Congress did have such a purpose, refusing to look at the actual congressional motives behind the investigation.

Barenblatt is the classic case of a FIRST AMENDMENT ad hoc BALANCING TEST. The Court held that the First Amendment protected individuals from compelled disclosure of their political associations. But Justice Harlan went on to say, "Where First Amendment rights are asserted to bar governmental interrogation, resolution of the issue always involved a balancing by the Courts of the competing private and public interest at stake in the circumstances shown." Then he balanced Barenblatt's interest in not answering questions about his communist associations against Congress's interest in frustrating the international communist conspiracy to overthrow the United States government. The interests thus defined, the Court had no trouble striking the balance in favor of the government. More than any other decision, *Barenblatt* establishes that the freedom of speech may be restricted by government if, in the Court's view, the government's interest in committing the infringement is sufficiently compelling.

MARTIN SHAPIRO

BARKER v. WINGO
407 U.S. 514 (1972)

The SPEEDY TRIAL right protects a defendant from undue delay between the time charges are filed and trial. When a defendant is deprived of that right, the only remedy is dismissal with prejudice of the charges pending against him. In *Barker*, the leading speedy trial decision, the Supreme Court discussed the criteria by which the speedy trial right is to be judged. The Court adopted a BALANCING TEST involving four factors to be weighed in each case where the issue arises. They are: (1) the length of the delay; (2) the reasons for the delay; (3) the defendant's assertion of his right; and (4) prejudice to the defendant, such as pretrial incarceration and inability to prepare a defense. In reaching its decision the Court noted that the speedy trial right is unique inasmuch as it protects societal rights as well as those of the accused. In many instances, delayed trials benefit a defendant because witnesses disappear or memories fade. The balancing takes into consideration the varied interests protected by that right.

WENDY E. LEVY

BARRON v. CITY OF BALTIMORE
7 Peters 243 (1833)

When JAMES MADISON proposed to the First Congress the amendments that became the BILL OF RIGHTS, he included a provision that no state shall violate FREEDOM OF RELIGION, FREEDOM OF PRESS, or TRIAL BY JURY in criminal cases; the proposal to restrict the states was defeated. The amendments constituting a Bill of Rights were understood to be a bill of restraints upon the United States only. In *Barron*, Chief Justice JOHN MARSHALL for a unanimous Supreme Court ruled in conformance with the clear history of the matter. *Barron* invoked against Baltimore the clause of the Fifth Amendment prohibiting the taking of private property without JUST COMPENSATION. The "fifth amendment," the Court held, "must be understood as restraining the power of the general government, not as applicable to the states."

LEONARD W. LEVY

BARROWS v. JACKSON
346 U.S. 249 (1953)

Following the decision in SHELLEY V. KRAEMER (1948), state courts could no longer constitutionally enforce racially RESTRICTIVE COVENANTS by INJUNCTION. The question remained whether the covenants could be enforced indirectly, in actions for damages. In *Barrows*, white neighbors sued for damages against co-covenantors who had sold a home to black buyers in disregard of a racial covenant. The Supreme Court held that the sellers had STANDING to raise the EQUAL PROTECTION claims on behalf of the black buyers, who were not in court, and went on to hold that the FOURTEENTH AMENDMENT barred damages as well as injunctive relief to enforce racial covenants. Chief Justice FRED M. VINSON, who had written the *Shelley* opinion, dissented, saying the covenant itself, "standing alone," was valid, in the absence of judicial ejectment of black occupants.

KENNETH L. KARST

BARTKUS v. ILLINOIS
359 U.S. 121 (1959)
ABBATE v. UNITED STATES
359 U.S. 187 (1959)

A 5–4 Supreme Court held in *Bartkus v. Illinois* that close cooperation between state and federal officials did not violate the DOUBLE JEOPARDY clause when

Illinois tried (and convicted) Bartkus for a robbery of which a federal court had acquitted him. Justice FELIX FRANKFURTER's majority opinion de-emphasized the connection between the prosecutions. Despite "substantially identical" INDICTMENTS and although the Federal Bureau of Investigation had given all its EVIDENCE to state authorities, Frankfurter could find no basis for the claim that Illinois was "merely a tool of the federal authorities" or that the Illinois prosecution violated the DUE PROCESS CLAUSE of the FOURTEENTH AMENDMENT. He rejected the assertion that the Fourteenth Amendment was a "short-hand incorporation" of the BILL OF RIGHTS and also cited the test of PALKO V. CONNECTICUT (1937) with approval.

Justice HUGO L. BLACK, joined by Chief Justice EARL WARREN and Justice WILLIAM O. DOUGLAS, dissented. Black found such prosecutions "so contrary to the spirit of our free country that they violate even the prevailing view of the Fourteenth Amendment." Justice WILLIAM J. BRENNAN, dissenting separately, presented convincing evidence that federal officers solicited, instigated, guided, and prepared the Illinois case, amounting to a second federal prosecution "in the guise of a state prosecution."

Justice Brennan joined the *Bartkus* majority in *Abbate v. United States,* decided the same day. The defendants here were indicted and convicted in both state and federal courts for the same act, the federal prosecution following the state conviction. Brennan, for the majority, relied squarely on UNITED STATES V. LANZA (1922), concluding that "the efficiency of federal law enforcement must suffer if the Double Jeopardy Clause prevents successive state and federal prosecutions." Black, for the same minority, relied on his *Bartkus* dissent and the distinction "that a State and the Nation can [not] be considered two wholly separate sovereignties for the purpose of allowing them to do together what, generally, neither can do separately."

DAVID GORDON

BASSETT, RICHARD
(1745–1815)

Richard Bassett represented Delaware at the CONSTITUTIONAL CONVENTION OF 1787 and signed the Constitution. Although there is no record of his speaking at the Convention, he was a leader in securing Delaware's ratification. He went on to become governor and chief justice of Delaware, and a United States senator.

DENNIS J. MAHONEY

BATES, EDWARD
(1793–1869)

A St. Louis attorney and Whig leader, Edward Bates, a moderate on slavery, opposed the LECOMPTON Constitution and repeal of the MISSOURI COMPROMISE. In 1860 he sought the Republican presidential nomination, and from 1861 to 1864 he was President ABRAHAM LINCOLN's ATTORNEY GENERAL and most conservative adviser. In response to EX PARTE MERRYMAN (1861) he defended Lincoln's suspension of HABEAS CORPUS on the weak rationale that the three branches of government were co-equal and that Chief Justice ROGER B. TANEY therefore could not order Lincoln to act. Bates personally disliked the suspension but thought it preferable to martial law. The CONFISCATION ACTS undermined Bates's sense of property rights, and his department rarely supported these acts. Bates strongly supported the EMANCIPATION PROCLAMATION, but he insisted it be limited to areas still under rebel control. He believed that free blacks could be United States citizens because he narrowly construed DRED SCOTT V. SANDFORD (1857) to apply only to Negroes "of *African* descent" suing in Missouri. Bates supplied legal opinions to support the legal tender statutes, but he opposed the admission of West Virginia on constitutional grounds. He also opposed the use of black troops and retaliation for atrocities by Confederates committed on black prisoners of war. Nevertheless, he urged Lincoln to give Negro soldiers equal pay once they were enlisted. Bates consistently urged Lincoln to assert his constitutional role as COMMANDER-IN-CHIEF when Union generalship was poor. Bates had a broad view of his office and exerted a greater control over the United States district attorneys than his predecessors.

PAUL FINKELMAN

Bibliography

CAIN, MARVIN E. 1965 *Lincoln's Attorney General: Edward Bates of Missouri.* Columbia: University of Missouri Press.

BATES v. STATE BAR OF ARIZONA
433 U.S. 350 (1977)

In 1976 two Phoenix lawyers ran newspaper advertisements offering "routine" legal services for "very reasonable" prices. A 5–4 Supreme Court declared here that the FIRST AMENDMENT protected this form of COMMERCIAL SPEECH. The majority rejected a number of "countervailing state interests" urged against the FREEDOM OF SPEECH protection, relying on VIRGINIA STATE BOARD OF PHARMACY V. VIRGINIA CITIZENS' CONSUMER COUNCIL (1976). The dissenters strenuously objected to the majority's equating intangible services—which they found impossible to standardize and rarely "routine"—with "prepackaged prescription drugs." The Court rejected, 9–0, a contention that the SHERMAN ANTITRUST ACT barred any restraint on such advertising.

DAVID GORDON

BAYARD v. SINGLETON
1 Martin (N. Car.) 42 (1787)

This was the first reported American state case in which a court held a legislative enactment unconstitutional. This and the TEN POUND ACT CASES are the only authentic examples of the exercise of JUDICIAL REVIEW carried to its furthest limit before the circuit work of the Justices of the Supreme Court of the United States in the 1790s. During the Revolution, North Carolina had confiscated and sold Tory estates; to protect the new owners, the legislature enacted that in any action to recover confiscated land, the courts must grant a motion to dismiss the suit. Bayard brought such a suit, and Singleton made a motion for dismissal. Instead of granting the motion, the high court of the state delayed decision and recommended a jury trial to settle the issue of ownership. The court seemed to be seeking a way to avoid holding the act unconstitutional and hoped that the legislature might revise it. The legislature summoned the judges before it to determine whether they were guilty of malpractice in office by disregarding a statute. The legislature found no basis for IMPEACHMENT but refused to revise the statute. On a renewed motion to dismiss, the court held the act void, on the ground that "by the constitution every citizen had undoubtedly a right to a decision of his property by TRIAL BY JURY." In defense of judicial review, the court reasoned that no statute could alter or repeal the state constitution, which was FUNDAMENTAL LAW. The court then submitted the case to a jury. The committee of the legislature that had heard the charges against the judges included RICHARD DOBBS SPAIGHT, a vehement antagonist of judicial review, and WILLIAM R. DAVIE, co-counsel for Bayard; shortly after, both men represented North Carolina at the CONSTITUTIONAL CONVENTION OF

1787. JAMES IREDELL, later one of the first Justices of the Supreme Court of the United States, also represented Bayard. Iredell published an address, "To the Public," in 1786, anticipating the doctrine of *Bayard v. Singleton,* and his correspondence with Spaight on judicial review best reflects the arguments at that time for and against the power of courts to hold enactments unconstitutional. Spaight's position, that such a power was a "usurpation" by the judiciary, accorded with the then prevailing theory and practice of legislative supremacy.

LEONARD W. LEVY

BEACON THEATRES, INC. v. WESTOVER
359 U.S. 500 (1964)

Fox West Coast Theatres, Inc., contending that it was being harassed and that its business was being impeded by the threats of a competitor, Beacon Theatres, Inc., to bring an ANTITRUST suit, brought an action for DECLARATORY JUDGMENT in the U.S. District Court. Beacon, in a countersuit, alleged conspiracy in restraint of trade, and asked treble damages under the SHERMAN ANTITRUST ACT.

Judge Westover, exercising his discretion under the Declaratory Judgment Act and the FEDERAL RULES OF CIVIL PROCEDURE, decided to hear first the declaratory judgment suit, which, as an action in EQUITY did not require a jury. Only if that suit were decided in favor of Beacon would the antitrust suit be tried.

The Supreme Court, in an opinion by Justice HUGO L. BLACK, held (5–3) that Westover's decision deprived Beacon of its right to TRIAL BY JURY in a civil case. Because trial by jury is a constitutional right, judicial discretion must be used to preserve it unless there is a showing that irreparable harm would result from the delay. "Only under the most imperative circumstances," Black wrote, ". . . can the right to a jury trial of legal issues be lost through prior determination of equitable claims."

DENNIS J. MAHONEY

BEARD, CHARLES A.
(1874–1948)

Charles Austin Beard, more than any other historian, shaped the way twentieth-century Americans look at the framing of the Constitution. He thus occupied, as he said a historian should, "the position of a statesman dealing with public affairs."

After being graduated at de Pauw and Columbia Universities, Beard continued his studies in Europe. His early writings reflect a theory of strict economic determinism; in *The Rise of American Civilization* (1927) he argued that the Civil War was less a struggle between SLAVERY and freedom than an epiphenomenon of emerging industrialism. Throughout his career as a teacher at Columbia University and the New School for Social Research and as a writer he maintained that historians cannot discover or describe the past as it actually was, but must instead reinterpret the past in order to shape their own times and the future.

Beard's most influential work was his *Economic Interpretation of the Constitution*. First published in 1913, the book was part of the Progressive movement's assault on such "undemocratic" constitutional obstacles to reform as the SEPARATION OF POWERS, CHECKS AND BALANCES, and FEDERALISM. The work was republished, with a new introduction, in 1935, when the forms of CONSTITUTIONALISM again seemed to frustrate attempts at reform legislation. The thesis of the book is that the Constitution was framed by large holders of personal property and capital (especially government securities) in order to further their own economic interests and to frustrate the majority will. The effect of the book at the time of each publication was to undermine the legitimacy of the Constitution in the public mind by ascribing base motives to its authors. Beard's assumptions about the amounts and types of property owned by the Framers have been thoroughly discredited; yet his thesis about the origin of the Constitution became the standard version taught in universities and public schools. Even his opponents have adopted Beard's analytical framework.

Besides the *Economic Interpretation*, Beard, alone or with his wife, Mary Ritter Beard, was author of some two dozen books on politics and history. He was also president both of the American Historical Association and of the American Political Science Association.

DENNIS J. MAHONEY

Bibliography

BROWN, ROBERT E. 1956 *Charles Beard and the Constitution.* Princeton, N.J.: Princeton University Press.

BEAUHARNAIS v. ILLINOIS
343 U.S. 250 (1952)

The Supreme Court upheld, 5–4, an Illinois GROUP LIBEL statute that forbade publications depicting a racial or religious group as depraved or lacking in virtue. Justice FELIX FRANKFURTER first argued that certain categories of speech including LIBEL had traditionally been excluded from FIRST AMENDMENT protection, and he then deferred to the legislative judgment redefining libel to include defamation of groups as well as individuals. By mixing excluded-categories arguments with arguments for judicial deference to legislative judgments for which there is a RATIONAL BASIS, the opinion moves toward a position in which the relative merits of a particular speech are weighed against the social interests protected by the statute, with the ultimate constitutional balance heavily weighted in favor of whatever balance the legislature has struck. Although *Beauharnais* has not been overruled, its continued validity is doubtful after NEW YORK TIMES v. SULLIVAN (1964).

MARTIN SHAPIRO

(SEE ALSO: *Freedom of Speech.*)

BECKER AMENDMENT
(1964)

The public indignation aroused by the Supreme Court's decisions on school prayer and Bible reading (ENGEL v. VITALE, 1962; ABINGTON TOWNSHIP v. SCHEMPP, 1963) provoked the introduction in Congress of over 160 proposals to amend the Constitution. When Chairman Emmanuel Celler, who opposed the amendments, bottled them up in his House Judiciary Committee, the proponents united behind a compromise measure drafted by Representative Frank J. Becker of New York.

The Becker Amendment was worded as a guide to interpretation of existing constitutional provisions rather than as new law. It had three parts. The first two provided that nothing in the Constitution should be deemed to prohibit voluntary prayer or scripture reading in schools or public institutions or the invocation of divine assistance in government documents or ceremonies or on coins or currency. The third part declared: "Nothing in this article shall constitute an ESTABLISHMENT OF RELIGION."

Under pressure of parliamentary maneuvering, Celler conducted hearings in 1964—at which many denominational leaders and constitutional scholars expressed opposition to the Becker Amendment—but his committee never reported any proposal to the House. Amendments similar to Becker's have been introduced in subsequent Congresses, but none has come close to the majority votes needed for submission to the states.

DENNIS J. MAHONEY

BEDFORD, GUNNING, JR.
(1747–1812)

Gunning Bedford, Jr., represented Delaware at the CONSTITUTIONAL CONVENTION OF 1787 and signed the Constitution. A spokesman for small-state positions, he vigorously advocated equal representation of the states in Congress; he also argued for easy removal of the president and against the VETO POWER. He was a delegate to Delaware's ratifying convention.

DENNIS J. MAHONEY

BEDFORD CUT STONE COMPANY v. JOURNEYMEN STONE CUTTERS ASSOCIATION
273 U.S. 37 (1927)

The company sought to destroy the union. The union's national membership of 5,000 men then refused to work on buildings made of the stone quarried by the company, which sought an INJUNCTION on the ground that the union's activities restrained INTERSTATE COMMERCE in violation of the ANTITRUST laws. Lower federal courts refused to enjoin the union. The Supreme Court commanded the injunction. The dissenting opinion of Justices LOUIS D. BRANDEIS and OLIVER WENDELL HOLMES revealed the significance of the case. When, Brandeis observed, capitalists combined to control major industries, the Court ruled that their restraints on commerce were "reasonable" and not violations of the antitrust acts. When, however, a small union, as its only means of self-protection, refused to work on products of an antiunion company, the Court forgot its RULE OF REASON and discovered unreasonable restraint. Brandeis might have added that the Court had made "antitrust" a synonym for "antilabor."

LEONARD W. LEVY

BELL v. MARYLAND
378 U.S. 226 (1964)

This case was the last SIT-IN case decided before the PUBLIC ACCOMMODATIONS provisions of the CIVIL RIGHTS ACT OF 1964 took effect. Twelve black students were convicted of criminal trespass for their participation in a sit-in demonstration in Baltimore. The Supreme Court reversed their conviction and remanded to the Maryland courts for clarification of state law. Six Justices, however, addressed the larger constitutional question that had been presented to the Court in case after case in the early 1960s: whether the FOURTEENTH AMENDMENT, in the absence of congressional legislation, provided a right to service in places of public accommodation. These six Justices divided 3–3.

Justices WILLIAM O. DOUGLAS and ARTHUR J. GOLDBERG, concurring in the reversal of the convictions, argued that racial SEGREGATION in public accommodations imposed a caste system that was inconsistent with the abolition of slavery and with the Fourteenth Amendment's establishment of CITIZENSHIP. The refusal to serve blacks, Douglas said, did not reflect any interest in the proprietor's associational RIGHT OF PRIVACY, but rather was aimed at promoting business. Because the restaurant was "property that is serving the public," it had a constitutional obligation not to exclude a portion of the public on racial grounds. Chief Justice EARL WARREN joined Goldberg's opinion, which focused on the rights of citizenship.

Justice HUGO L. BLACK dissented, joined by Justices JOHN MARSHALL HARLAN and BYRON R. WHITE. He indicated strongly his view that Congress, in enforcing the Fourteenth Amendment, could provide a right of access to public accommodations. In the absence of such a law, however, Black was unwilling to find in the Fourteenth Amendment a right to enter on the property of another against the owner's will. (At the ORAL ARGUMENT of the *Bell* case, Justice Black had observed, "But this was *private* property.") The state was entitled to protect the owner's decision by the ordinary processes of law without converting the owner's personal prejudices into state policy, and thus STATE ACTION.

KENNETH L. KARST

BELL v. WOLFISH

See: Right of Privacy

BELMONT, UNITED STATES v.
301 U.S. 324 (1937)

Belmont arose in the wake of President FRANKLIN D. ROOSEVELT's formal recognition of the Soviet Union in 1933 pursuant to an EXECUTIVE AGREEMENT between the two countries. In conjunction with this act of recognition, Soviet claims to assets located in the United States and nationalized by the Soviet Union in 1918 were assigned to the United States under a collateral agreement known as the "Litvinov Assignment." When the federal government sought to enforce these claims in the state of New York, however, the New York courts dismissed the suit, holding that to allow the federal government to enforce the assignment would contradict New York public policy against confiscation of private property.

The Supreme Court unanimously reversed, holding that the Litvinov Assignment, as part of the process of recognition, not only created international obligations but also superseded any conflicting state law or policy. In so holding, the Court affirmed the President's constitutional authority to speak "as the sole organ" of the national government in formally recognizing another nation and to take all steps necessary to effect such recognition. The Court stated that all acts of recognition unite as one transaction (here, in an "international compact" or executive agreement) which, unlike a formal TREATY, becomes a part of the "supreme Law of the Land" without requiring the ADVICE AND CONSENT of the Senate.

BURNS H. WESTON

(SEE ALSO: *Foreign Affairs and the Constitution; Pink, United States v.*)

Bibliography
HENKIN, LOUIS 1972 *Foreign Affairs and the Constitution.* Mineola, N.Y.: Foundation Press.

BENIGN RACIAL CLASSIFICATION

Although race must always be regarded as a SUSPECT CLASSIFICATION, there are circumstances in which official RACIAL DISCRIMINATION may be constitutionally permissible because the purpose is "benign and ameliorative." In *United States v. Montgomery County Board of Education* (1969), for example, the Supreme Court upheld a system of RACIAL QUOTAS for teachers imposed by a federal judge as part of a desegregation program. In REGENTS OF UNIVERSITY OF CALIFORNIA V. BAKKE (1978) the Court invalidated quotas but indicated that preferential treatment of minority applicants would be acceptable. The question remains whether the government can sponsor AFFIRMATIVE ACTION without denying any person EQUAL PROTECTION OF THE LAWS.

DENNIS J. MAHONEY

BENTON, THOMAS HART
(1782–1858)

A Missouri attorney, senator (1821–1851), and congressman (1853–1855), Thomas Hart Benton was an avid Jacksonian Democrat who led the opposition, on constitutional and economic grounds, to rechartering the second BANK OF THE UNITED STATES. A hard-money man, nicknamed "Old Bullion," Benton supported President ANDREW JACKSON's "specie circular" despite its adverse effects on his cherished goal of westward expansion. Benton opposed NULLIFICATION, and was ever after an enemy of JOHN C. CALHOUN and state sovereignty, allegedly saying in 1850 that Calhoun "died with TREASON in his heart and on his lips." Benton opposed extension of and agitation over SLAVERY, and he personally favored gradual emancipation. Thus, Benton opposed the ANNEXATION OF TEXAS, bellicose agitation over Oregon, war with Mexico (although he ultimately voted for the war), the WILMONT PROVISO, and HENRY CLAY's "Omnibus Bill" because all of these issues would impede western expansion and California statehood by involving them with slavery extension. Benton ultimately voted for some of the compromise measures in 1850, including the extension of slavery into some of the territories, but he opposed the new fugitive slave law. His opposition led to proslavery backlash and his defeat for reelection in 1850. In 1854 Benton published his senatorial memoirs, *Thirty Years View,* and in 1856–1857 *An Abridgement of the Debates of Congress.* While on his death bed, Benton wrote a long tract on DRED SCOTT V. SANDFORD in which he argued for the constitutionality of the MISSOURI COMPROMISE and savaged Chief Justice ROGER B. TANEY's opinion, which Benton believed was legally, historically, and constitutionally invalid, blatantly proslavery, and antiunion.

PAUL FINKELMAN

Bibliography
CHAMBERS, WILLIAM W. 1956 *Old Bullion Benton: Senator from the New West.* Boston: Little, Brown.

BENTON v. MARYLAND
395 U.S. 784 (1969)

This decision, one of the last of the WARREN COURT, extended the DOUBLE JEOPARDY provision of the Fifth Amendment to the states. (See INCORPORATION DOCTRINE.) A Maryland prisoner, having been acquitted on a larceny charge, successfully appealed his burglary conviction, only to be reindicted and convicted on both counts. A 7–2 Supreme Court, speaking through Justice THURGOOD MARSHALL, overruled PALKO V. CONNECTICUT (1937) and, relying on DUNCAN V. LOUISIANA (1968), declared that the Fifth Amendment guarantee "represents a fundamental ideal" which must be applied. Dissenting, Justices JOHN MARSHALL HARLAN and POTTER STEWART reiterated their opposition to incorporation, concluding that the WRIT OF CERTIORARI had been improvidently granted. In OBITER DICTUM they added that retrial here violated even the *Palko* standards.

DAVID GORDON

BEREA COLLEGE v. KENTUCKY
211 U.S. 45 (1908)

Berea College, founded half a century earlier by abolitionists, was fined $1,000 under a Kentucky statute forbidding the operation of racially integrated schools. The Supreme Court affirmed the conviction, 7–2, sustaining the law as an exercise of state power to govern CORPORATIONS. Justice JOHN MARSHALL HARLAN, a Kentuckian personally acquainted with the college, dissented, arguing that the law unconstitutionally deprived the school of liberty and property without DUE PROCESS OF LAW. His denunciation of state-enforced SEGREGATION also echoed his dissent in PLESSY V. FERGUSON (1896). The majority addressed neither issue.

KENNETH L. KARST

BERGER v. NEW YORK
388 U.S. 41 (1967)

A New York statute authorized electronic surveillance by police under certain circumstances. A conviction for conspiring to bribe a state official based on such surveillance was set aside because the statute did not meet FOURTH AMENDMENT requirements: (1) it did not require the police to describe in detail the place to be searched or the conversation to be seized, or to specify the particular crime being investigated; (2) it did not adequately limit the period of the intrusion; (3) it did not provide for adequate notice of the eavesdropping to the people overheard. These requirements were later incorporated in the OMNIBUS CRIME CONTROL AND SAFE STREETS ACT (1968).

HERMAN SCHWARTZ

BERMAN v. PARKER

See: Eminent Domain; Public Use; Taking of Property

BETTS v. BRADY
316 U.S. 455 (1942)

In *Betts* an INDIGENT defendant was convicted of robbery after his request for appointed counsel was denied. The Court held that the DUE PROCESS clause of the FOURTEENTH AMENDMENT required states to furnish counsel only when special circumstances showed that otherwise the trial would be fundamentally unfair. Here, because the defendant was of "ordinary intelligence" and not "wholly unfamiliar" with CRIMINAL PROCEDURE, the Court found no special circumstances.

Over the next two decades, *Betts* was consistently undermined by expansion of the "special circumstances" exception, resulting in the appointment of counsel in most FELONY cases, until it was finally overruled in GIDEON V. WAINWRIGHT (1963).

BARBARA ALLEN BABCOCK

(SEE ALSO: *Right to Counsel.*)

BEVERIDGE, ALBERT J.
(1862–1927)

Albert Jeremiah Beveridge of Indiana, a lawyer and orator of extraordinary talent and overweening ambition, served two terms in the United States Senate (1899–1911) as a Republican. He advocated imperialism to open new markets for American industry and favored permanent annexation of the insular TERRITORIES gained in the Spanish-American War, without extension of constitutional protections and self-government, for which their non-Anglo-Saxon inhabitants were unfit. An economic nationalist, Beveridge favored repeal of the SHERMAN ANTITRUST ACT, believing that trusts should not be broken up but regulated in the national interest. Defeated for reelection, Beveridge joined THEODORE ROOSEVELT's Progressive Party and was its candidate for governor in 1912. Defeated again, he turned to writing a long-planned biography of Chief Justice JOHN MARSHALL. The four-volume work, completed in 1919, won a Pulitzer Prize for biography. In the book Beveridge presents Marshall as the statesman who molded the Constitution to meet the needs of a vigorous, commercial nation, over the objections of petty agrarians and disunionists like THOMAS JEFFERSON.

DENNIS J. MAHONEY

Bibliography

BOWERS, CLAUDE G. 1932 *Beveridge and the Progressive Era.* New York: Literary Guild.

BIBB v. NAVAJO FREIGHT LINES, INC.
359 U.S. 520 (1959)

A unanimous Supreme Court here voided a state highway safety regulation because the state failed to demonstrate sufficient justification to balance the burden it imposed on INTERSTATE COMMERCE. An Illinois statute required trucks using its highways to employ a particular mudguard, outlawed in Arkansas and distinct from those allowed elsewhere. The Court said that cost and safety problems alone were insufficient reason for invalidation, given the "strong presumption of validity" owing to the statute. But, by creating a conflicting standard, the Illinois statute had seriously interfered with and imposed a "massive" burden on interstate commerce.

DAVID GORDON

(SEE ALSO: *State Regulation of Commerce.*)

BIBLE READING

See: Religion in Public Schools

BICAMERALISM

Bicameralism, the principle of CONSTITUTIONALISM that requires the legislature to be composed of two chambers (or houses), is a feature of the United States Constitution and of the constitution of every state except Nebraska. Bicameralism is supposed to guarantee deliberation in the exercise of the LEGISLATIVE POWER, by requiring that measures be debated in and approved by two different bodies before becoming law. It is also one of those "auxiliary precautions" by which constitutional democracy is protected from the mischiefs latent in popular self-government.

Bicameralism is not distinctively American; there were bicameral legislatures in the ancient republics of Greece and Rome, and there are bicameral legislatures in most countries of the world today. Bicameralism is found in the constitutions of nondemocratic countries (such as the Soviet Union) as well as of democratic countries. And, despite historical association with disparities of social class, both legislative chambers in democratic countries—emphatically including the United States—are typically chosen in popular elections; in countries where one house is chosen other than by election, that house is significantly less powerful than the elective house. Moreover, although it is the practice of most federal nations (such as Australia, Switzerland, and the Federal Republic of Germany) to reflect the constituent SOVEREIGNTY of the states in one house of the legislature, there are bicameral legislatures in countries where FEDERALISM is unknown.

The American colonists came originally from Britain and were familiar with the BRITISH CONSTITUTION. In Parliament, as the Framers knew it, there were two houses with equal power, reflecting two orders of society: the House of Lords comprising the hereditary aristocracy of England (together with representatives of the Scots nobility and the ecclesiastical hierarchy), and the House of Commons representing the freeholders of the counties and the chartered cities. Seats in the House of Commons were apportioned according to the status of the constituency (five seats per county, two per city), not according to population.

The local lawmaking bodies in the colonies were originally unicameral. Bicameralism was introduced in Massachusetts in 1644, in Maryland in 1650, and (in a unique form) in Pennsylvania in 1682; but in each case the "upper house" was identical with the governor's council, and so performed both legislative and executive functions. In the eighteenth century, all of the colonial legislatures but one were bicameral, with a lower house elected by the freeholders and an upper house generally comprising representatives of the wealthier classes. At the same time the upper houses (although retaining the name "council") became distinctly legislative bodies.

When the newly independent states began constructing constitutions after 1776, all but Pennsylvania and Georgia provided for bicameral legislatures. Typically, the upper house was elected separately from the lower and had higher qualifications for membership, but it was elected from districts apportioned on the same basis and by electorates with the same qualifications. In two states, Maryland and South Carolina, the upper houses were elected indirectly.

The CONTINENTAL CONGRESS, although it conducted a war, negotiated a peace, and directed the collective business of the United States, was never in form a national legislature. Even after its status was regularized by the ARTICLES OF CONFEDERATION, the Congress was a body composed of delegates selected by the state governments and responsible to them. A bicameral Congress was neither desirable nor feasible until Congress became the legislative branch of a national government.

The delegates to the CONSTITUTIONAL CONVENTION OF 1787 agreed at the outset on a bicameral national legislature. In the VIRGINIA PLAN, membership in the first house of Congress would have been apportioned according to the population of the states, and the second house would have been elected by the first. The GREAT COMPROMISE produced the Congress as we know it, with the House of Representatives apportioned by population (described by JAMES MADISON in THE FEDERALIST #39 as a "national" feature of the Constitution) and with equal REPRESENTATION of the states in the Senate (a "federal" feature), so that Congress itself reflects the compound character of American government.

The two principles of apportionment serve to insure that different points of view are brought to bear on deliberations in the two houses. That consideration is also advanced by having different terms for members of the two houses; a shorter term bringing legislators into more frequent contact with public opinion, a longer term permitting legislators to take a more extended view of the public interest. The priority of the House of Representatives with respect to revenue (taxing) measures and the association of the Senate with the executive in the exercise of the TREATY POWER and the APPOINTING POWER also tend to introduce different points of view into legislative deliberations. Until abolished by the SEVENTEENTH AMENDMENT, the election of senators by the state legislatures also contributed to the formation of different viewpoints.

The principal justification for bicameralism is that it increases and improves the deliberation on public measures. But bicameralism is also a device to protect constitutional government against the peculiar evils inherent in democratic government. One must guard against equating democracy, or even majority rule, with the immediate satisfaction of the short-term demands of transient majorities. As *The Federalist* #10 points out, a faction—a group whose aims are at odds with the rights of other citizens or with permanent and aggregate interests of the whole country—may at any given time amount to a majority of the popula-

tion. Although no mechanical device can guarantee that a majority faction will not prevail, the bicameral structure of Congress operates to make such a result less likely than it might otherwise be.

The Supreme Court cited the importance of bicameralism in the American constitutional system as one reason for striking down the LEGISLATIVE VETO in IMMIGRATION AND NATURALIZATION SERVICE V. CHADHA (1983). According to Chief Justice WARREN E. BURGER, that device permitted public policy to be altered by either house of Congress, contravening the belief of the Framers "that legislation should not be enacted unless it has been carefully and fully considered" lest special interests "be favored at the expense of public needs."

Bicameralism is also a principle of American constitutionalism at the state level. At one time representation of the lesser political units, typically the counties, was the rule for state upper houses. In REYNOLDS V. SIMS (1964), however, the Supreme Court held that such schemes of representation resulted in the overvaluation of the votes of rural citizens relative to those of urban and suburban citizens and that they therefore denied the latter the EQUAL PROTECTION OF THE LAWS in violation of the FOURTEENTH AMENDMENT. Some commentators, both scholars and politicians, predicted that imposition of the ONE PERSON, ONE VOTE standard would spell the doom of bicameralism at the state level. However, no state has changed to a unicameral system since the *Reynolds* decision.

Even more than to the innate reluctance of politicians to abolish any public office, this fact is testimony to the independent vitality of bicameralism as a constitutional principle. Even when territoriality is removed as a rationale, the desirability of having a second opinion on proposals before they become law cannot be gainsaid. Hence there is a tendency in the states to find ways of giving their upper houses a distinct perspective. The ordinary differentiation is by the size of the chambers and the length of the terms of office. Some states have tried, with the Supreme Court's approval, to preserve the territorial basis of the upper house by creating MULTIMEMBER DISTRICTS in the more populous territorial units.

The meaning of constitutionalism in a democratic polity is that the short-term interests of the majority will not be allowed to prevail if they are contrary to the rights of the minority or to the permanent and aggregate interests of the whole. The permanent and aggregate interests are not represented by any person or group of people, but they are protected by a constitutional system that requires prudent deliberation in the conduct of lawmaking. Bicameralism is an important constitutional principle because, and to the extent that, it institutionalizes such deliberation.

DENNIS J. MAHONEY

Bibliography

EIDELBERG, PAUL 1968 *The Political Philosophy of the American Constitution.* New York: Free Press.
WHEARE, KENNETH C. 1963 *Legislatures.* New York: Oxford University Press.

BICKEL, ALEXANDER M.
(1925–1974)

Alexander Bickel was a professor at Yale Law School from 1956 to 1974 and a prolific writer on law and politics. He became the most influential academic critic of the progressive liberal jurisprudence of his time, although he at first made only sympathetic refinements of that doctrine. Having served as a clerk for Justice FELIX FRANKFURTER and edited some unpublished judicial opinions of Justice LOUIS D. BRANDEIS, he, like they, rejected the old CONSTITUTIONALISM of private rights and unchanging FUNDAMENTAL LAW in favor of a living law, evolving with social conditions and with a progressive consciousness. His first important book, *The Least Dangerous Branch* (1962), advanced a variation of Frankfurter's prescription of judicial restraint. Bickel elaborated ways, such as avoiding a constitutional question, by which the SUPREME COURT might accommodate political democracy while enforcing the "principled goals" of a more open, humane, and free society.

In *The Supreme Court and the Idea of Progress* (1970), however, Bickel departed sharply from his role of political tactician for the rule of Supreme Court principle. He attacked the WARREN COURT's principles as themselves impolitic. In Bickel's view, the Court, confident that progress required nationalizing and leveling constitutional limits on the electoral process and an extension of desegregation to racial balancing, had imposed an egalitarianism that was subjective and arbitrary. As a result, Bickel argued, the Court had bred a legalistic authoritarianism and threatened the quality of public schools and distinctive communities.

The Morality of Consent (1975) was published posthumously. It examined the turmoil attending the VIETNAM WAR, student revolt, and WATERGATE, extended Bickel's critique, and attempted a reconstruction. Bickel portrayed the entire American order as

under siege and ill-defended. He saw universities as well as governments and corporations endangered by two extremes of theory—a committed moralism, which tended to a dictatorship of the self-righteous, and a permissive relativism, which would defend nothing and eroded the moral and social fabric. Bickel recurred to Edmund Burke's critique of the French Declaration of the Rights of Man, and then painstakingly set forth his own morality of consent, a morality to sustain not individual claims but the social process of communicating and governing.

ROBERT K. FAULKNER

Bibliography

FAULKNER, ROBERT K. 1978 Bickel's Constitution: The Problem of Moderate Liberalism. *American Political Science Review* 72:925–940.

BIDDLE, FRANCIS
(1886–1968)

Born to wealth and social position, Francis Biddle of Pennsylvania was graduated from Harvard College and Harvard Law School and became a law CLERK to Justice OLIVER WENDELL HOLMES. He entered public service in 1934 as FRANKLIN D. ROOSEVELT's chairman of the National Labor Relations Board. He also served as counsel for the congressional investigation of the Tennessee Valley Authority (1938); as a judge on the United States Court of Appeals for the Third Circuit (1939–1940); as solicitor general (1940–1941); and as attorney general (1941–1945). Biddle stoutly championed CIVIL LIBERTIES and, albeit unsuccessfully, opposed the evacuation of Japanese-Americans from the West Coast. He also served on the International Military Tribunal at Nuremberg, which tried the major German war criminals (1945–1946). Thereafter, Biddle retired to a life of writing and leisure. His chief books were *Fear of Freedom* (1951), an assault on McCarthyism; *Justice Holmes, Natural Law, and the Supreme Court* (1961); and *In Brief Authority* (1962), a record of his public service.

HENRY J. ABRAHAM

Bibliography

BIDDLE, FRANCIS 1962 *In Brief Authority: From the Years with Roosevelt to the Nürnberg Trial.* Garden City, N.Y.: Doubleday.

BILL OF ATTAINDER

In American constitutional law, a bill of attainder is any legislative act that inflicts punishment on designated individuals without a judicial trial. The term includes both the original English bill of attainder, which condemned a person to death for treason or felony and confiscated his property, and the bill of pains and penalties, used for lesser offenses and punishments. The first bill of attainder was passed by Parliament in 1459. They were common during the Tudor and Stuart reigns, and Cromwell's and William and Mary's parliaments also resorted to them. During the Revolutionary period, several state legislatures used bills of attainder to condemn Tories and to confiscate their property. THOMAS JEFFERSON in 1778 drafted, and the Virginia legislature passed, a bill of attainder against Josiah Philips, a notorious Tory brigand. The abuse of the procedure in English and American history foreshadowed the possibility of even greater abuse in the future. The bill of attainder, with its disregard of DUE PROCESS OF LAW, could be a potent weapon for the vengeful and covetous.

At the CONSTITUTIONAL CONVENTION OF 1787, ELBRIDGE GERRY proposed a prohibition against bills of attainder. The measure passed unanimously; it appears in Article I, section 9, as a limitation on Congress, and in Article I, section 10, as a limitation on the states. That the prohibition was meant to extend to all legislative punishments may be seen from a congressional debate in 1794. When Federalist Representative THOMAS FITZSIMONS introduced a resolution to censure the Jeffersonian Democratic Societies and to accuse them of fomenting the WHISKEY REBELLION, JAMES MADISON denounced it as a bill of attainder.

The Supreme Court first spoke to the question in the TEST OATH CASES (1867). The Court held unconstitutional both a Missouri requirement that practitioners of certain professions swear that they had not aided the Confederate cause and a federal requirement that lawyers take such an oath to practice before federal courts. Since former rebels could not take the oaths, they were effectively deprived of their livelihoods. The Missouri legislature and the Congress had therefore passed bills imposing punishment on the ex-Confederates without judicial trial or conviction of any crime.

No other federal law was held to violate the ban on bills of attainder until UNITED STATES v. LOVETT (1946). In that case the Court held unconstitutional a rider to an appropriations bill which prohibited any payment to three named PUBLIC EMPLOYEES, previously identified as subversives before a congressional committee, unless they were first discharged and reappointed. In *Lovett* the Court expanded on the definition it had given in the *Test Oath Cases,* making

clear that all legislative acts were covered, "no matter what their form."

In recent judicial interpretation of the bills-of-attainder clause a law prohibiting Communist party members from holding labor union office was declared unconstitutional (see UNITED STATES v. BROWN, 1965); but a law requiring subversive organizations to register with a government agency, and another commandeering the records of a disgraced ex-President were upheld.

DENNIS J. MAHONEY

(SEE ALSO: *Communist Party v. S.A.C.B., 1961; Nixon v. Administrator of General Services, 1977.*)

Bibliography

CHAFEE, ZECHARIAH 1956 *Three Human Rights in the Constitution of 1787.* Lawrence: University of Kansas Press.

BILL OF CREDIT

A bill of credit is a promissory note issued by a government on its own credit and intended to circulate as money. Under Article I, section 10, of the Constitution the states are prohibited from emitting bills of credit. The prohibition was regarded as essential by the Framers of the Constitution, and it was included without significant debate or dissent by the CONSTITUTIONAL CONVENTION OF 1787.

Bills of credit are, in fact, unsecured paper currency. Both ALEXANDER HAMILTON and JAMES MADISON, referring to the prohibition in THE FEDERALIST (#44 and #80), wrote of a prohibition on "paper money." In the years immediately preceding the adoption of the Constitution, many states had issued unsecured currency in a deliberately inflationary policy intended to benefit borrowers. As long as local politicians had the power to stimulate inflation, there could be no stable economy. The "more perfect union" required that money have essentially the same purchasing power in every state and region.

The MARSHALL COURT, in CRAIG v. MISSOURI (1830), held that a state issue of certificates acceptable for tax payments violated the prohibition on bills of credit, since they were "paper intended to circulate through the community for its ordinary purposes, as money." But the TANEY COURT held that notes issued by a state-chartered bank—of which the state was the sole stockholder—did not violate the prohibition, since they were not issued "on the faith of the state." (See BRISCOE v. BANK OF KENTUCKY, 1837.)

DENNIS J. MAHONEY

BILL OF RIGHTS (ENGLISH)
(December 16, 1689)

During the controversy with Great Britain, from 1763 to 1776, American editors frequently reprinted the English Bill of Rights, and American leaders hailed it as "the second MAGNA CARTA." After the DECLARATION OF INDEPENDENCE, Americans framing their first state constitutions drew upon the Bill of Rights; certain clauses of the national Constitution and our own BILL OF RIGHTS, the first ten amendments, can also be traced to the English statute of 1689. Its formal title was, "An act for declaring the rights and liberties of the subject, and settling the succession of the crown." Like Magna Carta, the PETITION OF RIGHT, and other constitutional documents safeguarding "liberties of the subject," the Bill of Rights imposed limitations on the crown only. Indeed, the document capped the Glorious Revolution of 1688–1689 by which England hamstrung the royal prerogative and made the crown subservient to Parliament, which remained unrestrained by any constitutional document. In effect the Bill of Rights ratified parliamentary supremacy, which is the antithesis of the American concept of a bill of rights as a bill of restraints upon the government generally. Notwithstanding its inflated reputation as a precursor of the American Bill of Rights, the English bill was quite narrow in the range of its protections even against the crown. In fact it established no new principles, except, perhaps, for the provision against standing armies in time of peace without parliamentary approval. Sir William S. Holdsworth, the great historian of English law, declared, "We look in vain for any statement of constitutional principle in the Bill of Rights," a judgment that is too severe.

The Bill of Rights confirmed several old principles of major significance. No TAXATION WITHOUT REPRESENTATION, which became the American formulation, here was limited to the assertion that levying money by royal prerogative "without grant of parliament" was illegal. The FREEDOM OF PETITION, protected by our FIRST AMENDMENT, and indirectly the FREEDOM OF ASSEMBLY go back to time immemorial, as the British say, but were here enshrined as part of the FUNDAMENTAL LAW. Article I, section 6, of the Constitution, protecting freedom of speech for members of Congress, derives from a clause in the Bill of Rights confirming a principle fought for by Parliament for a century and a half. Our Eighth Amendment follows closely the language of another provision of the Bill of Rights, which declares, "That excessive BAIL ought not to be required, no excessive fines imposed, nor CRUEL AND UNUSUAL PUNISHMENTS inflicted." The guarantee against excessive bail made the writ of HABEAS CORPUS effective by plugging the one loophole in the HABEAS CORPUS ACT OF 1679; the crown's judges had defeated that act's purpose by fixing steep bail that prisoners could not afford. The ACT OF TOLERATION OF 1689 preceded the Bill of Rights by a few months and is equally part of the constitutional inheritance of the Glorious Revolution.

The foremost significance of the English Bill of Rights, so called because it began as a declaration and ended as a bill enacted into law, probably lies in the symbolism of the name, conveying far more than the document itself actually protects. As an antecedent of the American Bill of Rights of 1791, the act of 1689 is a frail affair, though it achieved its purpose of cataloguing most of the rights that the Stuarts had breached. As a symbol of fundamental law and the RULE OF LAW it was a mighty precursor of the fuller catalogues of rights developed by the American states and in the Constitution.

LEONARD W. LEVY

Bibliography

SCHWOERER, LOIS G. 1981 *The Declaration of Rights, 1689.* Baltimore: Johns Hopkins University Press.

BILL OF RIGHTS (UNITED STATES)

On September 12, 1787, the only major task of the CONSTITUTIONAL CONVENTION OF 1787 was to adopt, engross, and sign the finished document reported by the Committee on Style. The weary delegates, after a hot summer's work in Philadelphia, were eager to return home. At that point GEORGE MASON remarked that he "wished the plan had been prefaced by a Bill of Rights," because it would quiet public fears. Mason made no stirring speech for CIVIL LIBERTIES; he did not even argue the need for a bill of rights or move the adoption of one, though he offered to second a motion if one were made. ELBRIDGE GERRY moved for a committee to prepare a bill, Mason seconded, and without debate the delegates, voting by states, defeated the motion 10–0. A motion to endorse FREEDOM OF THE PRESS was also defeated, after ROGER SHERMAN declared, "It is unnecessary. The power of Congress does not extend to the Press."

Not a delegate to the convention opposed a bill of rights in principle. The overwhelming majority believed "It is unnecessary." Although they were recommending a strong national government that could regulate individuals directly, Congress could exercise only ENUMERATED POWERS or powers necessary to carry out those enumerated. A bill of rights would restrain national powers, but, as Hamilton asked, "Why declare that things shall not be done which there is no power to do?" Congress had no power to regulate the press or religion.

Civil liberties, supporters of the Constitution believed, faced danger from the possibility of repressive state action, but that was a matter to be guarded against by state bills of rights. Some states had none, and no state had a comprehensive list of guarantees. That fact provided the supporters of ratification with another argument: if a bill were framed omitting some rights, the omissions might justify their infringement. The great VIRGINIA DECLARATION OF RIGHTS had omitted the FREEDOMS OF SPEECH, assembly, and petition; the right to the writ of HABEAS CORPUS; the right to GRAND JURY proceedings; the RIGHT TO COUNSEL; and freedom from DOUBLE JEOPARDY, BILLS OF ATTAINDER, and EX POST FACTO laws. Twelve states, including Vermont, had framed constitutions, and the only right secured by all was TRIAL BY JURY in criminal cases; although all protected religious liberty, too, five either permitted or provided for ESTABLISHMENTS OF RELIGION. Two passed over a free press guarantee. Four neglected to ban excessive fines, excessive BAIL, compulsory self-incrimination, and general SEARCH WARRANTS. Five ignored protections for the rights of assembly, petition, counsel, and trial by jury in civil cases. Seven omitted a prohibition on ex post facto laws. Nine failed to provide for grand jury proceedings, and nine failed to condemn bills of attainder. Ten said nothing about freedom of speech, while eleven were silent on double jeopardy. Omissions in a national bill of rights raised dangers that would be avoided if the Constitution simply left the rights of Americans uncatalogued. The Framers also tended to be skeptical about the value of "parchment barriers" against "overbearing majorities," as JAMES MADISON said. As realists they understood that the constitutional protection of rights would mean little during times of popular hysteria or war; any framer could cite examples of gross abridgments of civil liberties in states that had bills of rights.

The lack of a bill of rights proved to be the strongest argument of the opponents of ratification. The usually masterful politicians who dominated the Constitutional Convention had made a serious political error. Their arguments against including a bill of rights were neither politic nor convincing. A bill of rights could do no harm, and, as THOMAS JEFFERSON pointed out in letters persuading Madison to switch positions, might do some good. Moreover, the contention that listing some rights might jeopardize others not mentioned was inconsistent and easily answered. The inconsistency derived from the fact that the Constitution as proposed included some rights: no RELIGIOUS TEST for office; jury trials in criminal cases; the writ of habeas corpus; a tight definition of TREASON; and bans on ex post facto laws and bills of attainder. The argument that to include some rights would exclude others boomeranged; every right excluded seemed in jeopardy. Enumerated powers could be abused; the power to tax, opponents argued, might be used against the press or religion. Moreover, the argument that a bill of rights was unnecessary could not possibly apply to the rights of the criminally accused or to personal liberties of a procedural nature. The new national government would act directly on the people and be buttressed by an undefined executive power and a national judiciary to enforce laws made by Congress; and Congress had the authority to define crimes and prescribe penalties for violations of its laws. PATRICK HENRY contended that the proposed Constitution empowered the United States to torture citizens into confessing their violations of congressional enactments.

Mason's point that a bill of rights would quiet the fears of the people was unanswerable. Alienating him and his followers was bad politics and blunderingly handed them a stirring cause around which they could muster opposition to ratification. No rational argument—and the lack of a bill of rights created an extremely emotional issue not amenable to rational argument—could possibly allay the fears generated by demagogues like Henry and principled opponents like Mason.

In Pennsylvania, the second state to ratify, the minority demanded a comprehensive bill of rights. Massachusetts, the sixth state to ratify, was the first to do so with recommended amendments, although only two—jury trial in civil suits and grand jury INDICTMENT—belonged in a bill of rights. But Massachusetts led the way toward recommended amendments, and the last four states to ratify recommended comprehensive bills of rights. Every right that became part of the ten amendments known as the Bill of Rights was included in state recommendations, with the exception of JUST COMPENSATION for property taken.

Some Federalists—above all Madison, whose political position in Virginia deteriorated because of his opposition to a bill of rights—finally realized that statecraft and political expediency dictated a switch in position. In states where ratification was in doubt, especially New York, Virginia, and North Carolina, Federalists pledged themselves to subsequent amendments to protect civil liberties, as soon as the new government went into operation.

In the first Congress, Representative Madison sought to fulfill his pledge. His accomplishment in the face of opposition and apathy entitles him to be remembered as "father of the Bill of Rights" even more than as "father of the Constitution." Many Federalists thought that the house had more important tasks, like the passage of tonnage duties. The opposition party, which had capitalized on the lack of a bill of rights in the Constitution, hoped for either a second convention or amendments that would cripple the substantive powers of the government. They had used the bill of rights issue as a smokescreen for objections to the Constitution's provisions on DIRECT TAXES, the judicial power, and the commerce power; these objections could not be dramatically popularized, and now the Anti-Federalists sought to scuttle Madison's proposals. They began by stalling, then tried to annex amendments aggrandizing state powers, and finally depreciated the importance of the very protections of individual liberty that they had formerly demanded. Madison meant to prove that the new government was a friend of liberty, and he understood that his amendments, if adopted, would make extremely difficult the passage of genuinely Anti-Federalist proposals. He would not be put off; he was insistent, compelling, unyielding, and, finally, triumphant.

On June 8, 1789, he made his long masterful speech before an apathetic House, introducing amendments culled mainly from state constitutions and state ratification proposals. All power, he argued, is subject to abuse and should be guarded against by constitutional provisions securing "the great rights of mankind." The government had only limited powers, but it might, unless prohibited, use general warrants in the enforcement of its revenue laws. In Great Britain, bills of rights merely erected barriers against the powers of the crown, leaving the powers of Parliament "altogether indefinite," and in Great Britain, the constitution left unguarded the "choicest" rights of the press and of conscience. The great objective he had in mind, Madison declared, was to limit the powers of government, thus preventing legislative as well as executive abuse, and above all preventing abuses of power by "the body of the people, operating by the majority against the minority." Mere "paper barriers" might fail, but they raised a standard that might educate the majority against acts to which they might be inclined. To the argument that a bill or rights was not necessary because the states constitutionally protected freedom, Madison had two responses. One was that some states had no bills of rights, others "very defective ones." The states constituted a greater danger to liberty than the new national government. The other was that the Constitution should, therefore, include an amendment that "No State shall violate the equal rights of conscience, or the freedom of the press, or the trial by jury in criminal cases." This, Madison declared, was "the most valuable amendment in the whole list." To the contention that an enumeration of rights would disparage those not in the list, Madison replied that the danger could be guarded against by adopting a proposal of his composition that became the NINTH AMENDMENT. If his amendments were "incorporated" into the constitution, Madison said, using another argument borrowed from Jefferson, "independent tribunals of justice will consider themselves in a peculiar manner the guardians of those rights; they will be an impenetrable bulwark against every assumption of power in the legislative or executive; they will be naturally led to resist every encroachment upon rights expressly stipulated for in the constitution. . . ."

Supporters of Madison informed him that Anti-Federalists did not really want a bill of rights and that his proposals "confounded the Anties exceedingly. . . ." Madison's proposals went to a select committee, of which he was a member, though its chairman, John Vining of Delaware, thought the House had "more important business." The committee added freedom of speech to the recommended prohibitions on the states, made some stylistic changes, and urged the amendments, which the House adopted. Madison, however, had proposed to "incorporate" the amendments within the text of the Constitution at appropriate points. He did not, that is, recommend their adoption as a separate "bill of rights." Members objected that to incorporate the amendments would give the impression that the Framers of the Constitution had signed a document that included provisions not of their composition. Another argument for lumping the amendments together was that the matter of form was so "trifling" that the House should not squander its time debating the placement of the various amendments. Indeed, Aedanus Burke of South Carolina, an Anti-Federalist, thought the amendments were "not those solid and substantial amendments which the people expect; they are little better than whip-syllabub, frothy and full of wind . . . it will be better to drop the subject." Men of Burke's views in the Senate managed to kill the proposed restrictions on the states, and the Senate sought to cripple the clause against establishments of religion. A conference committee of the two houses, which included Madison, accepted the Senate's joining together several amendments but agreed to Madison's phrasing of the proposal that became the FIRST AMENDMENT. The House accepted the conference report on September 24, 1789, the Senate a day later. Virginia's senators, William Grayson and RICHARD HENRY LEE, both Anti-Federalists, opposed the amendments because they left "the great points of the Judiciary, direct taxation, &c to stand as they are. . . ." Lee informed Patrick Henry that they had erred in their strategy of accepting ratification on the promise of subsequent amendments. Grayson reported to Henry that the amendments adopted by the Senate "are good for nothing. . . ."

Within six months of the time the amendments, or Bill of Rights, were submitted to the states for approval, nine states ratified. Connecticut and Georgia refused to ratify on the ground that the Bill of Rights was unnecessary; they belatedly ratified on the sesquicentennial anniversary of the ratification of the Constitution in 1939. (Massachusetts ratified in 1939, too, although both houses of its legislature in 1790 had adopted most of the amendments, but they had failed to send official notice of ratification.) The admission of Vermont to the union in 1791 made necessary ratification by eleven states. Vermont's ratification of the amendments in November 1791 made Virginia's approval indispensable as the eleventh state. The battle there was stalled in the state senate, where the Anti-Federalists were in control. They first sought to sabotage the Bill of Rights and then, having failed in their chief objective to abolish the power of Congress to enact direct taxes, they irresolutely acquiesced two years later. Virginia finally ratified on December 15, 1791, making the Bill of Rights part of the Constitution.

The history of the framing and ratification of the Bill of Rights is sparse. We know almost nothing about what the state legislatures thought concerning the meanings of the various amendments, and the press was perfunctory in its reports, if not altogether silent. But for Madison's persistence the amendments would have died in Congress. Our precious Bill of Rights was in the main the result of the political necessity for certain reluctant Federalists to make their own a cause that had been originated, in vain, by the Anti-Federalists to vote down the Constitution. The party that had first opposed a Bill of Rights inadvertently wound up with the responsibility for its framing and ratification, while the party that had first professed to want it discovered too late that it was not only embarrassing but politically disastrous for ulterior party purposes.

LEONARD W. LEVY

Bibliography

BRANT, IRVING 1965 *The Bill of Rights: Its Origin and Meanings.* Indianapolis: Bobbs-Merrill.
DUMBAULD, EDWARD 1957 *The Bill of Rights and What It Means Today.* Norman: University of Oklahoma Press.
RUTLAND, ROBERT A. 1955 *The Birth of the Bill of Rights, 1776–1791.* Chapel Hill: University of North Carolina Press.
SCHWARTZ, BERNARD 1977 *The Great Rights of Mankind: A History of the American Bill of Rights.* New York: Oxford University Press.

BINGHAM, JOHN A.
(1815–1900)

An Ohio attorney, John Armor Bingham was a congressman (1855–1863, 1865–1873), Army judge advocate (1864–1865), solicitor of the COURT OF CLAIMS (1864–1865), and ambassador to Japan (1873–1885). After President ABRAHAM LINCOLN's assassination, President ANDREW JOHNSON appointed Bingham as a special judge advocate (prosecutor) to the military commission trying the accused assassination conspirators. Bingham was particularly effective in answering defense objections during the trials and in justifying the constitutionality of trying the civilian defendants in military courts.

From 1865 to 1867 Bingham served on the JOINT COMMITTEE ON RECONSTRUCTION. As a Republican moderate Bingham supported congressional reconstruction but demanded strict adherence to the Constitution and favored early readmission of the ex-Confederate states. He offered numerous amendments to moderate the CIVIL RIGHTS ACT OF 1866, and although these passed he still voted against the bill, because he believed Congress lacked the authority to protect freedmen in this manner. Bingham wanted very much to protect them, and during the debates over the civil rights bill he argued that a new constitutional amendment was the answer. Bingham believed that the results of the war—including the death of both SLAVERY and state SOVEREIGNTY, as well as the protection of CIVIL LIBERTIES for blacks—could be secured only by an amendment that would nationalize the BILL OF RIGHTS. By working to apply the Fifth and FIRST AMENDMENTS to the states Bingham linked the antislavery arguments of the antebellum period to postbellum conditions.

In 1865 Bingham suggested an amendment that would empower Congress "to secure to all persons in every State of the Union equal protection in their rights, life, liberty, and property." Bingham believed the THIRTEENTH AMENDMENT had not only freed blacks but also made them citizens. As citizens of the United States they were among "the People of the United States" referred to in the PREAMBLE to the Constitution and protected by the Fifth Amendment. However, Bingham was unsure whether the enforcement provision of the Thirteenth Amendment allowed Congress to guarantee and protect CIVIL RIGHTS. Johnson's veto of the 1866 Civil Rights bill only increased Bingham's determination to place such protection beyond the reach of a presidential veto or repeal by a future Congress. Bingham therefore drafted what became Section 1 of the FOURTEENTH AMENDMENT, protecting the freedmen by explicitly making them citizens, prohibiting states from abridging their PRIVILEGES AND IMMUNITIES as United States citizens, and guaranteeing all persons DUE PROCESS and EQUAL PROTECTION of the law. In 1871 Bingham reaffirmed his belief that the amendment was designed to protect those privileges and immunities "chiefly defined in the first eight amendments to the Constitution of the United States." Thus, as Bingham saw it, the ABOLITIONIST CONSTITUTIONAL THEORY of the antebellum period became part of the Constitution.

By 1867 Bingham was at least temporarily a Radical Republican. He supported THADDEUS STEVENS's bill for military reconstruction after the ex-Confederate states refused to ratify the Fourteenth Amendment and after numerous outrages had been perpetrated against freedom. Initially opposed to IMPEACHMENT, he was elected to the impeachment committee and was made chairman after threatening to resign unless given that position. Bingham vigorously pursued the prosecution of Johnson, and after it failed he attempted to investigate the seven Republican senators who voted against impeachment.

Bingham had initially opposed linking black suffrage to readmission to the Union, and opposed efforts by Stevens to create such a linkage. He argued that Congress lacked the constitutional authority to do this. But by 1870 he supported the FIFTEENTH AMENDMENT and sought to extend the franchise even further, by prohibiting religious, property, or nationality limitations on the ballot. In 1871, with the three new amendments legitimizing congressional action, Bingham supported the three "force bills," which prohibited states and individuals from violating the newly acquired constitutional rights of the freedmen, gave the federal government supervisory powers over national elections, and made numerous acts federal crimes under the Ku Klux Klan Act. (See FORCE ACTS.) Bingham, the careful constitutionalist and moderate Republican leader, defended these acts because they were a response to the terror being inflicted against blacks, and because they were now constitutional.

PAUL FINKELMAN

Bibliography
HYMAN, HAROLD M. and WIECEK, WILLIAM M. 1982 *Equal Justice under Law: Constitutional Development, 1835–1875.* New York: Harper & Row.
SWIFT, DONALD C. 1968 John A. Bingham and Reconstruction: The Dilemma of a Moderate. *Ohio History* 77:76–94.

BINNEY, HORACE
(1780–1875)

A leading Philadelphia attorney, Horace Binney edited six volumes of the Pennsylvania Supreme Court's decisions, covering the years 1799–1814. In 1862 Binney published two pamphlets entitled *The Privilege of the Writ of Habeas Corpus under the Constitution,* in which he defended President ABRAHAM LINCOLN's suspension of the writ. Binney argued that the President, and not Congress, had the power to suspend HABEAS CORPUS, and that each branch of the government had the right to interpret the Constitution independently. In 1865 Binney answered the many critics of his earlier work with a third pamphlet of the same title.

PAUL FINKELMAN

Bibliography
BINNEY, CHARLES CHAUNCEY 1903 *The Life of Horace Binney, with Selections from His Letters.* Philadelphia: Lippincott.

BIRNEY, JAMES G.
(1792–1857)

A slaveholder, James Gillespie Birney studied law under ALEXANDER DALLAS, was a mildly antislavery politician in Kentucky and Alabama, and was a spokesman for the American Colonization Society. In 1834 he freed his remaining slaves, abandoned colonization, and formed the Kentucky Anti-Slavery Society. Finding Kentucky too dangerous for an abolitionist, Birney moved to Cincinnati, and in 1836 began publishing an antislavery newspaper, *The Philanthropist.* Unlike WILLIAM LLOYD GARRISON, whom he bitterly opposed, Birney believed that the United States Constitution could be a useful tool for abolitionists. He also argued for abolitionist political activity. In 1840 he was the Liberty party candidate for the presidency, but he drew only 7,069 votes. Four years later he won 62,300 votes, helping set the stage for more successful antislavery parties.

Birney was involved in three legal cases that helped develop his antislavery constitutionalism. In 1836 an anti-abolitionist mob in Cincinnati destroyed his press. Birney hired SALMON P. CHASE in a successful suit against the mob leaders for damages to the press. In 1837 Birney sheltered and hired a runaway slave named Matilda, and when she was captured, Chase and Birney defended her on the ground that having voluntarily been brought to Ohio, she therefore was not a fugitive slave; they also made the dubious argument that slaves who escaped from Kentucky into Ohio could not be recaptured, because the NORTHWEST ORDINANCE provided only for the return of slaves who escaped from the "original states." Matilda was returned south, but Chase and Birney were more successful in appealing Birney's conviction for harboring slaves, which the Ohio Supreme Court overturned. (See ABOLITIONIST CONSTITUTIONAL THEORY.)

PAUL FINKELMAN

Bibliography

FLADELAND, BETTY L. 1955 *James Gillespie Birney: Slaveholder to Abolitionist.* Ithaca, N.Y.: Cornell University Press.

BIRTH CONTROL

The American birth control movement began in the early twentieth century as a campaign to achieve a right of REPRODUCTIVE AUTONOMY in the face of hostile legislation in many states. By the time that campaign succeeded in getting the Supreme Court to espouse a constitutional RIGHT OF PRIVACY which allowed married couples to practice contraception, there was not a single state in which an anticontraception law was being enforced against private medical advice or against drugstore sales. GRISWOLD V. CONNECTICUT (1965) and its successor decisions thus did not create the effective right of choice; they recog-

nized and legitimized the right, by subjecting restrictive legislation to strict judicial scrutiny and finding justifications wanting. (See FUNDAMENTAL INTERESTS.)

Contraception is only the most widely practiced method of birth control; others (apart from abstinence) are STERILIZATION and abortion. The Supreme Court, partly on the precedent of *Griswold*, recognized in ROE V. WADE (1973) a woman's constitutional right to have an abortion, qualified by the state's power to forbid abortion during the latter stages of pregnancy. The Court has had no occasion to recognize a person's right to choose to be sterilized, because the states have not sought to restrict that freedom. In any event the birth control movement has now won its most important constitutional battles; both married and single persons are free, both in fact and in constitutional theory, to choose not to beget or bear children.

"Birth control," however, has another potential meaning that is the antithesis of reproductive choice. The state may seek to coerce persons to refrain from procreating, either through compulsory sterilization or by other sanctions aimed at restricting family size. On present constitutional doctrine, the decision to procreate is "fundamental," requiring some COMPELLING STATE INTEREST to justify its limitation. (See SKINNER V. OKLAHOMA, 1942.) Although judicial recognition of such an interest is not inconceivable in some future condition of acute overpopulation, no such decision is presently foreseeable.

The constitutional right to choose whether to have a child or be a parent is properly rested today on SUBSTANTIVE DUE PROCESS grounds; "liberty" is precisely the point. Yet the interest in equality has also played a significant role in the development of these rights of choice. Justice BYRON R. WHITE, concurring in *Griswold*, pointed out how enforcement of an anticontraceptives law against birth control clinics worked to deny the disadvantaged from obtaining help in controlling family size. The well-to-do needed no clinics. And once *Griswold* recognized the right of married persons to practice contraception, the Supreme Court saw that EQUAL PROTECTION principles demanded extension of the right to be unmarried. (See EISENSTADT V. BAIRD, 1972; CAREY V. POPULATION SERVICES INTERNATIONAL, 1977.) Finally, judicial recognition of rights of reproductive choice has followed the progress of the women's movement. The breakdown of the traditional sexual "double standard" and the opening of new opportunities for women outside the "housewife marriage" have gone together, both socially and in constitutional development. No longer is the "erring woman" to be punished with unwanted pregnancy or parenthood. In 1920 Margaret Sanger wrote, "Birth control is woman's problem." Half a century later, the Supreme Court heard that message.

KENNETH L. KARST

Bibliography

CHARLES, ALAN F. 1980 Abortion and Family Planning: Law and the Moral Issue. Pages 331–356 in Ruth Roemer and George McKray (eds.), *Legal Aspects of Health Policy: Issues and Trends.* Westport, Conn.: Greenwood Press.

GREENAWALT, KENT 1971 Criminal Law and Population Control. *Vanderbilt Law Review* 24:465–494.

NOTE 1971 Legal Analysis and Population Control: The Problem of Coercion. *Harvard Law Review* 84:1856–1911.

BISHOP v. WOOD
426 U.S. 341 (1976)

Bishop worked a major change in the modern law of PROCEDURAL DUE PROCESS, enshrining in the law the view Justice WILLIAM H. REHNQUIST had unsuccessfully urged in ARNETT V. KENNEDY (1974): the due process right of a holder of a statutory "entitlement" is defined by positive law, not by the Constitution itself.

Here, a city ordinance that classified a police officer as a "permanent employee" was nonetheless interpreted by the lower federal courts to give an officer employment only "at the will and pleasure of the city." The Supreme Court held, 5–4, that this ordinance created no "property" interest in the officer's employment, and that, absent public disclosure of the reasons for his termination, he had suffered no stigma that impaired a "liberty" interest. The key to the majority's decision presumably lay in this sentence: "The federal court is not the appropriate forum in which to review the multitude of personnel decisions that are made daily by public agencies."

In dissent, Justice WILLIAM J. BRENNAN accurately commented that the Court had resurrected the "right/privilege" distinction, discredited in GOLDBERG V. KELLY (1970), and insisted that there was a federal constitutional dimension to the idea of "property" interests, not limited by state law and offering the protections of due process to legitimate expectations raised by government.

KENNETH L. KARST

BITUMINOUS COAL ACT
50 Stat. 72 (1937)

After CARTER V. CARTER COAL COMPANY (1936), Congress restored regulation of bituminous coal in INTERSTATE COMMERCE. The new act, designed to control the interstate sale and distribution of soft coal and to protect interstate commerce, levied a nineteen and one-half percent tax on all producers but remitted payment to those who accepted the new code. Price-fixing provisions constituted the crux of the act; Congress did not reenact any labor provisions, although it encouraged free COLLECTIVE BARGAINING.

The act established a National Bituminous Coal Commission to supervise an elaborate procedure for setting minimum prices. Unfair competition or sales below established prices violated the code. The act provided extensive PROCEDURAL DUE PROCESS and several means of enforcement, including CEASE-AND-DESIST ORDERS and private suits carrying treble damage awards for injured competitors.

An 8–1 Supreme Court sustained the act in *Sunshine Anthracite Coal Company v. Adkins* (1940). Conceding the tax was "a sanction to enforce the regulatory provisions of the Act," the majority held that Congress might nevertheless "impose penalties in aid of the exercise of any of its ENUMERATED POWERS." The Court thus upheld the act under the COMMERCE CLAUSE, declaring that the method of regulation was for legislative determination.

DAVID GORDON

BIVENS v. SIX UNKNOWN NAMED AGENTS OF THE FEDERAL BUREAU OF NARCOTICS
403 U.S. 388 (1971)

This is the leading case concerning IMPLIED RIGHTS OF ACTION under the Constitution. Federal agents conducted an unconstitutional search of Webster Bivens's apartment. Bivens brought an action in federal court seeking damages for a FOURTH AMENDMENT violation. Although no federal statute supplied Bivens with a cause of action, the Supreme Court, in an opinion by Justice WILLIAM J. BRENNAN, held that Bivens could maintain that action.

Two central factors led to the decision. First, violations of constitutional rights ought not go unremedied. The traditional remedy, enjoining unconstitutional behavior, plainly was inadequate for Bivens. And the

Court was unwilling to leave Bivens to the uncertainties of state tort law, his principal alternative source of action. Second, the implied constitutional cause of action makes federal officials as vulnerable as state officials for constitutional misbehavior. Prior to *Bivens*, state officials were subject to suits under SECTION 1983, TITLE 42, UNITED STATES CODE, for violating individuals' constitutional rights. An action against federal officials had to be inferred in *Bivens* only because section 1983 is inapplicable to federal officials.

Both factors emerged again in later cases. DAVIS v. PASSMAN (1979) recognized an implied constitutional cause of action for claims brought under the Fifth Amendment, and *Carlson v. Green* (1980) extended *Bivens* to other constitutional rights. BUTZ v. ECONOMOU (1978) extended to federal officials the good faith defense that state officials enjoy under section 1983.

Bivens raises important questions about the scope of federal JUDICIAL POWER. Chief Justice WARREN E. BURGER and Justices HUGO L. BLACK and HARRY BLACKMUN dissented on the ground that Congress alone may authorize damages against federal officials. The majority, and Justice JOHN MARSHALL HARLAN in a concurring opinion, required no congressional authorization. But they left open the possibility that Congress might have the last word in the area through express legislation.

THEODORE EISENBERG

BLACK, HUGO L.
(1886–1971)

When Hugo LaFayette Black was appointed to the Supreme Court in 1937, the basic tenets of his mature judicial philosophy had already been formed. Born in the Alabama hill country in 1886, Black received his law degree from the University of Alabama in 1906. He practiced law, largely handling personal injury cases, in Birmingham during the next twenty years and served brief terms as police court judge and county prosecutor. In 1926 he was elected to the United States Senate; after reelection in 1932 he became an outspoken advocate of the New Deal and a tenacious investigator. Throughout his career he read extensively in history, philosophy, and literary classics. From THOMAS JEFFERSON he took his view of the FIRST AMENDMENT. Aristotle, his "favorite author," and JOHN LOCKE offered appealing theoretical perspectives on the nature of government and society.

Coming to the bench in the aftermath of President FRANKLIN D. ROOSEVELT's Court-packing plan, which he vigorously espoused, Black searched for a jurisprudence of certainty, seeking clear, precise standards that would limit judicial discretion, protect individual rights, and give government room to operate. He saw the Constitution as a set of unambiguous commands designed to prevent the recurrence of historic evils. In its text and the intent of its Framers he found the authority for applying some provisions virtually open-ended, and others rather more strictly. All constitutional questions he considered open until he dealt with them; but when he came to a conclusion, he maintained it with single-minded devotion. His opinions never suggested that he entertained any doubts.

Black's Senate years left an indelible impression on his performance as Justice. Each of the popular branches must be left to carry out its duties according to the original constitutional understanding. Congress makes the laws, he noted in YOUNGSTOWN SHEET & TUBE COMPANY V. SAWYER (1952); the President's functions are limited to the recommending and vetoing of bills. Congress, Black believed, had the power to regulate whatever affected commerce. Likewise, unless states discriminated against INTERSTATE COMMERCE, they had the power to regulate in the absence of contrary congressional direction. Nor, under the DUE PROCESS clause of the FOURTEENTH AMENDMENT, might courts consider the appropriateness of legislation. In *Lincoln Federal Labor Union v. Northwestern Iron & Metal Company* (1949), he observed that the Court had rejected "the *Allgeyer-Lochner-Adair-Coppage* constitutional doctrine"; the states had power to legislate "so long as their laws do not run afoul of some specific federal constitutional provision, or of some valid federal law."

Black's adamant refusal to expand judicial power through the due process clause forced him to develop an alternative theory to protect the rights enumerated in the BILL OF RIGHTS. He had to overcome his initial "grave doubts" about the validity of JUDICIAL REVIEW. CHAMBERS V. FLORIDA (1940) was an early milestone. Courts, he stated in that case, "stand against any winds that blow as havens of refuge for those who might otherwise suffer because they are helpless, weak, outnumbered, or because they are non-conforming victims of prejudice and public excitement." Finally, in ADAMSON V. CALIFORNIA (1947), he laid down the formulation that guided him for the rest of his career:

My study of the historical events that culminated in the Fourteenth Amendment . . . persuades me that one of the chief objects that the provisions of the Amendment's first section, separately, and as a whole, were intended to accomplish was to make the Bill of Rights applicable to the States. . . . I fear to see the consequences of the Court's practices of substituting its own concepts of decency and fundamental justice for the language of the Bill of Rights as its point of departure in interpreting and enforcing that Bill of Rights. . . . To hold that his Court can determine what, if any, provisions of the Bill of Rights will be enforced, and if so to what degree, is to frustrate the great design of a written Constitution.

Only by limiting judges' discretion, and demanding that they enforce the textual guarantees, could the protection of these rights be ensured. Black feared that the "shock the conscience" test, which Justice FELIX FRANKFURTER employed for the Court in *Rochin v. California* (1952), with its "accordion-like qualities" and "nebulous" and "evanescent standards," "must inevitably imperil all the individual liberty safeguards specifically enumerated in the Bill of Rights."

Black applied his INCORPORATION DOCTRINE in scores of cases. From his early days as a public official he hated coerced confessions, and he viewed POLICE INTERROGATIONS without counsel as secret inquisitions in flat violation of the FIFTH AMENDMENT's guarantee of the RIGHT AGAINST SELF-INCRIMINATION. "From the time government begins to move against a man," he said when the Court considered MIRANDA V. ARIZONA (1966), "when they take him into custody, his rights attach." He led the Court in expanding the RIGHT TO COUNSEL from his first term, when he held in JOHNSON V. ZERBST (1938) that in a federal prosecution counsel must be appointed to represent a defendant who cannot afford to hire an attorney. To his supreme satisfaction he wrote the opinion in GIDEON V. WAINWRIGHT (1963), overruling BETTS V. BRADY (1942) and making similar assistance mandatory in state FELONY trials. More of his dissents eventually became law than those of any other Justice.

Given his approach of allowing free play to the spirit of the Constitution while resting his justifications largely on its words, the generalities of the EQUAL PROTECTION clause presented problems of interpretation for Black. In his view, Article I conferred on qualified voters the rights to vote and to have their votes counted in congressional elections. Dissenting in COLEGROVE V. GREEN (1946), he argued that both Article I and the equal protection clause required that congressional district lines be drawn "to give approximately equal weight to each vote cast." Black formally buried *Colegrove* in WESBERRY V. SANDERS (1963). In every REAPPORTIONMENT case, as in every case involving an INDIGENT prosecuted for crime, he supported the equal protection claim. He shared in the widespread agreement that the Fourteenth Amendment had been designed primarily to end RACIAL DISCRIMINATION, and made the first explicit reference to race as a SUSPECT CLASSIFICATION which must be subjected to the "most rigid scrutiny." Ironically, this came in one of the JAPANESE AMERICAN CASES (1943), in which he upheld, over biting dissents, a conviction for violating a military order during World War II excluding all persons of Japanese ancestry from the West Coast. But as the Court moved beyond race in applying the equal protection clause, Black refused to follow. Classifications based on wealth or poverty were not "suspect"; and even though the claims in VOTING RIGHTS cases were essential for the democratic process to reach its full potential, he denied them.

During the first twenty-five years of his tenure, Black's opinions had remarkable constancy as he unflaggingly pursued his goal of human advancement within the bounds of constitutional interpretation. But new issues confronted the Court and the country in the 1960s. Black was fighting old age, and Court work, he admitted, was harder. Because of cataract operations he did not read nearly so much as he had. References in his opinions to books and articles became infrequent, and the cases he cited were often his old ones as he repeatedly accused his colleagues of going beyond their province. No longer was he reading the words of the Constitution expansively; his interpretations were restraining and cramped; and his categories of permissible legal action narrowed. Increasingly, he had trouble adjusting to a world that was changing. His opinions took on an essay-like quality, with a new structure and tone, and a note of anger crept into them.

From the beginning Black consistently interpreted the FOURTH AMENDMENT as restrictively as any Justice in the Court's modern history. Refusing to examine the term "unreasonable" in SEARCH AND SEIZURE cases, he generally accepted law enforcement actions. Almost invariably he validated WARRANTLESS SEARCHES including SEARCHES INCIDENT TO ARREST. His Fourth Amendment opinions emphasized the guilt of the accused, often starting with detailed descriptions of the crime; and, oddly, he ignored the amendment's rich history. After calling the EXCLUSIONARY RULE "an extraordinary sanction, judicially imposed," in *United States v. Wallace & Tiernan Company* (1949), he changed his mind: by linking the Fourth and Fifth Amendments in MAPP V. OHIO (1961), he found that "a constitutional basis emerges which not only justifies but actually requires" the rule. But his enthusiasm waned as the Court enlarged the

FOURTH AMENDMENT's scope. In his last search and seizure case, COOLIDGE V. NEW HAMPSHIRE (1971), he converted this limitation on government into a grant of power: "The Fourth Amendment provides a constitutional means by which the Government can act to obtain EVIDENCE to be used in criminal prosecutions. The people are obliged to yield to a proper exercise of authority under that Amendment."

By the time the RIGHT OF PRIVACY matured as an issue, Black had tied himself to the text as a mode of constitutional interpretation. Two heated dissents indicated his narrow conception of the Fourth Amendment. Seemingly oblivious to the dangers of WIRETAPPING, he wrote in BERGER V. NEW YORK (1967): "Had the framers of this amendment desired to prohibit the use in court of evidence secured by an unreasonable search and seizure, they would have used plain appropriate language to say that conversations can be searched and words seized. . . ." Finding no mention of privacy in the Constitution, he dismissed it as a "vague judge-made goal" and denigrated it: "the 'right of privacy' . . . , like a chameleon, has a different color for every turning," he wrote in *Berger*. He accurately viewed its elevation to separate constitutional status in GRISWOLD V. CONNECTICUT (1965) as the revival of SUBSTANTIVE DUE PROCESS. "Use of any such broad, unbounded judicial authority would make of this Court's members a day-to-day constitutional convention." Black rejected the idea of a living Constitution. His *Adamson* dissent not only had expanded horizons but had set limits.

Black was most famous for his views on the First Amendment. In *Milk Wagon Drivers Union v. Meadowmoor Diaries* (1941), his initial opinion on the subject, he said, "Freedom to speak and write about public questions . . . is the heart of our government. If that be weakened, the result is debilitation; if it be stilled, the result is death." He ceaselessly implored the Court to expand the amendment's protections, and embellished his opinions with moving libertarian rhetoric. But as in other areas during his last half-dozen years or so, Black narrowed his construction and retreated from many of his previous positions.

He subscribed fully to the "preferred position" doctrine of the First Amendment. He used, and reworked, the CLEAR AND PRESENT DANGER test in BRIDGES V. CALIFORNIA (1941), adding words that he repeated often: "the First Amendment does not speak equivocally. It prohibits any law 'abridging the freedom of speech, or of the press.' It must be taken as a command of the broadest scope that explicit language . . . will allow." But slowly "clear and present

danger," with its inherent balancing of disparate interests, disillusioned Black. The First Amendment "forbids compromise" in matters of conscience, he argued in AMERICAN COMMUNICATIONS ASSOCIATION V. DOUDS (1950). The "basic constitutional precept" is that "penalties should be imposed only for a person's own conduct, not for his beliefs or for the conduct of those with whom he may associate"; those "who commit overt acts in violation of valid laws can and should be punished."

A new word began to appear as his opinions, invariably in dissent, grew more shrill and strident. "I think the First Amendment, with the Fourteenth, 'absolutely' forbids such laws without any 'ifs' or 'buts' or whereases,' " he wrote when the Court upheld a GROUP LIBEL statute in BEAUHARNAIS V. ILLINOIS (1952). The First Amendment "grants an absolute right to believe in any governmental system, discuss all governmental affairs, and argue for desired changes in the existing order," he proclaimed in *Carlson v. Landon* (1952)—"whether or not such discussion incites to action, legal or illegal," he added in YATES V. UNITED STATES (1957). He refined this speech-conduct distinction in BARENBLATT V. UNITED STATES (1959). Some laws "directly," while others "indirectly," affect speech; when in the latter cases the speech and action were intertwined, Black was willing to use a BALANCING TEST weighing "the effect on speech . . . in relation to the need for control of the conduct."

For many years Black voted to invalidate statutes as direct abridgments of First Amendment rights. He opposed such governmental actions as prescribing LOYALTY OATHS in WIEMAN V. UPDEGRAFF (1952); promulgating lists of "subversive" organizations in JOINT ANTI-FASCIST REFUGEE COMMITTEE V. MCGRATH (1952); demanding organizations' membership lists in GIBSON V. FLORIDA LEGISLATIVE INVESTIGATION COMMITTEE (1963); conducting LEGISLATIVE INVESTIGATIONS of suspected subversives in BARENBLATT V. UNITED STATES or prosecuting for subversive advocacy in DENNIS V. UNITED STATES (1951); and imposing penalties for Communist party membership in APTHEKER V. SECRETARY OF STATE (1965). Under his standard, OBSCENITY and LIBEL laws as well as the state's conditioning admission to the bar on an applicant's beliefs were unconstitutional. In cases of direct abridgment of speech, Black charged in UPHAUS V. WYMAN (1960), any balancing test substituted "elastic concepts" such as "arbitrary" and "unreasonable" for the Constitution's plain language, reducing the document's "absolute commands to mere admonitions." "Liberty, to be secure for any," he wrote in *Braden v. United States* (1961), "must be secure for all—even for the most miserable merchants of hated and unpopular ideas." The framers had ensured that liberty by doing all the balancing that was necessary.

Black was equally outspoken in RELIGIOUS LIBERTY cases, and played a key role in the development of the First Amendment's religious guarantees. He wrote the Court's opinion in EVERSON V. BOARD OF EDUCATION (1947), the first case declaring that the establishment clause applied to the states. After listing the clause's standards and stating that it was intended to erect, in Jefferson's words, "a wall of separation between Church and State," Black noted that government cannot "contribute tax-raised funds to the support of an institution which teaches the tenets and faith of any church." But for the state to pay the bus fares of all pupils, including those in parochial schools, served a secular purpose, and did not violate the establishment clause. In MCCOLLUM V. BOARD OF EDUCATION (1948), writing for the Court, he held unconstitutional a RELEASED TIME program in which religious instruction took place in a public school. In the school prayer case of ENGEL V. VITALE (1962), of all his opinions the one that produced the most vocal opposition, Black concluded that a state-sponsored "non-denominational" prayer was "wholly inconsistent" with the establishment clause. The clause prohibited any laws that "establish an official religion whether [they] operate directly to coerce non-observing individuals or not." Religion, he wrote, "is too personal, too sacred, too holy, to permit its 'unhallowed perversion' by a civil magistrate."

The direct action cases in the mid-1960s tested Black's First Amendment philosophy. He expounded the limitations that TRESPASS and BREACH OF THE PEACE statutes placed on FREEDOM OF SPEECH. Earlier, he had held, in GIBONEY V. EMPIRE STORAGE AND ICE COMPANY (1949), that legislatures could regulate PICKETING, but in *Barenblatt* he noted that they could not abridge "views peacefully expressed in a place where the speaker had a right to be." "Picketing," he now wrote in *Cox v. Louisiana* (1965), "though it may be utilized to communicate ideas, is not speech, and therefore is not of itself protected by the First Amendment." This was a very different Black from the one who in FEINER V. NEW YORK (1951) labeled the Court's decision sanctioning police action to silence a speaker as "a long step toward totalitarian authority."

New emphases emerged. The ownership of property became pivotal. A property owner, governmental or private, was under no obligation to provide a forum for speech; if owners could not control their property, Black feared, the result would be mob violence. The RULE OF LAW now took precedence over encouraging public discourse and protest. Focusing on maintaining "tranquility and order" in cases like *Gregory v. Chicago* (1969), Black deprecated protesters who "think they have been mistreated or . . . have actually been mistreated," and their supporters, who "do no service" to "their cause, or their country." Gone was much of his former admiration of dissenters, toleration of the unorthodox, and receptivity toward new ideas.

Nonetheless, Black remained uncompromising in protecting FREEDOM OF THE PRESS. In his view the people had the right to read any books or see any movies, regardless of content. In his final case, NEW YORK TIMES V. UNITED STATES (1971), he reexpressed his faith:

Both the history and language of the First Amendment support the view that the press must be left to publish news, whatever the source, without censorship, INJUNCTIONS, or PRIOR RESTRAINTS.

In the First Amendment the Founding Fathers gave the free press the protection it must have to fulfill its essential role in our democracy. The press was to serve the governed, not the governors. . . . The press was protected so that it could bare the secrets of government and inform the people. Only a free and unrestrained press can effectively expose deception in government. And paramount among the responsibilities of a free press is the duty to prevent any part of the government from deceiving the people and sending them off to distant lands to die of foreign fevers and foreign shot and shell.

Three months later he was dead.

Black is one of the handful of great judges in American history, second only to JOHN MARSHALL in his impact on the Constitution. Certain of his premises, and convinced that he and history were at one, he was a tireless, evangelical, constitutional populist. If the Court did not accept his most sweeping doctrines whole, it accepted them piece by piece. Incorporation stands as his monument, but equally enduring is his preeminence in sensitizing a whole generation to the value of the great freedoms contained in the Bill of Rights.

ROGER K. NEWMAN

Bibliography

FRANK, JOHN P. 1977 Hugo L. Black: Free Speech and the Declaration of Independence. *University of Illinois Law Forum* 2:577–620.

LANDYNSKI, JACOB W. 1976 In Search of Justice Black's

Fourth Amendment. *Fordham Law Review* 45:453–496.

REICH, CHARLES A. 1963 Mr. Justice Black and the Living Constitution. *Harvard Law Review* 76:673–754.

SNOWISS, SYLVIA 1973 The Legacy of Justice Black. *Supreme Court Review* 1973:187–252.

SYMPOSIUM 1967 Mr. Justice Black: Thirty Years in Retrospect. *UCLA Law Review* 14:397–552.

BLACK, JEREMIAH S.
(1810–1883)

Jeremiah S. Black served on the Pennsylvania Supreme Court (1851–1857), as U.S. attorney general (1857–1860), U.S. secretary of state (1860–1861), and U.S. Supreme Court reporter (1861–1862). He advised ANDREW JOHNSON during the early phase of his IMPEACHMENT, and defended Samuel Tilden's claim to the presidency in the disputed election of 1876. A lifelong Democrat, Black was particularly antagonistic to abolitionists. During the winter of 1860–1861 Black opposed SECESSION and urged President JAMES BUCHANAN to reinforce federal military bases in the South. Buchanan appointed Black to the Supreme Court of the United States, but the Senate refused to confirm him.

PAUL FINKELMAN

Bibliography

BRIGANCE, WILLIAM N. 1934 *Jeremiah Sullivan Black, a Defender of the Constitution and the Ten Commandments.* Philadelphia: University of Pennsylvania Press.

BLACK CODES

In 1865–1866, the former slave states enacted statutes, collectively known as the "Black Codes," regulating the legal and constitutional status of black people. The Black Codes attempted to accomplish two objectives: (1) to enumerate the legal rights essential to the status of freedom of blacks; and (2) to provide a special criminal code for blacks. The latter objective reflected the two purposes of the antebellum law of slavery: race control and labor discipline.

In the view of white Southerners, emancipation did not of its own force create a civil status or capacity for freedmen. The southern state legislatures accordingly specified the incidents of this free status: the right to buy, sell, own, and bequeath property; the right to make contracts; the right to contract valid marriages, including so-called common-law marriages, and to enjoy a legally recognized parent–child relationship; the right to locomotion and personal liberty; the right to sue and be sued, and to testify in court, but only in cases involving black parties.

But the Codes also reenacted elements of the law of slavery. They provided detailed lists of civil disabilities by recreating the race-control features of the slave codes. They defined racial status; forbade blacks from pursuing certain occupations or professions; prohibited blacks from owning firearms or other weapons; controlled the movement of blacks by systems of passes; required proof of residence; prohibited the congregation of groups of blacks; restricted blacks from residing in certain areas; and specified an etiquette of deference to whites, such as by prohibiting blacks from directing insulting words at whites. The Codes forbade racial intermarriage and provided the death penalty for blacks raping white women, while omitting special provisions for whites raping black women. (See MISCEGENATION.) They excluded blacks from jury duty, public office, and voting. Some Black Codes required racial SEGREGATION in public transportation or created Jim Crow schools. Most Codes authorized whipping and the pillory as punishment for freedmen's offenses.

The Codes salvaged the labor-discipline elements of slave law in master-and-servant statutes, VAGRANCY and pauper provisions, apprenticeship regulations, and elaborate labor contract statutes, especially those pertaining to farm labor. Other provisions permitted magistrates to hire out offenders unable to pay fines. These statutes provided a basis for subsequent efforts, extending well into the twentieth century, to provide a legal and paralegal structure forcing blacks to work, restricting their occupational mobility, and providing harsh systems of forced black labor, sometimes verging on PEONAGE.

The Black Codes profoundly offended the northern ideal of equality before the law. Northerners lost whatever sympathies they might have entertained for the plight of southern whites trying to make the revolutionary transition from a slave society, based on a legal regime of status, to a free, capitalist society based on will and contract. Northerners determined to force the former slave states to create new structures of racial equality. Consequently, the Black Codes were repealed or left unenforced during the congressional phase of Reconstruction. Later Redeemer and Conservative state legislatures reenacted the Jim Crow provisions and labor contract statutes to provide the statutory component of the twilight zone of semifreedom that characterized the legal status of southern blacks through World War I.

WILLIAM M. WIECEK

Bibliography

WILSON, THEODORE B. 1965 *The Black Codes of the South*. University: University of Alabama Press.

BLACKMUN, HARRY A.
(1908–   )

Nothing in Harry A. Blackmun's background presaged that within three years of his appointment he would write the most controversial Supreme Court opinion of his time—ROE v. WADE (1972)—providing significant constitutional protection to women and their doctors in the area of abortion.

After graduating from public school in St. Paul, Minnesota, where he and WARREN E. BURGER were elementary school classmates, young Blackmun attended Harvard College, having graduated in 1929 *summa cum laude*, and Harvard Law School, being graduated in 1932. He practiced law in St. Paul and then as resident counsel at the Mayo Clinic in Rochester, Minnesota. In 1959 President DWIGHT D. EISENHOWER appointed him to the Eighth Circuit, where he served for eleven unremarkable years until, in 1970, President RICHARD M. NIXON selected him to fill the vacancy on the Supreme Court created by the resignation of Justice ABE FORTAS.

Blackmun's early years on the Supreme Court did little to disturb his image as a judicial clone of his boyhood friend Warren Burger, at whose wedding he had served as best man. The two voted together so often that the press dubbed them the Minnesota Twins.

Blackmun's voting patterns shifted over the years until by the mid-1980s he was more likely to vote with Justices WILLIAM J. BRENNAN and THURGOOD MARSHALL in defense of a broad vision of constitutional rights than with Burger. When asked whether his views have changed, Blackmun asserts that he has remained constant while the Court has shifted, causing his recent opinions merely to appear more libertarian. If, however, one compares early and late Blackmun opinions, it is difficult to accept Blackmun's protestation that nothing has changed in his legal universe except the backdrop.

One widely held hypothesis seeking to explain Blackmun's apparent shift in views is linked to the stormy public reaction that greeted what is undoubtedly his most significant Supreme Court opinion—*Roe v. Wade*. In *Roe*, drawing on his years at the Mayo Clinic, Blackmun brought a medical perspective to the controversy over the constitutionality of state laws prohibiting abortion. In a now familiar construct, he divided pregnancy into trimesters, holding that the state had no compelling interest in preserving fetal life during the first two trimesters, but that the interest in viable fetal life became compelling in the final trimester. In the years following *Roe*, Blackmun vigorously defended the right of a pregnant woman, in consultation with her doctor, to decide freely whether to undergo an abortion, writing a series of opinions striking down state statutes designed to place obstacles in a woman's path and vigorously dissenting from the Court's willingness to uphold a ban on federal funds to poor women seeking abortions.

Public reaction to Blackmun's abortion decisions was intense. He was subjected to vigorous personal criticism by individuals who believe deeply in a moral imperative of preserving fetal life from the moment of conception. Critics called his opinion in *Roe* a classic example of judicial overreaching and even compared it to Chief Justice ROGER B. TANEY's infamous opinion in DRED SCOTT v. SANDFORD (1857).

Subjected to sustained personal and professional criticism after *Roe*, Blackmun was forced, according to one view, to confront fundamental questions about his role as a Supreme Court Justice. From the crucible of the personal and professional pressures generated by his abortion decisions, many believe that there emerged a Justice with a heightened commitment to the use of judicial power to protect individual freedom.

In fact, the linkage between Blackmun's defense of a woman's right to choose to undergo an abortion and his other major doctrinal innovation—the COMMERCIAL SPEECH doctrine—is a direct one. In *Bigelow v. Virginia* (1975) Blackmun wrote for the Court invalidating a ban on advertisements by abortion clinics and suggesting for the first time that a consumer's right to know might justify First Amendment protection for speech that merely proposed a commercial transaction. One year later, in VIRGINIA STATE BOARD OF PHARMACY v. VIRGINIA CITIZENS CONSUMER COUNCIL (1976) and BATES v. STATE BAR OF ARIZONA (1976), he struck down bans on advertising by pharmacists and lawyers, explicitly granting First Amendment protection for the first time to commercial speech. In his more recent commercial speech opinions, Blackmun's First Amendment analysis has become more trenchant, with his concurrence in CENTRAL HUDSON GAS & ELECTRIC CO. v. PUBLIC SERVICE COMMISSION (1980) ranking as a milestone in Supreme Court First Amendment theory.

Blackmun's third principal contribution to constitutional DOCTRINE—the defense of ALIENS—precedes his abortion decisions. In GRAHAM V. RICHARDSON, one of Blackmun's early majority opinions, he wrote the opinion that outlawed discrimination against resident aliens in granting WELFARE BENEFITS, holding that aliens, as a politically powerless group, were entitled to heightened judicial protection under the EQUAL PROTECTION clause. In later years, his majority opinions invalidated attempts to exclude aliens from all civil service jobs and from state-funded college scholarships; and, although he concurred in the Court's decision upholding the exclusion of aliens from the state police, he vigorously dissented from decisions upholding bans on alien public school teachers and deputy probation officers.

Blackmun's most significant FEDERALISM opinion dramatically illustrates his evolution on the Court. In 1976 he provided the crucial fifth vote for Justice WILLIAM H. REHNQUIST's opinion in NATIONAL LEAGUE OF CITIES V. USERY, invalidating congressional minimum wage protection for municipal employees as a violation of state SOVEREIGNTY. A decade later, however, Blackmun changed his mind and, abandoning the Rehnquist-Burger position, wrote the Court's opinion in GARCIA V. SAN ANTONIO METROPOLITAN TRANSPORTATION AUTHORITY (1985), rejecting their view of state sovereignty and overruling *Usery*.

The hypothesis that Blackmun's apparent drift toward the Brennan-Marshall wing of the Court is linked to the controversy over his abortion decisions is not wholly persuasive. It does not explain Justice Blackmun's pre-*Roe* decisions protecting aliens and it overlooks the fact that as a little known judge of the Eighth Circuit, Blackmun was among the first federal judges to declare prison conditions violative of the Eighth Amendment. Furthermore, it does not explain why, in the criminal law and CRIMINAL PROCEDURE area, Blackmun's post-*Roe* jurisprudence continues to construe Fourth, Fifth, and Sixth Amendment protections narrowly.

A more fruitful approach to Blackmun's voting patterns is to take seriously his protestation that a consistent judicial philosophy underlies his Supreme Court career. The task is difficult, for Blackmun's judicial philosophy defies easy categorization in terms of fashionable labels. He is "liberal" in cases involving racial minorities and aliens, but "conservative" in the criminal procedure area. His abortion decision in *Roe* has been called the most "activist" in the Court's history, but his *Garcia* federalism opinion counsels "judicial restraint." His commercial speech opinions are rigorously "libertarian," but his tax, antitrust law, and securities law opinions champion vigorous government in-

tervention. Not surprisingly, therefore, attempts to evaluate Blackmun's work using currently fashionable yardsticks often lead to a critical judgment that he is doctrinally inconsistent. In fact, Blackmun's Supreme Court work appears linked by a unifying thread—a reluctance to permit preoccupation with doctrinal considerations to force him into the resolution of an actual case on terms that fail to do intuitive justice to the parties before the Court.

Blackmun's commitment to a jurisprudence of just deserts is reflected in three characteristic motifs that pervade his opinions. First, he is openly mistrustful of rigidly doctrinaire analyses that force him into unfair or unreasonable resolutions of cases. In rejecting the Court's two-tier equal protection analysis in favor of a more "flexible" doctrine, or expressing skepticism about prophylactic EXCLUSIONARY RULES in the criminal process, or searching for a federalism compromise based more on pragmatism than on theory, or rejecting automatic use of the OVERBREADTH DOCTRINE in FIRST AMENDMENT cases, Justice Blackmun refuses to allow doctrine to force him into dispute resolutions that seem intuitively unfair or that give an unjust windfall to one of the parties before the Court.

Second, his opinions are fact-oriented, canvassing both adjudicative and LEGISLATIVE FACTS in an attempt to place the dispute before the Court in a realistic context. In his more recent opinions, he frequently scolds the Court for slighting a case's factual context, often complaining that the Court's desire to announce law has taken it beyond the actual dispute before the Court.

Finally, he insists upon results that accord with his view of the "real" world. His decisions have tended to support efforts to undo the consequences of RACIAL DISCRIMINATION and have demonstrated an increasing empathy for the plight of the powerless, while demonstrating little sympathy for lawbreakers. Such a personal vision of "reality" must ultimately inject a dose of subjectivism into the decision-making process. Yet Justice Blackmun's qualities of mind and heart serve to remind the Court that a doctrinaire, intellectualized jurisprudence needs to be balanced by a jurisprudence grounded in intuitive fairness to the parties, human warmth, and pragmatic realism.

BURT NEUBORNE

Bibliography
FUQUA, DAVID 1980 Justice Harry A. Blackmun: The Abortion Decisions. *Arkansas Law Review* 34:276–296.
NOTE 1983 The Changing Social Vision of Justice Blackmun. *Harvard Law Review* 96:717–736.

SCHLESSINGER, STEVEN R.   1980 Justice Harry Blackmun and Empirical Jurisprudence. *American University Law Review* 29:405–437.

SYMPOSIUM 1985 Dedication to Justice Harry A. Blackmun—Biography; Tributes. *Hamline Law Review* 8:1–149.

BLACKSTONE, WILLIAM
(1723–1780)

The influence of Sir William Blackstone's *Commentaries on the Laws of England,* first published at Oxford between 1765 and 1769, was pervasive in American jurisprudence for much of the nineteenth century, although the work affected constitutional thought more in the realm of philosophy rather than that of specific legal doctrine. The appeal of this four-volume summation of the COMMON LAW, in the beginning of the American federal system, may be explained in part by its highly readable style and its function as a ready reference for many lawyers and jurists whose professional preparation was often indifferent. The practical need for a comprehensive and coherent view of the parent stock more than offset a tentative effort to make the new nation entirely independent of English legal institutions; and after the first American annotations to Blackstone by ST. GEORGE TUCKER in 1804, the importing of successive English editions and the periodic publication of fresh American editions by jurists like THOMAS M. COOLEY of Michigan and scholars like William Draper Lewis of the University of Pennsylvania made the *Commentaries* a standard reference for more than a hundred years.

The almost instant appeal of Blackstone to the English New World colonies—soon to be arguing their entitlements to the "rights of Englishmen" which they finally concluded could be secured only through independence of England itself—lay not only in its comprehensiveness but also in its epitomizing of the creative mercantilist jurisprudence of Blackstone's friend and contemporary, WILLIAM MURRAY (Lord Mansfield), which demonstrated the adaptability of the common law to "modern" economic objectives. The colonial elite, who had devoted the last generation before independence to "Americanization" of the English law, had economic views substantially similar to the scions of the English ruling classes to whom Blackstone delivered his Oxford lectures as Vinerian professor of English law. It was not surprising, therefore, that the *Commentaries*—to be followed in the post-Revolutionary period by the published reports of Mansfield—should appeal to the ruling element in the new nation, which was eager to continue the rules of an ordered economy.

These American leaders, Edmund Burke reminded his listeners in his 1775 "Speech on Conciliation," had a sophisticated legal knowledge, and the proof was in the fact that at that date almost as many copies of the *Commentaries* had been sold in the colonies as in England. JOHN MARSHALL's father was a subscriber to the first Philadelphia printing of 1771–1772, and both the future Chief Justice and his great antagonist, THOMAS JEFFERSON, read assiduously in the volumes. Jefferson wrote that Blackstone's work was "the most elegant and best digested" of any English treatise, "rightfully taking [its] place by the side of the Justinian institutes." While he considered that its continuing popularity in the new nation encouraged a too-slavish reliance on English precedent, he applauded St. George Tucker's plan to bring out an edition with American annotations.

In constitutional thought, the obvious differences in the structure of British and American government stimulated Tucker and succeeding American editors to prepare elaborate essays distinguishing between the frames, although not necessarily the philosophies, of the two constitutional systems. Parliamentary supremacy, which Blackstone endorsed, was in one sense emulated in the organization of the legislative departments as provided in both state and national constitutions. The recent memory of arbitrary and preemptive authority exercised by royal governors led Tucker to make the "popular" branch dominant over the executive. Ironically, Chief Justice Marshall, however congenial he found Blackstone's definition of law in general, was to embody the general principles of the *Commentaries* into a judicial definition of American FEDERALISM which made the judicial an equal branch. Nevertheless, a succession of influential nineteenth-century jurists after Marshall converted the Blackstonian conservatism into the laissez-faire principles that dominated American constitutional law until the 1930s.

The Tucker interpretation of the *Commentaries* led, through his sons, NATHANIEL BEVERLEY TUCKER and HENRY ST. GEORGE TUCKER, to a strict constructionist or "STATES' RIGHTS" school of constitutional thought, which was brought to its zenith in the speeches and writings of Henry's son, John Randolph Tucker. His 1877 Saratoga Springs lecture on state-federal relations as affected by the post-Civil War amendments to the Federal Constitution culminated in his posthumously published *Commentaries on the Constitution* (1899). This view, merging with Cooley's edition of 1870, kept the conservative jurisprudence of Blackstone in a position of influence until the revolution in American constitutional doctrine in the New Deal crisis of the 1930s.

WILLIAM F. SWINDLER

Bibliography

BOORSTIN, DANIEL J.   (1941)1973   *The Mysterious Science of the Law: An Essay on Blackstone's Commentaries.* Cambridge, Mass.: Harvard University Press; reprint, Gloucester, Mass.: Peter Smith.

KATZ, STANLEY M., ed. [William Blackstone]   1979   *Commentaries on the Laws of England: A Facsimile of the First Edition.* Chicago: University of Chicago Press.

KENNEDY, DUNCAN   1979   The Structure of Blackstone's Commentaries. *Buffalo Law Review* 28:205–382.

BLAINE AMENDMENT
(1875)

Representative James G. Blaine of Maine, with the support of President ULYSSES S. GRANT, introduced, in December 1875, a proposed constitutional amendment to prohibit state financial support of sectarian schools. The amendment was intended to prevent public support of the Roman Catholic schools which educated a large percentage of the children of European immigrants.

The first clause of the proposed amendment provided that "no State shall make any laws respecting an ESTABLISHMENT OF RELIGION or prohibiting the free exercise thereof." This is an indication that Congress did not believe that the FOURTEENTH AMENDMENT incorporated the religion clauses of the FIRST AMENDMENT. (See INCORPORATION DOCTRINE.)

The second clause would have prohibited the use or control by a religious sect or denomination of any tax money or land devoted to public education. Together with the first clause this prohibition suggests the connection between support of church-related schools and establishment of religion recognized in twentieth-century Supreme Court opinions beginning with EVERSON V. BOARD OF EDUCATION (1947).

The Blaine Amendment was approved by the House of Representatives, 180–7; but even a heavily amended version failed to carry two-thirds of the Senate, and so the proposal died.

DENNIS J. MAHONEY

(SEE ALSO: *Government Aid to Sectarian Institutions.*)

BLAIR, JOHN
(1732–1800)

John Blair was a member of the Virginia House of Burgesses when the American Revolution began. In 1776, as a delegate to the state CONSTITUTIONAL CONVENTION, he served on the committee that drafted the VIRGINIA DECLARATION OF RIGHTS and the VIRGINIA CONSTITUTION. In 1777 he was appointed a judge, and in 1780 he became chancellor of Virginia. As a justice of the Court of Appeals he joined in deciding COMMONWEALTH V. CATON (1782). He was a delegate to both the CONSTITUTIONAL CONVENTION OF 1787—at which he never made a speech—and the Virginia ratifying convention. In 1789 President GEORGE WASHINGTON appointed him one of the original Justices of the Supreme Court of the United States. He served on the Supreme Court until 1796, a period during which the Court handed down few important decisions. In the most noteworthy, CHISHOLM V. GEORGIA (1793), Blair joined in the decision to hear a case brought against a state by a citizen of another state, arguing that to refuse to do so would be to "renounce part of the authority conferred, and, consequently part of the duty imposed by the Constitution."

DENNIS J. MAHONEY

Bibliography

ROSSITER, CLINTON   1966   *1787: The Grand Convention.* New York: Macmillan.

BLASPHEMY

Defaming religion by any words expressing scorn, ridicule, or vilification of God, Jesus Christ, the Holy Ghost, the doctrine of the Trinity, the Old or New Testament, or Christianity, constitutes the offense of blasphemy. In the leading American case, *Commonwealth v. Kneeland* (1838), Chief Justice LEMUEL SHAW of Massachusetts repelled arguments based on FREEDOM OF THE PRESS and on RELIGIOUS LIBERTY when he sustained a state law against blasphemy and upheld the conviction of a pantheist who simply denied belief in God, Christ, and miracles. In all the American decisions, the courts maintained the fiction that the criminality of the words consisted of maliciousness or the intent to insult rather than mere difference of opinion.

The Supreme Court has never decided a blasphemy case. In BURSTYN, INC. V. WILSON (1951) the Court relied on FREEDOM OF SPEECH to void a New York statute authorizing the censorship of "sacrilegious" films. Justice FELIX FRANKFURTER, concurring, observed that blasphemy was a far vaguer term than sacrilege because it meant "criticism of whatever the ruling authority of the moment established as the orthodox religious doctrine." In 1968, when the last prosecution of blasphemy occurred in the United States, an appellate court of Maryland held that the prosecution violated the First Amendment's ban on ESTABLISHMENT OF RELIGION and its protection of freedom of religion. Should a blasphemy case ever reach the Supreme Court, that Court would surely reach a similar result.

LEONARD W. LEVY

Bibliography

LEVY, LEONARD W. 1981 *Treason Against God: A History of the Offense of Blasphemy.* New York: Schocken Books.

BLATCHFORD, SAMUEL
(1820–1893)

Samuel Blatchford had been a federal judge for fifteen years when CHESTER A. ARTHUR appointed him to the Supreme Court in 1882. Like Horace Gray, Arthur's other appointee, Blatchford had initially made his mark on the profession as a reporter. Beginning in 1852, he published a volume of admiralty cases decided in the Southern District of New York, a volume of Civil War prize cases from the same JURISDICTION, and twenty-four volumes of Second Circuit decisions. He continued to report Second Circuit opinions following his appointment as district judge (1867), circuit judge (1872), and circuit justice. Blatchford's expertise in admiralty, PATENT, and construction of the national banking acts made him the Supreme Court's workhorse; he wrote 435 majority opinions during his eleven-year tenure, almost twenty percent more than his proportional share.

Two personal characteristics shaped Blatchford's modest contributions to American constitutional development. He was singularly uninterested in questions of statecraft, political economy, and philosophy; he was so committed to a collective conception of the judicial function that he dissented less frequently then any Justice since the era of JOHN MARSHALL. These attitudes, coupled with Chief Justice MORRISON R. WAITE's disinclination to assign him cases involving CONSTITUTIONAL INTERPRETATION, kept Blatchford out of the limelight during his first eight years on the Court. But his compromising tendency prompted

MELVILLE W. FULLER, Waite's successor, to regard him as the logical spokesman for narrow, unstable majorities in two controversial FOURTEENTH AMENDMENT cases. Blatchford's lackluster performances in CHICAGO, MILWAUKEE & ST. PAUL RAILWAY V. MINNESOTA (1890) and *Budd v. New York* (1892) underscored his stolid approach to constitutional law.

At issue in the *Chicago, Milwaukee* case was the validity of an 1887 Minnesota statute establishing a railroad commission authorized to set maximum rate schedules that would be "final and conclusive." Because this scheme left no role for courts in reviewing railroad rates, the briefs focused on two previous statements by Chief Justice Waite. In *Munn v. Illinois* (1877) Waite had explained that "the controlling fact" in rate controversies was "the power to regulate at all." And he had added that "for protection against abuses by legislatures the people must resort to the polls, not the courts." In the *Railroad Commission Cases* (1886), however, Justice STANLEY MATTHEWS had persuaded Waite to acknowledge that "under the pretense of regulating fares and freights, the State cannot require a railroad corporation to carry persons or property without reward; neither can it do that which in law amounts to a taking of private property for PUBLIC USE without JUST COMPENSATION, or without DUE PROCESS OF LAW." Speaking for a 6–3 majority, Blatchford concluded that Waite's majority opinion in the Railroad Commission Cases presupposed at least some role for the courts; it followed that the Minnesota law could not be sustained. At one point Blatchford came very close to equating due process with judicial process, but he cautiously retreated and ultimately said nothing about either the scope of JUDICIAL REVIEW or its rationale, which went beyond Waite's enigmatic OBITER DICTUM. Only the dissent by JOSEPH P. BRADLEY forthrightly summarized what seemed to be the majority's premise. "In effect," he complained, the Court had now held "that the judiciary, and not the legislature, is the final arbiter in the regulation of fares and freights."

Budd brought both of the central issues in *Munn* back to the Court for reconsideration. Speaking again for a majority of six, Blatchford reiterated the Court's conclusion that bulk storage and handling of grain was a "business AFFECTED WITH A PUBLIC INTEREST." Consequently rates of charge for these services might be regulated by state governments. But what of *Chicago, Milwaukee*, which Bradley had described as "practically overrul[ing]" *Munn*? The two cases were "quite distinguishable," Blatchford insisted, "for in this instance the rate of charges is fixed directly by the legislature." Blatchford apparently regarded this formulation as an appropriate means of reconciling all previous decisions on the subject. But the distinction between legislative and commission regulation was so artificial that Justice JOHN MARSHALL HARLAN simply ignored it in his characteristically robust opinion for the Court in SMYTH V. AMES (1898). Seymour D. Thompson, editor of the *American Law Review*, was less gracious. "It was no great disparagement of him," Thompson remarked in a critical appraisal of Blatchford's constitutional law opinions, "to say that he was probably a better reporter than Judge."

CHARLES W. MCCURDY

Bibliography

PAUL, ARNOLD 1969 Samuel Blatchford. Pages 1401–1414 in Leon Friedman and Fred L. Israel, eds., *The Justices of the United States Supreme Court, 1789–1969: Their Lives and Major Opinions*. New York: Chelsea House.

BLOCK GRANTS

See: Federal Grants-in-Aid; Revenue Sharing

BLOOD SAMPLES

See: Testimonial Compulsion

BLOUNT, WILLIAM
(1749–1800)

William Blount was a delegate to the CONSTITUTIONAL CONVENTION OF 1787 from North Carolina and a signer of the Constitution. Blount did not speak at the Convention and, disliking the result, signed the Constitution only to attest to the fact that it was consented to by all of the states represented.

DENNIS J. MAHONEY

BLUE RIBBON JURY

Under the laws of some states, cases of unusual importance or complexity may be tried to special juries chosen from a venire with qualifications higher than those for the ordinary jury panel. Such juries are commonly called "blue ribbon juries." In *Fay v. New York* (1947) the Supreme Court affirmed (5–4) the constitutionality of using a blue ribbon jury in a criminal prosecution. Whether such juries would meet the contemporary standard of being drawn from a source fairly representative of the community is uncertain. (See JURY DISCRIMINATION; TAYLOR V. LOUISIANA, 1975.) In any event, blue ribbon juries have fallen into disuse.

DENNIS J. MAHONEY

BLUM v. YARETSKY
457 U.S. 991 (1982)
RENDELL-BAKER v. KOHN
457 U.S. 830 (1982)

Following the Supreme Court's decision in BURTON V. WILMINGTON PARKING AUTHORITY (1961), commentators and lower courts began to ask whether a significant state subsidy to a private institution might make that institution's conduct into STATE ACTION, subject to the limitations of the Fourteenth Amendment. *Blum* and *Rendell-Baker* ended two decades of speculation; by 7–2 votes, the Court answered "No."

In *Blum* patients in private nursing homes complained that they had been transferred to facilities offering lesser care without notice or hearing, in violation of their rights to PROCEDURAL DUE PROCESS. Through the Medicaid program, the state paid the medical expenses of ninety percent of the patients; the state also subsidized the costs of the homes and extensively regulated their operation through a licensing scheme. The Court rejected each of these connections, one by one, as an argument for finding state action. The Constitution governed private conduct only when the state was "responsible" for that conduct; normally, such responsibility was to be found in state coercion or significant encouragement; these features were missing here.

In *Rendell-Baker* employees of a private school complained that they had been discharged for exercising their rights of FREEDOM OF SPEECH, and fired without adequate procedural protections. The Court reached neither issue, because it concluded that the action of the school did not amount to state action. Although the school depended on public funding, no state policy—no coercion or encouragement—influenced the employees' discharge.

Dissents in the two cases were written by Justices WILLIAM J. BRENNAN and THURGOOD MARSHALL, respectively. They argued that a consideration of all the interconnections between the institutions and the states, including the heavy subsidies, amounted to the kind of "significant state involvement" found in *Burton*. But considering the totality of circumstances in order to find state action is precisely what a majority of the BURGER COURT has been unwilling to do.

KENNETH L. KARST

BOARD OF CURATORS v. HOROWITZ
435 U.S. 78 (1979)

A state university medical student was dismissed during her final year of study for failure to meet academic standards. The Supreme Court unanimously held that she had not been deprived of her PROCEDURAL DUE PROCESS rights, but divided 5–4 on the reasons for that conclusion. For a majority, Justice WILLIAM H. REHNQUIST commented that the student had not asserted any "property" interest, and strongly hinted that she had not been deprived of a "liberty" interest. Nevertheless, assuming the existence of an interest entitled to due process protections, Rehnquist said that a dismissal for academic rather than disciplinary reasons required no hearing or opportunity to respond. Four concurring Justices disagreed with the remarkable conclusion that due process required a fair procedure for the ten-day suspension of an elementary school pupil in GOSS V. LOPEZ (1975) but not for the academic dismissal of a medical student. Here, however, the four Justices agreed that the student had been given a sufficient hearing.

Horowitz illustrates the artificiality of the Court's recent narrowing of the "liberty" or "property" interests to which the guarantee of procedural due process attaches. A student's interest in avoiding academic termination fits awkwardly into those categories, in their recent restrictive definitions. Yet the student plainly deserves protection against termination procedures that are arbitrary. The specter of judges' having to read examination papers is no more than a specter. The concern of procedural due process is not the fairness of a particular student's termination, but the fairness of the procedural system for depriving a person of an important interest.

KENNETH L. KARST

BOARD OF EDUCATION v. ALLEN
392 U.S. 236 (1968)

New York authorized the loan of state-purchased textbooks to students in nonpublic schools. Justice BYRON R. WHITE, speaking for the Supreme Court, relied heavily on the "pupil benefit theory" which

he purportedly derived from EVERSON V. BOARD OF EDUCATION (1947). If the beneficiaries of the governmental program were principally the children, and not the religious institutions, the program could be sustained.

Justice HUGO L. BLACK, the author of *Everson*, dissented. *Everson*, he recalled, held that transportation of students to church-related schools went "to the very verge" of what was permissible under the establishment clause. Justices WILLIAM O. DOUGLAS and ABE FORTAS also dissented.

Allen stimulated efforts to aid church-related schools in many state legislatures. Later opinions of the Court, invalidating many such aid programs, have limited *Allen's* precedential force to cases involving textbook loans.

RICHARD E. MORGAN

(SEE ALSO: *Government Aid to Religious Institutions.*)

BOARD OF EDUCATION v. PICO
457 U.S. 853 (1982)

Six students sued a school board in federal court, claiming that the board had violated their FIRST AMENDMENT rights by removing certain books from the high school and junior high school libraries. The board had responded to lists of "objectionable" and "inappropriate" books circulated at a conference of conservative parents. A fragmented Supreme Court, voting 5–4, remanded the case for trial.

Four Justices concluded that it would be unconstitutional for the school board to remove the books from the libraries for the purpose of suppressing ideas. Four others argued for wide discretion by local officials in selecting school materials, including library books. One Justice would await the outcome of a trial before addressing the constitutional issues. Thus, although the decision attracted national attention, it did little to solve the intractable constitutional puzzle of GOVERNMENT SPEECH.

KENNETH L. KARST

BOARD OF REGENTS v. ROTH
408 U.S. 564 (1972)

A nontenured state college teacher, hired for a one-year term, was told he would not be rehired for the following year. The Supreme Court held, 5–3, that he had not been deprived of PROCEDURAL DUE PRO-

CESS. Justice POTTER STEWART, for the majority, announced a restrictive view of the nature of the interests protected by the due process guarantee. Henceforth the Court would look for an impact on some "liberty" or "property" interest, rather than examine the importance of the deprivation imposed by the state. Here the teacher had no "property" interest beyond his one-year contract, and his nonrenewal required no hearing.

In a companion case, *Perry v. Sindermann* (1972), the Court found a "property" interest in an unwritten policy that was the equivalent of tenure for a state junior college teacher. Furthermore, the teacher had alleged that his contract had not been renewed because of his exercise of FIRST AMENDMENT freedoms—a "liberty" claim that did not depend on his tenured status.

KENNETH L. KARST

BOB JONES UNIVERSITY v. UNITED STATES
461 U.S. 574 (1983)

The Internal Revenue Service adopted a policy in 1969 of denying federal income tax exemption, available by statute to educational and religious institutions, to schools that practiced racial discrimination. Bob Jones University, an institution that had a multiracial student body but restricted interracial socializing, and Goldsboro Christian Schools, which practiced racial SEGREGATION on the basis of religious conviction, sought to have their tax-exempt status reinstated. In an opinion by Chief Justice WARREN E. BURGER, the Supreme Court held, 8–1, that the Internal Revenue Service had the power, even without explicit statutory authorization, to enforce by its regulations a "settled public policy" against racial discrimination in education. None of the Justices accepted the schools' claim that the regulations infringed on the First Amendment's guarantee of religious liberty, but Justice WILLIAM H. REHNQUIST, dissenting, warned of the danger of abrogating the SEPARATION OF POWERS.

DENNIS J. MAHONEY

BOB-LO EXCURSION COMPANY v. MICHIGAN
333 U.S. 28 (1948)

Although this decision unsettled interpretations of the COMMERCE CLAUSE, it nevertheless dealt SEGREGATION another blow. A Detroit steamship company vio-

lated a state CIVIL RIGHTS statute by refusing to transport a black girl to a local, though Canadian, destination. Justice WILEY RUTLEDGE's majority opinion distinguished MORGAN V. VIRGINIA (1946) and stressed the local nature of transportation in upholding the statute. Justices WILLIAM O. DOUGLAS and HUGO L. BLACK thought the law should be sustained because there could be no conflict with a congressional law; Chief Justice FRED M. VINSON and Justice ROBERT H. JACKSON dissented, arguing that *Morgan* and HALL V. DeCUIR (1878) governed.

DAVID GORDON

BODDIE v. CONNECTICUT
401 U.S. 371 (1971)

An INDIGENT sought to file for divorce in a state court but was unable to pay the $60 filing fee. The Supreme Court held, 8–1, that the state had unconstitutionally limited the plaintiff's ACCESS TO THE COURTS. For a majority, Justice JOHN MARSHALL HARLAN rested decision on a PROCEDURAL DUE PROCESS theory. The marriage relationship was "basic" in our society, and the state had monopolized the means for legally dissolving the relationship. Justice WILLIAM O. DOUGLAS, concurring, would have rested decision on an EQUAL PROTECTION theory.

Two subsequent 5–4 decisions, *United States v. Kras* (1971) and *Ortwein v. Schwab* (1971), made clear that *Boddie* had not implied a general right of access in all civil cases. *Boddie*'s due process approach, rather than equal protection, has guided the Court's subsequent dealings with WEALTH DISCRIMINATION in the civil litigation process.

KENNETH L. KARST

BOLLING v. SHARPE
347 U.S. 497 (1954)

In the four cases now known as BROWN V. BOARD OF EDUCATION (1954), the Supreme Court held that racial SEGREGATION of children in state public schools violated the FOURTEENTH AMENDMENT's guarantee of the EQUAL PROTECTION OF THE LAWS. *Bolling*, a companion case to *Brown*, involved a challenge to school segregation in the DISTRICT OF COLUMBIA. The equal protection clause applies only to the states. However, in previous cases (including the JAPANESE AMERICAN CASES, 1943–1944) the Court had assumed, at least for argument, that the Fifth Amendment's guarantee of DUE PROCESS OF LAW prohibited arbitrary discrimination by the federal government.

The Court in *Bolling* also drew on OBITER DICTA in the Japanese American Cases stating that racial classifications were suspect, requiring exacting judicial scrutiny. Because school segregation was "not reasonably related to any proper governmental objective," the District's practice deprived the segregated black children of liberty without due process. Chief Justice EARL WARREN wrote for a unanimous Court.

The Court concluded its Fifth Amendment discussion by remarking that because *Brown* had prohibited school segregation by the states, "it would be unthinkable that the same Constitution would impose a lesser duty on the Federal Government." Critics have suggested that what was "unthinkable" was the political implication of a contrary decision. But the notions of liberty and equality have long been understood to overlap. The idea of national CITIZENSHIP implies a measure of equal treatment by the national government, and the "liberty" protected by the Fifth Amendment's due process clause implies a measure of equal liberties. Doctrinally as well as politically, a contrary decision in *Bolling* would have been unthinkable.

KENNETH L. KARST

BOLLMAN, EX PARTE, v. SWARTWOUT
4 Cranch 75 (1807)

The Supreme Court discharged the prisoners, confederates in AARON BURR's conspiracy, from an INDICTMENT for TREASON. The indictment specified their treason as levying war against the United States. Chief Justice JOHN MARSHALL, for the Court, distinguished treason from a conspiracy to commit it. He sought to prevent the crime of treason from being "extended by construction to doubtful cases." To complete the crime of treason or levying war, Marshall said, a body of men must be "actually assembled for the purpose of effecting by force a treasonable purpose," in which everyone involved, to any degree and however remote from the scene of action, is guilty of treason. But the levying of war does not exist short of the actual assemblage of armed men. Congress had the power to punish crimes short of treason, but the Constitution protected Americans from a charge of treason for a crime short of it.

Bollman is also an important precedent in the law of federal JURISDICTION. In OBITER DICTUM, Marshall

stated that a federal court's power to issue a WRIT OF HABEAS CORPUS "must be given by written law," denying by inference that the courts have any inherent power to grant habeas corpus relief, apart from congressional authorization. (See EX PARTE McCARDLE, 1869; JUDICIAL SYSTEM.)

LEONARD W. LEVY

BOND, HUGH LENNOX
(1828–1893)

President ULYSSES S. GRANT on July 13, 1870, commissioned Hugh Lennox Bond judge of the newly created Fourth Circuit Court, a position he filled until his death. The Maryland judge was immediately called upon to hold court in an eleven-county section of South Carolina that had been plagued by the Ku Klux Klan's reign of terror. The judge fearlessly restored the rights of freedmen in South Carolina, but he did so in the belief that the states retained responsibility for preserving most CIVIL RIGHTS. Congress, he insisted, could only impede the traditional power of the states over the franchise when there was evidence of direct STATE ACTION resulting in discrimination based on race, color, or previous condition of servitude. Bond rejected the view that the Civil War amendments incorporated rights deriving from natural law; the protection of such rights, he concluded, remained squarely within state discretion.

He refused to allow the concept of dual CITIZENSHIP to erect an absolute bar to FEDERAL PROTECTION. In *United States v. Petersburg Judges of Elections* (1874), election officials were charged with preventing voting by freedmen without any overt act of RACIAL DISCRIMINATION. Bond acknowledged that under the concept of dual citizenship the states could take away certain rights, such as the franchise. He held, however, that so long as states continued to grant those rights, the federal government could protect freedmen by inferring discriminatory intent from acts depriving them of the rights that had been granted.

Bond insisted on the supremacy of the national government in its proper sphere. In 1876 he ordered the release of the Board of Canvassers of South Carolina who had been imprisoned by the state supreme court for attempting to report election returns favorable to RUTHERFORD B. HAYES. Bond held that Article I, section 2, protected the Canvassers in their capacity as federal officials.

During Reconstruction Bond courageously extended federal judicial protection to freedmen. Yet even this most vigorous champion in the circuit courts of freedmen's civil rights eschewed the Radical Republicans' CONSTITUTIONAL INTERPRETATION of the Civil War amendments.

KERMIT L. HALL

Bibliography

HALL, KERMIT L. 1984 Political Power and Constitutional Legitimacy: The South Carolina Ku Klux Klan Trials, 1871–1872. *Emory Law Journal* 33:921–951.

BONHAM'S CASE
8 Coke 113b (1610)

Although the issue in *Bonham's Case* concerned the power of the Royal College of Physicians to discipline nonmembers, its importance principally derives from its subsequent use as a precedent for JUDICIAL REVIEW and the subordination of LEGISLATION to a higher, constitutional law. Thomas Bonham, holder of a doctorate from Cambridge University, continued to practice in London after being refused permission by the College. Acting under powers conferred by royal charter and parliamentary statutes, the college authorities accordingly fined Bonham and secured his incarceration, thus triggering his suit for false imprisonment before the Court of Common Pleas.

Chief Justice Sir EDWARD COKE ruled in Bonham's favor. Although most of his numerous grounds were technical, Coke also criticized the statutory power of the college to be the original judge in a case to which it had itself been a party and concluded that the COMMON LAW courts could "control" and render void those acts of Parliament that were "against Common Right, and Reason, or repugnant, or impossible to be performed."

Coke, nevertheless, invoked no judicial power to invalidate legislation or measure its constitutionality. He advised only that the statute be construed strictly, not nullified, thus prescribing a rule of statutory construction rather than a doctrine of constitutional superintendence. Coke assumed, moreover, that the defect in the law inhered not in UNCONSTITUTIONALITY but in want of reasonableness and in impossibility of performance. The common law court intervened here as the handmaiden, not the antagonistic overseer, of Parliament, a brother court, and only for the purpose of recapturing a reasonableness that permeated the immutable laws sought by bench and Parliament alike.

Coke's use of evidence was also defective. Coke misquoted, for example, a major precedent, *Tregor's Case* (1334), by infusing into it language that it actually lacked to secure the desired result.

Two antagonistic streams of interpretation devolve from *Bonham's Case.* The Glorious Revolution of 1688 signaled the dominance of Parliament over court as well as crown and, thus, the demise of the spacious judicial interpretation of legislation advocated by Coke. In 1765 WILLIAM BLACKSTONE definitively stated that no power could control unreasonable statutes, for such control subverted all government by setting the judiciary over the legislature. Although Coke's opinion in *Bonham* retained wide currency in the seventeenth century, its erosion began almost immediately and accelerated in the following century. In *The Duchess of Hamilton's Case* (1712), for example, Sir Thomas Powys insisted that judges must "strain hard" to avoid interpretations of statutes that would nullify them.

As the American Revolution approached, however, *Bonham's Case* evolved in the American colonies in the opposite direction as a fixed constitutional barrier against Parliament. Thus, in PAXTON'S CASE (1761) JAMES OTIS urged the Massachusetts Superior Court to impose a disabling interpretation on the British statute of 1662 that had codified WRITS OF ASSISTANCE. Although only private parties, not bench and Parliament, had directly clashed in *Bonham's Case,* Otis advanced it as a firm precedent for judicial evisceration of legislation. Coke questioned only the reasonableness of a statute; Otis and his followers challenged a law's constitutionality.

WILLIAM J. CUDDIHY

Bibliography

CORWIN, EDWARD S. 1929 The "Higher Law" Background of American Constitutional Law. Ithaca, N.Y.: Cornell University Press.
THORNE, SAMUEL 1938 The Constitution and the Courts: A Reexamination of the Famous Case of Dr. Bonham. Pages 15–24 in Conyers Read (ed.), *The Constitution Reconsidered.* New York: Columbia University Press.

BONUS BILL

See: Internal Improvements

BORDER SEARCH

A search at an international boundary of a person, a vehicle, or goods entering the United States may be carried out without a SEARCH WARRANT and in the absence of PROBABLE CAUSE or even suspicion. In *United States v. Ramsey* (1977) the Supreme Court said that this extraordinary power, which also allows the government to open international mail entering the United States, "is grounded in the recognized right of the sovereign to control . . . who and what may enter the country." The First Congress, in 1789, authorized WARRANTLESS SEARCHES of vessels suspected of carrying goods on which customs duty had been evaded, and similar provisions have been enacted subsequently. As the Court held in ALMEIDA-SANCHEZ V. UNITED STATES (1973), such a search may be conducted not only at the border itself but also at its "functional equivalent," such as "an established station near the border," or "a point marking the confluence of two or more roads that extend from the border," or an airplane arriving on a nonstop flight from abroad.

Under *United States v. Brignoni-Ponce* (1975) an automobile may not be stopped by a roving patrol car miles from the border (in an area that is not its legal equivalent) to determine whether the occupants are illegal aliens unless there is reasonable suspicion. Under *United States v. Martinez-Fuerte* (1976) automobiles may be stopped for this purpose at fixed checkpoints; in these circumstances the opportunity of officers to act arbitrarily is limited.

JACOB W. LANDYNSKI

Bibliography
LaFave, Wayne R. 1978 *Search and Seizure: A Treatise on the Fourth Amendment.* Vol. 3:275–327. St. Paul, Minn.: West Publishing Co.

BORROWING POWER

Congress, under Article I, section 8, of the Constitution, may "borrow money on the credit of the United States." This power is ordinarily exercised through the sale of bonds or the issuance of BILLS OF CREDIT. The latter, sometimes called "treasury notes" or "greenbacks," are intended to circulate as currency and thus, in effect, to require the public to lend money to the government. In the GOLD CLAUSE CASES (1935) the Supreme Court held that the government, in borrowing, is bound by the terms of its contracts, but Congress, by invoking SOVEREIGN IMMUNITY, denied its creditors any legal remedy.

DENNIS J. MAHONEY

BOSTON BEER COMPANY v. MASSACHUSETTS
97 U.S. 25 (1878)

This case introduced the doctrine of INALIENABLE POLICE POWER, which weakened the CONTRACT CLAUSE's protections of property. The company's charter authorized it to manufacture beer subject to a reserved power of the legislature to alter, amend, or repeal the charter. The state subsequently enacted a prohibition statute. The RESERVED POLICE POWER should have been sufficient ground for the holding by the Court that the prohibition statute did not impair the company's chartered right to do business. However, Justice JOSEPH P. BRADLEY, in an opinion for a unanimous Court, found another and "equally decisive" reason for rejecting the argument that the company had a contract to manufacture and sell beer "forever." The company held its rights subject to the POLICE POWER of the state to promote the public safety and morals. "The Legislature," Bradley declared, "cannot, by any contract, devest itself of the power to provide for these objects." Accordingly the enactment of a statute prohibiting the manufacture and sale of intoxicating liquors did not violate the contract clause. Decisions such as this, by which the police power prevailed over chartered rights, produced a doctrinal response: the development of SUBSTANTIVE DUE PROCESS to protect property.

LEONARD W. LEVY

BOUDIN, LOUIS B.
(1874–1952)

Louis Boudianoff Boudin was a prominent New York attorney and the author of books and articles on constitutional law, jurisprudence, and government regulation of the economy. His most significant work was *Government by Judiciary* (2 vols., 1932), a massive, iconoclastic history of the doctrine of JUDICIAL REVIEW. Boudin argued that, beginning in 1803 with JOHN MARSHALL's opinion in MARBURY V. MADISON, the federal judiciary had gradually expanded its powers and authority at the expense of the legislative and executive branches, culminating in a "government by judiciary" hostile to the basic principles of the Constitution established by its Framers and to the tenets of democratic government. While Boudin's admirers praised his erudition and accepted his exposure of the weaknesses of the historical case for judicial review, his critics questioned his tendency to write as an advocate rather than as a historian and charged that his conclusions were not supported by an impartial examination of the historical evidence.

RICHARD B. BERNSTEIN

BOUNDS v. SMITH
430 U.S. 817 (1977)

Several state prisoners sued North Carolina prison authorities in federal court, claiming they had been denied legal research facilities in violation of their FOURTEENTH AMENDMENT rights. The Supreme Court, 6–3, upheld this claim in an opinion by Justice THURGOOD MARSHALL.

For the first time the Court explicitly recognized a "fundamental constitutional right of ACCESS TO THE COURTS." This right imposed on prison authorities the affirmative duty to provide either adequate law libraries or the assistance of law-trained persons, so that prisoners might prepare HABEAS CORPUS petitions and other legal papers. The three dissenters each wrote an opinion. Justice WILLIAM H. REHNQUIST complained that the majority had neither defined the content of "meaningful" access nor specified the source of the Fourteenth Amendment right; an EQUAL PROTECTION right, he pointed out, would conflict with ROSS v. MOFFITT (1974).

KENNETH L. KARST

BOWMAN v. CHICAGO & NORTHWESTERN RAILWAY COMPANY
125 U.S. 465 (1888)

The Supreme Court, by a vote of 6–3, held that a state statute prohibiting common carriers from importing intoxicating liquors into the state, except under conditions laid down by the state, violated the COMMERCE CLAUSE, because interstate transportation required a single regulatory system; the absence of congressional action made no difference.

LEONARD W. LEVY

(SEE ALSO: *State Regulation of Commerce.*)

BOYCOTT

A boycott is a group refusal to deal. Such concerted action is an effective way for society's less powerful members, such as unorganized workers or racial minorities, to seek fair treatment in employment, public accommodations, and public services. But as the Supreme Court recognized in *Eastern States Retail Lumber Dealers' Association v. United States* (1914): "An act harmless when done by one may become a public wrong when done by many acting in concert, for it then takes on the form of a conspiracy."

Boycotts by private entrepreneurs were illegal at common law as unreasonable restraints on commercial competition. The Sherman Act of 1890 made it a federal offense to form a "combination . . . in restraint of trade." The Supreme Court has interpreted that prohibition as covering almost every type of concerted refusal by business people to trade with others. The constitutionality of outlawing commercial boycotts has never seriously been questioned.

Employee boycotts may be either "primary" or "secondary." A primary boycott involves direct action against a principal party to a dispute. A union seeking to organize a company's work force may call for a strike, a concerted refusal to work, by the company's employees. A secondary boycott involves action against a so-called neutral or secondary party that is doing business with the primary party. The union seeking to organize a manufacturing company might appeal to the employees of a retailer to strike the retailer in order to force the retailer to stop handling the manufacturer's products.

Although early American law regarded most strikes as criminal conspiracies, modern statutes like the WAGNER NATIONAL LABOR RELATIONS ACT (NLRA) treat primary strikes in the private sector as "protected" activity, immune from employer reprisals. Even so, the Supreme Court has never held there is a constitutional right to strike. Furthermore, the Court sustained the constitutionality of statutory bans on secondary boycott strikes or related picketing in *Electrical Workers Local 501 v. NLRB* (1951). The use of group pressure to enmesh neutrals in the disputes of others was sufficient to enable government to declare such activity illegal.

Consumer boycotts present the hardest constitutional questions. Here group pressure may not operate directly, as in the case of a strike. Instead, the union or other protest group asks individual customers, typically acting on their own, not to patronize the subject firm. Yet if the appeal is to customers of a retailer not to shop there so long as the retailer stocks a certain manufacturer's goods, a neutral party is the target. The NLRA forbids union PICKETING to induce such a secondary consumer boycott. The Supreme Court held this limited prohibition constitutional in *NLRB v. Retail Clerks Local 1001* (1980), although there was no majority rationale. A plurality cited precedent concerning secondary employee boycotts, ignoring the differences between individual and group responses.

On the other hand, when a civil rights organization conducted a damaging boycott against white merchants to compel them to support demands upon elected officials for racial equality, the Supreme Court declared in *NAACP v. Claiborne Hardware Co.* (1982) that a state's right "to regulate economic activity could not justify a complete prohibition against a nonviolent, politically motivated boycott designed to force governmental and economic change and to effectuate rights guaranteed by the Constitution itself." The Court relied on the FIRST AMENDMENT rights of FREEDOM OF SPEECH, FREEDOM OF ASSEMBLY AND ASSOCIATION, and FREEDOM OF PETITION. The emphasis on the right to petition government raises the possibility of a different result if the merchants themselves, rather than the public officials, had been the primary target of the boycott. But that would appear incongruous. The Court needs to refine its constitutional analysis of consumer boycotts.

THEODORE J. ST. ANTOINE

Bibliography

HARPER, MICHAEL C. 1984 The Consumer's Emerging Right to Boycott: *NAACP v. Claiborne Hardware* and Its Implications for American Labor Law. *Yale Law Journal* 93:409–454.
KENNEDY, RONALD E. 1982 Political Boycotts, the Sherman Act, and the First Amendment: An Accommodation of Competing Interests. *Southern California Law Review* 55:983–1030.

BOYD v. UNITED STATES
116 U.S. 616 (1886)

Justice LOUIS D. BRANDEIS believed that *Boyd* will be remembered "as long as civil liberty lives in the United States." The noble sentiments expressed in JOSEPH P. BRADLEY's opinion for the Court merit that estimate, but like many another historic opinion, this one was not convincingly reasoned. To this day, however, members of the Court return to *Boyd* to grace their opinions with its authority or with an imperishable line from Bradley's.

Boyd was the first important SEARCH AND SEIZURE case as well as the first important case on the RIGHT AGAINST SELF-INCRIMINATION. It arose not from a criminal prosecution but from a civil action by the United States for the forfeiture of goods imported in violation of customs revenue laws. In such cases an 1874 act of Congress required the importer to produce in court all pertinent records tending to prove the charges against him or suffer the penalty of being taken "as confessed." The Court held the act unconstitutional as a violation of both the FOURTH and Fifth AMENDMENTS. The penalty made the production of the records compulsory. That compulsion, said Bradley, raised "a very grave question of constitutional law, involving the personal security and PRIVILEGES AND IMMUNITIES of the citizen. . . ." But did the case involve a search or a seizure, and if so was it "unreasonable," and did it force the importer to be a witness against himself in a criminal case?

Bradley conceded that there was no search and seizure as in the forcible entry into a man's house and examination of his papers. Indeed, there was no search here for evidence of crime. The compulsion was to produce records that the government required importers to keep; no private papers were at issue. Moreover, no property was confiscated as in the case of contraband like smuggled goods. The importer, who was not subject to a search, had merely to produce the needed records in court; he kept custody of them. But the Court treated those records as if they were private papers, which could be used as EVIDENCE against him, resulting in the forfeiture of his property, or to establish a criminal charge. Though the proceeding was a civil one, a different section of the same statute did provide criminal penalties for fraud.

Bradley made a remarkable linkage between the right against UNREASONABLE SEARCH and seizure and the right against self-incrimination. The "fourth and fifth amendments," he declared, "almost run into each other." That they were different amendments, protected different interests, had separate histories, and reflected different policies was of no consequence to Bradley. He was on sound ground when he found that the forcible production of private papers to convict a man of crime or to forfeit his property violated the Fifth Amendment and was "contrary to the principles of a free government." He was on slippery ground when he found that such a compulsory disclosure was "the equivalent of a search and seizure—and an unreasonable search and seizure—within the meaning of the fourth amendment." His reasoning was that though the case did not fall within the "literal terms" of either amendment, each should be broadly construed in terms of the other. Unreasonable searches and seizures "are almost always made for the purpose of compelling a man to give evidence against himself," and compulsion of such evidence "throws light on the question as to what is an 'unreasonable search and seizure.'. . ." In support of his reasoning Bradley quoted at length from Lord Camden's opinion (see WILLIAM PRATT) in ENTICK V. CARRINGTON (1765). Camden, however, spoke of a fishing expedition under GENERAL WARRANTS issued by an executive officer without authorization by Parliament. There was no warrant in this case, and there was authorization by Congress for a court to compel production of the specific records required by law to be kept for government inspection, concerning FOREIGN COMMERCE which Congress may regulate. In this case, however, Bradley thought meticulous analysis was out of place. He feared that unconstitutional practices got their footing in "slight deviations" from proper procedures, and the best remedy was the rule that constitutional protections "for the security of person and property should be liberally construed." Close construction, he declared, deprived these protections of their efficacy.

Justice SAMUEL F. MILLER, joined by Chief Justice MORRISON R. WAITE, concurred in the judgment that that offensive section of the act of Congress was unconstitutional. Miller found no search and seizure, let alone an unreasonable one. He agreed, however, that Congress had breached the right against self-incrimination, which he thought should be the sole ground of the opinion.

The modern Court no longer assumes that the Fifth Amendment is a source of the Fourth's EXCLUSIONARY RULE or that the Fourth prohibits searches for MERE EVIDENCE. Moreover, the production of private papers may be compelled in certain cases, as when the Internal Revenue Service subpoenas records in the hands of one's lawyer or accountant.

                                                                    LEONARD W. LEVY

Bibliography

GERSTEIN, ROBERT S. 1979 The Demise of Boyd: Self-Incrimination and Private Papers in the Burger Court. *UCLA Law Review* 27:343–397.
LANDYNSKI, JACOB W. 1966 *Search and Seizure and the Supreme Court.* Pages 49–61. Baltimore: Johns Hopkins University Press.

BRADLEY, JOSEPH P.
(1813–1892)

Joseph P. Bradley's appointment to the Supreme Court in 1870 by President ULYSSES S. GRANT was seen as part of Grant's supposed court-packing scheme. But whatever shadow that event cast on Bradley's reputation rapidly disappeared. For more than two decades on the bench, he commanded almost unrivaled respect from colleagues, lawyers, and legal commentators, and over time he consistently has been ranked as one of the most influential jurists in the Court's history.

When Bradley was appointed he already was a prominent railroad lawyer and Republican activist. Indeed, friends had been advocating his appointment to the Court nearly a year before his appointment. Shortly after Grant's inauguration in 1869, the Republicans increased the size of the court from eight to nine. While Grant and Congress haggled over the selection of a new Justice, the Court decided, 4–3, that the legal tender laws were unconstitutional. Justice ROBERT C. GRIER clearly was senile, and after he cast his vote against the laws his colleagues persuaded him to resign. That gave Grant two appointments and, on February 7, 1870, he nominated WILLIAM STRONG and Bradley—and the Court almost simultaneously announced its legal tender decision.

Within a year, Bradley and Strong led a new majority to sustain the constitutionality of greenbacks (unsecured paper currency). In his CONCURRING OPINION, Bradley saw the power to emit BILLS OF CREDIT as the essential issue in the case, and from that he contended that "the incidental power of giving such bills the quality of legal tender follows almost as matter of course." Bradley also emphasized the government's right to maintain its existence. He insisted it would be a "great wrong" to deny Congress the asserted power, "a power to be seldom exercised, certainly; but one, the possession of which is so essential, and as it seems to me, so undoubted." (See LEGAL TENDER CASES.)

Three months after his appointment, Bradley conducted circuit court hearings in New Orleans where he encountered the SLAUGHTERHOUSE CASES. He held unconstitutional the Louisiana statute authorizing a monopoly for slaughtering operations. Three years later, when the case reached the Supreme Court on appeal, Bradley dissented as the majority sustained the regulation. With Justice STEPHEN J. FIELD, Bradley believed that the creation of the monopoly and the impairment of existing businesses violated the PRIVILEGES AND IMMUNITIES clause of the FOURTEENTH AMENDMENT. Such privileges, Bradley had said earlier in his circuit court opinion, included a citizen's right to "lawful industrial pursuit—not injurious to the community—as he may see fit, without unreasonable regulation or molestation."

The antiregulatory views that Bradley advanced in *Slaughterhouse* did not persist as the major theme of his judicial career, as they did for Justice Field. JUDICIAL REVIEW and judicial superintendence of DUE PROCESS OF LAW could be maintained, he said, in *Davidson v. New Orleans* (1878), "without interfering with that large discretion which every legislative power has of making wide modifications in the forms of procedure." A year earlier, Bradley had vividly demonstrated his differences with Field when he provided Chief Justice MORRISON R. WAITE with the key historical sources and principles for the public interest doctrine laid down in *Munn v. Illinois* (1877). (See AFFECTATION WITH A PUBLIC INTEREST).

The Court largely gutted the *Munn* ruling when it held in WABASH, ST. LOUIS, AND PACIFIC RAILWAY V. ILLINOIS (1886) that states could not regulate interstate rates, even in the absence of congressional action. Bradley vigorously dissented, protesting that some form of regulation was necessary and that the Court had wrongly repudiated the public interest doctrine of the GRANGER CASES. Ironically, Bradley, the old railroad lawyer, found himself almost totally isolated when he dissented from the Court's finding that the judiciary, not legislatively authorized expert commisions, had the right to decide the reasonableness of railroad rates. That decision, in CHICAGO, MILWAUKEE AND ST. PAUL RAILWAY CO. V. MINNESOTA (1890), marked the triumph of Field's dissenting views in *Munn;* yet Bradley steadfastly insisted that rate regulation "is a legislative prerogative and not a judicial one."

Bradley insisted on responsibility and accountability from the railroads in numerous ways. In *New York Central R.R. v. Lockwood* (1873) he wrote that railroads could not, by contract, exempt themselves from liability for negligence. "The carrier and his customer do not stand on a footing of equality," he said. In *Railroad Company v. Maryland* (1875) he agreed that Maryland could compel a railroad to return one-fifth of its revenue in exchange for a right of way without compromising congressional control over commerce. But Bradley found clear lines of distinction between federally chartered and state chartered railroads. When the Court, in *Railroad Company v. Peniston* (1873), approved Nebraska's tax of a congressionally chartered railroad, Bradley disagreed, arguing that the carrier was a federal GOVERNMENT INSTRUMENTALITY; similarly, he joined Field in dissent in the SINKING FUND CASES (1879), arguing that Congress's requirement that the Union Pacific deposit some of its earnings to repay its debt to the federal govern-

ment was tantamount to the "repudiation of government obligations."

Bradley generally advocated a broad nationalist view of the COMMERCE CLAUSE. He wrote, for example, the opinion of the Court in *Robbins v. Shelby Taxing District* (1887), one of the most famous of the "drummer" cases of the period, holding that discriminatory state taxation of out-of-state salesmen unduly burdened interstate commerce. He also maintained that states could not tax the gross receipts of steamship companies or telegraph messages sent across state lines. Yet he steadfastly resisted the attempts of business to avoid their fair share of tax burdens, and he ruled that neither goods destined for another state nor goods that arrived at a final destination after crossing state lines were exempt from state taxing. (See STATE TAXATION OF COMMERCE.)

Despite Bradley's broad reading of the Fourteenth Amendment in the *Slaughterhouse Cases*, he voted with the Court majority that failed in various cases to sustain national protection of the rights of blacks. He ruled against the constitutionality of the FORCE ACT of 1870 while on circuit, and the Court sustained his ruling in UNITED STATES V. CRUIKSHANK (1876). He acquiesced in UNITED STATES V. REESE (1876), crippling enforcement of the FIFTEENTH AMENDMENT, and in HALL V. DeCUIR (1878) he agreed that a Louisiana law prohibiting racial segregation on railroads burdened interstate commerce. Unlike that of most of his colleagues, Bradley's interpretation of the commerce power was consistent, for he dissented with JOHN M. HARLAN when the Court in 1890 approved a state law requiring segregated railroad cars.

Bradley's most famous statement on racial matters came in the CIVIL RIGHTS CASES (1883). Speaking for all his colleagues save Harlan, Bradley held unconstitutional the CIVIL RIGHTS ACT OF 1875. He limited the scope of the Fourteenth Amendment when he wrote that it forbade only STATE ACTION and not private RACIAL DISCRIMINATION. Bradley eloquently—if unfortunately—captured the national mood when he declared: "When a man has emerged from slavery, and by the aid of beneficent legislation has shaken off the inseparable concomitants of that state, there must be some stage in the progress of his elevation when he takes the rank of a mere citizen and ceases to be the special favorite of the laws. . . ." Bradley concurred in BRADWELL V. ILLINOIS (1873), in which the Court held that Illinois had not violated the EQUAL PROTECTION clause of the Fourteenth Amendment when it refused to admit a woman to the bar. He stated that a woman's "natural and proper timidity" left her unprepared for many occupations, and he concluded that "the paramount destiny and mission of woman are to fulfill the noble and benign offices of wife and mother." Clearly, there were limits to the liberty that Bradley had so passionately advocated in the *Slaughterhouse Cases.*

The variety of significant opinions by Bradley demonstrates his enormous range and influence. In BOYD V. UNITED STATES (1886) he established the modern FOURTH AMENDMENT standard for SEARCH AND SEIZURE questions, advocating a narrow scope for governmental power: "It is the duty of courts to be watchful for the constitutional rights of the citizen, and against any stealthy encroachments thereon." In COLLECTOR V. DAY (1871) he dissented when the Court held that state officials were exempt from federal income taxes, and nearly sixty years later the Court adopted his position. He spoke for the Court in CHURCH OF JESUS CHRIST OF LATTER-DAY SAINTS V. UNITED STATES (1890), stipulating that forfeited Mormon property be applied to charitable uses, including the building of common schools in Utah. Finally, he helped resolve the Court's difficulties over the exercise of recently enacted JURISDICTION legislation and sustained the right of federal CORPORATIONS to remove their causes from state to federal courts. That opinion made possible a staggering number of new tort and corporate cases in the federal courts.

Bradley played a decisive role in the outcome of the disputed election of 1877 as he supported Rutherford B. Hayes's claims. He was the fifteenth member chosen on the Electoral Commission whose other members included seven Democrats and seven Republicans. Thus, Hayes and the Compromise of 1877 owed much to Bradley's vote.

Bradley, Field, Harlan, and SAMUEL F. MILLER are the dominant figures of late nineteenth-century judicial history. Field's reputation rests on his forceful advocacy of a conservative ideology that the Court embraced but eventually repudiated. Harlan's claims center on his CIVIL RIGHTS views. Miller's notions of judicial restraint continue to have vitality. But Bradley's range of expertise, his high technical competency, and the continuing relevance of his work arguably place him above those distinguished contemporaries. Indeed, a mere handful of Supreme Court Justices have had a comparable impact.

STANLEY I. KUTLER

Bibliography

FAIRMAN, CHARLES 1950 What Makes a Great Justice? *Boston University Law Review* 30:49–102.

MAGRATH, C. PETER 1963 *Morrison R. Waite: The Triumph of Character.* New York: Macmillan.

BRADWELL v. ILLINOIS
16 Wallace 130 (1873)

Bradwell is the earliest FOURTEENTH AMENDMENT case in which the Supreme Court endorsed sex discrimination. Mrs. Myra Bradwell, the editor of the *Chicago Legal News,* was certified by a board of legal examiners as qualified to be a member of the state bar. An Illinois statute permitted the state supreme court to make rules for admission to the bar. That court denied Mrs. Bradwell's application for admission solely on the ground of sex, although the fact that the applicant was married also counted against her: a married woman at that time was incapable of making binding contracts without her husband's consent, thus disabling her from performing all the duties of an attorney. She argued that the PRIVILEGES AND IMMUNITIES clause of the Fourteenth Amendment protected her CIVIL RIGHT as a citizen of the United States to be admitted to the bar, if she qualified.

Justice SAMUEL F. MILLER, speaking for the Court, declared that the right to be admitted to the practice of law in a state court was not a privilege of national CITIZENSHIP protected by the Fourteenth Amendment. Justice JOSEPH P. BRADLEY, joined by Justices NOAH SWAYNE and STEPHEN J. FIELD, concurred in the JUDGMENT affirming the state court, but offered additional reasons. History, nature, COMMON LAW, and the civil law supported the majority's reading of the privileges and immunities clause, according to Bradley. The "spheres and destinies" of the sexes were widely different, man being woman's protector; her "timidity and delicacy" unfit her for many occupations, including the law. Unlike Myra Bradwell, an unmarried woman might make contracts, but such a woman was an exception to the rule. "The paramount destiny and mission of woman are to fulfill the noble and benign offices of wife and mother. This is the law of the Creator." Society's rules, Bradley added, ought not be based on exceptions. Chief Justice SALMON P. CHASE dissented alone, without opinion, missing a chance to advocate the cause of SEX EQUALITY, at least in the legal profession.

LEONARD W. LEVY

BRANCH v. TEXAS

See: Capital Punishment Cases, 1972

BRANDEIS, LOUIS D.
(1856–1941)

The appointment of Louis D. Brandeis to the United States Supreme Court was not merely the crowning glory of an extraordinary career as a practicing lawyer and social activist. It was also the inauguration of an equally extraordinary career on the bench. In twenty-three years as a Justice, Brandeis acquired a stature and influence that few—before or since—could match. In part, this achievement reflected the fact that he was already a public figure when he ascended to the Court. But his skills as a jurist provided the principal explanation. He mastered details of procedure, remained diligent in researching the facts and law of the case, and, whatever the subject, devoted untold hours to make his opinions clear and logical. Perhaps the highest compliment came from colleagues who disagreed with his conclusions. "My, how I detest that man's ideas," Associate Justice GEORGE SUTHERLAND once observed. "But he is one of the greatest technical lawyers I have ever known."

Brandeis's opinions and votes on the Court were very much a product of his environment and experience. Born in Louisville, Kentucky, shortly before the Civil War, he grew up in a family that provided him with love and security. That background probably helped him in establishing skills as a tenacious lawyer in Boston, where he opened his office one year after graduating from Harvard Law School first in his class. Brandeis attained local and then national fame when he used his formidable talents to effect reform at the height of the Progressive movement in the early 1900s. He fought the establishment of a privately owned subway monopoly in Boston, was instrumental in developing a savings bank life insurance system to prevent exploitation of industrial workers by large insurance companies, developed the famed BRANDEIS BRIEF—a detailed compilation of facts and statistics—in defense of Oregon's maximum hour law for women, and even took on the legendary J. P. Morgan when the corporate magnate tried to monopolize New England's rail and steamship lines. Brandeis's renown as "the people's attorney" spread across the country when, in 1910, he led a team of lawyers in challenging Richard A. Ballinger's stewardship of the nation's natural resources as secretary of the interior in the administration of President WILLIAM HOWARD TAFT.

Because of Brandeis's well-known credentials as a lawyer who had single-handedly taken on the "trusts," WOODROW WILSON turned to him for advice in the presidential campaign of 1912. The relationship ripened, and after his election to the White House Wilson repeatedly called upon Brandeis for help in solving many difficult problems. Through these interactions Wilson came to appreciate Brandeis's keen intelligence and dedication to the public welfare. In January 1916 he nominated the Boston attorney to the Supreme Court. Brandeis was confirmed by the United States Senate almost six months later after a grueling and bitter fight.

For Brandeis, law was essentially a mechanism to shape man's social, economic, and political relations. In fulfilling that function, he believed, the law had to account for two basic principles: first, that the individual was the key force in society, and second, that individuals—no matter what their talents and aspirations—had only limited capabilities. As he explained to HAROLD LASKI, "Progress must proceed from the aggregate of the performances of individual men" and society should adjust its institutions "to the wee size of man and thus render possible his growth and development." At the same time, Brandeis did not want people coddled because of inherent limitations. Quite the contrary. People had to stretch themselves to fulfill their individual potentials.

In this context Brandeis abhorred what he often called "the curse of bigness." People, he felt, could not fully develop themselves if they did not have control of their lives. Individual control, however, was virtually impossible in a large institutional setting—whether it be a union, a CORPORATION, the government, or even a town. From this perspective, Brandeis remained convinced that democracy could be maintained only if citizens—and especially the most talented—returned to small communities in the hinterland and learned to manage their own affairs.

This commitment to individual development led Brandeis to assume a leadership position in the Zionist Movement in 1914 and retain it after he went on the Court. In Palestine, Brandeis believed, an individual could control his life in a way that would not be possible in the United States.

This theme—the need for individuals and local communities to control their own affairs—also threads the vast majority of Brandeis's major opinions on the Court. Some of the most controversial of Brandeis's early opinions concerned labor unions. Long before his appointment to the Court he had viewed unions as a necessary element in the nation's economy. Without them large CORPORATIONS would be able to exploit workers and prevent them from acquiring the financial independence needed for individual control. Brandeis made his views known on this matter in HITCHMAN COAL & COKE COMPANY V. MITCHELL

(1917). That case concerned the United Mine Workers' efforts to unionize the workers in West Virginia. As a condition of employment the mine owner forced his employees to sign a pledge not to join a union. A majority of the Court held that UMW officials had acted illegally in trying to induce the workers to violate that pledge.

Brandeis dissented. He could not accept the majority's conclusion that a union agreement would deprive the workers and mine owner of their DUE PROCESS rights under the FOURTEENTH AMENDMENT to FREEDOM OF CONTRACT. "Every agreement curtails the liberty of those who enter into it," Brandeis responded. "The test of legality is not whether an agreement curtails liberty, but whether the parties have agreed upon some thing which the law prohibits. . . ." Brandeis also saw no merit in the majority's concern with the UMW's pressure on workers to join the union. The plaintiff company's lawsuit was premised "upon agreements secured under similar pressure of economic necessity or disadvantage," he observed. "If it is coercion to threaten to strike unless plaintiff consents to a closed union shop, it is coercion also to threaten not to give one employment unless the applicant will consent to a closed non-union shop."

Brandeis adhered to these views in other labor cases that came before the Court. Eventually, the Court came around to Brandeis's belief that unions had a right to engage in peaceful efforts to push for a CLOSED SHOP. Brandeis himself added a finishing touch in an opinion he delivered in *Senn v. Tile Layers Union* (1937), where he upheld a state law restricting the use of INJUNCTIONS against PICKETING.

While concern for the plight of labor was vital to his vision of society, nothing concerned Brandeis more than the right of a state or community to shape its own environment. For this reason he voted to uphold almost every piece of social legislation that came before the Court. Indeed, he wanted to reduce federal JURISDICTION in part because, as he told FELIX FRANKFURTER, "in no case practically should the appellate federal courts have to pass on the construction of state statutes." Therefore, if the state wanted to regulate the practices of employment agencies, expand the disability protection to stevedores who worked the docks, or take other social actions, he would not stand in the way. As he explained for the Court in *O'Gorman & Young v. Hartford Insurance Company* (1931), "the presumption of constitutionality must prevail in the absence of some factual foundation of record for overthrowing the statute." This meant that the Court must abide by the legislature's

judgment even if the Court found the law to be of doubtful utility.

Only a few months after *O'Gorman* Brandeis applied this principle in NEW STATE ICE COMPANY V. LIEBMANN (1932). The Oklahoma Legislature had passed a law that prohibited anyone from entering the ice business without first getting a certificate from a state corporation commission showing that there was a public need for the new business. A majority of the Court struck the law down because the ice business was not so AFFECTED WITH A PUBLIC INTEREST to justify a measure that would, in effect, restrict competition.

Brandeis was all for competition. He had long believed that large corporations were dangerous because they often eliminated competition and with it the right of individuals to control their lives, a proposition he examined in detail in *Liggett Company v. Lee* (1933). Whatever misgivings he had about the merits of the Oklahoma law, Brandeis had no trouble accepting the state's right to make its own decisions, especially at a time when the nation was grappling with the problems of the Depression. "It is one of the happy incidents of the federal system," he wrote in dissent, "that a single courageous State may, if its citizens choose, serve as a laboratory; and try novel social and economic experiments without risk to the rest of the country. This Court has the power to prevent an experiment. . . . But in the exercise of this high power, we must be ever on our guard, lest we erect our prejudices into legal principles."

It was, in a way, an ironic warning. For Brandeis himself sometimes allowed personal prejudice to govern his opinions. There was no better example than *Nashville, Chattanooga & St. Louis Railway v. Walters* (1935). A railroad challenged the application of a Tennessee law that required it to pay half the cost of an underpass—not to eliminate existing safety hazards but to help improve the national highway system and thereby facilitate its use by newer, high-speed automobiles. The challenge found a sympathetic listener in Brandeis. He hated cars. To him they represented the extravagance and overcapitalization that contributed to the Depression. Brandeis also opposed the construction of the national highway system because its maintenance would require too much public money. Primarily for these reasons the Justice was willing to uphold the railway's argument and ask the state court to reconsider. Nathaniel Nathanson, Brandeis's law CLERK at the time, protested (as Brandeis had in other cases) that the Court had no business second-guessing the state, and here there were many conceivable reasons why Tennessee felt justified in asking railroads to assume half the tab for grade crossings. It was all to no avail. "I apply the test of OLIVER WENDELL HOLMES," Brandeis told his clerk, "Does it make you puke?" This case flunked the test. "It may be shocking to mention them in the same breath," Nathanson wrote to Frankfurter afterward, "but I sometimes wonder whether the Justice or [Associate Justice JAMES C.] MCREYNOLDS votes more in accordance with his prejudices. . . ."

The Tennessee case was an exception to Brandeis's general inclination to protect the states' right to legislate. In fact, he was so devoted to states' rights that he once openly disregarded one of his most-oft stated juridical principles—never decide constitutional matters that can be avoided. Brandeis relied on this principle when he refused to join the Court's opinion in ASHWANDER V. TENNESSEE VALLEY AUTHORITY (1936) upholding the constitutionality of federal legislation establishing the TVA. In a CONCURRING OPINION he argued that they should have dismissed the case without deciding the constitutional issue because the plaintiffs had no STANDING to bring the lawsuit.

Brandeis was willing to ignore the teachings of his TVA opinion, however, when Chief Justice CHARLES EVANS HUGHES asked the aging Justice to write the Court's opinion in ERIE RAILROAD V. TOMPKINS (1938). The Court had voted to overrule SWIFT V. TYSON (1842), a decision that concerned cases arising under DIVERSITY JURISDICTION. Specifically, *Swift* allowed federal courts to ignore the laws of the states in which they were located and instead to apply FEDERAL COMMON LAW. *Swift* thus enabled litigants in certain cases to shop for the best forum in filing a lawsuit, for a federal court under *Swift* could and often did follow substantive law different from that applied by local courts.

Brandeis had long found *Swift* offensive. Not only did it mean that different courts in the same state could come to different conclusions on the same question; of greater importance, *Swift* undermined the ability of the state to control its own affairs. He was no doubt delighted when Hughes gave him the chance to bury *Swift*; and he wanted to make sure there could be no resurrection by a later Court or Congress. He therefore wrote an opinion holding that *Swift* violated the Constitution because it allowed federal courts to assume powers reserved to the states. The constitutional basis for the opinion was startling for two reasons: first, Brandeis could have just as easily overturned *Swift* through a revised construction of the JUDICIARY ACT OF 1789; and second, none of the

parties had even raised the constitutional issue, let alone briefed it.

Brandeis would depart from his ready endorsement of state legislation if the law violated FUNDAMENTAL FREEDOMS and individual rights. It was not only a matter of constitutional construction. The BILL OF RIGHTS played a significant role in the individual's, and ultimately the community's, right to control the future. Brandeis knew, for example, that, without FIRST AMENDMENT protections, he never could have achieved much success as "the people's attorney" in battling vested interests. In those earlier times he had sloughed off personal attacks of the bitterest kind to pursue his goals. He knew that, in many instances, he would have been silenced if his right of speech had depended on majority approval. And he expressed great concern when citizens were punished—even during wartime—for saying or writing things someone found objectionable. "The constitutional right of free speech has been declared to be the same in peace and in war," he wrote in dissent in *Schaeffer v. United States* (1920). "In peace, too, men may differ widely as to what loyalty to our country demands; and an intolerant majority, swayed by passion or fear, may be prone in the future, as it has often been in the past, to stamp as disloyal opinions with which it disagrees." This point was later amplified in his concurring opinion in WHITNEY V. CALIFORNIA (1927). The Founding Fathers, Brandeis wrote, recognized "that fear breeds repression; that repression breeds hate; that hate menaces stable government; that the path of safety lies in the opportunity to discuss freely supposed grievances and proposed remedies; and that the fitting remedy for evil counsels is good ones."

Brandeis, then, often brought clear and deepseated convictions to the conference table. He was not one, however, to twist arms and engage in the lobbying that other Justices found so successful. "I could have had my views prevail in cases of public importance if I had been willing to play politics," he once told Frankfurter. "But I made up my mind I wouldn't—I would have had to sin against my light, and I would have hated myself. And I decided that the price was too large for the doubtful gain to the country's welfare."

Brandeis therefore tried to use established procedures to persuade his colleagues. To that end he would often anticipate important cases and distribute his views as a "memorandum" even before the majority opinion was written. In OLMSTEAD V. UNITED STATES (1928), for example, he tried to convince the Court that the federal government should not be allowed to use EVIDENCE in a criminal case that its agents had obtained by WIRETAPPING. The eavesdropping had been done without a judicial warrant and in violation of a state statute. Brandeis circulated a memorandum reflecting views that had not been debated at conference. The government should not be able to profit by its own wrongdoing, he said—especially when, as here, it impinged on the individual's RIGHT TO PRIVACY (a right he had examined as a lawyer in a seminal article in the *Harvard Law Review*). The memorandum could not command a majority, and Brandeis later issued an eloquent dissent that focused on the contention that warrantless wiretaps violated the FOURTH AMENDMENT's protection against UNREASONABLE SEARCHES and seizures.

At other times Brandeis would use the Saturday conferences to urge a view upon his colleagues. On one occasion—involving *Southwestern Bell Telephone Company v. Public Service Commission* (1923)—an entire day was devoted to a seminar conducted by Brandeis to explain why a utility's rate of return should be based on prudent investment and not on the reproduction cost of its facilities. Few, if any, Justices shared Brandeis's grasp of rate-making principles. Hence, it took more than two decades of experience and debate before the Court—without Brandeis—accepted the validity of his position.

Brandeis took his losses philosophically. He knew that progress in a democracy comes slowly, and he was prepared to accept temporary setbacks along the way. But he rarely faded in his determination to correct the result. If his brethren remained impervious to his reasoning, he was willing to use other resources. He peppered Frankfurter and others with suggestions on articles for the *Harvard Law Review*. He also turned to the numerous congressmen and senators who frequently dined with him. Were they interested in introducing legislation to restrict federal jurisdiction or some other objective? If the answer was affirmative, Brandeis often volunteered the services of Frankfurter (whose expenses in public interest matters were generally assumed by Brandeis).

Few of these extrajudicial activities produced concrete results. Brandeis was apparently pleased, consequently, when Hughes became Chief Justice in 1930. Brandeis felt that the former secretary of state had a better command of the law than did Taft, the preceding Chief Justice, and would be able to use that knowledge to expedite the disposition of the Court's growing caseload. Of greater significance, Hughes and some other new members of the Court had views that closely coincided with Brandeis's. In fact, in 1937, BENJAMIN N. CARDOZO, HARLAN FISKE STONE, and

Brandeis—the so-called liberal Justices—began to caucus in Brandeis's apartment on Friday nights to go over the cases for the Saturday conference.

With this kind of working relationship, plus the change in the times, Brandeis was able to join a majority in upholding New Deal legislation (he voted against only three New Deal measures). He also lived to see many of his earlier dissents become HOLDINGS of the Court, particularly in cases concerning labor and the right of states to adopt social legislation. After his death, many other dissents—including his First Amendment views and his contention that warrantless wiretaps were unconstitutional—would also become the law of the land. But Brandeis's overriding ambition—the desire to establish a legal framework in which individuals and communities could control their affairs—was frustrated by developments that would not yield to even the most incisive judicial opinion. Unions, like corporations and even government, continued to grow like Topsy. Almost everyone, it seemed, became dependent on a large organization. Brandeis, a shrewd realist, surely recognized the inexorable social, economic, and political forces that impeded the realization of his dreams for America. None of that, however, would have deterred him from pursuing his goals. As he once explained to his brother, the "future has many good things in store for those who can wait, . . . have patience and exercise good judgment."

LEWIS J. PAPER

Bibliography

BICKEL, ALEXANDER M. 1957 *The Unpublished Opinions of Mr. Justice Brandeis: The Supreme Court at Work.* Cambridge, Mass.: Harvard University Press.

FRANKFURTER, FELIX, ED. 1932 *Mr. Justice Brandeis.* New Haven, Conn.: Yale University Press.

FREUND, PAUL 1964 Mr. Justice Brandeis. In Allison Dunham and Philip B. Kurland, eds., *Mr. Justice.* Chicago: University of Chicago Press.

KONEFSKY, SAMUEL J. 1956 *The Legacy of Holmes and Brandeis: A Study in the Influence of Ideas.* New York: Macmillan.

MASON, ALPHEUS T. 1946 *Brandeis: A Free Man's Life.* New York: Viking Press.

PAPER, LEWIS J. 1983 *Brandeis.* Englewood Cliffs, N.J.: Prentice-Hall.

BRANDEIS BRIEF

The opinion of the Supreme Court in MULLER V. OREGON (1908) began with an unusual acknowledgment: the Court had found useful a brief by LOUIS D. BRAN-

DEIS, supporting Oregon's law regulating women's working hours. The brief had presented the views of doctors and social workers, the conclusions of various public committees that had investigated the conditions of women's labor, and an outline of similar legislation in the United States and overseas. The Court said that although these materials "may not be, technically speaking, authorities," they were "significant of a widespread belief that woman's physical structure, and the functions she performs in consequence thereof, justify special legislation." Its intimations of female dependency aside, this comment marked an important event: the Court's recognition of the utility of briefing and argument addressed to the factual basis for legislation.

Underlying the *Muller* opinion's comment lay a deeper change in the judiciary's conception of its proper role. Since around the time of the Civil War, lawyers and judges had commonly believed that the development of legal (including constitutional) doctrine was a pursuit of truth. In this view, there were answers to be found in authoritative documents such as laws and constitutions. The *Muller* opinion signaled a recognition that judges had a creative, legislative role, that they were properly concerned with the evaluation of the factual basis for legislation. This development, which sometimes bore the name of SOCIOLOGICAL JURISPRUDENCE and which culminated in the LEGAL REALISM of the 1920s and 1930s, represented a major shift in judicial attitudes. Judges came to see themselves as active participants in adapting the law to the needs of society. The technique of the Brandeis brief came to serve not only in cases involving ECONOMIC REGULATION but also in other constitutional contexts far removed. A famous modern example is BROWN V. BOARD OF EDUCATION (1954), in which an AMICUS CURIAE brief detailed the views of social scientists on the educational harm of racial SEGREGATION in schools.

It is possible to present such factual material as EVIDENCE in the trial of a constitutional case, and today it is not unusual for counsel to do so. However, the Brandeis brief has become a common technique in the Supreme Court and other appellate courts. In the *Muller* case, the Brandeis brief aimed at demonstrating that the Oregon legislature reasonably could have believed that certain evils existed and that a limit on women's working hours would mitigate them. Brandeis himself argued no more than that. The assumption was that the law was valid if there was a RATIONAL BASIS for the legislature's assumptions. Evidence on the other side of the factual questions would, in theory, be irrelevant. When the presumption of constitutionality is weaker—that is, when the state must justify its legislation by reference to a COMPELLING STATE INTEREST or some other heightened STANDARD OF REVIEW—the Brandeis brief technique may recommend itself to either side of the argument.

KENNETH L. KARST

(SEE ALSO: *Legislative Facts.*)

Bibliography
FREUND, PAUL A. 1951 *On Understanding the Supreme Court.* Chap. 3. Boston: Little, Brown.

BRANDENBURG v. OHIO
395 U.S. 444 (1969)

Libertarian critics of the CLEAR AND PRESENT DANGER test had always contended that it provided insufficient protection for speech because it depended ultimately on judicial guesses about the consequences of speech. Judges inimical to the content of a particular speech could always foresee the worst. Thus, to the extent that the test did protect speech, its crucial element was the imminence requirement, that speech was punishable only when it was so closely brigaded in time with unlawful action as to constitute an attempt to commit, or incitement of, unlawful action. When the Supreme Court converted clear and present danger to clear and probable danger in DENNIS V. UNITED STATES (1951) it actually converted the clear and present danger test into a BALANCING TEST that allowed judges who believed in judicial self-restraint to avoid enforcing the FIRST AMENDMENT by striking every balance in favor of the nonspeech interest that the government sought to protect by suppressing speech. The *Dennis* conversion, however, was even more damaging to the clear and present danger rule than a flat rejection and open replacement by the balancing standard would have been. A flat rejection would have left clear and present danger as a temporarily defeated libertarian rival to a temporarily triumphant antilibertarian balancing standard. The conversion to probable danger not only defeated the danger test but also discredited it among libertarians by removing the imminence requirement that had been its strongest protection for dissident speakers. Accordingly commentators, both libertarian and advocates of judicial self-restraint, were pleased to announce that *Dennis* had buried the clear and present danger test.

Some critics of the danger test had supported LEARNED HAND's approach in MASSES PUBLISHING

Co. v. Patten (1917), which had focused on the advocacy content of the speech itself, thus avoiding judicial predictions about what the speech plus the surrounding circumstances would bring. *Masses* left two problems, however: the "Marc Antony" speech which on the surface seems innocuous but in the circumstances really is an incitement, and the speech preaching violence in circumstances in which it is harmless. OLIVER WENDELL HOLMES himself had injected a specific intent standard alongside the danger rule, arguing that government might punish a speaker only if it could prove his specific intent to bring about an unlawful act.

Eighteen years after *Dennis,* carefully avoiding the words of the clear and present danger test itself, the Supreme Court brought together these various strands of thought in *Brandenburg v. Ohio,* a PER CURIAM holding that "the constitutional guarantees of free speech . . . do not permit a state to forbid or proscribe advocacy of the use of force or law violation except where such advocacy is directed to inciting or producing imminent lawless action and is likely to incite or produce such action." In a footnote the Court interpreted *Dennis* and YATES v. UNITED STATES (1957) as upholding this standard. The decision itself struck down the Ohio Criminal Syndicalism Act which proscribed advocacy of violence as a means of accomplishing social reform. The Court overruled WHITNEY v. CALIFORNIA (1927).

MARTIN SHAPIRO

BRANT, IRVING
(1885–1976)

Irving Newton Brant was a journalist, biographer, and constitutional historian. A strong supporter of President FRANKLIN D. ROOSEVELT, Brant published *Storm over the Constitution* in 1936; a vigorous defense of the constitutionality of the New Deal, it strongly influenced Roosevelt's later attempt to enlarge the membership of the Supreme Court. Brant's concentration in this book on the intent of the Framers of the Constitution led him to begin a biography of JAMES MADISON. Now regarded as definitive, his six-volume biography (1941–1961) had two aims: the rehabilitation of Madison's reputation as constitutional theorist and political leader, and the refutation of the STATES' RIGHTS interpretation of American history (which denied that the Revolutionary generation considered the newly created United States to be one

nation). Brant's other works include *The Bill of Rights* (1965), a history championing the absolutist interpretation of the BILL OF RIGHTS espoused by Justices HUGO L. BLACK and WILLIAM O. DOUGLAS, and *Impeachment: Trials and Errors* (1972).

RICHARD B. BERNSTEIN

BRANTI v. FINKEL
445 U.S. 507 (1980)

Branti v. Finkel tightened the FIRST AMENDMENT restrictions on the use of patronage in public employment first established in *Elrod v. Burns* (1976). Justice JOHN PAUL STEVEN's MAJORITY OPINION held that upon taking office a public defender could not constitutionally dismiss two assistants solely because they were affiliated with a different political party. The 6–3 majority held that these dismissals denied the employees' freedoms of belief and association. The employer had failed to show a sufficient connection between party loyalty and effective job performance.

Justice POTTER STEWART dissented, analogizing the public defender's office to private law practice. Justice LEWIS F. POWELL, joined by Justice WILLIAM H. REHNQUIST, also dissented, reiterating his dissenting view in *Elrod* that patronage plays an honorable, traditional role in American politics.

AVIAM SOIFER

BRANZBURG v. HAYES
408 U.S. 665 (1972)

Branzburg v. Hayes combined several cases in which reporters claimed a FIRST AMENDMENT privilege either not to appear or not to testify before grand juries, although they had witnessed criminal activity or had information relevant to the commission of crimes. The reporters' chief contention was that they should not be required to testify unless a GRAND JURY showed that a reporter possessed information relevant to criminal activity, that similar information could not be obtained from sources outside the press, and that the need for the information was sufficiently compelling to override the First Amendment interest in preserving confidential news sources.

Justice BYRON R. WHITE's opinion for the Court not only rejected these showings but also denied the very existence of a First Amendment testimonial privilege. Despite the asserted lack of any First Amendment privilege, the White opinion allowed that "news gathering" was not "without its First Amendment protections" and suggested that such protections would bar a grand jury from issuing SUBPOENAS to reporters "other than in good faith" or "to disrupt a reporter's relationship with his news sources." White rejected any requirement for a stronger showing of relevance, of alternative sources, or of balancing the need for the information against the First Amendment interest.

Nevertheless, Justice LEWIS F. POWELL, who signed White's 5–4 OPINION OF THE COURT, attached an ambiguous CONCURRING OPINION stating that a claim to privilege "should be judged on its facts by the striking of a proper balance between FREEDOM OF THE PRESS" and the government interest. Most lower courts have read the majority opinion through the eyes of Justice Powell. An opinion that emphatically denied a First Amendment privilege at various points seems to have created one after all.

STEVEN SHIFFRIN

(SEE ALSO: *Reporter's Privilege.*)

BRAUNFELD v. BROWN

See: Sunday Closing Laws

BREACH OF THE PEACE

Breach of the peace statutes are today popularly called disorderly conduct statutes. The wording of breach of the peace or disorderly conduct statutes varies significantly from one city or state to another. Generally, such statutes are violated if a person commits acts or makes statements likely to promote violence or disturb "good order" in a public place. Under modern statutes, as under the older COMMON LAW, it is possible to be guilty of committing a breach of the peace solely through the use of words likely to produce violence or disorder.

When a person is prosecuted for breach of the peace for his or her physical actions there is no significant FIRST AMENDMENT issue. Thus, if a person commits a breach of the peace by punching or shoving other persons in public no First Amendment issue arises. However, if a mixture of expression and physical activity forms the basis for the prosecution, the court must ask whether the person is being punished for the physical activity alone. Thus, a person might

be convicted of a breach of the peace for using SOUND-TRUCKS OR AMPLIFIERS if the statute punished any use of a sound amplification device, regardless of the message communicated.

When a person is accused of committing a breach of the peace by speaking to others, a court must determine whether the guarantees of FREEDOM OF SPEECH and assembly have been violated. In addition, the court must determine whether the statute is tailored to avoid punishing constitutionally protected speech.

Although the Supreme Court has held that the First Amendment does not prohibit the punishment of FIGHTING WORDS, it has upheld few convictions for breach of the peace based solely upon verbal conduct. A considerable number of breach of the peace and disorderly conduct statutes have been held unconstitutional under the doctrine of VAGUENESS and OVER-BREADTH.

A breach of the peace or disorderly conduct statute that can be constitutionally applied to persons who physically interfere with police officers engaged in police functions cannot constitutionally serve as the basis for punishing the use of insulting or annoying language to a police officer, short of actual interference with the officer's ability to perform police functions.

A person engaged in lawful speech in a public place may sometimes be confronted by a HOSTILE AUDIENCE. In such a situation the police must attempt to protect the individual speaker, or disperse the crowd, before ordering the speaker to cease his or her advocacy of the unpopular message. If it appears that the officers cannot otherwise prevent violence, they may order the speaker or speakers to cease their speech or assembly, and a refusal to comply can constitutionally be punished as disorderly conduct. Breach of the peace statutes may also be applied as consistent with the First Amendment to prohibit conduct that would interfere with the use of government property not traditionally open to speech. Thus, the state might prohibit activities near jails or school buildings if those activities interfere with the government's ability to operate the school or jail.

JOHN E. NOWAK

Bibliography

MONAGHAN, HENRY P. 1981 Overbreadth. *The Supreme Court Review* 1981:1–40.

NOWAK, JOHN E.; ROTUNDA, RONALD D.; and YOUNG, J. NELSON 1983 *Constitutional Law.* Pages 954–958, 973–987. St. Paul, Minn.: West Publishing Co.

BREARLY, DAVID
(1745–1790)

David Brearly represented New Jersey at the CONSTITUTIONAL CONVENTION OF 1787 and signed the Constitution. He was a spokesman for the small states, favoring equal representation of the states in Congress. He served on the Committee of Eleven on remaining matters, and delivered its reports to the Convention. He was later president of New Jersey's ratifying convention.

DENNIS J. MAHONEY

BRECKINRIDGE, JOHN
(1760–1806)

John Breckinridge studied law under Virginia's GEORGE WYTHE, then moved to Kentucky, serving as state attorney general (1795–1797), state representative (1798–1800), United States senator (1801–1805), and United States attorney general (1805–1806). During the ALIEN AND SEDITION ACT crisis Breckinridge traveled to Virginia, where he convinced THOMAS JEFFERSON, through an intermediary, that the vice-president's resolutions condemning the acts should be introduced in Kentucky, and not North Carolina, Jefferson's initial choice. Breckinridge revised Jefferson's draft by deleting the term NULLIFICATION, thus allowing Kentucky to condemn the acts and declare them unconstitutional without actually defying the federal government. Breckinridge then guided the resolutions through the Kentucky legislature while hiding Jefferson's authorship. In 1802 Breckinridge drafted and shepherded through the Senate an act to repeal the JUDICIARY ACT OF 1801—that eleventh-hour creation of the Federalists under JOHN ADAMS which allowed the outgoing President to appoint additional federal judges. Breckinridge argued that the repeal was constitutional, because if Congress had the power to create inferior courts, then Congress could also abolish them. He also contended against a judicial power to hold unconstitutional acts of Congress or of the President. Breckinridge initially doubted the constitutionality of the LOUISIANA PURCHASE, but in 1803 he introduced the Breckinridge Act which created territorial government for Louisiana. Like the Kentucky Resolutions, this act was secretly written by Jefferson.

PAUL FINKELMAN

(SEE ALSO: *Virginia and Kentucky Resolutions.*)

Bibliography
HARRISON, LOWELL H. 1969 *John Breckinridge: Jeffersonian Republican.* Louisville, Ky.: Filson Club.

BREEDLOVE v. SUTTLES
302 U.S. 277 (1937)

Georgia levied an annual POLL TAX of one dollar on every inhabitant between ages twenty-one and sixty except blind persons and women who did not register to vote. Voting registration was conditioned on payment of accrued poll taxes. A white male, denied registration for failure to pay poll taxes, challenged this scheme as a violation of the EQUAL PROTECTION and PRIVILEGES AND IMMUNITIES clauses of the FOURTEENTH AMENDMENT, and of the NINETEENTH AMENDMENT as well. In an opinion by Justice PIERCE BUTLER, a unanimous Supreme Court summarily rejected all these challenges and upheld the law. *Breedlove* was overruled in HARPER v. VIRGINIA BOARD OF ELECTIONS (1966).

KENNETH L. KARST

BREITHAUPT v. ABRAM
352 U.S. 432 (1957)

The taking of blood from an unconscious person to prove his intoxication and therefore his guilt for involuntary manslaughter was not conduct that "shocks the conscience" within the meaning of ROCHIN v. CALIFORNIA (1952), nor was it coercing a confession; accordingly the Supreme Court, in a 6–3 opinion by Justice TOM C. CLARK, found no violation of DUE PROCESS OF LAW.

LEONARD W. LEVY

BRENNAN, WILLIAM J.
(1906–)

William Joseph Brennan, Jr., was appointed an Associate Justice of the United States Supreme Court in October 1956. He quickly became, in both an intellectual and statistical sense, the center of gravity of what commentators have come to call the WARREN COURT, dissenting less than any other Justice, and fashioning many of that Court's most important opinions.

He came to the Court with more past judicial experience than any of his colleagues. For seven years he had been a New Jersey state judge, beginning his career at the trial level and rapidly advancing to the New Jersey Supreme Court. He had also been prominent in the movement to reform the antiquated New Jersey court system. He understood and cared about the practical workings of the justice system, and this concern was to prove important in the development of his constitutional perspective.

Brennan was a committed civil libertarian who believed in "providing freedom and equality of rights and opportunities, in a realistic and not merely formal sense, to all the people of this nation." He considered courts to be the particular guardians of constitutional rights. "[T]he soul of a government of laws," he once wrote, "is the judicial function, and that function can only exist if adjudication is understood by our people to be, as it is, the essentially disinterested, rational and deliberate element of our society." For Brennan, the judicial function demanded a continual effort to translate constitutional values into general doctrinal formulations. This emphasis on DOCTRINE distinguished Brennan from his colleague WILLIAM O. DOUGLAS, who was an equally committed civil libertarian.

Brennan viewed courts as the last resort of the politically disfranchised and the politically powerless. Constitutional litigation was for him "a form of political expression"; it was often, he wrote in NAACP V. BUTTON (1963), "the sole practicable avenue open to a minority to petition for redress of grievances." Litigation was thus an alternative, perhaps the only alternative, to social violence. For these reasons he seized every opportunity to enlarge litigants' access to federal courts. Exemplary is his opinion in BAKER V. CARR (1962), which held that the issue of unequal legislative representation was justiciable in federal court, and which Chief Justice EARL WARREN called "the most important case that we decided in my time." In opinion after opinion Brennan worked to open the doors of the federal courthouse, and to make available such federal judicial remedies for violations of the Constitution as HABEAS CORPUS, INJUNCTIONS, DECLARATORY JUDGMENTS, and DAMAGES. In later years Brennan dissented vigorously as many of these opinions were cut back by the BURGER COURT.

Because he believed that "the ultimate protection of individual freedom is found in judicial enforcement" of constitutional rights, Brennan did not flinch from the exercise of JUDICIAL POWER. When the time came, for example, to accelerate the ALL DELIBERATE SPEED with which BROWN V. BOARD OF EDUCATION (1955) had ordered the nation's public schools to be desegregated, Brennan, in GREEN V. NEW KENT COUNTY SCHOOL BOARD (1968), shattered the façade of southern "freedom-of-choice" plans and wrote that racial discrimination must end *"now"* and "be eliminated root and branch." In KEYES V. SCHOOL DISTRICT #1 OF DENVER (1973) Brennan took the lead in applying the requirement of *Brown* to northern school districts, and in cases like FRONTIERO V. RICHARDSON (1973) and CRAIG V. BOREN (1976) he played a major role in causing gender classifications to be subjected to substantial scrutiny under the EQUAL PROTECTION clause of the FOURTEENTH AMENDMENT.

Brennan was a nationalist. He believed in the power of Congress to define and protect CIVIL RIGHTS and to govern the national economy unrestrained by concerns of state SOVEREIGNTY. He disapproved of state regulations that interfered with interstate commerce. He favored the judicial imposition of national, constitutional values onto local decision-making processes. He believed, for example, that federal courts should fully incorporate almost all the guarantees of the BILL OF RIGHTS into the Fourteenth Amendment, and enforce them against the states. He dissented often and forcefully against the "federalist" leanings of the Burger Court. To Brennan the primary purpose of "the federal system's diffusion of governmental power" was to secure "individual freedom."

In his most enduring opinions, Brennan brought a unique and characteristic analysis to bear on the question of constitutional rights. Instead of inquiring into the power of government to regulate rights, he would instead focus on the manner in which the government's regulation actually functioned. The implications of this shift in focus were profound. They are perhaps most visible in the area of FIRST AMENDMENT adjudication.

To appreciate Brennan's contribution to First Amendment jurisprudence, it must be remembered that the Court to which Brennan was appointed was still reverberating from the effects of the constitutional crisis of the 1930s. It was, for example, groping for a means of reconciling judicial protection of First Amendment freedoms with the deep respect for majoritarian decision making that was the legacy of the Court's confrontation with President FRANKLIN D. ROOSEVELT's New Deal. At the time Brennan joined the Court, the Justices were embroiled in a vigorous but ultimately unproductive debate as to whether First Amendment freedoms were "absolutes" or whether they should be "weighed" against competing government interests in regulation. (See ABSOLUTISM and BALANCING TESTS.) Both sides of the debate viewed government interests and individual rights as locked in an indissoluble and paralyzing conflict.

Brennan's lasting contribution was to push the Court beyond this debate and to create a form of analysis in which this conflict receded from view. The essence of Brennan's approach was a precise and persistent focus on the processes and procedures through which government sought to regulate First Amendment freedoms.

Justice Brennan first used this approach in his second term on the Court in the modest but seminal case of SPEISER V. RANDALL (1958). The case involved a California law which denied certain tax exemptions to those who refused to execute an oath stating that they did "not advocate the overthrow of the United States or of the State of California by force of violence or other unlawful means." Significantly, Brennan did not approach the case in terms of an "absolute" right to engage in such advocacy. Nor did he inquire into California's "interests" in controlling such speech; he was willing to assume that California could deny tax exemptions to those who had engaged in proscribed speech.

Brennan focused his analysis instead on the procedures used to determine which taxpayers to penalize. He interpreted the California scheme as placing on taxpayers the burden of demonstrating that they had not engaged in unlawful speech. This procedure was unconstitutional, Brennan concluded, because it created too great a danger that lawful speech would be adversely affected. "The vice of the present procedure is that, where particular speech falls close to the line separating the lawful and the unlawful, the possibility of mistaken factfinding—inherent in all litigation—will create the danger that the legitimate utterance will be penalized. The man who knows that he must bring forth proof and persuade another of the lawfulness of his conduct necessarily must steer far wider of the unlawful zone than if the State must bear these burdens."

By focusing on the manner in which California had regulated speech, rather than on its power to do so, Brennan was led to inquire into the actual, practical effects of the regulatory scheme. He thus shifted the focus of judicial inquiry away from the particular speech of the litigant, and toward the impact of the legislation, as concretely embedded in its procedural setting, on concededly legitimate speech. This change in focus was central to Brennan's First Amendment jurisprudence, and it was the foundation of many of the Warren Court's innovations in this area. It had, for example, obvious relevance for the procedures used by government to regulate unprotected forms of speech like OBSCENITY. Brennan spelled out these implications in a series of influential obscenity decisions that demonstrated the substantive impact of such nominally procedural isses as BURDEN OF PROOF and the nature and timing of judicial HEARINGS.

Brennan's form of inquiry also led to a careful scrutiny of the VAGUENESS of government regulations of speech. Prior to *Speiser* the issue of "vagueness" was primarily conceived in terms of the rather weak NOTICE requirements of the DUE PROCESS clause. But Brennan's analysis offered a strict, new, and specifically First Amendment rationale for the doctrine. As Brennan explained in KEYISHIAN V. BOARD OF REGENTS (1967), a case involving a New York law prohibiting public school teachers from uttering "seditious" words, "[w]hen one must guess what conduct or utterance may lose him his position, one necessarily will 'steer far wider of the unlawful zone.'"

Brennan's focus on the practical impact of regulation also led him to the conclusion that the separation of legitimate from illegitimate speech had to be accomplished with "precision" and by legislation incapable of application to legitimate speech. As Brennan wrote in *Button*, First Amendment freedoms are "delicate and vulnerable," and "the threat of sanctions may deter their exercise almost as potently as the actual application of sanctions." In *Button* Brennan coined the term OVERBREADTH to capture this requirement that First Amendment regulations be narrowly tailored, and the term and the requirement have since become doctrinal instruments of major significance.

The framework of analysis developed by Brennan not only dominated the First Amendment jurisprudence of the Warren Court; it remained influential with the Burger Court that succeeded it. Its prominence was in large measure due to its apparent accommodation of government interests in regulation, if only the government could formulate its regulation more narrowly or more precisely. This accommodation, however, was in some respects illusory. The exact degree of constitutionally mandated precision or clarity was never specified, and the psychological assumptions that underlay the approach were not susceptible to empirical verification. As a result the requirements of clarity and precision could without explicit justification be loosened to uphold some government regulations, or tightened to strike down others. The indirection at the heart of this approach thus left it vulnerable to manipulation.

The approach was at its most compelling, therefore, when it was fused with an underlying substantive vision of the First Amendment. An illustration is the opinion which is Brennan's masterpiece, NEW YORK TIMES COMPANY V. SULLIVAN (1964). At issue in *Sullivan* was the Alabama law of LIBEL, which permitted a public official to recover damages for defamatory statements unless the speaker could prove that the statements were true. With reasoning similar to that in *Speiser* and *Button,* Brennan concluded that Alabama's allocation of the burden of proof was unconstitutional, because it "dampens the vigor and limits the variety of public debate" by inducing "self-censorship."

In *Sullivan,* however, Brennan took the unusual and penetrating step of lifting this analysis from its procedural setting and applying it to the substantive standards required by the First Amendment. Noting that the central purpose of the First Amendment was "the principle that debate on public issues should be uninhibited, robust, and wide-open," Brennan concluded that this purpose would be undermined if those who criticized public officials were subject to "any test of truth." He noted that an "erroneous statement is inevitable in free debate, and [it] must be protected if the freedoms of expression are to have the 'breathing space' that they 'need . . . to survive.' " The need for "breathing space" led Brennan to conclude that speech about public officials had to be constitutionally protected unless uttered with "actual malice"; that is, uttered "with knowledge that it was false or with reckless disregard of whether it was false or not." The actual malice standard thus incorporated into the substantive law of the First Amendment the insights Brennan had accumulated as a result of his prior focus on the process of regulation. The result, as ALEXANDER MEIKLEJOHN was moved to proclaim, was "an occasion for dancing in the streets."

Although Brennan's focus on process rather than power is most apparent in First Amendment opinions, it also pervades his entire approach to constitutional law. In *Speiser,* for example, California had argued that since a tax exemption was not a right but a privilege bestowed at the pleasure of the state, it could also be withdrawn by the state for any reason. The so-called RIGHT–PRIVILEGE DISTINCTION had a venerable judicial pedigree, and was supported by Supreme Court precedents as recent as *Barsky v. Board of Regents* (1954). Brennan, however, brought a fresh perspective to bear on this argument, for he was concerned not with California's power to withdraw the privilege but with the manner in which it did so. From this perspective the right–privilege distinction was beside the point.

Brennan repeatedly attacked the right–privilege

distinction, and many of his most important opinions, contributing to or originating major lines of doctrinal development, were predicated upon its rejection. Examples include SHERBERT V. VERNER (1963), which resuscitated the doctrine of "unconstitutional conditions" as applied to the denial of unemployment compensation; SHAPIRO V. THOMPSON (1969), which created the FUNDAMENTAL RIGHTS strand of equal protection analysis and applied it to durational RESIDENCY REQUIREMENTS for welfare recipients; and GOLDBERG V. KELLY (1970), which for the first time applied the protections of PROCEDURAL DUE PROCESS to the recipients of government entitlements such as WELFARE BENEFITS.

Brennan's focus on process deeply influenced both the Warren and the Burger courts. As the welfare state increased in complexity, Brennan's approach provided the basis for flexible yet far-reaching judicial review of government action. We can recognize the consequences of this approach in the shape of modern constitutional inquiry, with its characteristic scrutiny into whether government has acted through appropriate procedures and in a manner not unduly burdening the exercise of constitutional rights.

It is noteworthy that the results of this scrutiny depend upon an apprehension of the actual impact of government action. In later years Brennan's views on this subject were informed by a compassion and empathy that were not always shared by his colleagues. With the advent of the Burger Court, Brennan increasingly became a dissenter. His dissents, like his majority opinions, tended to be careful and lawyerly, without the eloquence or sting that mark the most memorable examples of the genre. Often, however, both Brennan and the majority were writing within doctrinal frameworks that Brennan himself had helped to create. His success in redefining the major questions of constitutional law is the measure of his achievement.

ROBERT C. POST

Bibliography

BRENNAN, WILLIAM JOSEPH, JR. 1969 Convocation Address. *Notre Dame Lawyer* 44:1029–1033.
—— 1981 Justice Thurgood Marshall: Advocate for Human Need in American Jurisprudence. *Maryland Law Review* 40:390–397.
HECK, EDWARD V. 1980 Justice Brennan and the Heyday of Warren Court Liberalism. *Santa Clara Law Review* 20:841–887.
HUTCHINSON, DENNIS J. 1983 Hail to the Chief: Earl Warren and the Supreme Court. *Michigan Law Review* 81:922–930.

KALVEN, HARRY, JR. 1964 The New York Times Case: A Note on "The Central Meaning of the First Amendment." *Supreme Court Review* 1964:191–221.

LEVY, LEONARD W., ED. 1972 *The Supreme Court under Earl Warren.* New York: Quadrangle Books.

BREWER, DAVID J.
(1837–1910)

David Josiah Brewer forged conservative socioeconomic beliefs into constitutional DOCTRINE. From the time he assumed his seat on the Supreme Court in December 1889, Brewer unabashedly relied on judicial power to protect private property rights from the supposed incursions of state and federal legislatures. Through more than 200 DISSENTING OPINIONS, most of which came during his last ten years on the bench, Brewer emerged as the conservative counterpart of the liberal "Great Dissenter," JOHN MARSHALL HARLAN.

Like his uncle, Justice STEPHEN J. FIELD, Brewer moved from moderate liberalism as a state judge to strident conservatism on the federal bench. Increasing doubts about the power of the Kansas legislature to regulate the manufacture and sale of alcohol punctuated his twelve-year career on the state supreme court. Brewer refrained from directly challenging a constitutional amendment that destroyed the livelihood of distillers without compensation, although, in *State v. Mugler* (1883), he expressed serious reservations about it. After President CHESTER A. ARTHUR appointed him to the Eighth Circuit in 1884, Brewer adopted a more aggressive position. He held that Kansas distillers deserved JUST COMPENSATION for losses suffered because of PROHIBITION, a position that the Supreme Court subsequently rejected in MUGLER V. KANSAS (1887).

Brewer's CIRCUIT COURT opinions on railroad rate regulation proved more prophetic. He ignored the Supreme Court's HOLDING in *Munn v. Illinois* (1877) that state legislatures could best judge the reasonableness of rates. (See GRANGER CASES.) Instead, Brewer asserted that judges had to inquire broadly into the reasonableness of rates and to overturn LEGISLATION that failed to yield a FAIR RETURN ON FAIR VALUE of investment.

These views persuaded President BENJAMIN HARRISON to appoint Brewer the fifty-first Justice of the Supreme Court. The new Justice immediately lived up to expectations by contributing to the emerging doctrine of SUBSTANTIVE DUE PROCESS OF LAW.

Brewer advocated use of the Fifth Amendment and the FOURTEENTH AMENDMENT to shelter corporate property rights from federal and state legislation. Three months after his appointment he joined the majority in the important case of CHICAGO, MILWAUKEE & ST. PAUL RAILWAY COMPANY V. MINNESOTA (1890) in striking down a state statute that did not provide for JUDICIAL REVIEW of rates established by an independent commission. More than other members of the Court, Brewer sought to expand the limits of substantive due process. Two years later, when the Court reaffirmed its *Munn* holding in *Budd v. New York* (1893), Brewer complained in dissent that the public interest doctrine granted too much discretion to the legislature. The Court ultimately accepted his position. In REAGAN V. FARMERS' LOAN AND TRUST COMPANY (1894) he spoke for a unanimous Court in holding that a state legislature could not force a railroad to carry persons or freight without a guarantee of sufficient profit. Brewer dramatically expanded the range of issues that the legislature had to consider when determining profitability, and, in so doing, he broadened the grounds for judicial intervention.

Brewer also applied judicial review to congressional acts. He joined the Court's majority in UNITED STATES V. E. C. KNIGHT COMPANY (1895) in narrowing Congress's power under the COMMERCE CLAUSE. He silently joined the same year with Chief Justice MELVILLE W. FULLER in POLLOCK V. FARMERS' LOAN AND TRUST COMPANY, a decision that obliterated more than one hundred years of PRECEDENT in favor of a federal income tax.

Brewer's important decision in IN RE DEBS (1895) coupled judicial power and property rights with a sweeping assertion of national power. The *Debs* case stemmed from the actions of the militant American Railway Union and its leader, Eugene V. Debs, in the Pullman strike of 1894. Debs had refused to obey an INJUNCTION granted by a lower federal court in Chicago that ordered the strikers to end their BOYCOTT of Pullman cars. President GROVER CLEVELAND dispatched troops to restore the passage of INTERSTATE COMMERCE and of the mails. The lower federal court then found Debs and other union members in contempt of court and imprisoned them. Debs petitioned the Supreme Court for a writ of HABEAS CORPUS on the ground that the lower court had exceeded its EQUITY power in issuing the injunction and that the subsequent EX PARTE contempt proceedings had resulted in conviction of a criminal offense without benefit of the procedural guarantees of the criminal law.

Brewer brushed aside Debs's claims with an opinion that blended morality, national supremacy, and the sanctity of private property. In JOHN MARSHALL-like strokes he concluded that the Constitution granted Congress ample power to oversee interstate commerce and the delivery of the mails. The President had acted properly in dispatching federal troops to quell the strikers, because the Constitution had pledged the power of the national government to preserve the social and economic order. The courts, Brewer concluded, had to protect property rights and this included the use of the CONTEMPT POWER to punish persons who refused to abide by injunctions. He disingenuously admonished Debs to seek social change through the ballot box.

Brewer in the post-*Debs* era retreated into STRICT CONSTRUCTION. This narrowing of his constitutional jurisprudence occurred at a time when most of the other Justices embraced the moderate middle class reformist ethos of the Progressive movement. Brewer, Chief Justice Fuller, and Justice RUFUS PECKHAM emerged as the conservative right wing of the Court.

Brewer disparaged Congress's resort to ENUMERATED POWERS to accomplish purposes not originally contemplated by the Framers. This contrasted sharply with his opinion in *Debs*. He dissented with Chief Justice Fuller in CHAMPION V. AMES (1903) on the ground that an act of Congress regulating interstate sale of lottery tickets threatened to destroy the TENTH AMENDMENT. More than issues of FEDERALISM troubled Brewer; his opinion reflected a socioeconomic agenda aimed at protecting property rights. In *South Carolina v. United States* (1905) he spoke for the Court in holding that the federal government could place an internal revenue tax on persons selling liquor, even though those persons acted merely as agents for the state. Brewer argued that state involvement, free from the federal TAXING POWER, in private business would lead inexorably to public ownership of important segments of the economy.

Brewer championed the concept of FREEDOM OF CONTRACT. He first articulated it for the Court in *Frisbie v. United States* (1895), and he joined with the majority two years later in ALLGEYER V. LOUISIANA when it struck down a Louisiana law affecting out-of-state insurance sales. Although the Court subsequently applied the concept unevenly, Brewer dogmatically clung to it. Between HOLDEN V. HARDY (1898) and McLean v. Arkansas (1909), Brewer routinely opposed state and federal laws designed to regulate labor. The single exception was MULLER V. OREGON (1908), and Brewer's opinion for a unanimous

Court in that case ironically contributed to the new liberalism of the Progressive era.

LOUIS D. BRANDEIS in *Muller* submitted a massive brief based on extensive documentary evidence about the health and safety of women workers. It openly appealed to judicial discretion, and Brewer took the opportunity to infuse his long-held views of the dependent condition of women into constitutional doctrine. He denied an absolute right of liberty of contract; instead he concluded that under particular circumstances state legislatures might intervene in the workplace. The supposed physical disabilities of women provided the mitigating circumstances that made the Oregon ten-hour law constitutional. He emphatically argued that the Court had not retreated from substantive due process. Nevertheless, the *Muller* decision and the BRANDEIS BRIEF encouraged constitutional litigation that three decades later shattered Brewer's most cherished conservative values.

The son of a Congregationalist minister and missionary, Brewer never lost touch with his Puritan sense of character and obligation. His jurisprudence forcefully, although naively, proclaimed that material wealth and human progress went hand in hand.

KERMIT L. HALL

Bibliography

CRAMER, RALPH E. 1965 Justice Brewer and Substantive Due Process: A Conservative Court Revisited. *Vanderbilt Law Review* 18:61–96.

PAUL, ARNOLD M. 1969 David J. Brewer. Pages 1515–1549 in Leon Friedman and Fred L. Israel, eds., *The Justices of the Supreme Court, 1789–1969.* New York: Chelsea House.

BREWER v. WILLIAMS
430 U.S. 378 (1977)

This highly publicized case produced three concurring and three dissenting opinions and Justice POTTER STEWART's opinion for a 5–4 majority. Williams, who had kidnapped and murdered a child, was being transported by police who had read the MIRANDA RULES to him. But the police played on his religious beliefs. Although they had agreed not to interrogate him and he had declared that he wanted the assistance of counsel and would tell his story on seeing his counsel, a detective convinced him to show where he had buried the body so that the child could have a Christian burial. The Court reversed his conviction, ruling that the use of EVIDENCE relating to or resulting from his incriminating statements violated his RIGHT OF COUNSEL once adversary proceedings against him had begun, and he had not waived his right. (See NIX V. WILLIAMS.)

LEONARD W. LEVY

BREWSTER v. UNITED STATES
408 U.S. 501 (1972)

A 6–3 Supreme Court held that the SPEECH OR DEBATE CLAUSE does not protect a United States senator from prosecution for accepting a bribe in return for a vote on pending legislation. The clause, said Chief Justice WARREN E. BURGER, only forbids inquiry into legislative acts or the motives behind those acts. Justices WILLIAM J. BRENNAN and WILLIAM O. DOUGLAS attacked the majority's distinction between money-taking and voting and joined Justice BYRON R. WHITE who contended that the only issue was the proper forum for the trial.

DAVID GORDON

BRICKER AMENDMENT
(1952)

Senator John Bricker of Ohio in 1952 introduced a proposed constitutional amendment designed to limit the TREATY POWER and the President's power to make EXECUTIVE AGREEMENTS. The proposal was an outgrowth of widespread isolationist sentiment following the KOREAN WAR, and of fear of the possible consequences of the DOCTRINE of MISSOURI V. HOLLAND (1920) when combined with the United Nations Charter or the so-called Universal Declaration of Human Rights. The amendment, as introduced, would have declared that "a provision of a treaty or other international agreement which conflicts with this Constitution shall not be of any force or effect," and would have prohibited "self-executing" treaties by requiring separate, independently valid congressional action before a treaty could have force as "internal law."

President DWIGHT D. EISENHOWER opposed the Bricker Amendment, arguing that it would make effective conduct of FOREIGN AFFAIRS impossible and deprive the President "of his historic position as the spokesman for the nation." In February 1954, the Senate defeated the Bricker Amendment, and later it failed by one vote to give the required two-thirds

approval to a weaker version written by Senator Walter F. George.

DENNIS J. MAHONEY

BRIDGES v. CALIFORNIA TIMES-MIRROR CO. v. CALIFORNIA
314 U.S. 252 (1941)

In these two companion cases, handed down by the Supreme Court on the same day, a bare majority of five Justices overturned exercises of the CONTEMPT POWER against Harry Bridges, a left-wing union leader, and the *Los Angeles Times,* then a bastion of the state's conservative business establishment, for their out-of-court remarks concerning pending cases. Bridges had been found in contempt for a telegram that predicted a longshoreman's strike in the event of a judicial decree hostile to his union; the *Times* had been punished for an editorial that threatened a judge with political reprisals if he showed leniency toward convicted labor racketeers.

Justice HUGO L. BLACK's majority opinion, joined by Justices WILLIAM O. DOUGLAS, FRANK MURPHY, STANLEY F. REED, and ROBERT H. JACKSON, held that both the telegram and the editorial had been protected by the FIRST AMENDMENT via the DUE PROCESS clause of the FOURTEENTH AMENDMENT against abridgment by the states; neither pronouncement constituted a CLEAR AND PRESENT DANGER to the administration of criminal justice in California courts. Justice FELIX FRANKFURTER, writing for himself and three others, dissented.

Frankfurter's dissent represented the original majority view when the cases were first argued in the spring of 1941. But the defection of Justice Murphy over the summer and the later addition of Justice Jackson produced a new majority for Black by October when the two cases were reargued.

MICHAEL E. PARRISH

BRIEF

Although the term may refer to a number of different kinds of legal documents, in American usage a "brief" ordinarily is a written summary of arguments presented by counsel to a court, and particularly to an appellate court. In the Supreme Court, counsel file briefs only after the Court has granted review of the case. Counsel's first opportunity to acquaint the Court with arguments in the case thus comes in the filing of a petition for a WRIT OF CERTIORARI (or, in the case of an APPEAL, a "jurisdictional statement"), and the papers opposing such a petition. By rule the Court prescribes the length and form of briefs, requires that they be printed (unless a party is permitted to proceed IN FORMA PAUPERIS, as one who cannot afford certain costs), and sets the number of copies to be filed. By the time of ORAL ARGUMENT, the Justices normally have had full opportunity to read and analyze the briefs (including reply briefs) of counsel for the parties and also for any AMICI CURIAE. At or after the argument, the Court may ask counsel to file supplemental briefs on certain issues.

KENNETH L. KARST

(SEE ALSO: *Brandeis Brief.*)

Bibliography

STERN, ROBERT L. and GRESSMAN, EUGENE 1978 *Supreme Court Practice*, 5th ed. Chaps. 6–7. Washington, D.C.: Bureau of National Affairs.

BRINEGAR v. UNITED STATES
338 U.S. 160 (1949)

In *Brinegar* the Supreme Court reaffirmed and broadened the rule in CARROLL V. UNITED STATES (1925) authorizing search of an automobile on the road where PROBABLE CAUSE exists to believe it contains contraband. The Court ignored the lack of congressional authorization for the WARRANTLESS SEARCH, a factor present, and emphasized, in *Carroll*.

JACOB W. LANDYNSKI

BRISCOE v. BANK OF COMMONWEALTH OF KENTUCKY
11 Peters 257 (1837)

This is one of the cases decided by the Supreme Court during the first term that ROGER B. TANEY was Chief Justice, and the decision panicked conservatives into the belief that the constitutional restraints which the MARSHALL COURT imposed on the states no longer counted. The case was decided during a depression year when an acute shortage of currency existed. Kentucky authorized a bank, which was state-owned and -operated, to issue notes that circulated as currency. Justice JOSEPH STORY made a powerful argument that the state notes violated the constitutional injunction against state BILLS OF CREDIT, but he spoke in lonely dissent. The Court, by a 6–1 vote, sustained the act authorizing the state bank notes. Justice JOHN MCLEAN, for the majority, assumed that the clause prohibiting bills of credit did not apply to notes not issued on the faith of a state by a CORPORATION chartered by the state. McLean's weak argument was dictated by the practical need for an expansion of the circulating medium. Economics rather than law governed the case.

LEONARD W. LEVY

BRITISH CONSTITUTION

Most eighteenth-century Englishmen believed that they were the freest people in the world. Foreign observers, such as MONTESQUIEU and Voltaire from France or Jean-Louis De Lolme from Geneva, concurred. Great Britain had somehow created and protected a unique heritage—a CONSTITUTION—that combined liberty with stability. This constitution was no single document nor even a collection of basic texts, although MAGNA CARTA, the BILL OF RIGHTS of 1689, and other prominent documents were fundamental to the tradition. It depended as much upon a series of informal understandings within the ruling class as upon the written word. And it worked. It "insures, not only the liberty, but the general satisfaction in all respects, of those who are subject to it," affirmed De Lolme. This "consideration alone affords sufficient ground to conclude without looking farther," he believed, "that it is also much more likely to be preserved from ruin." Not everyone agreed. English radicals insisted by the 1770s that only electoral reform and a reduction of royal patronage could preserve British liberty much longer. A vigorous press, the most open in Europe, subjected ministers to constant and often scathing criticism, which a literate and growing public thoroughly enjoyed. Yet until late in the pre-revolutionary crisis of 1763–1775, North Americans shared the general awe for the British constitution and frequently insisted that their provincial governments displayed the same virtues.

Apologists explained Britain's constitutional achievement in both legal and humanistic terms. The role of "mixed government" in preserving liberty appealed to a broad audience. Even lawyers used this theme to organize a bewildering mass of otherwise disparate information drawn from the COMMON LAW, parliamentary statutes, and administrative practice. "And herein indeed consists the true excellence of the English government, that all parts of it form a mutual check upon each other," proclaimed Britain's foremost jurist, Sir WILLIAM BLACKSTONE, in 1765. "In the legislature, the people are a check upon the nobility, and the nobility a check upon the people; . . . while the king is a check upon both, which preserves the executive power from encroachment. And this very executive power is again checked, and kept within due bounds by the two houses. . . ."

To work properly, mixed government (or a "mixed and balanced constitution") had to embody the basic elements of the social order: the crown, consisting not just of the monarch but of the army and navy, the law courts, and all other officeholders with royal appointments; the titled aristocracy with its numerous retainers and clients; and landholding commoners. Each had deep social roots, a fixed place in government, and the power to protect itself from the others. United as king, lords, and commons (or as the one, the few, and the many of classical thought), they became a sovereign power beyond which there was no appeal except to revolution, as American colonists reluctantly admitted by 1775.

Although the king could do no wrong, his ministers could. Every royal act had to be implemented by a minister who could be held legally accountable for what he did. Into the early eighteenth century, this principle generated frequent IMPEACHMENTS, a cumbersome device for attempting to achieve responsible government. By mid-century, impeachment, like the royal veto, had fallen into disuse. Crown patronage had become so extensive that a parliamentary majority hostile to the government almost never occurred in the century after the Hanoverian Succession of 1714. When it did, or even when it merely seemed inevitable, as against Sir Robert Walpole in 1742 and Lord North in 1782, the minister usually resigned, eliminating the need for more drastic measures. When William Pitt the Younger refused to resign in the face of an implacably hostile commons majority in 1783–1784, his pertinacity alarmed many contemporaries. It seemed to portend a major crisis of the constitution until Pitt vindicated himself with a crushing victory in the general election of 1784.

British CONSTITUTIONALISM took for granted a thoroughly aristocratic society. Mixed government theory rested upon the recognition of distinct social orders, linked in countless ways through patron–client relationships. Its boast, that it provided a government of laws and not of men, had real merit, which an independent judiciary assiduously sustained. In like manner the House of Commons really did check the ambitions of the crown. The quest for responsible ministers still had not reached its nineteenth-century pattern of cabinet government, but it had moved a long way from the seventeenth-century reliance upon impeachment.

The Revolution converted American patriots from warm admirers to critics of British constitutionalism. Some, such as Carter Braxton of Virginia, hoped to change the British model as little as possible. Others, especially THOMAS PAINE, denounced the entire system of mixed government as decadent and corrupt, fit only for repudiation. Most Americans fell between these extremes. They agreed that they needed formal written constitutions. In drafting them, they discovered the necessity for other innovations. Lacking fixed social orders, they simply could not sustain a mixed government. Patron–client relations were also much weaker among the Americans, who had come to regard most crown patronage as inevitably corrupt, a sign of the decay of English liberty. Americans built governments with no organic roots in European social orders. In nearly every state, they separated the government into distinct branches—legislative, executive, and judicial—to keep each behaving legally and correctly. The SEPARATION OF POWERS thus became the American answer to the mixed and balanced constitution. This rejection of government by king, lords and commons led inexorably to a redefinition of SOVEREIGNTY as well. Americans removed sovereignty from government and lodged it with the people instead. To give this distinction substance, they invented the CONSTITUTIONAL CONVENTION and the process of popular ratification. This transformation made true FEDERALISM possible. So long as sovereignty remained an attribute of government, it had to belong to one level or the other—to Parliament or the colonial legislatures. But once it rested with the people, they became free to grant some powers to the states and others to a central government. In 1787–1788, they finally took that step.

JOHN M. MURRIN

Bibliography

BLACKSTONE, WILLIAM (1765–1769)1979 *Commentaries on the Laws of England*, ed. by Stanley N. Katz et al. Chicago: University of Chicago Press.

BREWER, JOHN 1976 *Party Ideology and Popular Politics at the Accession of George III.* Cambridge: At the University Press.

DE LOLME, J. L. 1775 *The Constitution of England, or An Account of the English Government; In which it is compared with the Republican Form of Government, and occasionally with the other Monarchies in Europe.* London: T. Spilsbury for G. Kearsley.

POCOCK, J. G. A. 1975 *The Machiavellian Moment: Florentine Political Thought and the Atlantic Republi-*

can Tradition. Princeton, N.J.: Princeton University Press.

ROBERTS, CLAYTON 1966 *The Growth of Responsible Government in Stuart England.* Cambridge: At the University Press.

BROADCASTING

Broadcasting is the electronic transmission of sounds or images from a single transmitter to all those who have the appropriate receiving equipment. It is thus a powerful medium for communicating ideas, information, opinions, and entertainment. In many countries broadcasting has become an arm of government. In the United States, however, Congress established the Federal Radio Commission in 1927 and then the Federal Communications Commission (FCC) in 1934 to award broadcasting licenses to private parties. Although a number of licenses were also designated for "public broadcasting," most were allocated to qualified applicants who promised to serve the public interest by acting as public trustees of the airwaves.

The asserted basis for government intervention in the United States was, initially, to eliminate the interference created when many different parties broadcast over the same frequency in the same area. Yet this chaos could have been eliminated with a mere registration requirement and the application of property rights concepts, allocating broadcast licenses by deed, as land is allocated. Instead, the potential interference was used to justify a complex and comprehensive regulatory scheme, embodied in the COMMUNICATIONS ACT of 1934.

In 1952, the FCC established a pattern of allocating television licenses to ensure that the maximum number of local communities would be served by their own local broadcast stations, a departure from the more centralized broadcasting systems of most other countries. Although this decision has added additional voices of local news in many communities, most local television stations affiliated with national networks to share the cost of producing programs of higher technical quality. Thus, while broadcast regulation always has been premised on the primacy of these local outlets, much of it has focused on the relationship between local stations and the powerful national broadcasting networks.

Government regulation of broadcasting obviously presents dangers to the FREEDOM OF SPEECH. Notwithstanding a statutory prohibition on censorship in the Communications Act, the existence of the licensing scheme has significantly influenced the content of programs. Holders of valuable licenses are careful not to offend the FCC, lest they jeopardize their chances of a license renewal. Raised eyebrows and stated concerns about aspects of content prevent station management from acting as freely as newspapers or magazines do. (See FAIRNESS DOCTRINE.) Indeed, only in the last quarter-century have broadcasters come to understand the dominant role that they can play in the distribution of news and information in the United States.

Until recently, the distinct constitutional status of broadcast regulation was premised on the assumption that only a limited number of broadcasting frequencies existed and on the right of the federal government to insure that this scarce commodity was used in the public interest. But recent technological developments have belied this basis for special intervention. Clearly, policy and not physics created the scarcity of frequencies, and now that economic conditions have made alternative media practical, the FCC has begun to open the broadcasting spectrum to new entrants, such as direct broadcast satellites, low-power television, and microwave frequencies.

Nevertheless, in FCC V. PACIFICA FOUNDATION (1978) the Supreme Court suggested that the extraordinary impact of broadcasting on society is itself a possible basis for special rules, at least during hours when children are likely to be listening and watching. This rationale appears to be the only remaining basis for giving broadcasting special constitutional treatment. Technology is rendering obsolete all other distinctions between broadcasting and printed material. For the receiver of ideas at a home console, all manner of data—words and hard copy and soft images—will come through the atmosphere, or over cables, or both. Distinctions based on the mode of delivery of information will have less and less validity. FCC efforts to repeal broadcast regulations, however, have often met with congressional disapproval.

MONROE E. PRICE

(SEE ALSO: *CBS, Inc. v. Federal Communications Commission, 1981.*)

Bibliography

COASE, R. H. 1959 The Federal Communications Commission. *Journal of Law & Economics* 2:1–40.

BROAD CONSTRUCTION

Broad construction, sometimes called "loose construction," is an approach to CONSTITUTIONAL INTERPRETATION emphasizing a permissive and flexible reading of the Constitution, and especially of the powers of the federal government. Like its opposite, STRICT CONSTRUCTION, the phrase has political, rather than technical or legal, significance.

ALEXANDER HAMILTON advocated broad construction in his 1791 controversy with THOMAS JEFFERSON over the constitutionality of the bill to establish the Bank of the United States. The essence of Hamilton's position, which was accepted by President GEORGE WASHINGTON and endorsed by the Supreme Court in MCCULLOCH V. MARYLAND (1819), was the doctrine of IMPLIED POWERS: that the delegated powers implied the power to enact legislation useful in carrying out those powers. The broad constructionists also argued that the NECESSARY AND PROPER CLAUSE empowered Congress to make any law convenient for the execution of any delegated power. Similarly, broad construction justified enactment of the ALIEN AND SEDITION ACTS and expenditures for INTERNAL IMPROVEMENTS.

In his Report on Manufactures (1792) Hamilton advocated a broad construction of the TAXING AND SPENDING POWER that would authorize Congress to spend federal tax money for any purpose connected with the GENERAL WELFARE, whether or not the subject of the appropriation was within Congress's ordinary LEGISLATIVE POWER. Broad construction of the COMMERCE CLAUSE and of the taxing and spending power now forms the constitutional basis for federal regulation of the lives and activities of citizens. Proponents of broad construction argue that the Constitution must be adapted to changing times and conditions. However, a thoroughgoing broad construction is clearly incompatible with the ideas of LIMITED GOVERNMENT and CONSTITUTIONALISM.

The Constitution both grants power to the government and imposes limitations on the exercise of governmental power. Consistent usage would describe the expansive reading of either, and not just of the former, as broad construction. Indeed, President RICHARD M. NIXON frequently criticized the WARREN COURT for its "broad construction" of constitutional provisions guaranteeing the procedural rights of criminal defendants. The more common usage, however, reserves the term for constitutional interpretation permitting a wider scope for governmental activity.

In the late 1970s and the 1980s, broad construction was largely displaced by a new theory of constitutional jurisprudence called "noninterpretivism." Unlike broad construction, which depends upon a relationship between government action and some particular clause of the Constitution, noninterpretivism justifies

government action on the basis of values presumed to underlie the constitutional text and to be superior to the actual words in the document.

DENNIS J. MAHONEY

Bibliography

AGRESTO, JOHN   1984   *The Supreme Court and Constitutional Democracy.* Ithaca, N.Y.: Cornell University Press.

BROADRICK v. OKLAHOMA
413 U.S. 601 (1973)

The FIRST AMENDMENT doctrine of OVERBREADTH, developed by the WARREN COURT in the 1960s, came under increasing criticism from within the Supreme Court. In *Broadrick,* that criticism culminated in the invention of a "substantial overbreadth" DOCTRINE.

Oklahoma law restricted the political activities of state civil servants; such employees were forbidden to "take part in the management or affairs of any political party or in any political campaign," except to vote or express opinions privately. Three civil servants sued in a federal district court for a declaration that the law was unconstitutional for VAGUENESS and overbreadth. The district court upheld the law, and on direct review the Supreme Court affirmed, 5–4.

Justice BYRON R. WHITE, for the majority, concluded that the overbreadth doctrine should not be used to invalidate a statute regulating conduct (as opposed to the expression of particular messages or viewpoints) unless the law's overbreadth is "substantial, . . . judged in relation to the statute's plainly legitimate sweep." Although Oklahoma's law was theoretically capable of constitutionally impermissible application to some activities (the use of political buttons or bumper stickers were arguable examples), it was not substantially overbroad—not likely to be applied to a substantial number of cases of constitutionally protected expression. Thus the law's overbreadth did not threaten a significant CHILLING EFFECT on protected speech, and could be cured through "case-by-case analysis" rather than invalidation on its face. Appellants had conceded that their own conduct (campaigning for a superior state official) could be prohibited under a narrowly drawn statute.

Justice William J. Brennan, for three dissenters, called the decision "a wholly unjustified retreat" from established principles requiring facial invalidation of laws capable of applications to prohibit constitutionally protected speech. Justice WILLIAM O. DOUGLAS, dissenting, generally attacked the validity of laws restricting public employees' political activity.

On the same day the Court reaffirmed, 6–3, the validity of the HATCH ACT, which similarly restricts federal civil servants, in *Civil Service Commission v. National Association of Letter Carriers* (1973).

KENNETH L. KARST

BROCKETT v. SPOKANE ARCADES, INC.
472 U.S. (1985)

The *Brockett* opinion refined the DOCTRINE of OVER-BREADTH in FIRST AMENDMENT cases. A Washington statute provided both civil and criminal sanctions against "moral nuisances"—businesses purveying "lewd" matter. Various purveyors of sexually oriented books and films sued in federal district court for a DECLARATORY JUDGMENT that the law was unconstitutional and an INJUNCTION against its enforcement. That court denied relief, but the court of appeals held the law INVALID ON ITS FACE. The defect, the court said, was the law's definition of "lewd" matter, which followed the Supreme Court's formula defining OB-SCENITY, but defined the term "prurient" to include material that "incites lasciviousness or lust." That definition was substantially overbroad, the court said, because it included material that aroused only a normal, healthy interest in sex.

A 6–2 Supreme Court reversed, in an opinion by Justice BYRON R. WHITE. The Court agreed that, under MILLER V. CALIFORNIA (1973), a work could not be held obscene if its only appeal were to "normal sexual reactions" and accepted the lower court's interpretation that "lust" would embrace such a work. However, Justice White said, these plaintiffs were not entitled to a facial invalidation of the law. They had alleged that their own films and books were not obscene, but were constitutionally protected. In such a case, there is "no want of a proper party to challenge the statute, no concern that an attack on the statute will be unduly delayed or protected speech discouraged." The proper course would be to declare the statute's partial invalidity—here, to declare that the law would be invalid in application to material appealing to "normal . . . sexual appetites." In contrast, when the state seeks to enforce such a partially invalid statute against a person whose own speech or conduct is constitutionally *unprotected*, the proper course, assuming the law's substantial overbreadth, is to invalidate the law entirely. The result is ironic, but explainable. In the latter case, if the court did not hold the law invalid on its face, there would be a serious risk

of a CHILLING EFFECT on the potential protected speech of others who were not in court.

The propriety of partial invalidation depended on the SEVERABILITY of the Washington statute, but that issue was easily resolved: the law contained a severability clause, and surely the legislature would not have abandoned the statute just because it could not be applied to material appealing to normal sexual interests.

Justice SANDRA DAY O'CONNOR joined the OPIN-ION OF THE COURT but argued separately, joined by Chief Justice WARREN E. BURGER and Justice WIL-LIAM H. REHNQUIST, that the case was appropriate for federal court ABSTENTION, awaiting guidance from the state courts on the statutory meaning of "lust." Justice WILLIAM J. BRENNAN, joined by Justice THUR-GOOD MARSHALL, dissented, agreeing with the court of appeals.

KENNETH L. KARST

BRONSON v. KINZIE
1 Howard 311 (1843)

As a result of the depression of 1837 many states passed DEBTORS' RELIEF LEGISLATION to assist property holders who were losing their farms and homes by foreclosure. Illinois, for example, provided that foreclosed property could not be sold at auction unless it brought two-thirds of its appraised value, and that the property sold at foreclosure might be repurchased by the debtor within one year at the purchase price plus ten percent. Such legislation, which operated retroactively on existing contracts, did not directly affect their obligation, the duties of the contracting parties toward each other; it affected their remedies, the means by which the OBLIGATION OF CONTRACTS can be enforced.

By a vote of 7–1 the Supreme Court held the Illinois statutes unconstitutional on the ground that they violated the CONTRACT CLAUSE. The opinion of Chief Justice ROGER B. TANEY remained the leading one on the subject for ninety years, until distinguished away by HOME BUILDING LOAN ASSOCIATION V. BLAISDELL (1934). Taney conceded that the states have power to change the remedies available to creditors confronted by defaulting debtors, on condition that the changed remedy does not impair the obligation of existing contracts. "But if that effect is produced, it is immaterial whether it is done by acting on the remedy or directly on the contract itself." Taney reasoned that the rights of a contracting party could be "seriously impaired by binding the proceedings with new conditions and restrictions, so as to make the remedy hardly worth pursuing." In this case he found that if the state could allow the debtor to repurchase his lost property within a year, it might allow still more time, making difficult a determination of how much time the state might allow. Taney did not say why one year was too long, or why the Court could not fix a rule. He did say that the state requirement fixing two-thirds of the value as the minimum purchasing price "would frequently render any sale altogether impossible." He offered no test by which the state could know whether a change in the remedy adversely affected the obligation of a contract. Justice JOSEPH STORY privately wrote, "There are times when the Court is called upon to support every sound constitutional doctrine in support of the rights of property and of creditors."

LEONARD W. LEVY

BROOM, JACOB
(1752–1810)

Jacob Broom, a member of the CONSTITUTIONAL CONVENTION OF 1787 from Delaware, was a signer of the Constitution. He spoke briefly several times, exhibiting a desire to protect small-state interests and a distrust of a strong executive. When some delegates wanted to dissolve the Convention over the issue of REPRESENTATION, Broom argued against them.

DENNIS J. MAHONEY

BROWN, HENRY BILLINGS
(1836–1913)

Henry Billings Brown served on the Supreme Court from 1890 to 1906. During that period, he wrote more than 450 majority opinions and dissenting or CONCURRING OPINIONS in some fifty other cases, many of which had contemporary and historical significance. Justice Brown's jurisprudence revealed some hesitance, some ambivalence, even contradiction as he struggled to perform the judicial function.

The glorification of private property and free competition reflected one dimension of Brown's thought. He considered the right of private property "the first step in the emergence of the civilized man from the condition of the utter savage," and he joined the majority in LOCHNER V. NEW YORK (1905), striking down a state law that limited the hours of bakery workers to a maximum of sixty per week or ten per day. Yet

Brown usually construed the STATE POLICE POWER broadly and sanctioned legislative modification of laissez faire principles. In HOLDEN V. HARDY (1898) Brown upheld Utah's maximum hours act for miners, rejecting arguments that the state had violated the CONTRACT CLAUSE and denied property without DUE PROCESS. He looked realistically at the disparity in bargaining position between employer and employee, recognizing that fear of losing their jobs prompted laborers to perform work detrimental to their health. Concern for public health and inequality of bargaining power justified the state regulation.

POLLOCK V. FARMERS' LOAN & TRUST CO. (1895) also revealed Brown's willingness to permit legislative regulation of private property. When the Court struck down a congressional tax on incomes, Brown eloquently dissented, protesting that the decision ignored a century of "consistent and undeviating" precedent and represented "a surrender of the TAXING POWER to the moneyed class." Although opponents of the tax had raised the specter of socialism to dissuade Congress from raising funds, Brown construed *Pollock* as "the first step toward the submergence of the liberties of the people in a sordid despotism of wealth."

Brown supported the gradual development of federal power as a necessary concomitant to a modern industrial economy. He also wrote many of the Court's ADMIRALTY opinions, broadly interpreting federal JURISDICTION and the scope of federal maritime law. Brown similarly endorsed an expansive federal power under the COMMERCE CLAUSE, joining, for example, Justice OLIVER WENDELL HOLMES's classic statement of the STREAM OF COMMERCE doctrine in SWIFT & CO. V. UNITED STATES (1905).

Brown's CRIMINAL PROCEDURE and CIVIL LIBERTIES opinions reflected the general attitude of late nineteenth-, early twentieth-century America toward criminals, blacks, and women. In BROWN V. WALKER (1896) he held that the Fifth Amendment RIGHT AGAINST SELF-INCRIMINATION was not violated if the state coerced testimony and afforded IMMUNITY from criminal prosecution. Social disgrace and ridicule might result from invoking the Fifth Amendment, but a "self-confessed criminal" did not deserve protection from his neighbors' negative judgment.

Brown's callousness to CIVIL RIGHTS is manifest in one of the most infamous decisions of the nineteenth century—PLESSY V. FERGUSON (1896). For the Court, Brown upheld a Louisiana statute requiring railroads to provide "equal but separate accommodations" for "white" and "colored" patrons. In a remarkably disingenuous opinion, he reasoned that the statute had "no tendency to destroy the legal equality of the two races" and did "not necessarily imply the inferiority of either race to the other." Brown rejected a Fourteenth Amendment EQUAL PROTECTION challenge, citing as precedent state cases decided prior to passage of the FOURTEENTH AMENDMENT. To Brown the Louisiana law was a reasonable legislative decision consistent with "the established usages, customs and traditions of the people." In other words, Brown conceived civil rights as adequately protected in the legislative process; he did not envision civil rights as enforceable by a minority against the majority. *Plessy* mirrored the late nineteenth-century's belief in physical and social differences between the races. Contemporary scientific and social science thought considered the Negro and Caucasian races as biologically separate and the Caucasian race as superior. In *Plessy,* Brown constitutionalized the prevailing prejudices of his era.

ROBERT JEROME GLENNON

Bibliography

GLENNON, ROBERT JEROME 1973 Justice Henry Billings Brown: Values in Tension. *University of Colorado Law Review* 44:553–604.

BROWN v. ALLEN
344 U.S. 443 (1953)

In *Brown v. Allen* the Supreme Court rejected the claim that North Carolina practiced unconstitutional JURY DISCRIMINATION. Speaking through Justice STANLEY F. REED, the Court held that the state did not deny EQUAL PROTECTION to blacks by randomly selecting jury panels from lists of property taxpayers, even though there was still a significantly smaller proportion of black jurors than black citizens. The Court declined to consider whether selecting for jury duty those with the most property constituted WEALTH DISCRIMINATION. Justices HUGO L. BLACK, FELIX FRANKFURTER, and WILLIAM O. DOUGLAS, dissenting, argued that the tax-list selection technique was not a "complete neutralization of RACIAL DISCRIMINATION."

DENNIS J. MAHONEY

BROWN v. BOARD OF EDUCATION
347 U.S. 483 (1954)
349 U.S. 294 (1955)

In the dual perspectives of politics and constitutional development, *Brown v. Board of Education* was the Supreme Court's most important decision of the twentieth century. In four cases consolidated for decision,

the Court held that racial SEGREGATION of public school children, commanded or authorized by state law, violated the FOURTEENTH AMENDMENT's guarantee of the EQUAL PROTECTION OF THE LAWS. A companion decision, BOLLING V. SHARPE (1954), held that school segregation in the DISTRICT OF COLUMBIA violated the Fifth Amendment's guarantee of DUE PROCESS OF LAW.

Brown illustrates how pivotal historical events, viewed in retrospect, can take on the look of inevitability. To the actors involved, however, the decision was anything but a foregone conclusion. The principal judicial precedent, after all, was PLESSY V. FERGUSON (1896), which had upheld the racial segregation of railroad passengers, partly on the basis of an earlier Massachusetts decision upholding school segregation. More recent Supreme Court decisions had invalidated various forms of segregation in higher education without deciding whether *Plessy* should be overruled. Just a few months before the first *Brown* decision, Robert Leflar and Wylie Davis outlined eleven different courses open to the Supreme Court in the cases before it.

The four cases we now call *Brown* were the culmination of a twenty-year litigation strategy of the NAACP, aimed at the ultimate invalidation of segregation in education. (See SEPARATE BUT EQUAL DOCTRINE.) Part of that strategy had already succeeded; the Supreme Court had ordered the admission of black applicants to state university law schools, and had invalidated a state university's segregation of a black graduate student. The opinions in those cases had emphasized intangible elements of educational quality, particularly the opportunity to associate with persons of other races. (See SWEATT V. PAINTER, 1950). The doctrinal ground was thus prepared for the Court to strike down the segregation of elementary and secondary schools—if the Court was ready to occupy that ground.

The Justices were sensitive to the political repercussions their decision might have. The cases were argued in December 1952, and in the ordinary course would have been decided by the close of the Court's term in the following June or July. Instead of deciding, however, the Court set the five cases for reargument in the following term and proposed a series of questions to be argued, centering on the history of the adoption of the Fourteenth Amendment and on potential remedies if the Court should rule against segregation. The available evidence suggests that the Court was divided on the principal issue in the cases—the constitutionality of separate but equal public schools—and that Justice FELIX FRANKFURTER played a critical role in persuading his brethren to put the case over so that the incoming administration of President DWIGHT D. EISENHOWER might present its views as AMICUS CURIAE. It is clear that the discussion at the Court's CONFERENCE on the cases had dealt not only with the merits of the black children's claims but also with the possible reaction of the white South to a decision overturning school segregation. Proposing questions for the reargument, Justice Frankfurter touched on the same concern in a memorandum to his colleagues: ". . . for me the ultimate crucial factor in the problem presented by these cases is psychological—the adjustment of men's minds and actions to the unfamiliar and the unpleasant."

When Justice Frankfurter wrote of "the adjustment of men's minds," he had whites in mind. For blacks, Jim Crow was an unpleasant reality that was all too familiar. It is not surprising that the Justices centered their political concerns on the white South; lynchings of blacks would have been a vivid memory for any Justice who had come to maturity before 1930. In any event the Court handled the *Brown* cases from beginning to end with an eye on potential disorder and violence among southern whites.

Chief Justice FRED M. VINSON, who had written the opinions invalidating segregation in higher education, appeared to some of his brethren to oppose extending the reasoning of those opinions to segregation in the public schools. Late in the summer of 1953, five weeks before the scheduled reargument of *Brown,* Vinson died suddenly from a heart attack. With *Brown* in mind, Justice Frankfurter said, in a private remark that has since become glaringly public, "This is the first indication I have ever had that there is a God."

Vinson's replacement was the governor of California, EARL WARREN. At the *Brown* reargument, which was put off until December, he did not say much. In conference, however, Warren made clear his view that the separate but equal doctrine must be abandoned and the cases decided in favor of the black children's equal protection claim. At the same time, he though the Court should avoid "precipitous action that would inflame more than necessary." The conference disclosed an apparent majority for the Chief Justice's position, but in a case of such political magnitude, a unanimous decision was devoutly to be wished. The vote was thus postponed, while the Chief Justice and Justice Frankfurter sought for ways to unite the Court. Near-unanimity seems to have been achieved by agreement on a gradual enforcement of the Court's decision. A vote of 8–1 emerged late in the winter, with Justice ROBERT H. JACKSON preparing to file a

separate concurrence. When Jackson suffered a heart attack, the likelihood of his pursuing an independent doctrinal course diminished. The Chief Justice circulated a draft opinion in early May, and at last Justice STANLEY F. REED was persuaded of the importance of avoiding division in the Court. On May 17, 1954, the Court announced its decision. Justice Jackson joined his brethren at the bench, to symbolize the Court's unanimity.

The opinion of the Court, by Chief Justice Warren, was calculatedly limited in scope, unilluminating as to doctrinal implications, and bland in tone. The South was not lectured, and no broad pronouncements were made concerning the fate of Jim Crow. *Plessy* was not even overruled—not then. Instead, the opinion highlighted two points of distinction: the change in the status of black persons in the years since *Plessy,* and the present-day importance of public education for the individual and for American society. Borrowing from the opinion of the lower court in the Kansas case (*Brown* itself), the Chief Justice concluded that school segregation produced feelings of inferiority in black children, and thus interfered with their motivation to learn; as in the graduate education cases, such intangibles were critical in evaluating the equality of the educational opportunity offered to blacks. In *Plessy,* the Court had brushed aside the argument that segregation stamped blacks with a mark of inferiority; the *Brown* opinion, on the contrary, stated that modern psychological knowledge verified the argument, and in a supporting footnote cited a number of social science authorities. (See LEGISLATIVE FACTS.) Segregated education was inherently unequal; the separate but equal doctrine thus had no place in education.

In the ordinary equal protection case, a finding of state-imposed inequality is only part of the inquiry; the Court goes on to examine into justifications offered by the state for treating people unequally. In these cases the southern states had argued that segregation promoted the quality of education, the health of pupils, and the tranquillity of schools. The *Brown* opinion omitted entirely any reference to these asserted justifications. By looking only to the question of inequality, the Court followed the pattern set in earlier cases applying the separate but equal doctrine. However, in its opinion in the companion case from the District of Columbia, the Court added this remark: "Segregation in public education is not reasonably related to any proper governmental objective. . . ." With those conclusory words, the Court announced that further inquiry into justifications for school segregation was foreclosed.

The *Brown* opinion thus presented a near-minimum political target, one that could have been reduced only by the elimination of its social science citations. Everyone understood the importance of educational opportunity. Nothing was intimated about segregation in PUBLIC ACCOMMODATIONS or state courthouses, hospitals, or prisons. Most important of all, the Court issued no orders to the defendant school boards, but set the cases for yet another argument at the next term on questions of remedy: should segregation be ended at once, or gradually? Should the Supreme Court itself frame the decrees, or leave that task to the lower courts or a SPECIAL MASTER?

A full year passed before the Court issued its remedial opinion. *Brown II*, as that opinion is sometimes called, not only declined to order an immediate end to segregation but also failed to set deadlines. Instead, the Court told the lower courts to require the school boards to "make a prompt and reasonable start" toward "compliance at the earliest practicable date," taking into account such factors as buildings, transportation systems, personnel, and redrawing of attendance district lines. The lower courts should issue decrees to the end of admitting the plaintiff children to the schools "on a racially nondiscriminatory basis with ALL DELIBERATE SPEED. . . ."

This language looked like—and was—a political compromise; something of the sort had been contemplated from the beginning by Chief Justice Warren. Despite the Court's statement that constitutional principles could not yield to disagreement, the white South was told, in effect, that it might go on denying blacks their constitutional rights for an indefinite time, while it got used to the idea of stopping. Unquestionably, whatever the Court determined in 1954 or 1955, it would take time to build the sense of interracial community in the South and elsewhere. But in *Brown II* the Court sacrificed an important part of its one legitimate claim to political and moral authority: the defense of principle. A southern intransigent might say: after all, if *Brown* really did stand for a national principle, surely the principle would not be parceled out for separate negotiation in thousands of school districts over an indefinite time. The chief responses of the white South to the Court's gradualism were defiance and evasion. (See DESEGREGATION.) In 1956 a "Southern Manifesto," signed by nineteen Senators and 82 members of the House of Representatives, denounced *Brown* as resting on "personal political and social ideas" rather than the Constitution. One Mississippi senator, seeking to capitalize on the country's recent anticommunist fervor, called racial integration "a radical, pro-Communist political movement." President Eisenhower gave the decision no political support, promising only to carry out the law of the land.

Criticism of another sort came from Herbert Wechsler, a Columbia law professor with impressive credentials as a CIVIL RIGHTS advocate. Wechsler argued that the Supreme Court had not offered a principled explanation of the *Brown* decision—had not supported its repeated assertion that segregation harmed black school children. Charles L. Black, Jr., a Texan and a Yale professor who had worked on the NAACP briefs in *Brown*, replied that all Southerners knew that Jim Crow was designed to maintain white supremacy. School segregation, as part of that system, must fall before a constitutional principle forbidding states deliberately to disadvantage a racial group. This defense of the *Brown* decision is irrefutable. But the *Brown* opinion had not tied school segregation to the system of Jim Crow, because Chief Justice Warren's strategy had been to avoid sweeping pronouncements in the interest of obtaining a unanimous Court and minimizing southern defiance and violence.

Within a few years, however, in a series of PER CURIAM orders consisting only of citations to *Brown*, the Court had invalidated state-supported segregation in all its forms. In one case *Plessy* was implicitly overruled. Jim Crow was thus buried without ceremony. Yet the intensity of the southern resistance to *Brown* shows that no one had been deceived into thinking that the decision was limited to education. Not only did the occasion deserve a clear statement of the unconstitutionality of the system of racial segregation; political practicalities also called for such a statement. The Supreme Court's ability to command respect for its decisions depends on its candid enunciation of the principles underlying those decisions.

Both *Brown* opinions, then, were evasions. Even so, *Brown* was a great decision, a personal triumph for a great Chief Justice. For if *Brown* was a culmination, it was also a beginning. The decision was the catalyst for a political movement that permanently altered race relations in America. (See SIT-IN; CIVIL RIGHTS ACT OF 1964; VOTING RIGHTS ACT OF 1965.) The success of the civil rights movement encouraged challenges to other systems of domination and dependency: systems affecting women, ALIENS, illegitimate children, the handicapped, homosexuals. Claims to racial equality forced a reexamination of a wide range of institutional arrangements throughout American society. In constitutional/doctrinal terms, *Brown* was the critical event in the modern development of the equal protection clause as an effective guarantee of equal CITIZENSHIP, a development that led in turn to the rebirth of SUBSTANTIVE DUE PROCESS as a guarantee of fundamental personal liberties. After *Brown*, the federal judiciary saw itself in a new light, and all Americans could see themselves as members of a national community.

KENNETH L. KARST

Bibliography

BELL, DERRICK 1980 Brown v. Board of Education and the Interest-Convergence Dilemma. *Harvard Law Review* 93:518–533.

BLACK, CHARLES L., JR. 1960 The Lawfulness of the Segregation Decisions. *Yale Law Journal* 69:421–430.

KLUGER, RICHARD 1975 *Simple Justice.* New York: Knopf.

LEFLAR, ROBERT A. and DAVIS, WYLIE H. 1954 Segregation in the Public Schools—1953. *Harvard Law Review* 67:377–435.

WECHSLER, HERBERT 1959 Toward Neutral Principles of Constitutional Law. *Harvard Law Review* 73:1–35.

WILKINSON, J. HARVIE, III 1979 *From Brown to Bakke.* New York: Oxford University Press.

BROWN v. MARYLAND
12 Wheat. 419 (1827)

The Court, over the sole dissent of Justice SMITH THOMPSON, held unconstitutional a state act imposing an annual license tax of $50 on all importers of foreign merchandise. Since the state charged only $8 for a retailer's license, the Court could have found that the license tax on wholesalers of imported goods discriminated against FOREIGN COMMERCE, but Chief Justice JOHN MARSHALL, for the Court, expressly declined to give an opinion on the discrimination issue. Marshall rested his opinion partly on a finding that the license tax constituted a state IMPOST or customs duty on imports, contrary to the IMPORT-EXPORT CLAUSE of Article I, section 16, clause 2, of the Constitution. The sale of an import, Marshall reasoned, is inseparably related to bringing it into the country under congressional tariff acts and paying the duty on it.

Marshall had still greater interests to protect. He turned this simple case of a prohibited state impost, or of a state discrimination against foreign commerce, into an opportunity to lay down a rule explaining when federal authority over foreign commerce ceased and the state power to tax its internal commerce began: as long as the importer retained the property in his possession in the "original package" in which he imported it, federal authority remained exclusive; but when the importer broke the package and mixed the merchandise with other property, it became subject to STATE TAXATION. Marshall therefore found

that the state act was a violation of the COMMERCE CLAUSE interpreted as vesting an exclusive national power, as well as a violation of the import-export clause, and Marshall added, "we suppose the principles laid down in this case, to apply equally to importations from a sister State."

In the time of Chief Justice ROGER B. TANEY (who represented the state in *Brown*), the Court rejected that supposition and still later ruled that the ORIGINAL PACKAGE DOCTRINE applies only to foreign commerce. Although many imports, like crude oil and natural gas, no longer come in "packages," making the doctrine inapplicable, a state tax on foreign commerce still in transit remains an unconstitutional impost. But little remains today of the original package doctrine. In MICHELIN TIRE CORP. v. WAGES (1976) the Court abandoned the doctrine in cases involving nondiscriminatory *ad valorem* property taxes, ruling that such taxes, even on goods imported from abroad and remaining in their original packages, do not fall within the constitutional prohibition against state taxation of imports.

LEONARD W. LEVY

BROWN v. MISSISSIPPI
297 U.S. 278 (1936)

In this landmark decision, the Court for the first time held unconstitutional on DUE PROCESS grounds the use of a coerced confession in a state criminal proceeding. In a unanimous opinion reflecting outrage at the judicial system of Mississippi as well as at its law enforcement officers, Chief Justice CHARLES EVANS HUGHES found difficult to imagine methods "more revolting to the sense of justice" than those used by the state in this case. The record showed that prolonged "physical torture" of black suspects extorted their confessions; they were tried in a rush without adequate defense, were convicted solely on the basis of the confessions which they repudiated, and were quickly sentenced to death. The transcript read "like pages torn from some medieval account. . . ."

Yet the state supreme court, over dissenting opinions, had sustained the convictions on the basis of arguments later used by the state before the Supreme Court: under TWINING V. JERSEY (1908) the Constitution did not protect against compulsory self-incrimination in state courts, and counsel for the prisoners had not made a timely motion for exclusion of the confessions after proving coercion. To these arguments, Hughes replied, first, "Compulsion by torture to extort a confession is a different matter. . . . The rack and torture chamber may not be substituted for the witness stand" except by a denial of due process of law. The state could regulate its own CRIMINAL PROCEDURE only on condition that it observed the fundamental principles of liberty and justice. Second, Hughes regarded counsel's technical error as irrelevant compared to the fact that the wrong committed by the state was so fundamental that it made the whole proceeding a "mere pretense of a trial" and rendered the convictions void.

Brown did not revolutionize state criminal procedure or abolish third-degree methods. But it proved to be the foundation for thirty years of decisions on POLICE INTERROGATION AND CONFESSIONS, finally resulting in an overruling of *Twining* and a constitutional law intended by the FOURTEENTH AMENDMENT.

LEONARD W. LEVY

BROWN v. SOCIALIST WORKERS '74 CAMPAIGN COMMITTEE
459 U.S. 87 (1982)

In BUCKLEY V. VALEO (1976) the Supreme Court refused to recognize a blanket FIRST AMENDMENT right of minor political parties to keep their contributors and their disbursements confidential. The Court said, however, that such a right would be recognized in particular cases when parties could show that political privacy was essential to their exercise of First Amendment rights. *Brown* was such a case. The party had shown a "reasonable probability of threats, harassment, or reprisals" in the event of disclosure. The Court thus held, unanimously, that Ohio could not compel the disclosure of contributions to the party, and held, 6–3, that the same logic protected against compulsory disclosure of the party's expenditures, such as wages or reimbursements paid to party members and supporters.

KENNETH L. KARST

BROWN v. UNITED STATES
381 U.S. 437 (1965)

This decision revitalized the Constitution's prohibitions on BILLS OF ATTAINDER. The TAFT-HARTLEY Act had made it a crime for a member of the Communist party to be a labor union officer. Brown, convicted under this law, argued that it violated the FIRST AMENDMENT, the Fifth Amendment's DUE PROCESS clause, and Article I, section 9, which forbids Congress to pass a bill of attainder. A 5–4 Supreme Court agreed with the latter argument. Citing CUMMINGS V. MIS-

souri (1867), EX PARTE GARLAND (1867), and UNITED STATES V. LOVETT (1946), Chief Justice EARL WARREN said that the law amounted to legislative punishment of a specifically designated group. Congress might weed dangerous persons out of the labor movement, but it must use rules of general applicability, leaving adjudication to other tribunals. (See also IRREBUTTABLE PRESUMPTIONS.) Justice BYRON R. WHITE, for the dissenters, argued that Congress had shown no punitive purpose, but had intended to prevent future political strikes.

KENNETH L. KARST

BROWN v. WALKER
161 U.S. 591 (1896)

After COUNSELMAN V. HITCHCOCK (1892) Congress authorized transactional immunity to compel the testimony of anyone invoking the RIGHT AGAINST SELF INCRIMINATION in a federal proceeding. Appellant, despite a grant of immunity, refused to testify before a GRAND JURY investigating criminal violations of federal law. He argued that Congress could not supersede a constitutional provision by a mere statute and that the statute did not immunize him from all liabilities that might ensue from incriminating admissions. The Supreme Court, by a 5–4 majority, held that the act provided an immunity commensurate with the scope of the Fifth Amendment right and therefore constitutionally supplanted it.

Justice HENRY B. BROWN, for the Court, declared that if the compulsory disclosures could not possibly expose the witness to criminal jeopardy, the demand of the Fifth Amendment was satisfied. The statute did not have to protect him from every possible detriment that might result from his evidence, as long as it exempted the witness from prosecution for any crime to which he testified under compulsion. If his testimony "operates as a complete pardon for the offense to which it relates,—a statute absolutely securing to him such immunity from prosecution would satisfy the demands of the clause of question." But he could be compelled to be a witness against himself if a statute of limitations barred prosecution, if his evidence merely brought him into public disgrace, or if he had already received a pardon or absolute immunity and thus stood with respect to such offense "as if it had never been committed."

The dissenters argued that the act was unconstitutional because the amendment protected the witness from compulsory testimony that would expose him to INFAMY even in the absence of a prosecution. They added that the act also exposed the witness to a possible prosecution for perjury, which could not possibly be imputed if he did not have to testify. (See IMMUNITY GRANTS.)

LEONARD W. LEVY

BRYCE, JAMES
(1838–1922)

Educated at Oxford University and called to the bar at Lincoln's Inn, James Bryce was Regius Professor of Civil Law at Oxford from 1870 until 1893. A member of the Liberal party, he served in the House of Commons (1874–1906) and was a member of four cabinets. His writings on American government and politics were influential both in America and abroad and he was even elected president of the American Political Science Association.

Bryce's most noted work on America was *The American Commonwealth* (1888; last revised, 1910). Rejecting the model of ALEXIS DE TOCQUEVILLE's *Democracy in America,* Bryce set out to describe the American experience without deriving from it any general theories about democracy. A well-educated and widely traveled British politician, Bryce was most impressed by the very constitutional principles Americans frequently take for granted: FEDERALISM, SEPARATION OF POWERS, JUDICIAL REVIEW, and a fixed, written FUNDAMENTAL LAW beyond the amending power of the legislature. He thought the diffusion and limitation of governmental power in America were valuable safeguards against despotism, and that bicameralism and separation of powers provided the opportunity for full discussion of important measures; but he saw two great defects: the possibility that deadlock would prevent prompt action and the difficulty of fixing personal responsibility for policies and actions.

One of Bryce's important contributions as an empirical political scientist was his treatment of the POLITICAL PARTIES. The parties, he observed, constituted "a sort of second and unofficial government" directing the affairs of the legally constituted institutions. The party system counteracted the effects of federalism and separation of powers by linking the interests of legislative and executive officers and by making the results of local elections dependent upon national issues.

Bryce published thirteen other books, including *Studies in History and Jurisprudence* (1901) and *Modern Democracies* (1921), which present American gov-

ernment in comparative perspective, and numerous articles. He was the British ambassador to the United States from 1907 until 1913, and upon his retirement was elevated to the peerage as Viscount Bryce.

DENNIS J. MAHONEY

Bibliography
IONS, EDMUND S. 1970 *James Bryce and American Democracy, 1870–1920.* New York: Humanities Press.

BUCHANAN, JAMES
(1791–1868)

A Pennsylvania attorney, James Buchanan was a congressman (1821–1831), minister to Russia and Britain (1832–1834, 1853–1856), senator (1834–1845), secretary of state (1845–1849), and President (1856–1861). In 1831 Buchanan thwarted a repeal of the Supreme Court's APPELLATE JURISDICTION under section 25 of the JUDICIARY ACT OF 1789. The rest of his prepresidential career reflected his Democratic party regularity and support of STATES' RIGHTS. He attacked Chief Justice ROGER B. TANEY's nationalistic opinion in *Holmes v. Jennison* (1840), denounced the HOLDING in MCCULLOCH V. MARYLAND (1819), and urged a reduction in the number of Supreme Court Justices. In 1844 he declined an appointment to the Court. A close friend of many Southerners, Buchanan hated ABOLITIONISTS, always supported constitutional and congressional protection for slavery, and was the archetypal doughface—the northern man with southern principles. This outlook continued to his presidency and helped undermine it.

Before his inaugural address, Buchanan conversed with Chief Justice Taney while the audience looked on. In his address Buchanan observed that the question of SLAVERY IN THE TERRITORIES was of "little practical importance," in part because it was a "judicial question, which legitimately belongs to the Supreme Court of the United States, before whom it is now pending, and will, it is understood, be speedily and finally settled. To their decision, in common with all good citizens, I shall cheerfully submit. . . ." Two days later the decision was announced in DRED SCOTT V. SANDFORD (1857), and it appeared to many that Taney improperly had informed Buchanan of what the pending decision would hold. For over a month before the decision Buchanan had communicated with Justice JOHN CATRON of Tennessee and ROBERT C. GRIER of Pennsylvania about the case, successfully urging them to support Taney's position that the MISSOURI COMPROMISE was unconstitutional. Two years later, in his "House Divided Speech," ABRAHAM LINCOLN would accuse Buchanan of conspiring with Taney, President FRANKLIN PIERCE, and Senator STEPHEN A. DOUGLAS to force slavery into the territories. Although there was no conspiracy on this issue, Buchanan promoted slavery in the territories. In 1858 he unsuccessfully attempted to bring Kansas into the Union under the proslavery LECOMPTON CONSTITUTION. His support of slavery and southern Democrats helped split the party in 1860 over Douglas's nomination.

After Lincoln's election Buchanan presided over the disintegration of the Union, failing to act in any meaningful way. In December 1860 he blamed the crisis on the "long-continued and intemperate interference of the Northern people with the question of slavery in the Southern States. . . ." He asserted the Union "was intended to be perpetual," and that SECESSION "is revolution," but he also concluded that neither Congress nor the President had any constitutional authority "to coerce a State into submission which is attempting to withdraw" from the Union. The Union, he declared, rested "on public opinion." Buchanan spent his last few months in office vainly seeking a compromise which the South no longer wanted and whose terms the North found unacceptable. During these months Buchanan failed to protect military positions in the South, preserve national authority there, or prepare the nation for the impending war. Buchanan bequeathed to Lincoln a Union from which seven states had departed.

PAUL FINKELMAN

Bibliography

SMITH, ELBERT B. 1975 *The Presidency of James Buchanan.* Lawrence: University of Kansas Press.

BUCHANAN v. WARLEY
245 U.S. 60 (1917)

Buchanan was the most important race relations case between PLESSY V. FERGUSON (1896) and SHELLEY V. KRAEMER (1948). A number of southern border cities had adopted residential SEGREGATION ordinances. NAACP attorneys constructed a TEST CASE challenging the constitutionality of Louisville's ordinance, which forbade a "colored" person to move into a house on a block in which a majority of residences were occupied by whites, and vice versa. A black agreed to buy from a white a house on a majority-white block, provided that the buyer had the legal right to occupy the house. The seller sued to compel performance of the contract; the buyer defended on

the basis of the ordinance. The Kentucky courts upheld the ordinance. In the Supreme Court, both sides focused the argument on the constitutionality of neighborhood segregation. An unusual number of AMICUS CURIAE briefs attested to the case's importance.

A unanimous Supreme Court reversed, holding the ordinance invalid. Justice WILLIAM R. DAY's opinion discussed at length the rights to racial equality and the "dignity of citizenship" established in the THIRTEENTH and FOURTEENTH AMENDMENTS, as well as the rights to purchase and hold property, established by the CIVIL RIGHTS ACT OF 1866. He lamely distinguished *Plessy* as a case in which no one had been denied the use of his property. Ultimately, however, he rested decision on a theory of SUBSTANTIVE DUE PROCESS: the ordinance unconstitutionally interfered with property rights.

Day's curious opinion may have aimed at persuading two of his brethren. Justice JAMES C. MCREYNOLDS generally attached greater weight to claims of constitutional property rights than to claims to racial equality. And Justice OLIVER WENDELL HOLMES had prepared a draft DISSENTING OPINION that was not delivered, arguing that the white seller lacked STANDING to assert the constitutional right of blacks.

Despite the ground for decision, *Buchanan* was seen by the press as a major CIVIL RIGHTS victory for blacks. And when the Supreme Court faced ZONING in a nonracial context, it upheld an ordinance in VILLAGE OF EUCLID V. AMBLER REALTY CO. (1926). *Buchanan* plainly was more than a property rights decision.

KENNETH L. KARST

Bibliography

SCHMIDT, BENNO C., JR. 1982 Principle and Prejudice: The Supreme Court and Race in the Progressive Era. Part 1: The Heyday of Jim Crow. *Columbia Law Review* 82:444, 498–523.

BUCK v. BELL
274 U.S. 200 (1927)

In *Buck* the Supreme Court upheld, 8–1, a Virginia law authorizing the STERILIZATION of institutionalized mental defectives without their consent. Justice OLIVER WENDELL HOLMES, for the Court, wrote an opinion notable for epigram and insensitivity. Virginia's courts had ordered the sterilization of a "feeble minded" woman, whose mother and child were similarly afflicted, finding that she was "the probable potential parent of socially inadequate offspring," and that sterilization would promote both her welfare and society's. Holmes, the Civil War veteran, remarked that public welfare might "call upon the best citizens for their lives"; these "lesser sacrifices" were justified to prevent future crime and starvation. There was no violation of SUBSTANTIVE DUE PROCESS. Citing JACOBSON V. MASSACHUSETTS (1905), he said, "The principle that sustains compulsory VACCINATION is broad enough to cover cutting the Fallopian tubes. . . . Three generations of imbeciles are enough."

Turning to EQUAL PROTECTION, which he called "the usual last resort of constitutional arguments," Holmes saw no violation in the law's reaching only institutionalized mental defectives and not others: "the law does all that is needed when it does all that it can." Justice PIERCE BUTLER noted his dissent.

Although *Buck* continues to be cited, its current authority as precedent is doubtful. (See SKINNER V. OKLAHOMA, 1942.)

KENNETH L. KARST

Bibliography

CYNKAR, ROBERT J. 1981 Buck v. Bell: "Felt Necessities" v. Fundamental Values? *Columbia Law Review* 81:1418–1461.
GOULD, STEPHEN JAY 1984 Carrie Buck's Daughter. *Natural History* July:14–18.
LOMBARDO, PAUL A. 1985 Three Generations, No Imbeciles: New Light on *Buck v. Bell. New York University Law Review* 60:30–62.

BUCKLEY v. VALEO
424 U.S. 1 (1976)

In *Buckley* the Supreme Court dealt with a number of constitutional challenges to the complex provisions of the FEDERAL ELECTIONS CAMPAIGN ACT. The act provided for a Federal Elections Commission, members of which were to be appointed variously by the President and certain congressional leaders. The Court held the congressional appointment unconstitutional; Article 2, section 2, prescribes a process for appointing all officers who carry out executive and quasi-judicial duties: appointment by the President, with confirmation by the Senate. Congress subsequently amended the statute to meet the Court's objections.

Rejecting both FIRST AMENDMENT and EQUAL PROTECTION challenges, the Court upheld, 7–2, the provision of public funds for presidential campaigns in amounts that favored major parties over minor parties.

The Court used a BALANCING TEST in considering First Amendment challenges to the provisions limiting expenditures by candidates and contributions to candidates in congressional elections. For both expenditures and contributions the Court defined the government's interest as preventing corruption and appearance of corruption.

The Court placed the interest of the candidate in FREEDOM OF SPEECH on the other side of the balance in striking down the expenditure provisions. Limiting expenditure limited the amount of speech a candidate might make. The Court rejected the argument that another legitimate purpose of the statute was to equalize the campaign opportunities of rich and poor candidates. The PER CURIAM opinion said that the government might not seek to equalize speech by leveling down the rights of rich speakers. High expenditures by rich candidates created no risk of corruption. Indeed, the opinion demonstrated that such a candidate was not dependent on others' money.

In upholding the contribution limits, the Court characterized the First Amendment interest of contributors not as freedom of speech but freedom of association. It reasoned that the initial contribution of $1,000 allowed by the statute completed the act of association and that further contributions did not significantly enhance the association. Further contributions did, however, increase the risk of corruption.

The statute's requirement that all contributions over $100 be a matter of public record were challenged as violating the right to anonymous political association previously recognized in NAACP v. Alabama (1958). The Court upheld the reporting provisions but said that individual applications to contributors to small unpopular parties might be unconstitutional.

MARTIN SHAPIRO

Bibliography

POLSBY, DANIEL D. 1976 Buckley v. Valeo: The Special Nature of Political Speech. *Supreme Court Review* 1976:1–44.

BUDGET

The federal budget is the comprehensive annual program of income and expenditure of the federal government. The budget is not a constitutional requirement, nor does it answer to either the "appropriations made by law" or the "regular statement of account" of Article I, section 9, of the Constitution. Rather the budget is a legislatively created device to regularize the exercise of the TAXING AND SPENDING POWER.

In the nineteenth century there was no overall annual spending program. Appropriations bills were formulated by various congressional committees, which thereby exercised considerable control over the executive departments. A national budget process was first recommended by the Commission on Economy and Efficiency, appointed by President WILLIAM HOWARD TAFT in 1908; and the BUDGET AND ACCOUNTING ACT, which governed the budget process for over half a century, was enacted in 1921.

Because expenditure is an executive function, the President, as chief executive, was given authority to prepare and submit the budget. This represented a major shift of power within the government in favor of the executive branch. President FRANKLIN D. ROOSEVELT further consolidated presidential authority in 1939 by transferring the Bureau of the Budget (created by the 1921 act) from the Treasury Department to the Executive Office of the President. In 1969, President RICHARD M. NIXON restyled the bureau OFFICE OF MANAGEMENT AND BUDGET and increased its control over the operations of executive departments and agencies.

Congress reasserted its role in fiscal policymaking by the CONGRESSIONAL BUDGET AND IMPOUNDMENT CONTROL ACT (1974). The act created a permanent budget committee in each house of Congress, established the Congressional Budget Office to provide independent evaluation of executive economic planning, and prescribed a timetable for each phase of the budget and appropriations process. Even after passage of this act, however, the budget process is necessarily dominated by the chief executive.

DENNIS J. MAHONEY

Bibliography

BORCHERDING, THOMAS E., ed. 1977 *Budgets and Bureaucrats: The Sources of Government Growth.* Durham, N.C.: Duke University Press.

MARINI, JOHN 1978 The Politics of Budget Control: An Analysis of the Impact of Centralized Administration on the Separation of Powers. Unpublished Ph.D. dissertation, Claremont Graduate School.

BUDGET AND ACCOUNTING ACT
42 Stat. 20 (1921)

Among the aims of the reform movement of the early twentieth century was the creation of neutral processes and agencies to perform public functions, substituting administration for politics in the delivery of government services. One key reform was the introduction of the federal BUDGET. Proposed by President WILLIAM HOWARD TAFT's Commission on Economy and Efficiency, enactment of a federal budget law was delayed by World War I. When Congress finally passed a bill in 1920, President WOODROW WILSON, although a longtime advocate of a budget system, vetoed it rather than submit to its limitation of his REMOVAL POWER. A virtually identical bill was passed the following year and signed into law by President Warren Harding, who called it "the greatest reformation in governmental practice since the beginning of the Republic."

Under the act, the President alone was responsible for submitting to Congress each year a statement of the condition of the treasury, the estimated revenues and expenditures of the government for the year, and proposals for meeting revenue needs. The act created the Bureau of the Budget, to receive, compile, and criticize the estimates and requests of the various departments, and the General Accounting Office, to audit the government's fiscal activities.

The Budget and Accounting Act caused a major change in the balance of power within the government, giving the President, rather than Congress, effective control over government spending. The act provided the machinery through which, during the middle third of the twentieth century, the national executive managed the whole economy.

DENNIS J. MAHONEY

Bibliography

MARINI, JOHN 1978 The Politics of Budget Control: An Analysis of the Impact of Centralized Administration on the Separation of Powers. Unpublished Ph.D. dissertation, Claremont Graduate School.

BUNTING v. OREGON
243 U.S. 426 (1917)

This decision upheld maximum hour legislation and approved state regulations of overtime wages as a proper exception to the prevailing constitutional standards of FREEDOM OF CONTRACT. A 1913 Oregon law prescribed a ten-hour day for men and women alike, thus expanding the law regulating women's hours which had been upheld in MULLER V. OREGON (1908). In addition, the measure required time and a half wages for overtime up to three hours per day. Justice JOSEPH MCKENNA's opinion for the 5–3 majority (there was no written dissent) assumed the validity of the working hours regulations, thus ignoring LOCHNER V. NEW YORK (1905) as well as Justice DAVID J. BREWER's careful distinction in *Muller* that the status of women required special legislative concern. Lawyers for Bunting had attacked the law for its wage-fixing provisions and had invoked *Lochner* and *Muller* to demonstrate that the Oregon statute had no reasonable relation to the preservation of public health. McKenna, focusing on the overtime provision, denied that it was a regulation of wages. The statute, he contended, was designed as an hours law, and the Court was reluctant to consider it as a "disguise" for illegal purposes. Somewhat ingenuously, McKenna argued that the overtime provision was permissive and that its purpose was to burden and deter employers from using workers for more than ten hours. He admitted that the requirement for overtime might not attain that end, "but its insufficiency cannot change its character from penalty to permission." The Oregon Supreme Court had construed the overtime provision as reflecting a legislative desire to make the ten-hour day standard; beyond that, McKenna and his colleagues were not willing to inquire into legislative motive.

Bunting provided frail support in behalf of wage legislation. A few weeks later, the Court split 4–4 on Oregon's minimum wage law (STETTLER V. O'HARA), but in 1923 the Court struck down such legislation in ADKINS V. CHILDREN'S HOSPITAL.

STANLEY I. KUTLER

Bibliography

MASON, ALPHEUS T. 1946 *Brandeis: A Free Man's Life.* New York: Viking Press.

BURBANK v. LOCKHEED AIR TERMINAL
411 U.S. 624 (1973)

The Supreme Court, in a 5–4 vote, struck down a city ordinance regulating air traffic as a violation of the SUPREMACY CLAUSE. The ordinance prohibited jets from taking off between 11 P.M. and 7 A.M. and also forbade the airport operator from allowing such flights. The Court, speaking through Justice WILLIAM O. DOUGLAS, applied the PREEMPTION DOCTRINE and found the ordinance in conflict with two federal statutes which provided for the regulation of navigable airspace. Justice WILLIAM H. REHNQUIST, for the dis-

senters, contended that these statutes did not supersede the STATE POLICE POWER.

DAVID GORDON

BURCH v. LOUISIANA
441 U.S. 130 (1979)

In *Burch v. Louisiana,* the Supreme Court held that conviction by a 5–1 vote of a six-person jury in a state prosecution for a nonpetty offense violates the accused's right to TRIAL BY JURY under the Sixth and FOURTEENTH AMENDMENTS. *Burch* involved a prosecution for exhibiting two obscene motion pictures.

In two earlier cases, APOCADA V. OREGON (1972) and JOHNSON V. LOUISIANA (1972), the Court had sustained 10–2 and 9–3 verdicts, and it had also previously ruled in BALLEW V. GEORGIA (1978) that juries of less than six persons were unconstitutional. In *Burch,* the Court concluded that "having already departed from the strictly historical requirements of jury trial, it is inevitable that lines must be drawn somewhere if the substance of the jury trial right is to be preserved." It relied mainly upon "the same reasons that led us in *Ballew* to decide that use of a five person jury threatened the fairness of the proceeding and the proper role of the jury." *Burch* did not resolve the constitutionality of different majority verdict systems for juries composed of seven through eleven members or majorities of 8–4 or 7–5 on a jury of twelve.

NORMAN ABRAMS

(SEE ALSO: *Jury Size; Jury Unanimity.*)

BURDEN OF PROOF

Although the Constitution does not mention burden of proof, certain principles are widely accepted as having constitutional status. The first and most significant of these is the rule that in a criminal case the government must prove its case "beyond a REASONABLE DOUBT." This is the universal COMMON LAW rule, and was said by the Supreme Court in IN RE WINSHIP (1970) to be an element of DUE PROCESS. This standard is commonly contrasted with proof "by a preponderance of the evidence" or "by clear and convincing evidence." The standard of proof is in practice not easily susceptible to further clarification or elaboration.

To what matters does the burden apply? The *Win-*

ship Court said it extended to "every fact necessary to constitute the crime with which [a defendant] is charged." The government must prove its case beyond a reasonable doubt. But suppose the defendant raises a defense of ALIBI, insanity, duress, or diplomatic immunity? With respect to such defenses the usual rule is that the defendant may be required to produce some evidence supporting his claim; if he does not, that defense will not be considered by the jury. By what standard should the jury be instructed to evaluate such a defense? Should they deny the defense unless they are persuaded by a preponderance of the evidence that the defendant has established it? Or does the "burden of persuasion" on the issue raised by the defendant remain on the government, so that the jury must acquit unless persuaded beyond a reasonable doubt that the defense falls? On this complicated question there is no settled view. The answer should probably vary with the kind of defense: alibi, for example, is not really an affirmative defense but a denial of facts charged. Such a defense as diplomatic immunity, however, might be regarded as one upon which the defendant should bear the burden of proof.

The foregoing structure is complicated by the existence of "presumptions," that is, legislative or judicial statements to the effect that if one fact is proved— say, possession of marijuana—another fact essential to conviction may be "presumed"—say, that the marijuana was illegally imported. The Supreme Court has held such a legislative presumption valid when the proved fact makes the ultimate fact more likely than not.

The burden of proof beyond a reasonable doubt is a critical element of due process. Like the requirements that laws be public and their prohibitions comprehensible and prospective, that trials be public and by jury, and that the defendant have counsel, the burden of proof limits the power of the government to impose arbitrary or oppressive punishments. It reinforces the rights of the defendant not to be a witness against himself nor to take the stand, for it imposes upon the government the task of proving its whole case on its own. A lower standard of proof would pressure defendants to involve themselves in the process of their own condemnation.

In civil cases, the rule is simply stated: the legislature may decide upon the burden of proof as it wishes, usually choosing the "preponderance of the evidence" test. In specialized proceedings, such as motions to suppress evidence for criminal trials, special rules have evolved. (See STANDARDS OF REVIEW.)

JAMES BOYD WHITE

Bibliography
MCCORMICK, CHARLES 1954 *Handbook of the Law of Evidence.* Chap. 6. St. Paul, Minn.: West Publishing Co.

BUREAUCRACY

The Constitution creates an executive branch that neatly fits into the SEPARATION OF POWERS and CHECKS AND BALANCES system that the Framers devised. But the Constitution does not explicitly provide for the kind of administrative branch, or bureaucracy, that evolved beginning in the late nineteenth century. Congress created both independent commissions, such as the Interstate Commerce Commission (established in 1887), and other executive agencies that regulated a wide range of economic activities, and delegated to those bodies the authority both to make law through rule-making and to adjudicate cases arising under their JURISDICTION.

The Framers of the Constitution understandably did not foresee the development of an executive branch that would be a dominant force in lawmaking and adjudication, functions that they expected to be carried out by Congress and the courts. They conceived of "administration" as the "mere execution" of "executive details," to use ALEXANDER HAMILTON's description in THE FEDERALIST #72. Article II makes the President chief executive by giving him the responsibility to "take care that the laws be faithfully executed." He has the authority to appoint public ministers and other executive branch officials designated by Congress, subject to the ADVICE AND CONSENT of the Senate. He may "require the opinion in writing, of the principal officer in each of the executive departments, upon any subject relating to the duties of their respective offices. . . ." Hamilton concluded in *The Federalist* #72: "The persons, therefore, to whose immediate management the different administrative matters are committed ought to be considered as assistants or deputies of the Chief Magistrate and, on this account, they ought to derive their offices from his appointment, at least from his nomination, and ought to be subject to his superintendence."

Hamilton thought, as did most of the Framers, that the President would be, to use Clinton Rossiter's characterization in *The American Presidency* (1956), chief administrator. From a Hamiltonian perspective—one that later turned up in the presidential supremacy school of thought in public administration, reflected in the Report of the President's Committee on Administrative Management in 1937—the President is constitutionally responsible for the administrative branch.

Whatever may have been the intent of the Framers, the Constitution they designed allows and even requires both congressional and judicial intrusion into executive branch affairs. Two factors help to explain the constitutional ambiguities surrounding executive branch accountability. First, the system of separation of powers and checks and balances purposely gives Congress both the motivation and the authority to share with the President control over the executive branch. Congress jealously guards its position and powers, and its constitutional incentive to check the President encourages legislators to design an executive branch that will, in many respects, be independent of the White House. Other political incentives support those of the Constitution in encouraging Congress to hold the reins of the bureaucracy. Political pluralism has fragmented congressional politics into policy arenas controlled by committees. They form political "iron triangles" with agencies and special interests for their mutual benefit. The resulting executive branch pluralism is a major barrier to presidential control.

Agency performance of quasi-legislative and quasi-judicial functions is the second factor complicating the Hamiltonian prescription for the President to be chief administrator. From the standpoint of constitutional theory, Congress and the courts are the primary legislative and judicial branches, respectively. Each has a responsibility to oversee administrative activities that fall within their spheres. Congressional, not presidential, intent should guide agency rule-making. Moreover, the constitutional system, as it was soon to be interpreted by the Supreme Court, gave to the judiciary sweeping authority to exercise JUDICIAL REVIEW over Congress and, by implication, over the President and the bureaucracy as well. Chief Justice JOHN MARSHALL stated in MARBURY V. MADISON (1803): "It is emphatically the province and duty of the Judicial Department to say what the law is. Those who apply the rule to particular cases must, of necessity, expound and interpret that rule." In concrete CASES AND CONTROVERSIES, where administrative action is appropriately challenged by injured parties, courts interpret and apply both statutory and constitutional law.

The hybrid character of the bureaucracy confuses the picture of its place in the governmental scheme. Constitutional prescriptions apply to the bureaucracy as they do to other branches. The bureaucracy must conform to the norms of separation of powers and checks and balances, PROCEDURAL DUE PROCESS, and democratic participation. The formal provisions of the Constitution and the broader politics of the system have shaped the administrative branch in various ways, limiting and controlling its powers.

Ironically, although the President alone is to be chief executive, Congress actually has more constitutional authority over the bureaucracy than does the White House as the result of its extensive enumerated powers under Article I. These do not mention the executive branch explicitly but by application of the doctrine of IMPLIED POWERS give the legislature the authority to create administrative departments and agencies and determine their course of action. Under the TAXING AND SPENDING POWER, the commerce power, and the WAR POWERS, Congress has authorized the creation of a vast array of agencies to carry out its responsibilities. The Legislative Reorganization Act of 1946 mandated Congress to establish oversight committees to supervise the bureaucracy and see to it that agencies were carrying out legislative intent. More important than legislative oversight, a responsibility most committee chairmen eschew because of its limited vote-getting value, is the appropriations and authorization process carried out by dozens of separate committees on Capitol Hill. Committee chairmen and their staffs indirectly sway administrative policymaking through committee hearings and informal contact with administrators who know that Congress strongly influences agency budgets.

The President's executive powers under Article II mean little unless Congress acquiesces in their exercise and buttresses the President's position in relation to the bureaucracy. It is congressional DELEGATION OF POWER to the President as much as, if not more than, the Constitution that determines to what extent he will be chief administrator. But the bureaucracy is always a pawn in the executive–legislative power struggle. Congressional willingness to strengthen presidential authority over the executive branch depends upon political forces that dictate the balance of power between Capitol Hill and the White House. Presidents have valiantly struggled but only intermittently succeeded in obtaining from Congress the powers they have requested to give them dominance over the bureaucracy.

From the New Deal of FRANKLIN D. ROOSEVELT through the Great Society of LYNDON B. JOHNSON, Congress often agreed to requests for increased powers over the bureaucracy. During Roosevelt's administration, Congress for the first time gave the President authority to reorganize the executive Branch, subject to LEGISLATIVE VETO by a majority vote of either the House or the Senate. Roosevelt issued a historic EXECUTIVE ORDER in 1939 creating the presidential bureaucracy—the Executive Office of the President—to help him carry out his executive responsibilities. Laws granting the President reorganization authority were periodically renewed and acted upon until 1973 when Congress, in reaction to the WATERGATE revelations and concern over the "imperial presidency," allowed the reorganization act to expire. Although Congress renewed the reorganization law during the subsequent administration of President GERALD FORD, presidential authority over the bureaucracy had been impaired by the CONGRESSIONAL BUDGET AND IMPOUNDMENT CONTROL ACT of 1974 and other laws. Under the Congressional Budget Act the President could no longer permanently impound funds appropriated by Congress, as President RICHARD M. NIXON had done on over forty separate occasions. The law prevented the President from interfering with administrative implementation of legislative programs.

The courts, too, have claimed administrative turf, by exercising judicial review. Most of the statutes of individual agencies as well as the Administrative Procedure Act of 1946 set forth broad standards of procedural due process that administrators must follow when their decisions directly affect private rights, interests, and obligations. The courts not only interpret these statutory requirements but also apply to the administrative realm constitutional criteria for procedural fairness. For example, the Supreme Court held, in *Wong Yang Sung v. McGrath* (1950), that the Fifth Amendment's DUE PROCESS clause requires the Immigration Service to hold a full hearing with an independent judge presiding, before ordering the DEPORTATION of an illegal ALIEN whose life and liberty might be threatened if he were forced to return to his native land.

Involvement of the three original branches of government in the operations of the bureaucracy does not by itself solve the problem administrative agencies pose to the constitutional theory and practice of the separation of powers. Agencies performing regulatory functions combine in the same hands executive, legislative, and judicial powers. The Administrative Procedure Act of 1946 required a certain degree of separation of functions within agencies by creating an independent class of ADMINISTRATIVE LAW judges who initially decide formal rule-making and adjudicatory cases, which are those that by statute require trial-type hearings. Administrative judges must make their decisions on the record; *ex parte* consultations outside of the agency are forbidden entirely and, within the agency, can be made only in rule-making proceedings. Attempts to impose a judicial model on the administrative process, however, have not solved the constitutional dilemma posed by the fusion of powers within the bureaucracy. Commissions, boards, and agency heads have virtually unlimited discretion to overturn, on the basis of policy considerations, the decisions made by administrative law judges. Courts have supported the imposition of a judicial model on lower-level administrative rule-making and adjudicatory decisions, but have recognized the need for the heads of agencies to have discretion in interpreting legislative intent and flexibility in implementing statutory policy.

Another problem that the bureaucracy poses to the constitutional system is that of democratic control and accountability. An unelected, semi-autonomous administrative branch with the authority to make law arguably threatens to undermine the principles of representative government by removing lawmaking powers from Congress. The solution, in this view, is to restore the delegation of powers doctrine expressed by the Supreme Court in SCHECHTER POULTRY CORPORATION V. UNITED STATES (1935), holding that the primary legislative authority resides in Congress and cannot be delegated to the administrative branch. The *Schechter* rule was never strictly followed, and executive branch lawmaking increased and was even supported by the courts after that decision. However, judges did require that legislative intent be fairly clearly expressed, and they encouraged Congress to tighten agency procedural requirements to guarantee both fairness and compilation of records sufficient to permit effective judicial review.

Administrative discretion in lawmaking and adjudication remains a reality regardless of the intricate network of presidential, congressional, and judicial controls over the bureaucracy. But administrative agencies are not conspiracies to undermine individual liberties and rights, nor to subvert democratic government, a view that conservatives and liberals alike have of the enormous power of the executive branch. Political demands have led to the creation of executive departments and agencies that continue to be responsive to the interests in their political constituencies, a democratic accountability that is narrow but, nevertheless, an important part of the system of administrative responsibility.

The bureaucracy performs vital governmental functions that the three original branches cannot easily carry out. Essential to any modern government is a relatively large and complex administrative branch capable of implementing the wide array of the programs democratic demands produce. American bureaucracy has added an important new dimension to the constitutional system. Because it is so profoundly shaped by the separation of powers, by the process of checks and balances, and by democratic political forces, it does fit, although imperfectly, into the system of constitutional democracy the Framers desired.

PETER WOLL

Bibliography

FRIENDLY, HENRY J. 1962 *The Federal Administrative Agencies.* Cambridge, Mass.: Harvard University Press.

LANDIS, JAMES M. 1938 *The Administrative Process.* New Haven, Conn.: Yale University Press.

WOLL, PETER 1977 *American Bureaucracy.* New York: Norton.

BURFORD v. SUN OIL COMPANY

See: Abstention Doctrines

BURGER, WARREN E.
(1907–)

Warren Earl Burger was born in St. Paul, Minnesota. He attended the University of Minnesota and, in 1931, received a law degree from St. Paul College of Law (today known as the William Mitchell College of Law). After practicing law in St. Paul for several years, he became the assistant attorney general in charge of the Civil Division of the Department of Justice during the administration of DWIGHT D. EISENHOWER. In 1955, Burger was appointed a judge on the United States Court of Appeals for the District of Columbia Circuit. He served in that capacity until 1969, when he became the Chief Justice of the United States, having been nominated for that position by RICHARD M. NIXON.

In the years of his tenure as Chief Justice, the Supreme Court has been marked publicly as having a majority of Justices who hold a generally conservative orientation toward constitutional issues. Burger himself is widely viewed as a primary proponent of this conservative judicial posture and, at least during the early years of the BURGER COURT, he was expected to lead the other conservative Justices in a major, if one-sided, battle to undo as much as could be undone of the pathbreaking work of its predecessor, the quite distinctly liberal WARREN COURT.

To the surprise of many the record of the Burger Court has been extraordinarily complicated, or uneven, when viewed against both of its commonly as-

sumed objectives of overturning Warren Court decisions and of achieving what is often called a "nonactivist" judicial posture toward new claims for constitutional rights. Although it is true that a few Warren Court innovations have been openly discarded (for example, the recognition of a FIRST AMENDMENT right to speak in the context of privately owned SHOPPING CENTERS was overturned) and several other doctrines significantly curtailed (for example, the well-known 1966 ruling in MIRANDA V. ARIZONA has been narrowed as new cases have arisen), it is also true that many Warren Court holdings have been vigorously applied and even extended (for example, the principle of SEPARATION OF CHURCH AND STATE has been forcefully, if still confusingly, applied). What is perhaps most surprising of all, whole new areas of constitutional jurisprudence have been opened up. The foremost example here, of course, is the Court's highly controversial decision in ROE V. WADE (1973), which recognized a woman's constitutional right to have an abortion—subject to a set of conditions that rivaled in their legislation-like refinement the Warren Court's greatly maligned rules for the *Miranda* warnings. Against this history of overrulings, modifications, extensions, and new creations in the tapestry of decisions of its predecessor Courts, it is difficult to characterize the constitutional course steered by the modern Supreme Court under the stewardship of Warren Burger.

The same difficulty arises if one focuses more specifically on the constitutional thought of Burger himself. Burger may properly be regarded as one of the Court's most conservative members. In the field of criminal justice, he has tended to support police and prosecutors. He has joined in a large number of decisions limiting would-be litigants' access to the federal courts. Although he played an important role in the Court's recognition of constitutional rights in areas such as SEX DISCRIMINATION, discrimination against ALIENS, and SCHOOL BUSING, in each of these areas he has resisted extension of the rights initially recognized. Nonetheless, he has been inclined to accept the validity of congressional CIVIL RIGHTS legislation, and to read those laws generously. And he has been a strong supporter of claims of RELIGIOUS LIBERTY. Generally, he has joined the majority as it has pursued this surprisingly labyrinthine constitutional course. The starting point, therefore, for thinking about the constitutional thought of Warren Burger (just as it is for the Court as a whole during his tenure) is the realization that his opinions do not reflect an especially coherent vision of the Constitution and its contemporary significance.

But to say that the decisions and opinions of Burger, taken together, do not add up to a coherent whole does not mean that there are no important themes working their way through them. It is in fact quite possible to locate several distinct threads of thought: for example, a desire to return greater political power to the states in the federal system and to give greater protection to property interests is frequently reflected in Burger's constitutional opinions. But perhaps the most important characteristic of Warren Burger's opinions while Chief Justice is to be found in the area of individual rights and freedoms. It is there that one feels the strongest tension between a commitment to constitutional standards that control and limit the legislative process and a desire to maintain legislative control over the moral and intellectual climate of the community. It is in the resolution of that tension that one is able to determine what is most distinctive about Burger's constitutional jurisprudence.

Burger has frequently displayed a willingness to protect individual freedom at the expense of the interests of the state. His opinion for the Court in *Reed v. Reed* (1971), for example, was the first to subject gender classifications to more rigorous EQUAL PROTECTION scrutiny than had theretofore been the case. But, that said, it is also critical to an understanding of Burger's approach to the BILL OF RIGHTS to see that the depth of his commitment to individual liberties has been limited by a seemingly equal reluctance to extend constitutional protection to individuals or groups whose challenged behavior has gone beyond what may be called the customary norms of good behavior.

Two areas of First Amendment decisions are revealing here. In WISCONSIN V. YODER (1972), for example, Burger wrote an opinion for the Court upholding the right of members of an Amish religious community to refuse, on religious grounds, to comply with the Wisconsin compulsory school-attendance law. In his opinion Burger repeatedly emphasized the fact that the Amish had adopted a traditional lifestyle, saying at one point how "the Amish communities singularly parallel and reflect many of the virtues of THOMAS JEFFERSON's ideal of the 'sturdy yeoman.'" On the other hand, in every case in which a speaker who used indecent language has sought the protection of the First Amendment, Burger has rejected the claim (though in these cases, usually in dissent) and, in doing so, has stressed the importance of maintaining community norms about proper and improper behavior.

In Burger's opinions, therefore, the protection of a specific liberty is often tied to his assessment of the respectability of the behavior. Sometimes this underlying attitude for a decision has been misinterpreted for other motivations. For example, in COLUMBIA BROADCASTING SYSTEM, INC. V. DEMOCRATIC NATIONAL COMMITTEE (1973), a major decision rejecting the claim that individuals and groups have a constitutional and statutory right to purchase airtime from broadcast stations in order to discuss public issues, Burger emphasized the importance of preserving the "journalistic autonomy" or "editorial discretion" of broadcasters, a theme reported in the press accounts of the case at the time. But this suggestion that the decision rested on a heightened respect for editorial freedom, and a preparedness to live with the consequent risks of bad editorial behavior, was considerably undermined by an additional thought Burger expressed. Freedom for broadcast journalists was to be preferred, he said, because broadcasters were regulated and therefore "accountable," while "[n]o such accountability attaches to the private individual, whose only qualifications for using the broadcast facility may be abundant funds and a point of view."

It is a noteworthy feature of Burger's constitutional work that in the area of FREEDOM OF THE PRESS he has written many of the Court's most prominent decisions upholding claims of the print media for protection against various forms of government regulation. Burger wrote for the Court in MIAMI HERALD PUBLISHING CO. V. TORNILLO (1974), holding that states could not require a newspaper to provide access to political candidates who had been criticized in the newspaper's columns; in NEBRASKA PRESS ASSOCIATION V. STUART (1976), holding that courts could not enjoin the media from publishing in advance of trial purported confessions and other evidence "implicative" of an accused individual; and in RICHMOND NEWSPAPERS, INC. V. VIRGINIA (1980), holding that courts could not follow a course of generally excluding the media from attending and observing criminal trials.

Yet, despite this strong record of extending constitutional protection to the press, the Burger Court, and especially Burger himself, has been strongly criticized by various segments of the press for retreating from earlier precedents and for being generally hostile to press claims. Burger, it is true, has sometimes voted along with a majority to reject press claims, as, for example, in BRANZBURG V. HAYES (1972), when the press urged the Court to recognize a limited constitutional privilege for journalists against being compelled to give testimony to grand juries, or in GERTZ V. ROBERT WELCH, INC. (1974), when the press sought to extend the "actual malice" standard in libel actions to all discussions of public issues, not just to those discussions concerning public officials and PUBLIC FIGURES. But an objective assessment of the holdings of the Burger Court does not seem to warrant the general accusation of its hostility to the press. It is too easy to lose sight of the basic truth that in virtually every case that involved significant issues of press freedom Burger has supported the press, and in many of them has written the majority opinions.

Is it possible to account for this discrepancy between criticism and performance? Here again the best explanation is to be found in Burger's disinclination to extend constitutional protection to activity judged as falling below conventional standards of good behavior. But in the area of freedom of the press this disinclination has manifested itself less in the actual results Burger has reached in particular cases and more in the craftsmanship and the tone of his judicial opinions.

The contrast between the opinions of the Warren Court and of Burger in the freedom of press area is remarkable. With Warren Court opinions the tone struck is almost uniformly that of praise for the role performed by the press in the American democratic political system. They extol the virtues of an open and free press. Although the same theme is to be found in Burger's judicial work, one often encounters rather sharp criticism of the press as well. Burger has actively used the forum of the Supreme Court judicial opinion to ventilate his feelings about the condition of the American press, and not everything he has had to say in that forum has been complimentary. One should consider in this regard one of the major cases in the free press area just mentioned, *Miami Herald Publishing Co. v. Tornillo*. In that case Burger's opinion for the Court begins with a lengthy and detailed description of the argument advanced by the state of Florida in support of its statute, which guaranteed limited access for political candidates to the columns of newspapers. The press has grown monopolized and excessively powerful, the state contended: "Chains of newspapers, national newspapers, national wire and news services, and one-newspaper towns, are the dominant features of a press that has become noncompetitive and enormously powerful and influential in its capacity to manipulate popular opinion and change the course of events. . . . Such national news organizations provide syndicated 'interpretive reporting' as well as syndicated features and commentary, all of which can serve as part of the new school of 'journalism.' " While ultimately rejecting the legal conclusion that the state sought to draw from this assumed social reality, Burger's opinion nevertheless strongly intimates sympathy with the general portrait of the press

which the state's argument had painted. Thus, while the press may have had an ally in the constitutional result, it did not in the battle for public opinion generally.

Although Warren Burger retired from the Supreme Court at the end of the 1985–1986 term, what the lasting impact of his constitutional thought will be is of course impossible to tell. For the moment the most appropriate general assessment is that Burger's constitutional work displays a general disunity of character, while suggesting a responsiveness to generally conservative instincts, even when he is on the liberal side.

LEE C. BOLLINGER

Bibliography
BLASI, VINCENT, ED. 1983 *The Burger Court: The Counter-Revolution That Wasn't.* New Haven, Conn.: Yale University Press.
BOLLINGER, LEE C. 1986 *The Tolerant Society: Freedom of Speech and Extremist Speech in America.* New York: Oxford University Press.
CHOPER, JESSE 1980 *Judicial Review and the National Political Process.* Chicago: University of Chicago Press.
SYMPOSIUM 1980 The Burger Court: Reflections on the First Decade. *Law and Contemporary Problems* 43:1.

BURGER COURT
(1969–1986)

The roots of the Burger Court lie in the JUDICIAL ACTIVISM of the WARREN COURT. The social vision of the Supreme Court under EARL WARREN was manifested on many fronts—dismantling racial barriers, requiring that legislative apportionment be based upon population, and vastly expanding the range of rights for criminal defendants, among others. At the height of its activity, during the 1960s, the Warren Court became a forum to which many of the great social issues of the time were taken.

Such activism provoked sharp attacks on the Court. Some of the criticism came from the ranks of the academy, other complaints from political quarters. In the 1968 presidential campaign, RICHARD M. NIXON objected in particular to the Court's CRIMINAL PROCEDURE decisions—rulings which, he said, favored the country's "criminal forces" against its "peace forces."

During his first term as President, Nixon put four Justices on the Supreme Court—WARREN E. BURGER, HARRY A. BLACKMUN, LEWIS F. POWELL, JR., and WILLIAM H. REHNQUIST. Rarely has a President been given the opportunity to fill so many vacancies on the Court in so short a time. Moreover, Nixon was explicit about the ideological basis for his appointments; he saw himself as redeeming his campaign pledge "to nominate to the Supreme Court individuals who share my judicial philosophy, which is basically a conservative philosophy."

Thus was born the Burger Court. For a time, pundits, at least those of liberal persuasion, took to calling it "the Nixon Court." Reviewing the 1971 TERM, *The New Republic* lamented that the "single-mindedness of the Nixon team threatens the image of the Court as an independent institution."

Inevitably, the work of the Burger Court was compared with that of its predecessor, the Warren Court. During the early Burger years, there was evidence that, with Nixon's four appointees on the bench, a new, and more conservative, majority was indeed in the making on the Court.

By the summer of 1976, a conservative Burger Court seemed to have come of age. For example, near the end of the 1975 term the Court closed the doors of federal courts to large numbers of state prisoners by holding that a prisoner who has had a full and fair opportunity to raise a FOURTH AMENDMENT question in the state courts cannot relitigate that question in a federal HABEAS CORPUS proceeding. In other criminal justice decisions, the Court whittled away at the rights of defendants, showing particular disfavor for claims seeking to curb police practices.

Decisions in areas other than criminal justice likewise showed a conservative flavor. For example, in the same term the Court used the TENTH AMENDMENT to place limits on Congress's commerce power, rejected the argument that claims of AGE DISCRIMINATION ought to trigger the higher level of JUDICIAL REVIEW associated with SUSPECT CLASSIFICATIONS (such as race), and refused to hold that CAPITAL PUNISHMENT is inherently unconstitutional.

By the mid-1970s, a student of the Court might have summarized the Burger Court, in contrast with the Warren Court, as being less egalitarian, more sensitive to FEDERALISM, more skeptical about the competence of judges to solve society's problems, more inclined to trust the governmental system, and, in general, more inclined to defer to legislative and political processes. By the end of the 1970s, however, such generalizations might have been thought premature—or, at least, have to be tempered. As the years passed, it became increasingly more difficult to draw clean distinctions between the years of Earl Warren and those of Warren Burger.

Cases involving claims of SEX DISCRIMINATION furnish an example. In 1973 four Justices (WILLIAM J. BRENNAN, WILLIAM O. DOUGLAS, BRYON R. WHITE, and THURGOOD MARSHALL) who had been on the Court in the Warren era sought to have the Court rule that classifications based on sex, like those based on race, should be viewed as "inherently suspect" and hence subject to STRICT SCRUTINY. The four Nixon appointees (together with Justice POTTER STEWART) joined in resisting such a standard. Yet, overall, the Burger Court's record in sex discrimination cases proved to be one of relative activism, even though the Court applied an intermediate STANDARD OF REVIEW in those cases, rather than one of strict scrutiny. In the 1978 term, for example, there were eight cases that in one way or another involved claims of sex discrimination; in six of the eight cases the Justices voted favorably to the claim, either on the merits or on procedural grounds.

In the early 1980s, with the Burger Court in its second decade, there was evidence that a working majority, conservative in bent, was taking hold. Two more Justices from the Warren era (William O. Douglas and Potter Stewart) had retired. Taking their place were appointees of Republican presidents—JOHN PAUL STEVENS (appointed by President GERALD R. FORD) and SANDRA DAY O'CONNOR (named by President RONALD REAGAN). While Stevens tended to vote with the more liberal Justices, O'Connor appeared to provide a dependable vote for the more conservative bloc on the Court.

In the 1983 term the conservatives appeared to have firm control. The Court recognized a "public safety" exception to the MIRANDA RULES and a "good faith" exception to the EXCLUSIONARY RULE in Fourth Amendment cases. The Justices upheld a New York law providing for the PREVENTIVE DETENTION of juveniles and sustained the Reagan administration's curb on travel to Cuba. As one commentator put it, "Whenever the rights of the individual confronted the authority of government this term, government nearly always won." The AMERICAN CIVIL LIBERTIES UNION's legal director called it "a genuinely appalling term," one in which the Court behaved as a "cheerleader for the government."

No sooner had such dire conclusions been drawn than the Burger Court once again confounded the Court-watchers. The very next term saw the Court return to the mainstream of its jurisprudence of the 1970s. The Court's religion cases are an example. Between 1980 and 1984 the Court appeared to be moving in the direction of allowing government to "accommodate" religion, thus relaxing the barriers the FIRST AMENDMENT erects between church and state. The Court rebuffed challenges to Nebraska's paying a legislative chaplain and Pawtucket, Rhode Island's displaying a Christmas crèche. Yet in the 1984 term the Court resumed a separationist stance, invalidating major programs (both federal and state) found to channel public aid to church schools, invalidating an Alabama statute providing for a "moment of silence or prayer" in public schools, and striking down a Connecticut law making it illegal for an employer to require an employee to work on the employee's chosen Sabbath. The Reagan administration had filed briefs in support of the challenged laws in all four cases, and in each of the four cases a majority of the Justices ruled against the program.

Even so brief a sketch of the Burger Court's evolution conveys something of the dialectical nature of those years on the Court. In reading Burger Court opinions, one is sometimes struck by their conservative thrust, sometimes by a liberal result. Here the Burger Court is activist, there it defers to other branches or bodies. There is continuity with the Warren years, but discontinuity as well. One is struck, above all, by the way in which the Court in the Burger era has become a battleground on which fundamental jurisprudential issues are fought out.

No simple portrait of the Burger Court is possible. Some measure of the Burger years may be had, however, by touching upon certain themes that characterize the Burger Court—the questions which observers of the Court have tended to ask and the issues around which decision making on the Court has tended to revolve.

At the outset of the Burger era, many observers thought that a more conservative tribunal would undo much of the work of the Warren Court. This prophecy has been unfulfilled. The landmarks of the Warren Court remain essentially intact. Among those landmarks are BROWN V. BOARD OF EDUCATION (1954) (school desegregation), REYNOLDS V. SIMS (1964) (legislative REAPPORTIONMENT), and the decisions applying nearly all of the procedural protection of the BILL OF RIGHTS in criminal trials to the states.

In all of these areas, there have been, to be sure, important adjustments to Warren Court doctrine. Sometimes, a majority of the Burger Court's Justices have shown a marked distaste for the ethos underlying those precedents. Thus, while leaving such precedents as MIRANDA V. ARIZONA (1956) and MAPP V. OHIO (1961) standing, the Burger Court has frequently confined those precedents or carved out exceptions. Yet, despite criticisms, on and off the bench, of the INCORPORATION DOCTRINE, there has been no wholesale attempt to turn the clock back to the pre-Warren era.

In school cases, while the Burger Court has rebuffed efforts to provide remedies for de facto SEGREGATION, where de jure segregation is proved the Court has been generous in permitting federal judges to fashion effective remedies (it was an opinion of Chief Justice Burger, in SWANN V. CHARLOTTE-MECKLENBURG BOARD OF EDUCATION (1971) that first explicitly upheld lower courts' use of busing as a remedy in school cases). In legislative apportionment cases, the Burger Court has permitted some deviation from strict conformity to a population basis in drawing state and local government legislative districts, but the essential requirement remains that REPRESENTATION must be based on population.

A common complaint against the Warren Court was that it was too "activist"—that it was too quick to substitute its judgment for decisions of legislative bodies or other elected officials. In opinions written during the Burger years, it is common to find the rhetoric of judicial restraint, of calls for deference to policy judgments of legislatures and the political process generally.

Some Burger Court decisions reflect a stated preference for leaving difficult social issues to other forums than the courts. In rejecting an attack of Texas's system of financing public schools through heavy reliance on local property taxes, Justice Powell argued against judges' being too ready to interfere with "informed judgments made at the state and local levels."

Overall, however, the record of the Burger Court is one of activism. One of the hallmarks of activism is the enunciation by the Court of new rights. By that standard, no judicial decision could be more activist than the Burger Court's decision in ROE V. WADE (1973). There Justice Blackmun drew upon the vague contours of the FOURTEENTH AMENDMENT's DUE PROCESS clause to decide that the RIGHT TO PRIVACY (itself a right not spelled out in the Constitution) implies a woman's right to have an ABORTION.

In the modern Supreme Court, the Fourteenth Amendment's due process and EQUAL PROTECTION clauses have been the most conspicuous vehicles for judicial activism. The Warren Court's favorite was the equal protection clause—the so-called new equal protection which, through strict scrutiny and other such tests, produced such decisions as *Reynolds v. Sims*. With the advent of the Burger Court came the renaissance of SUBSTANTIVE DUE PROCESS.

An example of the Burger Court's use of substantive due process is Justice Powell's plurality opinion in MOORE V. EAST CLEVELAND (1977). There the Court effectively extended strict scrutiny to a local ordinance impinging on the "extended family." Powell sought to confine the ambit of substantive due process by offering the "teachings of history" and the "basic values that underlie our society" as guides for judging. It is interesting to recall that, only a few years before *Roe* and *Moore*, even as activist a Justice as Douglas had been uncomfortable with using substantive due process (hence his peculiar "emanations from a penumbra" opinion in GRISWOLD V. CONNECTICUT, 1965). The Burger Court, in opinions such as *Roe* and *Moore*, openly reestablished substantive due process as a means to limit governmental power.

Another index of judicial activism in the Supreme Court is the Court's willingness to declare an act of Congress unconstitutional. Striking down a state or local action in order to enforce the Constitution or federal law is common, but invalidation of congressional actions is rarer. The Warren Court struck down, on average, barely over one federal statute per term; the Burger Court has invalidated provisions of federal law at about twice that rate. More revealing is the significance of the congressional policies overturned in Burger Court decisions. Among them have been CAMPAIGN FINANCE (BUCKLEY V. VALEO, 1976), the eighteen-year-old vote in state elections (OREGON V. MITCHELL, 1970), special bankruptcy courts (NORTHERN PIPELINE CONSTRUCTION CO. V. MARATHON PIPE LINE CO., 1982), and the LEGISLATIVE VETO (IMMIGRATION AND NATURALIZATION SERVICE V. CHADHA, 1983).

Yet another measure of judicial activism is the Court's oversight of the behavior of coordinate branches of the federal government, apart from the substantive results of legislative or executive actions. The Burger Court thrust itself directly into the WATERGATE crisis, during Nixon's presidency. Even as the IMPEACHMENT process was underway in Congress, the Supreme Court, bypassing the Court of Appeals, expedited its hearing of the question whether Nixon must turn over the Watergate tapes. Denying Nixon's claim of EXECUTIVE PRIVILEGE, the Court set in motion the dénouement of the crisis, resulting in Nixon's resignation. The Burger Court has similarly been willing to pass on the ambit of Congress's proper sphere of conduct. For example, the Court's narrow view of what activity is protected by the Constitution's SPEECH OR DEBATE CLAUSE would have surprised WOODROW WILSON, who placed great emphasis on Congress's role in informing the nation.

Closely related to the question of judicial activism is the breadth and scope of the Court's business—the range of issues which the Court chooses to address. Justice FELIX FRANKFURTER used to warn against the Court's plunging into "political thickets" and was distressed when the Warren Court chose to treat legislative apportionment as appropriate for judicial resolution.

Reviewing the record of the Burger Court, one is struck by the new ground it has plowed. Areas that were rarely entered or went untouched altogether in the Warren years have since 1969 become a staple of the Court's docket. In the 1960s Justice ARTHUR J. GOLDBERG sought in vain to have the Justices debate the merits of capital punishment, but the Court would not even grant CERTIORARI. By contrast, not only did the Burger Court, in *Furman v. Georgia* (1972), rule that capital statutes as then administered were unconstitutional, but also death cases have appeared on the Court's calendar with regularity. (See CAPITAL PUNISHMENT CASES, 1972, 1976.)

Sex discrimination is another area that, because of Burger Court decisions, has become a staple on the Justices' table. In *Hoyt v. Florida* (1961) the Warren Court took a quite relaxed view of claims of sex discrimination in a decision upholding a Florida law making jury service for women, but not for men, completely voluntary. By the time Warren Burger became Chief Justice, in 1969, the women's movement had become a visible aspect of the American scene, and since that time the Burger Court has fashioned a considerable body of law on women's rights.

The Burger Court has carried forward—or has been carried along with—the "judicialization" or "constitutionalization" of American life. The victories won by blacks in court in the heyday of the CIVIL RIGHTS movement have inspired others to emulate their example. Prisoners, voters victimized by malapportionment, women, juveniles, inmates of mental institutions—virtually any group or individual failing to get results from the legislative or political process or from government bureaucracies has turned to the courts for relief. And federal judges have woven remedies for a variety of ills.

The Burger Court might have been expected to resist the process of constitutionalization. On some fronts, the Justices have slowed the process. SAN ANTONIO INDEPENDENT SCHOOL DISTRICT V. RODRIGUEZ (1973) represents a victory for a hands-off approach to SCHOOL FINANCE (although it is undercut somewhat by the Court's subsequent decision in *Plyler v. Doe*, 1982). But such decisions seem to be only pauses in the expansion of areas in which the judiciary is willing to inquire.

The Burger Court may sometimes reach a "liberal" result, sometimes a "conservative" one. In some cases the Justices may lay a restraining hand on the EQUITY powers of federal judges, and in some they may be more permissive. All the while, however, the scope of the Supreme Court's docket expands to include wider terrain. In constitutional litigation, there seems to be a kind of ratchet effect: once judges enter an area, they rarely depart. This pattern characterizes the Burger era as much as it does that of Warren.

Even in areas that seemed well developed in the Warren Court, the Burger Court has added new glosses. It was long thought that COMMERCIAL SPEECH fell outside the protection of the First Amendment; the Burger Court brought it inside. It was Burger Court opinions that enlarged press rights under the First Amendment to include, at least in some circumstances, a right of access to criminal trials. The jurisprudence by which government aid to sectarian schools is tested is almost entirely of Burger Court making. Most of the case law sketching out the contours of personal autonomy in such areas as abortion, BIRTH CONTROL, and other intimate sexual and family relations dates from the Burger era. If idle hands are the devil's workshop, the Burger Court is a temple of virtue.

The contour of rights consists not only of substantive doctrine; it also includes jurisdiction and procedure. Who shall have access to the federal forum, when, and for the resolution of what rights—these have been battlegrounds in the Burger Court. If a case may be made that the Burger Court has achieved a retrenchment in rights, it may be that the case is the strongest as regards the Court's shaping of procedural devices.

Warren Court decisions reflected a mistrust in state courts as forums for the vindication of federal rights. Burger Court decisions, by contrast, are more likely to speak of the COMITY owed to state courts. Thus, in a line of decisions beginning with YOUNGER V. HARRIS (1971), the Burger Court has put significant limitations on the power of federal judges to interfere with proceedings (especially criminal) in state courts. The Court also has sharply curtailed the opportunity for state prisoners to seek federal habeas corpus review of state court decisions.

Technical barriers such as STANDING have been used in a number of cases to prevent plaintiffs' access to federal courts. For example, in *Warth v. Selden* (1976) black residents of Rochester were denied standing to challenge exclusionary ZONING in the city's suburbs. Similarly, in SIMON V. EASTERN KENTUCKY WELFARE RIGHTS ORGANIZATION (1976) poor residents of Appalachia were held not to have standing to challenge federal tax advantages granted to private hospitals that refused to serve the INDIGENT.

By no means, however, are Burger Court decisions invariable in restricting access to federal courts or

in limiting remedies for the violation of federal law. Some of the Court's interpretations of SECTION 1983, OF TITLE 42, UNITED STATES CODE (a civil rights statute dating back to 1871) have made that statute a veritable font of litigation. The Warren Court had ruled, in 1961, that Congress, in enacting section 1983, had not intended that municipalities be among the "persons" subject to suit under the statute; in 1978, the Burger Court undertook a "fresh analysis" of the statute and concluded that municipalities are subject to suit thereunder.

Going further, the Court ruled, in 1980, that municipalities sued under section 1983 may not plead as a defense that the governmental official who was involved in the alleged wrong had acted in "good faith"; the majority disregarded the four dissenters' complaint that "ruinous judgments under the statute could imperil local governments." And in another 1980 decision the Court held that plaintiffs could use section 1983 to redress claims based on federal law generally, thus overturning a long-standing assumption that section 1983's reference to federal "laws" was to equal rights legislation. The Burger Court's section 1983 rulings have been a major factor in the "litigation explosion" which in recent years has been the subject of so much legal and popular commentary.

The reach of federal courts' equity powers has been another hotly debated issue in the Burger Court. CLASS ACTIONS seeking to reform practices in schools, prisons, jails, and other public institutions have made INSTITUTIONAL LITIGATION a commonplace. Such suits go far beyond the judge's declaring that a right has been violated; they draw the judge into ongoing supervision of state or local institutions (recalling the quip that in the 1960s federal district judge Frank Johnson was the real governor of Alabama). Institutional litigation in federal courts raises serious questions about federalism and often blurs the line between adjudication, legislation, and administration.

Some Burger Court decisions have attempted to curb federal judges' equity power in institutional cases. For example, in RIZZO V. GOODE (1976) Justice Rehnquist, for the majority, reversed a lower court's order to the Philadelphia police department to institute reforms responding to allegations of police brutality; Rehnquist admonished the judge to refrain from interfering in the affairs of local government. Similarly, in prison cases, the Burger Court has emphasized the importance of federal judges' deference to state prison officials' judgment about questions of prison security and administration.

In important respects, however, the Burger Court has done little to place notable limits on federal courts' equity powers. Especially is this true in school DESEG-REGATION cases. A wide range of remedies has been approved, including busing, redrawing of attendance zones, and other devices. Although the Court has maintained the distinction between DE FACTO AND DE JURE segregation (thus requiring evidence of purposeful segregation as part of a plaintiff's prima facie case), decisions such as those from Columbus and Dayton (both in 1979) show great deference to findings of lower courts used to support remedial orders against local school districts.

Painting a coherent portrait of the Burger Court is no easy task. An effort to describe the Court in terms of general themes, such as the Justices' attitude to judicial activism, founders on conflicting remarks in the Court's opinions. Likewise, an attempt to generalize about the Burger Court's behavior in any given area encounters difficulties.

Consider, for example, the expectation—understandable in light of President Nixon's explicit concern about the Warren Court's rulings in criminal justice cases—that the Burger Court would be a "law and order" tribunal. In the early years of the Burger Court (until about 1976), the Court, especially in its rulings on police practices, seemed bent on undermining the protections accorded in decisions of the Warren years. The majority showed their attitude to the exclusionary rule by referring to it as a "judicially created remedy," one whose benefits were to be balanced against its costs (such as to the functioning of a GRAND JURY). In the late 1970s, the Court seemed more sympathetic to *Miranda* and to other devices meant to limit police practices. But in the early 1980s, especially in SEARCH AND SEIZURE cases, the Court seemed once again markedly sympathetic to law enforcement.

Or consider the Court's attitudes to federalism. In some decisions, the Burger Court has seemed sympathetic to the interests of states and localities. In limiting state prisoners' access to federal writs of habeas corpus, the Court shows respect for state courts. In rebuffing attacks on inequalities in the financing of a state's public schools, the Court gives breathing room to local judgments about running those schools. In limiting federal court intervention in prison affairs, the Court gives scope for state judgments about how to run a prison.

Yet many Burger Court decisions are decidedly adverse to state and local governments' interests. The Court's section 1983 rulings have exposed municipalities to expensive damage awards. The Burger Court has been more active than the Warren Court in using the dormant COMMERCE CLAUSE to restrict state laws and regulations found to impinge upon national inter-

ests. And in the highly controversial decision of GARCIA V. SAN ANTONIO METROPOLITAN TRANSIT AUTHORITY (1985) the Court said that, if the states have Tenth Amendment concerns about acts of Congress, they should seek relief from Congress, not from the courts (in so ruling, the Court in *Garcia* overturned NATIONAL LEAGUE OF CITIES V. USERY, 1976, itself a Burger Court decision).

How does one account for such a mixed record, replete with conflicting signals about basic jurisprudential values? The temperament and habits of the Justices of the Burger Court play a part. Pundits often imagine the Justices coming to the Court's conference table with "shopping lists," looking for cases on which to hang doctrinal innovations. For most (although not necessarily all) of the Justices, this picture is not accurate. By and large, the Justices tend to take the cases as they come. This tendency is reinforced by the Court's workload pressures. Far more cases come to the Burger Court than came to the Warren Court. Complaints by the Chief Justice about the burden thus placed on the Court are frequent, and in 1975 it was reported that at least five Justices had gone on record as favoring the concept of a National Court of Appeals to ease the Supreme Court's workload.

The Burger years on the Court have lacked the larger-than-life figures of the Warren era, Justices like HUGO L. BLACK and Felix Frankfurter, around whom issues tended to polarize. Those were judges who framed grand designs, a jurisprudence of judging. Through their fully evolved doctrines, and their arm-twisting, they put pressure on their colleagues to think about cases in doctrinal terms. Since the departure of the great ideologues, the Justices have been under less pressure to fit individual cases into doctrinal tableaux. Ad hoc results become the order of the day.

The Burger Court has been a somewhat less ideological bench than was the Warren Court. Many of the Court's most important decisions have turned upon the vote of the centrists on the bench. It is not unusual to find, especially in 5–4 decisions, that Justice Powell has cast the deciding vote. Powell came to the bench inclined to think in the pragmatic way of the practicing lawyer; as a Justice he soon came to be identified with "balancing" competing interests to arrive at a decision. The Burger Court's pragmatism, its tendency to gravitate to the center, blurs ideological lines and makes its jurisprudence often seem to lack any unifying theme or principle.

A Burger Court decision—more often, a line of decisions—often has something for everyone. In *Roe v. Wade* the Court upheld the right of a woman to make and effectuate a decision to have an abortion. Yet, while invalidating state laws found to burden the abortion decision directly, the Court has permitted state and federal governments to deny funding for even therapeutic abortions while funding other medical procedures. In REGENTS OF THE UNIVERSITY OF CALIFORNIA V. BAKKE (1978) a majority of the Justices ruled against RACIAL QUOTAS in a state university's admissions process, but a university, consistent with *Bakke*, may use race as a factor among other factors in the admissions process.

Burger Court decisions show a distaste for categorical values. The Warren Court's fondness for prophylactic rules, such as *Miranda* or the Fourth Amendment exclusionary rule, is not echoed in the Burger Court. The Burger bench may not have jettisoned those rules outright, but most Justices of this era show a preference for fact-oriented adjudication rather than for sweeping formulae.

Burger Court opinions are less likely than those of the Warren Court to ring with moral imperatives. Even when resolving so fundamental a controversy as that over abortion, a Burger Court opinion is apt to resemble a legislative committee report more nearly than a tract in political theory. A comparison of such Warren Court opinions as *Brown v. Board of Education* and *Reynolds v. Sims* and a Burger Court opinion such as *Roe v. Wade* is instructive. Warren Court opinions often read as if their authors intended them to have tutorial value (Justice Goldberg once called the Supreme Court "the nation's schoolmaster"); Burger Court opinions are more likely to read like an exercise in problem solving.

For most of its existence, the Burger Court has been characterized by a lack of cohesive voting blocs. For much of its history, the Burger years have seen a 2–5–2 voting pattern—Burger and Rehnquist in one wing, Brennan and Marshall in the other wing, the remaining five Justices tending to take more central ground. Justice Stewart's replacement by Justice O'Connor (a more conservative Justice) tended to reinforce the Burger-Rehnquist wing, while Justice Stevens gravitated more and more to the Brennan-Marshall camp. Even so, the Burger Court was a long way from the sharp ideological alignments of the Warren years.

The Court's personalities and dynamics aside, the nature of the issues coming before the Burger Court help account for the mixed character of the Court's record. The Warren Court is well remembered for decisions laying down broad principles; *Brown, Mapp, Miranda,* and *Reynolds* are examples. The task of implementing much of what the Warren Court began fell to the Burger Court. Implementation, by its nature, draws courts into closer judgment calls. It is one thing to lay down the principle that public schools should not be segregated by race, but quite another to pick one's way through the thicket of de facto-de jure distinctions, interdistrict remedies, and shifting demographics. Had the Warren Court survived into the 1970s, it might have found implementation as difficult and splintering as has the Burger Court.

If the Warren Court embodied the heritage of progressivism and the optimistic expectations of post-World War II America, the Burger years parallel a period of doubt and uncertainty about solutions to social problems in the years after the Great Society, the VIETNAM WAR, and Watergate. In a time when the American people might have less confidence in government's capacity in other spheres, the Supreme Court might well intuitively be less bold in imposing its own solutions. At the same time, there appeared, in the Burger years, to be no turning back the clock on the expectations of lawyers and laity alike as to the place of an activist judiciary in public life. Debate over the proper role of the judiciary in a democracy is not insulated from debate over the role of government generally in a society aspiring to ORDERED LIBERTY. Judgments about the record of the Burger Court, therefore, tend to mirror contemporary American ideals and values.

A. E. DICK HOWARD

Bibliography

BLASI, VINCENT, ED. 1983 *The Burger Court: The Counter-Revolution That Wasn't.* New Haven, Conn.: Yale University Press.

FUNSTON, RICHARD Y. 1977 *Constitutional Counterrevolution?: The Warren Court and the Burger Court: Judicial Policy Making in Modern America.* Cambridge, Mass.: Schenkman.

LEVY, LEONARD W. 1974. *Against the Law: The Nixon Court and Criminal Justice.* New York: Harper & Row.

MASON, ALPHEUS T. 1979 *The Supreme Court from Taft to Burger,* 3rd ed. Baton Rouge: Louisiana State University Press.

WOODWARD, BOB and ARMSTRONG, SCOTT 1979 *The Brethren: Inside the Supreme Court.* New York: Simon & Schuster.

EMERSON, THOMAS I. 1980 First Amendment Doctrine and the Burger Court. *California Law Review* 68:422–481.

HOWARD, A. E. DICK 1972 Mr. Justice Powell and the Emerging Nixon Majority. *Michigan Law Review* 70:445–468.

REHNQUIST, WILLIAM H. 1980 The Notion of a Living Constitution. *Texas Law Review* 54:693–706.

SALTZBERG, STEPHEN A. 1980 Foreword: The Flow and Ebb of Constitutional Criminal Procedure in the Warren and Burger Courts. *Georgetown Law Journal* 69:151–209.

BURGESS, JOHN W.
(1842–1931)

John W. Burgess was professor of political science and constitutional law at Columbia University (1876–1912) where he founded America's first graduate department of political science. Trained in Germany, Burgess sought to develop an American political science based on historical determinism rather than the NATURAL RIGHTS assumptions of the DECLARATION OF INDEPENDENCE. He saw the Civil War as a necessary step in the process by which FEDERALISM gave way to nationalism. He understood the Constitution as creating the two spheres of government and liberty, and as granting rights to individuals rather than protecting preexisting rights. His most important book was *Political Science and Comparative Constitutional Law* (1890).

DENNIS J. MAHONEY

BURNS BAKING COMPANY v. BRYAN
264 U.S. 504 (1924)

The Supreme Court, speaking through Justice PIERCE BUTLER, declared unconstitutional a Nebraska statute that prohibited short-weighting as well as overweighting of bread as a violation of DUE PROCESS and an arbitrary interference with private business. Justice LOUIS D. BRANDEIS dissented, joined by OLIVER WENDELL HOLMES, decrying the decision as "an exercise of the powers of a super-legislature," and urging deference to the legislature's basis for state action.

DAVID GORDON

BURR, AARON
(1756–1836)

Aaron Burr of New York served as a Continental Army officer during the Revolutionary War and later practiced law in Albany and New York City. He was elected four times to the legislature and was for two years state attorney general before serving a term in the United States Senate (1791–1797). He organized the New York Republican party and was the first person to use the Tammany Society for political purposes.

In 1800 Burr was nominated for vice-president on the Republican ticket. Under the ELECTORAL COLLEGE system as it then existed, Burr received the same number of votes as his party's presidential nominee, THOMAS JEFFERSON. The House of Representatives took thirty-six ballots to break the tie and elect Jefferson President, and did so only after ALEXANDER HAMILTON interceded with Federalist congressmen.

After his term as vice-president ended in 1805, Burr became involved in a bizarre intrigue, generally supposed to have had as its object the creation of a separate nation southwest of the Appalachian Mountains. His expedition was thwarted, and Burr and several of his confederates were tried for TREASON. President Jefferson personally directed the prosecution and publicly proclaimed the conspirators guilty. In EX PARTE BOLLMAN AND SWARTOUT (1807) the Supreme Court released two of Burr's lieutenants on a writ of HABEAS CORPUS, refusing to extend the constitutional definition of treason to include conspiracy to commit the offense. A few months later Burr himself was tried before JOHN MARSHALL, sitting as circuit judge, and was acquitted on procedural grounds. The acquittal was the occasion of a renewed Jeffersonian assault against Marshall and the independence of the judiciary.

Burr spent the five years following his trial in European exile, and he never returned to public life.

DENNIS J. MAHONEY

Bibliography

LOMASK, MILTON 1979 *Aaron Burr: The Years from Princeton to Vice President, 1756–1805.* New York: Farrar, Straus & Giroux.
———— 1982 *Aaron Burr: The Conspiracy and Years of Exile, 1805–1836.* New York: Farrar, Straus & Giroux.

BURSTYN, INC. v. WILSON
343 U.S. 495 (1952)

The Supreme Court in this case unanimously overruled a 1915 decision that movies are a business "pure and simple," not entitled to constitutional protection as a medium for the communication of ideas. Justice TOM C. CLARK, for the *Burstyn* Court, ruled that expression by means of movies is included within the free speech and free press clauses of the FIRST AMENDMENT and protected against state abridgment by the FOURTEENTH. In this case New York authorized a state censor to refuse a license for the showing of any film deemed "sacrilegious," a standard that permitted unfettered and unprejudiced discretion.

(See VAGUENESS DOCTRINE.) The state, Clark declared, had no legitimate interest in protecting any religion from offensive views. Justice FELIX FRANKFURTER, concurring, emphasized the danger to the creative process and to RELIGIOUS LIBERTY from a standard so vague that it could be confused with BLASPHEMY.

LEONARD W. LEVY

BURTON, HAROLD
(1888–1964)

Probably no member of the United States Supreme Court enjoyed greater affection from his colleagues on the bench than Justice Harold Burton, whom FELIX FRANKFURTER once described as having "a kind of a boy scout temperament," and whom others praised for his kindness, reasonableness, and unfailing integrity. "There is no man on the bench now who has less pride of opinion," Frankfurter noted, ". . . or is more ready to change positions, if his mind can be convinced. And no vanity guards admission to his mind." Burton, a former mayor of Cleveland and United States senator from Ohio, enjoyed several other distinctions as well. Named to the Court in 1945, he was the only Republican appointed between 1933 and 1953; he also proved to be the most liberal of HARRY S. TRUMAN's four appointees, which, considering the nature of the competition, did not demand much liberalism.

Although dubbed by the press as one member of Truman's law firm, which also included FRED M. VINSON, TOM C. CLARK, and SHERMAN MINTON, Burton broke ranks with the President on the most crucial test of executive power during his tenure, when he joined Justice HUGO L. BLACK's opinion in YOUNGSTOWN SHEET & TUBE CO. V. SAWYER (1952), which declared Truman's seizure of the nation's steel mills illegal in the absence of congressional legislation.

With the notable exception of JOINT ANTI-FASCIST REFUGEE COMMITTEE V. MCGRATH (1951), however, Burton routinely upheld the Truman administration's efforts to destroy the American Communist party and to purge from the federal government suspected subversives during the high tide of the post-1945 Red Scare. He voted with the majority, for instance, in AMERICAN COMMUNICATIONS ASSOCIATION V. DOUDS (1950), in DENNIS V. UNITED STATES (1951), and in *Bailey v. Richardson* (1951), in which the VINSON COURT sustained the noncommunist oath provisions of the TAFT-HARTLEY ACT, the conviction of

eleven top Communist party leaders under the Smith Act, and the federal government's LOYALTY AND SECURITY PROGRAM.

Apart from Minton and STANLEY F. REED, Burton became the most virulent antiradical on the bench during the 1950s. In SLOCHOWER V. BOARD OF EDUCATION (1956) he dissented against Clark's opinion voiding the dismissal of a professor who had invoked his right AGAINST SELF-INCRIMINATION during an investigation into his official conduct. He also dissented in SWEEZY V. NEW HAMPSHIRE (1957), when the Court reversed the conviction of another professor for refusing to answer questions about his classes posed by the state's attorney general. And he, Minton, and Reed were the only dissenters in PENNSYLVANIA V. NELSON (1956), when the Court invalidated the SEDITION law of that state and, by implication, similar statutes in other states.

Generally, Burton followed an equally conservative standard with respect to criminal justice issues. Here, too, he usually endorsed the claims of government rather than those of the individual. In *Bute v. Illinois* (1948) he wrote for a majority of five that reaffirmed the rule of BETTS V. BRADY (1942), which permitted the states to prosecute noncapital felonies without appointing counsel for indigent defendants. He also tolerated forms of police conduct that offended even Frankfurter's conception of DUE PROCESS. (See RIGHT TO COUNSEL.)

Moments of compassion and insight redeemed Burton's otherwise lackluster record in CIVIL LIBERTIES cases. In *Louisiana ex rel. Francis v. Resweber* (1947), perhaps his most famous opinion, he rebelled against Louisiana's efforts to execute a convicted murderer after the first grisly attempt failed because of low voltage in the electric chair. He also joined Black and Frankfurter in their futile efforts to secure a full hearing before the Supreme Court for Julius and Ethel Rosenberg, who were convicted of espionage at the depths of the cold war with the Soviet Union.

By the conclusion of his judicial career in 1956, moreover, he had emerged as one of the Court's most outspoken foes of racial SEGREGATION, despite an unpromising beginning in MORGAN V. VIRGINIA (1946), where he had been the lone dissenter against Black's opinion invalidating the application of that state's Jim Crow law to interstate buses. Four years before BROWN V. BOARD OF EDUCATION, Burton had been prepared to overrule the SEPARATE BUT EQUAL DOCTRINE in *Henderson v. United States* (1950). Reluctantly, he bowed to the preference of several colleagues for invoking the COMMERCE CLAUSE to topple segregation on southern railroads in that case, but he joined Chief Justice EARL WARREN's opinion eagerly in *Brown.* Suffering from a debilitating illness that later claimed his life, Burton retired from the Court in 1958.

MICHAEL E. PARRISH

Bibliography

BERRY, MARY F.   1978   *Stability, Security, and Continuity: Mr. Justice Burton and Decision-Making in the Supreme Court, 1945–1958.* Westport, Conn.: Greenwood Press.

BURTON v. WILMINGTON PARKING AUTHORITY
365 U.S. 715 (1961)

Burton exemplifies the interest-balancing approach to the STATE ACTION limitation of the FOURTEENTH AMENDMENT used by the Supreme Court during the Chief Justiceship of EARL WARREN. A private restaurant, leasing space in a publicly owned parking structure, refused to serve Burton because he was black. In a state court action, Burton sought declaratory and injunctive relief, claiming that the restaurant's refusal amounted to state action denying him the EQUAL PROTECTION OF THE LAWS. The state courts denied relief, but the Supreme Court reversed, 7–2, holding the Fourteenth Amendment applicable to the restaurant's conduct.

Public agencies owned the land and the building, had floated bonds, were collecting revenues to pay for the building's construction and maintenance, and received rent payments from the restaurant. The restaurant could expect to draw customers from persons parking in the structure; correspondingly, some might park there because of the restaurant's convenience. Profits earned from the restaurant's RACIAL DISCRIMINATION, the Court said, were indispensable elements in an integral financial plan. All these interrelated mutual benefits taken together amounted to significant involvement of the state in the private racial discrimination. Justice TOM C. CLARK, for the majority, disclaimed any pretensions of establishing a general rule about state aid to private discrimination, or even for the leasing of state property. Under "the peculiar facts or circumstances" here, the state action limitation was satisfied.

Justice POTTER STEWART, concurring, said simply that a state statute permitting a restaurant's proprietor to refuse service to persons offensive to a majority of patrons amounted to official authorization of private discrimination—a theme explored later in REITMAN

v. MULKEY (1967). Justice JOHN MARSHALL HARLAN dissented, joined by Justice CHARLES E. WHITTAKER. Harlan complained that the majority had offered no guidance for determining when the state action limitation would be satisfied. Rather than pursue this inquiry, he urged a REMAND to the state courts for further illumination of the "authorization" question raised by Justice Stewart.

KENNETH L. KARST

BUSHELL'S CASE
6 State Trials 999 (1670)

A unanimous decision of the Court of Common Pleas, *Bushell's Case* stands for the proposition that a jury may not be punished for returning a verdict contrary to a court's direction. In medieval England, bribery and intimidation were commonly accepted methods of insuring "correct" verdicts, but the Privy Council and the Star Chamber had eliminated those practices by the sixteenth century. Nevertheless, the Star Chamber often handled as corrupt any acquittal that it felt contradicted the evidence. The popular view increasingly opposed punishment for jurors unless they returned a clearly corrupt verdict, and the House of Commons endorsed that position in 1667. The decision in *Bushell's Case* brought the law into line.

When jurors in a case against William Penn and other Quakers persisted in finding the defendants innocent—despite three days of starvation—Bushell and the other jurors were fined and imprisoned. Bushell obtained a writ of HABEAS CORPUS in the Court of Common Pleas and was subsequently discharged. Chief Justice John Vaughan delivered a powerful opinion distinguishing between the "ministerial" (administrative) and judicial functions of jurors. Violations of the former were finable but a verdict was judicial and therefore not subject to penalty. The Court only judged the law. The jury was obliged to deduce the facts from the evidence, and the court could not penalize them for disagreeing with its deductions and directions. Seventeenth-century jurors were expected and required to utilize their own knowledge of a case, private knowledge a judge likely did not have. Only by handpicking jurors could the Crown insure favorable verdicts.

DAVID GORDON

BUSING, SCHOOL

See: School Busing

BUTCHER'S UNION SLAUGHTERHOUSE v. CRESCENT CITY SLAUGHTERHOUSE
111 U.S. 746 (1884)

In this case the INALIENABLE POLICE POWER doctrine again defeated a VESTED RIGHTS claim based on the CONTRACT CLAUSE. Louisiana revoked a charter of monopoly privileges, which the Supreme Court had sustained in the first of the SLAUGHTERHOUSE CASES (1873). Although the contract was supposedly irrepealable for a period of twenty-five years, the Court, in an opinion by Justice SAMUEL F. MILLER, maintained that one legislature cannot bind its successors on a matter involving the GENERAL WELFARE, specifically the public health. No legislature can contract away the state's inalienable power to govern slaughterhouses, which affect the public health. Four Justices, concurring separately, argued that the original monopoly was unconstitutional and its charter revocable, because it violated the liberty and property of competing butchers; the four employed SUBSTANTIVE DUE PROCESS in construing the FOURTEENTH AMENDMENT.

LEONARD W. LEVY

BUTLER, BENJAMIN F.
(1818–1893)

A Massachusetts labor lawyer and Democratic politician, Benjamin Franklin Butler became a Union general in 1861. Butler declared that runaway slaves were "contrabands of war," and used them as noncombatants, refusing to return them to their masters. Later he supported the use of Negro soldiers and in 1864 forced the Confederacy to treat black Union prisoners of war according to the rules of war by retaliating against Confederate prisoners. In 1862 Butler directed the occupation of New Orleans, where his strict application of martial law kept a hostile population under control with virtually no violence. In 1865 Butler advocated that black veterans be given confiscated land and the franchise. After entering Congress in 1867, Butler was a manager of President ANDREW JOHNSON's IMPEACHMENT. Butler approached the trial as if he were prosecuting a horse thief. Butler's lack of dignity in presenting EVIDENCE probably contributed to Johnson's acquittal.

PAUL FINKELMAN

Bibliography

HOLZMAN, ROBERT S. 1978 *Stormy Ben Butler.* New York: Octagon Books.

BUTLER, PIERCE
(1744–1822)

Irish-born Pierce Butler represented South Carolina at the CONSTITUTIONAL CONVENTION OF 1787 and signed the Constitution. It was Butler who first proposed the Convention's secrecy rule. A frequent speaker, he favored a weak central government and championed the interests of slaveholders. He was later a United States senator.

DENNIS J. MAHONEY

BUTLER, PIERCE
(1866–1939)

President WARREN G. HARDING appointed Pierce Butler to the Supreme Court in 1922 in part because Harding wanted to name a conservative Democrat. He also preferred a Roman Catholic. As with other Harding judicial appointments, Chief Justice WILLIAM HOWARD TAFT had an influential role. Before his appointment, Butler had gained some fame as a railroad attorney, particularly for his defense of the carriers in the MINNESOTA RATE CASES (1913) and for his actions as a regent of the University of Minnesota, which led to the dismissal of faculty members who opposed World War I or who were socialists.

Progressive senators opposed Butler's confirmation, but marshaled only eight votes against him. The *New York Times* said that Butler's antagonists favored only judges who supported labor unions and opposed CORPORATIONS; the *St. Louis Post-Dispatch* countered that Butler's chief qualities were "bigotry, intolerance, narrowness, and partisanship." Taft predictably praised the appointment as "a most fortunate one." Until his death in 1939, Butler consistently followed the ideological direction friends and foes had anticipated.

Butler maintained his hostility to political dissenters while on the bench. He supported the majority in upholding a New York criminal anarchy law in GITLOW V. NEW YORK (1925). In UNITED STATES V. SCHWIMMER (1929) he sustained the government's denial of CITIZENSHIP to a sixty-year-old pacifist woman. In 1931 he broke with the majority in STROMBERG V. CALIFORNIA and in NEAR V. MINNESOTA to favor a state conviction of a woman who had displayed a red flag and a state court INJUNCTION against a newspaper editor who had harshly criticized public officials. In the *Near* case, Butler contended that FREEDOM OF THE PRESS should not protect an "insolent publisher who may have purpose and sufficient capacity to contrive and put into effect a scheme or program for oppression, blackmail, or extortion." Six years later Butler joined three others to protest the Court's revival of Justice OLIVER WENDELL HOLMES's CLEAR AND PRESENT DANGER doctrine in HERNDON V. LOWRY (1937). In one of his final statements, in *Kessler v. Strecker* (1939), he approved the DEPORTATION of an ALIEN who had once joined the Communist party but had never paid dues and long since had left the organization.

A Justice's views rarely are monolithic. In the area of CIVIL RIGHTS, for example, Butler stood alone in opposing state STERILIZATION of mental "defectives" in BUCK V. BELL (1927). Perhaps Butler's Catholicism motivated his vote; in any event, a half century later it was discovered that the sterilized woman had never been an imbecile, as Justice Holmes had callously characterized her. Butler also had strong views on the sanctity of the FOURTH AMENDMENT. In OLMSTEAD V. UNITED STATES (1928) he dissented from Taft's opinion upholding the use of WIRETAPPING for gaining evidence, and in another PROHIBITION case Butler insisted that the Fourth Amendment's prohibition of UNREASONABLE SEARCHES should be construed liberally. "Security against unlawful searches is more likely to be attained by resort to SEARCH WARRANTS than by reliance upon the caution and sagacity of petty officers," he wrote in *United States v. Lefkowitz* (1932).

His concern for the criminally accused, however, was not reflected in POWELL V. ALABAMA (1932), as he dissented with Justice JAMES C. MCREYNOLDS when the Court held that the "Scottsboro Boys" had been denied their RIGHT TO COUNSEL. He consistently opposed black claimants. For example, he dissented when the Court invalidated the Texas all-white primary election in NIXON V. CONDON (1932); he asserted in BREEDLOVE V. SUTTLES (1937) that payment of a POLL TAX as a condition to exercise VOTING RIGHTS did not violate the FOURTEENTH AMENDMENT; and he dissented when the Court first successfully attacked the SEPARATE BUT EQUAL DOCTRINE in MISSOURI EX REL. GAINES V. CANADA (1938). He also sustained state laws that prevented aliens from owning farm land in *Porterfield v. Webb* (1923).

Throughout the 1920s, Butler found the Court receptive to his conservative economic views. He was an aggressive spokesman for the claims of utilities, particularly in rate and valuation cases. He insisted on judicial prerogatives in such cases, relying on DUE PROCESS OF LAW to justify a court's determination of both law and facts. In general, Butler favored valuing utility property at reproduction costs in order to determine rate structures. He led the Court in striking down a state statute forbidding use of unsterilized material in the manufacture of mattresses in *Weaver v. Palmer Bros. Co.* (1924); and, in EUCLID V. AMBLER REALTY COMPANY (1926), he dissented when the Court, led by his fellow conservative, Justice GEORGE H. SUTHERLAND, sustained local zoning laws.

In the tumultuous New Deal years, Butler was one of the conservative "Four Horsemen," along with McReynolds, Sutherland, and WILLIS VAN DEVANTER. He opposed every New Deal measure that came before the Court. Butler rarely spoke in these cases, but before the Court reorganization battle he wrote the majority opinion narrowly invalidating a New York minimum wage law. Echoing LOCHNER V. NEW YORK (1905) and invoking ADKINS V. CHILDREN'S HOSPITAL (1923), Butler declared in MOREHEAD V. NEW YORK EX REL. TIPALDO (1936) that the state act violated the FOURTEENTH AMENDMENT's due process clause. Less than a year later, the *Tipaldo* decision was overturned. Thereafter, Butler and his fellow conservatives found themselves at odds with the new majority. To the end, however, they all resolutely kept the faith.

STANLEY I. KUTLER

Bibliography

BROWN, FRANCIS JOSEPH 1945 *The Social and Economic Philosophy of Pierce Butler.* Washington: Catholic University Press.

DANIELSKI, DAVID J. 1964 *A Supreme Court Justice Is Appointed.* New York: Random House.

BUTLER v. MICHIGAN
352 U.S. 380 (1957)

Michigan convicted Butler for selling to an adult an "obscene" book that might corrupt the morals of a minor. The Supreme Court unanimously reversed, in an opinion by Justice FELIX FRANKFURTER, who declared that the statute was not restricted to the evil with which it dealt; it reduced adults "to reading only what is fit for children," thereby curtailing their FIRST AMENDMENT rights as protected by the DUE PROCESS clause of the FOURTEENTH AMENDMENT.

LEONARD W. LEVY

BUTLER, UNITED STATES v.
297 U.S. 1 (1936)

In this historic and monumentally inept opinion, the Supreme Court ruled that the United States has no power to regulate the agrarian sector of the economy.

The AGRICULTURAL ADJUSTMENT ACT OF 1933 (AAA) sought to increase the purchasing power and living standards of farmers by subsidizing the curtailment of farm PRODUCTION and thus boosting farm prices. Congress raised the money for the subsidies by levying an EXCISE TAX on the primary processors of each crop, in this case a cotton mill, which passed on to the consumer the cost of the tax. AAA was the agricultural equivalent of a protective tariff. By a vote of 6–3 the Court held, in an opinion by Justice OWEN ROBERTS, that the statute unconstitutionally invaded the powers reserved to the states by the TENTH AMENDMENT. "It is a statutory plan," Roberts declared, "to regulate and control agricultural production, a matter beyond the powers delegated to the federal government. The tax, the appropriation of the funds raised, and the direction for their disbursement, are but parts of the plan. They are but means to an unconstitutional end." Roberts reached his DOCTRINE of DUAL FEDERALISM by simplistic MECHANICAL JURISPRUDENCE. He sought to match the statute with the Constitution and, finding that they did not square, seriously limited the TAXING AND SPENDING POWER.

Roberts did not question the power of Congress to levy an excise tax on the processing of agricultural products; he also conceded that "the power of Congress to authorize expenditures of public moneys for public purposes is not limited by the direct grants of legislative power found in the Constitution." He did not even deny that aiding the agrarian sector of the economy benefited the GENERAL WELFARE, in accord with the first clause of Article I, section 8; rather he reasoned that the Court did not need to decide whether an appropriation in aid of agriculture fell within the clause. He simply found that the Constitution did not vest in the government a power to regulate agricultural production. He ruled, too, that the tax was not really a tax, because Congress had not levied it for the benefit of the government; it expropriated money from processors to give to farmers. The tax power cannot, Roberts declared, be used as an instrument to enforce a regulation of matters belonging to the exclusive realm of the states, nor can the tax power be used to coerce a compliance which Congress has no power to command.

Despite Roberts's insistence on calling the crop curtailment program "coercive," it was in fact voluntary; a minority of farmers elected not to restrict production, foregoing subsidies. But Roberts added that even a voluntary plan would be unconstitutional as a "federal regulation of a subject reserved to the states." He added: "It does not help to declare that local conditions throughout the nation have created a situation

of national concern; for that is but to say that whenever there is a widespread similarity of local conditions, Congress may ignore constitutional limitations upon its own powers and usurp those reserved to the states."

Justice HARLAN FISKE STONE, joined by Justices LOUIS D. BRANDEIS and BENJAMIN N. CARDOZO, wrote a scathing, imperishable dissent, one of the most famous in the Court's history. Strongly defending the constitutionality of the AAA on the basis of the power to tax and spend, Stone lambasted Roberts's opinion as hardly rising "to the dignity of an argument" and as a "tortured construction of the Constitution." Stone's opinion confirmed President FRANKLIN D. ROOSEVELT's belief that it was the Court, not the Constitution, that stood in the way of recovery. The AAA decision helped provoke the constitutional crisis of 1937.

LEONARD W. LEVY

Bibliography

HART, HENRY M. 1936 Processing Taxes and Protective Tariffs. *Harvard Law Review* 49:610–618.
MURPHY, PAUL L. 1955 The New Deal Agricultural Program and the Constitution. *Agricultural History* 29:160–169.

BUTZ v. ECONOMOU
438 U.S. 478 (1978)

In an action against the Department of Agriculture and individual department officials for alleged constitutional violations, the Court united two previously separate doctrinal strands governing official liability. *Butz* indicated that immunity from personal liability of federal executive officials in direct actions under the Constitution would be available only under circumstances in which state executive officials would be immune from analogous constitutional actions under SECTION 1983, TITLE 42, UNITED STATES CODE. *Butz* also extended absolute immunity to judicial and prosecutorial officials within an administrative agency.

THEODORE EISENBERG

(SEE ALSO: *Executive Immunity; Judicial Immunity.*)

BYRNES, JAMES F.
(1879–1972)

Few members of the United States Supreme Court in this century have led more varied political lives than James F. Byrnes of South Carolina, who served as congressman, United States senator, and governor of his state, czar of production during World War II, and secretary of state. In these other roles, Byrnes left a larger historical legacy than he did on the Court, where he remained for only the October 1941 term.

He wrote sixteen opinions for the Court, never dissented, and did not write a CONCURRING OPINION. As a Justice, he is remembered chiefly for his opinion in EDWARDS V. CALIFORNIA (1942), where he and four others invalidated as a burden on INTERSTATE COMMERCE a California "anti-Okie" law that made it a MISDEMEANOR to bring into the state indigent nonresidents. Initially, Byrnes had been inclined to strike down the law as a violation of the PRIVILEGES AND IMMUNITIES clause of the FOURTEENTH AMEND-ment (a position held by four other Justices), but he finally rejected this approach under pressure from Chief Justice HARLAN FISKE STONE and Justice FELIX FRANKFURTER. Although he also wrote for the Court in *Taylor v. Georgia* (1942), where the Justices voided that state's debt-peonage law, Byrnes did not usually exhibit great sensitivity to the claims of CIVIL LIBER-TIES, or to the complaints of convicted felons and working-class people.

MICHAEL E. PARRISH

Bibliography

BYRNES, JAMES 1958 *All in One Lifetime.* New York: Harper & Row.

CABELL v. CHAVEZ-SALIDO

See: Aliens

CABINET

Whether or not the President should have a cabinet or council was a leading issue at the CONSTITUTIONAL CONVENTION. Such bodies were prevalent in the colonial governments and in the states that succeeded them. Another key element of the cabinet that also crystallized in the preconstitutional period was the concept of the department. Under the ARTICLES OF CONFEDERATION, Congress established four executive offices in 1781: a secretary of foreign affairs, a secretary of war, a superintendent of finance, and a secretary of marine.

At the Philadelphia Convention, GOUVERNEUR MORRIS proposed that there be a Council of State, consisting of the Chief Justice of the Supreme Court and the heads of departments or secretaries, of which there should be five, appointed by the President and holding office at his pleasure. The President should be empowered to submit any matter to the council for discussion and to require the written opinion of any one or more of its members. The President would be free to exercise his own judgment, regardless of the counsel he received. Morris's proposal was rejected in the late-hour efforts of the Committee of Eleven to complete the draft of the Constitution. Instead, the Committee made two principal provisions for advice for the President. Its draft specified that

"The President, by and with the ADVICE AND CONSENT of the Senate, shall appoint ambassadors, and other public ministers, judges of the Supreme Court, and all other officers of the United States, whose appointments are not herein provided for." This provision is attributed to the New York state constitution in which the governor shared the appointment power with the Senate. The draft by the Committee of Eleven also provided that the President "may require the opinion, in writing, of the principal officer of each of the Executive Departments upon any subject relating to the duties of their respective offices."

GEORGE MASON resisted this plan, declaring that omission of a council for the President was an experiment that even the most despotic government would not undertake. Mason proposed an executive council composed of six members, two from the eastern, two from the middle, and two from the southern states. BENJAMIN FRANKLIN seconded the proposal, observing that a council would check a bad President and be a relief to a good one. Gouverneur Morris objected that the President might induce such a council to acquiesce in his wrong measures and thereby provide protection for them. Morris's view prevailed and Mason's plan was defeated. Doubtless a potent factor in the outcome was the expectation that the venerated GEORGE WASHINGTON would become the first President and that a council of some power might impede his functioning. CHARLES PINCKNEY, who once had advocated a council, now argued that it might "thwart" the President.

With the Constitution's prescriptions so sparse, it remained for Washington's presidency to amplify the concept of the cabinet. Congress in 1789 created three departments (State, War, and Treasury) and an attorney general who was not endowed with a department. Washington's appointees—THOMAS JEFFERSON as secretary of state, ALEXANDER HAMILTON as secretary of treasury, Major General Henry Knox as secretary of war, and EDMUND RANDOLPH as attorney general—reflected Mason's emphasis on geographic representation, for they were drawn from the three principal sections of the country. Washington frequently requested the written opinions of his secretaries on important issues and asked them for suggestions for the annual address to Congress.

In 1793, the diplomatic crisis arising from the war between Britain and France caused the cabinet to take firmer shape as an institution. Washington and his secretaries gathered in a series of meetings, including a notable one of April 19 at which the issuance of the PROCLAMATION OF NEUTRALITY was agreed upon. Jefferson recorded that the meetings occurred "almost every day." Because the crisis persisted throughout 1793, the collegial character of the cabinet became well established. Jefferson, Randolph, and Madison referred to the assembled secretaries as the "cabinet," but Washington did not employ the term. Although "cabinet" was long employed in congressional discussion, it did not appear in statutes until the General Appropriation Act of 1907.

The Constitution's meager provisions left Washington largely free to tailor the cabinet to his own preferences. He selected his secretaries on the basis of their individual talents, without regard to their political or policy predispositions. This procedure proved costly, leading to continuous dispute between Hamilton and Jefferson that required a remaking of the cabinet. Washington then resolved not to recruit appointees strongly opposed to his policies. Presidents have applied this principle in constituting their cabinets ever since.

Washington did not consider himself limited by the Constitution to seeking advice only from his department heads. Congressman JAMES MADISON was a frequent adviser on Anglo-American diplomatic issues, on executive appointments, and on the President's reply to the formal addresses of the two houses of Congress. Chief Justice JOHN JAY provided counsel on diplomatic questions, addresses to Congress, and on the political aspects of a presidential tour of the New England states.

Washington was less successful in seeking counsel from the Senate and the Supreme Court. He visited the Senate to discuss issues arising from an Indian treaty under negotiation, and was rebuffed when legislators made clear that his presence constrained their deliberations. The SUPREME COURT, equally self-protective, declined to render ADVISORY OPINIONS.

Washington set the pattern for future presidencies in reaffirming the constitutional arrangement of a strong, independent, single executive, and in rejecting any division of responsibility between the President and the cabinet. Ever since, the view has prevailed that the Constitution confers upon the President the ultimate executive authority and responsibility, which he does not share with the department heads individually or collectively.

Like the President, the cabinet is subject to such basic principles as SEPARATION OF POWERS and CHECKS AND BALANCES, on which the Constitution was constructed. Consequently, both the cabinet and the President are susceptible to the influence of the other two branches. The paucity of constitutional provision and the circumstances of the cabinet's beginning in Washington's administration, together with its continuous presence in all succeeding administrations, cause the cabinet's institutional status to rest upon custom. Since its founding in 1793, the cabinet, as Richard F. Fenno, Jr., has written, has continued to be "an extra-legal creation, functioning in the interstices of the law, surviving in accordance with tradition, and institutionalized by usage alone." Its influence and, to a large degree, its form rest on the will of the President of the moment.

Not surprisingly, given its acute dependence on the President, the cabinet has varied widely in its functions and its importance. Jefferson recruited a cabinet of supportive fellow partisans, but JOHN QUINCY ADAMS drew into his cabinet representatives of his party's great factions who had contested his rise to the Presidency. JAMES MONROE used his cabinet for the arduous crafting of the MONROE DOCTRINE, but ABRAHAM LINCOLN is one of many Presidents who used his cabinet sparingly. ANDREW JACKSON preferred the counsel of his "kitchen cabinet," an informal, unofficial body of friends who did not hold high position. JOHN TYLER rejected the request of his Whig cabinet that matters be decided by majority vote, with each secretary and the President having but one vote. ANDREW JOHNSON added fuel to the flames of his IMPEACHMENT when he removed Secretary of War EDWIN M. STANTON. Johnson's congressional foes contended that he violated the TENURE OF OFFICE ACT of 1867, which purported to deny the President the right to remove civil officials, including members of his cabinet, without senatorial consent.

The twentieth century, too, has seen wide variation

in the demeanors of Presidents toward their cabinets, from WARREN G. HARDING, who considered it his duty to build a cabinet comprised of the "best minds" in the nation, to WOODROW WILSON and JOHN F. KENNEDY, who used their cabinets little and chafed under extended group discussion. DWIGHT D. EISENHOWER endeavored to make the cabinet a central force in his administration through innovations to enhance its operating effectiveness. He created the post of secretary of the cabinet, empowered to arrange an agenda for cabinet meetings and to oversee the preparation of "cabinet papers" by the departments and agencies presenting proposals for cabinet deliberation and presidential decision. The results of cabinet discussions were recorded, responsibilities for implementation were allotted among the departments and agencies, and a system of follow-up was installed to check on accomplishment.

RICHARD M. NIXON designated four members of his cabinet counselors to the President and empowered them to supervise clusters of activity in several or more departments and agencies. With his popularity dropping and an election looming, JIMMY CARTER reshuffled his administration on an unprecedented scale in 1979 by ejecting discordant cabinet secretaries and replacing them with more supportive appointees. RONALD REAGAN instituted a structure of cabinet councils for broad policy areas with memberships of department secretaries and White House staff, supported by subcabinet working groups.

The cabinet's lack of specific delineation in the Constitution contributes to its weakness in coordinating the far-flung activities of the executive branch and in producing innovative policy on the scale and at the pace the President requires. These shortcomings have caused the cabinet to be overshadowed by more recent institutions of the modern presidency that assist in policy development and coordination. These are largely concentrated in the Executive Office of the President, which includes, among other units, the White House Office, the OFFICE OF MANAGEMENT AND BUDGET, the National Security Council, and the Council of Economic Advisers.

The cabinet's frail constitutional base has made the development of the departments susceptible to forces inimical to the cohesiveness that the concept of a "cabinet" implies. Often departments, such as Labor, Agriculture, and Commerce, were brought into being more by the pressures of their client groups than by the President's preference, and without a clear concept of what a department should be. Frequently alliances are formed between the client groups, the department's bureaus, and congressional committees with jurisdiction over the department. These alliances' combined strength has often exceeded the President's and frustrated his will. Even department heads have sometimes proved more responsive to their alliances than to the President.

Because the doctrines of separation of powers and checks and balances bring the cabinet and its departments within reach of the courts and Congress, those branches too have shaped those executive institutions. The Supreme Court, for example, in *Kendall v. United States* (1838), circumscribed the President's discretionary power over the department head when it upheld a lower court decision ordering the postmaster general to pay a complainant money owed by the United States. The payment was a MINISTERIAL ACT which gave the President "no other control over the officer than to see that he acts honestly, with proper motives." Despite the silence of the Constitution concerning the power of removal, Presidents have long removed department heads for any cause they see fit, and in MYERS V. UNITED STATES (1926) the Court upheld an order of the postmaster general to remove a first-class postmaster despite a statute requiring that the removal be by the advice and consent of the Senate.

The cabinet departments depend on Congress for money, personnel, and other resources necessary to function. In effect, department secretaries look to Congress for the means of survival, sometimes straining their ties with the President. Much of the substance of cabinet rank is provided by Congress: salary, title, membership in bodies such as the National Security Council, place in the line of presidential succession. Members of Congress often assert that department heads, notwithstanding their relation with the President, have responsibilities to the legislators. The powers and functions of the department head are conferred by acts of Congress. Although Congress respects the cabinet secretary's advisory role to the President, he is not solely the President's aide in his extra-cabinet functions, but performs in a shadow area of joint executive-legislative responsibility, and struggles with the resulting dilemmas. It is virtually indispensable that a department secretary attract the confidence of Congress as well as that of the President.

The cabinet's few moorings in the Constitution make its relationships with the POLITICAL PARTIES uncertain and fluctuating. Wilson once conceived of the cabinet as a potential link between the President and his party in Congress. He subsequently abandoned this view and like many other Presidents emphasized loyalty and competence in cabinet selection. JOHN QUINCY ADAMS, Warren G. Harding, HARRY

S. TRUMAN, and other Presidents used the cabinet to diminish intraparty factionalism, chiefly by appointing their rivals for the presidential nomination to cabinet posts. Eisenhower allotted several posts to persons with ties to his rival, ROBERT A. TAFT. Parties, however, have considerably less influence on the cabinet than the chief executive or Congress.

LOUIS W. KOENIG

Bibliography

FENNO, RICHARD F., JR. 1959 *The President's Cabinet.* Cambridge, Mass.: Harvard University Press.

HINSDALE, MARY 1911 *A History of the President's Cabinet.* Ann Arbor: University of Michigan Press.

HORN, STEPHEN 1960 *The Cabinet and Congress.* New York: Columbia University Press.

CAHN, EDMOND
(1906–1964)

Edmond Cahn's civil libertarianism emphasized the importance of a written Constitution and the role of the judiciary in upholding the guarantees of the BILL OF RIGHTS. JUDICIAL REVIEW is a historically "legitimate" device, he believed, for "converting promises on parchment into living liberties," and the Supreme Court is "the nation's exemplar and disseminator of democratic values." "The firstness of the FIRST AMENDMENT" ensures "the indefinitely continuing right to be exposed to an ideological variety." SEPARATION OF CHURCH AND STATE strengthens both entities and places sovereignty of choice in the populace. The First Amendment, by securing the basis for participation in the democratic process, provides an indispensable moral link between the governed and the governors.

Cahn's fact-skepticism, continually questioning factual assumptions, led him to indict CAPITAL PUNISHMENT, because a mistake-laden legal system should not impose an irreversible penalty. He insisted that the morally neutral social sciences occupy a subordinate place in judicial decisions and that "a judge untethered by a text is a dangerous instrument." He shared much in common with his friend, Justice HUGO L. BLACK, whose off-Court advocacy of First Amendment ABSOLUTISM he did not explicitly adopt. Cahn, a professor of law at New York University, had great confidence in the democratic citizen, freed from false certainties and protected by the mandates of the Bill of Rights, to prevent or repair injustice.

ROGER K. NEWMAN

CALANDRA, UNITED STATES v.
414 U.S. 338 (1974)

In *Calandra* the Court refused to apply the EXCLUSIONARY RULE to bar a GRAND JURY from questioning a witness on the basis of unlawfully seized EVIDENCE. The Court pointed out that although grand juries are subject to certain constitutional limitations, they are not bound by the restrictive procedures that govern trials. Since the exclusionary rule is not a constitutional right that redresses an invasion of privacy, but rather a deterrent against future police misconduct, its application should be restricted to situations where it will be most effective as a remedy. Exclusion at the grand jury level would deter only those searches in which evidence is intended solely for grand jury use; if the evidence should be presented at a subsequent trial, it would be excluded.

JACOB W. LANDYNSKI

CALDER v. BULL
3 Dallas 386 (1798)

Calder is the leading case on the meaning of the constitutional injunction against EX POST FACTO LAWS. Connecticut had passed an act setting aside a court decree refusing to probate a will, and the plaintiff argued that the act constituted an ex post facto law. In the Court's main opinion Justice SAMUEL CHASE ruled that although all ex post facto laws are necessarily "retrospective," retrospective laws adversely affecting the citizen in his private right of property or contracts are not ex post facto laws. The prohibition against the latter extended only to criminal, not civil, cases. An ex post facto law comprehends any retrospective penal legislation, such as making criminal an act that was not criminal when committed, or aggravating the act into a greater crime than at the time it was committed, or applying increased penalties for the act, or altering the rules of EVIDENCE to increase the chances of conviction.

The case is also significant in constitutional history because by closing the door on the ex post facto route in civil cases, it encouraged the opening of another door and thus influenced the course of the DOCTRINE OF VESTED RIGHTS. The CONTRACT CLAUSE probably would not have attained its importance in our constitutional history, nor perhaps the DUE PROCESS clause substantively construed, if the Court had extended the ex post facto clause to civil cases. In *Calder*, Chase endorsed the judicial doctrine of vested rights drawn from the HIGHER LAW, as announced by Justice WILLIAM PATERSON in VAN HORNE'S LESSEE V. DORRANCE (1795). Drawing on "the very nature of our free Republican governments" and "the great first principles of the social compact," Chase declared that the legislative power, even if not expressly restrained by a written CONSTITUTION, could not constitutionally violate the right of an antecedent and lawful private contract or the right of private property. To assert otherwise, he maintained, would "be a political heresy," inadmissible to the genius and spirit of our governmental system.

Justice JAMES IREDELL concurred in the judgment as well as the definition of ex post facto laws but maintained that judges should not hold an act void "merely because it is, in their judgment, contrary to the principles of natural justice," which he thought undefinable by fixed standards. (See FUNDAMENTAL LAW; SUBSTANTIVE DUE PROCESS.)

LEONARD W. LEVY

CALHOUN, JOHN C.
(1782–1850)

John C. Calhoun, foremost southern statesman of his time, was a product of the great Scots-Irish migration that took possession of the southern backcountry before the American Revolution. Born near Abbeville, South Carolina, young Calhoun received a smattering of education at a local academy and in his twentieth year went "straight from the backwoods" to Yale College. He excelled by force of intellect and zeal. In 1805, not long after graduating, he attended Litchfield Law School. This New England Federalist education left a permanent impression on Calhoun's mind, though all his political associations were Jeffersonian. Returning to South Carolina, he was admitted to the bar and hung out his shingle in Abbeville. But Calhoun did not take to the law. After making it the stepping-stone to the political career he desperately wanted, he gave it up altogether. In 1807 he was elected to the legislature, taking the seat once held by his father. Sometime later he married Floride Bonneau Colhoun, who belonged to the wealthy lowcountry branch of the family, and brought her to the plantation he had acquired above the Savannah River. After two sessions at Columbia, Calhoun won election to the Twelfth Congress. He took his place with the "war hawks" and upon a brilliant maiden speech was hailed as "one of the master-spirits who stamp their name upon the age in which they live."

Calhoun's major biographer has conveniently divided his career into three phases: nationalist, nullifier, sectionalist. During the first, which ended in 1828, Calhoun was successively congressman, secretary of war, and vice-president. As a nationalist, he was the chief congressional architect of the Second Bank of the United States; he supported the tariff of 1816, including its most protective feature, the minimum duty on cheap cotton cloth; and he was a prominent advocate of INTERNAL IMPROVEMENTS. Many Republicans, headed by President JAMES MADISON, believed a constitutional amendment was necessary to sanction federally funded internal improvements. But Calhoun, speaking for his Bonus Bill to create a permanent fund for this purpose, declared that he "was no advocate for refined arguments on the Constitution. The instrument was not intended as a thesis for the logician to exercise his ingenuity on. It ought to be construed with plain, good sense. . . ." He held that the GENERAL WELFARE clause was a distinct power; to those who balked at that, he cited the ENUMERATED POWER to establish post roads. Deeply committed to a system of roads and canals and other improvements to strengthen the Union and secure its defenses, Calhoun, like Hamilton before him, viewed the Constitution as the starting-point for creative statesmanship. Later, when advocating internal improvements as secretary of war, he passed over the constitutional question in silence, thereby avoiding conflict with his chief, JAMES MONROE, who inherited Madison's scruples on the subject.

Calhoun made his first bid for the presidency in 1824 as an unabashed nationalist who professed "to be above all sectional or party feelings and to be devoted to the great interests of the country." He had to settle for the vice-presidency, however; and in that office he seized the first occasion to join the Jacksonian coalition against the National Republican administration of JOHN QUINCY ADAMS. Meanwhile, economic distress revolutionized the politics of South Carolina, driving Calhoun's friends off the nationalist platform and onto the platform of STATES' RIGHTS and STRICT CONSTRUCTION occupied for the past decade by his inveterate enemies. Calhoun was not a leader but a follower—a late one at that—in this movement. By 1827 he, too, had turned against the tariff as the great engine of "consolidation." It was unconstitutional, exploitative of the South, and, with other nationalist measures, it threatened "to make two of one nation." After the "tariff of abominations" the next year, Calhoun, at the request of a committee of the state legislature, secretly penned a lengthy argument against the tariff, showing its unconstitutionality, and expounded the theory of NULLIFICATION as the rightful remedy. (See EXPOSITION AND PROTEST.) The theory was speciously laid in the VIRGINIA AND KENTUCKY RESOLUTIONS. They, of course, were devised to secure the rule of the majority; Calhoun's theory, on the other hand, was intended to protect an aggrieved minority. Moreover, he was precise where those famous resolutions were ambiguous; and, unlike them, he invoked the constitution-making authority of three-fourths of the states. That authority might grant by way of amendment a federal power, such as the protection of manufactures, denied by any one of the states. Calhoun believed that the power of nullification in a single state would act as a healthy restraint on the lawmaking power of Congress; if not, and nullification occurred, the issue would be referred to a convention for decision. Each state being sovereign under this theory, SECESSION was always a last resort; but Calhoun argued that the Union would be strengthened, not weakened or dissolved, under the operation of nullification. Indeed, the Union could be preserved only on the condition of state sovereignty and strict construction—an exact reversal of his earlier nationalist position. The legislature published the *South Carolina Exposition* in December 1828. Although Calhoun's authorship was kept secret for several years, he had become the philosopher-statesman of a movement.

Calhoun hoped for reform from the new administration of ANDREW JACKSON, in which he was, again, the vice-president. But he was quickly disappointed. Personal differences, perhaps more than differences of principle or policy, caused his break with Jackson, completed early in 1831. Laying aside his presidential ambitions—he had hoped to be Jackson's successor—Calhoun issued his Fort Hill Address in July, publicly placing himself at the head of the nullification party in South Carolina. Named for the plantation near Pendleton that was ever after Calhoun's home, the address elaborated the theory set forth in the *Exposition*. When in the following year South Carolina nullified the tariff, it did so in strict conformity with the theory. Calhoun resigned the vice-presidency and was elected to the Senate to lead the state's cause in Washington. He denounced the President's FORCE BILL as a proposition to make war on a sovereign state. In a notable debate with DANIEL WEBSTER, he expounded the theory of the Union as a terminable compact of sovereign states and within that theory vindicated the constitutionality of nullification. (See UNION, THEORIES OF.) But Calhoun backed away from confrontation. He seized the olive branch of tariff reform HENRY CLAY dangled before him. The crisis was resolved peacefully. The nullifiers declared a victory, of course; and Calhoun vaunted himself on the basis of this illusion.

Henceforth, Calhoun abandoned nullification as a remedy and associated his constitutional theory with varying stratagems of sectional resistance to the alleged corruptions and majority tyranny of the general government. The idea of the "concurrent majority," in which the great geographical sections provided the balancing mechanism of estates or classes in classical republican theory, held a more and more important place in his thought. He came to believe that the government of South Carolina, with the balance of legislative power between lowcountry and upcountry established by "the compromise of 1808," embodied this theory. Slavery, of course, was at the bottom of the sectional interest for which Calhoun sought protection. In 1835 he proposed an ingenious solution to the problem of abolitionist agitation through the United States mail. Direct intervention, as Jackson proposed, was unconstitutional, Calhoun said; but the general government could cooperate in the enforcement of state laws that barred "incendiary publications." He thus invented the doctrine of "federal reenforcement" of state laws; and though his bill was defeated, his object was attained by administrative action. Calhoun led the fight in the Senate against the reception of petitions for the abolition of slavery in the DISTRICT OF COLUMBIA. He denied that there was an indefeasible right of petition. Regarding the attack on slavery in the District as an attack on "the outworks" of slavery in the states, he held that the mere reception of the petitions, even if they were immediately tabled, as would become the practice, amounted to an admission of constitutional authority over slavery everywhere. The fight was, therefore, the southern Thermopylae. In 1838, indulging his penchant for metaphysical solutions, Calhoun introduced in the Senate a series of six resolutions which, in principle, would throw a constitutional barricade around slavery wherever it existed—in the states, in the District, and in the territories (Florida then being the only territory). In an allusion to Texas, one resolution declared that refusal to annex territory lest it expand slavery violated the compact of equal sovereign states. This last resolution was dropped, others were modified, and as finally passed the resolutions advanced Calhoun's position by inches rather than yards.

Calhoun never naïvely believed that abolitionism constituted the chief danger to the South. The chief danger was from consolidation, from spoilsmen, from banks and other privileged interests fattening themselves at the public trough, and from the attendant corruption that undermined republican virtue and constitutional safeguards. The only remedy was to strip the government of its excessive revenues, powers, and patronage, and return to the Constitution as it came from the hand of the Framers. For a time, seeing Jackson as the immediate enemy, Calhoun worked with the Whigs; in 1840 he returned to the Democratic fold. He had become convinced that the Democratic party offered better prospects of security for the South. In addition, he hoped to realize his presidential ambition in succession to his old enemy, MARTIN VAN BUREN, in 1844. This was not to be.

The year 1844 found Calhoun secretary of state, engineering the ANNEXATION OF TEXAS, in the shattered administration of John Tyler. Returning to the Senate the following year, he lent his powerful voice to the Oregon settlement, opposed the Mexican War, then became the foremost champion of slavery in the new territories. He set forth his position in resolutions countering the WILMOT PROVISO in 1847: the territories are common property of the states; the general government, as the agent of the states, cannot discriminate against the citizens or institutions of any one in legislating for the territories; the restriction of slavery would be discriminatory; and finally, the people of the territories have the right to form state governments without condition as to slavery. Before long Calhoun repudiated the MISSOURI COMPROMISE and called for the positive protection of SLAVERY IN THE TERRITORIES. The leader of an increasingly militant South, he nevertheless acted, as in the past, to restrain disunionist forces. Secession was never an acceptable solution in his eyes.

The senator's last major speech—he was too ill to deliver it himself—occurred in March 1850 in response to Henry Clay's compromise plan. Calhoun did not so much oppose the measures of this plan as consider them inadequate. The balanced, confederate government of the Constitution had degenerated into a consolidated democracy before which the minority South was helpless. Only by restoring the sectional balance could the Union be saved, and he vaguely suggested a constitutional amendment for this purpose. Within the month he was dead. Two posthumous publications were his political testament. The *Disquisition on Government* contained his political theory, including the key idea of the concurrent majority. The *Discourse on the Constitution* specifically applied the theory to the American polity. After recommending various reforms, such as repeal of the 25th section of the JUDICIARY ACT OF 1789, the *Discourse* concluded with a proposal for radical constitutional

change: a dual executive, elected by North and South, each chief vested with the VETO POWER. This was a metaphysical solution indeed! Yet it was one that epitomized Calhoun's paradoxical relationship to the Constitution. Although he made a fetish of the Constitution, he could never accept its workings and repeatedly advocated fundamental reforms. Although he proclaimed his love of the Union, his embrace was like the kiss of death. And while exalting liberty, he based his ideal republic on slavery and rejected majority rule as incompatible with constitutional government.

MERRILL D. PETERSON

Bibliography

CRALLE, RICHARD K., ED. 1853–1857 *The Works of John C. Calhoun.* 6 Vols. New York: D. Appleton & Co.
MERIWETHER, ROBERT L.; HEMPHILL, W. EDWIN; WILSON, CLYDE N.; and others, eds. 1959–1980 *The Papers of John C. Calhoun.* 8 Vols. to date. Columbia: University of South Carolina Press.
WILTSE, CHARLES M. 1944 *John C. Calhoun: Nationalist, 1782–1828.* Indianapolis: Bobbs-Merrill.
———— 1949 *John C. Calhoun: Nullifier, 1829–1839.* Indianapolis: Bobbs-Merrill.
———— 1951 *John C. Calhoun: Sectionalist, 1840–1850.* Indianapolis: Bobbs-Merrill.

CALIFANO v. GOLDFARB
430 U.S. 199 (1977)
CALIFANO v. WEBSTER
430 U.S. 313 (1977)

These decisions illustrated the delicacy of distinguishing between "benign" gender classifications and unconstitutional ones. *Goldfarb* invalidated, 5–4, a SOCIAL SECURITY ACT provision giving survivor's benefits to any widow but only to a widower who actually had received half his support from his wife. *Webster*, decided three weeks later, unanimously upheld the same law's grant of a higher level of old age benefits to women than to men.

In *Goldfarb* four Justices, led by Justice WILLIAM J. BRENNAN, saw the law as a discrimination against women workers, whose surviving families received less protection. The provision had not been adopted to compensate widows for economic disadvantage but to provide generally for survivors; Congress had simply assumed that wives are usually dependent. Saving the cost of individualized determinations of dependency was also insufficient to justify the discrimination. Four other Justices, led by Justice WILLIAM H.

REHNQUIST, saw the law as a discrimination against male survivors; because the discrimination was not invidious, implying male inferiority or burdening a disadvantaged minority, it should be upheld as "benign." Justice JOHN PAUL STEVENS agreed with Justice Rehnquist that the discrimination ran against men; however, it was only "the accidental byproduct of a traditional way of thinking about females." Lacking more substantial justifications, it was invalid. (See Justice Stevens's concurrence in CRAIG V. BOREN, 1976).

All the Justices in *Webster* agreed that the gender discrimination was not the product of "archaic and overbroad generalizations" about women's dependency but was designed to compensate for women's economic disadvantages. The *Goldfarb* dissenters, concurring separately in *Webster*, suggested that the fine distinction between the two results would produce uncertainty in the law.

KENNETH L. KARST

(SEE ALSO: *Sex Discrimination.*)

CALIFANO v. WEBSTER

See: *Califano v. Goldfarb*

CALIFANO v. WESTCOTT
443 U.S. 76 (1979)

The Supreme Court unanimously found unconstitutional SEX DISCRIMINATION in a federal law providing WELFARE BENEFITS to families whose children were dependent because fathers (but not mothers) were unemployed. The discrimination was based on sexual stereotyping that assumed fathers were breadwinners and mothers homemakers, and was not substantially related to the goal of providing for dependent children. Four Justices would have invalidated the benefits granted by the statute. A majority of five, speaking through Justice HARRY A. BLACKMUN, instead construed the statute to extend benefits to children of unemployed mothers as well as fathers.

KENNETH L. KARST

CALVIN'S CASE
(The Case of the *Post-Nati*)
2 Howell's State Trials 559 (1608)

The assumption of the English throne by King James VI of Scotland in 1603 raised the question of what rights accrued in England to Scotsmen born subsequently (the *post-nati*). The English House of Commons wrecked James's plan for a union of the two kingdoms by refusing to permit the NATURALIZATION of Scotsmen dwelling in England and thereby their right to acquire property as native-born Englishmen did. In *Calvin's Case,* however, Lord Chancellor Ellesmere, speaking for the Courts of Chancery and King's Bench, held that the COMMON LAW conferred such naturalization and, thereby, the rights to inherit, sue, and purchase property. In the final stage of the controversy with Parliament that led to the American Revolution, Americans relied on *Calvin's case* when claiming that they owed allegiance only to George III personally and were not subject to the authority of Parliament.

WILLIAM J. CUDDIHY

CAMARA v. MUNICIPAL COURT
387 U.S. 523 (1967)

In *Camara* the Supreme Court held that the householder may resist warrantless ADMINISTRATIVE SEARCHES of dwellings by inspectors implementing fire, health, housing, and similar municipal codes. However, because the inspection is not a criminal investigation, PROBABLE CAUSE for a warrant may be found without information about the individual dwelling, on the basis of such factors as the date of the last inspection and the condition of the area. Similar protection was accorded to commercial premises in *See v. Seattle* (1967).

JACOB W. LANDYNSKI

CAMDEN, LORD

See: Pratt, Charles

CAMINETTI v. UNITED STATES

See: *Hoke v. United States*

CAMPAIGN FINANCE

Enlargement of the electorate and development of modern communications have heightened the importance of campaign funds for communicating with voters, a purpose less patently wicked or easily regulated than vote-buying and bribery, which have long been illegal.

Modern attempts to regulate campaign financing, which raise sweeping constitutional issues, have been largely centered on the FEDERAL ELECTION CAMPAIGN ACT of 1971 and its various amendments. Federal law has developed along six identifiable lines: prohibitions of bribery and corrupt practices; disclosures of campaign contributions and expenditures; limits on the amount of contributions from individuals and groups; prohibitions against contributions from certain sources, such as corporate or union treasuries; limits on total expenditures; and public financing.

Although the regulation of bribery and corrupt practices does not generally raise significant constitutional issues, all of the other elements of the Federal Election Campaign Act and of comparable state laws do. In BUCKLEY V. VALEO (1976), the landmark case on the constitutionality of political finance regulations, the Supreme Court held that expenditures to advocate the election or defeat of candidates are constitutionally protected speech and may not be limited. Subsequent decisions have held that no limit may be imposed on expenditures in REFERENDUM or INITIATIVE campaigns. And in *Common Cause v. Schmitt* (1982) an evenly divided Court sustained a lower court ruling that limits on expenditures by groups or individuals, acting independently, were impermissible, even when the candidate has agreed to limits as a condition for obtaining campaign public subsidies.

Campaign contributions embody a lesser element of constitutionally protected speech, but they are also an exercise of FREEDOM OF ASSEMBLY AND ASSOCIATION guaranteed in the FIRST AMENDMENT. Contributions may be limited to achieve COMPELLING STATE INTERESTS, such as avoidance of "the actuality and appearance of corruption." The Supreme Court has not yet identified any other compelling interest that justifies limits on campaign contributions. Hence, in *Buckley* the Court voided limits on a candidate's contributions to his own campaign and, in *Citizens Against Rent Control v. Berkeley* (1981), invalidated limits on contributions in referendum campaigns, because in neither case did the contributions pose a danger of corrupting candidates.

The rule against expenditures by and contributions from CORPORATIONS, labor unions, and other specified sources has not yet been tested in court, but its justification is largely undermined by FIRST NATIONAL BANK OF BOSTON V. BELLOTTI (1978), which struck down limits on referendum expenditures by corporations because First Amendment speech rights extend to corporations. Presumably the speech and association rights inherent in making contributions attach to corporations, unions, and other associations,

and only limits necessary to avoid the actuality or appearance of corruption could be applied.

Public subsidies of campaigns and parties have been adopted by Congress and several states. In *Buckley* the Court held that such expenditures are within the ambit of the spending power of the general welfare clause. The Court also sustained a limit on expenditures for candidates who voluntarily accept public subsidies. No unconstitutional discrimination was found in limiting eligibility for subsidies to parties that had received a specified percentage of the vote in a prior election.

The Court has acknowledged that some persons may be deterred from making contributions and others may be subject to harassment if they exercise their constitutional right to make contributions, but substantial governmental interests warrant disclosure because it assists voters to evaluate candidates, deters corruption, and facilitates enforcement of contribution limits. Minor parties and independent candidates, however, because they have only a modest likelihood of coming to power and because they are often unpopular, need show only "a reasonable probability that compelled disclosure . . . of contributors will subject them to threats, harassment, or reprisals" in order to obtain relief from the disclosure requirements. Minor-party expenditures were also held exempt from disclosure, in BROWN V. SOCIALIST WORKERS '74 CAMPAIGN COMMITTEE (1982), to protect First Amendment political activity.

Equality and liberty, both values rooted in the Constitution, come into conflict in regulation of political finance. Limitations on contributions and expenditures have been justified as efforts to equalize the influence of citizens and groups in the political process. Money and the control of technology, especially communications media, pose special problems of scale; the magnitude of potential inequality between citizens far exceeds that which occurs in traditional or conventional political participation.

In balancing First Amendment liberties and the concern for political equality, the Supreme Court has, in the area of campaign finance, consistently given preference to speech and association rights, with little reference to the inequality this may produce between citizens. The Court has sustained limits on contributions only to avoid corruption, not to achieve equality. Similarly, the Court has permitted public subsidies, which equalize funds available to candidates, and expenditure limits attached to such subsidies, which create an equal ceiling on spending. But equality is not the controlling principle; the Court has made clear that candidate participation in public subsidy-and-limitation schemes must be voluntary and that such schemes do not impose ceilings on expenditures by persons acting independently of candidates.

Although equality in the political process has constitutional imprimatur in voting, contemporary constitutional doctrines relating to campaign finance neither acknowledge the validity of equality interests nor provide means for effecting them.

DAVID ADAMANY

Bibliography

NICHOLSON, MARLENE 1977 Buckley v. Valeo: The Constitutionality of the Federal Election Campaign Act Amendments of 1974. *Wisconsin Law Review* 1977:323–374.

CAMPBELL, JOHN A.
(1811–1889)

John Archibald Campbell was the TANEY COURT's most thoughtful advocate of STATES' RIGHTS and, with the exception of JOSEPH STORY, its most penetrating legal scholar. Although never a constitutional doctrinaire like PETER V. DANIEL, Campbell rooted his constitutional jurisprudence in a southern exceptionalism antagonistic to corporate and federal judicial power. Appointed by President Franklin Pierce in March 1853, Campbell served until April 1861 when he resigned to return to Alabama and eventual support for the Confederacy.

Campbell analyzed constitutional disputes as clashes between sovereign entities. He dissented from successful efforts by the majority to expand federal ADMIRALTY JURISDICTION to river waters above the ebb and flow of the tide. In *Jackson v. Steamboat Magnolia* (1858) he ridiculed these efforts as factually incorrect, historically superficial, and purposefully intended to diminish state SOVEREIGNTY. Campbell only once won acceptance for his narrow view of federal admiralty jurisdiction when he persuaded a bare majority in *Taylor v. Carry* (1858) that, where claims against a vessel rested on conflicting state and federal JURISDICTION, the claimants had to proceed under the former.

Justice Campbell's most important decisions involved CORPORATIONS. The Taney Court recognized corporations as citizens, a status that enabled them to seek relief from unfavorable state legislative and judicial action through federal DIVERSITY JURISDICTION. Campbell in 1853 dissented when the Court reaffirmed this position in *Marshall v. Baltimore and Ohio Railroad*. He charged that the majority per- verted the meaning of CITIZENSHIP and crippled state economic regulation.

Campbell also dissented from the majority's view that corporate charters, even when narrowly construed, were contracts in perpetuity. In PIQUA BRANCH BANK V. KNOOP (1854) and DODGE V. WOOLSEY (1856) he insisted, respectively, that state legislatures and CONSTITUTIONAL CONVENTIONS could alter tax-exemption provisions of previously granted charters. The states, Campbell argued, had to retain sovereign power to tax corporations in order to promote the public interest. A political and economic agenda informed Campbell's thinking about corporate CITIZENSHIP and the CONTRACT CLAUSE: federal judicial protection of interstate corporations tilted the balance of national power in favor of northern manufacturing.

Campbell eased the dichotomy between state and federal sovereignty only on questions involving SLAVERY. In DRED SCOTT V. SANDFORD (1857) he concluded that the federal judiciary had a constitutional responsibility to protect slave property. He reiterated the primacy of federal judicial power in cases in the Fifth Circuit involving enforcement of the slave trade and neutrality laws. Like northern federal judges, who enforced the Fugitive Slave Acts, Campbell charged southern federal juries to adhere to a national RULE OF LAW.

During the post-Civil War era Campbell made his most lasting contribution to constitutional jurisprudence as an attorney for the corporations he once attacked. The Supreme Court in the SLAUGHTERHOUSE CASES (1873) narrowly rejected his arguments in behalf of the rights of corporate citizenship and SUBSTANTIVE DUE PROCESS under the FOURTEENTH AMENDMENT, but two decades later the Justices embraced them.

KERMIT L. HALL

Bibliography

SCHMIDHAUSER, JOHN R. 1958 Jeremy Bentham, the Contract Clause, and Justice John Archibald Campbell. *Vanderbilt Law Review* 11:801–820.

CANTWELL v. CONNECTICUT
310 U.S. 296 (1940)

Newton Cantwell and his sons, Jesse and Russell, were arrested in New Haven, Connecticut. As Jehovah's Witnesses and, by definition, ordained ministers, they were engaged in street solicitation. They distributed pamphlets, made statements critical of the Roman Catholic Church, and offered to play for passers-by a phonograph record including an attack on the Roman Catholic religion. The Cantwells were convicted of violating a Connecticut statute that prohibited persons soliciting money for any cause without a certificate issued by the state secretary of the Public Welfare Council. Jesse Cantwell was also convicted of the COMMON LAW offense of inciting a BREACH OF THE PEACE.

Justice OWEN J. ROBERTS delivered the opinion of a unanimous Court: although Connecticut had a legitimate interest in regulating the use of its streets for solicitation, the means the state had chosen infringed upon the RELIGIOUS FREEDOM of solicitors. The secretary appeared to have unlimited discretion to determine the legitimacy of a religious applicant and either issue or withhold the certificate. If issuance had been a "matter of course," the requirement could have been maintained, but so wide an official discretion to restrict activity protected by the free exercise clause was unacceptable. (See PRIOR RESTRAINT.)

The conviction of Jesse Cantwell for inciting breach of the peace was also constitutionally defective. Justice Roberts noted that the open-endedness of the common law concept of breach of the peace offered wide discretion to law enforcement officials. When such a criminal provision was applied to persons engaging in FIRST AMENDMENT-protected speech or exercise of religion there must be a showing of a CLEAR AND PRESENT DANGER of violence or disorder. Although Cantwell's speech was offensive to his listeners, it had not created such a danger.

As a religious freedom precedent, *Cantwell* is important in two ways: first, it made clear that the free exercise clause of the First Amendment applied to the states through the DUE PROCESS clause of the FOURTEENTH AMENDMENT; second, it suggested (in contrast to previous case law, for example, REYNOLDS V. UNITED STATES, 1879) that the free exercise clause protected not only beliefs but also some actions. The protection of belief was absolute, Roberts wrote, but the protection of action was not; it must give way in appropriate cases to legitimate government regulation. The implication was that at least some government regulations of religion-based conduct would be impermissible.

RICHARD E. MORGAN

CAPITAL PUNISHMENT

In 1971, the year before the Supreme Court began its long and tortured experiment in constitutional regulation of the death penalty, Justice JOHN MARSHALL HARLAN issued an ominous warning. In *McGautha*

v. California he said that because of the irreducible moral complexity and subjectivity of capital punishment, any effort to impose formal legal rationality on the choice between life and death for a criminal defendant would prove futile: "To identify before the fact those characteristics of criminal homicides and their perpetrators which call for the death penalty, and to express these characteristics in language which can be fairly understood and applied by the sentencing authority, appear to be tasks which are beyond present human ability."

A constitutional interpreter who accepted Justice Harlan's pronouncement could draw one of at least two possible implications from it. She could conclude that in the face of this moral uncertainty, courts cannot interfere in legislative decisions about capital punishment, for judges have no objective principles to correct legislators. On the other hand, she could conclude that capital punishment must be constitutionally forbidden, because this moral uncertainty means that legislators cannot make the death penalty process conform to the minimal constitutional principles of the RULE OF LAW. But a constitutional interpreter might also conclude that Justice Harlan was unnecessarily cynical, and that an enlightened judicial effort might achieve an acceptable moral and instrumental rationality in the administration of the death penalty. The erratic constitutional history of capital punishment both before and after *McGautha* reflects the stubborn difficulty of these questions. That history reveals a complex, often confused experiment in lawmaking. It also illuminates the fundamental, recurring dilemma that Justice Harlan described, and lends sobering support to his pronouncement.

The Fifth Amendment says that no person "shall be deprived of life . . . without DUE PROCESS OF LAW." Thus, a strict textual reader would easily conclude that the Constitution does not forbid capital punishment per se. And indeed in early America, execution was the automatic penalty for anyone convicted of murder or any of several other felonies. Well into the nineteenth century, a jury that believed a defendant to be guilty of murder had no legal power to save him from death. As the states began to draw distinctions among degrees of murder, a prosecutor had to win a conviction on an aggravated or first-degree murder charge to ensure execution, but, after conviction, the death penalty still lay beyond the legal discretion of the jury.

One potential constitutional restraint on the death penalty lay in the Eighth Amendment prohibition of CRUEL AND UNUSUAL PUNISHMENT. But at least in the Supreme Court's contemporary historical interpretation, *Gregg v. Georgia* (1976), the authors of the cruel and unusual punishment clause did not intend to forbid conventional capital punishment for serious crimes. Rather, the Eighth Amendment, drawing on the English BILL OF RIGHTS of 1689, was intended merely to prohibit any punishments not officially authorized by statute or not lying within the sentencing court's jurisdiction, and any torture or brutal, gratuitously painful methods of execution.

For most of the nineteenth century, American courts placed virtually no constitutional restrictions on capital punishment. Nevertheless, the state legislatures gradually rejected the automatic death penalty scheme. Some legislators may have believed that the automatic death laws were too harsh, and that at least some murderers merited legal mercy. Others, paradoxically, may have felt that the automatic death penalty law actually proved too lenient. A jury that believed a defendant was guilty of first-degree murder, but did not believe he deserved execution, could engage in "jury nullification"—it could act subversively by acquitting the defendant of the murder charge.

In any event, by the early twentieth century most of the states had adopted an entirely new type of death penalty law that gave juries implicit, unreviewable legal discretion in the choice between life and death sentences. The jury was instructed that if it found the defendant guilty of the capital crime, it must then decide between life and death. The jury had no legal guidance in this decision. Moreover, the jury rarely received any general information about the defendant's background, character, or previous criminal record that might be relevant to sentence; it only had the evidence proffered on the guilt issue. Although a few states eliminated capital punishment entirely late in the nineteenth century or early in the twentieth century, the new unguided discretion statute was essentially the model American death penalty law until 1972.

Executions of murderers and rapists were fairly frequent in the United States until the 1960s, though the rate of execution peaked at about 200 per year during the Depression and then dropped during World War II. By the 1960s, however, the long-standing practice of death sentencing through unguided jury discretion began to face increasing moral and political opposition. Beyond any fundamental change in moral attitudes toward state killing itself, the opposition sounded essentially three themes. First, early empirical studies by social scientists cast grave doubt on the major instrumental justification for the death penalty—its general deterrent power over murderers. Second, even informal data on the patterns of execu-

tion under the unguided discretion laws suggested that the criminal justice system in general, and sentencing juries in particular, acted randomly and capriciously in selecting defendants for capital punishment. The process did not treat like cases alike, and no rational principle emerged to explain why some defendants were executed and others of similar crimes or character were not.

Third, to the extent that any pattern emerged at all, it was the unacceptable pattern of race. Critics of the death penalty offered empirical evidence that the race of the defendant was an important factor in a jury's choice between life and death, and that the race of the victim was potentially a still greater factor. Blacks were sentenced to death more often than whites, and people who committed crimes against whites were executed far more often than those who committed crimes against blacks. The racial pattern was absolutely overwhelming in the instance of rape, where virtually all executed rapists were black men convicted of raping white women, but the pattern was powerfully suggestive for murder as well.

As these themes emerged in academic commentary, legal argument, and even public opinion in the late 1960s, the courts faced increasing pressure to impose some legal restraint on the death penalty. In the most important and most enigmatic decision on capital punishment in American history, *Furman v. Georgia* (1972), a muddled consensus of the Supreme Court ignored Justice Harlan's warning and accepted the challenge, if not the ultimate conclusion, of the arguments against capital punishment. All nine Justices wrote separate opinions in *Furman,* and by a vote of 5–4 the Court reversed the death sentences before them. But the five opinions for reversal achieved at best a vague, thematic consensus about the problems with the death penalty, and no majority position on the solution.

Justices WILLIAM J. BRENNAN and THURGOOD MARSHALL alone were clearly persuaded that the death penalty was categorically unconstitutional in all cases. Responding to the powerful textualist argument that the authors of the Constitution and the Bill of Rights contemplated a legal death penalty, the Justices chose to read the Eighth Amendment's cruel and unusual punishments clause as a flexible instrument that could adjust constitutional law to American society's moral development. Thus, "evolving standards of decency," reflected in public opinion, jury behavior, and legislative attitudes, had come to condemn the death penalty. Moreover, the Eighth Amendment authorized judges to examine the moral and instrumental justification for capital punishment, and neither retribution nor general deterrence withstood scrutiny. Retribution was an unworthy moral principle, and general deterrence had no empirical support.

But the *Furman* majority hinged on the more cautious and cryptic views of Justices WILLIAM O. DOUGLAS, BYRON R. WHITE, and POTTER STEWART. They avoided the question of whether capital punishment had become an absolutely forbidden penalty, and instead seemed to conclude that, as administered under the unguided discretion laws, capital punishment had achieved impermissibly random or racially discriminatory effects. Thus, the official signal from *Furman* seemed to be that the states could try yet again to develop sound capital punishment laws that would resolve the dilemma between legal guidance and discretion, though the Court certainly suggested no particular formula for doing so. (See CAPITAL PUNISHMENT CASES OF 1972.)

The immediate effect of *Furman* was to suspend all executions for a few years while about three-fourths of the state legislatures prepared their responses. The responses took two statutory forms. Ironically, a few states "solved" the problem of unguided discretion by completely eliminating discretion. Essentially, they returned to the early nineteenth-century model of the automatic death penalty, at least for those convicted of the most serious aggravated murders. Most of the states that restored the death penalty, however, chose a subtler, compromise approach, which might be called the "guided discretion" statute. A rough common denominator of these guided discretion statutes is a separate hearing on the question of penalty after a defendant is convicted of first degree murder. This hearing is a novel cross between the traditional discretionary sentencing hearing conducted by a trial judge in noncapital cases, and a formal, if abbreviated, criminal trial. In most states, the jury decides the penalty, though in a few states the judge either decides the penalty alone or has power to override a jury recommendation on penalty.

The matters at issue in this hearing consist of aggravating and mitigating factors which the two sides may establish. These factors partly overlap with the issues that would be resolved at the guilt trial, but comprehend new information about the defendant's character or background, which would normally be legally irrelevant at the guilt trial. Thus, the prosecution may establish that the defendant committed the murder in an especially heinous or sadistic way; that the victim was a specially protected person such as a police officer; that the murder was for hire or for some other form of pecuniary gain; that the murder was committed in the course of a rape, robbery, or burglary; or that the defendant had a substantial record of earlier violent crimes. Conversely, the defense may introduce evidence that the defendant, though unable to prove legal insanity, was emotionally impaired or under the influence of drugs at the time of the crime; that he was young, or had no serious criminal record; that he had suffered serious abuse or neglect as a child; or that since arrest he had demonstrated remorse and model prison behavior.

The sentencing judge or jury hears these factors and orders execution only if, according to some statutory formula, the aggravating circumstances outweigh the mitigating. Most of the statutes expressly enumerated these factors, and in addition provided for automatic appellate review of the death sentence. Many also required the state appellate court to conduct periodic "proportionality reviews" of death and life sentences in comparable murder cases, to ensure that the new system avoided the problem of caprice denounced in *Furman*.

In 1976 the states returned to the Supreme Court to learn whether they had properly met the obscure challenge of *Furman*. In a cluster of five cases handed down the same day, the Court once again failed to produce a majority opinion. Justices Brennan and Marshall would have struck down both types of statutes. Chief Justice WARREN E. BURGER and Justices HARRY A. BLACKMUN, BYRON R. WHITE, and WILLIAM H. REHNQUIST would have upheld both types of statutes. The swing plurality of Justices Potter Stewart, LEWIS F. POWELL, and JOHN PAUL STEVENS thus decided the constitutional fate of capital punishment, and the outcome, at least, of the 1976 cases was clear: the automatic death penalty statutes fell and the new guided discretion statutes survived.

First, in *Woodson v. North Carolina*, the plurality rejected the new automatic death laws as misguided solutions to the problem of discretion. These statutes were too rigid to capture the quality of individualized mercy required in death sentencing, and only revived the problem of "jury nullification" that had plagued the old automatic sentencing more than a century earlier. Second, in the key opinion in *Gregg v. Georgia* (1976) the plurality upheld the new guided discretion statutes as the proper solution to the complex of problems discerned in *Furman*. To do so, of course, the plurality had to reject the categorical arguments against the death penalty made by Justices Marshall and Brennan in *Furman*, and so it squarely held that the death penalty does not inevitably violate the BILL OF RIGHTS. The plurality opinion accepted retribution as a justifiable basis for execution, in particular because state-enacted revenge on murderers might prevent the more socially disruptive risk of private revenge. The plurality also found the empirical evidence of the general deterrent power of capital punishment to be equivocal, and declared that in the face of equivocal evidence, judges had to defer to popular and legislative judgments. Thus, the simple fact that three-fourths of the state legislatures had chosen to reenact the death penalty after *Furman* became a primary ground for the general constitutional legitimacy of capital punishment. The plurality relied on the curious principle that the state legislatures, which are supposedly subject to the Eighth Amendment, had become a major source of the evolving moral consensus that could determine the meaning of the Eighth Amendment.

The plurality then examined the Georgia guided discretion statute, as well as the statutes of Florida and Texas, in *Proffitt v. Florida* and *Jurek v. Texas*. It concluded that the substantive and procedural elements of the new concept of the penalty hearing, combined with the promise of strict appellate review, indicated that these statutes, on their face, were constitutionally sufficient to prevent the random and racist effects of the old unguided discretion laws. (See CAPITAL PUNISHMENT CASES OF 1976).

A year later, with the execution of Gary Gilmore in Utah, capital punishment was effectively restored in America. But because of the uncertain meaning of *Gregg*, the rate of execution, compared to the rate of death sentencing, remained very low for several years thereafter. While *Gregg* probably foreclosed any argument that capital punishment was fundamentally unconstitutional, it confirmed that the operation of the death penalty laws remained subject to very strict due process-style constraints. Thus, the death penalty defense bar quickly found numerous legal arguments for challenging particular death sentences or particular elements of the new state statutes. Some of the new legal claims involved state law issues: The new aggravating circumstances that entered the law of homicide after *Furman* had made state substantive criminal law doctrine far more complex than before.

Most of the new claims, however, were constitutional. In one series of cases, the court extended "Eighth Amendment due process" by imposing a sort of revived WARREN COURT criminal procedure jurisprudence on the state death penalty hearing. It gave capital defendants a CONFRONTATION right to rebut aggravating evidence in *Gardner v. Florida* (1977), and a COMPULSORY PROCESS right to present hearsay mitigating evidence in *Green v. Georgia* (1979); it

applied the due process "void-for-vagueness" principle to aggravating factors in *Godfrey v. Georgia* (1980) and the RIGHT AGAINST SELF-INCRIMINATION and RIGHT TO COUNSEL to penalty phase investigation in ESTELLE V. SMITH (1981); and it applied the principles of DOUBLE JEOPARDY to penalty phase determination in *Bullington v. Missouri* (1981). As the Court extended "Eighth Amendment due process," the defense bar pushed the lower courts still further to shape the penalty hearing into a formal criminal trial. It claimed, for example, that the Sixth and Eighth Amendments guaranteed the capital defendant a jury trial at the penalty phase, and that the jury had to apply the reasonable doubt standard to any choice of death over life.

At the same time, though it had foreclosed categorical arguments against the death penalty as a punishment for murder, the Court drew another line of decisions effectively limiting the death penalty to the crime of aggravated murder. In COKER V. GEORGIA (1977) the Court held that the death penalty was categorically disproportionate as a punishment for rape of adult women—and, by implication, for any non-homicidal crime. In so holding, it noted that the great majority of states had repealed the death penalty for rape, and thus continued the method of legislation—counting as a form of constitutional jurisprudence. Yet the Court also engaged in its own moral balancing of the severity of the crime of rape and the severity of the sentence of death, claiming under the Eighth Amendment some independent power to determine when a punishment was so disproportionate as to be "cruel and unusual." The Court further applied this jurisprudence of legislative consensus finding and moral reasoning in ENMUND V. FLORIDA (1982). There, the Court forbade the death penalty as punishment for certain attenuated forms of unintentional felony murder.

After the Court had refined the new constitutional law of the death penalty, the process of appellate litigation in the state supreme courts—and even more so in federal district courts on HABEAS CORPUS petitions—became increasingly complex. It also became increasingly prolonged: the vast majority of defendants sentenced to death under the new laws were likely never to suffer execution, and for those that did, the time between original sentence and execution was often as long as ten years. Meanwhile, the Supreme Court encountered an ever increasing caseload of death penalty cases, in which it was continually asked to fine-tune still further the new constitutional regulation of capital punishment. But the Court's effort at formal legal regulation began to seem self-perpetuating, endlessly creating new grounds for reversible error. The appellate and habeas corpus courts were increasingly overwhelmed with death cases.

The Court recognized that it had exacerbated, not resolved, the inescapable tension between rational legal constraint and subjective jury discretion in the administration of capital punishment, and it began an effort to change course. The result, however, was that it was soon moving confusingly in both directions at once as it faced the fundamental—and perennial—legal issue: the feasibility of strict statutory rules, rather than open-ended discretionary standards, in choosing which defendants should die.

Ironically, perhaps the key decision in explaining the apparent unraveling of the Court's effort at constitutional regulation in the death penalty was a great defense victory—*Lockett v. Ohio* (1978). There, the Court held that the state must permit the sentencing judge or jury to give independent consideration to any mitigating factors about the defendant's character, crime, or record that the defense could reasonably proffer, even if those factors fell outside the state statute's carefully enumerated list of mitigating factors. The Court took the view that the moral principles of individualized sentencing demanded a degree of jury discretion that no formal statutory list could capture. The echo of Justice Harlan's 1971 warning was obvious. The Court faced the argument that *Lockett* had, ironically, revived all the problems of unguided jury discretion it had denounced in *Furman* and purported to resolve in *Gregg*.

The defense bar quickly lent support to this view, inundating the lower courts with *Lockett* claims that exploited the vast moral relativism of the concept of mitigation. Defendants sought to introduce evidence unrelated to technical criminal responsibility yet vaguely related to their moral deserts, such as evidence of upright, citizenlike conduct in prison while awaiting trial, or of late-found literary promise. The proffered mitigating evidence sometimes was not about the defendant's character at all: a defendant had a loving family that would suffer terribly if he died young; or, however culpable the defendant was, he had an equally culpable accomplice who had managed to gain a plea to a noncapital charge. Other defendants argued that a jury could not make a sound normative judgment about penalty unless it heard detailed evidence about the gruesome physical facts of execution. Still others read *Lockett* as mandating that a jury must receive an explicit instruction that it had full legal power to exercise mercy. It could spare a defendant after consulting its subjective assessment of his moral deserts, regardless of the technical outcome of its measurement of formal aggravating and mitigating factors.

A few years after *Lockett*, facing the complaint that it had revived, at least on the defendant's side, the very unguided discretion that *Furman* purported to prohibit, the Court arrived at a crudely symmetrical solution. In a bizarrely obscure pair of decisions, *Zant v. Stephens* and *Barclay v. Florida* (1983), the Court held that the state, in effect, had its own *Lockett* rights: so long as the sentencing judge or jury established at least one statutorily defined aggravating factor, it could also take account of aggravating factors about the defendant's crime or character that did not appear on the statute's enumerated list. Having taken an important, if ambivalent, step toward regulating capital punishment, the Court, perhaps reflecting simply its own weariness at the overload of death cases before it, had embarked on deregulation. Along with *Zant* and *Barclay*, the Court began, in *California v. Ramos* (1983) and *Pulley v. Harris* (1984), to remove most formal restrictions on such things as prosecution closing argument in the penalty phase and state appellate proportionality review. In *Spaziano v. Florida* (1984) the Court made clear that the apparent trial-like formality of the penalty phase did not create any defense right to jury sentencing. Once again, Justice Harlan echoed ominously.

In any event, partly because the Court has begun to narrow the grounds on which capital defendants can claim legal error, the execution rate has begun a slow but steady increase, with the number of post-*Furman* executions passing fifty in 1985. For the foreseeable future, a tired and conservative Court is not likely to entertain many dramatic procedural or substantive attacks on the death penalty, and so capital punishment has achieved political, if not intellectual stability.

A remarkable irony, though, lies in one remaining possibility for a very broad attack on the death penalty. In the years since *Furman*, social scientists have conducted more sophisticated empirical studies of patterns of death sentencing and have uncovered evidence of random and racially disparate effects similar to the evidence that helped bring down the old unguided discretion laws in *Furman*. Most important, studies using multiple regression analysis have found significant evidence that, holding all other legitimate factors constant, murderers of whites are far more likely to suffer the death sentence than murderers of blacks.

One of the obvious implications of this evidence is that though the new guided discretion statutes reviewed in *Gregg* at first looked like they would meet the demands of *Furman,* they now may have proved failures. If so, there is no reason not to declare capital punishment unconstitutional yet again. It would seem politically unrealistic to think that the court would now accept this implication. But it is nevertheless important to consider how one might reconcile this evidence with the modern constitutional doctrine of capital punishment.

One could finesse the issue by taking the view that no system can be perfect and that the statistical discrepancy is insignificant. Or one could acknowledge that the discrepancy is significant and disturbing, but still ascribe it to the inevitable, often unconscious prejudices of jurors, rather than to any deliberate racist conduct by legislators or prosecutors. If so, one might conclude that the Constitution requires the states to do only what is morally possible, not what is morally perfect. To put the matter in doctrinal terms, one could engage in some mildly revisionist history of *Furman* and *Gregg.* That is, one could say that *Furman* only required the state legislatures to make their best efforts to devise rational, neutral death penalty laws, that *Gregg* had upheld the new guided discretion statutes on their face as proof that the state legislatures had made that effort successfully, and that constitutional law has no more to say about capital punishment. Whatever the conclusion, capital punishment has given constitutional doctrine making one of its most vexing challenges.

ROBERT WEISBERG

(SEE ALSO: *Barefoot v. Estelle, 1983.*)

Bibliography

BEDAU, HUGO ADAM (1967)1982 *The Death Penalty in America.* Oxford: Oxford University Press.

BERNS, WALTER 1979 *For Capital Punishment.* New York: Basic Books.

BOWERS, WILLIAM J., with PIERCE, GLENN L. 1984 *Legal Homicide: Death as Punishment in America, 1864–1982.* Boston: Northeastern University Press.

DEATH PENALTY SYMPOSIUM 1985 *U.C. Davis Law Review* 18:865–1480.

GRANUCCI, ANTHONY F. 1969 Nor Cruel and Unusual Punishments Inflicted: The Original Meaning. *California Law Review* 57:839–865.

GROSS, SAMUEL R. and MAURO, ROBERT 1985 Patterns of Death: An Analysis of Racial Disparities in Capital Sentencing and Homicide Victimization. *Stanford Law Review* 37:27–153.

LEMPERT, RICHARD 1981 Desert and Deterrence: An Assessment of the Moral Bases of the Case for Capital Punishment. *Michigan Law Review* 79:1177–1231.

WEISBERG, ROBERT 1983 Deregulating Death. *Supreme Court Review* 1983:304–395.

CAPITAL PUNISHMENT CASES OF 1972

Furman v. Georgia
Jackson v. Georgia
Branch v. Texas
408 U.S. 238 (1972)

The Eighth Amendment clearly and expressly forbids the infliction of CRUEL AND UNUSUAL PUNISHMENTS (a prohibition that since 1947 has applied to the states as well as to the national government), and opponents of CAPITAL PUNISHMENT have long argued that to execute a convicted criminal, whatever his crime, is such a punishment. It was obviously not so regarded by the persons who wrote and ratified the BILL OF RIGHTS. They acknowledged the legitimacy of the death penalty when, in the Fifth Amendment, they provided that no person "shall be held to answer for a capital . . . crime, unless on a PRESENTMENT or INDICTMENT of a GRAND JURY," and when in the same amendment they provided that no one shall, for the same offense, "be twice put in jeopardy of life or limb," and when they forbade not the taking of life as such but the taking of life "without DUE PROCESS OF LAW" (a formulation repeated in the FOURTEENTH AMENDMENT). The question of the original understanding of "cruel and unusual" is put beyond any doubt by the fact that the same First Congress that proposed the Eighth Amendment also provided for the death penalty in the first Crimes Act. In 1958, however, the Supreme Court, in the course of holding deprivation of CITIZENSHIP to be a cruel and unusual punishment, accepted the argument that the meaning of cruel and unusual is relative to time and place; the Eighth Amendment, the Court said in TROP V. DULLES (1958), "must draw its meaning from the evolving standards of decency that mark the progress of a maturing society." Implicit in this statement is the opinion that society, as it matures, becomes gentler, and as it becomes gentler, it is more disposed to regard the death penalty as cruel and unusual. According to one member of the five-man majority in the 1972 cases, that point had been reached: "capital punishment," wrote Justice THURGOOD MARSHALL, "is morally unacceptable to the people of the United States at this time in their history."

This assessment of the public's opinion could not reasonably provide the basis of the Court's judgment in these cases; contrary to Marshall, the polls showed a majority in favor of the death penalty and, more to the point, there were at that time some 600 persons on death row, which is to say, some 600 persons on whom the American people, acting through their federal and state courts, had imposed death sentences. Marshall's assessment was also belied by the reaction to the Court's decision: Congress and thirty-five states promptly enacted new death penalty statutes, and it is fair to assume that they did so with the consent of their respective popular majorities. The states remained authorized, or at least not forbidden, to do so, because the Court did not declare the death penalty as such to be a cruel and unusual punishment; only two members of the 1972 majority adopted that position. Justice WILLIAM J. BRENNAN said that the death penalty, for whatever crime imposed, "does not comport with human dignity." Marshall, in addition to finding it to be morally unacceptable, said its only possible justification was not that it was an effective deterrent (he accepted Thorsten Sellin's evidence that it was not) but as a form of retribution, a way to pay criminals back, and, he said, the Eighth Amendment forbade "retribution for its own sake." The other majority Justices found the death penalty to be cruel and unusual only insofar as the statutes permitted it to be imposed discriminatorily (WILLIAM O. DOUGLAS), or arbitrarily and capriciously (POTTER STEWART), or (because it is imposed infrequently) pointlessly or needlessly (BYRON R. WHITE).

That the death penalty has historically been imposed, if not capriciously, then at least in a racially and socially discriminatory fashion seems to be borne out by the statistics. Of the 3,859 persons executed in the United States during the years 1930–1967, when, for a time, executions ceased, 2,066, or fifty-four percent, were black. Georgia alone executed 366 persons, of whom 298 were black. Although American juries have shown increasing reluctance to impose the death penalty (despite the majority sentiment in favor of it in principle), they have been less reluctant to impose it on certain offenders, offenders characterized not by their criminality but by their race or class. "One searches our chronicles in vain for the execution of any members of the affluent strata in this society," said Douglas. "The Leopolds and Loebs are given prison terms, not sentenced to death." The three cases decided in 1972 illustrate his argument. The statutes (two from Georgia, one from Texas) empowered the juries to choose between death and imprisonment for

the crimes committed (murder in the one case and rape in the other two), and in each case the jury chose death. As crimes go, however, those committed here were not especially heinous. In the *Furman* case, for example, the offender entered a private home at about 2 A.M. intending to burglarize it. He was carrying a gun. When heard by the head of the household, William Micke, a father of five children, Furman attempted to flee the house. He tripped and his gun discharged, hitting Micke through a closed door and killing him. Furman was quickly apprehended, and in due course tried and convicted. The salient facts would appear to be these: the offender was black and the victim was white, which was also true in the other two cases decided that day.

By holding that the death penalty, as it has been administered in this country, is a cruel and unusual punishment, the Supreme Court challenged the Congress and the state legislatures, if they insisted on punishing by executing, to devise statutes calculated to prevent the arbitrary or discriminatory imposition of the penalty.

WALTER BERNS

Bibliography

BERNS, WALTER 1979 *For Capital Punishment: Crime and the Morality of the Death Penalty.* New York: Basic Books.

BLACK, CHARLES L., JR. 1974 *Capital Punishment: The Inevitability of Caprice and Mistake.* New York: Norton.

LEVY, LEONARD 1974 *Against the Law: The Nixon Court and Criminal Justice.* Pages 383–420. New York: Harper & Row.

SELLIN, THORSTEN 1980 *The Penalty of Death.* Beverley Hills, Calif.: Sage Publications.

VAN DEN HAAG, ERNEST 1975 *Punishing Criminals: Concerning a Very Old and Painful Question.* Pages 225–228. New York: Basic Books.

CAPITAL PUNISHMENT CASES OF 1976

Gregg v. Georgia, 428 U.S. 153
Jurek v. Texas, 428 U.S. 262
Proffitt v. Florida, 428 U.S. 242
Woodson v. North Carolina, 428 U.S. 280
Roberts v. Louisiana, 428 U.S. 325
Green v. Oklahoma, 428 U.S. 907

Writing for the Supreme Court in *McGautha v. California* (1971), only a year before the CAPITAL PUNISHMENT CASES OF 1972, Justice JOHN MARSHALL

HARLAN said, "To identify before the fact those characteristics of criminal homicides and their perpetrators which call for the death penalty, and to express these characteristics in language which can fairly be understood and applied by the sentencing authority, appear to be tasks which are beyond present human ability." Yet, in *Furman v. Georgia* (1972), by declaring unconstitutional statutes that permitted arbitrary, capricious, or discriminatory imposition of the death penalty, the Court challenged the Congress and the various state legislatures to write new statutes that did express in advance the characteristics that would allow the sentencing authorities to distinguish between what is properly a capital and what is properly a noncapital case. The statutes involved in the 1976 cases were drafted in the attempt to meet these requirements.

Three states (North Carolina, Louisiana, Oklahoma) attempted to meet them by making death the mandatory sentence in all first-degree murder cases, thereby depriving juries of all discretion, at least in the sentencing process. By the narrowest of margins, the Court found these mandatory sentencing laws unconstitutional. Justices WILLIAM J. BRENNAN and THURGOOD MARSHALL held to their views expressed in the 1972 cases that the death penalty is unconstitutional per se. In the 1976 cases they were joined by Justices POTTER STEWART, LEWIS F. POWELL, and JOHN PAUL STEVENS (new on the Court since the 1972 decisions) who held, in part, that it was cruel and unusual to treat alike all persons convicted of a designated offense. Their view was that no discretion is as cruel as unguided discretion.

The three statutes upheld in 1976 (those from Georgia, Texas, and Florida) permitted jury sentencing discretion but attempted to reduce the likelihood of abuse to a tolerable minimum. All three statutes, and especially the one from Georgia, embodied procedures intended to impress on judge and jury the gravity of the judgment they are asked to make in capital cases. For example, all three required the sentencing decision to be separated from the decision as to guilt or innocence. In one way or another, all three implied that a sentence of death must be regarded as an extraordinary punishment not to be imposed in an ordinary case, even an ordinary case of first-degree murder. For example, the Georgia law required (except in a case of treason or aircraft hijacking) a finding beyond a REASONABLE DOUBT of the presence of at least one of the aggravating circumstances specified in the statute (for example, that the murder "was outrageously and wantonly vile, horrible and inhuman"),

and required the sentencing authority to specify the circumstance found. In addition, the trial judge was required to instruct the jury to consider "any mitigating circumstances" (an element that was to play an important role in the 1978 capital punishment cases). Finally, Georgia required or permitted an expedited APPEAL to or review by the state supreme court, directing that court to determine whether, for example, "the sentence of death was imposed under the influence of passion, prejudice, or any other arbitrary factor," or was "excessive or disproportionate to the penalty imposed in similar cases, considering both the crime and the defendant."

These statutes went to great lengths to do what Harlan in *McGautha* had said could not be done but which, in effect, the Court in 1972 had said must be done: to characterize in advance the cases in which death is an appropriate punishment, or in which the sentencing authority (whether judge or jury) is entitled to decide that the death penalty is appropriate. With only Brennan and Marshall dissenting, the Court agreed that all three statutes met the constitutional requirements imposed four years earlier.

From the 1976 decisions emerged the following rules: the death penalty in and of itself is not a cruel and unusual punishment; a death sentence may not be carried out unless the sentencing authority is guided by reasonably clear statutory standards; in imposing the penalty, the sentencing authority must consider the characteristics of the offender and the circumstances of his offense; mandatory death sentences for murder (and presumably for all other offenses) are unconstitutional; the punishment must not be inflicted in a way that causes unnecessary pain; finally, the death penalty may not be imposed except for heinous crimes ("the punishment must not be grossly out of proportion to the severity of the crime").

The Court's decisions were a bitter disappointment not only to the hundreds of persons on death row who now seemingly faced the real prospect of being executed but also to the equally large number of persons who had devoted their time, talent, and in some cases their professional careers to the cause of abolishing the death penalty.

They had been making progress toward that end. In other Western countries, including Britain, Canada, and France, the death penalty had either been abolished by statute or been allowed to pass into desuetude; in the United States almost a decade had passed since the last legal execution. In this context it was easy for the opponents of capital punishment to see the Supreme Court's 1972 decision as a step along the path leading inevitably to complete and final abolition of the death penalty. This hope was dashed, at least temporarily, in 1976.

Not only did the Court for the first time squarely hold that "the punishment of death does not invariably violate the Constitution" but it also gave explicit support to the popular principle that punishment must fit the crime and that, in making this calculation, the community may pay back the worst of its criminals with death. Prior to 1976, the capital punishment debate had focused on the deterrence issue, and a major effort had been made by social scientists to demonstrate the absence of evidence showing the death penalty to be a more effective deterrent than, for example, life imprisonment. This opinion was challenged in 1975 by University of Chicago econometrician Isaac Ehrlich. Employing multiple regression analysis, Ehrlich concluded that each execution might have had the effect of deterring as many as eight murders. His findings were made available to the Court in an AMICUS CURIAE brief filed in a 1975 case by the solicitor general of the United States. In the 1976 opinion announcing the judgment of the Court, Stewart cited the Ehrlich study, acknowledged that it had provoked "a great deal of debate" in the scholarly journals, but nevertheless concluded that, at least for some potential murderers, "the death penalty undoubtedly is a significant deterrent." If this conclusion remains undisturbed, the focus of the capital punishment debate will shift to the issue of human dignity or the propriety of retribution. Thus, Stewart's statement on paying criminals back takes on added significance. With the concurrence of six Justices, he said, "the decision that capital punishment may be the appropriate sanction in extreme cases is an expression of the community's belief that certain crimes are themselves so grievous an affront to humanity that the only adequate response may be the penalty of death."

This sanctioning of the retributive principle especially disturbed Marshall, one of the two dissenters. Along with many opponents of the death penalty, he would be willing to allow executions if they could be shown to serve some useful purpose—for example, deterring others from committing capital crimes—but to execute a criminal simply because society demands its pound of flesh is, he said, to deny him his "dignity and worth." Why it would not deprive a person of dignity and worth to use him (by executing him) in order to influence the behavior of other persons, Marshall did not say; apparently he would be willing to accept society's calculations but not its moral judgments.

An unwillingness to accept society's moral judgments best characterizes the opposition to capital punishment, a fact reflected in the differences between popular and sophisticated opinion on the subject. Sophisticated opinion holds that the death penalty does not comport with human dignity because, as Brennan (the other dissenter) said, it treats "members of the human race as nonhumans, as objects to be toyed with and discarded." Popular opinion holds that to punish criminals, even to execute them, is to acknowledge their humanity, insofar as it regards them, as it does not regard other creatures, as responsible moral beings. Sophisticated opinion agrees with ABE FORTAS who, after he left the Supreme Court, argued that the "essential value" of our civilization is the "pervasive, unqualified respect for life"; this respect for life forbids the taking of even a murderer's life. Popular opinion holds that what matters is not *that* one lives but *how* one lives, and that society rightly praises its heroes, who sacrifice their lives for their fellow citizens, and rightly condemns the worst of its criminals who prey upon them.

In 1976, seven members of the Supreme Court agreed that society is justified in making this severe moral judgment, but this agreement on the principle may prove to be less significant than the Justices' inability to join in a common opinion of the Court. Embodied in that inability were differences in the extent to which the Justices were committed to the principle, and it could have been predicted that, in future cases, some of them would find reason not to apply it.

WALTER BERNS

Bibliography

BERNS, WALTER 1979 *For Capital Punishment: Crime and the Morality of the Death Penalty.* New York: Basic Books.

DAVIS, PEGGY C.; WOLFGANG, MARVIN E.; GIBBS, JACK P.; VAN DEN HAAG, ERNEST; and NAKELL, BARRY 1978 Capital Punishment in the United States: A Symposium. *Criminal Law Bulletin* 14:5–80.

EHRLICH, ISAAC 1975 The Deterrent Effect of Capital Punishment. *American Economic Review* 65:397–417.

ENGLAND, JANE C. 1977 Capital Punishment in the Light of Constitutional Evolution: An Analysis of Distinctions Between *Furman* and *Gregg. Notre Dame Lawyer* 52:596–610.

GILLERS, STEPHEN 1980 Deciding Who Dies. *University of Pennsylvania Law Review* 129:1–124.

LEMPERT, RICHARD O. 1981 Desert and Deterrence: An Assessment of the Moral Bases for Capital Punishment. *Michigan Law Review* 79:1177–1231.

CAPITATION TAXES

A capitation tax, or POLL TAX, is a tax levied on persons. A capitation tax takes a fixed amount for each person subject to it, without regard to income or property. Under Article I, section 9, any federal capitation tax must be apportioned among the states according to population, a restriction originally intended to prevent Congress from taxing states out of existence.

In the twentieth century some states made payment of capitation taxes a qualification for voting, usually in order to reduce the number of black voters. The TWENTY-FOURTH AMENDMENT and HARPER V. VIRGINIA BOARD OF ELECTIONS (1966) ended this practice.

DENNIS J. MAHONEY

(SEE ALSO: *Direct and Indirect Taxes; Excise Tax.*)

CAPTIVE AUDIENCE

The Supreme Court has encountered conflicts between FREEDOM OF SPEECH and PRIVACY. In some cases speech conflicts with a nonspeech interest, such as a claimed right to preserve one's peace and quiet. In other cases speech interests may be discerned on both sides; the listener objects to having to hear an uncongenial message. The notion of "captive audience" refers to both types of case. The right not to be compelled to listen to unwelcome messages may be viewed as a corollary to the right not to be compelled to profess what one does not believe, announced in WEST VIRGINIA BOARD OF EDUCATION V. BARNETTE (1943).

Justice WILLIAM O. DOUGLAS first argued the rights of captive auditors in a dissent in *Public Utilities Commission v. Pollak* (1952). His views reemerged in *Lehman v. Shaker Heights* (1974). There a city-owned transit system devoted transit advertising space solely to commercial and public service messages, refusing space to a political candidate. Four Justices held that placard space in city-owned buses and street cars did not constitute a PUBLIC FORUM because the space was incidental to a commercial transportation venture. Admitting, however, that city ownership implicated STATE ACTION, the four agreed that the transit system's advertising policies must not be "arbitrary, capricious, or invidious." The ban on political advertising was a reasonable means "to minimize chances of abuse, the appearance of favoritism and the risk of imposing upon a captive audience."

Justice Douglas concurred. His main point was that commuters, forced onto public transit as a economic

necessity, should not be made a captive audience to placard advertising they cannot "turn off." They have a right to be protected from political messages that they are totally without freedom of choice to receive or reject.

The dissenters argued that, whether or not buses and streetcars were special-purpose publically owned property that could be denied public forum status, the city could not constitutionally discriminate among placard messages on the basis of their content.

A finding that a public forum did exist would likely be decisive for the captive audience issue. Surely there is only the most attenuated "right not to receive" when one enters a public forum whose very definition is that it is open to all senders; those who do not wish to receive a particular visual message are expected to turn away their eyes. *Lehman* and COHEN V. CALIFORNIA (1971) illustrate this tension between the public forum and captive audience concepts.

MARTIN SHAPIRO

Bibliography

BLACK, CHARLES 1953 He Cannot Choose but Hear: The Plight of the Captive Auditor. *Columbia Law Review* 53:960–974.

CAHILL, SHEILA M. 1975 The Public Forum: Minimum Access, Equal Access and the First Amendment. *Stanford Law Review* 28:117–148.

CARDOZO, BENJAMIN N.
(1870–1938)

The towering professional and public reputation that OLIVER WENDELL HOLMES enjoyed when he retired from the Supreme Court in 1932 contributed to President HERBERT HOOVER's selection of Benjamin Nathan Cardozo as his successor despite the fact that there were already two New Yorkers and one Jew on the Supreme Court. Cardozo was one of the very few lawyers in the country whose reputation resembled that of Holmes. A series of famous opinions, his extrajudicial writings, especially *The Nature of the Judicial Process*, his position as chief judge of an able New York Court of Appeals, and his almost saintlike demeanor propelled him into prominence and combined with the usual exigencies of fate and political calculation to put him onto the Supreme Court.

During his five and one-half terms on the Supreme Court from 1932 to 1938, one of Cardozo's major contributions was his demonstration of the utility of COMMON LAW techniques to elaboration of the FOURTEENTH AMENDMENT. Ever since the passage of that amendment, a substantial body of constitutional thought has sought to prevent, or at least to limit, the substantive interpretation of its open-ended provisions. The line stretches from the SLAUGHTERHOUSE CASES (1873) through LEARNED HAND to the current day. The arguments in the 1980s are considerably more complex and theoretical than they were in the nineteenth century and in the 1920s and 1930s. Yet the underlying theme remains essentially the same: the inappropriateness in a democratic society of a nonelected court giving substantive content to broad constitutional phrases such as DUE PROCESS OF LAW and EQUAL PROTECTION OF THE LAWS because of the lack of appropriate sources of judicial law for such an endeavor. The controversies in Cardozo's day revolved around the use of the due process clauses and the equal protection clause to test both the economic legislation that marked an increasingly regulatory society and the numerous infringements by government of individual rights. Although Cardozo's political and social outlook differed somewhat from those of his predecessors on the Court, Holmes, LOUIS D. BRANDEIS, and HARLAN FISKE STONE, he shared the general substantive constitutional outlook that they had espoused for many years: great deference to legislative judgments in economic matters but a more careful scrutiny to constitutional claims of governmental violation of CIVIL RIGHTS in noneconomic matters.

Thus Cardozo was consistently to be found joining those members of the Court, especially Brandeis and Stone, who voted to uphold ECONOMIC REGULATION against attack on COMMERCE CLAUSE, due process, and equal protection grounds. He wrote some of the more eloquent dissents, *Liggett v. Lee* (1933) (Florida chain store tax), PANAMA REFINING COMPANY V. RYAN (1935) (the "hot oil" provision of the NATIONAL INDUSTRIAL RECOVERY ACT), *Stewart Dry Goods Company v. Lewis* (1935) (graduated taxes on gross sales), and CARTER V. CARTER COAL COMPANY (1936) (The Guffey-Snyder Act), and two of the major Court opinions after the Court reversed itself and adopted the constitutional views of the former dissenters. In STEWARD MACHINE COMPANY V. DAVIS (1937) and HELVERING V. DAVIS (1937) Cardozo's opinions upholding the SOCIAL SECURITY ACT expounded Congress's power under the TAXING AND SPENDING clause of the Constitution and provided the theoretical basis for upholding major legislative policies in a way that complemented the parallel recognition of expansive congressional power under the commerce clause. He also viewed the commerce clause as imposing broad limits on the power of individual states to solve their economic problems at the expense of their neighbors

(*Baldwin v. Seelig*, 1935), although he recognized at the same time that state financial needs required some tempering of those views (*Henneford v. Silas Mason Co.*, 1937).

Cardozo's special contribution lay in his discussion of the methodological approach to substantive results. Long before joining the Supreme Court, he had considered the appropriate factors that shape decision making for a judge, and although his primary experience was in the common law, he had considered the issue with respect to constitutional law as well. Many would sharply curtail the judiciary's role in constitutional, in contrast to common law, adjudication because of the legislature's inability to overturn most constitutional decisions, but Cardozo viewed the process of judicial decision making as unitary. In *The Nature of the Judicial Process* he had proposed a fourfold division of the forces that shape the growth of legal principles: logic or analogy (the method of philosophy); history (the historical or evolutionary method); custom (the method of tradition); and justice, morals, and social welfare (the method of sociology).

Those who have attacked the common law approach to Fourteenth Amendment adjudication have perceived the specter of subjectivism in employment of all these methods, but especially in the last. Cardozo saw "justice, morals, and social welfare," which he also labeled as "accepted standards of right conduct," as especially relevant in constitutional adjudication. He struggled to find an acceptable formula for deriving those standards, finally settling on "the principle and practice of the men and women of the community whom the social mind would rank as intelligent and virtuous."

Cardozo never directly met the charge of subjectivism, especially subjectivism in Fourteenth Amendment adjudication, for his message about judging was aimed at a different target: the regressive results produced by too slavish adherence to the so-called objective factors of precedent and logic. But he clearly did not believe that all was "subjective" or that complete reliance on "objective" factors was possible either. One did the best one could to avoid judging on the basis of purely personal values. "History or custom or social utility or some compelling sentiment of justice or sometimes perhaps a semi-intuitive apprehension of the pervading spirit of our law must come to the rescue of the anxious judge, and tell him where to go."

Cardozo brought these ideas with him to the Supreme Court and applied them to a number of notable issues. From its earliest days and notwithstanding bad experience with SUBSTANTIVE DUE PROCESS of law, epitomized by DRED SCOTT V. SANDFORD (1857) and LOCHNER V. NEW YORK (1905), the Court had become committed, in different guises and formulations, to the notion that various rights, liberties, privileges, or immunities existed that were not spelled out in the Constitution. Although there had been occasional discussion since the end of the nineteenth century of the question whether the Fourteenth Amendment "incorporated" specific provisions of the BILL OF RIGHTS (see INCORPORATION DOCTRINE), most major decisions in the twentieth century had used the due process clause on its own to assess whether a particular "liberty" had been denied. As the attack on the Court's use of the due process clause to strike down economic regulation increased throughout the 1930s, the Court began to refocus the issue of protection of noneconomic rights more in terms of incorporation of particular provisions of the Bill of Rights into the Fourteenth Amendment.

The classic reformulation was rendered by Cardozo in PALKO V. CONNECTICUT (1937). To be incorporated the claimed right must be "fundamental"; or one without which "neither liberty nor justice would exist"; or it must "be implicit in the concept of ORDERED LIBERTY." Without pursuing all the ramifications of the debate over "selective incorporation," as the *Palko* DOCTRINE came to be known, we should note that in the midst of the most severe attack on the Court's interpretation of the Fourteenth Amendment, Cardozo and the whole Court never questioned the notion that the amendment had a substantive content. The approach they chose, the selective incorporation doctrine, required the weighing of factors and building up of precedents in a common law fashion with only the general language of the Fourteenth Amendment as a starting point.

Two Fourteenth Amendment cases suffice to demonstrate specific attempts to apply a "common law" method of judging. In *Snyder v. Massachusetts* (1934) Cardozo wrote an opinion holding that due process was not violated when the defendant was not permitted to be present at a jury view of the scene of an alleged crime. After recognizing that the Fourteenth Amendment protected privileges "fundamental" to a FAIR TRIAL, he considered history, which showed that a view of the scene by a jury was not considered part of the "trial"; current practice in other states, which generally permitted the defendant to be present; and potential prejudice to defendant, which he found to be remote. The balance of these factors led him to conclude that there was nothing fundamental, on the facts of Snyder's case, about the right being asserted.

In GROSJEAN V. AMERICAN PRESS COMPANY

(1936), Cardozo wrote an opinion, never published, concerning a Louisiana statute that placed a tax on newspapers that carried advertising and had a circulation over 20,000. The majority had originally agreed to hold the statute unconstitutional on equal protection grounds. After Cardozo wrote an opinion concurring on grounds of violation of FREEDOM OF THE PRESS, Justice GEORGE SUTHERLAND substituted a new opinion for a unanimous Court adopting the free press rationale, although in an ambiguous formulation that suggests unconstitutional motivation as at least one of its rationales. The opinion that Cardozo then withdrew is one of his best, and it discusses his methodology and substantive rationale quite clearly. What is a law "abridging the freedom of the press" may be somewhat more specific than the question whether a law denies liberty without due process of law (or denies a PRIVILEGE OR IMMUNITY of national CITIZENSHIP), but it was not much more of a specific starting point for the Court in the context of the Louisiana statute.

Cardozo's draft opinion considered exhaustively the English use first of licenses and then of taxation to control the press as part of the history that led to adoption of the FIRST AMENDMENT. That history led him to conclude that the tax involved was a modern counterpart of those repressive tactics. But he also recognized the financial needs of government. He thus concluded unambiguously—and innovatively—that while the press was not immune from taxation and while classifications were normally a matter of legislative discretion, freedom of the press could be safeguarded only if the press was not subjected to discriminatory taxation vis-à-vis other occupations and through use of internal classifications. The opinion is a splendid example of the use of history and reason combined with a sympathetic appreciation of the setting in which the press functions and of modern needs to assure its "freedom."

Another interesting substantive view was his analysis, before coming to the Supreme Court, of three due process cases that have become increasingly important to modern constitutional theory: MEYER V. NEBRASKA (1923) and *Bartel v. Iowa* (1923) (state laws forbidding teaching of foreign languages to young children held unconstitutional) and PIERCE V. SOCIETY OF SISTERS (1928) (state requirement that all children attend public school through eighth grade held unconstitutional). In *The Paradoxes of Legal Science* he characterized the unconstitutional legislation and the nature of the "liberty" that was upheld in the following prophetic language. "Restraints such as these are encroachments upon the free development of personality in a society that is organized on the basis of family." This emphasis on "free development of personality" and "family" is a stunning extrapolation of a second level of generalization from the constitutional principle of "liberty"; it places Cardozo a half century ahead of his time, for such a conception of the "liberty" protected by the Fourteenth Amendment did not resurface until GRISWOLD V. CONNECTICUT (1965) and ROE V. WADE (1973); and it is a graphic (and controversial) example of the operation of the "method of sociology" in CONSTITUTIONAL INTERPRETATION.

Cardozo was a judge for twenty-four years and he thought hard about what he did. If he was not wholly successful in making a useful statement that would clarify the basis for the creative leap of judgment that enabled him to value certain arguments more than others and thus to reach a conclusion, no one in the half century that followed has been more successful. More important, he provided assistance in his extrajudicial writings and in the reasoning of his opinions for the position, which continues to have considerable support among constitutional theorists and especially among judges, that asserts the validity of applying techniques of common law adjudication to the elaboration of Fourteenth Amendment doctrine. Finally and perhaps even more controversially, he demonstrated that an able, conscientious judge who believed that substantive Fourteenth Amendment adjudication was different from legislating might so comport himself on the bench as to offer hope to his successors a half century later that that position is desirable and capable of achievement.

ANDREW L. KAUFMAN

Bibliography

Collected essays on Cardozo in joint 1939 issues of *Columbia Law Review*, 39, #1; *Harvard Law Review*, 52, #3; *Yale Law Journal*, 48, #3; and *Cardozo Law Review*, 1, #1.

KAUFMAN, ANDREW L. 1969 Benjamin Cardozo. In Leon Friedman and Fred L. Israel, eds., *The Justices of the Supreme Court of the United States, 1789–1969*, 3:2287–2307. New York: Chelsea House.

——— 1979 Cardozo's Appointment to the Supreme Court. *Cardozo Law Review* 1:23–53.

CAREY v. POPULATION SERVICES INTERNATIONAL
431 U.S. 678 (1977)

By a 7–2 vote the Supreme Court in *Carey* invalidated three New York laws restricting the advertisement and sale of birth control devices. Justice WILLIAM J.

BRENNAN wrote for a majority concerning two of the laws. First, he read GRISWOLD V. CONNECTICUT (1965) and ROE V. WADE (1973) to require STRICT SCRUTINY of laws touching the "fundamental" decision "whether to bear or beget a child." New York had limited the distribution of contraceptives to licensed pharmacists, and had not offered a sufficiently compelling justification. Second, he read the FIRST AMENDMENT to forbid a law prohibiting the advertising or display of contraceptives. (See COMMERCIAL SPEECH.)

The Court was fragmented in striking down the third law, which forbade distribution of contraceptives to minors under sixteen except under medical prescription. Justice Brennan, for himself and three other Justices, conceded that children's constitutional rights may not be the equivalent of adults' rights. Yet he found insufficient justification for the law in the state's policy of discouraging sexual activity among young people. He doubted that a limit on access to contraceptives would discourage such activity, and in any case the state could not delegate to doctors the right to decide which minors should be discouraged. Three concurring Justices expressed less enthusiasm for minors' constitutional rights to sexual freedom but found other paths to the conclusion that the New York law as written was invalid.

Chief Justice WARREN E. BURGER dissented without opinion, and Justice WILLIAM H. REHNQUIST filed a short dissent that was unusually caustic, even by his high standard for the genre.

Carey was not the last word on the troublesome problem of minors' rights concerning REPRODUCTIVE AUTONOMY; the Court has repeatedly returned to the issue in the ABORTION context. Yet *Carey*'s opinion invalidating the law limiting contraceptives sales to pharmacists was important for its recognition that *Griswold v. Connecticut* stood not merely for a right of marital PRIVACY but also for a broad FREEDOM OF INTIMATE ASSOCIATION.

KENNETH L. KARST

CAROLENE PRODUCTS COMPANY, UNITED STATES v.
Footnote Four
304 U.S. 144 (1938)

Footnote four to Justice HARLAN F. STONE's opinion in UNITED STATES V. CAROLENE PRODUCTS CO. (1938) undoubtedly is the best known, most controversial footnote in constitutional law. Stone used it to suggest categories in which a general presumption in favor of the constitutionality of legislation might be inappropriate. The issue of if and when particular constitutional claims warrant special judicial scrutiny has been a core concern in constitutional theory for nearly fifty years since Stone's three-paragraph footnote was appended to an otherwise obscure 1938 opinion.

The *Carolene Products* decision, handed down the same day as ERIE RAILROAD V. TOMPKINS (1938), itself reflected a new perception of the proper role for federal courts. It articulated a position of great judicial deference in reviewing most legislation. In his majority opinion, Stone sought to consolidate developing restraints on judicial intervention in economic matters, symbolized by WEST COAST HOTEL CO. V. PARRISH (1937). But in footnote four Stone also went on to suggest that legislation, if challenged with certain types of constitutional claims, might not merit the same deference most legislation should enjoy.

Stone's opinion upheld a 1923 federal ban on the interstate shipment of filled milk. The Court thus reversed a lower federal court and, indirectly, the Illinois Supreme Court, in holding that Congress had power to label as adulterated a form of skimmed milk in which butterfat was replaced by coconut milk. Today the decision seems unremarkable; at the time, however, not only was the result in *Carolene Products* controversial but the theory of variable judicial scrutiny suggested by its footnote four was new and perhaps daring.

Actually, only three other Justices joined that part of Stone's opinion which contained the famous footnote, though that illustrious trio consisted of Chief Justice CHARLES EVANS HUGHES, Justice LOUIS D. BRANDEIS, and Justice OWEN J. ROBERTS. Justice HUGO L. BLACK refused to agree to the part of Stone's opinion with the footnote because Black wished to go further than Stone in proclaiming deference to legislative judgments. Justice PIERCE BUTLER concurred only in the result; Justice JAMES C. MCREYNOLDS dissented; and Justices BENJAMIN N. CARDOZO and STANLEY F. REED did not take part.

In fact, the renowned footnote does no more than tentatively mention the possibility of active review in certain realms. The footnote is nonetheless considered a paradigm for special judicial scrutiny of laws discriminating against certain rights or groups. The first paragraph, added at the suggestion of Chief Justice Hughes, is the least controversial. The paragraph hints at special judicial concern when rights explicitly mentioned in the text of the Constitution are at issue.

This rights-oriented, interpretivist position involves less of a judicial leap than the possibility, suggested in the rest of the footnote, of additional grounds for judicial refusal or reluctance to defer to judgments of other governmental branches.

The footnote's second paragraph speaks of possible special scrutiny of interference with "those political processes which can ordinarily be expected to bring about repeal of undesirable legislation." To illustrate the ways in which clogged political channels might be grounds for exacting judicial review, Stone cites decisions invalidating restrictions on the right to vote, the dissemination of information, freedom of political association, and peaceable assembly.

The footnote's third and final paragraph has been the most vigorously debated. It suggests that prejudice directed against DISCRETE AND INSULAR MINORITIES may also call for "more searching judicial inquiry." For this proposition Stone cites two commerce clause decisions, MCCULLOCH V. MARYLAND (1819) and *South Carolina State Highway Dept. v. Barnwell Bros.* (1938), as well as FIRST AMENDMENT and FOURTEENTH AMENDMENT decisions invalidating discriminatory laws based on religion, national origin, or race. Judicial and scholarly disagreement since 1938 has focused mainly on two questions. First, even if the category "discrete and insular minorities" seems clearly to include blacks, should any other groups be included? Second, does paragraph three essentially overlap with paragraph two, or does it go beyond protecting groups who suffer particular political disadvantage? The question whether discrimination against particular groups or burdens on certain rights should trigger special judicial sensitivity is a basic problem in constitutional law to this day.

Footnote four thus symbolizes the Court's struggle since the late 1930s to confine an earlier, free-wheeling tradition of judicial intervention premised on FREEDOM OF CONTRACT and SUBSTANTIVE DUE PROCESS, on the one hand, while trying, on the other, to create an acceptable basis for active intervention when judges perceive political disadvantages or racial or other invidious discrimination.

Dozens of Supreme Court decisions and thousands of pages of scholarly commentary since *Carolene Products* have explored this problem. In EQUAL PROTECTION analysis, for example, the approach introduced in footnote four helped produce a two-tiered model of judicial review. Within this model, legislation involving social and economic matters would be sustained if any RATIONAL BASIS for the law could be found, or sometimes even conceived of, by a judge. In sharp contrast, STRICT SCRUTINY applied to classifications based on race, national origin, and, sometimes, alienage. Similarly, judicial identification of a limited number of FUNDAMENTAL RIGHTS, such as VOTING RIGHTS, sometimes seemed to trigger a strict scrutiny described accurately by Gerald Gunther as " 'strict' in theory and fatal in fact."

Though this two-tiered approach prevailed in many decisions of the WARREN COURT, inevitably the system became more flexible. "Intermediate scrutiny" is now explicitly used in SEX DISCRIMINATION cases, for example. The Court continues to wrestle with the problem suggested in footnote four cases involving constitutional claims of discrimination against whites, discrimination against illegitimate children, and total exclusion of some from important benefits such as public education. Parallel with footnote four, the argument today centers on the question whether it is an appropriate constitutional response to relegate individuals who claim discrimination at the hands of the majority to their remedies within the political process. Yet, as new groups claim discriminatory treatment in new legal realms, the meaning of "discrete and insular minorities" grows more problematic. Undeniably, however, the categories suggested in footnote four still channel the debate. A good example is John Hart Ely's *Democracy and Distrust* (1980), an influential book that expands upon footnote four's theme of political participation.

Justice LEWIS H. POWELL recently stated that footnote four contains "perhaps the most far-sighted dictum in our modern judicial heritage." Yet Powell also stressed that, in his view, it is important to remember that footnote four was merely OBITER DICTUM and was intended to be no more. Even so, the tentative words of footnote four must be credited with helping to initiate and to define a new era of constitutional development. The questions raised by footnote four remain central to constitutional thought; controversy premised on this famous footnote shows no sign of abating.

AVIAM SOIFER

Bibliography

BALL, MILNER S. 1981 Don't Die Don Quixote: A Response and Alternative to Tushnet, Bobbitt, and the Revised Texas Version of Constitutional Law. *Texas Law Review* 59:787–813.

ELY, JOHN HART 1980 *Democracy and Distrust.* Cambridge, Mass.: Harvard University Press.

LUSKY, LOUIS 1982 Footnote Redux: A *Carolene Products* Reminiscence. *Columbia Law Review* 82:1093–1105.

POWELL, LEWIS F., JR. 1982 *Carolene Products* Revisited. *Columbia Law Review* 82:1087–1092.

CARPENTER, MATTHEW H.
(1824–1881)

A Wisconsin lawyer and senator (1869–1875, 1879–1881), Matthew Hale Carpenter was a vigorous Douglas Democrat who favored compromise to prevent SECESSION. Nevertheless, believing secession treasonous, Carpenter supported the war and became a Republican. During Reconstruction Carpenter successfully argued *Ex Parte Garland* (1867) which held the FEDERAL TEST ACT of 1865 unconstitutional. (See TEST OATH CASES.) Subsequently General ULYSSES S. GRANT hired Carpenter as counsel for the Army in EX PARTE MCCARDLE (1868). Carpenter's successful defense of the Army and of the right of Congress to limit Supreme Court JURISDICTION led to his election to the Senate in 1869. There he was generally a strong supporter of Grant's administration, but he only mildly supported CIVIL RIGHTS. In 1872 Carpenter vigorously opposed federal legislation mandating integrated schools and juries because, among other reasons, the statute would violate STATES' RIGHTS. Similarly, as defense counsel he successfully argued for a narrow reading of the FOURTEENTH AMENDMENT in the SLAUGHTERHOUSE CASES (1873). As a former railroad lawyer, however, Carpenter was a leader in protecting business interests. He led the debates supporting the JURISDICTION ACT of 1875, which greatly expanded the JURISDICTION OF FEDERAL COURTS to hear cases in which CORPORATIONS might claim constitutional rights. In 1876 he successfully defended Secretary of War William Belknap in his IMPEACHMENT trial. In 1877 Carpenter unsuccessfully represented Samuel Tilden before the presidential electoral commission. He was defeated for reelection in 1875 because of his connection with Grant administration scandals, but was reelected to the Senate in 1879, serving until his death.

PAUL FINKELMAN

Bibliography

THOMPSON, EDWING BRUCE 1954 *Matthew Hale Carpenter: Webster of the West.* Madison: State Historical Society of Wisconsin.

CARR, ROBERT K.
(1908–1979)

Robert Kenneth Carr was an educator and political scientist; he taught at Dartmouth College (1937–1959) and was president of Oberlin College (1960–1970).

In 1947 Carr served as Executive Secretary of the President's Committee on Civil Rights appointed by HARRY S. TRUMAN and played a leading role in framing its report, *To Secure These Rights* (1947); this report's detailed presentation of the legal and social disabilities imposed on America's black population sparked nationwide controversy. Carr's own book on the subject, *Federal Protection of Civil Rights: Quest for a Sword* (1947), set forth the history of federal civil rights laws and their enforcement and demonstrated their inadequacy in theory and practice. In *The House Committee on Un-American Activities, 1946–1950* (1952), Carr argued that the carelessness and irresponsibility displayed by members and staff of the HOUSE COMMITTEE ON UN-AMERICAN ACTIVITIES outweighed the benefits of alerting the public to the dangers posed by communism at home and abroad; he concluded that the committee's record argued strongly for its own abolition. Carr also wrote two books on the Supreme Court for general readers, *Democracy and the Supreme Court* (1936) and *The Supreme Court and Judicial Review* (1942), and several other books on education and American government.

RICHARD B. BERNSTEIN

CARROLL, DANIEL
(1730–1796)

Daniel Carroll, a wealthy, European-educated Roman Catholic from Maryland, was a signer of both the ARTICLES OF CONFEDERATION and the Constitution. Carroll, who favored a strong national government, spoke often and served on three committees. He was subsequently elected to the first House of Representatives.

DENNIS J. MAHONEY

CARROLL v. PRESIDENT AND COMMISSIONERS OF PRINCESS ANNE
393 U.S. 175 (1968)

After a meeting of a "white supremacist" group at which "aggressively and militantly racist" speeches were made to a racially mixed crowd, the group announced another rally for the next night. Local officials obtained an EX PARTE order enjoining the group from holding a rally for ten days. The Supreme Court, reviewing this order two years later, held that the case fell within an exception to the doctrine of MOOTNESS: rights should not be defeated by short-term orders "capable of repetition, yet evading review."

A unanimous Court held that the *ex parte* order violated the FIRST AMENDMENT. An INJUNCTION against expressive activity requires NOTICE to the persons restrained and a chance to be heard, absent a showing that it is impossible to give them notice and a hearing.

KENNETH L. KARST

CARROLL v. UNITED STATES
267 U.S. 132 (1925)

In *Carroll* the Supreme Court held that an officer can stop and search an automobile without a warrant if there is PROBABLE CAUSE to believe the vehicle contains contraband.

The Court noted that national legislation had routinely authorized WARRANTLESS SEARCHES of vessels suspected of carrying goods on which duty had been evaded. The analogy was shaky; Congress's complete control over international boundaries would justify searching any imports even without probable cause. The Court also approved this warrantless search on a dubious interpretation of the National Prohibition Act. But the Court had independent grounds beyond history and congressional intent for its decision: the search was justified as an implied exception to the FOURTH AMENDMENT's warrant requirement, because the vehicle might be driven away before a warrant could be obtained. Given these EXIGENT CIRCUMSTANCES, probable cause rather than a warrant satisfied the constitutional test of reasonableness. Indeed, legislative approval was not considered in the later AUTOMOBILE SEARCH cases.

JACOB W. LANDYNSKI

CARTER, JAMES COOLIDGE
(1827–1905)

One of the preeminent legal philosophers of his time, James Coolidge Carter frequently appeared before the Supreme Court. Stressing that the FREEDOM OF CONTRACT limited the commerce power, Carter lost two 5–4 decisions in antitrust cases: UNITED STATES v. TRANS-MISSOURI FREIGHT ASSOCIATION (1897) and *United States v. Joint Traffic* (1898). He also defended the constitutionality of the income tax in POLLOCK v. FARMERS' LOAN & TRUST COMPANY (1895).

The clearest exposition of his views appears in *Law: Its Origin, Growth and Function* (1905) where he contended that law must harmonize with customary beliefs.

DAVID GORDON

CARTER, JIMMY
(1924–   )

As the first President elected after the WATERGATE scandal, Jimmy Carter was strongly oriented toward moral duties, Christian ethics, faith, trust, and personal rectitude. The "nobility of ideas" theme evoked in his inaugural address ranged broadly from human rights to the elimination of nuclear weapons. Missing from this pantheon of principles, however, was an understanding of the constitutional system and the mechanics of government needed to translate abstract visions into concrete accomplishments.

Carter considered himself an activist President and wanted to use the power of his office to correct social, economic, and political inequities. Some of his contributions to the legal system were long-lasting, such as the large number of women and persons from minority groups he placed on the federal courts. But comprehensive reforms for welfare, taxation, health, and energy became mired in Congress because of Carter's inability to articulate his beliefs and mobilize public opinion. He and his associates wrongly assumed that institutional resistance from Congress and the executive branch could be overcome simply by appealing to the people through the media.

Carter's congressional relations staff started off poorly and never recovered. By campaigning both against Congress and the bureaucracy, Carter had alienated the very centers of power he needed to govern effectively. He advocated "cabinet government" until the impression of departmental autonomy suggested weak presidential leadership. A major shake-up in July 1979 led to the firing or resignation of five cabinet secretaries, all with a history of friction with certain members of the White House staff. The abrupt nature of these departures cast doubt on Carter's judgment and stability, implying that in any contest between personal loyalty and professional competence, loyalty would prevail.

In foreign policy, the Camp David accord in 1978 marked a high point for Carter when he produced a "framework for peace" between Israeli Prime Minister Menachem Begin and Egyptian President Anwar Sadat. The ratification of the PANAMA CANAL TREA-

TIES also marked a personal triumph, although Carter required last-minute assistance from several senators. His recognition of the People's Republic of China seriously damaged his relations with a number of members of Congress, who were offended by his lack of consultation and the breach of faith with Taiwan. When some of the congressional opponents challenged the termination of the defense treaty with Taiwan, however, the Supreme Court in GOLDWATER V. CARTER (1979) ordered the case dismissed for lack of JUSTICIABILITY. The Iranian revolution and the seizure of the American Embassy in Teheran produced a bitter fourteen months of "America held hostage." This development, including the abortive rescue attempt in 1980, exacerbated Carter's problems of weak leadership and perceived helplessness.

Carter and his associates from Georgia arrived in office with the reputation of amateurs, an image they would never dispel. Carter had campaigned as an outsider, treating that title as a virtue that would set him apart from politicians tainted by the "establishment." He came as a stranger and remained estranged. Having carefully dissociated himself he could not form associations. Throughout his four years he demonstrated little understanding of or interest in legislative strategy, the levers of power, or political leadership.

LOUIS FISHER

Bibliography
JOHNSON, HAYNES 1980 *In the Absence of Power: Governing America.* New York: Viking.

CARTER v. CARTER COAL CO.
298 U.S. 238 (1936)

This was the New Deal's strongest case yet to come before the Supreme Court, and it lost. At issue was the constitutionality of the BITUMINOUS COAL ACT, which regulated the trade practices, prices, and labor relations of the nation's single most important source of energy, the bituminous industry in twenty-seven states. No industry was the subject of greater federal concern or of as many federal investigations. After the Court killed the NATIONAL INDUSTRIAL RECOVERY ACT (NIRA) and with it the bituminous code, Congress enacted a "Little NIRA" for bituminous coal. Although the statute contained no provision limiting the amount of bituminous that could be mined, the Court held it unconstitutional as a regulation of PRODUCTION.

The statute had two basic provisions, wholly separable and administered separately by independent administrative agencies. One agency supervised the price and trade-practices section of the statute; the other the labor section, dealing with MAXIMUM HOURS AND MINIMUM WAGES, and COLLECTIVE BARGAINING. In NEBBIA V. NEW YORK (1934) the Court had sustained against a due process attack the principle of price-fixing in the broadest language. The labor sections seemed constitutional, because strikes had crippled INTERSTATE COMMERCE and the national economy on numerous occasions and four times required federal troops to quell disorders. The federal courts had often enjoined the activities of the United Mine Workers as restraining interstate commerce.

The Court voted 6–3 to invalidate the labor provisions and then voted 5–4 to invalidate the entire statute. Justice GEORGE SUTHERLAND for the majority did not decide on the merits of the price-fixing provisions. Had he attacked them, he might have lost Justice OWEN J. ROBERTS, who had written the *Nebbia* opinion. The strategy was to hold the price provisions inseparable from the labor provisions, which were unconstitutional, thereby bringing down the whole act, despite the fact that its two sections were separable.

Sutherland relied mainly on the stunted version of the COMMERCE CLAUSE that had dominated the Court's opinions in UNITED STATES V. E. C. KNIGHT CO. (1895) and more recently in the NIRA and AGRICULTURAL ADJUSTMENT ACT cases: production is local; labor is part of production; therefore the TENTH AMENDMENT reserves all labor matters to the states. That the major coal-producing states, disavowing STATES' RIGHTS, had supported the congressional enactment and emphasized the futility of STATE REGULATION OF COMMERCE meant nothing to the majority. Sutherland rejected the proposition that "the power of the federal government inherently extends to purposes affecting the nation as a whole with which the states severally cannot deal." In fact the government had relied on the commerce power, not INHERENT POWERS. But Sutherland stated that "the local character of mining, of manufacturing, and of crop growing is a fact, whatever may be done with the products." All labor matters—he enumerated them—were part of production. That labor disputes might catastrophically affect interstate commerce was undeniable but irrelevant, Sutherland reasoned, because their effect on interstate commerce must always be indirect and thus beyond congressional control. The effect was indirect because production intervened between a strike and interstate commerce. All the evils, he asserted, "are local evils over which the federal government has no legislative control." (See EFFECTS ON COMMERCE.)

Chief Justice CHARLES EVANS HUGHES dissented on the question whether the price-fixing provisions of the statute were separable. Justice BENJAMIN N. CARDOZO, supported by Justices LOUIS D. BRANDEIS and HARLAN F. STONE, dissented on the same ground, adding a full argument as to the constitutionality of the price-fixing section. He contended too that the issue on the labor section was not ripe for decision, because Carter asked for a decree to restrain the statute's operation before it went into operation. Cardozo's broad view of the commerce power confirmed the Roosevelt administration's belief that the majority's antilabor, anti-New Deal bias, rather than an unconstitutional taint on the statute, explained the decision.

LEONARD W. LEVY

Bibliography

STERN, ROBERT L. 1946 The Commerce Clause and the National Economy, 1933–1946. *Harvard Law Review* 49:664–674.

CARY, JOHN W.
(1817–1895)

As the general counsel of the Chicago, Milwaukee & St. Paul Railway, John W. Cary was involved in some of the most important court cases on ECONOMIC REGULATION in the late 1800s. In briefs submitted in the GRANGER CASES (1877), Cary went beyond the doctrine of VESTED RIGHTS and the guarantee of JUST COMPENSATION relied on by other railroad attorneys such as WILLIAM EVARTS. Cary contended that state fixing of prices (including railroad rates) deprived stockholders not only of their property but also of their *liberty,* that is their freedom to use and control their property. A legislative power to fix prices, he argued, would be "in conflict with the whole structure and theory of our government, hostile to liberty. . . ."

In CHICAGO, MILWAUKEE & ST. PAUL RAILWAY V. MINNESOTA (1890) Cary, along with WILLIAM C. GOUDY, successfully argued that the reasonableness of state-fixed rates was subject to JUDICIAL REVIEW.

DENNIS J. MAHONEY

CASES AND CONTROVERSIES

Article III of the Constitution vests the JUDICIAL POWER OF THE UNITED STATES in one constitutionally mandated Supreme Court and such subordinate federal courts as Congress may choose to establish. Federal judges are appointed for life with salaries that cannot be diminished, but they may exercise their independent and politically unaccountable power only to resolve "cases" and "controversies" of the kinds designated by Article III, the most important of which are cases arising under the Constitution and other federal law. The scope of the federal judicial power thus depends in large measure on the Supreme Court's interpretations of the "case" and "controversy" limitation applicable to the Court itself and to other Article III tribunals.

That limitation not only inhibits Article III courts from arrogating too much power unto themselves; it also prevents Congress from compelling or authorizing decisions by federal courts in nonjudicial proceedings and precludes Supreme Court review of state court decisions in proceedings that are not considered "cases" or "controversies" under Article III. The limitation thus simultaneously confines federal judges and reinforces their ability to resist nonjudicial tasks pressed on them by others.

The linkage between independence and circumscribed power is a continuously important theme in "case" or "controversy" jurisprudence, as is the connection between "case" or "controversy" jurisprudence and the power of JUDICIAL REVIEW of government acts for constitutionality—a power that MARBURY V. MADISON (1803) justified primarily by the need to apply the Constitution as relevant law to decide a "case." During the CONSTITUTIONAL CONVENTION OF 1787, EDMUND RANDOLPH proposed that the President and members of the federal judiciary be joined in a council of revision to veto legislative excesses. The presidential VETO POWER was adopted instead, partly to keep the judiciary out of the legislative process and partly to insure that the judges would decide cases independently, without bias in favor of legislation they had helped to formulate. Similar concerns led the convention to reject CHARLES PINCKNEY's proposal to have the Supreme Court provide ADVISORY OPINIONS at the request of Congress or the President. Finally, in response to JAMES MADISON's doubts about extending the federal judicial power to expound the Constitution too broadly, the Convention made explicit its understanding that the power extended only to "cases of a Judiciary nature." The Framers understood that the judicial power of constitutional governance would expand if the concept of "case" or "controversy" did.

What constitutes an Article III "case," of a "judiciary nature," is hardly self-evident. No definition was articulated when the language was adopted, but only an apparent intent to circumscribe the federal judicial function, and to insure that it be performed independently of the other branches. In this century, Justice FELIX FRANKFURTER suggested that Article III precluded federal courts from deciding legal questions except in the kinds of proceedings entertained by the English and colonial courts at the time of the Constitution's adoption. But the willingness of English courts to give advisory opinions then—a practice clearly inconsistent with convention history and the Court's steadfast policy since 1793—refutes the suggestion. Moreover, from the outset the SEPARATION OF POWERS aspect of the "case" or "controversy" limitation has differentiated CONSTITUTIONAL COURTS (courts constituted under Article III) from others. Most fundamentally, however, the indeterminate historical contours of "cases" or "controversies" inevitably had to accommodate changes in the forms of litigation authorized by Congress, in the legal and social environment that accompanied the nation's industrial growth and the rise of the regulatory and welfare state, and in the place of the federal judiciary in our national life.

After two centuries of elaboration, the essential characteristics of Article III controversies remain imprecise and subject to change. Yet underlying the various manifestations of "case" or "controversy" doctrine are three core requirements: affected parties standing in an adverse relationship to each other, actual or threatened events that provoke a live legal dispute, and the courts' ability to render final and meaningful judgments. These criteria—concerning, respectively, the litigants, the facts, and judicial efficacy—have both independent and interrelated significance.

As to litigants, only parties injured by a defendant's behavior have constitutional STANDING to sue. COLLUSIVE SUITS are barred because the parties' interests are not adverse.

As to extant factual circumstances, advisory opinions are banned. This limitation not only bars direct requests for legal rulings on hypothetical facts but also requires dismissal of unripe or moot cases, because, respectively, they are not yet live, or they once were but have ceased to be by virtue of subsequent events. The parties' future or past adversariness cannot substitute for actual, current adversariness. Disputes that have not yet begun or have already ended are treated as having no more present need for decision than purely hypothetical disputes. (See RIPENESS; MOOTNESS).

The desire to preserve federal judicial power as

an independent, effective, and binding force of legal obligation is reflected both in the finality rule, which bars decision if the judgment rendered would be subject to revision by another branch of government, and in the rule denying standing unless a judgment would likely redress the plaintiff's injury. These two rules are the clearest instances of judicial self-limitation to insure that when the federal courts do act, their judgments will be potent. To exercise judicial power ineffectively or as merely a preliminary gesture would risk undermining compliance with court decrees generally or lessening official and public acceptance of the binding nature of judicial decisions, especially unpopular constitutional judgments. Here the link between the limitations on judicial power and that power's independence and effectiveness is at its strongest.

Historically, congressional attempts to expand the use of Article III judicial power have caused the greatest difficulty, largely because the federal courts are charged simultaneously with enforcing valid federal law as an arm of the national government and with restraining unconstitutional behavior of the coequal branches of that government. The enforcement role induces judicial receptivity to extensive congressional use of the federal courts, especially in a time of expansion of both the federal government's functions and the use of litigation to resolve public disputes. The courts' checking function, however, cautions judicial resistance to congressional efforts to enlarge the scope of "cases" or "controversies" for fear of losing the strength, independence, or finality needed to resist unconstitutional action by the political branches.

The early emphasis of "case" or "controversy" jurisprudence was on consolidating the judiciary's independence and effective power. The Supreme Court's refusal in 1793 to give President GEORGE WASHINGTON legal advice on the interpretation of treaties with France—the founding precedent for the ban on advisory opinions—rested largely on the desire to preserve the federal judiciary as a check on Congress and the executive when actual disputes arose. Similarly, HAYBURN'S CASE (1792) established that federal courts would not determine which Revolutionary War veterans were entitled to disability pensions so long as the secretary of war had the final say on their entitlement: Congress could employ the federal judicial power only if the decisions of federal courts had binding effect. In the mid-nineteenth century the concern for maintaining judicial efficacy went beyond finality of substantive judgment to finality of remedy. The Supreme Court refused to accept appeals from the Court of Claims, which Congress had established to hear monetary claims against the United States, because the statutory scheme forbade payment until the Court certified its judgments to the treasury secretary for presentation to Congress, which would then have to appropriate funds. The Court concluded that Congress could not invoke Article III judicial power if the judges lacked independent authority to enforce their judgments as well as render them.

Preserving judicial authority remains an important desideratum in the twentieth century, but the growing pervasiveness of federal law as a means of government regulation—often accompanied by litigant and congressional pressure to increase access to the federal courts—inevitably has accentuated the law-declaring enforcement role of the federal judiciary and tended to expand the "case" or "controversy" realm. MUSKRAT V. UNITED STATES (1911) cited the courts' inability to execute a judgment as a reason to reject Congress's authorization of a TEST CASE to secure a ruling on the constitutionality of specific statutes it had passed. Similarly, the Court initially doubted the federal courts' power to give DECLARATORY JUDGMENTS. Yet, by the late 1930s, the Supreme Court had upheld both its own power to review state declaratory judgment actions and the federal DECLARATORY JUDGMENT ACT of 1934. The declaratory judgment remedy authorizes federal courts to decide controversies before legal rights are actually violated. The judge normally enters no coercive order, but confines the remedy to a binding declaration of rights. So long as the controversy is a live one, between adverse parties, and the decision to afford a binding remedy rests wholly with the judiciary, the advisory opinion and finality objections pose no obstacles. A controversy brought to court too early may fail Article III ripeness criteria, but the declaratory remedy itself does not preclude the existence of a "case" or "controversy."

Congress has succeeded in expanding the reach of federal judicial power not only by creating new remedies for the federal courts to administer but also by creating new substantive rights for them to enforce. The Supreme Court maintains as a fundamental "case" or "controversy" requirement that a suing party, to have standing, must have suffered some distinctive "injury in fact." The injury must be particularized, not diffuse; citizen or taxpayer frustration with alleged government illegality is insufficient by itself. In theory, Congress cannot dispense with this requirement and authorize suits by individuals who are not injured. Congress may, however, increase the potential for an injury that will satisfy Article III, simply by legislating protection of new rights, the violation of which amounts to a constitutional "injury in fact." For example, *Trafficante v. Metropolitan Life Insurance Company* (1972) held that a federal CIVIL RIGHTS ban on housing discrimination could be enforced not only by persons refused housing but also by current tenants claiming loss of desired interracial associations; the Court interpreted the statute to create a legally protected interest in integrated housing. To a point, then, Article III "cases" or "controversies" expand correspondingly with the need to enforce new federal legislation. Yet the scope of congressional power to transform diffuse harm into cognizable Article III injury remains uncertain and apparently stops short of providing everyone a judicially enforceable generalized right to be free of illegal governmental behavior, without regard to more individualized effects.

The historically approved image is that federal judges decide politically significant public law issues only to resolve controversies taking the form of private litigation. Over the years, however, this picture has had to accommodate not only congressional creation of enforceable rights and remedies but also the modern realities of public forms of litigation such as the CLASS ACTION, the participation of organized public interest lawyers, and lawsuits aimed at reforming government structures and practices. (See INSTITUTIONAL LITIGATION.) Public law adjudication, especially constitutional adjudication, is certainly the most important function of the federal courts. The inclination to stretch the boundaries of "cases" or "controversies" to provide desired legal guidance on important social problems, although it has varied among federal judges and courts of different eras, increases in response to congressional authorization and the perception of social need. Offsetting that impulse, however, are two countervailing considerations. First, the judges realize that the more public the issues raised, the more democratically appropriate is a political rather than a judicial resolution. Second, they understand the importance of a litigation context that does not threaten judicial credibility, finality, or independence; that presents a realistic need for decision; and that provides adequate information and legal standards for confident, well-advised decision making. These competing considerations will continue to shape the meaning of "cases" and "controversies," setting the limits of the federal judicial function in ways that preserve the courts' checking and enforcement roles in the face of changes in the forms and objectives of litigation, in the dimensions of federal law, and in the expectations of government officials and members of the public.

JONATHAN D. VARAT

Bibliography

BRILMAYER, LEA   1979   The Jurisprudence of Article III: Perspectives on the "Case or Controversy" Requirement. *Harvard Law Review* 93:297–321.

MONAGHAN, HENRY P.   1973   Constitutional Adjudication: The Who and When. *Yale Law Journal* 82:1363–1397.

RADCLIFFE, JAMES E.   1978   *The Case-or-Controversy Provision.* University Park: Pennsylvania State University Press.

TUSHNET, MARK V.   1980   The Sociology of Article III: A Response to Professor Brilmayer. *Harvard Law Review* 93:1698–1733.

CATEGORICAL GRANTS-IN-AID

See: Federal Grants-in-Aid

CATO'S LETTERS

Between 1720 and 1723 John Trenchard and Thomas Gordon, collaborating under the pseudonym of "Cato," published weekly essays in the London newspapers, popularizing the ideas of English libertarians, especially JOHN LOCKE. Gordon collected 138 essays in four volumes which went through six editions between 1733 and 1755 under the title, *Cato's Letters: Essays on Liberty, Civil and Religious.* CLINTON ROSSITER, who rediscovered "Cato," wrote, "no one can spend any time in the newspapers, library inventories, and pamphlets of colonial America without realizing that *Cato's Letters* rather than Locke's *Civil Government* was the most popular, quotable, esteemed source of political ideas in the colonial period." The essays bore titles such as "Of Freedom of Speech . . . inseparable from publick Liberty," "The Right and Capacity of the People to judge of Government," "Liberty proved to be the unalienable Right of all Mankind," "All Government proved to be instituted by Men," "How free Governments are to be framed to last," "Civil Liberty produces all Civil Blessings," and "Of the Restraints which ought to be laid upon publick Rulers." Almost every colonial newspaper from Boston to Savannah anthologized *Cato's Letters*, and the four volumes were imported from England in enormous quantities. The most famous of the letters were those on the FREEDOM OF SPEECH and FREEDOM OF THE PRESS. Cato conceded that freedom posed risks, because people might express themselves irreligiously or seditiously, but restraints on expression resulted in injustice, tyranny, and ignorance. "Cato" would not prosecute criminal libels because prosecution was more dangerous to liberty than the expression of hateful opinions. The sixth edition is available in an American reprint of 1971.

LEONARD W. LEVY

Bibliography

JACOBSON, DAVID L. 1965 Introduction to *The English Libertarian Heritage.* Indianapolis: Bobbs-Merrill.

CATRON, JOHN
(c.1786–1865)

President ANDREW JACKSON appointed John Catron, his fellow Tennessean and political disciple, to the Supreme Court in 1837. A man who reflected Jackson's own views, Catron had been chief justice of Tennessee. While on the state bench, Catron had undoubtedly endeared himself to Jackson by opposing the BANK OF THE UNITED STATES and challenging JOHN MARSHALL's *Worcester v. Georgia* (1832) opinion on Indian rights. Jackson's appointment of Catron filled one of two new positions created by the Judiciary Act of 1837. JOHN McKINLEY of Alabama received the other appointment. The two decisively altered the geographic complexion of the Court, because five of the nine justices represented slaveholding circuits.

Catron's constitutional law decisions illustrated the judicial search for a balance between national and state power in the antebellum period. For example, in the LICENSE CASES (1847) Catron emphatically held that the commerce power could be exercised by Congress "at pleasure," but that absent such legislation, states might regulate INTERSTATE COMMERCE within their own boundaries. In the PASSENGER CASES (1849) he voted to strike down state taxes on immigrants because Congress had exercised its authority over foreign commerce.

Catron's opinions on the rights and powers of CORPORATIONS varied widely. He concurred in Chief Justice ROGER B. TANEY's opinion in BANK OF AUGUSTA V. EARLE (1839), holding that states could exclude foreign corporations, and he also agreed when the Court expanded federal court JURISDICTION over corporate activities in *Louisville Railroad Co. v. Letson* (1844). Except as a party to a diversity suit, however, a corporation, Catron insisted, was not a citizen within

the sense of the Constitution. Catron resisted the TANEY COURT's accommodation with corporate interests in the Ohio bank cases of the 1850s. In PIQUA BRANCH BANK V. KNOOP (1854) he vigorously opposed the use of the CONTRACT CLAUSE to protect state legislative tax exemptions in corporate charters. In a companion case, Catron saw the burgeoning power of corporations as threatening to subvert the state governments that had created them. He believed that the community rights doctrine of CHARLES RIVER BRIDGE V. WARREN BRIDGE COMPANY (1837) had become "illusory and nearly useless, as almost any beneficial privilege, property, or exemption, claimed by corporations" might be construed into a contract to the corporation's advantage. He also protested when the Court, in DODGE V. WOOLSEY (1856), invalidated Ohio's constitutional amendment repealing corporate tax exemptions.

Catron's role in DRED SCOTT V. SANDFORD (1857) was more prominent for his extrajudicial activities than for his opinion. Before the decision, he wrote several letters to President-elect JAMES BUCHANAN, notifying him of the Court's resolution to "decide and settle a controversy which has so long and seriously agitated the country, and which *must* ultimately be decided by the Supreme Court." He also urged Buchanan to pressure his fellow Pennsylvanian, Justice ROBERT GRIER, to join in the effort to decide the constitutional question of congressional control over SLAVERY IN THE TERRITORIES. Catron's political maneuverings have overshadowed his opinion which deviated in some significant respects from Taney's. For example, he did not think that the Court could review the plea in abatement and he thought Taney's discussion of black CITIZENSHIP unnecessary. He also differed from the Chief Justice on the scope of congressional power over the TERRITORIES, acknowledging that it was plenary, save for a few exceptions, such as slavery.

Catron closed his long career with some measure of distinction. Unlike his colleague, Justice JOHN CAMPBELL, who resigned, or Taney, who bitterly opposed the Union's war efforts and President ABRAHAM LINCOLN's conduct of the war, Catron clung to a Jacksonian faith in the Union. He carried out his circuit duties in Tennessee, Kentucky, and Missouri, often at great personal risk. He lost much of his property in Nashville when he failed to respond to a local demand that he resign. Although he opposed Lincoln's blockade policy when he dissented in the PRIZE CASES (1863), on circuit he upheld the confiscation laws and the government's suspension of the writ of HABEAS CORPUS. "I have to punish Treason, & will,"

Catron wrote. With that expression, and through his judicial decisions, Catron faithfully reflected the spirit of his patron, Andrew Jackson.

STANLEY I. KUTLER

Bibliography

GATTELL, FRANK OTTO 1969 John Catron. In Leon Friedman and Fred L. Israel, eds., *The Justices of the Supreme Court,* Vol. 1:737–768. New York: Chelsea House.
SWISHER, CARL B. 1935 *Roger B. Taney.* New York: Macmillan.

CEASE AND DESIST ORDER

In ADMINISTRATIVE LAW, cease and desist orders require the cessation of specific violations of law or government regulations. The power to issue such orders may be granted to REGULATORY COMMISSIONS by Congress. Cease and desist orders are issued only after FAIR HEARING and are subject to review in the federal courts.

DENNIS J. MAHONEY

CENSORSHIP

See: Prior Restraint and Censorship

CENTRAL HUDSON GAS & ELECTRIC CORP. v. PUBLIC SERVICE COMMISSION
447 U.S. 557 (1980)

Central Hudson is the leading decision establishing ground rules for the Supreme Court's modern protection of COMMERCIAL SPEECH under the FIRST AMENDMENT. New York's Public Service Commission (PSC), in the interest of conserving energy, forbade electrical utilities to engage in promotional advertising. The Supreme Court held, 8–1, that this prohibition was unconstitutional.

Justice LEWIS F. POWELL, for the Court, used an analytical approach to commercial speech that combined a TWO-LEVEL THEORY with a BALANCING TEST. First, he wrote, it must be determined whether the speech in question is protected by the First Amendment. The answer to that question is affirmative unless the speech is "misleading" or it is "related to illegal activity" (for example, by proposing an unlawful transaction). Second, if the speech falls within the zone of First Amendment protection, the speech can be regulated only if government satisfies all the elements of a three-part interest-balancing formula: the asserted governmental interest must be "substantial"; the regulation must "directly advance" that interest; and the regulation must not be "more extensive than is necessary to serve that interest."

This intermediate STANDARD OF REVIEW seems loosely patterned after the standard used under the EQUAL PROTECTION clause in cases involving SEX DISCRIMINATION. In those cases, the Court typically accepts that the governmental interest is important; when a statute is invalidated, the Court typically regards gender discrimination as an inappropriate means for achieving the governmental interest. The *Central Hudson* opinion followed this pattern: the promotional advertising was protected speech, and the state's interest in conservation was substantial and directly advanced by the PSC's regulation. However, prohibiting all promotional advertising, including statements that would not increase net energy use, was not the LEAST RESTRICTIVE MEANS for achieving conservation.

Concurring opinions by Justices HARRY A. BLACKMUN and JOHN PAUL STEVENS, both joined by Justice WILLIAM J. BRENNAN, adopted more speech-protective doctrinal positions. Justice WILLIAM H. REHNQUIST, in lone dissent, argued that the PSC's regulation was only an ECONOMIC REGULATION of a state-regulated monopoly, raising no important First Amendment issue.

KENNETH L. KARST

CENTRAL PACIFIC RAILROAD CO. v. UNITED STATES

See: Sinking Fund Cases

CERTIFICATION

Certification may refer to a broad range of acts of government officials high and low: a clerk may certify the accuracy of a copy of a document; the Federal Power Commission may issue a certificate that a natural gas pipeline will serve "public convenience and necessity." In federal courts, however, certification has a narrower meaning. A court may certify questions of law to another court for authoritative decision.

The UNITED STATES COURTS OF APPEALS are authorized by Congress to certify "distinct and definite" questions of law for decision by the Supreme Court. The practice has been criticized for influencing the Supreme Court to decide issues in the abstract, without a complete factual record, and for weakening the Court's control over the questions it will decide. Partly for these reasons, this form of certification is rarely used.

More frequently, federal district courts certify doubtful questions of state law for decision by state courts. About half the states expressly authorize their courts to answer such certified questions, and the Supreme Court has applauded the technique. This form of certification is merely a variant form of abstention.

KENNETH L. KARST

Bibliography
BATOR, PAUL M., MISHKIN, PAUL J., SHAPIRO, DAVID L., and WECHSLER, HERBERT, eds. 1973 *Hart and Wechsler's The Federal Courts and the Federal System,* 2nd ed. Pages 1582–1586. Mineola, N.Y.: Foundation Press.

CERTIORARI, WRIT OF

A writ of certiorari is an order from a higher court directing a lower court to transmit the record of a case for review in the higher court. The writ was in use in England and America before the Revolution. Unlike the WRIT OF ERROR, which was used routinely to review final judgments of lower courts, certiorari was a discretionary form of review that might be granted even before the lower court had given judgment.

When Congress established the circuit courts of appeals in 1891, it expressly authorized the Supreme Court to review certain of these courts' decisions, otherwise declared to be "final," by issuing the writ of certiorari, which remained discretionary. In 1925, Congress expanded the Court's certiorari JURISDICTION and reduced the availability of the writ of error (renamed APPEAL). Certiorari is today the chief mode of the Supreme Court's exercise of APPELLATE JURISDICTION. Proposals to abolish the Court's theoretically obligatory jurisdiction over appeals would leave appellate review entirely to certiorari, and thus to the Court's discretion.

By statute the Court is authorized to grant certiorari in any case that is "in" a federal court of appeals. Thus in an appropriate case the Court can bypass the court of appeals and directly review the action of the district court, as it did in the celebrated case of UNITED STATES V. NIXON (1974).

The Supreme Court's rules have long stated some considerations governing the Court's discretionary grant or denial of certiorari. Three factors are emphasized: (1) conflicts among the highest courts of the states or the federal courts of appeals; (2) the resolution of important unsettled issues of federal law; and (3) the correction of error. These factors do not exhaust but only illustrate the considerations influencing the Court's certiorari policy.

KENNETH L. KARST

Bibliography
LINZER, PETER 1979 The Meaning of Certiorari Denials. *Columbia Law Review* 79:1227–1305.

CHAE CHAN PING v. UNITED STATES
(Chinese Exclusion Case)
130 U.S. 581 (1889)

The CHINESE EXCLUSION ACT of 1882 authorized the issuance of certificates to Chinese ALIENS, guaranteeing their right to reenter the United States after leaving. In 1888 Congress amended that act to prohibit reentry by voiding all outstanding certificates, destroying the right of Chinese to land. Justice STEPHEN J. FIELD, for a unanimous Supreme Court, admitted that this act "is in contravention of express stipulations of the Treaty of 1868 (and other agreements) . . . but it is not on that account invalid or to be restricted in its enforcement. The treaties were of no greater legal obligation than the Act of Congress." He asserted that the treaties were equivalent to federal statutes and they might thus be "repealed or modified at the pleasure of Congress." Because "no paramount authority is given to one over the other" the government could constitutionally exclude aliens from the United States as "an incident of SOVEREIGNTY."

DAVID GORDON

CHAFEE, ZECHARIAH, JR.
(1885–1957)

Modern scholarship in the area of free speech is indelibly stamped with the ideas of Zechariah Chafee, Jr., a distinguished professor of law and University Professor at Harvard, and a CIVIL LIBERTIES activist.

Chafee, scion of a comfortable business-oriented New England family, left the family's iron business to enter Harvard Law School, returning there in 1916 to teach. Inheriting ROSCOE POUND's third-year EQUITY course, in which Pound dealt with INJUNCTIONS against libel, Chafee, uncertain as to the meaning of FREEDOM OF SPEECH, read all pre-1916 cases on the subject. He concluded that the few existing decisions reached results unsatisfactory to one seeking precedents for free speech protection. This realization, coupled with stringent new wartime espionage and SEDITION laws, and their often arbitrary enforcement, persuaded him of the importance of developing a modern law of free speech. Starting with articles in the *New Republic* and the *Harvard Law Review*, and a 1920 book, *Freedom of Speech*, Chafee attempted workable delineations between liberty, which he felt must be safeguarded carefully, and the restraints that emergency situations might warrant. Unhappy with the insensitivity of OLIVER WENDELL HOLMES's initial CLEAR AND PRESENT DANGER construct in SCHENCK V. UNITED STATES (1919), Chafee, with the assistance of Judge LEARNED HAND, set out to persuade Holmes that the test for speech should consider not only the individual's interest in freedom but also the social desirability of injecting provocative thought into the marketplace. "Tolerance of adverse opinion is not a matter of generosity, but of political prudence," Chafee argued. Holmes embraced this position in his dissent in ABRAMS V. UNITED STATES (1919), having been newly convinced that the FIRST AMENDMENT established a national policy favoring a search for truth, while balancing social interests and individual interests. Contemporary traditionalists reacted negatively with a move to oust Chafee from Harvard Law School. Such action was thwarted when Harvard President A. Lawrence Lowell rallied to Chafee's defense.

Chafee, as one of the nation's leading civil libertarians in the 1920s became involved with a number of vital issues. He served on commissions to probe owner autocracy and brutality in the mining regions of the East, and he spoke out publicly against excessive use of the labor injunction to curtail legitimate union activities. In 1929 he headed a subcommittee of the Wickersham Commission which looked into police use of the "third degree" and improper trial procedures. He played a prominent role in the American Bar Association's Commission on the BILL OF RIGHTS in the late 1930s, and in the 1940s served on the Commission on Freedom of the Press, afterward performing similar duties for the United Nations.

Chafee maintained a deep commitment to legal education. He personally regarded as his principal professional accomplishment the Federal Interpleader Act of 1936, a statute creating federal court JURISDICTION when persons in different states make conflicting claims to the same shares of stock or the same bank accounts. His chief influence can be seen, however, in the work of generations of attorneys and judges, nurtured on his free speech and civil liberties view, who have rewritten First Amendment doctrine along Chafee's lines.

PAUL L. MURPHY

Bibliography
MURPHY, PAUL L. 1979 *World War I and the Origin of Civil Liberties in the United States.* New York: Norton.

CHAMBERS v. FLORIDA
309 U.S. 227 (1940)

Chambers was the first coerced confession case to come before the Court since the landmark decision in BROWN V. MISSISSIPPI (1936). In *Brown*, the physical torture being uncontested, the state had relied mainly on the point that the RIGHT AGAINST SELF-INCRIMINATION did not apply to state proceedings. In *Chambers*, before the state supreme court finally affirmed the convictions it had twice reversed so that juries could determine whether the confessions had been freely and voluntarily made, and the record showed no physical coercion. Moreover, the state contested the JURISDICTION of the Supreme Court to review the judgments, arguing that there was no question of federal law to be denied. However, the Supreme Court, in an eloquent opinion by Justice HUGO L. BLACK, unanimously asserted jurisdiction and reversed the state court.

Black rejected the state's jurisdictional argument, declaring that the Supreme Court could determine for itself whether the confessions had been obtained by means that violated the constitutional guarantee of DUE PROCESS OF LAW. Reviewing the facts Black found that the black prisoners, having been arrested on suspicion without warrant, had been imprisoned in a mob-dominated environment, held incommunicado, and interrogated over five days and through a night until they abandoned their disclaimers of guilt and "confessed." POLICE INTERROGATION had continued until the prosecutor got what he wanted. On the basis of these facts Black wrote a stirring explanation of the relation between due process and free government, concluding that courts in our constitutional system stand "as havens of refuge for those who might otherwise suffer because they are helpless, weak, outnumbered, or because they are non-conforming victims of prejudice. . . ." Applying the exclusionary rule of *Brown*, the Court held that psychological as well as physical torture violated due process.

LEONARD W. LEVY

CHAMBERS v. MARONEY
399 U.S. 42 (1970)

In this important FOURTH AMENDMENT case involving the automobile exception to the SEARCH WARRANT clause, the police had seized a car without a warrant and had searched it later, without a warrant, after having driven it to the police station, where they impounded it. Justice BYRON R. WHITE for the Supreme Court acknowledged that the search could not be justified as having been conducted as a SEARCH INCIDENT TO ARREST; nor could he find EXIGENT CIRCUMSTANCES that justified the WARRANTLESS SEARCH.

White simply fudged the facts. He declared that there was "no difference between on the one hand seizing and holding a car before presenting the PROBABLE CAUSE issue to a magistrate and on the other hand carrying out an immediate search without a warrant." Either course was "reasonable under the Fourth Amendment," but the police had followed neither course in this case. Probable cause for the search had existed at the time of the search, and White declared without explanation that probable cause still existed later when the police made the search at the station, when the felons were in custody. However, the possibility that they might drive off in the car did not exist; that possibility had alone occasioned the automobile exception in the first place. Absent a risk that the culprits might use the vehicle to escape with the fruits of their crime, the constitutional distinction between houses and cars did not matter. White saw no difference in the practical consequences of choosing between an immediate search without a warrant, when probable cause existed, and "the car's immobilization until a warrant is obtained." That logic was irrefutable and irrelevant, because the failure of the police to obtain the warrant gave rise to the case. Only Justice JOHN MARSHALL HARLAN dissented from this line of reasoning.

Until this case mere probable cause for a search, as judged only by a police officer, did not by itself justify a warrantless search; the case is significant, too, because of its implied rule that exigent circumstances need not justify the warrantless search of a car. Following *Chambers*, the Court almost routinely assumed that if a search might have been made at the time of arrest, any warrantless search conducted later, when the vehicle was impounded, was a valid one.

LEONARD W. LEVY

CHAMPION v. AMES
188 U.S. 321 (1903)

As the twentieth century opened, the Supreme Court began to sustain use of the COMMERCE CLAUSE as an instrument to remedy various social and economic ills. (See NATIONAL POLICE POWER.) In 1895 Congress forbade interstate transportation of lottery tickets, seeking to safeguard public morals. Opponents challenged the act on three grounds: the tickets themselves were not SUBJECTS OF COMMERCE, Congress's power to regulate INTERSTATE COMMERCE did not extend to outright prohibition, and such a power would violate the TENTH AMENDMENT's reservation of certain powers to the states.

A 5–4 Court sustained the act, emphasizing Congress's plenary power over commerce. Because the tickets indicated a cash prize might be won, they were items liable to be bought or sold—thus, subjects of commerce and so subject to regulation. Citing the complete prohibition on FOREIGN COMMERCE in the EMBARGO ACT OF 1807, Justice JOHN MARSHALL HARLAN asserted that the power of regulation necessarily included the power of prohibition. Although he rejected the contention that "Congress may arbitrarily exclude from commerce among the states any article . . . it may choose," Harlan justified the ban on transporting lottery tickets on the ground that Congress alone had power to suppress "an evil of such appalling character," thus propounding the NOXIOUS PRODUCTS DOCTRINE. Harlan dismissed the Tenth Amendment objection: that provision was no bar to a power that had been "expressly delegated to Congress."

Chief Justice MELVILLE W. FULLER led Justices DAVID BREWER, RUFUS PECKHAM, and GEORGE SHIRAS in dissent. Fuller noted that the motive underlying the legislation was to suppress gambling, not to regulate commerce. He feared the disruption of distinct spheres of authority and the "creation of a centralized government." He also challenged Harlan's assertion that the commerce power included the right of prohibition. The Court, citing *Champion*, however, would soon uphold the PURE FOOD AND DRUG ACT (in HIPOLITE EGG COMPANY v. UNITED STATES, 1911), the MANN ACT (in HOKE v. UNITED STATES, 1913), and others, relying on its expansive view of the commerce clause.

DAVID GORDON

(SEE ALSO: *Hammer v. Dagenhart, 1918; United States v. Darby, 1941.*)

CHAMPION AND DICKASON v. CASEY
Cir. Ct., Rhode Island (1792)

Reported widely in newspapers in June 1792, this was the first case in which a federal court held a state act unconstitutional as a violation of the CONTRACT CLAUSE. Rhode Island had passed a stay law, postponing by three years the time for a debtor to pay his creditors.

The Circuit Court for the district, presided over by Chief Justice JOHN JAY, ruled that the stay law impaired the OBLIGATION OF CONTRACTS contrary to Article I, section 10.

LEONARD W. LEVY

CHANDLER v. FLORIDA
449 U.S. 560 (1981)

The Supreme Court here distinguished away ESTES v. TEXAS (1965), in which it had held that the televising of a criminal trial violated DUE PROCESS OF LAW because of the inherently prejudicial impact on criminal defendants. In *Chandler* an 8–0 Court ruled that the prejudicial effect must be actually shown by the facts of the particular case; Florida's statute, at issue here, imposed adequate safeguards on the use of electronic media in court, thereby insuring due process of law. Presumably the decision promoted FREEDOM OF THE PRESS and the principle of a PUBLIC TRIAL.

LEONARD W. LEVY

(SEE ALSO: *Free Press/Fair Trial.*)

CHAPLINSKY v. NEW HAMPSHIRE
315 U.S. 568 (1941)

In *Chaplinsky*, Justice FRANK MURPHY, writing for a unanimous Supreme Court, introduced into FIRST AMENDMENT jurisprudence the TWO-LEVEL THEORY that "There are certain well-defined and narrowly limited classes of speech, the prevention and punishment of which have never been thought to raise any constitutional problem. These include the lewd and obscene, the profane, the libelous, and the insulting or 'FIGHTING' WORDS—those which by their very utterance inflict injury or tend to incite an immediate breach of the peace." *Chaplinsky* itself arose under a "fighting words" statute, which the state court had interpreted to punish "words likely to cause an average addressee to fight." In this narrow context the decision can be seen as an application of the CLEAR AND PRESENT DANGER test. COHEN v. CALIFORNIA (1971), emphasizing this rationale, offered protection to an OBSCENITY that created no danger of violence.

In its broader conception of categories of speech excluded from First Amendment protection, the case served as an important doctrinal source for many later obscenity and libel decisions.

MARTIN SHAPIRO

CHAPMAN v. CALIFORNIA

See: Harmless Error

CHARLES RIVER BRIDGE v. WARREN BRIDGE COMPANY
11 Peters 420 (1837)

The Charles River Bridge case reflected the tension within ALEXIS DE TOCQUEVILLE's proposition that the American people desired a government that would allow them "to acquire the things they covet and which [would] . . . not debar them from the peaceful enjoyment of those possessions which they have already acquired." A metaphor for the legal strains that accompanied technological change, the case spoke more to the emerging questions of railroad development than to the immediate problem of competing bridges over the Charles River.

Following the Revolution, some investors petitioned the Massachusetts legislature for a charter to build a bridge over the Charles River, linking Boston and Charlestown. Commercial interests in both cities supported the proposal, and the state issued the grant in 1785. The charter authorized the proprietors to charge a variety of tolls for passage, pay an annual fee to Harvard College for the loss of its exclusive ferry service across the river, and then, after forty years, return the bridge to the state in "good repair."

Construction of the bridge began immediately, and in 1786, it was open to traffic, benefiting the proprietors, the communities, and the back country. The land route from Medford to Boston, for example, was cut from thirteen to five miles, and trade dramatically increased as the bridge linked the area-wide market. Success invited imitation, and other communities petitioned the legislature for bridge charters. When the state authorized the West Boston Bridge to Cambridge in 1792, the Charles River Bridge proprietors asked for compensation for the revenue losses they anticipated, and the state extended their charter from forty to seventy years. Ironically, that extension provided the basis for future political and legal assaults against the Charles River Bridge. Other bridges followed and no compensation was offered. The state specifically refuted any monopoly claims and the Charles River Bridge proprietors refrained from claiming any.

Increasing prosperity and population raised the collection of tolls to nearly $20,000 annually in 1805; the share values had increased over 300 percent in value. The toll rates having remained constant since 1786, profits multiplied. Swollen profits stimulated community criticism and animated a long-standing hostility toward monopolies. Opportunity was the watchword and special privilege its bane.

Beginning in 1823, Charlestown merchants launched a five-year effort to build a competing "free" bridge over the Charles. They argued that the existing facility was inadequate, overcrowded, and dangerous; but basically, they appealed for public support on the grounds that the tolls on the Charles River Bridge were "burdensome, vexatious, and odious." The proprietors, defending the bridge's utility, offered to expand and improve it. They consistently maintained that the legislature could not grant a new bridge franchise in the vicinity without compensating them for the loss of tolls. But the political climate persuaded legislators to support the new bridge, and in 1828, after rejecting various schemes for compensation, the legislature approved the Warren Bridge charter. The act established the bridge's termini at 915 feet from the existing bridge on the Boston side, and at 260 feet from it on the Charlestown side. The new bridge was given the same toll schedule as the Charles River Bridge, but the state provided that after the builders recovered their investment and five per cent interest, the bridge would revert to the commonwealth. In any event, the term for tolls could not exceed six years. Governor LEVI LINCOLN had previously vetoed similar legislation, but in 1828 he quietly acquiesced.

The new bridge, completed in six months, was an instant success—but at the expense of the Charles River Bridge. During the first six months of the Warren Bridge's operations, receipts for the old bridge rapidly declined. Net income for the Warren Bridge in the early 1830s consistently was twice that for the Charles River Bridge.

Counsel for the old bridge proprietors wasted little time in carrying their arguments to the courts. After DANIEL WEBSTER and LEMUEL SHAW failed to gain an INJUNCTION to prevent construction of the new bridge, they appeared in the state supreme court to argue the merits of the charter in 1829, nearly one year after the bridge's completion. Shaw and Webster contended that the Charles River Bridge proprietors were successors to the Harvard ferry's exclusive franchise. In addition, they argued that the tolls represented the substance of the 1785 charter. Although the charter for the new bridge did not take away the plaintiffs' franchise, the 1828 act effectively destroyed the tolls—the essence and only tangible property of the franchise. The lawyers thus contended that the new bridge charter violated the CONTRACT CLAUSE and the state constitutional prohibition against expropriation of private property without compensation. The Warren Bridge defendants denied the old bridge's monopoly claims and emphasized that the state had not deprived the Charles River Bridge proprietors' continued right to take tolls. They also maintained that the old bridge proprietors had waived exclusivity when they accepted an extension of their franchise in 1792 after the state had chartered the West Boston Bridge.

The state supreme court, dividing equally, dismissed the complaint to facilitate a WRIT OF ERROR to the United States Supreme Court. The Jacksonian Democrats on the state court supported the state and their Whig brethren opposed it. The former rejected monopoly claims and berated the Charles River Bridge proprietors for their failure to secure an explicit monopoly grant. Chief Justice Isaac Parker, acknowledging that the 1785 grant was not exclusive, agreed that the state could damage existing property interests for the community's benefit without compensation. But he insisted that "immutable principles of justice" demanded compensation when the forms of property were indistinguishable. He conceded that canals and railroads might legitimately destroy the value of a turnpike; but when the state chartered a similar franchise, then operators of the existing property could claim an indemnity.

The United States Supreme Court first heard arguments in the case in March 1831. Although absences and disagreements prevented any decision before JOHN MARSHALL's death in 1835, the Court's records offer good circumstantial evidence that he had supported the new bridge. Following several new appointments and ROGER B. TANEY's confirmation as Chief Justice, the Court heard reargument in January 1837. Webster again appeared for the plaintiffs; defendants engaged Simon Greenleaf of Harvard, a close associate of JOSEPH STORY and JAMES KENT. Both sides essentially continued the arguments advanced in the state court. Finally, in February 1837, after nearly nine years of litigation, the Court decisively ruled in behalf of the state's right to charter the new bridge.

Taney's opinion sought to balance property rights against community needs by strictly construing the old bridge charter. He rejected the proprietors' exclusivity claim, contending that nothing would pass by implication. "The charter . . . is a written instrument which must speak for itself," he wrote, "and be interpreted by its own terms." He confidently asserted that the "rule" of STRICT CONSTRUCTION was well settled and he particularly invoked Marshall's 1830 PROVIDENCE BANK V. BILLINGS opinion, rejecting a bank's claim to implied tax immunity. Like Marshall, Taney concluded that the implications of exclusivity constituted a derogation of community rights. He argued that the community's "interests" would be adversely affected if the state surrendered control of a line of travel for profit. Taney neatly combined old Federalist doctrines of governmental power with the leaven of Jacksonian rhetoric: "The continued existence of a government would be of no great value," he believed, "if by implications and presumptions, it was disarmed of the powers necessary to accomplish the ends of its creations; and the functions it was designed to perform, transferred to the hands of privileged CORPORATIONS."

But the touchstone of Taney's opinion was its practical response to the contemporary reality of public policy needs. Taking note of technological changes and improvements, such as the substitution of railroad traffic for that of turnpikes and canals, Taney argued that the law must be a spur, not an impediment, to change. If the Charles River Bridge proprietors could thwart such change, he feared that the courts would be inundated with suits seeking to protect established property forms. Turnpike companies, for example, "awakening from their sleep," would call upon courts to halt improvements which had taken their place. Railroad and canal properties would be jeopardized and venture capital would be discouraged. The Supreme Court, he concluded, would not "sanction principles" that would prevent states from enjoying the advances of science and technology. Taney thus cast the law with the new entrepreneurs and risk-takers as the preferred agents for material progress.

In his dissent Justice Story rejected Taney's reliance upon strict construction and advanced an imposing line of precedents demonstrating that private grants had been construed in favor of the grantees. "It would be a dishonour of the government," Story said, "that it should pocket a fair consideration, and then quibble as to the obscurities and implications of its own contract." But Story's dissent was not merely a defense of VESTED RIGHTS. Like Taney, he, too, was concerned with progress and public policy. But whereas Taney emphasized opportunity, Story maintained that security of title and the full enjoyment of existing property was a necessary inducement for private investment in public improvements. Story insisted that the proprietors were entitled to compensation. He thus discounted the potentially staggering social and economic costs implicit in a universal principle requiring JUST COMPENSATION when new improvement projects diminished the value of existing franchises.

Story's position reflected immediate reality. Several years earlier, the state's behavior in the bridge controversy had discouraged stock sales for the proposed Boston and Worcester Railroad. Lagging investment finally had forced the legislature to grant the railroad a thirty-year guarantee of exclusive privileges on the line of travel.

Given the materialism of the American people, Taney's arguments had the greater appeal and endurance. He allied the law with broadened entrepreneurial opportunities at the expense of past assets. Nothing threatened the economic aspirations of Americans more than the scarcity of capital; nothing, therefore, required greater legal encouragement than venture capital, subject only to the risks of the marketplace. These were the concerns that took a local dispute over a free bridge out of its provincial setting and thrust it into the larger debate about political economy. In a society that placed a premium on "progress" and on the release of creative human energy to propel that progress, the decision was inevitable. And throughout American economic development, the Charles River Bridge case has fostered the process that Joseph Schumpeter called "creative destruction," whereby new forms of property destroy old ones in the name of progress.

STANLEY I. KUTLER

Bibliography

KUTLER, STANLEY I. (1971)1977 *Privilege and Creative Destruction: The Charles River Bridge Case*, rev. ed. New York: Norton.

CHARTERS, COLONIAL

See: Colonial Charters; Particular Colonies

CHASE, SALMON P.
(1808–1873)

Born in New Hampshire, Salmon Portland Chase enjoyed an elite education as a private pupil of his uncle, Episcopal Bishop Philander Chase of Ohio, as a Dartmouth student (graduating 1826), and as an apprentice lawyer (1827–1830) to United States Attorney General WILLIAM WIRT. Subsequently, Chase rose quickly as a Cincinnati attorney, beginning also his numerous, seemingly opportunistic, successive changes in political party affiliations. Abandoning Whig, then Democratic ties, Chase became in turn a member of the Liberty party and of the Republican organizations, winning elections to the United States Senate (1848–1855, 1860–1861), and to Ohio's governorship (1856–1860). He was an unsuccessful candidate for the Republican presidential nomination in 1860. ABRAHAM LINCOLN appointed Chase secretary of the treasury (1861–1864), and Chief Justice of the United States (1864–1873). Yet in 1864 Chase tried to thwart Lincoln's second term, in 1868 he maneuvered for the Democratic presidential nomination, and in 1872 he participated in the "Liberal Republican" schism against ULYSSES S. GRANT.

Such oscillations reflected more than Chase's large personal ambitions. Constitutional, legal, and moral concerns gave his public life coherence and purpose. These concerns derived from Chase's early conviction that men and society were easily corrupted, that SLAVERY was America's primary spoiling agent, and that political corruption was a close second. Although Chase, observing Wirt in the *Antelope* litigation (1825), found the doctrine in SOMERSET'S CASE (1772) an acceptable reconciliation of slavery and the Constitution as of that year, later events, especially those attending fugitive slave recaptures, unpunished assaults on abolitionists, and increases in slave areas due especially to the Mexican War and the treaties that closed it off, brought him to accept ABOLITIONIST CONSTITUTIONAL THEORY. Chase concluded that slavery's expansion beyond existing limits would demoralize white labor.

The first steps on this ultimately abolitionist road came from Chase's association with and brave defenses of Ohio antislavery activists, including JAMES BIRNEY, and of fugitive slaves; such defenses won Chase the nickname "attorney general for runaway negroes." A merely opportunistic Cincinnati lawyer would have had easier routes to success than this. Defending runaways and their abettors, Chase abjured HIGHER LAW pleadings popular among abolitionists; he focused instead on technical procedures and on a carefully developed restatement of state-centered FEDERALISM in which he insisted that nonslave jurisdictions also enjoyed STATES' RIGHTS. Slave states were able to export their recapture laws into free states via the federal FUGITIVE SLAVERY statutes. Chase argued that residents of free states also deserved to have the laws of their states concerning the status of citizens enjoy reciprocal effect and respect within slavery jurisdictions. Such a traffic of free state laws and customs across the federal system was impossible (and was to remain so until Appomattox). Chase insisted that residents of free states possessed at least the right to protect their co-residents of any race within those states from being reduced to servitude without DUE PROCESS.

Chase's evolving ideas culminated in a "freedom national" position, a general program for resolving the dilemma that slavery posed to a federal society based on assumptions of legal remedies, CIVIL RIGHTS, and CIVIL LIBERTIES. In his thinking, free labor was more than a marketplace phenomenon. It was a moral imperative, a complex of ethical relationships that the nation, under the Constitution, must nurture. Reformed, corruption-free two-party politics, with even blacks voting, was the way Chase discerned finally to nationalize freedom, a nationalization based upon acceptance of the DECLARATION OF INDEPENDENCE and the BILL OF RIGHTS as minimum definitions of the nation's interest in private rights adversely affected by state wrongs or private inequities.

The Civil War and the wartime and post-Appomattox Reconstruction of the southern states were the contexts in which Chase refined his thinking about individuals' rights and the nation's duty to protect them. Lincoln found a place in his cabinet for every one of the major competitors for the Republican presidential nomination in 1860, and Chase became secretary of the treasury. Once the war started, Chase had responsibility to provide an adequate circulating medium for the suddenly ballooning marketplace needs of the government, of the banking and commercial communities of the Union states, and of the millions of urban and rural entrepreneurs who rushed to expand production. Chase helped key congressmen to shape the historic wartime laws on national banking, income taxation, and legal tender (the legitimacy of the last of which Chase himself was to question as Chief Justice, in the LEGAL TENDER CASES).

The most outspoken abolitionist in Lincoln's cabinet, Chase also carved out a role for Treasury officials, who were responsible for administering rebels' confiscated property, in the Army's coastal experiments for abandoned, runaway, or otherwise freed blacks. He applauded the CONFISCATION ACTS, the EMANCIPATION PROCLAMATION, the major elements in Lincoln's MILITARY RECONSTRUCTION, the FREEDMEN'S BUREAU statute, and the THIRTEENTH AMENDMENT. Upon ROGER B. TANEY's death in late 1864, Lincoln, well aware of Chase's antipathy to the decision in DRED SCOTT V. SANDFORD (1857) and his commitment to irreversible emancipation, both of which the President shared, named the Ohioan to be Chief Justice.

After Appomattox, Chase, for his first years as Chief Justice, found that the work of the Court was almost exclusively with white men's rights rather than with the momentous, race-centered public questions that faced the Congress and the new President, ANDREW JOHNSON. On circuit, however, Chase's *In re Turner* opinion sustained broadly, in favor of a black female claimant, the provisions of the 1866 CIVIL RIGHTS ACT for enforcing the Thirteenth Amendment. In his opinion, Chase insisted that federal rights against servitude were defendable in national courts as against both state or private action or inaction, and he emphasized that a state's standard of right could serve as an adequate federal standard so long as the state did not discriminate racially.

Some contemporaries applauded *In re Turner* as an articulation of the new, nationalized federal system of rights that the Thirteenth Amendment appeared to have won. Chase's other circuit opinions did not, therefore, disturb race egalitarians, and generally won favor in professional legal and commercial media. These opinions dealt with numerous litigations concerning private relationships such as marriage licenses, trusts and inheritances, business contracts, and insurance policies made under rebel state dispensation. Chase recognized the validity of these legal arrangements. His decisions helped greatly to stabilize commerce and family relationships in the South.

The course of post-Appomattox Reconstruction as controlled both by President Johnson and by Congress, troubled Chase deeply. He knew, from his work in Lincoln's cabinet, how narrowly the Union had escaped defeat and tended, therefore, to sustain wartime measures. Yet he revered both the CHECKS AND BALANCES of the national government and the state-centered qualities of the federal system reflected in the Constitution. Therefore, in EX PARTE MILLIGAN (1866), Chase, still new on the Court, joined in the unanimous statement that Milligan, who had been tried by a military court, should preferably have been prosecuted in a civilian court for his offenses. But Chase, with three other Justices, dissented from the majority's sweeping condemnation of any federal military authority over civilians in a nonseceded state. The dissenters insisted instead that Congress possessed adequate WAR POWER to authorize military courts.

Chase again dissented from the 5–4 decision in the TEST OATH CASES (1867). Though privately detesting oath tests, Chase held to a public position that legislators, not judges, bore the responsibility to prescribe professional qualifications and licensing standards. By this time Congress had decided on Military Reconstruction. Mississippi officials, appointed earlier by Johnson, asked the Court for an INJUNCTION against the President's enforcing Congress's reconstruction law, and for a ruling that it was unconstitutional. For an unanimous Court, Chase refused to honor the petition (MISSISSIPPI V. JOHNSON, 1867), relying on the POLITICAL QUESTION doctrine. He agreed with his colleagues also in *Georgia v. Stanton* (1867) in refusing to allow the Court to intrude into political questions involving enforcement of the Reconstruction statutes. Mississippians again tried to enlist the Court against Congress. In early 1868 EX PARTE McCARDLE raised *Milligan*-like issues of military trials of civilians, and of the Court's jurisdiction to hear such matters under the HABEAS CORPUS ACT OF 1867. Congress thereupon diminished the Court's APPELLATE JURISDICTION under that statute. Chase, for the Court, acquiesced in the diminution, though pointing out that all other habeas jurisdiction remained in the Court.

He supported Congress's Military Reconstruction as a statutory base for both state restorations and black suffrage, but he was offended by the Third Reconstruction Act (July 1867), providing that military decisions would control civil judgments in the South. The IMPEACHMENT of Andrew Johnson, with Chase presiding over the Senate trial, seemed to threaten the destruction of tripartite checks and balances. Chase drifted back toward his old Democratic states' rights position, a drift signaled by his advocacy of universal amnesty for ex-rebels and universal suffrage. He had tried, unsuccessfully, to have the FOURTEENTH

Amendment provide for both. His enhanced or renewed respect for states' rights was evident in *United States v. DeWitt* (1869), in which the Court declared a federal law forbidding the transit or sale of dangerous naphtha-adulterated kerosene, to be an excessive diminution of STATE POLICE POWERS.

This decision, the first in which the Court denied Congress a capacity to act for regulatory purposes under the COMMERCE CLAUSE, like the decisions on Reconstruction issues, suggests how far the CHASE COURT engaged in JUDICIAL ACTIVISM. Striking in this regard were the Legal Tender Cases. The first of these, *Hepburn v. Griswold* (1870), resulted in a 4–3 decision that the 1862 law authorizing greenbacks as legal tender was invalid as applied to contracts made before passage of the statute. Chase, for the thin majority, insisted that the statute violated the Fifth Amendment's due process clause, concluding that the spirit of the CONTRACT CLAUSE, though by its terms restraining only the states, applied also to the federal government. The trio of dissenters—all, like Chase, Republican appointees—saw the money and war powers as adequate authority for the statute.

Then, later in 1870, President ULYSSES S. GRANT named two new Justices to the Court: JOSEPH P. BRADLEY and WILLIAM STRONG. The new appointees created, in *Knox v. Lee* (1871), the second Legal Tender Case decision, a majority that overruled *Hepburn*. The new majority now upheld the nation's authority to make paper money legal tender for contracts entered into either before or after enactment of the statute, an authority not pinned necessarily to the war power.

Chase was in the minority in the SLAUGHTERHOUSE CASES (1873) in which the majority found no violation of the Thirteenth or Fourteenth Amendments in a state's assignment of a skilled-trade monopoly to private parties. The doctrine of *Slaughterhouse*, that the privileges of United States citizenship did not protect basic civil rights, signaled a sharp retreat from Chase's own *In Re Turner* position, and was a fateful step by the Court toward what was to become a general retreat from Reconstruction.

Slaughterhouse, along with Chase's anti-Grant position in 1872, closed off Chase's long and tumultuous career; he died in 1873. His career was consistent in its anticorruption positions and in its infusions of moral and ethical ideas into constitutional, legal, and political issues. Party-jumping was incidental to Chase's ends of a moral democracy, federally arranged in a perpetual union of perpetual states; he gave this concept effective expression in TEXAS V. WHITE (1869).

To be sure, neither Chase nor "his" Court created novel legal doctrines. But he, and it, helped greatly to reclaim for the Court a significant role in determining the limits of certain vital public policies, both national and state. In the tumults of Reconstruction, while avoiding unwinnable clashes with Congress, Chase bravely insisted that effective governmental power and individual rights could co-exist. He and his fellow Justices advanced novel constitutional doctrines drawn from the prohibitions against ex post facto laws and BILLS OF ATTAINDER, and from the commerce and money powers. In retrospect, such experiments with doctrine take on the quality of interim defenses of judicial authority between prewar reliance on the contract clause, as example, and the post-Chase development of the due process clause of the Fourteenth Amendment.

At the same time, Chase tried to focus the Court's attention on individuals' rights as redefined first by the Thirteenth and then by the Fourteenth Amendment, as against both private and public wrongs. As one who for years had observed at first hand the capacity of nation and states and private persons to wrong individuals, Chase, as Chief Justice, brought a particular sense of urgency to the goal of protecting individual rights. He failed to convert a majority of his brethren to this task. Instead, America deferred its constitutional commitments. (See CONSTITUTIONAL HISTORY, 1865–1877.)

HAROLD M. HYMAN

Bibliography

FAIRMAN, CHARLES 1971 *History of the Supreme Court of the United States: Reconstruction and Reunion, 1864–1888.* New York: Macmillan.
HUGHES, DAVID 1965 Salmon P. Chase: Chief Justice. *Vanderbilt Law Review* 18:569–614.
HYMAN, HAROLD M. and WIECEK, WILLIAM M. 1982 *Equal Justice under Law: Constitutional Development 1835–1875.* Chaps. 11–13. New York: Harper & Row.
WALKER, PETER F. 1978 *Moral Choices.* Chaps. 13–14. Baton Rouge: Louisiana State University Press.

CHASE, SAMUEL
(1741–1811)

Samuel Chase was one of the most significant and controversial members of America's revolutionary generation. Irascible and difficult, but also extremely capable, he played a central role in Maryland politics during the 1760s and 1770s, signed the DECLARATION OF INDEPENDENCE, and was a member of the Continental Congress from 1775 to 1778. In the latter year ALEXANDER HAMILTON denounced him for using confidential information to speculate in the flour market. During the 1780s Chase pursued various business interests, practiced law, rebuilt his political reputation, and became an important anti-Federalist leader. After the adoption of the Constitution, for reasons that remain unclear, he became an ardent Federalist.

In 1795 he was nominated for a position on the federal bench. President GEORGE WASHINGTON was at first wary of recommending him, but when he had trouble filling a vacancy on the United States Supreme Court, he offered the position to Chase, who accepted in 1796. As one of the better legal minds in the early republic, Chase delivered several of the Court's most important decisions in the pre-Marshall period. In WARE V. HYLTON (1796) he provided one of the strongest statements ever issued on the supremacy of national treaties over state laws. The decision invalidated a Virginia statute of 1777 that placed obstacles in the way of recovery of debts owed by Americans to British creditors, a law in clear violation of a specific provision of the treaty of peace with Great Britain (1783). In HYLTON V. UNITED STATES (1796) Chase and the Supreme Court for the first time passed upon the constitutionality of an act of Congress, upholding the carriage tax of 1794. Chase concluded that only CAPITATION TAXES were direct taxes subject to the constitutional requirement of apportionment among the states according to population. In CALDER V. BULL (1798), where the Supreme Court held that the prohibition against EX POST FACTO LAWS in the Constitution extended only to criminal, not civil, laws, Chase addressed the issue of constitutionality in natural law terms, presaging those late-nineteenth-century jurists who, in furthering the concept of SUBSTANTIVE DUE PROCESS, were to argue that the Supreme Court could properly hold laws invalid for reasons lying outside the explicit prohibitions of the constitutional text. Riding circuit, he ruled in *United States v. Worrall* (1798) that the federal courts had no jurisdiction over crimes defined by COMMON LAW. This position, which Chase abandoned, was adopted by the Supreme Court in *United States v. Hudson and Goodwin* (1812). (See FEDERAL COMMON LAW OF CRIMES.)

A fierce partisan, Chase refused to recognize the legitimacy of the Jeffersonian opposition in the party struggles of the late 1790s. He used his position on the bench to make speeches for the Federalists and he supported the passage of the ALIEN AND SEDITION ACTS in 1798. Riding circuit, he enforced the law with a vengeance when he presided over the trials of John Fries of Pennsylvania for TREASON and John Callendar

of Virginia for SEDITION, sentencing the former to death (Fries was eventually pardoned by President JOHN ADAMS) and the latter to a stiff fine and a prison sentence. When THOMAS JEFFERSON and the Republicans came to power in 1801 and repealed the JUDICIARY ACT OF 1801, Chase vigorously campaigned behind the scenes for the Supreme Court to declare the repeal law unconstitutional, but the other Justices did not go along with him. Chase, however, remained adamant in his opposition to the Jeffersonians, refusing to alter his partisan behavior. "Things," he argued, "must take their natural course, from *bad* to *worse.*" In May 1803, in an intemperate charge to a GRAND JURY in Baltimore, he launched yet another attack on the Republican party and its principles.

Shortly thereafter, President Jefferson urged that Chase be removed from office. The House of Representatives voted for his IMPEACHMENT, and he came to trial before the United States Senate. The Constitution authorizes impeachment and conviction of federal government officers for "Treason, Bribery, or other high Crimes and Misdemeanors." Many of the more militant Republicans, unhappy with Federalist control of the judiciary, favored an expansive view of what should constitute an impeachable offense. As one put it: "Removal by impeachment was nothing more than a declaration by Congress to this effect: You held dangerous opinions and if you are suffered to carry them into effect, you will work the destruction of the Union. We want your offices for the purpose of giving them to men who will fill them better." Others, including a number of Republicans, favored a narrow definition: impeachment was permitted only for a clearly indictable offense.

Chase proved to be a formidable opponent. Aided by a prestigious group of Federalist trial lawyers, he put up a strong defense, denying that any of his actions were indictable offenses under either statute or common law. His attorneys raised various complicated and even moot legal questions such as the binding quality of local custom; the reciprocal rights and duties of the judge, jury, and defense counsel; the legality of bad manners in a court room; the rules of submitting EVIDENCE; and the problems involved in proving criminal intent. The prosecution was led by JOHN RANDOLPH, an extreme Republican and highly emotional man who badly botched the legal part of his argument. Chase was acquitted on all counts, even though most senators disliked him and believed his conduct on the bench had been improper. The final result was not so much a vote for Chase as it was against a broad definition of the impeachment clause—a definition that might be used to remove other judges, perhaps even to dismantle the federal judiciary altogether. Even Jefferson appears to have come around to this point of view; he made no attempt to enforce party unity when the Senate voted, and he was not unhappy with the outcome of the trial.

Although Chase served on the Supreme Court for the rest of his life, he no longer played an important role. JOHN MARSHALL had begun his ascendancy, and although Marshall was a staunch nationalist, he was less overtly partisan than Chase and less inclined to provoke confrontations with the Jeffersonians.

RICHARD E. ELLIS

Bibliography

ELLIS, RICHARD E. 1981 The Impeachment of Samuel Chase. Pages 57–78 in Michal Belknap, ed., *American Political Trials*. Westport, Conn.: Greenwood Press.

HAW, JAMES, et al. 1981 *Stormy Patriot: The Life of Samuel Chase*. Baltimore: Johns Hopkins University Press.

CHASE COURT
(1864–1873)

The decade of SALMON P. CHASE's tenure as Chief Justice of the United States was one of the more turbulent in the history of the Supreme Court. Laboring under the cloud of hostility engendered by DRED SCOTT V. SANDFORD (1857), hurt by partisan attacks from without and divisions within, staggering under loads of new business, the Chase Court nevertheless managed to absorb and consolidate sweeping new jurisdictional grants to the federal courts and to render some momentous decisions.

The Chase Court displayed an unusual continuity of personnel, which was offset by political and ideological heterogeneity. Of the nine men Chase joined on his accession (the Court in 1864 was composed of ten members), seven served throughout all or nearly all his brief tenure. But this largely continuous body was divided within itself by party and ideological differences. JOHN CATRON, who died in 1865, JAMES M. WAYNE, who died in 1867, and ROBERT C. GRIER, who suffered a deterioration in his faculties that caused his brethren to force him to resign in 1870, were Democrats. NATHAN CLIFFORD, an appointee of President JAMES BUCHANAN, and STEPHEN J. FIELD were also Democrats, the latter a War Democrat. SAMUEL F. MILLER, DAVID DAVIS, and JOSEPH P. BRADLEY were Republicans. Chase himself was an ex-Democrat who had helped form the Republican party in 1854, but he drifted back to the Democratic party

after the war and coveted its presidential nomination. WILLIAM STRONG, Grier's replacement, and NOAH SWAYNE were also Democrats who turned Republican before the war. Like the Chief Justice, Davis never successfully shook off political ambitions; he accepted and then rejected the Labor Reform party's nomination for the presidency in 1872. From 1870, Republicans dominated the Court, which had long been controlled by Democrats.

The work of the Supreme Court changed greatly during Chase's tenure. In 1862 and 1866, Congress realigned the federal circuits, so as to reduce the influence of the southern states, which under the Judiciary Act of 1837 had five of the nine circuits. Under the Judiciary Act of 1866, the southern circuits were reduced to two. By the same statute, Congress reduced the size of the Court from ten to seven members, mainly to enhance the efficiency of its work, not to punish the Court or deprive President ANDREW JOHNSON of appointments to it. In 1869, Congress again raised the size of the Court to nine, where it has remained ever since. More significantly, the business of the Court expanded. By 1871, the number of cases docketed had doubled in comparison to the war years. This increase resulted in some measure from an extraordinary string of statutes enacted between 1863 and 1867 expanding the JURISDICTION OF THE FEDERAL COURTS in such matters as REMOVAL OF CASES from state to federal courts, HABEAS CORPUS, claims against the United States, and BANKRUPTCY.

The Chase Court was not a mere passive, inert repository of augmented jurisdiction: it expanded its powers of JUDICIAL REVIEW to an extent unknown to earlier Courts. During Chase's brief tenure, the Court held eight federal statutes unconstitutional (as compared with only two in its entire prior history), and struck down state statutes in thirty-six cases (as compared with thirty-eight in its prior history). The attitude that produced this JUDICIAL ACTIVISM was expressed in private correspondence by Justice Davis, when he noted with satisfaction that the Court in EX PARTE MILLIGAN (1866) had not "toadied to the prevalent idea, that the legislative department of the government can override everything." This judicial activism not only presaged the Court's involvement in policy during the coming heyday of SUBSTANTIVE DUE PROCESS; it also plunged the Chase Court into some of the most hotly contested matters of its own time, especially those connected with Reconstruction. The Court also attracted the public eye because of the activities of two of its members: Chase's and Davis's availability as presidential candidates, and Chase's firm, impartial service in presiding over the United

States Senate as a court of IMPEACHMENT in the trial of Andrew Johnson.

The Chase Court is memorable for its decisions in four areas: Reconstruction, federal power (in matters not directly related to Reconstruction), state regulatory and tax power, and the impact of the FOURTEENTH AMENDMENT.

Nearly all the cases in which the Supreme Court disposed of Reconstruction issues were decided during Chase's tenure. The first issue to come up was the role of military commissions. In EX PARTE VALLANDIGHAM, decided in February 1864 (ten months before Chase's nomination), the Court refused to review the proceedings of a military commission, because the commission is not a court. But that did not settle the issue of the constitutional authority of military commissions. The matter came up again, at an inopportune time, in *Ex parte Milligan*, decided in December 1866. Milligan had been arrested, tried, convicted, and sentenced to be hanged by a military commission in Indiana in 1864 for paramilitary activities on behalf of the Confederacy. The Court unanimously ruled that his conviction was illegal because Indiana was not in a theater of war, because the civil courts were functioning and competent to try Milligan for TREASON, and because he was held in violation of the provisions of the HABEAS CORPUS ACT OF 1863. But the Court split, 5–4, over an OBITER DICTUM in Justice Davis's MAJORITY OPINION stating that the Congress could never authorize military commissions in areas outside the theater of operations where the civil courts were functioning. The Chief Justice, writing for the minority, declared that Congress did have the power to authorize commissions, based on the several WAR POWERS clauses of Article I, section 8, but that it had not done so; hence Milligan's trial was unauthorized.

Milligan created a furor in Congress and deeply implicated the Court in the politics of Reconstruction. Assuming that military commissions were essential to the conduct of Reconstruction, Democrats taunted Republicans that *Milligan* implied that they were unconstitutional, and hence that proposed Republican measures providing for military trials in the CIVIL RIGHTS ACT OF 1866 and FREEDMEN'S BUREAU Act violated the Constitution. Taken together with subsequent decisions, *Milligan* caused Republicans some anxiety. But, as Justice Davis noted in private correspondence and as Illinois Republican LYMAN TRUMBULL stated on the floor of the Senate, the decision in reality had no application to the constitutional anomaly of Reconstruction in the South.

The Court next seemed to challenge congressional Reconstruction in the TEST OATH CASES, *Ex parte Garland* and *Cummings v. Missouri*, both 1867. The court, by 5–4 decisions, voided federal and state statutes requiring a candidate for public office or one of the professions to swear that he had never participated or assisted in the rebellion. The Court's holding, that they constituted BILLS OF ATTAINDER and EX POST FACTO LAWS, seemingly threatened programs of disfranchisement and oath qualification, another part of proposed Reconstruction measures. Then, in February 1868, the Court announced that it would hear arguments in EX PARTE McCARDLE, another challenge to military commissions. William McCardle had been convicted by a military commission for publishing inflammatory articles. A federal circuit court denied his petition for a writ of habeas corpus under the HABEAS CORPUS ACT OF 1867, a measure that had broadened the scope of the writ, and he appealed the denial to the Supreme Court. Alarmed, congressional Republicans enacted a narrowly drawn statute known as the McCardle repealer, denying the Supreme Court appellate jurisdiction in habeas petitions brought under the 1867 act. In 1869, the Court accepted the constitutionality of the repealer, because Article III, section 2, made the Court's APPELLATE JURISDICTION subject to "such Exceptions . . . as the Congress shall make." But Chief Justice Chase pointedly reminded the bar that all the rest of the Court's habeas appellate authority was left intact. This broad hint bore fruit in *Ex parte Yerger* (1869), where the Court accepted jurisdiction of a habeas appeal under the JUDICIARY ACT OF 1789. Chief Justice Chase chastised Congress for the McCardle repealer and reaffirmed the scope of the Great Writ.

In the meantime, the Court had turned to other Reconstruction issues. As soon as Congress enacted the MILITARY RECONSTRUCTION ACTS of 1867, southern attorneys sought to enjoin federal officials, including the President and the secretary of war, from enforcing them. In MISSISSIPPI V. JOHNSON (1867), the Court unanimously rejected this petition. Chief Justice Chase drew on a distinction, originally suggested by his predecessor Chief Justice JOHN MARSHALL in MARBURY V. MADISON (1803), between ministerial and discretionary responsibilities of the President, stating that the latter were not subject to the Court's injunctive powers. In *Georgia v. Stanton* (1867), the Court similarly dismissed a petition directed at the secretary of war and General ULYSSES S. GRANT, holding that the petition presented POLITICAL QUESTIONS resolvable only by the political branches of the government. But the words of Justice Nelson's opinion seemed to suggest that if the petition had alleged a threat to private property (rather than the state's property), there might be a basis for providing relief. In May 1867, Mississippi's attorneys moved to amend their petition to specify such a threat. The Court, in a 4–4 order (Justice Grier being absent), rejected the motion. This minor, unnoticed proceeding was probably the truest index to the attitudes of individual Justices on the substantive policy questions of Reconstruction.

The Court's final involvement with Reconstruction came with TEXAS V. WHITE (1869) and *White v. Hart* (1872). In the former case, decided on the same day that the Supreme Court acknowledged the validity of the McCardle repealer, the postwar government of Texas sought to recover some bonds that the Confederate state government had sold to defray military costs. Because a state was a party, this was an action within the ORIGINAL JURISDICTION of the Supreme Court. But one of the defendants challenged the jurisdictional basis of the action, claiming that Texas was not a state in the constitutional sense at the time the action was brought (February 1867). This challenge directly raised important questions about the validity of SECESSION and Reconstruction. Chief Justice Chase, writing for the six-man majority (Grier, Swayne, Miller, dissenting) met the issue head on. He first held that secession had been a nullity. The Union was "indissoluble," "an indestructible Union, composed of indestructible States" in Chase's resonant, memorable phrasing. But, he went on, though the relations of individual Texans to the United States could not be severed, secession had deranged the status of the state within the Union. In language suggestive of the "forfeited-rights" theory of Reconstruction propounded by Ohio congressman Samuel Shellabarger which had provided a conceptual basis for Republican Reconstruction, Chase stated that the rights of the state had been "suspended" by secession and war. Congress was responsible for restoring the proper relationship, in wartime because of its authority under the military and MILITIA CLAUSES of Article I, section 8, and in peacetime under the guarantee of a REPUBLICAN FORM OF GOVERNMENT in Article IV, section 4. This was preponderantly a question to be resolved by Congress rather than the President, and hence the Lincoln and Johnson governments in power before enactment of the Military Reconstruction Acts were "provisional." Congress enjoyed wide latitude in working out details of Reconstruction policy. The sweeping language of Chase's opinion strongly implied the constitutionality of military Reconstruction. The majority opinion also offered a useful distinction between legitimate acts of the Confederate government of Texas,

such as those designed to preserve the peace, and invalid ones in support of the rebellion.

In *White v. Hart* (1872) the Court reaffirmed its general position in *Texas v. White* and emphasized that the relationship of states in the union was a political question for the political branches to resolve. At the same time, the Court disposed of two lingering issues from the war in ways that reaffirmed the doctrine of *Texas v. White*. In *Virginia v. West Virginia* (1870) it accepted the creation of the daughter state, shutting its eyes to the obvious irregularities surrounding the Pierpont government's consent to the separation, and insisting that there had been a "valid agreement between the two States." And in *Miller v. United States* (1871), echoing THE PRIZE CASES (1863), a six-man majority upheld the constitutionality of the confiscation provisions of the Second Confiscation Act of 1862 on the basis of the Union's status as a belligerent.

The Chase Court decisions dealing with secession, war, and Reconstruction have stood well the test of time. *Milligan* and the *Test Oath Cases* remain valuable defenses of individual liberty against arbitrary government. The *McCardle* decision was a realistic and valid recognition of an explicit congressional power, while its sequel, *Yerger*, reaffirmed the libertarian implications of *Milligan*. The Court's position in the cases seeking to enjoin executive officials from enforcing Reconstruction was inevitable: it would have been hopeless for the Court to attempt to thwart congressional Reconstruction, or to accede to the Johnson/Democratic demand for immediate readmission of the seceded states. *Texas v. White* and *White v. Hart* drew on a sound prewar precedent, LUTHER V. BORDEN (1849), to validate actions by the dominant political branch in what was clearly a pure political question. Taken together, the Reconstruction cases evince a high order of judicial statesmanship.

The Chase Court made only tentative beginnings in issues of federal and state regulatory power, but those beginnings were significant. The first federal regulatory question to come up involved the currency. In VEAZIE BANK V. FENNO (1869) the Court sustained the constitutionality of sections of the Internal Revenue Acts of 1865 and 1866 that imposed a ten percent tax on state bank notes for the purpose of driving them out of circulation. Chase first held that the tax was not a DIRECT TAX (which would have had to be apportioned among the states) and then upheld Congress's power to issue paper money and create a uniform national currency by eliminating state paper.

The LEGAL TENDER CASES were more controversial. As secretary of the treasury, Chase had reluctantly acquiesced in the issuance of federal paper money. But when the issue came before the Court in the First Legal Tender Case (*Hepburn v. Griswold*, 1870), Chase, speaking for a 4–3 majority, held the Legal Tender Act of 1862 unconstitutional because it made greenbacks legal tender for preexisting debts. The division on the court was partisan: all the majority Justices were Democrats (Chase by this time had reverted to his Democratic antecedents), all the dissenters Republicans. Chase's reasoning was precipitate and unsatisfactory. He asserted that the act violated the OBLIGATION OF CONTRACTS, but the CONTRACT CLAUSE limited only the states. To this Chase responded that the act was contrary to the "spirit of the Constitution." He also broadly implied that the statute violated the Fifth Amendment's guarantee of DUE PROCESS.

An enlarged Court in 1871 reversed *Hepburn*, upholding the constitutionality of the 1862 statute in the Second Legal Tender Cases, with the two new appointees, Bradley and Strong, joining the three dissenters of the first case. Justice Strong for the majority averred that "every contract for the payment of money, simply, is necessarily subject to the constitutional power of the government over the currency." The Court's turnabout suggested to contemporaries that President Grant had packed the Court to obtain a reversal of the first decision. Grant was opposed to the decision, and he knew that Bradley and Strong were also opposed; but he did not secure from them any commitments on the subject, and he did not base his appointments solely on the single issue of legal tender.

Other Chase Court decisions involving federal power were not so controversial. In *United States v. Dewitt* (1870) Chase for the Court invalidated an exercise of what would come to be called the NATIONAL POLICE POWER, in this case a provision in a revenue statute prohibiting the mixing of illuminating oil with naphtha (a highly flammable mixture). Chase held that the COMMERCE CLAUSE conferred no federal power over the internal affairs of the states, and that the subject matter was remote from the topic of raising revenue. He simply assumed that there was no inherent national police power. In COLLECTOR V. DAY (1871) Justice Nelson for a divided Court held that federal revenue acts taxing income could not reach the salary of a state judge. Justice Bradley's dissent, maintaining the necessity of federal power to reach sources of income that included some functions of state government, was vindicated in GRAVES V. NEW YORK EX REL. O'KEEFE (1939), which overruled *Day*. In contrast to the foregoing cases, *The Daniel Ball*

(1871) upheld the power of Congress to regulate commerce on navigable waterways, even where these were wholly intrastate.

The Chase Court decisions passing on the regulatory and taxing authority of the states caused less controversy. These cases are significant principally as evidence that the Court continued unabated its prewar responsibility of monitoring the functioning of the federal system, inhibiting incursions by the states on national authority and the national market, while at the same time preserving their scope of regulation and their sources of revenue intact. The first case of this sort, GELPCKE V. DUBUQUE (1864), involved a suit on bonds, issued by a city to encourage railroad building, which the city was trying to repudiate. The state courts had reversed their prior decisions and held that citizens could not be taxed to assist a private enterprise such as a railroad. The Supreme Court, in an opinion by Justice Swayne, reversed the result below, thus upholding the validity of the bonds. Swayne intemperately declared that "We shall never immolate truth, justice, and the law, because a state tribunal has erected the altar and decreed the sacrifice." The decision was welcomed in financial circles, particularly European ones, and presaged a Court attitude sympathetic to investors and hostile to repudiation, especially by a public agency.

The Court displayed less passion in other cases. In *Crandall v. Nevada* (1868), it struck down a state CAPITATION tax on passengers of public conveyances leaving the state as an unconstitutional interference with the right of persons to move about the country. The commerce clause aspects of the case were left to be decided later. Another case involving personal liberty, *Tarble's Case* (1872), vindicated the Court's earlier position in ABLEMAN V. BOOTH (1859) by holding that a state court in a habeas corpus proceeding could not release an individual held in federal custody (here, an allegedly deserting army volunteer).

But most cases testing the scope of state regulatory power dealt with commerce. In PAUL V. VIRGINIA (1869) the Court, through Chase, held that the negotiation of insurance contracts did not constitute commerce within the meaning of the commerce clause, and hence that a state was free to regulate the conduct of insurance companies as it pleased. This doctrine lasted until 1944. But one aspect of Justice Field's concurring opinion in *Paul* had momentous consequences. He asserted that, for purposes of the PRIVILEGES AND IMMUNITIES clause of Article IV, CORPORATIONS could not be considered "citizens," and were thus not entitled to the privileges and immunities of natural PERSONS. This caused attorneys to look to other sources, such as the due process clause (with its term "person") as a source of protection for corporations. During the same term, in WOODRUFF V. PARHAM (1868), the Chase Court upheld a municipal sales tax applied to goods brought into the state in INTERSTATE COMMERCE even though they were still in their original package, thus limiting Marshall's ORIGINAL-PACKAGE DOCTRINE announced in BROWN V. MARYLAND (1827) to imports from other nations.

Three 1873 cases demonstrated the Court carefully adjusting the federal balance. In the State Freight Tax Case the Court struck down a state tax on freight carried out of the state. But in the *Case of the State Tax on Railway Gross Receipts* the Court upheld a state tax on a corporation's gross receipts, even when the taxpayer was a carrier and the tax fell on interstate business. And in the *Case of the State Tax on Foreign-Held Bonds* the Court struck down a tax on interest on bonds as applied to the securities of out-of-state bondholders.

The last category of major Chase Court cases dealt with the scope of the Reconstruction Amendments, and the extent to which they would alter the prewar balances of the federal system. One of Chase's circuit court decisions, *In re Turner* (1867), suggested that this potential might be broad. Chase there held a Maryland BLACK CODE's apprenticeship provision unconstitutional on the ground that it imposed a condition of involuntary servitude in violation of the THIRTEENTH AMENDMENT. This decision might have been the prelude to extensive federal involvement in matters that before the war would have been considered exclusively within the STATE POLICE POWER. But this possibility was drastically narrowed in the SLAUGHTERHOUSE CASES (1873), the last major decision of the Chase Court and one of the enduring monuments of American constitutional law. Justice Miller for the majority held that "the one pervading purpose" of the Reconstruction Amendments was the liberation of black people, not an extension of the privileges and rights of whites. Miller construed the privileges and immunities, due process, and EQUAL PROTECTION clauses of the Fourteenth Amendment in light of this assumption, holding that none of them had deranged the traditional balance of the federal system. The states still remained the source of most substantive privileges and immunities, and the states remained primarily responsible for securing them to individuals. This ruling effectively relegated the definition and protection of freedmen's rights to precisely those governments—Redeemer-dominated southern states—least likely to provide that protection. Because "we do not see in those [Reconstruction] amendments any

purpose to destroy the main features of the general system," Miller rejected a substantive interpretation of the new due process clause and restricted the equal protection clause to cases of "discrimination against the negroes as a class."

The future belonged to the *Slaughterhouse* dissenters, Justices Bradley and Field. Bradley articulated the doctrine of substantive due process, arguing that the right to pursue a lawful occupation is a property right which the state may not interfere with arbitrarily or selectively. Field, in a dissent in which Chase joined (Swayne dissented in a separate opinion) relied on the privileges and immunities clause of the Fourteenth Amendment, seeing in it a guarantee of "the fundamental rights" of free men, which cannot be destroyed by state legislation. His insistence on an "equality of right, with exemption from all disparaging and partial enactments, in the lawful pursuits of life" foreshadowed the doctrine of FREEDOM OF CONTRACT.

Yet Field's and Bradley's insistence on the right to follow a chosen occupation, free of arbitrary discrimination, did not avail Myra Bradwell in her effort to secure admission to the Illinois bar (BRADWELL V. ILLINOIS, 1873). Justice Miller for the majority (Chase being the lone dissenter) refused to overturn a decision of the Illinois Supreme Court denying her admission to the bar solely on the ground of her gender. "The paramount mission and destiny of woman are to fulfill the noble and benign offices of wife and mother. This is the law of the Creator," Bradley wrote in a concurrence. "And the rules of civil society . . . cannot be based upon exceptional cases." The emergent scope of the due process, equal protection, and privileges and immunities clauses were to have a differential application as a result of the *Slaughterhouse* dissents and *Bradwell* ruling, securing the rights of corporations and men in their economic roles, while proving ineffectual to protect others from discrimination based on race and gender. (See RACIAL DISCRIMINATION; SEX EQUALITY.)

During its brief span, the Chase Court made enduring contributions to American constitutional development. It handled the unprecedented issues of Reconstruction with balance and a due recognition of the anomalous nature of issues coming before it. Yet in those decisions, Chase and his colleagues managed to preserve protection for individual rights while at the same time permitting the victorious section, majority, and party to assure a constitutional resolution of the war consonant with its military results. In non-Reconstruction cases, the Chase court continued the traditional function of the Supreme Court in monitoring and adjusting the allocation of powers between nation and states. It was more activist than its predecessors in striking down federal legislation, while it displayed the same nicely balanced concern for state regulatory power and protection of the national market that was a characteristic of the TANEY COURT.

WILLIAM M. WIECEK

Bibliography

FAIRMAN, CHARLES 1939 *Mr. Justice Miller and the Supreme Court, 1862–1890.* Cambridge, Mass.: Harvard University Press.

———— 1971 *Reconstruction and Reunion, 1864–88, Part One* (vol. VI of the Oliver Wendell Holmes Devise *History of the Supreme Court of the United States*). New York: Macmillan.

HYMAN, HAROLD M. and WIECEK, WILLIAM M. 1982 *Equal Justice Under Law: Constitutional Development 1835–1875.* New York: Harper & Row.

KUTLER, STANLEY I. 1968 *Judicial Power and Reconstruction Politics.* Chicago: University of Chicago Press.

SILVER, DAVID M. 1957 *Lincoln's Supreme Court.* Urbana: University of Illinois Press.

SWISHER, CARL B. 1930 *Stephen J. Field: Craftsman of the Law.* Washington, D.C.: Brookings Institution.

WARREN, CHARLES 1937 *The Supreme Court in United States History*, rev. ed. Boston: Little, Brown.

CHATHAM, LORD

See: William Pitt

CHECKS AND BALANCES

In its precise meaning, "checks and balances" is not synonymous with SEPARATION OF POWERS; it refers instead to a system of rules and practices designed to maintain the separation of powers. The executive VETO POWER is considered part of this system, along with the power of JUDICIAL REVIEW, the IMPEACHMENT power, and other powers available to any of the branches of government for combating the encroachments of the others.

JAMES MADISON formulated the American theory of checks and balances in response to the Anti-Federalist charge that the proposed Constitution would contain an overlap of governmental functions, violating the principle of separated powers. Expressing a pessimistic view of human nature, he argued in THE FEDERALIST #10 that the way to avoid majority tyranny lay in creating a large national community of diverse and numerous economic interests, not in statesman-

ship or in religious and moral constraints. In *The Federalist* #47–49 Madison went on to argue that neither sharply drawn institutional boundaries nor appeals to the electorate could be relied upon to maintain the separation of powers. Both methods presupposed the virtues of official lawfulness and electoral nonpartisanship, virtues whose unreliability was attested by experience. Because such "external checks" were ineffective, said Madison in *The Federalist* #51, maintaining the separation of powers would require "internal checks" that linked the officeholders' personal ambitions to their duties. Officials would defend their constitutional prerogatives if they felt that doing so were a means to furthering their personal ambitions. "[A]mbition checking ambition"—not virtue—was the key to constitutional maintenance. And effective checks required each branch to have a hand in the others' functions. For example, the veto is the President's hand in the legislative function.

Madison knew, however, that this partial blending of power did not go far enough. Power might still be concentrated if all these branches were united in one interest or animated by the same spirit. Thinkers from Aristotle to MONTESQUIEU had taught that constitutions could be maintained at least partly through a balance of social groups such as estates or economic classes. But theorists with democratic pretensions could not institutionalize such social divisions. The problem for the Framers was to prevent a single interest from predominating in a society that had few official distinctions of status and class. Their answer was to rely on the different institutional psychologies of governmental branches whose personnel would represent the different constituencies and perspectives of a large and diverse society. Thus, Madison argued in *The Federalist* #62–63 that because of differences in age, period of CITIZENSHIP, tenure of office, constituency, and, to a lesser degree, legislative function, members of the House of Representatives and Senate would pursue different policies with different consequences for the long term and varying impact on local, national, and international opinion. ALEXANDER HAMILTON wrote in *The Federalist* #70–71 that presidential types would be likely to seek the acclaim that attends success in difficult tasks, especially tasks requiring leaders to stand against and change public opinion. Such differences in institutional psychology, compounded by the federal features of the electoral system and the pluralism of an essentially democratic, secular, and commercial society, were expected to impede the formation of political parties disciplined enough to overcome the moderating influence of separated institutions.

The American system of checks and balances envisions strong executive and judicial branches. Experience had taught the Framers that popular legislatures were a greater threat to the separation of powers than were executives or courts. Accordingly, *The Federalist* #51 rationalized the bicameralism of Congress and the independence of the executive and judicial branches as means of weakening the naturally strongest branch and strengthening the weaker ones. This positive feature of the system complements its negative function of preventing concentrations of power. The Framers thus sought to achieve separation of governmental institutions without sacrificing the capacity for coordinated leadership when times demanded.

The system of checks and balances has worked well in some respects, but not in all. It has discouraged concentrations of power through centralized and disciplined political parties. Although government is fragmented in normal times, the system does permit central leadership in times of crisis, as the presidencies of THOMAS JEFFERSON, ABRAHAM LINCOLN, and FRANKLIN D. ROOSEVELT attest. It has also helped to create a remarkable degree of judicial independence without producing a judiciary seriously at odds with public opinion on any given issue for too long. The system has not worked so well in the case of Congress, which has undermined its own position by a practice of broad DELEGATION OF POWER to the executive and independent agencies. Many such delegations are necessitated by the problems and complexities that have brought the triumph of the administrative state. But far too many delegations are little more than acts of political buckpassing explained by the perception that the way to reelection does not lie in clear positions on controversial questions, but in constituency services and publicity that is politically safe. After the Great Depression and before the Supreme Court's decision in IMMIGRATION AND NATURALIZATION SERVICE V. CHADHA (1983), Congress compounded avoidable offense to the separation of powers when it tried to straddle the question of legislative responsibility, limiting many of its buckpassing delegations of power with various versions of the LEGISLATIVE VETO.

Congress's experience shows that there is a limit to the ability of the system to maintain a constitutional arrangement through reliance on personal ambition. Personal ambition sometimes dictates surrendering institutional prerogatives. The same can be said when Presidents compromise firmness in anticipation of elections and when judges propose "judicial self-restraint" in response to threats like court-packing and withdrawals of JURISDICTION. Despite the Framers'

theory of checks and balances, officials must at some point respect constitutional duty as something other than mere means to personal ambition.

SOTIRIOS A. BARBER

Bibliography

FISHER, LOUIS 1978 *The Constitution Between Friends: Congress, the President, and the Law.* New York: St. Martin's Press.

SHARP, MALCOLM 1938 The Classical American Doctrine of "the Separation of Powers." In Association of American Law Schools, *Selected Essays on Constitutional Law.* Vol. 4:168–194. Chicago: Foundation Press.

VILE, M. J. C. 1967 *Constitutionalism and the Separation of Powers.* Oxford: Clarendon Press.

CHEROKEE INDIAN CASES

Cherokee Nation v. *Georgia*
5 Peters 1 (1831)

Worcester v. *Georgia*
6 Peters 515 (1832)

The Cherokee Indian Cases prompted a constitutional crisis marked by successful state defiance of the Supreme Court, the Constitution, and federal treaties. The United States had made treaties with the Georgia Cherokee, as if they were a sovereign power, and pledged to secure their lands. Later, in 1802, the United States pledged to Georgia that in return for its relinquishment of the Yazoo lands (see FLETCHER V. PECK, 1810) the United States would extinguish the Cherokee land claims in Georgia. The Cherokee, however, refused to leave Georgia voluntarily in return for wild lands west of the Mississippi. In 1824 Georgia claimed LEGISLATIVE JURISDICTION over all the Indian lands within its boundaries. The Cherokee, who had a written language and a plantation economy, then adopted a CONSTITUTION and declared their sovereign independence. Georgia, which denied that the United States had authority to bind the state by an Indian treaty, retaliated against the Cherokee by a series of statutes that nullified all Indian laws and land claims and divided Cherokee lands into counties subject to state governance. President ANDREW JACKSON supported the state against the Indians, and Congress, too, recognizing that the Indians could not maintain a separate sovereignty within the state, urged them to settle on federally granted land in the west or, if remaining in Georgia, to submit to state laws.

The Cherokee turned next to the Supreme Court.

Claiming to be a foreign state within the meaning of Article III, section 2, of the Constitution, the Indians invoked the Court's ORIGINAL JURISDICTION in a case to which a state was a party and sought an INJUNCTION that would restrain Georgia from enforcing any of its laws within Cherokee territory recognized by federal treaties. By scheduling a hearing the Court exposed itself to Georgia's wrath. Without the support of the political branches of the national government, the Court faced the prospect of being unable to enforce its own decree or defend the supremacy of federal treaties against state violation.

The case of Corn Tassel, which suddenly intervened, exposed the Court's vulnerability. He was a Cherokee whom Georgia tried and convicted for the murder of a fellow tribesman, though he objected that a federal treaty recognized the exclusive right of his own nation to try him. On Tassel's application Chief Justice JOHN MARSHALL issued a WRIT OF ERROR to the state trial court and directed the governor of the state to send its counsel to appear before the Supreme Court. Georgia's governor and legislature contemptuously declared that they would resist execution of the Court's writ with all necessary force, denounced the Court's infringement of state SOVEREIGNTY, and hanged Corn Tassel. Justice JOSEPH STORY spoke of "practical NULLIFICATION." Newspapers and politicians throughout the nation took sides in the dispute between the Court and the state, and Congress in 1831 debated a bill to repeal section 25 of the JUDICIARY ACT OF 1789. Although the House defeated the repeal bill, Whigs despondently predicted that the President would not support the Court if it decided the *Cherokee Nation* case contrary to his view of the matter.

The Court wisely decided, 4–2, to deny jurisdiction on the ground that the Cherokee were not a foreign state in the sense of Article III's use of that term. Although Marshall for the Court declared that the Cherokee were a "distinct political society" capable of self-government and endorsed their right to their lands, he candidly acknowledged that the Court could not restrain the government of Georgia "and its physical force." That, Marshall observed, "savors too much of the exercise of political power" and that was what the bill for an injunction asked of the Court.

A year later, however, the Court switched its strategy. At issue in *Worcester* was the constitutionality of a Georgia statute that prohibited white people from residing in Cherokee territory without a state license. Many missionaries, including Samuel Worcester, defied the act in order to bring a TEST CASE before the Supreme Court, in the hope that the Court would endorse Cherokee sovereignty and void the state's Cherokee legislation. Worcester and another, having been sentenced to four years' hard labor, were the only missionaries to decline a pardon; they applied to the Court for a writ of error, which Marshall issued. Georgia sent the records of the case but again refused to appear before a Court that engaged in a "usurpation" of state sovereignty. The state legislature resolved that a reversal of the state court would be deemed "unconstitutional" and empowered the governor to employ all force to resist the "invasion" of the state's administration of its laws. The case was sensationally debated in the nation's press, and nearly sixty members of Congress left their seats to hear the argument before the Supreme Court.

In an opinion by Marshall, with Justice HENRY BALDWIN dissenting, the Court reaffirmed its jurisdiction under section 25, upheld the exclusive power of the United States in Indian matters, endorsed the authority of the Cherokee Nation within boundaries recognized by federal treaties, declared that the laws of Georgia had no force within these boundaries, and held that the "acts of Georgia are repugnant to the Constitution, laws, and treaties of the United States." The Court also reversed the judgment of the Georgia court and commanded the release of Worcester.

Why did the Court deliberately decide on the broadest possible grounds and challenge Georgia? In a private letter, Justice Story, noting that the state was enraged and violent, expected defiance of the Court's writ and no support from the President. "The Court," he wrote, "has done its duty. Let the nation do theirs. If we have a government let its commands be obeyed; if we have not it is as well to know it. . . ." Georgia did resist and Jackson did nothing. He might have made the famous remark, "John Marshall has made his decision; now let him enforce it." But Jackson knew Marshall's reputation for political craftiness, knew that a majority of Congress resisted all efforts to curb the Court, and knew that public opinion favored the Court and revered its Chief as the nation's preeminent Unionist. Jackson did nothing because he did not yet have to act. The state must first refuse execution of the Court's writ before the Court could order a federal marshal to free Worcester, and it could not issue an order to the marshal without a record of the state court's refusal to obey the writ. Not until the next term of the Court could it decide whether it had a course of action that would force the President either to execute the law of the land or disobey his oath of office. Marshall believed that public opinion would compel Jackson to execute the law. In the fall of 1832, however, Marshall pessimistically wrote that "our Constitution cannot last. . . . The Union has been prolonged thus far by miracles. I fear they cannot continue."

A miracle did occur, making the Court's cause the President's before the Court's next term; the SOUTH CAROLINA ORDINANCE OF NULLIFICATION intervened, forcing Jackson to censure state nullification of federal law. Georgia supported Jackson against South Carolina, and he convinced Georgia's governor that the way to dissociate Georgia from nullification was to free Worcester. The governor pardoned him. Worcester, having won the Supreme Court's invalidation of the Georgia Cherokee legislation, accepted the pardon. The lawyers for the Cherokee persuaded them to desist from further litigation in order to preserve a Unionist coalition against nullificationists. In 1838, long after the crisis had passed, the Cherokees were forcibly removed from their lands. The Court could not save them. It never could. It had, however, saved its integrity ("The Court has done its duty") by defending the supreme law of the land at considerable risk.

LEONARD W. LEVY

Bibliography

BURKE, JOSEPH C. 1969 The Cherokee Cases: A Study of Law, Politics, and Morality. *Stanford Law Review* 21:500–531.
WARREN, CHARLES 1923 *The Supreme Court in United States History*, 3 vols. Vol. 2:189–229. Boston: Little, Brown.

CHEROKEE NATION v. GEORGIA

See: Cherokee Indian Cases

CHICAGO, BURLINGTON & QUINCY RAILROAD v. CHICAGO
166 U.S. 226 (1897)

A 7–1 Supreme Court here sustained a $1 award as JUST COMPENSATION for a TAKING OF PROPERTY, holding that the SEVENTH AMENDMENT precluded it from reexamining facts, decided by a jury, which dictated that amount. Although due process required compensation, a nominal sum did not deprive the railroad of either due process or EQUAL PROTECTION. The Court required a "fair and full equivalent for the thing taken by the public" and stressed the necessity for understanding the spirit of due process. "In determining what is DUE PROCESS OF LAW, regard must be had to substance, not to form."

DAVID GORDON

CHICAGO, MILWAUKEE & ST. PAUL RAILWAY v. MINNESOTA
134 U.S. 418 (1890)

This decision, making the courts arbiters of the reasonableness of railroad rates, presaged the Supreme Court's final acceptance of SUBSTANTIVE DUE PROCESS ten years later. The Minnesota legislature had established a commission to inspect rail rates and alter those it deemed unreasonable. A 6–3 Court struck down the statute as a violation of both substantive and PROCEDURAL DUE PROCESS. Justice SAMUEL BLATCHFORD found that the statute neglected to provide procedural due process: railroads received no notice that the reasonableness of their rate was being considered, and the commission provided no hearing or other chance for the railroads to defend their rates. Moreover, Blatchford said that a rate's reasonableness "is eminently a question for judicial investigation, requiring due process of law for its determination." A company, denied the authority to charge reasonable rates and unable to turn to any judicial mechanism for review (procedural due process) would necessarily be deprived "of the lawful use of its property, and thus, in substance, and effect, of the property itself, without due process of law" (substantive due process). In dissent, Justice JOSEPH P. BRADLEY declared that the majority had effectively overruled MUNN v. ILLINOIS (1877). Bradley's opinion explicitly rejected the assertion that reasonableness was a question for judicial determination; it is, he said, "pre-eminently a legislative one, involving considerations of policy as well as of remuneration." If the legislature could fix rates (as precedent had shown), why could it make no such delegation of power to a commission? Indeed, the Court's next step, in REAGAN v. FARMERS' LOAN & TRUST COMPANY (1894), would be the claim of power to void statutes by which the legislature itself directly set rates, and, in SMYTH v. AMES (1898), the Court would reach the zenith, actually striking down a state act for that reason.

DAVID GORDON

CHIEF JUSTICE, ROLE OF THE

The title "Chief Justice" appears only once in the Constitution. That mention occurs not in Article III, the judicial article, but in connection with the Chief Justice's role as presiding officer of the Senate during an IMPEACHMENT trial of the President. With such a meager delineation of powers and duties in the Constitution, the importance of the office was hardly obvious during the early days of the Republic. Despite President GEORGE WASHINGTON's great expectations for the post, his first appointee, JOHN JAY, left disillusioned and convinced that neither the Supreme Court nor the chief justiceship would amount to anything. Yet, a little over a century later, President WILLIAM HOWARD TAFT stated that he would prefer the office to his own. During that intervening century, an office of considerable power and prestige had emerged from the constitutional vacuum. Since then, the Chief Justice's role has continued to evolve. Today, the office is the product of both the personalities and the priorities of its incumbents and of the institutional forces which have become stronger as the Supreme Court's role in our government has expanded and matured.

Like the other Justices of the Supreme Court, the Chief Justice of the United States is appointed by the President with the ADVICE AND CONSENT of the Senate. He enjoys, along with all other full members of the federal judiciary, life tenure "during his GOOD BEHAVIOR." With respect to the judicial work of the Court, he has traditionally been referred to as *primus inter pares*—first among equals. He has the same vote as each Associate Justice of the Court. His judicial duties differ only in that he presides over the sessions of the Court and over the Court's private CONFERENCE at which the cases are discussed and eventually decided. When in the majority, he assigns the writing of the OPINION OF THE COURT. Like an Associate Justice, the Chief Justice also performs the duties of a circuit Justice. A circuit Justice must pass upon various applications for temporary relief and BAIL from his circuit and participate, at least in a liaison or advisory capacity, in the judicial administration of that circuit. By tradition, the Chief Justice is circuit Justice for the Fourth and District of Columbia Circuits.

In addition to his judicial duties, the Chief Justice has, by statute, responsibility for the general administration of the Supreme Court. While the senior officers of the Court are appointed by the entire Court, they perform their daily duties under his general supervision. Other employees of the Court must be approved by the Chief Justice.

The Chief Justice also serves as presiding officer of the Judicial Conference of the United States. The Conference, composed of the chief judge and a district judge from each circuit, has the statutory responsibility for making comprehensive surveys of the business of the federal courts and for undertaking a continuous study of the rules of practice and procedure. The Chief Justice, as presiding officer, must appoint the various committees of the Conference which under-

take the studies necessary for the achievement of those statutory objectives. He must also submit to the Congress an annual report of the proceedings of the Conference and a report as to its legislative recommendations. Other areas of court administration also occupy the Chief Justice's attention regularly. He has the authority to assign, temporarily, judges of the lower federal courts to courts other than their own and for service on the Panel on Multidistrict Litigation. He is also the permanent Chairman of the Board of the Federal Judicial Center which develops and recommends improvements in the area of judicial administration to the Judicial Conference.

From time to time, Congress has also assigned by statute other duties to the Chief Justice. Some are related to the judiciary; others are not. For instance, he must appoint some of the members of the Commission on Executive, Legislative, and Judicial Salaries; the Advisory Corrections Council; the Federal Records Council; and the National Study Commission on Records and Documents of Federal Officials. He also serves as Chancellor of the Smithsonian Institution and as a member of the Board of Trustees of both the National Gallery of Art and the Joseph H. Hirshhorn Museum and Sculpture Garden.

In addition to these formal duties, the Chief Justice is considered the titular head of the legal profession in the United States. He traditionally addresses the American Bar Association on the state of the judiciary and delivers the opening address at the annual meeting of the American Law Institute. He is regularly invited to other ceremonial and substantive meetings of the bar. Finally, as head of the judicial branch, he regularly participates in national observances and state ceremonies honoring foreign dignitaries.

The foregoing catalog of duties, while describing a burdensome role, does not fully indicate the impact of the Chief Justice on the Supreme Court's work. For instance, with respect to his judicial duties, the Chief Justice, while nominally only "first among equals," may exercise a significant influence on the Court's decision-making process and, consequently, on its final judicial work product. His most obvious opportunity to influence that process is while presiding at the Court's conference. He presents each case initially and is the first to give his views. Thus, he has the opportunity to take the initiative by directing the Court's inquiry to those aspects of the case he believes are crucial. Moreover, although the Justices discuss cases in descending order of seniority, they vote in the opposite order. Therefore, while speaking first, the "Chief," as he is referred to by his colleagues, votes last and commits himself, even preliminarily, only after all of the associates have explained their positions and cast their votes. If he votes with the majority, he may retain the opinion for himself or assign it to a colleague whose views are most compatible with his own. In cases where there is significant indecision among the Justices, it falls to the "Chief" to take the initiative with respect to the Court's further consideration of the case. He may, for instance, suggest that further discussion be deferred until argument of other related cases or he may request that several Justices set forth their views in writing in the hope that such a memorandum might form the basis of a later opinion.

There are also more indirect but highly significant ways by which the "Chief" can influence the decision-making process. As presiding officer during open session, he sets a "tone" which can make ORAL ARGUMENT either a formal, stilted affair or a disciplined but relaxed, productive dialogue between the Court and counsel. Even the Chief Justice's "administrative" duties within the Court can have a subtle influence on the Court's decision-making processes. The efficient administration of the Court's support services as well as the employment of adequate staff personnel can nurture an ambiance conducive to harmonious decision making.

While occupancy of the Court's center chair no doubt gives the incumbent an enhanced capacity to influence jurisprudential developments, there are clear limitations on the exercise of that power. The Court is a collegial institution; disagreement on important issues is a natural phenomenon. In such a context, as Justice WILLIAM H. REHNQUIST put it in a 1976 article: "The power to calm such naturally troubled waters is usually beyond the capacity of any mortal chief justice. He presides over a conference not of eight subordinates, whom he may direct or instruct, but of eight associates who, like him, have tenure during good behavior, and who are as independent as hogs on ice. He may at most persuade or cajole them." Political acumen is often as important as intellectual brilliance. Whatever the Chief's view of his power, he must remember that, in the eyes of the associates, "the Chief Justice is not entitled to a presumption that he knows more law than other members of the Court . . .," as Justice Rehnquist said in chambers in CLEMENTS v. LOGAN (1981). Other institutional concerns further constrain the Chief's ability to guide the Court's decisions. All Chief Justices have recognized, although to varying degrees, a responsibility to see not only that the Court gets its business done but also that it does so in a manner which maintains

the country's confidence. Sometimes, those objectives require that the Chief refrain from taking a strong ideological stance and act as a mediator in the formation of a majority. Similarly, while the assignment power can be a powerful tool, it must be exercised to ensure a majority opinion that advances, not retards, growth in the law. Even the prerogative of presiding over the conference has a price. The Chief Justice must spend significant additional time reviewing all the petitions filed with the Court. As the performance of Chief Justice CHARLES EVANS HUGHES demonstrated, perceiving those areas of ambiguity and conflict that are most troublesome in the administration of justice is essential to leading effectively the discussion of the conference. For the same reason, the Chief must take the time to master the intricacies of the Court's procedure.

The extrajudicial responsibilities of the Chief Justice can also place him at a distinct disadvantage in influencing the Court's jurisprudential direction. The internal decision-making process of the Court is essentially competitive. There is nothing so humble as a draft opinion with four votes and nothing so arrogant as one with six. Such a process does not easily take into account that one participant must regularly divert his attention because of other official responsibilities. Moreover, there is a special intellectual and physical cost in shifting constantly between the abstract world of the appellate judge and the pragmatic one of the administrator. A Chief Justice who takes all his responsibilities seriously must experience the fatiguing tension that inevitably results from such bifurcation of responsibilities. Here, however, there may be compensating considerations. Whatever advantage the Chief may lose in the judicial bargaining because of administrative distractions may well be partially recovered by the prestige gained by his accomplishments beyond the Court. The Court has benefited from a strong Chief Justice's defense against specific political threats such as President FRANKLIN D. ROOSEVELT's Court-packing plan. It has also benefited when the Chief's efforts have resulted in legislation making its own workload more manageable. Chief Justice Taft's support of the JUDICIARY ACT OF 1925, for instance, gave the Court more control over its own docket and, consequently, increased capacity to address, selectively, the most pressing issues. In modern times, the tremors of the litigation explosion that has engulfed the lower courts have been felt on the Supreme Court. The accomplishments of a Chief Justice in alleviating these problems cannot be overlooked by his associates.

Certainly, with respect to nonjudicial matters, a Chief Justice's special responsibility for institutional concerns has commanded respect from the associates. Even such greats as Justice LOUIS D. BRANDEIS regularly consulted the Chief on matters that might have an impact on the reputation of the Court as an institution. This same identification of the Chief Justice with the Supreme Court as an institution has made some Chief Justices the acknowledged spokesperson for both the Supreme Court and the lower federal courts before the other branches of government and, indeed, before the public.

With no specific constitutional mandate to fulfill, early Chief Justices, most especially JOHN MARSHALL, molded the office in which they served just as they molded the courts over which they presided. In those formative periods, the dominance of personal factors was understandable. Today, however, significant institutional forces also shape the office. In addition to the extrajudicial duties imposed by Congress, the Court, now a mature institution of American government, exerts through its traditions a powerful influence over every new incumbent of its bench—including the person in the center chair.

KENNETH F. RIPPLE

Bibliography

FRANKFURTER, FELIX 1953 Chief Justices I Have Known. *Virginia Law Review* 39:883–905.
FREUND, PAUL A. 1967 Charles Evans Hughes as Chief Justice. *Harvard Law Review* 81:4–43.
REHNQUIST, WILLIAM H. 1976 Chief Justices I Never Knew. *Hastings Constitutional Law Quarterly* 3:637–655.
SWINDLER, WILLIAM F. 1971 The Chief Justice and Law Reform. *The Supreme Court Review* 1971:241–264.

CHILD BENEFIT THEORY

Protagonists of aid to religious schools have sought to justify the practice constitutionally through what has become known as the child benefit theory. The establishment clause, they urge, forbids aid to the schools but not to the children who attend them. Recognizing that the schools themselves benefit from the action, they argue that the benefit is secondary to that received by the pupils, and note that the courts have long upheld governmental assistance to children as an aspect of the POLICE POWER.

The recognition is at least implicit in Supreme Court decisions through BOARD OF EDUCATION V. ALLEN (1968). Thus, in *Bradfield v. Roberts* (1899), the Court upheld the validity under the establishment clause of a grant of federal funds to finance the erection of a hospital in the DISTRICT OF COLUMBIA, to be maintained and operated by an order of nuns. The Court reasoned that the hospital corporation was a legal entity separate from its incorporators, and concluded that the aid was for a secular purpose. Later court decisions ignored this fiction, consistently upholding grants to religious organizations, corporate or noncorporate, to finance hospitals that, though owned and operated by churches, nevertheless were nonsectarian in their admission policies, and generally benefited the patients.

In EVERSON V. BOARD OF EDUCATION (1947) the Court upheld use of tax-raised funds to finance transportation to religious schools, in part because the program had the secular purpose to enable children to avoid the risks of traffic or hitchhiking in going to school. In COCHRAN V. LOUISIANA STATE BOARD OF EDUCATION (1930) and *Board of Education v. Allen* (1968) the Court similarly sustained laws financing the purchase of secular textbooks for use in parochial schools. The beneficiaries of the laws, the Court asserted, were not the schools but the children who attended them.

More recent decisions, however, manifest a weakening of the theory. In *Board of Education v. Nyquist* (1973) the Court refused to uphold a law to finance costs of maintenance and repair in religious schools, notwithstanding a provision that the program's purpose was to insure the health, welfare, and safety of the school children.

Two years later, in *Meek v. Pittenger*, the Court refused to extend *Allen* to encompass the loan of instructional materials to church-related schools, even though the materials benefited nonpublic school children and were provided for public school children. Finally, in WOLMAN V. WALTER (1977) the Court, unwilling to overrule either *Everson* or *Allen*, nevertheless refused to extend them to encompass educational field trip transportation to governmental, industrial, cultural, and scientific centers.

In these later cases, the Court has rejected the argument that if public funds were not used for these support services, many parents economically unable to pay for them would have to transfer their children to the public schools in violation of their own and of their children's religious conscience.

LEO PFEFFER

(SEE ALSO: *Establishment of Religion; Separation of Church and State.*)

Bibliography
DRINAN, ROBERT F., S.J. 1963 *Religion, the Courts, and Public Policy.* Chap. 5. New York: McGraw-Hill.
PFEFFER, LEO 1967 *Church, State and Freedom,* rev. ed. Chap. 14. Boston: Beacon Press.

CHILD LABOR AMENDMENT

Two years after BAILEY V. DREXEL FURNITURE CO. (1922) when for the second time the Supreme Court invalidated a federal child labor law, Congress approved a constitutional amendment empowering it to regulate on the subject. But from 1924 until 1938, the amendment languished in state legislatures, with only twenty-eight of the requisite thirty-six having ratified it by 1938.

Led by the National Association of Manufacturers, critics contended that the proposed amendment endangered traditional state powers and local control of PRODUCTION. The Granges also lobbied in agricultural states in the South and Midwest, arguing that such congressional power would threaten the use of children on family farms. Religious groups maintained that the amendment would lead to federal control of education and increase the costs of educating children. Newspapers overwhelmingly opposed the amendment on the grounds that they would be deprived of delivery boys.

The Court's decision in the WAGNER ACT CASES (1937) renewed interest in congressional legislation. The FAIR LABOR STANDARDS ACT in 1938 outlawed child labor, and in UNITED STATES V. DARBY (1941), the Court sustained the legislation and overturned its own precedents. The new law and the *Darby* decision combined to make the amendment unnecessary.

The lengthy ratification process prompted Congress to impose time limits on many subsequent amendments. The child labor amendment also raised a knotty constitutional problem when one state reversed its position (in a disputed vote) and approved ratification. That action was challenged in COLEMAN V. MILLER (1939), but the Court sidestepped the issue as a POLITICAL QUESTION and left its resolution to Congress.

STANLEY I. KUTLER

Bibliography
WOOD, STEPHEN 1968 *Constitutional Politics in the Progressive Era: Child Labor and the Law.* Chicago: University of Chicago Press.

CHILD LABOR CASE

See: *Hammer v. Dagenhart*

CHILD LABOR TAX ACT
40 Stat. 1138 (1918)

In HAMMER V. DAGENHART (1918), a 5–4 Supreme Court voided the Child Labor Act of 1916, which had forbidden carriers from transporting the products of child labor in INTERSTATE COMMERCE, as a prohibition, not a regulation, of commerce. This distinction had been thought rejected as early as CHAMPION V. AMES (1903). Progressive reformers, intent on abolishing child labor, had shifted the basis of their efforts from the COMMERCE CLAUSE to the TAXING POWER, thus invoking a new set of powerful precedents, notably MCCRAY V. UNITED STATES (1904).

In late 1918 Congress passed a Revenue Act to which had been added an amendment known as the Child Labor Tax Act. A ten percent EXCISE TAX was imposed on the net profits from the sale of child labor-produced items. This tax extended to any factory, mine, or mill employing children under fourteen, or to the age of sixteen under certain circumstances. Congressmen from the major cotton textile manufacturing states, southern Democrats, cast nearly all the negative votes.

In BAILEY V. DREXEL FURNITURE CO. (1922) an 8–1 Court invalidated the act, *McCray* and UNITED STATES V. DOREMUS (1919) notwithstanding, as a violation of the powers reserved to the states by the TENTH AMENDMENT.

DAVID GORDON

Bibliography
WOOD, STEPHEN B. 1968 *Constitutional Politics in the Progressive Era: Child Labor and the Law.* Chicago: University of Chicago Press.

CHILD LABOR TAX CASE

See: *Bailey v. Drexel Furniture Company*

CHILDREN'S RIGHTS

The law of childhood is complex, but as a general legal proposition, a child is someone who has not yet reached the age of civil majority. Each state has the authority to determine the age of majority for its own residents, and in most states that age is now eighteen. Prior to 1971, the age of majority was typically twenty-one, but after the ratification of the TWENTY-SIXTH AMENDMENT, which gave eighteen-year-olds the right to vote in federal elections, most states lowered the age of majority, as well as the voting age for state elections.

In general, children have less liberty than adults and are less often held accountable for their actions. Parents have legal power to make a wide range of decisions for the child, although they are held responsible by the state for the child's care and support. Children have a special power to avoid contractual obligations but are not normally entitled to their own earnings and cannot manage their own property. Moreover, persons younger than certain statutory limits are not allowed to vote, hold public office, work in various occupations, drive a car, buy liquor, or be sold certain kinds of reading material, quite apart from what either they or their parents may wish.

Although a variety of civic and personal rights accrue at the age of majority, rights to engage in various "adult" activities may occur either before or after the age of eighteen. For example, many states restrict the legal access of nineteen- and twenty-year-olds to alcoholic beverages. On the other hand, most states permit sixteen- and seventeen-year-olds to secure licenses to drive automobiles. State child labor laws typically permit young people who are sixteen or seventeen to work, particularly outside of school hours, although federal law prohibits the employment of children under eighteen in hazardous occupations. A minor who is self-supporting and living away from home may, through emancipation, obtain a broad range of adult rights.

When advocates speak of children's rights, they may have in mind either of two quite contradictory notions. One notion focuses on children's basic needs, and the obligations to satisfy those needs. The other focuses on autonomy and choice.

At times, the word "right" is used to describe the duties of others—typically parents or state officials—to satisfy what are seen as a child's basic needs. Thus, claims are made that a child has or should have a legal right to education, adequate food and shelter, and even love, affection, discipline, and guidance. The federal Constitution has not been interpreted to give a child a substantive right to adequate education or care, although state law sometimes creates such duties. For example, every state provides for free public education, typically through high school, and many

state constitutions require as much. Although the Supreme Court decided in SAN ANTONIO INDEPENDENT SCHOOL DISTRICT V. RODRIGUEZ (1973) that education is not a "fundamental" right, at least for purposes of requiring strict scrutiny under the EQUAL PROTECTION clause, the Court acknowledged in BROWN V. BOARD OF EDUCATION (1954) that education is "perhaps the most important function of state and local governments." There is no constitutional right to parental love, but opinions such as PIERCE V. SOCIETY OF SISTERS (1925) have suggested that children as well as parents have an interest of constitutional dimension in preserving the parent–child relationship. State child-neglect statutes do impose on parents an obligation to provide adequate custodial care. In all events, a child's "right" to such things as an education or minimally adequate care has little to do with the protection of choice on the part of a particular child. A judge usually does not ask a physically abused child whether she wants to remain with her parents when the responsible authorities believe they cannot protect her from further harm if she remains at home. Compulsory education laws and child labor laws do not give an unhappy eleven-year-old child the legal right to pursue an education by dropping out of school and taking a job.

A second, very different, notion of "children's rights" emphasizes autonomy, choice, and liberty. Claims asserting this sort of right have arisen in a variety of contexts: procedural claims in JUVENILE PROCEEDINGS and in schools (see GOSS V. LOPEZ, 1975); choices about abortion or BIRTH CONTROL; access to reading material (see GINSBERG V. NEW YORK, 1968); and involvement in political protests (see TINKER V. DES MOINES SCHOOL DISTRICT, 1969). Usually the challenge is to some form of state paternalism; but sometimes the minor's claim involves the assertion that he should have the "right" to act independently of his parents. Because the liberty of minors is much more restricted than that of adults, reformers have sometimes asserted that adolescents should have the right to adult status, at least in particular settings. A few have even suggested a children's liberation movement to end the double standard of morals and behavior for adults and children.

The definition of "children's rights" necessarily involves the allocation of power and responsibility among the child, the family, and the state. Taking contemporary constitutional doctrine at face value, three basic principles bear on this allocation. The first principle concerns the children themselves, and the notion that as individuals they have constitutional rights. The Supreme Court declared in IN RE GAULT (1967), the seminal children's rights case, "whatever may be their precise impact, neither the FOURTEENTH AMENDMENT nor the BILL OF RIGHTS is for adults alone."

The second principle concerns parents and the notion that parents have primary authority over the child. Children are part of families, and our traditions emphasize the primacy of the parental role in child-rearing. The rights of children cannot be defined without reference to their parents. The Court has suggested that parental authority also has a constitutional dimension: the state may not intrude too deeply into the parent–child relationship. Drawing on this principle, the Court held in WISCONSIN V. YODER (1972) that Wisconsin could not compel children to attend public schools when their old-order Amish parents believed that public schooling interfered with their raising of their children as their religion dictates. Nor may a state require all children to attend public school when there are private schools that meet legitimate regulatory standards.

The third principle concerns the state. It suggests that the state, in the exercise of its *parens patriae* power, has a special responsibility to protect children, even from their parents. The state's interest in protecting children has frequently been characterized as "compelling" and has been drawn on to justify a variety of child protective measures that constrain the liberty of parents and children alike. "Parents may be free," declared the Supreme Court in PRINCE V. MASSACHUSETTS (1944), "to become martyrs themselves. But it does not follow that they are free, under free and identical circumstances, to make martyrs of their children before they reach the age of full and legal discretion when they can make that choice for themselves."

Any one of these three principles, if taken very far, cuts deeply into the others. For example, to the extent that children, as individuals, are given autonomy rights, limits are necessarily imposed on parental rights to control their behavior or socialization. Recognition of child autonomy also limits the state's right to constrain a child's conduct in circumstances where adult conduct could not be similarly constrained. Some rights of child autonomy would disable the state from having special protective legislation for children. Broad interpretation of the state's *parens patriae* power to intervene to protect children necessarily will diminish both the parental role in child-rearing and the child's role in decision making. Similarly, an expansive interpretation of parents' rights to control

and govern their children necessarily limits the state's ability to protect children, or to ensure child autonomy.

The Supreme Court's decisions concerning children's rights evidence these tensions. For example, the *Tinker* decision, emphasizing child autonomy, declared that children have First Amendment rights to engage in peaceful political protest within the schools. On the other hand, the *Ginsberg* decision, emphasizing state protection of children, determined that the state could criminally punish the sale to minors of sexually explicit materials that an adult would have a constitutional right to receive. (See OBSCENITY.) In its decisions concerning juvenile delinquency proceedings, the Court has extended a broad range of procedural rights to minors, and yet also determined that a juvenile court need not provide an accused young person with TRIAL BY JURY. In PARHAM V. J. R. (1979) the Court held that due process does not require a hearing before the commitment of a minor by a parent to a state mental hospital. Similarly, although the *Pierce* and *Yoder* opinions emphasized the primacy of the parental role in child-rearing, *Prince*, in enforcing a child labor law, emphasized the state's *parens patriae* obligation to protect children.

The Supreme Court's decisions involving the abortion rights of minors suggest that a state may not give parents an absolute "veto" over a pregnant minor's decision to have an abortion (PLANNED PARENTHOOD OF CENTRAL MISSOURI V. DANFORTH, 1976), but may require parental notification, at least for younger pregnant teenagers still living at home (*H. L. v. Matheson*, 1981). And in *Planned Parenthood v. Ashcroft* (1983) the Court upheld a state law requiring either parental or judicial consent to a minor's abortion; under the law the court must approve the abortion if the minor is sufficiently mature to make the abortion decision, or, alternatively, if the abortion is in the minor's best interests.

In sum, the Constitution has not been interpreted to prohibit the state from treating children differently from adults. Because children often lack adult capacity and maturity and need protection, and because of the special relationship of children to their families, giving children the same rights and obligations as adults would often do them a substantial disservice. To assume adult roles, children need to be socialized. The Constitution does not prohibit the use of state or parental coercion in this task of socialization. But, because ours is a society where adults are socialized for autonomous choice, there are necessarily some limits, even for children. In determining the contour of children's constitutional rights, then, the Supreme Court appears to be seeking to recognize the moral autonomy of children as individuals without abandoning children to their rights.

ROBERT H. MNOOKIN

Bibliography

HAFEN, BRUCE C. 1976 Children's Liberation and the New Egalitarianism: Some Reservations about Abandoning Youth to Their "Rights." *Brigham Young University Law Review* 1976:605–658.

MNOOKIN, ROBERT H. 1978 *Child, Family and State.* Boston: Little, Brown.

———, ed. 1985 *In the Interest of Children.* New York: W. H. Freeman & Co.

TEITELBAUM, LEE E. 1980 Foreword: The Meaning of Rights of Children. *New Mexico Law Review* 10:235–253.

WALD, MICHAEL S. 1979 Children's Rights: A Framework for Analysis. *University of California, Davis, Law Review* 12:255–282.

YOUTH LAW CENTER 1982 Legal Rights of Children in the United States of America. *Columbia Human Rights Law Review* 13:675–743.

CHILLING EFFECT

Law is carried forward on a stream of language. Metaphor not only reflects the growth of constitutional law but nourishes it as well. Since the 1960s, when the WARREN COURT widened the domain of the FIRST AMENDMENT, Justices have frequently remarked on laws' "chilling effects" on the FREEDOM OF SPEECH. A statute tainted by VAGUENESS or OVERBREADTH, for example, restricts the freedom of expression not only by directly subjecting people to the laws' sanctions but also by threatening others. Because the very existence of such a law may induce self-censorship when the reach of the law is uncertain, the law may be held INVALID ON ITS FACE. The assumed causal connection between vague legislation and self-censorship was made by the Supreme Court as early as HERNDON V. LOWRY (1937); half a century later, circulating the coinage of Justice FELIX FRANKFURTER, lawyers and judges express similar assumptions in the language of chilling effects.

The assumption plainly makes more sense in some cases than it does in others. For a law's uncertainty actually to chill speech, the would-be speaker must be conscious of the uncertainty. Yet few of us go about our day-to-day business with the statute book in hand. A statute forbidding insulting language may be vague,

but its uncertainty is unlikely to have any actual chilling effect on speech in face-to-face street encounters. Yet a court striking that law down—even in application to one whose insults fit the Supreme Court's narrow definition of FIGHTING WORDS—is apt to speak of the law's chilling effects.

For chilling effects that are real rather than assumed, we must look to institutional speakers—publishers, broadcasters, advertisers, political parties, groups promoting causes—who regularly inquire into the letter of the law and its interpretation by the courts. Magazine editors, for example, routinely seek legal counsel about defamation. Here the uncertainty of the law's reach does not lie in any statutory language, for the law of libel and slander is largely the product of COMMON LAW judges. It was a concern for chilling effects, however, that led three concurring Justices in NEW YORK TIMES V. SULLIVAN (1964) to advocate an absolute rule protecting the press against damages for the libel of a public official. The majority's principle in the case, which would allow damages when a newspaper defames an official knowing that its statement is false, or in reckless disregard of its truth or falsity, may, indeed, chill the press. Even slight doubt about information may make an editor hesitate to publish it, for fear that it may turn out to be false—and that a jury years later will decide it was published recklessly. The concern is not to protect false information, but that doubtful editors will play it safe, suppressing information that is true.

Conversely, when the Justices are persuaded that the law's threat will not have the effect of chilling speech, they are disinclined to use the overbreadth doctrine. A prominent modern example is the treatment of COMMERCIAL SPEECH. Because advertising is profitable, and advertisers seem unlikely to be chilled by laws regulating advertising, such laws are not subject to challenge for overbreadth.

The worry, when a court discusses chilling effects, is that a law's uncertainty will cause potential speakers to censor themselves. Thus, an overly broad law is subject to constitutional challenge even by one whose own speech would be punishable under a law focused narrowly on speech lying outside First Amendment protection. The defendant in court stands as a surrogate for others whose speech would be constitutionally protected—but who have been afraid to speak, and thus have not been prosecuted, and cannot themselves challenge the law. Whether or not this technique amounts to a dilution of the jurisdictional requirements of STANDING or RIPENESS, it allows courts to defend against the chilling effects of unconstitutional statutes that would otherwise elude their scrutiny.

KENNETH L. KARST

Bibliography

AMSTERDAM, ANTHONY G. 1960 The Void-for-Vagueness Doctrine in the Supreme Court. *University of Pennsylvania Law Review* 109:67–116.
NOTE 1970 The First Amendment Overbreadth Doctrine. *Harvard Law Review* 83:844–927.
SCHAUER, FREDERICK 1978 Fear, Risk and the First Amendment: Unraveling the "Chilling Effect." *Boston University Law Review* 5:685–732.

CHIMEL v. CALIFORNIA
395 U.S. 752 (1969)

In *Chimel* the Supreme Court considerably narrowed the prevailing scope of SEARCH INCIDENT TO ARREST, by limiting the search to the person of the arrestee and his immediate environs. The Court thus ended a divisive, decades-long debate on the subject.

The principle that officers executing a valid arrest may simultaneously search the arrestee for concealed weapons or EVIDENCE has never been challenged; it is rooted in COMMON LAW, and was recognized by the Court in WEEKS V. UNITED STATES (1914) as an emergency exception to the FOURTH AMENDMENT's warrant requirement. That the search may extend beyond the person to the premises in which the arrest is made was recognized in AGNELLO V. UNITED STATES (1925). The extension, too, has never been challenged; it seems sensible to permit officers to eliminate the possibility of a suspect's seizing a gun or destroying evidence within his reach though not on his person. The permissible scope of a warrantless search of the premises has, however, embroiled the Court in controversy.

Some Justices would have allowed a search of the entire place, arguing that after an arrest, even an extensive search is only a minor additional invasion of privacy. The opposing camp, led by Justice FELIX FRANKFURTER, condemned such wholesale rummaging: to allow a search incident to arrest to extend beyond the need that justified it would swallow up the rule requiring a search warrant save in EXIGENT CIRCUMSTANCES. The latter view finally prevailed in *Chimel*, when the Court ruled that the search must be limited to the arrestee's person and "the area from which he might gain possession of a weapon or destructible evidence." It may not extend into any room other than the one in which the arrest is made, and even "desk drawers or other closed or concealed areas in that room itself" are off-limits to the officers if the suspect cannot gain access to them.

JACOB W. LANDYNSKI

CHINESE EXCLUSION ACT
22 Stat. 58 (1882)

Although Chinese IMMIGRATION to California probably raised both wages and living standards of white laborers, economic, political, and cultural arguments were adduced against the foreigners. Assimilation was said to be impossible: the Chinese were gamblers, opium smokers, and generally inferior. Anti-Chinese feeling became the hub for many political issues, and agitation for legislation increased. Senator John Miller of California contended that failure to enact exclusion would "empty the teeming, seething slave pens of China upon the soil of California." Although most of the nation was indifferent, opposition to exclusion was weak and disorganized; Congress thus passed its first exclusion law in 1882. The act prohibited Chinese laborers from entering the United States for ten years, although resident ALIENS might return after a temporary absence. Nonlaboring Chinese would be admitted only upon presentation of a certificate from the Chinese government attesting their right to come. Other sections provided for deportation of illegal immigrants and prohibited state or federal courts from admitting Chinese to CITIZENSHIP. Further exclusion acts or amendments passed Congress—eleven by 1902. The most important of these were the Scott Act of 1888 prohibiting the return of any departing Chinese and the Geary Act of 1892 which extended the 1882 law. (See CHAE CHAN PING V. UNITED STATES, 1889.)

DAVID GORDON

CHINESE EXCLUSION CASE

See: *Chae Chan Ping v. United States*

CHIPMAN, NATHANIEL
(1752–1843)

Federalist jurist and statesman Nathaniel Chipman was instrumental in securing Vermont's admission to the Union in 1791 as the first state with no history as a separate British colony. An ally and correspondent of ALEXANDER HAMILTON, Chipman was three times chief justice of Vermont and also the first federal judge in the Vermont district. He was professor of law at

Middlebury College (1816–1843) and author of *Principles of Government* (1793; revised edition 1833).

DENNIS J. MAHONEY

CHISHOLM v. GEORGIA
2 Dallas 419 (1793)

The first constitutional law case decided by the Supreme Court, *Chisholm* provoked opposition so severe that the ELEVENTH AMENDMENT was adopted to supersede its ruling that a state could be sued without its consent by a citizen of another state. Article III of the Constitution extended the JUDICIAL POWER OF THE UNITED STATES to all controversies "between a State and citizens of another State" and provided that the Supreme Court should have ORIGINAL JURISDICTION in all cases in which a state should be a party. During the ratification controversy, anti-Federalists, jealous of state prerogatives and suspicious about the consolidating effects of the proposed union, had warned that Article III would abolish state sovereignty. Ratificationists, including JOHN MARSHALL, JAMES MADISON, and ALEXANDER HAMILTON (*e.g.*, THE FEDERALIST #81) had argued that the clause intended to cover only suits in which a state had given its sovereign consent to being sued or had instituted the suit. Here, however, with Justice JAMES IREDELL alone dissenting, the Justices in SERIATIM OPINIONS held that the states by ratifying the Constitution had agreed to be amenable to the judicial power of the United States and in that respect had abandoned their SOVEREIGNTY.

The case arose when Chisholm, a South Carolinian executor of the estate of a Tory whose lands Georgia had confiscated during the Revolution, sued Georgia for restitution. The state remonstrated against the Court's taking jurisdiction of the case and refused to argue on the merits. The Justices, confronted by a question of sovereignty, discoursed on the nature of the Union, giving the case historical importance. Iredell, stressing the sovereignty of the states respecting reserved powers, believed that no sovereign state could be sued without its consent unless Congress so authorized. Chief Justice JOHN JAY and Justice JAMES WILSON, delivering the most elaborate opinions against Georgia, announced for the first time from the bench the ultra-nationalistic doctrine that the people of the United States, rather than the states or people thereof, had formed the Union and were the ultimate sovereigns. From this view, the suability of the states was compatible with their reserved sovereignty, and the clause in Article III neither excluded suits by outside citizens nor required state consent.

The decision, which seemed to open the treasuries of the states to suits by Tories and other creditors, stirred widespread indignation that crossed sectional and party lines. A special session of the Massachusetts legislature recommended an amendment that would prevent the states from being answerable in the federal courts to suits by individuals. Virginia, taking the same action, condemned the Court for a decision dangerous to the sovereignty of the states. The Georgia Assembly would have defied the decision by a bill providing that any United States officer attempting to enforce it should "suffer death, without benefit of clergy, by being hanged." Though the state senate did not pass the bill, Georgia remained defiant. Congress too opposed the decision and finally agreed on a remedy for it that took the form of the Eleventh Amendment.

LEONARD W. LEVY

Bibliography

MATHIS, DOYLE 1967 Chisholm v. Georgia: Background and Settlement. *Journal of American History* 54:19–29.

CHOATE, JOSEPH H.
(1832–1917)

A highly conservative lawyer and leader of the American bar, Joseph Hodges Choate often appeared before the Supreme Court in defense of property interests and removed from the concerns of a populace he inimitably referred to as the "Great Unwashed." In MUGLER V. KANSAS (1887), Choate sought in vain to convince the Court to embrace laissez-faire, but he succeeded in wresting, in OBITER DICTUM, future judicial examination of the reasonableness of exercises of STATE POLICE POWER. Choate unequivocally endorsed constitutional rights in private property, a position the Court would soon partly accept. Indeed, his most famous victory came in POLLOCK V. FARMERS' LOAN & TRUST COMPANY (1895), which he argued with WILLIAM GUTHRIE. Labeling the income tax "communistic" and heaping reactionary invective upon his opponent, JAMES COOLIDGE CARTER, Choate constructed a framework for the Court's decision; he attacked the tax as a DIRECT TAX on income from real property, history and judicial precedent to the contrary.

DAVID GORDON

Bibliography

HICKS, FREDERICK C. 1931 Joseph Hodges Choate. *Dictionary of American Biography*, Vol. 4. New York: Scribner's.

CHOICE OF LAW

In the system of American FEDERALISM, some transactions and phenomena are governed by supreme federal law and others by state law. In the latter situations, multistate transactions frequently raise the question which state's law is to be applied. "Choice of law" refers to the process of making this determination. Choice of law may usefully be viewed as an issue of distribution of legislative or lawmaking powers "horizontally" among the states in those areas not governed by overriding federal law.

A basic principle of choice of law theory under the Constitution is that determination of the allocation of lawmaking power among the states in such circumstances is, itself, an issue of state law. Each state has its own law on choice of law, which may differ from the choice of law doctrines of other states and which is applied in actions brought in that state both in state courts and in DIVERSITY JURISDICTION cases in federal courts. Thus the outcome of litigation involving a multistate transaction may in theory be determined by the choice of the forum in which the suit is brought. The basic principle might have been the contrary— that is, that conflicts of state laws within the federal system should be resolved by a comprehensive supreme federal law of choice of law, binding on the states. Such a body of national conflict of laws doctrine might have been derived from the FULL FAITH AND CREDIT clause, the COMMERCE CLAUSE, or the DUE PROCESS clause of the FOURTEENTH AMENDMENT. Alternatively, supreme federal choice of law doctrine might have been developed as FEDERAL COMMON LAW pertaining to the mutual relationships among the states in the federal union. Or Congress, under various ENUMERATED POWERS, might have enacted federal choice of law principles. None of these courses has been followed; the law of choice of law in the federal system has not developed, judicially or legislatively, as supreme federal law. The states remain the primary determiners of the legal aspects of their mutual relationships within the federal union.

A state's law of choice of law, like all state law, is subject to constitutional limitations. Two such provisions have occasionally been applied so as to limit state choice of law principles, but in general these are not significant limitations.

In an occasional early case the Supreme Court held that the application of the forum's own law to a multistate transaction violated due process, even though the forum state did have a legitimate interest in having its law prevail. Under more recent doctrine there would be no due process violation in such circumstances. The modern principle, enunciated in *Allstate Insurance Co. v. Hague* (1981), is that "for a State's substantive law to be selected in a constitutionally permissible manner, that State must have a significant contact or significant aggregation of contacts, creating state interests, such that choice of its law is neither arbitrary nor fundamentally unfair." The due process clause can also limit a state's choice of law doctrine where there would be unfair surprise to a litigant in the choice of law otherwise proposed to be made.

The Court also has occasionally held that the full faith and credit clause requires a state to apply the law of another state even though the forum state does have a legitimate interest in applying its own law. (Thus in a case of claims for benefits against a fraternal benefit association, the Court held that a national interest in having a single uniform law determine the mutual rights and obligations of members required all states to apply the law of the place where the association was incorporated.) In general, however, the full faith and credit clause does not require that a forum state apply the law of another state unless it would violate due process for the forum to apply its own law.

Other provisions of the Constitution are potentially applicable as limitations on state choice of law doctrine. The commerce clause might be the basis for channeling state choice of law principles regarding multistate commercial transactions. The EQUAL PROTECTION clause and the PRIVILEGES AND IMMUNITIES clause of Article IV might be held to limit distinctions made in state choice of law doctrine based upon the residence or domicile of parties to a transaction. These constitutional provisions have not been so developed.

HAROLD W. HOROWITZ

Bibliography

Symposium: Choice-of-Law Theory after *Allstate Insurance Co. v. Hague* 1981 *Hofstra Law Review* 10:1–211.
Symposium: Choice of Law 1981 *U. C. Davis Law Review* 14:837–917.

CHURCH OF JESUS CHRIST OF LATTER DAY SAINTS v. UNITED STATES
136 U.S. 1 (1890)

The Mormon Church was granted a charter of incorporation in February 1851 by the so-called State of Deseret; later an act of the territorial legislature of Utah confirmed the charter. In 1887 Congress, having plenary power over the TERRITORIES, repealed the charter and directed the seizure and disposal of church property.

Justice JOSEPH P. BRADLEY wrote for the Court. He held that the power of Congress over the territories was sufficient to repeal an act of incorporation. He also held that once the Mormon Church became a defunct CORPORATION, Congress had power to reassign its property to legitimate religious and charitable uses, as near as practicable to those intended by the original donors. The claim of RELIGIOUS FREEDOM could not immunize the Mormon Church against the congressional conclusion that, because of its sponsorship of polygamy, it was an undesirable legal entity.

Chief Justice MELVILLE WESTON FULLER dissented, joined by Justice STEPHEN J. FIELD and Justice L. Q. C. LAMAR. Fuller objected to according Congress such sweeping power over property.

RICHARD E. MORGAN

CIRCUIT COURTS

The JUDICIARY ACT OF 1789 fashioned a decentralized circuit court system. The boundaries of the three circuits coincided with the boundaries of the states they encompassed, a practice that opened them to state and sectional political influences and legal practices. The act assigned two Supreme Court Justices to each circuit to hold court along with a district judge in the state where the circuit court met. (After 1794, a single Justice and a district judge were a quorum.) The circuit-riding provision brought federal authority and national political views to the new and distant states, but also compelled the Justices to imbibe local political sentiments and legal practices.

For a century questions about the administrative efficiency, constitutional roles, and political responsibilities of these courts provoked heated debate. In the JUDICIARY ACT OF 1801, Federalists sought to replace the Justices with an independent six-person circuit court judiciary, but one year later the new Jeffersonian Republican majority in Congress eliminated the circuit judgeships and restored the Justices to circuit duties, although they left the number of circuits at six. (See JUDICIARY ACTS OF 1802.) Subsequent territorial expansion prompted the addition of new circuits and new Justices until both reached nine in the Judiciary Act of 1837. Slave state interests opposed further expansion because they feared the loss of their five-to-four majority on the high court. Congress in 1855 did create a special circuit court and judgeship for the Northern District of California to expedite land litigation.

Significant structural and jurisdictional changes accompanied the Civil War and Reconstruction. The Judiciary Act of 1869 established a separate circuit court judiciary and assigned one judge to each of the nine new circuits that stretched from coast to coast. Justices retained circuit-riding duties although the 1869 act and subsequent legislation required less frequent attendance.

Historically, these courts had exercised ORIGINAL and APPELLATE JURISDICTION in cases involving the criminal law of the United States, in other areas where particular statutes granted jurisdiction, and in cases resting on diversity of citizenship. The Judiciary Act of 1869 strengthened the appellate responsibilities of the circuit courts by denying litigants access to the Supreme Court unless the amount in controversy exceeded $5,000. The Jurisdiction and Removal Act of 1875 established a general FEDERAL QUESTION JURISDICTION and made it possible for, among others, interstate CORPORATIONS to seek the friendly forum of the federal as opposed to the state courts. The 1875 measure also transferred some of the original jurisdiction of the circuit courts to the district courts. However, because the circuit courts were given increased appellate responsibilities, along with only modest adjustments in staffing, their dockets became congested. The resulting delay in appeals, combined with similar congestion in the Supreme Court, persuaded Congress in 1891 to establish the Circuit Courts of Appeals which became the nation's principal intermediate federal appellate courts. (See CIRCUIT COURTS OF APPEALS ACT.) Although the old circuit courts became anachronisms, Congress delayed abolishing them until 1911.

Throughout the nineteenth century Supreme Court Justices held ambivalent attitudes toward circuit duty. The Justices complained about the rigors of circuit travel and the loss of time from responsibilities in the nation's capital, but most of them recognized that circuit judging offered a unique constitutional forum free from the immediate scrutiny of their brethren on the Court. "It is only as a Circuit Judge that the Chief Justice or any other Justice of the Supreme Court has, individually, any considerable power," Chief Justice SALMON P. CHASE observed in 1868.

Circuit court judges contributed to the nationalization of American law and the economy. Justice JOSEPH STORY, in the First Circuit, for example, broadly defined the federal ADMIRALTY AND MARITIME JURISDICTION. In perhaps the most important circuit court decision of the nineteenth century, Story held, in *De Lovio v. Boit* (1815), that this jurisdiction extended to all maritime contracts, including insurance policies, and to all torts and injuries committed on the high seas and in ports and harbors within the ebb and flow of the tide. This decision, coupled with Story's opinion eight years later in *Chamberlain v. Chandler* (1823), expanded federal control over admiralty and maritime-related economic activity and added certainty to contracts involving shipping and commerce.

The circuit courts extended national constitutional protection to property, contract, and corporate rights. Justice WILLIAM PATERSON's 1795 decision on circuit in VAN HORNE'S LESSEE V. DORRANCE was the first significant statement in the federal courts on behalf of VESTED RIGHTS. But in 1830 Justice HENRY BALDWIN anticipated by seven years the PUBLIC USE doctrine later embraced by the Supreme Court. In *Bonaparte v. Camden & A. R. Co.* he held that state legislatures could take private property only for public use, and that creation of a monopoly by a public charter voided its public nature. As new forms of corporate property emerged in the post-Civil War era, the circuit courts offered protection through the CONTRACT CLAUSE. In the early and frequently cited case of *Gray v. Davis* (1871) a circuit court held, and the Supreme Court subsequently affirmed, that a legislative act incorporating a railroad constituted a contract between the state and the company, and a state constitutional provision annulling that charter violated the contract clause.

The circuit courts' most dramatic nationalizing role involved commercial jurisprudence. Through their DIVERSITY JURISDICTION the circuit courts used SWIFT V. TYSON (1842) to build a FEDERAL COMMON LAW of commerce, thus encouraging business flexibility, facilitating investment security, and reducing costs to corporations. After the Civil War these courts eased limitations on the formation and operation of corporations in foreign states (*In Re Spain*, 1891), supported bondholders' rights, allowed forum shopping (*Osgood v. The Chicago, Danville, and Vincennes R. R. Co.*, 1875), and favored employers in fellow-servant liability cases.

Ambivalence, contradiction, and frustration typified circuit court decisions involving civil and political rights. In 1823 Justice BUSHROD WASHINGTON, in CORFIELD V. CORYELL, held that the PRIVILEGES AND IMMUNITIES clause guaranteed equal treatment of out-of-state citizens as to those privileges and immunities that belonged of right to citizens of all free governments, and which had at all times been enjoyed by citizens of the several states. After 1866 some circuit judges attempted to expand this narrow interpretation. Justice JOSEPH P. BRADLEY held, in *Live-Stock Dealers' & Butchers' Ass'n v. Crescent City Live-Stock Landing & Slaughter-House Co.* (1870), that the FOURTEENTH AMENDMENT protected the privileges and immunities of whites and blacks as national citizens against STATE ACTION. In 1871 the Circuit Court for the Southern District of Alabama, in *United States v. Hall*, decided that under the Fourteenth Amendment Congress had the power to protect by appropriate legislation all rights in the first eight amendments. And in *Ho Ah Kow v. Nunan* (1879) Justice STEPHEN J. FIELD struck down as CRUEL AND UNUSUAL PUNISHMENT, based on the Eighth Amendment and the EQUAL PROTECTION clause of the Fourteenth Amendment, a San Francisco ordinance that required Chinese prisoners to have their hair cut to a length of one inch from their scalps.

These attempts to nationalize civil rights had little immediate impact. The Supreme Court in 1873 rejected Bradley's reading of the Fourteenth Amendment, and in 1871 the Circuit Court for the District of South Carolina in *United States v. Crosby* concluded that the right of a person to be secure in his or her home was not a right, privilege, or immunity granted by the Constitution. Neither the Supreme Court nor any other circuit court adopted the theory of congressional power to enforce the Fourteenth Amendment set forth in *Hall*. Justice Field's *Nunan* opinion was most frequently cited in dissenting rather than majority opinions.

Political rights under the FIFTEENTH AMENDMENT fared only slightly better. In *United States v. Given* (1873) the Circuit Court for the District of Delaware held that the Fifteenth Amendment did not limit congressional action to cases where states had denied or abridged the right to vote by legislation. In the same year, however, Justice WARD HUNT, in *United States v. Anthony*, concluded that the right or privilege of voting arose under state constitutions and that the states might restrict it to males.

Despite a regional structure and diverse personnel, these circuit courts placed national over state interests, reinforced the supremacy of federal power, promoted national economic development, and enhanced the position of interstate corporations. However, in matters of civil and political rights they not only disagreed about the scope of federal powers but also confronted a Supreme Court wedded to a traditional state-centered foundation for these rights.

KERMIT L. HALL

Bibliography

FRANKFURTER, FELIX and LANDIS, JAMES M. 1927 *The Business of the Supreme Court: A Study in the Federal Judicial System.* Pages 3–86. New York: Macmillan.

HALL, KERMIT L. 1975 The Civil War Era as a Crucible for Nationalizing the Lower Federal Courts. *Prologue: The Journal of the National Archives* 7:177–186.

SWISHER, CARL B. 1974 *The Taney Period, 1836–1864.* Volume IV of *The Oliver Wendell Holmes Devise History of the Supreme Court of the United States.* Pages 248–292. New York: Macmillan.

CIRCUIT COURTS OF APPEALS ACT
26 Stat. 826 (1891)

The first substantial revision of the federal court system since its formation (except for the abortive JUDICIARY ACT OF 1801), this act established a badly needed level of courts just below the Supreme Court: the UNITED STATES COURTS OF APPEALS. Senator WILLIAM EVARTS led the reform movement to relieve pressure on the Supreme Court docket by providing intermediate appellate review for most district and circuit court decisions. By keeping the CIRCUIT COURTS but abolishing their APPELLATE JURISDICTION, Congress maintained two courts with substantially similar JURISDICTION, causing confusion until the circuit courts were abolished in the JUDICIAL CODE of 1911. The act established direct Supreme Court review, bypassing the courts of appeals, in cases of "infamous" crimes (an ill-considered description that actually increased the Court's business and had to be deleted in 1897), and introduced the principle of discretionary Supreme Court review by WRIT OF CERTIORARI.

The basic structure of today's system of appellate review of federal court decisions remains as it was established in the 1891 Act.

DAVID GORDON

Bibliography

FRANKFURTER, FELIX AND LANDIS, JAMES M. 1927 *The Business of the Supreme Court.* New York: Macmillan.

CITIES AND THE CONSTITUTION

Cities, unlike states, are not mentioned in the Constitution. Many other important collective institutions in our society, such as CORPORATIONS, are not mentioned in the Constitution either. In its effort to determine the constitutional status of cities, the Supreme Court has had to decide whether to treat cities like states or like corporations. In fact, the Court has been required to answer two separate questions concerning the constitutional status of cities. First, do cities, like private corporations, have rights that are protected from governmental power by the Constitution? Second, do cities, like states, exercise governmental power which is limited by the Constitution?

At the time the Constitution was written and adopted, there was no legal distinction between cities and other corporations. Neither WILLIAM BLACKSTONE's *Commentaries,* published the decade before the CONSTITUTIONAL CONVENTION OF 1787, nor the first treatise on corporations, published by Stuart Kyd in 1793, categorized corporations in a way that would distinguish the Corporation of the City of New York, for example, from manufacturing and commercial concerns or from universities. Each of these entities was considered a lay corporation, formed by its members and given legal status by a grant of power from the state. The ability of these corporations to pursue the purposes for which their charter was granted was a right that needed protection from governmental power. At the same time, however, all corporations wielded power delegated to them by the state and, therefore, posed a danger of abuse that required subjection to popular control.

The Supreme Court's first important attempt to settle the constitutional status of corporations created a distinction between cities and other corporations. In DARTMOUTH COLLEGE v. WOODWARD (1819) Justice JOSEPH STORY articulated a public/private distinction for American corporations, classifying cities with states and distinguishing them from private corporations. "Public corporations," he said, "are generally esteemed such as exist for public political purposes only, such as towns, cities, parishes, and counties; and in many respects they are so, although they involve some private interests; but strictly speaking, public corporations are such only as founded by the government for public purposes, where the whole interests belong also to the government."

When considering whether cities should have rights that protect them against state control, the Supreme Court has largely accepted Justice Story's proposition that the cities' whole interest belongs to the government; it has treated cities as if they were the state itself. At least insofar as they are considered "public" entities, cities, unlike private corporations, have virtually no constitutional protection against

STATE ACTION. The Supreme Court dramatically summarized the nature of state power over cities in *Hunter v. Pittsburg* (1907):

Municipal corporations are political subdivisions of the State created as convenient agencies for exercising such of the governmental powers of the State as may be entrusted to them. . . . The State, therefore, at its pleasure may modify or withdraw all such powers, may take without compensation such property, hold it itself, or vest it in other agencies, expand or contract the territorial area, unite the whole or part with another municipality, repeal the charter and destroy the corporation. . . . In all these respects the State is supreme, and its legislative body, conforming its actions to the state constitution, may do as it will, unrestrained by any provision of the Constitution of the United States.

The Court in *Hunter* indicated, however, that there might be a limit to state power over cities, one it articulated in terms of a public/private distinction within the concept of a city. To some extent, cities act like private corporations, and this private aspect of city government, the Court said, could receive the same constitutional protection as other private interests. Even Justice Story had recognized in *Dartmouth College* that cities are not purely public entities but "involve some private interests" as well. But the proposition that cities are entitled to protection from state power under the Constitution in their "proprietary" (as contrasted to their "governmental") capacities has not yielded them much constitutional protection. The Supreme Court has never struck down a state statute on the grounds that it invaded such a private sphere. Indeed, in *Trenton v. New Jersey* (1923) Justice PIERCE BUTLER, noting that such a sphere could not readily be defined, expressed doubt whether there was a private sphere that limited the states' power over their own municipalities.

Whatever limited protection the Court has given cities under the Constitution has involved their public and not their private capacities. In GOMILLION V. LIGHTFOOT (1960) the Court held that the FIFTEENTH AMENDMENT restricted the state's ability to define the boundaries of its cities in a way that infringed on its citizens' VOTING RIGHTS; the Court narrowed the extravagant description of state power over cities in *Hunter* by construing the Court's language in that case to be applicable only to the particular constitutional provisions considered there. But the Court has not subsequently expanded on its distinction between the Fifteenth Amendment and other constitutional provisions, such as the FOURTEENTH AMENDMENT and the contract clause, as vehicles for limiting state power over cities. No subsequent case has given cities constitutional protection against state power.

From 1976 to 1985, during the short life of NATIONAL LEAGUE OF CITIES V. USERY (1976), the Supreme Court articulated the most expansive constitutional protection ever given cities, again a protection for their public and not their private activities. By treating them as if they were states the Court limited the power of the federal government to regulate cities; it held that cities, like states, were immunized from federal control under the TENTH AMENDMENT insofar as federal interference "directly impaired their ability to structure integral operations in areas of traditional governmental functions." In GARCIA V. SAN ANTONIO METROPOLITAN TRANSIT AUTHORITY (1985), however, *National League of Cities* was overruled. One reason for OVERRULING *National League of Cities*, the Court said, was that there was no practical way to make a public/private distinction between "traditional governmental functions" and other state and city functions. Hence, the Court reasoned, there was no principled basis for choosing some areas of state or city activity over others to be immune from federal control as a constitutional matter.

There is a second question concerning the constitutional status of cities: to what extent are cities like states, and, therefore, subject to those constitutional provisions that affect the power of states? The Supreme Court's answer to this question has been complex.

For some purposes, the Court has treated cities like states. City power is like state power, for example, in that it is equally limited by the DUE PROCESS and EQUAL PROTECTION clauses of the Fourteenth Amendment and by the dormant commerce clause. On the other hand, the Court has held that cities are not like states for purposes of the ELEVENTH AMENDMENT (dealing with states' immunity from suits in federal court). In a number of nonconstitutional cases the Supreme Court has also sought to distinguish cities from states. "We are a nation not of city-states but of States," the Court said in *Community Communications Co. v. City of Boulder* (1982), holding cities, like private corporations but unlike states, liable to federal antitrust laws.

Indeed, sometimes the Court has treated cities in a way that distinguishes them from both states and corporations. In MONELL V. DEPARTMENT OF SOCIAL SERVICES (1978) the Supreme Court interpreted SECTION 1983 OF TITLE 42 OF THE UNITED STATES CODE to allow damage suits against cities when they commit constitutional violations. City action is like state action in that cities are subject to constitutional limitations applicable to states. But states, unlike cities, have immunities under the Eleventh Amendment against suits in federal court to enforce these constitutional limitations. Thus, under *Monell*, cities are liable under section 1983 for constitutional violations in situations in which neither the states (because of the Eleventh Amendment) nor private corporations (because their power is not subject to constitutional limitations) would be liable.

Finally, at times cities are considered like states and private corporations simultaneously. Both cities and states can act in the marketplace just as private corporations do. Thus in *White v. Massachusetts Council of Construction Employers* (1983) the Supreme Court held that the commerce clause does not restrict a city's ability to require its contractors to hire city residents as long as it is acting as a market participant and not as a market regulator. The Court thus extended to cities the immunity from commerce clause restrictions that it had previously provided states when they act as market participants. The practical effect of the *White* case, however, is limited. In *United Building & Construction Trades Council v. Camden* (1984) the Court held that the privileges and immunities clause, unlike the commerce clause, limited a city's ability to require its contractors to hire city residents whether or not it acts as a market participant. In *Camden* the Court treated cities like states but distinguished them from corporations; the power of states and cities, unlike that of corporations, is restrained by the privileges and immunities clause of the Constitution.

The cities' historic link with corporations and their assimilation in the nineteenth century to the status of states have given them a divided status under the Constitution. Although the predominant linkage has been between cities and states, there remain occasions when the prior linkage with corporations is emphasized. The Court's ability to conceptualize cities as either states or corporations (indeed, to conceptualize them as both simultaneously or as distinguishable from both) opens up a multitude of possibilities for the Court as it defines the relationship between cities and the Constitution in the future.

GERALD E. FRUG

Bibliography

CLARK, GORDON 1985 *Judges and the Cities: Interpreting Local Autonomy.* Chicago: University of Chicago Press.
FRUG, GERALD 1980 The City as a Legal Concept. *Harvard Law Review* 93:1059–1154.
HARTOG, HENDRIK 1983 *Public Property and Private Power: The Corporation of the City of New York in American Law, 1730–1870.* Chapel Hill: University of North Carolina Press.
MICHELMAN, FRANK 1977–1978 Political Markets and Community Self-Determination: Competing Judicial Models of Local Government Legitimacy *Indiana Law Journal* 53:145–206.

CITIZENSHIP
(Historical Development)

The concept of citizenship articulated during the American Revolution and adjusted to the special circumstances of an ethnically diverse federal republic in the nineteenth century developed from English theories of allegiance and of the subject's status. Enunciated most authoritatively by Sir EDWARD COKE in CALVIN'S CASE (1608), English law held that natural subject status involved a perpetual, immutable relationship of allegiance and protection between subject and king analogous to the bond between parent and child. All persons born within the king's allegiance gained this status by birth. Conquest or NATURALIZATION by Parliament could extend the status to the foreign-born, but subjects adopted in such a manner were by legal fiction considered bound by the same perpetual allegiance as the native-born. The doctrine "once a subject, always a subject" reflected Coke's emphasis on the natural origins of the subject–king relationship and militated against the emergence of concepts of voluntary membership and EXPATRIATION.

The appearance of new SOCIAL COMPACT ideas modified but did not entirely supersede traditional concepts. By the mid-eighteenth century, Lockean theorists derived subject status from the individual's consent to leave the state of nature and join with others to form a society. To such theorists the individual subject was bound by the majority and owed allegiance to the government established by that majority. Barring the dissolution of society itself or the consent of the majority, expressed through Parliament, individual subjects were still held to a perpetual allegiance.

Colonial conditions eroded these ideas. Colonial naturalization policies especially contributed to a subtle transformation of inherited attitudes. Provincial governments welcomed foreign-born settlers in order to promote population growth vital to physical security and economic prosperity. Offering political and economic rights in exchange for the ALIEN'S contribution to the general welfare of the community, the colonists underscored the contractual, consent-based aspects of membership that had been subordinated in English law to older notions of perpetual allegiance.

Imperial administrators, concerned to protect England's monopoly of colonial trade, declared in 1700 that colonial naturalization could confer subject status only within the confines of the admitting colony; although a parliamentary statute of 1740 established administrative procedures whereby a colonial court could vest an alien with a subject status valid throughout the empire, such actions merely reinforced the conclusion that the origins, extent, and effects of subject status were determined not by nature but by political and legal compacts.

When Americans declared independence in 1776 they initially relied on the traditional linkage of allegiance and protection to define citizenship in the new republican states. Congress's resolution of June 24, 1776, declared that all persons then resident in the colonies and deriving protection from the laws were members of and owed allegiance to those colonies. Lockean theory was also useful, for if each colony were considered a separate society merely changing its form of government, then loyalist minorities could still be considered subject to the will of patriot majorities. Yet forced allegiance clashed with the idea that all legitimate government required the free consent of the governed. Wartime TREASON prosecutions contributed to a gradual reformulation of the theory of citizenship that stressed the volitional character of allegiance. Employing a doctrine stated most clearly in the Pennsylvania case of *Respublica v. Chapman* (1781), American courts came to hold that citizenship must originate in an act of individual consent.

Republican citizenship required the consent of the community as well as of the individual, and legislators concerned with establishing naturalization policies concentrated on defining the proper qualifications for membership. This preoccupation obscured the ill-defined nature of the status itself. The Revolution had created a sense of community that transcended state boundaries; the ARTICLES OF CONFEDERATION implied that state citizenship carried with it rights in other states as well (Article IV). Framers of the United States Constitution perpetuated this ambiguity: section 2 of Article IV provided that "The citizens of each State shall be entitled to all PRIVILEGES AND IMMUNITIES of citizens in the several States." Questions concerning the nature and relationship of state and national citizenship would not be resolved until the Civil War.

The Revolutionary idea that citizenship began with the individual's consent extended logically to the idea of expatriation. Although some states acknowledged this principle, it raised delicate questions of federal relations after 1789. The problem appeared as early as 1795 in *Talbot v. Janson*, when the United States Supreme Court wrestled with the question whether a Virginia expatriation procedure could release a citizen from national as well as state allegiance. Unwilling to resolve that issue, the Court looked to Congress to provide a general policy of expatriation. Although the propriety of such a measure was discussed a number of times during the antebellum period, congressional action foundered on the same issue of federal relations. As long as the question of the primacy of state or United States citizenship remained open, the idea that citizenship rested on individual choice would be more valid for aliens seeking naturalization than for persons whose citizenship derived from birth.

The problematic character of dual state and national citizenship appeared in its most intractable form in disputes over the status of free blacks. Many northern states acknowledged free blacks as birthright citizens, though often at the cost of conceding that important political rights were not necessarily attached to that status. From the 1820s on, slave states increasingly resisted the contention that such citizenship carried constitutional guarantees of "privileges and immunities" in their own jurisdictions. ROGER B. TANEY's opinion in DRED SCOTT V. SANDFORD (1857) that national citizenship was restricted to white state citizens of 1789, persons naturalized by Congress, and their descendants alone marked the final effort, short of SECESSION, to restrict the scope of citizenship.

The FOURTEENTH AMENDMENT finally defined national citizenship as the product of naturalization or birth within the JURISDICTION of the United States, leaving state citizenship dependent upon residency. On July 27, 1868, Congress declared that the right of expatriation was a fundamental principle of American government, thus allowing persons born to citizenship the same right as aliens to choose their ultimate allegiance.

JAMES H. KETTNER

Bibliography

KETTNER, JAMES H. 1978 *The Development of American Citizenship, 1608–1870.* Chapel Hill: University of North Carolina Press.
ROCHE, JOHN P. 1949 *The Early Development of United States Citizenship.* Ithaca, N.Y.: Cornell University Press.

CITIZENSHIP
(Theory)

Article I, section B, of the Constitution authorizes Congress "to establish a uniform Rule of NATURALIZATION." The power afforded Congress in this spare textual authorization has long been interpreted as plenary, effectively insulating from constitutional challenge congressional decisions about whom to admit to the national community. The theory of national community expressed through this constitutional interpretation was summarily sketched by the Supreme Court nearly a century ago in *Nishimura Eiku v. United States* (1891): "It is an accepted maxim of international law, that every sovereign nation has the power, inherent in SOVEREIGNTY, and essential to self-preservation, to forbid the entrance of foreigners within its domain, or to admit them only in such cases and upon such conditions as it may see fit to prescribe."

This still regnant theory of sovereignty has become, for most people, entirely natural and unimposed. Its inchoate justification, articulated in abstract terms, does have a natural and necessary air: one can understand nations asserting an absolute right to decide whom to admit or to exclude as advancing the universal right to form communities and the right to keep them distinctive and stable. While nations have grown significantly more interconnected and while the world's creatures are one for some important purposes, the notion of protecting the right to form and maintain special communities within larger communities resonates with our understanding of how America became a nation. Still, even for one who believes in protecting the national community, a moral question remains: what constitutes membership in the political community to be protected?

In a strictly positive sense, the answer is that citizenship in this country has been conferred by birth (either in the United States or abroad to American parents) or by naturalization. Although only "a natural born Citizen" can be President, naturalized citizens are otherwise the formal equals of citizens by birth. Moreover, the Constitution extends many of its protections to "persons" or "people" so that ALIENS are protected in much the same way as citizens even before they are naturalized.

But the United States has been a national community not readily inclined to ask what constitutes membership in the political community—or perhaps more accurately, not genuinely curious about the answer or willing to give it constitutional significance. Congress has long presumed that those who currently share citizenship (citizens and, during most but not all historical periods, documented residents) constitute the community to be protected and maintained.

The judiciary, in turn, has long deferred to whatever Congress decides. This deference, while varying across the range of immigration law disputes, radically diverges from the political relationship between judiciary and legislature that informs most constitutional jurisprudence. Consider a range of congressional "membership" decisions and the corresponding judicial response: Exclusion decisions and procedures are treated as extraconstitutional; congressional power to classify aliens is effectively unconstrained by EQUAL PROTECTION values; DEPORTATION is treated as a civil and not a criminal proceeding, thereby denying certain constitutional protections expressly limited or interpreted to apply only to criminal proceedings; the power to detain remains unlimited by any coherent set of values, and is available effectively to imprison individuals and groups for long periods and under disreputable conditions; immigration judges remain intertwined with government agencies responsible for administering and enforcing immigration law. In so deferring to Congress, the judiciary either denies the constitutional relevance of the always amending character of the national community or indulges absolutely Congress's habitual response to what constitutes membership in the political community.

If together Congress and the courts "freed" us from being genuinely curious about ourselves, they were not without help in constructing this reality. It has been commonplace for many to deny that citizenship does or should play a central role in our political community. No less a figure in recent constitutional jurisprudence than ALEXANDER M. BICKEL insisted that citizenship "was a simple idea for a simple government"; others entirely ignored the question, as if a view on membership in the process of self-determination were not itself constitutive of the national community's very nature. But, of course, citizenship in the United States never has been a simple idea. Naturalization laws, implementing the FOURTEENTH Amendment, were not extended to persons of African descent until 1870; citizens of Mexican descent were deported in 1930 raids; citizens of Japanese descent were interned during World War II because of their ancestry; women citizens were not allowed to vote until 1920; Puerto Ricans and people of other conquered territories were afforded only second-class citizenship status. Yet the relationship of these and other events to our conception of United States citizenship has been far more often ignored than attended to, as if the denial of contradictory acts would somehow save the regnant theory of national community.

These efforts notwithstanding, the experience of community is beginning to challenge the prevailing constitutionalized attitude toward membership in the political community. The presence of millions of undocumented workers—sharing neighborhoods, burdens, and laws—has prompted intense and frequently conflicting responses to the general question of citizenship and its role in the political community. In PLYLER V. DOE (1982) the Supreme Court compelled the state of Texas to provide the children of undocumented workers with a free public education. At the same time, attention to the relationship of citizenship to the political community has led the Court to intensify its scrutiny of laws that deny documented residents access to certain occupations. State laws barring aliens from permanent civil service positions and from the practice of law and civil engineering have been struck down. But where the position is intimately related to the process of democratic self-government (the so-called political function exception), the Court has upheld laws requiring police, public teachers, and probation officers to be citizens.

What this communitarian challenge foreshadows defies facile forecasting; a theory so long dominant as ours toward community membership and sovereignty resists predictable or simple change. Still, in its unwillingness to be silenced, in its refusal to accept uncritically the regnant theory, today's challenge focuses attention on our history, and on the relationship of work to full political life. At least in this sense, there is the hope that we will no longer blithely disregard the values formally expressed in our vision of citizenship. After all, whom we acknowledge as full members of the political community tells us much about who we are and why we remain together as a nation.

GERALD P. LÓPEZ

CITY COUNCIL OF LOS ANGELES v. TAXPAYERS FOR VINCENT
466 U.S. 789 (1984)

A Los Angeles ordinance prohibited the posting of signs on public property. Supporters of a candidate for city council sued to enjoin city officials from continuing to remove their signs from utility poles; they were joined as plaintiffs by the company that made and posted the signs for them. Of the 1,207 signs removed during one week of the campaign, 48 supported the candidate; most were commercial signs. The Supreme Court, 6–3, rejected constitutional attacks on the ordinance on its face and as applied.

The case seemed to call for analysis according to the principles governing rights of access to the PUBLIC FORUM—rights particularly valuable to people of limited means. Instead, Justice JOHN PAUL STEVENS, for

the Court, applied the set of rules announced in UNITED STATES V. O'BRIEN (1968), suggesting the possibility that those rules might in the future be applied routinely to FIRST AMENDMENT cases involving regulations that are not aimed at message content. Here the government interest in aesthetic values was substantial; the city had no purpose to suppress a particular message; and the law curtailed no more speech than was necessary to its purpose. In a bow to public forum reasoning, Stevens noted that other means of communication remained open to the plaintiffs.

The dissenters, led by Justice WILLIAM J. BRENNAN, argued that the assertion of aesthetic purposes deserved careful scrutiny to assure even-handed regulation, narrowly tailored to aesthetic objectives that were both comprehensively carried out and precisely defined. The City had made no such showing here, they contended.

Critics of the decision have suggested that it is part of a larger inegalitarian trend in BURGER COURT decisions concerning the FREEDOM OF SPEECH and FREEDOM OF THE PRESS, a trend exemplified by BUCKLEY V. VALEO (1976) and HUDGENS V. N.L.R.B. (1976).

KENNETH L. KARST

CITY OF . . .

See: entry under name of city

CIVIL DISOBEDIENCE

Civil disobedience is a public, nonviolent, political act contrary to law usually done with the aim of bringing about a change in the law or policies of the government. The idea of civil disobedience is deeply rooted in our civilization, with examples evident in the life of Socrates, the early Christian society, the writings of Thomas Aquinas and Henry David Thoreau, and the Indian nationalist movement led by Gandhi.

The many occurrences of civil disobedience throughout American history have had a profound impact on the legal system and society as a whole. The Constitution does not provide immunity for those who practice civil disobedience, but because the United States is a representative democracy with deep respect for constitutional values, the system is uniquely responsive to acts of civil disobedience. Examples of civil disobedience in American history include the Quakers' refusal to pay taxes to support the colonial Massachusetts Church, the labor movement's use of the tactic in the early twentieth century, and citizens' withholding of taxes in protest of military and nuclear expenditures.

The fundamental justification for civil disobedience is that some persons feel bound by philosophy, religion, morality, or some other principle to disobey a law that they feel is unjust. As Martin Luther King, Jr., wrote in his *Letter from Birmingham Jail*, "I submit that an individual who breaks a law that his conscience tells him is unjust, and willingly accepts the penalty by staying in jail to arouse the conscience of the community over its injustice, is in reality expressing the very highest respect for law." Civil disobedience is most justifiable when prior lawful attempts to rectify the situation have failed; and when the acts of civil disobedience are done to force the society to recognize the problem; when performed openly and publicly; and when the actor will accept the punishment. Many proponents urge that civil disobedience be used only in the most extreme cases, arguing that the Constitution provides many opportunities to voice one's grievances without breaking the law.

Opponents of civil disobedience see it as a threat to democratic society and the forerunner of violence and anarchy. The premise of stable democracy, they contend, is that the minority will accept the will of the majority. Opponents argue that the lack of a coherent theory of civil disobedience can result in the abuse of the tactic.

Civil disobedience may be designed to change the Constitution itself. The responsiveness of the Constitution to the voice of dissent and civil disobedience is particularly evident in two movements in our history: the women's suffrage movement and the antislavery movement. These movements brought about great constitutional changes through a variety of political strategies, including civil disobedience.

The women's suffrage movement began in the first part of the nineteenth century. Increasing numbers of women were becoming active in political parties, humanitarian societies, educational societies, labor agitation groups, antislavery associations, and temperance associations. By 1848, the women had organized the National Women's Rights Convention at Seneca Falls where Elizabeth Cady Stanton and Lucretia Mott led the women in writing the Declaration of Sentiments. A main tenet of the declaration was that women should be granted the right to vote in order to preserve the government as one that has the consent of the governed. The women used a variety of tactics in their struggle to obtain the franchise, including conventional political tactics, lobbying at the national, state, and local levels, and petitions. An impor-

tant tactic in the women's fight was the use of civil disobedience, which helped gain support and publicity for their cause. The methods of civil disobedience included voting in elections (which was illegal), refusing to pay taxes, and PICKETING the White House.

A visible act of civil disobedience used by the women's movement was to register and vote in elections. A prominent example occurred in 1872 when Susan B. Anthony and fourteen other women registered and voted in Rochester, New York. They were accused and charged with a crime "of voting without the lawful right to vote." The women argued that the FOURTEENTH AMENDMENT and FIFTEENTH AMENDMENT gave them the legal right to vote. This legal argument was dismissed by the Supreme Court in MINOR V. HAPPERSETT (1875), when the Court held that women were CITIZENS but were not entitled to vote. Once the Court refused to recognize the argument based on existing amendments, the suffragist organization concentrated their efforts on the fight for passage of a constitutional amendment that would ensure women the right to vote.

Another, more isolated instance of civil disobedience was performed by activist Abby Smith. Abby Smith refused to pay her property taxes until she was given the right to vote at the town meeting. This simple instance of a woman standing up for her rights served to publicize the women's cause to a certain extent.

A final tactic of the women's suffrage movement that amounted to both civil disobedience and lawful dissent was the practice of picketing the White House in order to gain presidential support for the proposed amendment. Although the women had a legal right to picket, the policemen at the time treated them with contempt, as if they were lawbreakers. The women were jailed for exercising constitutional rights, and it was not until later that they were vindicated by the courts.

During the antislavery movement in the mid-1850s, civil disobedience gained considerable acceptance in some parts of the country. Opposition to slavery reached new peaks after the passage of the FUGITIVE SLAVE Law of 1850. The act provided for a simplified procedure to return escaped slaves to their masters, with provisions excluding TRIAL BY JURY and writs of HABEAS CORPUS from fugitive slave cases, and providing a financial incentive for federal commissioners to decide cases in favor of southern claimants. Throughout the North, meetings were held where citizens denounced the new law and vowed their disobedience to the act. Many based their views on philosophical, legal, or religious grounds. Those publicly opposing the act included Lewis Hayden, William C. Nell, Theodore Parker, Daniel Foster, and Henry David Thoreau. Some commentators believe that a clear and direct line runs from the antislavery crusaders to the Fourteenth Amendment. The acts of civil disobedience to the Fugitive Slave Act represented the feelings of a substantial portion of the country at the time. This opinion was eventually transformed into the THIRTEENTH, Fourteenth, and Fifteenth Amendments, which abolished slavery, guaranteed the former slaves' citizenship, and protected their right to vote. Civil disobedience remains a potentially significant tool for effecting constitutional change.

The Constitution has been used to justify civil disobedience. Examples in our recent history include the CIVIL RIGHTS movement and military resistance. Some of the best-known uses of civil disobedience occurred during the civil rights movements of the 1950s and 1960s. Martin Luther King, Jr., and his followers felt compelled to disobey laws that continued the practice of SEGREGATION; they opposed the laws on moral, ethical, and constitutional grounds. In fact, some of the laws they allegedly disobeyed were unconstitutional. Although the movement initially attempted to change the system through conventional legal and political channels, it eventually turned to the tactics of civil disobedience in order to bring national attention to its cause. By appealing to the Constitution as justification for their acts of civil disobedience, the civil rights leaders made important contributions to the development of constitutional law in the areas of EQUAL PROTECTION, DUE PROCESS, and FREEDOM OF SPEECH.

The civil rights movement's tactics included SIT-INS, designed to protest the laws and the practice of segregated lunch counters and restaurants. Black students entered restaurants and requested to be served in the white part of the establishment. When they refused to leave upon the owner's request, they were arrested on grounds of criminal TRESPASS.

Quite a few of these cases were heard by the Supreme Court, where the blacks argued that the equal protection clause of the Fourteenth Amendment made these laws unconstitutional. In *Peterson v. City of Greenville* (1963) ten black students had been arrested after they refused to leave a segregated restaurant. The Supreme Court reversed their convictions, holding that the laws requiring segregation violated the equal protection clause of the Fourteenth Amendment. The court reasoned that there was sufficient STATE ACTION because of the existence of the statute, which indicated the state policy in favor of segrega-

tion. Many factually similar cases were reversed on the authority of the *Peterson* decision. In addition to using the equal protection clause, the courts sometimes held that the laws as applied to black citizens were VOID FOR VAGUENESS or for lack of NOTICE.

The sit-ins, freedom rides, and continued demonstrations eventually swayed public opinion and contributed to the passage of the CIVIL RIGHTS ACT OF 1964, which prohibited discrimination in many areas of life. Under the act, many acts that had previously amounted to civil disobedience became protected by law.

In addition to the successes achieved in RACIAL DISCRIMINATION law, the civil rights movement and its acts of civil disobedience have contributed to the FIRST AMENDMENT law regarding freedom of speech and FREEDOM OF ASSEMBLY AND ASSOCIATION. For example, in COX V. LOUISIANA (1964) peaceful civil rights demonstrators were convicted of disturbing the peace. The Court struck down the BREACH OF THE PEACE statute for vagueness and OVERBREADTH, thus expanding constitutional rights to free speech and assembly.

Although the civil rights movement involved acts of civil disobedience on a massive scale, resistance to the country's military policy has traditionally involved more solitary acts. Still, the resisters have based many of their arguments on constitutional provisions. These arguments have not always been successful, but the protesters succeeded in calling attention to causes such as opposition to war and military policy.

Those opposed to the country's military policy have used both indirect and direct methods of civil disobedience. Examples of indirect methods include DRAFT CARD BURNING, supplying false information on tax forms, and trespassing on government grounds. Although the protesters gained publicity from these tactics, the disobedient's claims of freedom of speech and RELIGIOUS LIBERTY under the First Amendment usually have not been accepted by the courts. A well-known example of the use of indirect civil disobedience is the Catonsville Nine case in which protesters entered the office of the local Selective Service Board and destroyed government records. Their defense, based on philosophical and moral grounds, was held insufficient by the courts.

Direct forms of civil disobedience to war have included resistance to the draft and refusal to pay taxes. The disobedience surrounding the draft has taken many forms, but many legal challenges have focused on the SELECTIVE SERVICE ACT. In several cases, the men who refused induction argued that the CONSCIENTIOUS OBJECTION provision was unconstitutional as it applied to the individual. They argued that to construe the provision as requiring a belief in a supreme being was a violation of the free exercise clause of the First Amendment. The Court has avoided the constitutional questions in these cases by giving a broad construction to statutory exemptions of the conscientious objectors. Another direct form of civil disobedience used to protest the country's involvement in war has been to withhold the payment of taxes, arguing that to support a war that one does not believe in is in violation of the free exercise clause. The Supreme Court has never decided the constitutional issues in these cases. Although both direct and indirect forms of civil disobedience in resistance to military policy have been equally unsuccessful in presenting legal challenges to laws, they have been successful in publicizing the disobedients' grievances.

The debate concerning the morality or justification for the use of civil disobedience as a method of effecting change in society will never be fully resolved. However, civil disobedience remains a significant and often successful tactic used in many movements in American society. The use of civil disobedience, when incorporated with other conventional political strategies, can lead to profound changes in the Constitution itself or in the interpretation of the document. American society's positive response to certain acts of civil disobedience can be seen in the civil rights movement, the women's suffrage movement, and the antislavery movement. Although not all acts of civil disobedience yield substantial changes, our democratic system provides the opportunity for civil disobedience to contribute to significant changes in society.

ROBERT F. DRINAN, S.J.

Bibliography

FORTAS, ABE 1968 *Concerning Dissent and Civil Disobedience.* New York: World Publishing Co.

GREENBERG, JACK 1968 "The Supreme Court, Civil Rights, and Civil Dissonance." *Yale Law Journal* 77:1520–1544.

KALVEN, HARRY, JR. 1965 *The Negro and the First Amendment.* Columbus: Ohio State University Press.

WEBER, DAVID R., ED. 1978 *Civil Disobedience in America.* Ithaca, N.Y.: Cornell University Press.

CIVIL LIBERTIES

WILLIAM BLACKSTONE described civil liberty as "the great end of all human society and government . . . that state in which each individual has the power to pursue his own happiness according to his own views of his interest, and the dictates of his conscience, un- restrained, except by equal, just, and impartial laws." As a matter of law, civil liberties are usually claims of right that a citizen may assert against the state. In the United States the term "civil liberties" is often used in a narrower sense to refer to FREEDOM OF SPEECH, FREEDOM OF THE PRESS, FREEDOM OF ASSEMBLY AND ASSOCIATION, RELIGIOUS LIBERTY, personal privacy, and the right to DUE PROCESS OF LAW, or to other limitations on the power of the state to restrict individual freedom of action. In this sense, civil liberties may be distinguished from rights to equality (sometimes called "civil rights"), although the latter have increasingly been recognized as important elements of individual freedom because they permit participation in society without regard to race, religion, sex, or other characteristics unrelated to individual capacity.

The concept of civil liberties is a logical corollary to the ideas of LIMITED GOVERNMENT and RULE OF LAW. When government acts arbitrarily, it infringes civil liberty; the rule of law combats and confines these excesses of power. The concept "government of laws, not of men" reflects this idea as does the vision of justice as fairness.

Although civil liberties are usually associated in practice with democratic forms of government, liberty and democracy are distinct concepts. An authoritarian government structure may recognize certain limits on the capacity of the state to interfere with the autonomy of the individual. Correspondingly, calling a state democratic does not tell us about the extent to which it recognizes civil liberty. Thus, "civil liberties" does not refer to a particular form of political structure but to the relationship between the individual and the state, however the state may be organized. But civil liberties do presuppose order. As Chief Justice CHARLES EVANS HUGHES said in COX V. NEW HAMPSHIRE (1941), "Civil liberties imply the existence of an organized society maintaining public order without which liberty itself would be lost in the excesses of unrestrained abuses."

In the final analysis, civil liberties are based on the integrity and dignity of the individual. This idea was expressed by George C. Marshall, who was chief of staff to the American army in World War II and later served as secretary of state: "We believe that human beings have . . . rights that may not be given or taken away. They include the right of every individual to develop his mind and his soul in the ways of his own choice, free of fear and coercion—provided only that he does not interfere with the rights of others."

There are two principal justifications for preferring individual liberties to the interests of the general community—justice and self-interest. At the very least, justice requires norms by which persons in authority treat those within their power fairly and evenly. Self-interest suggests that our own rights are secure only if the rights of others are protected.

Because these two justifications for civil liberties are abstractions to most people, they are often subordinated to more immediate concerns of the state or the majority. In America, even administrations relatively friendly to civil liberty have perpetrated some of the worst violations. The administration of FRANKLIN D. ROOSEVELT interned Japanese Americans during World War II. ABRAHAM LINCOLN suspended the right of HABEAS CORPUS. And as Leonard W. Levy has reminded us, THOMAS JEFFERSON was far more of a libertarian as a private citizen than when he was in power. Nevertheless, civil liberties have been more broadly defined and fully respected in the United States than in other nations.

The roots of American civil liberties can be traced to ancient times. The city-state of Athens made a lasting contribution to civil liberty. In the sixth century B.C., Solon, the magistrate of Athens, produced a constitution that, while flawed, gave the poor a voice in the election of magistrates and the right to call public officials to account. Solon is also credited with first expressing the idea of the rule of law. But Athens knew no limits on the right of the majority to adopt any law it chose, and there was no concept of individual rights against the state. Greek philosophers introduced the idea of "natural law" and the derivative concept of equality; all Athenians (except slaves) were equal citizens, for all possessed reason and owed a common duty to natural law.

The Romans also contributed to civil liberties, first through a rudimentary SEPARATION OF POWERS of government and later by the further development of natural law. Justinian's *Institutes* recites, "Justice is the fixed and constant purpose that gives every man his due." Nevertheless, the Roman emperors were autocratic in practice; there were no enforceable rights against the state, which practiced censorship, restricted travel, and coerced religion.

In the Middle Ages there was little manifestation of civil liberties. But the idea of a pure natural law was carried forward in Augustine's *City of God*. On the secular side, the contract between feudal lords and their vassals established reciprocal rights and responsibilities whose interpretation was, in some places, decided by a body of the vassal's peers.

Among English antecedents of civil liberties, the starting point is MAGNA CARTA (1215), the first written instrument that exacted from a monarch rules

he was bound to obey. Although this document reflected the attempt of barons to secure feudal privileges, basic liberties developed from it—among them the security of private property, the security of the person, the right to judgment by one's peers, the right to seek redress of grievances from the sovereign, and the concept of due process of law. Above all, as Winston Churchill said, Magna Carta "justifies the respect in which men have held it" because it tells us "there is a law above the king."

Another great charter of English liberty was the 1628 PETITION OF RIGHT, a statute that asserted the freedom of the people from unconsented taxation and arbitrary imprisonment. The HABEAS CORPUS ACT OF 1679 was another major document of English liberty. The BILL OF RIGHTS of 1689, which also influenced American constitutional law, declared that parliamentary elections ought to be free and that Parliament's debates ought not to be questioned in any other place, and it condemned perversions of criminal justice by the last Stuart kings, including excessive BAIL and CRUEL AND UNUSUAL PUNISHMENTS.

The experience of the American colonies was important to the development of civil liberties in the United States. The COLONIAL CHARTERS set up local governments that built upon English institutions, and the colonists jealously opposed any infringements upon their rights. The VIRGINIA CHARTER OF 1606 reserved to the inhabitants "all liberties, Franchises and Immunities . . . as if they had been abiding and born, within this our Realm of England."

The MASSACHUSETTS BODY OF LIBERTIES of 1641 expressed in detail a range of fundamental rights later to be adopted in the American BILL OF RIGHTS. Rhode Island was the first colony to recognize religious liberty, largely through the efforts of its founder, ROGER WILLIAMS. The Puritans banished Williams from Massachusetts in 1635 for unorthodoxy, and he settled in Providence. There the plantation agreement of 1640 protected "liberty of Conscience," and this doctrine appeared in the Colony's charter in 1663. The Pennsylvania charter and those of other colonies were also influential in protecting individual rights. ZENGER'S CASE (1735), in which a jury acquitted a New York publisher on a charge of SEDITIOUS LIBEL, was a milestone in securing the freedom of the press.

By the time of the American Revolution, the colonists were familiar with the fundamental concepts of civil liberty that would be included in the Constitution and Bill of Rights. Unlike the contemporary French experience, where the promise of the Declaration of the Rights of Man went largely unfulfilled for want of institutional safeguards, the American Constitution of 1787 embodied a republican government elected by broad suffrage that was reinforced by judicial review and by CHECKS AND BALANCES among the three branches of government.

The original Constitution, a document devoted mainly to structure and the allocation of powers among the branches of the national government, contains some explicit safeguards for civil liberty. It provides that the "privilege" of habeas corpus, which requires a judge to release an imprisoned person unless he is being lawfully detained, may not be "suspended." The EX POST FACTO and BILL OF ATTAINDER clauses require the Congress to act prospectively and by general rule. Article III guarantees a jury trial in all federal criminal cases, defines TREASON narrowly, and imposes evidentiary requirements to assure that this most political of crimes will not be lightly charged.

Apart from the omission of a bill of rights, which was soon rectified, the Constitution's principal deficiency from a civil liberties standpoint was its countenance of slavery. Without mentioning the term, in several clauses it recognized the legality of that pernicious institution. DRED SCOTT V. SANDFORD (1857) cemented the legally inferior status of blacks and contributed to civil war by ruling that slaves or the descendants of slaves could not become citizens of the United States. The EMANCIPATION PROCLAMATION (1863) and the THIRTEENTH AMENDMENT (1865) freed the slaves, but the reaction that occurred after the end of Reconstruction in 1877 and decisions such as the CIVIL RIGHTS CASES (1883) and PLESSY V. FERGUSON (1896) undercut their purposes. The movement toward civil equality did not gain new momentum until the middle of the twentieth century.

The civil liberties of Americans are embodied primarily in the BILL OF RIGHTS (1791), the first ten amendments to the Constitution. JAMES MADISON proposed the amendments after the debates on RATIFICATION OF THE CONSTITUTION revealed wide public demand for additional protection of individual rights. The FIRST AMENDMENT guarantees the freedoms of speech, press, assembly, petition, and religious exercise, as well as the SEPARATION OF CHURCH AND STATE. The FOURTH AMENDMENT protects the privacy and security of home, person, and belongings and prohibits unreasonable SEARCHES AND SEIZURES. The Fifth, Sixth, and Eighth Amendments extend constitutional protection to the criminal process, including the right to due process of law, TRIAL BY JURY, CONFRONTATION of hostile witnesses, assistance of legal counsel, the RIGHT AGAINST SELF-INCRIMINATION, and protection against DOUBLE JEOPARDY and cruel and unusual punishment. The TENTH AMENDMENT reserves to the states and to the people powers not delegated to the federal government. Although the Bill of Rights was originally applicable only to the federal government, most of its provisions now have been applied to the states through the due process clause of the FOURTEENTH AMENDMENT. (See INCORPORATION DOCTRINE.) The amendment also provides a generalized guarantee of EQUAL PROTECTION OF THE LAWS as well as a virtually unenforced right to certain PRIVILEGES AND IMMUNITIES. Finally, the FIFTEENTH AMENDMENT and NINETEENTH AMENDMENT guarantee VOTING RIGHTS regardless of race or sex.

A practical understanding of civil liberties in the United States may be aided by illustrations of three main dimensions of the subject: freedom of speech, due process, and equal protection.

The First Amendment provides that "Congress shall make no law . . . abridging the freedom of speech, or of the press." The almost universal primacy given free speech as a "civil liberty" rests on several important values: the importance of freedom of speech for self-government in a democracy, its utility in probing for truth, its role in helping to check arbitrary government power, and its capacity to permit personal fulfillment of those who would express and receive ideas and feelings, especially unpopular ones, without fear of reprisal.

Consistent with the First Amendment, even revolutionary speech that is not "directed to inciting or producing imminent lawless action and is likely to incite or produce such action" is immunized from government control. (See INCITEMENT.) Similarly, highly offensive political speech and defamations of public officials and PUBLIC FIGURES that are not intentionally or recklessly false are protected. (See LIBEL AND THE FIRST AMENDMENT.) Because effective advocacy is enhanced by group membership, the First Amendment has also been interpreted to protect freedom of association from interference, absent a compelling state justification. The First Amendment provides particularly strong protection against PRIOR RESTRAINT—INJUNCTIONS or other means of preventing speech from ever being uttered or published.

Freedom of speech is not absolute. In addition to the limits just noted, OBSCENITY, child PORNOGRAPHY, and FIGHTING WORDS likely to provoke physical attacks are unprotected. All forms of speech, furthermore, are subject to reasonable time, place, and manner restrictions. The amendment has been interpreted to afford a lesser degree of protection to speech that is sexually explicit (although not obscene), to COMMERCIAL SPEECH, to SYMBOLIC SPEECH such as nonverbal displays intended to convey messages, and to

DEMONSTRATIONS (for example, PICKETING) that combine speech and action.

The concept of fair procedure, embodied in the due process clauses of the Fifth and Fourteenth Amendments, has been viewed as an element of civil liberties at least since Magna Carta, when the king was limited by "the LAW OF THE LAND." In principle, the guarantee of due process prevents government from imposing sanctions against individuals without sufficiently fair judicial or administrative procedures. Justice LOUIS D. BRANDEIS said: "In the development of our liberty insistence upon procedural regularity has been a large factor." Violations of this constitutional guarantee cover a wide range of official misconduct in the criminal process, from lynchings, to coerced confessions, to criminal convictions of uncounseled defendants, to interrogation of suspects without cautionary warnings. Beyond criminal cases, due process principles have been applied to protect juveniles accused of delinquency and individuals whose government jobs or benefits have been terminated. Whatever the context, civil liberty requires that individual interests of liberty and property not be sacrificed without a process that determines facts and liability at hearings that are fairly established and conducted. (See PROCEDURAL DUE PROCESS OF LAW, CRIMINAL; PROCEDURAL DUE PROCESS OF LAW, CIVIL).

The guarantee of equal protection is interpreted to forbid government, and in some cases private entities, to discriminate among persons on arbitrary grounds. The central purpose of the equal protection clause was to admit to civil equality the recently freed black slaves, and leading judicial decisions such as SHELLEY V. KRAEMER (1948) and BROWN V. BOARD OF EDUCATION (1954) and legislative enactments such as the CIVIL RIGHTS ACTS of 1866 and 1964 were particularly addressed to the condition of racial minorities. The constitutional guarantee of equality has been extended to women and to DISCRETE AND INSULAR MINORITIES—ethnic and religious groups, ALIENS, and children of unwed parents—whom the Supreme Court has deemed unable to protect their interests through the political process. In recent years, the Court has rejected attempts to broaden this category of specially protected groups. It has denied special protection to homosexuals, older persons, and the mentally retarded. The Court has also expressed the antidiscrimination ideal in holding that it is unconstitutional for a legislative districting system to accord votes in some districts significantly greater weight than votes in others.

A vexing equality issue is whether benign classifications of racial minorities or women are consistent with civil liberty on the theory that they prefer groups that historically were, and often still are, discriminated against. Against the background of slavery and legally enforced SEGREGATION, the Supreme Court has upheld AFFIRMATIVE ACTION programs for blacks that prefer them for employment and university admissions on the ground that a wholly "color blind" system would "render illusory the promise" of *Brown v. Board of Education.* It has also upheld some forms of preference for other minorities and for women. There is deep division over these programs. It is often charged that they are themselves an obnoxious use of racial or sexual classifications. Justice HARRY A. BLACKMUN responded to these contentions in REGENTS OF UNIVERSITY OF CALIFORNIA V. BAKKE (1978) by stating that "[i]n order to get beyond racism, we must first take account of race. . . . We cannot—we dare not—let the Equal Protection Clause perpetuate racial supremacy."

Some liberties in the United States are traceable to a natural law tradition that long antedated the Constitution and are only indirectly reflected in its text. In the American experience, for example, the VIRGINIA DECLARATION OF RIGHTS aserted that "all men are by nature equally free and independent, and have certain inherent rights . . . namely, the enjoyment of life and liberty, with the means of acquiring and possessing property." This sentiment was reflected in the DECLARATION OF INDEPENDENCE, which spoke of "inalienable rights," and in the Constitution itself, which embodied these principles. In CALDER V. BULL (1798) Justice SAMUEL CHASE expressed his view that NATURAL RIGHTS "form the very nature of our free Republican governments." Over the years the Supreme Court has recognized a number of rights not explicitly grounded in the constitutional text, including, for a season, FREEDOM OF CONTRACT, and, in recent years, the RIGHT TO TRAVEL, and the FREEDOM OF ASSOCIATION. The Court's most celebrated recent decisions of this kind have recognized a series of rights that reflect values of personal privacy and autonomy. These include the rights to marriage and to BIRTH CONTROL, to family relationships and to ABORTION. These liberties are fundamental conditions of the ability of a person to master his or her life. (See FREEDOM OF INTIMATE ASSOCIATION.)

The Supreme Court's decisions enunciating some of these rights have been challenged as unrooted in the original intention of the Framers and therefore subjective and illegitimate. But the Constitution was not frozen in time. Chief Justice JOHN MARSHALL said in McCULLOCH V. MARYLAND (1819) for a unanimous

Court that it is an instrument "intended to endure for ages to come and, consequently, to be adapted to the various crises of human affairs." In the twentieth century, Justice BENJAMIN N. CARDOZO agreed: "The great generalities of the Constitution have a content and a significance that vary from age to age." Further, the NINTH AMENDMENT contemplated that the provisions of the Bill of Rights explicitly safeguarding liberty were not meant to be exhaustive: "The enumeration in the Constitution, of certain rights, shall not be construed to deny or disparage others retained by the people." Finally, the structure of the Constitution, and the premises of a free society, imply certain liberties, such as the freedom of association and the right to travel.

The uncertainty and even illogic of Supreme Court decisions protecting certain groups and rights—why illegitimate children and not homosexuals, why a right to travel and not a right to housing—should not be viewed as merely the product of politics or prejudice. There are inevitably disagreements and inconsistencies over the proper boundaries of civil liberties and the proper judicial role in their recognition. Filling in the "majestic generalities" of the Constitution has always been a long-range and uncertain task.

An example of the difficulty is CAPITAL PUNISHMENT—the question whether there is a constitutional right not to be executed even for a heinous crime. This liberty is widely accepted throughout the world, but the United States Supreme Court has not recognized it as a constitutional right, instead permitting states to impose sentences of death for murder, subject to due process limitations. Many consider capital punishment inherently a violation of civil liberties because of the randomness in its application, its finality in the face of inevitable trial errors, its disproportionate use against racial minorities, and its dehumanizing effect on both government and the people. The struggle over this and other claims of civil liberty continues in public opinion, legislatures, and the courts.

Another source of American civil liberties is the doctrine of separation of governmental powers, illuminated most notably in the eighteenth century by the *philosophe* MONTESQUIEU. Anticipating John Acton's dictum that absolute power corrupts absolutely, the Supreme Court recognized in LOAN ASSOCIATION V. TOPEKA (1875) that the "theory of our governments, State and National, is opposed to the deposit of unlimited power anywhere. The executive, the legislative, and the judicial branches of these governments are all of limited and defined powers." In the same vein, individual rights are enhanced by the existence of a diverse population. THE FEDERALIST #51

states: "In a free government the security for civil rights [consists] in the multiplicity of interests."

The Supreme Court has enforced the principle of separation of powers. In YOUNGSTOWN SHEET & TUBE CO. v. SAWYER (1952) it denied that the President had constitutional power, even in time of national emergency, to seize private companies without legislative authorization. Two Justices rested on the separation of powers doctrine in NEW YORK TIMES CO. V. UNITED STATES (1971) by holding that under all but extraordinary circumstances the President lacks inherent power to enjoin news organizations from publishing classified information. And in UNITED STATES V. NIXON (1974), while ruling that Presidents possess an EXECUTIVE PRIVILEGE to maintain the secrecy of certain communications, the Court rebuffed President RICHARD M. NIXON's attempt to withhold White House tapes from the Watergate special prosecutor. In form, these decisions dealt with questions of allocation of governmental powers; in fact they were civil liberties decisions effectuating a structure designed, in Justice Brandeis's words, "to preclude the exercise of arbitrary power."

Neither the original Constitution nor the Bill of Rights guaranteed the right to vote, a cornerstone of democratic government as well as a civil liberty; slaves, women, and those without property were disfranchised. During the early nineteenth century states gradually rescinded property qualifications; the Fifteenth Amendment (1868) barred voting discrimination by race or color, and the Nineteenth Amendment (1920) outlawed voting discrimination on the ground of sex. Nevertheless, various devices were employed to prevent nonwhites from voting. These were curtailed by the VOTING RIGHTS ACT of 1965, the TWENTY-FOURTH AMENDMENT's invalidation of POLL TAXES as a qualification for voting, and the Supreme Court's decision in HARPER V. VIRGINIA BOARD OF ELECTIONS (1966). The TWENTY-SIXTH AMENDMENT (1971) extended the franchise to all citizens eighteen years of age and older.

A controversial question is presented by the relationship between the right to property and civil liberties. As the Supreme Court stated in GRIFFIN V. ILLINOIS (1956), "Providing equal justice for poor and rich, weak and powerful alike is an age-old problem." Although some would reject any such link between economics and liberty, others disagree. ALEXANDER HAMILTON stated that "a power over a man's subsistence is a power over his will." More recently, Paul Freund, recognizing that economic independence provides a margin of safety in risk or protest, commented that the effective exercise of liberty may require "a degree of command over material resources."

To a limited extent the Supreme Court has concurred. It has prohibited discrimination against the poor in cases involving voting rights and ACCESS TO THE COURTS. It has also afforded procedural protection against loss of government entitlements, including a government employee's interest in his job and a recipient's interest in welfare benefits. On the other hand, the Court has refused to recognize a generalized constitutional right to economic security. The Court has permitted reduction of welfare benefits below a standard of minimum need, has permitted courtroom filing fees to keep indigents from obtaining judicial discharge of debts, and has refused to recognize a constitutional right to equalized resources for spending on public education. The Court said in DANDRIDGE V. WILLIAMS (1970): "In the area of economics and social welfare, a State does not violate [equal protection] merely because the classifications made by its laws are imperfect." The idea that civil liberties imply a degree of economic security is not yet a principle of constitutional law.

Invasions of liberty are usually committed by government. But individuals may also be victimized by private power. The authority of medieval lords over their vassals was not merely economic. Today large institutions such as corporations, labor unions, and universities may seek to limit the speech or privacy of individuals subject to their authority. For this reason federal and state legislation bars RACIAL DISCRIMINATION and other forms of arbitrary discrimination in the hiring, promotion, and firing of employees, in the sale and rental of private housing, and in admission to academic institutions. The courts likewise have recognized that private power may defeat civil liberties by barring the enforcement of private RESTRICTIVE COVENANTS not to sell real estate to racial minorities and by barring private censorship and interference with freedom of association when those restrictions are supported by STATE ACTION.

Civil liberties can never be entirely secure. Government and large private institutions often seek to achieve their goals without scrupulous concern for constitutional rights. In the eighteenth century Edmund Burke wrote: "Of this I am certain, that in a democracy the majority of citizens is capable of exercising the most cruel oppression upon the minority." More recently, Charles Reich observed that civil liberties are an "unnatural state for man or for society because in a short-range way they are essentially contrary to the self-interest of the majority. They require the majority to restrain itself." The legal rights of minorities and the weak need special protection, particularly under conditions of stress.

The first such condition is economic stringency. Mass unemployment and high inflation exacerbate ethnic rivalries and discrimination, and at times are offered to justify the repression of dissent. Minorities pay the heaviest price. The victims include the dependent poor, whose government benefits are often among the first casualties during economic recession.

War also strains the Bill of Rights, for a nation threatened from without is rarely the best guardian of civil liberties within. As noted, President Abraham Lincoln suspended habeas corpus during the Civil War and President Franklin D. Roosevelt approved the internment of Japanese Americans during World War II. In addition, President WOODROW WILSON presided over massive invasions of free speech during World War I; McCARTHYISM, the virulent repression of dissent, was a product of the Cold War of the late 1940s and early 1950s; and President LYNDON B. JOHNSON authorized prosecution of protestors during the VIETNAM WAR. More recently, the deterioration of détente in the 1980s has led to interference with peaceful demonstrations, widespread surveillance of Americans, politically motivated travel bans and visa denials, and censorship of former government officials.

A third perennial source of trouble for civil liberties in America has been religious zeal. Anti-Catholic and Anti-Semitic nativism paralleled slavery during the nineteenth and twentieth centuries. The Scopes trial (STATE V. SCOPES, 1925), in which a public school teacher was convicted for teaching evolution, was the result of fundamentalist excesses. On the other hand, religious sentiments have often buttressed civil liberties by, for example, supporting the extension of civil rights to racial and other minorities and endorsing the claims of conscientious objectors to conscription in the armed services, even during wartime. But zealous groups threaten to infringe civil liberties when they seek government support to impose their own religious views on nonadherents. This has taken many forms, including attempts to introduce organized prayer in public schools, to outlaw birth control and abortion, and to use public tax revenues to finance religious schools.

If civil liberties exist simply as abstractions, they have no more value than the barren promises entombed in many totalitarian constitutions. To be real, rights must be exercised and respected. The political branches of government—legislators and executive officials—can be instrumental in protecting fundamental rights, and especially in preventing their sacrifice to the supposed needs of the nation as a whole. Yet majoritarian pressures on elected representatives are great during times of crisis, and the stress on liberty is most acute.

The vulnerability of politically accountable officials teaches that freedom is most secure when protected by life-tenured judges insulated from electoral retribution. The doctrine of JUDICIAL REVIEW, which gives the courts final authority to define constitutional rights and to invalidate offending legislation or executive action, is the most important original contribution of the American political system to civil liberty.

Since Chief Justice John Marshall wrote for a unanimous Supreme Court in MARBURY V. MADISON (1803) that the power of judicial review is grounded in the Constitution, tension has existed between this checking authority and the nation's commitment to majority rule. Challenges to the legitimacy of judicial review have been rejected with arguments based on the SUPREMACY CLAUSE in Article VI of the Constitution, on the pragmatic need for national uniformity, and on history. Thus, ROSCOE POUND, the long-time dean of Harvard Law School, concluded that the claim that judicial review is usurpation is refuted by the "clear understanding of American Lawyers before the Revolution, based on the seventeenth-century books in which they had been taught, the unanimous course of decision after independence and down to the adoption of the Constitution, not to speak of the writings of the two prime movers in the convention which drafted the instrument."

Judicial review reinforces the principle that even in a democracy the majority must be subject to limits that assure individual liberty. This principle is the essential premise of the Bill of Rights—the need to counteract the majoritarian pressures against liberty that existed in the eighteenth century and have persisted throughout American history. In the words of the Spanish writer José Ortega y Gassett, "[Freedom] is the right which the majority concedes to minorities and hence it is the noblest cry that has ever resounded in this planet." Further, the democratic political process requires civil liberties in order to function—the rights to vote, to speak, and to hear others. Elected legislatures and executive officials cannot be relied on to protect these rights fully and thus to assure the integrity of the democratic process; an insulated judiciary is essential to interpret the Constitution.

The role of the Supreme Court and other courts in exercising judicial review is valid even though their decisions may not reflect the view of the people at a given time. American democracy contemplates limitations on transient consensus and imposes long-term restrictions on the power of legislative majorities to act, subject to a constitutional amendment, because the democracy established by the Constitution is concerned not merely with effectuating the majority's will but with protecting minority rights. Further, as Burt Neuborne has pointed out, federal judges have a democratic imprimatur: "They are generally drawn from the political world; they are appointed by the President and must be confirmed by the Senate." It is for these reasons that James Madison viewed courts as the "natural guardian for the Bill of Rights."

The central role of independent courts in the enforcement of civil liberties has provoked efforts to weaken judicial review. The abolitionists, dissatisfied with federal judges who protected the rights of slaveholders, clamored for jury trials for alleged fugitive slaves; populists have long urged the popular election of judges; and Franklin D. Roosevelt sought to pack the Supreme Court to bend it to popular will. More recently, bills have been introduced in Congress to limit the JURISDICTION OF THE FEDERAL COURTS and to bar some legal remedies that are indispensable to the effectuation of certain constitutional rights. Whatever the perceived short-term advantages of such schemes to one group or another, the long-term effect would be erosion of judicial review and a consequent undermining of civil liberty.

The centrality of courts to the constitutional plan must not obscure the equally important role of legislatures. They can enhance or weaken civil liberty and, absent a declaration of unconstitutionality, their actions are final. During the period of the WARREN COURT, it was widely assumed that the judiciary alone would defend individual rights because legislatures were subject to immediate pressures from the electorate that prevented them from taking a long and sophisticated view of American liberties and protecting minorities and dissenters. But during the 1960s Congress prohibited discrimination in employment, housing, access to PUBLIC ACCOMMODATIONS, and voting; it passed the FREEDOM OF INFORMATION ACT; and it provided legal services for the poor. A few years later it enacted laws aimed at protecting the privacy of personal information. Congress can authorize expenditures, create and dismantle administrative agencies, and enact comprehensive legislation across broad subject areas—powers beyond the institutional capacity of courts.

Legislatures can also impair civil liberties in ways other than restricting judicial review. In recent years battles have raged in Congress over the Legal Services Corporation, the FREEDOM OF INFORMATION ACT, the VOTING RIGHTS ACT, school prayer, tuition tax credits to support private schools, the powers of the Central Intelligence Agency and the Federal Bureau of Investigation, and many other issues. This congressional agenda reflects an intense national debate over the meaning and scope of civil liberties in the 1980s.

Whatever the forum, the security of civil liberty requires trained professionals to press the rights of people. Throughout American history the services of paid counsel have been supplemented by lawyers who volunteer out of ideological commitment or professional obligation. Publicly supported legal services organizations and legislative provision for awarding attorneys' fees to prevailing plaintiffs in CIVIL RIGHTS cases have encouraged the growth of a sophisticated bar that litigates constitutional issues. Vital support for the defense of civil liberties is also provided by private organizations such as the AMERICAN CIVIL LIBERTIES UNION (ACLU) and more specialized groups such as the National Association for the Advancement of Colored People, the National Organization for Women, and public interest law firms ranging across the political spectrum. These bodies engage in litigation, legislative lobbying, and public education in order to advance the rights of their constituencies or constitutional rights generally.

History shows that civil liberties are never secure, but must be defended again and again, in each generation. Examples of frequently repetitive violations of civil liberties involve police misconduct, school book censorship, and interference with free speech and assembly. For instance, the ACLU found it necessary to assert the right of peaceful demonstration when that right was threatened by Mayor Frank Hague's ban of labor organizers in New Jersey in the 1930s, by Sheriff Bull Connor's violence to civil rights demonstrators in Alabama in the 1960s, by the government's efforts to stop antiwar demonstrators in Washington in the 1970s, and by the 1977–1978 effort of the city of Skokie, Illinois, to prevent a march by American Nazis.

The continuing defense of civil liberties is indispensable if often thankless. Strong and determined opponents of human rights have always used the rhetoric of patriotism and practicality to subvert liberty and to dominate the weak, the unorthodox, and the despised. Government efficiency, international influence, domestic order, and economic needs are all important in a complex world, but none is more important than the principles of civil liberties. As embodied in the Constitution and the Bill of Rights, these princi-ples reflect a glorious tradition extending from the ancient world to modern times.

NORMAN DORSEN

Bibliography

BRANT, IRVING 1965 *The Bill of Rights.* Indianapolis: Bobbs-Merrill.

CHAFEE, ZECHARIAH, JR. 1956 *The Blessings of Liberty.* Philadelphia: Lippincott.

——— 1941 *Free Speech in the United States.* Cambridge, Mass.: Harvard University Press.

DEWEY, ROBERT E. AND GOULD, JAMES A., eds. 1970 *Freedom: Its History, Nature, and Varieties.* London: Macmillan.

DORSEN, NORMAN, ed. 1984 *Our Endangered Rights.* New York: Pantheon.

——— 1970 *The Rights of Americans: What They Are— What They Should Be.* New York: Pantheon.

EMERSON, THOMAS I. 1970 *The System of Freedom of Expression.* New York: Random House.

HAIMAN, FRANKLYN 1981 *Speech and Law in a Free Society.* Chicago: University of Chicago Press.

HAND, LEARNED 1960 *The Spirit of Liberty.* New York: Knopf.

MARSHALL, BURKE, ed. 1982 *The Supreme Court and Human Rights.* Washington, D.C.: Forum Series, Voice of America.

MULLER, HERBERT J. 1963 *Freedom in the Western World from the Dark Ages to the Rise of Democracy.* New York: Harper & Row.

SCHWARTZ, BERNARD 1971 *The Bill of Rights: A Documentary History.* New York: Chelsea House/McGraw-Hill.

TRIBE, LAURENCE H. 1978 *American Constitutional Law.* Mineola, N.Y.: Foundation Press.

CIVIL LIBERTIES AND THE ANTISLAVERY CONTROVERSY

Two civil liberties issues linked the freedom of communication enjoyed by whites with the cause of the slave: the mails controversy of 1835–1837 and the gag controversy of 1836–1844.

By 1835, southern political leaders, anxiety-ridden by threats to the security of slavery, were in no mood to tolerate a propaganda initiative of the American Anti-Slavery Society, which began weekly mailings of illustrated antislavery periodicals throughout the South. The first mailing was seized and burned by a Charleston, South Carolina, mob, an action condoned by Postmaster General Amos Kendall. President AN-DREW JACKSON recommended legislation that would prohibit mailings of antislavery literature to the slave states. Senator JOHN C. CALHOUN denounced this as a threat to the SOVEREIGNTY of the states, while some northern political leaders objected to it on the grounds that it inhibited the FIRST AMENDMENT rights of FREEDOM OF SPEECH and FREEDOM OF THE PRESS of their constituents. In ensuing debates, the POSTAL POWER under Article I, section 8, and the First Amendment became the center of debates on Jackson's counterproposal, which would have mandated interstate cooperation in suppressing abolitionist mailings. Ironically, in 1836, Congress apparently inadvertently enacted legislation making it a misdemeanor to delay delivery of mail. But by 1837, abolitionists abandoned the campaign for more promising antislavery ventures.

The gag controversy proved to be longer-lived. Opponents of slavery had been petitioning Congress ever since 1790 on various subjects relating to slavery, such as the international and interstate slave trade. Such petitions were routinely either tabled or shunted to the oblivion of committees. Southerners in Congress were extremely inhospitable to such petitions, especially when the Anti-Slavery Society discontinued its mails campaign in favor of a stepped-up petition and memorial drive in 1836 focusing on the abolition of slavery in the DISTRICT OF COLUMBIA. To cope with the resulting flood of unwelcome petitions, Calhoun proposed that each house, acting under the rules of proceedings clause of Article I, section 5, refuse to receive petitions concerning slavery, rather than receiving and then tabling them. More moderate congressmen, however, adopted alternate resolutions providing for automatic tabling of such petitions. This only stimulated the antislavery societies to more successful petition drives. In response, each house annually adopted evermore stringent gag rules, the House of Representatives making its a standing rule in 1840.

Congressman JOHN QUINCY ADAMS, the former President who represented a Massachusetts district in the House, carried on an eight-year struggle to subvert the gags; he slyly introduced abolitionist petitions despite the standing rule. Enraged southern congressmen determined to stop his impertinence by offering a motion to censure him in 1842. The move backfired because it gave Adams a splendid forum to defend the First Amendment FREEDOM OF PETITION and to dramatize the threat to whites' CIVIL LIBERTIES posed by the attempted suppression of the antislavery movement. The Adams censure resolution failed. Proslavery congressmen then succeeded in censuring another antislavery Whig, Joshua Giddings of Ohio, for introducing antislavery resolutions in the House in 1842. He resigned his seat, immediately ran for reelection in what amounted to a referendum on his anti-

slavery position, and was overwhelmingly reelected. Recognizing that the gags were not only tattered and ineffectual but now also counterproductive, stimulating the very debate they were meant to choke, Congress let them lapse in 1844.

WILLIAM M. WIECEK

Bibliography

WIECEK, WILLIAM M. 1977 *The Sources of Antislavery Constitutionalism in America, 1760–1848.* Ithaca, N.Y.: Cornell University Press.

CIVIL–MILITARY RELATIONS

The Constitution has a twofold impact on civil–military relations: first, through its specific provisions on this subject: and second, through the overall structure of government and division of powers it prescribes.

Several provisions of the Constitution deal directly with civil–military relations. The second clause of Article I, section 6, prohibits members of Congress from simultaneously holding other federal office. Article I, section 8, gives Congress the power to declare war, to grant LETTERS OF MARQUE AND REPRISAL, to make rules concerning captures, to raise and to support armies, to provide and to maintain a navy, to make rules for the regulation of the armed forces, to provide for calling the militia into federal service, and to provide for organizing, arming, and disciplining the militia. Article I, section 10, limits the military powers of the states. Article II, section 2, makes the President COMMANDER-IN-CHIEF of the armed forces and authorizes the appointment of officers. The SECOND AMENDMENT protects the right of the people to keep and bear arms, in order to constitute a "well-regulated militia." And the THIRD AMENDMENT severely restricts the quartering of troops in private homes.

These provisions constitute only a skeletal framework for the relations between civil government and military forces and between the military and society. Some of them (for example, those dealing with the quartering of troops, the two-year limit on appropriations for the army, the incompatibility of congressional and military office) have become obsolete, meaningless, or unobserved in practice. When written, however, these provisions reflected a broad consensus, expressed in the debates and actions of the CONSTITUTIONAL CONVENTION and the state ratifying conventions. Three key views underlay that consensus. The Framers believed that military power and military usurpation should be feared, that soldiering should be an aspect of citizenship, and that control of military power should be divided between state and national governments and between President and Congress.

The "supremacy of the civil over the military," said Justice FRANK MURPHY in DUNCAN V. KAHANAMOKU (1945), "is one of our great heritages." At the time of the framing of the Constitution, everyone agreed on the need to insure civil authority over the military. One of the indictments of George III in the DECLARATION OF INDEPENDENCE was that he had "affected to render the Military independent of and superior to the Civil Power." Several state constitutions, including the Virginia and Massachusetts Bills of Rights, contained declarations that the military should in all cases and at all times be subordinate to and governed by the civil power. CHARLES PINCKNEY vainly proposed inclusion of similar language in the federal Constitution, and the lack of such a provision was the target of much criticism in the state conventions. Objections were also raised because the Constitution had no provision guarding against the dangers of a peacetime standing army.

In practice civil supremacy prevailed for two reasons: the deeply ingrained antimilitary attitudes continuously prevalent in American political culture, and the equally deeply ingrained ideal of the apolitical, nonpartisan, impartial military professional that gained ascendancy in the officer corps after the Civil War. In the early nineteenth century, the line between professional officer and professional politician was unclear, and individual military officers were often involved in politics. After World War II many military officers were appointed to high civil positions in government. Yet at no time, in peace or war, did serious challenges to civilian authority issue from the central military institutions. When, as in the Civil War and the KOREAN WAR, individual military leaders challenged or seemed to challenge the authority of the President, they were removed from command. The Supreme Court, in EX PARTE MILLIGAN (1866), also limited military power by holding that martial law may operate only in situations where actual conflict forces civil courts to close. The Court has also narrowly defined the extent to which American civilians accompanying the armed forces overseas are subject to military justice, as in REID V. COVERT (1957).

In the 1780s there was general agreement that the militia should be the principal source of defense for a free society. Some members of the Constitutional Convention proposed prohibiting a standing army in peacetime or limiting the size of such an army. These proposals were rebutted both in the debates and in THE FEDERALIST by arguments that there was no way to prevent another nation with a standing army from threatening the United States, and that inability to maintain such a force would invite aggression. Everyone agreed, however, that in keeping with the tradition dating from the English BILL OF RIGHTS of 1689, the power to establish military forces rested with Congress. There was widespread belief that appropriations for the army should be limited to one year, and a two-year limit was approved only because it seemed likely that Congress might assemble only once every two years. The Constitution is silent on the means Congress may employ to recruit military manpower. CONSCRIPTION was, however, an accepted eighteenth-century practice, and the Supreme Court has held that the power to "raise and support" armies included, "beyond question," the power "to classify and conscript manpower for military service" in peace or in war.

The early consensus on the central role of the militia did not extend to the question of who should control it. Traditionally, the militias had been state forces, and it was widely accepted that they should remain under state control in time of peace. The national government, however, needed the power to call on the militia to deal with invasions or insurrections. Experience in the Revolution also had demonstrated the need to insure that the militia meet minimum national standards. JAMES MADISON remarked that control over the militia "did not seem in its nature to be divisible between two distinct authorities," but in the end that control was divided: the national government took responsibility for organizing, arming, and disciplining the militia, and the state governments were responsible for the appointment of officers and training. In the debates that led to this shared control, the most repeated and persuasive argument of the nationalists was the need to have a well-organized and disciplined militia under national control so as to reduce reliance on a standing army. Support in the state conventions for what subsequently became the SECOND AMENDMENT was based on similar reasoning.

In the Militia Act of 1792, Congress did not effectively exercise its powers to organize, arm, and discipline the militia. In effect, the states retained sole control over the militia in peacetime. When required, the militia was called into federal service for the limited constitutional purposes of executing the laws, suppressing insurrections, and repelling invasions. Even in wartime, however, the assertion of federal control was controversial because the states guarded their power to appoint officers. In addition, militia units could not be used outside the United States. Thus in the nineteenth century the militia was under state control in peace and under dual control in war. Laws passed between 1903 and 1933 in effect put the militia, now called the National Guard, under dual control in peace and national control in war. Federal support was greatly expanded, federal standards were more effectively imposed, and provision was made to order the National Guard into federal service in war under the army clause of the Constitution, thus precluding any assertion of state power.

In Great Britain the king was the COMMANDER-IN-CHIEF of the army and navy and in some states the governors played similar roles. The Federal Convention gave the President command of the national military forces and of the militia when in federal service. War Presidents, most notably ABRAHAM LINCOLN, FRANKLIN ROOSEVELT, and LYNDON B. JOHNSON, actively directed military operations. The commander-in-chief clause is unique in the Constitution in assigning power in terms of an office rather than a function. It is, consequently, unclear to what extent it gives the President powers extending beyond military command. In *The Federalist*, ALEXANDER HAMILTON wrote that the clause grants "nothing more than the supreme command and direction of the military and naval forces"; yet he also wrote that the clause makes the executive responsible for the "direction of war" and gives him "the power of directing and employing the common strength." The latter definition might justify a President's seizing a steel plant to insure the continuation of war production; the former clearly would not. Beginning with Lincoln, Presidents have, however, used the clause to justify the exercise of a wide range of war powers.

The ineligibility clause of the Constitution expressly prohibits appointment of congressmen to civil positions created while they are in Congress. The Framers specifically exempted military positions, because, in case of a war, citizens capable of conducting it might be members of Congress. The incompatibility clause, on the other hand, applies to both civil and military offices. Enforced in the nineteenth century, this prohibition against simultaneously holding legislative position and military office has been frequently and systematically violated in the twentieth century by congressmen holding reserve commissions in the military services.

The more fundamental provisions in the Constitution regarding the distribution of power have had an equal effect on shaping civil–military relations, complicating, and at times frustrating, the achievement of civilian control over the military. FEDERALISM required that authority over the militia be divided between state and national governments. This division has enhanced the power of the militia by giving them two masters that might be played off against each other. The division of control over the national forces between Congress and President has worked in comparable fashion. Military officers testifying before congressional committees have some freedom to determine how far they should go in defending the policies of their commander-in-chief and how far they should go in expressing their own views. Military officers working in implicit cooperation with influential members of Congress may be able to undermine policies of the President. In addition, the commander-in-chief clause has at times been interpreted to encourage a direct relationship between the President and the uniformed heads of the armed services, bypassing the civilian secretaries of those departments. The Framers clearly intended to establish firm civilian control over the military, and many specific provisions are designed to secure that goal. Yet, by limiting the power of each branch of the government, the constitutional system effectively limits the power those branches can exercise over the military.

SAMUEL P. HUNTINGTON

Bibliography

HUNTINGTON, SAMUEL P. 1957 *The Soldier and the State: The Theory and Politics of Civil–Military Relations.* Cambridge, Mass.: Harvard University Press.
RIKER, WILLIAM H. 1957 *Soldiers of the States: The Role of the National Guard in American Democracy.* Washington, D.C.: Public Affairs Press.
SMITH, LOUIS 1951 *American Democracy and Military Power.* Chicago: University of Chicago Press.

CIVIL RIGHTS

The core of the concept "civil rights" is freedom from RACIAL DISCRIMINATION. Although the term, not improperly, often refers to freedom from discrimination based on nationality, alienage, gender, age, sexual preference, or physical or mental handicap—or even RELIGIOUS LIBERTY, immunity from official brutality, FREEDOM OF ASSEMBLY AND ASSOCIATION, FREEDOM OF THE PRESS, FREEDOM OF SPEECH, the RIGHT OF PRIVACY, and additional rights found in the Constitution or elsewhere—other terms can characterize these rights. Sometimes they are referred to as CIVIL LIBERTIES or by particular names (for example, gender or handicap discrimination). Although the racial discrimination cases have influenced doctrinal development in many of these other areas, standards governing them often differ at the levels of both judicial scrutiny and appropriate remedies. Racial discrimination deserves separate treatment.

The constitutional law of civil rights begins in the THIRTEENTH, FOURTEENTH, and FIFTEENTH AMENDMENTS. These "Civil War Amendments" were adopted during Reconstruction to effect a radical revision of the status of blacks and a sharp change in relations between national and state governments. Until the end of the Civil War, the situation of black people had been dominated by SLAVERY in the South and a regime under which, in the words of the Supreme Court in DRED SCOTT V. SANDFORD (1857), they had no rights that a white man was bound to respect. Their legal rights or disabilities derived from state law, subject to no meaningful control by the national government. The Civil War amendments changed that. The Thirteenth Amendment abolished slavery; the Fourteenth, among other things, prohibited states from denying to any person DUE PROCESS OF LAW or EQUAL PROTECTION OF THE LAWS. (Other provisions of the Fourteenth Amendment had little practical effect). The Fifteenth Amendment protected VOTING RIGHTS against governmentally imposed racial discrimination.

Each amendment empowered Congress to adopt enforcing legislation. Such laws were enacted—most notably the CIVIL RIGHTS ACT OF 1866—but they were not implemented, were interpreted restrictively, or fell into disuse following the COMPROMISE OF 1877 which assured the Presidential election of RUTHERFORD B. HAYES in exchange for his pledge to withdraw Union troops from the South and end Reconstruction. During the same period southern states, effectively free from national control, implemented BLACK CODES, and later Jim Crow laws, which returned black people to a status that was only nominally free. No significant national civil rights law was adopted again until the mid-1960s.

Between Reconstruction and the mid-twentieth century, the judiciary sporadically found significant content in the Civil War Amendments; yet racial SEGREGATION and discrimination remained pervasive in the South and widespread elsewhere. During the same period, the Fourteenth Amendment was interpreted expansively to protect burgeoning business enterprise. Between BROWN V. BOARD OF EDUCATION (1954) and the CIVIL RIGHTS ACT OF 1964, the main period of the modern civil rights revolution, the doctrinal potential of the amendments to advance the cause of black people became largely realized. Implementation became the main task, taking the form of comprehensive civil rights statutes, lawsuits brought by the United States and private parties, and adminis-

trative enforcement. As a result of this process, some whites have charged that remedies for blacks violate *their* constitutional rights: for example, that AFFIRMATIVE ACTION constitutes "reverse discrimination," or that SCHOOL BUSING for integration injures them. Justice OLIVER WENDELL HOLMES's aphorism, "the life of the law has not been logic: it has been experience," is as least as true of civil rights law as of any other branch of law.

The concept of "equal protection of the laws" underwent its greatest evolution between 1896, when PLESSY V. FERGUSON upheld a state law requiring SEPARATE BUT EQUAL segregation of whites and blacks in intrastate rail travel, and 1954, when *Brown v. Board of Education* held that segregated public EDUCATION denied equal protection. Although *Plessy* dealt only with intrastate transportation and *Brown* only with education, each was quickly generalized to other aspects of life.

The very factors which the Supreme Court invoked to uphold segregation in 1896 were reassessed in *Brown* and used to justify a contrary result. The *Plessy* majority held that the framers of the Civil War Amendments did not intend to eliminate segregation in rail travel which the Court characterized as a social, not a political activity. It thereby distinguished STRAUDER V. WEST VIRGINIA (1880), in which the Supreme Court had held that excluding blacks from juries violated the Fourteenth Amendment because it stigmatized them. *Plessy* dismissed the argument that segregating blacks from whites could justify segregating Protestants from Catholics, because that would be unreasonable; racial segregation was reasonable, for state court decisions and statutes had authorized segregation in schools. Finally, the Court addressed what today is called social psychology, writing that although *Plessy* claimed segregation connoted black inferiority, whites would not consider themselves stigmatized if they were segregated by a legislature controlled by blacks. Any harmful psychological effects of segregation were self-inflicted.

Plessy became so deeply ingrained in jurisprudence that as late as 1927, in GONG LUM V. RICE, a Court in which Holmes, LOUIS D. BRANDEIS, and HARLAN F. STONE sat unanimously agreed that racial segregation in education "has been many times decided to be within the constitutional power of the state legislature to settle, without the intervention of the federal courts under the Federal Constitution."

Other Supreme Court decisions, however, offered hope that some day the Court might come to a contrary conclusion. In YICK WO V. HOPKINS (1886) the Court invalidated as a denial of equal protection a city ordinance which, under the guise of prohibiting laundries from operating in wooden buildings, where virtually all Chinese laundries were located, excluded Chinese from that business. In BUCHANAN V. WARLEY (1917) it invalidated racial zoning of urban land under the due process clause. Later it struck down state laws prohibiting blacks from participating in primary elections. By 1950, in SWEATT V. PAINTER and MCLAURIN V. OKLAHOMA STATE REGENTS, the Court invalidated segregation in law school and graduate education, without holding segregation unconstitutional per se and without abandoning the separate-but-equal formula. These and other decisions foreshadowed *Brown* and undermined precedents approving segregation.

Brown contradicted or distinguished *Plessy* on every score. It read the legislative history of the Civil War Amendments as inconclusive on the question of school segregation, pointing out that although after the Civil War public education had been undeveloped and almost nonexistent for blacks, it had become perhaps the most important function of state government. In effect the amendment was treated as embodying a general evolutionary principle of equality which developed as education became more important. The Court treated early precedents as not controlling school segregation and drew from the 1950 graduate school cases support for a contrary result.

In contrast to *Plessy*'s dismissal of the psychological effects of segregation, *Brown* held that "to segregate them [black children] from others of similar age and qualifications solely because of their race generates a feeling of inferiority as to their status in the community that may affect their hearts and minds in a way unlikely ever to be undone." The Court cited social science literature in support of this response to *Plessy*. This portion of the opinion provoked much adverse commentary, some condemning the decision as based on social science, not law. But of course, *Plessy* had come to its sociological conclusions without any evidence at all.

In BOLLING V. SHARPE, a companion case to *Brown*, the Court decided that the Fifth Amendment's due process clause prohibited school segregation in the District of Columbia. Any other result, the Court said, would be "unthinkable."

The contending arguments in *Plessy* and *Brown* not only exemplify the possibilities of legal advocacy but also raise the question how "equal protection" could be interpreted so differently at different times. After all, the arguments remained the same, but first one side prevailed, then the other. The reason for the change lies in the development of American history. Indeed, *Brown* suggests as much in describing how much public education had changed between Reconstruction and 1954, how essential education had become for personal development, and how much blacks had achieved. By 1954 black citizens had fought for their country in two major World Wars, the more recent of which was won against Nazi racism; had moved from concentration in the South to a more even distribution throughout the country; and had achieved much socially, politically, economically, and educationally, even though their status remained below that of whites.

The courtroom struggle leading to *Brown* showed that blacks were ready to participate effectively in securing their full liberation. It culminated a planned litigation campaign, building precedent upon precedent, directed by a group of mostly black lawyers headed by THURGOOD MARSHALL, then head of the NAACP LEGAL DEFENSE AND EDUCATIONAL FUND and later a Justice of the United States Supreme Court. This campaign had many ramifications, not the least of which was to become a model for development of public interest law, which grew rapidly in the 1970s.

The nation owed black people a debt which it acknowledged officially in several ways. In the late 1940s and in *Brown* itself the solicitor general of the United States joined counsel for black litigants in calling upon the Supreme Court to declare segregation unconstitutional. That the country was generally prepared to accept this argument was further evidenced in the 1947 Report of President HARRY S. TRUMAN's Committee on Civil Rights. The committee called for the end of racial segregation and discrimination in education, PUBLIC ACCOMMODATIONS, housing, employment, voting, and all other aspects of American life.

Despite the storm of controversy stirred by the 1954 decisions, they are firmly rooted in constitutional law and nowadays there is no longer significant criticism of their results. *Brown* was quickly followed by decisions applying its principles to all other forms of state imposed racial segregation. Courts soon ordered desegregation of parks, beaches, sporting events, hospitals, publically owned or managed accommodations, and other public facilities.

But *Brown* could not affect the rights of blacks against privately imposed discrimination, for the equal protection clause is a directive to the states. The admonition that "no state" shall deny equal protection was not addressed to private employers, property owners, or those who managed privately owned public accommodations. In the CIVIL RIGHTS CASES (1883) the Supreme Court made clear not only that the equal protection clause did not apply to private action but that Congress in enforcing the Fourteenth Amendment might not prohibit private persons from discriminating. As a consequence, national civil rights laws could not apply to private restaurants, hotels, transportation, employment, and housing—places where people spend most of their lives.

In 1960 the SIT-INS, freedom rides, and DEMONSTRATIONS burst upon the national scene, aimed first at racial exclusion from privately owned public accommodations and then at other forms of discrimination. This phase of the civil rights struggle sought to move antidiscrimination precepts beyond the limitation of state power to prohibitions against private discrimination. The cases arising out of these efforts necessarily examined the distinction between what is private and what is STATE ACTION, an issue long debated in political theory and constitutional law. On the one hand, it has been argued that privately asserted rights derive from power conferred and enforced by the state and that at bottom there is no such thing as a "private" right. According to this reasoning, applying the TRESPASS laws to enforce an owner's privately held preference against black patronage of his lunch counter would be prohibited by the Fourteenth Amendment: the owner's property interest is a function of state law; the law of trespass is a state creation; prosecution and its consequences are state conduct. Pursuing such reasoning, lawyers for sit-in demonstrators identified the governmental components of otherwise private action, arguing that the Fourteenth Amendment, therefore, protected blacks who were denied service on racial grounds and later prosecuted for refusing to leave the premises. They had some legal support for this argument. Even before 1954 the Supreme Court had held in MARSH V. ALABAMA (1946) that religious proselytizing on company town property was protected by the FIRST AMENDMENT against prosecution for trespass because the town was a governmental entity, notwithstanding private ownership. Similarly, the equal protection clause had been interpreted to forbid enforcement by state courts or racially RESTRICTIVE COVENANTS against purchase or occupancy of real estate by blacks or other minorities. These cases, and their rationales, followed to the end of their logic, would mean that governmental enforcement of private discrimination violates the equal protection clause.

But the courts were not prepared to follow the reasoning to its logical conclusion. In cases in which blacks were arrested and prosecuted for entering or remaining on privately owned public accommodations where they were not wanted because of race, the Supreme Court first avoided deciding whether there was state action by ruling for the defendants on various other grounds, for example, lack of evidence or VAGUENESS of the law. In other cases the Court found state action in special circumstances: a private owner segregated because required by law; an ordinance required segregated toilets, which tended to encourage exclusion of blacks; a private restaurant leased premises from a state agency; private security guards who enforced segregation were also deputy sheriffs. But the Court balked at finding state action in prosecution for trespass to enforce a proprietor's personal decision to discriminate. The resistance grew out of a fear that to extend the state action doctrine would make most private decisions subject to government control. Moreover, if one could not call upon the state to enforce private preferences, personal force might be employed.

Other legal theorists would have differentiated between conduct prohibited by the amendment and that which is not by factoring into the decision-making process the concept of privacy. They would find, for example, that impermissible state action existed in racial exclusion from a restaurant but not from a private home. The policy against racial discrimination would prevail in the restaurant case, where there was no countervailing interest of privacy, but in the private home case the privacy interest would outweigh strictures against racial discrimination.

In 1964 the Court held that the Civil Rights Act of that year invalidated convictions of sit-in demonstrators, even those convicted before its passage. The fundamental question of precisely what level of state involvement in private conduct constitutes state action was left undecided.

The uncertain scope of the state action doctrine was underscored by the constitutional basis advanced for congressional power to pass the 1964 Civil Rights Act. Congress relied on the COMMERCE CLAUSE in addition to the Fourteenth Amendment because the commerce clause does not require state action to justify congressional regulation. The initial Supreme Court decisions upholding the 1964 Civil Rights Act, HEART OF ATLANTA MOTEL V. UNITED STATES (1964) and KATZENBACH V. McCLUNG (1964), relied on the commerce clause, and upheld applications of the law in cases of minimal effect upon commerce.

The impulse to define fully the meaning of state action was further damped by developments in Thirteenth Amendment law. The Thirteenth Amendment has no state action limitation and, therefore, covers private as well as state action. But early efforts to apply it to discrimination as a BADGE OF SERVITUDE were rejected by the Court, which held that the amendment forbade only slavery itself. The Civil Rights Act of 1866 had made illegal private racially discriminatory refusals to contract or engage in real estate transactions. But not until 1968 did the Supreme Court interpret these laws to forbid private discrimination. By the mid-1960s, through the civil rights acts of that period and the new judicial interpretation of Reconstruction legislation, it was no longer necessary to discover state action in ostensibly private conduct in order to prevent discrimination. With the passing of this need, concerted efforts to expand the courts' views of the state action concept came to a halt.

The contrast between the promise of the Constitution and its performance was nowhere better highlighted than in *Brown* itself. The Supreme Court treated constitutional right and remedy in two separate opinions, *Brown I* and *Brown II*, decided in 1955. *Brown I* decided only that racial segregation was unconstitutional, postponing decisions on the means and the pace of school desegregation. *Brown II* proclaimed that school segregation need not end immediately; it had to be accomplished with ALL DELIBERATE SPEED. The Court required a "prompt and reasonable" start, and permitted delay only for the time necessary for administrative changes. Opposition to desegregation, the Court said, would not justify delay. Nevertheless, southern schools actually integrated at an extremely slow pace. Not until 1969, when the Court announced that the time for "deliberate speed" had passed, did school integration proceed rapidly.

While the "deliberate speed" decision contributed to a sense that desegregation was not urgent and procrastination was tolerable, it is difficult to believe that a different formula would have materially affected the pace of integration. Armed physical opposition in Little Rock and elsewhere in the South was aimed at integration at any time, with or without deliberate speed. One hundred members of Congress signed the SOUTHERN MANIFESTO denouncing the Supreme Court, and Congress came within a single vote of severely restricting the Court's JURISDICTION. Congressional legislation implementing *Brown* would not be adopted until after the civil rights movement of the 1960s.

The refusal of school districts to desegregate was not susceptible to remedy because there was almost no one who would bring integration suits. No southern white lawyers would bring school suits until the 1970s; in many a southern state, there was only a handful of black lawyers with minimal resources; civil rights organizations were few, small, and overburdened; the United States Justice Department and the Department of Health, Education, and Welfare had no authority to bring suit. As a consequence, where school boards resisted or claimed to be in compliance with *Brown*, there was hardly any way to compel change. These conditions, not "deliberate speed," kept school segregation in place. Real opportunities for the judiciary to speed the pace of integration had to await political change. That change came in the 1960s, with the pro-civil rights policies of Presidents JOHN F. KENNEDY and LYNDON B. JOHNSON, culminating in the Civil Rights Act of 1964.

Supreme Court opinions stating in OBITER DICTUM that integration must be achieved rapidly began to be issued at the end of the 1960s. In the 1970s courts began to hand down detailed orders requiring the end of segregation "root and branch." Because black and white families were segregated residentially, the only way to integrate schools in many communities was to combine in single attendance zones areas separated by some distance, thus employing SCHOOL BUSING. Numerical standards also were employed to measure whether acceptable levels of integration had been reached. These techniques—particularly busing and RACIAL QUOTAS—have stimulated controversy and political opposition.

The integration of the 1970s in most instances was carried out as quickly as possible when courts ordered it. Although the deliberate speed doctrine had by then been overruled, such rapid desegregation met its literal requirements. In a typical case, the revision of boundaries and regulations and the reassignment of students and teachers took a few months. Conditions in the nation, not "deliberate speed," caused the long delay.

Brown, of course, concerned states where segregation had been required or permitted by statute. By the 1970s the Supreme Court faced the issue of northern segregation which was not caused by state statute. It differentiated between "de facto" segregation (resulting from racially segregated housing patterns) and "de jure" segregation (resulting from deliberate official decisions). Some commentators argued that there is no such thing as de facto segregation, for children always are assigned to schools by governmental action. But only where some intent to discriminate was demonstrated did the courts require desegregation. However, where an intent to discriminate has been shown in part of a district, a presumption has been held to arise that single-race schools elsewhere in the district have been the product of such intent. Under this doctrine many northern districts have been desegregated.

Often a city school district is nearly all black and

surrounded by white suburban districts. The Court held in MILLIKEN V. BRADLEY (1974) that integration across district lines may not be ordered without proof of an interdistrict violation. A number of lower courts have found such violations and have ordered integration across district lines.

All of these standards were implemented, particularly in the 1970s, by the Departments of Justice and Health, Education, and Welfare (later the Department of Education). The private bar brought a considerable number of cases facilitated by congressional legislation authorizing the award of counsel to prevailing parties in school segregation, to be paid by defendants. But the intimate relation between politics and implementation of constitutional civil rights became apparent once more in the 1980s when a new administration opposed to busing and numerical standards for gauging integration virtually ceased bringing school cases to court, undertook to modify or revoke INJUNCTIONS in already decided cases, and opposed private plaintiffs in others.

Following *Brown* and in response to the demonstrations of the 1960s, the Civil Rights Acts of 1964, 1965, and 1968 were enacted with the goal of implementing the ideals of the Civil War amendments. But results of these laws varied according to their political, social, and legal settings. Public accommodations, for example, integrated easily; housing has been intractable. Affirmative action policies have been devised to assure certain levels of minority participation, but they have stimulated opposition by whites who claim they are being disfavored and illegally so. Controversy has also developed over the question of whether antidiscrimination orders might be entered only upon a showing of official discriminatory intent, or whether such orders are also justified to remedy the racially discriminatory effects of official policies. Affirmative action and discriminatory intent, the twin central legal issues of civil rights in the 1980s, have in common a concern with distributive fairness. Both issues have been contested in political, statutory, and constitutional arenas.

In general, the courts have sustained the constitutionality of affirmative action as a congressional remedy for past discriminations and as an appropriate judicial remedy for past statutory or constitutional violations. In medical school admissions, for example, four Justices of the Supreme Court thought a fixed racial quota favoring minorities violated the Civil Rights Act of 1964, and a fifth Justice found an equal protection violation; a different majority, however, concluded that an admissions policy favoring racial and other diversity, which assured the admission of a substantial but not fixed number of minorities, would be valid as an aspect of a university's First Amendment exercise of academic freedom. The Court, with three dissents, has sustained a congressionally mandated quota assuring ten percent of certain government contracts to minority contractors. And in school integration numerical measures of integration have been commonplace. In employment and voting as well, affirmative action has been incorporated into efforts to undo discrimination and has been upheld by the courts. [See REGENTS OF UNIVERSITY OF CALIFORNIA V. BAKKE (1978), and FULLILOVE V. KLUTZNICK 1980).]

The courts usually have required a showing of discriminatory intent in order to establish an equal protection violation, but intent may be inferred from conduct. In any event, the intent requirement may be dispensed with where Congress has legislated to make discriminatory results adequate to trigger corrective action.

The public accommodations portions of the 1964 Act prohibited discrimination in specific types of establishments (typified by those providing food or amusement) that affect INTERSTATE COMMERCE. An exception for private clubs reflected uncertainty about the lack of power (perhaps arising out of countervailing constitutional rights of association) and the desirability of controlling discrimination in such places. But the meaning of "private" in this context has not been explicated. Clubs where a substantial amount of business is conducted may not be exempt and an amendment has been proposed to make this clear.

Immediately following passage of the law the Department of Justice and private plaintiffs brought successful suits against recalcitrant enterprises. Most public accommodations complied rapidly. Large national enterprises that segregated in the South integrated because they could not afford the obloquy of resistance, threat of boycott, and consequent loss of business in the North. Many small southern businesses opened to all without problems. Even proprietors who wished to continue discriminating soon bowed to the law's commands. Today one rarely hears of public accommodations discrimination.

Before adoption of the civil rights legislation of the 1960s, the only significant federal regulations of employment discrimination were the Fifth Amendment and Fourteenth Amendment, which prohibited federal and state employment discrimination, and executive order prohibition of discrimination by certain government contractors. The Railway Labor Act and the NATIONAL LABOR RELATIONS ACT were construed to forbid discrimination by covered unions. But all such limitations were difficult to enforce. The Civil Rights Act of 1964 and the 1968 Equal Employment Opportunity (EEO) Act were the first effective prohibitions against discrimination in employment. Private suits (with counsel fees payable to prevailing plaintiffs), suits by the Equal Employment Opportunity Commission against private defendants, and suits by the Justice Department against state and local government are the primary mechanisms of enforcement. As elsewhere in modern civil rights law, the two most important issues with constitutional overtones under this law have been whether a plaintiff must prove that discrimination was intentional and whether courts may award affirmative relief, including racial quotas. As to intent, the EEO statute has been interpreted to forbid hiring and promotion criteria that have an adverse impact on a protected group but bear no adequate relationship to ability to perform the job. Thus, an intelligence test for coal handlers, or a height requirement for prison guards, which screen out blacks or women and do not indicate ability to do the job, violate the statute even absent a showing of intent to discriminate. On the other hand, when the statute is not applicable, a plaintiff can secure relief under the Constitution only by showing intentional discrimination.

Affirmative action in the form of hiring and promotion goals and timetables have been prescribed by courts and all branches of the federal government with enforcement responsibility. Moreover, some private employers have adopted these techniques as a matter of social policy or to head off anticipated charges of discrimination. The legality of such programs has been upheld in the vast majority of cases. Affirmative action has substantially increased minority and female participation in jobs it covers but continues to be attacked by nonprotected groups as unconstitutional, illegal, or unwise. In 1984 the Supreme Court held that the EEO Act prohibits enjoining layoffs of black beneficiaries of a consent decree requiring certain levels of black employment where that would result in discharging whites with greater seniority.

Although the Fifteenth Amendment expressly protects the right to vote against racial discrimination and the Fourteenth Amendment's equal protection clause also has been interpreted to do so, voting discrimination was widespread and blatant well into the 1960s, and to some extent it still persists. Apart from physical violence and intimidation, which lasted until the mid-1960s, a long line of discriminatory devices has been held to be in violation of the Constitution

and statutes, only to be succeeded by new ones. Very early, southern states adopted GRANDFATHER CLAUSES, requiring voters to pass literacy tests but exempting those who were entitled to vote in 1866, along with their lineal descendants—which meant whites only. When the courts struck down the grandfather clause, it was succeeded by laws permitting registration only during a very brief period of time without passing a literacy test. Thereafter even those who could pass the test were not permitted to register. Very few blacks could take advantage of this narrow window, but the stratagem was not outlawed until 1939. Most southern states through the 1920s had laws prohibiting blacks from voting in party PRIMARY ELECTIONS. In the South, the Democratic party excluded blacks, and the winner of the Democratic primary always was elected. These laws were held unconstitutional in the 1940s and 1950s on the grounds that the party primary was an integral part of the state's electoral system, despite its nominal autonomy. As the white primary fell, laws and practices were widely adopted requiring registrants to read and understand texts like the Alabama State Constitution or to answer registrars' questions such as "how many bubbles are there in a bar of soap." These tests were held unconstitutional. Racial GERRYMANDERING, a not uncommon practice where blacks in fact voted, also was enjoined as unconstitutional. Other impediments to voting were not motivated solely by racial considerations but affected blacks disproportionately, such as the POLL TAX, later prohibited by constitutional amendment. LITERACY TESTS also lent themselves to discriminatory administration.

The VOTING RIGHTS ACT OF 1965 invalidated any and all racially discriminatory tests and devices. But, more important, states in which there was a history of voting discrimination (identified by low registration or voter turnout) could not adopt new voting standards unless those standards were certified as nondiscriminatory by the Department of Justice. This prohibition ended the tactic of substituting one discriminatory device for another. Where they were needed, federal officials could be sent to monitor registration and voting or, indeed, to register voters.

Although the 1965 law significantly reduced racial discrimination in the electoral process, abuses persisted in the forms of inconvenient registration procedures, gerrymandering, occasional intimidation, and creation of MULTIMEMBER DISTRICTS. This last device has its roots in post-Reconstruction efforts to dilute black voting strength. The use of single-member districts to elect a city council would result in the election of blacks from those districts where blacks constitute a majority. By declaring the entire city a multimember district, entitled to elect a number of at-large candidates, the majority white population can, if votes are racially polarized, elect an all-white council—a result that has occurred frequently. The Supreme Court required a showing of discriminatory intent if such a voting system were to be held unconstitutional. But the interplay between Court and Congress produced an amendment of the Voting Rights Act in 1982, permitting proof of a violation of the act by a showing of discriminatory effect.

Affirmative action has been an issue in voting as in other areas. The Supreme Court has held that, upon a showing of past voting discrimination, the attorney general may condition approval of legislative redistricting upon a race-conscious drawing of district lines to facilitate election of minority candidates.

Until 1968, the most important federal prohibition of housing discrimination was the equal protection clause, which was held in SHELLEY V. KRAEMER (1948) to prohibit judicial enforcement of restrictive covenants among property owners forbidding occupancy of property by members of racial minorities. The Fifth and Fourteenth Amendments prohibit racial segregation in public housing, but the construction of public housing has virtually ceased.

The Fair Housing Act of 1968 marked the completion of the main statutory efforts to satisfy the prescriptions of President HARRY S. TRUMAN's 1947 Committee on Civil Rights. On the eve of the law's passage, the Supreme Court interpreted the Civil Rights Act of 1866 to forbid refusals to engage in real property transactions on racial grounds. Nonetheless, the 1866 and 1968 acts have been the least effective of the civil rights acts. Their failure owes to deep, persistent opposition to housing integration, to a lack of means of enforcement commensurate with the extent of the problem, and to a shortage in the housing market of houses in the price range which most minority buyers can afford. Because the housing market is atomized, a single court order cannot have widespread effect. (Housing is thus unlike education, where an entire district may be desegregated, or employment, where government agencies and other large employers can be required to take steps affecting thousands of employees.)

An effort to address the relationship between race and economics in housing foundered at the constitutional level when the Court held that large-lot zoning—which precluded construction of inexpensive housing, thereby excluding minorities—was not invalid under the Constitution absent a demonstration of racially discriminatory intent. The 1968 Fair Housing Act authorizes judicial relief when such laws produce discriminatory effects, without demonstration of intent. Nevertheless, economic factors and political opposition have prevented the statutory standard from having a significant practical impact. In several states where state law has invalidated such zoning, the actual change in racial housing patterns has been slight.

Some legislative efforts to desegregate housing have run into constitutional obstacles. A municipality's prohibition of "For Sale" signs to discourage panic selling by whites in integrated neighborhoods has been held to violate the First Amendment. A judge's award of damages for violation of the Fair Housing Act has been held to violate the Sixth Amendment right of TRIAL BY JURY (subsequently, contrary to civil rights lawyers' expectations, jury verdicts often have been favorable to plaintiffs). A large governmentally assisted housing development's racial quota, set up with the aim of preventing "tipping" (whites moving out when the percentage of blacks exceeds a certain point), was still being contested in the mid-1980s.

From constitutional adoption, through interpretation, and judicial and statutory implementation, the law of civil rights has interacted with the world that called it into being. No great departures from settled doctrine are to be anticipated in the near future. But similar assertions might have been made confidently at various points in the history of civil rights, only to be proved wrong in years to come.

JACK GREENBERG

Bibliography

BLACK, CHARLES L., JR. 1967 Foreword: State Action, Equal Protection, and California's Proposition 14. *Harvard Law Review* 81:69–109.

EASTLAND, TERRY and BENNETT, WILLIAM J. 1979 *Counting by Race.* New York: Basic Books.

GREENBERG, JACK 1968 The Supreme Court, Civil Rights and Civil Dissonance. *Yale Law Journal* 77:1520–1544.

JOINT CENTER FOR POLITICAL STUDIES 1984 *Minority Vote Dilution*, Chandler Davidson, ed. Washington, D.C.: Howard University Press.

KIRP, DAVID L. 1983 *Just Schools: The Idea of Racial Equality in American Education.* Berkeley: University of California Press.

KLUGER, RICHARD 1975 *Simple Justice: The History of Brown v. Board of Education and Black America's Struggle for Equality.* New York: Knopf.

KONVITZ, MILTON R. 1961 *Century of Civil Rights.* New York: Columbia University Press.

KUSHNER, JAMES A. 1983 *Fair Housing: Discrimination*

in Real Estate, Community Development, and Revitalization. New York: Shepard's/McGraw-Hill.

SCHLEI, BARBARA and GROSSMAN, PAUL 1983 *Employment Discrimination Law,* 2nd ed. Washington, D.C.: Bureau of National Affairs.

U.S. COMMISSION ON CIVIL RIGHTS 1981 *Affirmative Action in the 1980's: Dismantling the Process of Discrimination.* Washington, D.C.: U.S. Commission on Civil Rights.

CIVIL RIGHTS ACT OF 1866
(Framing)
14 Stat. 27

Responding to the Black Codes, Congress in 1866 passed its first CIVIL RIGHTS bill to enforce the THIRTEENTH AMENDMENT. The bill's definition of national CITIZENSHIP superseded the decision in DRED SCOTT v. SANDFORD (1857), which had excluded blacks. A citizen was any person not an Indian or of foreign allegiance born in any state or territory, regardless of color. All citizens were to enjoy full and EQUAL PROTECTION of all laws and procedures for the protection of persons and property, and be subject to like punishments without regard to former slave status. In all jurisdictions citizens were to have equal rights to sue, contract, witness, purchase, lease, sell, inherit, or otherwise convey personal or real property. Anyone who, "under color of any law . . . or custom," prevented any person from enjoying those rights, or who subjected any person to discriminatory criminal punishments because of race or previous involuntary servitude, was subject to MISDEMEANOR prosecutions in federal courts. Congress further authorized the REMOVAL OF CASES from state to federal courts of persons denied civil rights and of federal officer defendants, prosecuted by states, protecting civil rights; that provision connected the civil rights bill to the FREEDMEN'S BUREAU and the HABEAS CORPUS statutes. All federal officials could initiate proceedings under the bill. Federal judges were to appoint special commissioners to enforce judgments under the bill (a use of fugitive slave law processes for opposite purposes). Alternatively, judges could employ the army or state militias, under the President's command, as posses. Last, Congress expanded the Supreme Court's APPELLATE JURISDICTION to include questions of law arising from the statute.

President ANDREW JOHNSON's powerful veto of the Civil Rights Bill, though overridden by Congress, touched both honorable traditions of the states' monopoly of rights and ignoble concepts of race hierarchy. He insisted that the bill would create a centralized military despotism and invoked the recent EX PARTE MILLIGAN (1866) decision. Congress, he argued, was creating black citizens of the same states it was excluding from representation.

Though trenchant, the veto never touched on the question of the remedies available to injured citizens or the nation, when states failed to carry out their duty to treat their own citizens equally. If no statutory remedies existed, then both nation and states were returned to the conditions of 1860. Anxious to make clear the fact of the nation's advance from that pitiable condition, the Congress pushed ahead with a FOURTEENTH AMENDMENT proposal and, in 1867, resorted to military reconstruction as a desperate stop-gap.

But the Fourteenth Amendment, unlike the Thirteenth (which the Civil Rights Act enforced) constrained only STATE ACTION, at least according to Supreme Court judgments commencing with the *Slaughterhouse* case (1873). In May 1870, the Congress "re-enacted" the 1866 Civil Rights law, this time under the Fourteenth and FIFTEENTH AMENDMENTS (though section 16 of the 1870 law still punished discriminatory felonious private acts). In 1874, a revision of the federal statutes appeared, breaking up the text of the 1866 statute into scattered sections.

HAROLD M. HYMAN

(SEE ALSO: *Section 1983, Title 42, United States Code.*)

Bibliography

HOWE, M. A. DEWOLFE 1965 Federalism and Civil Rights. [Massachusetts Historical Society] *Proceedings* 77:15–27.

HYMAN, HAROLD M. and WIECEK, WILLIAM M. 1982 *Equal Justice under Law: Constitutional Development 1835–1875.* Chaps. 9–11. New York: Harper & Row.

KACZOROWSKI, ROBERT J. 1971 Nationalization of Civil Rights: Theory and Practice in a Racist Society, 1866–1883. Ph.D. diss., University of Minnesota.

CIVIL RIGHTS ACT OF 1866
(Judicial Interpretation)

Judicial interpretation has transformed the Civil Rights Act of 1866 from a simple effort to dismantle the BLACK CODES into one of the most important existing CIVIL RIGHTS laws. In assessing judicial treatment of the act, it is helpful to consider section one of the act separately from section three. Other sections have not led to noteworthy judicial development. Section one of the act, which granted all persons the same rights as white persons to make and enforce contracts, sue, be parties, give EVIDENCE, inherit, purchase, lease, sell, hold, and convey real and personal property, and to the full and equal benefit of all laws and proceedings for the security of person and property, was reenacted in modified form by the Civil Rights Act of 1870, was divided into two sections by the REVISED STATUTES OF 1874, and survives as sections 1981 and 1982 of Title 42, United States Code. Section three of the act, which set forth the procedures for vindicating rights protected by section one, was scattered throughout the United States Code. Portions of it survive as CIVIL RIGHTS REMOVAL statutes and as part of section 1988 of Title 42. Judicial interpretation of the 1866 act is not unrelated to these statutory reshufflings. Cut adrift from their moorings in the entire 1866 act, the act's remnants are amenable to many more interpretations than the original provision.

Cases decided in the years immediately following the 1866 act's passage are particularly important in ascertaining its original meaning. The REVISED STATUTES of 1874 would strip the act's descendants of any close resemblance to the original measure. And once the courts became accustomed to applying the FOURTEENTH AMENDMENT, much of the 1866 act would become superfluous. In addition, ratification of the Fourteenth Amendment eliminated most doubts about the act's constitutionality.

Prior to ratification of the Fourteenth Amendment, most courts were willing to sustain the act under Congress's THIRTEENTH AMENDMENT power to proscribe SLAVERY. But at least Kentucky's highest court in *Bowlin v. Commonwealth* (1867) declared the act unconstitutional. Other courts avoided such a declaration only by interpreting the act not to prohibit some forms of RACIAL DISCRIMINATION that the act's words arguably covered.

In the reported interpretations of the act, for example, courts divided over whether states could continue to outlaw marriages between whites and blacks. State courts in Tennessee (1871), Indiana (1871), and Alabama (1878) found marriage not to be a contract within the meaning of section 1, and therefore rejected attacks on antimiscegenation laws that relied on the 1866 act. State courts in Louisiana (1874) and Alabama (1872) relied at least in part on the 1866 act to find intermarriage legal, but the Alabama case was soon overruled. Not until LOVING v. VIRGINIA (1967) did the Supreme Court hold the Fourteenth Amendment to ban antimiscegenation laws.

State courts also divided over whether the 1866 act abrogated state laws prohibiting blacks from testifying against whites. The Kentucky court found Congress's effort to do so unconstitutional, but an 1869 Arkansas decision found the act to authorize such testimony. In 1869, the California Supreme Court relied on the 1866 act's evidentiary provision to dismiss an INDICTMENT against a mulatto, because Chinese witnesses had testified at his trial and state law prohibited them from testifying against white men. But a year later, despite the 1866 act, the California court sustained the state's evidentiary ban on testimony by Chinese against whites.

After the 1870s, section 1 diminished in importance. The state laws against which it most successfully operated, laws mandating racial discrimination in areas covered by section 1, could also be attacked directly under the Fourteenth Amendment. And with section 1 and the Fourteenth Amendment undermining the most egregious provisions of the Black Codes, there remained only one important area to which section 1 might be applied—private discrimination. When the CIVIL RIGHTS CASES (1883), UNITED STATES V. HARRIS (1883), and UNITED STATES V. CRUIKSHANK (1876) limited Congress's Thirteenth and Fourteenth Amendment power to legislate against private racial discrimination, there was doubt about whether section 1 constitutionally could be applied to private discrimination. One early lower federal court opinion, *United States v. Morris* (1903), suggested the 1866 act's applicability to private discrimination, but Supreme Court statements in *Virginia v. Rives* (1880) and CORRIGAN V. BUCKLEY (1926) suggested that the act did not apply to private conduct. (See STRAUDER V. WEST VIRGINIA, 1880.)

Hurd v. Hodge (1948), a companion case to SHELLEY V. KRAEMER (1948), gave section 1 some new life. The court applied section 1 to prohibit courts in the DISTRICT OF COLUMBIA from enforcing a racially RESTRICTIVE COVENANT. The breakthrough came in JONES V. ALFRED H. MAYER CO. (1968), where the Court held both that Congress meant the 1866 act to proscribe private discrimination and that Congress constitutionally could outlaw private discrimination under the Thirteenth Amendment. As the result of *Jones, Johnson v. Railway Express Co.* (1974), and RUNYON V. MCCRARY (1976), the remnants of the 1866 act were transformed from historical relics into federal laws broadly prohibiting private racial discrimination in the sale or lease of all housing, in schools, in employment and in virtually all other contracts. In many respects the 1866 act's newly discovered coverage exceeds that of comprehensive modern civil rights laws. *General Building Constructors Association, Inc. v. Pennsylvania* (1982) limited the 1866 act's reach by holding that liability may not be imposed under the act without proof of intentional discrimination.

Section 3 of the 1866 act traveled a less visible path through the courts. Its primary significance has been to determine when a violation of former section 1 authorizes an original or removal action in federal court. (See REMOVAL OF CASES.) In *Blyew v. United States* (1872), over the dissents of Justices JOSEPH P. BRADLEY and NOAH SWAYNE, the Court held that Kentucky's testimonial disqualification of black witnesses did not confer ORIGINAL JURISDICTION on a lower federal court to hear a state murder case at which the black witnesses were to testify. In a series of civil rights removal cases, the Court held that what had been section 3 authorized removal to federal court where state laws expressly mandated a racial distinction that prevented blacks from receiving equal justice, as when blacks were excluded from juries. But the Court found removal not to be authorized where the same result was achieved through other than formal state statutory command.

Under section 3's remnants, actions that arise under state law but are removed to federal court are tried in federal court by applying state law. In *Robertson v. Wegmann* (1978), however, the Court misconstrued the shred of the 1866 act commanding this result to require application of state law to cases arising under *federal* law. The same remnant, section 1988, also has been relied on in *Sullivan v. Little Hunting Park, Inc.* (1969) to authorize damages for violations of section 1 rights and in *Tomanio v. Board of Regents* (1980) to require the use of state statutes of limitations in federal civil rights cases.

THEODORE EISENBERG

Bibliography

BARDOLPH, RICHARD 1970 *The Civil Rights Record.* Pages 84–87, 94–96, 200–201, 532–533. New York: Thomas Y. Crowell.
CARR, ROBERT K. 1947 *Federal Protection of Civil Rights.* Ithaca, N.Y.: Cornell University Press.
EISENBERG, THEODORE 1981 *Civil Rights Legislation.* Charlottesville, Va.: Michie Co.

CIVIL RIGHTS ACT OF 1875
18 Stat. 335

On his deathbed Senator CHARLES SUMNER (Republican, Mass.) implored a congressional friend, "You must take care of the civil rights bill,—my bill, the civil rights bill, don't let it fail." Since 1870 Sumner had sought to persuade Congress to enact a law guaranteeing to all people, regardless of race or religion, the same accommodations and facilities in public schools, churches and cemeteries incorporated by public authority, places of public amusement, hotels licensed by law, and common carriers. Sumner had contended that racial SEGREGATION was discriminatory, that SEPARATE BUT EQUAL facilities were inherently unequal, and that compulsory equality would combat prejudice as much as compulsory segregation fostered it. Opponents claimed that the FOURTEENTH AMENDMENT protected the privileges of United States CITIZENSHIP only, not those of state citizenship to which the bulk of CIVIL RIGHTS attached. Opponents also claimed that Congress had no constitutional power to protect civil rights from violation by private persons or businesses.

School DESEGREGATION was unpopular among northern Republicans and hated by southern Democrats. After the election of 1874 resulted in a Democratic victory in the House, supporters of Sumner's bill settled for "half a loaf" by consenting to the deletion of the provisions on education, churches, and cemeteries. A black congressman from South Carolina agreed to the compromise because the school clause jeopardized the Republican party in the South and subordinated the educational needs of blacks to their right to be desegregated. Teaching the "three Rs" to the children of former slaves was more important than risking their educational opportunities by demanding their admission to "white" schools.

In February 1875 the lame-duck 43rd Congress, 2nd session, voting along party lines in both houses, passed the modified bill which President ULYSSES S. GRANT signed into law on March 1. The Civil Rights Act of 1875, the last Reconstruction measure and the last civil rights act until 1957, was the most important congressional enactment in the field of PUBLIC ACCOMMODATIONS until the CIVIL RIGHTS ACT OF 1964. The act of 1875 affirmed the equality of all persons in the enjoyment of transportation facilities, in hotels and inns, and in theaters and places of public amusement. Theoretically such businesses, though privately owned and operated, were like public utilities, exercising public functions for the benefit of the public and subject to public regulation. Anyone violating the statute was civilly liable for $500 damages and, on conviction in federal court, subject to a fine of not more than $1,000 or imprisonment for not more than one year. In 1883 the Supreme Court held the statute unconstitutional in the CIVIL RIGHTS CASES.

LEONARD W. LEVY

Bibliography

KONVITZ, MILTON R. 1961 *A Century of Civil Rights.* New York: Columbia University Press.

CIVIL RIGHTS ACT OF 1957
71 Stat. 634

Although this law marked the end of an eighty-two-year period of congressional inactivity in the field of CIVIL RIGHTS, it accomplished little. The act created the CIVIL RIGHTS COMMISSION but granted it only investigative and reporting powers. The act also created a separate CIVIL RIGHTS DIVISION within the Department of Justice to be headed by an additional assistant attorney general. More substantively, the act made it unlawful to harass those exercising their VOTING RIGHTS in federal elections and provided for federal initiation of proceedings against completed or potential violations. Offenders receiving more than slight penalties were entitled to TRIAL BY JURY, a watering-down provision inserted by Senate opponents.

The act is as significant for important deletions from the original bill as for what was ultimately enacted. Southern senators managed to eliminate a provision authorizing the ATTORNEY GENERAL to seek injunctive relief against all civil rights violators, a provision opponents feared would enhance the federal presence in school DESEGREGATION disputes and one they characterized as reimposing Reconstruction on the South. The emasculated act was viewed as a victory for southern segregationists. It was not even worth a filibuster.

THEODORE EISENBERG

Bibliography

BRAUER, CARL M. 1977 *John F. Kennedy and the Second Reconstruction.* New York: Columbia University Press.

CIVIL RIGHTS ACT OF 1960
74 Stat. 86

The insignificance and ineffectiveness of the CIVIL RIGHTS ACT OF 1957 generated pressure in the next Congress to enact a more effective CIVIL RIGHTS law. And the CIVIL RIGHTS COMMISSION established by the 1957 act added to the pressure by issuing a report documenting the abridgment of black VOTING RIGHTS in the South.

As enacted, the 1960 act required state election officers to retain for twenty-two months records relating to voter registration and qualifications in elections of federal officials. Where courts found patterns or practices of abridgment of the right to vote on account of race, they were authorized to declare individuals qualified to vote and to appoint federal voting referees to take EVIDENCE and report to the court on the treatment of black voters.

In a provision originally aimed at interference with school DESEGREGATION decrees, the act imposed criminal penalties for obstruction of all court orders. It also created a federal criminal offense of interstate flight to avoid prosecution for destroying buildings or other property.

Like the 1957 act, the 1960 act is noteworthy for its failure to include a proposed provision authorizing the United States to initiate actions on behalf of persons deprived of civil rights.

THEODORE EISENBERG

Bibliography

BRAUER, CARL M. 1977 *John F. Kennedy and the Second Reconstruction.* New York: Columbia University Press.

CIVIL RIGHTS ACT OF 1964
78 Stat. 241

The Civil Rights Act of 1964 signified many changes. For JOHN F. KENNEDY, prompted by southern resistance to DESEGREGATION orders and violent responses to peaceful CIVIL RIGHTS protests, proposing the measure symbolized an aggressive new attitude toward RACIAL DISCRIMINATION. For LYNDON JOHNSON, who supported the act after Kennedy's assassination, it marked a turn away from southern regionalism and toward national leadership on civil rights matters. For Congress, the act ended a century of nonexistent or ineffective civil rights laws and was the first civil rights measure with respect to which the Senate invoked CLOTURE. For blacks, the act was the first major legislative victory since Reconstruction and the most far-reaching civil rights measure in American history.

The act consists of eleven titles. Titles I and VIII reinforce voting rights provisions of the CIVIL RIGHTS ACTS OF 1957 and 1960 and limit the use of LITERACY TESTS to measure voter qualifications. (See also VOTING RIGHTS ACT OF 1970.) Titles III and IV, in provisions deleted from the bills that became the 1957 and 1960 acts, authorize court actions by the ATTORNEY GENERAL to challenge segregated public facilities and schools. Title V amends provisions governing the CIVIL RIGHTS COMMISSION. Title IX authorizes appeal from orders remanding to state courts civil rights cases that have been removed to federal court and authorizes the Attorney General to intervene in EQUAL PROTECTION cases. Title X establishes a Community

Relations Service to assist communities in resolving discrimination disputes. Title XI deals with miscellaneous matters. The most important parts of the law are Title II, forbidding discrimination in PUBLIC ACCOMMODATIONS; Title VI, forbidding discrimination in federally assisted programs; and Title VII, forbidding EMPLOYMENT DISCRIMINATION. In 1972, Congress extended Title VII's coverage to most government employees. It does not cover religious institutions.

Congress shaped the 1964 act with a keen awareness of previously declared constitutional limitations on ANTIDISCRIMINATION LEGISLATION. Title II's ban on discrimination in public accommodations and Title VII's ban on employment discrimination are limited to those entities whose operations affect INTERSTATE COMMERCE. By limiting these provisions to establishments and employers affecting commerce, Congress sought to avoid the CIVIL RIGHTS CASES' (1883) determination that Congress lacks power under the FOURTEENTH AMENDMENT to outlaw discrimination by private citizens, even in such a quasi-public area as that of public accommodations. Unlike its power to enforce the Fourteenth Amendment, Congress's COMMERCE CLAUSE power is not limited to STATE ACTION. In HEART OF ATLANTA MOTEL, INC. V. UNITED STATES (1964) and KATZENBACH V. MCCLUNG (1964) the Court upheld Title II as a valid exercise of the commerce power and the power to regulate interstate travel. Under the Court's subsequent decision in JONES V. ALFRED H. MAYER CO. (1968), much of Title II and Title VII would be valid as congressional enforcement of the THIRTEENTH AMENDMENT. Title VI's ban on discrimination in federally assisted programs was tied to another constitutional provision, Congress's TAXING AND SPENDING POWER.

Judicial interpretation seems to have avoided another potential constitutional problem attending Title VII. Under a 1972 amendment to Title VII, employers must accommodate an employee's religious practices if the employer is able to do so without undue hardship. In *Trans World Airlines, Inc. v. Hardison* (1977), the Supreme Court held that the statute does not require an employer to bear more than a DE MINIMIS cost to accommodate an employee's religious preferences. If Title VII were interpreted to mandate substantial concessions to religiously based employee work preferences, it might raise serious problems under the FIRST AMENDMENT'S ESTABLISHMENT OF RELIGION clause.

With the 1964 act's constitutional vulnerability minimized shortly after enactment, the way was clear for its development. Title II, banning racial discrimi-

nation in public accommodations, was the act's symbolic heart, providing immediate and highly visible evidence that blacks, as equal citizens, were entitled to equal treatment in the public life of the community. But Title II generated little litigation, for compliance was swift throughout the South once the principle of equal access was established. Equalizing employment opportunity was a goal that would take longer to accomplish. Thus in operation, Title VII has dwarfed all other titles combined, frequently generating a huge backlog of cases in the agency charged with Title VII's administration, the Equal Employment Opportunity Commission (EEOC), and leading to thousands of judicial decisions.

The proof necessary to establish a Title VII violation repeatedly occupies the Supreme Court. Two leading cases, *McDonnell Douglas Corp. v. Green* (1973) and GRIGGS V. DUKE POWER CO. (1971), approve alternative methods of proof in Title VII cases. Under *McDonnell Douglas*, a plaintiff alleging discrimination by an employer must, after exhausting the necessary remedies with the EEOC or a state antidiscrimination agency, show that the plaintiff applied and was rejected for a job for which the plaintiff was qualified, and that the employer continued to try to fill the position. An employer must then justify its actions. Under *Griggs*, in an extension of Title VII not necessarily contemplated by the 1964 Congress, proof that an employment selection criterion has a disproportionate adverse impact on minorities requires the employer to show that the selection standard is required by business necessity. After *Griggs*, statistically based Title VII cases, and threats to bring such cases, became a widespread method for pressuring employers to hire more minority and female workers. Few employers are both able to prove the business necessity of employment tests or other hiring criteria and willing to incur the expense of doing so.

The 1964 act, particularly Title VII, is not without its ironies. First, opponents of the act amended it to include sex discrimination in the hope that such an amendment would weaken the bill's chances for passage. But the bill passed with the additional ban that revolutionized at least the formal status of female workers. And in the case of sex discrimination, Title VII reaches beyond traditional refusals to hire or obvious pay disparities. When the Court held in *General Electric Co. v. Gilbert* (1976) that excluding pregnancy from a health plan does not constitute discrimination on the basis of sex, Congress amended Title VII to overturn the result. *Los Angeles Department of Water and Power v. Manhart* (1978) marks some sort of outer limit on Title VII's protection of female workers. The Court held Title VII to proscribe a requirement that females, who live longer than males and therefore can expect to receive greater total retirement benefits from a pension plan, contribute more to a pension than males contribute. In the case of sex, religion, or national origin discrimination, Title VII provides a defense if these factors constitute a bona fide occupational qualification, a defense sometimes difficult to separate from that of business necessity. The Supreme Court found in *Dothard v. Rawlinson* (1977) that a bona fide occupational qualification justifies requiring male prison guards for at least some classes of male prisoners.

Second, although the BURGER COURT generally has been viewed as conservative in the field of civil rights, Title VII owes much of its practical importance to Chief Justice WARREN E. BURGER's opinion for the Court in *Griggs v. Duke Power Co. Griggs* removed the requirement that discriminatory intent be an element of Title VII cases. This holding, in addition to its significance for Title VII, has been incorporated in other areas, including discrimination in housing under the CIVIL RIGHTS ACT OF 1968. *New York City Transit Authority v. Beazer* (1979), in which the Court refused to invalidate an employment selection standard (exclusion of drug users) with disparate impact on minorities, may signify some retrenchment from the full force of the *Griggs* principle. And in *International Brotherhood of Teamsters v. United States* (1977), the Court refused to extend *Griggs* to invalidate seniority systems that predate Title VII. But the Court never has directly questioned *Griggs*. In UNITED STEELWORKERS OF AMERICA V. WEBER (1979), the Burger Court concluded that Title VII permitted at least some private AFFIRMATIVE ACTION employment programs.

Although Title VII deservedly receives most of the attention paid to the 1964 act, Title VI is also an important antidiscrimination law. In REGENTS OF THE UNIVERSITY OF CALIFORNIA V. BAKKE (1978) it provided the setting for the Court's first important pronouncement on affirmative action programs. Many subsequent antidiscrimination laws, such as Title IX of the EDUCATION AMENDMENT OF 1972, the AGE DISCRIMINATION ACT OF 1975, and the REHABILITATION ACT of 1973 are modeled after Title VI. Title VI is the principal antidiscrimination measure for programs receiving federal funds that are not affected by other antidiscrimination measures. In the case of public institutions, however, there is much overlap between Title VI's prohibitions and those contained in the Fourteenth Amendment. The Supreme Court has been ambiguous in describing the relationship be-

tween the two. In *Bakke,* a majority of Justices suggested that Title VI and the Constitution are coterminous, but it did not purport to overturn the Court's earlier holding in LAU V. NICHOLS (1974), widely read as extending Title VI to cases of discrimination not banned by the Constitution.

The contributions of the 1964 act to racial equality defy precise measurement, but surely they have been weighty. Beyond the tangible changes the act brought to the public life of southern communities and to the entire American workplace lie enormous changes in attitudes and everyday personal relations. Those who believe that "you can't legislate morality" would do well to ponder the lessons of the Civil Rights Act of 1964.

THEODORE EISENBERG

(SEE ALSO: *Firefighters Local #1784 v. Stotts, 1984.*)

Bibliography
DORSEN, NORMAN; BENDER, PAUL; NEUBORNE, BURT; and LAW, SYLVIA 1979 *Emerson, Haber and Dorsen's Political and Civil Rights in the United States,* 4th ed. Vol. II:581–608, 902–1062, 1172–1220. Boston: Little, Brown.
LARSON, ARTHUR and LARSON, LEX K. 1981 *Employment Discrimination.* New York: Matthew Bender.
SCHLEI, BARBARA L. and GROSSMAN, PAUL 1976 *Employment Discrimination Law.* Washington, D.C.: Bureau of National Affairs.
SULLIVAN, CHARLES A.; ZIMMER, MICHAEL J.; and RICHARDS, RICHARD F. 1980 *Federal Statutory Law of Employment Discrimination.* Indianapolis: Bobbs-Merrill.

CIVIL RIGHTS ACT OF 1968
82 Stat. 696

This act capped the modern legislative program against RACIAL DISCRIMINATION that included the CIVIL RIGHTS ACT OF 1964 and the VOTING RIGHTS ACT of 1965. Title VIII of the act, which constitutes the nation's first comprehensive OPEN HOUSING LAW, prohibits discrimination in the sale, rental, financing, and advertising of housing, and in membership in real estate brokerage organizations. Ironically, soon after Title VIII's enactment, the Supreme Court, in JONES V. ALFRED H. MAYER CO. (1968), construed a remnant of the CIVIL RIGHTS ACT OF 1866 to outlaw private racial discrimination in housing. In dissent in *Jones,* Justice JOHN M. HARLAN, joined by Justice BYRON R. WHITE, relied in part on Title VIII's passage to challenge the need for the Court's decision. The 1968 act also contained criminal penalties to protect civil rights activity and comprehensive measures to protect rights of AMERICAN INDIANS. Different portions of the act, including antiriot provisions, represented a backlash against antiwar demonstrations, CIVIL RIGHTS protest, and other forms of domestic unrest.

Like the Civil Rights Act of 1964, the 1968 act survived a southern filibuster in the Senate. Efforts by House opponents to delay consideration of the bill backfired. The delay led to the bill's consideration in the aftermath of DR. MARTIN LUTHER KING, JR.'S assassination. Given that the bill passed the House by a small margin, the delay may have made all the difference.

THEODORE EISENBERG

Bibliography

HARVEY, JAMES C. 1973 *Black Civil Rights During the Johnson Administration.* Jackson, Miss.: University and College Press of Mississippi.

CIVIL RIGHTS CASES
109 U.S. 3 (1883)

In an opinion by Justice JOSEPH P. BRADLEY, with only Justice JOHN MARSHALL HARLAN dissenting, the Supreme Court ruled that Congress had no constitutional authority under either the THIRTEENTH or the FOURTEENTH AMENDMENT to pass the CIVIL RIGHTS ACT OF 1875. Holding that act unconstitutional proved to be one of the most fateful decisions in American history. It had the effect of reinforcing racist attitudes and practices, while emasculating a heroic effort by Congress and the President to prevent the growth of a Jim Crow society. The Court also emasculated the Fourteenth Amendment's enforcement clause, section five. The tragedy is that the Court made the Constitution legitimize public immorality on the basis of specious reasoning.

The *Civil Rights Cases* comprised five cases decided together, in which the act of 1875 had been enforced against innkeepers, theater owners, and a railroad company. In each of the five, a black citizen was denied the same accommodations, guaranteed by the statute, as white citizens enjoyed. The Court saw only an invasion of local law by the national government, contrary to the powers reserved to the states under the TENTH AMENDMENT. Bradley began his analysis with the Fourteenth Amendment, observing that its first section, after declaring who shall be a citizen, was prohibitory: it restrained only STATE ACTION. "Individual invasion of individual rights is not the subject-matter of the amendment." Its fifth section empowered Congress to enforce the amendment

by appropriate legislation. "To enforce what? To enforce the prohibition," Bradley answered. He ignored the fact that the enforcement section applied to the entire amendment, including the CITIZENSHIP clause, which made all persons born or naturalized in the United States and subject to its jurisdiction citizens of the United States and of the states in which they reside. As Harlan pointed out, citizenship necessarily imports "equality of civil rights among citizens of every race in the same state." Congress could guard and enforce rights, including the rights of citizenship, deriving from the Constitution itself. Harlan reminded the Court of its opinion in STRAUDER V. WEST VIRGINIA (1880), where it had said that "a right or immunity created by the constitution or only guarantied by it, even without any express delegation of power, may be protected by congress."

But Bradley took the view that the legislative power conferred upon Congress by the Fourteenth Amendment does not authorize enactments on subjects "which are within the domain of state legislation. . . . It does not authorize congress to create a code of municipal law for regulation of private rights." Congress can merely provide relief against state action that violates the amendment's prohibitions on the states. Thus, only when the states acted adversely to the rights of citizenship could Congress pass remedial legislation. But its legislation could not cover the whole domain of CIVIL RIGHTS or regulate "all private rights between man and man in society." Otherwise, Congress would "supersede" the state legislatures. In effect the Court was saying that the Reconstruction amendments had not revolutionized the federal system. In effect the Court also warned the states not to discriminate racially, lest Congress intervene, as it had in the CIVIL RIGHTS ACT OF 1866, which the Court called "corrective" legislation against state action. In the cases under consideration, however, the discrimination derived from purely private acts unsupported by state authority. "The wrongful act of an individual, unsupported by any such authority, is simply a private wrong" that Congress cannot reach. Congress can, of course, reach and regulate private conduct in the normal course of legislation, penalizing individuals; but, Bradley explained, in every such case Congress possesses under the Constitution a power to act on the subject.

Under the Thirteenth Amendment, however, Congress can enact any legislation necessary and proper to eradicate SLAVERY and "all badges and incidents of slavery," and its legislation may operate directly on individuals, whether their acts have the sanction of state authority or not. The question, then, was whether the Thirteenth Amendment vested in Congress the authority to require that all persons shall have equal accommodations in inns, public conveyances, and places of public amusement. The Court conceded that the amendment established "universal civil and political freedom throughout the United States" by abolishing slavery, but it denied that distinctions based on race or color abridged that freedom. Where, Bradley asked, does slavery, servitude, or badges of either arise from race discrimination by private parties? "The thirteenth amendment," he declared, "has respect, not to distinctions of race, or class, or color, but to slavery." The act of the owner of an inn, or theater, or transportation facility in refusing accommodation might inflict an ordinary civil injury, recognizable by state law, but not slavery or an incident of it. "It would be running the slavery argument into the ground," Bradley insisted, "to make it apply to every act of discrimination which a person may see fit to make" as to his guests, or those he will take in his coach, or those he will admit to his concert. On the theory that mere discrimination on account of race or color did not impose badges of slavery, the Court held that the Thirteenth Amendment, like the Fourteenth, did not validate the Civil Rights Act of 1875.

The case involved questions of law, history, and public policy. Harlan, dissenting, had the weight of argument as to all three, but Bradley had the weight of numbers. It was an 8–1 decision, and the eight scarcely bothered to answer the dissenter. Ignoring him might have been more discreet than trying to rebut him. He met their contentions head-on, starting with a strenuous objection to their parsimonious interpretation of national powers under the Thirteenth and Fourteenth Amendments, both of which expressly made affirmative grants of power. By contrast, Harlan demonstrated, the Court had generously construed the Constitution to support congressional enactments on behalf of slaveholders. The fugitive slave acts, which operated on private individuals, were based on a clause in the Constitution, Article 4, section 2, paragraph 3, that did not empower Congress to legislate at all. The clause merely provided that a fugitive slave be delivered up upon the claim of his owner, yet the Court sustained the acts of 1793 (PRIGG V. PENNSYLVANIA, 1842) and of 1850 (ABLEMAN V. BOOTH, 1859), implying a national power to enforce a right constitutionally recognized. The Thirteenth Amendment, as the majority admitted, established a constitutional right: civil freedom for citizens throughout the nation. And, as the majority admitted, the abolition of slavery reached the BADGES OF SERVI-

TUDE, so that the freedmen would have the same rights as white men. Similarly, the act of 1875 reached badges of servitude, because it, like the amendments to the Constitution, aimed at erasing the assumption that blacks were racially inferior. For Harlan, RACIAL DISCRIMINATION was a badge of servitude. Bradley had distinguished the act of 1866 from the act of 1875 on the ground that the earlier statute aimed at protecting rights that only the states might deny. Harlan replied that citizens regardless of race were entitled to the same civil rights.

Harlan also demonstrated that the rights allegedly violated by purely private parties were denied by individuals and CORPORATIONS that exercised public functions and wielded power and authority under the state. Relying on a broad concept of state action, he sought to prove that the parties whom the majority regarded as private were, in contemplation of law, public or quasi-public. A railroad corporation, an innkeeper, and a theater-manager had denied accommodations to black citizens. Railroads and streetcars were common carriers, that is, they were public highways, performing state functions; they were public conveyances which, though privately owned, had been established by state authority for a public use and were subject to control by the state for the public benefit. Free citizens of any race were entitled to use such facilities. Similarly, the COMMON LAW defined innkeepers as exercising a quasi-public employment that obligated them to take in all travelers, regardless of race. Theaters were places of public amusement, licensed by the public, of which the "colored race is a part," and theaters were clothed with a public interest, in accord with MUNN V. ILLINOIS (1877). Congress had not promiscuously sought to regulate the entire body of civil rights nor had it entered the domain of the states by generally controlling public conveyances, inns, or places of public amusement. Congress had simply declared that in a nation of universal freedom, private parties exercising public authority could not discriminate on ground of race; in effect the statute reached state instrumentalities whose action was tantamount to state action.

Under the Thirteenth Amendment, Congress could reach badges of servitude; under the Fourteenth, it could reach racial discrimination by state agencies. Contrary to the Court's assertion, Congress had not outlawed racial discrimination imposed by purely private action. It had aimed at such discrimination only in public places chartered or licensed by the state, in violation of the rights of citizenship which the Fourteenth Amendment affirmed. The amendment's fifth section empowered Congress to pass legislation enforcing its affirmative as well as its prohibitory clauses. Courts, in the normal exercise of JUDICIAL REVIEW, could hold unconstitutional state acts that violated the prohibitory clauses. Accordingly, section five was not restricted to merely corrective or remedial national legislation. Congress, not the Court, said Harlan, citing MCCULLOCH V. MARYLAND (1819), might choose the means best adopted to implementing the ends of the two amendments. Harlan insisted that Congress

may, without transcending the limits of the constitution, do for human liberty and the fundamentals of American citizenship, what it did, with the sanction of this court, for the protection of slavery and the rights of the masters of fugitive slaves. If fugitive slave laws, providing modes and prescribing penalties whereby the master could seize and recover his fugitive slave, were legitimate exertions of an implied power to protect and enforce a right recognized by the constitution, why shall the hands of congress be tied, so that—under an express power, by appropriate legislation, to enforce a constitutional provision granting citizenship—it may not, by means of direct legislation, bring the whole power of this nation to bear upon states and their officers, and upon such individuals and corporations exercising public functions, assumed to abridge the supreme law of the land.

Some old abolitionists, deploring a ruling that returned the freedmen to a "reign of contempt, injury, and ignominy," denounced the "new DRED SCOTT decision," but most were resigned to defeat. Racial segregation was common throughout the country. Not surprisingly *The Nation* magazine, which approved of the decision, observed that the public's general unconcern about the decision indicated "how completely the extravagant expectations as well as the fierce passions of the war have died out." The Court served "a useful purpose in thus undoing the work of Congress," said the *New York Times,* and *Harper's Weekly* agreed. Public opinion supported the Court, but justice and judicial craftsmanship were on the side of Harlan, dissenting.

LEONARD W. LEVY

Bibliography
KONVITZ, MILTON R. 1961 *A Century of Civil Rights.* New York: Columbia University Press.
WESTIN, ALAN F. 1962 The Case of the Prejudiced Doorkeeper. Pages 128–144 in Garraty, John A., *Quarrels That Have Shaped the Constitution.* New York: Harper & Row.

CIVIL RIGHTS COMMISSION

THE CIVIL RIGHTS ACT OF 1957 created the Commission on Civil Rights to investigate alleged deprivations of VOTING RIGHTS, to study and collect information concerning denials of EQUAL PROTECTION, and to appraise federal laws and policies with respect to equal protection of the laws. Subsequent legislation restated and expanded the commission's concerns to include denials of rights on the basis of color, race, religion, national origin, sex, age, or handicap. Initially, the commission was to issue a series of reports and expire upon issuance of its final report, but Congress repeatedly has extended the commission's reporting duties and life. The commission lacks power to enforce any antidiscrimination or other CIVIL RIGHTS laws.

By the standards of later civil rights legislation, creation of the commission seems an innocuous event. But at the time even this mild gesture drew substantial southern opposition. The commission's "snoopers," one southern congressman argued, "would cause inestimable chaos, confusion, and unrest among [the South's] people and would greatly increase the tension and agitation between the races there."

Because of the commission's advisory nature, measuring its accomplishments is difficult. In the 1960s, the commission's early reports helped to inform Congress about the need for voting rights legislation. And it clearly has served the function, added to its mandate in 1964, of a national clearinghouse for information about denials of equal protection. But the commission also has played a somewhat larger political role. In most administrations the commission's views are more egalitarian than the President's. The commission thus serves as a gadfly that both makes official sounding pronouncements and commands media attention. Administrations hear the commission even if they do not always listen to it.

THEODORE EISENBERG

Bibliography
United States Commission on Civil Rights 1961 *Report.* Pages xv–xviii. Washington, D.C.: U.S. Government Printing Office.

CIVIL RIGHTS DIVISION

Created by Order of the Attorney General No. 3204, February 3, 1939, the Civil Rights Section (originally named the Civil Rights Unit) of the Justice Department became the federal government's principal CIVIL RIGHTS litigation unit. The order creating the Section called for a study of federal law to assess its utility in enforcing civil rights. The study, which stated the legal basis and goals of the Section's early civil rights enforcement efforts, suggested the need for TEST CASES to resolve uncertainties about the scope and constitutionality of the only statutory weapons then available to the Section, the surviving Reconstruction-era civil rights legislation. The Section's test cases include UNITED STATES V. CLASSIC (1941), an important precedent establishing authority to prosecute offenses relating to PRIMARY ELECTIONS, and SCREWS V. UNITED STATES (1945), which allowed the application of the criminal provisions of the CIVIL RIGHTS ACT OF 1866 to misconduct by state police officers.

The Civil Rights Section's growth reflects a general increase in national concern with civil rights matters. As of 1947, the Section is reported never to have had more than eight or ten lawyers and professional workers on its staff. In 1950, the section more than doubled in size. The CIVIL RIGHTS ACT OF 1957 upgraded the Section to the status of Division by providing for an additional assistant attorney general. By 1965, the Division had eighty-six attorneys and ninety-nine clerical workers. By 1978, there were 178 attorneys and 203 support personnel.

The Division's principal activity consists of litigation. It enforces the CIVIL RIGHTS ACTS OF 1957, 1960, 1964, and 1968, the VOTING RIGHTS ACT OF 1965, the Equal Credit Opportunity Act, the 1866 act's criminal provisions, laws prohibiting PEONAGE and involuntary servitude, and various other laws. It does so through direct actions or through AMICUS CURIAE appearances in private cases. An administration's civil rights priorities are reflected in the categories of cases emphasized by the Division. In the early 1960s the Division emphasized voting rights cases. From 1965 to 1967, DESEGREGATION of education was its priority issue. By 1967, employment litigation became a priority item. Creation of a Task Force on Sex Discrimination in 1977 reflected a growing concern with sex discrimination.

THEODORE EISENBERG

Bibliography

CARR, ROBERT K. 1947 *Federal Protection of Civil Rights: Quest for a Sword.* Ithaca, N.Y.: Cornell University Press.

CIVIL RIGHTS REMOVAL

Since the CIVIL RIGHTS ACT OF 1866, federal CIVIL RIGHTS laws have allowed REMOVAL OF CASES from state to federal courts. The 1866 and 1870 acts provided for removal to federal court of state criminal or civil cases affecting persons who were denied or could not enforce in state court rights guaranteed by the acts. In the REVISED STATUTES of 1874, Congress restated the removal power to encompass violations of "any law providing for . . . equal civil rights." Early removal cases, typified by STRAUDER V. WEST VIRGINIA (1880), allowed removal when state courts denied rights by enforcing state statutes but refused removal when state courts denied rights by following uncodified practices. With the vanishing of the BLACK CODES, removal became an insignificant remedy.

In the 1960s, civil rights protesters often were arrested under state TRESPASS, traffic, and other minor laws and were subjected to unfair state court proceedings. After a pause of eighty years, the Court again considered civil rights removal. In *Georgia v. Rachel* (1966) civil rights SIT-IN demonstrators being prosecuted for trespass in state court sought removal. The Court held removal authorized only for violations of "any law providing for specific civil rights stated in terms of racial equality." But, bending the *Strauder-Rives* line, the Court did not require that a state statute be the basis for the alleged deprivation of federal rights. The Court allowed removal on the grounds that the state prosecution violated the CIVIL RIGHTS ACT OF 1964, which outlaws even attempts to punish persons exercising rights of equal access to PUBLIC ACCOMMODATIONS.

On the same day, however, the Court decided in *City of Greenwood v. Peacock* (1966) that workers engaged in a voter registration drive could not rely on various voting statutes that prohibit RACIAL DISCRIMINATION to remove their state prosecutions for obstructing the public streets. The mere likelihood of prejudice was not enough to justify removal under the statute. The majority evidently shrank from the prospect of wholesale removal of criminal prosecutions of black defendants from southern state courts to federal courts. *Peacock* effectively precludes widespread modern use of civil rights removal.

THEODORE EISENBERG

Bibliography

AMSTERDAM, ANTHONY G. 1965 Criminal Prosecutions Affecting Federally Guaranteed Civil Rights: Federal Removal and Habeas Corpus Jurisdiction to Abort State Court Trial. *University of Pennsylvania Law Review* 113:793–912.

CIVIL RIGHTS REPEAL ACT
28 Stat. 36 (1894)

From the middle of the 1860s to 1875, Congress was favorably disposed toward ANTIDISCRIMINATION LEGISLATION and even enacted some such measures over presidential veto. But many of the provisions enacted encountered restrictive interpretations to outright invalidation in the Supreme Court. The Repeal Act of 1894 symbolizes formal reconvergence of congressional and judicial attitudes towards CIVIL RIGHTS statutes.

In 1892 the Democratic party, for the first time after the Civil War, gained control of both houses of Congress and the presidency. In the Repeal Act of 1894, which repealed portions of the Enforcement Act of 1870 and the FORCE ACT OF 1871, Congress eliminated most civil rights measures that had not already been undermined by the Court. The repealed provisions had provided for federal control of federal elections through the appointment of federal election officials, a control method revived in the CIVIL RIGHTS ACTS OF 1960 and 1964 and the VOTING RIGHTS ACT OF 1965.

THEODORE EISENBERG

Bibliography
EISENBERG, THEODORE 1981 *Civil Rights Legislation.* Page 741. Charlottesville, Va.: Michie Co.

CIVIL WAR AMENDMENTS

See: Fifteenth Amendment; Fourteenth Amendment; Thirteenth Amendment

CLAIMS COURT

The Claims Court hears actions for money damages against the United States, except for tort claims. The court thus hears claims for contract damages, tax refunds, and JUST COMPENSATION for property taken. With the consent of all parties to an action against the government under the FEDERAL TORT CLAIMS ACT, the court can substitute for a court of appeals and review the decision of a federal district court.

Under the doctrine of SOVEREIGN IMMUNITY, the United States cannot be sued without its consent. At first, persons with claims against the government had to ask Congress for relief under private acts. This practice became burdensome, and in 1855 Congress established the Court of Claims to hear nontort money claims against the United States, and report its recommendations to Congress. Much of the congressional burden remained; thus, in 1863, Congress empowered the court to give judgments against the government. In 1866 the process became fully "judicial" when Congress repealed a provision delaying payment of such

a judgment until the Treasury estimated an appropriation.

The Court of Claims retained the nonjudicial function of giving ADVISORY OPINIONS on questions referred to it by the houses of Congress and heads of executive departments. However, its judges from the beginning had life tenure during GOOD BEHAVIOR. In 1933 the question arose whether the Court of Claims was a CONSTITUTIONAL COURT. Congress, responding to the economic depression, reduced the salaries of federal employees, except for judges protected by Article III against salary reductions. In *Williams v. United States* (1933), the Supreme Court, taking the preposterous position that claims against the government fell outside the JUDICIAL POWER OF THE UNITED STATES, held that the Court of Claims was a LEGISLATIVE COURT whose judges' salaries could constitutionally be reduced.

In 1953 Congress declared explicitly that the Court of Claims was established under Article III. In *Glidden v. Zdanok* (1962) the Supreme Court accepted this characterization on the basis of two separate (and incompatible) theories, pieced together to make a majority for the result. Two Justices relied on the 1953 Act; three others would have overruled *Williams* and held that the court had been a constitutional court since 1866 when Congress allowed its judgments to be paid without executive revision, and its business became almost completely "judicial." (The same decision confirmed that the COURT OF CUSTOMS AND PATENT APPEALS was a constitutional court.) The Court of Claims transferred new congressional reference cases to its chief commissioner, and Congress ratified this practice. The court's business became wholly "judicial."

In the FEDERAL COURTS IMPROVEMENT ACT (1982) Congress reorganized a number of specialized federal courts. The Court of Claims disappeared, and its functions were reallocated. The commissioners of that court became judges of a new legislative court, the United States Claims Court. They serve for fifteen-year terms. The Article III judges of the Court of Claims became judges of a new constitutional court, the UNITED STATES COURT OF APPEALS FOR THE FEDERAL CIRCUIT. That court hears appeals from a number of specialized courts, including the Claims Court.

The availability of a suit for damages in the Claims Court serves to underpin the constitutionality of some governmental action that might otherwise raise serious constitutional problems. Some regulations, for example, are arguable TAKINGS OF PROPERTY; if the regulated party can recover compensation in the

Claims Court, however, the constitutional issue dissolves (*Blanchette v. Connecticut General Insurance Corps.*, 1974).

                                        KENNETH L. KARST

Bibliography

Symposium: The Federal Courts Improvement Act   1983
    Cleveland State Law Review 32:1–116.

CLARK, CHARLES E.
(1889–1963)

Charles Edward Clark, the son of a Connecticut farmer and a graduate of Yale College, achieved distinction as a legal educator and a federal judge. In 1919 he began teaching at Yale Law School, where he had earned his law degree, and became its dean in 1929. Within the year he had modernized the curriculum, stressing interdisciplinary studies. Originally a Republican, Clark became a New Dealer and in 1937 was the only law school dean to testify in favor of President FRANKLIN D. ROOSEVELT's court reorganization plan. In 1939 Roosevelt appointed him to the UNITED STATES COURT OF APPEALS, Second Circuit. As a federal judge for twenty-five years he tended to be a liberal activist even though his opinions on the rights of the criminally accused strongly supported prosecutorial positions. But Clark's opinions favored trade unions, CIVIL RIGHTS, and government regulation of the economy. As a FIRST AMENDMENT absolutist, he eloquently and ardently championed views that Justices HUGO L. BLACK and WILLIAM O. DOUGLAS of the Supreme Court later endorsed.

                                        LEONARD W. LEVY

Bibliography

SCHICK, MARVIN 1970 *Learned Hand's Court.* Baltimore: Johns Hopkins University Press.

CLARK, TOM C.
(1899–1977)

Tom Campbell Clark, Associate Justice of the Supreme Court and ATTORNEY GENERAL of the United States, was born September 23, 1899, in Dallas, Texas. He was educated at the University of Texas at Austin, receiving his B.A. in 1921 and his LL.B. in 1922. Admitted to the Texas Bar in 1922, he joined his family's firm in Dallas.

Clark began his twelve-year career with the Department of Justice in 1937 as a special assistant to the attorney general. He held a number of posts in the department, capped by his 1945 appointment as attorney general by President HARRY S. TRUMAN. With this promotion, Clark became the first person to become attorney general by working himself up from the lower ranks of the department.

Four years later, President Truman appointed Clark Associate Justice of the Supreme Court; he took his oath of office on August 24, 1949. His tenure on the bench spanned eighteen years, and he served on both the VINSON COURT and WARREN COURT. He retired from the Court on June 12, 1967, to avoid the appearance of a conflict of interests when his son, Ramsey Clark, was appointed attorney general by President LYNDON B. JOHNSON. Clark, however, continued to sit as a judge in the various courts of appeal, and to be a vigorous and vocal advocate of judicial reform until his death on June 13, 1977.

On the Supreme Court, Clark built a reputation as a pragmatic jurist. Early on, he voted regularly with Chief Justice FRED M. VINSON and the other Truman appointees. In time, however, he began to assert his independence. In YOUNGSTOWN SHEET AND TUBE COMPANY V. SAWYER (1952), the steel seizure case, Clark voted against Vinson and Truman, concurring in the Court's decision holding unconstitutional Truman's order for governmental seizure of the nation's steel mills.

While Clark was generally viewed as politically conservative, he was relatively nonideological, and his views changed throughout his tenure, especially during the years of the Warren Court (1953–1969). He was a nationalist, a liberal on racial matters, and, in general, a conservative on issues of CRIMINAL PROCEDURE and CIVIL LIBERTIES.

Clark's most significant opinions in the area of FEDERALISM are his landmark opinion on STATE REGULATION OF COMMERCE in DEAN MILK COMPANY V. MADISON (1951), and his dissent in *Williams v. Georgia* (1955), which provided the classic definition of "independent and ADEQUATE STATE GROUNDS" that insulate state court decisions from the Supreme Court. In the racial area, speaking for the Court in BURTON V. WILMINGTON PARKING AUTHORITY (1961), he rejected as unlawful STATE ACTION racial discrimination by private persons who had leased public property. In addition, he wrote for the Court in HEART OF ATLANTA MOTEL, INC., V. UNITED STATES (1964) where, in a case involving both national power and racial justice, a unanimous Court upheld the PUBLIC ACCOMMODATIONS provisions of the CIVIL RIGHTS ACT OF 1964.

In the areas of criminal procedure and civil liberties Clark was less consistent. Although he may be best known for his controversial opinion in MAPP V. OHIO (1961), declaring that illegally seized evidence must be excluded from a state criminal prosecution, this opinion was atypical. More often, especially in his later years on the bench, he disagreed with the liberalization of criminal procedure wrought by the Warren Court. For instance, he dissented strongly—indeed almost violently—in MIRANDA V. ARIZONA (1966).

Similarly, Clark's record on civil liberties, though generally conservative, was not completely consistent. Probably Clark was most consistent as to those issues arising out of anticommunist and LOYALTY-SECURITY PROGRAMS. As attorney general, he had been instrumental in setting up some of these programs, and as a Justice he continued to support government efforts to suppress what he regarded as the communist conspiracy. Thus, he dissented in WATKINS V. UNITED STATES (1957) and joined the majority in BARENBLATT V. UNITED STATES (1959). In addition, he was the sole dissenter in *Greene v. McElroy* (1959), a decision which badly damaged the loyalty-security program for employees of private companies.

On the other hand, Clark was generally less sympathetic to efforts by the states to cope with what he regarded as a national problem. Thus, he wrote for a unanimous Court in WIEMAN V. UPDEGRAFF (1952), which held unconstitutional an Oklahoma LOYALTY OATH statute requiring state employees to swear that they were not members of organizations designated by the attorney general as subversive or a "Communist front." Clark emphasized that under the Oklahoma law an individual could be guilty of perjury even though he did not know the character of the organization that he had innocently joined. And he joined the majority in PENNSYLVANIA V. NELSON (1956), which invalidated state SEDITION laws on the ground that Congress had preempted the field.

In other areas of civil liberties, Justice Clark tended more often to vote in favor of asserted constitution rights. Thus, in the area of church–state relations, he wrote the opinion in ABINGTON TOWNSHIP SCHOOL DISTRICT V. SCHEMPP (1963), which held unconstitutional a Pennsylvania statute that required that each school day start with the reading of at least ten verses from the Bible. Similarly, he voted with the majority in a series of cases that drastically narrowed court-martial jurisdiction over civilians, the most significant of which was *Kinsella v. Singleton* (1960).

JOHN KAPLAN

Bibliography

KIRKENDALL, RICHARD 1969 Tom C. Clark. In Leon Friedman and Fred L. Israel, eds., *The Justices of the United States Supreme Court, 1789–1969.* New York: Chelsea House.

CLARK DISTILLING CO. v. WESTERN MARYLAND RAILWAY CO.
242 U.S. 311 (1917)

With Justices OLIVER WENDELL HOLMES and WILLIS VAN DEVANTER dissenting without opinion, the Court upheld the WEBB-KENYON ACT. Chief Justice EDWARD D. WHITE, for the majority, rejected the assertion that the act constituted an unconstitutional legislative DELEGATION OF POWER to the states. No delegation occurred because Congress provided for uniform regulation throughout the states.

DAVID GORDON

CLARKE, JOHN H.
(1857–1945)

With the exception of OLIVER WENDELL HOLMES and LOUIS D. BRANDEIS, John H. Clarke was the most consistently progressive member of the Supreme Court during the final years of EDWARD D. WHITE's chief justiceship and the early tenure of WILLIAM HOWARD TAFT. A prosperous newspaper publisher and attorney who defended many midwestern railroads, Clarke belonged to the moderate wing of the Democratic Party in Ohio which defended the gold standard in 1896 and looked skeptically upon reform programs. WOODROW WILSON appointed Clarke to the federal district court in 1914 and two years later elevated him to the Supreme Court to fill the vacancy left by Wilson's presidential rival, CHARLES EVANS HUGHES.

Intellectually, Clarke could not fill Hughes's shoes, but he surprised many critics by his voting record in cases involving CORPORATIONS and labor. Despite his earlier representation of big business, Clarke became a strong judicial supporter of the antitrust laws. He dissented in the two leading cases of the period, *United States v. United Shoe Machinery Company* (1918) and *United States v. United States Steel Corporation* (1920), when the WHITE COURT spurned the government's efforts to convict these industrial giants for monopolistic behavior.

In 1920, however, Clarke won a majority to his side when the Justices ordered the dissolution of a major railroad monopoly in *United States v. Lehigh Valley Railroad,* and found the Reading Railroad guilty of restraint of trade in the anthracite coal industry. Over a powerful dissent by Holmes, Clarke also wrote for the Court that upheld indictments for open price agreements in the hardwood lumber industry.

Clarke rejected the dominant judicial ideology of FREEDOM OF CONTRACT, which had been used to stifle legislative reforms to benefit labor. He endorsed Oregon's ten-hour law for all industrial workers in BUNTING V. OREGON (1917), approved of the federal ADAMSON ACT which mandated an eight-hour day for railroad workers in WILSON V. NEW (1917), and refused to endorse the INJUNCTION at issue in the YELLOW DOG CONTRACT case of HITCHMAN COAL & COKE CO. V. MITCHELL (1917). He voted as well to sustain the constitutionality of the KEATING-OWEN CHILD LABOR ACT in HAMMER V. DAGENHART (1918), refused to sanction the prosecution of labor unions under the antitrust laws in UNITED MINE WORKERS V. CORONADO COAL CO. (1922), and upheld a union's right to conduct a SECONDARY BOYCOTT in the notorious case of DUPLEX PRINTING CO. V. DEERING (1921).

Despite his progressive record with respect to ECONOMIC REGULATION and the rights of labor, Clarke will probably always be remembered as the Justice who wrote for the majority in the case of ABRAMS V. UNITED STATES (1919), which sustained the conviction of pro-Bolshevik pamphleteers under the wartime ESPIONAGE ACT and SEDITION ACT. Clarke's opinion provoked Holmes's famous and biting dissent. Arguing that "men must be held to have intended and to be accountable for the effects which their acts were likely to produce," Clarke transformed Holmes's CLEAR AND PRESENT DANGER test into something approximating the BAD TENDENCY TEST that came to dominate the Court's FIRST AMENDMENT jurisprudence for several decades.

MICHAEL E. PARRISH

Bibliography

WARNER, HOYT L. 1959 *Life of Mr. Justice Clarke.* Cleveland, Ohio: Western Reserve University Press.

CLASS ACTION

The class action is a procedural device aggregating the claims or defenses of similarly situated individuals so that they may be tried in a single lawsuit. In recent decades the class action has frequently served as the vehicle by which various groups have asserted constitutional claims. For example, all the minority-race school children in various districts have sued (through their parents) to rectify alleged RACIAL DISCRIMINATION on the part of school authorities; or, to illustrate a nonconstitutional claim, the buyers of home freezers have sued as a group claiming that the dealer had made fraudlent misrepresentations. In both examples the members of the class could have sued separately. The class action pulled these potential individual actions into a single lawsuit making litigation feasible for the members of the class (by permitting a single lawyer to try all their claims together). For the party opposing the class the suit has the advantage of providing a single adjudication of all similar claims and the disadvantage, especially marked in suits for money damages, that the entire potential liability to a large group turns on a single suit.

The class action depends on representation, and that concept draws the Constitution into the picture. In the class action most class members are represented by an active litigant whose success or failure binds the class members. Opinions interpreting the DUE PROCESS clauses of the Constitution (in the Fifth and FOURTEENTH ADMENDMENTS) suggest that normally one may not be bound by the results of litigation to which one is not a party. Yet the class action purports to do just that—to bind the absentee class members to the results of a suit in which they played no active role.

The Supreme Court and the drafters of state and federal class action rules have supplied two solutions to this apparent tension. The Supreme Court's answer came in *Hansberry v. Lee* (1940), in which the justices indicated that class actions could bind absentee class members if the active litigants *adequately represented* the class. If not, the Court reasoned, binding the absentees would deprive them of due process of law.

Adequate representation has two aspects, competence and congruence of interests. All would agree that adequate representation implies some absolute level of competence and diligence on the part of the class representative and attorney. Though few cases have specifically discussed the question, it seems virtually a matter of definition that an adequate representative must pursue the cause with some minimum level of professional skill.

The second aspect of adequate representation presents a more difficult problem, forcing us to decide whether such representation requires the class members to have *agreed* that the action is in their interests, or whether it is possible to define such interests abstractly, without specific consent. Such an abstract definition relies on common intuitions about what would benefit persons in the class's circumstances. In *Hansberry* the Court did not need to decide between these definitions of interest because the attempted class representation failed on either count. Subsequent cases and procedural rules have not clearly resolved the question.

Contemporary procedural rules require that a judge presiding over a class action suit consider initially whether the action is in the class's interest, abstractly considered; that much seems constitutionally required. Beyond that, some rules also require that the absentee members receive individual notice permitting them to exclude themselves from the litigation.

Founded on the constitutional proposition that some form of representation will suffice to bind members of a class, the class suit has come to play an important role in twentieth-century American litigation.

STEPHEN C. YEAZELL

Bibliography

KALVEN, HARRY JR. and ROSENFIELD, MAURICE 1941 The Contemporary Function of the Class Suit. *University of Chicago Law Review* 8:684–721.

WRIGHT, CHARLES A. and MILLER, ARTHUR 1972 *Federal Practice and Procedure*, Vols. 7 & 7A. St. Paul, Minn.: West Publishing Co.

YEAZELL, STEPHEN C. 1980 From Group Litigation to Class Action; Part II: Interest, Class and Representation. *U.C.L.A. Law Review* 28:1067–1121.

CLASSIC, UNITED STATES v.
313 U.S. 299 (1941)

This became a TEST CASE used by the United States Attorney in Louisiana and the newly created CIVIL RIGHTS DIVISION of the Department of Justice to ascertain the federal government's power to protect VOTING RIGHTS in PRIMARY ELECTIONS. Louisiana election commissioners charged with willfully altering and falsely counting congressional primary election ballots were indicted under what are now sections 241 and 242 of Title 18, United States Code. To analyze the INDICTMENT under section 241, the Supreme Court had to determine whether the right to have one's ballot counted in a state primary election was a right or a privilege secured by the Constitution. Relying in part on Article I, section 2, of the Constitution, the Court held, 4–3, that the right to choose a congressman was "established and guaranteed" by the Constitution and hence secured by it. The Court then reaffirmed earlier holdings that Congress could pro-

tect federally secured voting rights against individual as well as STATE ACTION and squarely held that those rights included participation in state primary elections for members of Congress, thus overruling *Newberry v. United States* (1921).

In articulating those rights "secured by the Constitution" within the meaning of section 241, *Classic* forms a link between early interpretations of the phrase, as in EX PARTE YARBROUGH (1884), and later consideration of it, as in UNITED STATES V. GUEST (1966) and GRIFFIN V. BRECKENRIDGE (1971), the latter case decided under the civil counterpart to section 241, section 1985(3) of Title 42, United States Code. *Classic* also constitutes an important link in the chain of precedents specifically pertaining to federal power over elections. Later cases from the 1940s include SMITH V. ALLWRIGHT (1944) and *United States v. Saylor* (1944).

Because the *Classic* indictment also charged a violation of section 242, which requires action "under COLOR OF LAW," the case provides an early modern holding on the question whether action in violation of state law can be action under color of law. With virtually no discussion of the issue, the Court held such action to be under color of law, a holding later used to support similar holdings in *Screws v. United States* (1945) and MONROE V. PAPE (1961). Dissenters in *Screws* and *Monroe* would object to reliance on *Classic* because of its abbreviated consideration of the issue.

THEODORE EISENBERG

CLAY, HENRY
(1777–1852)

Henry Clay, distinguished politician and legislator, was a product of the Jeffersonian Republicanism that took possession of the Trans-Appalachian West, fought a second war against Great Britain, and was nationalized in the process. Born in Hanover County, Virginia, young Clay clerked for Chancellor GEORGE WYTHE and read law in Richmond before emigrating to Kentucky in his twentieth year. Settling in the rising metropolis of Lexington, Clay was promptly admitted to the bar, and by virtue of extraordinary natural talent, aided by the fortune of marriage into a prominent mercantile family, he soon became a leading member of the Bluegrass lawyer-aristocracy.

The chaos of land titles in Kentucky—a legacy of the state's Virginia origins—made it a paradise for lawyers. Clay mastered this abstruse branch of jurisprudence but earned his reputation as a trial lawyer in capital cases, in which he was said never to have lost a client. He rode the circuit of the county courts, acquiring a character for high spirits and camaraderie; he practiced before the court of appeals and also before the United States district court at Frankfort. When he first went to Congress in 1806, Clay was admitted to the bar of the Supreme Court. Occasionally in years to come he argued important constitutional cases before the court. He was chief counsel for the defendant in OSBORN V. BANK OF THE UNITED STATES (1824), for instance, in which the Court struck down a prohibitive state tax on branches of the bank. At about the same time he conducted Kentucky's defense of its Occupying Claimants Law, enacted years earlier in order to settle thousands of disputed land titles. Here Clay was unsuccessful, as the Court, in GREEN V. BIDDLE (1823), found the Kentucky law in violation of the CONTRACT CLAUSE. Justice JOSEPH STORY remarked after hearing Clay in this case that, if he chose, Clay might achieve "great eminence" at the bar. This interesting judgment would never be tested, however, for Clay sought eminence in politics rather than law.

Clay entered politics in 1798 as a Jeffersonian Republican protesting the ALIEN AND SEDITION ACTS and seeking liberal reform of the state constitution. Elected to the legislature in 1803, he became chief spokesman and protector of the Lexington-centered "court party." He was also very popular, rising rapidly to the speakership of the lower house. In 1806 he was sent to the United States Senate to complete three months of an unexpired term; this experience was repeated, upon the resignation of another incumbent, in 1810. Clay distinguished himself as a bold patriot and orator, as an advocate of federal INTERNAL IMPROVEMENTS and encouragement of domestic manufactures, both of great interest to Kentucky, and as the leading opponent of recharter of the national bank on strict Jeffersonian grounds. He then sought and won election to the Twelfth Congress. Upon its meeting in November 1811, he achieved recognition as chief of the "war hawks" who, though a small minority, took command of the House and elected Clay speaker. Whether or not the war hawks caused, in some significant degree, the War of 1812 is a matter in dispute among historians; but there is no doubt that they brought fresh westerly winds of nationalism into Congress and that Clay, as speaker, mobilized congressional action behind the JAMES MADISON administration's prosecution of the war. Clay transformed this constitutional office, the speakership, from that of an impartial moderator into one of political

leadership. Five times he would be reelected speaker, always virtually without opposition; and when he finally retired from the House there was no one to fill his shoes.

After the Peace of Ghent, which he had helped negotiate as an American commissioner, Clay supported President Madison's national Republican platform with its broad constitutional principles. This support required an about-face on the constitutionality of a national bank. Clay candidly chalked up his error to experience, saying that the financial exigencies of the war had shown the necessity of a national bank; he now agreed with Madison on the need for a central institution to secure a stable and uniform currency. Henceforth, certainly, Clay's principal significance with respect to the Constitution lay in the affirmation of congressional powers.

The protective tariff was the core of the maturing national system of political economy that Clay named "the AMERICAN SYSTEM." The country ought not any longer, he argued, look abroad for wealth, but should turn inward to the development of its own resources. Manufactures would rise and flourish behind the tariff wall, consuming the growing surplus of American agriculture; and a balanced, sectionally based but mutually supportive, economy of agriculture, commerce, and manufactures would be the result. Because the system premised a positive role for the national government in economic development, it carried immense implications for the Constitution. When the protective tariff was first attacked on constitutional grounds in 1824, Clay rejected the narrow view that limited the TAXING POWER to raising revenue and continued the liberal interpretation of the COMMERCE CLAUSE that began with Jefferson's embargo. The infrastructure of the "home market" would be provided by a national system of INTERNAL IMPROVEMENTS. Madison, in his surprising veto of the Bonus Bill in 1817, interposed the constitutional objection that neither the funding nor the building of roads and canals was among the enumerated powers. When Madison's successor, JAMES MONROE, persisted in this view, Clay mounted a campaign to overturn it. He appealed to the Jeffersonian precedent of the National (Cumberland) Road; he appealed to the WAR POWERS (transportation as an element of national defense), to the power of Congress to establish post roads, and, above all, to the commerce power. To the old fears of a runaway Constitution Clay opposed his trust in democratic elections and the balance of interests to keep order. Monroe finally conceded the unlimited power of Congress to appropriate money for internal improvements, though not to build or operate them.

Clay protested that the concession was of greater scope than the principle he had advocated. But he took satisfaction in the result, most immediately in the General Survey Act of 1824.

Clay's coalition with JOHN QUINCY ADAMS in 1825, in which he secured the New Englander's election to the presidency and accepted appointment as his secretary of state, contributed to a growing sectional and partisan opposition to the American System and the constitutional doctrines that supported it. South Carolina's NULLIFICATION of the protective tariff in 1832 provoked a crisis that Clay, now in the Senate, helped to resolve with his Compromise Tariff Act. Under it protective duties would be gradually lifted until in 1842 they would be levied for revenue only. Without surrendering any constitutional principle, Clay nevertheless seemed to surrender the policy of protectionism. Some politicians said he courted southern votes in his quest for the presidency. As the National Republican candidate against President ANDREW JACKSON in the recent election, he had been badly defeated, winning nothing in the South, and he may have seen in this crisis an opportunity for a useful change of political direction. But Clay insisted he acted, first, to save the Union from the disaster of nullification, which was compounded by Jackson's threatened vengeance, and second, to save what he could of the American System. A high protective tariff could no longer be sustained in any event. The national debt was about to be paid off; the treasury faced an embarrassing surplus unless the revenue was drastically reduced. Clay sought to offset the impact of the surplus on the tariff by diverting the soaring revenue of public land sales to the states. Although Congress passed Clay's Distribution Bill in 1833, Jackson vetoed it.

This veto, with many others, above all JACKSON'S VETO OF THE BANK BILL, fueled Clay's assault on the alleged executive usurpations and monarchical designs of the President. The senator proposed to curtail the powers of the presidency. The abuse of the veto power should be corrected by a constitutional amendment allowing override by a majority of both houses. The despotic potential of the office, which Jackson was the first to disclose, should be curbed further by an amendment limiting the president to a single term, perhaps of six years. Clay also rejected the 1789 precedent on the REMOVAL POWER, arguing that the power of removal in the President effectively negated the Senate's agency in appointment. Removal, like appointment, should be a joint responsibility. The Whig Party, under Clay's leadership, consistently advocated these measures. None was ever enacted. Clay contin-

ued the campaign even after the Whigs came to power in 1841, assailing President John Tyler as he had earlier assailed Jackson.

Although Clay usually supported national authority in the debates of his time, he became increasingly cautious and protective of the Constitution under the threats posed, first, by reckless Jacksonian Democracy, and second, by the combination of abolitionism in the North and aggressive slavocracy in the South. He accepted the "federal consensus" on slavery: it was a matter entirely within the JURISDICTION of the states. Nevertheless, he raised no bar to the use of federal funds to advance gradual emancipation and colonization by the states, indeed advocated it in certain contexts. In the controversy over the right of petition for abolition of slavery in the DISTRICT OF COLUMBIA, he held that a gag was not only indefensible in principle but impolitic in practice, because it would make libertarian martyrs of the abolitionists. Clay opposed the ANNEXATION OF TEXAS, believing that the expansion of slavery it entailed must seriously disrupt the Union. When he seemed to equivocate on the issue in the election of 1844—his third run for the presidency—he lost enough northern votes to ensure his defeat. Returning to the Senate in 1849, he proposed a comprehensive plan for settlement of critical issues between North and South. It eventually became the COMPROMISE OF 1850. Here, as in all of his constructive legislative endeavors, Clay evaded spurious questions of constitutional law and sought resolution on the level of policy in that "spirit of compromise" which, he said, lay at the foundation of the American republic. From his earlier part in effecting the MISSOURI COMPROMISE (1820–1821) and the Compromise of 1833, he had earned the title of The Great Pacificator. The Compromise of 1850 added a third jewel to the crown.

Henry Clay was the most popular American statesman of his generation and one of the most respected. He helped to shape the course of constitutional development during forty years, not as a lawyer, judge, or theorist, but as a practical politician and legislator in national affairs.

MERRILL D. PETERSON

Bibliography

COLTON, CALVIN, ED. (1856)1904 *The Works of Henry Clay.* 10 Vols. New York: G. P. Putnam's.

HOPKINS, JAMES F. and HARGREAVES, MARY W. M., EDS. 1959–1981 *The Papers of Henry Clay.* Vols. 1–6. Lexington: University of Kentucky Press.

SEAGER, ROBERT II; WINSLOW, RICHARD E., III; and HAY, MELBA PORTER, EDS. 1982–1984 *Papers of Henry Clay.* Vols. 7–8. Lexington: University of Kentucky Press.

VAN DEUSEN, GLYNDON G. 1937 *The Life of Henry Clay.* Boston: Houghton, Mifflin.

CLAYTON ACT
38 Stat. 730 (1914)

Mistakenly hailed by Samuel Gompers as labor's MAGNA CARTA, the Clayton Act represented a new generation's attempt to deal with trusts. Acclaimed for its specificity, the new act in reality contained crucial ambiguities as vague as the SHERMAN ANTITRUST ACT it was intended to supplement. WOODROW WILSON'S ANTITRUST policy included both the FEDERAL TRADE COMMISSION ACT and the Clayton Act; in his view the latter would leave the Sherman Act intact while specifying conduct henceforth prohibited. Framed by Representative Henry Clayton, chairman of the House Judiciary Committee, the antitrust bill pleased no one: labor objected to the absence of an explicit guarantee of immunity for unions, many congressmen found the list of restraints of trade incomplete, and agrarian radicals believed that the bill betrayed Democratic pledges. In the face of this opposition, Wilson abandoned the Clayton bill in Congress. The House, unhappy over the vagueness of the Sherman Act and wishing to leave businessmen no loopholes, sought as specific a bill as possible. The Senate objected, but a compromise was reached naming only a few, particularly pernicious, practices which were declared unlawful "where the effect may be to substantially lessen competition or tend to create monopoly"—hardly a model of certainty. Four provisions of the Clayton Act contain this operative phrase. Section 7 prohibited the acquisition of stock by one corporation of another or mergers, but, by neglecting to forbid acquisitions of assets as well as stock, it provided a loophole not plugged until 1950. The act also placed strict limitations on interlocking directorates (section 8), and outlawed price discrimination (section 2) and exclusive dealing and tying contracts (section 3). The Federal Trade Commission would enforce these provisions by procedures paralleling those in the F.T.C. Act. In addition, the act rendered individual officers personally liable for corporate violations, permitted private individuals to secure INJUNCTIONS and to file treble damage suits, and allowed final judgments in government suits to be considered *prima facie* EVIDENCE in private cases.

Of two labor provisions, section 6, which declared that labor was "not a commodity or article of commerce" and that antitrust laws could not be used to forbid legitimate organizing activities, conceded nothing new. Section 20 prohibited the issuance of injunctions in labor cases unless "necessary to prevent irreparable injury to property." Together with a further clause which declared that peaceful strikes and boycotts were not in violation of federal antitrust laws, this section represented the only victory labor gained in this act.

DAVID GORDON

(SEE ALSO: *Labor and the Constitution.*)

Bibliography
NEALE, A. D. and GOYDER, D. G. 1980 *The Antitrust Laws of the United States of America,* 3rd ed. Cambridge: At the University Press.

CLEAN AIR ACT

See: Environmental Regulation

CLEAR AND PRESENT DANGER

The clear and present danger rule, announced in SCHENCK V. UNITED STATES (1919), was the earliest FREEDOM OF SPEECH doctrine of the Supreme Court. Affirming Schenck's conviction, Justice OLIVER WENDELL HOLMES concluded that a speaker might be punished only when "the words are used in such circumstances and are of such a nature as to create a clear and present danger that they will bring about the substantive evils that Congress has a right to prevent." Holmes was drawing on his own earlier Massachusetts Supreme Judicial Court opinion on the law of attempts. There he had insisted that the state might punish attempted arson only when the preparations had gone so far that no time was left for the prospective arsonist to change his mind, so that the crime would have been committed but for the intervention of the state. In the free speech context, Holmes and Justice LOUIS D. BRANDEIS assimilated this idea to the MARKETPLACE OF IDEAS rationale, arguing that the best corrective of dangerous speech was more speech rather than criminal punishment; government should intervene only when the speech would do an immediate harm before there was time for other speech to come into play.

In the context of *Schenck,* the danger rule made particular sense; the federal statute under which the defendant was prosecuted made the *act* of espionage a crime, not the speech itself. The danger rule in effect required that before speech might be punished under a statute that forbade action, a close nexus between the speech and the action be shown. The concentration of the rule on the intent of the speaker and the circumstances surrounding the speech also seem most relevant in those contexts in which speech is being punished as if it constituted an attempt at a criminal act. Opponents of the danger rule have often insisted that Holmes initially intended it not as a general FIRST AMENDMENT test but only for cases in which a statute proscribing action was applied to a speaker.

In *Schenck*, Holmes wrote for the Court. The most extended statement of the danger rule came some months later in ABRAMS V. UNITED STATES (1919), but by then it was to be found in a Holmes dissent, joined by Brandeis. In GITLOW V. NEW YORK (1925) the Court used the BAD TENDENCY TEST which openly rejected the imminence or immediacy element of the danger rule—again over dissents by Holmes and Brandeis. Brandeis kept the danger rule alive in a concurrence in WHITNEY V. CALIFORNIA (1927) in which he added to the immediacy requirement that the threatened evil be serious. The danger of minor property damage, for example, would not justify suppression of speech.

In the 1930s and 1940s the Court was confronted with a series of cases involving parades and street corner speakers in which the justification offered for suppressing speech was not concern for the ultimate security of the state but the desire to maintain peaceful, quiet, and orderly streets and parks free of disturbance. Behind the proffered justifications usually lurked a desire to muzzle unpopular speakers while leaving other speakers free. In this context the clear and present danger rule was well designed to protect unpopular speakers from discrimination. It required the community to prove that the particular speaker whom it had punished or denied a license did in fact constitute an immediate threat to peace and good order. In such cases as HERNDON V. LOWRY (1937) (subversion), THORNHILL V. ALABAMA (1941) (labor PICKETING), *Bridges v. California* (1941) (contempt of court), WEST VIRGINIA BOARD OF EDUCATION V. BARNETTE (1943) (compulsory flag salute), and *Taylor v. Mississippi* (1943) (state sedition law), the clear and present danger rule became the majority constitutional test governing a wide range of circumstances, not only for statutes punishing conduct but also those regulating speech itself.

Even while enjoying majority status the rule came under attack from two directions. The "absolutists" led by ALEXANDER MEIKLEJOHN criticized the rule for allowing too broad an exception to First Amendment protections. The rule made the protection of speech dependent on judicial findings whether clear and present danger existed; judges had notoriously broad discretion in making findings of fact, as FEINER V. NEW YORK (1951) and TERMINIELLO V. CHICAGO (1949) illustrated. When applied to radical or subversive speech, the danger test seemed to say that ineffectual speech would be tolerated but that speech might be stifled just when it showed promise of persuading substantial numbers of listeners. On the other hand, those favoring judicial self-restraint, led by Justice FELIX FRANKFURTER, argued that the rule was too rigid in its protection of speech and ought to be replaced by a BALANCING TEST that weighed the interests in speech against various state interests and did so without rendering the immediacy of the threat to state interests decisive.

Later commentators have also argued that the distinction between speech and conduct on which the danger rule ultimately rests is not viable, pointing to picketing and such SYMBOLIC SPEECH as FLAG DESECRATION which intermingle speech and action. The danger rule also engenders logically unresolvable HOSTILE AUDIENCE problems. If Holmes's formula had demanded a showing of the specific intent of the speaker to bring about violence or of specific INCITEMENT to crime in the content of the speech, it might have afforded greater protection to some speakers. The independent weight the danger formula gives to surrounding circumstances may permit the stifling of speakers because of the real or imagined act or threats of others. Yet focusing exclusively upon intent or upon the presence of the language of incitement may lead to the punishment of speakers whose fervently revolutionary utterances in reality have little or no chance of bringing about any violent action at all.

In DENNIS V. UNITED STATES (1951) the clear and *present* danger test was converted overtly into a clear and *probable* danger test and covertly into a balancing test. As its origin in the law of attempts reminds us, the cutting edge of Holmes's test had been the imminence or immediacy requirement. Speech might be punished only if so closely brigaded in time and space with criminal action that no intervening factor might abort the substantive evil. The probable danger test held that if the anticipated evil were serious enough the imminence requirement might be greatly relaxed. In practice this evisceration of the danger test left the Court free to balance the interests to be protected against the degree of infringement on speech, as the proponents of judicial self-restraint argued the Court had always done anyway under the danger standard.

Since *Dennis* the Court has consistently avoided the precise language of the clear and present danger test and with few exceptions commentators announced its demise. In BRANDENBURG V. OHIO (1969), however, the Court announced that "constitutional guarantees of free speech . . . do not permit a State to forbid . . . advocacy of the use of force or of law violation except where such advocacy is directed to inciting or producing imminent lawless action and is likely to incite or produce such action." The text and footnotes surrounding this pronouncement, its careful avoidance of the literal clear and present danger formula itself, plus the separate opinions of several of the Justices indicate that *Brandenburg* did not seek to revive Holmes's danger rule per se. Such earlier proponents of the rule as HUGO L. BLACK and WILLIAM O. DOUGLAS, feeling that it had been too corrupted by its *Dennis* conversion to retain any power to protect speech, had moved to the position of Meiklejohnian absolutism and its rejection of the danger standard. On the other hand, those Justices wishing to preserve low levels of protection for subversive speech and the high levels of judicial self-restraint toward legislative efforts to curb such speech that had been established in *Dennis* and YATES V. UNITED STATES (1957), shied away from the danger test because they knew that, in its Holmesian formulation, it was antithetical to the results that had been achieved in those cases. Apparently, then, Holmes's formula was avoided in *Brandenburg* because some of the participants in the PER CURIAM opinion thought the danger rule protected speech too little and others thought it protected speech too much.

Yet *Brandenburg* did revive the imminence requirement that was the cutting edge of the danger test, and it did so in the context of subversive speech and of OVERRULING *Whitney v. California,* in which the Brandeis and Holmes clear and present danger "concurrence" was in reality a dissent. Even when the danger test was exiled by the Supreme Court it continued to appear in state and lower federal court decisions and in popular discourse. Although the distinction between speech and action—like all distinctions the law seeks to impose—is neither entirely logical nor entirely uncontradicted by real life experience, clear and present danger reasoning survives because most decision makers do believe that the core of the First Amendment is that people may be punished for what they do, not for what they say. Yet even from this basic rule that speech alone must not be punished, we are compelled to make an exception when speech becomes part of the criminal act itself or a direct incitement to the act. Even the most

absolute defenders of free speech would not shy from punishing the speaker who shouts at a mob, "I've got the rope and the dynamite. Let's go down to the jail, blow open the cell and lynch the bastard." However imperfectly, the Holmesian formula captures this insight about where the general rule of free speech ends and the exception of punishment begins. It is for this reason that the danger rule keeps reappearing in one form or another even after its reported demise.

The danger rule is most comforting when the speech at issue is an open, particular attack by an individual on some small segment of government or society, such as a street corner speech denouncing the mayor or urging an end to abortion clinics. In such instances the general government and legal system clearly retain the strength to intervene successfully should the danger of a substantive evil actually become clear and present. The emasculation of the danger test came in quite a different context, that of covert speech by an organized group constituting a general attack on the political and legal system as a whole. Unlike the situation in particularized attacks, where the reservoir of systemic power to contain the anticipated danger remains intact, should subversive speech actually create a clear and present danger of revolution the system as a whole might not have the capacity to contain the danger. It is one thing to wait until the arsonist has struck the match and quite another to wait until the revolution is ready to attack the police stations. For this reason the Court in *Dennis* reverted to the *Gitlow*-style reasoning that the government need not wait until the revolutionaries had perfected their campaign of conversion, recruitment, and organization. *Dennis* and *Yates* carve out a Communist party exception to the immediacy requirement of the clear and present danger rule. They say that where the speech is that of a subversive organization, the government need not prove a present danger of revolution but only that the organization intends to bring about the revolution as speedily as circumstances permit. Thus the government is permitted to intervene early enough so that its own strength is still intact and that of the revolutionaries still small. When in defense of the danger rule Holmes argued that time had overthrown many fighting faiths, he did so with a supreme confidence that it was the American, democratic, fighting faith that time favored and that subversive movements would eventually peter out in America's liberal climate. It was a failure of that faith in the face of the communist menace that led to the emasculation of the danger rule during the Cold War of the 1950s. With hindsight we can see that Holmes's confidence remained justified, and that communist subversion could not have created even a probable, let alone a present danger. Nonetheless American self-confidence has eroded sufficiently that the Supreme Court remains careful not to reestablish the full force of the danger rule lest it handicap the political and legal system in dealing with those who organize to destroy it.

MARTIN SHAPIRO

(SEE ALSO: *Judicial Activism and Judicial Restraint.*)

Bibliography

ANTIEAU, CHESTER JAMES 1950 "Clear and Present Danger"—Its Meaning and Significance. *Notre Dame Lawyer* 1950:3–45.

———— 1950 The Rule of Clear and Present Danger: Scope of Its Applicability. *Michigan Law Review* 48:811–840.

MENDELSON, WALLACE 1952 Clear and Present Danger—From Schenck to Dennis. *Columbia Law Review* 52:313–333.

———— 1953 The Degradation of the Clear and Present Danger Rule. *Journal of Politics* 15:349–355.

———— 1961 Clear and Present Danger—Another Decade. *Texas Law Review* 39:449–456.

STRONG, FRANK 1969 Fifty Years of "Clear and Present Danger": From Schenck to Brandenburg—And Beyond. *Supreme Court Review* 1969:427–480.

CLERKS

Each Justice of the Supreme Court employs two or more law clerks. (In recent years, typically each Justice, other than the CHIEF JUSTICE, has employed four clerks.) Most of the clerks are not long-term career employees, but honor law school graduates who have previously served for a year as clerk to a lower federal judge. Typically, the term of service for these non-career clerks is one year.

The practice of employing recent law school graduates as short-term clerks began with Justice HORACE GRAY. Gray employed a highly ranked Harvard Law School graduate each year at his own expense while serving on the Massachusetts Supreme Judicial Court. He continued to do so when appointed to the United States Supreme Court in 1882. Congress assumed the cost of Justices' law clerks in 1886, but only Gray and his sucessor, OLIVER WENDELL HOLMES, continued the pattern of employing recent law school graduates. The widespread use of the Holmes-Gray practice began in 1919, when Congress authorized each Justice to employ both a "law clerk" and a "stenographic clerk." The use of young law school graduates as judges' law clerks for one- or two-year periods is now

the prevailing pattern in most lower federal courts. A clerkship position with a Supreme Court Justice is prestigious, and former clerks have become prominent in the legal profession, government, the judiciary and academe. Three Justices had themselves served as law clerks to Supreme Court Justices (BYRON R. WHITE, WILLIAM H. REHNQUIST, and JOHN PAUL STEVENS).

The employment of noncareer clerks has been defended as exposing the Justices to fresh ideas and the new theories current in their clerks' law schools. Concern that clerks have too large a role in decisions has been expressed, but this is exaggerated, given the clerks' brief tenure and what is known of the Court's decision process. A distinct concern is that with employment of more clerks, they increasingly play an inappropriately large part in the drafting of opinions. That concern is not so easily rebutted, since each Justice has used clerks' services in a distinct fashion, and there is insufficient reliable public information of the roles played by the Court's current clerks. Court opinions, however, have become longer, more elaborate in their arguments, and studded with citations. The opinions of several Justices appear to be written in a uniform law review style, suggesting that staff plays a large part in their drafting.

WILLIAM COHEN

Bibliography

OAKLEY, JOHN B. and THOMPSON, ROBERT S. 1980 *Law Clerks and the Judicial Process.* Berkeley: University of California Press.

CLEVELAND, GROVER
(1837–1908)

The first Democratic President since JAMES BUCHANAN, Grover Cleveland supported civil service reform and tariff reduction. Cleveland devoted much of his two terms (1884–1888, 1892–1896) to eliminating corruption, inefficiency, and the exploitation of government for private benefit. Generally STATES' RIGHTS and probusiness in viewpoint, he insisted that the federal government function within constrained constitutional limits. As the first executive in decades willing to fight Congress, he frequently used the VETO POWER. A 6–3 Supreme Court sustained Cleveland's view of presidential removal power in *McAllister v. United States* (1891). (See APPOINTING AND REMOVAL POWER.)

Cleveland played almost no part in passage of the INTERSTATE COMMERCE ACT. He had no public reaction to the unpopular decision in POLLOCK V. FARMERS' LOAN & TRUST COMPANY (1895), voiding the income tax, for he believed criticism of the Court unseemly.

Cleveland was the second President with an opportunity to enforce the SHERMAN ANTITRUST ACT, but he expressed serious doubts about the act's effectiveness. Cleveland promised action "to the extent that [trusts] can be reached and restrained by Federal power," although he contended that state action provided the proper remedy. What antitrust successes his administration won (such as UNITED STATES V. TRANS-MISSOURI FREIGHT ASSOCIATION, 1897, and *United States v. Addyston Pipe & Steel Corp.*, 1899) belong to his second attorney general, Judson Harmon. Cleveland's last annual message even contains an exculpatory announcement about the "thus far . . . ineffective" act.

Cleveland and his first attorney general, RICHARD OLNEY, helped secure a federal INJUNCTION against the Pullman strike in 1894. Over the Illinois governor's objections, Cleveland sent 2,000 troops to Chicago to protect the mails and insure the free flow of INTERSTATE COMMERCE, purposes specifically approved by the Court in IN RE DEBS (1895). The troops broke the strike, killing twelve workers; this incident gave rise to the epithet "government by injunction."

Cleveland appointed four men to the Court—L. Q. C. LAMAR, MELVILLE FULLER, EDWARD WHITE, and RUFUS PECKHAM—but he was also the first President to suffer the embarrassment of having two successive appointments rejected by the Senate.

DAVID GORDON

Bibliography
MERRILL, HORACE 1957 *Bourbon Leader: Grover Cleveland*. Boston: Little, Brown.

CLEVELAND BOARD OF EDUCATION v. LAFLEUR
414 U.S. 632 (1974)

The Cleveland school board required a pregnant school teacher to take maternity leave, without pay, for five months before the expected birth of her child. A Virginia county school board imposed a similar four-month leave requirement. The Supreme Court, 7–2, held these rules unconstitutional. Justice POTTER STEWART, for the majority, invoked the IRREBUTTABLE PRESUMPTIONS doctrine. The school boards, by assuming the unfitness of pregnant teachers during the mandatory leave periods, had denied teachers individualized hearings on the question of their fitness, in violation of the guarantee of PROCEDURAL DUE PROCESS. Justice WILLIAM O. DOUGLAS concurred in the result, without opinion. Justice LEWIS F. POWELL rejected the irrebuttable presumptions ground as an EQUAL PROTECTION argument in disguise, but concluded that the boards' rules lacked rationality and denied equal protection. Justice WILLIAM H. REHNQUIST, for the dissenters, aptly characterized the irrebuttable presumptions doctrine as "in the last analysis nothing less than an attack upon the very notion of lawmaking itself."

KENNETH L. KARST

CLIFFORD, NATHAN
(1803–1881)

Nathan Clifford came to the Supreme Court in 1858 after an active political career. He served in the Maine legislature in the 1830s and in the House of Representatives in the early 1840s. He was JAMES K. POLK's attorney general, and during his term he represented (in a private capacity) the rebellious Dorr faction before the Supreme Court in LUTHER V. BORDEN (1849). Clifford's most significant political achievement came in 1848 when Polk dispatched him to persuade Mexico to accept the TREATY OF GUADALUPE HIDALGO as amended by Congress. A decade later, President JAMES BUCHANAN selected him to succeed Justice BENJAMIN R. CURTIS. At a time when the Court was perceived in many quarters as an instrument of southern and Democratic party interests, the choice of a Northerner with southern principles was viewed as blatant partisanship. After a lengthy confirmation battle, the Senate narrowly approved him.

Clifford, a "doughface" in politics, regarded himself as a Jeffersonian "strict constructionist" in constitutional matters. He resolutely opposed the centralization of governmental power during the 1860s and early 1870s. But in ABLEMAN V. BOOTH (1859) he voted to affirm federal judicial supremacy. During the war, Clifford generally supported the government. He wrote opinions upholding the seizure of slave-trading ships; he joined his colleagues in declining to decide any constitutional questions involving the legal tender laws; and he supported the Court's refusal to consider the martial law issues in EX PARTE VALLANDIGHAM (1864). In the PRIZE CASES (1863), however, Clifford joined the dissenters who questioned the legality of President ABRAHAM LINCOLN's blockade of southern ports.

Following the war, Clifford consistently opposed Republican Reconstruction policy. He joined the majority opinion in EX PARTE MILLIGAN (1866), which struck down trials by military commissions where the civil courts were functioning; he supported the majority in the TEST OATH CASES (1867); he agreed with the majority's narrow construction of the FOURTEENTH AMENDMENT in the SLAUGHTERHOUSE CASES (1873); and in separate opinions in several VOTING RIGHTS cases, including UNITED STATES V. REESE (1876) and UNITED STATES V. CRUIKSHANK (1876), he went beyond the majority opinions to condemn federal interference with state elections. Finally, he joined the Court's majority that overturned the legal tender laws in *Hepburn v. Griswold* (1870), but when that decision was reversed a year later in *Knox v. Lee* (1871), he dissented in a strict construction of Congress's power to regulate currency. (See LEGAL TENDER CASES.)

In HALL V. DECUIR (1878) Clifford wrote for the Court, nullifying a Louisiana law prohibiting segregation of steamboat passengers. "Governed by the laws of Congress," he wrote, "it is clear that a steamer carrying passengers may have separate cabins and dining saloons for white persons and persons of color, for the plain reason that the laws of Congress contain nothing to prohibit such an arrangement." In short, the absence of federal policy negated state policy— a strange position for an old STATES' RIGHTS Democrat.

Clifford generally supported state regulatory policies. His concurrence in *Slaughterhouse* signified his unwillingness to embrace a nationalizing interpretation of the Fourteenth Amendment; likewise, it reflected Clifford's traditionalist views of the STATE POLICE POWER. In *Munn v. Illinois* (1877), for example, he joined the majority to sustain Illinois's regulation of grain elevators. (See GRANGER CASES.) Clifford's most articulate statements on state powers came in his dissent in LOAN ASSOCIATION V. TOPEKA (1875). Rejecting the majority's invalidation of a state bonding authorization, Clifford struck at the Court's invocation of natural law doctrine and notions of judicial superintendence. Contending that state legislative power was "practically absolute," subject only to specific state and federal constitutional prohibitions, Clifford protested against JUDICIAL REVIEW that went beyond such limitations in tones reminiscent of older Jeffersonian doctrine: such power, he said, "would be to make the courts sovereign over both the constitution and the people, and convert the government into a judicial despotism."

Clifford dissented ninety-one times during his tenure, an extraordinarily high figure for the time. To some extent, it reflected his isolation and his archaic views. Throughout his judicial career, he consistently was perceived as a partisan Democrat. He served as president of the Electoral Commission to resolve the disputed election of 1876, and most accounts generally credit him with fairness in his conduct of the meetings. Nevertheless, the political purpose of his appointment in 1858 shadowed his work. He did not disappoint his benefactors; yet it was a career best characterized as dull and mediocre.

STANLEY I. KUTLER

Bibliography

CLIFFORD, PHILIP Q. 1922 *Nathan Clifford, Democrat.* New York: Putnam's.
FAIRMAN, CHARLES 1939 *Mr. Justice Miller and the Supreme Court, 1862–1890.* Cambridge, Mass.: Harvard University Press.

CLOSED SHOP

A workplace is a closed shop if, by virtue of a labor contract, only the members of a particular union may be hired. After passage of the TAFT-HARTLEY ACT (1947), the closed shop was replaced by the "union shop" wherein one must join the union after being hired.

DENNIS J. MAHONEY

CLOTURE

Cloture terminates debate in a legislative body. The rules of the Senate encourage extended debates and, by taking advantage of those rules, sectional or ideological cliques can prevent action on bills they oppose. Only after rules reforms in the early 1960s made cloture easier did Congress pass effective CIVIL RIGHTS ACTS.

DENNIS J. MAHONEY

CLYMER, GEORGE
(1739–1813)

George Clymer, who represented Pennsylvania at the CONSTITUTIONAL CONVENTION OF 1787, was a signer of both the DECLARATION OF INDEPENDENCE and the Constitution. Clymer did not speak often, but he was a member of the committees on state debts and the slave trade.

DENNIS J. MAHONEY

COCHRAN v. LOUISIANA
281 U.S. 370 (1930)

Louisiana provided books to all public and private school children. The private school support was challenged on FOURTEENTH AMENDMENT grounds as a use of public money for private purposes. Chief Justice CHARLES EVANS HUGHES held that the state's purpose was public.

Cochran is sometimes cited as an accommodationist precedent, but it was not decided under the establishment clause, which was not considered to apply to the states at that time.

RICHARD E. MORGAN

CODISPOTI v. PENNSYLVANIA
418 U.S. 506 (1974)

A 5–4 Court here extended its decision in DUNCAN V. LOUISIANA (1968) to persons receiving serious punishment for criminal contempt. Following their trial, two defendants were cited for contempt and given several consecutive sentences for contempt of court. *Bloom v. Illinois* (1968) served as the basis for Justice BYRON R. WHITE's opinion that the defendants were entitled to a TRIAL BY JURY. Even though no single sentence exceeded six months, the consecutive sentences could not be separated; they all stemmed from one trial conducted as a single proceeding by one judge.

DAVID GORDON

COEFFICIENT CLAUSE

See: Necessary and Proper Clause

COERCED CONFESSION

See: Police Interrogation and Confessions

COERCIVE ACTS

See: Constitutional History before 1776; First Continental Congress

COHEN, MORRIS R.
(1880–1947)

Morris Raphael Cohen came to the United States from Russia in 1892. After receiving his doctorate from Harvard in 1906, Cohen taught philosophy at the City College of New York from 1912 until 1938, when he retired to devote the rest of his life to writing.

A disciple of Justice OLIVER WENDELL HOLMES, Cohen rejected the conventional belief that judges decide cases by mechanical application of independently existing legal rules; he argued that the process of judicial lawmaking should be guided by the scientific method, a thorough understanding of the social consequences of judicial decisions, and a hierarchical set of social values. Believing natural law to be the measure of justice and advocating the philosophical analysis of legal systems, Cohen attacked such proponents of LEGAL REALISM as JEROME FRANK and THURMAN ARNOLD for their refusal to recognize any external standard by which positive law could be criticized. Cohen's legal writings are collected in *Law and the Social Order* (1933) and *Reason and Law* (1950).

RICHARD B. BERNSTEIN

Bibliography
HOLLINGER, DAVID A. 1975 *Morris R. Cohen and the Scientific Ideal.* Cambridge, Mass.: M.I.T. Press.

COHEN v. CALIFORNIA
403 U.S. (1971)

Cohen was convicted of disturbing the peace. He wore a jacket bearing the words "Fuck the draft" while walking down a courthouse corridor. In overturning the conviction, a 5–4 Supreme Court held that the FIGHTING WORDS exception to FIRST AMENDMENT protection did not apply where "no individual . . . likely to be present could reasonably have regarded the words . . . as a direct personal insult," and there was no showing that anyone who saw Cohen was in fact violently aroused or that . . . [he] . . . intended such a result." Both majority and dissenters suggested that the failure to show that violence was imminent as the result of the words was fatal to the state's case. The Court thus made clear that words, in the abstract, cannot be read out of the First Amendment; the "fighting words" doctrine depends on the context in which words are uttered.

The state's assertion of other justifications for punishing Cohen were similarly rejected: the jacket's message was not OBSCENITY, because it was not erotic; the privacy interests of offended passers-by were insubstantial in this public place, and anyone offended might look away; there was no CAPTIVE AUDIENCE.

Cohen's chief doctrinal importance lies in its rejection of the notion that speech can constitutionally be prohibited by the state because it is offensive. Because offensiveness is an "inherently boundless" category, any such prohibition would suffer from the vice of VAGUENESS. And the First Amendment protects not only the cool expression of ideas but also "otherwise inexpressible emotions."

MARTIN SHAPIRO

COHENS v. VIRGINIA
6 Wheat. 265 (1821)

In the rancorous aftermath of McCULLOCH v. MARYLAND (1819), several states, led by Virginia and Ohio, denounced and defied the Supreme Court. State officers of Ohio entered the vaults of a branch of the Bank of the United States and forcibly collected over $100,000 in state taxes. (See OSBORN v. BANK OF THE UNITED STATES, 1824.) Virginia's legislature resolved that the Constitution be amended to create "a tribunal for the decision of all questions, in which the powers and authorities of the general government and those of the States, where they are in conflict, shall be decided." Widespread and vitriolic attacks on the Court, its doctrine of IMPLIED POWERS, and section 25 of the JUDICIARY ACT OF 1789 showed that MARTIN V. HUNTER'S LESSEE (1816) and *McCulloch* were not enough to settle the matters involved, especially as to the JURISDICTION of the Court over state acts and decisions in conflict with the supreme law of the land as construed by the Court. Accordingly a case appears to have been contrived to create for Chief Justice JOHN MARSHALL an opportunity to reply officially to his critics and to reassert both national supremacy and the supreme appellate powers of his Court.

Two brothers surnamed Cohen sold lottery tickets in Norfolk, Virginia, contrary to a state act prohibiting their sale for a lottery not authorized by Virginia. The Cohens sold tickets for a lottery authorized by an act of Congress to benefit the capital city. In Norfolk the borough court found the defendants guilty and fined them $100. By Virginia law, no appeal could be had to a higher state court. The Cohens, prosperous Baltimore merchants who could easily afford the paltry fine, claimed the protection of the act of Congress and removed the case on WRIT OF ERROR from the local court to the highest court of the land; moreover they employed the greatest lawyer in the nation, WILLIAM PINCKNEY, whose usual fee was $2,000 a case, and another distinguished advocate, David B. Ogden, who commanded a fee of $1,000. More was at stake

than appeared. "The very title of the case," said the Richmond *Enquirer*, "is enough to stir one's blood"— a reference to the galling fact that the sovereign state of Virginia was being hauled before the Supreme Court of the United States by private individuals in seeming violation of the ELEVENTH AMENDMENT. The state governor was so alarmed that he notified the legislature, and its committee, referring to the states as "sovereign and independent nations," declared that the state judiciaries were as independent of the federal courts as the state legislatures were of Congress, the twenty-fifth section of the 1789 notwithstanding. The legislature, having adopted solemn resolutions of protest and repudiating federal JUDICIAL REVIEW, instructed counsel representing Virginia to argue one point alone: that the Supreme Court had no jurisdiction in the case. Counsel, relying on the Eleventh Amendment to argue that a state cannot be sued without its consent, also contended that not a word in the Constitution "goes to set up the federal judiciary above the state judiciary."

Marshall, for a unanimous Court dominated by Republicans, conceded that the main "subject was fully discussed and exhausted in the case of *Martin v. Hunter*," but that did not stop him from writing a fifty-five-page treatise which concluded that under section 25 the Court had jurisdiction in the case. Marshall said little that was new, but he said it with a majestic eloquence and a forcefulness that surpassed JOSEPH STORY's, and the fact that the Chief Justice was the author of the Court's nationalist exposition, addressed to STATES RIGHTS' advocates throughout the country, added weight and provocation to his utterances. He was sublimely rhapsodic about the Constitution and the Union it created, sarcastic and disparaging in restating Virginia's position. Boldly he piled inference upon inference, overwhelming every particle of disagreement in the course of his triumphs of logic and excursions into the historical record of state infidelity. And he had a sense of the melodramatic that Story lacked, as when Marshall began his opinion by saying that the question of jurisdiction "may be truly said vitally to affect the Union." The defendant in error—Virginia—did not care whether the Constitution and laws of the United States had been violated by the judgment of guilt that the Cohens sought to have reviewed. Admitting such violation, Virginia contended that the United States had no corrective. Virginia, Marshall continued, maintained that the nation possessed no department capable of restraining, peaceably and by authority of law, attempts against the legitimate powers of the nation. "They maintain," he added, "that the constitution of the United States has provided no tribunal for the final construction of itself, or of the laws or treaties of the nation; but that this power may be exercised in the last resort by the courts of every state of the Union." Virginia even maintained that the supreme law of the land "may receive as many constructions as there are states. . . ." Marshall confronted and conquered every objection.

Quickly turning to Article III, Marshall observed that it authorizes Congress to confer federal jurisdiction in two classes of cases, the first depending on the character of the case and the second on the character of the parties. The first class includes "all" cases involving the Constitution and federal laws and treaties, "whoever may be the parties," and the second includes all cases to which states are parties. By ratifying the Constitution the states consented to judicial review in both classes of cases, thereby making possible the preservation of the Union. That Union is supreme in all cases where it is empowered to act, as Article VI, the SUPREMACY CLAUSE, insures by making the Constitution and federal law the supreme law of the land. The Court must decide every case coming within its constitutional jurisdiction to prevent the supreme law of the land from being prostrated "at the feet of every state in the Union" or being vetoed by any member of the Union. Collisions between the United States and the states will doubtless occur, but, said Marshall, "a constitution is framed for ages to come, and is designed to approach immortality as nearly as human institutions can approach it." To prevail, the government of the Union derived from the Constitution the means of self-preservation. The federal courts existed to secure the execution of the laws of the Union. History proved, Marshall declared, that the states and their tribunals could not be trusted with a power to defeat by law the legitimate measures of the Union. Thus the Supreme Court can take APPELLATE JURISDICTION even in a case between a state and one of its own citizens who relied on the Constitution or federal law. Otherwise Article III would be mere surplusage, as would Article VI. For the Court to decline the jurisdiction authorized by Article III and commanded by Congress would be "treason to the Constitution."

Although Marshall's rhetoric certainly addressed itself, grandiosely, to the question of jurisdiction, his critics regarded all that he had declared thus far as OBITER DICTA, for he had not yet faced the Eleventh Amendment, which Virginia thought concluded the case on its behalf. Upon finally reaching the Eleventh Amendment question, Marshall twisted a little history and chopped a little logic. The amendment, he said, was adopted not to preserve state dignity or sovereignty but to prevent creditors from initiating suits against states that would raid their treasuries. The amendment did not, therefore, apply to suits commenced by states and appealed by writ of error to the Supreme Court for the sole purpose of inquiring whether the judgment of a state tribunal violated the Constitution or federal law.

The argument that the state and federal judiciaries were entirely independent of each other considered the Supreme Court as "foreign" to state judiciaries. In a grand peroration, Marshall made his Court the apex of a single judicial system that comprehended the state judiciaries to the extent that they shared a concurrent jurisdiction over cases arising under the supreme law of the land. For most important purposes, Marshall declared, the United States was "a single nation," and for all those purposes, its government is supreme; state constitutions and laws to the contrary are "absolutely void." The states "are members of one great empire—for some purposes sovereign, for some purposes subordinate." The role of the federal judiciary, Marshall concluded, was to void state judgments that might contravene the supreme law; the alternative would be "a hydra in government."

Having sustained the jurisdiction of the Court, Marshall offered a sop to Virginia: whether the congressional lottery act intended to operate outside the DISTRICT OF COLUMBIA, he suggested, depended on the words of that act. The case was then reargued on its merits, and Marshall, again for a unanimous Court, quickly sustained the Cohens' conviction: Congress had not intended to permit the sale of lottery tickets in states where such a sale was illegal.

Virginia "won" its case, just as Madison had in *Marbury v. Madison* (1803), but no one was fooled this time either. The governor of Virginia in a special message to his legislature spoke of the state's "humiliation" in having failed to vindicate its sovereign rights. A legislative committee proposed amendments to the Constitution that would cripple not only the JUDICIAL POWER OF THE UNITED STATES but also (reacting to *McCulloch*) the powers of Congress in passing laws not "absolutely" necessary and proper for carrying out its ENUMERATED POWERS. In the United States Senate, enemies of the Court proposed constitutional amendments that would vest in the Senate appellate jurisdiction in cases where the laws of a state were impugned and in all cases involving the federal Constitution, laws, or treaties. Intermittently for several years senators introduced a variety of amendments to curb the Court or revoke section 25, but those who shared a common cause did not share a common remedy, though GREEN V. BIDDLE (1823) and OSBORN V. BANK OF THE UNITED STATES (1824) inflamed their cause.

In Virginia, where the newspapers published Marshall's long opinion to the accompaniment of scathing denunciations, SPENCER ROANE and JOHN TAYLOR returned to a long battle that had begun with the *Martin* case and expanded in the wake of *McCulloch*. Roane, as "Algernon Sydney," published five articles on the theme that *Cohens* "negatives the idea that the American states have a real existence, or are to be considered, in any sense, as sovereign and independent states." He excoriated federal judicial review, implied powers, and the subordination of the states, by judicial construction, to "one great consolidated government" that destroyed the equilibrium of the Constitution, leaving that compact of the states nonexistent except in name. Taylor's new book, *Tyranny Unmasked* (1822), continued the themes of his *Construction Construed* (1820), where he argued that the "federal is not a national government: it is a league of nations. By this league, a limited power only over persons and property was given to the representatives of the united nations." The "tyranny" unmasked by the second book turned out to be nationalist programs, such as the protective tariff, and nationalist powers, including the power of the Supreme Court over the states.

THOMAS JEFFERSON read Roane and Taylor, egged them on, and congratulated them for their orthodox repudiation of the Court's "heresies." To Justice WILLIAM JOHNSON, who had joined Marshall's opinion, Jefferson wrote that Roane's articles "appeared to me to pulverize every word which had been delivered by Judge Marshall, of the extra-judicial part of his opinion," and to Jefferson "all was extra-judicial"—and he was not wholly wrong—except the second *Cohens* opinion on the merits. Jefferson also wrote that the doctrine that courts are the final arbiters of all constitutional questions was "dangerous" and "would place us under the despotism of an oligarchy." Recommending the works of Roane and Taylor to a friend, Jefferson militantly declared that if Congress did not shield the states from the dangers originating with the Court, "the states must shield themselves, and meet the invader foot to foot." To Senator NATHANIEL MACON of Virginia, Jefferson wrote that the Supreme Court was "the germ of dissolution of our federal government" and "an irresponsible body," working, he said, "like gravity, by day and night, gaining a little today and a little tomorrow, and advancing its noiseless step, like a thief over the fields of jurisdiction, until all shall be usurped from the States, the government of all becoming a consolidated one."

JAMES MADISON deplored some of the Court's tactics, especially its mingling of judgments with "comments and reasoning of a scope beyond them," often at the expense of the states; but Madison told Roane flatly that the judicial power of the United States "over cases arising under the Constitution, must be admitted to be a vital part of the System." He thought Marshall wrong on the Eleventh Amendment and extreme on implied powers, but, he wrote to Roane, on the question "whether the federal or the State decisions ought to prevail, the sounder policy would yield to the claims of the former," or else "the Constitution of the U.S. might become different in every State."

The public reaction to *Cohens* depressed Marshall, because, as he wrote to Story, the opinion of the Court "has been assaulted with a degree of virulence transcending what has appeared on any former occasion." Roane's "Algernon Sydney" letters, Marshall feared, might be believed true by the public, and Roane would be hailed as "the champion of state rights, instead of being what he really is, the champion of dismemberment." Marshall saw "a deep design to convert our government into a mere league of States. . . . The attack upon the Judiciary is in fact an attack upon the Union." The whole attack originated, he believed, with Jefferson, "the grand Lama of the mountains." An effort would be made, predicted Marshall, accurately, "to repeal the 25th section of the Judiciary Act." Doubtless the personal attacks on him proved painful. A bit of anonymous doggerel, which circulated in Virginia after *Cohens*, illuminates public feeling.

> Old Johnny Marshall what's got in ye
> To side with Cohens against Virginny.
> To call in Court his "Old Dominion."
> To insult her with your foul opinion!
> I'll tell you that it will not do
> To call old Spencer in review.
> He knows the law as well as you.
> And once for all, it will not do.
> Alas! Alas! that you should be
> So much against State Sovereignty!
> You've thrown the whole state in a terror,
> By this infernal "Writ of Error."

The reaction to *Cohens* proves, in part, that the Court's prose was overbroad, but Marshall was reading the Constitution in the only way that would make the federal system operate effectively under one supreme law.

LEONARD W. LEVY

Bibliography

BEVERIDGE, ALBERT J. 1916–1919 *The Life of John Marshall*, 4 vols. Vol. IV: 340–375. Boston: Houghton-Mifflin.

HAINS, CHARLES GROVE 1944 *The Role of the Supreme Court in American Government and Politics, 1789–1835.* Pages 427–461. Berkeley: University of California Press.

KONEFSKY, SAMUEL J. 1964 *John Marshall and Alexander Hamilton.* Pages 93–111. New York: Macmillan.

COKE, EDWARD
(1552–1634)

Edward Coke (pronounced Cook) was an English lawyer, judge, and parliamentarian who influenced the development of English and American constitutional law by promoting the supremacy of the COMMON LAW in relation to parliamentary powers and the royal prerogative.

After studying at Trinity College, Cambridge, Coke entered the Inner Temple and was called to the Bar in 1578. His career was outstanding from the start. He was elected to Parliament in 1589 and in 1593 he became Speaker of the House of Commons. Appointed attorney-general in 1594, he prosecuted several notable TREASON cases, including that of Sir Walter Raleigh in 1603.

In 1600, Coke began publication of his *Reports.* Eleven volumes had been published by 1615; two additional volumes appeared after his death. These were not collections of appellate opinions; rather, they consisted of case notes made by Coke, legal history, and general criticism. Coke had mastered the precedents, and he brought symmetry to scattered authority. Thereafter, *The Reports,* as they were usually called, were the authoritative common law precedents in England and colonial America.

Coke was appointed Chief Justice of the Court of Common Pleas in 1606, serving until 1613, when he was appointed Chief Justice of the Court of King's Bench. His judicial career was terminated in 1616 when King James I removed him from office. During these years Coke began enunciating ideas concerning the supremacy of the common law, foreshadowing modern concepts of government under law.

Coke's judicial pronouncement most influential on the American doctrine of JUDICIAL REVIEW came in BONHAM'S CASE (1610). The College of Physicians had fined and imprisoned Dr. Bonham for practicing medicine without a license. The court held that because the College would share in the fine, the charter and parliamentary act conferring this authority were contrary to the common law principle that no man can be a judge in his own case. Coke stated: "And it appears in our books, that in many cases, the common law will control acts of parliament, and sometimes adjudge them to be utterly void: for when an act of parliament is against common right and reason, or repugnant, or impossible to be performed, the common law will control it, and adjudge such act to be void. . . ." Coke believed that the common law contained a body of fundamental, although not unchangeable, principles to be ascertained and enunciated by judges through the "artificial reason" of the law. In *Bonham's Case* he seemed to be reasoning that parliamentary acts must be interpreted consistently with those principles. Whatever Coke's precise meaning, however, the statement foreshadowed the American DOCTRINE of judicial review; it was influential in the developing concept of the supremacy of law as interpreted and applied by the judiciary.

Another incident of Coke's judicial career that contributed to the modern idea of government under law came in 1608 during a confrontation with James I. The king had claimed authority to withdraw cases from the courts and decide them himself. In a dramatic Sunday morning meeting convened by the king and attended by all the judges and bishops, Coke maintained that there was no such royal authority. He asserted, quoting Bracton, that the king was not under man "but under God and law," one of the earliest and most quoted expressions of this concept.

Coke returned to Parliament in 1620 and in the final phase of his career made two major contributions to constitutional government and English and American law.

Drawing on the provision in MAGNA CARTA that "no free man shall be taken [or] imprisoned . . . except by the . . . law of the land," he launched the concept of "due process of law." Coke asserted that this provision referred to the established processes of the common law. He expressed this view in the parliamentary debates leading to the PETITION OF RIGHT in 1628, raising Magna Carta to new heights with statements such as "Magna Carta is such a fellow that he will have no sovereign." Coke's arguments presaged the later American concept of a written constitution superior to other law. He also linked Magna Carta with HABEAS CORPUS, although there was little historical support for the connection. He believed that there must be a remedy for imprisonment contrary to common law process and the remedy was to be had through the writ of habeas corpus.

Coke's other major contribution in his last years was the writing of his *Institutes.* This four-part work, published in 1641, became a basic text in the education of lawyers in England and America. In America, where law books were few, the *Institutes* were the standard work before the publication of WILLIAM BLACKSTONE's *Commentaries* in 1767. As noted by the Supreme Court in one of its several twentieth-century references to Coke (KLOPFER V. NORTH CAROLINA, 1967): "Coke's Institutes were read in the American Colonies by virtually every student of the law. Indeed, THOMAS JEFFERSON wrote that at the time he studied law (1762–1767), *Coke Lyttleton* was the universal elementary book of law students. And to JOHN RUTLEDGE of South Carolina, the Institutes seemed to be almost the foundation of our law." Because few lawyers in England and America had either the inclination or the resources to go behind Coke's *Institutes* and his *Reports,* these works, despite historical inaccuracies revealed by later scholarship, became the authoritative legal source on both sides of the Atlantic.

Coke represents a transition from medieval to modern law. He lived in the dawn of the modern constitutional era, when the British colonization of North America was beginning. As the colonists later sought authority to support their arguments that royal power was limited by law, they found it in Coke. Since the American Revolution, Coke has been regarded as an early authority for the proposition that all government is under law and that it is ultimately for the courts to interpret the law.

DANIEL J. MEADOR

Bibliography

BOUDIN, LOUIS B. 1929 Lord Coke and the American Doctrine of Judicial Power. *New York University Law Review* 6:223–246.
BOWEN, CATHERINE D. 1957 *The Lion and the Throne: The Life and Times of Sir Edward Coke.* Boston: Little, Brown.
MULLETT, CHARLES F. 1932 Coke and the American Revolution. *Economica* 12:457–471.

COKER v. GEORGIA
433 U.S. 584 (1977)

Ehrlich Coker, an escaped felon, was convicted of rape with aggravating circumstances and sentenced to die. The Supreme Court, in a 7–2 decision, overturned the sentence. Justice BYRON R. WHITE, in a PLURALITY OPINION, argued that CAPITAL PUNISHMENT is "grossly disproportionate and excessive pun-

ishment for the crime of rape," and therefore unconstitutional under the Eighth Amendment, binding on the states through the FOURTEENTH AMENDMENT. Justice LEWIS F. POWELL's concurring opinion was applicable to the facts of this case only, while Justice WILLIAM J. BRENNAN and THURGOOD MARSHALL would have held the death penalty unconstitutional in any case whatsoever. Chief Justice WARREN E. BURGER and Justice WILLIAM H. REHNQUIST dissented, arguing that Coker's sentence was within the reserved power of the State.

DENNIS J. MAHONEY

COLEGROVE v. GREEN
328 U.S. 549 (1946)

Colegrove v. Green and BAKER V. CARR (which all but overruled *Colegrove* in 1962) bracket the passage of the ONE PERSON, ONE VOTE movement from failure to success. Migration had drastically enlarged urban electoral districts and reduced rural ones in most states, but legislators and voters were slow to reapportion, and reapportionists turned to courts for relief. But courts were wary of tampering with legislators' seats.

The Supreme Court dismissed Colegrove's suit to enjoin Illinois congressional elections in "malapportioned" districts. The Justices gave two reasons: the case wanted EQUITY to make an INJUNCTION appropriate, and it presented a POLITICAL QUESTION reserved for decision of the elected branches both by constitutional mandate and by lack of judicially appropriate standards of judgment. "Courts," said Justice FELIX FRANKFURTER, "ought not to enter this political thicket." Three Justices dissented, arguing that the case did not lack equity, that the question was not political, and that constitutional mandate and standards could be found in Article I, section 2, and the EQUAL PROTECTION clause of the FOURTEENTH AMENDMENT—a debatable assertion little argued in either *Colegrove* or *Baker.* Justice WILEY RUTLEDGE, the tiebreaker, thought the question nonpolitical but joined in the vote for dismissal for want of equity.

Though the Court dismissed all REAPPORTIONMENT cases for sixteen years, citing *Colegrove,* Rutledge's discretionary rationale left room for the debate between Justices WILLIAM J. BRENNAN and Frankfurter in *Baker,* and for the intervention that led to the reapportionment revolution. The applicability of the equal protection clause to reapportionment was not seriously debated until REYNOLDS V. SIMS (1964) and OREGON V. MITCHELL (1970). Justices HUGO L. BLACK and JOHN MARSHALL HARLAN debated the applicability of Article I, section 2, in WESBERRY V. SANDERS (1964), which finally overruled *Colegrove*.

WARD E. Y. ELLIOTT

Bibliography
AUERBACH, CARL A. 1964 The Reapportionment Cases: One Person, One Vote—One Vote, One Value." *Supreme Court Review* 1964:1–87.

COLEMAN v. MILLER
307 U.S. 433 (1939)

The lieutenant governor of Kansas had broken a tie vote in the Kansas senate to endorse a CHILD LABOR AMENDMENT, which Kansas had previously rejected. The losing senators, opponents of the amendment, challenged the vote because the lieutenant governor was not a part of the state "legislature" within the meaning of Article V and because the previous rejection of the amendment, plus the lapse of thirteen years, had cost the amendment its "vitality."

Over objections from dissenting Justices PIERCE BUTLER and JAMES C. MCREYNOLDS that the lapse of time issue had not been briefed or argued, Chief Justice CHARLES EVANS HUGHES declined to hear the challenge, citing the ratification of the FOURTEENTH AMENDMENT and arguing that efficacy of ratification—both as to lapse of time and as to the prior rejection—was a POLITICAL QUESTION, requiring "appraisal of a great variety of relevant conditions, political, social, and economic," not "within the appropriate range of EVIDENCE receivable in a court." Dominant considerations in political questions, he noted, are the "appropriateness of final action" by the elected branch and the "lack of satisfactory criteria for judicial determination."

Justice HUGO L. BLACK, writing for four concurring Justices, thought that Hughes had not sufficiently emphasized Congress's "exclusive power to control submission of constitutional amendments." An evenly divided Court expressed no opinion as to whether counting the lieutenant governor as part of the legislature was a political question.

WARD E. Y. ELLIOTT

Bibliography
SCHARPF, FRITZ W. 1966 Judicial Review and the Political Question: A Functional Analysis. *Yale Law Journal* 75:517–597.

COLGATE v. HARVEY
296 U.S. 404 (1935)

This case is a historical curiosity. Vermont taxed the income from money loaned out of state but exempted from taxation any income from money loaned in the state at not more than five percent interest. The Supreme Court, in an opinion by Justice GEORGE SUTHERLAND, held the act unconstitutional as a violation of the EQUAL PROTECTION and PRIVILEGES AND IMMUNITIES clauses of the FOURTEENTH AMENDMENT. Justices HARLAN F. STONE, LOUIS D. BRANDEIS, and BENJAMIN N. CARDOZO, in dissent, found difficulty in perceiving a privilege of national CITIZENSHIP which the state had violated, especially because the Court had decided forty-four cases since 1868 in which state acts had been attacked as violating the privileges and immunities clause and until this case had held none of them unconstitutional. MADDEN V. KENTUCKY (1940) overruled *Colgate*.

LEONARD W. LEVY

COLLATERAL ATTACK

As a general proposition a litigant gets one chance to present his case to a trial court; if he is dissatisfied with the result, he may APPEAL. What he cannot do, however, is to attack it "collaterally," starting the lawsuit all over again at the bottom, not so much asserting error in the first proceeding as ignoring it or trying to have the second trial court undo its results. This COMMON LAW doctrine forbidding collateral attack exists independently of the Constitution, which makes no direct mention of it. But the Constitution is frequently incomprehensible without some reference to its common law background. In this instance the document at three points implicates the doctrine of collateral attack. One section, the FULL FAITH AND CREDIT clause, seems to forbid collateral attack in civil cases (except where DUE PROCESS may require otherwise); the HABEAS CORPUS clause, by contrast, seems to require it in at least some criminal cases.

What constitutes collateral attack is itself often a difficult question; different JURISDICTIONS attach different significance to their judgments. As a general proposition, though, the full faith and credit clause requires that State A give the JUDGMENTS of State B the same effect State B would; to that extent the clause prohibits collateral attack in the interstate context. (A federal statute imposes the same requirements on federal courts.) The due process clause, however, limits the full faith and credit clause; if the courts of the state rendering the first judgment lacked jurisdiction over the defendant, the full faith and credit clause does not bar collateral attack. Due process requires that a defendant be able collaterally to attack a judgment rendered by a court that lacked authority over him. The due process clause, however, requires a court to permit collateral attack only when the party using it has not previously litigated the issue of jurisdiction; if he has, that question, like all others, is closed. Moreover, one who engages in litigation without raising the question of jurisdiction is generally treated as if he had done so and lost; the justification for such treatment is that the litigant had an opportunity to do so: due process does not require giving a second chance to one who has actually engaged in a lawsuit. The operation of this proposition leaves open to collateral attack only those judgments entered without any participation by the defendant—default judgments.

Collateral attack is thus available but is rather tightly circumscribed in civil cases; those held in detention on criminal charges have a somewhat wider scope of collateral attack available to them. The habeas clause requires federal courts (and arguably also those of the states) to entertain challenges to detention. Interpreting the federal statutes implementing the clause, federal courts have permitted those in custody to complain of various basic constitutional defects in the trials leading to their conviction; courts in some circumstances have permitted such collateral attack even though the asserted constitutional defect could have been raised in a direct appeal. To that extent present habeas practice, like the due process clause, requires courts to permit collateral attack. Unlike the due process clause, however, the habeas statute has been interpreted to permit litigants in some circumstances to raise again issues already litigated in the criminal trial.

At one level, then, the Constitution appears to issue contradictory commands: recognize judgments as conclusive—except when they are not. At another level the contradiction disappears, for both commands flow from the same impulse: under normal conditions only direct attack by appeal is permissible, but when the basic prerequisites of proper adjudication are absent (the basis of judicial authority or the incidents of a fair criminal trial), the normal rules must give way.

STEPHEN C. YEAZELL

Bibliography

AMERICAN LAW INSTITUTE 1971 *Restatement of the Law 2d, Conflicts of Laws.* St. Paul, Minn.: American Law Institute Publishers.

EISENBERG, THEODORE 1981 *Civil Rights Legislation.* Charlottesville, Va.: Michie Co.

NOTE 1957 The Value of the Distinction between Direct and Collateral Attacks on Judgments. *Yale Law Journal* 66:526–544.

COLLECTIVE BARGAINING

Collective bargaining is the process of negotiation between employers and labor unions to establish the wages, hours, and working conditions of employees. Collective bargaining has been regulated by the federal government since passage of the WAGNER (NATIONAL LABOR RELATIONS) ACT (1935) and the TAFT-HARTLEY ACT (1947).

DENNIS J. MAHONEY

(SEE ALSO: *Labor and the Constitution.*)

COLLECTOR v. DAY
11 Wallace 113 (1871)

In MCCULLOCH V. MARYLAND (1819) the Supreme Court had held unconstitutional a state tax on an instrumentality of the national government, and in *Dobbins v. Commissioners* (1842) the Court had forbidden a state to tax the salary of a federal officer. The Court had reasoned that a sovereign government must be immune from the taxes of another government to preserve its independence. Here the Court applied that doctrine reciprocally, holding that the United States had no constitutional power to tax the salary of a state judge. In GRAVES V. NEW YORK EX REL. O'KEEFE (1939) the Court overruled both *Dobbins* and *Collector*, vitiating the DOCTRINE of reciprocal tax immunities.

LEONARD W. LEVY

(SEE ALSO: *Intergovernmental Immunities.*)

COLLUSIVE SUIT

Article III of the Constitution limits the federal courts to the decision of CASES OR CONTROVERSIES. One component of that limitation bars adjudication of the merits of a claim absent a real dispute between parties who have conflicting interests. If nominally opposing parties manufacture a lawsuit to secure a judicial ruling, if one party controls or finances both sides of a case, or if both parties in fact desire the same ruling, the suit will be dismissed as collusive. The issues in a case need not be contested, so long as the parties' ultimate interests in the litigation are opposed. Hence, a default judgment can be entered, or a guilty plea accepted. Nor are all TEST CASES forbidden as collusive—only those where the contestants seek the same outcome. Of course, other JUSTICIABILITY barriers may prevent adjudication.

Like the ban on ADVISORY OPINIONS, the rule banning collusive suits saves judicial resources for disputes that need resolution, helps assure that federal courts act only on the basis of the information needed for sound decision making, and, in constitutional cases, prevents premature judicial intervention in the political process. The rule also may block efforts by supposed adversaries (but actual allies) to procure a ruling detrimental to opponents who are not represented in the collusive action.

JONATHAN D. VARAT

COLONIAL CHARTER

Perhaps no other American constitutional topic has been subject to such changing and contrary interpretations as has that of colonial charters. For example, GEORGE BANCROFT, who in 1834 had written that the Massachusetts charter of 1629 "established a CORPORATION, like other corporations within the realm," wrote in 1883 that the charter "constituted a body politic by the name of the Governor and Company of the Massachusetts Bay." Bancroft's apparent inconsistency is less contradiction than part of a constitutional controversy. Even during the colonial period constitutional experts disagreed about the legal nature of charters.

A few North American colonies (Plymouth, New Haven) had no charters. Most did, however, and the earliest charters were of two types. The first (Virginia, Massachusetts Bay), modeled on trading company charters granted to merchants, stressed commerce and settlement. The second (Maryland, Maine, Carolina) was based on the palatinate bishopric of Durham County, England. Later, a third type of charter was issued: "royal" charters for colonies in which the governor and other designated officers were appointed by the Crown. Containing more provisions directing government functions, royal charters generally defined a colony's relations with the mother country, not its internal constitution. No matter the type, charters were statements of privileges, not organic acts of government; they conferred immunities from prosecution and did not define structures of governance. Colonial charters, therefore, did not contribute signifi-

cantly to constitutional law or history except when Americans claimed immunity from parliamentary authority.

American legal theory held that charters were contracts by which the king promised to protect and defend his American subjects in exchange for the subjects' allegiance. A better theory was that charters were evidence of a contract between the English crown and the first settlers of America. By either theory charters were not CONSTITUTIONS but one of the sources of constitutional rights along with the ancient English constitution, the current British constitution, the original contract, the second original contract, COMMON LAW, custom, and, to a minor degree, natural law. The first charter of Virginia stated a principle, repeated in later Virginia charters and in the charters of several other colonies, that the colonists "shall have and enjoy all Liberties, Franchises, and Immunities . . . to all Intents and Purposes as if they had been abiding and born within this our Realm of England. . . ." Americans of the Revolutionary period read such provisions as supporting their constitutional arguments against Britain. The legal theory subscribed to on the imperial side of the controversy held that charters created corporations not unlike municipal and commercial corporations in the mother country. As JOSEPH GALLOWAY declared, the colonies were only "corporations, or subordinate bodies politic, vested with *legislative* powers, to regulate their own internal police, under certain regulations and restrictions, and no more." A more extreme imperial theory held that charters were irrelevant; that the powers and limitations of colonial government came not from charters but from the instructions that British ministers issued to colonial governors. This theory, which American legislatures repudiated, contributed to the coming of the Revolution.

The American theory that charters were inviolable contracts confirming inalienable rights was premised on Old Whig constitutional definitions of LIMITED GOVERNMENT which still enjoyed some support in Britain during the second half of the eighteenth century and found expression in arguments that Parliament lacked constitutional authority to revoke or amend charters. This argument had little support in Britain, where all charters were viewed as revocable. In fact, a majority of colonies had their charters revoked and regranted at various times by the British government. Indeed, no single action so provoked the American Revolution as the Massachusetts Government Act asserting the authority of Parliament to amend colonial charters by unilateral decision.

When the Revolution commenced there were only two proprietary charters (Pennsylvania, Maryland) and two corporate charters (Connecticut, Rhode Island). Remaining colonies had royal charters, except Quebec and Georgia, which were governed by instructions. When Americans began to draft organic acts, they came more and more to think of charters as constitutions. To resist the Massachusetts Government Act, which revoked the charter of 1691, colonial leaders gave consideration to "resuming" the original charter of 1629 granted by Charles I. Connecticut and Rhode Island retained their charters as state constitutions, Connecticut until 1818 and Rhode Island until 1843.

JOHN PHILLIP REID

Bibliography

REID, JOHN PHILLIP 1976 In the First Line of Defense: The Colonial Charters, the Stamp Act Debate and the Coming of the American Revolution. *New York University Law Review* 51:177–215.

COLOR OF LAW

Some CIVIL RIGHTS statutes proscribe only behavior "under color of" state law, and this requirement has played an important role in the development of FEDERAL PROTECTION OF CIVIL RIGHTS. Ironically, civil rights statutes have been interpreted in a manner that strips the color of law requirement of most of its contemporary significance. Judicial interpretation usually equates the color of law requirement with STATE ACTION. Because in most contexts in which the color of law requirement appears state action also is required, there is no obvious independent role for the color of law requirement.

The phrase "under color of . . . law" appears in the nation's first civil rights act, the CIVIL RIGHTS ACT OF 1866. There it seemed to limit the act's coverage to actions taken pursuant to—under color of— the post-Civil War southern BLACK CODES. Subsequent revisions of the 1866 act and civil rights statutes modeled after it retained the concept as a way of limiting their coverage. It currently appears in section 242 of the federal criminal code, SECTION 1983, TITLE 42, UNITED STATES CODE, and section 1343(3) of the judicial code, the jurisdictional counterpart to section 1983.

In deciding what constitutes action under color of law, two extreme readings have been rejected. One view, advocated in dissenting opinions by Justices OWEN ROBERTS, FELIX FRANKFURTER, and ROBERT H. JACKSON in SCREWS V. UNITED STATES (1945) and by Justice Frankfurter in MONROE V. PAPE (1961), deems behavior to be under color of state law only when it is authorized by state law. In this view, any action by state officials in violation of state law cannot be under color of law. Where, as in *Screws*, a law officer murders his prisoner, in clear violation of state law, the officer's act would not be regarded as being under color of law and, therefore, would not be subject to civil or criminal penalties under federal statutes containing the requirement. This view of the color of law requirement would limit the significance of modern civil rights statutes, for much official behavior that civil rights litigants allege to violate the Constitution or federal law also violates state law. This view, however, would make the color of law requirement meaningful in the context of the times during which the requirement first appeared. During the post-Civil War era, much of the most disturbing official behavior, particularly behavior aimed at recently freed blacks, was authorized by state law.

The expansive extreme view of color of law arises not in interpreting the phrase itself but in interpreting it in conjunction with a series of nouns that accompany it. Section 1983, for example, refers to action "under color of any statute, ordinance, regulation, custom or usage." In *Adickes v. S. H. Kress & Co.* (1970), Justices WILLIAM J. BRENNAN and WILLIAM O. DOUGLAS interpreted "color of custom" to include virtually all segregative activity in the South, public or private, because the activity sprang from widespread custom. The majority in *Adickes* interpreted color of custom to include only action that constituted state action. Color of custom thus encompasses private behavior only to the extent that private persons act sufficiently in concert with public officials to render their action state action. This interpretation, combined with rejection in *Screws* and *Monroe* of the view limiting color of law to action authorized by law, leaves the color of law concept with little independent meaning. In general, action is under color of law if and only if the action satisfies the state action requirement.

There are, however, two areas in which it is useful to differentiate between state action and action under color of law. First, some constitutional rights, such as the THIRTEENTH AMENDMENT right not to be enslaved, are protected against both governmental and private infringement. A private person who caused the deprivation of such a right would be liable under statutes containing the "color of law" requirement even though his action was not state action. In these rare cases, action that is under color of law but that is not state action would lead to federal civil rights liability. Second, where a constitutional right, such as the right to DUE PROCESS, can be violated only by the government, private behavior authorized by statute may be action under color of law but, for want of state action, it may not subject the actor to civil rights liability. For example, when, pursuant to state statutes, creditors repossessed property without judicial proceedings, the Court in FLAGG BROS., INC. V. BROOKS (1978) held that the action taken was under color of law but that it was not state action.

In the pre-Civil War era, Congress employed the color of law requirement in a fashion related to its later use in civil rights statutes. States upset with expanding federal power and the behavior of federal officials would go so far as to initiate in state court criminal or civil proceedings against federal officers. Fearful of a biased forum, Congress, in a series of provisions commencing in 1815, provided federal officials with a right to remove these proceedings to federal court. (See REMOVAL OF CASES.) But Congress limited the power of removal to instances when the state proceedings were attributable to action by the officers under color of their office or of federal law. In this sense, as the Court noted in *Tennessee v. Davis* (1880), the color of law requirement clearly meant only action authorized by law, a point emphasized by the dissenters in *Screws.*

Nevertheless, it may be consistent with the purposes of both the removal and civil rights provisions to interpret color of law as limited to action authorized by law only in the case of the removal statute. If one views Congress in each case as desiring to protect only lawful behavior, it makes sense to interpret color of law in the removal statute to require action authorized by law and to interpret color of law in civil rights statutes to encompass official action, whether or not authorized by law. Use of the broad civil rights interpretation of color of law would immunize from state process action by federal officers not authorized by federal law. And in the context of civil rights statutes, adhering to the interpretation given the removal provision would immunize from federal remedies action by state officers not authorized by state law. The different interpretations serve a common function, subjecting a wrongdoer to liability.

THEODORE EISENBERG

Bibliography

EISENBERG, THEODORE 1982 Section 1983: Doctrinal Foundations and an Empirical Study. *Cornell Law Review* 67:507–510.

COLUMBIA BROADCASTING SYSTEM v. DEMOCRATIC NATIONAL COMMITTEE
412 U.S. 94 (1973)

The Supreme Court here considered a FIRST AMENDMENT challenge to a broadcaster's refusal to accept editorial advertisements except during political campaigns. Some Justices maintained that the broadcaster's action did not amount to governmental action, but the Court did not reach the question. Even assuming STATE ACTION, it held that the First Amendment permitted broadcasters to discriminate between commercial and political advertisements. Broadcasters, the Court observed, were obligated by the FAIRNESS DOCTRINE to cover political issues, and their choice to cover such issues outside of commercials protected CAPTIVE AUDIENCES and avoided a threat that the wealthy would dominate broadcast decisions about political issues.

STEVEN SHIFFRIN

COLUMBIA BROADCASTING SYSTEM, INC. v. FEDERAL COMMUNICATIONS COMMISSION
453 U.S. 367 (1981)

A 1971 amendment to the COMMUNICATIONS ACT OF 1934 permits the Federal Communications Commission (FCC) to revoke a broadcaster's license for failure to allow reasonable access to a candidate for federal office. The Supreme Court here interpreted this provision to create a right of access for an individual candidate. Further, reaffirming the much criticized precedent of RED LION BROADCASTING CO. V. FCC (1969), the Court sustained the law, as so interpreted, against a FIRST AMENDMENT challenge. The dissenters argued that the statute created no right of access.

KENNETH L. KARST

COLUMBUS BOARD OF EDUCATION v. PENICK
443 U.S. 449 (1979)
DAYTON BOARD OF EDUCATION v. BRINKMAN
433 U.S. 406 (1977); 443 U.S. 526 (1979)

These cases demonstrated the artificiality of the DE FACTO/DE JURE distinction in school DESEGREGATION litigation. Both cases arose in cities in Ohio, where racially segregated schools had not been prescribed by law since 1888. In both, however, blacks charged another form of de jure segregation: intentional acts by school boards aimed at promoting SEGREGATION.

When the *Dayton* case first reached the Supreme Court, a related doctrinal development was still a fresh memory. WASHINGTON V. DAVIS (1976) had held that RACIAL DISCRIMINATION was not to be inferred from the fact that governmental action had a racially disproportionate impact; rather the test was whether such an impact was intended by the legislative body or other officials whose conduct was challenged. (See LEGISLATION.) *Dayton I* in 1977 applied this reasoning to school segregation, emphasizing that a constitutional violation was to be found only in cases of established segregative intent. The Court remanded the case for more specific findings on the question of intent, and said that any remedy must be tailored to the scope of the segregation caused by any specific constitutional violations.

Many observers took *Dayton I* to portend the undermining of KEYES V. SCHOOL DISTRICT NO. 1 (1973). In *Keyes* the Court had held that, once a significant degree of de jure segregation was established, systemwide desegregation remedies (including SCHOOL BUSING) were appropriate unless the school board showed that any remaining racially separate schools were the product of something other than the board's segregative intent. When the case returned to the Supreme Court two years later, these predictions were confounded.

Dayton II came to the Court along with the *Columbus* case, and they were decided together. *Columbus*, decided by a 7–2 vote, provided the main opinions. Writing for a majority of five, Justice BYRON R. WHITE applied the *Keyes* presumptions approach so vigorously that the dissenters remarked that the de facto/de jure distinction had been drained of most of its meaning. None of the Justices disputed the finding that in 1954–1955, when BROWN V. BOARD OF EDUCATION was decided, the Columbus school board had deliberately drawn boundary lines and selected school sites to maintain racial segregation in a number of schools. What divided the Court was the question of inferences to be drawn from these undisputed facts.

Justice White reasoned that this de jure segregation placed the school board under an affirmative duty to dismantle its dual system. Its actions since 1954, however, had aggravated rather than reduced segregation; the foreseeability of those results helped prove the board's segregative intent. A districtwide busing remedy was thus appropriate under *Keyes*. Justice WILLIAM H. REHNQUIST, dissenting, pointed out the

tension between this decision and *Dayton I*. Here there was no showing of a causal relationship between pre-1954 acts of intentional segregation and current racial imbalance in the schools. Thus present-day de facto segregation was enough to generate districtwide remedies, so long as some significant pre-1954 acts of deliberate segregation could be shown.

It will be a rare big-city school district in which such acts cannot be found—with a consequent presumption of current de jure segregation. A school board cannot overcome this presumption merely by relying on a neighborhood school policy and showing that the city's residences are racially separated. This analysis obviously blurs the de facto/de jure distinction.

Dayton II made clear that a school board's segregative purpose was secondary to its effectiveness in performing its affirmative duty to terminate a dual system—and that effectiveness was to be measured in the present-day facts of racial separation and integration. Justice White again wrote for the majority, but now there were four dissenters. Justice POTTER STEWART, the Court's one Ohioan, concurred in Columbus but dissented in *Dayton II*, deferring in each case to the district court's determination as to a continuing constitutional violation. In *Dayton II*, the district court had found pre-1954 acts of deliberate segregation, but had found no causal connection between those acts and present racial separation in the schools. That separation, the district judge concluded, resulted not from any segregative purpose on the part of the school board but from residential segregation. Justice Stewart would have accepted that judgment, but the majority, following the *Columbus* line of reasoning, held that the board had not fulfilled its affirmative duty to dismantle the dual system that had existed in 1954. Chief Justice WARREN E. BURGER joined Justice Stewart in both cases; Justice Rehnquist dissented in *Dayton II* chiefly on the basis of his *Columbus* dissent.

Justice LEWIS F. POWELL joined Justice Rehnquist's dissents, and also wrote an opinion dissenting in both cases. Justice Powell had argued in *Keyes* for abandoning the de facto/de jure distinction, and he did not defend that distinction here. Rather he repeated his skepticism that court orders could ever end racial imbalance in large urban school districts and his opposition to massive busing as a desegregation remedy. Justice Powell, a former school board president, argued that, twenty-five years after *Brown*, the federal courts should be limiting rather than expanding their control of public school operations.

KENNETH L. KARST

Bibliography

KITCH, EDMUND W. 1979 The Return of Color-Consciousness to the Constitution: Weber, Dayton, and Columbus. *Supreme Court Review* 1979:1–15.

COMITY, JUDICIAL

Comity is the deference paid by the institutions of one government to the acts of another government—not out of compulsion, but in the interest of cooperation, reciprocity, and the stability that grows out of the satisfaction of mutual expectations. When the courts of one nation give effect to foreign laws and the orders of foreign courts, that deference is called judicial comity. (See ACT OF STATE DOCTRINE.)

The states of the United States are, for many purposes, separate sovereignties. A state court, in deciding a case, starts from the assumption that it will apply its own state law. When it applies the law of another state, normally it does so as a matter of comity. (See CHOICE OF LAW, CONSTITUTIONAL LIMITS UPON.) Because comity is not so much a rule as an attitude of accommodation, state courts generally feel free to refuse to apply a law that violates their own state's public policy. In *Nevada v. Hall* (1979) California courts upheld a million-dollar verdict against the State of Nevada in an automobile injury case, rejecting Nevada's claim of SOVEREIGN IMMUNITY; the Supreme Court affirmed, saying that the Constitution left to California's courts the degree of comity they should afford to Nevada law.

A state court's enforcement of the valid judgment of a court of another state is not merely a matter of comity but is required by the FULL FAITH AND CREDIT CLAUSE. Similarly, the SUPREMACY CLAUSE binds state courts to enforce valid federal laws and regulations, along with the valid judgments of federal courts.

Notions of comity have recently taken on increased significance in the federal courts themselves. A federal court may, under some circumstances, stay its proceedings because another action between the same parties is pending in a state court. The Supreme Court in *Fair Assessment of Real Estate Association v. McNary* (1981) discovered in the Tax Injunction Act (1937) a general principle of comity forbidding federal courts not only to enjoin the collection of state taxes but also to award DAMAGES in state tax cases. And comity has been a major consideration in the development of the "equitable restraint" doctrine of YOUNGER V. HARRIS (1971), which generally forbids a federal court to grant an INJUNCTION against the continuation of a pending state criminal prosecution.

KENNETH L. KARST

(SEE ALSO: *Abstention Doctrine.*)

COMITY CLAUSE

See: Full Faith and Credit

COMMANDER-IN-CHIEF

In every state, the command of the armed forces is the ultimate component of executive power. Article II of the Constitution, adapting British practice, designates the President commander-in-chief both of the nation's armed forces and of the state militia when it is called into national service. Article IV, guaranteeing each state a REPUBLICAN FORM OF GOVERNMENT, somewhat qualifies that authority. It provides that the national force be used to suppress domestic violence only on application of the state legislature or of the governor when the state legislature cannot be convened.

With regard to domestic (and republican) tranquillity, it became apparent soon after 1789 that the deference of Article IV to STATES' RIGHTS did not permit the national government fully to protect the peace of the United States. Although state governments dealt with most episodes of domestic disorder—and still do—some of those episodes had a national dimension. As early as 1792, Congress declared that "it shall be lawful for the President" to use national troops or call forth the militia whenever he deems such action necessary to protect the functioning of the government or the enforcement of its laws. President GEORGE WASHINGTON leading more than 12,000 national guardsmen to suppress the WHISKEY REBELLION of 1793 is the classic symbol of an independent national power to enforce what the President, echoing Jean-Jacques Rousseau, called "the general will." This power has been invoked regularly, most notably during and after the Civil War, but also in major strikes affecting the national economy (IN RE DEBS, 1895) and in the enforcement of judicial decisions ordering racial DESEGREGATION during the 1950s and 1960s. President WILLIAM HOWARD TAFT used the national force to protect Asian ALIENS threatened by a local mob, relying on his duty as President to carry out the international responsibility of the United States for the safety of aliens.

The formula of the 1792 statute, like that used in

later statutes, straddles an unresolved controversy between the President and Congress. Congress insists that its power to pass laws NECESSARY AND PROPER to implement the President's authority as commander-in-chief includes the right to restrict the President's capacity to act. All Presidents, on the other hand, while recognizing the necessity for legislation in many situations, claim that statutes cannot subtract from their constitutional duty and power to preserve the Constitution and enforce the laws. Although the pattern of usage is by no means uniform, Presidents generally conform to statutes that purport to reinforce and structure the President's use of the armed forces in domestic disorders, at least as a matter of courtesy, unless "sudden and unexpected civil disturbances, disasters, or calamities," in the language of Army regulations, leave no alternative. Some Presidents have even paid lip service to the POSSE COMITATUS ACT (1878), a dubious relic of the end of Reconstruction. That act prohibits the use of the Army in suppressing domestic turbulence unless "expressly" authorized. Presidents have evaded this restriction by employing marines for the purpose.

Modern statutes usually retain the ancient requirement of a public proclamation before force is used to restore order, although Presidents sometimes ignore the tradition. The use of force by the President (or by a governor) in dealing with civil disorder does not alone justify suspending the writ of HABEAS CORPUS. According to the DOCTRINE of EX PARTE MILLIGAN (1867) and other cases, the writ cannot be suspended so long as the courts remain capable of carrying out their duties normally.

The use of force as an instrument of diplomacy, or of war and other extended hostilities, does not involve issues of dual SOVEREIGNTY but has presented significant constitutional conflicts both between Congress and the President, and between individuals and the state. (See WAR, FOREIGN AFFAIRS, AND THE CONSTITUTION.) The President's power as commander-in-chief under such circumstances goes far beyond the conduct of military operations. As the Supreme Court declared in *Little v. Barreme* (1804), it is also the President's prerogative to deploy troops and weapons at home and abroad in times of peace and war, and to use them when no valid law forbids him to do so. The purposes for which the President may use the armed forces in carrying on the intercourse of the United States with foreign nations are infinite and unpredictable. They include diplomatic ceremony and demonstrations of power; the employment of force in self-defense in order to deter, anticipate, or defeat armed attack against the interests of the United States, or any other act in violation of international law that would justify the use of force in time of peace; and the prosecution of hostilities after a congressional DECLARATION OF WAR. In actual hostilities, it is the President's sole responsibility to negotiate truces, armistices, and cease-fires; to direct the negotiation of peace treaties or other international arrangements terminating a condition of war; and to govern foreign territory occupied in the course of hostilities until peace is restored.

These powers are extensive. The use, threat, or hint of force is a frequent element of diplomacy. Military occupations lasted for years during and after the Civil War, the Philippine campaign, a number of Caribbean episodes, and both World Wars. The Cold War has required the apparently permanent deployment abroad of American armed forces on a large scale; novel legal arrangements have developed to organize these activities. Although the broad political and prudential discretion of both the President and Congress is taken fully into account by the courts in reviewing such exercises of the commander-in-chief's authority, constitutional limits have nonetheless emerged.

In recent years Congress has effectively employed its appropriation power to qualify the President's discretion as commander-in-chief in conducting military or intelligence operations that are not "public and notorious" general wars under international law. While such contests between the power of the purse and the power of the sword are largely political, they raise the principle of the SEPARATION OF POWERS applied in IMMIGRATION AND NATURALIZATION SERVICE V. CHADHA (1983). The judicial response to these contests can be expected further to clarify a particularly murky part of the boundary between the President and Congress.

EUGENE V. ROSTOW

Bibliography

BISHOP, JOSEPH W., JR. 1974 *Justice under Fire.* New York: Charter House.
CORWIN, EDWARD S. (1940)1957 *The President: Office and Powers 1787–1957.* New York: New York University Press.
WILCOX, FRANCIS 1971 *Congress, the Executive, and Foreign Policy.* New York: Harper & Row.

COMMENTATORS ON THE CONSTITUTION

The first important analysis of the Constitution appeared during the ratification contests of 1787 and 1788. ALEXANDER HAMILTON and JAMES MADISON, who had participated in the CONSTITUTIONAL CONVENTION, collaborated with JOHN JAY on THE FEDERALIST (1788), a series of essays defending the proposed new plan of government. Appealing to the rationalistic temper of the eighteenth century, they justified the creation of a strong central government on logical and philosophical grounds, and developed a model of CONSTITUTIONALISM that relied upon structural CHECKS AND BALANCES to promote harmony within the system. Ultimate SOVEREIGNTY, they argued, inhered in the American people; the Constitution, as an instrument of the popular will, defined and limited the powers of both the national government and the states. *The Federalist* provided valuable insights into the thinking of the Founding Fathers and established the guidelines for further constitutional commentary down to the Civil War.

Between 1789 and 1860 two major groups of commentators emerged in response to recurring political crises and sectional tensions. Legally trained publicists from New England and the middle states espoused a national will theory of government to justify the expansion of federal power, while southern lawyers and statesmen formed a state compact school of constitutional interpretation that championed decentralization and state sovereignty. Each group approached constitutional issues in a formal and mechanistic way, and relied upon close textual analysis to support its position.

The nationalists argued that the American people, acting in a collective national capacity, had divided sovereign power between the nation and the states and established the Constitution as the supreme LAW OF THE LAND. Under the resulting federal system, the states retained control of their internal affairs but were subordinate to the general government in all important national concerns, including taxation, INTERSTATE COMMERCE, and FOREIGN AFFAIRS. The Constitution, moreover, created a permanent union, whose basic features could be changed only by resort to a prescribed AMENDING PROCESS. Although several nationalists conceded that the Constitution had originated in a compact of the people of the several states, they insisted that such a compact, once executed, was inviolate, and could not be modified thereafter by the parties. Such was the message of NATHANIEL CHIPMAN's *Sketches of the Principles of Government* (1793) and William Alexander Duer's *Lectures on Constitutional Jurisprudence* (1843).

Other advocates of national supremacy rejected contractual assumptions altogether, and moved toward an organic theory of the Union. Nathan Dane, in *A General Abridgment and Digest of American Law* (1829), contended that the states had never been truly sovereign, because they owed their independence from British rule to the actions of the CONTINENTAL CONGRESS, a national body that represented the American people. The people, not the states, had ratified the Constitution through the exercise of majority will; therefore, any state efforts to nullify federal law or to withdraw from the Union amounted to illegal and revolutionary acts. JAMES KENT's *Commentaries on American Law* (1826–1830) and Timothy Walker's *Introduction to American Law* (1837) further noted that the Constitution provided for the peaceful resolution of federal–state disputes through the Supreme Court's power of JUDICIAL REVIEW.

In attacking the compact model of constitutionalism, these commentators stressed the noncontractual language of the PREAMBLE and the SUPREMACY CLAUSE. A similar preoccupation with formal textual analysis characterized JOSEPH STORY's *Commentaries on the Constitution of the United States* (1833), the most influential and authoritative statement of the nationalist position. Story, an associate Justice of the Supreme Court, interpreted the Constitution on a line-by-line basis, in light of the nationalistic jurisprudence of JOHN MARSHALL. Like Marshall, he insisted that the powers of the federal government had to be construed broadly, as the Framers had intended. On both theoretical and pragmatic grounds, Story defended the power of the Supreme Court to strike down unconstitutional state laws. Yet he also emphasized the limits of national authority, noting that the states retained control over matters of internal police that affected the daily lives of their citizens. Although Congress alone could regulate interstate commerce, for example, state legislatures might pass health and safety measures that indirectly affected such commerce. By focusing upon questions of terminology and classification, Story sought to demonstrate the stability of the federal system and to place the Constitution above partisan politics.

Nationalist historians described the formation of the Union in similarly legalistic and reverential terms. GEORGE TICKNOR CURTIS's *History of the Origin, Formation, and Adoption of the Constitution of the United States* (1854–1858), the first work to deal exclusively with a constitutional topic, quoted at length from the journals of the Continental Congress and other public records, but largely ignored surrounding political and economic circumstances. For Curtis and other romantic nationalists, the Founding Fathers were disinterested and divinely inspired patriots, who enjoyed the full confidence and support of the American people. Only RICHARD HILDRETH's *History of* the United States of America (1849–1852) presented a contrary view. Hildreth stressed the importance of conflicting economic groups in the new nation and pointed out that the Constitution had been ratified by conventions representing only a minority of American voters.

Although state compact theorists shared the prevailing belief in a fixed and beneficent Constitution, they deplored what they perceived as the aggrandizing tendencies of the national government. St. George Tucker's "View of the Constitution of the United States," appended to his edition of WILLIAM BLACKSTONE's Commentaries (1803), established the basic premises of the southern constitutional argument. The states and their respective citizens, Tucker contended, had entered into a compact—the Constitution—and had delegated some of their sovereign powers to the resulting federal government for specific and limited purposes. Because the Union remained subordinate to its creators, the states, and depended upon their cooperation for its continued existence, all positive grants of national power had to be construed strictly. If the federal government overstepped its constitutional powers, Tucker suggested that individuals might look to the state or federal courts for redress, while violations of STATES' RIGHTS would be answered by appropriate action from the state legislatures.

Later commentators refined Tucker's ideas and fashioned new remedies for the protection of state rights. The Philadelphia lawyer WILLIAM RAWLE introduced the possibility of peaceable SECESSION through the action of state CONSTITUTIONAL CONVENTIONS in A View of the Constitution of the United States (1825). Rawle's reasoning was hypothetical: because the people of each state had agreed to form a permanent union of representative republics, they could withdraw from their compact only by adopting a new state constitution based upon nonrepublican principles. A more realistic assessment of the nature and consequences of secession appeared in HENRY ST. GEORGE TUCKER's Lectures on Constitutional Law (1843). In Tucker's view, secession provided the only mode of resistance available to a state after a controversial federal law had been upheld by the judiciary. Secession was a revolutionary measure, however, because the Constitution had established the courts as the permanent umpires of federal–state relations.

Advocates of NULLIFICATION proposed a more extreme version of the state sovereignty argument, whose origins went back to JOHN TAYLOR of Caroline's Construction Construed; and Constitutions Vindicated (1820) and New Views of the Constitution of the United States (1823). Unlike the southern moderates, Taylor insisted that sovereignty was indivisible and inhered exclusively in the states. Each "state nation" thus retained the power to construe the terms of the federal compact for itself, and to interpose its authority at any time to protect its citizens against the consolidating tendencies of the federal government. Whenever a federal law violated the Constitution, asserted Abel Parker Upshur in A Brief Inquiry into the Nature and Character of Our Federal Government (1840), a state might summon its citizens to a special convention and declare the act null and void within its borders.

As the influence of the slaveholding South continued to decline in national politics, some commentators sought to preserve the Union by adding still more checks and balances to the constitutional structure. In A Disquisition on Government and A Discourse on the Constitution and Government of the United States (1851), JOHN C. CALHOUN called for amendments that would establish a dual executive and base REPRESENTATION upon broad interest groups, any one of which might block the enactment of undesirable congressional legislation. ALEXANDER H. STEPHENS's A Constitutional View of the Late War Between the States (1868–1870) and JEFFERSON DAVIS's The Rise and Fall of the Confederate Government (1881) confirmed the mechanistic cast of southern constitutional thought, as they summed up the case for secession in its final form. With the defeat of the Confederacy, the secessionist option ceased to exist, and later commentators treated the issue as a historical footnote. During the 1950s conservative Southerners tried unsuccessfully to circumvent federal CIVIL RIGHTS policy by reviving the idea of INTERPOSITION in such works as William Old's The Segregation Issue: Suggestions Regarding the Maintenance of State Autonomy (1955).

For Civil War Unionists the exercise of sweeping WAR POWERS by the President and Congress provoked vigorous constitutional debate. Conservative publicists, committed to a restrictive view of federal power, insisted that no departure from prewar constitutional norms was permissible, despite the wartime emergency. Former Supreme Court Justice BENJAMIN R. CURTIS charged in Executive Power (1862) that President ABRAHAM LINCOLN had acted illegally in authorizing the military to arrest and imprison suspected disloyal civilians in areas removed from a war zone. Joel Parker's The War Powers of Congress, and of the President (1863) denounced the EMANCIPATION PROCLAMATION and related CONFISCATION

ACTS for impairing property rights and revolutionizing federal–state relations.

A rival group of Lincolnian pragmatists defended the actions of federal authorities by appealing to an organic theory of constitutional development. Evolving national values and practices had shaped the Constitution far more than abstract legal rules, asserted FRANCIS LIEBER in *What Is Our Constitution— League, Pact, or Government?* (1861). The Founding Fathers had not anticipated the problem of secession; therefore, the Lincoln administration might, in conformity with natural law principles, take whatever measures it deemed necessary to preserve the nation. Sidney George Fisher's *The Trial of the Constitution* (1862) discovered new sources of federal power in the doctrine of popular sovereignty and other unwritten democratic dogmas. Charging that adherence to the checks and balances of the formal Constitution had immobilized the government in practice, Fisher urged Congress to create a new constitutional tradition by transforming itself into an American parliament immediately responsive to the popular will. William Whiting, solicitor of the War Department, contended that existent constitutional provisions authorized the federal government to pursue almost any wartime policy it chose. In *The War Powers of the President and the Legislative Powers of Congress in Relation to Rebellion, Treason, and Slavery* (1862), Whiting looked to the GENERAL WELFARE CLAUSE and other statements of broad national purpose to legitimize controversial Union measures.

The leading commentators of the late nineteenth century carried forward an organic view of the Constitution, but linked it to a laissez-faire ideology that sharply restrained the exercise of governmental power at all levels. Influenced by the conservative Darwinism of Herbert Spencer and William Graham Sumner, these economic libertarians feared legislative innovation and called upon the judiciary to preserve the fundamental economic rights of the individual against arbitrary state action. In *A Treatise on the Constitutional Limitations Which Rest upon the Legislative Power of the States of the American Union* (1868), THOMAS MCINTYRE COOLEY argued that a libertarian tradition stretching back to MAGNA CARTA protected private property from harmful regulation, even in the absence of specific constitutional guarantees. By appealing to these historic liberties, Cooley sought to broaden the scope of the DUE PROCESS clause, transforming it into a substantive restraint upon economic legislation. JOHN FORREST DILLON's *A Treatise on Municipal Corporations* (1872) discovered implied limits to the taxing power. Taxes could only be levied for a PUBLIC PURPOSE, Dillon maintained, and could not benefit one social class at the expense of another. CHRISTOPHER G. TIEDEMAN took an equally restrictive view of state and federal POLICE POWER in *A Treatise on the Limitations of Police Power in the United States* (1886), condemning usury laws and efforts to control wages and prices.

In the area of civil rights, commentators opposed "paternalistic" legislation and insisted that the Civil War had not destroyed the traditional division of power between the nation and the states. Amendments must conform to the general principles underlying the Constitution, asserted John Norton Pomeroy in *An Introduction to the Constitutional Law of the United States* (1868); and these principles included FEDERALISM, as defined by the Founding Fathers. Despite the broad language of the FOURTEENTH AMENDMENT, therefore, Congress lacked power to remedy most civil rights violations, which remained subject to state control. JOHN RANDOLPH TUCKER's *The Constitution of the United States* (1899) warned that federal attacks on customary racial practices in the South would undermine local institutions and create a dangerous centralization of power in the national government. The racist assumptions shared by most libertarians surfaced clearly in John Ordronaux's *Constitutional Legislation in the United States* (1891). Noting that national progress depended upon "race instincts," Ordronaux suggested that blacks, Orientals, and other non-Aryans were unfit for the full responsibilities of democratic CITIZENSHIP.

Constitutional historians of the late nineteenth century used a Darwinian model of struggle and survival to explain the rise of the American nation. HERMANN VON HOLST, the first scholar to make systematic use of the records of congressional debates, combined antislavery moralism with a laissez-faire attitude toward northern business in his ponderous *Constitutional and Political History of the United States* (1876–1892). Equally moralistic and libertarian was JAMES SCHOULER's *History of the United States under the Constitution* (1880–1913). In the growth of republican institutions and the triumph of Union arms Schouler discerned the unfolding of a divine plan. From a Social Darwinist perspective, William A. Dunning's *The Constitution of the United States in Civil War and Reconstruction, 1860–1867* (1885) and JOHN W. BURGESS's *Reconstruction and the Constitution, 1866– 1876* (1902) criticized federal policymakers for enfranchising blacks at the expense of their Anglo-Saxon superiors.

In its mature form libertarian theory created a twilight zone on the borders of the federal system, within which neither the national government not the states could act. While the TENTH AMENDMENT prevented Congress from regulating local economic activities, state legislatures found their police powers circumscribed by the restrictive principles defined by Cooley and his associates. These extraconstitutional restraints also limited the federal government when it sought to exercise its express powers over taxation and commerce. Twentieth-century economic and racial conservatives have continued to defend the libertarian viewpoint and to protest the expansion of federal regulatory power. In *Neither Purse Nor Sword* (1936), James M. Beck and Merle Thorpe condemned early New Deal legislation for violating property rights and invading the reserved powers of the states. Charles J. Bloch's *States' Rights—The Law of the Land* (1958), written in the aftermath of the *Brown* decision, charged that the VINSON COURT and WARREN COURT had subverted the meaning of the Fourteenth Amendment in civil rights cases, and called upon Congress to revitalize the Tenth Amendment, "the cornerstone of the Republic."

As the excesses of a period of industrial growth threatened the welfare of workers and consumers, however, other commentators condemned the laissez-faire model of constitutionalism as archaic and unsuited to the needs of a modern democracy. Impressed by the empiricism of the emerging social sciences, these democratic instrumentalists approached constitutional questions from a pragmatic and reformist perspective. Although they did not deny the existence of fundamental principles, they argued that these principles needed to be adapted to changing environmental conditions. Through intelligent social planning, they maintained, federal and state lawmakers might control an expanding economy in accordance with the popular will.

Mechanistic eighteenth-century concepts, such as SEPARATION OF POWERS, impaired the efficiency of modern government, charged WOODROW WILSON in *Congressional Government* (1885) and *Constitutional Government in the United States* (1908). Constitutional grants of power to the national government established only "general lines of definition," he added, and should be broadly construed by the courts in response to developing societal needs. In a similar vein, WESTEL W. WILLOUGHBY's *The Constitutional Law of the United States* (1910) and FRANK J. GOODNOW's *Social Reform and the Constitution* (1911) criticized judges for obstructing progressive reforms through their continued adherence to laissez-faire idealism.

The advent of the welfare state in the 1930s magni-

fied disagreements between libertarians and instrumentalists, and provoked a major confrontation between President FRANKLIN D. ROOSEVELT and the Supreme Court. EDWARD S. CORWIN, the most influential constitutional commentator of the time, applauded the programs of the early New Deal for establishing a new COOPERATIVE FEDERALISM. In *The Twilight of the Supreme Court* (1934), Corwin urged the Justices to uphold legislative policymaking in economic matters, and pointed to the nationalistic decisions of John Marshall as appropriate precedents. When judicial intransigence persisted, according to Attorney General ROBERT H. JACKSON in *The Struggle for Judicial Supremacy* (1941), the administration adopted a court-packing plan as the only apparent means of restoring the full constitutional powers of the national government. Although the plan failed, a majority of Justices began to redefine congressional power in more liberal terms. Corwin welcomed the Court's belated acceptance of sweeping federal regulation in *Constitutional Revolution, Ltd.* (1941), and correctly predicted that the Justices would thereafter focus their review power on protection of CIVIL LIBERTIES and the rights of minorities.

Instrumentalist historians tended to seek the causes of constitutional change in underlying social and economic developments. CHARLES A. BEARD's pathbreaking study, *An Economic Interpretation of the Constitution of the United States* (1913), encouraged Progressive reformers by demythologizing the work of the Philadelphia Convention. Using previously neglected Treasury and census records, Beard presented the Founding Fathers as a conspiratorial elite who had devised an undemocratic Constitution to protect their property from the attacks of popular legislative majorities. In *American Constitutional Development* (1943) CARL BRENT SWISHER drew upon other nontraditional sources to explain, and justify, the emergence of the positive state. With comparable erudition WILLIAM W. CROSSKEY's *Politics and the Constitution in the History of the United States* (1953) used linguistic analysis to demonstrate the legitimacy of New Deal regulatory measures. After an exhaustive inquiry into the eighteenth-century meaning of "commerce" and other key words, Crosskey concluded that the Framers had intended to create a unitary, centralized system in which "the American people could, through Congress, deal with any subject they wished, on a simple, straightforward, nation-wide basis."

Although the instrumentalists emphasized the need to adapt the Constitution to changing socioeconomic conditions, they remained committed to the RULE OF LAW and acknowledged the binding force of constitutional norms. This moderate position failed to satisfy a small group of radical empiricists, who argued that written codes were meaningless in themselves and merely served to rationalize the political decisions of legislators and judges. "The language of the Constitution is immaterial since it represents current myths and folklore rather than rules," asserted THURMAN W. ARNOLD in *The Folklore of Capitalism* (1937). "Out of it are spun the contradictory ideals of governmental morality." Howard L. McBain's *The Living Constitution: A Consideration of the Realities and Legends of Our Fundamental Law* (1927) similarly contended that law had no life of its own, but depended for its substance on the unpredictable actions of men. Because the American people believed the fiction of a government of law, they had grown politically apathetic, charged J. ALLEN SMITH in *The Growth and Decadence of Constitutional Government* (1930). Although constitutionalism had been designed to limit arbitrary power, he noted, it protected an irresponsible governing elite from popular scrutiny and control.

The empiricists were more successful in diagnosing ills than in prescribing remedies. Because they stressed the determining influence of ideology and personality upon decision making, they could find no satisfactory way to limit the discretionary power of public officials. The scope of administrative discretion must necessarily broaden as society grows more complex, contended William B. Munro in *The Invisible Government* (1928). He welcomed the trend, which promised to give government agencies greater flexibility in dealing with contemporary problems. Yet unrestrained power might also encourage irresponsible behavior, such as judges so often displayed in reviewing legislative measures. Both LOUIS B. BOUDIN's *Government by Judiciary* (1932) and Fred Rodell's *Nine Men: A Political History of the Supreme Court of the United States from 1790 to 1955* (1955) reduced jurisprudence to politics, and charged that judges wrote their conservative policy preferences into law under the guise of legal principles. The only remedy they could suggest, however, was the appointment to the bench of liberals who would promote the public welfare in a more enlightened, albeit equally subjective, fashion.

During the past quarter-century commentators, preeminently ALEXANDER M. BICKEL, have continued to debate the nature and scope of JUDICIAL REVIEW, in the context of the Supreme Court's enlarged role as guardian of individual and minority rights. The timely aspects of such recent studies attest to the constructive role that commentators have historically played in the shaping of American constitutional law. Responsive to changing trends in social and political thought, they have often helped to redefine and clarify the terms of constitutional discourse. As Corwin once quipped, "If judges make law, so do commentators."

MAXWELL BLOOMFIELD

Bibliography

BAUER, ELIZABETH K.   1952   *Commentaries on the Constitution, 1790–1860.* New York: Columbia University Press.

BELZ, HERMAN   1971   The Realist Critique of Constitutionalism in the Era of Reform. *American Journal of Legal History* 15:288–306.

HYMAN, HAROLD M.   1973   *A More Perfect Union: The Impact of the Civil War and Reconstruction on the Constitution.* New York: Knopf.

KONEFSKY, ALFRED S.   1981   Men of Great and Little Faith: Generations of Constitutional Scholars. *Buffalo Law Review* 30:365–384.

LARSEN, CHARLES E.   1959   Nationalism and States' Rights in Commentaries on the Constitution after the Civil War. *American Journal of Legal History* 3:360–369.

MURPHY, PAUL L.   1963   Time to Reclaim: The Current Challenge of American Constitutional History. *American Historical Review* 69:64–79.

NEWTON, ROBERT E.   1965   Edward S. Corwin and American Constitutional Law. *Journal of Public Law* 14:198–212.

COMMERCE CLAUSE

The commerce clause is the small part of the Constitution that provides that "The Congress shall have power . . . to regulate commerce with foreign nations, and among the several states, and with the Indian tribes."

The phrase relating to the Indians was derived from the provision in the 1781 ARTICLES OF CONFEDERATION which gave the federal congress "the sole and exclusive right and power of . . . regulating the trade and managing all affairs with the Indians." Despite the elimination of the sweeping second phrase, there never has been any question that the Indian part of the commerce clause (plus the TREATY and WAR POWERS) gave Congress power over all relations with the Indians, and no more need be said about it.

Nor has there been much question as to the scope of the federal power to regulate foreign commerce. Combined with the tax and WAR POWERS and the provisions prohibiting the states from entering treaties and agreements with foreign powers and from imposing duties on imports and exports, this power clearly gave the federal government complete authority over relations with foreign nations.

The short clause relating to "commerce among the several states," however, has become one of the most significant provisions in the Constitution. It has been in large part responsible for the development of the United States as a single integrated economic unit, with no impediments to the movement of goods or people at state lines.

The draftsmen of the commerce clause could not have envisaged the eventual magnitude of the national commercial structure or the breadth of the CONSTITUTIONAL INTERPRETATION which that structure would produce. Nevertheless the need for a national power over commerce led to the calling of the CONSTITUTIONAL CONVENTION OF 1787, and the seed for the growth of the power was planted in the early years.

In 1786 the Virginia General Assembly, and then a commission representing five states meeting at Annapolis, called for the appointment of commissioners to consider "the trade of the United States" and "how far a uniform system in their commercial regulation may be necessary to their common interest and their permanent harmony." The Congress created under the Articles of Confederation thereupon approved the calling of a convention to meet in Philadelphia in May 1787 for the purpose of revising the Articles and reporting its recommendations to the Congress and the States.

The Convention, after considerable debate, adopted a resolution generally describing the powers to be given the National Legislature, in the form proposed by the Virginia delegation led by GEORGE WASHINGTON, Governor EDMUND RANDOLPH, and JAMES MADISON. It was resolved that "the national legislature ought . . . to legislate in all cases for the general interests of the Union, and also in those to which the states are separately incompetent, or in which the harmony of the United States may be interrupted by the exercise of individual legislation." This and other resolutions were sent to a drafting committee, which reported out the commerce clause and other powers to be conferred on Congress in substantially the form finally adopted.

Although the needs of commerce had been principally responsible for the calling of the Convention, the clause was accepted with hardly any debate. The same was true in the state ratifying conventions. All reflected the view that in general the new Constitution gave the federal government power over matters of national but not of local concern.

The same view was expressed in the first commerce clause case in 1824 (GIBBONS V. OGDEN), written for a unanimous Supreme Court by Chief Justice JOHN MARSHALL, who had been a member of the Virginia ratifying convention. The Court declared that the commerce power did not extend to commerce that is completely internal, and "which does not extend to or affect other states." It "may very properly be restricted to that commerce which concerns more states than one. . . . The genius and character of the whole government seems to be, that its action is to be applied to all the concerns of the nation, and to these internal concerns which affect the States generally."

Of course, neither in 1787 nor in 1824 did those who wrote or ratified or interpreted the Constitution contemplate the tremendous and close-knit economic structure that exists today and the accompanying inability of the states, or of any agency but the nation, to meet the governmental problems that structure presents. Indeed, in the 1820s and into the 1850s many persons regarded even the construction of the principal highways within each state as purely internal matters not subject to federal power, as appeared from President JAMES MONROE's veto on constitutional grounds of an appropriation to construct what is now Interstate 70 from Maryland to the Western states. Although the MARSHALL COURT would not have agreed, some of the more STATES' RIGHTS-minded Supreme Court Justices of the 1840s and 1850s did.

In general, during the century from 1787 to 1887, the only national commercial problems concerned foreign trade and navigation and the removal of state-imposed barriers to interstate trade. Affirmative federal regulation applied almost entirely to matters of navigation on the oceans, lakes, and rivers. An early statute required vessels engaged in coastal traffic to obtain federal licenses. Reasonably enough, none of these were challenged as falling outside the commerce power.

All of the commerce clause cases during the first 100 years, and a great many of them thereafter, were concerned with the negative effect of the clause upon state legislation—even though the clause did not mention the states. The Constitution merely said that Congress should have the power to regulate commerce. Other clauses imposed specific prohibitions upon the states, but the commerce clause did not. On the other hand, it was well known during the early period that the principal evil at which the commerce clause was directed was state restrictions upon the free flow of commerce.

The issue first came before the Supreme Court in

GIBBONS V. OGDEN (1824). New York had granted Robert Fulton and ROBERT LIVINGSTON the exclusive right for thirty years to operate vessels propelled by steam in New York waters, thereby excluding steamboats coming from neighboring states. New Jersey, Connecticut, and Ohio had promptly passed retaliatory legislation forbidding the New York monopoly from operating in their waters. The case presented an example (though unforeseeable in 1787) of the type of interstate commercial rivalry which the commerce clause had been designed to prevent.

A unanimous Supreme Court held that Congress's commerce power extended to all commercial intercourse among the states, rejecting arguments that it did not apply to navigation and passenger traffic. The Court, speaking through Marshall, further concluded that Congress had exercised its power in the Coastal Licensing Act, that Gibbons's vessels were operating in compliance with that statute, and that New York's attempt to prohibit them from operating in New York waters was inconsistent with the federal statute and therefore unconstitutional under the SUPREMACY CLAUSE of the Constitution. The Court did not find it necessary to decide whether the power of Congress to regulate interstate commerce was exclusive or whether the states had CONCURRENT POWER in the absence of a conflicting federal law, although Marshall seemed to favor the former view. But Marshall recognized that, although the states had no power to regulate interstate or FOREIGN COMMERCE as such, they could exercise their preexisting powers to enact laws on such subjects as health, quarantine, turnpikes and ferries, and other internal commerce, even though that might overlap the subjects that Congress could reach under the commerce clause. Thus, as a practical matter, the Court recognized that the states had concurrent powers over many aspects of commerce, or of internal matters that might affect external commerce.

After ROGER B. TANEY became Chief Justice in 1835, a number of the Justices, including Taney, took the flat position that only state laws inconsistent with acts of Congress were preempted, and that the commerce clause itself had no preemptive effect. But in none of the cases could a majority of the Court agree on any theory.

This unhappy and unhealthy state of the law was formally resolved in 1852, when, speaking through newly appointed Justice BENJAMIN R. CURTIS, the Court sustained a Pennsylvania law governing the use of pilots in the port of Philadelphia in COOLEY V. BOARD OF WARDENS OF PHILADELPHIA (1852). Six Justices agreed that whatever subjects of this power are in their nature national, or admit only of one uniform system, or plan of regulation, may justly be said to be of such a nature as to require exclusive legislation by Congress. Where there was no need for regulation on a national scale, only state laws inconsistent with federal would fall.

The Court still cites the *Cooley* principle with approval, although the *Cooley* formula has been largely superseded by an interest-balancing approach to STATE REGULATION OF COMMERCE. (See SELECTIVE EXCLUSIVENESS; STATE POLICE POWER; STATE TAXATION OF COMMERCE.) But in a number of cases during the years following *Cooley,* the Court adopted a more simplistic approach. If the subject of the state regulation was interstate commerce, only Congress could regulate it; if it was not, only the states could. In these cases the Court held—or at least said—that the United States could not tax or regulate manufacturing or PRODUCTION because they were beyond the scope of the federal commerce power, a pronouncement that later caused substantial difficulty but was not explicitly disavowed until *Commonwealth Edison Co. v. Montana* (1981).

During the twenty years after the Civil War, the Court held that states could not directly tax or regulate interstate commerce, but that they could, for example, fix railroad rates between points in the same state. (See GRANGER CASES, 1877.) When, however, Illinois attempted to apply its prohibition against charging more for a shorter rail haul than a longer one to freight between Illinois cities and New York, the Court, applying the *Cooley* formula, held in WABASH, ST. LOUIS & PACIFIC RAILWAY V. ILLINOIS (1886) that the state had no such power. The opinion made it clear that interstate rates, even for the part of a journey within a state, were not subject to state regulation. Such transportation was "of that national character" that can be "only appropriately" regulated by Congress rather than by the individual states.

Because leaving shippers subject to unregulated rail rates was unthinkable at that time, Congress reacted in 1887 by adopting the INTERSTATE COMMERCE ACT, the first affirmative federal regulation of land transportation.

Three years later, in response to a similar public reaction against uncontrolled monopolies, Congress enacted the SHERMAN ANTITRUST ACT, which prohibited combinations that restrained or monopolized interstate and foreign trade or commerce. The Court easily upheld the applicability of the statute to interstate railroads, but, amazingly, by a vote of 8–1, held the act inapplicable to the Sugar Trust which combined all the sugar refiners in the United States.

UNITED STATES V. E. C. KNIGHT CO. (1895) held that such a combination concerned only manufacture and production, and not "commerce," as the act (and, presumably, the Constitution) used the word. This ruling left the country remediless against national monopolies of manufacturers. Since interstate manufacturers are of course engaged in interstate trade—selling, buying, and shipping—as well as manufacture, this was a strange decision. It was soon devitalized, though not expressly OVERRULED, in SWIFT & COMPANY V. UNITED STATES (1905), STANDARD OIL COMPANY V. UNITED STATES (1911), and UNITED STATES V. AMERICAN TOBACCO COMPANY (1911), which similarly involved combinations of manufacturers.

In a number of cases the Court upheld congressional regulation of interstate transportation for noncommercial reasons. Federal statutes forbidding the interstate sale of lottery tickets, the interstate transportation of women for immoral purposes, stolen motor vehicles, diseased cattle which might range across state lines, misbranded food and drugs, and firearms were all held valid, usually without much question. The effect was to establish that the commerce clause applied to things or persons moving across state lines, whether or not they had anything to do with trade or commerce in the usual sense. (See NATIONAL POLICE POWER.) This conclusion was consistent with Marshall's original definition of commerce as intercourse in GIBBONS V. OGDEN.

The Court's narrow approach to the commerce power in the early twentieth century was demonstrated by its invalidation in 1908 of a law creating a WORKER'S COMPENSATION system for all railroad employees, because it included those doing intrastate shop and clerical work, and a law prohibiting railroads from discharging employees because of membership in a labor organization. (See EMPLOYERS' LIABILITY CASES, 1908; ADAIR V. UNITED STATES, 1908.) In HAMMER V. DAGENHART (1918) the Court even held that Congress could not prohibit the interstate transportation of child-made goods because the prohibition's purpose was to prevent child labor in manufacturing plants within the states.

Decisions other than the monopoly cases during the same period recognized that the congressional commerce power could apply to intrastate transactions that had an effect upon or relation to interstate commerce. Although strikes blocking interstate shipments from manufacturing plants were found to affect interstate commerce only indirectly, the result was different when an intent to restrain interstate commerce was found, or when a SECONDARY BOYCOTT extended to other states. (See LOEWE V. LAWLOR,

1908.) Intrastate trains were held subject to federal safety regulations because of the danger to interstate trains on the same tracks. Intrastate freight rates were held subject to federal control when a competitive relationship to interstate rates or a general effect on all rail rates could be shown. (See SHREVEPORT DOCTRINE.) In 1930 the Court sustained the application of the Railway Labor Act to clerks performing intrastate work so as to protect the right to COLLECTIVE BARGAINING and thereby avert strikes disrupting interstate commerce, contrary to the *Adair* decision in 1908.

Perhaps of greatest significance were cases sustaining federal regulation of the stockyards and the Chicago Board of Trade which, even though located in a single city, were found to control interstate prices for agricultural products. (See STAFFORD V. WALLACE, 1922; CHICAGO BOARD OF TRADE V. OLSEN, 1923.) The Court was not disturbed by the fact that the sales of grain futures which had such an effect were often completely local, since most of them were not followed by any shipments of physical products.

Thus by 1930 there were lines of cases saying that the federal power did not extend to business activity occurring in a single state, and other cases holding the contrary where some kinds of relationship to interstate commerce were shown.

The Great Depression running from 1929 through the 1930s brought the nation its severest economic crisis. Inaction during HERBERT HOOVER's administration proved ineffective and left thirteen million persons unemployed, prices and wages dropping in a self-perpetuating spiral, and banks, railroads, and many other businesses insolvent. The amount of revenue freight carried by railroad, a fair measure of the quantity of interstate commerce, had fallen by fifty-one percent. The public expected FRANKLIN D. ROOSEVELT, who took office in March 1933, to do something about the Depression. Although no one was sure what would work—and no one is yet quite sure what, if anything, did work—the President and Congress tried. Obviously the economy could not be restored by states acting separately. Only measures taken on a national scale could possibly be effective.

To stop the downward spiral in wages and prices, and to increase employment by limiting the number of hours a person could work, MAXIMUM HOURS AND MINIMUM WAGES were prescribed for industry generally, not merely for employees in interstate commerce. Collective bargaining was made mandatory, and protected against employer interference. The object was to increase national employment, national purchasing power, and the demand for and consumption of all products, which would benefit employers, employees, and the flow of commodities in interstate commerce. All this was originally sought to be accomplished by the NATIONAL INDUSTRIAL RECOVERY ACT (NIRA), which authorized every industry to prepare a code of competition designed to accomplish the above purposes; the code would become effective and enforceable when approved by the President.

The same statute and the AGRICULTURAL ADJUSTMENT ACT OF 1933 (AAA) attempted to cope with the overproduction of petroleum and agricultural products, which had forced prices down to absurd levels, such as five cents per barrel of crude oil and thirty-seven cents per bushel of wheat. The petroleum code under the NIRA and programs adopted under the AAA provided for the fixing of production quotas for oil producers and farmers.

The two lines of authorities summarized above supported opposing arguments as to the constitutionality of these measures under the commerce clause. For Congress to prescribe wages, hours, and production quotas for factories, farms, and oil wells undoubtedly would regulate intrastate activities, which prior opinions had frequently said were regulable only by the states.

On the other hand, the reasoning of opinions sustaining federal regulation of intrastate features of railroading and the intrastate marketing practices of stockyards and grain exchanges also supported the use of the commerce power to regulate intrastate acts that had an effect upon interstate commerce. The same was true of many of the antitrust cases referred to above. None of the relationships previously found insufficient to support federal regulation had involved general economic effects that halved the flow of interstate trade. But Congress had never sought to regulate the main body of manufacturing, mining, and agricultural production.

In the mid-1930s the Supreme Court included four Justices—WILLIS VAN DEVANTER, JAMES McREYNOLDS, GEORGE SUTHERLAND, and PIERCE BUTLER—who looked askance at any enlargement of the scope of governmental power over business and who steadily voted against extension of the congressional commerce power, and also voted to invalidate both federal and state regulation under the due process clauses. Chief Justice CHARLES EVANS HUGHES and Justice OWEN J. ROBERTS sometimes voted with these four, while Justices LOUIS D. BRANDEIS, HARLAN FISKE STONE, and BENJAMIN N. CARDOZO usually voted to sustain the legislative judgments as to how to deal with economic problems.

In a series of cases in 1935 and 1936, passing upon the validity of the NIRA, the AAA, and the GUFFEY-SNYDER (BITUMINOUS COAL CONSERVATION) ACT regulating the bituminous coal industry, Hughes and Roberts joined the conservative four to hold these acts unconstitutional.

The government had hoped and planned to test the constitutionality of the NIRA in a case involving the nationally integrated petroleum industry, PANAMA REFINING CO. V. RYAN (January 1935). But the Court found it unnecessary to decide the commerce issue in the *Panama* case. Instead, that question came before the Court in SCHECHTER POULTRY CORP. V. UNITED STATES (May 1935), in which the defendant had violated the provisions of the Live Poultry Code with respect to wages and hours and marketing practices of seemingly little consequence. The poultry slaughtered and sold by the defendant had come to New York City from other states, but there was nothing in the record to show that this interstate movement was greatly affected by the practices in question.

The only persuasive argument supporting the constitutionality of the Poultry Code was that the depressed state of the entire economy and of interstate commerce in general could be remedied only by increasing national purchasing power, and that prescribing minimum wages and maximum hours for all employees, whether or not in interstate industries, was a reasonable method of accomplishing that purpose. None of the Justices was willing to go that far. Indeed, the opinion of Chief Justice Hughes for the Court and the concurring opinion of Justice Cardozo emphasized as a principal defect in the argument that it would extend federal power to all business, interstate or intrastate. The fact that little would be left to exclusive state control, rather than the magnitude of the effect on interstate commerce from a national perspective, was treated as decisive. On the same day, in RAILROAD RETIREMENT BOARD V. ALTON, an act establishing a retirement program for railroad employees was held, by a vote of 5–4, not to be within the federal commerce power.

In theory, the *Schechter* decision left open the power of Congress to regulate production in major interstate industries such as petroleum or coal. But that opening, if it existed, seemed to be closed by two decisions in 1936. Because of the foreseeable risks from reliance on the commerce power, Congress had utilized the taxing power to "persuade" farmers to limit the production of crops in order to halt the collapse of farm prices. In UNITED STATES V. BUTLER (1936), over Justice Stone's vigorous dissent, six Justices, speaking through Justice Roberts and including Chief Justice Hughes, thought it unnecessary to determine whether this legislative scheme came within the ENUMERATED POWERS of Congress. The majority avoided this inquiry by concluding that the law intruded upon the area of production reserved to the states by the TENTH AMENDMENT, which reserves to the states or the people "the powers not delegated to the United States." The Court invoked the same theory a few months later in CARTER V. CARTER COAL COMPANY (1936) to invalidate the Guffey Act's regulation of wages, hours, and collective bargaining in the coal industry. Although the evidence submitted in a long trial proved indisputably the obvious fact that coal strikes could and did halt substantially all interstate commerce moving by rail, as most commerce then did, five Justices, speaking through Justice Sutherland, found decisive not the magnitude of an effect on interstate commerce but whether the effect was immediate, without an intervening causal factor. Even Chief Justice Hughes concurred to this extent, although not in other parts of the majority opinion. Only Justices Brandeis, Stone, and Cardozo challenged the reasoning of the majority.

The *Butler* and *Carter* cases made it plain—or so it seemed—that the Constitution as construed by the Court completely barred the federal government from endeavoring to resolve the national economic problems which called for control of intrastate transactions at the production or manufacturing stage. As an economic matter, individual states were unable to set standards for their own industries that were in competition with producers in other states. The result was that in the United States no government could take action deemed necessary to deal with such matters no matter how crippling their effect upon the national economy might be.

In early 1937 the same type of collective bargaining regulation which the *Carter* case had stricken for the coal industry was on its way to the Supreme Court in the first cases under the WAGNER (NATIONAL LABOR RELATIONS) ACT of 1935. That statute by its terms applied to unfair labor practices that burdened or obstructed interstate commerce or tended to lead to a labor dispute that had such an effect. The courts of appeals, following the *Carter* case, had held that the act could not constitutionally reach a steel manufacturing company, a trailer manufacturer, and a small clothing manufacturer.

Three days before the arguments in these cases in the Supreme Court were to commence, President Roosevelt, who had recently been reelected by a tremendous majority, announced a plan to add up to six new Justices to the Supreme Court, one for each Justice over seventy years of age, purportedly for the purpose of providing younger judges who could enable the Court to keep up with its workload. The Court and many others vigorously opposed the plan. Two months later, in the WAGNER ACT CASES (1937), Chief Justice Hughes and Justice Roberts joined Justices Brandeis, Stone, and Cardozo to sustain the applicability of the National Labor Relations Act to the three manufacturers. The evidence as to the effect of their labor disputes upon interstate commerce was obviously much weaker than that presented in the *Carter* case as to the entire bituminous coal industry. Within the next few months, Justices Van Devanter and Sutherland retired, to be succeeded by Senator HUGO L. BLACK and Solicitor General STANLEY F. REED, and the court-packing plan gradually withered away, even though for a long time President Roosevelt refused to abandon it. No one can be certain whether the plan influenced the Chief Justice and Justice Roberts, but many persons thought the facts spoke for themselves.

Chief Justice Hughes's opinion for the Court in NATIONAL LABOR RELATIONS BOARD V. JONES & LAUGHLIN STEEL CORP. (1937) flatly declared that practices in productive industry could have a sufficient effect upon interstate commerce to justify federal regulation under the commerce clause. The test was to be "practical," based on "actual experience." The reasoning of the *Carter* and *Butler* cases was repudiated, although the majority opinion did not say so.

In 1938 a revised AGRICULTURAL ADJUSTMENT ACT and a new FAIR LABOR STANDARDS ACT were enacted. Under the former, the secretary of agriculture, after obtaining the necessary approval of two-thirds of the tobacco growers in a referendum, prescribed marketing quotas determining the maximum quantity of tobacco each grower could sell. Although the practical effect was to limit what would be produced, the object was to stabilize prices by keeping an excessive supply off the market. In MULFORD V. SMITH (1939), the Court, speaking through Justice Roberts, found that because interstate and intrastate sales of tobacco were commingled at the auction warehouses where tobacco was sold, Congress clearly had power to limit the amount marketed by each farmer. HAMMER V. DAGENHART, UNITED STATES V. BUTLER, and the Tenth Amendment were mentioned only in the dissenting opinion of Justice McReynolds and Butler.

The Fair Labor Standards Act of 1938 in substance reenacted the minimum wage and maximum hour provision of the NIRA for employees engaged in interstate commerce or the production of goods for such commerce, and also forbade the shipment in interstate commerce of goods produced under the proscribed labor conditions. The minimum wage then prescribed was twenty-five cents per hour. The prevailing wage in the lumber industry in the South ranged from ten cents to twenty-seven and a half cents per hour, which made it difficult for employers paying more than the lowest amount to compete. A case involving a Georgia sawmill (UNITED STATES V. DARBY LUMBER COMPANY) came to the Supreme Court late in 1940, and was decided in early 1941 after Justice Butler had died and Justice McReynolds had retired. By that time Justices FELIX FRANKFURTER and WILLIAM O. DOUGLAS had replaced Cardozo and Brandeis, and Justice FRANK MURPHY had succeeded Butler.

The Supreme Court, speaking unanimously through Justice Stone, upheld the statute. The Court held that Congress had the power to exclude from interstate commerce goods that were not produced in accordance with prescribed standards, and to prescribe minimum wages and maximum hours for employees producing goods which would move in interstate commerce. Overruling HAMMER V. DAGENHART, the Court declared that the power of Congress to determine what restrictions should be imposed upon interstate commerce did not exclude regulations whose object was to control aspects of industrial production. The Court invoked the interpretation of the NECESSARY AND PROPER CLAUSE in MCCULLOCH V. MARYLAND (1819): the commerce power extended not merely to the regulation of interstate commerce but also "to those activities intrastate which so affect interstate commerce or the exercise of the power of Congress over it as to make regulation of them appropriate means to the attainment of a legitimate end, the exercise of the granted power of Congress to regulate interstate commerce." The emphasis was not on direct or indirect effects, a judge-made concept not tied to constitutional language, or even to the substantiality of an effect. The Court found it sufficient that the establishment of federal minimum labor standards was a reasonable means of suppressing interstate competition based on substandard labor conditions. In KIRSCHBAUM V. WALLING (1942) the Court broadly construed the commerce clause to make the Fair Labor Standards Act apply to service and maintenance employees who were not directly engaged in the production of goods for commerce but in the performance of services ancillary to such production.

A year and a half after *Darby*, in WICKARD V. FILBURN (1942), a unanimous Court, speaking through Justice ROBERT H. JACKSON, upheld marketing quotas under the amended Agricultural Adjustment Act, even though they limited the amount of wheat allowed to be consumed on the farm as well as the amount sold. The object was to reduce the supply of wheat in order to increase the price—and the total supply of wheat, including the twenty percent of the crop consumed on the farm for feed or seed, not only was in at least potential competition with wheat in commerce but had a substantial influence on prices and market conditions for the wheat crop throughout the nation. Reviewing the prior law, and explicitly noting the cases that were being disapproved—*E. C. Knight, Employers' Liability, Hammer v. Dagenhart, Railroad Retirement Board, Schechter,* and *Carter*—Justice Jackson's opinion laid to rest the prior controlling effect attributed to nomenclature such as "production" and "indirect," as distinct from the actual economic effect of an activity upon interstate commerce. Even if an "activity be local" and not itself commerce, "it may still, whatever its nature, be reached by Congress if it exerts a substantial economic effect on interstate commerce." The proper point of reference was "what was necessary and proper to the exercise by Congress of the granted power." The Court further declared, as it had in *Darby*, that the magnitude of the contribution of each individual to the EFFECT ON COMMERCE was not the criterion but the total contribution of persons similarly situated, which meant that the insignificant effect of the amount consumed on any particular farm was not decisive.

In 1944 and 1946, in cases holding that Congress could regulate the insurance industry and public utility holding companies (UNITED STATES V. SOUTHEASTERN UNDERWRITERS ASSOCIATION, 1944; *North American Co. v. Securities and Exchange Commission,* 1946), the Court broadly summarized the teachings of its prior cases beginning with the words of Chief Justice Marshall in *Gibbons v. Ogden:*

Commerce is interstate . . . when it "concerns more States than one.". . . The power granted is the power to legislate concerning transactions which, reaching across State boundaries, affect the people of more states than one;—to govern affairs which the individual states, with their limited territorial jurisdictions, are not fully capable of governing. This federal power to determine the rules of intercourse across state lines was essential to weld a loose confederacy into a single, indivisible Nation; its continued existence is equally essential to the welfare of that Nation.

Since these decisions there has been no doubt that Congress possesses full power to regulate all aspects of the integrated national economy. The few commerce clause cases of importance since that time concerned the use of the commerce power for noncommercial purposes: to combat racial SEGREGATION, crime, and environmental problems.

In *Katzenbach v. McClung* (1964) the Court sustained the provisions of the CIVIL RIGHTS ACT OF 1964 prohibiting RACIAL DISCRIMINATION by restaurants serving interstate travelers or obtaining a substantial portion of their food from outside the state, both because discrimination had a highly restrictive effect upon interstate travel by Negroes and because it reduced the amount of food moving in interstate commerce (which seems quite doubtful). (See also HEART OF ATLANTA MOTEL V. UNITED STATES, 1964.)

PEREZ V. UNITED STATES (1971) upheld the application of the federal loanshark statute to purely intrastate extortion on the ground that Congress had rationally found that organized crime was interstate in character, obtaining a substantial part of its income from loansharking which to a substantial extent was carried on in interstate and foreign commerce or through instrumentalities of such commerce. Unmentioned rationales might have been the difficulty of proving that loansharking in a particular case had an interstate connection and the belief that it was necessary to prohibit all loansharking as an appropriate means of prohibiting those acts that did affect interstate commerce.

In *Hodel v. Virginia Surface Mining and Reclamation Association* (1981) the Court unanimously upheld federal regulation of surface or strip coal mining operations, rejecting the contention that this was merely a regulation of land use not committed to the federal government. There had been legislative findings that surface coal mining causes water pollution and flooding of navigable streams and that it harms productive farm land and hardwood forests in many parts of the country. The Court found, following *Darby*, that this was a means of preventing destructive interstate competition favoring the producers with the lowest mining and reclamation standards, that Congress can regulate the conditions under which goods shipped in interstate commerce are produced when that in itself affects interstate commerce, and that the commerce power permits federal regulation of activities causing air or water pollution, or other environmental hazards that may have effects in more than one state.

The more recent decisions, which in some respects went far beyond the classical statements as to the modern scope of the commerce power in *Darby* and *Wickard v. Filburn,* were expected and accepted with little comment or concern. The country now appears to recognize that the national government should have and does have power under the commerce clause to deal with problems that do not limit themselves to individual states—as Chief Justice Marshall had declared in 1824, though doubtless with no idea of how far that principle would eventually be carried.

The enlargement of the commerce power since 1789 is attributable not to the predilections of judges but to such inventions as steamboats, railroads, motor vehicles, airplanes, the telegraph, telephone, radio, and television. When the nation was young, composed mainly of farms and small towns, there was little interstate trade, except by water or near state lines. Now persons and goods can cross the continent in less time than a traveler in 1789 would have taken to reach a town thirty miles away. Business and the economy have adjusted to these changes. Somewhat more slowly than the people and Congress, the Supreme Court has recognized that an integrated national economy is predominantly interstate or related to interstate commerce, and must be subject to governmental control on a national basis.

The expansion of the concept of interstate commerce and of the subjects which Congress can regulate under the commerce power was not accompanied by a contraction of the powers of the states. Only those state laws that discriminate against or unduly burden interstate commerce are forbidden.

ROBERT L. STERN

Bibliography

CORWIN, EDWARD S. 1959 *The Commerce Power versus States Rights.* Princeton, N.J.: Princeton University Press.

FRANKFURTER, FELIX 1937 *The Commerce Clause under Marshall, Taney and Waite.* Chapel Hill: University of North Carolina Press.

GAVIT, BERNARD C. 1932 *Commerce Clause of the United States Constitution.* Bloomington, Ind.: Principia Press.

STERN, ROBERT L. 1934 That Commerce Which Concerns More States Than One. *Harvard Law Review* 47:1335–1366.

—— 1946 The Commerce Clause and the National Economy, 1933–1946. *Harvard Law Review* 59:645–693, 883–947.

—— 1951 The Problems of Yesteryear—Commerce and Due Process. *Vanderbilt Law Review* 4:446–468.

—— 1955 The 1955 Ross Prize Essay: The Scope of the Phrase "Interstate Commerce." *American Bar Association Journal* 41:823–826, 871–874.

—— 1973 The Commerce Clause Revisited—The Federalization of Interstate Crime. *Arizona Law Review* 15:271–285.

COMMERCE COURT

In 1910 Congress established the Commerce Court, with the JURISDICTION, formerly held by the district courts and courts of appeals, to review decisions of the Interstate Commerce Commission (ICC). Although the ICC acquiesced in the establishment of the new court, acceptance soon turned to opposition. The Commerce Court reversed the ICC's decisions in a number of important cases, and congressional Democrats saw the court as a threat to the program of railroad regulation. Two 1912 bills to abolish the court were vetoed by President WILLIAM HOWARD TAFT. In 1913, a third abolition bill received President WOODROW WILSON's blessing.

The creation of specialized federal courts is often proposed but not often enacted. The short, unhappy life of the Commerce Court is regularly offered as a cautionary tale.

KENNETH L. KARST

Bibliography

DIX, GEORGE E. 1964 The Death of the Commerce Court: A Study in Institutional Weakness. *American Journal of Legal History* 8:238–260.

COMMERCIAL SPEECH

Until 1976 "commercial speech"—a vague category encompassing advertisements, invitations to deal, credit or financial reports, prospectuses, and the like—was subject to broad regulatory authority, with little or no protection from the FIRST AMENDMENT. The early decisions, epitomized by *Valentine v. Chrestensen* (1942), followed the then characteristic judicial approach of defining certain subject-matter categories of expression as wholly outside the scope of First Amendment protection. Under this TWO-LEVEL THEORY, a "definitional" mode of First Amendment adjudication, commercial speech was considered to be, along with FIGHTING WORDS, OBSCENITY, and LIBEL, outside First Amendment protection.

When facing combinations of unprotected commercial speech and protected political speech in subsequent cases, the Court made First Amendment protection turn on the primary purpose of the advertisement. Thus, in MURDOCK V. PENNSYLVANIA (1943), the Court struck down an ordinance requiring solicitors of orders for goods to get a license and pay a fee as it applied to Jehovah's Witnesses who sold religious pamphlets while seeking religious converts. On the other hand, in *Bread v. Alexandria* (1951) the Court held that a door-to-door salesman of national magazine subscriptions was subject to a town ordinance barring such sales techniques, because his primary purpose was to sell magazines rather than to disseminate ideas.

The "primary purpose" test unraveled in NEW YORK TIMES V. SULLIVAN (1964), more prominently known for another rejection of the definitional approaches in its holding that defamation is not beyond First Amendment protection. In *Sullivan*, the *New York Times* had printed an allegedly defamatory advertisement soliciting funds for civil rights workers. Although the advertisement's primary purpose was, arguably, to raise money, the Court held that it was protected by the First Amendment because it "communicated information, expressed opinion, recited grievances, protested claimed abuses, and sought financial support on behalf of a movement whose existence and objectives are matters of the highest public interest and concern."

Recent decisions have gone well beyond *Sullivan* and moved advertising and other commercial speech—political or not—within the protection of the First Amendment. In the leading case, VIRGINIA PHARMACY BOARD V. VIRGINIA CITIZENS CONSUMER COUNCIL (1976), the Court struck down a state ban on prescription drug price advertising. The Court rejected the state's "highly paternalistic approach," preferring a system in which "people will perceive their own best interests if only they are well enough informed, and that the best means to that end is to open the channels of communication rather than to close them." The Court cautioned, however, that because untruthful speech has never been protected for its own sake government may take effective action against false and misleading advertisements. And it indicated a greater scope for regulating false or misleading commercial speech than is permitted in relation to false political statements, such as defamations of public officials, because advertising is more easily verifiable and is less likely to be "chilled" by regulation because it is a commercial necessity.

Virginia Pharmacy Board fixed the principle that advertising may be controlled when it is false, misleading, or takes undue advantage of its audience; but the case left open the issue whether whole categories of commercial speech deemed inherently misleading or difficult to police can be suppressed. This issue divided the Supreme Court with respect to lawyers' advertising, when a narrow majority extended First Amendment protection to price advertising of routine legal services, rejecting the dissenters' claim that the complex and variegated nature of legal services gave lawyers' advertising a high potential for deception and impeded effective regulation of particular deceptions. However, the Court held that "ambulance chasing"—in-person solicitation of accident victims for pecuniary gain—could be barred entirely because of its potential for deception and overbearing.

Where regulation of commercial expression is not directed at potential deception but intended to advance other interests such as aesthetics or conservation, the Supreme Court has followed a relatively permissive approach to state regulatory interests, while becoming hopelessly fragmented about the First Amendment principles that ought to govern. Thus, in METROMEDIA, INC. V. SAN DIEGO (1981) a shifting majority coalition of Justices made clear that commercial billboards could be entirely banned in a city for aesthetic or traffic safety reasons. Recent decisions, following CENTRAL HUDSON GAS & PUBLIC SERVICE COMMISSION (1980), have fashioned a four-part test to appraise the validity of restrictions on commercial speech. Protection will not be extended to commercial speech that is, on the whole, misleading or that encourages unlawful activity. Even protected commercial speech may be regulated if the state has a substantial interest, if the regulation directly advances that interest, and if the regulation is no broader than necessary to effectuate the state's interest. The elastic properties of this four-part test in actual application have generated considerable disarray within the Supreme Court.

The commercial speech decisions of the BURGER COURT have made clear that freedom of expression principles extend beyond political and religious expression, protecting not only the MARKETPLACE OF IDEAS but expression in the marketplace itself. Second, in affirming relatively broad regulatory power over commercial speech, even though it is deemed to be protected by the First Amendment, the Court has reinforced the notion that the First Amendment extends different levels of protection to different types of speech. The commercial speech decisions thus lend support to Justice ROBERT H. JACKSON's OBITER DICTUM in KOVACS V. COOPER (1949) that under the First Amendment each type and medium of expression "is a law unto itself."

BENNO C. SCHMIDT, JR.

Bibliography

JACKSON, THOMAS H. and JEFFRIES, J. C., JR. 1979 Commercial Speech: Economic Due Process and the First Amendment. *Virginia Law Review* 65:1–41.
WEINBERG, JONATHAN 1982 Constitutional Protection of Commercial Speech. *Columbia Law Review* 82:720–750.

COMMITTEE FOR PUBLIC EDUCATION AND RELIGIOUS LIBERTY v. NYQUIST
413 U.S. 752 (1973)
SLOAN v. LEMON
413 U.S. 825 (1973)

These cases, said Justice LEWIS F. POWELL in his opinion for a 6–3 SUPREME COURT, "involve an intertwining of societal and constitutional issues of the greatest importance." After LEMON V. KURTZMAN (1971), New York State sought to aid private sectarian schools and the parents of children in them by various financial plans purporting to maintain the SEPARATION OF CHURCH AND STATE. Avowing concern for the health and safety of the children, the state provided direct financial grants to "qualifying" schools for maintenance costs. But as Justice Powell observed, "virtually all" were Roman Catholic schools, and the grants had the inevitable effect of subsidizing religious education, thus abridging the FIRST AMENDMENT's prohibition against an ESTABLISHMENT OF RELIGION. New York, as well as Pennsylvania, also provided for the reimbursement of tuition paid by parents who sent their children to nonpublic sectarian schools; New York also had an optional tax relief plan. The Court found that the reimbursement plans constituted grants whose effect was the same as grants made directly to the institutions, thereby advancing religion. The tax benefit plan had the same unconstitutional result, because the deduction, like the grant, involved an expense to the state for the purpose of religious education. The Court distinguished outright tax exemptions of church property for reasons given in WALZ V. TAX COMMISSION (1970). By distinguishing *Nyquist* in MUELLER V. ALLEN (1983), the Court sustained the constitutionality of a tax benefit plan that aided the parents of children in nonpublic sectarian schools.

LEONARD W. LEVY

COMMITTEE FOR PUBLIC EDUCATION AND RELIGIOUS LIBERTY v. REGAN
444 U.S. 646 (1980)

A New York statute directed the reimbursement to nonpublic schools of costs incurred by them in complying with certain state-mandated requirements, including the administration of standardized tests. The participation of church-related schools in this program was challenged as an unconstitutional ESTABLISH-MENT OF RELIGION, but the Supreme Court rejected the challenge.

Justice BYRON R. WHITE, writing for a narrowly divided Court, noted that a previous New York law authorizing reimbursement for test services performed by nonpublic schools had been found unconstitutional in *Levitt v. Committee* (1973). However, the new statute, unlike its predecessor, provided for state audit of school financial records to insure that public monies were used only for secular purposes.

Justice HARRY BLACKMUN, with whom Justices WILLIAM J. BRENNAN and THURGOOD MARSHALL joined, dissented. Blackmun stressed that New York's program involved direct payments by the state to a school engaged in a religious enterprise. Justice JOHN PAUL STEVENS also filed a brief dissent.

Committee v. Regan is another illustration of the blurred nature of the line the Court has attempted to draw between permissible and impermissible state support to church-related schools.

RICHARD E. MORGAN

COMMON LAW
(Anglo-American)

The common law is a system of principles and rules grounded in universal custom or natural law and developed, articulated, and applied by courts in a process designed for the resolution of individual controversies. In this general sense, the common law is the historic basis of all Anglo-American legal systems. It is also an important element in the origin and plan of the United States Constitution.

Though sometimes characterized as "unwritten" in reference to their ultimate source, the principles and rules of the Anglo-American common law are in fact found in thousands of volumes of written judicial opinions reporting the grounds of decision in countless individual cases adjudicated over the course of centuries. The process that produced this body of law has three important aspects. First, common law principles and rules derive their legitimacy from the adversary process of litigation. They are valid only if they are HOLDINGS, that is, propositions necessary to the resolution of actual controversies. Second, the common law is applied through a characteristic reasoning process that compares the facts of the present case to the facts of earlier cases. The holdings of those earlier cases are PRECEDENTS, which must be followed unless their facts can be distinguished or unless they

can be overruled because their grounds are deemed unsound in light of changing social conditions or policy. In the latter situation, or if no existing precedent is applicable, a new rule may be fashioned from the logic of related rules or underlying principle. Third, the common law is a process in the procedural sense. Litigation is governed by rules designed to shape issues of fact and law so that a case may be fairly and efficiently presented to and decided by the jury, the traditional mode of trial.

The principles and rules of the common law grow and change within this threefold process at the initiative of parties to litigation as they bring forward issues falling outside, or challenging, existing precedents. The common law may also be changed by legislative enactment, but in Anglo-American countries legislation is relied on chiefly to supplement or revise or codify the common law in specific situations.

The Anglo-American common law evolved from decisions of the three great English courts of King's Bench, Common Pleas, and Exchequer, which were firmly established by the end of the thirteenth century. These courts, though created under the royal prerogative, became effectively independent by virtue of their ancient origins and the prestige and life tenure of their judges.

By the time of the American Revolution, two strands were apparent in the English common law. The private law, which developed in actions between subjects, included complex DOCTRINES of property, contract, and tort appropriate to a sophisticated landed and commercial society. The public law, product of actions in which the king was a litigant, consisted of rules defining and limiting his political and fiscal prerogatives, defining criminal conduct as a reflection of his role as peacekeeper, and establishing a series of procedural rights accorded to the criminally accused. In the largely unwritten English constitution, Parliament as supreme sovereign had power to alter or abolish even the most fundamental common law rules, but by convention basic governmental institutions and individual rights were ordinarily beyond legislative change.

The English common law had by 1776 been received in the American colonies. The full array of English law books was the source of common law principles and rules, and the courts followed the common law process. Though the colonists argued otherwise, the English view was that colonial reception of the common law was a matter of grace, not right. In legal theory, the colonies, as the king's dominions, were directly governed by the prerogative, free of common law constraints. Colonial governmental powers were expressly granted and defined by charter or statute. King and Parliament, when England's interests demanded, would set aside rights guaranteed by the common law. As the DECLARATION OF INDEPENDENCE shows, the Revolution was in part fought to rectify violations of charter grants of legislative and judicial power and invasions of individual rights such as TRIAL BY JURY and freedom from unreasonable SEARCH AND SEIZURE.

In reaction to the prerevolutionary experience, the people of the United States asserted SOVEREIGNTY through the federal and state constitutions, under which the executive, legislative, and judiciary were separate branches subject to the written FUNDAMENTAL LAW. The constitutions, however, were adopted against a common law backdrop. The states had expressly received the common law, assuming that their courts would develop it through application of the common law process. The federal Constitution contained no express reception provision, but it did authorize Congress to establish federal courts with JURISDICTION over cases arising under federal law and between citizens of diverse citizenship. Once the federal courts were established, important and difficult questions arose concerning their power to develop a FEDERAL COMMON LAW.

The result of two centuries of learned disputation is that today there is little federal common law. The Supreme Court in ERIE RAILROAD V. TOMPKINS (1938) settled the most enduring controversy by holding that in diversity-of-citizenship cases federal courts must apply the common law as though they were courts of the states where they sit, overruling Justice JOSEPH STORY's famous contrary decision in SWIFT V. TYSON (1842). Earlier the Court had concluded, as DUE PROCESS might have required, that there was no FEDERAL COMMON LAW OF CRIMES, even where federal interests were involved. In civil matters affecting federal interests the Court has held that there is no general federal common law, but the federal courts may articulate common law rules to supplement a comprehensive federal statutory scheme or implement an EXCLUSIVE JURISDICTION. These results are consistent with the basic premise of FEDERALISM that the national government is one of limited powers and other powers are reserved to the states, or to the people.

While the federal Constitution did not adopt the common law as a general rule of decision, many of its specific provisions were of common law origin. In its delineation of the SEPARATION OF POWERS, the Constitution incorporated common law limitations upon the prerogative and Parliament which had been honored in England and disregarded in the colonies. The BILL OF RIGHTS, adopted in part because of doubts about the existence and efficacy of a federal common law, codified specific common law procedural rights accorded the criminally accused. It also incorporated common law protections of more fundamental interests, including that basic guarantee of reason and fairness in governmental action, the right to due process of law.

Most important, the common law process has enabled the federal judiciary to attain its intended position in the constitutional plan. Chief Justice JOHN MARSHALL's opinion in MARBURY V. MADISON (1803), asserting judicial power to review legislation and declare it unconstitutional, was founded on the common law obligation of courts to apply all the relevant law, including the Constitution, in deciding cases. A declaration of unconstitutionality in one case is effective in other similar situations because of the force of precedent. In refining *Marbury*'s principle, the Supreme Court more recently has developed the doctrine of JUSTICIABILITY, designed to establish in constitutional cases the existence of a truly adversary CASE OR CONTROVERSY, to which decision of a constitutional issue is necessary. Together, these rules, by proclaiming that the federal courts are confined to the traditional common law judicial role, provide both legitimacy and effectiveness to court enforcement of the Constitution's limits upon the powers of the other branches and the states.

L. KINVIN WROTH

Bibliography

GOEBEL, JULIUS, JR. 1971 *Antecedents and Beginnings to 1801.* Volume 1 of *The Oliver Wendell Holmes Devise History of the Supreme Court of the United States.* New York: Macmillan.
LLEWELLYN, KARL N. 1960 *The Common Law Tradition: Deciding Appeals.* Boston: Little, Brown.
PLUCKNETT, THEODORE F. T. (1929)1956 *A Concise History of the Common Law.* Boston: Little, Brown.
TRIBE, LAURENCE H. 1978 *American Constitutional Law.* Mineola, N.Y.: Foundation Press.

COMMON LAW, CONSTITUTIONAL

See: Constitutional Common Law

COMMON LAW, FEDERAL CIVIL

See: Federal Common Law, Civil

COMMON LAW, FEDERAL CRIMINAL

See: Federal Common Law of Crimes

COMMONWEALTH v. ALGER

See: State Police Power

COMMONWEALTH v. AVES
18 Pickering (Mass.) 193 (1836)

This became the nation's leading case on sojourner slaves. It posed an unprecedented question: can a slave brought temporarily into a free state be restrained of liberty and be removed from the state on the master's return? Chief Justice LEMUEL SHAW rejected the contention that COMITY between the states compelled recognition of the laws of the master's domicile. SLAVERY, Shaw replied, was so odious that only positive local law recognized it. (See SOMERSET'S CASE, 1772.) In Massachusetts slavery was unconstitutional. Any nonfugitive slave entering Massachusetts became free because no local law warranted restraint and local laws could prevent involuntary removal.

LEONARD W. LEVY

COMMONWEALTH v. CATON
4 Call's (Va.) Reports (1782)

Decided by the highest court of Virginia in 1782, this case is a disputed precedent for the legitimacy of JUDICIAL REVIEW. The state constitution of 1776, which did not empower courts to void enactments in conflict with the constitution, authorized the governor to grant pardons except in impeachment cases. A statute on TREASON deprived the governor of his PARDONING POWER and vested it in the general assembly. Caton, having been sentenced to death for treason, claimed a pardon granted by the lower house, though the upper house refused to concur. The court had only to rule that the pardon was not valid.

Call's unreliable report of the case, a reconstruction made in 1827, indicates that the court considered the constitutionality of the statute on treason and that seven of the eight judges were of the opinion that the court had the power to declare an act of the legislature unconstitutional, though the court unanimously held the act constitutional. In fact, only one of the eight judges ruled the act unconstitutional, one held that it had no power to so rule, and another, GEORGE WYTHE, declared that the court had the power but need not exercise it in this case; he decided that the pardon had no force of law because it was not in conformity with the disputed act, which he found constitutional. A majority of the court, including Chief Justice EDMUND PENDLETON and Chancellor JOHN BLAIR, declined to decide the question whether they had the power to declare an act unconstitutional. Writing to JAMES MADISON a week later, Pendleton reported, "The great Constitutional question . . . was determined . . . by 6 Judges against two, that the Treason Act was not at variance with the Constitution but a proper exercise of the Power reserved to the Legislature by the latter. . . ." Both houses subsequently granted the pardon. The legitimacy of the case as a precedent for judicial review is doubtful.

LEONARD W. LEVY

COMMONWEALTH v. JENNISON
(Massachusetts, 1783, Unreported)

In 1781 Quock Walker, a Massachusetts slave, left his master, Nathaniel Jennison, to work as a hired laborer for Seth and John Caldwell. Jennison went to the Caldwell farm, seized Walker, beat him severely, and brought him home where he was locked up.

Three legal cases resulted from this event. In *Walker v. Jennison* (1781) Walker sued his former master for assault and battery. A jury ruled Walker was a free man and awarded him fifty pounds in damages. Jennison then successfully sued the Caldwells for twenty-five pounds for enticing away his "slave property." This decision was overturned by a jury in *Caldwell v. Jennison* (1781). Here attorney LEVI LINCOLN paraphrased arguments from SOMERSET V. STEWART (1772) in a stirring speech against slavery. In 1783 Jennison was convicted under a criminal INDICTMENT for assault and battery against Walker (*Commonwealth v. Jennison*). Chief Justice WILLIAM CUSHING charged the jury that the Massachusetts Constitution of 1780 abolished slavery by declaring "All men are born free and equal. . . ." Although some blacks were held as slaves after these cases, the litigation, known collectively as the "Quock Walker Cases," was instrumental in ending the peculiar institution in Massachusetts.

PAUL FINKELMAN

Bibliography

FINKELMAN, PAUL 1981 *An Imperfect Union: Slavery, Federalism, and Comity.* Chapel Hill: University of North Carolina Press.

COMMONWEALTH v. SACCO AND VANZETTI
(Massachusetts, 1921)

On August 23, 1927, the Commonwealth of Massachusetts electrocuted two Italian immigrants, Nicola Sacco and Bartolomeo Vanzetti, for the crimes of armed robbery and murder. The executions stirred angry protest in the United States and throughout the world by millions of people who believed that the two men had been denied a fair trial because of their ethnic background and political opinions.

Sacco and Vanzetti, ALIENS and anarchists who had fled to Mexico to avoid the draft during World War I, were arrested in 1920 and quickly brought to trial in Dedham, Massachusetts, for the murder of a paymaster and a guard during the robbery of a shoe factory. The trial took place at the end of the postwar Red Scare in a political atmosphere charged with hysteria against foreigners and radicals. Although the ballistics evidence was inconclusive and many witnesses, most of them Italian, placed the two men elsewhere at the time of the robbery, the jury returned guilty verdicts after listening to patriotic harangues from the chief prosecutor, Frederick Katzmann, and the trial judge, Webster Bradley Thayer.

During his cross-examination of the two defendants, Katzmann constantly emphasized their unorthodox political views and their flight to Mexico during the war. Thayer tolerated a broad range of political questions, mocked the two men's anarchism, and urged the members of the jury to act as "true soldiers . . . in the spirit of supreme American loyalty."

A diverse coalition of Bay State aristocrats, law professors such as FELIX FRANKFURTER, Italian radicals, and New York intellectuals attempted to secure a new trial for the condemned men during the next seven years. They marshaled an impressive amount of evidence pointing to Thayer's prejudice, the doubts of key prosecution witnesses, and the possibility that the crime had been committed by a gang of professional outlaws. The Massachusetts Supreme Judicial Court, however, relying on principles of trial court discretion that made it virtually impossible to challenge any of Thayer's rulings, spurned these appeals and refused to disturb either the verdict or the death sentences. A similar conclusion was reached by a special commission appointed by Governor Alvan T. Fuller and headed by Harvard University president A. Lawrence Lowell.

Last-minute efforts to secure a stay of execution from federal judges, including Supreme Court Justices OLIVER WENDELL HOLMES and LOUIS D. BRANDEIS, also proved unavailing. Attorneys for Sacco and Vanzetti argued that because of Thayer's hostility their clients had been denied a FAIR TRIAL guaranteed by the DUE PROCESS clause of the FOURTEENTH AMENDMENT. But with the exception of MOORE v. DEMPSEY (1923), where a state murder trial had been intimidated by a mob, the Supreme Court had shown great reluctance to intervene in local criminal proceedings. "I cannot think that prejudice on the part of a presiding judge however strong would deprive the Court of jurisdiction," wrote Holmes, "and in my opinion nothing short of a want of legal power to decide the case authorizes me to interfere. . . ." Whether Sacco and Vanzetti received a fair trial is questionable; however, Francis Russell has shown how illusory is the old contention that they were wholly innocent.

MICHAEL E. PARRISH

Bibliography

JOUGHN, G. LOUIS and MORGAN, EDMUND M. 1948 *The Legacy of Sacco and Vanzetti.* New York: Harcourt, Brace.

RUSSELL, FRANCIS 1962 *Tragedy in Dedham: The Story of the Sacco-Vanzetti Case.* New York: Harper & Row.

COMMONWEALTH STATUS

Commonwealths are TERRITORIES in free association with the United States, enjoying virtual autonomy in internal affairs but subject to the United States in foreign and defense matters. Citizens of commonwealths are citizens of the United States: they pay federal taxes and may move freely to, from, and within the United States. Public officials are elected by the people of the commonwealths and neither the officials nor their acts require approval by the President or Congress. Constitutional limitations on state legislation are applicable to commonwealth legislation; and APPEAL lies from the highest court of a commonwealth to the Supreme Court of the United States. When Congress established commonwealth status for the Philippines in 1934 it intended an interim state en route to independence, but commonwealth status has become a practically permanent condition for PUERTO RICO and the Northern Marianas.

The basis of the commonwealth relationship is a "covenant" between the American people and the people of the territory. Since Congress's authority to ratify the covenant derives from its plenary power over territories (Article IV, section 3, clause 2), most legal authorities maintain that Congress could repeal the covenant and impose direct rule. But any attempt to do so would constitute a grievous breach of faith and would excite overwhelming domestic and international political opposition.

DENNIS J. MAHONEY

COMMUNICATIONS ACT
48 Stat. 1064 (1934)

The Communications Act of 1934, enacted under Congress's COMMERCE POWER, provides the statutory basis for federal regulation of BROADCASTING and electronic communication. The act describes the electromagnetic spectrum as a national resource and permits private parties to use portions of it only as trustees in the public interest. To administer its provisions the act established the seven-member Federal Communications Commission (FCC), authorizing it to make regulations with the force of law and to issue licenses to broadcasters that may be granted, renewed, or revoked in accordance with "public interest, convenience, and necessity." Under the authority of the act the FCC has promulgated the FAIRNESS DOCTRINE, requiring broadcasters to provide equal time for replies to controversial messages, as well as regulations to prohibit the broadcasting of OBSCENITY.

The act was based on both technological and ideological considerations. The assumption that broadcasting channels are extremely limited has been disproved by improvements in technology; however, the ideological bias in favor of public ownership and regulation has not yet been overcome. Because of the Supreme Court's deference to Congress's findings of LEGISLATIVE FACT regarding the scarcity of broadcasting channels, as embodied in the Communications Act, in the face of the manifest reality that such channels are far more numerous than, for example, presses capable of producing a major metropolitan newspaper or an encyclopedia, the protection afforded broadcasters' FREEDOM OF SPEECH and FREEDOM OF THE PRESS is significantly reduced.

DENNIS J. MAHONEY

COMMUNIST CONTROL ACT
68 Stat. 775 (1954)

This measure marked the culmination of the United States government's program to prevent subversion from within during the loyalty-security years. Conservative senators, eager to facilitate removal of communists from positions of union leadership, and Senator HUBERT H. HUMPHREY, tired of hearing liberals smeared as "soft on communism," pushed the measure through Congress with large majorities in each chamber. Clearly tied to the 1954 elections, the act outlawed the Communist party as an instrumentality conspiring to overthrow the United States government. The bill as initially drafted made party membership a crime. Responding to criticism of the DWIGHT D. EISENHOWER administration that the membership clause would make the provisions of the 1950 INTERNAL SECURITY ACT unconstitutional, because compulsory registration would violate the RIGHT AGAINST SELF-INCRIMINATION, the bill's sponsors removed its membership clause. However, Congress deprived the Communist party of all "rights, privileges, and immunities attendant upon legal bodies created under the jurisdiction of the laws of the United States or any political subdivision thereof." The act added a new category of groups required to register—"communist-infiltrated" organizations. These, like communist and "front" organizations, although outlawed, were expected to register with the SUBVERSIVE ACTIVITIES CONTROL BOARD.

The measure, virtually inoperative from the beginning, raised grave constitutional questions under the FIRST AMENDMENT, the Fifth Amendment, and the ban against BILLS OF ATTAINDER. The Justice Department ignored it and pushed no general test of its provisions in the court. The act summarized well the official policy toward the Communist party at the time—to keep it legal enough for successful prosecution of its illegalities.

PAUL L. MURPHY

Bibliography
AUERBACH, CARL 1956 The Communist Control Act of 1954. *University of Chicago Law Review* 23:173–220.

COMMUNIST PARTY

See: Subversive Activities and the Constitution

COMMUNIST PARTY OF THE UNITED STATES v. SUBVERSIVE ACTIVITIES CONTROL BOARD
367 U.S. 1 (1961)

The Supreme Court upheld application to the Communist party of provisions of the Subversive Activities Control Act requiring "any organization . . . substantially controlled by the foreign government . . . controlling the world Communist movement" to register with the Board, providing lists of officers and members. The Court postponed considering self-incrimination objections, held that where an individual might escape regulation merely by ceasing to engage in the regulated activity no BILL OF ATTAINDER existed, and deferred to the congressional balance between national security and the FREEDOM OF ASSOCIATION arguing that any inhibition on communists' associational freedom caused by exposure was incidental to regulation of their activities on behalf of foreign governments.

MARTIN SHAPIRO

COMPACT THEORY

See: Social Compact Theory; Theories of the Union

COMPANION CASE

Cases decided by the Supreme Court on the same day are called companion cases when they involve the same issues or issues that are closely related. Sometimes a single opinion is used to explain two or more companion cases, and sometimes separate opinions are written. Occasionally a Justice writing for the Court will select the strongest of a group of companion cases for explanation in a full opinion, leaving the weaker cases to be discussed only briefly, with heavy reliance on the conclusions in the full opinion.

KENNETH L. KARST

COMPELLING STATE INTEREST

When the Supreme Court concludes that STRICT SCRUTINY is the appropriate STANDARD OF REVIEW, it often expresses its searching examination of the justification of legislation in a formula: the law is invalid unless it is necessary to achieve a "compelling state interest." The inquiry thus touches not only legislative means but also legislative purposes.

Even the permissive RATIONAL BASIS standard of review demands that legislative ends be legitimate. To say that a governmental purpose must be one of compelling importance is plainly to demand more. How much more, however, is something the Court has been unable to say. What we do know is that, once "strict scrutiny" is invoked, only rarely does a law escape invalidation.

Any judicial examination of the importance of a governmental objective implies that a court is weighing interests, engaging in a kind of cost-benefit analysis as a prelude to deciding on the constitutionality of legislation. Yet one would be mistaken to assume that the inquiry follows such a neat, linear, two-stage progression. Given the close correlation between employing the "strict scrutiny" standard and invalidating laws, the very word "scrutiny" may be misleading. A court that has embarked on a search for compelling state interests very likely knows how it intends to decide.

In many a case a court does find a legislative purpose of compelling importance. That is not the end of the "strict scrutiny" inquiry; there remains the question whether the law is necessary to achieve that end. If, for example, there is another way the legislature might have accomplished its purpose, without imposing so great a burden on the constitutionally protected interest in liberty or equality, the availability of that LEAST RESTRICTIVE MEANS negates the necessity for the legislature's choice. The meaning of "strict scrutiny" is that even a compelling state interest must be pursued by means that give constitutional values their maximum protection.

The phrase "compelling state interest" originated in Justice FELIX FRANKFURTER's concurring opinion in *Sweezy v. New Hampshire* (1957), a case involving the privacy of political association: "For a citizen to be made to forego even a part of so basic a liberty as his political autonomy, the subordinating interest of the State must be compelling." The Supreme Court uses some variation on this formula not only in FIRST AMENDMENT cases but also in cases calling for "strict scrutiny" under the EQUAL PROTECTION clause or under the revived forms of SUBSTANTIVE DUE PROCESS. The formula, in short, is much used and little explained. The Court is unable to define "compelling state interest" but knows when it does not see it.

KENNETH L. KARST

Bibliography

TRIBE, LAURENCE H. 1978 *American Constitutional Law.* Pages 1000–1002. Mineola, N.Y.: Foundation Press.

COMPETITIVE FEDERALISM

This is a term often used in analysis of constitutional DOCTRINE or working governmental practice. Competitive federalism is closely related to DUAL FEDERALISM, and in contrast with COOPERATIVE FEDERALISM stresses the conflict between the national government and the states.

HARRY N. SCHEIBER

COMPROMISE OF 1850

The Compromise of 1850 comprised a related series of statutes enacted by Congress in an attempt to settle sectional disputes related to SLAVERY that had flared since 1846, with the outbreak of the Mexican War and the introduction of the WILMOT PROVISO. After California's 1849 demand for admission as a free state and the concurrent appearance of southern disunionist sentiment, what had begun as a contest over the constitutional status of SLAVERY IN THE TERRITORIES absorbed other issues related to the security of slavery in the extant states and expanded into a crisis of the Union.

From proposals submitted by President Zachary Taylor and Senator HENRY CLAY, Senator STEPHEN A. DOUGLAS marshaled measures through Congress that admitted California as a free state; established the Texas-New Mexico boundary and compensated Texas and holders of Texas securities for territory claimed by Texas but awarded to New Mexico; abolished the slave trade in the DISTRICT OF COLUMBIA (but Congress rejected a proposal to abolish slavery itself there); amended the Fugitive Slave Act of 1793 by the drastic new measure known as the Fugitive Slave Act of 1850; and created Utah and New Mexico Territories. (See FUGITIVE SLAVERY.)

Both major parties hailed the Compromise as a final settlement of all problems relating to slavery. Southern disunion sentiment abated, while the Free Soil coalition, which had made a respectable beginning in the 1848 election, began to disintegrate. FRANKLIN PIERCE was elected President in 1852 on a platform extolling the finality of the Compromise and condemning any further agitation of the slavery issue.

But the territorial and fugitive-slave measures only extended and inflamed the slavery controversy. The New Mexico and Utah acts were couched in ambiguous language that left the status of slavery in those two immense territories unsettled, though Congress did decisively reject the Free Soil solution embodied in the Wilmot Proviso of 1846. The acts also contained sections providing for APPEAL of slavery controversies from the TERRITORIAL COURTS directly to the United States Supreme Court, an effort to resolve a politically insoluble problem by nonpolitical means.

The Fugitive Slave Act of 1850 was a harsh and provocative measure that virtually legitimated the kidnapping of free blacks. It thrust the federal presence into northern communities in obtrusive ways by potentially forcing any adult northern male to serve on slave-catching posses, by creating new pseudo-judicial officers encouraged by the fee structure to issue certificates of rendition, and by authorizing use of federal military force to enforce the act. It was therefore widely unpopular in the northern states. Subsequent recaptures, renditions, and rescues provided numerous real-life counterparts to the fictional drama of *Uncle Tom's Cabin.*

The finality supposedly achieved by the Compromise of 1850 was shattered by the controversy over the KANSAS-NEBRASKA ACT of 1854. But as ALEXANDER STEPHENS noted back in 1850, "the present adjustment may be made, but the great question of the permanence of slavery in the Southern states will be far from being settled thereby."

WILLIAM M. WIECEK

Bibliography
POTTER, DAVID M. 1976 *The Impending Crisis, 1848–1861.* New York: Harper & Row.

COMPROMISE OF 1877

Four of the sectional compromises in nineteenth-century America were efforts to settle quarrels by mutual concessions and forestall danger of violence. Three of the four efforts were temporarily successful, and only the fourth, that of 1861, broke down in failure. For the next sixteen years, during the Civil War and Reconstruction, differences were resolved by resort to force. The Compromise of 1877 differed from the earlier ones in several ways, one of them being that its main purpose was to foreclose rather than to forestall resort to armed force. Since the Republican party was committed to force when necessary to protect freedmen's rights under the constitutional amendments and CIVIL RIGHTS acts of the Reconstruction period, any repudiation of such commitments had to be negotiated discreetly.

Under President ANDREW JOHNSON and President ULYSSES S. GRANT, the government had been backing away from enforcement of freedmen's rights almost from the start. In part the result of white resistance in the South, this retreat from Reconstruction was also a consequence of the prevalence of white-supremacy sentiment in the North. In the elections of

1874, regarded by some as a referendum on Reconstruction, the Republican House majority of 110 was replaced by a Democratic majority of sixty. And in the ensuing presidential election of 1876 the Democratic candidate, Samuel J. Tilden, won a majority of the popular votes and was conceded 184 of the 185 electoral votes required for election. He also claimed all the nineteen contested votes of South Carolina, Florida, and Louisiana, the only southern states remaining under Republican control. But so did his Republican opponent, Rutherford B. Hayes, who also claimed the election. The impasse was solved by an agreement between the two political parties (not the sections) to create a bipartisan electoral commission of fifteen to count the votes. An unanticipated last minute change of one member of the commission gave the Republicans a majority of one, and by that majority they counted all contested votes for Hayes. That eliminated Tilden, but to seat Hayes required formal action of the House. The Democratic majority, enraged over what they regarded as a "conspiracy" to rob them of their victory, talked wildly of resistance and started a filibuster.

Foreseeing the victory of Hayes, southern Democrats sought to salvage whatever they could out of defeat. Their prime objective was "home rule," which meant not only withdrawal of troops that sustained Republican rule in South Carolina and Louisiana but also a firm Republican commitment to abandon use of force in the future for defending rights of freedmen, carpetbaggers, and scalawags. This amounted to the virtual nullification of the FOURTEENTH and FIFTEENTH AMENDMENTS and the CIVIL RIGHTS ACT. In return southern conservatives promised to help confirm Hayes's election, and many Democrats of the old Whig persuasion promised to cooperate with the new administration, but not to defect to the Republican party unless it abandoned "radicalism."

With control of the army and the submission of enough northern Democrats, Republicans could have seated Hayes anyway. But the southerners exploited Republican fears of resistance and skillfully played what they later admitted was "a bluff game." An old Whig himself, Hayes fell in with the idea of reconstituting his party in the South under conservative white leaders in place of carpetbaggers. He not only pledged "home rule" but promised to appoint a conservative southern Democrat to his cabinet and sweetened his appeal to that constituency by publicly pledging generous support to bills for subsidizing "INTERNAL IMPROVEMENTS of a national character" in the South. Hayes's election was confirmed only two days before he took office.

As in earlier sectional compromises, not all the terms of that of 1877 were fulfilled, but the main ones were. Hayes appointed a southern Democrat his postmaster general, chief dispenser of patronage, and placed many other white conservatives in southern offices. Bills for federal subsidies to internal improvements met with more success than ever before. The troops sustaining Republican rule in the two states were removed and Democrats immediately took over. In the CIVIL RIGHTS CASES (1883) the Supreme Court erected the STATE ACTION barrier, severely limiting the reach of the Fourteenth Amendment. The Court's opinion was written by Justice JOSEPH P. BRADLEY, who had been a member of the 1877 electoral commission. More important than all this was the pledge against resort to force to protect black rights. That commitment held firm for eighty years, until the military intervention at Little Rock, Arkansas, in 1957. This set a record for durability among sectional compromises.

C. VANN WOODWARD

Bibliography

GILLETTE, WILLIAM 1980 *Retreat from Reconstruction, 1869–1879.* Baton Rouge: Louisiana State University Press.

POLAKOFF, KEITH J. 1973 *The Politics of Inertia: The Election of 1876 and the End of Reconstruction.* Baton Rouge: Louisiana State University Press.

WOODWARD, C. VANN 1966 *Reunion and Reaction: The Compromise of 1877 and the End of Reconstruction.* Boston: Little, Brown.

COMPULSORY PROCESS, RIGHT TO

The first state to adopt a constitution following the Declaration of Independence (New Jersey, 1776) guaranteed all criminal defendants the same "privileges of witnesses" as their prosecutors. Fifteen years later, in enumerating the constitutional rights of accused persons, the framers of the federal BILL OF RIGHTS bifurcated what New Jersey called the "privileges of witnesses" into two distinct but related rights: the Sixth Amendment right of the accused "to be confronted with the witnesses against him," and his companion Sixth Amendment right to "compulsory process for obtaining witnesses in his favor." The distinction between witnesses "against" the accused and witnesses "in his favor" turns on which of the parties—the prosecution or the defense—offers the witness's statements in evidence as a formal part of its case. The CONFRONTATION clause establishes the government's obligations regarding the production and examination of witnesses whose statements the prosecution puts into evidence either in its case in chief or in rebuttal. The compulsory process clause establishes the government's obligations regarding the production and examination of witnesses whose statements the defendant seeks to put into evidence in his respective case.

The constitutional questions of compulsory process are twofold: What is "compulsory process?" Who are the "witnesses in his favor" for whom a defendant is entitled to compulsory process? The first is the easier of the two questions to answer. "Compulsory process" is a term of art used to denominate the state's coercive devices for locating, producing, and compelling evidence from witnesses. A common example is the SUB-POENA *ad testificandum,* a judicial order to a person to appear and testify as a witness, or suffer penalty of CONTEMPT for failing to do so. The right of compulsory process, in turn, is the right of a defendant to invoke such coercive devices at the state's disposal to obtain evidence in his defense. The right of compulsory process is therefore no guarantee that defendants will succeed in locating, producing, or compelling witnesses to testify in their favor; it does not entitle defendants to the testimony of witnesses who have died or otherwise become unavailable to testify through no fault of the state. Rather, it assures defendants that the state will make reasonable, good-faith efforts to produce such requested witnesses as are available to testify at trial. It gives a defendant access to the same range of official devices for producing available evidence on his behalf as the prosecution enjoys for producing available evidence on its behalf.

The more significant question for a defendant is: Who are the witnesses for whom a defendant is entitled to compulsory process? What law defines "witnesses in his favor"? Early commentators argued that a defendant might claim compulsory process only with respect to witnesses whose testimony had already been determined to be admissible, according to the governing rules of evidence in the respective jurisdiction. The Supreme Court in its seminal 1967 decision in *Washington v. Texas* rejected that narrow interpretation of "witnesses in his favor." The defendant had been tried in state court for a homicide that he asserted his accomplice alone had committed. The accomplice, who had already been convicted of committing the murder, had appeared at the defendant's trial and offered to testify that he, the accomplice, had acted alone in committing the homicide. The trial court, invoking a state rule of evidence disqualifying accomplices from testifying for one another in crimi-

nal cases, refused to allow the accomplice to testify in Washington's favor, and Washington was convicted. The Supreme Court held, first, that the compulsory process clause of the Sixth Amendment, like other clauses of the Sixth Amendment, had become applicable to the states through the DUE PROCESS clause of the FOURTEENTH AMENDMENT. Second, and more significantly, the Court held that the meaning of "witnesses in [a defendant's] favor" was to be determined not by state or federal evidentiary standards of admissibility but by independent constitutional standards of admissibility. The compulsory process clause, it said, directly defines the "witnesses" the defendant is entitled to call to the witness stand. The state in *Washington* violated the defendant's right of compulsory process by "arbitrarily" preventing him from eliciting evidence from a person "who was physically and mentally capable of testifying to events that he had personally observed, and whose testimony would have been relevant and material to the defense."

Having determined that the compulsory process clause operates to render exculpatory evidence independently admissible on a defendant's behalf, the Court found *Washington* to be an easy case; the accomplice's proffered testimony was highly probative of the defendant's innocence, and the state's reasons for excluding it were highly attenuated. The Court has since invoked the authority of *Washington* to prohibit a trial judge from silencing a defense witness by threatening him with prosecution for perjury; to prohibit a state from invoking state HEARSAY RULES to exclude highly probative hearsay evidence in a defendant's favor; and to prohibit a trial judge from instructing a jury that defense witnesses are less worthy of belief than prosecution witnesses. Lower courts have invoked the compulsory process clause to compel the government to disclose the identity of informers; to compel defense witnesses to testify over claims of EVIDENTIARY PRIVILEGES; and to compel the prosecution to grant use IMMUNITY to defense witnesses asserting the RIGHT AGAINST SELF-INCRIMINATION. Although the Supreme Court in *Washington* did not define the outer limits of the compulsory process clause, it subsequently emphasized in *Chambers v. Mississippi* (1973) that "few rights are more fundamental than the right of an accused to present witnesses in his defense."

The companion clause to compulsory process, the confrontation clause, is the more widely known and the more often litigated of the Sixth Amendment witness clauses. The issues of confrontation can be grouped into two questions: What does the right "to be confronted" with witnesses mean? Who are the "witnesses against him" whom a defendant is entitled to confront? The answer to the first question has become relatively clear in recent years. Some commentators, including JOHN HENRY WIGMORE, once argued that the right to be "confronted" with witnesses meant no more than the right of a defendant to be brought face to face with the state's witnesses and to cross-examine them in accord with the ordinary (nonconstitutional) rules of evidence. The Supreme Court in 1974 rejected that position in *Davis v. Alaska.* Davis was convicted in a state court on the basis of testimony for the prosecution by a juvenile delinquent. On cross-examination, the witness refused to answer impeaching questions relating to his current delinquency status, invoking a state-law privilege for the confidentiality of juvenile court records. The Supreme Court held that the right to be confronted with prosecution witnesses creates an independent right in defendants, overriding state rules of evidence to the contrary, to elicit probative evidence from the state's witnesses by cross-examining them for exculpatory evidence they may possess. The Court has yet to decide how far the right to examine prosecution witnesses extends in circumstances other than those presented in *Davis.* The parallel right of compulsory process suggests, however, that the confrontation clause entitles a defendant to elicit by cross-examination from prosecution witnesses the same range of probative evidence that the compulsory process clause entitles him to elicit by direct examination from defense witnesses. Both witness clauses serve the same purpose—to enable an accused to defend himself by examining witnesses for probative evidence in his defense.

The more difficult, and still uncertain, question of confrontation is the meaning of "witnesses against him." A defendant certainly has a right to face and cross-examine whichever witnesses the prosecution actually produces in court. The question is whether the confrontation clause also defines the "witnesses" whom the prosecution must call to the witness stand. Does the confrontation clause specify which witnesses the prosecution must produce in person? Or does it merely entitle a defendant to confront whichever witnesses the prosecution in its discretion chooses to produce? These questions arise most frequently in connection with hearsay, that is, evidence whose probative value rests on the perception, memory, narration, or sincerity of a "hearsay declarant," someone not present in court—and thus not subject to cross-examination. Most jurisdictions address the hearsay problem by treating hearsay as presumptively inadmissible, subject to numerous exceptions for particular kinds of hearsay that are admissible either because of their reliability or for other reasons. The Sixth Amendment potentially comes into play whenever the prosecution invokes such an exception to introduce hearsay evidence against the accused. The confrontation question is whether the hearsay declarant is a "witness against" the defendant, within the meaning of the Sixth Amendment, who must be produced for cross-examination under oath and in the presence of the jury.

The Supreme Court held in *Bruton v. United States* (1968) that a prosecutor must produce in person a declarant whose out-of-court statements are being offered against an accused, not to prove him guilty but to spare the state the administrative burden of conducting separate trials. The more difficult question is what other declarants are "witnesses" against an accused for constitutional purposes.

Some authorities have argued that hearsay declarants are always witnesses against the accused for Sixth Amendment purposes and, hence, must always be produced in person as a predicate for using their out-of-court statements against an accused, even if they are no longer available to appear or testify in person. Other authorities argue that hearsay declarants are never witnesses against the accused for Sixth Amendment purposes. The Supreme Court appears to have adopted a middle position. *Ohio v. Roberts* (1980) arguably held that although the state has a Sixth Amendment obligation to produce in person available hearsay declarants whom it can reasonably assume the defendant would wish to examine in person at the time their out-of-court statements are introduced into evidence, the state has no Sixth Amendment obligation to produce hearsay declarants who have become unavailable through no fault of the state. The state remains constitutionally free to use the hearsay statements of these declarants, provided that the statements possess sufficient "indicia of reliability" to afford the trier of fact "a satisfactory basis" for evaluating their truth—such as statements that fall within "firmly rooted hearsay exceptions." Significantly, the state's burden of production under the confrontation clause thus parallels its burdens under the compulsory process clause. Both clauses require the state to make reasonable, good-faith efforts to produce in person witnesses the defendant wishes to examine for evidence in his defense. Yet neither clause requires the state to produce witnesses whom a defendant is not reasonably expected to wish to examine for evidence in his defense, or witnesses who have died, disappeared, or otherwise become unavailable through no fault of the state.

Although the confrontation clause does not require the state to produce declarants who are unavailable to testify in person or whom a defendant is not reasonably expected to wish to examine in person, other constitutional provisions do regulate the state's use of their hearsay statements. *Manson v. Brathwaite* (1977) held that the due process clauses of the Fifth and Fourteenth Amendments require the state to ensure that every item of evidence it uses against an accused, presumably including hearsay evidence, possesses sufficient "features of reliability" to be rationally evaluated by the jury for its truth. The compulsory process clause, in turn, requires states to assist the defendant in producing every available witness, including available hearsay declarants, whose presence the defendant requests and who appears to possess probative evidence in his favor. It follows, therefore, that although the state has no obligation under the confrontation clause to produce hearsay declarants who are unavailable to testify in person, it has a residual due process obligation to ensure that their hearsay statements possess sufficient "indicia of reliability" to support a conviction of the accused. Although the state has no obligation under the confrontation clause to produce as prosecution witnesses available declarants whom it does not reasonably believe the defendant would wish to examine in person at the time their out-of-court statements are introduced into evidence, it has a residual obligation under the compulsory process clause to assist him in producing such declarants whenever the defendant indicates that he wishes to call and examine them as witnesses in his defense.

PETER WESTEN

Bibliography

WELLBORN III, OLIN GUY 1982 The Definition of Hearsay in the Federal Rules of Evidence. *Texas Law Review* 61:49–93.

WESTEN, PETER 1974 The Compulsory Process Clause. *Michigan Law Review* 73:73–184.

———— 1978 Confrontation and Compulsory Process: A Unified Theory of Evidence for Criminal Cases. *Harvard Law Review* 91:567–628.

———— 1979 The Future of Confrontation. *Michigan Law Review* 77:1185–1217.

CONCORD TOWN MEETING RESOLUTIONS
(October 21, 1776)

The people of Concord, Massachusetts, at a town meeting in 1776, were the first to recommend a CONSTITUTIONAL CONVENTION as the only proper body to frame a CONSTITUTION. Earlier that year the provisional legislature of Massachusetts had requested permission from the people of the state to draw up a constitution. The legislature had recommended that the free males of voting age assemble in all the towns to determine that issue and also to decide whether the constitution should be made public for the towns to consider before the legislature ratified it. Nine towns objected to the recommended procedure on the grounds that a legislature was not competent for the purpose. Among the nine, Concord best described the procedure that should be followed.

Concord's resolutions declared that the legislature was not competent for three reasons: a constitution is intended to secure the people in their rights against the government; the body that forms a constitution has the power to alter it; a constitution alterable by the legislature is "no security at all" against the government's encroachment on the rights of the people. Accordingly, Concord resolved, a convention representing the towns should be chosen by all the free male voters. The sole task of the convention should be to frame the constitution. Having completed its task, the convention should publish the proposed constitution "for the Inspection and Remarks" of the people. One week later the town of Attleboro, endorsing the Concord principle of a convention, recommended that the constitution be ratified by the people of the towns rather than by the legislature.

The legislature, ignoring the dissident towns, framed a constitution but submitted it for ratification. The people overwhelmingly rejected it. In 1780 the people ratified a state constitution that was framed by a constitutional convention, the first in the history of the world to be so framed. Concord had designed an institution of government that conformed with the SOCIAL COMPACT theory of forming a FUNDAMENTAL LAW.

LEONARD W. LEVY

CONCURRENT JURISDICTION

The Constitution does not require Congress to create lower federal courts. The Framers assumed that state courts would be competent to hear the cases included in Article III's definition of the JUDICIAL POWER OF THE UNITED STATES. When Congress does choose to confer some of the federal judicial power on lower federal courts, state courts normally retain their JURISDICTION as well. This simultaneous or concurrent jurisdiction of state and federal courts normally exists unless Congress enacts a law stating that the federal power shall be exclusive. Only in unusual circumstances, as when state jurisdiction would gravely disrupt a federal program, has the Supreme Court required an explicit grant of congressional authority for concurrent state jurisdiction to exist. Indeed, in the limited instance of DIVERSITY JURISDICTION, the Framers intended concurrent jurisdiction to be mandatory, so that Congress could not divest state courts of judicial power they possessed before adoption of the Constitution.

Concurrent jurisdiction allows plaintiffs initial choice of a forum more sympathetic to their claims. In many circumstances, however, a defendant may supplant that choice by exercising a right under federal law to remove the case from state to federal court. (See REMOVAL OF CASES.)

State courts need not always agree to exercise their concurrent jurisdiction. If a state court declines to hear a federal claim for nondiscriminatory reasons tied to the sound management of the state judicial system, the Supreme Court will respect that decision.

When concurrent jurisdiction exists, state and federal courts may be asked to adjudicate the same rights or claims between parties at the same time. Ordinarily neither the federal nor the state court is required to stay its proceeding in such situations. However, the federal courts do possess a limited statutory power to enjoin pending state proceedings, and a state or federal court that is the first to obtain custody of property that is the subject of the dispute may enjoin the other.

CAROLE E. GOLDBERG-AMBROSE

Bibliography

CURRIE, DAVID 1981 *Federal Jurisdiction in a Nutshell*, 2nd ed. St. Paul, Minn.: West Publishing Co.

CONCURRENT POWERS

In THE FEDERALIST, JAMES MADISON wrote that in fashioning the federal relationship "the convention must have been compelled to sacrifice theoretical propriety to the force of extraneous circumstances." These sacrifices which produced a "compound republic, partaking both of the national and federal character" were "rendered indispensable" by what Madison termed "the peculiarity of our political situation." An important feature of the compound republic is the idea of concurrent powers.

Concurrent powers are those exercised independently in the same field of legislation by both federal and state governments, as in the case of the power to tax or to make BANKRUPTCY laws. As ALEXANDER HAMILTON explained in *The Federalist* #32, "the State governments would clearly retain all the rights of SOVEREIGNTY which they before had, and which were not, by that act, *exclusively* delegated to the United States." Hamilton goes on to explain that this "alienation" would exist in three cases only: where there is in express terms an exclusive delegation of authority to the federal government, as in the case of the seat of government; where authority is granted in one place to the federal government and prohibited to the states in another, as in the case of IMPOSTS; and where a power is granted to the federal government "to which a similar authority in the States would be absolutely and totally *contradictory* and *repugnant*, as in the case of prescribing naturalization rules." This last, Hamilton notes, would not comprehend the exercise of concurrent powers which "might be productive of occasional interferences in the *policy* of any branch of administration, but would not imply any direct contradiction or repugnancy in point of constitutional authority." The only explicit mention of concurrent power in the Constitution occurred in the ill-fated EIGHTEENTH AMENDMENT which provided that "the Congress and the several States shall have concurrent power to enforce this article."

The story of concurrent power in modern American constitutional history has largely been the story of federal PREEMPTION. The concurrent authority of the states is always subordinate to the superior authority of the federal government and generally can be exercised by the states only where the federal government has not occupied the field, or where Congress has given the states permission to exercise concurrent powers. Thus in MCCULLOCH V. MARYLAND (1819), Maryland's concurrent power of taxation had to give way when the state sought to tax a federal instrumentality, because such a tax was utterly repugnant to federal supremacy.

In the years since *McCulloch* the Supreme Court has devised an intricate system for determining when a federal exercise of power has implicitly or explicitly worked to diminish or extinguish the concurrent powers of the states. The federal government's steady expansion of power over the years has, of course, placed more restrictions on concurrent action by the states as, in more and more areas, the federal government has occupied the whole field of legislation.

The Court's decision in *Pacific and Electric Company v. Energy Resources Commission* (1983) provides a useful summary of the factors that determine whether federal preemption may be said to have taken place: whether Congress is acting within constitutional limits and explicitly states its intention to preempt state authority; whether the scheme of federal regulation is so pervasive as to make reasonable the inference that Congress intended for the state to be excluded from concurrent regulation; whether, even though the regulation of Congress is not pervasive, the operation of concurrent powers on the part of the state would actually conflict with federal law; and whether, in the absence of pervasive legislation, state law stands as an obstacle to the accomplishment of the full purposes and objectives of Congress. It is not difficult to see that most of the states' concurrent powers today exist at the forbearance of the federal legislature. This result was not entirely anticipated by the Framers of the Constitution; but it was the inevitable consequence of the centripetal forces embodied in the national features of the compound republic.

EDWARD J. ERLER

Bibliography

DODD, WALTER F. 1963 Concurrent Powers. In Edwin R. Seligman, ed., *Encyclopedia of the Social Sciences*, Vol. 4:173–174. New York: Macmillan.
STORY, JOSEPH 1833 *Commentaries on the Constitution of the United States*, Vol. 1:407–433. Boston: Hilliard, Gray & Co.

CONCURRENT RESOLUTION

Concurrent resolutions adopted by the Congress, unlike JOINT RESOLUTIONS, do not require the president's signature and do not ordinarily have the force of law. Concurrent resolutions may be used to express the "sense of Congress" or to regulate the internal affairs of Congress (such as expenditure of funds for congressional housekeeping).

Since 1939, concurrent resolutions have been the normal means of expressing the LEGISLATIVE VETO when by law that limit on PRESIDENTIAL ORDINANCE-MAKING POWER requires action by both houses. Recent examples of this requirement are found in the WAR POWERS ACT (1973) and the CONGRESSIONAL BUDGET AND IMPOUNDMENT CONTROL ACT (1974).

DENNIS J. MAHONEY

CONCURRING OPINION

When a member of a multi-judge court agrees with the DECISION reached by the majority but disagrees with the reasoning of the OPINION OF THE COURT or wishes to add his own remarks, he will customarily file a concurring opinion. The concurring opinion usually proposes an alternative way of reaching the same result. Once relatively rare, separate concurrences have become, in the late twentieth century, a normal part of the workings of the Supreme Court of the United States.

A concurring opinion may diverge from the majority opinion only slightly or only on technical points, or it may propose an entirely different line of argument. One example of the latter sort is found in ROCHIN V. CALIFORNIA (1952) in which the concurring opinions staked out a much bolder course of constitutional interpretation than the majority was willing to follow. In a constitutional system in which great issues of public policy are decided in controversies between private litigants, the principles of law enunciated in the opinions are usually of far greater importance than the decision with respect to the parties to the case. Sometimes dissenting Justices are closer to the majority on principles than are concurring Justices.

In the most important cases, several Justices may write separate opinions, even though there is substantial agreement on the grounds for deciding the case. DRED SCOTT V. SANDFORD (1857) and the CAPITAL PUNISHMENT CASES (1972) are examples of cases in which every Justice filed a separate concurring or DISSENTING OPINION.

Scholars generally agree that separate concurrences often diminish the authority of the court's decision and reduce the degree of certainty of the law. Some critics have suggested elimination of concurring opinions, especially when they are filed by Justices who also subscribe to the MAJORITY OPINION. But concurring opinions, no less than dissenting opinions, provide alternative courses for future constitutional development.

DENNIS J. MAHONEY

CONFEDERATE CONSTITUTION

The Constitution of the Confederate States of America, adopted in 1861, closely followed, and was in a sense a commentary upon, the Constitution of the United States. The most important points of divergence were: provision for the heads of executive departments to sit and speak in the Congress, a single six-year term for the President, a line-item VETO POWER over appropriations, explicit provision for presidential power to remove appointed officials, and the requirement of a two-thirds vote in each house to admit new states.

The Confederate Constitution prohibited laws impairing the right of property in slaves; but it also prohibited the foreign slave trade (except with the United States). Other innovations included a ban on federal expenditures for INTERNAL IMPROVEMENTS and provision for state duties on sea-going vessels, to be used for improvement of harbors and navigable waters. The AMENDING PROCESS provided for a convention of the states to be summoned by Congress upon the demand of state conventions; Congress did not have the power to propose amendments itself.

The provisions of the BILL OF RIGHTS of the United States Constitution were written into the body of the Confederate Constitution, as were those of the ELEVENTH and TWELFTH AMENDMENTS.

DENNIS J. MAHONEY

Bibliography
COULTER, E. MERTON 1950 *The Confederate States of America, 1861–1865.* Baton Rouge: Louisiana State University Press.

CONFERENCE

When the Justices of the Supreme Court refer to themselves in the aggregate as "the Conference"—as distinguished from "the Court"—they are alluding to their deliberative functions in reaching decisions. The Conference considers, discusses, even negotiates; the Court acts.

The name comes from the Justices' practice of meeting to discuss cases and vote on their disposition. Two kinds of questions are considered at these Conferences: whether the Court should review a case, and how to decide a case under review. Just before the beginning of each TERM, the Conference considers a great many applications for review. (See APPEAL; CERTIORARI, WRIT OF; APPELLATE JURISDICTION; ORIGINAL JURISDICTION.) During the term, in weeks when ORAL ARGUMENTS are scheduled, the Conference generally meets regularly to consider the cases argued within the preceding few days.

The Conference is limited to the nine Justices. Clerks and secretaries do not attend, and if messages are passed into the room, tradition calls for the junior Justice to be doorkeeper. By another tradition, each Justice shakes hands with all the other Justices before the Conference begins. The CHIEF JUSTICE presides.

The Chief Justice calls a case for discussion, and normally speaks first. The other Justices speak in turn, according to their seniority. (Interruptions are not unknown.) The custom has been for Justices to vote in inverse order of seniority, the Chief Justice voting last. Recent reports, however, suggest flexibility in this practice; when the Justices' positions are already obvious, a formal vote may be unnecessary. The vote at the Conference meeting is not final. Once draft opinions and memoranda "to the Conference" have begun to circulate, votes may change, and even the Court's decision may change.

KENNETH L. KARST

(SEE ALSO: *Opinion of the Court; Dissenting Opinion; Concurring Opinion.*)

Bibliography
HUGHES, CHARLES EVANS 1928 *The Supreme Court of the United States: Its Foundation, Methods and Achievements: An Interpretation.* New York: Columbia University Press.
WOODWARD, BOB and ARMSTRONG, SCOTT 1979 *The Brethren: Inside the Supreme Court.* New York: Simon & Schuster.

CONFESSIONS

See: Police Interrogation and Confessions

CONFIRMATIO CARTARUM
1297

Within two centuries after its adoption MAGNA CARTA was reconfirmed forty-four times. The reconfirmation of 1297 is significant because it was the first made after representatives of the commons were admitted to Parliament; because it embodied the inchoate principle that TAXATION WITHOUT REPRESENTATION is unlawful; and because it regarded Magna Carta as FUNDAMENTAL LAW. By one section the king agreed to exact certain taxes only "by the common assent of the realm. . . ." Another section declared that any act by the king's judges or ministers contrary to the great charter "shall be undone, and holden for nought." WILLIAM PENN ordered the charter and its reconfirmation of 1297 reprinted in the colonies for the first time in 1687. JOHN ADAMS, THOMAS JEFFERSON, and other lawyers of the era of the American Revolution were familiar with the principles of the statute of 1297, and in MARBURY V. MADISON (1803) the Supreme Court declared that any act contrary to the fundamental law of the written constitution is void.

LEONARD W. LEVY

Bibliography
PERRY, RICHARD L., ed. 1959 *Sources of Our Liberties.* Pages 23–31. New York: American Bar Foundation.

CONFISCATION ACTS
12 Stat. 319 (1861)
12 Stat. 589 (1862)

Congress enacted the Confiscation Acts "to insure the speedy termination of the present rebellion." Both statutes liberated the slaves of certain rebels and authorized the confiscation of other types of property by judicial procedures based on admiralty and revenue models. Both statutes were compromise measures, influenced by the progressive goal of emancipation of slaves and by a respect for the rights of private property.

The Supreme Court upheld the constitutionality of the acts in the 6–3 decision of *Miller v. United States* (1871), finding congressional authority in the WAR POWERS clauses of Article I. The majority shrugged off Fifth and Sixth Amendment objections on the grounds that the statutes were not ordinary punitive legislation but rather were extraordinary war measures.

The acts were indifferently and arbitrarily enforced, producing a total of less than $130,000 net to the Treasury. Property of Confederates was also virtually confiscated in proceedings for nonpayment of the wartime direct tax, under the Captured and Abandoned Property Act of 1863, and through President ABRAHAM LINCOLN's contraband emancipation policies.

WILLIAM M. WIECEK

Bibliography

RANDALL, JAMES G. 1951 *Constitutional Problems under Lincoln.* Urbana: University of Illinois Press.

CONFRONTATION, RIGHT OF

The confrontation clause of the Sixth Amendment, which guarantees an accused person the right "to be confronted with the witnesses against him," is one of the two clauses in the BILL OF RIGHTS that explicitly address the right of criminal defendants to elicit evidence in their defense from witnesses at trial. The other clause is its Sixth Amendment companion, the COMPULSORY PROCESS clause, which guarantees the accused the right to "compulsory process for obtaining witnesses in his favor." Together these two clauses provide constitutional foundations for the right of accused persons to defend themselves through the production and examination of witnesses at trial.

PETER WESTEN

(SEE ALSO: *Hearsay Rules.*)

CONGRESS AND THE SUPREME COURT

The delegates to the CONSTITUTIONAL CONVENTION OF 1787 confronted two fundamental problems in their quest to correct the political defects of the ARTICLES OF CONFEDERATION. First, they needed to bolster the powers of government at the national level so as to transform the "league of friendship" created by the Articles into a government with all the coercive powers requisite to government. Second, the Framers sought to create energetic but limited powers that would enable the new national government to govern, but in ways safe to the rights of the people. As JAMES MADISON put it in THE FEDERALIST #51, the task was to "enable the government to control the governed, but in the next place oblige it to control itself."

Their successful solution to this political problem was to separate the powers of government. Because the primary source of trouble in a popular form of government would be the legislative branch, the object was to bolster the coordinate executive and judicial branches, to offer "some more adequate defence . . . for the more feeble, against the more powerful members of the government." The arrangement of checked and balanced institutions would at once avoid "a tyrannical concentration of all the powers of government in the same hands" while rendering the administration of the national government more efficient.

When the Framers examined the existing federal system under the Articles to determine precisely what it was that rendered it "altogether unfit for the administration of the affairs of the Union," the want of an independent judiciary "crown[ed] the defects of the confederation." As ALEXANDER HAMILTON put it in *The Federalist* #22, "Laws are a dead letter without courts to expound and define their true meaning and operation." Thus the improved science of politics offered by the friends of the Constitution prominently included provision for "the institution of courts composed of judges, holding their offices during good behavior."

But to some Anti-Federalist critics of the Federalist-backed Constitution, the judiciary was too independent and too powerful. To the New York Anti-Federalist "Brutus," the proposed judiciary possessed such independence as to allow the courts to "mould the government into almost any shape they please." The "Federal Farmer" was equally critical: his fellow citizens were "more in danger of sowing the seeds of arbitrary government in this department than in any other." With such unanticipated criticism, the Federalists were forced to defend the judicial power more elaborately than had been done in the early pages of *The Federalist.*

So compelling were the Anti-Federalist arguments that Hamilton saw fit to explain and defend the proposed judicial power in no fewer than six separate essays (#78–83) in *The Federalist.* His task was to show how an independent judiciary was not only *not* a threat to safe popular government but was absolutely essential to it. In making his now famous argument in *The Federalist* #78 that the judiciary would be that branch of the new government "least dangerous to the political rights of the Constitution," Hamilton made the case that the courts were "designed to be an intermediate body between the people and the legislature, in order, among other things, to keep the latter within the limits assigned to their authority." By exercising neither force nor will but merely judgment, the courts would prove to be the "bulwarks of a limited constitution." Such an institution, Hamilton argued, politically independent yet constitutionally rooted, was essential to resist the overwhelming power of the majority of the community. Only with such a constitutional defense could the rights of individuals and of minor parties be protected against majority tyranny; only an independent judiciary could allow the powers of the national government to be sufficiently enhanced, while simultaneously checking the unhealthy impulses of majority rule that had characterized politics at the state level under the Articles.

To counter the Anti-Federalist complaint that the courts would be imperiously independent, Hamilton reminded them that the courts would not be simply freewheeling sources of arbitrary judgments and decrees. The Constitution, in giving Congress the power to regulate the APPELLATE JURISDICTION of the Supreme Court "with such exceptions, and under such regulations, as the Congress shall make," hedged against too expansive a conception of judicial power. "To avoid an arbitrary discretion in the courts," Hamilton noted, "it is indispensable that they should be bound down by strict rules and precedents, which serve to define and point out their duty in every particular case that comes before them." Thus the stage was set for a history of political confrontation between the Congress and the Court.

The tension between Congress and the Court has been a constant part of American politics at least since CHISHOLM V. GEORGIA (1793) led to the ELEVENTH AMENDMENT. Each generation has seen dramatic Supreme Court rulings that have prompted political cries to curb the courts. JOHN MARSHALL's now celebrated opinions in MARBURY V. MADISON (1803) and MCCULLOCH V. MARYLAND (1819), for example, caused him a good bit of political grief when he wrote them; the decision in DRED SCOTT V. SANDFORD (1857) soon came to be viewed as a judicially "self-inflicted wound" that weakened the Court and exacerbated the conflict that descended into civil war; and more recently, protests against the rulings in BROWN V. BOARD OF EDUCATION (1954) and ROE V. WADE (1973) have caused not only political demands for retaliation against the Court but social conflict and even violence as well. But through it all the Court has weathered the hostility with its independence intact.

Only once were the critics successful in persuading Congress to act against the Court, and the Court validated that move. In EX PARTE MCCARDLE (1869) the Court confirmed Congress's power to withdraw a portion of the Court's appellate jurisdiction. Fearing that the Court would use William McCardle's petition for a writ of HABEAS CORPUS under the HABEAS CORPUS ACT OF 1867 as a vehicle for invalidating the Reconstruction Acts *in toto*, the Congress repealed that portion of the act under which McCardle had brought his action—and after the Court had heard arguments in the case. The Court upheld the constitutionality of Congress's action in repealing this particular part of the Court's JURISDICTION. The extent of Congress's power to withdraw the Court's appellate jurisdiction remains a matter of constitutional controversy.

The constitutional relationship between Congress and the Court is one thing; their political relationship is another matter. Although there are often loud cries for reaction against the Court, the critics usually lack sufficient force to achieve political retribution. The reason is most often explained as a matter of political prudence. The courts by their decisions frequently irritate a portion of the community—but usually only a portion. For most decisions will satisfy certain public constituencies that are as vociferous as the critics. Even the most errant exercises of judicial decision making are rarely sufficient to undermine the public respect for the idea of an independent judiciary.

The reason for this is simple enough: an independent judiciary makes good political sense. To make the judiciary too much dependent upon "popularity" as that popularity may be reflected in Congress would be to lower the constitutional barriers to congressional power, barriers generally agreeable to most people most of the time. The arguments of Hamilton in *The Federalist* still carry considerable weight.

Thus in the constitutional design of separating the powers of government through the device of "partial agency"—mingling the powers enough to give each branch some control over the others—is to be found the inevitable gulf between legitimate power and prudent restraint. For Congress to be persuaded to restrict judicial power, the case must first be made that such restrictions are both necessary and proper.

Despite the dangers of legislative power, it was still considered by the Framers to be the cardinal principle of POPULAR SOVEREIGNTY. Basic to this principle is the belief that it is legitimate for the people through the instrumentality of law to adjust, check, or enhance certain institutions of the government. This belief embraces the power of the legislature to exert some control over the structure and administration of the executive and judicial branches.

The qualified power of the legislature to tamper with the judiciary is not so grave a danger to the balance of the Constitution as some see it. For even when a judicial decision runs counter to particular—and perhaps pervasive—political interests, the institutional arrangements of the Constitution are such as to slow down the popular outrage and give the people time for "more cool and sedate reflection." And given the distance between the people and LEGISLATION afforded by such devices as REPRESENTATION (with its multiplicity of interests), BICAMERALISM, and the executive VETO POWER, an immediate legislative backlash to judicial behavior is unlikely. Experience demonstrates that any backlash at all is likely to be "weak and ineffectual." But if the negative response is not merely transient and is widely and deeply felt, then the Constitution wisely provides well-defined mechanisms for a deliberate political reaction to what the people hold to be intolerable judicial excesses.

But ultimately the history of court-curbing efforts in America, from the failed IMPEACHMENT of Justice SAMUEL CHASE to the Court-packing plan of FRANKLIN D. ROOSEVELT, teaches one basic lesson: the American political system generally operates to the advantage of the judiciary. Presidential court-packing is ineffective as a means of exerting political influence, and impeachment is too difficult to use as an everyday check against unpopular decisions. Not since John Marshall saw fit pseudonymously to defend his opinion in *McCulloch v. Maryland* (1819) in the public press has any Justice or judge felt obliged to respond to public outrage over a decision.

Political responses to perceived excesses of judicial power tend to take one of two forms: either a policy response against a particular decision or an institutional response against the structure and powers of the courts. In either event, the response may be either partisan or principled. Usually a policy response will take the form of a proposed constitutional amendment or statute designed to overrule a decision. An institutional response will generally seek to make jurisdictional exceptions, to create special courts with specific jurisdiction, or to make adjustments regarding the personnel, administration, or procedures of the judicial branch. Whatever the response, court-curbing is difficult. Although a majority of one of the houses of Congress may object to particular cases of "judicial impertinence," as one congressman viewed Justice DAVID DAVIS's controversial opinion in EX PARTE MILLIGAN (1866), a variety of objections will issue in different views of what should be done.

On the whole, there has consistently been a consensus that tampering with judicial independence is a serious matter and that rash reprisals against the Court as an institution may upset the constitutional balance. Underlying the occasional outbursts of angry public sentiment against the court is that "moral force" of the community of which ALEXIS DE TOCQUEVILLE wrote. On the whole, the American people continue to view the judiciary as the "boast of the Constitution."

For any political attempt to adjust or limit the judicial power to be successful it is necessary that it be—and be perceived to be—a principled rather than a merely partisan response. Only then will the issue of JUDICIAL ACTIVISM be met on a ground high enough to transcend the more common—and generally fruitless—debates over judicial liberalism and conservatism. The deepest issue is not whether a particular decision or even a particular court is too liberal for some and too conservative for others; the point is whether the courts are exercising their powers capably and legitimately. Keeping the courts constitutionally legitimate and institutionally capable benefits both the liberal and the conservative elements in American politics.

The system the Framers devised is so structured that the branch the Framers thought "least dangerous" is not so malleable in the hands of Congress as to be powerless. Yet the threat of congressional restriction of the Court remains, a threat that probably helps to keep an otherwise largely unfettered institution within constitutional bounds.

GARY L. McDOWELL

Bibliography

BERGER, RAOUL 1969 *Congress versus the Supreme Court.* Cambridge, Mass.: Harvard University Press.

BRECKENRIDGE, A. C. 1971 *Congress Against the Court.* Lincoln: University of Nebraska Press.

MORGAN, DONALD L. 1967 *Congress and the Constitution.* Cambridge, Mass.: Harvard University Press.

MURPHY, WALTER F. 1962 *Congress and the Courts.* Chicago: University of Chicago Press.

CONGRESSIONAL BUDGET AND IMPOUNDMENT CONTROL ACT
88 Stat. 297 (1974)

President RICHARD M. NIXON's IMPOUNDMENT of billions of dollars appropriated by Congress for purposes which he did not approve amounted to the assertion of virtually uncontrollable power to block any federal program involving monetary expenditures. Nixon used impoundment as a weapon to alter legislative policy rather than to control the total level of government spending.

Congress, in the 1974 act, strengthened its own budgeting process, establishing new budget committees in each house and creating the Congressional Budget Office to give Congress assistance comparable to that given the President by the OFFICE OF MANAGEMENT AND BUDGET. The act required the President to recommend to Congress, in a special message, any proposal to impound funds. Thereafter, either house might veto the impoundment proposal by resolution, thereby forcing release of the funds. If the President refused to comply, the Comptroller General was authorized to seek a court order requiring the President to spend the money. The constitutionality of the LEGISLATIVE VETO was thrown into doubt by the IMMIGRATION AND NATURALIZATION SERVICE V. CHADHA (1983).

PAUL L. MURPHY

(SEE ALSO: *Constitutional History, 1961–1977.*)

CONGRESSIONAL INVESTIGATIONS

See: Legislative Investigations

CONGRESSIONAL MEMBERSHIP

Congress under the ARTICLES OF CONFEDERATION was a unicameral body representing thirteen states. But delegates to the CONSTITUTIONAL CONVENTION, influenced by the example of the British Parliament and almost all of the states, agreed rather early to the principle of a two-house legislature. Members of the House of Representatives were to be popularly elected, with each state's members proportionate to population. But membership in the Senate and selection of senators caused intense controversy.

The large states wanted the Senate also to represent population, but the smaller states were adamantly opposed. They forced a compromise under which every state would have two senators, elected by the state legislatures for six-year terms. This solution gave effect to the federal principle, the Senate representing the states and the House providing popular representation. However, legislative election of senators ultimately proved unacceptable. During the nineteenth century the elections were often marked by scandals and deadlocks, and a rising progressive temper in the country led to adoption of the SEVENTEENTH AMENDMENT in 1913 providing for direct popular election of senators.

The size of the House was initially set by Article I at sixty-five, to be revised thereafter on the basis of decennial censuses. As the population grew and more states were admitted to the Union, Congress increased the number of seats until it reached 435 after the 1910 census. Congress then concluded that further enlargement would make the House unwieldy, and by statute in 1929 fixed 435 as the permanent size of the House.

After each census the 435 House seats are apportioned among the states according to a statutory formula. It is then the responsibility of each state legislature to draw the lines for congressional districts. There was initially no legal obligation to assure equality of population among districts. Particularly in the early twentieth century rural-dominated state legislatures refused to revise district lines to provide equitable representation for growing urban areas. Judicial relief failed when the Supreme Court in COLEGROVE V. GREEN (1946) ruled that drawing the boundary lines of congressional districts was a POLITICAL QUESTION for decision by the state legislatures and Congress, not the courts. This HOLDING was implicitly overruled by the Court in BAKER V. CARR (1962), and in WESBERRY V. SANDERS (1964) the Court made equality of population in congressional districts a constitutional requirement.

The drawing of congressional district lines typically generates bitter legislative controversy as the majority party endeavors to protect its dominance by gerrymandering and incumbents of both parties seek to safeguard their own districts. In numerous states since 1964 legislative deadlocks have required the courts to intervene and draw the district lines.

Members of the House have two-year terms. Proposals for extending the term to four years have been made because of the increased costs of campaigning, longer sessions of Congress, and more complex legislative problems. In the Senate, the fact that only one-third of the seats fall vacant every two years gives it the status of a "continuing body," in contrast to the House which must reconstitute itself and elect its officers every two years.

The presiding officer of the House is its Speaker, chosen by the majority party from among its members. The Speaker has a vote and may on rare occasions participate in debate. The Senate's presiding officer is the vice-president; when serving in this capacity his title is President of the Senate. He has no vote except in case of a tie. The Constitution authorizes the Senate to choose a president *pro tempore* to preside in the absence of the vice-president. The president *pro tempore* is typically the senior member of the majority party.

Article I requires that a senator be thirty years of age, nine years a citizen of the United States, and an inhabitant of the state from which elected. A representative need be only twenty-five years of age and a citizen for seven years. By custom a representative should reside in the district from which elected. Members of Congress are disqualified for appointment to executive office, a provision that prevents the development of anything approaching a parliamentary system. To accept an executive post, a member of Congress must resign.

Each house is authorized to "be the judge of the elections, returns and qualifications of its own members" (Article I, section 5). The "qualifications," it has been established by POWELL V. MCCORMACK (1969), are only the age, residence, and CITIZENSHIP requirements stated in the Constitution. However, on several occasions both houses have in effect enforced additional qualifications by refusing to seat duly elected members who met the constitutional qualifications. In 1900 the House refused to seat a Utah polygamist; similar action was taken in 1919 against a Wisconsin socialist who had been convicted under the ESPIONAGE ACT for opposing American participation in World War I. The most prominent black member of Congress, Adam Clayton Powell, was denied his seat in 1967. There was a judgment of criminal contempt outstanding against him, and his conduct as a committee chairman had been irregular. The Supreme Court ruled, however, that he possessed the constitutional qualifications and so could not be denied his seat. Members of Congress cannot be impeached, but they are subject to vote of censure by their chamber, and to expulsion by two-thirds vote. The Court indicated that the House might have expelled Powell for his

alleged conduct. Vacancies in the Senate can be filled by the state governor, but in the House only by special election.

Members of Congress have immunity from arrest during legislative sessions except for cases of "TREASON, FELONY and breach of the peace" (Article I, section 6). They are guaranteed FREEDOM OF SPEECH by the provision that "for any speech or debate in either house, they shall not be questioned in any other place." (See SPEECH OR DEBATE CLAUSE.) The purpose is to prevent intimidation of legislators by the executive or threat of prosecution for libel or slander. They can be held accountable for statements or actions in their legislative capacity only by their own colleagues. This immunity covers not only speeches in Congress but also written reports, resolutions offered, the act of voting, and all other things generally done in a legislative session. However, immunity does not extend to press releases, newsletters, or telephone calls to executive agencies, the Supreme Court held in HUTCHINSON V. PROXMIRE (1979). Also, taking a bribe to influence legislation is not a "legislative act," according to BREWSTER V. UNITED STATES (1972).

C. HERMAN PRITCHETT

Bibliography

DAVIDSON, ROGER H. and OLESZEK, WALTER J. 1985 *Congress and Its Members*, 2nd ed. Washington, D.C.: Congressional Quarterly.

CONGRESSIONAL PRIVILEGES AND IMMUNITIES

The Constitution specifically protects members of Congress against interference with their deliberative function. The special privileges and immunities attendant on CONGRESSIONAL MEMBERSHIP are contained in the first clause of Article I, section 6, of the Constitution. The Framers of the Constitution, familiar with the devices used by the British king against members of Parliament and by royal governors against members of the provincial legislatures, sought to insulate the members of the federal legislature against pressures that might preclude independence of judgment.

The PRIVILEGE FROM ARREST, other than for TREASON, FELONY, or BREACH OF THE PEACE, has been known in Anglo-American constitutional history since the advent of parliaments; WILLIAM BLACKSTONE cited an ancient Gothic law as evidence of the privilege's immemorial origins. The English Parliament claimed freedom of debate, that is, immunity from prosecution or civil lawsuit resulting from utterances in Parliament, at least from the thirteenth century; that immunity was finally established in the English BILL OF RIGHTS (1689). In America, privilege from arrest during legislative sessions was first granted in Virginia in 1623, and freedom of debate was first recognized in the FUNDAMENTAL ORDERS OF CONNECTICUT (1639).

The ARTICLES OF CONFEDERATION extended both the privilege from arrest and the freedom of debate to members of Congress, in words transcribed almost verbatim from the English Bill of Rights: "Freedom of speech and debate in Congress shall not be impeached or questioned in any court, or place out of Congress, and the members of Congress shall be protected in their persons from arrests and imprisonments, during the time of their going to and from, and attendance on Congress, except for treason, felony, or breach of the peace." At the CONSTITUTIONAL CONVENTION, these congressional privileges and immunities first appeared in the report of the Committee of Detail; they were agreed to without debate and without dissent. The Committee of Style gave final form to the wording of the clause.

The privilege from arrest, limited as it is to arrest for debt, no longer has any practical application. The immunity from having to answer in court, or in any other place out of Congress, for congressional SPEECH OR DEBATE is now primarily a shield against civil actions by private parties rather than against an executive jealous of his prerogative. That shield has been expanded to protect the whole legislative process, but not, as one senator learned to his chagrin in HUTCHINSON V. PROXMIRE (1979), to every public utterance of a member of Congress concerning a public issue.

DENNIS J. MAHONEY

Bibliography

WORMSER, MICHAEL D., ED. 1982 *Guide to Congress*, 3rd ed. Pages 850–855. Washington, D.C.: Congressional Quarterly.

CONGRESSIONAL VETO

See: Legislative Veto

CONKLING, ROSCOE
(1829–1888)

A New York attorney, congressman (1859–1863, 1865–1867), and senator (1867–1881), Roscoe Conkling in 1861 initiated legislation creating the Joint Committee on the Conduct of the War. In 1865, as a member of the JOINT COMMITTEE ON RECONSTRUCTION, Conkling supported CIVIL RIGHTS for blacks. In 1867 he sponsored military reconstruction legislation. Conkling and other supporters of the bill argued that the South was still in the "grasp of war" and only a military occupation and Reconstruction would insure protection of the freedmen. After Reconstruction Conkling continued to support civil rights and helped Frederick Douglass become the first black Recorder of Deeds in Washington, D.C. Douglass placed Conkling alongside ULYSSES S. GRANT, CHARLES SUMNER, and BENJAMIN F. BUTLER as a protector of freedmen. In 1880 Conkling led a movement to renominate Grant because of disagreements with President RUTHERFORD B. HAYES over Reconstruction and patronage. In 1881 Conkling resigned his Senate seat to protest JAMES A. GARFIELD's appointments in New York State. As the undisputed leader of the New York Republican party, Conkling thought he, and not the President, should dispense patronage in the Empire State. Earlier he had opposed Hayes's attempts to remove federal officeholders in New York and had defended CHESTER A. ARTHUR from corruption charges. In 1873 Conkling declined Grant's offer of the Chief Justiceship of the United States; in 1882 the Senate confirmed him for an Associate Justiceship, but he declined to serve.

PAUL FINKELMAN

Bibliography

JORDON, DAVID M. 1971 *Roscoe Conkling of New York: Voice in the Senate.* Ithaca, N.Y.: Cornell University Press.

CONNALLY, THOMAS T. (TOM)
(1877–1963)

A conservative Texas Democrat and internationalist, Tom Connally, as he officially called himself, served twelve years in the House of Representatives and twenty-four in the Senate. When he retired from politics in 1953, he said he was most proud of his leadership against FRANKLIN D. ROOSEVELT's Court-packing plan of 1937 and in favor of the creation of the United Nations. Connally's main achievements were in the field of FOREIGN AFFAIRS, from managing the Lend Lease Act to confirmation of the NORTH ATLANTIC TREATY. He was cool toward much of the New Deal, except when it benefited Texas cattle, oil, and cotton interests. The Supreme Court struck down the Connally "Hot Oil" Act in PANAMA REFINING CO.

v. RYAN (1935), but he secured a revised measure that constitutionally prohibited the shipment in INTERSTATE COMMERCE of oil produced in excess of government quotas. He opposed every CIVIL RIGHTS measure that came before the Senate and joined every southern filibuster, preventing the enactment of anti-lynching and anti-POLL TAX bills. Connally was one of the last of colorful, powerful, demagogic, and grandiloquent southern politicians who affected a drawl, string-tie, frock coat, and flowing hair.

LEONARD W. LEVY

Bibliography
CONNALLY, TOM and STEINBERG, ALFRED 1954 *My Name Is Tom Connally.* New York: Crowell.

CONNECTICUT COMPROMISE

See: Great Compromise

CONQUERED PROVINCES THEORY

"Conquered provinces" was one of a half dozen constitutional theories concerning the relationship of the seceded states and the Union. Representative THADDEUS STEVENS (Republican, Pennsylvania), the principal exponent of conquered provinces, argued that SECESSION had been de jure as well as de facto effective, and destroyed the normal constitutional status of the seceded states. Union victory required that they be governed under the principles of international law, which would have authorized essentially unlimited congressional latitude in setting Reconstruction policy. Congressional legislation for the ex-states had to be based on the premise that "the foundation of their institutions, both political, municipal, and social, must be broken up and relaid." This was to be accomplished through extensive confiscation of Confederates' properties and the abolition of slavery. The state constitutions would have to be rewritten and submitted to Congress, which would then readmit each "province" as a new state.

Other principal theories of Reconstruction were: territorialization, popular among some Republicans since 1861, which would have treated the seceded states as territories; STATE SUICIDE, expounded by CHARLES SUMNER since 1862; state indestructibility, the basis of varying southern and presidential views, and being the central assumption of ABRAHAM LINCOLN's programs; Richard Henry Dana's "Grasp of War" theory of 1865, which would have sanctioned congressional policy under the WAR POWERS; and forfeited rights, a theory propounded by Rep. Samuel Shellabarger (Republican, Ohio), which ultimately came as close as any to being the constitutional basis of congressional Republican Reconstruction.

Stevens's conquered provinces theory was logically consistent with Republican objectives, and Lincoln's policies concerning the wartime Reconstruction of Louisiana, Arkansas, and Tennessee resembled parts of Stevens's program. But because the idea of conquered provinces was widely considered unconstitutional and draconian, it was never adopted as the basis of Republican policy.

WILLIAM M. WIECEK

Bibliography
MCKITRICK, ERIC L. 1960 *Andrew Johnson and Reconstruction.* Chicago: University of Chicago Press.

CONSCIENTIOUS OBJECTION

A conscientious objector is a person who is opposed in conscience to engaging in socially required behavior. Since the genuine objector will not be easily forced into acts he abhors and since compelling people to violate their own moral scruples is usually undesirable in a liberal society, those who formulate legal rules face the question whether conscientious objectors should be excused from legal requirements imposed on others. The issue is most striking in relation to compulsory military service: should those whose consciences forbid killing be conscripted for combat? Historically, conscientious objection has been considered mainly in that context, and the clash has been understood as between secular obligation and the sense of religious duty felt by members of pacifist sects. The Constitution says nothing directly about conscientious objection, and for most of the country's existence Congress was thought to have a free hand in deciding whether to afford any exemption and how to define the class of persons who would benefit. By now, it is evident that the religion clauses of the FIRST AMENDMENT impose significant constraints on how Congress may draw lines between those who receive an exemption from military service and those who do not. The Supreme Court has never accepted the argument that Congress is constitutionally required to establish an exemption from military service, but it has indicated that the Constitution does entitle some individuals to exemption from certain other sorts of compulsory laws.

The principle that society should excuse conscientious objectors from military service was widely recognized in the colonies and states prior to adoption of the Constitution. JAMES MADISON's original proposal for the BILL OF RIGHTS included a clause that "no person religiously scrupulous of bearing arms shall be compelled to render military service in person," but that clause was dropped, partly because conscription was considered a state function. The 1864 Draft Act and the SELECTIVE SERVICE ACT of 1917 both contained exemptions limited to members of religious denominations whose creeds forbade participation in war. The 1917 act excused objectors only from combatant service, but the War Department permitted some of those also opposed to noncombatant military service to be released for civilian service.

The 1940 Selective Service Act set the basic terms of exemption from the system of compulsory military service that operated during World War II, the KOREAN WAR, and the Vietnam War, and during the intervening periods of uneasy peace. A person was eligible "who, by reason of religious training and belief, [was] conscientiously opposed to participation in war in any form." Someone opposed even to noncombatant service could perform alternate civilian service. In response to a court of appeals decision interpreting "religious training and belief" very broadly, Congress in 1948 said that religious belief meant belief "in relation to a Supreme Being involving duties superior to those arising from any human relation. . . ." What Congress had attempted to do was relatively clear. It wanted to excuse only persons opposed to participation in all wars, not those opposed to particular wars, and it wanted to excuse only those whose opposition derived from religious belief in a rather traditional sense. The important Supreme Court cases have dealt with these lines of distinction.

By dint of strained interpretation of the statute, the Court has avoided a clear decision whether Congress could limit the exemption to traditional religious believers. First, in UNITED STATES V. SEEGER (1965), a large majority said that an applicant who spoke of a "religious faith in a purely ethical creed" was entitled to the exemption because his belief occupied a place in his life parallel to that of a belief in God for the more orthodox. Then, in Welsh v. United States (1970), four Justices held that someone who laid no claim to being religious at all qualified because his ethical beliefs occupied a place in his life parallel to that of religious beliefs for others. Four other Justices acknowledged that Congress had explicitly meant to exclude such applicants. Justice JOHN MARSHALL HARLAN urged that an attempt to distinguish religious objectors from equally sincere nonreligious ones constituted a forbidden ESTABLISHMENT OF RELIGION; the three other Justices thought that Congress could favor religious objectors in order to promote the free exercise of religion. Because the plurality's view of the statute was so implausible, most observers have supposed that its members probably agreed with Justice Harlan about the ultimate constitutional issue, but this particular tension between "no establishment" and "free exercise" concepts has not yet been decisively resolved.

In Gillette v. United States (1971), a decision covering both religious and nonreligious objectors to the Vietnam War, the Court upheld Congress's determination not to exempt those opposed to participation in particular wars. Against the claim that the distinction between "general" and "selective" objectors was impermissible, the Court responded that the distinction was supported by the public interest in a fairly administered system, given the difficulty officials would have dealing consistently with the variety of objections to particular wars. The Court also rejected the claim that the selective objector's entitlement to free exercise of his religion created a constitutionally grounded right to avoid military service.

In other limited areas, the Court has taken the step of acknowledging a free exercise right to be exempt from a generally imposed obligation. Those religiously opposed to jury duty cannot be compelled to serve, and adherents of traditional religious groups that provide an alternative way of life for members cannot be required to send children to school beyond the eighth grade. (See WISCONSIN V. YODER, 1972.) Nor can a person be deprived of unemployment benefits when an unwillingness to work on Saturday is religiously based, though receptivity to jobs including Saturday work is a usual condition of eligibility. (See SHERBERT V. VERNER, 1963.) What these cases suggest is that if no powerful secular reason can be advanced for demanding uniform compliance, the Constitution may require that persons with substantial religious objections be excused. To this degree the Constitution itself requires special treatment for conscientious objectors. Beyond that, its recognition of religious liberty and of governmental impartiality toward religions provides a source of values for legislative choice and constrains the classifications legislatures may make.

KENT GREENAWALT

Bibliography

FINN, JAMES, ED. 1968 A Conflict of Loyalties. New York: Pegasus.

GREENAWALT, KENT 1972 All or Nothing At All: The Defeat of Selective Conscientious Objection. *Supreme Court Review* 1971: 31–94.

SIBLEY, MULFORD QUICKERT and JACOB, PHILIP E. 1952 *Conscription of Conscience: The American State and the Conscientious Objector, 1940–1947.* Ithaca, N.Y.: Cornell University Press.

CONSCRIPTION

The power of the federal government to conscript may derive either from its power to raise armies or, more debatably, from its broadly interpreted power to regulate commerce. It is restricted by the THIRTEENTH AMENDMENT's prohibition of involuntary servitude or, conceivably, by the Fifth Amendment's guarantee of liberty. The manner in which conscription is conducted must comport with a familiar range of constitutional protections, notably those that guarantee EQUAL PROTECTION and RELIGIOUS LIBERTY.

Though the nation has employed systems of military conscription during the Civil War, both World Wars, and for all but twelve months between 1945 and 1972, the interplay of these different constitutional considerations has been remarkably underdeveloped. Two hundred years after the Constitution was written, at least two fundamental questions about conscription remain unresolved. What is the power of Congress (or the states) to conscript for civilian purposes? How, if at all, is a conscription system obliged to take account of CONSCIENTIOUS OBJECTION?

The ambiguity surrounding these questions derives in part from the fact that although the constitutionality of military conscription is well settled, the issue has not been settled well. In SELECTIVE DRAFT LAW CASES (1917) the Supreme Court reviewed the World War I military conscription statute and declared that it was "unable to conceive" how the performance of the "supreme and noble duty" of military service in time of war "can be said to be the imposition of involuntary servitude." Therefore, in its view, this contention was "precluded by its mere statement."

This terse comment establishes no conceptual basis for the analysis of later questions. Unfortunately, also, history is not a particularly helpful guide. The intention of the Framers is not clear. At the time of the Constitution, it was accepted that state militias could conscript soldiers, but the central government could not do so. At the same time, the Constitution gave the Congress the power to "raise armies" and it was widely recognized that it could not tenably rely on volunteers. On the basis of this evidence some scholars have argued that to conclude that conscription (as opposed to enlistment) was a power given to Congress is logical, and others have called this conclusion absurd.

Legislative history and judicial PRECEDENT in this first century of the Republic are similarly uninformative. When the Supreme Court decided the *Selective Draft Law Cases* it had only two precedents for a military draft: first, Secretary of War JAMES MONROE's proposal for conscription during the War of 1812, a proposal still under compromise deliberation by Congress when peace arrived; and, second, the Civil War Enrollment Act, the constitutionality of which had been ruled on only by a sharply divided and perplexed Supreme Court of Pennsylvania.

The most significant judicial precedent, *Butler v. Perry* (1916), had been decided only a year before by the Supreme Court itself. Here the Court rejected a Thirteenth Amendment challenge to a Florida statute requiring adult men to work one week a year on public roads: "from colonial days to the present time, conscripted labor has been much relied on for the construction and maintenance of public roads," and the Thirteenth Amendment "certainly was not intended to interdict enforcement of those duties which individuals owe to the state."

No subsequent Supreme Court decision limits this sweeping view of the power to conscript. To the contrary, the Court held in *United States v. Macintosh* (1931) that the right of conscientious objection is only statutory and in ROSTKER V. GOLDBERG (1981) that the government can compel an all-male military registration in the face of equal protection contentions founded on a theory of SEX DISCRIMINATION.

Notwithstanding these decisions, it seems likely that a major constitutional issue would arise if the power to conscript were asserted more aggressively. Such an issue might arise if, for example, participation were coerced in a system of civilian national service or if the statutory right of conscientious objection were abolished. In that event, the question thus far begged—what "duties . . . individuals owe to the state"—would have to be, for the first time, seriously addressed.

RICHARD DANZIG
IRA NERKEN

Bibliography

ANDERSON, MARTIN and BLOOM, VALERIE 1976 *Conscription: A Select and Annotated Bibliography.* Stanford, Calif.: Hoover Institution Press.

FRIEDMAN, LEON 1969 Conscription and the Constitution: The Original Understanding. *Michigan Law Review* 67:1493–1552.

MALBIN, MICHAEL J. 1972 Conscription, the Constitution, and the Framers: An Historial Analysis. *Fordham Law Review* 40:805–826.

CONSENT DECREE

In a civil suit in EQUITY, such as a suit for an INJUNCTION or a DECLARATORY JUDGMENT, the court's order is called a decree. By negotiation, the plaintiff and the defendant may agree to ask the court to enter a decree that they have drafted. If the court approves, its order is called a consent decree. Federal courts frequently enter consent degrees in actions to enforce regulatory laws in fields such as antitrust, EMPLOYMENT DISCRIMINATION, and ENVIRONMENTAL REGULATION.

KENNETH L. KARST

(SEE ALSO: *Antitrust Law and the Constitution; Plea Bargaining.*)

CONSENT SEARCH

When an individual consents to a search, he effectively waives his rights under the FOURTH AMENDMENT and makes it unnecessary for the police to obtain a SEARCH WARRANT. In determining the validity of such a consent, the trial court must determine whether the consent was voluntary. The consent of a person illegally held is not considered voluntary. However, an explicit warning about one's constitutional rights, which MIRANDA V. ARIZONA (1966) made mandatory for custodial interrogation, is not a condition for effective consent to a search, under the decision in SCHNECKLOTH V. BUSTAMONTE (1973).

Consent must obviously be obtained from a person entitled to grant it. Not ownership of the premises but the right to occupy and use them to the exclusion of others is the decisive criterion. Thus, the consent of a landlord to search premises let to others is worthless. The consenting party controls the terms of the consent: it may be as broad or as narrow as he wishes to make it, allowing a search of an entire dwelling or merely of one small item.

For a consent by another person to be valid as against a defendant, it must be shown that the consenting party possessed common authority in the place or things searched. Anyone with joint access or control of the premises may consent to a search.

JACOB W. LANDYNSKI

Bibliography
LAFAVE, WAYNE R. 1978 *Search and Seizure: A Treatise on the Fourth Amendment.* Vol. 2:610–774. St. Paul, Minn.: West Publishing Co.

CONSPIRACY

See: Criminal Conspiracy

CONSTITUTION

At the time of the Stamp Act controversy, a British lord told BENJAMIN FRANKLIN that Americans had wrong ideas about the British constitution. British and American ideas did differ radically. The American Revolution repudiated the British understanding of the constitution; in a sense, the triumph in America of a novel concept of "constitution" *was* the "revolution." The British, who were vague about their unwritten constitution, meant by it their system of government, the COMMON LAW, royal proclamations, major legislation such as MAGNA CARTA and the BILL OF RIGHTS, and various usages and customs of government animating the aggregation of laws, institutions, rights, and practices that had evolved over centuries. Statute, however, was the supreme part of the British constitution. After the Glorious Revolution of 1688–1689, Parliament dominated the constitutional system and by ordinary legislation could and did alter it. Sir WILLIAM BLACKSTONE summed up parliamentary supremacy when he declared in his *Commentaries* (1766), "What Parliament doth, no power on earth can undo."

The principle that Parliament had unlimited power was at the crux of the controversy leading to the American Revolution. The American assertion that government is limited undergirded the American concept of a constitution as a FUNDAMENTAL LAW that imposes regularized restraints upon power and reserves rights to the people. The American concept emerged slowly through the course of the colonial period, yet its nub was present almost from the beginning, especially in New England where covenant theology, SOCIAL COMPACT THEORY, and HIGHER LAW theory blended together. THOMAS HOOKER in 1638 preached that the foundation of authority lay in the people who might choose their governors and "set bounds and limitations on their powers." A century later Jared Elliot of Massachusetts preached that a "legal government" exists when the sovereign power "puts itself under restraints and lays itself under limitations. This is what we call a legal, limited, and well constituted government." Some liberal theologians viewed God himself as a constitutional monarch, limited in power because he had limited himself to the terms of his covenant with mankind. Moreover God ruled a constitutional universe based on immutable natural laws that also bound him. Jonathan Mayhew preached in Boston that no one has a right to exercise a wanton SOVEREIGNTY over the property, lives, and consciences of the people—"such a sovereignty as some inconsiderately ascribe to the supreme governor of the world." Mayhew explained that "God himself does not govern in an absolute, arbitrary, and despotic manner. The power of this almighty king is limited by law; not indeed, by acts of Parliament, but by the eternal laws of truth, wisdom, and equity. . . ."

Political theory and law as well as religion taught that government was limited; so did history. But the Americans took their views on such matters from a highly selective and romanticized image of seventeenth-century England, which they perpetuated in America even as England changed. Seventeenth-century England was the England of the great struggle for constitutional liberty by the common law courts and Puritan parliaments against despotic Stuart kings. Seventeenth-century England was the England of EDWARD COKE, JOHN LILBURNE, and JOHN LOCKE. It was an England in which religion, law, and politics converged with theory and experience to produce limited monarchy and, ironically, parliamentary supremacy. To Americans, however, Parliament had bound itself by reaffirming Magna Carta and passing the HABEAS CORPUS ACT, the Bill of Rights, and the TOLERATION ACT, among others. Locke had taught the social contract theory; advocated that taxation without representation or consent is tyranny; written that "government is not free to do as it pleases," and referred to the "bounds" which "the law of God and Nature have set to the legislative power of every commonwealth, in all forms of government."

Such ideas withered but did not die in eighteenth-century England. CATO'S LETTERS popularized Locke on both sides of the Atlantic; Henry St. John (Viscount Bolingbroke) believed that Parliament could not annul the constitution; Charles Viner's *General Abridgment of Law and Equity* endorsed Coke's views in Dr. BONHAM'S CASE (1610); and even as Parliament debated the Declaratory Act (1766), which asserted parliamentary power to legislate for America "in all cases whatsoever," CHARLES PRATT (Lord Camden) declared such a power "absolutely illegal, contrary to the fundamental laws of . . . this constitution. . . ."

Richard Price and Granville Sharpe were two of the many English radicals who shared the American view of the British constitution.

TAXATION WITHOUT REPRESENTATION provoked Americans to clarify their views. JAMES OTIS, arguing against the tax on sugar, relied on *Dr. Bonham's Case* and contended that legislative authority did not extend to the "fundamentals of the constitution," which he believed to be fixed. THOMAS HUTCHINSON, a leading supporter of Parliament, summed up the American constitutional reaction to the stamp tax duties by writing, "The prevailing reason at this time is, that the Act of Parliament is against Magna Charta and the NATURAL RIGHTS of Englishmen, and therefore according to Lord Coke, null and void." The TOWNSHEND ACT duties led to American declarations that the supreme legislature in any free state derives its power from the constitution, which limits government. JOHN DICKINSON, in an essay reprinted throughout the colonies, wrote that a free people are not those subject to a reasonable exercise of government power but those "who live under a government so constitutionally checked and controlled, that proper provision is made against its being otherwise exercised." J. J. Zubly of Georgia was another of many who argued that no government, not even Parliament, could make laws against the constitution any more than it could alter the constitution. An anonymous pamphleteer rhapsodized in 1775 about the "glorious constitution worthy to be engraved in capitals of gold, on pillars of marble; to be perpetuated through all time, a barrier, to circumscribe and bound the restless ambition of aspiring monarchs, and the palladium of civil liberty. . . ." TOM PAINE actually argued that Great Britain had no constitution, because Parliament claimed to exercise any power it pleased. To Paine a constitution could not be an act of the government but of "people constituting government. . . . A constitution is a thing antecedent to a government; a government is only the creature of the constitution."

Thus, by "constitution," Americans meant a supreme law creating the government, limiting it, unalterable by it, and above it. When they said that an act of government was unconstitutional, they meant that the government had acted lawlessly because it lacked the authority to perform that act. Accordingly the act was not law; it was null and void, and it could be disobeyed. By contrast when the British spoke of a statute being unconstitutional, they meant only that it was impolitic, unwise, unjust, or inexpedient, but not that it was beyond the power of the government to enact. They did not mean that Parliament was limited in its powers and had exceeded them.

The American view of "constitution" was imperfectly understood even by many leaders of the revolutionary movement as late as 1776. The proof is that when the states framed their first constitutions, the task was left to legislatures, although some received explicit authorization from the voters. THOMAS JEFFERSON worried because Virginia had not differentiated fundamental from ordinary law. Not until Massachusetts framed its constitution of 1780 by devising a CONSTITUTIONAL CONVENTION did the American theory match practice. When the CONSTITUTIONAL CONVENTION OF 1787 met in Philadelphia, the American meaning of a constitution was fixed and consistent.

LEONARD W. LEVY

Bibliography
ADAMS, RANDOLPH G. (1922)1958 3rd ed. *Political Ideas of the American Revolution.* New York: Barnes & Noble.
BAILYN, BERNARD 1967 *Ideological Origins of the American Revolution.* Cambridge, Mass.: Harvard University Press.
BALDWIN, ALICE M. (1928) 1958 *The New England Clergy and the American Revolution.* New York: Frederick Ungar.
MCLAUGHLIN, ANDREW C. 1932 *The Foundations of American Constitutionalism.* New York: New York University Press.
MULLETT, CHARLES F. 1933 *Fundamental Law and the American Revolution.* New York: Columbia University Press.

CONSTITUTIONAL COMMON LAW

"Constitutional common law" refers to a theory about the lawmaking competence of the federal courts. The theory postulates that much of what passes as constitutional adjudication is best understood as a judicially fashioned COMMON LAW authorized and inspired, but not compelled, by the constitutional text and structure. Unlike the "true" constitutional law exemplified by MARBURY V. MADISON (1803), constitutional common law is ultimately amenable to control and revision by Congress. The theory originated in an effort to explain how the Supreme Court could legitimately insist upon application of the EXCLUSIONARY RULE in state criminal proceedings, once the Court had recast the exclusionary rule as simply a judicially fashioned remedy designed to deter future unlawful police conduct rather than as part and parcel of a criminal defendant's underlying constitutional rights or a necessary remedy for the violation thereof. On this view of the exclusionary rule, why does the state court have a constitutional obligation to do more than provide an "adequate" remedy for the underlying constitutional violation, such as an action for DAMAGES? The source of the Supreme Court's authority to insist that the state courts follow any rule not required by the constitution or authorized by some federal statute is not evident. ERIE RAILROAD V. TOMPKINS (1938) makes plain that the federal courts have no power to create a general FEDERAL COMMON LAW. This limitation exists not simply because of Congress's express statutory command, applicable to civil cases in the federal district courts, but because of the perception that there is no general federal judicial power to displace state law. To the contrary, the courts must point to some authoritative source—a statute, a treaty, a constitutional provision—as explicitly or implicitly authorizing judicial creation of substantive federal law. That federal statutes can constitute such authority has long been clear, and the result has been in many areas judicial creation of a federal common law designed to implement federal statutory policies. There is no a priori reason to suppose that the Constitution itself should differ from statutes in providing a basis for the generation of an interstitial federal common law. Not surprisingly, therefore, a significant body of federal common law has been developed on the basis of constitutional provisions. For example, the Supreme Court has developed bodies of federal substantive law on the basis of the constitutional (and statutory) grants of jurisdiction to hear cases in ADMIRALTY, as well as cases involving disputes among the states or implicating FOREIGN AFFAIRS. Because the Court's decisions are ultimately reversible by Congress, its decisions holding statutes to be invalid burdens upon INTERSTATE COMMERCE are also best understood as federal common law created by the Court on the authority of the COMMERCE CLAUSE.

In the foregoing examples, constitutional common law has been created to govern situations where state interests are subordinated to interests of special concern to the national government, and thus come within the reach of the plenary national legislative power. They are FEDERALISM cases, in that the federal common law implements and fills out the authority that has been committed to the national government by the constitutional text and structure. Thus, the principle of these cases arguably is limited to the generation of federal constitutional common law in support of national legislative competence. These "federalism" cases do not by themselves establish that the Court may fashion a common law based solely upon constitutional provisions framed as *limitations* on governmental power in order to vindicate CIVIL LIBERTIES, such as those protected by the FIRST AMENDMENT and FOURTH AMENDMENT. Such a judicial rule-making authority—which seeks to create federal rules in areas of primary *state* concern—intersects with federalism concerns in ways that sets these cases apart from the federalism cases. Moreover, at the national level judicial creation of common law implicates SEPARATION OF POWERS considerations. Nonetheless, the Court's constitutionally based common law decisions in areas of plenary national legislative authority at least invite inquiry whether the specific constitutional guarantees of individual liberty might also authorize the creation of a substructure of judicially fashioned rules to carry out the purposes and policies of those guarantees. Several COMMENTATORS have, directly or indirectly, argued for acceptance of judicial power to fashion such a subconstitutional law of civil liberties. They argue that recognition of such a power is the most satisfactory way to rationalize a large and steadily growing body of judicial decision, not only in the criminal procedure area but also with many of the Court's administrative DUE PROCESS cases, while at the same time recognizing a coordinate and controlling authority in Congress. There has, however, been no significant judicial consideration of this theory apart from the decision in *Turpin v. Mailet* (2d Cir., *en banc*, 1978–1979).

Whatever its perceived advantages, a theory that posits a competence in the courts to fashion a constitutionally inspired constitutional common law of civil liberties must deal adequately with a series of objections: that development of such a body of law is inconsistent with the original intent of the Framers; that the line between true constitutional interpretation and constitutional common law is too indeterminate to be useful; and that the existence of such judicial power is inconsistent with the autonomy of the executive department in enforcing law as well as the rightful independence of the states in the federal system. The theory of constitutional common law bears a family resemblance to the views of those commentators who hold that the Court may legitimately engage in "noninterpretive" review—that is, the Court may properly impose values on the political branches not fairly inferrable from the constitutional text or the structure it creates—but who insist that Congress may control those decisions by regulating the JURISDICTION of the Supreme Court. Other differences aside,

the constitutional common law view would permit Congress to overrule the noninterpretive decisions directly, bypassing the awkward theoretical and political problems associated with congressional attempts to manipulate jurisdiction for substantive ends.

HENRY P. MONAGHAN

Bibliography

MONAGHAN, HENRY P. 1975 The Supreme Court, 1974 Term—Foreword: Constitutional Common Law. *Harvard Law Review* 89:1–45.
SCHROCK, THOMAS S. and WELSH, ROBERT C. 1978 Reconsidering the Constitutional Common Law. *Harvard Law Review* 91:1117–1176.

CONSTITUTIONAL CONVENTION

Constitutional conventions, like the written constitutions that they produce, are among the American contributions to government. A constitutional convention became the means that a free people used to put into practice the SOCIAL COMPACT THEORY by devising their FUNDAMENTAL LAW. Such a convention is a representative body acting for the sovereign people to whom it is responsible. Its sole commission is to frame a CONSTITUTION; it does not pass laws, perform acts of administration, or govern in any way. It submits its work for popular ratification and adjourns. Such a convention first came into being during the American Revolution. The institutionalizing of constitutional principles during wartime was the constructive achievement of the Revolution. The Revolution's enduring heroics are to be found in constitution-making. As JAMES MADISON exultantly declared, "Nothing has excited more admiration in the world than the manner in which free governments have been established in America; for it was the first instance, from the creation of the world . . . that free inhabitants have been seen deliberating on a form of government and selecting such of their citizens as possessed their confidence, to determine upon and give effect to it."

Within a century of 1776 nearly two hundred state constitutional conventions had been held in the United States. The institution is so familiar that we forget how novel it was even in 1787. At the CONSTITUTIONAL CONVENTION, which framed this nation's constitution, OLIVER ELLSWORTH declared that since the framing of the ARTICLES OF CONFEDERATION (1781), "a new sett [sic] of ideas seemed to have crept in. . . . Conventions of the people, or with power derived expressly from the people, were not then thought of. The Legislatures were considered as competent."

Credit for understanding that legislatures were not competent for that task belongs to JOHN LILBURNE, the English Leveller leader, who probably originated the idea of a constitutional convention. In his *Legall Fundamentall Liberties* (1649), he proposed that specially elected representatives should frame an Agreement of the People, or constitution, "which Agreement ought to be above Law; and therefore [set] bounds, limits, and extent of the people's Legislative Deputies in Parliament." Similarly, Sir Henry Vane, once governor of Massachusetts, proposed, in his *Healing Question* (1656), that a "convention" be chosen by the free consent of the people, "not properly to exercise the legislative power" but only to agree on "fundamentall constitutions" expressing the will of the people "in their highest state of soveraignty. . . ." The idea, which never made headway in England, was reexpressed in a pamphlet by Obadiah Hulme in 1771, recommending that a constitution should "be formed by a convention of delegates of the people, appointed for the express purpose," and that the constitution should never be "altered in any respect by any power besides the power which first framed [it]." Hulme's work was reprinted in Philadelphia in 1776 immediately before the framing of the PENNSYLVANIA CONSTITUTION by a specially elected convention. That convention, however, in accordance with prevailing ideas, simultaneously exercised the powers of government and after promulgating its constitution remained in session as the state legislature. Until 1780 American legislatures wrote constitutions.

The theory underlying a constitutional convention, but not the actual idea of having one, was first proposed in America by the town meeting of Pittsfield, Massachusetts, on May 29, 1776. Massachusetts then had a provisional revolutionary extralegal government. Pittsfield asked, "What Compact has been formed as the foundation of Government in this province?" The collapse of British power over the colonies had thrown the people, "the foundation of power," into "a state of Nature." The first step to restore civil government on a permanent basis was "the formation of a fundamental Constitution as the Basis & ground work of Legislation." The existing legislature, Pittsfield contended, although representative, could not make the constitution because, "They being but servants of the people cannot be greater than their Masters, & must be responsible to them." A constitution is "above the whole Legislature," so that the "legislature cannot certainly make it. . . ." Pittsfield understood the difference between fundamental and ordinary law, yet inconsistently concluded that the legislature should frame the constitution on condition that it be submitted to the people for ratification.

Pittsfield was merely inconsistent, but the Continental Congress was bewildered. The provisional government of Massachusetts, requesting advice from Congress on how to institute government, said that it would accept a constitution proposed by Congress. That was in May 1775. Many years later, when his memory was not to be trusted, JOHN ADAMS recalled in his autobiography that congressmen went around asking each other, "How can the people institute government?" As late as May 1776, Congress, still lacking an answer, merely recommended that colonies without adequate governments should choose representatives to suppress royal authority and exercise power under popular authority. By then the temporary legislatures of New Hampshire and South Carolina, without popular authorization, had already framed and promulgated constitutions as if enacting statutory law, and continued to operate as legislatures. Adams, however, credited himself with knowing how to "realize [make real] the theories of the wisest writers," who had urged that sovereignty resides in the people and that government is made by contract. "This could be done," he explained, "only by conventions of representatives chosen by the people in the several colonies. . . ." How, congressmen asked him, can we know whether the people will submit to the new constitutions, and he recalled having replied, if there is doubt, "the convention may send out their project of a constitution, to the people in their several towns, counties, or districts, and the people may make the acceptance of it their own act." Congress did not follow his advice, he wrote, because of his "new, strange, and terrible doctrines."

Adams had described a procedure followed only in Massachusetts, and only after the legislature had asked the people of the towns for permission to frame a constitution and submit it for popular ratification. Several towns, led by Concord (see CONCORD TOWN MEETING RESOLUTIONS) protested that the legislature was not a competent body for the task, because a constitution had been overwhelmingly rejected in 1778. Concord had demanded a constitutional convention. In 1779 the legislature asked the towns to vote on the question whether a state constitution should be framed by a specially elected convention. The towns, voting by universal manhood suffrage, overwhelmingly approved. In late 1779 the delegates to the first constitutional convention in world history met in Cambridge and framed the MASSACHUSETTS CONSTITUTION of 1780, which the voters ratified after an intense public debate. With pride Thomas Dawes declared in an oration, "The people of Massachusetts have reduced to practice the wonderful theory. A numerous people have convened in a state of nature, and, like our ideas of the patriarchs, have authorized a few fathers of the land to draw up for them a glorious covenant." New Hampshire copied the procedure when revising its constitution in 1784, and it rapidly became standard procedure. Within a few years American constitutional theory had progressed from the belief that legislatures were competent to compose and announce constitutions, to the belief that a convention acting for the sovereign people is the only proper instrument for the task and that the sovereign must have the final word. A constitution, then, in American theory, is the supreme fundamental law that creates the legislature, authorizes its powers, and limits the exercise of its powers. The legislature is subordinate to the Constitution and cannot alter it.

LEONARD W. LEVY

Bibliography

ADAMS, WILLI PAUL 1980 *The First American Constitutions: Republican Ideology and the Making of the State Constitutions in the Revolutionary Era.* Chapel Hill: University of North Carolina Press.

DODD, WALTER F. 1910 *The Revision and Amendment of State Constitutions.* Baltimore: Johns Hopkins University Press.

JAMESON, JOHN ALEXANDER 1887 *A Treatise on Constitutional Conventions: Their History, Powers, and Modes of Proceeding.* 4th ed. Chicago: Callahan & Co.

MCLAUGHLIN, ANDREW C. 1932 *The Foundations of American Constitutionalism.* New York: New York University Press.

WOOD, GORDON S. 1969 *The Creation of the American Republic, 1776–1787.* Chapel Hill: University of North Carolina Press.

CONSTITUTIONAL CONVENTION OF 1787

Over the last two centuries, the work of the Constitutional Convention and the motives of the Founding Fathers have been analyzed under a number of different ideological auspices. To one generation of historians, the hand of God was moving in the assembly; under a later dispensation, the dialectic replaced the Deity: "relationships of production" moved into the niche previously reserved for Love of Country. Thus, in counterpoint to the Zeitgeist, the Framers have undergone miraculous metamorphoses: at one time acclaimed as liberals and bold social engineers, today they appear in the guise of sound Burkean conservatives.

The "Fathers" have thus been admitted to our best circles; the revolutionary generation that confiscated all Tory property in reach and populated New Brunswick with outlaws has been converted into devotees of "consensus" and "prescriptive rights." Indeed, there is one fundamental truth about the Founding Fathers that every generation of Zeitgeisters has done its best to obscure: they were first and foremost superb democratic politicians. They were political men—not metaphysicians, disembodied conservatives, or agents of history—and, as recent research into the nature of American politics in the 1780s confirms, they were required to work within a democratic framework. The Philadelphia Convention was not a council of Platonic guardians working within a manipulative, predemocratic framework; it was a nationalist reform caucus which had to operate with great delicacy and skill in a political cosmos full of enemies to achieve the one definitive goal—popular approbation.

Perhaps the time has come, to borrow WALTON HAMILTON's fine phrase, to promote the Framers from immortality to mortality, to give them credit for their magnificent demonstration of the art of democratic politics: they made history and they did it within the limits of consensus. What they did was hammer out a pragmatic compromise that would both bolster the "national interest" and be acceptable to the people. What inspiration they got came from collective experience as politicians in a democratic society. As JOHN DICKINSON put it to his fellow delegates on August 13, "Experience must be our guide. Reason may mislead us."

When the Constitutionalists went forth to subvert the ARTICLES OF CONFEDERATION, they employed the mechanisms of political legitimacy. Although the roadblocks confronting them were formidable, they were also endowed with certain political talents. From 1786 to 1790 the Constitutionalists used those talents against bumbling, erratic behavior by the opponents of reform. Effectively, the Constitutionalists had to induce the states, by democratic techniques, to cripple themselves. To be specific, if New York should refuse to join the new Union, the project was doomed; yet before New York was safely in, the reluctant state legislature had to take the following steps: agree to send delegates to the Convention and maintain them there; set up the special ratifying convention; and accept that convention's decision that New York should ratify the Constitution. The same legal hurdles existed in every state.

The group that undertook this struggle was an interesting amalgam of a few dedicated nationalists and self-interested spokesmen of various parochial bailiwicks. Georgians, for example, wanted a strong central authority to provide military protection against the Creek Confederacy; Jerseymen and Connecticuters wanted to escape from economic bondage to New York; Virginians sought a system recognizing that great state's "rightful" place in the councils of the Republic. These states' dominant political figures therefore cooperated in the call for the Convention. In other states, the cause of national reform was taken up by the "outs" who added the "national interest" to their weapons systems; in Pennsylvania, for instance, JAMES WILSON's group fighting to revise the state Constitution of 1776 came out four-square behind the Constitutionalists.

To say this is not to suggest that the Constitution was founded on base motives but to recognize that in politics there are no immaculate conceptions. It is not surprising that a number of diversified private interests promoted the nationalist public interest. However motivated, these men did demonstrate a willingness to compromise in behalf of an ideal that took shape before their eyes and under their ministrations.

What distinguished the leaders of the Constitutionalist caucus from their enemies was a "continental" approach to political, economic, and military issues. Their institutional base of operations was the Continental Congress (thirty-nine of the fifty-five designated delegates to the Convention had served in Congress), hardly a locale that inspired respect for the state governments. One can surmise that membership in the Congress had helped establish a continental frame of reference, particularly with respect to external affairs. The average state legislator was probably about as concerned with foreign policy then as he is today, but congressmen were constantly forced to take the broad view of American prestige, and to listen to the reports of Secretary JOHN JAY and their envoys in Europe. A "continental" ideology thus developed, demanding invigoration of our domestic institutions to assure our rightful place in the international arena. Indeed, an argument with the force of GEORGE WASHINGTON as its incarnation urged that our very survival in the Hobbesian jungle of world politics depended upon a reordering and strengthening of our national SOVEREIGNTY.

MERRILL JENSEN seems quite sound in his view that to most Americans, engaged as they were in self-sustaining agriculture, the "Critical Period" was not particularly critical. The great achievement of the Constitutionalists was their ultimate success in convincing the elected representatives of a majority of the white male population that change was imperative. A small group of political leaders with a continental vision and essentially a consciousness of the United States' international impotence, was the core of the movement. To their standard rallied other leaders' parallel ambitions. Their great assets were active support from George Washington, whose prestige was enormous; the energy and talent of their leadership; a communications "network" far superior to the opposition's; the preemptive skill which made "their" issue The Issue and kept the locally oriented opposition on the defensive; and the new and compelling credo of American nationalism.

Despite great institutional handicaps, the Constitutionalists in the mid-1780s got the jump on the local oppositions with the demand for a Convention. Their opponents were caught in an old political trap: they were not being asked to approve any specific reform but only to endorse a meeting to discuss and recommend needed reforms. If they took a hard line, they were put in the position of denying the need for any changes. Moreover, because the states would have the final say on any proposals that might emerge from the Convention, the Constitutionalists could go to the people with a persuasive argument for "fair play."

Perhaps because of their poor intelligence system, perhaps because of overconfidence generated by the failure of all previous efforts to alter the Articles, the opposition awoke too late. Not only did the Constitutionalists manage to get every state but Rhode Island to appoint delegates to Philadelphia but they also dominated the delegations. The fact that the delegates to Philadelphia were appointed by state governments, not elected by the people, has been advanced as evidence of the "undemocratic" character of the gathering, but this argument is specious. The existing central government under the Articles was considered a creature of the states—not as a consequence of elitism or fear of the mob but as a logical extension of STATES' RIGHTS doctrine. The national government was not supposed to end-run the state legislatures and make direct contact with the people.

With delegations named, the focus shifted to Philadelphia. While waiting for a quorum to assemble, JAMES MADISON drafted the so-called VIRGINIA PLAN. This was a political masterstroke: once business got underway, this plan provided the framework of discussion. Instead of arguing interminably over the agenda, the delegates took the Virginia Plan as their point of departure, including its major premise: a new start on a Constitution rather than piecemeal amendment. This proposal was not necessarily revolutionary—a new Constitution might have been formulated as "amendments" to the Articles of Confederation—but the provision that amendments take effect after approval by nine states was thoroughly subversive. The Articles required unanimous state approval for any amendment.

Standard treatments of the Convention divide the delegates into "nationalists" and "states' righters" with various shadings, but these latter-day characterizations obfuscate more than they clarify. The Convention was remarkably homogeneous in ideology. ROBERT YATES and JOHN LANSING, Clinton's two chaperones for ALEXANDER HAMILTON, left in disgust on July 10. LUTHER MARTIN left in a huff on September 4; others went home for personal reasons. But the hard core of delegates accepted a grinding regimen throughout a Philadelphia summer precisely because they shared the Constitutionalist goal.

Basic differences of opinion emerged, of course, but these were not ideological; they were structural. If the so-called states' rights group had not accepted the fundamental purposes of the Convention, they could simply have pulled out and aborted the whole enterprise. Instead of bolting, they returned day after day to argue and to compromise. An index of this basic homogeneity was the initial agreement on secrecy: these professional politicians wanted to retain the freedom of maneuver that would be possible only if they were not forced to take public stands during preliminary negotiations. There was no legal means of binding the tongues of the delegates: at any stage a delegate with basic objections to the emerging project could have denounced the convention. Yet the delegates generally observed the injunction; Madison did not even inform THOMAS JEFFERSON in Paris of the course of the deliberations. Secrecy is uncharacteristic of any assembly marked by ideological polarization. During the Convention the *New York Daily Advertiser* called the secrecy "a happy omen, as it demonstrates that the spirit of party on any great and essential point cannot have arisen to any height."

Some key Framers must have been disappointed. Commentators on the Constitution who have read THE FEDERALIST but not Madison's record of the actual debates (secret until after his death in 1836), have credited the Fathers with a sublime invention called "Federalism." Yet the Constitution's final balance between the states and the nation must have dissatisfied Madison, whose Virginia Plan envisioned a unitary national government effectively freed from and dominant over the states. Hamilton's unitary views are too well known to need elucidation.

Under the Virginia Plan the general government was freed from state control in a truly radical fashion, and the scope of its authority was breathtaking. The national legislature was to be empowered to disallow the acts of state legislatures, and the central government would be vested, in addition to the powers of the nation under the Articles of Confederation, with plenary authority "wherever . . . the separate States are incompetent or in which the harmony of the United States may be interrupted by the exercise of individual legislation." Finally, the national Congress was to be given the power to use military force on recalcitrant states.

The Convention was not scandalized by this militant program for a strong autonomous central government. Some delegates were startled, some leery of so comprehensive a reform, but nobody set off any fireworks and nobody walked out. Moreover, within two weeks the general principles of the Virginia Plan had received substantial endorsement. The temper of the gathering can be deduced from its unanimous approval, on May 31, of a resolution giving Congress authority to disallow state legislation "contravening in its opinion the Articles of Union."

Perhaps the Virginia Plan was the delegates' ideological Utopia, but as discussions became more specific many of them had second thoughts. They were practical politicians in a democratic society, and they would have to take home an acceptable package and defend it—and their own political futures—against predictable attack. June 14 saw the breaking point between dream and reality. Apparently realizing that under the Virginia Plan, Massachusetts, Virginia, and Pennsylvania could virtually dominate the national government, the delegates from the small states demanded time for a consideration of alternatives. John Dickinson reproached Madison: "You see the consequences of pushing things too far. Some of the members from the small States wish for two branches in the General Legislature and are friends to a good National Government; but we would sooner submit to a foreign power than . . . be deprived of an equality of suffrage in both branches of the Legislature, and thereby be thrown under the domination of the large States."

Now the process of accommodation was put into action smoothly—and wisely, given the character and strength of the doubters. Madison had the votes, but mechanical majoritarianism could easily have destroyed the objectives of the majority: the Constitutionalists sought a qualitative as well as a quantitative consensus, a political imperative to attain ratification.

According to the standard script, the "states' rights" group now united behind the NEW JERSEY PLAN, which has been characteristically portrayed as no more than a minor modification of the Articles of Confederation. The New Jersey Plan did put the states back into the institutional picture, but to do so was a recognition of political reality rather than an affirmation of states' rights.

Paterson, the leading spokesman for the project, said as much: "I came here not to speak my own sentiments, but the sentiments of those who sent me. Our object is not such a Government as may be best in itself, but such a one as our Constituents have authorized us to prepare, and as they will approve." This is Madison's version; in Yates's transcription, a crucial sentence follows: "I believe that a little practical virtue is to be preferred to the finest theoretical principles, which cannot be carried into effect."

The advocates of the New Jersey Plan concentrated their fire on what they held to be the political liabilities of the Virginia Plan—which were matters of institutional structure—rather than on the proposed scope of national authority. Indeed, the SUPREMACY CLAUSE of the Constitution first saw the light of day in Paterson's Sixth Resolution; for Paterson, under either the Virginia or the New Jersey system the general government would "act on individuals and not on states." From the states' rights viewpoint, this was heresy.

Paterson thus reopened the agenda of the Convention, but within a distinctly nationalist framework. Paterson favored a strong central government but opposed putting the big states in the saddle. As evidence for this there is an intriguing proposal among Paterson's preliminary drafts of the New Jersey Plan:

Whereas it is necessary in Order to form the People of the U.S. of America in to a Nation, that the States should be consolidated, . . . it is therefore resolved, that all the Lands contained within the Limits of each state individually, and of the U.S. generally be considered as constituting one Body or Mass, and be divided into thirteen or more integral parts.

Resolved, That such Divisions or integral Parts shall be styled Districts.

He may have gotten the idea from his New Jersey colleague Judge DAVID BREARLEY, who on June 9 had commented that the only remedy to the dilemma over representation was "that a map of the U.S. be spread out, that all the existing boundaries be erased, and that a new partition of the whole be made into 13 equal parts." According to Yates, Brearley added

at this point, "then a government on the present [Virginia Plan] system will be just."

Thus, the delegates from the small states announced that they were unprepared to be offered up as sacrificial victims to a "national interest" that reflected Virginia's parochial ambition. Caustic CHARLES PINCKNEY was not far off when he remarked sardonically that "the whole conflict comes to this: Give New Jersey an equal vote, and she will dismiss her scruples, and concur in the National system." What he rather unfairly did not add was that the Jersey delegates were not free agents who could adhere to their private convictions; they had to stake their reputations and political careers on the reforms approved by the Convention—in New Jersey, not Virginia.

Paterson spoke on Saturday, and the weekend must have seen a good deal of consultation, argument, and caucusing. One delegate prepared a full-length address: on Monday Alexander Hamilton, previously mute, rose and delivered a six-hour oration. It was a remarkably apolitical speech; the gist of his position was that both the Virginia and New Jersey Plans were inadequately centralist, and he detailed a reform program reminiscent of the Protectorate under the Cromwellian *Instrument of Government* of 1653. He wanted, to take a striking phrase from a letter to George Washington, a "strong well mounted government."

From all accounts this was a compelling speech, but it had little practical effect; the Convention adjourned, admired Hamilton's rhetoric, and returned to business. Hamilton, never a patient man, stayed another ten days and then left in disgust for New York. Although he returned to Philadelphia sporadically and attended the last two weeks of the Convention, Hamilton played no part in the laborious task of hammering out the Constitution. His day came later when he led the New York Constitutionalists into the savage imbroglio over ratification—an arena in which his unmatched talent for political infighting surely won the day.

On June 19 James Madison led off with a long, carefully reasoned speech analyzing the New Jersey Plan; although intellectually vigorous in his criticisms, Madison was quite conciliatory in mood: "The great difficulty lies in the affair of REPRESENTATION; and if this could be adjusted, all others would be surmountable." When he finished, a vote was taken on whether to continue with the Virginia Plan as the nucleus for a new constitution: seven states voted yes; New York, New Jersey, and Delaware voted No; and Maryland was divided.

Paterson, it seems, lost decisively; yet in a fundamental sense he and his allies had achieved their purpose: from that day onward, it could never be forgotten that the state governments loomed ominously in the background. Moreover, nobody bolted the convention. Paterson and his colleagues set to work to modify the Virginia Plan, particularly with respect to representation in the national legislature. They won an immediate rhetorical bonus; when OLIVER ELLSWORTH of Connecticut moved that the word "national" be expunged from the Third Virginia Resolution ("Resolved that a *national* Government ought to be established consisting of a *supreme* Legislative, Executive and Judiciary"), Randolph agreed and the motion passed unanimously. The process of compromise had begun.

For two weeks the delegates circled around the problem of legislative representation. The Connecticut delegation appears to have evolved a possible compromise early in the debates, but the Virginians, particularly Madison, fought obdurately against providing for equal representation of states in the second chamber. There was enough acrimony for BENJAMIN FRANKLIN to propose institution of a daily prayer, but on July 2, the ice began to break when the majority against equality of representation was converted into a dead tie. The Convention was ripe for a solution and the South Carolinians proposed a committee. Madison and James Wilson wanted none of it, but with only Pennsylvania dissenting, a working party was established to cope with the problem of representation.

The members of this committee, one from each state, were elected by the delegates. Although the Virginia Plan had held majority support up to that date, neither Madison nor Randolph was selected. This was not to be a "fighting" committee; the members could be described as "second-level political entrepreneurs."

There is a common rumor that the Framers divided their time between philosophical discussions of government and reading the classics in political theory. In fact, concerns were highly practical; they spent little time canvassing abstractions. A number of them had some acquaintance with the history of political theory, and it was a poor rhetorician indeed who could not cite JOHN LOCKE, MONTESQUIEU, or James Harrington in support of a desired goal. Yet up to this point no one had expounded a defense of states' rights or the SEPARATION OF POWERS on anything resembling a theoretical basis. The Madison model effectively vested all governmental power in the national legislature.

Because the critical fight was over representation

of the states, once the GREAT COMPROMISE was adopted on July 17 the Convention was over the hump. Madison, James Wilson, and GOUVERNEUR MORRIS fought the compromise all the way in a last-ditch effort to get a unitary state with parliamentary supremacy. But their allies deserted them and after their defeat they demonstrated a willingness to swallow their objections and get on with the business. Moreover, once the compromise had carried (by five states to four, with one state divided), its advocates threw themselves into the job of strengthening the general government's substantive powers. Madison demonstrated his devotion to the art of politics when he later prepared essays for *The Federalist* in contradiction to the basic convictions he expressed in the Convention.

Two ticklish issues illustrate the later process of accommodation. The first was the institutional position of the executive. Madison argued for a chief magistrate chosen by the national legislature, and on May 29 this proposal had been adopted with a provision for a seven-year nonrenewable term. In late July this was reopened; groups now opposed election by the legislature. One felt that the states should have a hand in the process; another small but influential circle urged direct election by the people. There were a number of proposals: election by the people, by state governors, by electors chosen by state legislatures, by the national legislature. There was some resemblance to three-dimensional chess in the dispute because of the presence of two other variables: length of tenure and eligibility for reelection. Finally the thorny problem was consigned to a committee for resolution.

The Brearley Committee on Postponed Matters was a superb aggregation of talent and its compromise on the Executive was a masterpiece of creativity. Everybody present knew that under any system devised, George Washington would be the first President; thus they were dealing in the future tense. To a body of working politicians the merits of the Brearley proposal were obvious: everyone could argue to his constituents that he had really won the day. First, the state legislatures had the right to determine the mode of selection of the electors; second, the small states were guaranteed a minimum of three votes in the ELECTORAL COLLEGE while the big states got acceptance of the principle of proportional power; third, if the state legislatures agreed (as six did in the first presidential election), the people could be involved directly in the choice of electors; and finally, if no candidate received a majority in the College, the decision passed to the House of Representatives with each state having one vote.

This compromise was almost too good to be true, and the Framers snapped it up with little debate or controversy. Thus the Electoral College was neither an exercise in applied Platonism nor an experiment in indirect government based on elitist distrust of the masses. It was merely an improvisation which was subsequently, in *The Federalist* #68, endowed with high theoretical content.

The second issue on which some substantial bargaining took place was SLAVERY. The morality of slavery was, by design, not an issue; but in its other concrete aspects, slavery influenced the arguments over taxation, commerce, and representation. The THREE-FIFTHS RULE—that three-fifths of the slaves would be counted both for representation and for purposes of DIRECT TAXATION—had allayed some northern fears about southern overrepresentation, but doubts remained. Southerners, on the other hand, were afraid that congressional control over commerce would lead to the exclusion of slaves or to their prohibitive taxation as imports. Moreover, the Southerners were disturbed over "navigation acts" (tariffs), or special legislation providing, for example, that exports be carried only in American ships. They depended upon exports, and so urged inclusion of a proviso that navigation and commercial laws require a two-thirds vote in Congress.

These problems came to a head in late August and, as usual, were handed to a committee in the hope that, in Gouverneur Morris's words, "these things may form a bargain among the Northern and Southern states." The Committee reported its measures of reconciliation on August 25, and on August 29 the package was wrapped up and delivered. What occurred can best be described in George Mason's dour version. Mason anticipated JOHN C. CALHOUN in his conviction that permitting navigation acts to pass by majority vote would put the South in economic bondage to the North. Mainly on this ground, he refused to sign the Constitution. Mason said:

The Constitution as agreed to till a fortnight before the Convention rose was such a one as he would have set his hand and heart to. . . . Until that time the 3 New England States were constantly with us in all questions . . . so that it was these three States with the 5 Southern ones against Pennsylvania, Jersey and Delaware. With respect to the importation of slaves, [decision making] was left to Congress. This disturbed the two Southernmost States who knew that Congress would immediately suppress the importation of slaves. Those two States therefore struck up a bargain with the three New England States. If they would join to admit slaves for some years, the two Southernmost States would join in changing the clause which required the ⅔ of

the Legislature in any vote [on navigation acts]. It was done.

On the floor of the Convention there was a love-feast. When Charles Pinckney of South Carolina attempted to overturn the committee's decision, by insisting that the South needed protection from the imperialism of the northern states, General CHARLES COTEWORTH PINCKNEY arose to spread oil on the waters:

It was in the true interest of the S[outhern] States to have no regulation of commerce; but considering the loss brought on the commerce of the Eastern States by the Revolution, their liberal conduct towards the views of South Carolina [on the regulation of the slave trade] and the interests the weak South. States had in being united with the strong Eastern states, he thought it proper that no fetters should be imposed on the power of making commercial regulations; and that his constituents, though prejudiced against Eastern States, would be reconciled to this liberality. He had himself prejudices against the Eastern States before he came here, but would acknowledge that he had found them as liberal and candid as any men whatever.

Drawing on their vast collective political experience, employing every weapon in the politician's arsenal, looking constantly over their shoulders at their constituents, the delegates put together a Constitution. It was a makeshift affair; some sticky issues they ducked entirely; others they mastered with that ancient instrument of political sagacity, studied ambiguity, and some they just overlooked. In this last category probably fell the matter of the power of the federal courts to determine the constitutionality of acts of Congress. When the judicial article was formulated, deliberations were still at the stage where the legislature was endowed with broad authority which by its own terms was scarcely amenable to JUDICIAL REVIEW. In essence, courts could hardly determine when "the separate States are incompetent or . . . the harmony of the United States may be interrupted"; the national legislature, as critics pointed out, was free to define its own jurisdiction. Later the definition of legislative authority was changed into the form we know, a series of stipulated powers, but the delegates never seriously reexamined the jurisdiction of the judiciary under this new limited formulation. All arguments on the intention of the Framers in this matter are thus deductive and *a posteriori*.

The Framers were busy and distinguished men, anxious to get back to their families, their positions, and their constituents, not members of the French Academy devoting a lifetime to a dictionary. They were trying to do an important job, and do it in such a fashion that their handiwork would be acceptable to diverse constituencies. No one was rhapsodic about the final document, but it was a beginning, a move in the right direction, and one they had reason to believe the people would endorse. In addition, because they had modified the impossible amendment provisions of the Articles of Confederation to one demanding approval by only three-quarters of the states, they seemed confident that gaps in the fabric which experience would reveal could be rewoven without undue difficulty.

So, with a neat phrase introduced by Benjamin Franklin that made their decision sound unanimous and an inspired benediction by the Old Doctor urging doubters to question their own infallibility, the delegates accepted the Constitution. Curiously, Edmund Randolph, who had played so vital a role throughout, refused to sign as did his fellow Virginian George Mason and ELBRIDGE GERRY of Massachusetts. Presumably, Randolph wanted to check the temper of the Virginia populace before he risked his reputation, and perhaps his job, in a fight with PATRICK HENRY. Events lend some justification to this speculation: after much temporizing and use of the conditional tense, Randolph endorsed ratification in Virginia and ended up getting the best of both worlds.

Madison, despite his reservations about the Constitution, was the campaign manager for ratification. His first task was to get the Congress in New York to light its own funeral pyre by approving the "amendments" to the Articles and sending them on to the state legislatures. Above all, momentum had to be maintained. The anti-Constitutionalists, now thoroughly alarmed and no novices in politics, realized that their best tactic was attrition rather than direct opposition. Thus they settled on a position expressing qualified approval but calling for a second Convention to remedy various defects (the one with the most demagogic appeal was the lack of a BILL OF RIGHTS). Madison knew that to accede to this demand would be equivalent to losing the battle, nor would he agree to conditional approval (despite wavering even by Hamilton). This was an all-or-nothing proposition: national salvation or national impotence, with no intermediate position possible. Unable to get congressional approval, he settled for second best: a unanimous resolution of Congress transmitting the Constitution to the states for whatever action they saw fit to take. The opponents then moved from New York and the Congress, where they had attempted to attach amendments and conditions, to the states for the final battle.

At first, the campaign for RATIFICATION went beautifully: within eight months after the delegates set their names to the document, eight states had ratified. Theoretically, a ratification by one more state convention would set the new government in motion, but in fact until Virginia and New York acceded to the new Union, the latter was a fiction. New Hampshire was the next to ratify; "Rogues' Island" was involved in its characteristic political convulsions; North Carolina's convention did not meet until July and then postponed a final decision. Finally in New York and Virginia, the Constitutionalists outmaneuvered their opponents, forced them into impossible political positions, and won both states narrowly.

Victory for the Constitution meant simultaneous victory for the Constitutionalists; the anti-Constitutionalists either capitulated or vanished into limbo—soon Patrick Henry would be offered a seat on the Supreme Court and Luther Martin would be known as the Federalist "bull-dog." And, irony of ironies, Alexander Hamilton and James Madison would shortly accumulate a reputation as the formulators of what is often alleged to be our political theory, the concept of "federalism." Arguments would soon appear over what the Framers "really meant"; although these disputes have assumed the proportions of a big scholarly business in the last century, they began almost before the ink on the Constitution was dry. One of the best early ones featured Hamilton versus Madison on the scope of presidential power.

The Constitution, then, was not an apotheosis of "constitutionalism," a triumph of architectonic genius; it was a patchwork sewn together under the pressure of time and events by a group of extremely talented democratic politicians. They refused to attempt the establishment of a strong, centralized sovereign on the principle of legislative supremacy for the excellent reason that the people would not accept it. They risked their political fortunes by opposing the established doctrines of state sovereignty because they were convinced that the existing system was leading to national impotence and, probably, to foreign domination. For two years, they worked to get a convention established. For over three months, in what must have seemed to the faithful participants an endless process of give-and-take, they reasoned, cajoled, threatened, and bargained amongst themselves. The results were a Constitution which the voters, by democratic processes, did accept, and a new and far better national government.

JOHN P. ROCHE

Bibliography

BROWN, ROBERT E. 1956 *Charles Beard and the Constitution.* Princeton, N.J.: Princeton University Press.

DINKIN, ROBERT J. 1977 *Voting in Provincial America.* Westport, Conn.: Greenwood Press.

ELKINS, STANLEY AND MCKITRICK, ERIC 1961 The Founding Fathers: Young Men of the Revolution. *Political Science Quarterly* 76:181–203.

FARRAND, MAX (ED.) 1937 *Records of the Federal Convention of 1787.* New Haven, Conn.: Yale University Press.

KENYON, CECELIA M. 1955 Men of Little Faith: The Anti-Federalists on the Nature of Representative Government. *William and Mary Quarterly,* 3rd series, 12: McDonald, Forrest T. 1958 *We the People.* Chicago: University of Chicago Press.

ROCHE, JOHN P. 1961 The Founding Fathers: A Reform Caucus in Action. *American Political Science Review* 55:799–816.

ROSSITER, CLINTON 1966 *1787: The Grand Convention.* New York: Macmillan.

WARREN, CHARLES (1928)1937 *The Making of the Constitution.* Boston: Little, Brown.

CONSTITUTIONAL COURT

Article III vests the federal judicial power in the Supreme Court and in any lower courts that Congress may create. The judiciary so constituted was intended by the Framers to be an independent branch of the government. The judges of courts established under Article III were thus guaranteed life tenure "during GOOD BEHAVIOR" and protected against the reduction of their salaries while they held office. The federal courts so constituted are called "constitutional courts." They are to be distinguished from LEGISLATIVE COURTS, whose judges do not have comparable constitutional guarantees of independence.

Constitutional courts, sometimes called "Article III courts," are limited in the business they can be assigned. They may be given JURISDICTION only over CASES AND CONTROVERSIES falling within the JUDICIAL POWER OF THE UNITED STATES. For example, Congress could not constitutionally confer jurisdiction on a constitutional court to give ADVISORY OPINIONS, or to decide a case that fell outside Article III's list of cases and controversies included within the judicial power. That list divides into two categories of cases: those in which jurisdiction depends on the issues at stake (for example, FEDERAL QUESTION JURISDICTION) and those in which jurisdiction depends on the parties to the case (for example, DIVERSITY JURISDICTION).

Congress can, of course, create bodies other than constitutional courts and assign them the function of deciding cases—even cases falling within the judicial power, within limits that remain unclear even after NORTHERN PIPELINE CONSTRUCTION CO. V. MARATHON PIPE LINE CO. (1982). Such a legislative court is not confined by Article III's specification of the limits of the federal judicial power, any more than an administrative agency would be so confined. However, a legislative court's decisions on matters outside the limits of Article III cannot constitutionally be reviewed by the Supreme Court or any other constitutional court.

KENNETH L. KARST

Bibliography

WRIGHT, CHARLES ALAN 1983 *The Law of Federal Courts,* 4th ed. Pages 39–52. St. Paul, Minn.: West Publishing Co.

CONSTITUTIONAL HISTORY BEFORE 1776

The opening words of the United States Constitution, "We the People," startled some of the old revolutionaries of 1776. PATRICK HENRY, after expressing the highest veneration for the men who wrote the words, demanded "What right had they to say, *We the People. . . .* Who authorized them to speak the language of *We, the People,* instead of *We, the States?*" It was a good question and, as Henry knew, not really answerable. No one had authorized the members of the CONSTITUTIONAL CONVENTION to speak for the people of the United States. They had been chosen by the legislatures of thirteen sovereign states and were authorized only to act for the governments of those states in redefining the relationships among them. Instead, they had dared not only to act for "the people of the United States" but also to proclaim what they did as "the supreme law of the land," supreme apparently over the actions of the existing state governments and supreme also over the government that the Constitution itself would create for the United States. Because those governments similarly professed to speak and act for the people, how could the Constitution claim supremacy over them and claim it successfully from that day to this, however contested in politics, litigation, and civil war? The answer lies less in logic than in the centuries of political experience before 1787 in which Englishmen and Americans worked out a political faith that gave to "the people" a presumptive capacity to constitute governments.

The idea that government originates in a donation by the people is at least as old as classical Greece. Government requires some sort of justification, and a donation of power by the governed or by those about to be governed was an obvious way of providing it. But such a donation has seldom if ever been recorded as historical fact, because it is virtually impossible for any substantial collection of people to act as a body, either in conveying powers of government or in prescribing the mode of their exercise. The donation has to be assumed, presumed, supposed, imagined—and yet be plausible enough to be acceptable to the supposed donors.

In the Anglo-American world two institutions have lent credibility to the presumption. The first to emerge was the presence in government of representatives chosen by a substantial portion of the people. With the powers of government thus shared, it became plausible to think of the representatives and the government as acting for the people and deriving powers from them. But as these popular representatives assumed a dominant position in the government, it was all too easy for them to escape from the control of those who chose them and to claim unlimited power in the name of the almighty people. A second device was necessary to differentiate the inherent sovereign powers of the people from the limited powers assigned to their deputed agents or representatives. The device was found in written CONSTITUTIONS embodying the people's supposed donation of power in specific provisions to limit and define the government.

Such written constitutions were a comparatively late development; the United States Constitution was one of the first. They came into existence not simply out of the need to specify the terms of the putative donation of power by the people but also out of earlier attempts by representatives or spokesmen of the people to set limits to governments claiming almighty authority from a different source. Although the idea of a popular donation was an ancient way of justifying government, it was not the only way. Indeed, since the fall of Rome God had been the favored source of authority: earthly rulers, whether in church or state, claimed His commission, though the act in which He granted it remained as shadowy as any donation by the people. Up to the seventeenth century, the persons who spoke for the people spoke as subjects, but they spoke as subjects of God as well as of God's lieutenants. While showing a proper reverence for divinely ordained authority, they expected those commissioned by God to rule in a godlike manner, that is, to abide by the natural laws (discernible in God's government of the world) that were supposed to guide human conduct and give force to the specific "positive" laws of nations derived from them. Even without claiming powers of government, those who spoke for

the people might thus set limits to the powers of government through "fundamental" laws that were thought to express the will of God more reliably than rulers who claimed His commission. The link is obvious between such FUNDAMENTAL LAWS and written constitutions that expressed the people's will more reliably than their elected representatives could. The one grew out of the other.

Written constitutions were a deliberate invention, designed to overcome the deficiencies of representative government, but representative government itself was the unintended outcome of efforts by kings to secure and extend their own power. The story begins with the creation of the English House of Commons in the thirteenth century, when the English government centered in a hereditary king who claimed God-given authority but had slender means for asserting it. The king, always in need of funds, summoned two representatives from each county and from selected boroughs (incorporated towns) to come to his court for the purpose of consenting to taxes. He required the counties and boroughs in choosing representatives, by some unspecified electoral process, to give them full powers of attorney, so that no one could later object to what they agreed to. Although only a small part of the adult population shared in the choice of representatives, the House of Commons came to be regarded as having power of attorney for the whole body of the king's subjects; every man, woman, and child in the country was held to be legally present within its walls.

The assembly of representatives, thus created and identified with the whole people, gradually acquired an institutional existence, along with the House of Lords, as one branch of the king's Parliament. As representatives, the members remained subjects of the king, empowered by other subjects to act for them. But from the beginning they were somewhat more than subjects: in addition to granting the property of other subjects in taxes, they could petition the king for laws that would direct the actions of government. From petitioning for laws they moved to making them: by the sixteenth century English laws were enacted "by authority" of Parliament. Theoretically that authority still came from God through the king, and Parliament continued to be an instrument by which English monarchs consolidated and extended their government, never more so than in the sixteenth century. But in sharing their authority with Parliament the kings shared it, by implication, with the people. By the time the first American colonies were founded in the early seventeenth century, the king's instrument had become a potential rival to his authority, and the people had become a potential alternative to God as the immediate source of authority.

The potential became actual in the 1640s when Parliament, discontented with Charles I's ecclesiastical, military, and fiscal policies, made war on the king and itself assumed all powers of government. The Parliamentarians justified their actions as agents of the people; and at this point the presumption of a popular origin of government made its appearance in England in full force. The idea, which had been overshadowed for so long by royal claims to a divine commission, had been growing for a century. The Protestant Reformation had produced a contest between Roman Catholics and Protestants for control of the various national governments of Europe. In that contest each side had placed on the people of a country the responsibility for its government's compliance with the will of God. The people, it was now asserted, were entrusted by God with creating proper governments and with setting limits on them to insure protection of true religion. When the limits were breached, the people must revoke the powers of rulers who had betrayed their trust. For Roman Catholics, Protestant rulers fitted the definition, and vice versa.

When Englishmen, mostly Protestant, challenged their king, who leaned toward Catholicism, these ideas were ready at hand for their justification, and the House of Commons had long been recognized as the representative of the people. The House, the members now claimed, to all intents and purposes *was* the people, and the powers of the people were supreme. Both the king and the House of Lords, lacking these powers, were superfluous. In 1649 the Commons killed the king, abolished the House of Lords, and made England a republic.

By assuming such sweeping powers the members of the House of Commons invited anyone who felt aggrieved by their conduct of government not only to question their claim to represent the people but also to draw a distinction between the powers of the people themselves and of the persons they might choose, by whatever means, to represent them.

The first critics of the Commons to draw such a distinction were, not surprisingly, the adherents of the king, who challenged the Commons in the public press as well as on the field of battle. The House of Commons, the royalists pointed out, had been elected by only a small fraction of the people, and even that fraction had empowered it only to consent to positive laws and taxes, not to alter the government. Parliament, the royalists insisted, must not be confused with the people themselves. Even if it were granted that the people might create a government and set limits

on it in fundamental laws, the House of Commons was only one part of the government thus created and could not itself change the government by eliminating the king or the Lords.

More radical critics, especially the misnamed Levellers, called not only for a reform of Parliament to make it more truly representative but also for a written "Agreement of the People" in which the people, acting apart from Parliament, would reorganize the government, reserving certain powers to themselves and setting limits to Parliament just as Parliament had formerly set limits to the king. Although the Levellers were unsuccessful, other political leaders also recognized the need to elevate supposed acts of the people, in creating a government and establishing its fundamental laws, above acts of the government itself. They also recognized that even a government derived from popular choice needed a SEPARATION OF POWERS among legislative, executive, and judicial branches, not merely for convenience of administration but in order to prevent government from escaping popular control.

Although the English in these years generated the ideas that have guided modern republican government, they were unable to bring their own government into full conformity with those ideas. By the 1650s they found that they had replaced a monarch, whose powers were limited, first with a House of Commons that claimed unlimited powers and refused to hold new elections, and then with a protector, Oliver Cromwell, whose powers knew only the limits of his ability to command a conquering army. In 1660 most Englishmen were happy to see the old balance restored with the return of a hereditary king and an old-style but potent Parliament to keep him in line. In 1688 that Parliament again removed a king who seemed to be getting out of control. This time, instead of trying to eliminate monarchy, they replaced one king with another who promised to be more tractable than his predecessor. William III at the outset of his reign accepted a parliamentary declaration of rights, spelling out the fundamental laws that limited his authority.

JOHN LOCKE, in the classic defense of this "Glorious Revolution," refined the distinction made earlier by the Levellers between the people and their representatives. Locke posited a SOCIAL COMPACT in which a collection of hitherto unconnected individuals in a "state of nature" came together to form a society. Only after doing so did they enter into a second compact in which they created a government and submitted to it. This second compact or constitution could be broken—the government could be altered or replaced—without destroying the first compact and throwing the people back into a state of nature. Society, in other words, came before government; and the people, once bound into a society by a social compact, could act without government and apart from government in order to constitute or change a government.

Locke could point to no historical occurrence that quite fitted his pattern. Even the Glorious Revolution was not, strictly speaking, an example of popular constituent action; rather, one branch of an existing government had replaced another branch. And the Declaration of Rights, although binding on the king, was no more than an act of Parliament that another Parliament might repeal. Moreover, the authority of the king remained substantial, and he was capable of extending his influence over Parliament by appointing members to lucrative government offices.

Locke's description of the origin of government nevertheless furnished a theoretical basis for viewing the entire British government as the creation of the people it governed. That view was expressed most vociferously in the eighteenth century by the so-called commonwealthmen, who repeated the call for reforms to make Parliament more representative of the whole people and to reduce the king's influence on its members. But it was not only commonwealthmen who accepted Locke's formulation. By the middle of the eighteenth century the doctrine of the divine right of kings was virtually dead in England, replaced by the sovereignty of the people, who were now accepted as the immediate source of all authority whether in king, lords, or commons.

In England's American colonies the idea that government originates in the people had been familiar from the outset, nourished not only by developments in England but also by the special conditions inherent in colonization. Those conditions were politically and constitutionally complex. The colonies were founded by private individuals or corporations under charters granted by the king, in which Parliament had no part. In the typical colony the king initially conveyed powers of government to the founders, who generally remained in England and directed the enterprise through agents. As time went on, the king took the powers of government in most colonies to himself, acting through appointed governors. But whether the immediate source of governmental authority in a colony rested in the king or in royally authorized corporations or individual proprietors, it proved impossible to govern colonists at 3,000 miles' distance without current information about changing local conditions. That kind of information could best be obtained

through a representative assembly of the settlers, empowered to levy taxes and make laws. As a result, in each of England's colonies, within a short time of the founding, the actual settlers gained a share in the choice of their governors comparable to that which Englishmen at home enjoyed through their Parliament.

England's first permanent colony in America, Virginia, was the first to exhibit the phenomenon. The Virginia Company of London, which founded the colony in 1607 and was authorized to govern it in 1609, did so for ten years without participation of the actual settlers. The results were disastrous, and in 1618 the company instructed its agents to call a representative assembly. The assembly met in 1619, the first in the present area of the United States. When the king dissolved the Virginia Company and resumed governmental authority over the colony in 1624, he declined to continue the assembly, but the governors he appointed found it necessary to do so on their own initiative until 1639, when the king recognized the need and made the Virginia House of Burgesses an official part of the government.

In most other colonies representatives were authorized from the beginning or came into existence spontaneously when colonists found themselves beyond the reach of existing governments. The Pilgrims who landed at Plymouth in 1620 provided for their own government by the MAYFLOWER COMPACT, with a representative assembly at its center. The initial governments of Rhode Island and Connecticut began in much the same way. In these Puritan colonies religious principle worked together with pragmatic necessity to emphasize the popular basis of government. Puritans believed that government, though ordained by God, must originate in a compact (or covenant) between rulers and people, in which rulers promised to abide by and enforce God's laws, while the people in return promised obedience. Even in Massachusetts, where from the beginning the government rested officially on a charter from the king, Governor John Winthrop took pains to explain that he regarded emigration to Massachusetts as a tacit consent to such a covenant on the part of everyone who came. The emigrants themselves seem to have agreed; and because the king's charter did not spell out the laws of God that must limit a proper government, the representative assembly of the colony in 1641 adopted the MASSACHUSETTS BODY OF LIBERTIES, which did so.

The model for the colonial representative assemblies was the House of Commons of England; but from the beginning the colonial assemblies were more representative than the House of Commons, in that a much larger proportion of the people shared in choosing them. In England REPRESENTATION was apportioned in a bizarre fashion among the towns and boroughs, with nearly empty villages sending members while many populous towns sent none. In the colonies, although the extension of representation did not everywhere keep up with the spread of population westward, the imbalance never approached that in England, where virtually no adjustments to shifts of population were made after the sixteenth century and none at all between 1675 and the nineteenth century. And while in England a variety of property qualifications and local regulations excluded the great majority of adult males from voting, in the colonies, because of the abundance of land and its widespread ownership, similar restrictions excluded only a minority of adult males.

In addition to its broader popular base, representation in the colonies retained more of its original popular function than did the English counterpart. Representatives in both England and the colonies were initially identified more with a particular group of subjects than with their rulers. As representatives assumed a larger and larger role in government, they necessarily came to consider themselves as acting more in an authoritative capacity over the whole people and less as the designated defenders of their immediate constituents. This conception grew more rapidly in England, as the power of the king declined and that of Parliament increased, than it did in the colonies, where representatives continued to champion the interests of their constituents against unpopular directives from England. The divergence in the American conception of representation was to play a key role both in the colonies' quarrel with England and in the problems faced by the independent Americans in creating their own governments.

By 1763, when France surrendered its North American possessions, Great Britain stood at the head of the world's greatest empire. But the place of the American colonists in that empire remained constitutionally uncertain. Officially their governments still derived authority not from popular donation but directly or indirectly from the king. In two colonies, Rhode Island and Connecticut, the king had conveyed power to the free male inhabitants to choose their own governor, governor's council, and legislative assembly. In two more the king had conveyed governmental power to a single family, the Penns in Pennsylvania and the Calverts in Maryland, who exercised their authority by appointing the governor and his council. In the rest of the colonies the king appointed the governor and (except in Massachusetts) his council, which in all colonies except Pennsylvania doubled as the upper house of the legislature. Thus in every colony except Rhode Island, Connecticut, and Massachusetts, a representative assembly made laws and levied taxes, but neither the governor nor the members of the upper house of the legislature owed their positions even indirectly to popular choice.

It might have been argued that the king himself owed his authority to some sort of popular consent, however tacitly expressed, but it would have been hard to say whether the people who gave that consent included those living in the colonies. It would have been harder still to say what relationship the colonists had to the king's Parliament. In England the king's subordination to Parliament had become increasingly clear. It was Parliament that recognized the restoration of Charles II in 1660; it was Parliament that, in effect, deposed James II in 1688; it was Parliament that placed George I on the throne in 1714 and established the succession of the House of Hanover. Insofar as England's kings ruled Great Britain after 1714 they ruled through Parliament. But they continued to rule the colonies through royal governors and councils, and Parliament still had no hand officially in the choice of royal governors and councils or in the formulation of instructions to them.

Because each colony had its own little parliament, its representative assembly, the people of each colony could have considered themselves as a separate kingdom and a separate people, separate not only from the people who chose the representative assemblies of the other colonies but separate also from the people of Great Britain who chose the British Parliament. If any colonist thought that way—and probably few did before the 1760s or 1770s—he would have had to consider a complicating fact: the British Parliament did on occasion legislate for the colonies and the colonies submitted to that legislation, most notably to the Navigation Acts of 1660 and 1663, which limited the trade of the colonies for the benefit of English merchants. Did this submission mean that the people of the colonies, who elected no representatives to Parliament, were subordinate to, as well as separate from, the people of Great Britain?

In one sense the answer had to be yes: if the king was subordinate to Parliament and the colonists were subordinate to the king, that would seem to make the colonists subordinate to Parliament and thus to the people who elected Parliament. But since Parliament had so seldom legislated for the colonies, it could be argued that the colonists' subordination to it was restricted to those areas where it had in fact legislated for them, that is, in matters that concerned their trade. In other areas, they would be subordinate to Parliament only through the king, and the subordination of the colonial representative assemblies to the king was by no means unlimited. Through the taxing power the colonial assemblies had achieved, over the years, a leverage in the operation of their respective governments comparable to that which had raised Parliament above the king in Great Britain. To be sure, they had not arrived at so clear a position of superiority over their royal governors as Parliament enjoyed over the king. For example, while Queen Anne was the last monarch to veto an act of Parliament, royal governors regularly vetoed acts of colonial assemblies; and even an act accepted by the king's governor could still be vetoed by the king himself. The assemblies nevertheless enjoyed considerable power; by refusing to authorize taxation or to appropriate funds, they could thwart royal directives that they considered injurious to the interests or rights of their constituents. And in some ways they enjoyed a greater independence of royal influence than did Parliament. Because there were few sinecures or places of profit in colonial governments within the appointment of the king or his governors, it was difficult for a governor to build a following in an assembly through patronage.

Despite its constitutional and political ambiguities the British imperial system worked. It continued to work until the power of Parliament collided with the power of the colonial assemblies, thus requiring a resolution of the uncertainties in their relationship. The collision occurred when Parliament, facing a doubled national debt after the Seven Years War, passed the Revenue Act of 1764 (usually called the Sugar Act), levying duties on colonial imports, and the Stamp Act of 1765, levying direct taxes on legal documents and other items used in the colonies. In these acts, probably without intending to, Parliament threatened to destroy the bargaining power through which the colonial assemblies had balanced the authority of the king and his governors. If Parliament could tax the colonists directly, it might free the king's governors from dependence on the assemblies for funds and ultimately render the assemblies powerless.

In pamphlets and newspaper articles the colonists denounced the new measures. The assemblies, both separately and in a STAMP ACT CONGRESS, to which nine colonies sent delegates, spelled out in resolutions and petitions what they considered to be fundamental constitutional rights that Parliament had violated. In doing so the assemblies were obliged to define their constitutional relationship to Parliament with a precision never before required.

Parliament, it must be remembered, had been regarded for centuries as the bulwark of English liberties. It was the representative body of the English people, and through it the English had tamed their king as no other Europeans had. To question its supremacy might well seem to be a reactionary retreat toward absolute monarchy by divine right. The colonists were therefore hesitant to deny all subordination to Parliament. Yet, if they were to enjoy the same rights that other British subjects enjoyed in Great Britain, they must reserve to their own assemblies at the very least the power to tax. They acknowledged, therefore, the authority of Parliament to legislate for the whole empire as it had hitherto done in regulating colonial trade, but they drew a distinction between the power to legislate and the power to tax.

The colonists associated legislation with the sovereign power of a state, and they wanted to consider themselves as remaining in some still undefined way under the sovereign power of the British government. But taxation had from the time of England's first Parliaments been a function of representatives, authorized by those who sent them to give a part of their property to the king in taxes. Taxation, the colonial assemblies affirmed, was not a part of the governing or legislative power, but an action taken in behalf of the king's subjects. This distinction could be seen, they pointed out, in the form given to Parliamentary acts of taxation: such acts originated in the House of Commons and were phrased as the gift of the commons to the king.

Now the difference between American and British conceptions of representation began to appear. The colonists did not think of the English House of Commons as representing them, for no county or town or borough in the colonies sent members. The British government had never suggested that they might, and the colonists themselves rejected the possibility as impracticable. Given their conception of the representative's subservient relation to his constituents, it would have been impossible, they felt, to maintain adequate control over representatives at 3,000 miles' distance. Thus the colonists had not authorized and could not authorize any representative in Parliament to give their property in taxes. When Parliament taxed them, therefore, it deprived them of a fundamental right of Englishmen, sacred since before the colonies were founded. For a Parliament in which the colonists were not represented to tax them was equivalent to the king's taxing Englishmen in England without the consent of the House of Commons. The colonists called in vain on English courts to nullify this violation of fundamental law.

In answering the colonial objections, British spokesmen did not claim that the colonists could be taxed without the consent of their representatives. Thomas Whately, speaking for the ministry that sponsored the taxes, went even further than the colonists by denying that any legislation affecting British subjects anywhere could be passed without consent of their representatives. But he went on to affirm what to the colonists was an absurdity, that the colonists were represented in the House of Commons. Although they did not choose members, they were *virtually* represented by every member chosen in Britain, each of whom was entrusted with the interests not merely of the few persons who chose him but of all British subjects. The colonists were represented in the same way as Englishmen in towns that sent no members, in the same way also as English women and children.

However plausible this reasoning may have been to Englishmen, to the colonists it was sheer sophistry. They made plain in resolutions of their assemblies, as for example in Pennsylvania, "That the only legal Representatives of the Inhabitants of this Province are the Persons they annually elect to serve as Members of Assembly." Pamphlets and newspapers were even more scathing in rejecting the pretensions of Parliament to represent Americans. In Massachusetts JAMES OTIS asked, "Will any man's calling himself my agent, representative, or trustee make him so in fact?" On that basis the House of Commons could equally pretend "that they were the true and proper representatives of all the common people upon the globe." (See TAXATION WITHOUT REPRESENTATION.)

In reaction to the objections of the colonists and of the English merchants who traded with them, Parliament in 1766 repealed the Stamp Act and revised the Sugar Act. But at the same time it passed a Declaratory Act, affirming its right to legislate for the colonies "in all cases whatsoever." The framers of the act deliberately omitted specific mention of the power to tax, but in the following year Parliament again exercised that presumed power in the TOWNSHEND ACTS, levying more customs duties on colonial imports. The colonists again mounted protests, but they were still reluctant to deny all Parliamentary authority over them and clung to their distinction between legislation and taxation, which the great William Pitt himself had supported (unsuccessfully) in Parliamentary debate. Parliament, they said, could regulate their trade, even by imposing customs duties, but must not use the pretext of trade regulation for the purpose of raising revenue.

Once again the colonial protests, backed by boycotts, secured repeal of most of the offending taxes, but once again Parliament reaffirmed the principle of its unlimited power, not in a declaration, but by retaining a token tax on tea. The colonists, relieved of any serious burden, were left to ponder the implications of their position. In one sense Parliament was treating them as part of a single people, over all of whom, whether in England or elsewhere, Parliament reigned supreme. In rejecting the notion that they were, or even could be, represented in Parliament, the colonists implied that they were a separate people or peoples.

A reluctance to face this implication had prompted their continued recognition of some sort of authority in Parliament. If Parliament in the past had secured the rights of Englishmen, was it not dangerous (as Whately had indeed said it was) to rely instead on the powers of their own little assemblies? If they were a separate people, or peoples, not subject to Parliament, would they not be foregoing the rights of Englishmen, the very rights they were so vigorously claiming? Could they expect their own assemblies to be as effective defenders of those rights as the mighty British Parliament?

As the quarrel over taxation progressed, with the Boston Tea Party of 1773 and Parliament's punitive Coercive Act of 1774 against Massachusetts, more and more Americans overcame the doubts raised by such questions. The Coercive Acts regulated trade with a vengeance by interdicting Boston's trade, and the acts also altered the government of Massachusetts as defined by its royal charter (ending the provincial election of the governor's council), thereby showing once and for all that guarantees given by the king could not stand before the supremacy claimed by Parliament. In the treatment of Massachusetts the other colonies read what was in store for them, and the various colonial assemblies sent delegates to the FIRST CONTINENTAL CONGRESS in 1774 in order to concert their response.

As in the earlier Stamp Act Congress, the delegates had to determine what they considered to be the limits of Parliament's authority. This time, abandoning their distinction between legislation and taxation (which Parliament had never recognized), they denied that Parliament had or had ever had constitutional authority over them. As a last conciliatory gesture, they expressed a willingness voluntarily to submit to bona fide regulations of trade, but made clear that Parliament had no constitutional right to make such regulations. Following the lead given in tracts by JOHN ADAMS, JAMES WILSON, and THOMAS JEFFERSON, they elevated their separate representative assemblies to a constitutional position within their respective jurisdictions equal to that of Parliament in Great Britain. The only remaining link connecting them with the mother country was their allegiance to the same king, who must be seen as the king of Virginia, Massachusetts, and so on, as well as of England, Scotland, Wales, and Ireland. (Ireland, it was noted, also had its separate Parliament.) Over his peoples beyond the seas the king exercised his powers through separate but equal governments, each with its own governor, council, and representative assembly.

The king did not, of course, rule by divine right. In the colonies as in England he derived his authority from the people themselves, that is, from the separate consent or constituent act of each of the peoples of his empire. John Adams of Massachusetts, perceiving the need to identify such an act, pointed to the Glorious Revolution of 1688 as an event in which each of the king's peoples participated separately. "It ought to be remembered," he said, "that there was a revolution here, as well as in England, and that we as well as the people of England, made an original, express contract with King William." That contract, as Adams and other colonists now saw it, limited royal power in the same way it was limited in England and guaranteed in each colony the exclusive legislative and taxing authority of the representative assembly.

Although the First Continental Congress gave a terminal clarity to the colonists' views of their constitutional position in the empire, it looked forward uncertainly toward a new relationship among the colonies themselves. The membership of the Congress reflected the uncertainty. Some of the members had been chosen by regularly constituted assemblies; others had been sent by extralegal conventions or committees; and a few were self-appointed. What authority, if any, the members had was not clear. Given the view of representation that had guided colonial reaction to Parliamentary taxation, no one was ready to claim for Congress the powers denied to Parliament. Though delegates from every colony except Georgia were present, they had not been chosen by direct popular elections and therefore were not, by their own definition, representatives. At best, as one of them put it, they were "representatives of representatives."

Yet they had not come together simply for discus-sion. Boston was under military occupation and Massachusetts was under military government. Regular royal government throughout the colonies was fast approaching dissolution. It was time for action, and the Congress took action. Without pausing to determine by what authority, it adopted an ASSOCIATION forbidding not only exports to and imports from Great Britain but also the consumption of British goods. And it called for the creation of committees in every county, city, and town to enforce these restrictions.

In the misnamed Association (membership in which was scarcely voluntary) the Congress took the first steps toward creating a national government separate from that of the (not yet independent) states. If the members believed, as presumably they did, that the authority of government derives from the people, they implied, perhaps without quite realizing what they were doing, that there existed a single American people, distinct not only from the people of Great Britain but also from the peoples of the several colonies and capable of conveying a political authority distinct from that either of Great Britain or of the several colonies.

The implication would not become explicit until the Constitution of 1787, but the Second Continental Congress, which assembled in May 1775, looked even more like the government of a single people than had the First. Fighting had already broken out in April between British troops and Massachusetts militiamen, and Congress at once took charge of the war and began the enlistment of a Continental Army. It sent envoys to France to seek foreign assistance. It opened American commerce to foreign nations. It advised the peoples of the several colonies to suppress all royal authority within their borders. And finally, after more than a year of warfare, it declared the independence of the United States.

Despite the boldness of these actions, the DECLA-RATION OF INDEPENDENCE itself betrayed the ambiguities that Americans felt about their own identity. It unequivocally put an end to royal authority (parliamentary authority had already been rejected) and consequently to all remaining connection with the people of Great Britain. But it was not quite clear whether the independence thus affirmed was of one people, or of several, or of both one and several. While the preamble spoke of "one people" separating from another, the final affirmation was in the plural, declaring that "these United Colonies are, and of Right ought to be Free and Independent States." Yet in stating what constituted free and independent statehood, the Declaration specified only "power to levy war, conclude peace, contract alliances, establish commerce." These were all things, with the possible exception of the last, that had been done or would be done by the Congress.

But if the Congress sometimes acted like the government of a single free and independent state, the members still did not recognize the implication that they represented a single free and independent people. They did not consider their Declaration of Independence complete until it had been ratified by each of the separate states whose freedom and independence it declared. And when they tried to define their own authority, they found it difficult to reach agreement. ARTICLES OF CONFEDERATION, first drafted in 1776, were not ratified by the several states until 1781. The Articles entrusted Congress with the powers it was already exercising but declined to derive those powers from a single American people. The old local committees of the Association of 1774, tied directly to Congress, were now a thing of the past, and the enactments of Congress became mere recommendations, to be carried out by the various states as they saw fit.

Even before the Declaration of Independence, in response to the recommendation of the Congress, the states had begun to create governments resting solely on the purported will of the people within their existing borders. In every state a provisional government appeared, usually in the form of a provincial congress resembling the old colonial representative assembly. In most of the states, beginning with Virginia in June 1776, these provincial congresses drew up and adopted, without further reference to the people, constitutions defining the structure of their governments and stating limitations on governmental powers in bills of rights. In every case the constitution was thought or proclaimed to be in some way an act of the people who were to be governed under it, and therefore different from and superior to acts of representatives in a legislative assembly. But often the provincial congress that drafted a state constitution continued to act as the legislative body provided in it. Although a constitution might affirm its own superiority to ordinary legislation, the fact that it was created by legislative act rendered doubtful its immunity to alteration by the body that created it.

A similar doubt surrounded the principle, also enunciated in most of the constitutions, that (as in Virginia) "The legislative, executive, and judiciary departments shall be separate and distinct, so that neither exercise the powers properly belonging to the other." The several provincial congresses that drafted the constitutions inherited the aggressiveness of the colonial assemblies against executive and, to a lesser degree, judicial powers, which had hitherto rested in an overseas authority beyond their reach. In spite of the assertion of the separation of powers, and in spite of the fact that executives and judges would now derive authority solely from the people they governed, the state constitutions generally gave the lion's share of power in government to the representative assemblies.

The result was to bring out the shortcomings of the view of representation that had directed the colonists in their resistance to British taxation. For a decade the colonists had insisted that a representative must act only for the particular group of persons who chose him. They occasionally recognized but minimized his responsibility, as part of the governing body, to act for the whole people who were to be governed by the laws he helped to pass. Now the representative assemblies were suddenly presented with virtually the entire powers of government, which they shared only with a weak executive and judiciary and with a Continental Congress whose powers remained uncertain, despite Articles of Confederation that gave it large responsibilities without the means to perform them. Undeterred by any larger view of their functions, too many of the state assemblymen made a virtue of partiality to their particular constituents and ignored the long-range needs not only of their own state but of the United States.

The solution lay ahead in 1787. By 1776 the inherited ingredients of the settlement then adopted were in place. A rudimentary distinction between the constituent actions of a putative people and the actions of their government had been recognized, though not effectively implemented, in the state governments. All government officers were now selected directly or indirectly by popular choice, with their powers limited, at least nominally, by a reservation to the people of powers not specifically conveyed. And a national center of authority, not quite a government but nevertheless acting like a government, was in operation in the Continental Congress.

What was needed—and with every passing year after 1776 the need became more apparent—was a way to relieve popular government from the grip of short-sighted representative assemblies. Two political inventions filled the need. The first was the constitutional convention, an assembly without legislative powers, entrusted solely with the drafting of a constitution for submission to popular ratification, a constitution that could plausibly be seen as the embodiment of the popular will superior to the ordinary acts of representative assemblies. Massachusetts provided this invention in 1779, in the convention that drafted the state's first constitution. (See MASSACHUSETTS CONSTITUTION.)

The first invention made way for the second, which was supplied by JAMES MADISON and his colleagues at Philadelphia in 1787. They invented the American people. It was, to be sure, an invention waiting to be made. It had been prefigured in the assumptions behind the Continental Association and the Declaration of Independence. But it reached fulfillment only in the making of the Constitution. By means of a national constitutional convention the men at Philadelphia built a national government that presumed and thus helped to create an American people, distinct from and superior to the peoples of the states.

The idea of popular SOVEREIGNTY was, as we have seen, an old one, but only occasionally had it dictated the formation of popular governments, governments in which all the officers owed their positions directly or indirectly to popular election. Though the idea surfaced powerfully in the England of the 1640s and 1650s, it eventuated there in a restored monarchy, and it won only partial recognition in England's Revolution of 1688. In the American Revolution it had seemingly found full expression in thirteen separate state governments, but by 1787 the actions of those governments threatened once again to discredit the whole idea. The signal achievement of the constitutional convention was expressed in the opening words of the document it produced: "We the People of the United States." The United States Constitution rescued popular sovereignty by extending it. It inaugurated both a new government and a new people.

EDMUND S. MORGAN

Bibliography

ADAMS, WILLI PAUL 1980 *The First American Constitutions.* Chapel Hill: University of North Carolina Press.
BAILYN, BERNARD 1967 *The Ideological Origins of the American Revolution.* Cambridge, Mass.: Harvard University Press.
———— 1968 *The Origins of American Politics.* New York: Knopf.
FIGGIS, JOHN NEVILLE 1914 *The Divine Right of Kings.* Cambridge: At the University Press.
GREENE, JACK P. 1963 *The Quest for Power.* Chapel Hill: University of North Carolina Press.
KANTOROWICZ, ERNST H. 1957 *The King's Two Bodies.* Princeton: N.J.: Princeton University Press.
LABAREE, LEONARD W. 1930 *Royal Government in America.* New Haven, Conn.: Yale University Press.
MCILWAIN, CHARLES H. 1923 *The American Revolution.* New York: Macmillan.
MORGAN, EDMUND S. and MORGAN, HELEN M. 1953 *The Stamp Act Crisis.* Chapel Hill: University of North Carolina Press.
POCOCK, JOHN G. A. 1957 *The Ancient Constitution and the Feudal Law.* Cambridge: At the University Press.
RUSSELL, CONRAD 1979 *Parliaments and English Politics 1621–1629.* Oxford: Clarendon Press.
SCHUYLER, ROBERT L. 1929 *Parliament and the British Empire.* New York: Columbia University Press.
SKINNER, QUENTIN 1978 *The Foundations of Modern Political Thought.* Cambridge: At the University Press.
TUCKER, ROBERT W. and HENDRICKSON, DAVID C. 1982 *The Fall of the First British Empire.* Baltimore: Johns Hopkins University Press.

CONSTITUTIONAL HISTORY, 1776–1789

On July 4, 1776, King George III wrote in his diary, "Nothing of importance this day." When the news of the DECLARATION OF INDEPENDENCE reached him, he still could not know how wrong he had been. The political philosophy of SOCIAL COMPACT, NATURAL RIGHTS, and LIMITED GOVERNMENT that generated the Declaration of Independence also spurred the most important, creative, and dynamic constitutional achievements in history; the Declaration itself was merely the beginning. Within a mere thirteen years Americans invented or first institutionalized a bill of rights against all branches of government, the written CONSTITUTION, the CONSTITUTIONAL CONVENTION, FEDERALISM, JUDICIAL REVIEW, and a solution to the colonial problem (admitting TERRITORIES to the Union as states fully equal to the original thirteen). RELIGIOUS LIBERTY, the SEPARATION OF CHURCH AND STATE, political parties, SEPARATION OF POWERS, an acceptance of the principle of equality, and the conscious creation of a new nation were also among American institutional "firsts," although not all these initially appeared between 1776 and 1789. In that brief span of time, Americans created what are today the oldest major republic, political democracy, state constitution, and national constitution. These unparalleled American achievements derived not from originality in speculative theory but from the constructive application of old ideas, which Americans took so seriously that they constitutionally based their institutions of government on them.

From thirteen separate colonies the Second Continental Congress "brought forth a new nation," as ABRAHAM LINCOLN said. In May 1776, Congress urged all the colonies to suppress royal authority and adopt permanent governments. On that advice and in the midst of a war the colonies began to frame the world's first written constitutions. When Congress triggered the drafting of those constitutions, Virginia instructed its delegates to Congress to propose that Congress should declare "the United Colonies free and independent states." Neither Virginia nor Congress advocated state sovereignty. Congress's advice implied the erection of state governments with sovereign powers over domestic matters or "internal police."

On June 7, 1776, Congressman RICHARD HENRY LEE of Virginia introduced the resolution as instructed, and Congress appointed two committees, one to frame the document that became the Declaration of Independence and the other to frame a plan of confederation—a constitution for a continental government. When Lincoln declared, "The Union is older than the States, and in fact created them as States," he meant that the Union (Congress) antedated the states. The Declaration of Independence, which stated that the colonies had become states, asserted the authority of the "United States of America, in General Congress, Assembled."

The "spirit of '76" tended to be strongly nationalistic. The members of Congress represented the states, of course, and acted on their instructions, but they acted for the new nation, and the form of government they thought proper in 1776 was a centralized one. As a matter of fact BENJAMIN FRANKLIN had proposed such a government on July 21, 1775, when he presented to Congress "ARTICLES OF CONFEDERATION and perpetual Union." Franklin urged a congressional government with an executive committee that would manage "general continental Business and Interests," conduct diplomacy, and administer finances. His plan empowered Congress to determine war and peace, exchange ambassadors, make foreign alliances, settle all disputes between the colonies, plant new colonies, and, in a sweeping omnibus clause, make laws for "the General Welfare" concerning matters on which individual colonies "cannot be competent," such as "our general Commerce," "general Currency," the establishment of a post office, and governance of "our Common Forces." Costs were to be paid from a common treasury supplied by each colony in proportion to its male inhabitants, but each colony would raise its share by taxing its inhabitants. Franklin provided for an easy amendment process: Congress recommended amendments that would become part of the Articles when approved by a majority of colonial assemblies. Franklin's plan of union seemed much too radical in July 1775, when independence was a year away and reconciliation with Britain on American terms was the object of the war. Congress simply tabled the Franklin plan.

As the war continued into 1776, nationalist sentiment strengthened. THOMAS PAINE's *Common Sense* called for American independence and "a Continental form of Government." Nationalism and centralism were twin causes. JOHN LANGDON of New Hampshire favored independence and "an American Constitution" that provided for appeals from every colony to a national congress "in everything of moment relative to governmental matters." Proposals for a centralized union became common by the spring of 1776, and these proposals, as the following representative samples suggest, tended to show democratic impulses. Nationalism and mitigated democracy, not nationalism and conservatism, were related. A New York newspaper urged the popular election of a national congress with a "superintending power" over the individual colonies as to "all commercial and Continental affairs," leaving to each colony control over its "internal policy." A populistic plan in a Connecticut newspaper recommended that the congress be empowered to govern "all matters of general concernment" and "every other thing proper and necessary" for the benefit of the whole, allowing the individual colonies only that which fell "within the territorial jurisdiction of a particular assembly." The "Spartacus" essays, which newspapers in New York, Philadelphia, and Portsmouth printed, left the state "cantons" their own legislatures but united all in a national congress with powers similar to those enumerated by Franklin, including a paramount power to "interfere" with a colony's "provincial affairs" whenever required by "the good of the continent." "Essex" reminded his readers that "the strength and happiness of America must be Continental, not Provincial, and that whatever appears to be for the good of the whole, must be submitted to by every Part." He advocated dividing the colonies into many smaller equal parts that would have equal representation in a powerful national congress chosen directly by the people, including taxpaying widows. Carter Braxton, a conservative Virginian, favored aristocratic controls over a congress that could not "interfere with the internal police or domestic concerns of any Colony . . . ."

Given the prevalence of such views in the first half of 1776, a representative committee of the Continental Congress probably mirrored public opinion when it framed a nationalist plan for confederation. On July 12, one month after the appointment of a thirteen-member committee (one from each state) to write a draft, JOHN DICKINSON of Pennsylvania, the committee chairman, presented to Congress a plan that borrowed heavily from Franklin's. The Committee of the Whole of Congress debated the Dickinson draft and adopted it on August 20 with few changes. Only one was significant. Dickinson had proposed that Congress be empowered to fix the western boundaries of states claiming territory to the Pacific coast and to form new states in the west. The Committee of the Whole, bending to the wishes of eight states with extensive western claims, omitted that provision from its revision of the Dickinson draft. That omission became a stumbling block.

On August 20 the Committee of the Whole reported the revised plan of union to Congress. The plan was similar to Franklin's, except that Congress had no power over "general commerce." But Congress, acting for the United States, was clearly paramount to the individual states. They were not even referred to as "states." Collectively they were "the United States of America"; otherwise they were styled "colonies" or "colony," terms not compatible with sovereignty, to which no reference was made. Indeed, the draft merely reserved to each colony "sole and exclusive Regulation and Government of its internal police, in all matters that shall not interfere with the Articles of this Confederation." That crucial provision, Article III, making even "internal police" subordinate to congressional powers, highlighted the nationalist character of the proposed confederation.

The array of congressional powers included exclusive authority over war and peace, land and naval forces, treaties and alliances, prize cases, crimes on the high seas and navigable rivers, all disputes between states, coining money, borrowing on national credit, Indian affairs, post offices, weights and measures, and "the Defence and Welfare" of the United States. Congress also had power to appoint a Council of State and civil officers "necessary for managing the general Affairs of the United States." The Council of State, consisting of one member from each of the thirteen, was empowered to administer the United States government and execute its measures. Notwithstanding this embryonic executive branch, the government of the United States was congressional in character, consisting of a single house whose members were to be elected annually by the legislatures of the colonies. Each colony cast one vote, making each politically equal in Congress. On all important matters, the approval of nine colonies was required to pass legislation. Amendments to the Articles needed the unanimous approval of the legislatures of the various colonies, a provision that later proved to be crippling.

The Articles reported by the Committee of the Whole provoked dissension. States without western land claims opposed the omission of the provision in the Dickinson draft that gave Congress control over western lands. Large states opposed the principle of one vote for each state, preferring instead proportionate representation with each delegate voting. Sharp differences also emerged concerning the rule by which each state was to pay its quota to defray common expenses. Finally some congressmen feared the centralizing nature of the new government. Edward Rutledge of South Carolina did not like "the Idea of destroying all Provincial Distinctions and making every thing of the most minute kind bend to what they call the good of the whole. . . ." Rutledge resolved "to vest the Congress with no more Power than what is absolutely necessary." JAMES WILSON of Pennsylvania could declare that Congress represented "all the individuals of the states" rather than the states, but ROGER SHERMAN of Connecticut answered, "We are representatives of states, not individuals." That attitude would undo the nationalist "spirit of '76."

Because of disagreements and the urgency of prosecuting the war, Congress was unable to settle on a plan of union in 1776. By the spring of 1777 the nationalist momentum was spent. By then most of the states had adopted constitutions and had legitimate governments. Previously, provisional governments of local "congresses," "conventions," and committees had controlled the states and looked to the Continental Congress for leadership and approval. But the creation of legitimate state governments reinvigorated old provincial loyalties. Local politicians, whose careers were provincially oriented, feared a strong central government as a rival institution. Loyalists no longer participated in politics, local or national, depleting support for central control. By late April of 1777, when state sovereignty triumphed, only seventeen of the forty-eight congressmen who had been members of the Committee of the Whole that adopted the Dickinson draft remained in Congress. Most of the new congressmen opposed centralized government.

James Wilson, who was a congressman in 1776 and 1777, recalled what happened when he addressed the Constitutional Convention on June 8, 1787:

Among the first sentiments expressed in the first Congs. one was that Virga. is no more. That Massts. is no more, that Pa. is no more &c. We are now one nation of brethren. We must bury all local interests and distinctions. This language continued for some time. The tables at length began to turn. No sooner were the State Govts. formed than their jealousy & ambition began to display themselves. Each endeavored to cut a slice from the common loaf, to add to its own morsel, till at length the confederation became frittered down to the impotent condition in which it now stands. Review the progress of the articles of Confederation thro' Congress & compare the first and last draught of it [Farrand, ed., *Records,* I, 166–67].

The turning point occurred in late April 1777 when Thomas Burke of North Carolina turned his formidable localist opinions against the report of the Committee of the Whole. Its Article III, in his words, "expressed only a reservation [to the states] of the power of regulating the internal police, and consequently resigned every other power [to Congress]." Congress, he declared, sought even to interfere with the states' internal police and make its own powers "unlimited." Burke accordingly moved the following substitute for Article III, which became Article II of the Articles as finally adopted: "Each State retains its sovereignty, freedom and independence, and every power, jurisdiction and right, which is not by this confederation expressly delegated to the United States in Congress assembled." Burke's motion carried by the votes of eleven states, vitiating the powers of the national government recommended by the Committee of the Whole.

In the autumn of 1777 a Congress dominated by state-sovereignty advocates completed the plan of confederation. Those who favored proportionate representation in Congress with every member entitled to vote lost badly to those who favored voting by states with each state having one vote. Thereafter the populous wealthy states had no stake in supporting a strong national government that could be controlled by the votes of lesser states. The power of Congress to negotiate commercial treaties effectively died when Congress agreed that under the Articles no treaty should violate the power of the states to impose tariff duties or prohibit imports and exports. The power of Congress to settle all disputes between states became merely a power to make recommendations. The permanent executive branch became a temporary committee with no powers except as delegated by the votes of nine states, the number required to adopt any major measure. Congress also agreed that it should not have power to fix the western boundaries of states claiming lands to the Pacific.

After the nationalist spurt of 1776 proved insufficient to produce the Articles, the states made the Confederation feckless. Even as colonies the states had been particularistic, jealous, and uncooperative. Centrifugal forces originating in diversity—of economics, geography, religion, class structure, and race—produced sectional, provincial, and local loyalties that could not be overcome during a war against the centralized powers claimed by Parliament. The controversy with Britain had produced passions and principles that made the Franklin and Dickinson drafts unviable. Not even these nationalist drafts empowered Congress to tax, although the principle of no TAXATION WITHOUT REPRESENTATION had become irrelevant as to Congress. Similarly, Congress as late as 1774 had "cheerfully" acknowledged Parliament's legitimate "regulation of our external commerce," but in 1776 Congress denied that Parliament had any authority over America, and by 1777 Americans were unwilling to grant their own central legislature powers they preferred their provincial assemblies to wield. Above all, most states refused to repose their trust in any central authority that a few large states might dominate, absent a constitutionally based principle of state equality.

Unanimous consent for amendments to the Articles proved to be too high a price to pay for acknowledging the "sovereignty" of each state, although that acknowledgment made Maryland capable of winning for the United States the creation of a national domain held in common for the benefit of all. Maryland also won the promise that new states would be admitted to the union on a principle of state equality. That prevented the development of a colonial problem from Atlantic to Pacific, and the NORTHWEST ORDINANCE OF 1787 was the Confederation's finest and most enduring achievement.

The Constitution of 1787 was unthinkable in 1776, impossible in 1781 or at any time before it was framed. The Articles were an indispensable transitional stage in the development of the Constitution. Not even the Constitution would have been ratified if its Framers had submitted it for approval to the state legislatures that kept Congress paralyzed in the 1780s. Congress, representing the United States, authorized the creation of the states and ended up, as it had begun, as their creature. It possessed expressly delegated powers with no means of enforcing them. That Congress lacked commerce and tax powers was a serious deficiency, but not nearly so crippling as its lack of sanctions and the failure of the states to abide by the Articles. Congress simply could not make anyone, except soldiers, do anything. It acted on the states, not on people. Only a national government that could execute its laws independently of the states could have survived.

The states flouted their constitutional obligations. The Articles obliged the states to "abide by the determinations of the United States, in Congress assembled," but there was no way to force the states to comply. The states were not sovereign, except as to their internal police and tax powers; rather, they behaved unconstitutionally. No foreign nation recognized the states as sovereign, because Congress possessed the external attributes of sovereignty especially as to FOREIGN AFFAIRS and WAR POWERS.

One of the extraordinary achievements of the Articles was the creation of a rudimentary federal system. It failed because its central government did not operate directly on individuals within its sphere of authority. The Confederation had no independent executive and judicial branches, because the need for them scarcely existed when Congress addressed its acts mainly to the states. The framers of the Articles distributed the powers of government with remarkable acumen, committing to Congress about all that belonged to a central government except, of course, taxation and commercial regulation, the two powers that Americans of the Revolutionary War believed to be part of state sovereignty. Even ALEXANDER HAMILTON, who in 1780 advocated that Congress should have "complete sovereignty," excepted "raising money by internal taxes."

Congress could requisition money from the states, but they did not pay their quotas. In 1781 Congress requisitioned $8,000,000 for the next year, but the states paid less than half a million. While the Articles lasted, the cumulative amount paid by all the states hardly exceeded what was required to pay the interest on the public debt for just one year.

Nationalists vainly sought to make the Articles more effective by both interpretation and amendment. Madison devised a theory of IMPLIED POWERS by which he squeezed out of the Articles congressional authority to use force if necessary against states that failed to fulfill their obligations. Congress refused to attempt coercion just as it refused to recommend an amendment authorizing its use. Congress did, however, charter a bank to control currency, but the opposition to the exercise of a power not expressly delegated remained so intense that the bank had to be rechartered by a state. Congress vainly sought unanimous state consent for various amendments that would empower it to raise money from customs duties and to regulate commerce, foreign and domestic. In 1781 every state but Rhode Island approved an amendment empowering Congress to impose a five percent duty on all foreign imports; never again did an amendment to the Articles come so close to adoption. Only four states ratified an amendment authorizing a congressional embargo against the vessels of any nation with whom the United States had no treaty of commerce. Congress simply had no power to negotiate commercial treaties with nations such as Britain

that discriminated against American shipping. Nor had Congress the power to prevent states from violating treaties with foreign nations. In 1786 JOHN JAY, Congress's secretary of foreign affairs, declared that not a day had passed since ratification of the 1783 treaty of peace without its violation by at least one state. Some states also discriminated against the trade of others. Madison likened New Jersey, caught between the ports of Philadelphia and New York, "to a cask tapped at both ends." More important, Congress failed even to recommend needed amendments. As early as 1784 Congress was so divided it defeated an amendment that would enable it to regulate commerce, foreign and domestic, and to levy duties on imports and exports. Often Congress could not function for lack of a quorum. The requisite number of states was present for only three days between October 1785 and April 1786. In 1786 Congress was unable to agree on any amendments for submission to the states.

The political condition of the United States during the 1780s stagnated partly because of the constitutional impotence of Congress and the unconstitutional conduct of the states. The controversy with Britain had taught that liberty and localism were congruent. The 1780s taught that excessive localism was incompatible with nationhood. The Confederation was a necessary point of midpassage. It bequeathed to the United States the fundamentals of a federal system, a national domain, and a solution to the colonial problem. Moreover the Articles contained several provisions that were antecedents of their counterparts in the Constitution of 1787: a free speech clause for congressmen and LEGISLATIVE IMMUNITY, a PRIVILEGES AND IMMUNITIES clause, a clause on the extradition of FUGITIVES FROM JUSTICE, a FULL FAITH AND CREDIT clause, and a clause validating United States debts. The Confederation also started an effective government bureaucracy when the Congress in 1781 created secretaries for foreign affairs, war, marine, and finance—precursors of an executive branch. When the new departments of that branch began to function in 1789, a corps of experienced administrators, trained under the Articles, staffed them. The courts established by Congress to decide prize and admiralty cases as well as boundary disputes foreshadowed a national judiciary. Except for enactment of the great Northwest Ordinance, however, the Congress of the Confederation was moribund by 1787. It had successfully prosecuted the war, made foreign alliances, established the national credit, framed the first constitution of the United States, negotiated a favorable treaty of peace, and created a national domain. Congress's accomplishments were monumental, especially during wartime, yet in the end it failed.

By contrast, state government flourished. Excepting Rhode Island and Connecticut, all the states adopted written constitutions during the war, eight in 1776. Madison exultantly wrote, "Nothing has excited more admiration in the world than the manner in which free governments have been established in America, for it was the first instance, from the creation of the world that free inhabitants have been seen deliberating on a form of government, and selection of such of their citizens as possessed their confidence to determine upon and give effect to it."

The VIRGINIA CONSTITUTION OF 1776, the first permanent state constitution, began with a Declaration of Rights adopted three weeks before the Declaration of Independence. No previous bill of rights had restrained all branches of government. Virginia's reflected the widespread belief that Americans had been thrown back into a state of nature from which they emerged by framing a social compact for their governance, reserving to themselves certain inherent or natural rights, including life, liberty, the enjoyment of property, and the pursuit of happiness. Virginia's declaration explicitly declared that as all power derived from the people, for whose benefit government existed, the people could reform or abolish government when it failed them. On the basis of this philosophy Virginia framed a constitution providing for a bicameral legislature, a governor, and a judicial system. The legislature elected a governor, who held office for one year, had no veto power, and was encumbered by an executive council. The legislature chose many important officials, including judges.

Some states followed the more democratic model of the PENNSYLVANIA CONSTITUTION OF 1776, others the ultraconservative one of Maryland, but all state constitutions prior to the MASSACHUSETTS CONSTITUTION OF 1780 were framed by legislatures, which in some states called themselves "conventions" or assemblies. Massachusetts deserves credit for having originated a new institution of government, a specially elected constitutional convention whose sole function was to frame the constitution and submit it for popular ratification. That procedure became the standard. Massachusetts's constitution, which is still operative, became the model American state constitution. The democratic procedure for making it fit the emerging theory that the sovereign people should be the source of the constitution and authorize its framing by a constitutional convention, rather than the legislature to which the constitution is paramount. Massachusetts was also the first state to give more than lip service to the principle of separation of powers. Everywhere else, excepting perhaps New York, unbalanced government and legislative supremacy prevailed. Massachusetts established the precedent for a strong, popularly elected executive with a veto power; elsewhere the governor tended to be a ceremonial head who depended for his existence on the legislature.

The first state constitutions and related legislation introduced significant reforms. Most states expanded VOTING RIGHTS by reducing property qualifications, and a few, including Vermont (an independent state from 1777 to 1791), experimented with universal manhood suffrage. Many state constitutions provided for fairer apportionment of REPRESENTATION in the legislature. Every southern state either abolished its ESTABLISHMENT OF RELIGION or took major steps to achieve separation of church and state. Northern states either abolished SLAVERY or provided for its gradual ending. Criminal codes were made more humane. The confiscation of Loyalist estates and of crown lands, and the opening of a national domain westward to the Mississippi, led to a democratization of landholding, as did the abolition of feudal relics such as the law of primogeniture and entail. The pace of democratic change varied from state to state, and in some states it was nearly imperceptible, but the Revolution without doubt occasioned constitutional and political developments that had long been dammed up under the colonial system.

The theory that a constitution is supreme law encouraged the development of judicial review. Written constitutions with bills of rights and the emerging principle of separation of powers contributed to the same end. Before the Revolution appellate judges tended to be dependents of the executive branch; the Revolution promoted judicial independence. Most state constitutions provided for judicial tenure during good behavior rather than for a fixed term or the pleasure of the appointing power. Inevitably when Americans believed that a legislature had exceeded its authority they argued that it had acted unconstitutionally, and they turned to courts to enforce the supreme law as law. The dominant view, however, was that a court holding a statute unconstitutional insulted the sovereignty of the legislature, as the reactions to HOLMES V. WALTON (1780) and TREVETT V. WEEDEN (1786) showed. COMMONWEALTH V. CATON (1782) was probably the first case in which a state judge declared that a court had power to hold a statute unconstitutional, though the court in that case sustained the act before it. In RUTGERS V. WADDINGTON (1784) Alexander Hamilton as counsel argued that a state act violating a treaty was unconstitutional, but the court declared that the judicial power advocated by counsel was "subversive of all government." Counsel in *Trevett* also contended that the court should void a state act. Arguments of counsel do not create precedents but can reveal the emergence of a new idea. Any American would have agreed that an act against a constitution was void; although few would have agreed that courts have the final power to decide matters of constitutionality, that idea was spreading. The TEN POUND ACT CASES (1786) were the first in which an American court held a state enactment void, and that New Hampshire precedent was succeeded by a similar decision in the North Carolina case of BAYARD v. SINGLETON (1787). The principle of MARBURY v. MADISON (1803) thus originated at a state level before the framing of the federal Constitution.

The Constitution originated in the drive for a strong national government that preceded the framing of the Articles of Confederation. The "critical period" of 1781–1787 intensified that drive, but it began well before the defects of the Articles expanded the ranks of the nationalists. The weaknesses of the United States in international affairs, its inability to enforce the peace treaty, its financial crisis, its helplessness during SHAYS' REBELLION, and its general incapacity to govern resulted in many proposals—in Congress, in the press, and even in some states—for national powers to negotiate commercial treaties, regulate the nation's commerce, and check state policies that adversely affected creditor interests and impeded economic growth. Five states met at the Annapolis Convention in 1786, ostensibly to discuss a "uniform system" of regulating commerce, but those who masterminded the meeting had a much larger agenda in mind—as Madison put it, a "plenipotentiary Convention for amending the Confederation."

Hamilton had called for a "convention of all the states" as early as 1780, before the Articles were ratified, to form a government worthy of the nation. Even men who defended state sovereignty conceded the necessity of a convention by 1787. William Grayson admitted that "the present Confederation is utterly inefficient and that if it remains much longer in its present State of imbecility we shall be one of the most contemptible Nations on the face of the earth. . . ." LUTHER MARTIN admitted that Congress was "weak, contemptibly weak," and Richard Henry Lee believed that no government "short of force, will answer." "Do you not think," he asked GEORGE MASON, "that it ought to be declared . . . that any State act of legislation that shall contravene, or oppose, the authorized acts of Congress, or interfere with the expressed rights of that body, shall be *ipso facto* void,

and of no force whatsoever?" Many leaders, like THOMAS JEFFERSON, advocated executive and judicial branches for the national government with "an appeal from state judicatures to a federal court in all cases where the act of Confederation controlled the question. . . ." RUFUS KING, who also promoted a "vigorous Executive," thought that the needed power of Congress to regulate all commerce "can never be well exercised without a Federal Judicial." A consensus was developing.

The Annapolis Convention exploited and nurtured that consensus when it recommended to all the states and to Congress that a constitutional convention to "meet at Philadelphia on the second Monday in May next (1787), to take into consideration the situation of the United States, to devise such further provisions as shall appear to them necessary to render the constitution of the federal government adequate to the exigencies of the Union. . . ." Several states, including powerful Virginia and Pennsylvania, chose delegates for the Philadelphia convention, forcing Congress to save face on February 21, 1787, by adopting a motion in accord with the Annapolis recommendation, although Congress declared that the "sole and express purpose" of the convention was "revising the articles of confederation."

The CONSTITUTIONAL CONVENTION OF 1787, which formally organized itself on May 25, lasted almost four months, yet reached its most crucial decision almost at the outset. The first order of business was the nationalistic VIRGINIA PLAN (May 29), and the first vote of the Convention, acting as a Committee of the Whole, was the adoption of a resolution "that a *national* Government ought to be established consisting of a *supreme* legislative, Executive and Judiciary" (May 30). Thus the Convention immediately agreed on abandoning, rather than amending, the Articles; on writing a new Constitution; on creating a national government that would be supreme; and on having it consist of three branches.

The radical character of this early decision may be best understood by comparing it with the Articles. The Articles failed mainly because there was no way to force the states to fulfill their obligations or to obey the exercise of such powers as Congress did possess. "The great and radical vice in the construction of the existing Confederation," said Alexander Hamilton, "is the principle of legislation for states or governments, in their corporate capacities, and as contradistinguished from the individuals of which they consist." The Convention remedied that vital defect in the Articles, as George Mason pointed out (May 30), by agreeing on a government that "could directly operate on individuals." Thus the framers solved the critical problem of sanctions by establishing a national government that was independent of the states.

On the next day, May 31, the Committee of the Whole made other crucial decisions with little or no debate. One, reflecting the nationalist bias of the Convention, was the decision to establish a bicameral system whose larger house was to be elected directly by the people rather than by the state legislatures. Mason, no less, explained, "Under the existing confederacy, Congress represent the States not the people of the States; their acts operate on the States, not on the individuals. The case will be changed in the new plan of Government. The people will be represented; they ought therefore to choose the Representatives." Another decision of May 31 was to vest in the Congress the sweeping and undefined power, recommended by the Virginia Plan, "to legislate in all cases to which the separate States are incompetent; or in which the harmony of the U.S. may be interrupted by the exercise of individual [state] legislation; to negative all laws passed by the several States contravening in the opinion of the National Legislature the articles of Union, or any treaties subsisting under the authority of the Union." Not a state voted "nay" to this exceptionally nationalistic proposition. Nor did any state oppose the decision of the next day to create a national executive with similarly broad, undefined powers.

After deliberating for two weeks, the Committee of the Whole presented the Convention with its recommendations, essentially the adoption of the Virginia Plan. Not surprisingly, several of the delegates had second thoughts about the hasty decisions that had been made. ELBRIDGE GERRY reiterated "that it was necessary to consider what the people would approve." Scrapping the Articles contrary to instructions and failing to provide for state equality in the system of representation provoked a reconsideration along lines described by WILLIAM PATERSON of New Jersey as "federal" in contradistinction to "national." Yet injured state pride was a greater cause of dissension than were the powers proposed for the national government. Some delegates were alarmed, not because of an excessive centralization of powers in the national government but because of the excessive advantages given to the largest states at the expense of the others. Three states—Virginia, Massachusetts, and Pennsylvania—had forty-five percent of the white population in the country. Under the proposed scheme of proportionate representation, the small states feared that the large ones would dominate the others by controlling the national government.

On June 15, therefore, Paterson submitted for the Convention's consideration a substitute plan. It was a small states plan rather than a STATES' RIGHTS one, for it too had a strong nationalist orientation. Contemplating a revision, rather than a scrapping, of the Articles, it retained the unicameral Congress with its equality of state representation, thus appeasing the small states. But the plan vested in Congress one of the two critical powers previously lacking: "to pass Acts for the regulation of trade and commerce," foreign and interstate. The other, the power of taxation, appeared only in a stunted form; Congress was to be authorized to levy duties on imports and to pass stamp tax acts. Except for its failure to grant full tax powers, the PATERSON PLAN proposed the same powers for the national legislature as the finished Constitution. The Plan also contained the germ of the national SUPREMACY CLAUSE of the Constitution, Article Six, by providing that acts of Congress and United States treaties "shall be the supreme law of the respective States . . . and that the Judiciary of the several States shall be bound thereby in their decisions, any thing in the respective laws of the Individual States to the contrary notwithstanding." The clause also provided for a federal judiciary with extensive jurisdiction and for an executive who could muster the military of the states to compel state obedience to the supreme law. Compulsion of states was unrealistic and unnecessary. Paterson himself declared that the creation of a distinct executive and judiciary meant that the government of the Union could "be exerted on individuals."

Despite its nationalist features, the Paterson Plan retained a unicameral legislature, in which the states remained equal, and the requisition system of rising a revenue, which had failed. "You see the consequence of pushing things too far," said John Dickinson of Delaware to Madison. "Some of the members from the small States wish for two branches in the General Legislature and are friends to a good National Government; but we would sooner submit to a foreign power than submit to be deprived of an equality of suffrage in both branches of the Legislature, and thereby be thrown under the domination of the large states." Only a very few dissidents were irreconcilably opposed to "a good National Government." Most of the dissidents were men like Dickinson and Paterson, "friends to a good National Government" if it preserved a wider scope for small state authority and influence.

When Paterson submitted his plan on June 15, the Convention agreed that to give it "a fair deliberation" it should be referred to the Committee of the Whole and that "in order to place the two plans in due comparison, the other should be recommitted." After debating the two plans, the Committee of the Whole voted in favor of reaffirming the original recommendations based on the Virginia Plan "as preferable to those of Mr. Paterson." Only three weeks after their deliberations, had begun the Framers decisively agreed, for the second time, on a strong, independent national government that would operate directly on individuals without the involvement of states.

But the objections of the small states had not yet been satisfied. On the next day, Connecticut, which had voted against the Paterson Plan, proposed the famous GREAT COMPROMISE: proportionate representation in one house, "provided each State had an equal voice in the other." On that latter point the Convention nearly broke up, so intense was the conflict and deep the division. The irreconcilables in this instance were the leaders of the large-state nationalist faction, otherwise the most constructive and influential members of the Convention: Madison and James Wilson. After several weeks of debate and deadlock, the Convention on July 16 narrowly voted for the compromise. With ten states present, five supported the compromise, four opposed (including Virginia and Pennsylvania), and Massachusetts was divided. The compromise saved small-state prestige and saved the Convention from failure.

Thereafter consensus on fundamentals was restored, with Connecticut, New Jersey, and Delaware becoming fervent supporters of Madison and Wilson. A week later, for example, there was a motion that each state should be represented by two senators who would "vote per capita," that is, as individuals. Luther Martin of Maryland protested that per capita voting conflicted with the very idea of "the States being represented," yet the motion carried, with no further debate, 9–1.

On many matters of structure, mechanics, and detail there were angry disagreements, but agreement prevailed on the essentials. The office of the presidency is a good illustration. That there should be a powerful chief executive provoked no great debate, but the Convention almost broke up, for the second time, on the method of electing him. Some matters of detail occasioned practically no disagreement and revealed the nationalist consensus. Mason, of all people, made the motion that one qualification of congressmen should be "citizenship of the United States," and no one disagreed. Under the Articles of Confederation, there was only state citizenship; that there should be a concept of national citizenship seemed natural to men framing a constitution for a nation.

Even more a revelation of the nationalist consensus was the fact that three of the most crucial provisions of the Constitution—the taxing power, the NECESSARY AND PROPER CLAUSE, and the supremacy clause—were casually and unanimously accepted without debate.

Until midway during its sessions, the Convention did not take the trouble to define with care the distribution of power between the national government and the states, although the very nature of the "federal" system depended on that distribution. Consensus on fundamentals once again provides the explanation. There would be no difficulty in making that distribution; and, the framers had taken out insurance, because at the very outset, they had endorsed the provision of the Virginia Plan vesting broad, undefined powers in a national legislature that would act on individuals. Some byplay of July 17 is illuminating. ROGER SHERMAN of Connecticut thought that the line drawn between the powers of Congress and those left to the states was so vague that national legislation might "interfere . . . in any matters of internal police which respect the Government of such States only, and wherein the general welfare of the United States is not concerned." His motion to protect the "internal police" of the states brought no debaters to his side and was summarily defeated; only Maryland supported Connecticut. Immediately after, another small-state delegate, GUNNING BEDFORD of Delaware, shocked even EDMUND RANDOLPH of Virginia, who had presented the Virginia Plan, by a motion to extend the powers of Congress by vesting authority "to legislate in all cases for the general interest of the Union." Randolph observed, "This is a formidable idea indeed. It involves the power of violating all the laws and constitution of the States, of intermeddling with their police." Yet the motion passed.

On July 26 the Convention adjourned until August 6 to allow a Committee on Detail to frame a "constitution conformable to the Resolutions passed by the Convention." Generously construing its charge, the committee acted as a miniature convention and introduced a number of significant changes. One was the explicit enumeration of the powers of Congress to replace the vague, omnibus provisions adopted previously by the Convention. Although enumerated, these powers were liberally expressed and formidable in their array. The committee made specific the spirit and intent of the Convention. Significantly the first enumerated power was that of taxation and the second that of regulating commerce among the states and with foreign nations: the two principal powers that had been withheld from Congress by the Articles.

When the Convention voted on the provision that Congress "shall have the power to lay and collect taxes, duties, imposts and excises," the states were unanimous and only one delegate, Elbridge Gerry, was opposed. When the Convention next turned to the commerce power, there was no discussion and even Gerry voted affirmatively.

Notwithstanding its enumeration of the legislative powers, all of which the Convention accepted, the Committee on Detail added an omnibus clause that has served as an ever expanding source of national authority: "And to make all laws that shall be necessary and proper for carrying into execution the foregoing powers." The Convention agreed to that clause without a single dissenting vote by any state or delegate. The history of the great supremacy clause, Article Six, shows a similar consensus. Without debate the Convention adopted the supremacy clause, and not a single state or delegate voted nay. Finally, Article One, Section 10, imposing restrictions on the economic powers of the states with respect to paper money, ex post facto laws, bills of credit, and contracts also reflected a consensus in the Convention. In sum, consensus, rather than compromise, was the most significant feature of the Convention, outweighing in importance the various compromises that occupied most of the time of the delegates.

But why was there such a consensus? The obvious answer (apart from the fact that opponents either stayed away or walked out) is the best: experience had proved that the nationalist constitutional position was right. If the United States was to survive and flourish, a strong national government had to be established. The Framers of the Constitution were accountable to public opinion; the Convention was a representative body. That its members were prosperous, well-educated political leaders made them no less representative than Congress. The state legislatures, which elected the members of the Convention, were the most unlikely instruments for thwarting the popular will. The Framers, far from being able to do as they pleased, were not free to promulgate the Constitution. Although they adroitly arranged for its ratification by nine state ratifying conventions rather than by all state legislatures, they could not present a plan that the people of the states would not tolerate. They could not control the membership of those state ratifying conventions. They could not even be sure that the existing Congress would submit the Constitution to the states for ratification, let alone for ratification by state conventions that had to be specially elected. If the Framers got too far astray from public opinion, their work would have been wasted. The consensus

in the Convention coincided with an emerging consensus in the country that recaptured the nationalist spirit of '76. That the Union had to be strengthened was an almost universal American belief.

For its time the Constitution was a remarkably democratic document framed by democratic methods. Some historians have contended that the Convention's scrapping of the Articles and the ratification process were revolutionary acts which if performed by a Napoleon would be pronounced a coup d'état. But the procedure of the Articles for constitutional amendment was not democratic, because it allowed Rhode Island, with one-sixtieth of the nation's population, to exercise a veto power. The Convention sent its Constitution to the lawfully existing government, the Congress of the Confederation, for submission to the states, and Congress, which could have censured the Convention for exceeding its authority, freely complied—and thereby exceeded its own authority under the Articles! A coup d'état ordinarily lacks the deliberation and consent that marked the making of the Constitution and is characterized by a military element that was wholly lacking in 1787. A Convention elected by the state legislatures and consisting of many of the foremost leaders of their time deliberated for almost four months. Its members included many opponents of the finished scheme. The nation knew the Convention was considering changes in the government. The proposed Constitution was made public, and voters in every state were asked to choose delegates to vote for or against it after open debate. The use of state ratifying conventions fit the theory that a new fundamental law was being adopted and, therefore, conventions were proper for the task.

The Constitution guaranteed to each state a republican or representative form of government and fixed no property or religious qualifications on the right to vote or hold office, at a time when such qualifications were common in the states. By leaving voting qualifications to the states the Constitution implicitly accepted such qualifications but imposed none. The Convention, like the Albany Congress of 1754, the Stamp Act Congress, the Continental Congresses, and the Congresses of the Confederation, had been chosen by state (or colonial) legislatures, but the Constitution created a Congress whose lower house was popularly elected. When only three states directly elected their chief executive officer, the Constitution provided for the indirect election of the President by an ELECTORAL COLLEGE that originated in the people and is still operative. The Constitution's system of separation of powers and elaborate CHECKS AND BALANCES was not intended to refine out popular influence on government but to protect liberty; the Framers divided, distributed, and limited powers to prevent one branch, faction, interest, or section from becoming too powerful. Checks and balances were not undemocratic, and the Federalists were hard pressed not to apologize for checks and balances but to convince the Anti-Federalists, who wanted far more checks and balances, that the Constitution had enough. Although the Framers were not democrats in a modern sense, their opponents were even less democratic. Those opponents sought to capitalize on the lack of a BILL OF RIGHTS, and RATIFICATION OF THE CONSTITUTION became possible only because leading Federalists committed themselves to amendments as soon as the new government went into operation. At that time, however, Anti-Federalists opposed a Bill of Rights because it would allay popular fears of the new government, ending the chance for state sovereignty amendments.

Although the Framers self-consciously refrained from referring to slavery in the Constitution, it recognized slavery, the most undemocratic of all institutions. That recognition was a grudging but necessary price of Union. The THREE-FIFTHS CLAUSE of Article I provided for counting three-fifths of the total number of slaves as part of the population of a state in the apportionment of REPRESENTATION and DIRECT TAXATION. Article IV, section 2, provided for rendition of fugitive slaves to the slaveholder upon his claim. On the other hand, Article I, section 9, permitted Congress to abolish the slave trade in twenty years. Most delegates, including many from slaveholding states, would have preferred a Constitution untainted by slavery; but Southern votes for ratification required recognition of slavery. By choosing a Union with slavery, the Convention deferred the day of reckoning.

The Constitution is basically a political document. Modern scholarship has completely discredited the once popular view, associated with CHARLES BEARD, that the Constitution was undemocratically made to advance the economic interests of personalty groups, chiefly creditors. The largest public creditor at the Convention was Elbridge Gerry, who refused to sign the Constitution and opposed its ratification, and the largest private creditor was George Mason who did likewise. Indeed, seven men who either quit the Convention in disgust or refused to sign the Constitution held public securities that were worth over twice the holdings of the thirty-nine men who signed the Constitution. The most influential Framers, among them Madison, Wilson, Paterson, Dickinson, and Gouverneur Morris, owned no securities. Others, like Washington, who acted out of patriotism, not profit, held trifling amounts. Eighteen members of the Convention were either debtors or held property that depreciated after the new government became operative. On crucial issues at the Convention, as in the state ratifying conventions, the dividing line between groups for and against the Constitution was not economic, not between realty and personalty, or debtors and creditors, or town and frontier. The restrictions of Article I, section 10, on the economic powers of the states were calculated to protect creditor interests and promote business stability, but those restrictions were not undemocratic; if impairing the obligations of contracts or emitting bills of credit and paper money were democratic hallmarks, the Constitution left Congress free to be democratic. The interest groups for and against the Constitution were substantially similar. Economic interests did influence the voting on ratification, but no simple explanation that ignores differences between states and even within states will suffice, and many noneconomic influences were also at work. In the end the Constitution was framed and ratified because most voters came to share the vision held by Franklin in 1775 and Dickinson in 1776; those two, although antagonists in Pennsylvania politics, understood for quite different reasons that a strong central government was indispensable for nationhood.

LEONARD W. LEVY

Bibliography

ADAMS, WILLI PAUL 1980 *The First American Constitutions.* Chapel Hill: University of North Carolina Press.

BEARD, CHARLES 1935 *An Economic Interpretation of the Constitution of the United States.* New York: Macmillan.

BROWN, ROBERT E. 1956 *Charles Beard and the Constitution: A Critical Analysis of "An Economic Interpretation of the Constitution."* Princeton, N.J.: Princeton University Press.

BURNETT, EDMUND C. 1941 *The Continental Congress.* New York: Macmillan.

CROSSKEY, WILLIAM W. and JEFFREY, WILLIAM, JR. 1980 *Politics and the Constitution in the History of the United States.* Volume III: "The Political Background of the Federal Convention." Chicago: University of Chicago Press.

FARRAND, MAX, ed. 1937(1966) *The Records of the Federal Convention of 1787.* New Haven, Conn.: Yale University Press.

JENSEN, MERRILL 1940 *The Articles of Confederation.* Madison: University of Wisconsin Press.

KENYON, CECILIA, ed. 1966 *The Antifederalists.* Indianapolis: Bobbs-Merrill.

MCDONALD, FORREST 1958 *We the People: The Eco-*

nomic Origins of the Constitution. Chicago: University of Chicago Press.

McLaughlin, Andrew C. 1905 *The Confederation and the Constitution, 1783–1789.* New York: Harper & Brothers.

Murphy, William P. 1967 *The Triumph of Nationalism: State Sovereignty, the Founding Fathers, and the Triumph of the Constitution.* Chicago: Quadrangle Books.

Racove, Jack N. 1979 *The Beginnings of National Politics: An Interpretation of the Continental Congress.* New York: Knopf.

Warren, Charles 1928 *The Making of the Constitution.* Boston: Little, Brown.

CONSTITUTIONAL HISTORY, 1789–1801

GEORGE WASHINGTON was inaugurated the first President of the United States on April 30, 1789, in New York City. The First Congress, having been elected in February, was already at work. Most of the members were supporters of the Constitution. Fifty-four of them had sat either in the CONSTITUTIONAL CONVENTION or in one of the state ratifying conventions; only seven were Anti-Federalists. A new government had been established. But in 1789 it was only a blueprint. The first business of the President and Congress was to breathe life into the Constitution. For a document of some 5,000 words, the Constitution was remarkably explicit and complete. Yet it left a great deal to the discretion and decision of the men entrusted with its care. They, too, were "founding fathers," for they transformed words engrossed on parchment into living institutions and defined the terms of debate on the Constitution.

JAMES MADISON was the Federalist leader in the House of Representatives, where most of the formative legislation of the new government originated. Among the first statutes were those establishing the three executive departments: state, treasury, and war. Madison wrote into his bill for the department of state a provision authorizing the President to remove the department head, thereby precipitating the first congressional debate over interpretation of the Constitution. The document was clear on the President's power to appoint, with the advice and consent of the Senate, but silent on his power to remove executive officers. Removal being the reverse of appointment, some congressmen argued that it should follow the same course. But Madison contended, successfully, that the President's responsibility to see that the laws were faithfully executed necessarily included the re-moval power. The action of the House set an enduring precedent. Thus it was that in the first year of the new government an UNWRITTEN CONSTITUTION, unknown to the Framers, grew up alongside the written constitution. (See APPOINTING AND REMOVAL POWER.)

Article II, it was sometimes said, had been framed with General Washington in mind; and so great was the confidence in him that Congress showed little jealousy of the chief executive. The act creating the treasury department, however, made its head responsible to Congress as well as to the President. This was recognition that "the power of the purse" was fundamentally a legislative power, and therefore the secretary of the treasury must answer to Congress in financial matters.

The JUDICIARY ACT OF 1789, which gave life to Article III, originated in the Senate. The act provided for an elaborate system of federal courts, created the office of ATTORNEY GENERAL, and in Section 25 authorized the Supreme Court to review on APPEAL decisions of state courts concerning questions of federal law involving the United States Constitution and the laws and treaties made under it. None of this had been settled in the Constitution itself, though Federalists said that Article III together with the SUPREMACY CLAUSE of Article VI implicitly sanctioned Section 25.

The Federalists, with Madison in the lead, kept the promise made during the ratification campaign to add a BILL OF RIGHTS to the Constitution. Even before North Carolina and Rhode Island entered the new union, Congress approved twelve amendments and sent them to the states. Ten were ratified and on December 15, 1791, became part of the Constitution. In the founding of the nation the Bill of Rights was important less because it secured fundamental rights and liberties against the national government, which was without DELEGATED POWER in this sphere, than because it strengthened public confidence in the government without impairing its powers as many Anti-Federalists had wished.

The principal executive offices were filled by THOMAS JEFFERSON at state, ALEXANDER HAMILTON in the treasury, Henry Knox in the war department, and EDMUND RANDOLPH as the part-time attorney general. The unity of the executive was one of the claims made for it in THE FEDERALIST. Washington worked closely with his subordinates, and depended on them for initiative and advice, but there was never any doubt that the executive power belonged exclusively to him. The Constitution made no provision for a "cabinet," nor was one contemplated at first. The President seemed to think, on the basis of the ADVICE AND

CONSENT clause, that the Senate was meant to function as an advisory council. In August he appeared personally in the Senate to ask its advice on a proposed treaty with an Indian tribe. But the process proved awkward and cumbersome. It was not repeated. The President, instead, conducted his business with the Senate in writing, and met his need for collective consultation and advice, particularly in FOREIGN AFFAIRS, through the development of the cabinet. By 1793 it was an established institution. There were suggestions in the First Congress of a movement toward a generalized ministerial responsibility on the model of the treasury act; but this did not materialize. On the whole, the first presidency decisively enforced the theory of SEPARATION OF POWERS, associated with congressional government, rather than the ministerial responsibility characteristic of parliamentary government. In 1791 the President exercised the VETO POWER for the first time. The veto was potentially a means for controlling legislation, but Washington did not use it in that fashion (he vetoed only one other measure in eight years), and in the first forty years of the government Presidents used the veto sparingly.

The most important political and constitutional issues of Washington's first administration arose out of Hamilton's financial program. Exploiting his special relationship with Congress—conceiving of himself, indeed, as a kind of prime minister—Hamilton submitted a series of reports to Congress recommending measures to put the country's fiscal house in order, strengthen the government by appealing to the cupidity of the moneyed class, and stimulate the commercial and manufacturing sectors of the economy. His plan to fund the national debt at face value raised questions of equity between debtor and creditor interests but did not present a constitutional issue. The expectation of funding on the part of creditor groups had, of course, been a vital source of Federalist support for the Constitution. But Hamilton's plan also called for the assumption of the state debts. This proposal surprised many and aroused intense opposition in Congress, especially among Southerners sensitive to Anti-Federalist fears of undue concentration of power in the national government. Madison opposed Hamilton's plan, though on other grounds, and in doing so disclosed a division in the Federalist ranks on the direction of the new government. He was joined by his Virginia friend, Jefferson, who had just taken up his duties as secretary of state in the spring of 1790. Both were disposed to be conciliatory on this issue, however, and entered into a sectional bargain with Hamilton that would fix the permanent seat of government on the Potomac in exchange for the nec-

essary southern votes to secure passage of the assumption bill. Still, the compromise failed to quiet Anti-Federalist fears. In December the Virginia legislature adopted a series of resolutions condemning the assumption of state debts as inimical to federal and republican institutions and pointedly questioning the constitutionality of the measure. Hamilton responded angrily. "This," he said, "is the first symptom of a spirit which must either be killed, or will kill the Constitution."

The constitutional question was brought to the fore a few months later on the bill to charter the BANK OF THE UNITED STATES. A national bank, as conceived and proposed by Hamilton, would function as the financial arm of the government and multiply the active capital of the country by mounting a large paper circulation. Because three-fourths of the initial bank capital would come in the form of public securities—securities issued to fund the debt—the institution was obviously an integral part of the funding system and would directly benefit the same creditor class. Madison vigorously opposed the bill in the House, less on grounds of policy than on grounds of unconstitutionality. The power to incorporate a bank was not among the powers delegated to Congress, nor could it be considered NECESSARY AND PROPER to execute those powers. But Congress adopted the bill and sent it to the President. Uncertain whether to sign or return it, Washington first sought the attorney general's opinion, which was adverse, and then requested Jefferson's. The secretary of state agreed with Madison and offered an even more emphatically STRICT CONSTRUCTION of the Constitution. The government was one of strictly delegated powers, as declared in the TENTH AMENDMENT still in the course of ratification. "To take a single step beyond the boundaries thus specifically drawn around the powers of Congress," Jefferson warned, "is to take possession of a boundless field of power, no longer susceptible to definition." To these objections Hamilton replied in a powerful opinion founded on the doctrine of IMPLIED POWERS. "Every power vested in a government is in its nature *sovereign*, and included, by *force* of the *term*, a right to employ all *means* requisite and fairly applicable to the attainment of the *ends* of such power, and which are not precluded by restrictions and exceptions specified in the Constitution . . ." (italics in original). The utility of a national bank in the execution of powers to tax, borrow money, and regulate commerce could not be denied. It was decisive in Hamilton's judgment. Washington concurred, and signed the Bank Bill into law.

In his Report on Manufactures, presented to the

Second Congress, Hamilton extended his nationalist program by way of the GENERAL WELFARE CLAUSE. Believing that extensive domestic manufactures were necessary to the wealth and welfare of the nation, Hamilton proposed a comprehensive system of aid and encouragement—tariffs, bounties, inspections, export controls, drawbacks—which he justified under the power to provide for the general welfare. No legislation resulted from the report, but it produced consternation in opposition ranks. "If not only the *means*, but the *objects* [of the government] are unlimited," Madison wrote, "The parchment had better be thrown into the fire at once" (italics in original). Virginia's two senators introduced constitutional amendments to limit the application of the clause to the ENUMERATED POWERS and deny the power of Congress to charter corporations.

Although the widening debate took its shape from the constitutional question, it involved much more. It involved the conflict of economic interests: debtors and creditors, landed property and fluid capital, the mass of people engaged in agriculture, and the enterprising class of merchants, bankers, and manufacturers. The fact that the former tended to be concentrated in the South, the latter in the Northeast, particularly in the coastal cities, gave the conflict a sectional character as well. The debate also involved competing strategies of economic development in the new nation, as well as contrasting ideas of the nature of freedom, the Union, and republican government. To an extent, certainly, the conflict was epitomized in the clash between the leading cabinet secretaries, Jefferson and Hamilton, who increasingly appeared as the protagonists of opposing doctrines and parties in the public eye. One despised, the other idolized governance. One located the strength of the republic in the diffuse energies of a free society, the other in the consolidation of the government's power. One believed that private interest corrupted public good, the other conscripted private interest for public benefit. One viewed the Constitution as a superintending rule of political action, the other, as a point of departure for heroic statesmanship. In the balance between authority and liberty, Hamilton was an apologist for the former, Jefferson for the latter. Hamilton feared most of the ignorance and turbulence of the people, while Jefferson preached "trust the people" and feared rulers independent of them.

The division on foreign policy deepened the division on domestic policy. Jefferson, Madison, and those who began to call themselves Republicans opposed British power and influence and openly championed the French Revolution. Hamilton and the Federalists,

on the other hand, relied upon British trade, credit, and power to nurture American development; they feared the contagion of French ideas. The controversy over foreign policy assumed a constitutional dimension after Britain and France went to war in 1793. President Washington issued a proclamation pledging "a conduct friendly and impartial" toward the belligerents and warning citizens against hostile acts. Jefferson opposed this PROCLAMATION OF NEUTRALITY, as it came to be known, principally because it tended to defeat his foreign policy objectives to oppose Britain and support France. As an ally, France had a right to expect friendship from the United States; Britain, on the other hand, might have been made to pay a price for American neutrality, as in recognition of "free ships make free goods" and related guarantees of neutral rights. Viewing a declaration of neutrality as the negative side of a DECLARATION OF WAR, Jefferson also held that the proclamation invaded the authority of Congress. The popular reception of the new French minister to the United States, Edmond Genet, fueled criticism of the proclamation. Genet himself took advantage of this sentiment by arming privateers in American ports and issuing military commissions to American citizens. Hamilton, under the pseudonym "Pacificus," wrote a series of newspaper articles in defense of the presidential proclamation. Broadly construing Article II, Hamilton maintained that all executive power is vested in the President unless specifically qualified or withheld. The power to declare war belonged to Congress, of course, but did not preclude unilateral actions by the President bearing on the exercise of that power. To Republicans such a power looked suspiciously like the British royal prerogative in foreign affairs. Taking up his pen in reply, Madison, as "Helvidius," argued that all matters touching on the WAR POWER are necessarily legislative; the executive, therefore, cannot initiate a course of action that, in effect, confronts Congress with a *fait accompli.* Whatever the abstract merits of Madison's argument, it gave too little weight to realities in the conduct of foreign affairs, which inevitably favored the executive.

In the absence of statute, executive officers decided difficult questions of neutrality as they arose. Thus it was that the cabinet became a permanent institution. Jefferson and Hamilton were usually at odds, causing many split decisions. On July 18, 1793, the officers submitted to the Supreme Court a list of twenty-nine questions about international law. The Justices declined to rule, however, thereby setting a precedent against ADVISORY OPINIONS. The cabinet hammered out its own ADMINISTRATIVE LAW of neutrality, which prevailed until Congress convened and enacted the Neutrality Act of 1794.

Long before that the firebrand French minister had been recalled and Jefferson had retired from the government, ensuring Hamilton the same ascendancy in foreign affairs he had earlier enjoyed in domestic affairs. The upshot was JAY'S TREATY, negotiated in London in November 1794 and ratified by the Senate six months later. The treaty preserved peace with Britain but, in Republican opinion, at the cost of submission to British maritime power and risk of war with France. Like every great issue of Washington's presidency, the treaty caused significant constitutional debate. Because some provisions required appropriations to carry them into effect, the treaty came under the scrutiny of the House of Representatives. In this connection a Republican majority demanded that the President lay before the House a copy of the instructions given to JOHN JAY and other pertinent documents. The President emphatically rejected the call, holding that the House had no constitutional power with respect to treaties. The House, after reiterating its position and carefully differentiating the appropriation power from the TREATY POWER, which it disclaimed, proceeded to vote the money requested by the President.

The protracted battle over Jay's Treaty set the stage for the presidential election of 1796. Washington's decision to retire after two terms lifted the last restraint on partisanship, and two infant POLITICAL PARTIES, each with its own standard bearer, JOHN ADAMS for the Federalists, Jefferson for the Republicans, contested the election. The Constitution had been intended to work without parties. Parties, the Framers reasoned, fed the natural turbulence of the populace and served the ambitions of demagogues; they caused implacable rivalries in legislative councils, usurping the place of reason and moderation; they introduced whole networks of partisan allegiance at cross-purposes with the national welfare. Washington had attempted to govern independently of parties, but in an increasingly polarized political environment even he became a partisan. When the Republicans sought to channel popular enthusiasm for the French cause into "democratic societies," Washington publicly condemned the societies as illicit political engines, thereby betraying intolerance of political opposition from outside the constitutional channels of authority. WASHINGTON'S FAREWELL ADDRESS pointedly warned the people against the "baneful" effects of parties. The Republicans, however, were rapidly discovering in party organization outside the government the appropriate means for wresting power from the Federalists who, in their eyes, were the real bane of the country.

Adams was elected President by a slender ELECTORAL COLLEGE majority. Crisis with France, mounting since the British treaty, set the course of the administration. Angrily denouncing French decrees against American commerce, Adams sent a special commission to negotiate in Paris under threat of war. Intriguing agents of the French foreign ministry demanded money as the price of negotiations. The Americans indignantly refused. This affair—the XYZ Affair—then exploded in the United States, and the Federalists converted foreign crisis into domestic crisis. Under cover of whipped-up war hysteria, they assailed the patriotism of the Republicans, portraying them as Jacobin disorganizers in the country's bowels whose ultimate treachery only awaited the signal of an invading French army. Although the President refrained from asking for a declaration of war, he inflamed the war spirit. Congress abrogated the French treaties, expanded the army, established the Navy Department, and authorized an undeclared naval war against France. The Republicans fought this policy to no avail. Two years later the Supreme Court, in a prize case, *Bas v. Tingey* (1800), upheld the power of the government to make war without declaring it.

The war hysteria found domestic expression in the ALIEN AND SEDITION ACTS. The Republicans attacked the laws restrictive of ALIENS on grounds of policy and the Alien Act, in particular, for violating the Constitution by authorizing the President summarily to deport aliens deemed dangerous to the nation. The Sedition Act, the Republicans argued, was without congressional authority and directly violated the FIRST AMENDMENT. Despite the smokescreen of war, TREASON, and subversion, Republicans believed that the law aimed at suppressing their presses and crippling their party. Political freedom, as well as FREEDOM OF SPEECH and FREEDOM OF THE PRESS, was at stake. When the federal courts, manned by partisan Federalist judges, cooperated in enforcing the Sedition Act, closing off the judicial channel of redress, Jefferson and Madison turned to two Republican state legislatures to arouse opposition. The VIRGINIA AND KENTUCKY RESOLUTIONS interposed the authority of these states to declare the Alien and Sedition Acts unconstitutional and urged other states to join in forcing their repeal. The resolutions were especially significant as landmark statements of the THEORY OF THE UNION as a compact of sovereign states and of the right of a state, whether by INTERPOSITION or NULLIFICATION, to judge the constitutionality of acts of Congress. Northern state legislatures, in response, rejected the theory together with the appeal. Although the resolutions contributed to rising popular opposition against the administration, they did not force repeal of the hated laws. Whatever their later significance for the issue of STATES' RIGHTS and Union—the constitutional issue over which the Civil War would be fought—the resolutions originated in a struggle for political survival and addressed the fundamental issue of freedom and self-government descending from the American Revolution.

The foreign crisis passed in 1800. Adams seized the olive branch extended by France, broke with the Hamiltonian faction in his administration, and dispatched another commission to negotiate peace. The result was the Convention of 1800, which restored normal relations and formally terminated the Franco-American alliance of 1778. From the standpoint of the "war system," Adams's decision to make peace drove a sword into the Federalist party. In the ensuing presidential election, Hamilton and his friends conspired to defeat Adams.

The election of 1800 was bitterly contested by two organized political parties. The Republicans achieved unprecedented unity behind their ticket of Jefferson and AARON BURR. By party organization and electioneering tactics they turned the election of the President into a test of public opinion. This, of course, made a mockery of the Constitution, under which a body of electors separated from the people was to choose the President and vice-president. Electoral tickets became party tickets, and every presidential elector became an agent of the popular majority that elected him.

Jefferson won a decisive victory over Adams. Although the Federalists swept New England, took two of the small middle states (New Jersey and Delaware), and picked up scattered votes in three others, the Republicans won everything else, south, west, and north. The electoral vote, 73–65, failed to reflect the wide Republican margin at the polls. But the victory was jeopardized by political developments that played havoc with the electoral system. Under the Constitution each elector cast two votes for different candidates; the one with the most votes became President, while the runner-up became vice-president. The rise of political parties made the system an anachronism, for electors chosen on a party ticket would cast both votes for the party candidates, thereby producing a tie between them. So it happened in 1800: Jefferson and Burr received an equal number of electoral votes. The choice was thus thrown into the House of Representatives. There the lame-duck Federalist majority

plotted to annul the popular verdict either by creating an interregnum or by dealing Burr into the presidency. Finally, on the thirty-sixth ballot, the stalemate was broken and Jefferson was elected.

The new Republican majority moved rapidly to amend the Constitution to prevent a similar occurrence in the future. The TWELFTH AMENDMENT (1804) provided for separate ballots for President and vice-president. The elaborate machinery devised by the Framers for the election of the President was thus radically revised in response to changing political realities. Not only was this an effective use of the AMENDING PROCESS, but it seemed to suggest frequent change by amendment in the future. However, the next amendment of the Constitution came only after the passage of sixty-one years and the convulsions of civil war.

MERRILL D. PETERSON

Bibliography

BUEL, RICHARD, JR.   1972   Securing the Revolution: Ideology and American Politics, 1789–1815. Ithaca, N.Y.: Cornell University Press.
MALONE, DUMAS   1962   Jefferson and the Ordeal of Liberty. Boston: Little, Brown.
MILLER, JOHN C.   1960   The Federalist Era: 1789–1801. New York: Harper & Row.
STOURZH, GERALD   1970   Alexander Hamilton and the Idea of Republican Government. Stanford, Calif.: Stanford University Press.
WHITE, LEONARD D.   1948   The Federalist: A Study in Administrative History, 1789–1801. New York: Free Press.

CONSTITUTIONAL HISTORY, 1801–1829

THOMAS JEFFERSON entered the presidency in 1801 with a rhetoric of return to constitutional first principles. Inaugurated in the new permanent capital on the Potomac, he offered a brilliant summation of these principles together with a lofty appeal for restoration of harmony and affection. "We are all republicans: we are all federalists," he declared. He hoped to achieve "a perfect consolidation" of political sentiments by emphasizing principles that ran deeper than party names or doctrines. He spoke of preserving "the whole constitutional vigor" of the general government yet called for "a wise and frugal government, which shall restrain men from injuring one another, which shall leave them otherwise free to regulate their own pursuits of industry and improvement, and shall not take from the mouth of labor the bread it has earned." Jefferson never doubted that "constitutional vigor" and individual liberty were perfectly compatible, indeed that the strength of republican government rested upon the freedom of the society. He named "absolute acquiescence in the decisions of the majority the vital principle of republics, from which there is no appeal but to force." This principle demanded freedom of opinion and debate, including the right of a minority to turn itself into a new majority, as the Republican party had done. "If there be any among us," Jefferson said, alluding to the delusions of 1798, "who would wish to dissolve this Union or to change its republican form, let them stand undisturbed as monuments of the safety with which error may be tolerated where reason is left free to combat it." He thus announced a commitment to ongoing change through the democratic process. Because of that commitment the Constitution became an instrument of democracy, change became possible without violence or destruction, and government went forward on the continuing consent of the governed.

The "revolution of 1800," as Jefferson later called it, introduced no fundamental changes in the structure or machinery of the general government but made that government a more effective instrument of popular leadership. Jefferson himself possessed great popular authority. Combining this with the constitutional authority of the office, he overcame Whiggish monarchical fears and gave the presidency a secure place in the republican system. Jefferson dominated his administration more surely and completely than even GEORGE WASHINGTON had done. The cabinet, which was composed of moderate Republicans, enjoyed unprecedented harmony, stability, and unity. It was the main agency of policy and decision making.

Jefferson also dominated Congress. For the first time, in 1801, the Republicans controlled both houses of Congress. The Federalists were a shrinking minority, though by no means powerless. In republican theory Congress should control the executive. Jefferson honored the theory in official discourse. Thus he declined to appear before Congress in person and sent his annual "State of the Union" message to be read by a clerk, setting a precedent that remained unbroken for 112 years. Practically, however, Jefferson recognized that the government demanded executive leadership if any majority, Federalist or Republican, was to carry out its program. How could he overcome the constraints of republican theory and the constitutional SEPARATION OF POWERS? The solution was found partly through the personal influence Jefferson

commanded and partly through a network of party leadership outside constitutional channels. As the unchallenged head of the Republican party, Jefferson acted with an authority he did not possess, indeed utterly disclaimed, in his official capacity. Leaders of both houses of Congress were the President's political lieutenants. Despite the weak structural organization of the Republican party in Congress—the only formal machinery was the presidential nominating caucus which came into being every four years—the party was a pervasive functional reality. The President was chief legislator as well as chief magistrate. Nearly all the congressional legislation during eight years originated with the President and his cabinet. Lacking staff support, Congress depended on executive initiatives and usually followed them. Federalists complained of the "backstairs" influence of the President; eventually some Republicans, led by JOHN RANDOLPH, rebelled. But the system of presidential leadership worked with unerring precision during Jefferson's first term. It faltered during his second term when the Republicans, with virtually no opposition to contend with, began to quarrel among themselves; and it would not work at all under Jefferson's successor, JAMES MADISON, who lacked Jefferson's popular prestige and personal magnetism.

In matters of public policy, the Jefferson administration sought reform within the limits of moderation and conciliation. More doctrinaire Republicans, still infected with Anti-Federalism, were not satisfied with a mere change of leadership and demanded restrictive constitutional amendments to place the true principles of government beyond reversal or contradiction. While rejecting this course, Jefferson was never entirely happy with the consequences of his temporizing policies. Republican reform was bottomed on fiscal policy. The Hamiltonian system of public debt, internal taxes, and a national bank was considered an evil of the first magnitude. Secretary of the Treasury ALBERT GALLATIN developed a plan to extinguish the debt, which had increased under the Federalists, by large annual appropriations, yet, amazingly, reduce taxes at the same time. All internal taxes would be repealed and government would depend solely on revenue from the customs houses. The plan required deep retrenchment, especially in the army and navy departments. Of course, it was premised on peace. Congress embarked on it; and although the debt was dramatically reduced during the next seven years, the plan was initially upset by the exigencies of the Tripolitan War, then derailed by the Anglo-American crisis that led to the War of 1812. Jefferson agonized over

ALEXANDER HAMILTON's fiscal system. "When the government was first established," he wrote in 1802, "it was possible to have kept it going on true principles, but the contracted, English, half-lettered ideas of Hamilton destroyed that hope in a bud. We can pay off his debt in 15 years, but we can never get rid of his financial system. It mortifies me to be strengthening principles which I deem radically vicious, but the vice is entailed on us by the first error. . . . What is practicable must often control pure theory." A case in point was the Bank of the United States. Jefferson thought it an institution of "the most deadly hostility" to the Constitution and republican government. Yet he tolerated the Bank, in part because its charter ran to 1811 (when Republicans would refuse to renew it) and also because Gallatin found the bank highly useful to the government's operations.

Jefferson's "war on the judiciary" featured three main battles and several skirmishes, ending in no very clear outcome. The first battle was fought over the JUDICIARY ACT OF 1801. Republicans were enraged by this blatantly partisan measure passed in the waning hours of JOHN ADAMS's administration. It created a new tier of courts and judgeships, extended the power of the federal judiciary at the expense of state courts, and reduced the number of Supreme Court Justices beginning with the next vacancy, thereby denying the Republicans an early opportunity to reshape the Court. Jefferson promptly targeted the act for repeal. The Federalists had retreated to the judiciary as a stronghold, he said, from which "all the works of Republicanism are to be beaten down and erased." The Sedition Act had demonstrated the prostration of the judiciary to partisan purposes. After taking office Jefferson acted to pardon victims of the act, which he considered null and void, and to drop pending prosecutions. He often spoke of making judges more responsible to the people, perhaps by periodic review of their tenure; and although he recognized the power of JUDICIAL REVIEW, he did not think it binding on the executive or the legislature. According to his theory of "tripartite balance" each of the coordinate branches of government is supreme in its sphere and may decide questions of constitutionality for itself. The same theory was advanced by Republicans in Congress, as against the Federalist claim of exclusive power of the Supreme Court to declare legislation unconstitutional. Congress did not settle this issue; but after heated debate it repealed the offensive act and, with minor exceptions, returned the judiciary to its previous footing.

The second battle involved the case of MARBURY v. MADISON (1803). Although the Supreme Court's decision would later be seen as the cornerstone of judicial review, the case was understood at the time primarily as a political duel between the President and the Court, one in which Chief Justice JOHN MARSHALL took a gratuitous stab at the executive but then deliberately backed away from a confrontation he knew the Court could not win.

The third battle featured the IMPEACHMENT of federal judges. In 1803 Congress impeached, tried, and convicted Judge JOHN PICKERING of the district court in New Hampshire. The case was a hard one because Pickering's bizarre conduct on the bench stemmed from intoxication and possible insanity; but in the absence of any constitutional authorization for the removal of an incompetent judge, the Republicans took the course of impeachment and convicted him of "high crimes and misdemeanors." The subsequent impeachment of Supreme Court Justice SAMUEL J. CHASE was clearly a political act. A high-toned Federalist, Chase had earned Republican enmity as the convicting judge in several SEDITION trials and by harangues to grand juries assailing democracy and all its works. Nevertheless, his trial in the Senate ended in a verdict of acquittal in 1805. Jefferson and the Republican leaders turned away from impeachment in disgust. Although it may have produced salutary restraint in the federal judiciary, and enhanced the President's role as a popular leader, neither impeachment nor any other Jeffersonian action disturbed the foundations of judicial power.

During his second term, Jefferson used the TREASON trial of AARON BURR to renew the attack on the judiciary but without success. The former vice-president was charged with treason for leading a military expedition to separate the western states from the Union. Determined to convict him, Jefferson again faced an old enemy, John Marshall, who presided in the trial at Richmond. At Burr's request, Marshall subpoenaed Jefferson to appear in court with papers bearing on the case. Jefferson refused, citing his responsibility as chief executive. "The Constitution enjoins his constant agency in the concerns of six millions of people. Is the law paramount to this, which calls on him on behalf of a single one?" he asked. The court backed off. Nothing required Jefferson's presence. He offered to testify by deposition, but this was not requested. When the trial ended in Burr's acquittal, Jefferson denounced its whole conduct as political. He laid the proceedings before Congress and urged that body to furnish some remedy for judicial arrogance and error. Several Republican state legislatures instructed their delegations to seek amendment making judges removable on the address of both houses of Congress. Both President and Congress were preoccupied with FOREIGN AFFAIRS in the fall of 1807, however, and nothing came of this effort.

The first foreign crisis of the Jefferson administration culminated in the LOUISIANA PURCHASE. It was an ironic triumph for a President, an administration, and a party that made a boast of constitutional purity. For the Constitution made no provision either to acquire foreign territory or, as the purchase treaty mandated, to incorporate that territory and its inhabitants into the Union. Jefferson, therefore, proposed to sanction the acquisition retroactively by amendment of the Constitution. Actually, such an authorization was the lesser part of the amendment he drafted; the larger part undertook to control the future of the Trans-Mississippi West by prohibiting settlement above the thirty-third parallel. But neither part interested congressional Republicans, and Jefferson, though he said failure of the amendment made the Constitution "a blank paper by construction," acquiesced. A revolution in the Union perforce became a revolution in the Constitution as well. The expansion of the treaty-making power was only the beginning of the revolution. A series of acts for the government of the new territory vested extraordinary power in the President; and the President proposed, with the sanction of a constitutional amendment, a national system of INTERNAL IMPROVEMENTS to unite this far-flung "empire of liberty."

The foreign crisis of Jefferson's second administration continued under Madison and finally terminated in the War of 1812. With the formation of the Third Coalition against Napoleonic France in 1805, all Europe was engulfed in war. The United States became the last neutral nation of consequence—to the profit of its carrying trade. Unfortunately, each side, the British and the French, demanded the trade on its own terms, and submission to one side's demands entailed conflict with the other. Britain, the dominant sea power, was the greater problem. British ships attacked American carriers under interpretations of rules of blockade, contraband, and neutral commerce that were rejected by the United States. Britain claimed the right of impressment of seamen aboard American ships on the ground that they were actually British subjects who had deserted from His Majesty's Navy and shipped aboard American vessels with government connivance. There was some truth in this claim, but thousands of American citizens were, in fact, impressed by Britain. And every seizure was a stinging reminder of past colonial servitude. Diplomatic efforts to settle these issues proved abortive. Relations rapidly deteriorated after the *Chesapeake-Leopard* Affair in June 1807. The attack of HMS *Leopard* on an American naval vessel after its captain refused to permit boarding and search for deserters inflamed the entire country against Britain. Jefferson might have taken the country to war. Instead, in December, he proposed, and Congress swiftly passed, the EMBARGO ACT. Essentially a self-blockade of American commerce, the act was in some part a preparation for war and in some part an experiment to test the theory of "peaceable coercion." The idea that the United States might enforce reason and justice on European belligerents by withholding its commerce was a first principle of Jeffersonian statecraft. Under the trial now begun, that idea failed. While the policy had comparatively little effect abroad, it produced serious economic, political, and perhaps even constitutional damage at home.

The embargo raised a host of constitutional issues, all hotly debated by Federalists and Republicans, though the parties seemed to have changed places. First, and broadest, was the issue of the commerce power. Republicans said the power to regulate commerce included the power to prohibit it. Federalists, who were closely allied with eastern merchants and shipmasters, limited regulation to encouragement and protection. Yet it was a Federalist, John Davis, the United States District Judge for Massachusetts, who upheld the constitutionality of the embargo on a broad view of the commerce power backed up by the "inherent SOVEREIGNTY" of the United States. Second, wholesale violation of the embargo in the Lake Champlain region led the President to proclaim an insurrection and authorize military force to suppress it under the same law George Washington had earlier used to put down the WHISKEY REBELLION over Republican opposition. Third, enforcement of the embargo required ever tighter measures of control. The fourth in the series of five embargo acts empowered customs collectors to search without a SEARCH WARRANT and to detain vessels merely on suspicion of intent to violate the law. The FOURTH AMENDMENT, a part of the Bill of Rights, was thus jeopardized. Fourth, before Congress adjourned in April 1808 it authorized the President to suspend the embargo against either or both belligerents—an unprecedented DELEGATION OF POWER. Federalists, of course, denounced the embargo in terms that recalled the VIRGINIA AND KENTUCKY RESOLUTIONS.

A storm of protest in New England led Congress, at the end of Jefferson's presidency, to repeal the embargo. The Non-Intercourse Act, which replaced it, reopened trade with all the world except Britain and France. That course, too, failed; and for the next three years under the new president, Madison, the country drifted toward war. In the end, war was declared because both diplomacy and "peaceable coercion" had failed to resolve the conflict over neutral rights. But that conflict was a symbol of much more: the honor and independence of the nation, the freedom of its commerce, the integrity of American nationality, the survival of republican government. The war was thus morally justified as the second war for American independence. The nation was ill-prepared for war, however, and its conduct produced one disaster after another. One section of the Union, New England, vigorously opposed the war from the start.

This opposition gave rise to the principal constitutional controversy of the time. The governors of the New England states challenged congressional power to provide for organizing and calling forth the militia. The chief justice of Massachusetts's highest court advised the governor that the right to decide when the militia should be called belonged to him, not to Congress or the President; and later, in 1814, when the militia was activated it was in the state rather than the national service. Years later, in *Luther v. Mott* (1827), the Supreme Court fully sustained national authority over the militia. Interference with the prosecution of the war was accompanied by a steady stream of denunciation. Madison called this a "seditious opposition," but unlike his Federalist predecessors he made no move to restrain or suppress it. Ultra-Federalists had been hinting at disunion since the Louisiana Purchase threatened New England's power in the Union; some of them had plotted to establish a Northern Confederacy in 1804. Now, a decade later, Federalist delegates from all the New England states met secretly in the HARTFORD CONVENTION, not to plot disunion, for moderate forces were in control, but to organize resistance against "Mr. Madison's War." Resolutions adopted by the convention recommended a series of constitutional amendments, including elimination of the THREE-FIFTHS CLAUSE for the apportionment of representation and direct taxes, limitation of presidential tenure to one term, a two-thirds vote in Congress to admit new states and to declare war, and the disqualification of naturalized citizens from federal office.

The commissioners of the Hartford Convention arrived in Washington with their resolutions in the midst of jubilation over the Battle of New Orleans. They were ridiculed, of course; and from this nadir the Federalist party never recovered. News of the Peace of Ghent quickly followed. While it resolved none of the issues over which the war had begun, the treaty placed American independence on impregnable foundations and confirmed the strength of republican government. The American people erased the shame from a war so meager in victories, so marked by defeat, division, and disgrace, and put upon it the face of glory. In December 1815 Madison laid before Congress a nationalistic program that featured measures, such as a national bank, formerly associated with the defeated party. Yet the program was not a case of "out-Federalizing Federalism." The Republican nationalism that matured with the Peace of Ghent had nothing to do with Federalist nationalism, with its vitiating Anglophobia, its narrow class and sectional views, and its distrust of popular government. The American political experiment had vindicated itself, exorcising earlier fears for its survival and making possible the incorporation of principles of national improvement and consolidation into the Republican party.

A new era dawned in American politics in 1815. For a quarter-century the nation had directed its industry and commerce toward a Europe ravaged by war and revolution; now that era had ended, and with it the opportunity of rearing American prosperity on the misfortunes of the Old World. For almost as long, government had been carried on by party spirit; now one of the two parties, the Federalist, around which the rivalry of men, issues, and principles had turned, ceased to be a factor in national affairs, and it was by no means clear what political force would replace the force of party. A country that had hugged the Atlantic seaboard and sought its prosperity in foreign trade was about to explode in the Trans-Appalachian West. During the next six years five new western states would enter the Union. A wider Union and the rise of the West as a self-conscious section raised difficult problems of economic development, constitutional principle, and political power. Since its Revolutionary birth the nation had enjoyed astonishing continuity of leadership. Thomas Jefferson, author of the Declaration of Independence, was a gray eminence at Monticello; James Madison, Father of the Constitution, was the President who had finally, irrevocably, secured that independence in a second war against Great Britain. But a new generation of political leaders had burst on the scene during the war, and the fate of the nation now lay in their hands.

Nearly all Republicans united on the program of national improvement and consolidation that Madison laid before the Fourteenth Congress in December. This "Madisonian Platform" proceeded from an enlarged view of the general government's responsibility for the nation's welfare. A national bank had previously been recommended to Congress as an agency for financing the war. Now, facing the chaos of runaway state banking, Madison recommended it as a permanent institution to secure the constitutional object of a stable and uniform national currency. Madison, of course, had opposed the original Bank of the United States as unconstitutional, and Republicans in Congress had defeated its recharter in 1811. But conditions and needs had changed, and Madison, with most of these same Republicans, considered that experience had settled the question of constitutionality in favor of a national bank. The Madisonian platform called for continuing in peacetime high tariff duties on imports in order to protect the infant industries that had grown up behind the sheltering wall of war and embargo. The President called for a comprehensive system of internal improvements—roads and canals to bind the nation together, secure its defenses, and facilitate internal commerce. Any deficiency of constitutional power should be overcome by amendment. In a final appeal to the liberality of American patriotism, Madison proposed the establishment of a national university, in Washington, which would be "a central resort of youth and genius from every part of their country, diffusing on their return examples of those national feelings, those liberal sentiments, and those congenial manners which contribute cement to our union and strength to [its] great political fabric."

Congress responded with legislation to charter a national bank, establish a system of tariff protection, and create a permanent fund for financing a vast network of roads, canals, and other improvements. The last measure, dubbed the Bonus Bill because the fund was founded on the bonus to be paid for the bank charter, was vetoed by Madison on constitutional grounds in the last act of his presidency. In this surprising retreat to the doctrine of strict construction, Madison delivered the first shock to the postwar nationalism he had himself championed. His successor, JAMES MONROE, took the same position on internal improvements, holding that a constitutional amendment was necessary to authorize them. Republican leaders in Congress disagreed. They found sufficient constitutional warrant to build as well as to fund internal improvements in the commerce, post road, and general welfare clauses, and they declined to seek an amendment lest by the failure to obtain it the Constitution be weakened. In the end, however, Monroe conceded the unlimited power of Congress to appropriate money for internal improvements, while continuing to deny the power to construct and operate them.

This concession provided a constitutional justification for the General Survey Act of 1824. Although the same argument supported important projects in the ensuing administration, no national system of internal improvements was ever realized. In the absence of constructive national action, the several states embarked upon ambitious projects of their own (New York's Erie Canal, for instance, begun in 1817); and soon the government even relinquished its one great enterprise, the National Road, to the states.

The period of Monroe's presidency was signalized as "The Era of Good Feelings." This reflected the dissolution of old party ties and feelings. The Republican party had become the grand party of the nation. In 1820 Monroe ran unopposed for reelection and only one erratic electoral vote was cast against him. But his success had little to do with party or popularity, nor did it translate into effective power and leadership. Power and leadership had shifted to Congress, particularly to the House of Representatives where HENRY CLAY had converted the office of speaker from that of an impartial moderator to one of policymaking leadership. To an extent, certainly, executive power receded because foreign affairs had taken a distant second place to domestic affairs on the nation's agenda. Interestingly, Monroe is best remembered not for any initiative or achievement in domestic affairs but for a masterly stroke of foreign policy, the Monroe Doctrine. But Clay even challenged the President in foreign policy; and congressional ascendancy owed much to the boldness and address of young leaders like Clay who sought to command the popular feeling and power of the country. Partly for this reason the postwar Republicans consensus was soon shattered and "good feelings" vanished on the winds of change. Great issues, such as the Missouri Compromise, split the nationalizing Republican party along its sectional seams. The Panic of 1819, which led to the first major depression in the country's history, released powerful currents that shriveled the bright hopes of 1815.

Although the Panic of 1819 broke banks, bankrupted merchants, idled workers, and emptied factories everywhere, it was centered in American agriculture, especially in the freshly burgeoning lands of the South and West. Many purchasers of these lands had availed themselves of the credit allowed by the Harrison Land Act of 1800. Also important to frontier farmers and planters, of course, was bank credit. State banks had generally met this need, but now they were aided and abetted by the new Bank of the United States, which established most of its branches in the South and West. Agricultural prices collapsed worldwide in 1818. A severe contraction of bank credit followed. The Bank of the United States barely survived, and did so only at the expense of bankrupting many thousands of farmers, merchants, and local bankers. Several western states enacted legislation in the interest of debtors. The controversy over the constitutionality of debtor relief laws rocked Kentucky for a decade. All along the frontier, in wheat lands and in cotton lands, people tended to blame their troubles on the Bank. There were calls for repeal of its charter, and state legislatures acted to restrain "The Monster." Ohio levied a prohibitive tax on resident branches; when it was not paid the state auditor seized $100,000 of the Bank's funds, thereby giving birth to the case of OSBORN V. THE BANK OF THE UNITED STATES (1824). Wherever the depression caused hostility to the Bank, it weakened the spring of support for economic nationalism generally. To nationalist leaders, on the other hand, the depression offered further confirmation of the colonial character of the American economy and pointed up the imperative need for higher protective tariffs and other government assistance to bring about a flourishing "home market" for the products of American industry. This AMERICAN SYSTEM, as Clay named it, had its fulfillment in the Tariff of 1824.

While the Panic was at its height, in March 1819, the Supreme Court handed down its unanimous decision in MCCULLOCH V. MARYLAND, upholding the constitutionality of the Bank and its freedom to operate without state interference. Chief Justice John Marshall drew upon the Hamiltonian doctrine of IMPLIED POWERS not only for the congressional authority to charter a bank but also for a sweeping vindication of national supremacy. In the same momentous term, which established the high-water mark of judicial nationalism, the court invoked the CONTRACT CLAUSE to strike down laws of two states. In DARTMOUTH COLLEGE V. WOODWARD it extended the protection of that clause to corporate charters; and in STURGES V. CROWNINSHIELD it struck down a New York law for the relief of debtors whose contracts antedated the law. Quite aside from their implications for national versus state authority, all these decisions placed the court unreservedly on the side of propertied interests against popular majorities in state legislatures.

The Bank case, in particular, provoked attack on the Supreme Court and more broadly on the growth of national power. In Virginia opposition to the Supreme Court, which Jefferson called a "subtle corps of sappers and miners constantly working under ground to undermine the foundations of our confederated fabric," sparked revival of the STATES' RIGHTS doctrines of the Virginia and Kentucky Resolutions and offered powerful reinforcement of the state's challenge to the court's appellate jurisdiction. The challenge had ridden on an old case involving the confiscation of Loyalist lands during the American Revolution. Taking the case on appeal from the Virginia Court of Appeals, the Supreme Court had overturned the state's confiscation law and found for the right of the English heir. To this Judge SPENCER ROANE, head of the Virginia court, responded by denying the Supreme Court's appellate jurisdiction, declaring section 25 of the Judiciary Act of 1789 unconstitutional, and refusing to execute the Supreme Court's decree. The court again took up the case, MARTIN V. HUNTER'S LESSEE (1816), and through Justice JOSEPH STORY reasserted the constitutionality of the appellate jurisdiction over state courts together with the judicial supremacy that went with it. But for the Bank case the controversy would have been quickly forgotten. As Marshall observed, however, that case "roused the Sleeping Giant of Virginia." Under the pseudonym "Hampden," in the columns of the Richmond *Enquirer*, Roane advanced a DUAL FEDERALISM philosophy of the Constitution. Under it there could be no ultimate appeal from the state courts to the Supreme Court. Marshall replied at length as "Friend of the Constitution" in the Alexandria *Gazette*. The veteran Old Republican JOHN TAYLOR of Caroline expounded the Virginia doctrines *ad nauseum* in *Construction Construed and Constitutions Vindicated* (1820). The doctrines still had a long course to run, but the controversy over appellate jurisdiction drew to a close in COHENS V. VIRGINIA (1821). In this arranged case Virginia became the defendant when the Cohens appealed their conviction in state court to the Supreme Court under Section 25. The Virginia assembly adopted resolutions backing the state cause. Surprisingly, perhaps because the case resulted in a nominal victory for the state, Marshall's broad assertion of national judicial supremacy provoked no official reaction in Virginia, and opposition collapsed in 1822.

The Missouri Compromise was enacted in the midst of these events and communicated its own passions to them. The proposal to restrict slavery in Missouri as a condition of statehood raised difficult questions about the constitutional authority of Congress, the nature of the Union, the future of the West, the morality of slavery, and the sectional balance of power. Congress had previously restricted SLAVERY IN THE TERRITORIES. That power was not seriously in dispute. But the Missouri constitution would provide for slavery, and it was by no means clear that Congress could overrule it, especially as slavery had always been considered an institution under local jurisdiction. The compromise resolved the issue by allowing Missouri to enter the Union as a slave state. A new problem arose, however, when the proffered Missouri constitution contained a provision for excluding "free negroes and mulattoes" from the state. Opponents of the compromise charged that this violated the PRIVILEGES AND IMMUNITIES clause of the United States Constitution, because Negroes who were citizens of northern states would be denied citizenship in Missouri. Laboriously, a new compromise had to be constructed to save the original one. Under it Missouri would be admitted to the Union only after the legislature agreed, despite the constitutional provision, never to pass a law that might abridge the privileges and immunities of citizens. Missouri acquiesced and gained admission to the Union in August 1821. Not for many years would the harmony of the Union again be disturbed by slavery. The Missouri Compromise, therefore, contributed mightily to peace and union. Yet to Thomas Jefferson, contemplating the exclusion of slavery above the 36' 30" parallel, the compromise was "like a fire-ball in the night," sounding "the knell of the Union." "It is hushed, indeed, for the moment. But this is a reprieve only, not the final sentence. A geographical line, once conceived and held up to the angry passions of men, will never be obliterated; and every new irritation will mark it deeper and deeper."

The Republican consensus vanished during Monroe's second term. The Missouri question had raised fears of sectional parties and politics that were not dispelled by the compromise. The growth of the West, with a maturing sectional consciousness of its own, and the scramble of economic interests for the bounty and favor of the general government put the National Republican system under heavy strain. While nationalists continued to believe that the Union would survive and prosper only through measures of consolidation, growing numbers of Republicans, inspired by the Virginia "Old Republicans," believed consolidation must tear the Union apart. They called for return to Jeffersonian austerity and states' rights.

In this unstable political environment, the contest for the presidential succession was especially disturbing. Monroe's chief cabinet officers, JOHN QUINCY ADAMS, William H. Crawford, and JOHN C. CALHOUN, were in the race from the start, and they were soon joined by Henry Clay and ANDREW JACKSON. In the absence of a single dominant leader or a clear line of succession, such as the Virginia dynasty had afforded, the Republican party split into personal followings and factions. The congressional caucus of the party, which had been the mechanism for nominating candidates for President and vice-president, could no

longer be relied upon. The caucus itself had become an issue. In an increasingly democratic electorate it was assailed as a closed, elitist institution. Politicians grew wary of the caucus but saw no obvious substitute for it. "We are putting to the proof the most delicate part of our system, the election of the Executive," DANIEL WEBSTER remarked. What was most distressing about the present contest, among men nourished on traditional Whig fears of executive power, was that it made the presidency the center of gravity in the government. Great issues of public policy were submitted to the artifice and caprice of presidential politics; and senators and representatives, if elected on the basis of presidential preferences, must necessarily compromise their independence. This threatened subordination of the legislative to the executive power was an inversion of the proper constitutional order.

Given the multiplicity of candidates, each with his own following, and none able to command a majority of votes, the election of the President inevitably wound up in the House of Representatives. There Clay, the speaker, having been eliminated, threw his support to Adams, who was chosen over Jackson, the popular vote leader. Adams's subsequent appointment of Clay as secretary of state, the cabinet post which had furnished the President for the third successive time, brought cries of "corrupt bargain" from the Jacksonians, and from this canard the Adams administration never recovered. Boldly, in his first message to Congress, Adams proposed to rally the country behind a great program of national improvement, one which took conventional internal improvements—rivers and harbors, roads and canals—only as a starting point. "Liberty is power," Adams declared. A nation of liberty should be a nation of power, provided, of course, power is used beneficently. The Constitution presents no obstacle. Indeed, to refrain from exercising legitimate powers for good ends would be treachery to the people. "While foreign nations less blessed with that freedom which is power . . . are advancing with gigantic strides in the career of public improvement," Adams said, "were we to slumber in indolence or to fold up our arms and proclaim to the world that we are palsied by the will of our constituents, would it not be to cast away the bounties of Providence and doom ourselves to perpetual inferiority?"

In response to the message, all the old artillery of states' rights and STRICT CONSTRUCTION was hauled out and turned on the administration. Liberty is power? What dangerous nonsense. Liberty is the jealous restraint of power. Individuals, not governments, are the best judges of their own interests; and the national interest consists only in the aggregate of individual interests. These ideas had been employed in the attack on the American System. Now they entered deeply into the ideology of the emerging Jacksonian coalition. A new recruit to the coalition was Vice-President Calhoun, who began to shed the liberality and nationalism that had characterized his political career. In part, certainly, he was influenced by the rising states' rights frenzy in South Carolina. This movement was orchestrated by Calhoun's enemies in the Crawford faction. In 1825 they drove through the legislature resolutions declaring the protective tariff and federal internal improvements unconstitutional. This "Revolution of 1825," as it came to be known, showed how far out of step Calhoun was with the opinion of his state, and he hurried to catch up.

In Congress the anticonsolidation movement provided most of the rhetoric and some of the substance of opposition on every issue with the administration but was especially evident in debates on the judiciary and the tariff. Report of a bill in the House to reorganize the federal judiciary, mainly by the addition of three circuits—and three new judges—in the West, furnished a forum for advocates of reforming the judiciary. There was still no consensus on the role and authority of the Supreme Court. The Court had been a powerful ally of consolidation. Between 1816 and 1825 it had ruled in favor of national power seventeen times and of states' rights only six times, when they were at issue; and by 1825 it had invalidated in whole or in part the statutes of ten states. Various measures, most of them involving constitutional amendment, had been offered to curb judicial power: the withdrawal of opinions, or removal of Justices, on the address of both houses of Congress; the requirement of seriatim opinions; the use of the Senate as a tribunal of last resort on federal questions; and the repeal of section 25 of the Judiciary Act. All were aired in the 1826 debate. Nothing of substance emerged; the reorganization bill itself, after passing the House, failed in the Senate. Yet the debate, which was the "last hurrah" of reform, may have contributed to the increasing moderation of the Marshall Court after 1825.

The tariff had been a constitutional issue since the great debate on the American System in 1824. The power to tax, Virginia congressman PHILIP P. BARBOUR had then argued, was not a power to promote one industry over another, nor did any such power exist in the Constitution. Controversy was reignited three years later by demands for additional protection, particularly on behalf of the rising wool and woolens industry of the Northeast. Jacksonian politicians, who came into control of the new Congress, could not ignore the demand. Under the leadership of MAR-TIN VAN BUREN of New York they framed a tariff bill that was a political stratagem rather than a serious piece of economic legislation. Moreover, they persuaded their southern friends to go along with the bill on the spurious plea that it would finally fail because of provisions designed to trigger overwhelming New England opposition, thereby enabling the Jacksonians to claim credit in the North for protectionist efforts without inflicting further injury on the South. But in the Senate, where it was named the Tariff of Abominations, the bill was amended to become less objectionable to New England, and its great spokesman, Webster, heretofore a free-trader, dramatically declared his support. The TARIFF ACT OF 1828 became law. The South felt betrayed. In South Carolina, which had grasped the flagging torch of states' rights from Virginia, there were demands to "calculate the value of the Union." The legislature, in December, enacted a series of resolutions declaring the tariff oppressive and unconstitutional. It also published the South Carolina Exposition and Protest, which Calhoun had authored secretly at the invitation of a legislative committee. The Exposition repeated, with some elaboration, the litany of antitariff arguments South Carolina radicals had been urging for several years and it offered the first authoritative statement of "the Carolina doctrine" of nullification.

A motley coalition—western agrarians, southern planters, northern democrats—swept Andrew Jackson into the presidency in 1828. His inaugural address gave no clear sign of the direction his administration would take; but the dominant pressure of the men, ideas, and interests gathered around the President was toward dissolution of the National Republican platform and toward the rebirth of party government on specious Jeffersonian principles.

MERRILL D. PETERSON

Bibliography

ADAMS, HENRY 1891–1893 History of the United States during the Administrations of Jefferson and Madison. 9 Vols. New York: Scribner's.

BEVERIDGE, ALBERT J. 1919 The Life of John Marshall, vol. IV. Boston: Houghton Mifflin.

CUNNINGHAM, NOBLE E., JR. 1978 The Process of Government under Jefferson. Princeton, N.J.: Princeton University Press.

DANGERFIELD, GEORGE 1952 The Era of Good Feeling. New York: Harcourt, Brace.

GOODRICH, CARTER, ED. 1967 The Government and the Economy: 1783–1861. Indianapolis: Bobbs-Merrill.

JOHNSTONE, ROBERT M., JR. 1978 Jefferson and the Presidency: Leadership in the Young Republic. Ithaca, N.Y.: Cornell University Press.

KETCHAM, RALPH 1984 *Presidents above Party: The First American Presidency, 1789–1829.* Chapel Hill: University of North Carolina Press.

SOFAER, ABRAHAM D. 1976 *War, Foreign Affairs and Constitutional Power: The Origins.* Cambridge, Mass.: Ballinger.

TURNER, FREDERICK JACKSON 1906 *Rise of the New West, 1819–1829.* New York: Macmillan.

WHITE, LEONARD D. 1951 *The Jeffersonians: A Study in Administrative History, 1801–1829.* New York: Macmillan.

CONSTITUTIONAL HISTORY, 1829–1848

Constitutional change in the Jacksonian era began with the Virginia CONSTITUTIONAL CONVENTION of 1829–1830, and climaxed in the election controversies of 1848. Between these dates, the American people tried to renovate their constitutional order, especially with respect to the great issues of FEDERALISM, democratization, and slavery.

Virginia's venerable Constitution of 1776, like other early constitutions, had come to enshrine the related evils of malapportionment and disfranchisement. THOMAS JEFFERSON denounced these and other defects in the document from the founding of the commonwealth to his death. His criticism produced the convention of 1829, where the badly underrepresented Western delegates demanded reform, including white manhood suffrage and a REAPPORTIONMENT that would fairly represent the growing population of their region. The convention was a showcase of Virginia's political leadership, including as delegates JAMES MADISON (who had also been a delegate at the 1776 convention), JOHN MARSHALL, JAMES MONROE, JOHN RANDOLPH, as well as emergent conservative leaders like JOHN TYLER, Benjamin Watkins Leigh, and Abel Parker Upshur. The conservatives from the tidewater region, representing the interests of slaveholders, held the reformers at bay, conceding only a limited modification of the old freehold suffrage to include householders and leaseholders, far less than the taxpayer-militia qualification representing a compromise conceded by the western delegates. Reapportionment similarly fell short of western demands, as the convention adopted a complex system of regional representation. The conservative triumph on these two issues was assured partly because many delegates heeded Leigh's warning that reform would produce "the annihilation of all state rights." Implicit in this response were fears for the security of slavery. Those fears were bloodily confirmed by Nat Turner's 1831 slave insurrection in Southampton County, and reawakened the next year as the Virginia General Assembly debated and ultimately voted down a proposal for the gradual abolition of slavery.

Slavery, only hinted at in the 1828 Virginia debates, soon surfaced as a constitutional topic throughout the South. In *State v. Mann* (1829) Chief Judge Thomas Ruffin of the North Carolina Supreme Court held that the absolute subjection characteristic of slavery was "essential to the value of slaves as property, to the security of the master, and [to] the public tranquility." The South Carolina Court of Appeals later held that "a slave can invoke neither MAGNA CHARTA nor COMMON LAW. . . . In the very nature of things, he is subject to despotism." The political counterpart of this new proslavery jurisprudence was the "positive good" thesis, first advanced by South Carolina Governor George McDuffie in 1835 and amplified thereafter by JOHN C. CALHOUN in the United States Senate.

Southern judicial and political leaders found themselves compelled to erect defenses for the internal security of slavery after 1830 in part because a new cadre of abolitionists appeared in the northern states, led at first by William Lloyd Garrison. Repudiating both gradualism and projects for the colonization of free blacks in Liberia, this new generation of antislavery workers demanded the immediate and uncompensated abolition of slavery. They tried their hand at constitutional challenges to slavery. Although they conceded that the federal government had no power to interfere with slavery in the states, they found many areas for legitimate federal action, such as exclusion of slavery from the territories, abolition of slavery in the DISTRICT OF COLUMBIA, abolition of the interstate slave trade, and refusal to admit new slave states. At the state level, they sought, unsuccessfully, to have slavery declared unconstitutional in New Jersey, persuaded the Massachusetts and New York legislatures to enact PERSONAL LIBERTY LAWS, and provided invaluable support for fugitive slave rescues. In 1832, when they got their first taste of constitutional litigation in the Connecticut prosecution of Prudence Crandall, they attempted to define and secure the rights of free blacks under the PRIVILEGES AND IMMUNITIES CLAUSE of Article IV, section 2, of the Constitution.

By 1830 it was obvious that the South Carolinians were counting the costs of the Union, and weighing their alternatives. The fundamental concepts of state

SOVEREIGNTY and the right of SECESSION were commonplace at the time. Thus in the Webster-Hayne debates of 1830, South Carolina Senator Robert Y. Hayne was closer to orthodoxy than DANIEL WEBSTER when he supported a cluster of theories derived or extrapolated from the VIRGINIA AND KENTUCKY RESOLUTIONS of 1798–1799: he condemned the consolidationist tendencies of the federal government, asserted state sovereignty, insisted on a STRICT CONSTRUCTION of the Constitution, reiterated the compact theory of the Union (by which the Constitution and the national Union were the creation of a compact of sovereign states), and defended the legitimacy of INTERPOSITION and NULLIFICATION. Webster's famous rhetorical reply is better known but less analytical than other rebuttals by EDWARD LIVINGSTON, JOHN QUINCY ADAMS, and JOSEPH STORY between 1830 and 1833. These maintained that sovereignty had effectively been transferred to the national government by the Constitution, that the Union created thereby was perpetual, and that secession was extralegal. In his *Commentaries on the Constitution* (1833), Story flatly denied that the Constitution was a compact among sovereign states. James Madison joined his venerable voice to theirs, condemning all theories of nullification as perversions of the doctrines he and Thomas Jefferson had propounded in 1798 and 1799. All maintained that because the Union was perpetual, it was therefore indissoluble. But John Quincy Adams had the ominous last word when he wrote in 1831 that "it is the odious nature of [this] question that it can be settled only at the cannon's mouth." South Carolina's attempted nullification of the TARIFF ACT of 1828 and its 1832 revision forced a resolution of these conflicts that came close to the mode Adams had predicted.

Though ostensibly aimed at the tariff, and the larger but more nebulous problem of the "consolidation" of the federal government's powers, the nullification controversy at its heart concerned the security and perpetuity of slavery. The tariff controversy nonetheless provided a convenient vehicle for the Carolinians to reconfirm their traditional THEORIES OF THE UNION and state sovereignty. In November 1832 a specially elected convention adopted the SOUTH CAROLINA ORDINANCE OF NULLIFICATION, which prohibited collection of the tariff and appeals to the United States Supreme Court. President ANDREW JACKSON responded with his "Proclamation to the People of South Carolina," drafted by Secretary of State Livingston, which refuted nullification theories, asserted federal supremacy, insisted on obedience to federal laws,

warned that "Disunion by armed force is treason," and, surprisingly in view of his Bank Veto Message five months earlier, maintained that the Supreme Court was the proper and final arbiter of disputes under the United States Constitution and laws. The FORCE ACT of 1833 gave teeth to the proclamation, while a compromise tariff assuaged Carolina's nominal grievance. The Carolinians suspended, then rescinded the ordinance of nullification, which had been universally condemned by other states. But the state convention consoled itself with the empty gesture of a second ordinance nullifying the Force Act. On this equivocal note, the nullification crisis dissolved. Both sides in reality suffered a long-term defeat. Nationalists led by Jackson had failed to quash ideas of state sovereignty and secession; Calhoun and the nullifiers had failed to forge a united front of slave states and had promoted the federal "consolidation" they feared and condemned.

The second party system, emergent at the time of the nullification crisis, produced its own constitutional controversies. HENRY CLAY had announced the basis of what he called the AMERICAN SYSTEM in 1824: a protective tariff, federal aid to INTERNAL IMPROVEMENTS, and support for the second Bank of the United States. In a decade this became the program of the Whig Party. Jacksonian Democrats denounced all three elements as being of dubious constitutionality. In 1830 President Andrew Jackson vetoed the MAYSVILLE ROAD BILL partly because he doubted that federal aid for internal improvements, at least those lying wholly within a state, was constitutional. Two years later, in his veto of the recharter bill for the second Bank of the United States, he similarly expressed reservations about the constitutional power of Congress to charter a bank. He brushed aside the binding force of Chief Justice John Marshall's decision on the subject in MCCULLOCH V. MARYLAND (1819) by asserting that "the authority of the Supreme Court must not, therefore, be permitted to control the Congress or the Executive when acting in their legislative capacities. . . ." In 1833 Jackson ordered his subordinates to remove all federal deposits from the bank, and to redistribute them in selected state-chartered banks.

The democratization of American politics was advanced by the Whigs' development of mass electioneering techniques in the 1840 presidential campaign. Whig success was short-lived, however, because of President William Henry Harrison's death in 1841. JOHN TYLER, a conservative Virginia Democrat, succeeded to the office, and in doing so established the important precedent that he was not merely the "acting President" but President in fact. One of the few positive accomplishments of the Whigs' brief accession to power was the enactment of the nation's second Bankruptcy Act in 1841. Its repeal in 1843 returned the matter of insolvency legislation to the states, where it was to remain until 1898. Direction of the nation's economy was to remain chiefly the responsibility of the states until the Civil War. (See BANKRUPTCY POWER.)

In the 1830s the states encouraged and subsidized economic development in numerous ways. Their role was almost entirely promotional; during the Jacksonian era, they essayed only the most diffident beginnings of ECONOMIC REGULATION. The state legislatures granted charters and franchises for banking, insurance, railroad, and manufacturing CORPORATIONS. Encouraged by the remarkable but unduplicated success of New York's Erie Canal in the 1820s, other states provided direct financial support for construction of turnpikes, canals, and railroads.

State jurists likewise supported economic development, sometimes by creating whole new domains of law (torts, nonmarine insurance), and sometimes by reworking traditional legal doctrines to provide instrumentalist approaches supportive of entrepreneurs. In 1831 Chancellor Reuben Walworth of New York upheld the power of the legislature to grant EMINENT DOMAIN powers to railroads, and Chief Justice LEMUEL SHAW of the Massachusetts Supreme Judicial Court afterward approved the extension of that power to manufacturing corporations as well. Chief Judge JOHN BANNISTER GIBSON of the Pennsylvania Supreme Court helped refashion the law of contracts in favor of the doctrine of *caveat emptor,* an impersonal and seller-oriented approach presumably suited to a national market. The new orientation of the law of contracts and sales emphasized the autonomy of the individual and private will, dismissing earlier insistence on equitable dealing and community standards of fairness.

But the public law of the states in the 1830s was not exclusively concerned with succoring nascent industrial capitalism. In fact, the common law itself, as well as its judicial exemplars, came under reformist attack. In the Jacksonian period, the movement toward an elective judiciary decisively gained ground, as Mississippi led the way in 1832 by making its entire bench elective. Other states followed suit, so that by the twentieth century only the federal judiciary remained wholly appointive and life-tenured. An even stronger assault on judge-made law emerged from the movement to codify all laws. Even legal conservatives

like Joseph Story conceded that some restatement of law in certain areas (EVIDENCE, criminal law, and commercial law) might be both feasible and useful. More thoroughgoing codifiers, such as Edward Livingston and Robert Rantoul, condemned the common law as antidemocratic, mysterious, and prolix.

Meanwhile, the controversy over slavery intensified. From 1835 to 1840, mobs in all sections of the country harassed abolitionists and free blacks. The beleaguered abolitionists, for their part, mounted a propaganda campaign against slaveholding by weekly mailings of abolitionist literature throughout the South. Democrats and southern political leaders reacted violently, with Postmaster General Amos Kendall condoning destruction of mail in Charleston. President Jackson recommended congressional prohibition of abolitionist mailing in the southern states, but Senator John C. Calhoun objected, partly because such federal legislation would invade rights reserved to the states. The controversy dissipated when abolitionists redirected their energies to a petition campaign, garnering signatures throughout the north on petitions to Congress demanding various antislavery measures, such as abolition in the District of Columbia, interdiction of the interstate slave trade, and refusal to annex the slaveholding republic of Texas or to admit new slave states.

Abolitionists were active in legal-constitutional efforts against slavery at the state level, too. In Massachusetts, they scored a striking victory against the ingress of sojourners' slaves in COMMONWEALTH V. AVES (1836), when Chief Justice Shaw expounded an American version of the doctrine of SOMERSET'S CASE (King's Bench, 1772). Shaw held that a sojourning slave could not be held in slavery against her will in Massachusetts because no state law supported slavery and because the "all men are free and equal" provision of the 1780 Massachusetts Declaration of Rights was "precisely adapted to the abolition of negro slavery." Abolitionists enjoyed less success the next year in Ohio and Pennsylvania, however. Chief Judge Gibson held in 1837 that, under the Pennsylvania constitution, blacks were not "freemen" and hence could not vote. A state constitutional convention meeting that year took no action to reverse this holding. In Ohio, the abolitionist lawyers SALMON P. CHASE and JAMES G. BIRNEY developed an impressive range of legal and constitutional arguments in *Matilda's Case* (1837) to demonstrate that the 1793 federal Fugitive Slave Act was unconstitutional under the FOURTH AMENDMENT, the Fifth Amendment's DUE PROCESS clause, and the NORTHWEST ORDINANCE's guarantees of TRIAL BY JURY and HABEAS CORPUS. These arguments failed then, but they furnished an impressive stock of ideas to expanding ABOLITIONIST CONSTITUTIONAL THEORY.

At the national level, defenders of slavery launched a counterattack against this assault. The United States House of Representatives in 1836 adopted the first of the congressional "gag resolutions," declaring that all petitions coming into the House as a result of the antislavery petition campaign would be automatically tabled, without being referred or read. In subsequent years, the Senate adopted a similar rule, and the House made it a standing rule. But the gags proved insufficient bars to the determined evasions of a handful of antislavery congressmen, led by John Quincy Adams, who repeatedly introduced antislavery petitions. (See CIVIL LIBERTIES AND THE SLAVERY CONTROVERSY.)

Observing such assaults on slavery with alarm, Calhoun introduced into the Senate in 1837 a series of resolutions that in effect restated the nature of the Union and slavery's relation to it. These resolutions condemned antislavery agitation as "subversive"; declared that the federal government was the "common agent" of the states, bound to protect all their institutions, including slavery; that slavery was an "essential element" in the organization of the Union; that any congressional interference with slavery in the District of Columbia or the territories would be an "attack on the institutions" of the slave states; and that Congress could not discriminate against the interests of the slave states in the territories. Congress declined to adopt the last two, but its endorsement of the others threatened to give the slave states a constitutional predominance in the Union.

Abolitionists responded with innovative constitutional thinking of their own. In 1839 the hitherto unified movement began to split apart. The antislavery mainstream became involved in political action, forming the Liberty Party. They conceded exclusive state power over slavery in the states where it existed, but called for congressional action elsewhere, as, for example, by refusing to admit new slave states and by repealing the Fugitive Slave Act. Two splinter groups of the movement challenged this moderate position. Followers of William Lloyd Garrison, embracing the theological doctrine of perfectionism, by 1842 came to denounce the Constitution as a proslavery compact, and called for disunion. Radical abolitionists, led by the New York lawyer Alvan Stewart, discarded previous assumptions about slavery's legitimacy and contended that slavery was everywhere unconstitutional as a violation of various constitutional provisions, including the Fifth Amendment's due process clause

(considered both in procedural and substantive senses), Article IV's guarantee of a REPUBLICAN FORM OF GOVERNMENT, and the same article's privileges and immunities clause.

Abolitionists harked back to the DECLARATION OF INDEPENDENCE and to the tenets of republican ideology of the Revolutionary era. So did contemporary suffrage reformers in Rhode Island, who faced the same problems of malapportionment and disenfranchisement as had Virginia two decades earlier. After concluding that the existing conservative regime would never concede reform, they called an extralegal constitutional convention to modernize the state's constitution, which until then had been the 1662 Charter. This "People's Constitution" was ratified by universal male suffrage. Its supporters then elected a new government for the state, with Thomas W. Dorr as governor. The existing regime refused to cede power, so for several months in 1842, Rhode Island had two governments, each claiming a different source of constitutional legitimacy: the Dorrites, a do-it-yourself, implicitly revolutionary popular sovereignty; and the extant regime, legality backed by force. With behind-the-scenes support of President Tyler, the regular government suppressed its opponents, then inaugurated the substance of what the reformers had demanded. The failure of the Dorr Rebellion demonstrated that the guarantees of self-government and equality in the Declaration of Independence would not be taken literally or programmatically in the Jacksonian era.

Constitutional change came to other states less turbulently in the 1840s. In neighboring Massachusetts, Chief Justice Shaw placed the Supreme Judicial Court in the forefront of legal and constitutional innovation in a series of decisions from 1842 to 1850 that created new doctrines and revolutionized old ones. In COMMONWEALTH V. HUNT (1842) Shaw legitimated labor union organization in the United States. The Philadelphia and New York *Cordwainers Cases* (1806, 1810), reaffirmed by New York decisions in the mid-1830s, had held labor organization and strikes to be CRIMINAL CONSPIRACIES at common law and illegal under state statutes prohibiting injury to commerce. But in *Hunt,* Shaw held that neither the objectives of the workers nor their means—unions and strikes—were inherently unlawful. Because it removed the taint of per se illegality from unions, the *Hunt* decision has been extravagantly called the "Magna Carta of organized labor."

Another Shaw decision of the same year, *Farwell v. Boston and Worcester Railroad,* proved as damaging to the cause of industrial workers as *Hunt* had been beneficial. In exempting an employer from liability for the injury to one of its employees caused by the negligence of another employee, Shaw enunciated the fellow-servant rule that stood as a bar to recovery in such situations.

Because Massachusetts was in the vanguard of industrialization, Shaw had an opportunity to influence the law of railroads and common carriers more than any other contemporary jurist, leading one scholar to conclude that he "practically established the railroad law for the country." In cases involving eminent domain and taxation, Shaw held railroads to be "a public work, established by public authority" whose property is held "in trust for the public." Shaw thereby hoped to secure legislative benefits granted railroads, while at the same time leaving open the possibility of some degree of public control through legislation. Yet he was solicitous to exempt railroads from forms of liability that would have drained investment capital.

The temperance movement proved to be as prolific a source of judicial lawmaking as innovations in transportation technology. Throughout the antebellum period, state appellate courts had kept alive the HIGHER LAW tradition enunciated by Justice SAMUEL CHASE in his opinion in CALDER V. BULL (1798). State judges, especially those of Federalist and Whig antecedents, readily struck down various state laws for the inconsistency with "the great principles of eternal justice" or "the character and genius of our government." In his *Commentaries on the Constitution* (3rd ed., 1858), Joseph Story summed up "the strong current of judicial opinion" that "the fundamental maxims of a free government seem to require, that the rights of personal liberty and private property should be held sacred." The Delaware Supreme Court used such nebulous concepts derived from the nature of republican government to void a local-option PROHIBITION statute in 1847. Higher law constitutional doctrine became all the more important after the United States Supreme Court's 5–4 decision in the LICENSE CASES (1847), upholding Massachusetts, Rhode Island, and New Hampshire statutes taxing and regulating liquor imported from outside the state. This trend culminated in the celebrated case of WYNEHAMER V. PEOPLE (1856), where the New York Court of Appeals struck down a state prohibition statute under the state constitution's LAW OF THE LAND and due process clauses.

Chief Justice Shaw was the author of a doctrine that provided a powerful offset to such higher law tendencies: the POLICE POWER. In COMMONWEALTH V. ALGER (1951) he stated that all property is held "under the implied liability that . . . use of it may be so regulated, that it shall not be injurious . . . to the rights of the community." He accorded the legislature sweeping power to subject property to "reasonable limitations." After the Civil War, the police power doctrine constituted the basis for an alternative to the dogmas of SUBSTANTIVE DUE PROCESS and FREEDOM OF CONTRACT.

Courts were by no means the sole font of constitutional innovation in the 1840s. State legislatures and constitutional conventions also modified the constitutional order. Reflecting the movement of the age from status to contract, as noted by Sir Henry Maine, the state legislatures in the 1840s extended some measure of control to married women over their own property through the married women's property acts. State courts sometimes reacted with hostility to these measures, seeing them either as a deprivation of the husband's property rights protected by higher law or as deranging gender and marital relationships.

Four New England states experimented with embryonic railroad regulatory commissions (Rhode Island, 1839; New Hampshire, 1844; Connecticut, 1850; Massachusetts, various ad hoc special commissions), but none of these proved successful or permanent. New York in the 1840s had to confront the legal consequences of the emergent nativist controversy. Roman Catholics sought public funding for parochial schools and objected to use of the King James Bible for devotional sessions in public schools. Nativists, for their part, demanded that the predominantly Catholic immigrants of the period be disfranchised.

The most significant state constitutional event of the decade was the drafting and ratification of the New York Constitution of 1846. This document was a compendium of constitutional trends of the era and profoundly influenced subsequent constitutions, especially those of Michigan and Wisconsin. It capped the decade's long movement toward general incorporation acts by restricting the granting of special corporate charters, and, for good measure, made all legislation respecting corporations, both general and special, subject to repeal or amendment at any time. It put to rest the controversies of the rent wars of the previous decade by abolishing all feudal real property tenures and perpetual leases, converting all long-term leaseholds into freeholds. It made the entire New York bench elective, and required appointment of a three-member commission to draw up a reformed procedural code.

Despite the sweep of innovation in the 1846 New York Constitution and its daughters in the west, the needs of certain groups in American society remained unmet. Chief among these were women. Feminists convened in Seneca Falls, New York, in 1848 and issued a manifesto on women's rights modeled on the Declaration of Independence, demanding VOTING RIGHTS, the recognition by law of full legal capacity, revision of male-biased divorce laws, access to the professions and to educational opportunity, and abolition of all discriminatory legislation.

Blacks in the northern states were no better off. After 1842, their situation, especially in areas near the slave states, became more precarious because of Justice Story's opinion in PRIGG V. PENNSYLVANIA (1842), upholding the constitutionality of the Fugitive Slave Act of 1793 and striking down inconsistent state legislation. After *Prigg*, most state personal liberty laws, such as those assuring jury trial to alleged fugitives or extending the writ of habeas corpus to them, were suspect. Abolitionists seized on a Story dictum in *Prigg*, stating that the states did not have to assist in fugitive recaptures under the federal act. They induced several state legislatures to enact statutes prohibiting state facilities from being used for temporary detention of alleged fugitives.

The slavery question briefly returned to Congress in 1842, in the form of the "*Creole* Resolutions" offered by Representative Joshua Giddings (Whig, Ohio). Slaves aboard the *Creole*, an American-flag vessel, mutinied on the high seas and made their way to the Bahamas, where most of them were freed by British authorities. Secretary of State Daniel Webster protested and demanded compensation for the liberated slaves. Giddings, despite the gag rule, introduced resolutions setting forth the *Somerset*-based position that the slaves had merely resumed their natural status, freedom, and could not be reenslaved. The federal government lacked authority to protect or reimpose their slave status, which was derived solely from Virginia law and hence confined to this JURISDICTION. The House defeated the resolutions and censured Giddings. But he was reelected by a landslide, in effect forcing and winning a REFERENDUM on his antislavery positions. This, together with the earlier and ignominious failure of an effort to censure Representative John Quincy Adams for flouting the gag, led to the demise of the gag rules in both houses in 1844.

Such inconclusive sparring between slavery and abolition might have gone on indefinitely had it not been for the Mexican War. But proslavery ambitions to expand into the southwestern empire fundamentally altered the character of the American Union, destabilizing extant constitutional settlements and requiring new constitutional arrangements to replace the now obsolete MISSOURI COMPROMISE.

ANNEXATION OF TEXAS had been controversial ever since Texan independence in 1836. When the issue reestablished itself on the national agenda in 1844, opponents of annexation, including Daniel Webster, Joseph Story, and John Quincy Adams, argued that annexation was not constitutionally permissible under the territories clause of Article IV, section 3, because previous annexations had been of dependent territories of sovereign nations, whereas Texas was itself an independent nation. Proponents dismissed this as an insignificant technicality, under the broad reading of the FOREIGN AFFAIRS power by Chief Justice Marshall in AMERICAN INSURANCE CO. V. CANTER (1828). Political opposition blocked ratification of an annexation treaty until President Tyler hit on the expedient of annexation by JOINT RESOLUTION of both houses, which required only a majority vote in each, rather than the two-thirds required for treaties in the Senate. Texas was thereby annexed in 1845.

Annexation hastened the deterioration of relations with Mexico, but Tyler was cautious and circumspect in his deployment of American forces in the areas disputed between Mexico and the United States. But the new President, JAMES K. POLK, ordered American ground forces into the area. After Mexican forces captured American soldiers, and the United States declared war, the question of the extent of the President's power to order American troops into combat areas reappeared regularly in congressional debates over military appropriations. In 1847, Whig Representative ABRAHAM LINCOLN offered the SPOT RESOLUTIONS, demanding to know the spot on American soil where, according to Polk, Mexican troops had attacked Americans. This led to House passage of a resolution early in 1848 declaring that the Mexican War had been "unconstitutionally begun by the President." Military victories and the TREATY OF GUADALUPE HIDALGO (1848) obviated this partisan measure, without providing any resolution to the question originally debated by James Madison and ALEXANDER HAMILTON in the Helvidius-Pacificus exchange of 1793 over whether there is an inherent executive prerogative that would embrace the power to commit troops to belligerent situations without explicit authorization by Congress. (See WAR, FOREIGN AFFAIRS, AND THE CONSTITUTION.)

In 1846, northern public opinion coalesced with remarkable unity behind the WILMOT PROVISO, which would have prohibited the extension of slavery into any territories to be acquired as a result of the Mexican War. Alarmed by the extent and fervor of grassroots support for such exclusion in the free states, administration Democrats and southern political leaders offered three alternatives to it, plus an expedient designed to depoliticize the whole question. The earliest proposal was to extend the old Missouri Compromise line of 36° 30′ all the way to the Pacific coast with slavery excluded north of the line and permitted south of it. After a short-lived flurry of interest in 1847, this suggestion withered. The northern Democratic alternative to the Wilmot Proviso was widely known as POPULAR SOVEREIGNTY or, pejoratively, "squatter sovereignty." First proposed by Vice-President George M. Dallas and then associated with Michigan Senator Lewis Cass, popular sovereignty called on Congress to refrain from taking any action concerning SLAVERY IN THE TERRITORIES, leaving it to the settlers of the territories to determine the future of slavery there. The idea's principal appeal derived from its superficial and simplistic democratic appearance. But its vitality was due to an ambiguity that could not be indefinitely postponed, namely, *when* were the settlers to make that determination? By the southern interpretation, that decision could not be made until the eve of statehood, by which time, presumably, slaveholders could avail themselves of the opportunity of settling there with their slaves and thus give the territory a proslavery impetus it would never lose. (All prior American territorial settlements had either guaranteed property rights in extant slaves, such as the LOUISIANA PURCHASE TREATY, or, like the Northwest Ordinance, had left existing pockets of slavery undisturbed as a practical matter despite their theoretical prohibition of slavery.) The northern assumption concerning popular sovereignty was that the territorial settlers could make their choice concerning slavery at any time in the territorial period, a position unacceptable to the South, which correctly believed that such an interpretation would exclude slavery.

The third alternative was embodied in resolutions offered by Calhoun in 1847. He proposed that the territories were the common property of all the states, and that Congress therefore could not prohibit citizens of any state from taking their property (including slaves) with them when they migrated into a territory. He also asserted that Congress could not refuse to admit a new state because it permitted slavery. After Calhoun's death in 1850, others advocated that Congress would have to protect the rights of slaveholders in all territories.

This selection of alternatives naturally influenced the presidential election of 1848. Democrats nominated Cass, thus providing some oblique endorsement of popular sovereignty, with its yet unresolved ambiguity. Whigs nominated the apolitical General ZACHARY TAYLOR and refused to endorse any party position at all on the various alternatives. Disgruntled elements of both parties in the northern states joined hands with the moderate, political-action abolitionists of the Liberty party to form the Free Soil party, which adopted the Wilmot Proviso as its basic plank, supplemented by the old Liberty party program of "divorce" of the federal government from support of slavery. Free Soil was an implicitly racist program, calling for the exclusion of all blacks from the territories to keep them open to white settlement, but that made it no less abominable to southern political leaders. The Whig victory in 1848 on its nonplatform merely postponed the resolution of what was rapidly becoming an urgent constitutional confrontation.

The American Union was in a far different condition in 1848 from what it had been at the onset of the Jacksonian era. The nation had increased in geographical extent by half. Such an immense increase necessitated a new or wholly revised constitutional order that could accommodate, if possible, the conflicting sectional expectations for the future of the western empire. All major constitutional events that had occurred at the national level since 1831 had made John Quincy Adams's prediction of that year all the more pertinent: the questions came ever closer to being settled at the cannon's mouth.

WILLIAM M. WIECEK

Bibliography

BLOOMFIELD, MAXWELL 1976 *American Lawyers in a Changing Society, 1776–1876.* Cambridge, Mass.: Harvard University Press.

DUMOND, DWIGHT L. 1961 *Antislavery: The Crusade for Freedom in America.* Ann Arbor: University of Michigan Press.

FRIEDMAN, LAWRENCE M. 1973 *A History of American Law.* New York: Simon & Schuster.

HAAR, CHARLES M., ED. 1965 *The Golden Age of American Law.* New York: Braziller.

HORWITZ, MORTON J. 1977 *The Transformation of American Law, 1780–1860.* Cambridge, Mass.: Harvard University Press.

HURST, JAMES WILLARD 1956 *Law and the Conditions of Freedom in the Nineteenth-Century United States.* Madison: University of Wisconsin Press.

HYMAN, HAROLD M. and WIECEK, WILLIAM M. 1982 *Equal Justice under Law: Constitutional Development, 1835–1875.* New York: Harper & Row.

LEVY, LEONARD W. 1957 *The Law of the Commonwealth and Chief Justice Shaw: The Evolution of American Law, 1830–1860.* Cambridge, Mass.: Harvard University Press.

WIECEK, WILLIAM M. 1977 *The Sources of Antislavery*

Constitutionalism in America, 1760–1848. Ithaca, N.Y.: Cornell University Press.

ZAINALDIN, JAMIL 1983 *Law in Antebellum Society: Legal Change and Economic Expansion.* New York: Knopf.

CONSTITUTIONAL HISTORY, 1848–1861

In American constitutional history, the years 1848 to 1861 ordinarily appear as a prelude to revolution, a time of intense controversy without significant change. Yet in at least two respects this impression is mistaken. First, constitutional change, though minimal in the national government, was widespread and vigorous among the states during the antebellum period. Second, if the structure of party politics is included (as it should be) in one's purview of the American constitutional system, then the 1850s, like the 1860s, were a decade of revolution.

Powerful social forces exerted pressure upon the constitutional order at mid-century. Mass immigration reached its first crest, with more than two million persons arriving in the years 1849–1854. This great influx caused much concern about the effects of ethnic diversity upon the quality of national life and upon the American experiment in self-government. At the same time, the progress of industrialization and business enterprise was rapidly changing the economic face of the agricultural nation for which the Constitution had been written. The railroads alone, as they tripled their mileage in the 1850s and thus accelerated their transformation of domestic commerce, confronted government with a host of new issues and problems, ranging from the regulation of capital formation to the determination of corporate liability in tort law. Still another major force at work was the continuing westward expansion of American SOVEREIGNTY and American people. The United States in 1848 was a transcontinental nation that had acquired forty percent of all its territory in the preceding three years. Occupation and assimilation of this new Western empire, extending from the mouth of the Rio Grande to the waters of Puget Sound, would absorb much national energy throughout the rest of the century. The process in itself placed no heavy strains upon the constitutional system. For the most part, it required only the further use of already tested forms and practices, such as territorial organization. But in the antebellum period, westward expansion became irredeemably entangled with still another formidable social force—the increasingly ominous sectional conflict over slavery.

The federal government, while extending its rule to the Pacific Ocean in the antebellum period, underwent little structural change. The Constitution had not been amended since 1803. Far fewer amendments than usual were proposed from 1848 to 1860, and none of them passed either house of Congress. (Prominent among those introduced were proposals for the popular election of senators and postmasters.) During the secession winter of 1860–1861, however, Congress received nearly two hundred proposed amendments. Most of them were aimed at dampening the crisis by offering concessions or guarantees to the South on such subjects as SLAVERY IN THE TERRITORIES and the DISTRICT OF COLUMBIA, the domestic slave trade, FUGITIVE SLAVES, and the right to travel with slaves in free states. Only one of these efforts proved successful to the point of passing both houses, but RATIFICATION in the states had scarcely begun before it was interrupted and canceled by the outbreak of hostilities. This abortive "Thirteenth Amendment" would have forbidden any amendment authorizing Congress to interfere with slavery as it existed in the states, thereby presumably fixing a double lock on the constitutional security of the institution. (See CORWIN AMENDMENT.)

Besides formal amendment, constitutional change may be produced by other means, such as legislative enactment and judicial decision. Congress altered the structure of the executive branch in 1849, for instance, by establishing a Department of the Interior. To it were transferred a number of agencies previously housed in other departments, notably those administering PATENTS, public lands, military pensions, and Indian affairs. Congress in 1849 also created the new office of "assistant secretary" for the Treasury Department, adding a similar position to the Department of State four years later. The federal bureaucracy as a whole grew appreciably in the antebellum period, but largely because of the necessary expansion of the postal system. Of the 26,000 civilian employees in 1851 and 37,000 in 1861, eighty percent were in the postal service. Only six percent performed their duties in the capital. On the eve of the Civil War, the whole Washington bureaucracy numbered about 2,200. The Department of State got along throughout the 1850s with a staff of thirty persons or fewer. The presidency remained a very simple affair with practically no official staff. Not until 1857 did Congress provide funds even for a private secretary and a messenger.

The federal government accepted few new responsibilities during the antebellum period. Enlargement of its role was inhibited by the economic principle of laissez-faire, by the constitutional principles of STRICT CONSTRUCTION and FEDERALISM, and by the inertial influence of custom. Most of the governmental activity affecting the lives of ordinary citizens was carried on by the states and their subdivisions. Any effort to extend national authority usually met resistance from Southerners worried about the danger of outside interference with slavery. Congressional reluctance to expand federal power is well illustrated in the history of the first successful telegraph line, run between Washington and Baltimore in the mid-1840s. Built with federal money and put in commercial operation as a branch of the postal system, it was very soon turned over to private ownership. When Congress did occasionally become venturesome, presidential disapproval might intervene. JAMES K. POLK and Franklin Pierce, citing constitutional reasons, vetoed several INTERNAL IMPROVEMENTS bills. JAMES BUCHANAN expressed similar scruples in vetoing homestead legislation and land grants for the support of colleges. Sometimes a new social problem or need did evoke federal intervention, such as laws providing for safety inspection of steamboats and for minimum health standards on ocean-going passenger ships. Perhaps most significant was the expanded use of federal subsidies, in the form of land grants or mail contracts, to support railroad construction, steamship lines, and overland stagecoach service to the Pacific.

Although the three branches of the federal government remained fairly stable in their relationships to one another during the antebellum period, there was some shift of power from the presidency to Congress. The change is commonly viewed as a decline in presidential leadership, but it must be attributed to other factors as well, including the intensity of the sectional conflict. Congress could quarrel violently over slavery, then arrange some kind of truce, and thus perform admirably its function as a deliberative assembly. The President, on the other hand, could take no vigorous action, make no substantial proposal in respect of slavery without infuriating one side or the other.

For various reasons, none of the Presidents between ANDREW JACKSON and ABRAHAM LINCOLN served more than a single term, and only one, MARTIN VAN BUREN, was even renominated. Polk's energetic foreign policy and successful prosecution of the war with Mexico strengthened the presidency for a time, but by 1848 sectional strains and party dissension had put his administration in disarray. Zachary Taylor and Millard Fillmore were committed as Whigs to the principle of limited executive power. They did not exercise the VETO POWER, for instance, and were the last Presidents in history to refrain from doing so. Tay-

lor, to be sure, proved unexpectedly stubborn on the slavery issue and seemed headed for a collision with Congress until his sudden death in the summer of 1850 cleared the way for compromise. During the great sectional crisis of 1846–1850, the Senate reached its peak of oratorical splendor and national influence. JOHN C. CALHOUN, HENRY CLAY, and DANIEL WEBSTER were the most famous men in America, and the outstanding political figure of the decade that followed was not a President but a senator—STEPHEN A. DOUGLAS. Most of the leading cabinet members of the 1840s and 1850s (Webster, Calhoun, Buchanan, Robert J. Walker, John M. Clayton, JEFFERSON DAVIS, Lewis Cass) were recruited directly from the Senate. Lincoln, after his election in 1860, filled the three top cabinet positions with Republican senators. The appearance of presidential weakness in the 1850s was therefore partly a reflection of senatorial prestige.

If Pierce and Buchanan were among the most ineffectual of American Presidents, as they are commonly portrayed, it was not for lack of trying to be otherwise. Both men regarded themselves as Jacksonian executives. Together they exercised the veto as often as Jackson in his two terms (though Pierce's negatives were usually overridden). Both took stern attitudes toward groups whom they labeled rebellious—namely, the free-state forces in Kansas and the Mormons in Utah. Both conducted a vigorously expansionist foreign policy, having in mind especially the acquisition of Cuba. Both made energetic use of patronage to coerce votes from Congress on critical measures—the KANSAS-NEBRASKA ACT in 1854 and the admission of Kansas with a proslavery constitution in 1858. (See LECOMPTON CONSTITUTION.) Their fatal mistake was in misjudging the moral and political strength of the antislavery crusade. Seeking to discredit and dissipate the movement rather than accommodate it, they pursued policies that disastrously aggravated the sectional conflict and thereby brought the Presidency into disrepute. Then, in the final crisis of 1860–1861, Buchanan's constitutional scruples and his reluctance to use presidential power without specific congressional authorization lent substance to the *fainéant* image that history has fixed upon him. Again, as in 1850, the fate of the country seemed to rest primarily with the Senate, and when compromise failed in that body, little hope remained for peaceable preservation of the Union.

Meanwhile, the Supreme Court had tried its hand at resolving the slavery question and in the process had reasserted its power to review congressional legislation. The famous decision in DRED SCOTT V. SANDFORD (1857) invalidated a law that had been repealed three years earlier—the 36°30' restriction of the MIS-SOURI COMPROMISE. Consequently, it did not put the Court into confrontation with Congress. Like the policies of Pierce and Buchanan, however, the decision outraged antislavery opinion and aggravated the sectional conflict. Thus the Court, like the presidency, entered the Civil War with lowered prestige.

At the level of state rather than national government, antebellum Americans acted very much in accord with the Jeffersonian credo that every generation should write its own fundamental law. The period 1830 to 1860 has been called "the high water mark for the making of constitutions among the states." During those three decades, ten new states framed their first constitutions, and eighteen of the other twenty-four revised their constitutions by means of conventions. In addition, many states added amendments from time to time through legislative action. The voters of Massachusetts, for instance, rejected a new constitution drafted by a convention in 1853, but they approved of six amendments in 1855, three in 1857, one in 1859, and two in 1860.

State constitutions became longer in the antebellum period, not only describing in greater detail the structure and functions of government but also incorporating many specific instructions and prohibitions intended to set public policy and control the substance of governmental action. The machinery for constitutional change remained heterogeneous, generally cumbersome, and, in some states, poorly defined. There was a clear trend, however, toward popular participation at every stage. Typically, voters decided whether a convention should be called, elected its members, and passed judgment on its handiwork. Legislative amendment, which bypassed the convention process and often had to be approved by two successive legislatures, was always submitted to the voters for ratification.

Democratization of the state constitutional systems, begun earlier in the century, proceeded unremittingly during the antebellum period. Two major categories of change were further extension of the franchise and further lengthening of the list of elective offices. With but a few exceptions, the old religious and property-holding qualifications for suffrage disappeared, although some states continued to require that voters be taxpayers. Under nativist influence, Connecticut in 1855 and Massachusetts in 1857 sought to curtail immigrant participation in politics by installing an English literacy test. But a stronger contrary tendency, exemplified in the constitutions of Wisconsin (1848), Michigan (1850), Indiana (1851), and Kansas (1859), was to expand the immigrant vote by enfranchising foreigners as soon as they had declared their intention to become citizens. Women were everywhere excluded from the polls, except in a few local elections, and blacks could vote only in a half-dozen northeastern states, but white male suffrage had become almost universal. The shift from appointive to elective offices was most dramatic in the case of the judiciary. Until 1846, only a few states had elective judgeships of any kind, and only in Mississippi were all judges elected. In that year both New York and Iowa followed the Mississippi example, and then the rush began. By 1861, twenty-four of the thirty-four states had written the election of judges into their constitutions, though in five of them the change did not extend to their supreme courts.

The antebellum state constitutions, like those written earlier, were primarily constructive. They established or redesigned systems of government and endowed them with appropriate powers. But in many there was also a conspicuous strain of negativism, reflecting disillusionment with state government and a determination to curb extravagance, corruption, and favoritism. Notably, the framers often placed new restrictions on legislative authority, particularly with reference to public finance, banks, and corporations. These subjects were political issues, of course, but then every CONSTITUTIONAL CONVENTION became to some extent a party battle. As a rule, Democrats were more hostile than their opponents to corporate enterprise and government promotion of it. Attitudes varied according to local circumstances, however, and much depended upon which party in the state had the upper hand at the time. The states of the Old Northwest, where prodigal internal improvement policies in the 1830s had proved disastrous, were especially emphatic in their restraint of legislative power. Their new constitutions approved in the years 1848–1851 forbade state investment in private enterprise and put strict limits on public indebtedness. They also restricted banking in various ways, such as ordering double liability for stockholders, prohibiting the suspension of specie payments, and requiring that any general banking act must be submitted to a popular REFERENDUM.

State constitutional change occurred in many ways and resulted from the work of many hands, including those of voters, convention delegates, legislators, governors, and judges. Appellate courts particularly often shaped or reshaped the fundamental law in the course of performing their routine duties, although JUDICIAL REVIEW of state legislation by state courts was a fairly rare occurrence until after the Civil War. Despite all the constitutional activity, innovation was by no means the dominant mode in the antebellum period. States borrowed much from one another, and old forms were sometimes retained well beyond the limits of their appropriateness. Vermont in 1860 still had its quaint Council of Revision, elected every seven years to examine the condition of the constitution and propose amendments. North Carolina had not yet given its governor a veto power, and in South Carolina, the legislature continued to choose the state's presidential electors. Yet the new problems of the age did encourage some experimentation. For example, certain states had begun to develop the quasi-judicial regulatory commission as an extra branch of government, and framers of the Kansas constitution in 1859 introduced the item veto, a device that most states would eventually adopt.

Although federal and state constitutional development proceeded in more or less separate grooves, the fundamental constitutional problem of the age was the relation between the nation and its constituent parts. The problem had been present and intermittently urgent since the birth of the republic, but after 1846 it became associated much more than ever before with the interrelated issues of slavery and expansion and with the dynamics of party politics.

In the federal system established by the Constitution, the national government and the state governments were each supreme within their respective spheres. This principle of DUAL FEDERALISM, even though it accorded rather well with the actual structure and distribution of governmental power in antebellum America, was by no means universally accepted as a true design of the Republic. Nationalists like Webster and Lincoln asserted the primacy of the nation, the sovereignty of its people, and the perpetuity of the Union. Sectionalists like Calhoun and Davis lodged sovereignty with the states, insisted upon strict construction of federal authority, and viewed the Union as a compact that could be abrogated. Logical consistency was not a characteristic of the intersectional debate, however. Both proslavery and antislavery forces invoked federal power and appealed to states' rights whenever either strategy suited their purposes. With regard to the recovery of fugitive slaves, for instance, Southerners demanded expansion and vigorous use of national authority, while the resistance to that authority of some northern state officials amounted to a revival of nullification. (See UNION, THEORIES OF THE.)

Most Americans agreed that slavery was a state institution, but from that premise they drew conflicting inferences. In the radical antislavery view of SALMON P. CHASE, the institution had no standing beyond the bounds of slave-state JURISDICTION, and the federal government had no constitutional power to establish it, protect it, or even acknowledge its legal existence. In short, slavery was local and freedom national. (See ABOLITIONIST CONSTITUTIONAL THEORY.) According to Calhoun, however, the federal government, as the mere agent of the states, was constitutionally obligated to give slavery as much protection as it gave any other kind of property recognized by state law. Only the sovereign power of a state could restrict or abolish the institution. In short, slavery was national and antislavery the local exception.

The practice of the United States government over the years ran closer to Calhoun's theory than to Chase's. All three branches recognized property rights in slaves and extended aid of some kind to their masters. Congress went beyond the requirements of the Constitution in making the recovery of fugitive slaves a federal business, and under congressional rule the national capital became a slave state in miniature, complete with a slave code, whipping posts, and a thriving slave trade. The image of the nation consistently presented in diplomatic relations was that of a slaveholding republic. With a persistence amounting to dedication, the Department of State sought compensation for owners of slaves escaping to foreign soil, and repeatedly it tried to secure Canadian cooperation in the return of fugitives. In the *Dred Scott* decision, Chief Justice ROGER B. TANEY laid down the one-sided rule that the federal government had no power over slavery except "the power coupled with the duty of guarding and protecting the owner in his rights."

To be sure, national authority was also used for antislavery purposes. In outlawing the foreign slave trade, Congress plainly acted within the letter and intent of the Constitution. In prohibiting slavery throughout much of the Western territory, however, the lawmakers probably drew as much sanction from the example of the NORTHWEST ORDINANCE as from the somewhat ambiguous passage in Article IV, section 3, that seemed to be relevant—namely, "The Congress shall have Power to dispose of and make all needful Rules and Regulations respecting the Territory or other Property belonging to the United States." By 1840, such prohibition had been enacted in six territorial organic acts, as well as in the Missouri Compromise. Furthermore, Chief Justice JOHN MARSHALL in AMERICAN INSURANCE COMPANY v. CANTER (1828) had given the territory clause a broad construction. In legislating for the TERRITORIES, he declared, "Congress exercises the combined powers of the general and of a State government." Since the authority of a state government to establish or abolish slavery was generally acknowledged, Marshall's words seemed to confirm Congress in possession of the same authority within the territories.

The constitutionality of legislation excluding slavery from federal territory did not become a major issue in American public life until after introduction of the WILMOT PROVISO in 1846. Although the question had arisen at times during the Missouri controversy of 1819–1820, the famous 36°30′ restriction had been approved without extensive discussion and with the support of a majority of southern congressmen. The subject had arisen again during the 1830s, but only as a secondary and academic consideration in the debate over abolitionist attacks upon slavery in the District of Columbia. As a practical matter, the Missouri Compromise had presumably disposed of the problem by reviving and extending a policy of having two different policies, one on each side of a dividing line. North of that line (first the Ohio River and then 36°30′), slavery was prohibited; south of the line, slavery was permitted if desired by the white inhabitants.

In the summer of 1846, with Texas annexed and admitted to statehood, with title to Oregon secured by treaty, and with the war against Mexico under way, the United States found itself engaged in territorial expansion on a grand scale. Texas entered the Union as a slaveholding state, and Oregon was generally understood to be free soil, but what about New Mexico and California, if they should be acquired by conquest? To many Americans, including President Polk, the obvious answer seemed to be extending the Missouri Compromise line to the Pacific Ocean. But the issue arose at a time when sectional antagonism had been inflamed by a decade of quarreling over abolitionist petitions, the GAG RULE, and the Texas question. Furthermore, whereas the 36°30′ line had meant partial abolition in a region previously open to slavery, extension of the line through New Mexico and California would have meant a partial rescinding of the abolition already achieved there by Mexican law. So David Wilmot's proposal to forbid slavery in any territory that might be acquired from Mexico won the overwhelming approval of northern congressmen when it was introduced in the House of Representatives on August 8, 1846. Southerners were even more united and emphatic in their opposition; for the Proviso would have completed the exclusion of slaveholders from all the newly acquired land in the Far West. Such injustice, they warned, could not fail to end in disunion.

The Proviso principle of "no more slave territory" quickly became the premier issue in American politics

and remained so for almost fifteen years. Virtually the raison d'être of the Free Soil and Republican parties, the principle was rejected by Congress in 1850 and again in 1854, deprived of its legitimacy by the Supreme Court in 1857, and supported by less than forty percent of the electorate in the presidential contest of 1860. Yet forty percent proved sufficient to put a Republican in the White House and thereby precipitate SECESSION. During those years of intermittent sectional crisis from 1846 to 1861, the Southerners and northern conservatives who controlled government policy sought desperately and sometimes discordantly for a workable alternative to the Proviso. One thing that complicated their task was the growing tendency of all elements in the controversy to constitutionalize their arguments.

Southerners especially felt the need for constitutional sanction, partly because of their vulnerability as a minority section but also in order to offset the moral advantage of the antislavery forces. It was not enough to denounce the Proviso as unfair; they must also prove it to be unconstitutional despite the string of contrary precedents running back to the venerated Northwest Ordinance. One way of doing so was to invoke the Fifth Amendment, arguing that any congressional ban on slavery in the territories amounted to deprivation of property without DUE PROCESS OF LAW. But this argument, though used from time to time and incorporated rather vaguely in Taney's *Dred Scott* opinion, did not become a significant part of anti-Proviso strategy. For one thing, the Fifth Amendment had another cutting edge, antislavery in its effect. Free Soilers and Republicans could and did maintain that slavery was illegal in federal territory because it amounted to deprivation of *liberty* without due process of law.

More in keeping with the strict constructionism generally favored by Southerners was the principle of "nonintervention," that is, congressional nonaction with respect to slavery in the territories. Actually, nonintervention had been government policy in part of the West ever since 1790, always with the effect of establishing slavery. But in earlier years the policy had been given little theoretical underpinning. Then, after the introduction of the Wilmot Proviso, there were strenuous efforts to convert nonintervention into a constitutional imperative. The emerging argument ignored Marshall's opinion in *American Insurance Company v. Canter* and held that the territory clause of the Constitution referred only to disposal of public land. In providing government for a territory, Congress could do nothing more than what was absolutely necessary to prepare the territory for statehood. That did not include either the prohibition or the establishment of slavery. Thus nonintervention became a doctrine of federal incapacity. It left open, however, the question of what authority prevailed in the absence of congressional power. One answer, associated with Calhoun, was that property rights in slavery were silently legitimized in every territory by the direct force of the Constitution. Another answer, associated with Lewis Cass and Douglas, was that nonintervention meant leaving the question of slavery to be decided by the local territorial population. The latter theory, given the name POPULAR SOVEREIGNTY, had the advantage of seeming to be in tune with the spirit of Jacksonian democracy.

Thus, by 1848, when American acquisition of New Mexico and California was confirmed in the TREATY OF GUADALUPE HIDALGO, four distinct solutions to the problem of slavery in the territories had emerged. At one political extreme was the free soil doctrine requiring enactment of the Wilmot Proviso. At the other extreme was the Calhoun property rights doctrine legitimizing slavery in all federal territory by direct force of the Constitution. Between them were two formulas of compromise: extension of the 36°30′ line and the principle of popular sovereignty. Presumably the choice rested with Congress, but the constitutionalizing of the argument opened up another possibility—that of leaving the status of slavery in the territories to judicial determination. Legislation facilitating referral of the question to the Supreme Court was proposed in 1848 and incorporated in the historic set of compromise measures enacted two years later. The COMPROMISE OF 1850 admitted California as a free state, but for the rest of the Mexican Cession it adopted the principle of nonintervention. The effect was to reject the 36°30′ and Proviso solutions while leaving the field still open to popular sovereignty, the property rights doctrine, and judicial disposition.

Although neither of the major parties took a formal stand on the territorial question in the elections of 1848 and 1852, it was the Democrats who became closely associated with the principle of nonintervention. Cass, their presidential nominee in 1848, declared that Congress lacked the power to prohibit slavery in the territories and that the territorial inhabitants should be left free to regulate their internal concerns in their own way. This seemed to endorse popular sovereignty as the appropriate corollary to nonintervention, but for about a decade the Democratic party managed to invest both terms with enough ambiguity to accommodate both its northern and southern wings. More specifically, Southerners found that they could assimilate popular sovereignty

to their own purposes by viewing it as the right of a territorial population to accept or reject slavery *at the time of admission to statehood.* That would presumably leave the Calhoun doctrine operative during the territorial period. At the same time, northern Democrats like Douglas went on believing that popular sovereignty meant the right of a territorial legislature to make all decisions regarding slavery, within the limits of the Constitution. The Whigs failed to achieve any such convenient doctrinal ambiguity, and that failure may have contributed to the disintegration of their party.

In 1854, a heavily Democratic Congress organized the territories of Kansas and Nebraska, repealing the antislavery restriction of the Missouri Compromise and substituting the principle of nonintervention. "The true intent and meaning of this act," the measure declared, "[is] not to legislate slavery into any Territory or State, nor to exclude it therefrom, but to leave the people thereof perfectly free to form and regulate their domestic institutions in their own way, subject only to the Constitution of the United States." This passage, since it could be interpreted to mean either the northern or the southern brand of popular sovereignty, preserved the ambiguity so necessary for Democratic unity. But of course the Kansas-Nebraska Act, by removing a famous barrier to slavery, provoked a storm of anger throughout the free states and set off a political revolution.

The crisis of the late 1850s was in one respect a confrontation between the emerging Republican party and the increasingly united South—that is, between the Wilmot Proviso and the principles of Calhoun. Yet it was also a struggle within the Democratic party over the meaning of nonintervention and popular sovereignty. The *Dred Scott* decision in March 1857 cleared the air and intensified the crisis. In ruling that Congress had no power to prohibit slavery in the territories, the Supreme Court officially constitutionalized the principle of nonintervention and virtually rendered illegal the main purpose of the Republican party. But Chief Justice Taney went further and disqualified the northern Democratic version of popular sovereignty. If Congress had no such power over slavery, he declared, then neither did a territorial legislature. Douglas responded with his FREEPORT DOCTRINE, insisting that a territorial government, by unfriendly legislation, could effectively exclude slavery, no matter what the Court might decide to the contrary. Southern Democrats, in turn, demanded federal protection of slavery in the territories, and on that issue the party split at its national convention in 1860.

By 1860 it had become apparent that slavery was

not taking root in Kansas or in any other western territory. Yet when secession began after Lincoln's election, the efforts at reconciliation concentrated on the familiar territorial problem. The centerpiece of the abortive Crittenden compromise was an amendment reviving and extending the 36°30′ line, so recently outlawed by the Supreme Court. This continued fascination with an essentially empty issue was not so foolish as it now may seem; for the territorial question had obviously taken on enormous symbolic meaning. Because of the almost universal agreement that slavery in the states was untouchable by the federal government, the territories had come to be the limited battleground of a fierce and fundamental struggle. Thus the sectional conflict of the 1850s, whatever its origins and whatever its substance, was decisively shaped by constitutional considerations.

DON E. FEHRENBACHER

Bibliography

BESTOR, ARTHUR 1961 State Sovereignty and Slavery: A Reinterpretation of Proslavery Constitutional Doctrine, 1846–1860. *Illinois State Historical Society Journal* 54:117–80.
DEALEY, JAMES QUAYLE 1915 *Growth of American State Constitutions.* Boston: Ginn & Co.
FEHRENBACHER, DON E. 1978 *The Dred Scott Case: Its Significance in American Law and Politics.* New York: Oxford University Press.
PARKINSON, GEORGE PHILLIP, JR. 1972 "Antebellum State Constitution-Making: Retention, Circumvention, Revision." Ph.D. dissertation, University of Wisconsin.
POTTER, DAVID M. 1976 *The Impending Crisis, 1848–1861.* Completed and edited by Don E. Fehrenbacher. New York: Harper & Row.
WHITE, LEONARD D. 1954 *The Jacksonians: A Study in Administrative History, 1829–1861.* New York: Macmillan.

CONSTITUTIONAL HISTORY, 1861–1865

If expediency and ideology ordinarily conflict with the constitutionalist desire for procedural regularity and limitations on government, in time of war they pose a fundamental challenge to CONSTITUTIONALISM and the RULE OF LAW. The first fact to be observed about the constitutional history of the Civil War, therefore, is that the federal Constitution, as in the prewar period, served as both a symbol and a source of governmental legitimacy and as a normative standard for the conduct of politics. Because the rule of the Constitution continued without interruption, it is easy to overlook the pressures that the war generated to institute a regime based exclusively on necessity and the public safety. To be sure, considerations of public safety entered into wartime constitutionalism, and there were those who believed passionately that the Union government in the years 1861 to 1865 did indeed cast aside the Constitution and resort to arbitrary rule. Yet, considered from either a comparative or a strictly American perspective, this judgment is untenable. The record abundantly demonstrates the persistence of constitutional controversy in Congress, in the executive branch, in the courts, and in the forum of public opinion—evidence that the nation's organic law was taken seriously in time of war, even if it was not applied in the same manner as in time of peace. Indeed, a constitutionalizing impulse may be said to have manifested itself in the business of warfare itself. General Order No. 100 for the government of Union armies in the field, promulgated by President ABRAHAM LINCOLN in 1863, was an attempt to limit the destructiveness of modern war that had resulted from developments in weaponry and from the emergence of other aspects of total war.

The most important constitutional question resolved by the events of the war concerned the nature of the Union. (See THEORIES OF THE UNION.) The Framers of the Constitution had created a mixed regime that in some respects resembled a confederation of autonomous states and in others a centralized unitary government. Its distinguishing feature—the chief characteristic of American FEDERALISM—was the division of SOVEREIGNTY between the federal government and the state governments. In constitutional law several decisions of the Supreme Court under Chief Justice JOHN MARSHALL had confirmed this dual-sovereignty system; yet periodically it was questioned by political groups who insisted that the Union was simply a league of sovereign states, and that the federal government possessed no sovereignty whatsoever except as the agent of the states. From 1846 to 1860 defenders of slavery asserted this state-sovereignty theory of the Union; although they never secured a congressional majority for the theory, they did force northern Democrats to adopt positions that virtually abandoned any claim to federal sovereignty in matters concerning slavery. The SECESSION policy of President JAMES BUCHANAN, which regarded secession as illegal but nonetheless tolerated the existence of the newly forming Confederate States of America, signified the constitutional and political bankruptcy of Democratic DUAL FEDERALISM and the practical repudiation of federal sovereignty.

The constitutional results of the Civil War must

be measured against the effective triumph of proslavery state sovereignty which permitted the disintegration of the Union in 1860–1861. Northern victory in the war established federal sovereignty in political fact and in public policy, and by the same token repudiated the state-sovereignty theory of the Union. From the standpoint of constitutional law, this result vindicated the divided-sovereignty concept of federalism asserted in the early national period. From the standpoint of federal–state relations in the field of public policy, the war produced a significant centralizing trend, evident principally in military recruitment and organization, internal security, the regulation of personal liberty and CIVIL RIGHTS, and the determination of national economic policy.

The changes in federalism produced by the war have usually been described—sometimes in almost apocalyptic terms—as the destruction of STATES' RIGHTS and the old federal Union and their replacement by a centralized sovereign nation. In fact, however, the changes in federal–state relations that occurred between 1861 and 1865 did not seriously erode or alter the decentralized constitutional system and political culture of the United States. The centralizing of policy was based on military need rather than the appeal of a new unitary constitutional model, and it was of limited scope and duration. In no comprehensive way did the federal government become supreme over the states, nor were states' rights obliterated either in law or in policy. The theoretical structure of American federalism, as explicated by John Marshall, persisted; the actual distribution of power between the states and the federal government, the result of policy struggles on questions raised by the war, was different.

Perhaps the best way to describe the change in federalism that occurred during the Civil War is to say that after a long period of disinclination to use the constitutional powers assigned to it, the federal government began to act like an authentic sovereign state. Foremost among its achievements was the raising of armies and the providing and maintaining of a navy for the defense of the nation.

At the start of the war the decision to resist secession was made by the federal government, but the task of raising a military force fell largely upon the states. The regular United States Army, at approximately 16,000 men, was inadequate for the government's military needs, and federal authorities were as yet unprepared to call for United States volunteers. To meet the emergency it was necessary to rely on the militia, a form of military organization that, while subject to national service, was chiefly a state institu-

tion. Accordingly President Lincoln on April 15, 1861, acting under the Militia Act of 1795, issued a call to the state governors to provide 75,000 militia for three months of national service. By August 1861, in pursuance of additional presidential requests, the War Department had enrolled almost 500,000 men for three years' duty. Yet, although carried out under federal authority, the actual recruiting of troops and to a considerable extent their preparation for combat were done by the state governors, acting as a kind of war ministry for the nation.

This arrangement did not last long. Within a year declining popular enthusiasm and the utility of centralized administrative management severely impeded state recruiting efforts and led to greater federal control. Eventually national CONSCRIPTION was adopted. Congress took a half-way step toward this policy in the Militia Act of July 1862, authorizing the President, in calling the militia into national service, to make all necessary rules and regulations for doing so where state laws were defective or inadequate. Under this statute a draft was planned by the War Department, to be enforced by provost marshals nominated by state governors and appointed by the department. Political resistance in the states prevented implementation of this plan. At length, in the Enrollment Act of March 1863, Congress instituted an exclusively national system of conscription. Directed at male citizens ages twenty to forty-five and foreigners who declared their intention to become citizens, the draft law omitted all reference to the state militia. Conscription was to be enforced by federal provost marshals under a Provost Marshal General, operating under an administrative structure organized according to congressional districts. The Civil War draft, which permitted substitutes and money commutation, aroused widespread and often violent opposition and was directly responsible for inducting only six percent of the total Union military force. Nevertheless, it proved to be a decisive constitutional precedent on which the federal government relied in meeting its manpower needs in the wars of the twentieth century. (See SELECTIVE SERVICE ACTS.)

Closely related to the raising of armies was the task of maintaining internal security on the home front against the treasonable and disloyal acts of persons interfering with the war effort. In this sphere too the Union government exercised previously unused powers, asserting an unwonted sovereignty in local affairs that challenged the states' exclusive power to regulate civil and political liberty.

The law against TREASON, the elements of which had been defined in the Constitution, was the most formidable instrument for protecting national security outside the theater of war. Yet in its various manifestations—the Treason Act of 1790 requiring the death penalty and the Seditious Conspiracies Act of 1861 and the treason provisions of the CONFISCATION ACT of 1862 imposing less severe penalties—it was inapplicable in the South as long as federal courts could not operate there. It was also unsuited to the task of containing the less than treasonable activities of Confederate sympathizers and opponents of the war in the North. Loyalty oaths were a second internal security measure. The third, and by far the most important, component of Union internal security policy was military detention of persons suspected of disloyal activities, suspension of the writ of HABEAS CORPUS, and the imposition of martial law.

In April 1861 and on several occasions thereafter, President Lincoln authorized military commanders in specific areas to arrest and deny the writ of habeas corpus to persons engaging in or suspected of disloyal practices, such as interfering with troop movements or discouraging enlistments. In September 1862 the President issued a general proclamation that such persons were liable to trial by military commission or court-martial. Initially the State Department supervised civilian arrests made by secret service agents, federal marshals, and military officers. In February 1862 the War Department assumed responsibility for this practice and created a commission to examine the causes of arrests and provide for the release of persons deemed to be political prisoners. Congress further shaped internal security policy in the HABEAS CORPUS ACT of March 1863, requiring the secretaries of war and state to provide lists of prisoners to federal courts for GRAND JURY consideration. If no indictment for violation of federal law should be forthcoming, a prisoner was to be released upon taking an oath of allegiance.

The Union government arrested approximately 18,000 civilians, almost all of whom were released after brief detention for precautionary rather than punitive purposes. The policy was extremely controversial, however, for what Unionists might consider a precaution to prevent interference with the war effort could easily be regarded by others as punishment for political dissent. Evaluation of internal security policy depended upon conflicting interpretations of CIVIL LIBERTIES guarantees under the Constitution, and differing perceptions of what critics and opponents of the government were in reality doing. As with conscription, however, there was no denying that internal security measures had a significant impact on federal–state relations.

In carrying out this policy the federal government for the first time intervened significantly in local regulation of civil and political liberty. Not only did the federal government make arbitrary or irregular arrests but it also temporarily suspended the publication of many newspapers. Not surprisingly, considering the traditional exclusivity of state power over civil liberty and the partisan context in which the internal security question was debated, the states resisted this extension of federal authority. In several states persons adversely affected by internal security measures, or by enforcement of federal laws and orders concerning conscription, trade restrictions, internal revenue, or emancipation, initiated litigation charging federal officers with violations of state law, such as false arrest, unlawful seizure, kidnaping, assault, and battery. Under prewar federalism no general recourse was available to national officials involved as defendants in state litigation of this sort. Congress remedied this defect, however, in the Habeas Corpus Act of 1863.

The 1863 act provided that orders issued by the President or under his authority should be a defense in all courts against any civil or criminal prosecution for any search, seizure, arrest, or imprisonment undertaken in pursuance of such an order. The law further authorized the removal of litigation against national officers from state to federal courts, and it imposed a two-year limit on the initiation of such litigation. On only two previous occasions, in 1815 and 1833 in response to state interference with customs collection, had Congress given protection for federal officers acting under authority of a specific statute by permitting removal of litigation from state to federal courts. The Habeas Corpus Act of 1863, by contrast, protected actions taken under any federal law or EXECUTIVE ORDER. Critics argued that the law gave immunity rather than indemnity, denied citizens judicial remedies for wrongs done by the government, and usurped state power. The logic of even a circumscribed national sovereignty demanded some means of protection against state JURISDICTION, however, and during reconstruction Congress extended the removal remedy and the federal judiciary upheld its constitutionality. The wartime action marked an important extension of federal jurisdiction that made the national government, at least in time of national security crisis, more able to compete with the states in the regulation of civil liberty.

The most novel and in the long run probably the most important exercise of federal sovereignty during the Civil War led directly to the abolition of slavery and the protection of personal liberty and civil rights by the national government. No constitutional rule was more firmly established than that which prohibited federal interference with slavery in the states that recognized it. The outbreak of hostilities did not abrogate this rule, but it did create the possibility that, under the war power, the federal government might emancipate slaves for military purposes. After prohibiting slavery where it could under its peacetime constitutional authority (in the DISTRICT OF COLUMBIA and in the TERRITORIES), Congress struck at slavery in the Confederacy itself. In the Confiscation Act of 1862, it declared "forever free" slaves belonging to persons in rebellion, those who were captured, or who came within Union army lines. Executive interference with slavery went considerably farther. After trying unsuccessfully in 1862 to persuade loyal slaveholding states to accept a federally sponsored plan for gradual, compensated emancipation to be carried out by the states themselves, Lincoln undertook military emancipation. In the EMANCIPATION PROCLAMATION of January 1, 1863, he declared the freedom of all slaves in states still in rebellion and pledged executive-branch protection of freedmen's personal liberty.

Federal power over personal liberty was further made manifest in the work of local police regulation undertaken by Union armies as they advanced into southern territory. All persons in occupied areas were affected by the rule of federal military commanders, and none more so than freed or escaped slaves. From the first incursions of national force in May 1861, War and Treasury Department officials protected blacks' personal liberty, provided for their most pressing welfare needs in refugee camps, and assisted their assimilation into free society by organizing their labor on abandoned plantations and by recruiting them into the army. In March 1865 Congress placed emancipation-related federal police regulation on a more secure footing by creating the Bureau of Refugees, Freedmen, and Abandoned Lands. Authorized to control all subjects relating to refugees and freedmen for a period of one year after the end of the war, the FREEDMEN'S BUREAU throughout 1865 established courts to protect freedmen's personal liberty and civil rights, in the process superseding the states in their most traditional and jealously guarded governmental function.

Federal emancipation measures, based on the war power, did not accomplish the permanent abolition of slavery as it was recognized in state laws and constitutions. To accomplish this momentous change, and the invasion of state power that it signified, amendment of the Constitution was necessary. Accordingly, Congress in January 1865 approved for submission to the states a constitutional amendment prohibiting slavery or involuntary servitude, except as a punishment for crime, in the United States or any place subject to its jurisdiction. Section 2 of the amendment gave Congress authority to enforce the prohibition by appropriate legislation.

Controversy surrounded this terse, seemingly straightforward, yet rather delphic pronouncement, which became part of the Constitution in December 1865. Though it appeared to be a legitimate exercise of the amending power under Article V, Democrats argued that the THIRTEENTH AMENDMENT was a wrongful use of that power because it invaded state jurisdiction over local affairs, undermining the sovereign power to fix the status of all persons within a state's borders and thus destroying the unspoken premise on which the Constitution and the government had been erected in 1787. The Republican framers of the amendment for their part were uncertain about the scope and effect of the guarantee of personal liberty that they would write into the nation's organic law. At the least, the amendment prohibited chattel slavery, or property in people; many of its supporters believed it also secured the full range of civil rights appurtenant to personal liberty that distinguished a free republican society. No determination of this question was required in order to send the amendment to the states, however, and when a year later the precise scope of the guarantees provided and congressional enforcement power became issues in reconstruction, more detailed and specific measures, such as the CIVIL RIGHTS ACT OF 1866 and the FOURTEENTH AMENDMENT, were deemed necessary. Constitutionally speaking, the Thirteenth Amendment played a minor role in reconstruction.

The federal government further exercised sovereignty characteristic of a nation-state in the sphere of economic policy. This development raised few questions of constitutional propriety; the instruments for accomplishing it lay ready to hand in the ALEXANDER HAMILTON-John Marshall doctrines of BROAD CONSTRUCTION and IMPLIED POWERS. These doctrines had fallen into desuetude in the Jacksonian era, when mercantilist-minded state governments effectively determined economic policy. The exodus of Southerners from the national government in 1861 altered the political balance, however, and Republicans in control of the wartime Congress seized the opportunity to adopt centralizing economic legislation. They raised the tariff for protective purposes, authorized construction of a transcontinental railway, facilitated settlement on the public domain (HOMESTEAD ACT), provided federal aid to higher education (MORRILL ACT), established a uniform currency, asserted federal control over the nation's banking institutions, and taxed the American people in innovative ways (income tax, DIRECT TAX). These measures laid the foundation for increasing federal ECONOMIC REGULATION in the late nineteenth and early twentieth centuries. Yet they did not make the determination of economic policy an exclusively national function. In this field, as in civil rights, the federal government's acquisition of a distinct and substantial share of sovereignty diminished, but by no means obliterated, state power.

As the federal government gained power relative to the states during the war, so within the SEPARATION OF POWERS structure of the national government the executive expanded its authority relative to the other branches. Lincoln was the instrument of this constitutional change. Unlike his predecessor Buchanan, Lincoln was willing to acknowledge the necessity of an inflexible defense of the Union during the secession crisis, and after the bombardment of Fort Sumter he acted swiftly and unhesitatingly to commit the nation to arms.

To raise a fighting force Lincoln called the state militia into national service, ordered—without authority from Congress—a 40,000-man increase in the regular army and navy, requested 42,000 volunteers, and proclaimed a blockade of ports in the seceded states. He also instituted the main elements of the internal security program previously described, closed the postal service to treasonable correspondence, directed that $2,000,000 be paid out of the federal treasury, and pledged the credit of the United States for $250,000,000. Lincoln did all this without congressional authority, but not without regard for Congress. Ordering the militia into national service, he called Congress into session to meet in mid-summer. Directing the enlargement of the army and navy, he said he would submit these actions to Congress. He did so, and Congress voted approval of the President's military orders, "as if they had been done under the previous express authority and direction of the Congress." Thereafter Lincoln was ever mindful of the lawmaking branch, and in some respects deferential to it. Yet in war-related matters he continued to take unilateral actions. Thus he proclaimed martial law, suspended habeas corpus, suppressed newspaper publication, issued orders for the conduct of armies in the field, ordered slave emancipation, and directed the political reorganization of occupied southern states.

How could these extraordinary actions be rationalized under the nation's organic law? The question aroused bitter controversy at the time, giving rise to charges of dictatorship which continued to find echo in scholarly debate. No more penetrating analysis of the problem has ever been offered than that presented by Lincoln himself.

In his message to Congress of July 4, 1861, Lincoln said his actions were required by "public necessity" and "popular demand." Referring to suspension of the writ of habeas corpus, he stated that if he violated "some single law," his doing so was justified on the ground that it would save the government." . . . are all the laws, *but one*, to go unexecuted, and the government itself go to pieces, lest that one be violated?" he asked. On another occasion Lincoln posed the question whether it was possible to lose the nation and yet preserve the Constitution. "By general law life and limb must be protected," he reasoned, "yet often a limb must be amputated to save a life; but a life is never wisely given to save a limb." This appears to mean that the Constitution might be set aside, as a limb is amputated, to save the life of the nation. The inference can be drawn that emergency action, while expedient, is unconstitutional.

What is required to understand the lawfulness of the emergency measures in question, however, is not legalistic analysis of the constitutional text but rather consideration of the fundamental relationship between the nation and the Constitution. Lincoln's principal argument was that the steps taken to defend the government were constitutional because the Constitution implicitly sanctioned its own preservation. The Constitution in this view was not a mere appendage of the living nation or a derivative expression or reflection of national life, as a legal code might be considered to be. Coeval and in an ultimate political sense coterminous with it, the Constitution *was* the nation. This conception is present in Lincoln's statement of April 1864 that "measures, otherwise unconstitutional, might become lawful, by becoming indispensable to the preservation of the constitution, through the preservation of the nation." "Is there," he asked in his message of July 1861, "in all republics, this inherent and fatal weakness? Must a government, of necessity, be too *strong* for the liberties of its own people, or too *weak* to maintain its own existence?" Not that Lincoln conceded to his critics at the level of positivistic, text-based constitutional argument. Concerning habeas corpus suspension, for example, he tenaciously insisted that as the Constitution did not specify who might exercise this power, he was justified in doing so when Congress was not in session. Congress, in fact, subsequently ratified Lincoln's suspension of habeas corpus. Although his argument conformed to the requirements of American constitutional politics, his principal justification of emergency actions was that they were necessary to preserve the substance of political liberty, which was the end both of the Constitution and the Union.

It is sometimes said that Lincoln established in American public law the principle of constitutional dictatorship. Yet at no time did Lincoln exercise unlimited power. The notion of constitutional dictatorship also obscures the fact that although Lincoln applied military power on a far wider scale than previous Presidents, in doing so he merely accelerated a tendency toward expansion of the executive's defensive war-making capability. In 1827 the Supreme Court, in MARTIN V. MOTT, had upheld the President's power under the Militia Act of 1795 to call out the militia (and by extension the army and navy) in the event of actual or imminent invasion. President JAMES K. POLK had used this defensive war-making power to commit the nation to war against Mexico, and Presidents Millard Fillmore and Franklin Pierce had employed military force in circumstances that could have led to wars with foreign states. In his exercise of executive power Lincoln merely widened a trail blazed by his predecessors.

Yet in minor matters unrelated to the war, emancipation, and reconstruction, Lincoln was a passive President. Although as party leader he made effective use of his patronage powers, he did little to influence congressional legislation aside from formal suggestions in annual messages. Moreover he exercised the veto sparingly, gave broad latitude to his department heads, and made little use of the cabinet for policy-making purposes. Lincoln's respect for legislative independence complemented and encouraged another important nineteenth-century constitutional trend—the strengthening of congressional power.

To an extent that is difficult to appreciate in the late twentieth century, nineteenth-century government was preeminently legislative in nature. Lawmakers shaped public policy, resolved constitutional controversies through debate and legislation, controlled the TAXING AND SPENDING process, and exercised significant influence over administration. The years between the presidencies of THOMAS JEFFERSON and ANDREW JACKSON had been a period of legislative assertiveness, and although the struggle over slavery had brought Congress to near-paralysis, still the political foundation existed for wartime exertions of power that anticipated the era of congressional government during and after reconstruction.

Although Congress approved Lincoln's emergency measures in 1861, its action by no means signified general deference to executive power. On the contrary, reciting constitutional provisions that gave Congress power to declare war and regulate the military establishment, members made vigorous claim to exercise the WAR POWER. Accordingly, they raised men and supplies for the war, attempted through the Joint Committee on the Conduct of the War to influence military strategy, modified internal security policy, and enacted laws authorizing confiscation, emancipation, and reconstruction. The need for party unity notwithstanding, the Republican majority in Congress insisted on civilian control over the military, monitored executive department administration, and, in an unusual maneuver in December 1862, even tried to force a change in the cabinet. Tighter internal organization and operational procedures made Congress more powerful as well as more efficient during the war. The speaker of the House, for example, assumed greater control over committee memberships and the flow of legislative business; the party caucus became a more frequent determinant of legislative behavior; and standing committees and their chairmen enjoyed enhanced prestige and influence, gradually superseding select committees as the key agencies for accomplishing legislative tasks. Exercising power conferred by statute in 1857 to punish recalcitrant or uncooperative witnesses, Congress used its investigative authority to extend its governmental grasp.

In the 1930s and 1940s, Civil War historiography regarded conflict between a radical-dominated Congress and the soberly conservative Lincoln administration as the central political struggle of the war. Recent research has shown, however, that disagreement between the Democratic and Republican parties was more significant in shaping the course of political and constitutional events than was the radical versus moderate tension within the Republican party. Conflict occurred between the executive and legislative branches, as much as a result of institutional rivalry inherent in the structure of separated powers as of programmatic differences. Congressional–presidential relations were not notably more strained than they have been in other American wars. Although Lincoln demonstrated the potentially vast power inherent in the presidency, his wartime actions did not measurably extend the executive office beyond the sphere of crisis government. He evinced no tendency toward the so-called stewardship conception of the presidency advanced by THEODORE ROOSEVELT in the early twentieth century. The power of Congress waxed, its wartime achievements in policymaking and internal organization providing a solid basis for a subsequent era of congressional government.

A significant portion of American constitutional history from 1861 to 1865 occurred south of the Potomac, where were manifested many of the same problems and tendencies that appeared in the wartime experience of the United States government. The CONFEDERATE CONSTITUTION, modeled closely on that of the United States, revealed the most bitterly contested issues that had led to the war. It recognized and protected the right of slave property; proclaimed state sovereignty as the basis of the Confederacy; omitted the GENERAL WELFARE clause and the TAXING AND SPENDING POWER contained in the United States Constitution; stated that all federal power was expressly delegated; and prohibited a protective tariff and INTERNAL IMPROVEMENTS appropriations. Yet the right of secession was not recognized, evidence that the Confederacy was intended to be a permanent government.

Confederate constitutional history was marked by war-induced centralization and conflicts between federal and state authority. The Confederate government conscripted soldiers; suspended the writ of habeas corpus and declared martial law; confiscated enemy property and seized for temporary use the property of its own citizens; taxed heavily and imposed tight controls on commerce and industry; and owned and operated munitions, mining, and clothing factories. These actions and policies aroused strong opposition as expressed in the rhetoric of states' rights and through the institutions of state government. Some governors refused to place their troops under the Confederacy's authority and challenged conscription and internal security measures. Many state judges granted writs of habeas corpus that interfered with military recruitment. Lack of effective leverage over the states seriously hampered the Confederate war effort.

The most significant difference between Union and Confederate constitutionalism centered on POLITICAL PARTIES. Driven by the desire to create national unity, Southerners eschewed political party organization as unnecessary and harmful. When political differences arose, they had to find resolution in the conflict-inducing methods of the system of states' rights. In the North, by contrast, political parties continued to compete, with beneficial results. Political disagreements between the government and its Democratic critics were kept within manageable bounds by the concept of a loyal opposition, while among members of the governing party differences were directed into policy alternatives. Moreover, party organization encouraged federal–state cooperation in the implementation of controversial measures like conscription, thus helping to minimize the centrifugal effects of federal organization. Indeed, the persistence of organized party

competition, even in the critical year of 1864 when military success was uncertain and the Democratic party campaigned on a platform demanding a cessation of hostilities, was perhaps the most revealing fact in Civil War constitutional history. It showed that despite important changes in federal–state relations and reliance on techniques of emergency government, the American commitment to constitutionalism was firm, even amidst events that tested it most severely.

HERMAN BELZ

Bibliography

BELZ, HERMAN 1978 *Emancipation and Equal Rights: Politics and Constitutionalism in the Civil War Era.* New York: Norton.

CURRY, LEONARD P. 1968 *Blueprint for Modern America: Nonmilitary Legislation of the First Civil War Congress.* Nashville, Tenn.: Vanderbilt University Press.

FEHRENBACHER, DON E. 1979 Lincoln and the Constitution. In Cullom Davis, ed., *The Public and Private Lincoln: Contemporary Perspectives.* Carbondale: University of Southern Illinois Press.

HYMAN, HAROLD M. 1973 *A More Perfect Union: The Impact of the Civil War and Reconstruction on the Constitution.* New York: Knopf.

MCKITRICK, ERIC 1967 Party Politics and the Union and Confederate War Efforts. In Walter Dean Burnham and William N. Chambers, eds., *The American Party System: Stages of Political Development.* New York: Free Press.

MCLAUGHLIN, ANDREW C. 1936 Lincoln, the Constitution, and Democracy. *International Journal of Ethics* 47:1–24.

RANDALL, JAMES G. (1926)1951 *Constitutional Problems under Lincoln,* rev. ed. Urbana: University of Illinois Press.

WEIGLEY, RUSSELL F. 1967 *A History of the United States Army.* New York: Macmillan.

CONSTITUTIONAL HISTORY, 1865–1877

The great political and constitutional issue of the period 1865–1877 was the Reconstruction of the Union after the Civil War. Reconstruction presented several closely related issues. There were issues involving the nature of the federal system. One of these arose even before the war ended: what was the constitutional relationship to the Union of the states that had attempted to secede? Another arose after the southern states were restored to normal relations: what powers did the national government retain to protect the rights of its citizens? There was the problem of defining the constitutional status of black Americans—a problem that finally forced Americans to define American CITIZENSHIP and the rights incident to it. Also, because the President and Congress disagreed on these issues, Reconstruction brought about a crisis in legislative–executive relations that culminated in the only impeachment of an American President. Finally, the Reconstruction controversy had a powerful effect upon Americans' conception of the proper role of government, laying the groundwork for the development of laissez-faire constitutionalism.

These issues would be adjusted in the context of the established party system. During the war, the Republican party worked diligently and fairly successfully to broaden its support. Renaming their organization the Union party, Republican leaders accepted as colleagues men who had been influential Democrats until the outbreak of war. In 1864 the party nominated Tennessee's Democratic former governor and senator, ANDREW JOHNSON, to the vice-presidency. Despite this, the Union party, which would revive the name Republican after the war, was the heir to the governmental activism of the old Federalist and Whig parties. Likewise Republicans inherited nationalist theories of the federal system. (See UNION, THEORIES OF THE.) The war confirmed and extended their distrust of STATES' RIGHTS doctrines; yet many Republicans would resist going too far in the direction of "consolidation" of the Union at the expense of traditional areas of state jurisdiction. On the other hand, the majority of Democrats had remained loyal to their party and its heritage of states' rights and small government. Naturally, the Reconstruction issue, which involved both questions, found the two parties ranged against one another.

Northerners faced a paradox when they considered the status of the Confederate states at war's end. They had denied that a state could leave the Union, but few wanted the same governments that had attempted secession to return as if nothing had happened. Only so-called Peace Democrats argued that the Union should be restored through negotiations between the Confederate state governments and the national government. Somehow, Republicans and War Democrats insisted, the national government must have power to secure some changes in the South and in the federal system before final restoration. As the war progressed, and especially in 1865 and 1866, when they were forced to grapple with the problem, Republicans propounded a variety of constitutional justifications for such power. Unlike Democrats, who insisted that state government had existed before the Union and independent of it, Republicans insisted that states could exist only in the Union and by virtue of their connection with it. Thus, by trying to secede,

the southern states had committed STATE SUICIDE, in the graphic language of Senator CHARLES SUMNER; or, as other Republicans put it, they had "forfeited their rights." Given this view, there were several ways to justify national power over Southerners. Many Republicans argued that if Southerners now lacked state governments, Congress must restore them under the clause of the Constitution requiring the national government to guarantee a REPUBLICAN FORM OF GOVERNMENT to each state. Moreover, in the 1849 case of LUTHER V. BORDEN the Supreme Court, citing this clause, had seemed to concede to the "political branches" of the government the power to recognize whether a state government was legitimate in case of doubt. The Court had held that the admission of state representatives to Congress was conclusive. With state governments defunct, Republicans argued, the Court's holding meant that the political branches of the national government would have final say about what government would be recognized as restored to the Union and when that recognition would take place. Implicit in this power was the authority to determine what sort of government would be acceptable.

But when some Republicans insisted that the GUARANTEE CLAUSE entitled the national government to require changes it believed necessary for states to be considered republican, most of their colleagues rebelled. Such an interpretation would give the national government power to modify "unrepublican" political and civil laws in states that had never left the Union.

Other Republicans found a safer source of power over states that had forfeited their rights: the national government had recovered control over the territory and citizens of the South through exercise of its WAR POWERS, which had overridded the peacetime provision of the Constitution that guaranteed citizens' and states' rights. The government could continue to hold Southerners in this "grasp of war" until they agreed to meet the government's conditions for the restoration of peace. On this theory, national power would be temporary, providing no precedent for intruding in states that had not been in rebellion.

Finally, other Republicans—those who wanted the most radical changes in southern society—argued that, having broken away from national authority de facto, the southern states were conquered provinces no different from any other newly acquired territory. Thus Southerners were subject to the direct control of the national government, which ought to provide ordinary territorial governments through which they could govern themselves under the revisory power of Congress. In this way the national government would retain authority to legislate directly for the South until new states were created there—establishing a public school system, for example, or confiscating the great landed estates and distributing them among the people as small farms. But this theory also seemed too radical for most Northerners, and most Republicans endorsed the more limited "grasp-of-war" doctrine.

Congress was adjourned in April and May 1865, as Lincoln was assassinated and the war ended. Lincoln's successor, the former Democrat Johnson, accepted the key elements of the WADE-DAVIS BILL developed during the war, but he followed Lincoln's policy of carrying it out under presidential authority, rather than calling Congress back into session to enact Reconstruction legislation. Johnson called for white, male voters in each southern state to elect a state constitutional convention as soon as fifty percent of them had taken a loyalty oath that would entitle them to AMNESTY. Thus blacks would have to depend on governments elected by whites for protection of life and property. The conventions were required to pronounce their states' SECESSION ordinances null and void, repudiate debts incurred by their Confederate state governments, and abolish slavery. Finally, the southern states would have to ratify the proposed THIRTEENTH AMENDMENT, which abolished slavery throughout the land. Then the conventions could organize elections to ratify the new constitutions, elect state officials, and elect congressmen. By December 1865, as Congress reconvened, this process had been completed in most of the southern states and would soon be completed in the remainder.

At first Johnson was vague about his constitutional theory of Reconstruction, but as congressional opposition developed his supporters articulated a position that left little power to Congress. Secession had merely "suspended" the operation of legal governments in the South, they insisted. As COMMANDER-IN-CHIEF of the armed forces, the President had the duty under the government's war powers to reanimate state governments. War powers were inherently presidential, Johnson insisted. He had exercised them in such a way as to preserve the traditional federal system. Congress could do no more than exercise its constitutional power to "judge of the elections, returns and qualifications of its own members" by deciding whether individual congressmen-elect were disqualified by their roles in the war; it could not deny REPRESENTATION to whole states. Gaining the support of northern Democrats for this states'-rights-oriented policy, Johnson set the stage for a bitter struggle over the relative powers of the branches of the national government.

A majority of congressmen might have acquiesced in the President's position had they been confident that loyalists would control the southern state governments or that the rights of the newly freed slaves would be respected there. However, it soon became apparent that the states were controlled by former rebels and that the rights of the freedmen would be severely circumscribed. Compounding the problem, the ex-Confederate-dominated South would increase its congressional representation now that slavery was abolished; the constitutional provision counting only three-fifths of the slave population would no longer apply. All this persuaded congressional Republicans to refuse immediate admission of southern state representatives to Congress and to seek a compromise with the President.

There were two thrusts to the congressional policy: protection of freedmen's rights and a new system of apportionment of representation in Congress. Most congressional leaders believed that the Thirteenth Amendment automatically conferred citizenship upon the freedmen when it abolished slavery. Moreover, the amendment's second section authorized Congress to pass legislation appropriate to enforce abolition. Republicans acted upon this understanding by passing a new FREEDMEN'S BUREAU bill, augmenting one passed during the war, and proposing the bill that became the CIVIL RIGHTS ACT OF 1866. The first, a temporary measure justified under the war powers, authorized an Army bureau to supervise the transition from slave to free labor, protecting the rights and interests of the freedmen in the process. The second was designed to secure permanent protection for the freedmen in their basic rights. Few Republicans thought that Americans would accept so drastic a change in the federal system as to give Congress instead of the states the job of protecting people in their ordinary rights. Therefore they adopted the idea of leaving that job to the states but requiring them to treat all groups equally. At the same time, Republicans intended to require equality only in the protection of *basic* rights of citizenship. This goal forced them to define just what those rights were. So the Civil Rights Act declared all persons born in the United States, except Indians who did not pay taxes, to be citizens of the United States; it granted all citizens, regardless of race, the same basic rights as white citizens. What were these basic rights of citizenship? "To make and enforce contracts; to sue, be parties, and give evidence; to inherit, purchase, lease, sell, hold, and convey real and personal property; and to full and equal benefit of all laws and proceedings for the security of persons and property" and to "be subject to like punishment, pains, and penalties." To secure these rights without centralizing power of ordinary legislation in Washington, the bill permitted citizens to remove legal cases from state to federal court jurisdiction in any state that did not end discrimination. (See CIVIL RIGHTS REMOVAL.) The idea was to force states to abolish RACIAL DISCRIMINATION in their own laws in order to preserve their jurisdictions. As its author explained, the act would "have no operation in any State where the laws are equal, where all persons have the same civil rights without regard to color or race."

At the same time Republicans prepared a fourteenth amendment to define citizenship and its rights; to change the way seats in Congress were apportioned, so as to reflect the number of voters rather than gross population; to disqualify leading Confederates from holding political office; and to guarantee payment of the United States debt while repudiating the Confederate debt. Congress was to have power to enforce this amendment, too, by "appropriate" legislation.

Republicans expected Johnson to endorse these measures, which after all did not attempt to replace the governments he had instituted in the South, and they expected Southerners to signify their acceptance of these "terms of peace" by ratifying the new amendment. However, Johnson insisted that the Republican program would revolutionize the federal system. He vetoed the legislation and urged Southerners to reject the proposed amendment. At the same time he attacked the Republicans bitterly. Republicans responded by passing the Civil Rights Act over Johnson's veto, enacting the new Freedman's Bureau Act, and sending the FOURTEENTH AMENDMENT to the states for RATIFICATION. To the voters, they stressed the moderation of their proposals, and Johnson's supporters were badly beaten in the congressional elections of 1866. Nonetheless, Southerners followed Johnson's advice and refused to ratify the amendment.

This refusal angered and frightened Republican congressmen. If the conflict drifted into stalemate, northern voters might tire of it and blame the Republicans for not completing restoration. Outraged at southern recalcitrance and Johnson's "betrayal," the Republicans passed new Reconstruction laws over his veto early in 1867. Designating Johnson's southern governments as temporary only, the Republicans instructed Southerners to begin the process anew. This time many leading Confederates would be disfranchised while the freedmen were permitted to vote.

New state conventions would have to be elected to write new constitutions banning racial discrimination in civil and political rights. The voters would have to ratify these constitutions, and then newly elected state officials would have to ratify the Fourteenth Amendment. In 1869 the Republican Congress proposed to the states the FIFTEENTH AMENDMENT, banning racial discrimination in voting; southern states that had not yet finished the process of being readmitted would be required to ratify this amendment, too. In some ways the new program was a relief to Republicans. They expected that once southern blacks could vote, their state governments would have to provide them with the protection of the laws, thus rendering unnecessary the exercise of national power and preserving the old balance of the federal system.

Until the southern states complied with the new Reconstruction laws, they were to be under the control of the Army, subject to martial law and, if necessary, military courts. Southerners insisted that this whole program was unconstitutional, and they tried to persuade the Supreme Court to declare it so. In 1867 and 1868 representatives of Johnson's state governments asked the Supreme Court to enjoin Johnson and his secretary of war, respectively, from enforcing the MILITARY RECONSTRUCTION ACTS. They hoped for success, because the majority of the Justices were suspected of opposing the Republican program. In earlier cases, including EX PARTE MILLIGAN (1866), a narrow majority had held that military courts could not operate upon civilians where civil courts were functioning, and in the TEST OATH CASES the Court had ruled unconstitutional laws requiring persons to swear oaths of past loyalty in order to follow certain professions. However, even Johnson would not sustain an effort to secure Court intervention in so plainly a political issue, and the Court dismissed both suits. (See MISSISSIPPI V. JOHNSON, 1867.)

Southerners tried again in EX PARTE McCARDLE (1869), where a Southerner convicted of murder in a military court asked for a write of HABEAS CORPUS, citing the Supreme Court's Milligan decision. At least some Reconstruction laws might be jeopardized if the Court endorsed this argument, and Republicans responded by repealing the law under which McCardle had brought his suit. The Court grudgingly acquiesced in the repeal but virtually invited a new application for the writ under another law.

These developments produced ambivalent feelings about the courts among Republicans. Before the war the judiciary had tended to sustain laws protecting slavery and discrimination against black Americans. During the war Chief Justice ROGER B. TANEY had seemed to obstruct the military effort, and the Court's course since the war had hardly been reassuring. Fearing judicial interference, several leading Republicans proposed narrowing the Court's jurisdiction and requiring a two-thirds majority of Justices to rule a congressional law unconstitutional, or denying that power altogether. On the other hand, the judiciary was the only national institution besides the military capable of enforcing the new laws protecting the rights of American citizens. Not only did Congress refrain from passing the court-limitation bills but it also expanded judicial authority by making the national judiciary the forum in which citizens and even businesses were to secure justice if their rights were denied in the states. Indeed, even as Republicans worried whether the Court would impair Reconstruction, in their roles as circuit court judges the Justices were upholding the power of the national government to protect rights under the Thirteenth and Fourteenth Amendments. Altogether, the Reconstruction era witnessed a great expansion of the jurisdiction and activity of the federal courts.

While the southern attack on the Reconstruction laws failed in the Supreme Court, Johnson was able to use against the laws the fact that they employed the military in their enforcement. As COMMANDER-IN-CHIEF of the armed forces, Johnson sought to limit the authority of military commanders and to give command of occupying forces to officers sympathetic to his position. When Secretary of War EDWIN M. STANTON resisted these efforts, Johnson suspended him from office and appointed the popular General ULYSSES S. GRANT in his place. By late 1867 Johnson's obstruction was so successful that Reconstruction was grinding to a halt, with white Southerners ready to prevent ratification of their new, egalitarian constitutions.

Many Republicans denied that the President had the constitutional right to obstruct legislation in this way, and they urged the House of Representatives to impeach him. However, most Republicans were frightened of taking so radical a step, and many insisted that IMPEACHMENT lay only for indictable crimes. Despite his obstructionism, Johnson had not clearly broken any law, and they would not support impeachment until he did. Therefore in December 1867 the first impeachment resolution failed.

However, in February 1868 Johnson did finally seem to break a law. As noted, Johnson had earlier suspended Secretary of War Stanton. He had done this while the Senate was adjourned, conforming to the TENURE OF OFFICE ACT, passed in 1867, which made all removals of government officers temporary

until the Senate confirmed a successor, or, in certain circumstances, voted to accept the President's reasons for removal. In Stanton's case, the Senate in 1867 refused to concur in the removal, and Stanton returned to office. Now Johnson defied the Senate and the law, ordering Stanton's permanent removal. The House impeached him immediately, and from March through May the Senate established rules of procedure, heard arguments and testimony, and deliberated.

Although many questions were raised during Johnson's trial in the Senate, the decision finally turned for most senators on whether they believed Stanton was in reality covered by the Tenure of Office Act. Despite Johnson's initial compliance with the act, his lawyers persuaded just enough Republican senators that the act did not cover Stanton, and Johnson was acquitted. But the price for acquittal was Johnson's promise to end his obstruction of the Reconstruction laws. With that interference ended, most southern states adopted new state constitutions, and in nearly all those states Republicans took control of the governments.

The new southern constitutions and Republican governments were among the most progressive in the nation. Elected mainly by black voters, southern Republican leaders thought they could secure enough white support to guarantee continued victory by using government power to promote prosperity and provide services. Thus they emulated northern Republican policies, using state taxes and credit to subsidize railroads and canals, to develop natural resources, and to control flooding along the Mississippi River. They created the first centralized state public school systems and opened state hospitals and asylums. At the same time southern Republicans were committed to improving the conditions of former slaves, both on principle and to keep the support of their largest constituency. They passed laws to provide them with the same state services that whites received, put blacks in important positions, banned discrimination in many businesses, shaped labor laws to protect workers' interests, and appointed local judges who would be sympathetic to blacks in disputes with whites.

All these activities required the states to spend and borrow far more money than they had before the war. Because it was primarily whites who owned enough property to pay taxes, the Republican policies redistributed wealth, something not acceptable to nineteenth-century Americans. Bitterly, white Southerners charged that "ignorant," "brutal" voters were being duped by venal politicians with promises of "class legislation." Southern whites denied that such governments were really democratic. Unable to defeat Republicans at the polls in most states, they turned to violence and fraud. From 1868 through 1872, midnight riders, known by such names as the Ku Klux Klan, terrorized local Republican leaders. After 1872 the violence became more organized and more closely linked to anti-Republican political organizations.

A few southern Republican governors were at first able to suppress the violence. But by 1870 they were appealing to the national government for help, thus causing serious problems for national Republican leaders. Republicans had hoped that enfranchising the freedmen would protect them without a massive expansion of national power. Moreover, everyone believed that legislation must be based on the Fourteenth and Fifteenth Amendments, ignoring the earlier view that the Thirteenth Amendment gave power to protect citizens' basic rights. But the language of the two later amendments only protected rights against STATE ACTION, and Republicans had a difficult time justifying laws protecting blacks and white Republicans from attacks by private individuals. Nonetheless, in 1871 Republicans passed such laws and also authorized President Grant to take drastic action to crush violence, including suspension of the writ of habeas corpus. They insisted that the Fourteenth Amendment required states to protect their residents; failure to do so would amount to state denial of EQUAL PROTECTION.

At first this response seemed successful, and violence abated. However, it soon flared anew. In many southern states Republicans claimed that Democratic violence and intimidation should nullify apparent Democratic majorities in elections, and they refused to count Democratic votes from areas where violence was most intense. In return Democrats organized armed militia to press their claims. In state after state Republicans had to appeal for national troops to protect them against such opponents. Where it was difficult to afford protection, the Democratic militias—often called "White Leagues"—drove Republican officials from office.

It became ever more difficult for national Republicans to respond. More and more Northerners feared that continued national intervention in the South was undermining the federal system. At the same time the Supreme Court manifested its concern to preserve a balance between state and national authority. In *Texas v. White* (1869) the Justices emphasized the importance of states in the Union, and in *Collector v. Day* (1871) they seemed to endorse the doctrine of DUAL FEDERALISM, by denying the national government's power to tax the incomes of officers of the "sovereign" states. In the SLAUGHTERHOUSE CASES (1873) the Court, in an implicitly dual federalist opinion, ruled that national and state citizenships were distinct. The Fourteenth Amendment protected only a limited number of rights inherent in national citizenship; those rights usually identified as basic remained the sole province of the states. This decision severely curtailed national power to protect black Southerners and southern Republicans from violence. In UNITED STATES V. CRUIKSHANK (1876) the Court held invalid indictments against white conspirators who had massacred blacks, in part on the grounds that the Fourteenth Amendment was aimed only at state action and could not justify prosecution of private individuals.

At the same time a growing number of Northerners were coming to share Southerners' concern about "class legislation." To these Northerners, calls for a protective tariff, for artificial inflation of the currency, for repudiation of state-guaranteed railroad bonds, for regulation of railroad rates, and for government imposition of an eight-hour work day all indicated a growing clamor for "class legislation" in the North. City political organizations, which taxed urban property holders to provide services to the less wealthy, seemed to be engaging in the same kind of "plunder" that southern whites alleged against their Republican governments. Many Northerners began to argue that the state and national constitutions required judges to overturn class legislation. They had some initial successes. The Supreme Court ruled part of the Legal Tender Act unconstitutional, only to overrule itself a year later (see LEGAL TENDER CASES, 1870), and state courts ruled that business and railroad promotion laws exceeded legislative power. However, the courts generally declined the invitation to write the doctrine of "laissez faire" into the Constitution. The majority in the *Slaughterhouse Cases* rejected the argument, and the Court sustained broad state regulatory power over businesses AFFECTED WITH A PUBLIC INTEREST—railroads, grain warehouses, and others that were left undefined. (See GRANGER CASES, 1877.)

Nonetheless, the conviction was growing that the sort of wealth-redistributing policies followed by southern Republicans was fundamentally wrong and so was fear that such ideas might spread north. More and more Northerners agreed with southern whites that southern proponents of such policies were "carpetbaggers" and "scalawags." By 1875 President Grant was refusing to help his beleaguered political allies; all but three southern states had returned to Democratic control, often through force and intimidation; and white Southerners were planning similarly violent campaigns to "redeem" the last three in 1876. Their effort to do so led to one of the greatest political and constitutional crises in American history.

In the presidential election of 1876 the violence and fraud endemic in the South threatened to engulf the nation. In the three remaining Republican states in the South—South Carolina, Louisiana, and Florida—Democrats engaged in campaigns of violence and intimidation. Republican officials threw out votes from districts they claimed Democrats had carried by force. Democrats once again charged fraud and armed to confront Republicans; southern Republicans once again appealed to the national government for protection. However, this time the outcome of the presidential election itself turned upon who had carried these three states. Without them, Democrat Samuel J. Tilden was one electoral vote short of victory. Republican RUTHERFORD B. HAYES needed the electoral votes of all three to win.

As the time drew near to count the electoral vote and declare a winner, two sets of electoral votes were sent to Congress from each of the contested states—the Republican votes certified by appropriate state agencies, and Democratic competitors. The Constitution requires electoral votes to be counted by the president of the Senate (normally the vice-president of the United States) in the presence of both houses of Congress. Republicans insisted that, absent a specific congressional resolution governing the subject, the Republican president pro tempore of the Senate would have the power to decide which set of votes were the correct ones to count (the vice-president having died in office). Controlling the Senate, Republicans prepared to block any contrary resolution that might come from the Democratic House. Democrats, on the other hand, insisted that if the two houses of Congress could not agree upon which set of votes was legitimate, neither could be counted. Then no candidate would have a majority, and according to the Constitution the House would name the winner.

With no clear precedent, and with the Supreme Court not yet accepted as the usual arbiter of such constitutional disputes, it seemed that the conflict might be resolved by force. Republican President Grant controlled the Army; if he recognized a President counted in by the Republicans, a competitor named by the House would have a hard time pressing his claim. To counter this Republican program, Democrats threatened forcible resistance.

As Americans demanded a peaceful end to the crisis, the two sides were forced to compromise. Congress passed a resolution turning all disputed electoral votes over to an Electoral Commission of ten congressmen and five Supreme Court Justices for decision. The commission decision would stand in each case unless *both* houses voted to disagree to it—an early example of a LEGISLATIVE VETO.

To the Democrats' dismay, the three Republican Supreme Court Justices joined the five Republican congressmen on the commission to decide every disputed vote in favor of the Republican candidate. In each case the majority accepted the votes certified by the agency authorized by state law. Republicans insisted the commission had no power "to go behind" these returns.

Furious, Democrats charged that this was a partisan decision. Many of them urged Democratic congressmen to prevent the completion of the count by filibustering, saying that the House could name the President if the count were not completed by the constitutional deadline of March 3. But most Democrats felt that Americans would not support such a radical course after Democrats had agreed to the compromise. To strengthen these moderates, Hayes promised not to help southern Republicans against rival claimants for state offices. As a result Hayes was declared President just within the deadline. When he honored his commitment to the Democrats, the last southern Republican governments collapsed, even though the Republicans had claimed state victories based on the same election returns that elected Hayes. (See COMPROMISE OF 1877.)

The collapse of Reconstruction was related directly to the development of constitutional commitments that would dominate the last quarter of the nineteenth century. It marked a renewal of a state-centered federalism that would characterize succeeding years. Furthermore, it was a direct result of the growing fear of "class legislation" that would lead to the acceptance of "laissez-faire constitutionalism" in the 1890s.

MICHAEL LES BENEDICT

Bibliography

BENEDICT, MICHAEL LES 1975 *A Compromise of Principle: Congressional Republicans and Reconstruction, 1863–1869.* New York: W. W. Norton.
FAIRMAN, CHARLES 1971 *Reconstruction and Reunion, 1864–88—Part One,* Volume 6 of *The History of the Supreme Court of the United States.* New York: Macmillan.
GILLETTE, WILLIAM 1979 *Retreat from Reconstruction, 1869–1879.* Baton Rouge: Louisiana State University Press.
HYMAN, HAROLD M. 1973 *A More Perfect Union: The Impact of the Civil War and Reconstruction upon the Constitution.* New York: Knopf.

McKitrick, Eric L. 1960 *Andrew Johnson and Reconstruction.* Chicago: University of Chicago Press.

Stampp, Kenneth M. 1965 *The Era of Reconstruction, 1865–1877.* New York: Knopf.

CONSTITUTIONAL HISTORY, 1877–1901

American public life during the Civil War-Reconstruction years was dominated by clashes over constitutional issues of the most basic sort: race and CITIZENSHIP; FEDERALISM, STATES' RIGHTS, and the Union; the power of the President, Congress, and the courts; and the bounds of military and civil authority. This was a time when the interpretation of the Constitution held center stage in American public life. The resolution of fundamental issues was sought in Congress and the courts, in party politics and elections, ultimately through force of arms. Merely to list the milestones of the period—the great debate over SLAVERY IN THE TERRITORIES; DRED SCOTT V. SANDFORD (1857); SECESSION and CIVIL WAR; the THIRTEENTH, FOURTEENTH, and FIFTEENTH AMENDMENTS; the CIVIL RIGHTS, Reconstruction, and Enforcement Acts; and the IMPEACHMENT OF ANDREW JOHNSON—is to make the point that during the years from 1850 to 1877 the Constitution provided the context in which Americans expressed, and fought over, their most fundamental social beliefs.

How different was the period that followed! The structure of government—the relationship of the states and territories to the Union; the powers of Congress, the courts, and the President; the role of the POLITICAL PARTIES—often was a matter of political but rarely of constitutional concern. Nor were the major economic and social issues of the time confronted primarily in constitutional terms. It is revealing that no amendment to the Constitution was adopted between 1870 and 1913.

This does not mean, though, that constitutional issues had no place in American public policy between 1877 and 1900. Rather, what happened was that a sea change was taking place in American life, and the issues generated by this change took time to assume a full-fledged constitutional guise. Just as the basic constitutional issues of states' rights and slavery did not fully emerge until the 1850s, so too the constitutional issues generated by the rise of an urban-industrial society did not come into their own until after 1900, in many respects not until the 1930s.

Where should we look, in the late nineteenth century, for the seeds of the great twentieth-century effort to adapt the Constitution to the realities of an urban-industrial society? The primary structural concern of the time was over the role of the judiciary, and here was a foreshadowing of the conflict between the administrative state and the representative state that would assume such great importance after 1900. Second, economic issues—in particular, those involving the regulation of large enterprises—were a fruitful area of contention in the late nineteenth century. And finally, questions of citizenship and race—partly a legacy of the Civil War-Reconstruction years but also a product of the social strains generated by an industrializing society—continued to engage the attention of the public and of policymakers.

Frank Goodnow in his *Comparative Administrative Law* (1893) observed that while constitutional issues set the terms of debate over the character of American government before the Civil War, administrative issues took center stage afterward. Certainly it seemed that, as much as anything could, the war had settled the question of the relationship of the states to the Union. Nor did the desuetude of the post-Reconstruction Presidency, the dominance of Congress, or the still-nascent administrative state generate much in the way of constitutional debate.

Late nineteenth-century Presidents were caught up in party politics and patronage and did relatively little to formulate and conduct public policy. But America's evolution into a powerful industrial nation began to leave its mark. RUTHERFORD B. HAYES and GROVER CLEVELAND used federal troops to restore order during the railroad strikes of 1877 and 1894. The federal bureaucracy, though small, was growing; and something like a professional civil service took form, in part under the aegis of the Civil Service Commission established by the PENDLETON ACT of 1883. Tariff and fiscal policy came to be more closely identified with presidential leadership. But in constitutional terms the chief executive at the end of the century was little changed from what he had been in 1877.

Congress, however, became a considerably more powerful and effective branch of government during this period. WOODROW WILSON in 1885 called "Congressional Government" the "predominant and controlling force, the centre and source of all motive and of all regulative power." This enhanced authority came from the fact that state and local party leaders served as senators and representatives; from congressional control over budgetary and fiscal policy; and from the increasing regularity and stability of congressional leadership and procedure.

Perhaps the most striking change in the balance of governmental powers during the late nineteenth century was the rise of JUDICIAL ACTIVISM. The Supreme Court found only two federal laws unconstitutional between 1790 and 1864, but it voided federal acts in seven cases between 1868 and 1877 and in eleven cases between 1878 and 1899. The Court voided state acts in thirty-eight cases before 1865, in thirty-five cases between 1865 and 1873, and in ninety-one cases between 1874 and 1899. A debate as old as the Constitution heated up once again in the 1890s: what were the proper limits of JUDICIAL REVIEW?

The belief was then widespread—and has been gospel since—that the late nineteenth-century courts declared open season on laws threatening corporate interests. The *American Law Review* observed in 1894 that "it has come to be the fashion . . . for courts to overturn acts of the State legislatures upon mere economical theories and upon mere casuistical grounds." Federal and state courts found in the DUE PROCESS and EQUAL PROTECTION clauses of the Fourteenth Amendment and in the doctrine of FREEDOM OF CONTRACT grounds for voiding laws that regulated working conditions or taxed CORPORATIONS. This judicial conservatism culminated in an unholy trinity of Supreme Court decisions in the mid-1890s: IN RE DEBS (1895), which sustained a federal INJUNCTION against striking railroad workers; UNITED STATES V. E. C. KNIGHT COMPANY (1895), which severely limited the scope of the SHERMAN ANTITRUST ACT; and POLLOCK V. FARMERS' LOAN AND TRUST (1895), which struck down the 1894 federal income tax law. Arnold Paul has called these decisions "related aspects of a massive judicial entry into the socioeconomic scene, . . . a conservative oriented revolution."

But the extent of the courts' antilabor and antiregulatory decision making has been exaggerated; and its purpose has been distorted. A review in 1897 of 1,639 state labor laws enacted during the previous twenty years found that 114 of them—only seven percent—were held unconstitutional. The STATE POLICE POWER to regulate working conditions was widely accepted legal doctrine: in ninety-three percent of 243 Fourteenth Amendment challenges before 1901 the Supreme Court upheld the state laws. By the late 1890s the influential New York and Massachusetts courts looked favorably on laws affecting the conditions of labor, as did the Supreme Court in HOLDEN V. HARDY (1898).

Nor did judicial policy rest only on a tender concern for the rights of property. The desire to foster a national economy was evident in many federal court decisions. And many Justices shared the widespread public sense that American society was being wrenched beyond recognition by industrialism and its consequences. Justice STEPHEN J. FIELD and jurist THOMAS M. COOLEY were as ill at ease with large corporate power as they were with legislative activism. The influential judge and treatise writer JOHN F. DILLON, who called all attempts "to pillage and destroy" private property "as baneful as they are illegal," insisted "with equal earnestness upon the proposition that such property is under many important duties toward the State and society, which the owners generally fail to appreciate."

By far the most important applications of the Constitution to issues of public policy during the late nineteenth century involved large corporate enterprise, that increasingly conspicuous and troubling presence on the American scene. Railroads led the way both in the scale of their corporate organization and in the consequent public, regulatory, and judicial response.

The roads were great beneficiaries of private and state loans before the Civil War. In the years after 1865, they received substantial federal and state land grants, and loans and subsidies from counties and townships. There were 35,000 miles of track in 1865; 93,000 in 1880. But by the mid-1870s railroads were staggering beneath the weight of their expansion. Fierce competition in the East and Midwest forced down rates and earnings. The overcapitalized lines, with high fixed costs, suffered also from the price deflation of the time. Bankruptcies and reorganizations, rate discrimination, and price-fixing pools were among the consequences. All had the effect of feeding popular anti-railroad sentiment.

That great Civil War venture in mixed enterprise, the Union Pacific Railroad, was a prolific breeder of controversy. Political and constitutional difficulties sprang up around the federal government's role in the capitalization and direction of the road. Congressmen bitterly assailed the Union Pacific's inability (or disinclination) to meet its financial obligations to the government. But not until the SINKING FUND CASES (1879) did the Supreme Court sustain the right of Congress to require this and other transcontinental lines to repay their debts. The Credit Mobilier scandal of 1872, in which stock in the construction company that built the Union Pacific was distributed to a number of influential politicians, epitomized the difficulty of fitting a semipublic enterprise into the American system of government. The Pacific Railroad Commission finally concluded: "The sovereign should not be mated with the subject."

Railroad land grants were no less a source of contention. The House unanimously resolved in 1870 that "the policy of granting subsidies in public lands to railroads and other corporations ought to be discontinued." Once again, the very principle of such aid came under attack: "These grants . . . have been made on the theory that government is an organized benevolence, and not merely a compact for the negative function of repelling a public enemy or repressing disorders."

The consequences of state and local railroad aid also were distressing, and were equally productive of doubts as to whether such aid was part of the proper role of government. The Supreme Court heard more than 350 bonding cases between 1870 and 1896. While the courts felt constrained to enforce most of those obligations, they made clear their displeasure with government subsidization. John F. Dillon condemned subsidies as "a coercive contribution in favor of private railway corporations" which violated "the general spirit of the Constitution as to the sacredness of private property." Thomas M. Cooley objected to railroad subsidies on similar grounds, arguing that "a large portion of the most urgent needs of society are relegated exclusively to the law of demand and supply." In LOAN ASSOCIATION V. TOPEKA (1875) the Supreme Court used this argument to block direct government subsidization of private enterprise.

During the years from 1880 to 1900, public, political, and (inevitably) judicial attention shifted from subsidization to regulation of the economy. The prevailing economic thought of the time, the weakness of government supervision, and the power of private interests worked against an effective system of ECONOMIC REGULATION. But inevitably the strains and conflicts attending the rise of an industrial economy produced demands on the state to intervene.

Journalist E. L. Godkin observed in 1873: "The locomotive is coming in contact with the framework of our institution. In this country of simple government, the most powerful centralizing force which civilization has yet produced must, within the next score years, assume its relation to that political machinery which is to control and regulate it." Nor surprisingly the railroads, the biggest of America's national enterprises, were the first to come under federal regulation.

During the 1870s, state railroad policy had moved from subsidy to containment. The 1870 Illinois constitution required the legislature to "pass laws establishing maximum rates of charges for the transportation of passengers and freight." That body in 1871 set maximum freight and grain elevator rates, forbade price discrimination, and created a railroad commission with supervisory and enforcement powers. Similar laws were adopted in Minnesota, Wisconsin, and Iowa.

Because Grange members often were prominent advocates of rate regulation, these acts came to be known as the Granger laws.

The Supreme Court in *Munn v. Illinois* (1877), the first of the GRANGER CASES, upheld the regulatory power of the legislatures and opened up yet another path to regulation by resurrecting the old COMMON LAW doctrine that when private property was AFFECTED WITH A PUBLIC INTEREST it was subject to public accountability and control. But at the same time the Court conceded that "under some circumstances" legislation might be held to violate the Fourteenth Amendment: a portent of the conservative jurisprudence of later years.

Whatever constitutional authority might adhere to state regulation, its effectiveness was severely limited by compliant state railroad commissions, the political and legal influence of the roads, and above all the national character of the enterprise. From the mid-1880s on, federal courts increasingly struck down state railroad tax and rate laws that in their view interfered with the flow of INTERSTATE COMMERCE. The implicit policy decision was that ratemaking should be in the hands of the railroads—and be subject to the review of federal courts, not state courts and legislatures. One observer thought that "long tables of railway statistics, with the accompanying analyses, look strangely out of place in a volume of United States Reports": testimony to the fact that the courts of necessity were taking on a quasi-administrative role.

The scale and complexity of the interests affected by the railroads, the competitive problems of the lines themselves, the limited effectiveness of state regulation, and the growing intervention of the federal courts all fed a movement for national railroad regulation culminating in the INTERSTATE COMMERCE ACT of 1887. That act defined and laid down penalties for rate discrimination, and created an Interstate Commerce Commission (ICC) with the power to investigate and prosecute violators. Its primary purpose was negative: to block pooling and other cartel practices, not to secure a stable railroad rate structure. What the ICC gained thereby in constitutionality it lost in administrative effectiveness. Its early performance showed how difficult it was—given the power of private interests, popular distrust of government, and constitutional limits on the exercise of public power—to establish a bureaucratic mode of regulation. Instead, the ICC adopted what was in fact the only functioning American mode of economic supervision, that of the judiciary. Cooley, the judge and treatise writer who became the ICC's first chairman, announced: "The Commissioners realize that they are a new court,

. . . and that they are to lay the foundations of a new body of American law."

During the first ten years of its existence the ICC handed down rulings on more than 800 rate controversies. But the Commission's impact was limited by the size, complexity, and competitiveness of the railroad business and by its lack of supervisory power. Demands rose in the 1890s for government ownership and operation of the lines, or at least for more rigorous supervision by a national Department of Transportation. But, as Cooley observed, these proposals were beyond the range of the late nineteenth-century American polity: "The perpetuity of free institutions in this country requires that the political machine called the United States Government be kept from being overloaded beyond its strength. The more cumbrous it is the greater is the power of intrigue and corruption under it."

The regulation of large enterprise in general posed the same problems, and produced the same response, as did that of the railroads. Mid-nineteenth-century general incorporation acts, and the competition among states to attract corporation charters, guaranteed that the terms of incorporation would remain easy, the regulation of company affairs loose and permissive. In theory the internal affairs of corporations were the business of the states; in practice, the states exercised little control.

But as in the case of the railroads, the growth of business corporations into national enterprises created a demand for federal regulation. Once again, judicial interpretation fostered the growth of a national economy. State and federal courts strengthened the legal status of foreign (out-of-state) corporations, in effect reversing the severe constraints imposed on them by PAUL V. VIRGINIA (1869). In *Barron v. Burnside* (1887) the Supreme Court for the first time held that state regulation of foreign corporations could be of doubtful constitutionality. By the turn of the century the "liberal theory" of foreign corporations was the prevailing one.

Even more dramatic was the courts' use of the Fourteenth Amendment to protect corporate rights and privileges. During the 1870s, said Howard Jay Graham, "the rule that corporations were *not* to be regarded as constitutional 'PERSONS' theoretically was the LAW OF THE LAND." But this rule was more theory than fact, and during the late nineteenth century the judiciary explicitly brought corporations under the protection afforded to persons by the due process and equal protection clauses of the Amendment.

The rise of large enterprise in the late nineteenth century took forms that roused public concern and ultimately evoked a legislative and judicial response. The urge to override the limitations of state chartering led to the invention of the corporate trust and then the holding company. Although only about ten trusts were created during the 1880s, the word in the generic sense of a "huge, irrepressible, indeterminate" corporation came to be the object of great public concern. By 1890 several states had ANTITRUST laws, and six state supreme courts had held that trust agreements were against public policy or were illegal as monopolies or conspiracies in RESTRAINT OF TRADE. And public pressure grew for a federal antitrust law, as it had for railroad regulation.

The SHERMAN ANTITRUST ACT of 1890, passed overwhelmingly by Congress, relied on the legislature's power under the COMMERCE CLAUSE to outlaw "every contract, combination in the form of trust or otherwise, or conspiracy, in restraint of trade or commerce." The breadth of the law's formulation, and its dependence on the courts rather than on an administrative agency to define its provisions, testified to the still underdeveloped state of federal regulation. But in other ways the statute was sophisticated. By relying on the old common law concept of the illegality of conspiracies in restraint of trade, the drafters minimized the risk of having the law declared unconstitutional. And the Sherman Act was widely understood to be aimed at great combinations, not to fix an unrealistic standard of small-unit competition on the economy.

Even so, enforcement was full of difficulty. The Department of Justice in the 1890s lacked the manpower, the money, and the inclination to prosecute vigorously. The courts, too, severely limited the utility of the act. They held that a firm could come to dominate a sector of the economy without doing anything illegal, and they developed distinctions between reasonable and unreasonable restraint of trade, between legitimate business practices and "illegal commercial piracy." And in its Sugar Trust decision of 1895 (*United States v. E. C. Knight Company*) the Supreme Court dealt the law a heavy blow, holding that the Sherman Act applied only to "commerce" and not to manufacturing, and that the activities of the American Sugar Refining Company lay outside the act's coverage even though that firm controlled over ninety percent of the nation's sugar refining capacity.

The *American Law Review* called this decision "the most deplorable one that has been rendered in favor of incorporated power and greed . . . since the Dartmouth College case." In fact, the Court did take a narrow and mechanical view of interstate commerce. On that premise, its decision reflected a long-held distinction between state regulation of manufacturing and federal responsibility for interstate commerce. When private parties brought suit against trade and price cartels (particularly by those prime instances of enterprises in interstate commerce, the railroads), the Supreme Court was not reluctant to find that they violated the Sherman Act.

By the turn of the century it was apparent that the problem of corporate regulation was "rapidly assuming phases which seem beyond the scope of courts of justice." The rise of corporate capitalism, and the question of what to do about it, called as much for political-administrative will and wisdom as for legal-constitutional power and propriety.

The primary legal and, ultimately, constitutional justification for late nineteenth-century state regulation was the police power: the obligation of the states to protect the health, morals, safety, and welfare of their citizens. Many thought that the potential of that power was great indeed. The president of the American Bar Association estimated in 1897 that more than ninety percent of state legislation rested on the police power. CHRISTOPHER TIEDEMAN's *Limitations of the Police Power in the United States* (1886) was an elaborate attempt to find constitutional grounds for containing what he took to be a widely applied principle of government intervention. OLIVER WENDELL HOLMES caustically said of the police power: "We suppose the phrase was invented to cover certain acts of the legislature which are seen to be unconstitutional, but which are believed to be necessary."

The police power had its greatest appeal when public health and morals appeared to be at stake. A case in point was regulation of the liquor business. The Supreme Court upheld the right of the states to forbid the manufacture and sale of alcohol, and refused to accept the due process clause of the Fourteenth Amendment as a defense against state liquor legislation. (See INALIENABLE POLICE POWER.) Still more dramatic was judicial acceptance of extensive regulation—indeed, the near-crippling—of the oleomargarine industry. By 1886, twenty-two states either heavily taxed that product or required unattractive packaging or labeling. An 1886 federal law—"protection run mad," said an outraged critic—required that the product be called "oleo" (rather than "butterine" or other enticing names), and subjected it to a high license and manufacturing tax. The Supreme Court in *Powell v. Pennsylvania* (1888) upheld a similar Pennsylvania statute on the basis of the state's police power to protect public health.

The insufficiency of the state police power as a basis of state economic regulation became more and more apparent as the century neared its end. Corporate interests effectively espoused a laissez-faire, SUBSTANTIVE DUE PROCESS constitutionalism. More fundamentally, courts recognized the growing imbalance between state supervision and an economy that was becoming national in scope.

By 1899 the Supreme Court had held twenty-nine state laws unconstitutional because they conflicted with the commerce clause of the Constitution. In LEISY V. HARDIN (1890) the Court voided an Iowa law blocking the entry of liquor into the state, holding that the movement of an original package was protected by the national commerce power, so long as Congress had not authorized the state regulation. Responding to this invitation, Congress quickly passed the Wilson Act, which made liquor subject to state law regardless of where it was packaged. The Court validated the law on the grounds that "the common interest did not require entire freedom in the traffic in ardent spirits." But without similar congressional authorization, it continued to apply the original package doctrine against state laws restricting the entry of oleomargarine and cigarettes. And in CHAMPION V. AMES (1903) the Court upheld a statute forbidding the interstate transportation of lottery tickets, thus opening the prospect of NATIONAL POLICE POWER.

The constraints that limited the application of government authority to economic problems were at least as evident in the realm of social policy. During the period of the Civil War and Reconstruction, citizenship and race had been issues of prime importance not only in constitutional law but in politics and legislation as well. In the twentieth century these and other social concerns—education, crime, poverty, social mores, CIVIL LIBERTIES—would draw comparable attention from the public, Congress, and the courts. But such was not the case during the years between 1871 and 1900. With American society in transit from its small-unit agrarian past to its large-unit urban, industrial future, the political or constitutional standing of individual or social rights was largely ignored.

These years saw relatively little redefinition—in either constitutional law or legislative action—of the status of women, Orientals, blacks, or AMERICAN INDIANS. Legal barriers to female equality occasionally fell, but by legislation, not constitutional adjudication. Opposition to women's suffrage remained strong. Between 1870 and 1910 suffrage advocates conducted 480 campaigns in thirty-three states to get the issue on the ballot. Seventeen state REFERENDA (all but three west of the Mississippi) were held; only two were successful, in Colorado in 1893 and in Idaho in 1896.

The position of Orientals and blacks in society worsened. Organized labor agitated for the exclusion of Chinese immigrants, and anti-Chinese riots in the West testified to the intensity of public feeling. An 1882 federal law banned Chinese immigration for ten years. Supplementary acts in 1884 and 1888 tightened the exclusion law and imposed restrictions on Chinese already in the country. The Supreme Court in 1887 refused to apply the Civil Rights and Enforcement Acts of the Reconstruction period to Chinese, and in 1889 the Court upheld the restriction of Chinese immigration.

In 1892 Congress overwhelmingly renewed Chinese exclusion for another decade; it also required the registration of every resident Chinese laborer, with affidavits by one or more whites that the registrant had entered the country legally. The Supreme Court upheld this law in 1893. These policies had palpable consequences. About 100,000 lawful Chinese immigrants were in the United States in 1880; there were about 85,000 in 1900. In 1902 Chinese immigration was suspended indefinitely.

An even more pervasive white public opinion supported—or at least remained unconcerned about—discrimination against blacks. Late nineteenth-century northern courts generally upheld state laws that forbade discrimination in theaters, restaurants, and other public places, as a proper exercise of the police power. (The degree to which those laws were enforced is another matter.) But on similar grounds the courts accepted the growing number of SEGREGATION statutes. State laws separating the races in public transportation and accommodation, forbidding racial intermarriage, limiting access to the vote, and segregating schools met with no judicial obstacle.

In this sense the Supreme Court's acceptance of a Louisiana railroad segregation law in PLESSY V. FERGUSON (1896) represented the approval of an already widely established public policy, not the promulgation of new constitutional doctrine. When in 1903 the Court refused to agree that the Fifteenth Amendment might be used against Alabama officials who kept blacks from voting, Holmes suggested that relief "from a great political wrong" must come from "the legislative and political department of the government of the United States." At the same time the Court's invention of the STATE ACTION limitation on congressional power encouraged Congress to refrain from remedying private RACIAL DISCRIMINATION. (See CIVIL RIGHTS CASES, 1883.)

On the face of things, Indian public policy in the late nineteenth century had a different goal: it sought not to foster but to reduce separatism. Indian Commissioner Thomas J. Morgan declared in 1891: "The end

at which we aim is that the American Indians shall become as speedily as possible Indian-Americans; that the savage shall become a citizen." But majority sentiment still regarded even nontribal Indians as inferior, and the Supreme Court went along. In *Elk v. Wilkins* (1884)—coterminous with the CIVIL RIGHTS CASES that invalidated the CIVIL RIGHTS ACT OF 1875—the Court held that Indians were not citizens within the understanding of the Fourteenth Amendment.

At the end of the century the acquisition of noncontiguous territory with substantial populations (Hawaii, the Philippines, Puerto Rico) raised old problems of statehood and citizenship in new forms. The Supreme Court in the INSULAR CASES (1901) limited the degree to which the Constitution applied to these peoples, much as the Court had been inclined to do with regard to Orientals, blacks, and Indians.

In most of the areas of social policy—education, crime, FIRST AMENDMENT freedoms—that in the twentieth century became important battlegrounds of public policy and constitutional law, there was little or no late nineteenth-century constitutional controversy. Only two such issues—prohibition and religion—raised substantial questions of constitutionality. New Hampshire Senator Henry W. Blair first proposed a national prohibition amendment to the Constitution in 1876, and a proposal to this effect was before Congress continuously until its adoption in 1918. State and local restrictions on the distribution and sale of liquor increased, and in general the courts sustained them against Fourteenth Amendment attacks, as proper applications of the police power.

The place of RELIGION IN THE PUBLIC SCHOOLS led to much political and legal conflict. State courts frequently dealt with the thorny issue of school Bible reading. Most states allowed this practice without exegesis, and the courts approved so long as attendance or participation was voluntary. The Iowa Supreme Court upheld a law that forbade the exclusion of Bible reading from the schools. But the Wisconsin court denied the constitutionality of such reading: "The connection of church and state corrupts religion, and makes the state despotic."

Protestant–Roman Catholic hostility underlay much of the conflict over school Bible reading, as it did the issue of state aid to parochial schools. Maine Republican James G. Blaine sought a constitutional amendment forbidding aid in the 1870s (see BLAINE AMENDMENT), and by 1900 twenty-three states had banned public grants to parochial schools. But the interrelationship of religion and education did not come before the Supreme Court until well into the twentieth century.

FELIX FRANKFURTER once told of a distinguished professor of property law who was called on to teach a course in constitutional law. Dutifully he did so. But he soon abandoned the effort, on the ground that the subject was "not law at all but politics." At no time in American history did this pronouncement seem more justified than in the period from 1877 to 1901. Except for the regulation of large enterprise, Americans debated the problems of a developing industrial society more in political than in constitutional terms. After 1900 the fit—or lack of fit—between those problems and the American constitutional system would be faced more directly.

MORTON KELLER

Bibliography

BETH, LOREN P.   1971   *The Development of the American Constitution 1877–1917.* New York: Harper & Row.

GRAHAM, HOWARD J.   1968   *Everyman's Constitution: Historical Essays on the Fourteenth Amendment, The 'Conspiracy Theory,' and American Constitutionalism.* Chaps. 10–13. Madison, Wisc.: State Historical Society.

KELLER, MORTON   1977   *Affairs of State: Public Life in Late Nineteenth Century America.* Cambridge, Mass.: Harvard University Press.

PAUL, ARNOLD M.   1960   *Conservative Crisis and the Rule of Law.* Ithaca, N.Y.: Cornell University Press.

SKOWRONEK, STEPHEN   1982   *Building a New American State: The Expansion of National Administrative Capacities 1877–1920.* Cambridge: At the University Press.

CONSTITUTIONAL HISTORY, 1901–1921

American public life profoundly changed during the early twentieth century. The policy agenda during the Progressive era stands in dramatic contrast, both quantitatively and qualitatively, to its nineteenth-century predecessors. A substantial body of state and national legislation sought to subject large corporations and public utilities to far greater regulation than had been the case before. A comparable surge of enactments dealt with social issues ranging from the hours and working conditions of women and children to housing, the quality of food and drugs, the conservation of land, and the control of drinking and prostitution.

More than at any time since the Civil War and Reconstruction, Americans paid substantial attention to the structure of their government. The pace of lawmaking that dealt with politics and government quickened, stimulated by the dual motives (not always complementary) of expanding popular democracy and of bringing greater honesty and efficiency to the workings of the American state. A burst of innovation led to the creation of direct PRIMARY ELECTIONS, the INITIATIVE and REFERENDUM, and new registration and voting laws, as well as to the direct election of senators and to women's suffrage. A flood of discussion and a lesser flow of administrative, judicial, and legislative action sought to increase the effectiveness of the executive branch and the BUREAUCRACY, to improve the workings of Congress and the functioning of the courts, and to modernize the relationship between federal and state authorities and the governance of the nation's cities.

American involvement in World War I was the capstone to the Progressive era. Federal involvement in the American economy and society reached new heights; and in both technique and spirit wartime governance drew heavily on the immediate prewar experience.

THEODORE ROOSEVELT, WILLIAM HOWARD TAFT, and WOODROW WILSON were far more activist than their predecessors both in leadership styles and in domestic and foreign policy. But perhaps the most dramatic result of the quickened pace of government and the new policy agenda was the adoption between 1913 and 1920 of four constitutional amendments, providing for a federal income tax, the direct election of senators, PROHIBITION, and women's suffrage. Only at the beginning of the Republic and during the Reconstruction era had constitutional revision occurred on so large a scale.

Insofar as there was a common denominator to the public policy of the Progressive era, it lay in the belief that the time had come to deal with some of the more chaotic and unjust aspects of a mature industrial society; to bring public policy (and the nation's political and governing institutions) into closer accord with new social and economic realities. This impulse cannot be simply explained away by the once fashionable label of "reform," or the now fashionable label of "social control." A quest for social justice coexisted in complex ways with a search for order. Some Progressives wanted society (and the polity) to be more efficient: more honest and economical, less wasteful and corrupt. Others sought policies that would make society safer: more secure from the threats of big business and corrupt political machines, or from the vagaries of competition and the business cycle, or from radicals, immigrants, or blacks. Still others wanted society to be fairer: more humane and less inequitable.

This was not solely an American development.

H. G. Wells observed in 1906 that "the essential question for America, as for Europe, is the rescue of her land, her public service, and the whole of her great economic process from the anarchic and irresponsible control of private owners . . . and the organization of her social life upon the broad, clear, humane conceptions of modern science."

Could it be said that a substantially changed constitutional order was one consequence of American Progressivism? Did the complex structure of ECONOMIC REGULATION embodied in the Interstate Commerce Commission, enforcement of the SHERMAN ACT, the Federal Trade Commission, railroad regulation, and a host of other economic measures fundamentally alter the relationship of the state to the economy? Did the interventionism embodied in the growing body of social legislation, accumulating restrictions on IMMIGRATION, the CIVIL LIBERTIES onslaught of the war years, and the passage of national prohibition fundamentally alter the relationship of government to American society and the individual rights of its citizens? Did the sequence of interventionist foreign policy actions, delimited at one end by the acquisition of overseas colonies after the Spanish-American War of 1898, and at the other by American intervention in World War I, fundamentally alter the place of FOREIGN AFFAIRS in the American political order?

In sum, did the early twentieth-century outburst of legislation, executive leadership, new agencies, and new government functions lead to what has been called "a qualitatively different kind of state"? Did a corporate-bureaucratic system of government supplant the nineteenth-century American "state of courts and parties"? JOHN W. BURGESS held in 1923 that the past generation had seen the transformation of American constitutional law from a stress on the protection of individual liberty to the imposition of "autocratic" governmental power over property, persons, and thought.

The distinctive American style of government that took form during the first century of the nation's history rested on the balance and SEPARATION OF POWERS among the executive, legislative, and judicial branches; on a FEDERALISM that rendered (through the POLICE POWER) to the states the things that were social; and on a conception of individual rights that, for all its abuses and distortions (the sacrifice of southern blacks to the not-so-tender mercies of southern whites; the use of the DUE PROCESS clause of the FOURTEENTH AMENDMENT to spare CORPORATIONS the indignity of state regulation and taxation), arguably gave nineteenth-century Americans more individual freedom from the interposition of the state than any other people in the world. To what degree was that constitutional order changed between 1901 and 1921?

Of course there can be no definitive answer: the glass of change inevitably will remain partially filled for some, partially empty for others. But an obscure chapter in the constitutional history of the United States may come into clearer focus if we abandon the traditional historiographical emphasis on Progressive "reform" in favor of an examination of the major instrumentalities of government: Congress, the presidency, the bureaucracy, and the mechanisms governing federal–state relations.

Congress was the branch of government that underwent the most overt and formal alteration during the early twentieth century. Two major changes, the popular election of senators through the passage of the SEVENTEENTH AMENDMENT, and the reduction of the powers of the speaker of the House of Representatives, came about in these years. These changes were products of the widespread view that Congress, like the parties, was under the control of corrupt, machine-bound politicos and sinister business interests.

Six times between 1893 and 1911 the House approved a direct election amendment. Finally, spurred by an arrangement whereby progressive Republicans agreed to drop the cause of black voting in the South in return for southern Democratic support, the Senate accepted the change. The Southerners assured that control of the time, place, and manner of holding senatorial elections would remain the province of each state.

A 1911 law sought also to assure that congressional districts would be compact, contiguous, and of roughly equal populations. But enforcement was so difficult, and the courts were so loath to intervene, that it had little effect. And although the direct election of senators gradually reversed the tendency (at least until recent times) for the Senate to become a "millionaires's club," it cannot be said that that body's role in the governmental process was substantially different in the 1920s from what it had been before 1900.

The controversy over the House speaker's authority was more intense. Joseph G. Cannon, the speaker from 1901 to 1911, appointed and was himself one of the five-member Committee on Rules, thus controlling assignments to the key committees of the House, which he populated with like-thinking conservatives. His power to expedite the work of an unwieldy legislature had been a late-nineteenth-century reform, designed to keep a boss-ridden legislature from working its will. Now it appeared to a majority of congressmen as an obstacle to the more programmatic demands of Progressive government. In 1910–1911 a coalition of Democrats and insurgent Republicans deprived Cannon of his power to serve on and appoint the Rules Committee, to choose standing committees, and to recognize members on the floor.

The seniority system came into general use as a more equitable means of choosing committee chairmen—a "reform" of the sort that Finley Peter Dunne's Mr. Dooley presumably had in mind when he commented on the Progressive predilection for structural change: "I wisht I was a German, and believed in machinery." But by the 1920s the House was as much under the control of the majority party leadership as it had ever been. During most of the decade, the Republican speaker, rules committee chairman, and floor leader ran the GOP Steering Committee and, hence, Congress. Surely Cannon would have nodded approval of floor leader John G. Tilson's estimate of his role in the 69th Congress (1929): "It will probably be said with truth that the most important work I have done during the session has been in the direction of preventing the passage of bad or unnecessary laws."

Much of the constitutional controversy of the early twentieth century focused on the character of the presidency—and of the Presidents. The Spanish-American War and the governance of territories afterward gave WILLIAM MCKINLEY's administration some of the attributes of the modern presidency, and led to concern over "The Growing Power of the President." But it was the chief executives of the Progressive years who gave a dramatically new shape to the office.

Theodore Roosevelt's executive vigor, his flamboyant efforts to turn the presidency into a "bully pulpit," his concern with issues such as the relations between capital and labor, the trusts, and conservation, and his assertiveness in foreign policy gave his presidency a cast of radicalism. Critics often spoke of him—more so than of any president since ABRAHAM LINCOLN—as having stretched the Constitution to its limits and beyond. Roosevelt himself thought that the power of the presidency enabled him "to do anything that the needs of the nation demanded. . . . Under this interpretation of executive power, I did and caused to be done many things not previously done. . . . I did not usurp power, but I did greatly broaden the use of executive power." But Roosevelt's innate conservatism, the traditionalist goals that informed most of his actions, and his political skill meant that few of his initiatives ran into constitutional difficulties. The

most serious congressional objections on constitutional grounds came in the debate over the HEPBURN ACT expanding the power of the Interstate Commerce Commission (ICC); and Roosevelt adroitly compromised by leaving untouched the courts' power to review the ICC's decisions.

A contemporary said that the difference between Roosevelt and his successor, William Howard Taft, was that when a desirable course of action was proposed to Roosevelt he asked if the law forbade it; if not, then it should be done. Taft, on the other hand, tended to ask if the law allowed it; if not, then Congress must be asked. Taft brought a judicial temperament and experience (and almost no elective experience) to his office. He was thus a more self-conscious advocate of a limited presidency, and celebrator of the supremacy of law and of constitutional limitations, than any of his Republican predecessors.

Yet these views did not prevent his administration from adopting a more vigorous antitrust policy than that of Roosevelt. And Taft advocated innovations such as the establishment of a COMMERCE COURT to review ICC decisions and the institution of a federal BUDGET drawn up by the executive branch. The realities of early-twentieth-century American public life weighed more heavily than the niceties of constitutional theory.

Woodrow Wilson as a scholar of American government had long been critical of the traditional relationship between President and Congress. He often praised the British system of ministerial responsibility; his ideal President resembled the British Prime Minister. But as chief executive Wilson more closely followed Roosevelt's conception of the presidency as a bully pulpit (though perhaps with less bullying and more pulpit-pounding). And even more than Roosevelt he took the lead in formulating and seeing to the passage of legislation, a course symbolized by his breaking a tradition that dated from the time of THOMAS JEFFERSON by personally proposing legislation in a message to Congress.

The scope and coherence of Wilson's legislation was far greater than that of his predecessors. But it is worth noting that of the numerous major bills passed in his administration, including the FEDERAL RESERVE ACT, the FEDERAL TRADE COMMISSION ACT, the CLAYTON ANTITRUST ACT, the WEBB-KENYON ACT, the ESPIONAGE ACT, and the SEDITION ACT, only the KEATING-OWEN CHILD LABOR ACT was struck down by the Supreme Court.

With the entry of the United States into World War I, Wilson assumed presidential leadership of a sort that had not been seen since the time of Lincoln and the Civil War. The mobilization of American agriculture, industry, military manpower, and public opinion led to federal intervention into private activity on a massive scale. The creation of agencies such as the War Industries Board, the Food, Fuel, and Railroad Administrations, the War Finance Corporation, the National War Labor Board, and the Committee on Public Information, and statutes such as the SELECTIVE SERVICE ACT, the ESPIONAGE ACT, the Webb-Pomerene Act (which allowed exporters to organize cartels), and the Overman Act (which greatly expanded the President's power over federal bureaus and agencies) amounted to an unprecedented increase of federal power and its concentration under the President.

Did these circumstances in fact add up to a basic change in the constitutional character of the presidency? Certainly the administrations of WARREN G. HARDING and CALVIN COOLIDGE did not suggest so: they would have been comfortable with the most ardent (and least efficacious) practitioners of the limited presidency of the nineteenth century. Nor did HERBERT HOOVER, whose ambitions resembled those of his Progressive predecessors, exercise effective executive leadership on a bold new scale. And when FRANKLIN D. ROOSEVELT came into office in the trough of the Depression in 1933, he found it necessary to rest his call for a "temporary departure from [the] normal balance" of "executive and legislative authority" on the need for a "broad executive power to wage a war against the emergency as great as the power that would be given me if we were in fact invaded by a foreign foe."

For all the pressures of early-twentieth-century social, economic, and cultural change, the executive branch's constitutional position altered little if at all. After 1921, as before 1900, the powers of the presidency depended not upon alterations in Article II of the Constitution, or upon what the Supreme Court made of that article, but on the political skills of the incumbent and on the course of events: war and peace, prosperity and depression, the growth and alteration of government itself.

The argument that the character of American government underwent major change during the early twentieth century rests on the rise of an administrative state. Certainly one distinguishing characteristic of this period was the proliferation of administrative courts, boards, and commissions, with an attendant expansion of the powers, rules, and regulations of the public administration sector of the American state.

The ideal of expert administrators functioning through (or above) restraints such as party politics,

federalism, or the balance of powers had a strong appeal to the Progressive generation. Abbot Lawrence Lowell warned: "If democracy is to be conducted with the efficiency needed in a complex modern society it must overcome its prejudice against permanent expert officials as undemocratic."

The courts had performed a number of essentially administrative and regulatory duties during the nineteenth century. Now, as economic and social problems became more complex and technical, so grew routinized and prescribed administrative processes, in which rule replaced discretion in public law. State laws and constitutions became ever more detailed and codelike; state regulatory agencies multiplied and gained substantially in independence. Federal laws increasingly left to administrative officers the "power to make supplementary law through rules and regulations."

The American involvement in World War I led to an exponential growth of administrative agencies and their power. The War Industries Board and its allied commissions had control over the American economy of a sort only dreamed of in Theodore Roosevelt's New Nationalism. Under the wartime ESPIONAGE ACT, the Post Office Department, the Department of Justice, and the Committee on Public Information wielded powers of suppression and persuasion over American thought and opinion that had no analogue in the nation's past.

Just where administrative law and its accompanying instrumentalities stood in the constitutional system was a matter of continuing concern. Woodrow Wilson observed in his pioneering 1887 essay "The Study of Administration" that "the field of administration is a field of business. It is removed from the hurry and strife of politics; it at most points stands apart even from the debatable ground of constitutional study." But administration was political in its relationship to law, to policy, and to interest group pressures; and it had an intimate relationship to—indeed, was very much a part of—the constitutional system of American government. In many ways the history of American public administration between 1900 and 1921 was a painful instruction in those home truths.

Administrative law of a sort had been part of the American constitutional system since the nineteenth century. Pensions, customs, internal revenue, land grants, and patents were administered by governmental agencies subject to little or no JUDICIAL REVIEW. There was continuing resistance to the idea that public administration had a distinct place in the constitutional order. Bruce Wyman, in one of the earliest systematic discussions of administrative law, set the subject in the context of Anglo-American COMMON LAW rather than constitutional law, holding that the central issue was whether public administration was subject to the same rules of law as governed the relations of citizens with one another.

Adolph Berle took another tack, arguing that administrative law was in fact the application of the will of the state by all three branches, for modern conditions made the traditional differentiation of functions impossible. Administrative law's constitutionality, he implied, rested on the proposition that all of the branches of government were essentially instruments for the expression of the popular will. Thus administrative law was "not a supplement to constitutional law. It is a redivision of the various bodies of law which previously had been grouped under the head of constitutional law."

The courts created evasive categories—"quasi-legislative," "quasi-judicial"—which enabled them to accept administrative powers without addressing the question of whether or not these threatened the separation of powers. By 1914 it appeared that "the exercise of certain discretionary power by administrative officers formally considered legislative is now held unobjectionable."

The growth of the federal bureaucracy, its increasing adherence to its own norms and standards, the fact that it was more and more under the civil service rather than political patronage—all of this has been taken to herald the arrival on the American scene of an autonomous administrative state. But the continuing subservience of government and public policy to the dictates of party politics, the competing governmental units of Congress and the courts, and underlying it all the persisting individualism, hostility to the state, and diversity of American life and thought, meant that the administrative expansion of the early twentieth century did not go on unchecked.

During the war, and immediately after, a number of intellectuals put forward schemes of postwar domestic economic and social reconstruction; they thought that the wartime infrastructure of governmental control and direction might be turned to more basic postwar problems. It soon became apparent, however, that both ideology and politics were working in another direction. Wilson himself told Congress in December 1918: "Our people . . . do not want to be coached and led. . . . [f]rom no quarter have I seen any general scheme of 'reconstruction' which . . . we could force our spirited businessmen and self conscious laborers to accept with due pliancy and obedience."

Similar forces worked to constrain the outward reach of postwar foreign policy embodied in the League of Nations. Both courts and legislatures after the mid-1920s began to turn from the radical-bashing of the Espionage Acts and the 1919–1920 Red Scare to begin the erection of the broad definition of FIRST AMENDMENT freedoms that would come to prevail in the modern American definition of civil liberties. A 1918 survey of American ADMINISTRATIVE LAW (probably by the young HAROLD LASKI, surely no enemy of the active state) warned that "with the great increase of state activity . . . there never was a time" when the value of the BILL OF RIGHTS "will have been so manifest."

As in so many other areas of American government, surface changes did not necessarily alter underlying continuities. Congressmen and party leaders may no longer have had the patronage power that once had been theirs. Yet Congress as an institution, and congressmen as party politicians, remained intensely sensitive to the political implications of administrative appointments, activities, and, perhaps most of all, budgets.

Attempts by the Presidents of the time to extend the control of the executive branch over the bureaucracy frequently ran afoul of congressional opposition. By 1921 it was an arguable point—as, indeed, it always had been—whether the bureaucracy was more subject to the direction of the President or to the will of Congress. One thing was certain: the autonomy of the bureaucracy—from Congress, from the parties, from politics—was not markedly greater than it had been a generation before.

True, administrative law as a field of theoretical concern and practical application would continue to develop. The New Deal did not spring fully armed from the brow of Franklin Roosevelt, but was built on a solid foundation of national and state precedents. From an international (and a later American) perspective, the New Deal's experiments did not seem especially bold and revolutionary. But the scale and passion of the charges of a broached constitutionalism raised by the New Deal's opponents in the 1930s suggests just how limited was the pre-1933 acceptance of an American administrative state.

One more aspect of the evolution (or non-evolution) of the American Constitution during the early twentieth century demands attention. That is the hoary principle of federalism: the distribution of functions between the state and federal governments.

In theory the Civil War and the postwar amendments had settled the nagging early-nineteenth-century question as to the degree to which the states were independent governmental entities. Relatively little attention was paid to the question of federalism during the late nineteenth century, in large part because the issues that most engaged the national government—tariff and currency policy, foreign relations, Indian affairs—were of marginal concern to the states. But as the full force of industrialism and urbanism began to change public policy in the early twentieth century, the relative roles of the federal and state governments once again became a matter of constitutional importance. The police power over health, safety, morals, and (from the late nineteenth century on) welfare, was the major legal basis for state social and economic legislation. For the most part the court accepted this; as ZECHARIAH CHAFEE, JR., observed in 1920, "The health, comfort, and general welfare of the citizens are in charge of the state governments, not of the United States."

But of the 194 Supreme Court decisions that invalidated state laws between 1899 and 1921, 102 were explained on the ground that the laws violated the distribution of powers embodied in the principle of federalism. By the 1920s and the early 1930s there was much talk of a judicial DUAL FEDERALISM that had created a "twilight zone" in which neither state nor federal power applied. And the attempt of the New Deal to create a new level of national intervention in the realms of economic regulation and social welfare led to one of the great constitutional controversies in American history. Once again, it would appear that the policy changes of the 1900–1921 period were not accompanied by a significant alteration of the constitutional order.

MORTON KELLER

Bibliography

BERLE, A. A., JR. 1916–1917 The Expansion of American Administrative Law. *Harvard Law Review* 30:430–448.
BETH, LOREN 1971 *The Development of the American Constitution 1877–1917.* New York: Harper & Row.
BLUM, JOHN M. 1954 *The Republican Roosevelt.* Cambridge, Mass.: Harvard University Press.
BURGESS, JOHN W. 1923 *Recent Changes in American Constitutional Theory.* New York: Columbia University Press.
HASBROUCH, PAUL D. 1927 *Party Government in the House of Representatives.* New York.
LOWELL, A. LAWRENCE 1913 Expert Administrators in Popular Government. *American Political Science Review* 7:45–62.
NOTE 1915 Delegation of Legislative Power to Administrative Officials. *Harvard Law Review* 28:95–97.
NOTE 1918 The Growth of Administrative Law in America. *Harvard Law Review* 31:644–646.
SKOWRONEK, STEPHEN 1982 *Building a New American State: The Expansion of National Administrative Capacities, 1877–1920.* Cambridge: At the University Press.
WYMAN, BRUCE 1903 *The Principles of Administrative Law Governing the Relations of Public Officers.* St. Paul, Minn.: Keefe-Davidson Co.

CONSTITUTIONAL HISTORY, 1921–1933

If reverence for the federal Constitution had diminished in the Progressive era, it was revitalized in the 1920s, as the Constitution again became a symbol of national unity and patriotism. Organizations such as the American Bar Association and the National Security League launched national campaigns of patriotism, circulating leaflets and pamphlets by the hundreds of thousands, encouraging Constitution worship, promoting an annual Constitution Day, and working for state laws to require Constitution instruction in the public schools. Forty-three states passed laws mandating the study of the the Constitution; often such laws required loyalty oaths for teachers. Such laws were intended to affirm one hundred percent Americanism from every public school instructor.

The Constitution which was so apotheosized, however, was one geared primarily to the service of property interests. This meant, on the one hand, the protection of business from government regulation and from assault by radical and liberal critics; and, on the other, active intervention of courts and the executive branch to see that constitutional ways were found to insure that the free use of one's property be protected by positive government policies, both formal and informal. Thus, while constitutional changes did occur during the decade and new emphases were developed, these modulations were contained within the dominant ideological construct of free enterprise and individual property rights—rights, it was argued, that had been secured for all time by the sacred document and its amendments.

The most influential constitutionalist of the 1920s was Chief Justice WILLIAM HOWARD TAFT. Taft set the tone for national political leadership. He was fully committed to the protection of a social order explained and justified by the tenets of JOHN LOCKE, Adam Smith, the Manchester Economists, WILLIAM BLACKSTONE, THOMAS COOLEY, and Herbert Spencer. Espousing a social ethic that stressed self-reliance, individual initiative and responsibility, and the survival of the fittest, Taft emphasized the virtually uninhibited privilege of private property and rationalized the growth of corporate collectivism in terms of individual liberty and private enterprise. For Taft it was time to move away from Progressive expansivism and restore the country to its traditional constitutional bases through a legal system that rested primarily upon judicial defense of a static Constitution and an immutable natural law.

In specific constitutional terms, these goals required restrictive, although selectively restrictive, interpretations of the federal government's taxing and commerce power; an emphasis upon the TENTH AMENDMENT as an instrument for precluding federal intrusion into the reserved powers of the states; and a limitation on the states themselves, through an interpretation of the FOURTEENTH AMENDMENT that emphasized SUBSTANTIVE DUE PROCESS and FREEDOM OF CONTRACT. These constitutional constructs would protect property against restrictive state laws but leave the states free through their police power to legislate against private activities that might threaten that property.

Operating from these assumptions, the Supreme Court majority in this period was activist in its hostility to legislative enactments that threatened or constrained the rights or privileges of the "haves" of society. Thus, between 1921 and 1933, that body ruled unconstitutional fourteen acts of Congress, 148 state laws placing governmental restraints on one or another form of business activity, and twelve city ordinances. Conversely, its majority had no trouble sustaining federal measures that aided business and sanctioning numerous state laws and city ordinances that abridged the CIVIL LIBERTIES of labor, radicals, too outspoken pacifists, and other critics of the capitalist system. In 1925, Taft took the further step of lobbying through Congress a new JUDICIARY ACT, granting the Supreme Court almost unlimited discretion to decide for itself what cases it would hear. (See CERTIORARI, WRIT OF.) Henceforth the Court could choose to take no more cases than it could handle expediently and could restrict adjudication to matters of more general interest. The result was an upgrading of the importance of the cases that the body did agree to hear and a commensurate enhancement of the Court's own prestige and power. Such a looming judicial presence dampened the enthusiasm of activist legislators, state and national, for pushing social reform legislation and made progressive members of REGULATORY COMMISSIONS cautious about exercising their frequently lim-

ited authority. Hence bodies such as the Interstate Commerce Commission and the Federal Trade Commission remained largely passive during the period, except when their business-oriented majorities sought to act solicitiously toward those being regulated.

The three presidential administrations of the period, while sharing a common constitutional philosophy, differed in concrete legislative and policy accomplishments. WARREN G. HARDING had begun his presidency with an ambitious legislative docket. His proposals included a National BUDGET AND ACCOUNTING ACT (previously vetoed by WOODROW WILSON), a new farm credit law, the creation of a system of national highways, the enactment of a Maternity Bill, the immediate development and effective regulation of aviation and radio, the passing of an antilynching law, and the creation of a Department of Public Welfare. A surprised Congress was confused over priorities and wound up passing little legislation. The PACKERS AND STOCKYARDS ACT of 1921 made it unlawful for packers to manipulate prices, create monopolies, and award favors to any person or locality. The regulation of stockyards provided for nondiscriminatory services, reasonable rates, open schedules, and fair charges. The measure, which was constitutionally based on a broad interpretation of the COMMERCE CLAUSE, gave the secretary of agriculture authority to entertain complaints, hold hearings, and issue CEASE AND DESIST ORDERS. The bill was a significant part of the agrarian legislation of the early 1920s, and its validation by the Supreme Court in STAFFORD V. WALLACE (1922) provided a constitutional basis for later New Deal legislation. The 1921 Congress also passed the FESS-KENYON ACT, appropriating money for disabled veteran rehabilitation, and the SHEPPARD-TOWNER MATERNITY ACT, subsidizing state infant and maternity welfare activities. Aside from the bill setting up a Budget Bureau in the Treasury Department with a director appointed by the President, little else was forthcoming. By the end of 1921 the *New York Times* observed: "It is evident, and it is clearly admitted in Washington, that the public is not counting any longer upon sound and constructive legislation from Congress." Indeed, Congress supported only occasional further legislation through the decade. One effect of such congressional inaction, along with the increasingly desultory Harding leadership and the even more quiescent CALVIN COOLIDGE presidency, was to direct the attention of reformers to the AMENDING PROCESS.

The immediate post-World War I years had seen the ratification of the EIGHTEENTH AMENDMENT (prohibition) and the NINETEENTH AMENDMENT (woman suffrage). In the 1920s certain fallout from both occurred. Prohibition was unpopular from the start. In fact, noncompliance became such a problem that by the late 1920s President HERBERT HOOVER appointed a special commission, headed by former Attorney General GEORGE WICKERSHAM to "investigate problems of the enforcement of prohibition under the 18th Amendment." As the report of the commission stated, "the public was irritated at a constitutional 'don't' in a matter where the people saw no moral question." More specifically, the commission pointed to enforcement problems, emphasizing the lack of an American tradition of concerned action between independent government instrumentalities. This, it felt, was now being painfully demonstrated by the Eighteenth Amendment's policy of state enforcement of federal laws, with responsibility too often falling between the two stools and enforcement occurring not at all. Not surprisingly, during the twelve years that the Eighteenth Amendment was in force, more than 130 amendments affecting the Eighteenth in some manner were introduced. Most of these amendments provided for outright repeal; others weakened the amendment in varying degrees. When FRANKLIN D. ROOSEVELT opposed prohibition in 1932, he attracted wide support. The TWENTY-FIRST AMENDMENT repealing the Eighteenth was ratified in December 1933, although prohibition's legal residue took some years to settle. (This measure came only nine months after passage of the relatively uncontroversial TWEN-TIETH AMENDMENT, eliminating the "lame duck" session of Congress and changing the time for the inauguration of presidents from March to January).

The momentum that carried woman suffrage to a successful amendment continued to some degree into the early 1920s. Some feminist leaders continued to push for improved working conditions for women, for minimum wage laws, and for laws bettering the legal status of women in marriage and DIVORCE. In 1922, Congress passed the Cable Act, providing that a married woman would thereafter retain and determine her own citizenship and make her own application for naturalization after lawful admission for permanent residence, which the Act reduced to three years. Supporters of the political emancipation of women, especially the National Women's Party, got the EQUAL RIGHTS AMENDMENT (ERA) introduced in Congress in 1923 and worked for its adoption by lobbying and exerting political pressure in the early years of the decade. At that time the ERA was opposed by most of the large women's organizations, by trade unions, and by the Women's Bureau primarily because it was seen as a threat to labor-protective legislation. Opponents contended that the ERA would deprive most working women and the poor of hard-won economic gains and would mainly benefit middle and upper class women. Thus the measure floundered at the time, not to be revived until toward the end of World War II. The same period saw all native-born American Indians granted full citizenship through the Curtis Act of 1924. The measure, however, did not automatically entitle them to vote, and some states still disfranchised Indians as "persons under guardianship." In 1925 Congress passed the Federal Corrupt Practices Act, extending federal regulation of political corruption to the choice of presidential electors.

A CHILD LABOR AMENDMENT fared only slightly better. With the Supreme Court striking down federal child labor laws as unconstitutional under both the commerce and the taxing powers, advocates of children's rights turned to the amending process and Congress adopted a proposed Child Labor Amendment in June 1924. Opposed by manufacturers' associations and certain religious groups, the measure, by 1930, had secured ratification in only five states. More than three-fourths had rejected it, with the greatest hostility coming from the south and from agricultural regions, where child labor was seen as essential to family economic stability. The measure was eventually superseded by the FAIR LABOR STANDARDS ACT of 1938. By that time the evils of child exploitation were no longer felt to be beyond the constitutional reach of federal legislative power.

Other amendments were proposed: providing minimum wages for women; establishing uniform national marriage and divorce laws; giving the president an item veto in appropriation bills; abolishing congressional immunity for speeches and debates in either house; providing representation for the DISTRICT OF COLUMBIA; changing the amending process itself; providing for the election of judges; providing for the independence of the Philippine Islands; prohibiting sectarian legislation; defining the right of states to regulate employment of ALIENS; requiring teachers to take an oath of allegiance; preventing governmental competition with private enterprise; conferring upon the House of Representatives coordinate power for the ratification of treaties; limiting the wealth of individual citizens; providing for legislation by INITIA-TIVE; extending the civil service merit system; regulating industry; and prohibiting loans to any except allies. Varying support for all reflected, to a greater or lesser degree, public discontent with aspects of the political-constitutional system of the time. A segment of this discontent crystallized in the La Follette Progressive Party's 1924 platform, which even proposed the RECALL of judges, much to the alarm and ire of Chief Justice Taft. Such straws in the wind did not, however, portend a successful assault upon property-oriented constitutional interpretation. That assault would await the depths of the Depression.

The middle to later years of the decade saw continued congressional hostility to government interference in economic and personal activities, but no reluctance to use power when the result supported President Coolidge's aphorism that "the business of America is business." Antilynching legislation failed during the decade; northern conservatives joined white southerners in deploring it as an assault upon STATES' RIGHTS and individual freedom. In 1927, Congress enacted the McNary-Haugen Farm Bill, an elaborate measure calling for federal support for agricultural prices. The measure countered the prevailing temper of constitutional conservatism, for it extended national regulatory authority over agricultural PRODUCTION and thus not only invaded a sphere of authority traditionally reserved to the states but also interfered extensively with private property rights. President Coolidge vetoed the measure, denouncing it as "economically and constitutionally unsound." When Congress persisted, he vetoed a second McNary-Haugen Bill the following year on the same grounds.

Somewhat similar antistatist sentiments emerged when, in 1925, newly appointed Attorney General HARLAN FISKE STONE took the Bureau of Investigation out of politics and terminated its pursuit of radicals. "There is always the possibility," Stone stated in taking the action, "that a secret police may become a menace to free government and free institutions because it carries with it the possibility of abuses of power which are not always quickly apprehended or understood. The Bureau . . . is not concerned with political or other opinions of individuals. It is concerned with their conduct, and then only with such conduct as is forbidden by the laws of the United States." Store's action was popular with all but some patriotic and right-wing groups for whom radical, or even unorthodox, ideas were a threat which the government did have a responsibility actively to check.

On the other hand, Congress met little opposition when it enacted a broad, restrictive IMMIGRATION Act in 1924 imposing stringent quotas on entry to the United States, heavily biased against southern and eastern European and Asiatic peoples. Such action was consonant with the strong tendency of the courts in the period to define the rights of aliens narrowly, with an eye to keeping such people in their proper place, particularly as easily exploitable members of the work force.

To the extent that an alternative constitutional tradition existed or was developed in the 1920s, its impact was not fully felt until Depression days. There were undertones of protest, however, coming from disparate sources. Justice LOUIS D. BRANDEIS, in his dissent in *Gilbert v. Minnesota* (1920), a decision sustaining a sedition conviction for criticism of the government's wartime policies, had stated: "I cannot believe that liberty guaranteed by the Fourteenth Amendment includes only liberty to acquire and to enjoy property." Others quickly picked up on the contradiction in this double standard, particularly when the same "liberty" was not then deemed applicable to FREEDOM OF SPEECH, FREEDOM OF THE PRESS, and FREEDOM OF ASSEMBLY. The AMERICAN CIVIL LIBERTIES UNION (ACLU), a product of the war, itself an opponent of strong government intervention in people's personal lives, worked through the decade to strengthen the power of labor and working people. The ACLU operated on the assumption that BILL OF RIGHTS freedoms flowed from economic power and that artificial impediments to the achievement of that power had to be removed. The National Association for the Advancement of Colored People was active in the decade in behalf of the constitutional rights of minorities, although its successes in producing constitutional change were decidedly limited. Similarly, organized labor saw itself as a beleaguered "minority" throughout the decade, attributing its position partly to conservation constitutionalism. Samuel Gompers stated shortly before his death: "The Courts have abolished the Constitution as far as the rights and interest of the working people are concerned."

The impact of such criticism ultimately was not so great as that from popularly elected constitutional liberals and an influential segment of the legal community. Senators William E. Borah and GEORGE NORRIS openly opposed the appointment of CHARLES EVANS HUGHES to the Chief Justiceship, arguing that there was a need for judges who would stop treating the Fourteenth Amendment only as a protection of property and recognize it as a guarantee of individual liberty. Although this opposition failed, partly because of Hughes's constitutional record and the public image of him as more progressive than reactionary, the Senate did block the subsequent nomination of John J. Parker, a prominent North Carolina Republican, to the Supreme Court in 1930; opponents particularly emphasized his racist and antilabor record. Both actions constituted unignorable Depression calls for constitutional liberalization, echoed increasingly by liberal lawyers, particularly in the law schools, many of which has been influenced by the LEGAL REALISM movement of the times. Such criticism combined with growing disillusionment with the business establishment and cynicism about a Supreme Court that could be aggressively activist in the protection of property rights and a paragon of self-restraint when it came to protecting human rights. Pressure for altered uses of government power mounted fairly early in Depression days.

Herbert Hoover was undoubtedly the most competent of the 1920s Presidents. A successful mining engineer and government bureaucrat, he had served effectively as war-time food administrator under Woodrow Wilson and as secretary of commerce in the Harding and Coolidge administrations. Hoover was eager to overhaul the executive branch of the government and reorganize it in ways that would achieve greater efficiency and greater economies in government. Saddled quickly with the worst depression in American history, Hoover was pressed to launch a large-scale national attack on the depression through federal governmental action. Such action had to fit his constitutional views, which were decidedly Taftian. For Hoover, "unless the enterprise system operated free from popular controls, constitutional freedoms would die." "Under the Constitution it was impossible to attempt the solution of certain modern social problems by legislation." "Constitutional change must be brought about only by the straightforward methods provided by the Constitution itself." Such a commitment to laissez faire economics and constitutional conservatism precluded sweeping federal actions and permitted only such remedial legislation as the AGRICULTURAL MARKETING ACT of 1929, designed to assist in the more effective marketing of agricultural commodities. Congress created the Reconstruction Finance Corporation in 1932 to rescue commercial, industrial, and financial institutions through direct government loans. Both measures so limited the scope of permissible federal activity that neither proved adequate to the challenge of providing successful depression relief.

A more specific example of Hoover's constitutionalism involved congressional enactment of the Muscle Shoals Bill of 1931. In 1918 President Wilson had authorized, as a war-time measure, the construction of government plants at Muscle Shoals on the Tennessee River for the manufacture of nitrates and of dams to generate electric power. After the war the disposition of these plants and dams produced bitter national controversy. Conservatives insisted that they be turned over to private enterprise. Congress twice enacted measures providing for government ownership and operation for the production and distribution of power and the manufacture of fertilizers. In vetoing the second of these bills (Coolidge had vetoed the first in 1928), Hoover reiterated his belief that government ownership and operation was an approach to socialism designed to break down the initiative and enterprise of the American people. He argued that such a measure was an unconstitutional federal entrance into the field of powers reserved to the states and as such deprived the people of local communities of their liberty.

A growing number of congressmen and senators, however, were convinced that such constitutional negativism was no longer useful. In 1932, Congress passed and sent to a reluctant President the NORRIS-LaGUARDIA ACT, probably the most important measure of the period. Ever since the 1890s, labor had protested against business's turn to the courts for INJUNCTIONS to prohibit its legitimate activities. Congress's only response was a Railway Labor Act, in 1926, giving railway labor the right to bargain collectively through its own representatives. By the late 1920s, a national campaign against the labor INJUNCTION was launched with liberal congressional leaders joined by groups as disparate as the ACLU, the Federal Council of Churches, and the American Federation of Labor, all protesting the unfairness and unconstitutionality of enjoining labor's legitimate use of speech, press, and assembly. The Great Depression intensified this discontent. The Norris-LaGuardia Act made YELLOW DOG CONTRACTS unenforceable in federal courts; forbade the issuance of injunctions against a number of hitherto outlawed union practices; and guaranteed jury trials in criminal prosecutions based on violations of injunctions. The act thus removed the machinery for a variety of informal antilabor devices.

Hoover's response was to seek assurance from his attorney general, William Mitchell, that the more rigorous terms of the measure could be successfully bypassed. Having gained such assurance, he signed the bill, leaving Senator Norris to remark, bitterly, that the President dared not veto but did everything he could to weaken its effect. Yet the measure was generally popular, as was its symbolism, which presaged a more active role for the federal government in the achievement of social justice.

Such response was not lost on Franklin D. Roosevelt. During the presidential campaign of 1932, he called for a new, more liberal view of the Constitution and a BROAD CONSTRUCTION of congressional legislative power as a way of solving the nation's difficult problems. His overwhelming election victory seemed to assure that the minority liberal constitutional arguments of the 1920s would become majority ones when the New Deal program was enacted.

PAUL L. MURPHY

Bibliography

HICKS, JOHN D. 1960 *Republican Ascendancy, 1921–1933.* New York: Harper & Row.

LEUCHTENBURG, WILLIAM E. 1958 *The Perils of Prosperity, 1914–1932.* Chicago: University of Chicago Press.

MURPHY, PAUL L. 1972 *The Constitution in Crisis Times, 1918–1969.* New York: Harper & Row.

———— 1972 *The Meaning of Freedom of Speech: First Amendment Freedoms from Wilson to F.D.R.* Westport, Conn.: Greenwood Press.

CONSTITUTIONAL HISTORY, 1933–1945

With the exception of the Civil War-Reconstruction era and the turbulent decade of the 1960s, no period in our history generated more profound changes in the constitutional system than the years of the Great Depression and World War II. Although the tenure of a Chief Justice of the United States often marks the boundary of a particular constitutional epoch, in this period it was a single President, FRANKLIN D. ROOSEVELT, whose personality and policies dominated the nation's political landscape, first as the leader of a domestic "war" against economic chaos, and, finally, as the architect of victory over the Axis powers. "Most of us in the Army have a hard time remembering any President but Franklin D. Roosevelt," remarked one soldier at the time of Roosevelt's death in April 1945. "He was the COMMANDER-IN-CHIEF, not only of the armed forces, but of our generation."

Roosevelt, described by Justice OLIVER WENDELL HOLMES as having a "second-rate intellect, but a first-rate temperament," was a charming, politically astute country squire from Hyde Park, New York. Crippled by polio at thirty-nine, elected President a decade later, he presided over five momentous revolutions in American life. The first, arising from his confrontation with the Supreme Court, has been aptly termed the "constitutional revolution" of 1937. The Court abandoned its long campaign, dating from the 1880s, to shape the content of the nation's economic policy by means of the judicial veto. The second revolution elevated the presidency, already revitalized by THEO-

DORE ROOSEVELT and WOODROW WILSON in the Progressive era, to the pinnacle of leadership within the American political system. FDR did not invent the "imperial presidency," but his mastery of the radio, his legislative skills, and his twelve-year tenure went far toward institutionalizing it, despite several notable setbacks at the hands of Congress and the Court.

The third revolution, symbolized by the expansion of FEDERAL GRANT-IN-AID programs, the SOCIAL SECURITY ACT of 1935, and the efforts by the Department of Justice to protect CIVIL RIGHTS under the old Reconstruction-era statutes, significantly transformed American FEDERALISM by making the national government the chief custodian of economic security and social justice for all citizens. The fourth, marked by the revitalization of old independent REGULATORY COMMISSIONS such as the Interstate Commerce Commission, saw the final denouement of laissez-faire capitalism and the birth of state capitalism, managed by a bureaucratic elite drawn from the legal profession, the academic world, and private business. And the fifth revolution, characterized by the unionization of mass-production industries, the growing influence of urban-labor representatives in the Congress, and Roosevelt's successful effort to attract support from ethnic minorities, brought a major realignment in voting blocs and party strength that lasted three decades.

The triumph of Roosevelt and the Democratic party in the 1932 elections represented both the outcome of short-term political forces and the culmination of voting realignments that began much earlier. The inability of the HERBERT HOOVER administration to stop the slide into economic depression after the stock market crash of 1929 represented the most obvious and immediate source of Roosevelt's appeal. More significantly, his victory ended an era of Republican domination in national politics that began with WILLIAM McKINLEY in 1896, and it ushered in a Democratic reign that lasted well into the 1980s. From McKinley to Hoover, the Republicans controlled the White House, except for Wilson's two terms (1913–1921), a Democratic interlude that rested mostly upon divisions in Republican ranks.

The Republicans also controlled both houses of Congress for twenty-eight of the thirty-six years between McKinley and Franklin Roosevelt, elected a majority of the nation's governors and state legislators outside the South, and even enjoyed great popularity in big cities among trade unionists, middle class professionals, and many ethnic-religious minorities. On a platform of high tariffs, sound money, low taxes, and rising prosperity, the GOP built a formidable national coalition.

The Republican coalition developed signs of collapse during the WARREN G. HARDING–CALVIN COOLIDGE–Herbert Hoover years as economic distress increased among farmers and industrial workers despite the vaunted prosperity of the Republican New Era. In 1924, running as an independent on the Progressive party ticket, the aging Senator Robert LaFollette garnered a healthy share of votes from both urban workers and staple-crop farmers, who protested with their ballots against the economic conservatism of Coolidge and his Democratic rival, John W. Davis, a prosperous Wall Street lawyer. Hoover easily defeated New York governor Alfred E. Smith in 1928, but Smith—Irish, Roman Catholic, opposed to prohibition, and urban to the core—detached millions of ethnic, working class voters from the Republican party. Three years of economic distress which also alienated farmers, businessmen, and the once-affluent middle classes, completed the realignment process and assured Roosevelt victory in 1932.

From 1932 until his death, Roosevelt forged his own national coalition. Anchored in the lily-white South and the big cities where the Democratic party had been powerful since the days of ANDREW JACKSON and MARTIN VAN BUREN, Roosevelt welded together a collection of social, ethnic, regional, and religious minorities into a new political majority. In peace and war, the New Deal gave power, status, and recognition to those who had been outsiders in American society before the Great Depression—Irishmen, Jews, Slavs, white Southerners, and blacks.

Within this broad, diverse "Roosevelt coalition," the power and influence of organized labor and the urban wing of the Democratic party grew impressively, especially after the elections of 1934 and 1936 and the passage of the WAGNER (NATIONAL LABOR RELATIONS) ACT in 1935. Roosevelt's nomination in 1932 had been made possible by the support of key southern leaders. The success of the New Deal after 1934 and Roosevelt's electoral victories in 1940 and 1944, however, rested upon the political acumen and money provided by big labor through the political action committees of the Congress of Industrial Organizations. Roosevelt built well. His coalition ran both houses of Congress in every year but eight during the next half century. It elected HARRY S. TRUMAN in 1948, JOHN F. KENNEDY in 1960, LYNDON B. JOHNSON in 1964, and JIMMY CARTER in 1976.

Neither of the two amendments to the Constitution ratified during this period owed their inspiration directly to Roosevelt or the New Deal, although the TWENTIETH AMENDMENT, eliminating the lame-duck session of Congress, had been pushed by leading progressives for over a decade, and the TWENTY-FIRST AMENDMENT, repealing national PROHIBITION of liquor, had been endorsed by the Democratic party in its 1932 platform. Both amendments were proposed in 1932, the first time since 1789 that a single Congress had sent to the states for RATIFICATION more than one amendment. Congress also specified an unusual ratification procedure for the Twenty-First Amendment, requiring the states to convene special ratifying conventions instead of submitting the measure to their legislatures. Proponents of prohibition repeal feared that the legislatures, most of them malapportioned in favor of rural constituencies, would not be sympathetic to ratification.

Supporters of the Twentieth Amendment, led by the venerable progressive senator from Nebraska, GEORGE NORRIS, argued that the existing short session of Congress which met from December until March was a barrier to effective majoritarian democracy. By an accident of history, Congresses elected in November of even-numbered years did not meet in regular session until December of the odd-numbered year. Norris's amendment, first passed by the Senate in 1923, proposed to correct this situation by moving forward to January 3 from December the date on which sessions of Congress began and shifting back to January 3 and 20 from March 4 the date on which the terms of office began for members of Congress, and the President and Vice-President, respectively. A newly elected Congress, reflecting the fresh mandate of the people, would meet two months after an election rather than thirteen months later.

The Senate passed the Norris plan five times after 1923, but it failed to advance in the Republican-dominated House of Representatives, where the Speaker, Nicholas Longworth, opposed it. Longworth wished to keep the lame-duck session as a check upon the turbulent masses and he also objected to a provision in the Norris amendment that allowed Congress to determine the date of its own adjournment each year. Such flexibility, he believed, would only encourage more lawmaking by Congress, a prospect that he and other conservatives viewed with great distaste. The 1930 elections returned Democratic majorities to both houses of Congress, who quickly passed the Twentieth Amendment and sent it on to the states where it was ratified three years later.

American temperance organizations struggled for more than a century to achieve their goal with the adoption of the EIGHTEENTH AMENDMENT in 1919. It took the "wet" forces little more than a decade to bring the brewery, the distillery, and the saloon back to American life through ratification of the Twenty-First Amendment nine months after Roosevelt took office. Like the resurgence of the Democratic party, the repeal of national prohibition reflected a fundamental shift in political forces. The Congress that passed the Eighteenth Amendment during World War I was overwhelmingly rural, with House seats apportioned on the basis of the 1910 census, the last to record a majority for the countryside rather than the cities. The 72nd Congress, on the other hand, reflected the reapportionment of the House in 1929, where twenty-one states (mostly from the rural South and West) lost representation and eleven states (mostly in Eastern metropolitan areas) increased their share of seats.

In addition to providing urban-ethnic voters with a measure of symbolic revenge for the inconvenience of a "dry" decade, the repeal of prohibition had wide appeal in a nation reeling from economic depression and plagued by criminal violence. Sponsors argued that repeal would boost employment, raise tax revenues, and permit law enforcement personnel to concentrate upon the apprehension of major criminals such as John Dillinger. With equal vehemence, defenders of the "dry" faith claimed that repeal had been hatched by millionaires and rich corporations, eager to shift their tax burdens onto poor consumers of alcohol, and that Satan would conquer America. Thirty-six states, more concerned for the nation's fiscal problems than for the wiles of Satan, ratified the repeal amendment by December 1933.

The legislative program of the New Deal had a more direct impact upon the fate of the old CHILD LABOR AMENDMENT, which had passed Congress in 1924 but had failed to secure ratification by three-fourths of the states. As late as 1937, only twenty-eight state legislatures had ratified the proposal which would have authorized Congress to regulate or prohibit the labor of persons under eighteen years of age. Fifteen states, mostly in the South and border regions, had rejected it; five had failed to act. The amendment became moot, however, when Congress in 1938 passed the FAIR LABOR STANDARDS ACT, which contained a similar restriction, and when the Supreme Court upheld its constitutionality in UNITED STATES V. DARBY LUMBER COMPANY (1941).

As usual, formal constitutional revision on the state level during these years was more extensive and diverse than for the federal government, although only three states (New York, Missouri, and Georgia) entirely rewrote their constitutions. At one extreme were states such as Tennessee and Illinois, where constitutional innovation remained minimal. The fundamental law of Tennessee had not been amended since 1870, while the Illinois Constitution of 1890 had been revised only twice since that date. On the other hand, voters in Louisiana were asked to adopt twenty-eight constitutional amendments in 1938, nineteen in 1940, ten in 1942, and nineteen in 1944, creating an organic law that filled nearly 300 pages with 200,000 words. California ran a distant second. By the end of World War II, its constitution of 1879 had been amended 250 times and totaled close to 50,000 words.

Unlike the United States Constitution with its broad, sweeping language, most state charters in this period included detailed declarations of public policies; the amendment process often served as a surrogate for statutory changes. In 1944, for instance, 100 proposed amendments were put before the voters in thirty different states. In California, Arizona, Oregon, and Washington the electorates defeated amendments to enact old-age pension schemes. Arkansas and Florida adopted right-to-work amendments that banned union shops, while California spurned a similar amendment. In the same year voters in other states were asked to pass upon amendments dealing with the location of airports, POLL TAXES, dog racing, and preferential civil service hiring for veterans.

Because of the era's economic crisis, which combined high unemployment, business failures, and falling tax revenues, all of the states confronted similar constitutional crises, because their organic laws usually limited state indebtedness. Escalating relief burdens placed a severe strain upon the states' fiscal resources, especially before the New Deal picked up a larger share of these costs after 1935. Legislatures and governors often found paths around these obstacles through constitutional experimentation: amendment, REFERENDUM, and judicial interpretation.

The age of Roosevelt, marked by class conflict and intense political controversy over both the economy and FOREIGN AFFAIRS, spawned many durable myths about the presidency, the growth of federal authority, and the relationship between government and the private sector. Roosevelt's critics, who hated the New Deal and distrusted his diplomacy, accused him of erecting a Presidential dictatorship. The New Deal and the mobilization of the war economy, it has been argued, also transformed the federal union as well as business–government relationships by subjecting local government and business corporations to the despotism of Washington bureaucrats. There is some truth in these generalizations but also considerable exaggeration.

Few political leaders in our history could match

Roosevelt's oratorical gifts, his skill at dispensing patronage, and his deft manipulation of subordinates, the press, Congress, and opponents. But Roosevelt also experienced a number of profound setbacks between 1933 and 1939 that limited presidential power even during the unparalleled economic crisis of the Great Depression. It was World War II that shifted the balance decisively in his favor, but even during those turbulent years he usually functioned within boundaries set by Congress and public opinion.

Under the New Deal, the years of presidential preeminence in the shaping of domestic policy were remarkably fertile but brief. During the so-called Hundred Days, from Roosevelt's inauguration to early June 1933, Congress rubber-stamped dozens of White House proposals, including new banking laws, the first federal securities statute, a complete overhaul of the nation's monetary system, legislation creating the Tennessee Valley Authority, as well as laws setting up the controversial National Recovery Administration and the New Deal's basic farm program. Acting under the dubious authority of the World War I Trading with the Enemy Act, Roosevelt banned gold exports and all foreign exchange transactions until Congress approved of the administration's monetary plans that nullified gold clauses in private and public contracts and devalued the dollar by almost twenty-five percent. Equating the Depression with war, Roosevelt asked for and received from Congress the resources appropriate for a military commander battling a foreign invader.

The 1934 elections gave the President even larger majorities in Congress. This mandate encouraged a second burst of New Deal reforms in 1935. Again responding to presidential initiatives, Congress adopted a series of path-breaking laws, including the Social Security Act, the Wagner National Labor Relations Act, a $4.8 billion relief and public works measure, and a significant revision of the federal tax code that closed many loopholes and levied new surcharges on the very rich. Despite the judicial mutilation of key administration measures in 1935–1936, executive power probably stood at its peacetime zenith after Roosevelt's crushing reelection victory in 1936.

Even during these years of strong presidential leadership, Roosevelt's claims to authority did not go unchallenged. The federal courts remained a bastion of conservative Republicanism. Federal judges had issued hundreds of INJUNCTIONS against New Deal programs by early 1935, when the Supreme Court began to invalidate many of the laws of the Hundred Days, including the NATIONAL INDUSTRIAL RECOVERY ACT (NIRA) and the AGRICULTURAL ADJUSTMENT ACT.

The most serious rebuff to the President came in the *Schechter* case, where the Justices invalidated the NIRA on the ground of improper DELEGATION OF POWER to the executive, and HUMPHREY'S EXECUTOR V. UNITED STATES (1935), where they curbed the President's power to remove members of independent regulatory commissions.

These judicial affronts to presidential authority became a war during FDR's second term, beginning with his ill-devised scheme to "pack" the Supreme Court with additional Justices. His proposed "Judicial Reform Act of 1937" inspired criticism both from conservatives and from many of the President's liberal friends in the Congress as well. This bitter legislative struggle divided the New Deal coalition, squandered much of the political capital that Roosevelt had accumulated during the previous four years, and gave rise to cries of "dictatorship," "tyranny," and "fascism." When the dust settled, the Court-packing plan had been defeated by Chief Justice CHARLES EVANS HUGHES and opponents in the Congress, but the Supreme Court never again seriously challenged the New Deal.

The economic recession of 1937–1938 and Roosevelt's attempt to restructure the executive branch dealt new blows to presidential leadership and prestige. Having taken credit for the economic upturn in 1935–1936, the President had to absorb the blame for the "Roosevelt recession," which had been triggered in part by his own desire to cut federal expenditures and balance the budget. Congress also scuttled his plans to reorganize the executive branch which rested upon the recommendations of a blue-ribbon committee on administrative management. The original bill called for an enlargement of the White House staff, creation of the Executive Office of the President to include the Bureau of the Budget, and a consolidation of existing bureaus, agencies, and commissions into twelve superdepartments under the President's control. The independent regulatory commissions such as the Federal Trade Commission, the Interstate Commerce Commission, and the Securities Exchange Commission would have been regrouped under the authority of these executive departments.

Congressional opponents denounced the plan as another presidential power grab. Working in tandem with rebellious bureaucrats who hoped to protect their own fiefdoms from the White House, they easily defeated the most controversial features of the plan. Roosevelt got his Bureau of the Budget and a larger staff, but little more. His political fortunes hit rock bottom in the 1938 elections, when several conservative Democratic senators won reelection despite Roosevelt's effort to purge them during bitter primary campaigns. Confronted by an emerging conservative congressional coalition of southern Democrats and midwestern Republicans, Roosevelt had lost the initiative on domestic policy by the time German troops marched into Austria and Czechoslovakia.

The growth of presidential power, checked at the end of the 1930s, received new impetus after 1938 from the coming of World War II. Although the Supreme Court had reaffirmed in the broadest possible terms the President's constitutional authority over foreign policy in UNITED STATES v. CURTISS-WRIGHT EXPORT CORPORATION (1936), the actual limits of that authority remained to be tested. Sometimes alone and sometimes with congressional support, between 1939 and 1945 Roosevelt enlarged presidential power to an extent unknown even during World War I and the early New Deal.

Facing substantial isolationist sentiment both in Congress and among the public, Roosevelt initially attempted to counter Germany and Japan by means of EXECUTIVE AGREEMENTS and EXECUTIVE ORDERS that rested exclusively upon his claims to inherent presidential authority to conduct foreign relations and command the armed forces. He applied economic sanctions against Japan, terminating a 1911 commercial treaty, banning sales of scrap iron and steel, and freezing all Japanese financial assets in the United States. He ordered naval patrols of the western Atlantic—virtually assuring hostilities with German U-boats—and he ordered the military occupation of Iceland, with attendant naval convoys to protect ships supplying the occupation troops. In brief, Roosevelt waged an economic war in Asia and shooting war in the Atlantic without the consent of Congress.

The most extraordinary assertion of presidential power before Pearl Harbor was the destroyer-bases executive agreement in September 1940, by which Roosevelt transferred fifty over-age American destroyers to the British government in return for leases on seven naval bases in the Caribbean. This transaction, through which the President gave away a substantial portion of the United States Navy, rested upon a generous interpretation of an old nineteenth-century statute which permitted the President to dispose of worn-out ships. Most observers have believed that this action subverted the intention of Congress and violated a 1917 law specifically prohibiting the President in any foreign war "to send out of the jurisdiction of the United States any vessel built, armed, or equipped as a vessel of war." Attorney General ROBERT H. JACKSON, who advised Roosevelt on the legality of the transfer, dismissed this statute on the grounds that it applied only to ships built with the specific intention of giving them to a nation at war.

After the Japanese attack on Pearl Harbor Congress rapidly augmented presidential control over both military policy and the domestic economy. By means of the renewal of Lend-Lease, the Second WAR POWERS ACT, the EMERGENCY PRICE CONTROL ACT, the War Labor Dispute Act, and other laws, Congress gave the President the discretion, among other things, to allocate $50 billion of war supplies to America's allies, to reorganize all executive departments and agencies at will, to fix rents and prices throughout the land, and to seize industrial plants closed by strikes. In 1935, invalidating the NIRA, the Supreme Court had scolded Congress for vesting unbridled authority in the President to regulate the economy. Ten years later, as World War II drew to a close, executive discretion over the nation's economic structure far transcended that of the NIRA years.

A substantial enlargement of presidential discretion was essential for effective prosecution of World War II, but the growth of executive power carried with it threats to CIVIL LIBERTIES and unfathomable dangers to the survival of the human race. The Congress that permitted the President to restructure the executive branch also approved of the administration's plans to remove Japanese Americans from the West Coast. (See JAPANESE AMERICAN CASES.) The Congress that permitted the President to ration sugar and gasoline also gave the Commander-in-Chief a blank check for research, development, and potential use of nuclear weapons. This was truly, in Justice BENJAMIN N. CARDOZO's memorable phrase, "delegation run riot."

The expansion of federal responsibility for economic management and social services paralleled the growth of presidential power between 1933 and 1945. In a series of cases beginning with the WAGNER ACT CASES (1937) and ending with WICKARD v. FILBURN (1942), the Supreme Court laid to rest the antiquated notions of DUAL FEDERALISM, which had postulated the existence of rigid constitutional boundaries separating appropriate federal activities from those reserved exclusively to the states. In the wake of these decisions and those upholding the Social Security Act, there seemed to be no constitutional limitation upon the authority of Congress to regulate INTERSTATE COMMERCE and to tax and spend on behalf of the GENERAL WELFARE, even where these federal efforts intruded deeply into areas of social and economic life traditionally left to local government. Practice often preceded formal doctrinal legitimation. In 1934, for instance, the Bureau of Biological Survey in the Department of Commerce eradicated over seven million disease-carrying rodents in three states with a $8.7 million grant from the Civil Works Administration. Although this project produced no constitutional objection, a more sweeping federal intrusion into the domain of local health authorities is hard to imagine.

The most far-reaching instrument of expanding federal policymaking became the myriad programs of FEDERAL GRANTS-IN-AID which provided federal money for specific activities to be administered by state officials under federal guidelines. As early as 1862, the MORRILL ACT had conveyed federal lands to the states on condition that they be used for the construction and support of colleges and universities. In the Weeks Act of 1911, Congress had extended this principle to include cash grants to the states for fighting forest fires in the watersheds of navigable streams. Similar grant-in-aid programs flourished during the Wilson administration for vocational education, highways, and agricultural extension work, but budget-conscious Republican administrations had put a cap on new programs during the 1920s.

In their efforts to fight the depression, both the Hoover and Roosevelt administrations increasingly used the grant-in-aid technique. The Emergency Relief and Construction Act of 1932, approved reluctantly by Hoover, offered over $600 million in federal loans to the states for work-relief projects. The Roosevelt administration substituted grants for loans in the relief programs of the New Deal. By 1940, in addition to these vast relief activities and the continuation of old programs from the Progressive era, the New Deal had undertaken grant-in-aid programs for employment services and unemployment compensation, old age assistance, child welfare services, and maternity care. Social Security, the largest New Deal grant-in-aid program, assisted the blind, the disabled, and the unemployed through combined federal–state efforts.

The growth of federal grant-in-aid programs during the New Deal years rested upon the realization that many social and economic problems required national attention and that only the federal government commanded the fiscal resources to deal with them. Between 1932 and the end of World War II, the federal government's share of total taxes collected rose from twenty-four percent to nearly seventy-four percent. At the same time, grant-in-aid programs avoided the growth of an even larger federal bureaucracy and left many important administrative decisions in the hands of state and local officials.

In addition to grant-in-aid programs, state and local elites played a major role in the implementation of other New Deal efforts as well, a pattern of political decision making that refuted simplistic ideas about rampant centralization of power in federal bureaucrats. The heart of the New Deal's farm program, the domestic allotment system, vested important decisions in county committees composed of farmers and extension-service personnel chosen by local authorities. Under the Taylor Grazing Act, local livestock ranchers determined the extent of grazing rights on the vast public lands in the western states. And the most coercive federal program in this period, the SELECTIVE SERVICE ACT of 1940, left life-and-death decisions about the drafting of millions of American citizens in the hands of local draft boards appointed by state governors. Without the active participation of state and local officials, the wartime rationing programs for gasoline, sugar, coffee, and butter would have broken down for lack of enforcement.

When New Deal reformers ignored the interests and sensibilities of local elites, they provoked instant political protest and retaliation. Roosevelt quickly dismantled the innovative Civil Works Administration in 1934 because it drew intense criticism from governors, county supervisors, and mayors who objected to the complete nationalization of its extensive work-relief efforts. The subsequent Works Projects Administration program gave a larger share of decision making to local officials, who systematically used the machinery to punish political enemies and to discriminate against racial minorities, especially in the South. When idealistic young lawyers in the Agricultural Adjustment Administration attempted to protect sharecroppers and tenants from wholesale eviction under the farm program, they stirred up a revolt by commercial farmers, who forced their removal from the agency. Much of the opposition from southern Democrats to the New Deal after 1935 grew out of their anger at the Department of Justice for attempting to protect blacks from local violence under the old Reconstruction-era civil rights laws. The New Deal nourished a new brand of COOPERATIVE FEDERALISM in many areas of American life, but it was not a federalism without conflict and tensions, especially when national reformers challenged entrenched local customs and power relationships.

While encouraging the growth of big labor and ministering to the needs of the elderly and the poor, the New Deal also provided substantial benefits to American capitalists. Business opposition to Roosevelt was intense, but it was narrowly based in labor-intensive corporations in textiles, automobiles, and steel which had the most to lose from collective bargaining. The New Deal found many business allies among firms in the growing service industries of banking, insurance, and stock brokerage where government regulations promised to reduce cutthroat competition and to weed out marginal operators. Because of its aggressive policies to expand American exports and investment opportunities abroad, the New Deal also drew support from high-technology firms and from the large oil companies who were eager to penetrate the British monopoly in the Middle East.

Sophisticated businessmen discovered that they could live comfortably in a world of government regulation. The "socialistic" Tennessee Valley Authority lowered the profits of a few utility companies, but cheap electric power for the rural South translated into larger consumer markets for the manufacturers of generators, refrigerators, and other appliances. In addition to restoring public confidence in the stock exchanges and the securities industry, the Securities and Exchange Commission promoted self-regulation among over-the-counter dealers. Motor trucking firms received a helping hand from the Interstate Commerce Commission in reducing rate wars, and the major airlines looked to the Civil Aeronautics Board to protect them from the competitive rigors of the marketplace. When "Dr. Win-the-War" replaced "Dr. New Deal" after 1942, businessmen began to play key roles as well in the wartime agencies that regulated production, manpower, and the allocation of raw materials. The New Deal thus laid the foundations of both the welfare state and the permanent warfare state.

MICHAEL E. PARRISH

Bibliography

CAREY, JANE PERRY 1865 *The Rise of a New Federalism: Federal–State Cooperation in the United States.* New York: Russell & Russell.
HAWLEY, ELLIS P. 1965 *The New Deal and the Problem of Monopoly.* Princeton, N.J.: Princeton University Press.
LEUCHTENBURG, WILLIAM E. 1963 *Franklin D. Roosevelt and the New Deal.* New York: Harper & Row.
PATTERSON, JAMES T. 1969 *The New Deal and the States: Federalism in Transition.* Princeton, N.J.: Princeton University Press.
POLENBERG, RICHARD 1972 *War and Society: The United States 1941–1945.* Philadelphia: Lippincott.
SCHLESINGER, ARTHUR M., JR. 1957, 1959, 1960 *The Age of Roosevelt,* 3 vols. Boston: Houghton Mifflin.

CONSTITUTIONAL HISTORY, 1945–1961

Reconversion to a peacetime society required reestablishing balance among the branches of the government and a careful reassessment of the role of each.

The same process occasioned a reexamination of the relations between government and private power. These immediate problems of reconstruction were joined by the emergence of a "cold war" with the Communist bloc of nations. Americans defined that struggle as one against totalitarian rule—the antithesis of constitutional democracy.

The wartime period had seen massive government regulation of the economy and the personal lives of citizens. Congress had authorized governmental reorganization in 1941, reenacting a World War I measure giving the President almost unlimited power to reorganize federal agencies directing the nation's resources in wartime. (See WAR POWERS ACT.) At the end of World War II, Congress created a bipartisan Commission on Organization of the Executive Branch of the government headed by ex-President HERBERT HOOVER. It recommended reforms designed to reduce administrative disorder and bureaucracy. Congress in 1947 proposed the TWENTY-SECOND AMENDMENT (ratified in 1951) limiting presidential service to two terms.

Although many congressional conservatives hoped to roll back various New Deal programs, few were prepared to return the nation's economy to the unregulated control of private business leaders. Depression lessons had been painful. The FULL EMPLOYMENT ACT of 1946 declared that it was the government's task to take all steps necessary to maximize employment, production, and purchasing power. And while certain conservative congressmen were disturbed by the economic management this measure obviously necessitated, few opposed its goal of securing national economic stability. The Housing and Rent Act of 1947, continuing the wartime Price Control Act, raised an important question: does the WAR POWER continue after the shooting has ceased? The Supreme Court, in WOODS V. MILLER (1948), answered affirmatively as to legislation responding to wartime dislocations.

The issue of restraints on organized labor dissolved presidential–congressional harmony. President HARRY S. TRUMAN in 1946 vetoed the TAFT-HARTLEY ACT, an amendment to the 1935 WAGNER ACT, the nation's principal labor law. Taft-Hartley sought to eliminate an alleged prolabor bias by arming management with new rights and imposing limitations on long-established trade union practices. Truman called the act "completely contrary to the national policy of economic freedom," and "a threat to the successful working of our democratic society." But Congress passed it over his veto, and thirty states also enacted antilabor statutes, including RIGHT-TO-WORK LAWS and antipicketing measures. The LANDRUM-GRIFFIN ACT of 1959 sought to combat growing charges of union scandal, extortion, and deprivation of members' rights by imposing more direct federal authority over internal union procedures.

Executive-legislative cooperation resulted in passage of the Cellar-Kefauver Act of 1950, authorizing more rigid enforcement of the antitrust laws against corporate mergers. Two years later, following a Supreme Court ruling striking at "fair trade" laws, Congress passed the McGuire Act exempting state-approved fair trading from the federal antitrust laws. Seen as a consumer protection law, the measure was politically acceptable at the time.

In the FOREIGN AFFAIRS area, Congress and the President clashed. Truman had inherited a presidency whose prerogatives in foreign policy had been greatly expanded. Committed to the realization of Roosevelt's postwar programs, Truman backed American participation in the new United Nations. Such action entailed expanding presidential prerogatives at the expense of congressional power. American participation meant applying military sanctions against an aggressor state at the discretion of the United States delegate to the Security Council, who was under the control of the President. By the United Nations Participation Act of 1945 Congress recognized that the President could not commit the United States to participation in United Nations military sanctions without congressional consent, but it acknowledged implicitly that Congress's warmaking power was conditioned by the necessity of international security action. Similarly, when the United States joined the NORTH ATLANTIC TREATY Organization in 1950, it pledged automatic intervention if any member suffered armed attack. The question was raised whether such a commitment upset the traditional balance between the executive and legislative branches in questions of war and peace.

With the invasion of South Korea by Communist forces, presidential discretion rather than congressional action provided a dramatic answer. Truman, on June 25, 1950, without asking for a formal DECLARATION OF WAR or consulting Congress, ordered United States POLICE ACTION in the area. This order brought charges from Senator ROBERT A. TAFT that Truman had "usurped power and violated the Constitution and the laws of the United States." In the "great debate" that followed, Truman's actions and presidential war power generally were condoned, but not without a strong attempt, led by Senator John Bricker, to curb the treaty-making power of the President by constitutional amendment. One form of the unsuccessful BRICKER AMENDMENT would have declared:

"A provision of a treaty or other international agreement which conflicts with this Constitution shall not be of any force or effect."

The Supreme Court ultimately eased the minds of Bricker's supporters. The circumstances were constitutionally significant. As new treaties of alliance grew in the late 1940s and early 1950s, American military and civilian personnel spanned the globe. Questions grew regarding the legal status of American citizens living abroad. Did the Constitution follow the flag? In REID V. COVERT (1957) the Court held that an EXECUTIVE AGREEMENT was subject to the limits of the Constitution, and thus could not confer on Congress power to authorize trial by COURT-MARTIAL of a civilian dependent of a serviceman stationed overseas. "We must not," wrote Justice HUGO L. BLACK, "break faith with this nation's tradition of keeping military power subservient to civilian authority."

Earlier, Congress had enacted a NATIONAL SECURITY ACT, creating the National Security Council and reorganizing the means by which war powers were exercised. The measure constricted the President's foreign policy prerogatives by requiring him to consult Congress before taking certain actions. In practice, however, it did not constrain willful Presidents. The ATOMIC ENERGY ACT of 1946 sought to insure civilian control over atomic energy production and precluded dissemination of technical information to other nations. By the 1950s, however, President Eisenhower sought and obtained an amendment, as the basis for an international cooperation program, to develop peaceful applications of nuclear energy. Nuclear power was apparently to become an important bargaining chip in the international arena.

One incident growing out of the KOREAN WAR revealed public feelings regarding the swelling authority of the executive and the proper nature of constitutional government. During the war, the President felt that constitutional history was on his side, given earlier validated presidential interventions in national emergency crises. He authorized his secretary of commerce to seize and operate struck steel mills, thereby insuring production of vital defense materials. His executive order was not based on statutory authority, but only on the ground that a threatened strike of the nation's steelworkers created a national emergency. When the steel companies sought an INJUNCTION against the government, federal spokesmen argued that the seizure was based upon Article II of the Constitution, and "whatever inherent, implied, or residual powers may flow therefrom." The President's actions drew sharp criticism, especially his refusal to use the Taft-Hartley Act provisions hated by his labor constituency. Before the Supreme Court, government counsel stressed expanded presidential prerogative during national emergencies, but the Supreme Court drew a line between public regulation and governmental operation of private business. In one of its most celebrated postwar constitutional decisions, the Court, speaking through Justice Black, rejected claims for presidential EMERGENCY POWERS and INHERENT POWERS in domestic affairs. Truman promptly announced compliance with the ruling, and the public reacted favorably to JUDICIAL ACTIVISM in curtailing excessive federal power. (See STEEL SEIZURE CONTROVERSY; YOUNGSTOWN SHEET & TUBE V. SAWYER.)

Constitutional development in the Truman years had been heavily influenced by considerations of national security at home and abroad, some serious, some specious, and all heavily political. Republican and conservative southern Democratic opponents of the New Deal had begun in 1938 to "red-bait" the Roosevelt administration by associating its personnel with un-Americanism or by representing the government's extension of powers as socialistic or communistic. Wartime investigations of federal employees and postwar revelations of inadequate security procedures intensified conservative demands for a housecleaning of the executive branch. Capitalizing on this issue during the 1946 congressional elections, the Republicans secured control of both houses of Congress, insuring that the subsequent Congress would investigate the loyalty of federal employees. During this period, the HOUSE COMMITTEE ON UN-AMERICAN ACTIVITIES (HCUA) was given permanent committee status, and between 1947 and 1948 Congress instituted thirty-five committee investigations of federal personnel and policies.

Lacking Roosevelt's political capital, and alarmed by leaks of classified information, Truman moved quickly to take control of the loyalty issue. In November 1946 he appointed a special presidential commission to investigate the problem, and in 1947 he formally instituted, by EXECUTIVE ORDER 9835, a permanent federal employee LOYALTY-SECURITY PROGRAM. To disarm congressional opposition further, Truman appointed conservatives to the loyalty program's major administrative positions. Under this program, negative information from any source was the potential basis for a security dismissal or the denial of government service. An ATTORNEY GENERAL'S LIST of subversive organizations was drawn up, with membership a basis for dismissal. The only guideline the order provided was that a designated organization must be "totalitarian, Fascist, Communist, or subversive," or one adopting a policy "approving the com-

mission of acts of force or violence to deny to others their constitutional rights."

Civil libertarians attacked the program on constitutional grounds, charging that it presumed employees to be subversive and subject to dismissal unless they could prove themselves innocent. Critics of the program also charged that it lacked procedural protections, a charge raised chronically against HCUA. However, the administration moved with regard for justice and fair play during its loyalty probes, and by early 1951 the Civil Service Commission had cleared more than three million federal employees; the Federal Bureau of Investigation had made 14,000 investigations of doubtful cases; over 2,000 employees had resigned, although in very few cases because of the investigation; and 212 persons had been dismissed because of reasonable doubts of their loyalty. In 1948 the executive branch also sought to demonstrate concern for national security by obtaining indictments of the eleven national leaders of the Communist party under the Smith Act. A long and bombastic trial followed, ending in convictions for conspiracy to advocate overthrow of the government by force and violence. (See DENNIS V. UNITED STATES.)

Conservative critics claimed that the Truman administration's loyalty efforts were window dressing to divert attention from more serious problems. The sensational Alger Hiss-Whittaker Chambers hearings and the resultant conviction of Hiss, a former New Deal official, for perjury in connection with disclosures of secret security information, catalyzed Congress into launching its own loyalty program. The MUNDT-NIXON BILL, seeking to force communists out into the open by requiring them to register with the Justice Department, was caught in 1948 election year politics and failed passage; but by 1950, following the reelection of Truman, the INTERNAL SECURITY ACT, a similar measure, was passed resoundingly over the President's veto. The act went beyond the Truman loyalty program for government employees. It attempted to extend loyalty probes into nongovernmental areas of American life and generally assumed a need to shift the authority for security matters to congressional leadership. Civil libertarians challenged the measure as violative particularly of FIRST AMENDMENT guarantees. But in the Korean War period, with burgeoning security apprehensions fed aggressively by Senator JOSEPH R. MCCARTHY of Wisconsin, the possibility of launching a successful test case of even the act's most extreme provisions promised little success. Instead, Senator Patrick A. McCarran of Nevada, one of the measure's principal champions, persuaded Congress in 1952 to pass, over another Truman veto, a revised immigration law. The act contained provisions to prevent the admission of possible subversives, and it authorized DEPORTATION of immigrants with communist affiliations even after they had become citizens.

The expanded activities of congressional committees in LEGISLATIVE INVESTIGATIONS of loyalty and security raised important constitutional questions about committee prerogatives and behavior. While practice varied, some of the more flamboyant committees, such as HCUA, Senator McCarthy's Committee on Governmental Operations, or McCarran's Senate Internal Security Committee with large, aggressive, and ruthless staffs, pried into federal activities and even investigated subversion in the movie and entertainment industries, various private organizations, the academic community, and the churches. Committee actions alarmed civil libertarians, because of growing disregard for the type of procedural guarantees and safeguards of individual liberty normally afforded any citizen in a court of law. The committees browbeat witnesses, denied a RIGHT TO COUNSEL, and afforded no opportunity to examine charges, which were often irresponsible and from dubious sources. Opportunity to cross-examine witnesses was denied. Individuals' past affiliations and activities were used as evidence of guilt, and they were expected to prove themselves innocent to an obviously biased congressional "jury." As a result many witnesses invoked the Fifth Amendment, refusing to testify on the grounds that any statement made might tend to incriminate them. This led to charges that such citizens were "Fifth Amendment Communists." Congress in 1954 passed a FEDERAL IMMUNITY ACT to force testimony in return for promises of immunity from prosecution. (See IMMUNITY GRANT.) Generally the courts, including the Supreme Court, were cautious about thwarting government measures, deciding cases on the narrowest of grounds and proscribing only the most overt abuses.

Postwar demands for greater constitutional protections for minorities within American society expanded CIVIL RIGHTS. Many Americans believed that the United States should extend first class CITIZENSHIP to all. The struggle with the Communist world for the minds of Third World people added urgency. Early in 1946, President Truman established a Committee on Civil Rights affirming that "the preservation of civil rights, guaranteed by the Constitution, is essential to domestic tranquillity, national security, the general welfare, and the continued existence of our free institutions." In 1947 the committee proposed extension of an approach initiated by Attorney General FRANK MURPHY in the late 1930s, stressing that the federal government should be a shield in protecting citizens against those who would endanger their rights, and a sword to cut away state laws violating those rights. The report called for strengthening the CIVIL RIGHTS DIVISION of the Justice Department, using the Federal Bureau of Investigation in cases involving violations of civil rights, enacting antilynching and anti-POLL TAX laws, and establishing a permanent Fair Employment Practices Commission. However, with Southerners dominating many key congressional committees, prospects were dim for any program extending full civil rights to black Americans.

Truman determined to make the effort. In early 1948 he sent Congress a message calling for prompt implementation of the commission's report. A southern revolt in the Congress culminated in the secession of members from the Democratic Party. These "Dixiecrats" ran their own presidential candidate, J. Strom Thurmond, on a STATES' RIGHTS platform calling for "segregation of the races" and denouncing national action in behalf of civil rights as a "totalitarian concept, which threatens the integrity of the states and the basic rights of their citizens." Although Truman won the election, in the civil rights area he had available only executive remedies. These he utilized, strengthening the Civil Rights Division and encouraging the Justice Department to assist private parties in civil rights cases. He also ordered that segregation be ended in federal employment and that the armed services be fully integrated. (See EXECUTIVE ORDERS 9980 AND 9981.) These developments encouraged civil rights activists to look to the courts for constitutional action in behalf of minority rights. Truman's Supreme Court appointees, however, were consistently conservative and espoused a narrow view of the judicial power. Only a few cautious rulings proscribed some forms of RACIAL DISCRIMINATION. (See SHELLEY V. KRAEMER, 1948; SWEATT V. PAINTER, 1950.)

Although DWIGHT D. EISENHOWER shared many of Truman's views regarding the President's vital and dominant leadership role in foreign policy, he conceived the domestic presidency in a different light. No social crusader, Eisenhower also had no desire to undo major programs of the New and Fair Deals. Rather he saw the presidency as a mediating agency, harmonizing the functioning of the team, and ratifying decisions and policies carefully prepared by responsible subordinates or by congressional leadership. Thus during Eisenhower's eight years in office Congress reasserted considerable domestic initiative, and when the President acted he usually complemented congressional desires.

During the 1952 campaign, Republicans made much of the "Communists in government" issue. Eisenhower realized that loyalty-security actions had to be taken to satisfy a nervous public. In 1953, he established a new executive loyalty program that expanded the criteria of the earlier Truman program. Discharge from federal service was now based on a simple finding that the individual's employment "may not be clearly consistent with the interests of national security." Several thousand "security risks" were dismissed. HCUA, cheering from the sidelines, then attempted to subpoena former President Truman to explain his security inadequacies. Truman responded with a polite letter giving the committee a lecture on SEPARATION OF POWERS and the independence of the executive.

Critics of the program focused on the absence of PROCEDURAL DUE PROCESS, the prevalence of GUILT BY ASSOCIATION, and the use of "faceless informers" as sources of damaging accusations. As long as Senator McCarthy was riding high such allegations remained just that. Tired of being smeared as "soft on Communists," frustrated liberal Democrats pushed through Congress a COMMUNIST CONTROL ACT in 1954, outlawing the party and initially seeking to make party membership a crime. The act proved virtually unenforceable. With the Senate censure and eventual demise of Senator McCarthy and the growing lack of enthusiasm of the Eisenhower administration for fueling the loyalty hysteria, security issues drifted into the background. By the late 1950s respectable bodies such as the New York City Bar Association and the League of Women Voters called for more precise standards for the federal government's loyalty-security program. With the Supreme Court also questioning aspects of that program's constitutional insensitivity, the President in early 1960 established a new industrial security program with vastly improved procedural safeguards. It included FAIR HEARINGS, the right of CONFRONTATION, and the right to examine all charges under ordinary circumstances. The same spirit came to prevail in the operation of other security programs.

The Eisenhower administration showed concern for state prerogatives and the need for balancing them against the rights of the individual. The federal government's growth in size and power since the late 1930s had been paralleled in state governments. During this period the states collected more money, spent more, employed more people, and engaged in more activities than ever before. When the expenditure and employment were assisted by FEDERAL GRANTS-IN-AID, lack of state compliance with federal standards meant potential loss of federal revenues. But states acted enthusiastically on their own in areas ranging from education and social services to a struggle with the federal government over control of natural resources. In 1947 the Supreme Court ruled that the United States had dominion over the soil under the marginal sea adjoining California. That state had maintained it was entitled, by virtue of the "equal footing" clause in the act admitting it to the Union, to the rights enjoyed by the original states and that those states owned such offshore areas. The Court concluded that such ownership had not been established at the time of the Constitution, and the interests of SOVEREIGNTY favored national dominion. But following the victorious Eisenhower campaign of 1952, in which the Republicans had courted the West and the South with promises of offshore riches, Congress passed the Submerged Lands Act of 1953, vesting in the states the ownership of lands beneath the marginal sea adjacent to the respective states. The Supreme Court subsequently denied leave to file complaints challenging the statute's constitutionality.

At another level, states and municipalities became so concerned in the 1950s with employees' loyalty that they enacted restrictive security measures. These included prohibiting the employment of Communist party members, LOYALTY OATHS as a condition of employment for teachers, service personnel, and candidates for public office, and measures authorizing state prosecution for SEDITION against the United States. State bar associations in turn moved to exclude from admission candidates who were allegedly former Communist party members or who refused to answer questions regarding former suspect affiliations. When the Supreme Court struck at such state sedition laws (PENNSYLVANIA V. NELSON, 1956) and bar restraints (SCHWARE V. NEW MEXICO BOARD OF BAR EXAMINERS, 1958; KONIGSBERG V. CALIFORNIA STATE BAR, 1957) its actions were denounced by the Conference of Chief Justices of the States as "the high-water mark . . . in denying to a state the power to keep order in its own house." Bills were introduced in Congress to deny the Court APPELLATE JURISDICTION in cases of this kind.

In this atmosphere, national leaders were hesitant to push for early implementation of the Supreme Court's DESEGREGATION mandate, and preferred to interpret the command "with ALL DELIBERATE SPEED" by emphasizing deliberation. A pattern of "massive resistance" emerged in the southern states, constituting a crazy quilt of INTERPOSITION proclamations, pupil-assignment or placement laws, freedom-of-choice laws, TUITION GRANT plans, and state statutes prescribing discipline of teachers for violation of state policies on the school segregation question. Meanwhile, federal authorities sat on their hands until after the 1956 election. Then they took cautious steps to bring the federal government more directly into the civil rights area. Eisenhower's attorney general proposed a federal statute to authorize an investigation of rights violations, particularly VOTING RIGHTS. The CIVIL RIGHT ACT OF 1957 passed after Southerners had so amended it as to make it virtually toothless. When Eisenhower signed the act into law early in September, he could have used a much stronger bill. One week earlier Governor Orville Faubus of Arkansas, an acknowledged segregationist, had ordered state troops into Little Rock to prevent implementation of a federal court order approving the admission of a handful of black students into that city's Central High School. Confronted with military defiance of federal authority, Eisenhower had no choice but to respond. He reluctantly dispatched several companies of the United States Army to Little Rock, under a provision of the United States Code, which authorized the suppression of insurrection and unlawful combinations that hindered the execution of either state or federal law. (See POSSE COMITATUS ACT.) He also nationalized and thus neutralized the Arkansas National Guard. Black children attended school for a year under military protection and Arkansas's massive resistance was held at bay by bayonets.

After the Little Rock case was decided by the Supreme Court in COOPER V. AARON (1958), which sustained the school desegregation order, Congress also acted. The CIVIL RIGHTS ACT OF 1960 made it a federal crime for a person to obstruct or interfere with a federal court order, or to attempt to do so by threats of force. Other provisions expanded federal remedies for enforcing voting rights. The measure, for which the Republicans claimed credit in their 1960 platform, put Congress and the executive branch on record as committed to push ahead with rights enforcement.

For minority groups without the political constituency of blacks, little positive action was forthcoming. Women's rights in this period was a subliminal theme at best. Women's work in World War II had gone a long way toward shattering the stereotype of the helpless, weaker sex in need of protective legislation. Some leaders in Congress moved toward proposal of the EQUAL RIGHTS AMENDMENT as a vote of thanks to women for their magnificent wartime performance. Both parties endorsed the measure at war's end, and Harry Truman spoke publicly in its support. But Eleanor Roosevelt, with the support of organized labor, insisted that protective legislation was more valuable for working women than the establishment of an abstract principle of legal rights. Despite two attempts in the Senate to pass a bill proposing the amendment in the late 1940s, and a third in 1953 with a rider specifying that no protective legislation was to be affected, the measure was not seriously revived in this period.

The rights of American Indians suffered even more. In 1953, the Eisenhower administration set out on a policy of "termination," supporting a program designed to reduce the federal government's involvement in Indian affairs and to "free" Indians from federal supervision. Specifically, termination sought to end the existing supportive federal–tribal relationship and transfer almost all responsibilities and powers from the federal government to the states. The effects on "terminated" tribes was disastrous; many tribal members were soon on public assistance rolls. Indians detested the law embodying this policy, seeing it as an instrument for tribal extinction. They expended their energies to defeat it, and finally achieved victory in 1968. The Indian Civil Rights Act of that year encouraged Indian self-determination with continuing government assistance and services.

The judicial branch in the period from 1945 to 1961 changed from a cautious and accommodating agency, under Chief Justice FRED M. VINSON, to an active, aggressive, and controversial storm-center under Chief Justice EARL WARREN. Just as WILLIAM HOWARD TAFT had made the Supreme Court the principal instrument for the determination of constitutionality in the 1920s, Earl Warren, who assumed the chief justiceship 1953, came to play a similar role in the late 1950s. Often backlash resulted, but in Warren's case, from conservatives and not liberals. Statistically, the WARREN COURT'S record was not so activist as that of the 1920s. Four acts of Congress, eighty-five state acts, and sixteen ordinances were ruled unconstitutional from 1945 through 1960, with the Justices overruling twenty-two prior decisions. But the activist image was strong because the Court entered explosive areas of sensitive public policy.

The Court's unanimous decision in BROWN V. BOARD OF EDUCATION (1954) had shocked southern states-righters into defensive and retaliatory actions. The Court's consistent pushing ahead in the civil rights area sustained and intensified this antipathy. But Warren, supported by a liberal majority, was not prepared to stop. In the loyalty-security area, the Court limited the more sweeping provisions of the Smith Act, the Internal Security Act of 1950, and state loyalty measures. The rights of individuals and their protection from the abuses of government seemed to come first to the Justices' minds. The Court struck at departures from fair procedure by congressional committees. In *Jencks v. United States* (1957) it ruled that a defendant in a criminal case should have access to prior recorded statements of witnesses against him. Congress promptly sought to limit that ruling by the passage of the JENCKS ACT. By the late 1950s, the Justices began the process of critically examining state anti-OBSCENITY and censorship laws. In Congress there was talk of the need to curtail the Court's authority through legislation limiting its appellate jurisdiction. National action by right-wing groups quickly emerged to bolster such a movement, contributing to a broad public dialogue on the Court's proper function.

Defenders and critics of the Warren Court's liberal activism debated the proper role of the Constitution in the American polity. Champions of liberal judicial activism defended the legitimacy of judicial activity to shape constitutional law in accordance with democratic values. Supporters of judicial restraint advocated deference to popularly elected legislatures with courts confined to a narrowly circumscribed role. To conservative constitutionalists, the rule of law meant more than the imposition by a liberal Court of its own ethical imperatives, with little concern for orthodox doctrinal consistency.

There were no winners in this debate. But it proved apropos to the developments of the 1950s and to the institutional interrelationships of those years.

PAUL L. MURPHY

Bibliography

MURPHY, PAUL L. 1969 *The Constitution in Crisis Times, 1918–1969.* New York: Harper & Row.

MURPHY, WALTER F. 1962 *Congress and the Court.* Chicago: University of Chicago Press.

PRITCHETT, C. HERMAN 1954 *Civil Liberties and the Vinson Court.* Chicago: University of Chicago Press.

CONSTITUTIONAL HISTORY, 1961–1977

An examination of nonjudicial constitutional development from the administration of President JOHN F. KENNEDY to that of President GERALD R. FORD reveals at the outset an unusual amount of constitutional change through the process of constitutional amendment. Indeed, counting the adoption of the BILL OF RIGHTS in 1791 as only one episode of constitutional change via the AMENDMENT PROCESS, the period from 1961 to 1977 was characterized by an exceptionally high level of constitutional amending activity, with four amendments adopted during the period. In contrast, again counting the adoption of the Bill of Rights as one amendment episode, there were thirteen constitutional amendments adopted between 1789 and 1961.

Three of the constitutional amendments adopted during the 1961–1977 period were clear reflections of the expansion of egalitarianism that found expression in other fields in the policies of DESEGREGATION, REAPPORTIONMENT, and the enlargement of the protection of CIVIL RIGHTS. The TWENTY-THIRD AMENDMENT, adopted on March 19, 1961, extended the right to vote in presidential elections to the residents of the DISTRICT OF COLUMBIA although restricting the District to the number of electoral votes allotted to the least populous state. The TWENTY-FOURTH AMENDMENT, ratified on January 23, 1964, outlawed the imposition of POLL TAXES in presidential and congressional elections and therefore removed a form of WEALTH DISCRIMINATION in federal elections. The addition of this amendment to the Constitution was subsequently rendered superfluous by the Supreme Court's holding in HARPER V. VIRGINIA BOARD OF ELECTIONS (1966) that poll taxes were a form of INVIDIOUS DISCRIMINATION prohibited by the Constitution. Further extension of VOTING RIGHTS occurred with the adoption of the TWENTY-SIXTH AMENDMENT on June 30, 1971, which extended the right to vote in both federal and state elections to eighteen-year-old citizens. The Twenty-Sixth Amendment was necessitated by the Supreme Court's holding in OREGON V. MITCHELL (1974) that Congress lacked the constitutional power to legislate the eighteen-year-old vote in state and local elections.

In contrast with the Twenty-Third, Twenty-Fourth, and Twenty-Sixth Amendments, the Twenty-Fifth Amendment, relating to PRESIDENTIAL SUCCESSION and disability and adopted in 1967, was the result of years of debate with regard to the problems that might arise if an incumbent president were temporarily or permanently disabled. Serious consideration of such an amendment to the Constitution was prompted by the illnesses afflicting President DWIGHT D. EISENHOWER during his term of office, and additional impetus for constitutional change in this area was created by the assassination of President Kennedy in 1963.

Under the provisions of the Twenty-Fifth Amendment, the President may declare his own disability to perform the duties of the office by informing the president pro tempore of the Senate and the speaker of the House of Representatives in writing of his own disability. Alternatively, the President's disability may be declared in writing to the same congressional officers by the vice-president and a majority of the Cabinet. In either instance, the vice-president assumes the duties of the presidency as acting President. A period of presidential disability may be ended either by the President's informing the congressional officers in writing of the termination of his disability, or if there is disagreement between the President and the vice-president and a majority of the Cabinet on the issue of the President's disability, the Congress may resolve the dispute. A two-thirds majority of both houses of Congress, however, is required to declare the President disabled; otherwise, the President resumes the duties of his office.

Although the disability provisions of the Twenty-Fifth Amendment have not been applied, Section 2 of the amendment had an important impact on the succession to the presidency during the administration of President RICHARD M. NIXON. Section 2 provides that whenever a vacancy in the office of vice-president occurs, the President shall appoint a new vice-president with the approval of a majority of both houses of Congress. These provisions of the Twenty-Fifth Amendment came into play when Vice-President Spiro T. Agnew resigned his office in 1973 under the threat of prosecution for income tax evasion. Pursuant to Section 2, President Nixon appointed Congressman Gerald R. Ford of Michigan as Agnew's successor, and the Congress confirmed Ford as vice-president. Subsequently, President Nixon resigned his office on August 9, 1974, when his IMPEACHMENT for his involvement in the WATERGATE affair and other abuses of office seemed imminent, and Vice-President Ford succeeded Nixon in the office of President. Under the provisions of the Twenty-Fifth Amendment, Ford thus became the first appointed vice-president as well as the first unelected vice-president to assume the office of the presidency.

The Watergate affair that led to President Nixon's resignation involved not only charges of bugging the Democratic National Committee headquarters, and the obstruction by the executive of the subsequent investigation of that incident, but also more generalized abuses of power by the executive. In addition to the issue of the scope of EXECUTIVE PRIVILEGE, which was ultimately resolved by the Supreme Court adversely to the President's claims in UNITED STATES v. NIXON (1974), the Watergate affair raised major constitutional issues concerning the nature of the impeachment process, as the impeachment of a President was seriously considered by the Congress for the first time since the impeachment of President AN-DREW JOHNSON in 1868. Because the Constitution provides that governmental officers including the President may be removed from office on impeachment for TREASON, bribery, or other high crimes and MISDEMEANORS, the consideration of the impeachment of President Nixon by the Congress involved the determination of what constituted an impeachable offense, an issue that had also been at the heart of the debate over the Johnson impeachment.

In the deliberations of the Judiciary Committee of the House of Representatives regarding ARTICLES OF IMPEACHMENT against President Nixon, the President's supporters argued that the President could be impeached only within the meaning of the Constitution for an indictable criminal offense. The President's opponents, on the other hand, contended that articles of impeachment could embrace political offenses, such as the abuse of power by the President, which were not indictable under the criminal law. The latter position ultimately prevailed among a majority of the Judiciary Committee when the committee adopted three articles of impeachment against President Nixon that contained charges that were essentially political, abuse of power offenses which were not indictable.

Article one of the articles of impeachment charged the President with obstruction of justice and with violating his oath of office requiring him to see to it that the laws were faithfully executed, but the second and third articles charged him with violating the constitutional rights of citizens, impairing the administration of justice, misusing executive agencies, and ignoring the SUBPOENAS of the Judiciary Committee through which it had sought EVIDENCE related to its impeachment inquiry. Although these charges included some indictable offenses, in adopting the articles the majority of the committee obviously construed the words "high crimes and misdemeanors" to include offenses that did not involve indictable crimes. In reaching this conclusion, the committee majority took a position that conformed with the view of the nature of the impeachment process that the House of Representatives had adopted in the Johnson impeachment proceedings in 1868.

Whether this broad view of the nature of impeachable offenses would have been sustained by a majority of the House of Representatives or the required two-thirds majority in the Senate remained an unanswered question because of President Nixon's resignation in August 1974. The Supreme Court rejected the President's claim of executive privilege and ordered the disclosure of the White House tape recordings relevant to the trial of those indicted in the Watergate affair. On the tapes thus released there appeared conversations clearly indicating President Nixon's participation in a conspiracy to obstruct justice, an indictable offense. In light of almost certain impeachment by the House of Representatives and likely conviction in the Senate, President Nixon resigned. With the impeachment process thus aborted, the answer to what properly could be considered an impeachable offense was left unresolved, as it had been in the proceedings against President Johnson over a hundred years earlier.

The Watergate affair and the abuses of presidential power associated with it, along with the involvement of the United States in the Vietnam War, had a profound impact upon the principal nonjudicial constitutional issue during the 1961–1977 period—the issue of the proper relation between the powers of the executive branch of the government and the powers of the Congress. Beginning at least as early as the administrations of FRANKLIN D. ROOSEVELT in the 1930s and 1940s, the presidency had increasingly become the dominant political institution at the national level, and Roosevelt's successors refined and added to the assertions of PRESIDENTIAL POWER that had characterized his administrations. By the late 1960s and early 1970s, therefore, the "Imperial Presidency" had become the focus of considerable attention and constitutional controversy, and a reassertion of congressional power against the aggrandizement of presidential power had clearly begun.

This reassertion of congressional power was to a great extent a reaction to the expansion of the powers of the presidency to new extremes during the administration of President Nixon. Although previous presidents had asserted the power to impound and to refuse to expend funds appropriated by Congress in limited areas, President Nixon asserted a much broadened IMPOUNDMENT power as a presidential prerogative. Instead of the relatively isolated instances of presidential refusals to spend congressionally appropriated monies that had occurred previously, during the 1970s the Nixon administration impounded billions of dollars in congressional appropriations and effectively asserted a presidential power to enforce only those congressionally authorized programs that received the president's approval.

The involvement of the United States in the war in Vietnam and Southeast Asia contributed to further controversy regarding the scope of presidential power to commit the armed forces to foreign military conflicts in the absence of a DECLARATION OF WAR by the Congress. The involvement of the United States in Vietnam had begun under President Kennedy with the dispatch of military advisers to the South Vietnamese armed forces, but under Presidents LYNDON B. JOHNSON and Nixon the American military presence in Southeast Asia grew to hundreds of thousands of troops. The failure of the American military efforts in Southeast Asia and the high cost of those efforts in lives and resources bolstered the arguments of critics that the power of the President to commit the United States to foreign military conflicts must be reined in.

Because of the impoundment policy of the Nixon administration and the presidential war in Southeast Asia, a reassertion of congressional power occurred in the field of domestic as well as FOREIGN AFFAIRS. The congressional response to the impoundment controversy was the enactment of the CONGRESSIONAL BUDGET AND IMPOUNDMENT CONTROL ACT OF 1974. This legislation provided that if the President resolved to eliminate the expenditure of funds appropriated by Congress, he was required to inform both houses of Congress of: the amounts involved; the agencies and programs affected; and the fiscal, budgetary, and economic effects of, and the reasons for, the proposed impoundment of funds. Both houses of Congress, the act provided, must approve the impoundment within forty-five days. If the President proposed instead to defer the spending of congressionally authorized appropriations, the act provided that he must similarly inform Congress of his intention to defer expenditures, and within forty-five days either house of Congress could require the expenditure of the funds by passing a resolution disapproving the President's proposed action. If the President refused to abide by congressional disapproval of impoundments, the act further authorized the Comptroller General to initiate legal action in the federal courts to force compliance with the will of the Congress.

In addition to addressing the problem of presidential impoundments, the Congressional Budget and Impoundment Control Act was directed at strengthening the powers of Congress over the budgetary process. To replace the practice of enacting appropriations without regard to the total amount that should be appropriated in a given fiscal year, the act provided that the Congress should agree upon a BUDGET resolution at the outset of the appropriations process, setting the total amount of money to be appropriated during the fiscal year. The amount so specified would then govern the actions of Congress in considering individual appropriations bills.

Finally, the act created a new agency, the Congressional Budget Office, and authorized that agency to advise Congress regarding revenue estimates, the likely amount of deficits or revenue surpluses and other economic data important to the budgetary process. Congress thus created a congressional agency, beyond the control of the executive, which would be an independent source of economic and budgetary information in competition with the executive branch's Treasury Department and Office of Management and Budget.

This reassertion of congressional power over domestic policy was matched in the field of foreign policy by the WAR POWERS RESOLUTION of November 7, 1973, passed over the veto of President Nixon. In the War Powers Resolution, Congress sought to deal with the problem of presidential wars such as the military involvement of the United States in Southeast Asia. Congress therefore not only imposed restrictions upon the power of the President to commit the country's armed forces in foreign conflicts but also sought to define the war-making powers of both the President and the Congress.

With regard to the war-making power of the President, the War Powers Resolution declared that the President could introduce United States armed forces into hostilities, or into a situation in which imminent involvement in hostilities was clearly indicated by the circumstances, only pursuant to a declaration of war, or under specific statutory authorization, or in response to a national emergency created by an attack upon the United States, its territories or possessions, or its armed forces. The language of the resolution thus clearly repudiated the argument, frequently asserted in the past, that the President was constitutionally authorized to take whatever action deemed necessary to protect the national interest. The impact of the resolution as an authoritative congressional interpretation of the President's constitutional war-making power was diluted, however, by the decision of Congress to include the interpretation of the President's war-making power in the "Purpose and Policy" section of the act, with the result that it did not purport to have legally binding effect.

The parts of the War Powers Resolution that did purport to be legally binding required the President to consult with Congress in every possible instance before committing the armed forces in hostilities or hostile situations. If the armed forces are introduced by the President into hostilities or hostile situations in the absence of a declared war, the resolution provided, the President must report the situation in writing to the presiding officers of the Congress within forty-eight hours and continue to report every six months thereafter. The resolution further required that in the absence of a declared war, the introduction

of the armed forces must be terminated within sixty days, or ninety days if the military situation makes their safe withdrawal impossible within sixty days. Finally, in the absence of a declared war or congressional authorization, the President must withdraw the armed forces from hostilities occurring outside the territory of the United States if Congress directs him to do so by CONCURRENT RESOLUTION, which is not subject to the President's veto power.

Although the War Powers Resolution was plainly an attempt by Congress to reassert its authority over presidential war-making and over the conduct of foreign affairs generally, its impact upon presidential power did not appear to have been so great as its supporters hoped or it critics feared at the time of its passage. During the administration of President Ford, American armed forces were introduced into hostile situations during the evacuation of Vietnam as well as during the recapture of the American merchantman *Mayaguez* and its crew from Cambodia. President Ford nevertheless did not feel bound in these actions by the terms of the War Powers Resolution but rather made plain his conviction that he was acting under his constitutional powers as COMMANDER-IN-CHIEF and as chief executive. The War Powers Resolution was thus subjected to early challenge as an authoritative construction of the President's war-making power. Given the ability of Presidents to marshal public support for their actions in foreign affairs, particularly in times of crisis, it was clear that the act could not be considered the last word regarding the relative power of Congress and the President in the field of foreign policy and war-making.

Just as the War Powers Resolution and the Congressional Budget and Impoundment Control Act symbolized the reassertion of congressional power in relation to the executive, both also embodied the device which Congress increasingly used in reasserting power over executive policymaking—the LEGISLATIVE VETO. The legislative veto first emerged as a congressional device for controlling the executive during the 1930s when Congress reserved the right to veto presidential proposals to reorganize the executive branch, but by the 1970s the legislative veto in various forms had proliferated and had been embodied in almost two hundred statutes enacted by Congress. The increased use of the legislative veto reflected Congress's dissatisfaction with its relationship with the executive and a desire to reassert policymaking power that had been eroded during the previous decades of heightened executive power.

Congress employed the legislative veto to disapprove proposed presidential actions, to disapprove rules and regulations proposed by the executive branch or administrative agencies, and to order the termination of presidential actions. The device took several forms, with some statutes requiring a resolution of approval or disapproval by only one house of Congress, others requiring both houses to act through a concurrent resolution, and still others conferring upon congressional committees the power to exercise the legislative veto.

Despite its increased use by Congress, the legislative veto was frequently opposed by the executive branch since its introduction in the 1930s on the grounds that the practice violates the Constitution. The executive and other critics of the legislative veto argued that the practice violated the principle of SEPARATION OF POWERS, ignored the principle of bicameralism in the exercise of legislative power, and allowed Congress to avoid the President's veto power which is normally applicable to legislation passed by Congress.

The constitutional principle of separation of powers, critics of the legislative veto noted, permits Congress to shape national policy by passing statutes, but, properly construed, does not permit Congress to interfere in the enforcement or administration of policy—a power properly belonging to the executive branch. The legislative veto, it was argued, thus violated a fundamental constitutional principle, especially insofar as it was used to allow Congress to veto rules and regulations proposed by executive or administrative agencies under DELEGATIONS OF POWER from the Congress.

Opponents also argued that the Constitution contemplates that Congress's policy-making role ordinarily requires the passage of statutes by both houses of Congress with the presentation of the statutes to the President for his approval or disapproval. By allowing the approval or disapproval of national policy through single house resolutions, JOINT RESOLUTIONS, or decisions of congressional committees, it was argued, the legislative veto ignored the bicameral legislative process contemplated by the Constitution and in addition permitted congressional policymaking through mechanisms not subject to the President's veto power, as the Constitution also contemplated.

Congress, on the other hand, clearly viewed the legislative veto as a useful weapon in exercising oversight over the executive and the bureaucracy, both of which were recipients of massive delegations of legislative power since the 1930s. Striking at another source of the imperial presidency, Congress thus em-

bodied the legislative veto in the National Emergencies Act of 1976, which terminated national emergencies declared by the President in 1933, 1950, 1970, and 1971, and required the President to inform the Congress of the existence of national emergencies and the powers the executive intends to use in managing the emergency. Such emergencies, the act provided, could be terminated at any time by Congress via a concurrent resolution. (See EMERGENCY POWERS.)

Despite the long-standing controversy regarding the constitutional legitimacy of the legislative veto, the Supreme Court did not pass upon the validity of the device until 1983. In IMMIGRATION AND NATURALIZATION SERVICE V. CHADHA (1983), however, the Court declared the legislative veto invalid on the ground that it violated the constitutional principles requiring legislative enactments to be passed by both houses of Congress and to be subject to the veto powers of the President.

Just as the period from the administration of President Kennedy to that of President Ford witnessed significant readjustments of presidential–congressional relations, dramatic changes also occurred during the period in the nature of the political party system and the electoral process. Perhaps the most significant development was the decline in the power and influence of the major political parties. The decline in the percentage of the public who identified with the Republican and Democratic parties that began in the 1950s continued during the 1960s and 1970s. In 1952 twenty-two percent of the voters indicated a strong identification with the Democratic party, while thirteen percent indicated such an identification with the Republican party. By 1976, these percentages had declined to fifteen and nine percent, respectively, while the number of voters identifying themselves as independents had risen significantly.

This decline in voter identification with the two major political parties was accompanied by a decline in the importance of the national conventions of the two parties in the selection of presidential candidates. In 1960, only sixteen states selected their delegations to the national party conventions through presidential primaries, but by 1976 thirty states used the primary system for the selection of national party convention delegates, with the result that almost three-quarters of the Democratic national convention delegates and well over sixty percent of the Republican delegates were selected through the presidential primary process. Nominations of presidential candidates were consequently no longer the products of negotiations among party leaders at the national conventions;

rather the national conventions merely ratified the selection of a presidential candidate as determined in the presidential primaries. And this decline in the significance of the national conventions was furthered, in the Democratic party, by the adoption of rules during the 1970s diminishing the power of party leaders and requiring proportional representation of women, minority groups, and other constituent groups within the party.

The decline of power of the political parties was furthered by the adoption of federal CAMPAIGN FINANCING laws in 1971, 1974, and 1976 which limited the amounts that could be contributed to election campaigns by individuals and groups and provided for federal financing of presidential elections. The result was a further diminution of the importance of traditional party organizations to presidential candidates, who increasingly relied upon personal campaign organizations both to win nomination and to conduct their national election campaigns. In a governmental system based upon the separation of powers, the decline of the party system, which traditionally had served to bridge the gap between the executive and legislative branches, could only have profound effects upon the capacity of Presidents to lead as well as upon the formation of national policy.

The period between 1961 and 1977 witnessed an acceleration of a long-term trend toward the centralization of power in the national government, although by the end of the period a significant reaction to this trend had become apparent. Two primary factors contributed to this centralizing trend: increased subsidization by the national government of programs at the state and local levels, and the assumption of responsibility by the national government over vast areas that had traditionally been left to state and local governments.

When John F. Kennedy was elected in 1960, for example, FEDERAL GRANTS-IN-AID to state and local governments stood at just over seven billion dollars and accounted for approximately fifteen percent of the total expenditures of state and local governments. By 1976, these federal grants-in-aid had mushroomed to almost sixty billion dollars and constituted almost twenty-five percent of total state and local expenditures.

Not only did state and local governments become increasingly dependent financially upon federal largess during this period but the character of federal grant-in-aid programs was also significantly altered. Before the 1960s, federal aid was primarily directed at subsidizing programs identified by state and local governments, but during the 1960s the identification of program needs increasingly shifted to the national government, with federal funds allocated according to national priorities. In addition, many federal grants, especially during President Johnson's War on Poverty program, were distributed at the local community level, by-passing state governors and officials who had traditionally had a voice in the administration of federal grants. As a result of the ensuing outcry from state and local officials, during the late 1960s and 1970s the federal government resorted to the device of block grants to state and local governments, grants involving fewer nationally imposed restrictions on their use and thus allowing the exercise of greater discretionary power by state and local officials. In 1972, Congress also adopted the State and Local Fiscal Assistance Act, which embraced the principle of federal revenue sharing with state and local governments. Despite the greater flexibility allowed state and local decision makers under REVENUE SHARING and block grants, the financial dependence of state and local governments on the national government in 1976 was eight times what it had been in 1960.

During the same period, the federal government's power was significantly expanded through congressional passage of a host of new statutes that expanded the regulatory role of the federal government in numerous new fields. Civil rights, the environment, occupational safety, consumer protection, and many other fields for the first time were subjected to extensive federal regulation. Since almost all of the new regulatory statutes involved extensive delegation of legislative power by Congress to the bureaucracy, the new expansion of federal regulatory authority involved a massive increase in administrative rules and regulations, as the bureaucracy exercised the legislative powers that had been delegated to it.

This increased intrusion of the federal government into the lives and affairs of the public ultimately produced a backlash of hostility toward the federal bureaucracy. John F. Kennedy had campaigned for the presidency in 1960 with the promise to get the country moving again, a promise suggesting an activist role for the national government. Because of the backlash against the expansion of the regulatory role of the federal government, however, presidential candidates in 1976 found that attacks on the federal bureaucracy and the national government as a whole hit a responsive chord with the public and proved to be popular campaign rhetoric.

This unpopularity of the bureaucracy, however, was only one symptom of the American public's shaken confidence in its major political institutions that had become manifest by the mid-1970s. Between 1961 and 1976, one President had been assassinated, one had resigned in disgrace, the long and costly war in Vietnam had concluded in disaster, and the Watergate affair had revealed the betrayal of the public trust at the highest levels of the government as well as abuses of power with sinister implications for the liberties of the American people. Such traumatic events not only undermined public confidence in political institutions but also profoundly affected the course of constitutional development. The office of the presidency, which since the 1930s had evolved into the dominant political institution at the national level, was consequently diminished considerably by 1976 in both power and prestige. Although a resurgence of congressional power had occurred in the 1970s, there was little evidence that Congress was institutionally capable of assuming the role of national leadership previously performed by the presidency, and effective national leadership had been made even more difficult by the decline of the political party system.

The most basic problem confronting the American polity by 1976 was nevertheless the problem of the loss of public confidence in governmental institutions. And the restoration of that confidence was the most profoundly difficult and fundamentally important task American public leadership faced as this period of constitutional development came to a close.

RICHARD C. CORTNER

Bibliography

ALEXANDER, HERBERT 1976 *Financing Politics: Money, Elections and Political Reform.* Washington, D.C.: Congressional Quarterly.
DRY, MURRAY 1981 The Congressional Veto and the Constitutional Separation of Powers. In Bessette, Joseph M. and Tulis, Jeffry, *The Presidency in the Constitutional Order.* Baton Rouge: Louisiana State University Press.
JACOB, HERBERT AND VINES, KENNETH N., eds. 1976 *Politics in the American States: A Comparative Analysis*, 3rd ed. Boston: Little, Brown.
KEECH, WILLIAM R. AND MATTHEWS, DONALD R. 1977 *The Party's Choice.* Washington, D.C.: Brookings Institution.
KURLAND, PHILIP B. 1977 *Watergate and the Constitution.* Chicago: University of Chicago Press.
SCHLESINGER, ARTHUR M., JR. 1973 *The Imperial Presidency.* Boston: Houghton Mifflin.
SCIGLIANO, ROBERT 1981 The War Powers Resolution and the War Powers. In Bessette, Joseph M. and Tulis, Jeffry, *The Presidency in the Constitutional Order.* Baton Rouge: Louisiana State University Press.
SUNDQUIST, LEONARD D. 1981 *The Decline and Resur-gence of Congress.* Washington, D.C.: Brookings Institution.

CONSTITUTIONAL HISTORY, 1977–1985

As America moved from commemorating the bicentennial of the DECLARATION OF INDEPENDENCE to commemorating the bicentennial of the Constitution, the political order was in apparent disarray. Constitutional history is, primarily, an account of changes in the distribution of power and authority within a regime. At least since 1933, political power in the American regime had shifted toward the federal government, and, within the federal government, toward the executive branch. Commentators referred to an "imperial presidency"; and yet no one since DWIGHT D. EISENHOWER had held the presidential office for two full terms. JOHN F. KENNEDY had been assassinated; LYNDON B. JOHNSON had abandoned the quest for reelection; RICHARD M. NIXON had been forced to resign; GERALD R. FORD, the appointed vice-president who succeeded Nixon, lost his bid for election in his own right. JIMMY CARTER, who defeated Ford, was to prove unable to carry the burden of the presidency, and so to be crushed in his bid for reelection by the landslide that elected RONALD REAGAN.

The national consensus about what the government should be and should do, at bottom a consensus about the meaning of the Constitution, was breaking down. No longer did national majorities automatically form behind the notions of positive government, of redistribution of wealth and incomes, or of solving anything identified as a "national problem" by creating a new administrative agency within the federal BUREAUCRACY. There were indications that a new consensus was forming, but it was not yet fully formed. Less clearly than in the past—say, in 1800, 1832, 1860, or 1932—was the new consensus readily identified with the program of a particular POLITICAL PARTY, although the revitalization of the Republican party gave it the better claim to such identification.

Constitutional history can be understood either broadly or narrowly. In the broad sense, the constitution is the arrangement of offices and the distribution of powers in a country, it is how the country governs itself. In a narrow sense, the Constitution is a document in which the framework for self-government is spelled out. The process of constitutional change in the United States most often involves redistribution of power without constitutional amendment.

Formal amendment of the Constitution is a rare

event. Only thirty-two amendments have ever been proposed by Congress, and two of those were pending as 1977 began; by 1985 both had died for want of RATIFICATION. The EQUAL RIGHTS AMENDMENT (ERA), ostensibly a guarantee that women and men would be treated equally under the law, but potentially a blank check for expansion of federal and judicial power, had been proposed in 1972. The DISTRICT OF COLUMBIA REPRESENTATION AMENDMENT, which would have made the national capital the equivalent of a STATE for most purposes, had been proposed in 1978. Even as those proposals failed to obtain the necessary votes in state legislatures, there was popular demand for more amendments: to mandate a balanced federal BUDGET; to proscribe SCHOOL BUSING as a remedy for de facto school segregation; to permit prayer in public schools; and to overturn the Supreme Court's proclamation of a constitutional right to abortion.

Amendments to accomplish each of these objectives were introduced in Congress, and the ERA was reintroduced, but none was proposed to the states. Indeed, only one amendment received a two-thirds vote in either house of Congress: the balanced budget amendment passed the Senate, but died when the House of Representatives failed to act on it. In the case of the balanced budget amendment, there were petitions from thirty-three states (one less than constitutionally required) calling for a convention to frame the proposal. Although there was much speculation among politicians, academicians, and pundits about how such a convention might work and whether it could be restricted in its scope, the failure of a thirty-fourth state to act made the speculation at least temporarily moot.

For three decades, constitutional innovation had been centered on the judicial branch. Between 1977 and 1985, however, constitutional development centered on the contest between Congress and the executive branch for predominance. The most important constitutional decision of the Supreme Court during the period, IMMIGRATION AND NATURALIZATION SERVICE V. CHADHA (1983), passed on a phase of that contest.

The only uniquely American constitutional doctrine is that of the SEPARATION OF POWERS attended by CHECKS AND BALANCES. The embodiment of that doctrine in the Constitution set up a constant rivalry for preeminence between the political branches and an intense jealousy of powers and prerogatives. Beginning in the FRANKLIN D. ROOSEVELT era, the President—or the institutionalized presidency—seemed to acquire ever more power within the political system,

and appeared to have acquired a permanent position of dominance. But the VIETNAM WAR and the WATERGATE crisis led to a resurgence of Congress, represented especially in the War Powers Resolution of 1973 and the CONGRESSIONAL BUDGET AND IMPOUNDMENT CONTROL ACT of 1974.

The seizure of the American embassy in Iran by Islamic revolutionary guards in 1979 set the stage for reassessment of the constitutional status of the WAR POWERS. President Carter in April 1980 ordered the armed forces to attempt a rescue of the American citizens held hostage in Tehran. The secrecy necessarily surrounding such an attempt precluded the "consultations" mandated by the War Powers Resolution. When, through the coincidence of bad planning and bad weather, the operation proved a costly failure, congressional critics were quick to denounce Carter for his defiance of the law—some going so far as to call for his IMPEACHMENT. The hostages subsequently were released as the result of an EXECUTIVE AGREEMENT by which Carter canceled the claims of some Americans against the revolutionary government of Iran and caused other claims to be submitted to an international tribunal rather than to American courts. This settlement of the hostage crisis appeared to some observers to exceed the scope of presidential power, but it was upheld by the Supreme Court in DAMES & MOORE V. REGAN (1981).

The War Powers Resolution continued to bedevil presidential conduct of FOREIGN AFFAIRS during the Reagan administration; but the real character of that controversial resolution was revealed by the contrast between two incidents involving American military forces. In 1981 President Reagan, at the request of all of the governments of the region, and in conjunction with two foreign allies, detailed a battalion of marines to Beirut, Lebanon, as part of an international peacekeeping force. The operation was not of the sort explicitly covered by the War Powers Resolution, and Reagan, although he communicated with members of Congress, did not take steps to comply with the consultation or reporting requirements of the resolution. Congress, however, unilaterally acted to approve the President's course of action rather than precipitate a confrontation over either the applicability of the resolution or its constitutionality. Several months after a suicide bomber killed more than 200 marines, the President withdrew the rest of the marines from Lebanon, conceding a major foreign policy failure; but Congress, because it had acted affirmatively to approve the operation, was in no position to condemn the President for that failure.

Subsequently, in 1984, the President authorized

a military operation to rescue American citizens trapped in the small Carribean nation of Grenada and to liberate that country from a Cuban-sponsored communist dictatorship. Such an operation was precisely within the terms of the War Powers Resolution, but it was planned and executed in secrecy and, again, the President complied with neither the consultation nor the reporting requirements of the resolution. However, because the operation was perceived as a success, most members of Congress refrained from complaining about the breach of the War Powers Resolution.

As the War Powers Resolution represented the resurgence of Congress in the foreign policy arena, the Congressional Budget Act was designed to reassert congressional control over government spending priorities. The federal budgetary process had been introduced in the 1920s to replace the chaotic amalgam of uncoordinated appropriations by which Congress had theretofore allocated federal revenues. But the executive budget, while coordinating expenditures and subjecting them to a common annual plan, remained detached from the appropriations process; hence disputes arose between the branches, especially when the aggregate of appropriations exceeded the executive's estimate of revenues. The deferral and cancellation of appropriated expenditures—called IMPOUNDMENT—became especially controversial when President Nixon was accused of using them for political, rather than economic, reasons.

The 1974 act purported to solve the problem by making budget planning a congressional function and by linking budgeting and appropriations in a single process. But, because the internal structure of Congress is not conducive to unified decision making and because the executive branch has not conceded that the detailed planning of expenditures is properly a legislative activity, the revised budget process has not been successful. The national government commonly operates for most of the year on the basis of resolutions authorizing continued spending at some percentage increase over the previous year's spending plus numerous special appropriations.

Between 1977 and 1985, as, to a lesser degree, between World War II and 1977, one of the great tests of constitutional government in America was the fiscal crisis resulting from persistent excesses of governmental expenditures over governmental revenues. Under constant political pressure to maintain or increase expenditure levels, but facing the unpopularity of increases in taxation (combined with the economic difficulty that increased tax rates may, by diminishing the tax base, actually result in lower revenues), Congress has resorted to borrowing to finance chronic deficits. At the end of 1985, Congress enacted, and President Reagan signed, a law providing for automatic reductions of appropriations when projected deficits reached specified levels. However, the ink was hardly dry before that measure (the GRAMM-RUDMAN-HOLLINGS ACT) was challenged as unconstitutional, even by some members of Congress and some representatives of the administration.

State legislatures, commonly required by their state constitutions to balance their own annual budgets, have petitioned Congress for a convention to propose a balanced budget amendment to the federal constitution. How even a constitutional mandate could be enforced to make Congress do what it seems unable to do, that is, to make difficult choices about public affairs, remains unclear. Meanwhile, the Congressional Budget Act exists to frustrate any attempt of the executive branch to supply the decision making.

Yet another device by which Congress attempted to reassert itself in the contest for dominance under a constitution that separates powers was the LEGISLATIVE VETO. Long before 1977, the DELEGATION OF POWER to the executive branch and to various INDEPENDENT REGULATORY AGENCIES was so great that the published volumes of federal regulations exceeded in number by many times the volumes of federal statutes. In statutes delegating legislative power to administrative bodies, Congress began to include provisions allowing Congress, or one house of Congress, to deprive agency actions of effect by simple resolution. In June 1983 the Supreme Court, in IMMIGRATION AND NATURALIZATION SERVICE V. CHADHA, held that the legislative veto, in some or all of its forms, was unconstitutional. The effect of the *Chadha* decision on legislative veto provisions that differed significantly from that in the Immigration and Nationality Act remained unclear for some time after the decision, and Congress continued to enact new legislative veto provisions after the decision. The real winner in that struggle for power, however, was not the President, but the bureaucracy.

Congress also asserted itself in more traditional ways, especially by exploiting the constitutional requirement that certain presidential actions have the Senate's ADVICE AND CONSENT. One category of such action is treaty making. President Carter suffered embarrassment over the PANAMA CANAL TREATIES and defeat on the second Strategic Arms Limitation Treaty. The Panama Canal debate was the first extended debate on a major treaty since that on the

Treaty of Versailles in 1919. The treaty was signed in September 1977 but the Senate did not consent to its ratification until the spring of 1978. The vote was 68–32 (only one affirmative vote more than required) and the Senate attached a "reservation" to the treaty, asserting that the United States could intervene militarily if the canal should ever be closed; the reservation nearly caused Panama to rescind its ratification of the treaty. President Carter signed the strategic arms treaty in July 1979 at a summit meeting with President Leonid Brezhnev of the Soviet Union. Although trumpeted as a major foreign policy achievement, the treaty was delayed in Senate hearings and finally shelved in 1980 after the Soviet Union invaded Afghanistan.

President Carter vigorously asserted the presidential treaty power when, after recognizing the People's Republic of China in Beijing as the lawful government of all of China he unilaterally abrogated the long-standing mutual defense treaty between the United States and the Republic of China on Taiwan. An affronted Congress immediately provided for a United States Institute to represent American interests in the Republic of China while delaying for over a year Carter's request that trade preferences be granted to the mainland regime. Congress was unable to salvage the mutual defense treaty, however; and the Supreme Court held in GOLDWATER V. CARTER (1979) that members of Congress lacked STANDING to challenge the President's action in court.

The other category of action requiring Senate approval is appointments. The Senate, although nominally controlled by the President's own party, frequently used confirmation hearings and votes to express disapproval of certain Reagan administration policies, especially the administration's reluctance to impose and enforce AFFIRMATIVE ACTION requirements. The Senate delayed for over a year appointment of Edwin Meese to be ATTORNEY GENERAL, and rejected outright the promotion of William Bradford Reynolds to be associate attorney general. Although Reagan's nomination of SANDRA DAY O'CONNOR to the Supreme Court (the only nomination to the Court between 1977 and 1985) was approved rapidly and without serious controversy, several other judicial appointments were delayed or rejected.

Another signal characteristic of American constitutionalism is FEDERALISM. From the mid-1930s on, the balance of power between the national government and the states has been shifting steadily in favor of the national government. President Reagan came to office pledging a reversal of that trend. However, his proposal for a "new federalism," in which governmental functions assumed by the national government would be relinquished to the states, was coolly received not only by Congress but also by state politicians, who feared that their responsibilities would increase even as their revenues continued to decrease. Somewhat more successful was Reagan's proposal to replace the myriad of categorical FEDERAL GRANTS-IN-AID, by which the national government partially funded certain mandated programs and set the standards by which the programs were to be run, with block grants.

Congress, however, has increasingly imposed conditions and restrictions on the use of block grant funds; so even the limited victory may prove hollow. Although conservatives like President Reagan frequently express a principled aversion to the use of conditional grants of money as a means to coerce the states into acceding to federal goals and programs, they have not been so averse in practice. Examples of new uses of the TAXING AND SPENDING POWER to accomplish legislative goals not strictly within Congress's ENUMERATED POWERS include: a requirement that hospitals receiving federal funds perform certain lifesaving measures on behalf of handicapped newborn children; a requirement that states, as a condition of receiving highway building funds, enact certain provisions to counter drunken driving; and a requirement that schools, as a condition of receiving federal aid, permit religious groups to meet in their facilities on the same basis as do other extracurricular organizations.

Whether the election of 1980 wrought an enduring change in the constitution of American government remains an open question. Although President Reagan decisively defeated former Vice-President Walter F. Mondale in 1984, the House of Representatives remained under the control of Carter's and Mondale's party. And the Senate, even with a Republican majority, did not prove to be so committed as the President to reduction of the role of the federal government in American society. Nevertheless, Reagan had considerable success in achieving the deregulation of some kinds of businesses and in returning to private enterprise some activities that had come under the ownership and management of the federal government. On the other hand, the heralded "new federalism" did not cause a resurgence in the relative importance of the state governments, and federal control continued to be maintained through the use of conditions attached to grants-in-aid. At the bicentennial of the Constitution, it is still too early to say whether

Reagan effected, as he said he would, "another American revolution."

DENNIS J. MAHONEY

Bibliography

CARTER, JIMMY 1984 *Keeping the Faith.* New York: Bantam.

FISHER, LOUIS 1984 *Congressional Conflicts between Congress and the President.* Princeton, N.J.: Princeton University Press.

GINSBERG, BENJAMIN 1987 *Reconstituting American Politics: Cleavages and Coalitions in the Age of Ronald Reagan.* New York: Oxford University Press.

HOWITT, ARNOLD M. 1984 *Managing Federalism: Studies in Intergovernmental Relations.* Washington: Congressional Quarterly.

SCHRAMM, PETER W. and MAHONEY, DENNIS J., EDS. 1986 *The 1984 Election and the Future of American Politics.* Durham, N.C.: Carolina Academic Press.

CONSTITUTIONAL INTERPRETATION

"Constitutional interpretation" comprehends the methods or strategies available to people attempting to resolve disputes about the meaning or application of the Constitution. The possible sources for interpretation include the text of the Constitution, its "original history," including the general social and political context in which it was adopted as well as the events immediately surrounding its adoption, the governmental structures created and recognized by the Constitution, the "ongoing history" of interpretations of the Constitution, and the social, political, and moral values of the interpreter's society or some subgroup of the society. The term "originalist" refers to interpretation concerned with the first three of these sources.

The extraordinary current interest in constitutional interpretation is partly the result of controversy over the SUPREME COURT's expansive readings of the FOURTEENTH AMENDMENT; it also parallels developments in literary theory and more generally the humanities. Received notions about the intrinsic meaning of words or texts, access to an author's intentions, and the very notion of "validity" in interpretation have been forcefully attacked and vehemently defended by philosophers, literary theorists, social scientists, and historians of knowledge. Legal writers have imported scholarship from these disciplines into their own, and some humanists have become interested in legal interpretation.

Issues of interpretive methodology have always been politically charged—certainly so in constitutional law. JOHN MARSHALL's foundational decisions asserting the power of the central government were met by claims that he had willfully misconstrued the document. In our own time, modernist interpretive theories tend to be invoked by proponents of JUDICIAL ACTIVISM, and more conventional views by its opponents. The controversy within the humanities and the social sciences is itself deeply political, for the modernist assertion that truth or validity is socially constructed and hence contingent is often perceived as destabilizing or delegitimating.

The Constitution is a political document; it serves political ends; its interpretations are political acts. Any theory of constitutional interpretation therefore presupposes a normative theory of the Constitution itself—a theory, for example, about the constraints that the words and intentions of the adopters should impose on those who apply or interpret the Constitution. As Ronald Dworkin observed, "Some parts of any constitutional theory must be independent of the intentions or beliefs or indeed the acts of the people the theory designates as Framers. Some part must stand on its own political or moral theory; otherwise the theory would be wholly circular."

The eclectic practices of interpreters and the continuing debate over the appropriate methods or strategies of constitutional interpretation suggest that we have no unitary, received theory of the Constitution. The American tradition of constitutional interpretation accords considerable authority to the language of the Constitution, its adopters' purposes, and the implications of the structures created and recognized by the Constitution. But our tradition also accords authority to precedents and the judicial exegesis of social values and practices, even when these diverge from plausible readings of the text and original understandings.

Any theory of constitutional interpretation must start from the fact that we have a written Constitution. Why is the written Constitution treated as binding? Because, as Chief Justice Marshall asserted in MARBURY V. MADISON (1803), it is law—the supreme law of the land—and because since 1789 public institutions and the citizenry have treated it as an authoritative legal document. It is no exaggeration to say that the written Constitution lies at the core of the American "civil religion."

Doubtless, the most frequently invoked canon of textual interpretation is the "plain meaning rule." Marshall wrote in STURGES V. CROWNINSHIELD (1819):

[A]lthough the spirit of an instrument, especially of a constitution, is to be respected not less than its letter, yet the spirit is to be collected chiefly from its words. . . . [I]f, in any case, the plain meaning of a provision, not contradicted by any other provision in the same instrument, is to be disregarded, because we believe the framers of that instrument could not intend what they say, it must be one in which the absurdity and injustice of applying the provision to the case, would be so monstrous that all mankind would, without hesitation, unite in rejecting the application.

Marshall did not equate "plain" meaning with "literal" meaning, but rather (as Justice OLIVER WENDELL HOLMES later put it) the meaning that it would have for "a normal speaker of English" under the circumstances in which it was used. The distinction is nicely illustrated by Chief Justice Marshall's opinion in McCULLOCH V. MARYLAND (1819), decided the same year as *Sturges*. Maryland had argued that the NECESSARY AND PROPER clause of Article I authorized Congress only to enact legislation "indispensable" to executing the ENUMERATED POWERS. Marshall responded with the observation that the word "necessary," as used "in the common affairs of the world, or in approved authors, . . . frequently imports no more than that one thing is convenient, or useful, or essential to another." He continued:

Such is the character of human language, that no word conveys to the mind, in all situations, one single definite idea; and nothing is more common than to use words in a figurative sense. Almost all compositions contain words, which, taken in their rigorous sense, would convey a meaning different from that which is obviously intended. It is essential to just construction that many words which import something excessive, should be understood in a more mitigated sense—in that sense which common usage justifies. . . . This word, then, like others, is used in various senses; and in its construction, the subject, the context, the intention of the person using them, are all to be taken into view.

To read a provision without regard to its context and likely purposes will yield either unresolvable indeterminacies or plain nonsense. An interpreter could not, for example, decide whether the FIRST AMENDMENT's "FREEDOM OF SPEECH" encompassed singing, flag-waving, and criminal solicitation; or whether the "writings" protected by the COPYRIGHT clause included photographs, sculptures, performances, television broadcasts, and computer programs. She would not know whether the provision in Article II that "No person except a natural born Citizen . . . shall be eligible to the Office of President" disqualified persons born abroad or those born by Caesarian section. We can identify interpretations as compelling, plausible, or beyond the pale only because we think we understand the concerns that underlie the provisions.

One's understanding of a provision, including the concerns that underlie it, depends partly on the ideological or political presuppositions one brings to the interpretive enterprise. Marshall could so readily label Maryland's construction of the word "necessary" as excessive because of his antecedent conception of a "constitution" as essentially different from a legal code—as a document "intended to endure for ages to come"—and because of his beliefs about the structure of FEDERALISM implicit in the United States Constitution. A judge starting from different premises might have found Maryland's construction more plausible.

A meaning thus is "plain" when it follows from the interpreter's presuppositions and when these presuppositions are shared within the society or at least within the relevant "community of interpretation"—for example, the legal profession. Kenneth Abraham has remarked, "The plain is plain because it is constantly recurring in similar contexts and there is general agreement about the meaning of language that may be applied to it. In short, meaning is a function of agreement. . . ."

When a provision is interpreted roughly contemporaneously with its adoption, an interpreter unconsciously places it in the social and linguistic context of her society. Over the course of several centuries, however, even a relatively stable nation will undergo changes—in social and economic relations, in technology, and ultimately in values—to an extent that a later interpreter cannot readily assume that she has direct access to the contexts in which a constitutional provision was adopted. This poses both a normative and a methodological question for the modern interpreter: should she attempt to read provisions in their original social and linguistic contexts, or in a modern context, or in some way that mediates between the two? And, to the extent that the original contexts are relevant, how can she ascertain them?

Original history includes "legislative history"—the debates and proceedings in the conventions and legislatures that proposed and adopted constitutional provisions—and the broader social, economic, and political contexts surrounding their adoption. Although it is widely acknowledged that original history should play a role in constitutional interpretation, there is little agreement over the aims and methods of historical inquiry. The controversy centers on the level of generality on which an interpreter should try to apprehend the adopters' intentions. On the highest or broadest level, an interpreter poses the questions: "What was the general problem to which this provision was responsive and how did the provision respond to it?" On the most specific level, she inquires: "How would the adopters have resolved the particular issue that we are now considering?"

The first or "general" question elicits answers such as: "The purpose of the COMMERCE CLAUSE was to permit Congress to regulate commerce that affects more than one state, or to regulate where the states are separately incompetent to regulate." Or: "The purpose of the EQUAL PROTECTION clause was to prohibit invidious discrimination." These characterizations do not purport to describe the scope of a provision precisely. On the contrary, they are avowedly vague or open-ended: the claim is not that the equal protection clause forbids every conceivable invidious discrimination (it may or may not) but that it is generally concerned with preventing invidious discriminations.

The general question is an indispensable component of any textual interpretation. The interpreter seeks a "purpose" that she can plausibly attribute to everyone who voted for the provision, and which, indeed, must have been understood as their purpose even by those who opposed its adoption. The question is often couched in objective-sounding terms: it seeks the "purpose of the provision" rather than the "intent of the framers." And its answer is typically sought in the text read in the social and linguistic context in which it was adopted. As Marshall wrote in *McCulloch*, "the spirit of an instrument . . . is to be collected chiefly from its words." If the status of the written Constitution as "law" demands textual interpretation, it also entails this general inquiry, without which textual interpretation cannot proceed.

The second inquiry, which can be called "intentionalist," seeks very specific answers, such as: "Did the adopters of the Fourteenth Amendment intend to prohibit school SEGREGATION?" or "Did they intend to prohibit 'reverse' discrimination?" One rationale for this focus was asserted by Justice GEORGE H. SUTHERLAND, dissenting in HOME BUILDING & LOAN ASSOCIATION V. BLAISDELL (1934): "[T]he whole aim of construction, as applied to a provision of the Constitution, is . . . to ascertain and give effect to the intent of its framers and the people who adopted it." Another rationale is that recourse to the adopters' intentions constrains the interpreter's discretion and hence the imposition of her own values. Some methodological problems are presented by any interpretive strategy that seeks to specify the adopters' intentions.

The procedures by which the *text* of a proposed constitutional provision is adopted are usually straightforward and clear: a text becomes a law if it is adopted by the constitutionally prescribed procedures and re-

ceives the requisite number of votes. For example, an amendment proposed in Congress becomes a part of the Constitution when it is approved by two-thirds of the members of each House and ratified by the legislatures in three-fourths of the states, or by conventions in three-fourths of the states, as Congress may prescribe.

How does an *intention* acquire the status of law? Some interpreters assume, without discussion, that by ratifying the framers' language, the thousands of people whose votes are necessary to adopt a constitutional provision either manifest their intent to adopt, or are somehow bound by, the intentions of certain of the drafters or framers—even if those intentions are not evident from the text itself. This view is not supported by anything in the Constitution, however, or by eighteenth- or nineteenth-century legal theory or practice.

If one analogizes the adoption of "an intention" concerning the text of the Constitution to the adoption of a text, an intention would become binding only when it was held by the number and combination of adopters prescribed by Article V. This poses no particular difficulty for an interpreter who wishes to understand the general aims or purposes of a provision. Statements by framers, proponents, and opponents, together with the social and political background against which the provision was adopted, often indicate a shared understanding. But these sources cannot usually answer specific questions about the adopters' intentions. The intentionalist interpreter thus often engages in a degree of speculation that undermines the very rationale for the enterprise.

The adopters of a provision may intend that it prohibit or permit some activity, or that it *not* prohibit or permit the activity; or they may have no intentions at all regarding the matter. An intentionalist interpreter must often infer the adopters' intentions from opaque sources, and must try to describe their intentions with respect to situations that they probably never thought about.

The effort to determine the adopters' intentions is further complicated by the problem of identifying the intended specificity of a provision. This problem is nicely illustrated by an example of Ronald Dworkin's. Consider the possible intentions of those who adopted the CRUEL AND UNUSUAL PUNISHMENT clause of the Eighth Amendment. They might have intended the language to serve only as a shorthand for the Stuart tortures which were their exemplary applications of the clause. Somewhat more broadly, they might have intended the clause to be understood to incorporate the principle of *ejusdem generis*—to include their exemplary applications and other punishments that they found, or would have found, equally repugnant.

More broadly yet, they might have intended to delegate to future decision makers the authority to apply the clause in light of the general principles underlying it. To use Dworkin's terms, they might have intended future interpreters to develop their own "conceptions" of cruel and unusual punishment within the framework of the adopters' general "concept" of the clause. If so, then the fact that they viewed a certain punishment as tolerable does not imply that they intended the clause "not to prohibit" such punishments. Like parents who instill values in their children both by articulating and applying a moral principle, the adopters may have accepted the eventuality that the principle would be applied in ways that diverged from their own particular views.

Whether or not such a motivation seems likely with respect to applications of the clause in the adopters' contemporary society, it may be more plausible with respect to applications by future interpreters, whose understandings of the clause would be affected by changing knowledge, values, and forms of society. On the other hand, the adopters may have thought of themselves as more virtuous or less corruptible than unknown future generations, and for that reason may have intended this and other clauses to be construed narrowly.

How can an interpreter determine the breadth of construction intended by the adopters of any particular provision? Primarily, if not exclusively, from the language of the provision itself. Justice FELIX FRANK-FURTER wrote in *National Mutual Insurance Company v. Tidewater Transfer Company* (1949):

The precision which characterizes [the jurisdictional provisions] . . . of Article III is in striking contrast to the imprecision of so many other provisions of the Constitution dealing with other very vital aspects of government. This was not due to chance or ineptitude on the part of the Framers. The differences in subject-matter account for the drastic difference in treatment. Great concepts like "Commerce among the several states," "due process of law," "liberty," "property," were purposely left to gather meaning from experience. For they relate to the whole domain of social and economic fact, and the statesmen who founded this nation knew too well that only a stagnant society remains unchanged. But when the Constitution in turn gives strict definition of power or specific limitations upon it we cannot extend the definition or remove the translation. Precisely because "it is a *constitution* we are expounding," M'Culloch v. Maryland, we ought not to take liberties with it.

Charles Curtis put the point more generally: "Words in legal documents are simply delegations to others of authority to give them meaning by applying them to particular things or occasions. . . . And the more imprecise the words are, the greater is the delegation, simply because then they can be applied or not to more particulars. This is the only important feature of words in legal draftsmanship or interpretation."

This observation seems correct. Yet it is worth noting that the relative precision of a word or clause itself depends both on context and on interpretive conventions, and is often uncertain and contestable. For example, in UNITED STATES V. LOVETT (1946) Justice Frankfurter characterized the BILL OF AT-TAINDER clause as among the Constitution's very "specific provisions." Yet he construed that clause to apply to punishments besides death, ignoring the technical eighteenth-century distinction between a bill of attainder, which imposed the death penalty, and a bill of "pains and penalties," which imposed lesser penalties.

The effort to characterize clauses as relatively open or closed confronts a different sort of historical problem as well. The history of interpretation of written constitutions was not extensive in 1787. Marshall's assertion that it is the nature of a constitution "that only its great outlines should be marked" (*McCulloch*) drew more on theory than on practice. But Marshall and his successors practiced this theory. Whatever assumptions the adopters of the original Constitution might have made about the scope of their delegations of authority, the Reconstruction amendments were adopted in the context of decades of "latitudinarian" constitutional interpretation. What bearing should this context have on the interpretation of provisions adopted since the original Constitution?

The intentionalist interpreter's initial task is to situate the provision and documents bearing on it in their original linguistic and social contexts. She can draw on the accumulated knowledge of American social, political, and intellectual history. Ultimately, however, constitutional interpretation is subject to the same limitations that attend all historical inquiry. Quentin Skinner has described the most pervasive of these:

[I]t will never in fact be possible simply to study what any given classic writer has *said* . . . without bringing to bear some of one's own expectations about what he must have been saying. . . . [T]hese models and preconceptions in terms of which we unavoidably organize and adjust our perceptions and thoughts will themselves tend to act as determinants of what we think or perceive. We must classify in order to understand, and we can only classify the unfamiliar in terms of the familiar. The perpetual danger, in our attempts to enlarge our historical understanding, is thus that our expectations about what someone must be saying or doing will themselves determine that we understand the agent to be doing something which he would not—or even could not—himself have accepted as an account of what he *was* doing.

Trying to understand how the adopters intended a provision to apply in their own time and place is, in essence, doing history. But the intentionalist interpreter must take the further step of translating the adopters' intentions into the present. She must decide how the commerce power applies to modes of transportation, communication, and economic relations not imagined—perhaps not imaginable—by the adopters; how the cruel and unusual punishment clause applies to the death penalty in a society that likely apprehends death differently from a society in which death was both more commonplace and more firmly integrated into a religious cosmology. The Court invoked difficulties of this sort when it concluded that the history surrounding the adoption of the Fourteenth Amendment was "inconclusive" with respect to the constitutionality of school DESEGREGATION almost a century later. Noting the vastly different roles of public education in the mid-nineteenth and mid-twentieth centuries, Chief Justice EARL WARREN wrote in BROWN V. BOARD OF EDUCATION (1954): "[W]e cannot turn back the clock to 1868 when the Amendment was adopted. . . . We must consider public education in the light of its full development and its present place in American life throughout the Nation. Only in this way can it be determined if segregation in public schools deprives these plaintiffs of the equal protection of the laws." In sum, even the historian who attempts to meet and understand the adopters on their own ground is engaging in a creative enterprise. To project the adopters into a world they could not have envisioned borders on fantasy.

In an important lecture given in 1968, entitled "Structure and Relationship in Constitutional Law," Professor Charles L. Black, Jr., described a mode of constitutional interpretation based on "inference from the structure and relationships created by the constitution in all its parts or in some principal part." Professor Black observed that in *McCulloch v. Maryland,* "Marshall does not place principal reliance on the [necessary and proper] clause as a ground of decision. . . . [Before] he reaches it he has already decided, on the basis of far more general implications,

that Congress possesses the power, not expressly named, of establishing a bank and chartering corporations: . . . [h]e addresses himself to the necessary and proper clause only in response to counsel's arguing its *restrictive* force." Indeed, the second part of *McCulloch,* which held that the Constitution prohibited Maryland from levying a tax on the national bank, rested exclusively on inferences from the structure of the federal system and not at all on the text of the Constitution. Similarly, *Crandall v. Nevada* (1868) was not premised on the PRIVILEGES AND IMMUNITIES clause of either Article IV or the Fourteenth Amendment. Rather, the Court inferred a right of personal mobility among the states from the structure of the federal system: "[The citizen] has the right to come to the seat of government to assert any claim he may have upon that government, or to transact any business he may have with it . . . and this right is in its nature independent of the will of any State over whose soil he must pass to exercise it."

Citing examples like these, Professor Black argued that interpreters too often have engaged in "Humpty-Dumpty textual manipulation" rather than relying "on the sort of political inference which not only underlies the textual manipulation but is, in a well constructed opinion, usually invoked to support the interpretation of the cryptic text."

Institutional relationships are abstractions from the text and the purposes of provisions—themselves read on a high level of abstraction. The implications of the structures of government are usually vague, often even ambiguous. Thus, while structural inference is an important method of interpretation, it shares the limitations intrinsic to other interpretive strategies. It seldom yields unequivocal answers to the specific questions that arise in the course of constitutional debates.

For the most part, the Supreme Court—the institution that most systematically and authoritatively interprets and articulates the meaning of the Constitution—has construed the language, original history, and structure of the Constitution on a high level of abstraction. It has treated most provisions in the spirit suggested by Chief Justice Marshall in *McCulloch v. Maryland.* This view of the Constitution is partly a political choice, based on the desire to accommodate a venerated and difficult-to-amend historical monument with changing circumstances, attitudes, and needs. But it is no less a consequence of the nature of language and history, which necessarily leave much of the meaning of the Constitution to be determined by its subsequent applications.

Constitutional disputes typically arise against the

background of earlier decisions on similar subjects. A complete theory of constitutional interpretation therefore must deal with the role of precedent. Interpreting a judicial precedent is different from interpreting the constitutional provision itself. A precedent consists of a JUDGMENT based on a particular set of facts together with the court's various explanations for the judgment. The precedent must be read, not only in terms of its own social context, but against the background of the precedents it invokes or ignores. Lon Fuller wrote:

In the common law it is not too much to say that the judges are always ready to look behind the words of a precedent to what the previous court was trying to say, or to what it would have said if it could have foreseen the nature of the cases that were later to arise, or if its perception of the relevant factors in the case before it had been more acute. There is, then, a real sense in which the written words of the reported decisions are merely the gateway to something lying behind them that may be called, without any excess of poetic license, "unwritten law."

The American doctrine of STARE DECISIS accords presumptive but not indefeasible authority to precedent. Courts sometimes have overruled earlier decisions to return to what is said to be the original understanding of a provision. They have also overruled precedents that seem inconsistent with contemporary norms. For example, in HARPER v. VIRGINIA STATE BOARD OF ELECTIONS (1966), the Supreme Court overruled a twenty-year-old precedent to invalidate, under the equal protection clause, a state law conditioning the right to vote in state election on payment of an annual POLL TAX of $1.50. After surveying intervening decisions protecting political participation and other interests, Justice WILLIAM O. DOUGLAS concluded: "In determining what lines are unconstitutionally discriminatory, we have never been confined to historic notions of equality, any more than we have restricted due process to a fixed catalogue of what was at a given time deemed to be the limits of fundamental rights. . . . Notions of what constitutes equal treatment for purposes of the Equal Protection clause *do* change."

The process of constitutional adjudication thus has a dynamic of its own. It creates an independent force which, as a DOCTRINE evolves, may compete with the text and original history as well as with older precedents. Whether or not, as Justice JOHN MARSHALL HARLAN argued in dissent, *Harper* was inconsistent with the original understanding of the Fourteenth Amendment, the decision would have been inconceivable without the intervening expansion of doc-

trine beyond applications contemplated by the adopters of the Fourteenth Amendment.

Disagreements about the propriety of this evolutionary process are rooted in differing theories of constitutional law. To a strict intentionalist like Raoul Berger, the process appears to be simply the accretion of errors, which should be corrected to the extent possible. Others hold that the process properly accommodates the Constitution to changing needs and values. As Justice Holmes wrote in MISSOURI v. HOLLAND (1920):

[W]hen we are dealing with words that are also a constituent act, like the Constitution of the United States, we must realize that they have called into life a being the development of which could not have been foreseen completely by the most gifted of its begetters. It was enough for them to realize or to hope that they had created an organism; it has taken a century and cost their successors much sweat and blood to prove that they created a nation. The case before us must be considered in the light of our entire experience and not merely in that of what was said a hundred years ago. . . . We must consider what this country has become in deciding what the Amendment has reserved.

Chief Justice CHARLES EVANS HUGHES's opinion in *Home Building & Loan* stands as the Court's most explicit assertion of the independent force of precedents and of the changing values they reflect. The Court upheld a law, enacted during the Depression, which postponed a mortgagor's right to foreclose against a defaulting mortgagee. In dissent, Justice Sutherland argued that the CONTRACT CLAUSE, which had been adopted in response to state debtor-relief legislation enacted during the depression following the Revolutionary War, was intended to prohibit precisely this sort of law. Given his intentionalist premise this disposed of the case. Hughes did not dispute Sutherland's account of the original history. Rather, he reviewed the precedents interpreting the contract clause to conclude:

It is manifest . . . that there has been a growing appreciation of public needs and of the necessity of finding ground for a rational compromise between individual rights and public welfare. The settlement and consequent contraction of the public domain, the pressure of a constantly increasing density of population, the interrelation of the activities of our people, and the complexity of our economic interests, have inevitably led to an increased use of the organization of society in order to protect the very bases of individual opportunity. . . . [T]he question is no longer merely that of one party to a contract as against another, but of the use of reasonable means to safeguard the economic structure upon which the good of all depends.

The views articulated by Holmes, Hughes, and Douglas reflect the Court's actual practice in adjudication under the BILL OF RIGHTS, the Fourteenth Amendment, and other provisions deemed relatively open-textured. The process bears more resemblance to COMMON LAW adjudication than to textual exegesis.

In an influential essay, Thomas Grey observed that the American constitutional tradition included practices of nonoriginalist adjudication purportedly based on principles of natural rights or FUNDAMENTAL LAW, or on widely shared and deeply held values not readily inferred from the text of the written Constitution. Several of the Supreme Court's contemporary decisions involving procreation and the family have invoked this tradition, and have given rise to a heated controversy over the legitimacy of adjudication based on "fundamental values."

Originalist and nonoriginalist adjudication are not nearly so distinct as many of the disputants assume. Constitutional provisions differ enormously in their closed- or open-texturedness. Indeed, a provision's texture is not merely a feature of its language or its original history, but of the particular situation in which it is applied. One's approach to a text is determined by tradition and by social outlooks that can change over time. Depending on one's political philosophy, one may bemoan this inevitability, or embrace it. For better or for worse, however, Terrance Sandalow described an important feature of our constitutional tradition when he remarked that "[t]he Constitution has . . . not only been read in light of contemporary circumstances and values; it has been read *so that* the circumstances and values of the present generation might be given expression in constitutional law."

Most disputes about constitutional interpretation and fundamental values concern interpretation in particular institutional contexts. Today's disputes center on the judicial power to review and strike down the acts of legislatures and agencies and are motivated by what ALEXANDER M. BICKEL dubbed the "countermajoritarian difficulty" of JUDICIAL REVIEW. Urgings of "judicial restraint" or of a more expansive approach to constitutional adjudication tend to reflect differing opinions of the role of the judiciary in a democratic polity and, more crudely, differing views about the substantive outcomes that these strategies yield. The question, say, whether Congress, the Supreme Court, or the states themselves should take primary responsibility for elaborating the equal protection clause is essentially political and cannot be resolved by abstract principles of interpretation. But this observation also cautions against taking interpretive positions based on particular institutional concerns and generalizing them beyond the situations that motivated them.

Constitutional interpretation is as much a process of creation as one of discovery. If this view is commonplace among postrealist academics, it is not often articulated by judges and it probably conflicts with the view of many citizens that constitutional interpretation should reflect the will of the adopters of the Constitution rather than its interpreters.

So-called STRICT CONSTRUCTION is an unsatisfactory response to these concerns. First, the most frequently litigated provisions do not lend themselves to "strict" or unambiguous or literal interpretation. (What are the strict meanings of the privileges or immunities, due process, and equal protection clauses?) Second, attempts to confine provisions to their very narrowest meanings typically produce results so ludicrous that even self-styled strict constructionists unconsciously abandon them in favor of less literal readings of texts and broader conceptualizations of the adopters' intentions. (No interpreter would hold that the First Amendment does not protect posters or songs because they are not "speech," or that the commerce clause does not apply to telecommunications because the adopters could not have foreseen this mode of commerce.) An interpreter must inevitably choose among different levels of abstraction in reading a provision—a choice that cannot itself be guided by any rules. Third, the two modes of strict interpretation—literalism and strict intentionalism—far from being synergistic strategies of interpretation, are often antagonistic. (Although the adopters of the First Amendment surely did not intend to protect obscene speech, the language they adopted does not exclude it.) A strict originalist theory of interpretation must opt either for literalism or for intentionalism, or must have some extraconstitutional principle for mediating between the two.

To reject these strategies is not to shed constraints. The text and history surrounding the adoption of a provision originate a line of doctrine, set its course, and continue to impose limitations. Some interpretations are more plausible than others; some are beyond the pale. And the criteria of plausibility are not merely subjective. Rather, they are intersubjective, constituted by others who are engaged in the same enterprise. Beyond the problem of subjectivity, however, the demographic characteristics of the legal interpretive community gives rise to an equally serious concern: the judiciary and the bar more generally have tended to be white, male, Anglo-Saxon, and well-to-do, and one might well wonder whether their interpretations do not embody parochial views or class interests. The concerns cannot be met by the choice of interpretive strategies, however, but only by addressing the composition and structure of the institutions whose interpretations have the force of law.

PAUL BREST

Bibliography

ABRAHAM, KENNETH 1981 Three Fallacies of Interpretation: A Comment on Precedent and Judicial Decision. *Arizona Law Review* 23:771–783.

BERGER, RAOUL 1977 *Government by Judiciary: The Transformation of the Fourteenth Amendment.* Cambridge, Mass.: Harvard University Press.

BLACK, CHARLES L., JR. 1969 *Structure and Relationship in Constitutional Law.* Baton Rouge: Louisiana State University Press.

CURTIS, CHARLES 1950 A Better Theory of Legal Interpretation. *Vanderbilt Law Review* 3:407–437.

DWORKIN, RONALD 1981 The Forum of Principle. *New York Law Review* 56:469–518.

ELY, JOHN HART 1980 *Democracy and Distrust.* Cambridge, Mass.: Harvard University Press.

FULLER, LON 1968 *Anatomy of Law.* New York: Praeger.

GREY, THOMAS 1975 Do We Have an Unwritten Constitution? *Stanford Law Review* 27:703–718.

HOLMES, OLIVER W. 1899 The Theory of Interpretation. *Harvard Law Review* 12:417.

MONAGHAN, HENRY 1981 Our Perfect Constitution. *New York University Law Review* 56:353–376.

SANDALOW, TERRANCE 1981 Constitutional Interpretation. *Michigan Law Review* 79:1033–1072.

SKINNER, QUENTIN 1969 Meaning and Understanding in the History of Ideas. *History & Theory* 8:3–53.

SYMPOSIUM 1985 Constitutional Interpretation. *University of Southern California Law Review* 58:551–725.

SYMPOSIUM ON LAW AND LITERATURE. 1982 *Texas Law Review* 60:373–586.

TEN BROEK, JACOBUS 1938–1939 Admissibility and Use by the Supreme Court of Extrinsic Aids in Constitutional Construction. *California Law Review* 26:287–308, 437–454, 664–681; 27:157–181, 399–421.